Praise for Previous Editions

"*Mastering AutoCAD 2002* is an excellent book for architects and engineers that presents information in a tutorial manner."

—*Joseph Lombardo, Sybex reader*

"The more I read your new book, the more I appreciate the huge effort that you have put into it. It is really a treasure trove for me. This book is really the reason people like me become recognized as "experts" where we work...."

—*Mario Ramirez, AutoCAD Consultant, Philippines*

"I have recently purchased [*Mastering AutoCAD 2000*] and find it extremely helpful...it covers a complex subject with a clear and lucid style—thank you."

—*Bill Warren, Warren Design, UK*

"I am incredibly impressed with this book—it has much more information that the user's guide that comes with the program. The CD-ROM alone is worth the money....Well organized, well indexed, and very readable; you won't be able to find another book like this."

—*A reader from Houston, Texas, courtesy of Amazon.com*

"Enjoyable, easy to read—a book with excellent explanations—an indispensable AutoCAD 2000 reference."

—*A reader for Bangkok, Thailand, courtesy of Amazon.com*

Praise for Previous Editions

Mastering™

AutoCAD® 2004 and AutoCAD LT® 2004

George Omura

SYBEX®

San Francisco London

Associate Publisher: Dan Brodnitz

Acquisitions and Developmental Editor: Willem Knibbe

Production Editor: Jennifer L. Campbell

Technical Editor: Mike Gunderloy

Copyeditor: Pat Coleman

Compositor: Jill Niles

Graphic Illustrator: Scott Benoit

CD Coordinator: Dan Mummert

CD Technician: Kevin Ly

Proofreaders: Nancy Riddiough, Laurie O'Connell, Emily Hsuan, Darcy Maurer, Monique van den Berg

Indexer: Ted Laux

Book Designer: Maureen Forys, Happenstance Type-O-Rama

Cover Designer: Design Site

Cover Illustrator: Sergie Loobkoff

Library of Congress Card Number: 2003101649

ISBN: 0-7821-4188-9

Manufactured in the United States of America

10 9 8 7 6 5

Software License Agreement: Terms and Conditions

The media and/or any online materials accompanying this book that are available now or in the future contain programs and/or text files (the "Software") to be used in connection with the book. SYBEX hereby grants to you a license to use the Software, subject to the terms that follow. Your purchase, acceptance, or use of the Software will constitute your acceptance of such terms.

The Software compilation is the property of SYBEX unless otherwise indicated and is protected by copyright to SYBEX or other copyright owner(s) as indicated in the media files (the "Owner(s)"). You are hereby granted a single-user license to use the Software for your personal, noncommercial use only. You may not reproduce, sell, distribute, publish, circulate, or commercially exploit the Software, or any portion thereof, without the written consent of SYBEX and the specific copyright owner(s) of any component software included on this media.

In the event that the Software or components include specific license requirements or end-user agreements, statements of condition, disclaimers, limitations or warranties ("End-User License"), those End-User Licenses supersede the terms and conditions herein as to that particular Software component. Your purchase, acceptance, or use of the Software will constitute your acceptance of such End-User Licenses.

By purchase, use or acceptance of the Software you further agree to comply with all export laws and regulations of the United States as such laws and regulations may exist from time to time.

Software Support

Components of the supplemental Software and any offers associated with them may be supported by the specific Owner(s) of that material, but they are not supported by SYBEX. Information regarding any available support may be obtained from the Owner(s) using the information provided in the appropriate read.me files or listed elsewhere on the media.

Should the manufacturer(s) or other Owner(s) cease to offer support or decline to honor any offer, SYBEX bears no responsibility. This notice concerning support for the Software is provided for your information only. SYBEX is not the agent or principal of the Owner(s), and SYBEX is in no way responsible for providing any support for the Software, nor is it liable or responsible for any support provided, or not provided, by the Owner(s).

Warranty

SYBEX warrants the enclosed media to be free of physical defects for a period of ninety (90) days after purchase. The Software is not available from SYBEX in any other form or media than that enclosed herein or posted to www.sybex.com. If you discover a defect in the media during this warranty period, you may obtain a replacement of identical format at no charge by sending the defective media, postage prepaid, with proof of purchase to:

SYBEX Inc.
Product Support Department
1151 Marina Village Parkway
Alameda, CA 94501
Web: `http://www.sybex.com`

After the 90-day period, you can obtain replacement media of identical format by sending us the defective disk, proof of purchase, and a check or money order for $10, payable to SYBEX.

Disclaimer

SYBEX makes no warranty or representation, either expressed or implied, with respect to the Software or its contents, quality, performance, merchantability, or fitness for a particular purpose. In no event will SYBEX, its distributors, or dealers be liable to you or any other party for direct, indirect, special, incidental, consequential, or other damages arising out of the use of or inability to use the Software or its contents even if advised of the possibility of such damage. In the event that the Software includes an online update feature, SYBEX further disclaims any obligation to provide this feature for any specific duration other than the initial posting.

The exclusion of implied warranties is not permitted by some states. Therefore, the above exclusion may not apply to you. This warranty provides you with specific legal rights; there may be other rights that you may have that vary from state to state. The pricing of the book with the Software by SYBEX reflects the allocation of risk and limitations on liability contained in this agreement of Terms and Conditions.

Shareware Distribution

This Software may contain various programs that are distributed as shareware. Copyright laws apply to both shareware and ordinary commercial software, and the copyright Owner(s) retains all rights. If you try a shareware program and continue using it, you are expected to register it. Individual programs differ on details of trial periods, registration, and payment. Please observe the requirements stated in appropriate files.

Copy Protection

The Software in whole or in part may or may not be copy-protected or encrypted. However, in all cases, reselling or redistributing these files without authorization is expressly forbidden except as specifically provided for by the Owner(s) therein.

To my friends and family…

Acknowledgments

MANY HARDWORKING PEOPLE GAVE their best effort to produce *Mastering AutoCAD 2004 and AutoCAD LT 2004*. I'd like to offer my sincerest gratitude to those people who helped bring this book to you.

Heartfelt thanks go to the editorial and production teams at Sybex for their efforts in getting this book to press on an incredible schedule. Willem Knibbe made sure things got off to a great start and offered encouragement throughout the writing process. Leslie Light, production editor, kept the project moving with skill and patience. Pat Coleman, copy editor, made sure that the book made sense. Mike Gunderloy, technical editor, provided helpful suggestions and kept things on the right track. Jill Niles and Scott Benoit, electronic publishing specialists, created the pages you see before you and innumerable proofreaders checked every one of those pages. Dan Mummert coordinated the ever-important permissions for software reproduction. Finally, Kevin Ly compiled the CD and made it easy and fun to use.

I also want to thank the many contributors to this book. A big thanks to Mike Gunderloy who not only provided his expertise for our technical review but also wrote the original drafts of the chapters on ActiveX Automation and VBA.

You can see the handiwork of Paul Richardson and Christine Merredith of Technical Publications in the sidebars that discuss the San Francisco Main Library. Thanks also go to the architectural firms of Pei Cobb Freed & Partners and Simon Martin-Vegue Winkelstein Moris Associated Architects for generously granting permission to reproduce drawings from their design of the San Francisco Main Library.

At Autodesk, Christine Kalb and Evie LaHaie aided in obtaining permissions to include the trial versions of AutoCAD 2004 and VIZ 4 on our CD. Thanks also go to Denis Cadu who has given his continued support of our efforts over many projects. Jim Quanci, as usual, gave generous assistance to the ever needful author.

And as usual, a great big thanks to my family who have always been a source of inspiration and support.

Contents at a Glance

Contents

Introduction

WELCOME TO *Mastering AutoCAD 2004 and AutoCAD LT 2004*. As many readers have already discovered, this book is a unique blend of tutorial and reference that includes everything you need to get started and stay ahead with AutoCAD. With this edition, you get coverage of the latest features of both AutoCAD 2004 and AutoCAD LT 2004, plus expanded coverage of 3D modeling and customization.

How to Use This Book

Rather than just showing you how each command works, *Mastering AutoCAD 2004 and AutoCAD LT 2004* shows you AutoCAD 2004 in the context of a meaningful activity. You will learn how to use commands while working on an actual project and progressing toward a goal. This book also provides a foundation on which you can build your own methods for using AutoCAD and become an AutoCAD expert. For this reason, I haven't covered every single command or every permutation of a command response. You should think of this book as a way to get a detailed look at AutoCAD as it is used on a real project. As you follow the exercises, I encourage you to also explore AutoCAD on your own, applying the techniques you learn to your own work.

Both experienced and beginning AutoCAD users will find this book useful. If you are not an experienced user, the way to get the most out of this book is to approach it as a tutorial—chapter by chapter, at least for the first two parts of the book. You'll find that each chapter builds on the skills and information you learned in the previous one. To help you navigate, the exercises are shown in numbered steps. To address the needs of all readers worldwide, the exercises provide both U.S. (feet/inches) and metric measurements.

Once you've mastered the material in Parts I and II, you can follow your interests and explore other parts of the book in whatever order you choose. Part III takes you to a more advanced skill level. There, you'll learn more about storing and sharing drawing data and how to create more complex drawings. If you're interested in 3D, check out Part IV. If you want to start customizing right away, go to Part V. You can check out Chapter 22 at any time as it gives you general information on sharing AutoCAD files with your co-workers and consultants. Chapter 22 also discusses many of the newest features in AutoCAD 2004. You can also use this book as a ready reference for your day-to-day problems and questions about commands. Optional exercises at the end of each chapter will help you review and look at different ways to apply the information you've learned. Experienced users will also find this book to be a handy reference tool.

Finally, if you run into problems using AutoCAD, see the "Troubleshooting" section in Appendix C. You'll find a listing of the most common issues that readers face when first learning AutoCAD.

AutoCAD 2004 and AutoCAD LT 2004

This time around, Autodesk has released both AutoCAD 2004 and AutoCAD LT 2004 simultaneously. Not surprisingly, they are nearly identical in the way they look and work. You can share files between the two programs with complete confidence that you won't lose data or corrupt files. The main differences are that LT does not support all the 3D functions of AutoCAD 2004; nor does it support the customization tools of AutoLISP and VBA. But LT still has plenty to offer in both the productivity and customization areas. And because they are so similar, I can present material for both programs with only minor adjustments.

When a feature is discussed that is only available in AutoCAD 2004, you will see the AutoCAD Only icon.

ACAD only

You'll also see warning messages when tutorials vary between AutoCAD 2004 and LT. If only minor differences occur, you will see either a warning message or directions embedded in the tutorial indicating the differences between the two programs.

In the few instances where LT has a feature that is not available in AutoCAD 2004, you will see the LT Only icon.

LT only

I've also provided work-around instructions wherever possible when LT does not offer a feature found in AutoCAD 2004.

Getting Information Fast

I've included plenty of tips and warnings:

TIP *Tips are designed to make practice easier.*

WARNING *Warnings steer you away from pitfalls.*

Also, in each chapter you will find more extensive tips and discussions in the form of sidebars set off from the main text. To encourage you along the way, some of the sidebars show you how topics in each chapter were applied to a real-world project, the San Francisco Main Library. Together the tips, warnings, and sidebars provide a wealth of information I have gathered over years of using AutoCAD on a variety of projects in different office environments. You may want to browse through the book, just reading these notes, to get an idea of how they might be useful to you.

Another quick reference you'll find yourself turning to often is Appendix D, which contains tables of all the system variables and dimension variables with comments on their uses. If you experience any problems, you can consult the "Troubleshooting" section in Appendix C.

What to Expect

Mastering AutoCAD 2004 and AutoCAD LT 2004 is divided into five parts, each representing a milestone in your progress toward becoming an expert AutoCAD user. Here is a description of those parts and what they will show you.

Part 1: The Basics

As with any major endeavor, you must begin by tackling small, manageable tasks. In this first part, you will become familiar with the way AutoCAD looks and feels. Chapter 1, *This Is AutoCAD,* shows you how to get around in AutoCAD. In Chapter 2, *Creating Your First Drawing,* you will learn how to start and exit the program and how to respond to AutoCAD commands. Chapter 3, *Learning the Tools of the Trade,* tells you how to set up a work area, edit objects, and lay out a drawing. In Chapter 4, *Organizing Your Work,* you will explore some tools unique to CAD: symbols, blocks, and layers. As you are introduced to AutoCAD, you will also get a chance to make some drawings that you can use later in the book and perhaps even in future projects of your own.

Part 2: Building on the Basics

Once you have the basics down, you will begin to explore some of AutoCAD's more subtle qualities. Chapter 5, *Editing for Productivity,* tells you how to reuse drawing setup information and parts of an existing drawing. In Chapter 6, *Enhancing Your Drawing Skills,* you will learn how to assemble and edit a large drawing file. Chapter 7, *Printing and Plotting,* shows you how to get your drawing onto hard copy. Chapter 8, *Adding Text to Drawings,* tells you how to annotate your drawing and edit your notes. Chapter 9, *Using Dimensions,* gives you practice in using automatic dimensioning (another unique CAD capability), which has been enhanced in AutoCAD 2004 with the true associative dimensioning feature. Along the way, I will be giving you tips on editing and how to solve problems you may encounter as you begin to use AutoCAD for more complex tasks.

Part 3: Becoming an Expert

At this point, you will be on the verge of becoming a real AutoCAD expert. Part III is designed to help you polish your existing skills and give you a few new ones. Chapter 10, *Attributes—Storing Data with Graphics,* tells you how to attach information to drawing objects and how to export that information to database and spreadsheet files. Chapter 11, *Working with External Databases,* continues with the data exchange theme by showing you how to link drawings to existing database files. In Chapter 12, *Copying Pre-existing Drawings into AutoCAD,* you will learn techniques for transferring paper drawings to AutoCAD. In Chapter 13, *Power Editing,* you will complete the apartment building tutorial. During this process you will learn how to integrate what you've learned so far and gain some tips on working in groups. Chapter 14, *Drawing Curves and Solid Fills,* gives you an in-depth look at some special drawing objects, such as splines and fitted curves. In Chapter 15, *Getting and Exchanging Data from Drawings,* you will practice getting information about a drawing and learn how AutoCAD can interact with other applications, such as spreadsheets and desktop-publishing programs. You'll also learn how to copy and paste data.

Part 4: 3D Modeling and Imaging

Although 2D drafting is AutoCAD's workhorse application, AutoCAD's 3D capabilities give you a chance to expand your ideas and look at them in a new light. Chapter 16, *Introducing 3D*, covers AutoCAD's basic features for creating three-dimensional drawings. Chapter 17, *Using Advanced 3D Features*, introduces you to some of the program's more powerful 3D capabilities. Chapter 18, *Rendering and Animating 3D Drawings*, shows how you can use AutoCAD to produce lifelike views of your 3D drawings. Chapter 19, *Mastering 3D Solids*, is a guided tour of AutoCAD 2004's solid-modeling feature. On the CD, you'll find *Architectural Solid Modeling*, which takes you deeper into the world of 3D solid modeling where you will model a classic building to learn the finer points of AutoCAD 3D. *Advanced Surface Modeling*, also on the CD, shows you how to make full use of AutoCAD's surface modeling tools to create more complex, free-form shapes.

Part 5: Customization and Integration

One of AutoCAD's greatest strengths is its openness to customization. Chapter 20, *Introduction to Customization*, gives you a gentle introduction to the world of AutoCAD customization. You'll learn how to load and use existing Express Tools that expand AutoCAD's functionality, and you'll be introduced to AutoLISP as a tool to create macros. Chapter 21, *Integrating AutoCAD into Your Projects and Organization*, shows you how to customize menus, toolbars, line types, and hatch patterns. Chapter 22, *Managing and Sharing Your Drawings*, shows you how you can adapt AutoCAD to your own work style. You'll learn about the tools that help you exchange drawings with others and how to secure your drawings to prevent tampering. If you're really serious about customization, you'll want to take a look at additional bonus chapters on the CD that offer in-depth coverage of customization topics. *Exploring VBA*, covers the basic concepts of Visual Basic Automation for AutoCAD. Visual Basic lets you build custom applications that work with AutoCAD and other Windows programs. Two more chapters about VBA and ActiveX are also on the CD. And if you are more interested in AutoLISP, the classic *ABCs of AutoLISP* is an entire book that gives you the basic foundation in AutoLISP programming.

The Appendices

Finally, this book has four appendices. Appendix A, *What's on the Companion CD?*, covers everything you need to know about the software and example files included on this book's CD. Appendix B, *Installing and Setting Up AutoCAD*, contains an installation and configuration tutorial. If AutoCAD is not already installed on your system, you should follow this tutorial before starting Chapter 1. Appendix C, *Hardware and Software Tips*, offers information on hardware related to AutoCAD. It also provides tips on improving AutoCAD's performance and troubleshooting and provides more detailed information on setting up AutoCAD's plotting feature. Appendix D, *System and Dimension Variables*, provides a reference to system and dimension variables, as well as detailed information regarding dimension style settings.

The Minimum System Requirements

This book assumes you have an IBM-compatible computer with at least a Pentium II or equivalent CPU. Your computer should have at least one CD drive and a hard disk with 170MB or more free space for the AutoCAD program files and about 100MB of additional space for sample files and workspace. In addition to these requirements, you should also have enough free disk space to allow for a Windows virtual memory page file of at least 256MB. Consult your Windows manual or Appendix A of this book for more on virtual memory. Finally, AutoCAD requires 220MB of free space on your C drive for temporary installation files.

AutoCAD 2004 runs best on systems with at least 256MB or more of RAM, though you can get by with 128MB. Your computer should also have a high-resolution monitor and an up-to-date display card. An SVGA display with a resolution of 1024 × 768 or greater will work fine with AutoCAD. If you intend to use a digitizer tablet, you'll want to have one free USB, or serial, port available. I also assume you are using a mouse and have the use of a printer or a plotter. A CD or DVD is needed to install AutoCAD and the software from this book. Finally, you'll want an Internet connection to take full advantage of the support offerings from Autodesk.

If you want a more detailed explanation of hardware options with AutoCAD, see Appendix C. You will find a general description of the available hardware options and their significance to AutoCAD.

TIP *If you intend to use a digitizer tablet in place of a mouse, Autodesk also provides you with a digitizer template in the form of a drawing file called* `Tablet.dwg`*. You can open and print this file and then place it on your tablet. Once the digitizer template is properly configured, you can select commands directly from the template. See Appendix B for instructions on configuring the digitizer template.*

Doing Things in Style

Much care has been taken to see that the stylistic conventions in this book—the use of uppercase or lowercase letters, italic or boldface type, and so on—will be the ones most likely to help you learn AutoCAD. On the whole, their effect should be subliminal. However, you may find it useful to be conscious of the following rules:

- Pull-down selections are shown by a series of menu options separated by the ➢ symbol (for example, choose File ➢ New).
- Keyboard entries are shown in boldface (for example, enter **Rotate**).
- Command-line prompts are shown in a monospaced font (for example, `Select objects:`).

For most functions, this book describes how to select options from toolbars and the menu bar. In addition, where applicable, I include related keyboard shortcuts and command names in parentheses. These command names provide continuity for readers accustomed to working at the command prompt.

Finally, to help the first time user, I show more graphics in the first part of the book. For example, full toolbars are shown to give you a better idea of where to find a tool in a toolbar. Later in the book, you'll see margin icons that show the specific tool you are being asked to use.

What's on the CD?

A CD included with this book contains a wealth of utilities, symbols libraries, and sample programs that can greatly enhance your use of AutoCAD. The CD includes the drawing files from all the exercises throughout this book so that you can pick up an exercise anywhere in the book, without having to work through the book from front to back. You can also use these sample files to repeat exercises or to just explore how files are organized and put together.

Further, the CD even includes a trial version of AutoCAD 2004, in case you don't have access to the software. For readers who want to learn more about customization, you'll find three chapters that cover ActiveX and additional information on VBA. An online book—*The ABCs of AutoLISP*—functions as an easy-to-use, online reference for AutoLISP, the AutoCAD macro-programming language. And *AutoCAD 2004 Instant Reference* is the definitive companion to *Mastering AutoCAD 2004 and AutoCAD LT 2004*; it's full of detailed descriptions of AutoCAD's commands and tools. The CD also additional includes 3D utilities and a 3D parts library. See Appendix A for a more extensive rundown of what's available on the CD.

WARNING *AutoCAD now allows side-by-side installation of AutoCAD 2004 with earlier releases. However, if you purchase an upgrade version of AutoCAD 2004, you must remove the previous version of AutoCAD within 60 days.*

New Features of AutoCAD 2004

AutoCAD 2004 offers a higher level of speed, security, and ease of use. File sizes have been greatly reduced, which means that you can load projects faster and store them easier. The interface offers some great productivity tools such as multiple Undo and Redo. Tool palettes offer a greatly simplified way to help you implement your custom libraries, and full, True Color support gives you greater flexibility in producing presentation graphics.

Other new features include the following:

- Productivity-enhancing AutoCAD Express Tools
- Password protection for DWG files
- Digital signatures for data security
- Support for printing shaded and rendered views
- True Color, PANTONE®, and RAL color support
- Gradient fills for enhanced 2D presentations
- More accurate hidden-line 3D views that display surface intersections accurately
- Cloud tool to allow easy revision cloud drawing
- In-place multiline text editing with enhanced control for indents and tabs
- Improved DWF file format for secure sharing of multipage documents
- Automatic notification of Xref changes or missing Xrefs
- New tool palettes for easy access to frequently used content
- Wipeout command to hide portions of a drawing
- Improved optional right-click functionality

- Improved Properties palette with Auto-hide feature
- Autodesk DesignCenter Online for quick and easy connection to online content
- AutoCAD Express Viewer for the exchange and viewing of DWF files with non-AutoCAD users
- Communication Center for opt-in notifications of product updates, extensions, news, and support information

Finally, AutoCAD offers one of the most easily customizable versions yet, with customization options through the new Tool palettes, as well as a simplified dialog box for toolbar customization.

TIP *AutoCAD continues to improve its Windows compatibility with standard keyboard shortcuts for copy, paste, and delete functions. For example, you can move or copy drawing elements within a drawing or between open drawings using the Ctrl+C and Ctrl+V copy and paste shortcut keys. Ctrl+O opens a file, and Ctrl+N creates a new file. OLE has also improved by lifting the data size limit for exchanges between Office XP Pro applications and AutoCAD 2004.*

Contact the Author

I hope that *Mastering AutoCAD 2004 and AutoCAD LT 2004* will be of benefit to you and that, once you have completed the tutorials, you will continue to use the book as a reference. If you have comments, criticisms, or ideas about how the book can be improved, you can send e-mail to me at the address below. And thanks for choosing *Mastering AutoCAD 2004 and AutoCAD LT 2004.*

George Omura
`gomura@yahoo.com`

Part 1

The Basics

In this part:

Chapter 1

This Is AutoCAD

AutoCAD HAS BEEN AROUND since 1983 when version 1.4 was introduced. Its longevity is the result of a solid product and a steadily expanding set of capabilities. The latest iteration, AutoCAD 2004, is faster, has an improved interface, and includes new features based on the more popular end-user wish-list items. AutoCAD 2004 also offers something that won't be visible at first glance. Autodesk wanted to make sure that their latest version of AutoCAD would be one of the most reliable ever, so AutoCAD 2004 has been through one of the most extensive beta-testing programs in the history of AutoCAD. Users have always cited reliability as one of AutoCAD's most important features, and AutoCAD 2004 should prove to be a solid performer.

Before you can start to make use of AutoCAD 2004's new capabilities, you'll need to become familiar with the basics. If you are completely new to AutoCAD, you'll want to read this first chapter carefully. It introduces you to many of AutoCAD's basic operations, such as opening and closing files, getting a close-up look at part of a drawing, and changing a drawing. If you are familiar with earlier versions of AutoCAD, you might want to read through this chapter anyway to get acquainted with new AutoCAD 2004 features. So let's get started!

Topics in this chapter include the following:

- The AutoCAD Window
- Opening an Existing File
- Getting a Closer Look with the Zoom Command
- Saving a File As You Work
- Making Changes and Opening Multiple Files
- If You Want to Experiment…

TIP *In this chapter, and throughout the rest of the book, when we say "AutoCAD," we mean both AutoCAD and AutoCAD LT. Some topics will only apply to AutoCAD. In those situations, you'll see an icon indicating that the topic does not apply to AutoCAD LT. If you are using AutoCAD 2004 LT, these icons can help you focus on the topics that are more relevant to your work.*

Taking a Guided Tour

First, you will get a chance to familiarize yourself with the AutoCAD screen and how you communicate with AutoCAD. As you do the exercises in this chapter, you will also get a feel for how to work with this book. Don't worry about understanding or remembering everything that you see in this chapter. You will get plenty of opportunities to probe the finer details of the program as you work through the later chapters. To help you remember the material, you will find a brief exercise at the end of each chapter. For now, just enjoy your first excursion into AutoCAD.

WARNING *AutoCAD 2004 is designed to run on Windows NT4 with service pack 6, Windows 2000 and Windows XP. It is not designed to run on Windows 98 or Windows Me though some users have reported running it successfully on Windows 98. If you are using a network license version of AutoCAD, you may also use Windows 2000 server edition or Windows NT4 server edition with service pack 5. This book was written using AutoCAD 2004 on Windows XP Professional with a Windows Classic desktop theme.*

If you already installed AutoCAD and are ready to jump in and take a look, proceed with the following steps to launch the program:

1. Choose Start ➢ All Programs ➢ Autodesk ➢ AutoCAD 2004 ➢ AutoCAD 2004. You can also double-click the AutoCAD 2004 icon on your Windows Desktop. LT users will use AutoCAD LT 2004 in place of AutoCAD 2004.
2. The opening greeting, called a *splash screen*, tells you which version of AutoCAD you are using, to whom the program is registered, and the AutoCAD dealer's name and phone number, should you need help.
3. After the splash screen closes, you see the AutoCAD Window with a blank default document named `Drawing1.dwg` as shown in Figure 1.1.

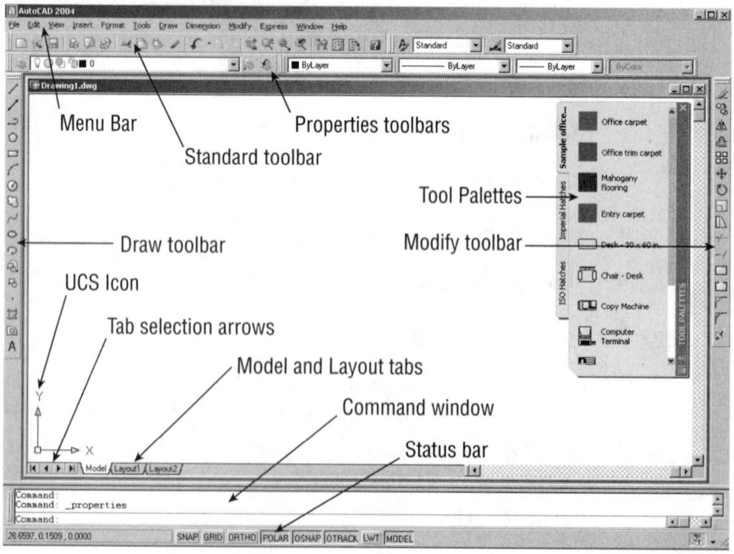

FIGURE 1.1
A typical arrangement of the elements in the AutoCAD window

NOTE *If you see the Startup dialog box after step 3, click Cancel. AutoCAD displays a default document as shown in Figure 1.1. You'll learn more about the Startup dialog box in Chapter 2.*

Let's take a look at the AutoCAD window in detail. Don't worry if it seems like a lot of information. You don't have to memorize it all, but by looking at all the parts, you'll be aware of what is available in a general way.

LT only

AutoCAD LT users will see the Active Assistance window. This window is an aid to new users, and it provides immediate help with AutoCAD commands. For now, you can close it by clicking the Close button in the upper-right corner. To prevent the Active Assistance window from appearing automatically, right-click the Active Assistance icon in the Windows tool tray (it is a question mark icon in the lower-right corner of the computer screen), and choose Settings from the shortcut menu to open the Active Assistance Settings dialog box. Click the On Demand radio button, and then click OK. You can open the Active Assistance window at any time by choosing Help ➢ Active Assistance from the AutoCAD menu bar.

Message to Veteran AutoCAD Users

AutoCAD, like many popular programs, is continually evolving. Quite often, that evolution forces us to change some old and cherished habits.

If you've been using AutoCAD for a while, and you've grown accustomed to certain behaviors, you can take certain steps to make AutoCAD 2004 a more familiar environment.

You can, for example, restore the Enter (↵) function to the mouse right-click instead of using the newer shortcut menu. Follow these steps:

1. Choose Tools ➢ Options to open the Options dialog box.
2. Click the User Preference tab.
3. In the Windows Standard Behavior group, click the Right-Click Customization button to open the Right-Click Customization dialog box.
4. Click the ENTER radio button in the Command Mode group, and then click the Apply & Close button.

Another option is to turn on the time-sensitive right-click option at the top of the Right-Click Customization dialog box. With this option, a quick right-click is the same as pressing the Enter ↵ key but you can still access the right-click shortcut menus by holding down the right mouse button a bit longer. You can even set the duration required to open the right-click shortcut menus.

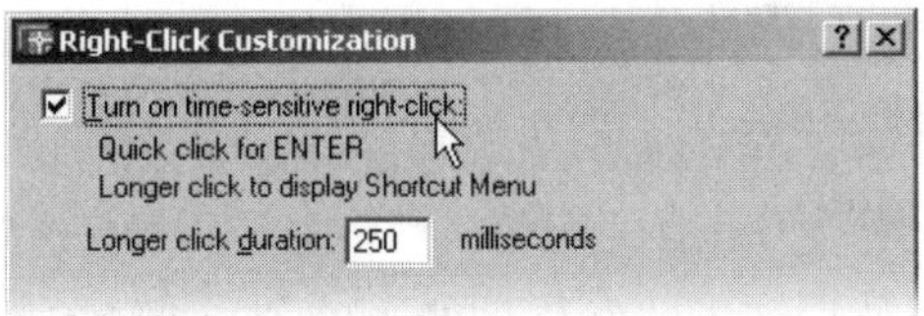

Continued on next page

MESSAGE TO VETERAN AUTOCAD USERS *(continued)*

If you prefer to enter commands and command options through the keyboard instead of using dialog boxes, you can do so for a number of commands. Here is a list of commands that normally produce a dialog box.

Array	Attdef	Attedit
Bhatch	Boundary	Group
HatcheditImage	Insert	Image
Layer	Layout	Linetype
MtextBlock	Osnap	Pan
Partialopen	Purge	Rename
Style	Units	View
Wblock	Xbind	Xref

To use these commands from the command prompt, add a minus sign (–) to the beginning of the command name. For example, to use the old Layer command, enter **–layer** at the command prompt. To use the old Pan command, enter **–pan** at the command prompt. (By the way, when you enter **–pan** from the command prompt, the command reverts to the "classic" method of panning in AutoCAD, in which you click two points to indicate the direction and displacement, instead of the "real time" pan. This "classic" method is useful when you want to pan your view a specific distance because it allows you to enter the pan distance and direction.)

Even if you don't care to enter commands from the keyboard, knowing about the use of the minus sign can help you create custom macros. See Chapter 20 for more on AutoCAD customization.

The AutoCAD Window

The AutoCAD program window is divided into six parts:

- Menu bar
- Docked and floating toolbars
- Drawing area
- Command window
- Status bar
- Tool Palettes

TIP A seventh hidden component, the Properties palette, gives you detailed information about the objects in your drawing. You can also use it to modify some of those properties. You'll learn more about the Properties palette in Chapter 4.

Figure 1.1 shows a typical layout of the AutoCAD program window. Along the top is the *menu bar*, and at the bottom are the *Command window* and the *status bar*. Just below the menu bar and to either side of the window are the *toolbars*. The *drawing area* occupies the rest of the screen. (By the way, your screen may show the drawing area in black. You can set the drawing area background color using the Options dialog box. Appendix B describes how to do this. (The figures in this book show the drawing area background in white for clarity.)

You can easily move and reshape many of the elements in the AutoCAD window. Figure 1.2 demonstrates how different AutoCAD can look after some simple rearranging of window components. You can move toolbars from their default locations to any location on the screen. When they are in their default location, they are in their *docked* position. When they are moved to a location where they are free-floating, they are *floating*.

FIGURE 1.2

An alternative arrangement of the elements in the AutoCAD window

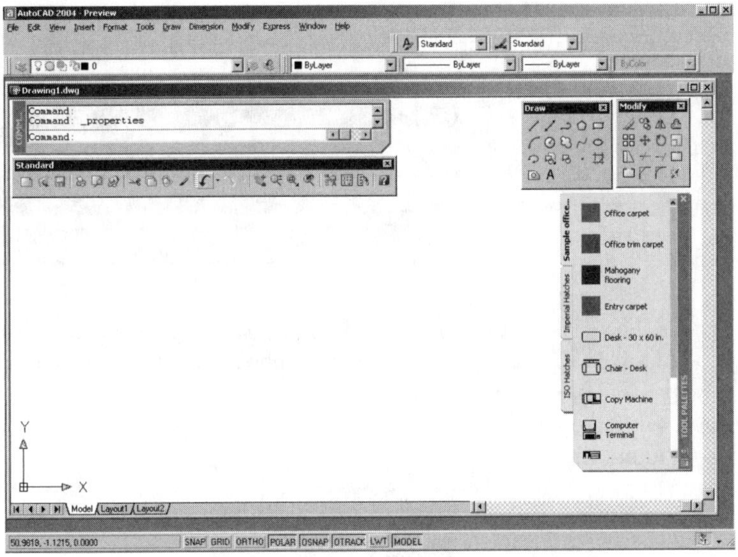

The menu bar at the top of the drawing area (as shown in Figure 1.3) offers pull-down menus from which you select commands in a typical Windows fashion. The toolbars offer a variety of commands through tool buttons and drop-down lists. For example, the name or number of the *layer* that you are currently working on is displayed in a drop-down list in the Properties toolbar. To the right of the layer name are icons for tools you can use to work with the layer. The tools and lists on the toolbar are plentiful, and you'll learn more about all of them later in this chapter and as you work through this book.

TIP *A layer is like an overlay that allows you to separate different types of information. AutoCAD allows an unlimited number of layers. On new drawings, the default layer is 0. You'll get a detailed look at layers and the meaning of the Layer tools in Chapter 4.*

FIGURE 1.3

The components of the menu bar and the Standard toolbar.

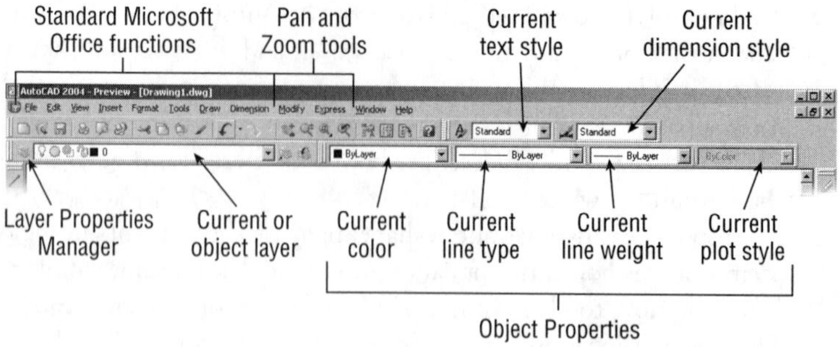

The Draw and Modify toolbars, which are normally docked on either side of the drawing area, offer commands that create new objects and edit existing ones. These are just two of many toolbars available to you. Figure 1.4 shows these two toolbars in their floating state.

FIGURE 1.4

The Draw and Modify toolbars as they appear when floating

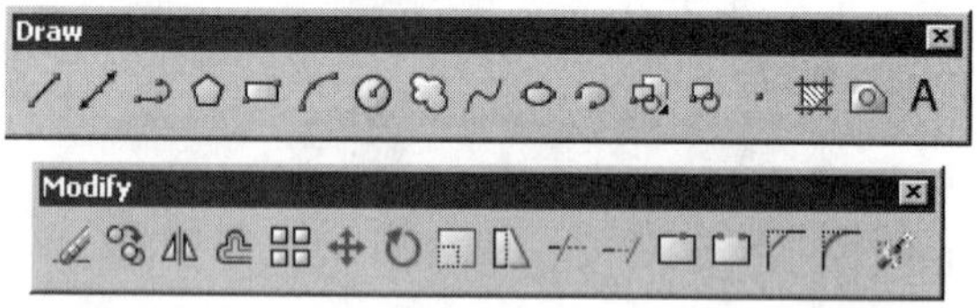

The Tool palettes offer a quick way to gain access to frequently used symbols, known as *blocks* in AutoCAD. You can create your own symbols and add them to the palettes. You'll get a closer look at the Tool palettes in Chapter 2.

FIGURE 1.5

The Tool palettes

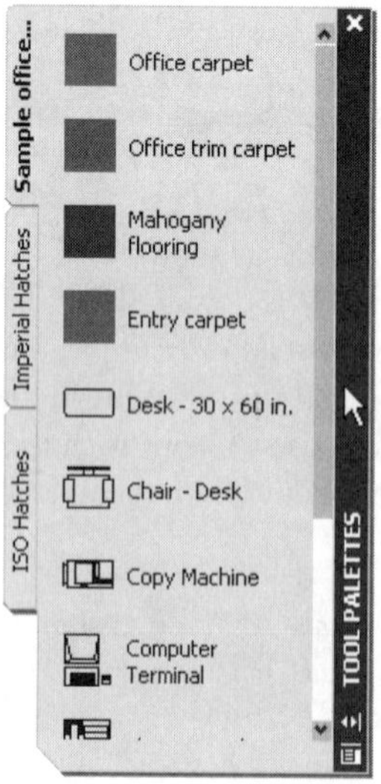

The drawing area—your workspace—occupies most of the screen. Everything you draw appears in this area. As you move your mouse around, crosshairs appear to move within the drawing area. This is the drawing cursor that lets you point to locations in the drawing area.

At the bottom of the drawing area, you'll see a set of tabs. These tabs give you access to the Layout views of your drawing. These views let you lay out your drawing as in a desktop publishing program. You'll learn about the Layout tabs in Chapter 7. The arrows to the left of the tabs let you navigate the tabs when there are more tabs than can fit in the AutoCAD window.

The Command window, located just below the drawing area, gives you feedback about AutoCAD's commands as you use them. You can move and resize this window just as you move and resize toolbars. By default, the Command window is in its docked position, as shown in Figure 1.6.

FIGURE 1.6

The status bar and the Command window

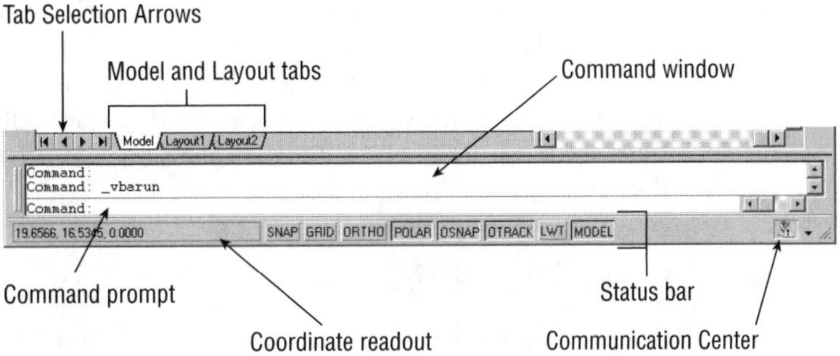

Below the Command window is the status bar (see Figure 1.6)The status bar gives you information at a glance about the state of the drawing. For example, the coordinate readout toward the far left of the status line tells you the location of your cursor.

TIP *In a new installation of AutoCAD, you will see a message balloon in the bottom right corner of AutoCAD. This message balloon alerts you to the latest news and information regarding AutoCAD through a feature called the Communication Center. You'll learn more about the Communication Center in Chapter 2.*

PICKING POINTS IN THE DRAWING AREA

Let's practice using the coordinate readout and the drawing cursor.

1. Move the cursor around in the drawing area. As you move, notice how the coordinate readout changes to tell you the cursor's location. It shows the coordinates in an X,Y, Z format.
2. Now place the cursor in the middle of the drawing area and click the left mouse button. You have just picked a point. Move the cursor, and a rectangle follows. This is a *selection window*; you'll learn more about this window in Chapter 2.
3. Move the cursor a bit in any direction; then click the left mouse button again. Notice that the selection window disappears.
4. Try picking several more points in the drawing area. Notice that as you click the mouse, you alternately start and end a selection window.

If you accidentally click the right mouse button, the shortcut menu appears. A right mouse click frequently opens a menu that contains options that are *context sensitive*. This means that the contents of the shortcut menu depend on where you right-click as well as the command that is active at the time of your right-click. If there are no appropriate options at the time of the right-click, AutoCAD treats the right-click as a ↵. You'll learn more about these options as you progress through the book. For now, if you happen to open this menu by accident, press the Esc key to close it.

TIP *The ↵ symbol is used in this book to denote the Enter key. Whenever you see it, press the Enter key, also known as the Return key.*

THE UCS ICON

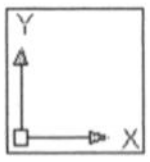

In the lower-left corner of the drawing area, you see an L-shaped arrow. This is the *User Coordinate System (UCS)* icon, which tells you your orientation in the drawing. This icon becomes helpful as you start to work with complex 2D drawings and 3D models. The X and Y arrows indicate the x- and y-axes of your drawing. The little square at the base of the arrows tells you that you are in what is called the *World Coordinate System*. Chapter 17 discusses this icon in detail. For now, you can use it as a reference to tell you the direction of the axes.

IF YOU CAN'T FIND THE UCS ICON...

The UCS icon can be turned on and off, so if you are on someone else's system and you don't see the icon, don't panic. It also changes shape depending on whether you are in Paper Space mode in a Layout tab or in Model Space! If you don't see the icon or it doesn't look as it does in this chapter, see Chapter 13 for more information on Paper Space and Model Space. Chapter 17 gives you more information on the UCS icon.

THE COMMAND WINDOW

At the bottom of the screen, just above the status bar, is a small horizontal window called the *Command window*. Here AutoCAD displays responses to your input. By default, it shows three lines of text. The bottom line shows the current messages, and the top two lines show messages that have scrolled by or, in some cases, components of the current message that do not fit in a single line. Right now, the bottom line displays the message `Command` (see Figure 1.6 earlier in this chapter). This *prompt* tells you that AutoCAD is waiting for your instructions. As you click a point in the drawing area, you'll see the message `Specify Opposite Corner`. At the same time, the cursor starts to draw a selection window that disappears when you click another point.

As a new user, pay special attention to messages displayed in the Command window because this is how AutoCAD communicates with you. Besides giving you messages, the Command window records your activity in AutoCAD. You can use the scroll bar to the right of the Command window to review previous messages. You can also enlarge the window for a better view. (Chapter 2 discusses these components in more detail.)

TIP *You can think of the Command window as similar to the Address or Location input box found in web browsers. It allows you to manually input data through the keyboard. It also tells you what's going on in the program. As you become more familiar with AutoCAD, you may find you don't need to rely on the Command window as much. For new users, however, the Command window can be quite helpful in understanding what steps to take as you work.*

Now let's look at AutoCAD's window components in detail.

The Pull-Down Menus

As in most Windows programs, the pull-down menus on the menu bar offer an easy-to-understand way to access the general controls and settings for AutoCAD. Within these menus you'll find the commands and functions that are the heart of AutoCAD. By clicking menu items, you can cut and paste items to and from AutoCAD, change the settings that make AutoCAD work the way you want it to, set up the measurement system you want to use, access the help system, and much more.

TIP *To close a pull-down menu without selecting anything, press the Esc key. You can also click any other part of the AutoCAD window or click another pull-down menu.*

The pull-down menu options perform four basic functions:

- Display additional menu choices
- Display a dialog box that contains settings you can change
- Issue a command to create or modify your drawing
- Offer an expanded set of the same tools found in the Draw and Modify toolbars

As you point to commands and options in the menus or toolbars, AutoCAD provides additional help for you in the form of brief descriptions of each menu option, which appear in the status bar.

Here's an exercise to let you practice with the pull-down menus and get acquainted with the way you issue AutoCAD commands:

1. Click View in the menu bar. The list of items that appears includes the commands and settings that let you control the way AutoCAD displays your drawings. Don't worry if you don't understand them yet; you'll get to know them in later chapters.

2. Move the highlight cursor slowly down the list of menu items. As you highlight each item, notice that a description of it appears in the status line at the bottom of the AutoCAD window. These descriptions help you choose the menu option you need.
3. Some of the menu items have triangular pointers to their right. This means the command has additional choices. For instance, highlight the Zoom item, and you'll see another set of options appear to the right of the menu.

TIP *If you look carefully at the command descriptions in the status bar, you'll see an odd word at the end. This is the keyboard command equivalent to the highlighted option in the menu or toolbar. You can actually type these keyboard commands to start the tool or menu item that you are pointing to. You don't have to memorize these command names, but knowing them will be helpful to you later if you want to customize AutoCAD.*

This second set of options is called a *cascading menu*. Whenever you see a pull-down menu item with the triangular pointer, you know that this item opens a cascading menu offering a more detailed set of options.

You might have noticed that other pull-down menu options are followed by an ellipsis (…). This indicates that the option displays a dialog box, as the following exercise demonstrates:

1. Move the highlight cursor to the Tools option in the menu bar.

TIP *If you prefer, you can click and drag the highlight cursor over the pull-down menu to select an option.*

ACAD only

2. Click the Options item at the bottom of the menu to open the Options dialog box. (LT users will not see a Profiles tab.)

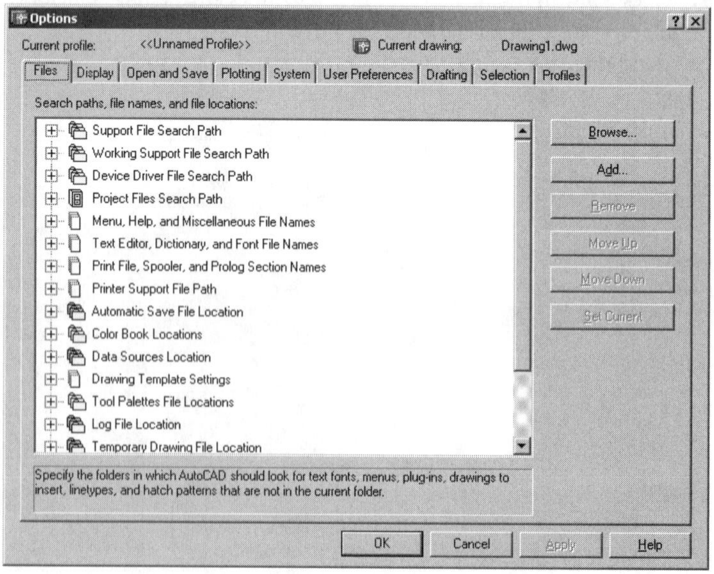

TIP *The list in the Files tab of the Options dialog box works much like Windows Explorer. Clicking the plus sign to the left of the items in the list expands the option to display more detail.*

This dialog box contains several "pages," indicated by the tabs across the top, that contain settings for controlling what AutoCAD shows you on its screens, where you want it to look for special files, and other "housekeeping" settings. You needn't worry about what these options mean at this point. Appendix B describes the Options dialog box in more detail.

ACAD only

3. In the Options dialog box, click the Open And Save tab. The options change to reveal new options. (LT users will not see the Object ARX Applications group, and the Allow Other Users To Refedit Current Drawing option in the External References (Xref) group is also not available.)

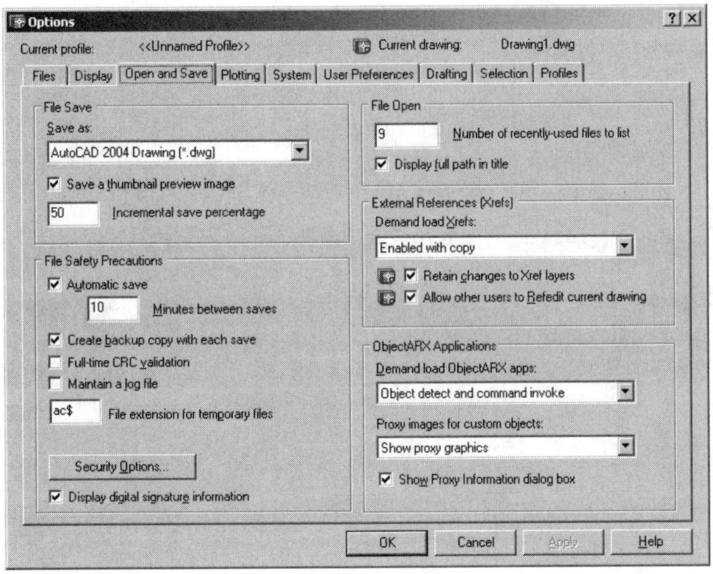

In the middle-left side of the dialog box, you'll see the Automatic Save check box, with the Minutes Between Saves input box set to 10 minutes. This setting controls how frequently AutoCAD performs an automatic save.

4. Change the 10 to 20, and then click OK. You have just changed AutoCAD's Automatic Save feature to automatically save files every 20 minutes instead of every ten.

TIP *If you want to know more about the settings in the Options dialog box, check out Appendix B.*

The third type of item you'll find on pull-down menus is a command that directly executes an AutoCAD operation. Let's try an exercise to explore these commands.

1. Click the X in the upper-right corner of the Tool palettes to close it. You won't be using it for a while.

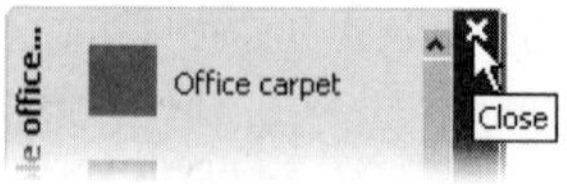

2. Click the Draw option from the menu bar, and then click the Rectangle command. Notice that the Command window now shows the following prompt:

```
Specify first corner point or [Chamfer/Elevation/Fillet/Thickness/Width]:
```

AutoCAD is asking you to select the first corner for the rectangle, and in brackets, it is offering a few options that you can take advantage of at this point in the command. Don't worry about those options right now. You'll have an opportunity to learn about command options in Chapter 2.

3. Click a point roughly in the lower-left corner of the drawing area, as shown in Figure 1.7. Now as you move your mouse, you'll see a rectangle follow the cursor with one corner fixed at the position you just selected. You'll also see the following prompt in the Command window:

```
Specify other corner point or [Dimensions]:
```

FIGURE 1.7

Selecting the first point of a rectangle

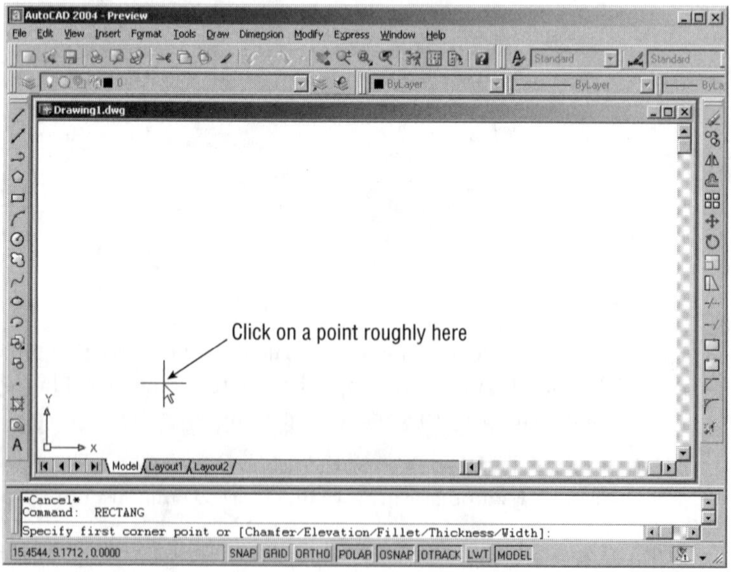

3. Click another point anywhere in the upper-right region of the drawing area. A rectangle appears (see Figure 1.8). You'll learn more about the different cursor shapes and what they mean in Chapter 2.

FIGURE 1.8

Once you've selected your first point of the rectangle, you see a rectangle follow the motion of your mouse.

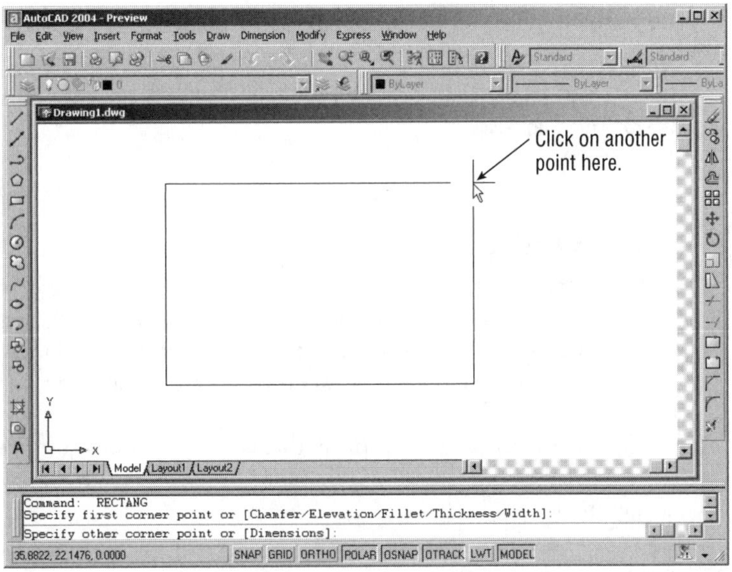

At this point, you've seen how most of AutoCAD's commands work. Many drawing and editing functions display messages in the Command window. You'll find that dialog boxes are offered when you want to change settings. Also, be aware that many of the pull-down menu items are duplicated in the toolbars, which you will explore next.

COMMUNICATING WITH AUTOCAD

AutoCAD is the perfect servant: It does everything you tell it to, and no more. You communicate with AutoCAD using the pull-down menus and the toolbars. These devices invoke AutoCAD commands. A command is a single-word instruction you give to AutoCAD telling it to do something, such as draw a line (the Line tool in the Draw toolbar) or erase an object (the Erase tool in the Modify toolbar). Whenever you invoke a command, by either typing it or selecting a menu or toolbar item, AutoCAD responds by presenting messages to you in the Command window or by displaying a dialog box.

The messages in the Command window often tell you what to do next, or they offer a list of options, usually shown within square brackets. A single command often presents several messages, which you answer to complete the command. These messages serve as an aid to new users who need a little help. If you ever get lost while using a command or forget what you are supposed to do, look at the Command window for clues. As you become more comfortable with AutoCAD, you will find that you won't need to refer to these messages as frequently.

As an additional aid, you can right-click to display a context-sensitive shortcut menu. If you are in the middle of a command and are not selecting points, this menu offers a list of options specifically related to that command. For example, if you right-click your mouse before picking the first point for the rectangle command in the previous exercise, a menu appears, offering the same options that are listed in the command prompt, plus some additional options.

Continued on next page

COMMUNICATING WITH AUTOCAD *(continued)*

A dialog box is like a form you fill out on the computer screen. It lets you adjust settings or make selections from a set of options pertaining to a command. You'll get a chance to work with commands and dialog boxes later in this chapter.

The Toolbars

Although the pull-down menus offer a full range of easy-to-understand options, they require some effort to navigate. The toolbars, on the other hand, offer quick, single-click access to the most commonly used AutoCAD features. In the default AutoCAD window arrangement, you see only the most commonly used toolbars. Other toolbars are available, but they are hidden from view until you open them.

The tools in the toolbars perform three types of actions, just like the pull-down menu commands: They display further options, open dialog boxes, and issue commands that require keyboard or cursor input.

THE TOOLBAR TOOL TIPS

AutoCAD's toolbars contain tools that represent commands. To help you understand each tool, a *tool tip* appears just below the arrow cursor when you rest the cursor on a tool. Each tool tip helps you identify the tool with its function. A tool tip appears when you follow these steps:

1. Move the arrow cursor onto one of the toolbar tools and leave it there for a moment. Notice that a brief description of the tool appears nearby—this is the tool tip. In the status bar, a more detailed description of the tool's purpose appears (see Figure 1.9).

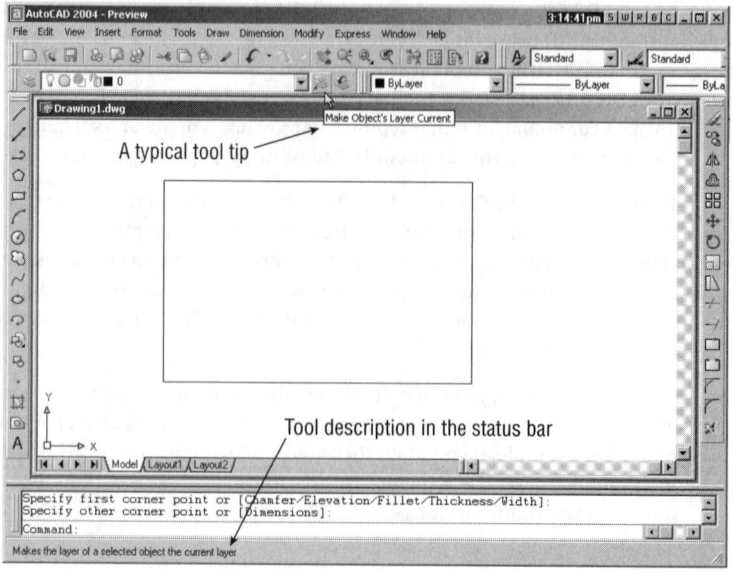

FIGURE 1.9

Tool tips show you the function of each tool in the toolbar. AutoCAD also displays a description of the tool in the status bar.

2. Move the cursor across the toolbar. As you do, notice that the tool tips and status bar descriptions change to describe each tool. The keyboard command equivalent of the tool is also shown in the status bar at the end of the description.

WORKING WITH FLYOUTS

Most toolbar tools start a command as soon as you click them, but a few tools display a set of additional tools (similar to the cascading menus in the menu bar) that are related to the tool you selected. This set of additional tools is called a toolbar *flyout*. If you've used other Windows graphics programs, chances are you've seen flyouts. Look closely at the tools just below the Express or Dimension pull-down menu options on your screen or in Figure 1.8 earlier in this chapter. You'll be able to identify which toolbar tool has a flyout; it has a small right-pointing arrow in the lower-right corner of the tool.

The following steps show you how a flyout works:

1. Move the cursor to the Zoom Window tool in the Standard toolbar. Click and hold the left mouse button to display the flyout. Don't release the mouse button.

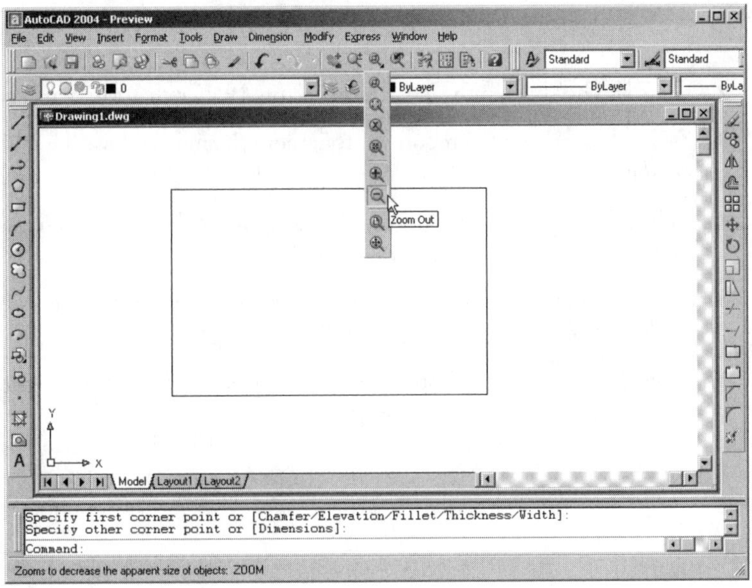

2. Still holding down the left mouse button, move the cursor over the flyout; notice that the tool tips appear here as well. Also, notice the description in the status bar.

3. Move the cursor to the Zoom Window tool at the top of the flyout and release the mouse button.

4. You don't need to use this tool yet, so press the Esc key to cancel this tool.

As you can see from this exercise, you get a lot of feedback from AutoCAD!

MOVING THE TOOLBARS

One characteristic of AutoCAD's toolbars is their mobility. They can be either floating anywhere on the AutoCAD window or in a docked position. *Docked* means the toolbar is placed against the top and side borders of the AutoCAD window so that the toolbar occupies a minimal amount of space. If you want to, you can move the toolbar to any location on your desktop, thus turning it into a floating toolbar.

Later in this section you'll find descriptions of all of AutoCAD's toolbars, but first try the following exercise to move the Standard toolbar away from its current position in the AutoCAD window.

1. Move the arrow cursor so that it points to the vertical bars, called *grab bars,* to the far left of the Standard toolbar, as shown here:

2. Click and hold down the left mouse button. Notice that a gray rectangle appears by the cursor.
3. Still holding down the mouse button, move the mouse downward. The gray box follows the cursor.
4. When the gray box is over the drawing area, release the mouse button and the Standard toolbar—now a floating toolbar—moves to its new location.

You can now move the Standard toolbar to any location on the screen that suits you. You can also change the shape of the toolbar. Try the following steps:

1. Place the cursor on the bottom-edge border of the Standard toolbar. The cursor becomes a double-headed arrow, as shown here:

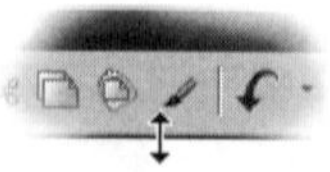

2. Click and drag the border downward. The gray rectangle jumps to a new, taller rectangle as you move the cursor.
3. When the gray rectangle changes to the shape you want, release the mouse button to reshape the toolbar.

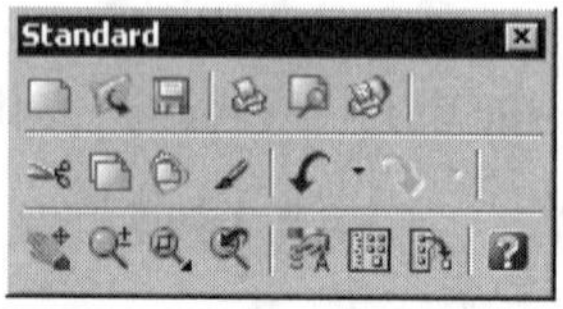

4. To move the toolbar back into its docked position, place the arrow cursor on the toolbar's title bar and slowly click and drag so that the cursor is in position in the upper-left corner of the AutoCAD window. Notice how the gray outline of the toolbar changes as it approaches its docked position.

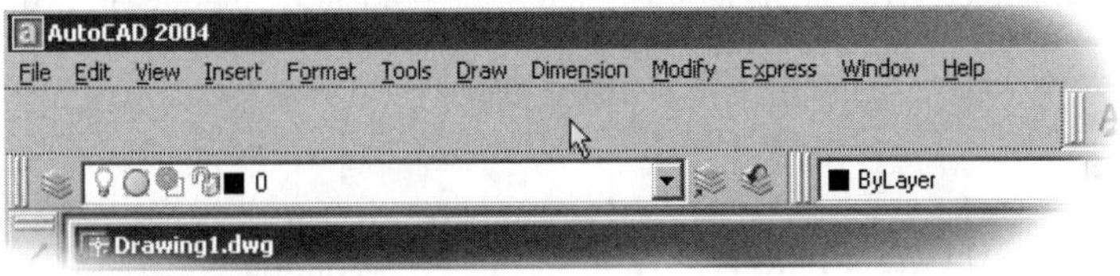

5. When the outline of the Standard toolbar is near its docked position, release the mouse button. The toolbar moves back into its previous position in the AutoCAD window.

TIP *You can also move a toolbar from a docked position to a floating one by double-clicking the toolbar's grab bar. Double-click the title bar of a floating toolbar to move the toolbar to its docked position.*

You can move and reshape any of AutoCAD's toolbars to place them out of the way and still have them ready to give you quick access to commands. You can also put them away altogether when you don't need them and bring them back at will, as shown in the following steps:

1. Click and drag the Draw toolbar from its position at the left of the AutoCAD window to a point near the center of the drawing area. Remember to click and drag the grab bars at the top of the toolbar.
2. Click the Close button in the upper-left corner of the Draw floating toolbar. This is the small square button with the X in it. The toolbar disappears.
3. To recover the Draw toolbar, right-click the border or grab bar of any toolbar—but not a toolbar button. A shortcut menu of toolbars appears.
4. Locate and select Draw in the shortcut menu. The Draw toolbar reappears.
5. Click and drag the Draw toolbar back to its docked position in the far-left side of the AutoCAD window.

TIP *If you do not want the toolbar to dock but instead want it to appear "floating" near the border of the AutoCAD Window, you can press the Ctrl key before you click and drag the toolbar into position. This prevents toolbars from automatically falling into a docked position.*

AutoCAD remembers your toolbar arrangement between sessions. When you exit and then reopen AutoCAD later, the AutoCAD window appears just as you left it.

TERMINOLOGY TO REMEMBER: CASCADING MENU

When this book asks you to select an option from the pull-down menu, you will see the notation *Menu ➢ Option*. For cascading menus, the notation will be *Menu ➢ Option ➢ Option*; the second *➢ Option* is in a cascading menu. In either case, the selected menu option issues a command that performs the function being discussed. As mentioned earlier, the actual command name appears in the status bar when you point to a menu option or toolbar tool.

You may have noticed several other toolbars listed in toolbar shortcut menu that don't appear in the AutoCAD window. To keep the screen from becoming cluttered, many of the toolbars are not placed on the screen by default. The toolbars you'll be using most often are displayed first; others that are less frequently used are kept out of sight until you need them and select them from the list. Here are brief descriptions of all the toolbars available:

3D Orbit Tools to control 3D views (not available in LT).

CAD Standards Tools that let you check the layer, dimension, and text styles against standards that you have created (not available in LT).

Dimension Commands that help you dimension your drawings. Many of these commands are duplicated in the Dimension pull-down menu. See Chapter 9.

Draw Commands for creating common objects, including lines, arcs, circles, curves, ellipses, and text. This toolbar appears in the AutoCAD window by default. Many of these commands are duplicated in the Draw pull-down menu.

Draw Order Commands that let you arrange the order of overlapping objects. If an object covers another object that you need to have visible, you can use the Draw Order to "move" an object behind another or to the back of a set of objects (not available in LT).

Inquiry Commands for finding distances, point coordinates, object properties, mass properties, and areas.

Insert Commands for importing other drawings, raster images, and OLE objects.

Layer Drop-down list and tools for controlling layer properties located just below the Standard toolbar.

Layouts Tools that let you set up drawing layouts for viewing, printing, and plotting.

Modify Commands for editing existing objects. You can move, copy, rotate, erase, trim, extend, and so on. Many of these commands are duplicated in the Modify pull-down menu.

Modify II Commands for editing special complex objects such as polylines, multilines, 3D solids, and hatches.

Properties for a set of drop-down lists and tools for manipulating the properties of objects. This toolbar is normally docked to the right of the Layer toolbar, just below the Standard toolbar.

Object Snap Tools to help you select specific points on objects, such as endpoints and midpoints. See Chapter 3.

Refedit Tools that allow you to make changes to symbols or background drawings that are imported as external reference drawings. See Chapter 13 for more about external references (not available in LT).

Reference Commands that control cross-referencing of drawings. See Chapters 6 and 13.

Render Commands to operate AutoCAD's rendering feature. See Chapter 18 (not available in LT).

Shade Offers tools to control the way 3D models are displayed. See Chapter 16 for more on Shade (not available in LT).

Solids Commands for creating 3D solids. See Chapter 19 (not available in LT).

Solids Editing Command for editing 3D solids. See Chapter 19 (not available in LT).

Standard The most frequently used commands for view control, file management, and editing. This toolbar is normally docked below the menu bar.

Styles Tools that control style options such as text styles and dimension styles.

Surfaces Commands for creating 3D surfaces. See Chapters 16 and 17 (not available in LT).

Text Tools for creating and editing text.

UCS Tools for setting up a plane on which to work. UCS stands for User Coordinate System. This is most useful for 3D modeling, but it can be helpful in 2D drafting, as well. See Chapter 17.

UCS II Tools for selecting from a set of predefined user coordinate systems.

View Offers tools to control the way you view 3D models. See Chapter 16 for more on 3D views.

Viewports Tools that let you create and edit multiple views to your drawing. See Chapter 13 for more about viewports.

Web Tools for accessing the World Wide Web, as discussed in Chapter 22.

Zoom Commands that allow you to navigate your drawing.

You'll get a chance to work with all the toolbars over the course of this book. If you use the book simply as a reference, be sure to read through the exercises for explanations of which tools to use for specific operations.

MENUS VERSUS THE KEYBOARD

Throughout this book, you will be told to select commands and command options from the pull-down menus and toolbars. For new and experienced users alike, menus and toolbars offer an easy-to-remember method for accessing commands. If you are an experienced AutoCAD user who is used to the earlier versions of AutoCAD, you still have the option of entering commands directly from the keyboard. Most of the keyboard commands you know and love still work as they did.

Another method for accessing commands is to use accelerator keys, which are special keystrokes that open and activate pull-down menu options. You might have noticed that the commands in the menu bar and the items in the pull-down menus all have an underlined character. By pressing the Alt key followed by the key corresponding to the underlined character you activate that command or option, without having to engage the mouse. For example, to issue File ➢ Open, press Alt, then F, and then finally O (Alt+F+O).

Many tools and commands have keyboard shortcuts; shortcuts are one-, two-, or three-letter abbreviations of a command name. As you become more proficient with AutoCAD, you may find these shortcuts helpful. As you work through this book, the shortcuts will be identified for your reference.

Finally, if you are feeling adventurous, you can create your own accelerator keys and keyboard shortcuts for executing commands by adding them to the AutoCAD support files. Chapter 21 discusses how to customize menus, toolbars, and keyboard shortcuts.

Working with AutoCAD

Now that you've been introduced to the AutoCAD window, let's try using a few of AutoCAD's commands. First, you'll open a sample file and make a few simple modifications to it. In the process, you'll become familiar with some common methods of operation in AutoCAD.

Opening an Existing File

In this exercise, you will get a chance to see and use a typical Select File dialog box. To start with, you will open an existing file.

1. From the menu bar, choose File ➢ Close. A message appears asking you if you want to save the changes you've made to the current drawing. Click No.
2. Choose File ➢ Open to open the Select File dialog box. This is a typical Windows file dialog box, with an added twist. The large Preview box on the right allows you to preview a drawing before you open it, thereby saving time while searching for files. To the left is a panel known as the Places List in which you can find frequently used locations on your computer or the Internet.

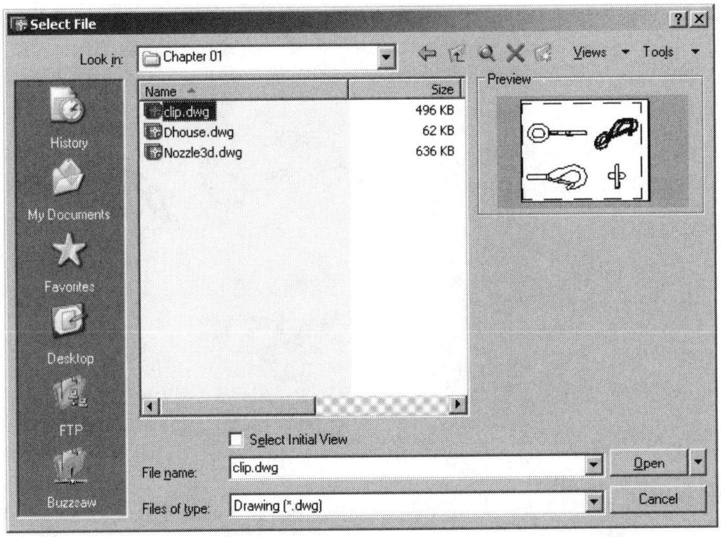

TIP *If you don't see a Preview box in the Select File dialog box, click the word View in the upper-right corner, and then select Preview from the list that appears.*

3. In the Select File dialog box, open the Look In drop-down list and locate the `\AutoCAD2004\Projects\Chapter 01` folder. (You may need to explore the list to find it.) The file list changes to show the contents of the `\AutoCAD2004\Projects\Chapter 01` folder.

4. Move the arrow to the `Clip.dwg` file and click it. Notice that the `Clip.dwg` filename now appears in the File Name input box above the file list. Also, the Preview box now shows a thumbnail image of the file.

TIP *The* `Clip.dwg` *drawing is included on the companion CD. If you cannot find this file, be sure you installed the sample drawings from the companion CD. See the Readme file on the CD for installation instructions.*

5. Click the OK button at the bottom of the Select File dialog box. AutoCAD opens the `Clip.dwg` file, as shown in Figure 1.10.

FIGURE 1.10

The Layout view of the `Clip.dwg` file

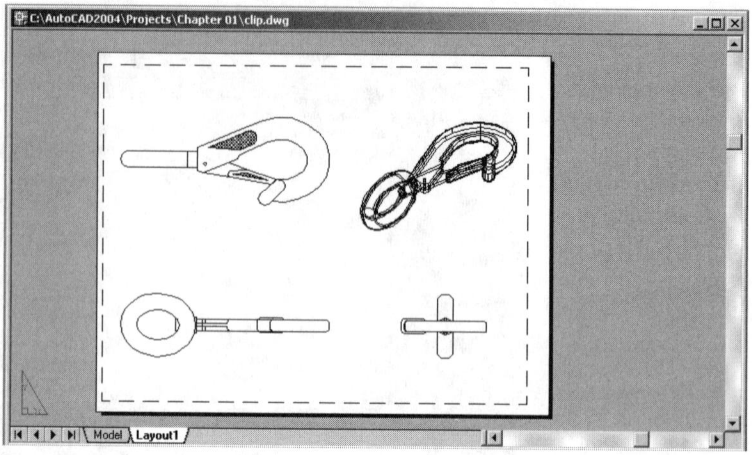

The `Clip.dwg` file opens to display a Layout tab view of the drawing. You will know this by looking at the tabs at the bottom of the AutoCAD Window. Currently, the Layout1 tab is highlighted.

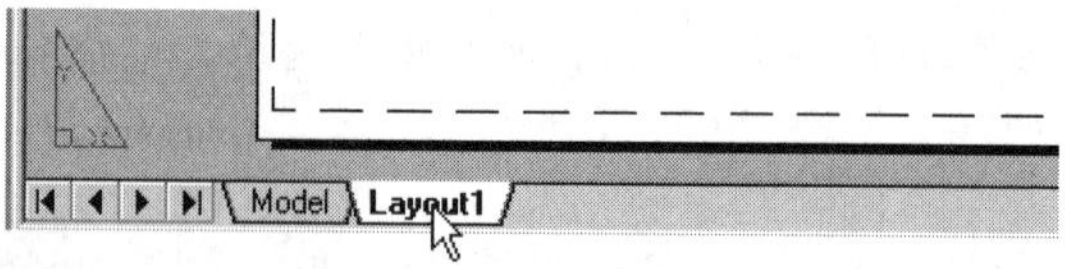

You may recall that a layout is a type of view that lets you lay out different views of your drawing in preparation for printing. Also notice that the AutoCAD window's title bar displays the name of the drawing. This offers easy identification of the file.

This particular file contains both 2D drawings and a 3D model of a typical locking clip. The Layout tab view shows a top, front, and right side view as well as an isometric view.

Getting a Closer Look

One of the most frequently used commands is Zoom, which gives you a closer look at a part of your drawing. It offers a variety of ways to control your view. Now you'll enlarge a portion of the clip drawing to get a more detailed look. To tell AutoCAD what area you want to enlarge, you use what is called a *zoom window*.

You'll start by switching to a Model Space view of the drawing. The Model tab places you in a workspace where you do most of your drawing creation and editing.

1. Click the Model tab at the bottom of the AutoCAD window.

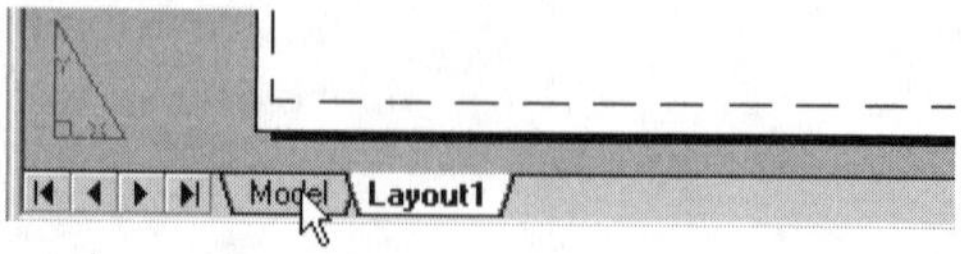

Your view changes to show the full 3D model with the 2D representations of the model.

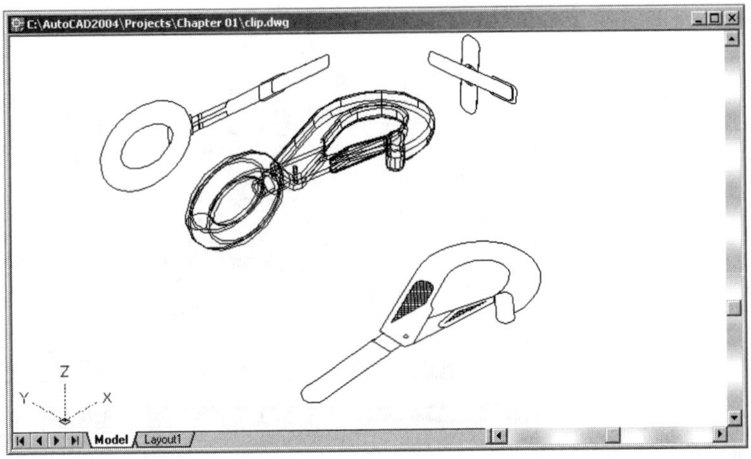

2. Choose View ➢ 3D Views ➢ Plan View ➢ World UCS. You can also type **Plan↵ ↵**. Your display changes to a two-dimensional view looking down on the drawing.

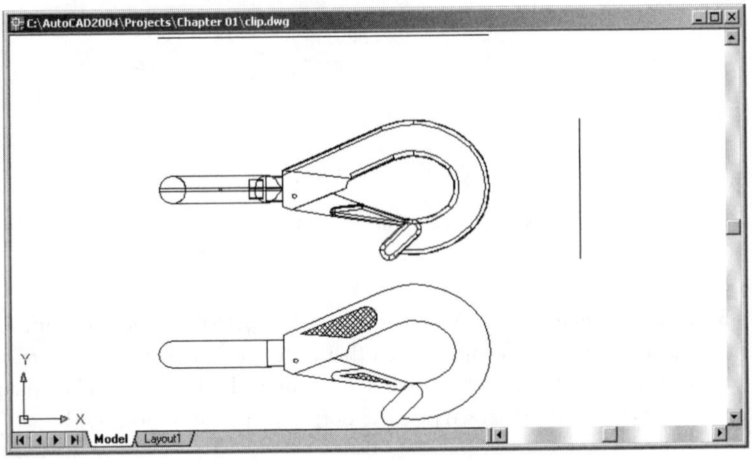

3. Click the Zoom Window button on the Standard toolbar.

   You can also choose View ➢ Zoom ➢ Window from the pull-down menu or type the command: **Z↵ W↵**.

4. The Command window displays the `First corner:` prompt. Look at the top image in Figure 1.11. Move the crosshair cursor to a location similar to the one shown in the figure; then left-click the mouse. Move the cursor and the rectangle appears, with one corner fixed on the point you just picked, while the other corner follows the cursor.

FIGURE 1.11
Placing the zoom window around the clip

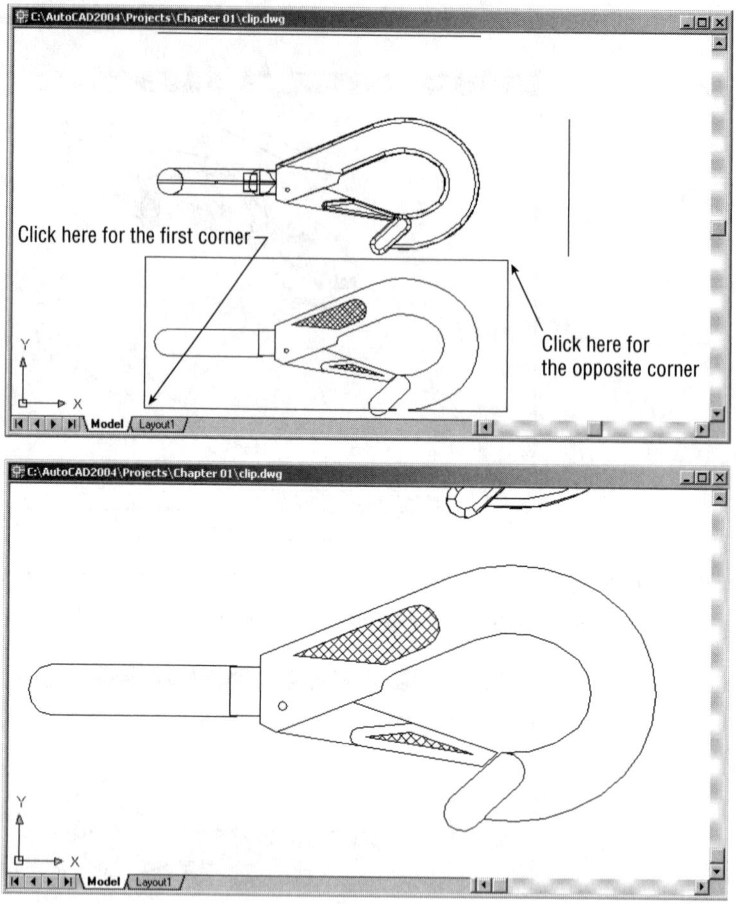

5. The Command window now displays the `Specify first corner:` and `Specify opposite corner:` prompts. Position the other corner of the window so it encloses the lower image of the clip, as shown in the top image in Figure 1.11, and left-click the mouse again. The clip enlarges to fill the screen (see the bottom image in Figure 1.11).

TIP *If you decide that you don't like the position of the first point you pick while defining the zoom window, you can right-click the mouse and re-select the first point. This only works when you enter **Z↵ W↵** to issue the Zoom Window command or when you select Zoom Window from the Standard toolbar.*

In this exercise, you used the Window option of the Zoom command to define an area to enlarge for your close-up view. You saw how AutoCAD prompts you to indicate first one corner of the selection window and then the other. These messages are helpful for first-time users of AutoCAD. You will use the Window option frequently—not just to define views, but also to select objects for editing.

Getting a close-up view of your drawing is crucial to working accurately, but you'll often want to return to a previous view to get the overall picture. To do so, click the Zoom Previous button on the Standard toolbar.

Do this now, and the previous view—one showing the entire clip—returns to the screen. You can also get there by choosing View ➢ Zoom ➢ Previous.

You can quickly enlarge or reduce your view using the Zoom Realtime button on the Standard toolbar.

TIP *You can also zoom in and out using the Zoom In and Zoom Out buttons in the Zoom Window flyout of the Standard toolbar. The Zoom In button shows a magnifying glass with a plus sign; the Zoom Out button shows a minus sign. If you have a mouse equipped with a scroll wheel, you can zoom in and out just by turning the wheel. The location of the cursor at the time you move the wheel will determine the center of the zoom. A click-and-drag of the scroll wheel will let you pan your view.*

1. Click the Zoom Realtime button on the Standard toolbar. You can also right-click and choose Zoom from the shortcut menu. The cursor changes to a magnifying glass.
2. Place the Zoom Realtime cursor slightly above the center of the drawing area, and then click and drag downward. Your view zooms out to show more of the drawing.
3. While still holding the left mouse button, move the cursor upward. Your view zooms in to enlarge your view. When you have a view similar to the one shown in Figure 1.12, release the mouse button. (Don't worry if you don't get *exactly* the same view as the figure. This is just for practice.)

FIGURE 1.12

The final view you want to achieve in step 3 of the exercise

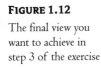

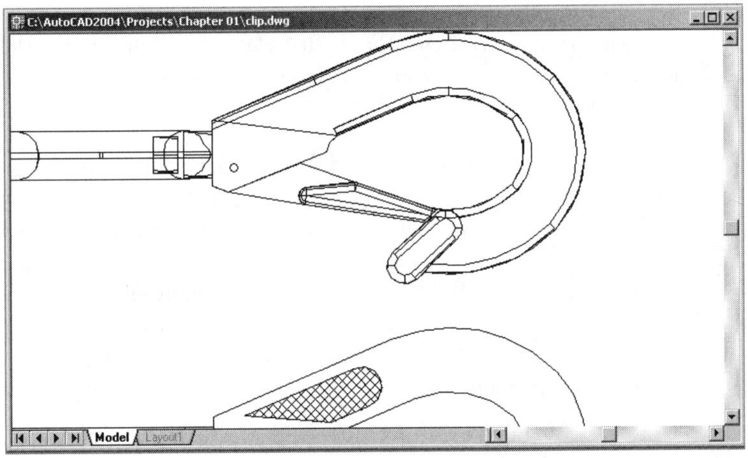

4. You are still in Zoom Realtime mode. Click and drag the mouse again to see how you can further adjust your view. To exit, you can select another command besides a Zoom or Pan command, press the Esc key, or right-click your mouse.

5. Right-click now, and choose Exit from the shortcut menu to exit the Zoom Realtime command.

As you can see from this exercise, you have a wide range of options for viewing your drawings, just by using a few buttons. In fact, these buttons, along with the scroll bars at the right side and bottom of the AutoCAD window, are all you need to control the display of 2D drawings.

THE AERIAL VIEW WINDOW

The *Aerial View* window is an optional AutoCAD display tool. It gives you an overall view of your drawing, regardless of the magnification you are using for the drawing editor. Aerial View also makes it easier to get around in a large-scale drawing. You'll find that this feature is best suited to complex drawings that cover great areas, such as site plans, topographical maps, or city planning documents.

You'll find a detailed description of the Aerial View window in Chapter 6. As you become more comfortable with AutoCAD, you might want to try it.

Saving a File As You Work

It is a good idea to save your file periodically as you work on it. You can save it under its original name (choose File ➢ Save) or under a different name (choose File ➢ Save As), thereby creating a new file.

By default, AutoCAD automatically saves your work at 10-minute intervals under the name `AUTO.SV$`; this is known as the *Automatic Save* feature. Using settings in the Options dialog box or system variables, you can change the name of the autosaved file and control the time between autosaves. See Chapter 3 for details.

TIP *By default, in Windows XP, the* `AUTO.SV$` *file is stored in the* `C:\Documents and Settings\User Name\Local Settings\Temp\`. *You can find the exact location for your system by entering* ***Savefilepath*** *↵ at the command prompt.*

Let's first try the Save command. This quickly saves the drawing in its current state without exiting the program.

Choose File ➢ Save. You will notice some disk activity while AutoCAD saves the file to the hard disk, and you'll see a progress indicator in the status bar. As an alternative to choosing File ➢ Save, you can press **Alt+F S**. This is the accelerator key combination, also called *hotkey*, for the File ➢ Save command.

Now try the Save As command. This command displays a dialog box that allows you to save the current file under a new name.

1. Choose File ➢ Save As or type **Saveas**↵ at the command prompt to open the Select File dialog box. Notice that the current filename, `Clip.dwg`, is highlighted in the File Name input box.

2. Type **Myfirst**. As you type, the name `Clip.dwg` disappears from the input box and is replaced by `Myfirst`. You don't need to enter the .dwg filename extension. AutoCAD adds it to the filename automatically when it saves the file.

3. Click the Save button. The dialog box closes, and you will notice some disk activity.

You now have a copy of the clip file under the name `Myfirst.dwg`. The name of the file displayed in the AutoCAD window's title bar has changed to `Myfirst`. From now on, when you use the File ➢ Save option, your drawing will be saved under its new name. Saving files under a different name can be useful when you are creating alternatives or when you just want to save one of several ideas you have been trying out.

TIP *If you are working with a small monitor, you might want to consider closing the Draw and Modify toolbars. The Draw and Modify pull-down menus offer the same commands, so you won't lose any functionality by closing these toolbars. If you really want to maximize your drawing area, you can also turn off the scroll bars and reduce the Command window to a single line. Appendix B shows how to do this. You can also gain some extra drawing space by clicking the Maximize button in the upper-right corner of the drawing area.*

Making Changes

You will frequently make changes to your drawings. In fact, one of AutoCAD's primary advantages is the ease with which you can make changes. The following exercise shows you a typical sequence of operations involved in making a change to a drawing:

1. From the Modify toolbar, click the Erase tool (the one with a pencil eraser touching paper). This activates the Erase command. You can also choose Modify ➢ Erase from the pull-down menu.

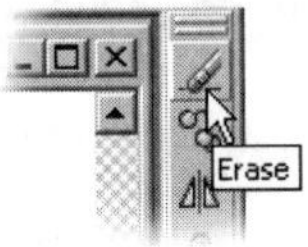

Notice that the cursor has turned into a small square; this square is called the *pickbox*. You also see `Select objects:` in the command prompt area. This message helps remind new users what to do.

2. Place the pickbox on the cross hatch pattern of the clip (see Figure 1.13) and click it. The cross hatch of the clip becomes highlighted. The pickbox and the `Select object:` prompt remain, telling you that you can continue to select objects.

3. Now press ↵. The cross hatch disappears. You have just erased a part of the drawing.

In this exercise, you first issued the Erase command, and then you selected an object by clicking it using a pickbox. The pickbox tells you that you must select items on the screen. Once you've done that, press ↵ to move on to the next step. This sequence of steps is common to many of the commands you will work with in AutoCAD.

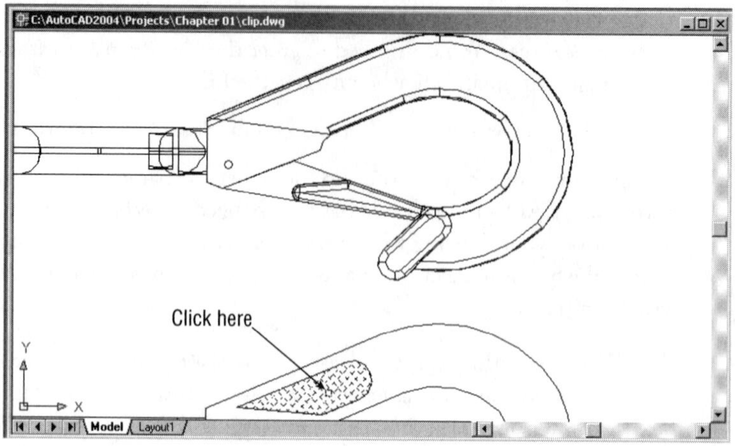

FIGURE 1.13
Erasing a portion of the clip

TIP *You can also click an object or a set of objects and then press the Delete key.*

Opening Multiple Files

You can have multiple documents open at the same time in AutoCAD. This can be especially helpful if you want to exchange parts of drawings between files or if you just want another file open for reference. Try the following exercise to see how multiple documents work in AutoCAD.

1. Choose File ➢ New to open the Select Template dialog box.

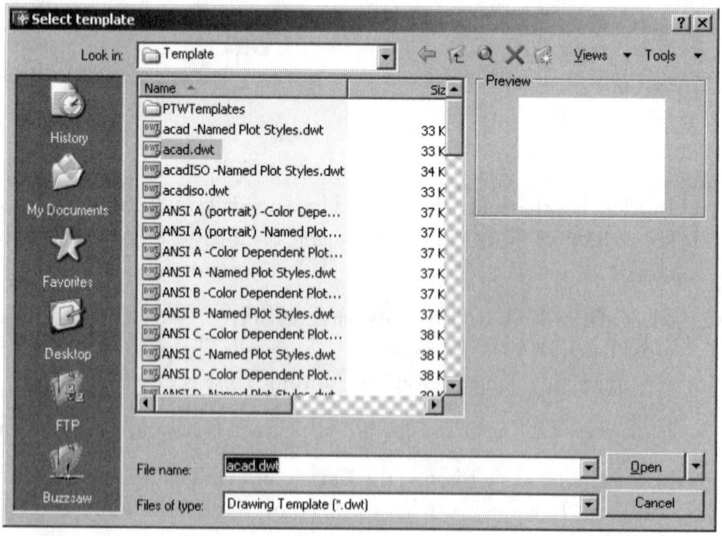

2. Make sure `acad.dwt` is selected, and then click Open.

NOTE *If you see the Create New Drawing dialog box after step 2, click the Start From Scratch button and select* ***Imperial****, then click OK and AutoCAD will display a default document. You'll learn more about the Create New Drawing dialog box in Chapter 2.*

3. Choose Window ➢ Tile Vertically to get a view of both drawing files. The options in the Window pull-down menu act just like their counterparts in other Windows programs that allow multiple document editing.

TIP *When you create a new file in AutoCAD, you are actually opening a copy of a template file as you saw in step 1. A template file is a blank file that is set up for specific drawing types. The* `acad.dwt` *file is a generic template set up for imperial measurements. Another template file called* `acadiso.dwt` *is a generic template useful for metric measurements. Other templates are set up for specific drawing sheet sizes and measurement systems. You'll learn more about templates in Chapter 6.*

You can now see both of the files you have open. Let's see what can be done with these two files.

1. Click in the window with the clip drawing to make it active.
2. Choose View ➢ Zoom ➢ All to get an overall view of the drawing.
3. Click the 2D version of the clip at the bottom of the clip drawing to select it. A series of squares appears on the drawing. These are called handles, and you'll learn more about them in the next chapter.
4. Click and drag the selected object, but avoid clicking any of the blue squares. You'll see a small rectangle appear next to the cursor.

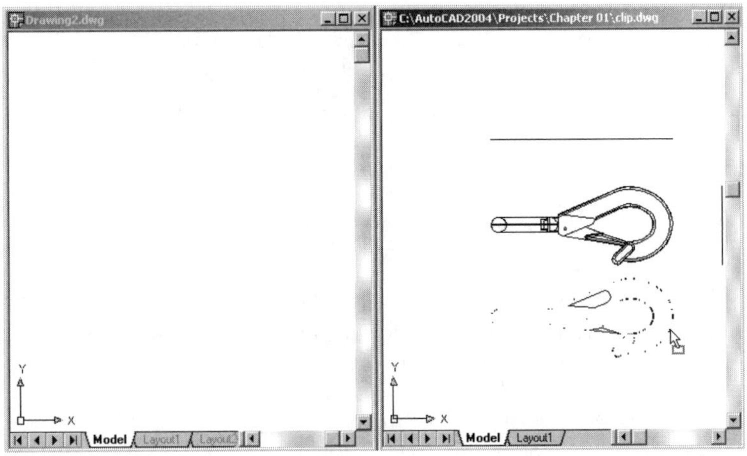

5. While still holding the left mouse button, drag the cursor to the new file window. When you see the clip appear in the new drawing window, release the mouse button. You've just copied part of a drawing from one file to another.

Now you have two files open at once. You can have as many files open as you want, as long as you have adequate memory to accommodate them. You can control the individual document windows as you would any window, using the Window pull-down menu or the window control buttons in the upper-right corner of the document window.

Adding a Pre-Drawn Symbol with the Tool Palette

In the last exercise, you saw how you can easily copy an object from one file to another using a click-and-drag method. Now let's take a look at another tool that lets you click and drag symbols into your drawings.

1. Click the Tool Palettes tool in the Standard toolbar to open the Tool palettes.
2. Make sure the Sample Office Project tab is selected in the Tool palettes, and then click and drag the Chair - Desk symbol from the Tool palettes into the new file window. The chair symbol appears in the window.
3. Click the Imperial Hatch tab, and then click and drag any of the solid patterns into the chair. The chair is filled with the solid pattern.

While you've got the Tool palettes open, let's look at some of its unique features.

1. Right-click the Tool palettes, and then choose Transparency from the shortcut menu to open the Transparency dialog box.

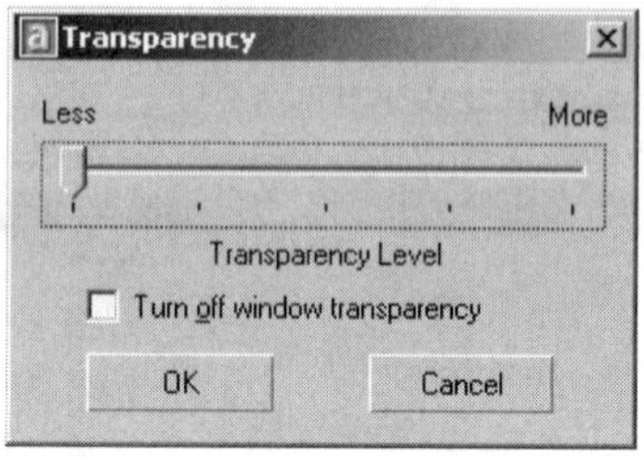

2. Move the Transparency Level slider to the middle of the dialog box, and then click OK. You now see objects that are "behind" the Tool palettes.

You can't actually select points that are "behind" the palettes as you draw, but the Transparency feature can help you visualize your drawing more easily while the palettes are open.

Let's take another look at a display feature of the Tool palettes.

TIP *The Command window also has a Transparency option. To use it, you must first move the Command window to an undocked position toward the middle of the AutoCAD window. You can then right-click the Command window title bar and choose Transparency. You will see the same Transparency dialog box you see when you right-click the Tool palettes and choose Transparency.*

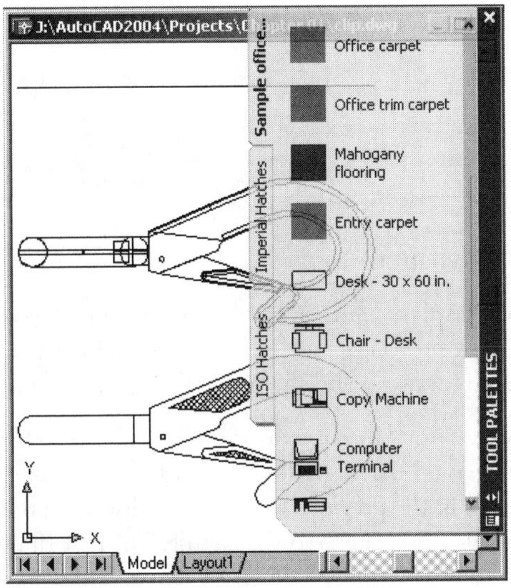

1. Right-click the Tool palettes again, and choose Auto-Hide.
2. Move the cursor away from the Tool palettes. The Tool salettes close so that just the Tool palettes title bar is visible.
3. Move the cursor on top of the Tool palettes title bar. The palette opens to reveal the palettes.
4. Turn the Auto-Hide feature off by right-clicking the Tool palettes and selecting Auto-Hide.
5. Click the X in the upper-right corner of the Tool palettes.

The Tool palettes offer a way to quickly add fill patterns and pre-drawn symbols to your drawing. It is a great tool to help you manage your library of custom, pre-drawn symbols. You've just gotten a taste of what it can do, but to make full use of its capabilities, you'll need to learn about blocks, hatch patterns, and the AutoCAD DesignCenter. You won't see much of this tool in the beginning of this book, but keep it in the back of your mind as you begin to learn more about AutoCAD. After finishing the first part of this book, you can skip ahead to Chapter 22 to learn how to use and customize the Tool palettes.

Closing AutoCAD

When you are done with your work on one drawing, you can open another drawing, temporarily leave AutoCAD, or close AutoCAD entirely. To close all the open files at once and exit AutoCAD, choose File ➢ Exit.

1. Choose File ➢ Exit, the last item in the File menu. A dialog box appears, asking you if you want to "Save Changes to `Myfirst.dwg`?" and offering three buttons labeled Yes, No, and Cancel.

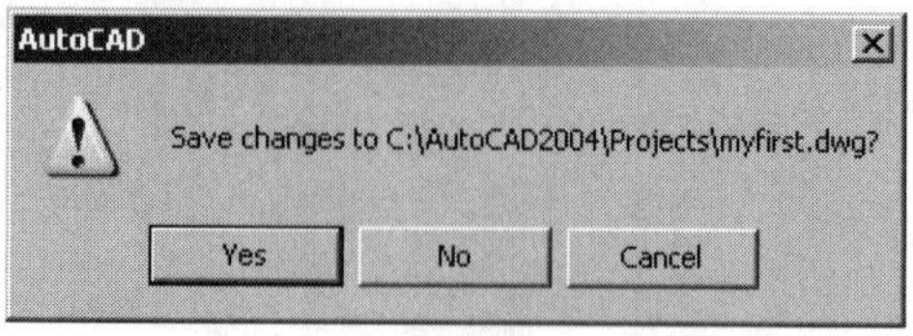

2. Click the No button.

3. AutoCAD displays another message asking you if you want to save `Drawing2.dwg`, which is the new drawing you opened in the last exercise. Click the No button again. AutoCAD closes both the clip drawing and the new drawing and exits without saving your changes.

Whenever you attempt to exit a drawing that has been changed, you get this same inquiry box. This request for confirmation is a safety feature that lets you change your mind and save your changes before you exit AutoCAD. In the previous exercise, you discarded the changes you made, so the clip drawing reverts to its state before you erased the handle. The new drawing is completely discarded, and no file is saved.

If you only want to exit AutoCAD temporarily, you can minimize it so it appears as a button on the Windows XP or Windows2000 status bar. You do this by clicking the Minimize button in the upper-right corner of the AutoCAD window; the Minimize button is the title-bar button that looks like an underscore (_). Alternatively, you can use the Alt+Tab key combination to switch to another program.

TIP *The AutoCAD Express Tools offer the Close All Drawings and Quick Exit tools that let you close multiple .dwg files at one time. See Chapter 20 for more on the Express tools.*

If You Want to Experiment...

Try opening and closing some of the sample drawing files on the accompanying CD.

1. Start AutoCAD by choosing Start ➢ Programs ➢ AutoCAD 2004 ➢ AutoCAD 2004.

2. Close the AutoCAD 2004 window, and then choose File ➢ Open.

3. Use the dialog box to open the `Myfirst` file again. Notice that the drawing appears on the screen with the handle enlarged. This is the view you had on screen when you used the Save command in the earlier exercise.

4. Erase the cross hatch, as you did in the earlier exercise.

5. Choose File ➢ Open again. This time, open the `Dhouse` file from the `Figures` folder. The 3D `Dhouse` drawing opens.

6. Choose File ➢ Exit. Notice that you exit AutoCAD without getting the Save Changes dialog box for the Dhouse drawing. This is because you didn't make any changes to the `Dhouse` file.

Chapter 2

Creating Your First Drawing

THIS CHAPTER EXAMINES SOME of AutoCAD's basic functions. You will get a chance to practice with the drawing editor by building a simple drawing to use in later exercises. You'll learn how to give input to AutoCAD, interpret prompts, and get help when you need it. This chapter also covers the use of coordinate systems to give AutoCAD exact measurements for objects. You'll see how to select objects you've drawn and how to specify base points for moving and copying.

If you're not a beginning AutoCAD user, you might want to move on to the more complex material in Chapter 3. You can use the files supplied on the companion CD to continue the tutorials at that point.

Topics include the following:

- Getting to Know the Draw Toolbar
- Starting Your First Drawing
- Specifying Distances with Coordinates
- Interpreting the Cursor Modes and Understanding Prompts
- Selecting Objects and Editing with Grips
- Getting Help
- If You Want to Experiment…

Getting to Know the Draw Toolbar

Your first task in learning how to draw in AutoCAD is simply to draw a line. But before you begin drawing, take a moment to familiarize yourself with the toolbar you'll be using more than any other to create objects with AutoCAD: the Draw toolbar.

1. Start AutoCAD just as you did in the first chapter, by choosing Start ➢ All Programs ➢ Autodesk ➢ AutoCAD 2004 ➢ AutoCAD 2004. If you see the Startup dialog box, click Cancel to go directly to the default Drawing1 document. You'll get a chance to work with the Startup dialog box later in this chapter.

2. In the AutoCAD window, move the arrow cursor to the top icon in the Draw toolbar, which is the vertical toolbar at the far left of the AutoCAD window, and rest it there so that the tool tip appears.

3. Slowly move the arrow cursor downward over the other tools in the Draw toolbar, and read each tool tip.

In most cases, you'll be able to guess what each tool does by looking at its icon. The icon with an arc, for instance, indicates that the tool draws arcs; the one with the ellipse shows that the tool draws ellipses; and so on. For further clarification, the tool tip gives you the name of the tool. In addition, the status bar at the bottom of the AutoCAD window gives you information about a tool. For example, if you point to the Multiline Text tool at the bottom of the Draw toolbar, the status bar reads `Creates a multiple-line text object`. It also shows you the actual AutoCAD command name: `MTEXT`. This command is what you type in the Command window to invoke the Multiline Text tool. You also use `MTEXT` if you are writing a macro or creating your own custom tools.

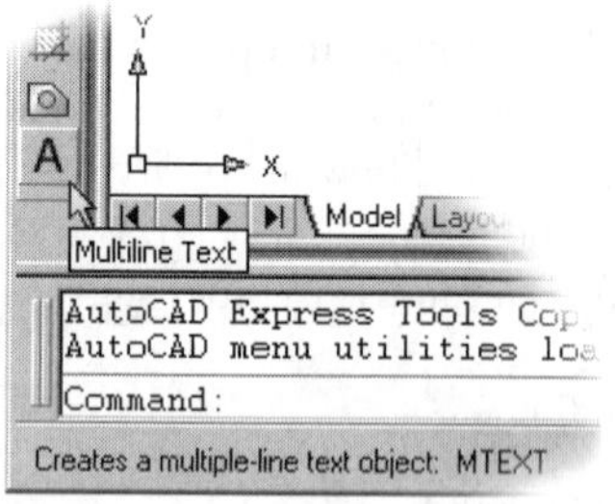

Table 2.1 will aid you in navigating the two main toolbars, Draw and Modify. You'll get experience with many of AutoCAD's tools as you work through this book.

TABLE 2.1: THE OPTIONS ON THE DRAW AND MODIFY TOOLBARS

Draw: Icon	Draw: Tool	Modify: Icon	Modify: Tool
	Line		Erase
	Construction Line (Xline)		Copy Object
	Polyline (Pline)		Mirror
	Polygon		Offset
	Rectangle		Array
	Arc		Move

Continued on next page

TABLE 2.1: THE OPTIONS ON THE DRAW AND MODIFY TOOLBARS *(continued)*

DRAW		**MODIFY**	
ICON	**TOOL**	**ICON**	**TOOL**
	Circle		Rotate
	Revcloud (new)	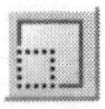	Scale
	Spline		Stretch
	Ellipse	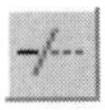	Trim
	Ellispse Arc (new since 2000)		Extend
	Insert Block	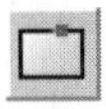	Break at Point
	Make Block	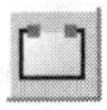	Break
	Point		Chamfer
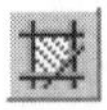	Hatch		Fillet
	Region	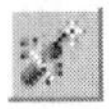	Explode
	Multiline Text		

As you saw in Chapter 1, clicking a tool issues a command. Clicking and dragging some tools opens a flyout. A flyout offers further options for that tool. If a tool has a flyout, you'll see a small triangle in the lower-right corner of the tool.

1. Click and drag the Zoom Window tool on the Standard toolbar. A flyout appears with an additional set of tools. These tools allow you to adjust your view in various ways.

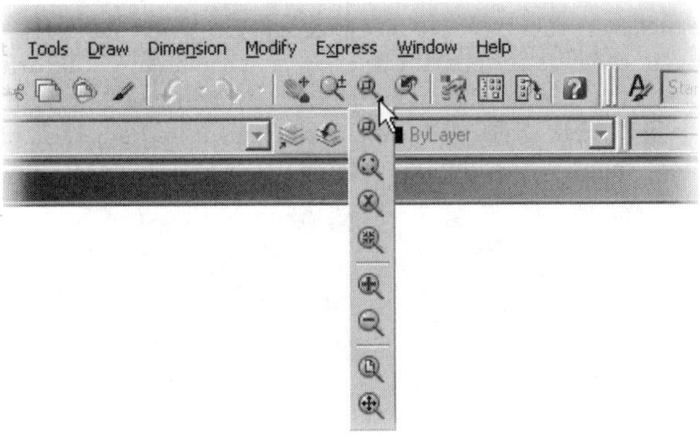

2. Move the cursor down the flyout to the last tool, until the tool tip reads "Zoom Extents"; then let go of the mouse button. Notice that the icon representing the Zoom Window tool now changes and becomes the icon from the flyout that represents Zoom Extents.

By selecting the Zoom Extents tool, you also issue the Zoom Extents command. This command adjusts the view of the drawing so that it fills the drawing area. Since nothing is currently in the drawing, the view doesn't change. You'll use Zoom Extents in Chapter 3 and see how it behaves when there are objects in the drawing.

3. For now, you'll want to keep the Zoom Window tool visible in the Standard toolbar, so click and drag the Zoom Extents tool, and then select Zoom Window from the top of the flyout. Press the Escape key to cancel the Zoom Window command. You'll get a chance to use Zoom Window in Chapter 3.

By making the most recently selected option on a flyout the default option for the toolbar tool, AutoCAD gives you quick access to frequently used commands. A word of caution, however: This feature can confuse the first-time AutoCAD user. Also, the grouping of options on the flyout menus is not always self-explanatory—even to a veteran AutoCAD user.

TIP *If you find you are working a lot with one particular flyout, you can easily open a version of the flyout as a floating toolbar so that all the flyout options are readily available with a single click. For example, to open the Zoom flyout you just used as a toolbar, right-click any toolbar and choose Zoom from the shortcut menu.*

WORKING WITH TOOLBARS

As you work through the exercises, this book will show you the tools to choose, along with the toolbar or flyout that contains the tool. Don't be alarmed, however, if the toolbars you see in the examples don't look exactly like those on your screen. To save page space, in some places I have oriented the toolbars and flyouts horizontally for the illustrations; the ones on your screen might be oriented vertically, like the Draw and Modify toolbars to the left and right of the AutoCAD window. Although the shape of your toolbars and flyouts may differ from the ones you see in this book, the contents are the same. So when you see a graphic showing a tool, focus on the tool icon itself with its tool tip name, along with the name of the toolbar in which it is shown.

Starting Your First Drawing

In Chapter 1, you looked at a pre-existing sample drawing. This time you will begin to draw on your own drawing, by creating a door that will be used in later exercises. First, though, you must learn how to tell AutoCAD what you want, and, even more important, you must understand what AutoCAD wants from you.

TIP *In this chapter, you'll start to see instructions for both Imperial measurement and metric users. In general, you will see the instructions for Imperial measurement first, followed by the metric instructions. You won't be dealing with inches or centimeters yet, however. You're just getting to know the AutoCAD system.*

Start by opening the Create New Drawing dialog box. This dialog box helps new user set up drawings quickly.

1. Choose Tools ➢ Options to open the Options dialog box.

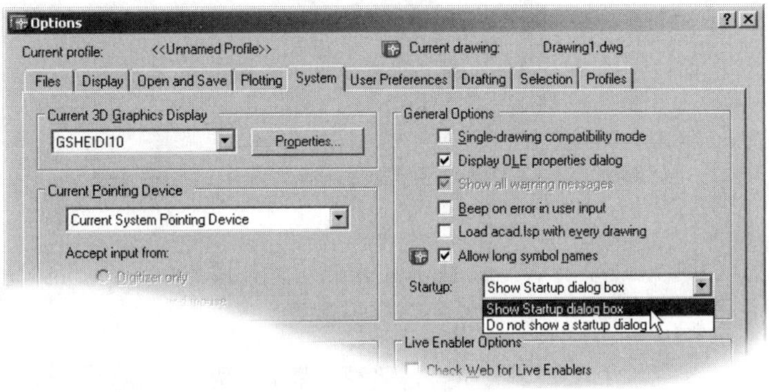

2. Click the System tab.
3. In the General Options group, click the Startup drop-down list and select Show Startup Dialog Box.
4. Click OK to apply the new setting and exit the dialog box.

Selecting the Show Startup Dialog Box option causes AutoCAD to open the Create New Drawing dialog box whenever you start a new drawing. You'll use this dialog box in the early stages of the book. If you decide you don't need the wizard as you become more comfortable with AutoCAD, you can easily turn it off by taking the previous steps again, and instead of choosing Show Startup Dialog Box in step 3, choose Do Not Show A Startup Dialog.

NOTE *With the Show Startup Dialog Box option turned on, you will also see the Startup dialog box when you first open AutoCAD. The Startup dialog box is basically the same as the New Drawing dialog box.*

Now let's create a new file.

1. Choose File ➢ Close to close the current file. In the Save Changes dialog box, click No. Notice that the toolbars disappear and the AutoCAD drawing window appears blank when no drawings are open.

2. Choose File ➢ New to open the Create New Drawing dialog box.

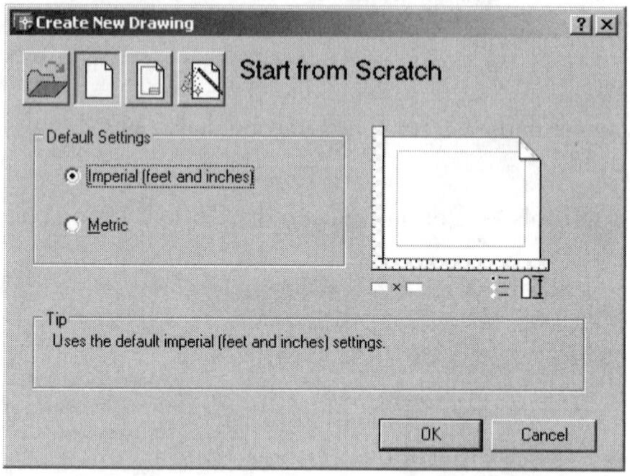

3. Click the Use A Wizard button in the dialog box. Two options appear in the Select A Wizard listbox: Quick Setup and Advanced Setup.

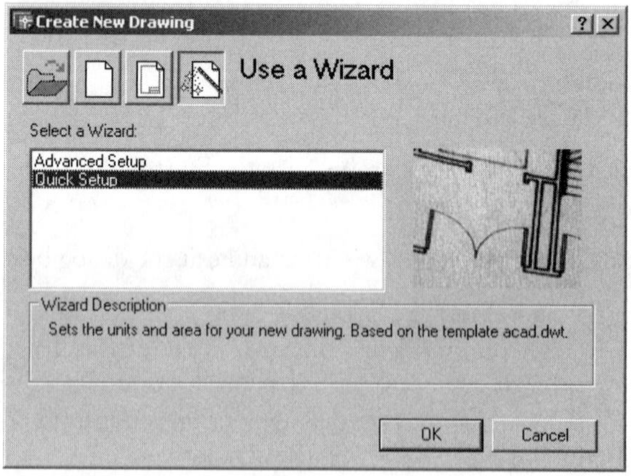

4. Click the Quick Setup option, and then click OK to open the Quick Setup Units dialog box.

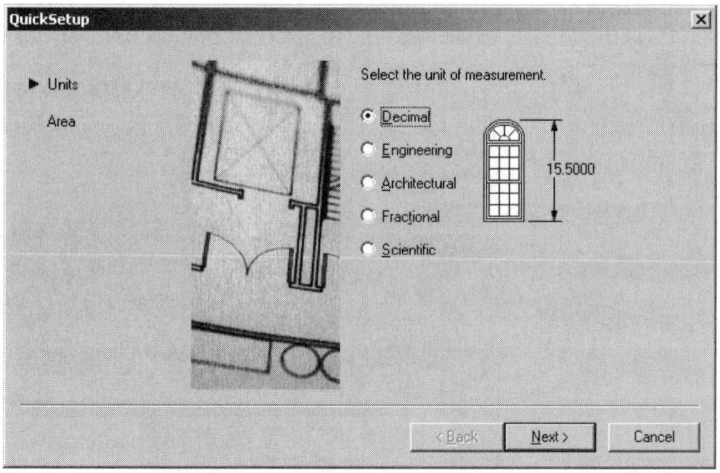

5. For now, you'll use the default decimal units as indicated by the radio buttons. You'll learn more about these options in the next chapter. Click Next to open the Quick Setup Area dialog box.

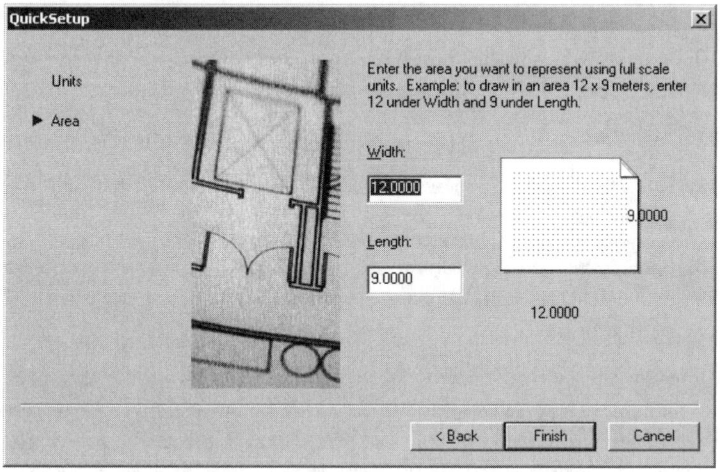

6. If the Width text box doesn't already show 12, double-click it and enter **12**. Metric users should enter **40**.

7. Press the Tab key to move to the Length text box and enter **9**. Metric users should enter **30**.

8. Click Finish. A new drawing file appears in the AutoCAD window.

9. From the menu bar, choose View ➢ Zoom ➢ All. This ensures that your display covers the entire area you specified in steps 6 and 7.

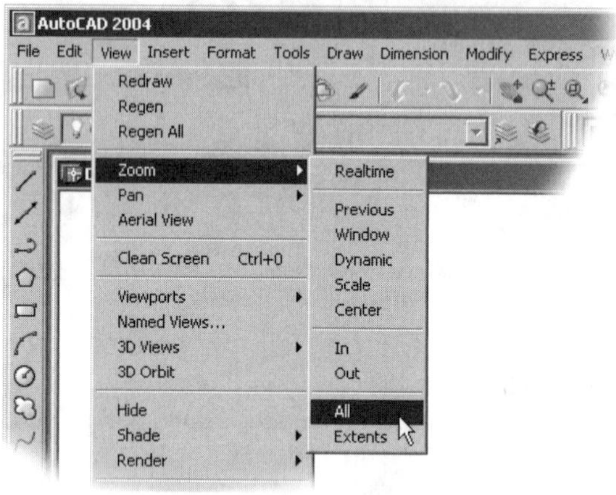

10. To give your new file a unique name, choose File ➢ Save As to open the Save Drawing As dialog box.

11. Type **Door**. As you type, the name appears in the File Name text box.

12. Double-click the `Sample` folder shown in the main file list of the dialog box to open the `Sample` subfolder.

13. Click Save. You now have a file called `Door.dwg`, located in the `Sample` subfolder of your `AutoCAD2004` folder. Of course, your drawing doesn't contain anything yet. You'll take care of that next.

The new file shows a drawing area roughly 12 inches wide by 9 inches high. Metric users will have a file that shows an area roughly 40 mm wide by 30 mm high. This area is your workspace, though you're not limited to it in any way. No visual clues indicate the size of the area. To check the area size for yourself, move the crosshair cursor to the upper-right corner of the screen, and observe the value in the coordinate readout. This is the standard AutoCAD default drawing area for new drawings.

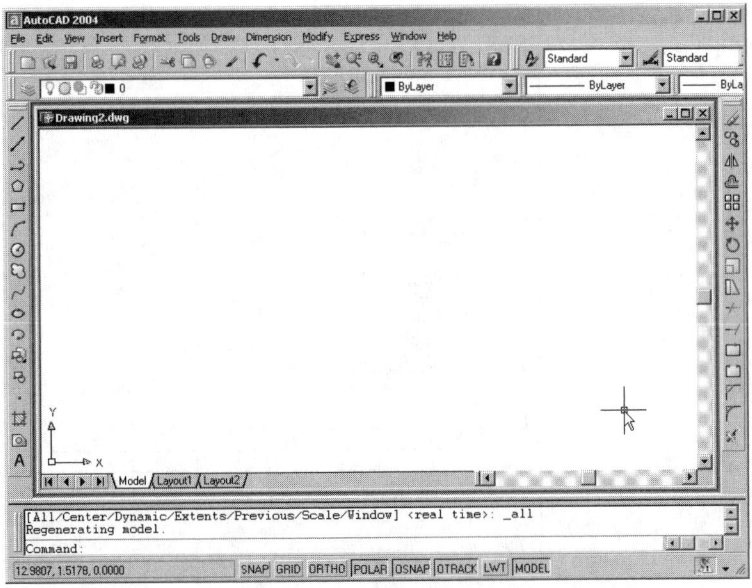

WARNING *The coordinate readout won't show exactly 12 inches by 9 inches, or 40 mm by 30 mm for metric, because the proportions of your drawing area are not likely to be exactly 12 x 9 or 40 x 30. AutoCAD does try to optimize the display for the drawing area when you choose View ➢ Zoom ➢ All.*

To begin a drawing, follow these steps:

1. Click the Line tool on the Draw toolbar, or type **L↵**.

   You've just issued the Line command. AutoCAD responds in two ways. First, you see the message

   `Specify first point:`

   in the command prompt, asking you to select a point to begin your line. Also, the cursor has changed its appearance; it no longer has a square in the crosshairs. This is a clue telling you to pick a point to start a line.

TIP *Throughout this book, you'll be given the option to use the keyboard shortcuts for commands. For example, in step 1, you were given the option to type* ***L↵*** *in the Command window to start the Line command.*

2. Using the left mouse-button, select a point on the screen near the center. As you select the point, AutoCAD changes the prompt to

   `Specify next point or [Undo]:`

   Now as you move the mouse around, notice a line with one end fixed on the point you just selected and the other end following the cursor (see the first image in Figure 2.1). This action is called *rubber-banding*.

FIGURE 2.1

A rubber-banding line

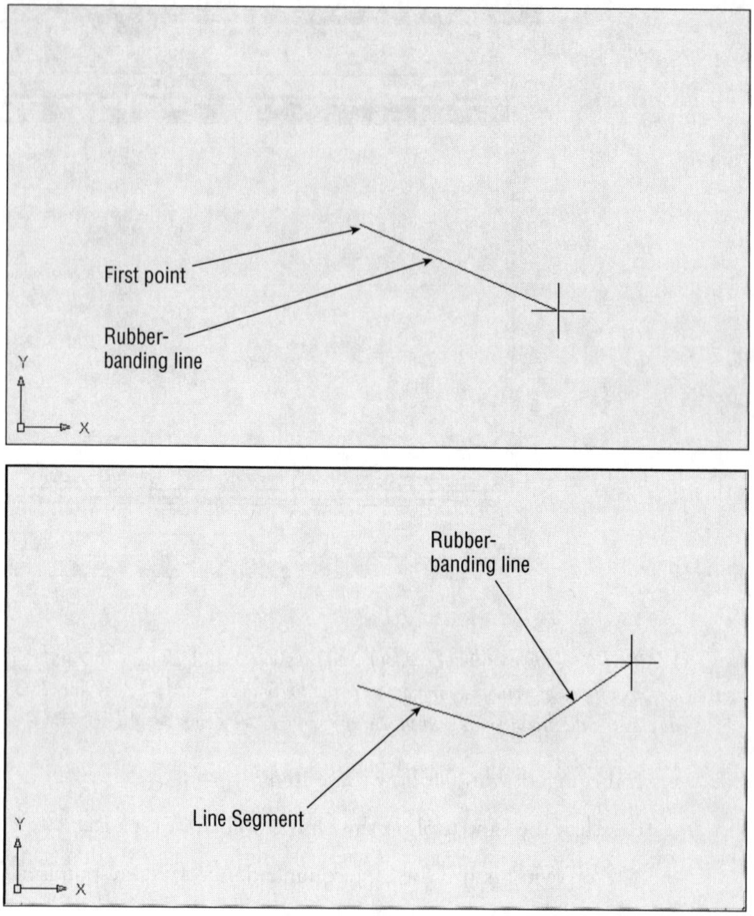

If you move the cursor to a location directly to the left or right of the point you clicked, you'll see a dotted horizontal line appear, along with a message at the cursor. This action also occurs when you point directly up or down. In fact, your cursor will seem to jump to a horizontal or vertical position.

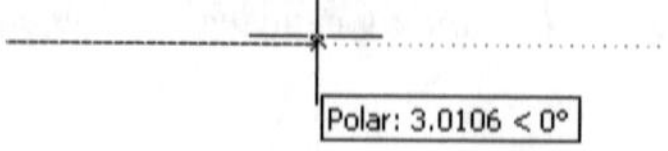

This feature is called Polar Tracking. It helps to restrict your line to an exact horizontal or vertical direction like a T-square and triangle. You can turn Polar Tracking on or off by clicking the Polar button in the status bar. If you don't see it, chances are it's just been turned off. You'll learn more about Polar Tracking in Chapter 3.

TIP *Although you won't learn how to use Polar Tracking in this chapter, you will learn about the notation that appears by the cursor when Polar Tracking is active.*

Now continue with the Line command:

3. Move the cursor to a point below and to the right of the first point you selected, and click the left mouse button again. The first rubber-banding line is now fixed between the two points you selected, and a second rubber-banding line appears (see the second image in Figure 2.1).

4. If the line you drew isn't the exact length you want, you can back up during the Line command and change it. To do this, click Undo in the Standard toolbar, or type **U↵**.

TIP *The Undo tool in the Standard toolbar offers an Undo drop-down list from which you can select the exact command that you want to undo. See the "Getting Out of Trouble" sidebar in this chapter for more information.*

Now the line you drew previously will rubber-band as if you hadn't selected the second point to fix its length. You've just drawn, and then undrawn, a line of an arbitrary length. The Line command is still active. Two things tell you that you are in the middle of a command. If you don't see the word `Command` in the bottom line of the Command window, a command is still active. Also, the cursor will be the plain crosshair without the box at its intersection.

TIP *From now on, I will refer to the crosshair cursor without the small box as the point selection mode of the cursor. If you look ahead to Figure 2.7, you'll see all the modes of the drawing cursor.*

GETTING OUT OF TROUBLE

Beginners and experts alike are bound to make a few mistakes. Before you get too far into the tutorial, here are some powerful yet easy-to-use tools to help you recover from accidents.

Backspace (←) If you make a typing error, press the Backspace key to back up to your error, and then retype your command or response. The Backspace key is in the upper-right corner of the main keyboard area.

Escape (Esc) This is perhaps the single most important key on your keyboard. When you need to quickly exit a command or a dialog box without making changes, just press the Esc key in the upper-left corner of your keyboard. In previous versions of AutoCAD, you had to press Esc twice in some instances. Beginning with AutoCAD 2000, you need to press Esc only once, though it won't hurt to press it twice. (Press Esc before editing with grips or issuing commands through the keyboard.)

U↵ If you accidentally change something in the drawing and want to reverse that change, click the Undo tool in the Standard toolbar (the left-pointing curved arrow). You can also type **U↵** at the command prompt. Each time you do this, AutoCAD undoes one operation at a time, in reverse order. The last command performed is undone first, then the next-to-last command, and so on. The prompt displays the name of the command being undone, and the drawing reverts to its state prior to that command. If you need to, you can undo everything back to the beginning of an editing session.

Continued on next page

GETTING OUT OF TROUBLE *(continued)*

Undo↵ If you decide that you want to back up a few steps of an operation you just performed, you can use the Undo tool (the right-pointing curved arrow) in the Standard toolbar. Or type **Undo↵**. Each click of the Undo tool steps you back one operation. In AutoCAD 2004, you may also select the exact command to undo by using the Undo drop-down list. You can open the Undo drop-down list by clicking the downward pointing arrow found to the right of the Undo tool.

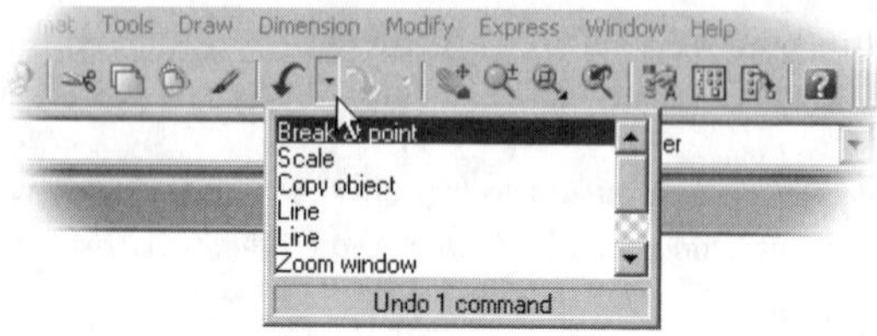

Redo↵ If you accidentally Undo one too many commands, you can redo the last undone command by clicking the Redo tool (the right-pointing curved arrow) in the Standard toolbar. Or type **Redo↵**. In AutoCAD 2004, Redo allows you to redo several operations that you might have undone with the Undo command. You can also select the exact command to redo by using the Redo drop-down list. To open the Redo drop-down list, click the downward pointing arrow found to the right of the Redo tool.

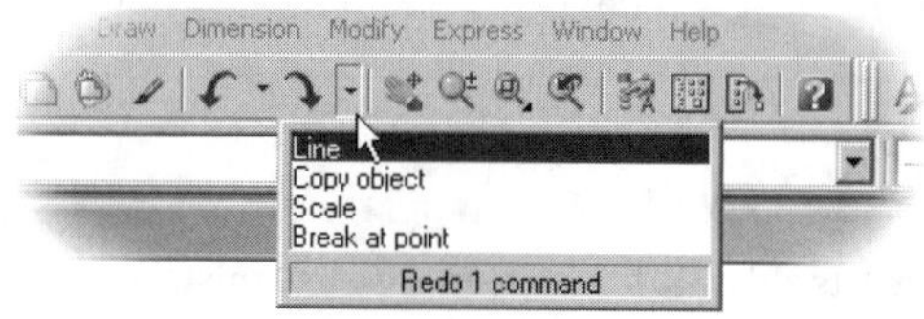

Specifying Distances with Coordinates

Next, you will continue with the Line command to draw a plan view (an overhead view) of a door, to no particular scale. Later, you will resize the drawing to use in future exercises. The door will be 3.0 units long and 0.15 units thick. For metric users, the door will be 9 units long and 0.5 units thick. To specify these exact distances in AutoCAD, you can use either relative polar coordinates or Cartesian coordinates.

WARNING *The Imperial and metric distances are not equivalent in the exercises in this chapter. For example, 3 units in the Imperial-based drawing is not equal to 9 metric units. These distances are arbitrary and based on how they will appear in the figures in this chapter.*

Specifying Polar Coordinates

To enter the exact distance of 3 (or 9 metric) units to the right of the last point you selected, do the following:

1. Type **@3<0**. Metric users should type **@9<0**. As you type, the letters appear at the command prompt.
2. Press ↵. A line appears, starting from the first point you picked and ending 3 units to the right of it (see Figure 2.2). You have just entered a relative polar coordinate.

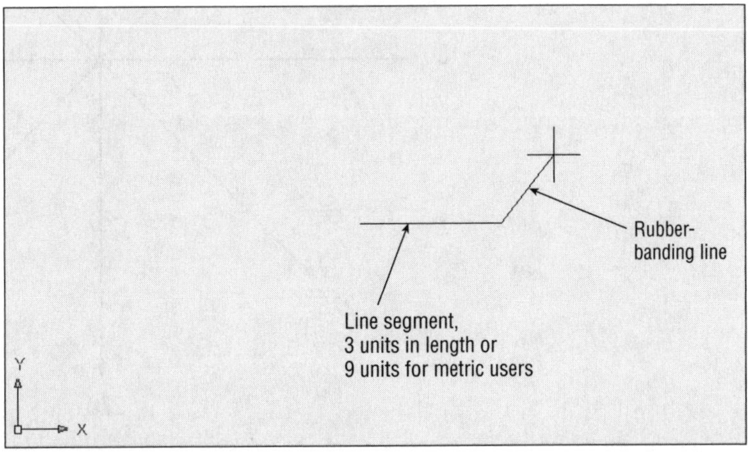

FIGURE 2.2

Notice that the rubber-banding line now starts from the last point selected. This tells you that you can continue to add more line segments.

The "at" sign (@) you entered tells AutoCAD that the distance you are specifying is from the last point you selected. The 3 (or 9 metric) is the distance, and the less-than symbol (<) tells AutoCAD that you are designating the angle at which the line is to be drawn. The last part is the value for the angle, which in this case is 0. This is how to use polar coordinates to communicate distances and directions to AutoCAD.

TIP *If you are accustomed to a different method for describing directions, you can set AutoCAD to use a vertical direction or downward direction as 0°. See Chapter 3 for details.*

Angles are given based on the system shown in Figure 2.3, in which 0° is a horizontal direction from left to right, 90° is straight up, 180° is horizontal from right to left, and so on. You can specify degrees, minutes, and seconds of arc if you want to be that exact. I'll discuss angle formats in more detail in Chapter 3.

FIGURE 2.3

AutoCAD's default system for specifying angles

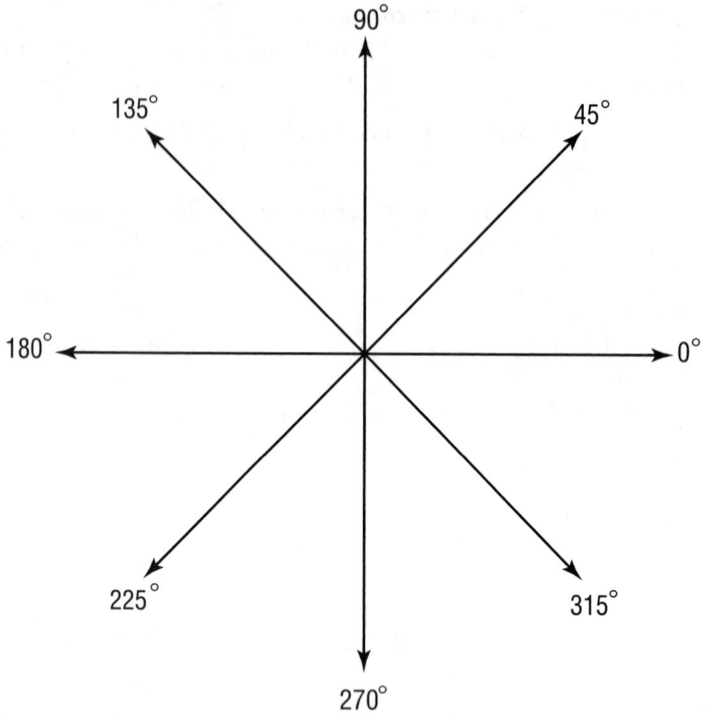

Specifying Relative Cartesian Coordinates

For the next line segment, let's try another method for specifying exact distances.

1. Enter **@0,0.15↵**. Metric users should enter **@0,0.5↵**. A short line appears above the endpoint of the last line.

TIP *Step 1 indicates that metric users should enter **@0,0.5↵** for the distance. You can also enter **0,.5** (zero comma point five). The leading zero is included for clarity. European metric users should be aware that the comma is used as a separator between the x and y components of the coordinate. In AutoCAD, commas are not used for decimal points; you must use a period to denote a decimal point.*

Once again, the @ tells AutoCAD that the distance you specify is from the last point picked. But, in this example, you give the distance in x and y values. The x distance, 0, is given first, followed by a comma, and then the y distance, 0.15. This is how to specify distances in relative Cartesian coordinates.

2. Enter **@-3,0↵**. Metric users should enter **@-9,0↵**. The result is a drawing that looks like Figure 2.4.

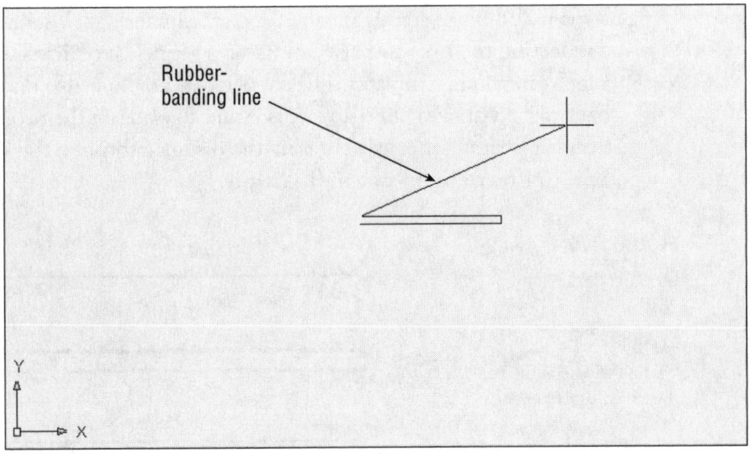

FIGURE 2.4

These three sides of the door were drawn using the Line tool. Points are specified using either relative Cartesian or polar coordinates.

The distance you entered in step 2 was also in x,y values, but here you used a negative value to specify the x distance. Positive values in the Cartesian coordinate system are from left to right and from bottom to top (see Figure 2.5). (You may remember this from your high school geometry class!) If you want to draw a line from right to left, you must designate a negative value. It is also helpful to know where the origin of the drawing lies. In a new drawing, the origin, or coordinate 0,0, is in the lower-left corner of the drawing.

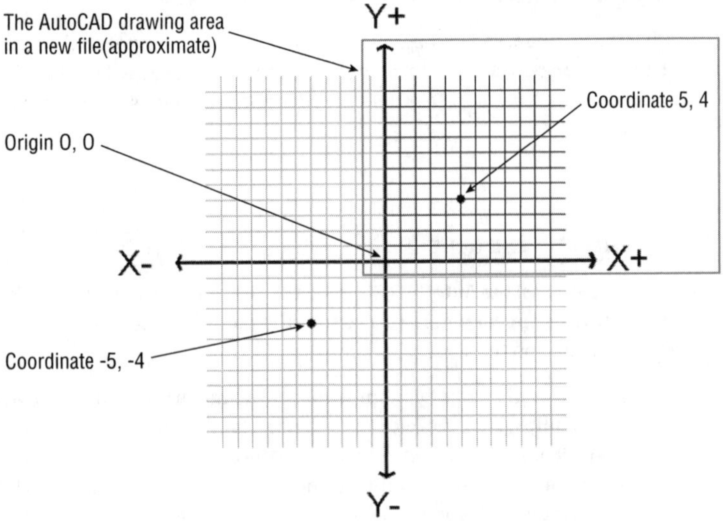

FIGURE 2.5

Positive and negative Cartesian coordinate directions

TIP *To finish drawing a series of lines without closing them, you can press Esc, ↵, or the spacebar.*

3. Type C↵. This C stands for the Close command. It closes a sequence of line segments. A line connecting the first and last points of a sequence of lines is drawn (see Figure 2.6), and the Line command terminates. The rubber-banding line also disappears, telling you that AutoCAD has finished drawing line segments. You can also use the rubber-banding line to indicate direction while simultaneously entering the distance through the keyboard. See the sidebar "A Fast Way to Enter Distances" in this chapter.

FIGURE 2.6
Distance and direction input for the door. Distances for metric users are shown in brackets.

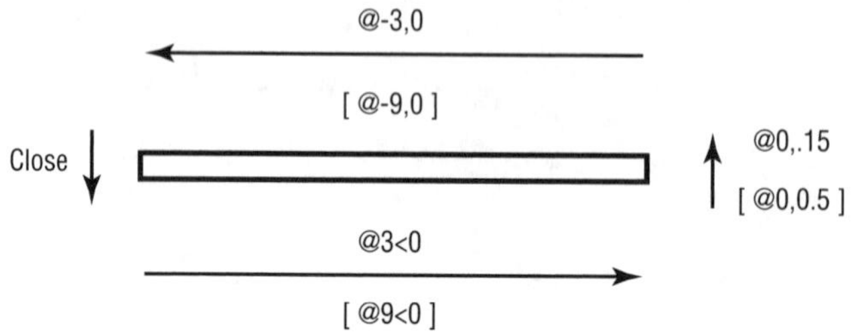

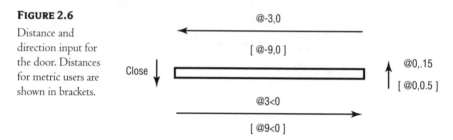

A FAST WAY TO ENTER DISTANCES

A third method for entering distances is to simply point in a direction with a rubber-banding line and then enter the distance through the keyboard. For example, to draw a line 3 units long from left to right, click the Line tool on the Draw toolbar, click a start point, and then move the cursor so the rubber-banding line points to the right at some arbitrary distance. While holding the cursor in the direction you want, type **3**↵. The rubber-banding line becomes a fixed line 3 units long.

Using this method, called the Direct Distance method, along with the Ortho mode or Polar Snap described in Chapter 3, can be a fast way to draw objects of specific lengths. Use the standard Cartesian or polar coordinate methods when you need to enter exact distances at angles other than those that are exactly horizontal or vertical.

CLEANING UP THE SCREEN

On some systems, the AutoCAD Blipmode setting may be turned on. This causes tiny cross-shaped markers, called blips, to appear where you've selected points. These blips can be helpful to keep track of the points you've selected on the screen.

Blips aren't actually part of your drawing and do not print. Still, they can interfere with your work. To clear the screen of blips, click the Redraw tool in the toolbar (it's the one that looks like a pencil point drawing an arc), or type **R**↵. The screen quickly redraws the objects, clearing the screen of the blips. You can also choose View ➢ Redraw View to accomplish the same thing. As you will see later in this book, Redraw can also clear up other display problems.

Another command, Regen, does the same thing as Redraw, but it also updates the drawing display database—which means it takes a bit longer to restore the drawing. Regen is used to update certain types of changes that occur in a drawing. You will learn about Regen in Chapter 7.

To turn Blipmode on and off, type **blipmode**↵ at the command prompt, and then enter **on**↵ or **off**↵.

Interpreting the Cursor Modes and Understanding Prompts

The key to working with AutoCAD successfully is understanding the way it interacts with you. This section will help you become familiar with some of the ways AutoCAD prompts you for input. Understanding the format of the messages in the Command window and recognizing other events on the screen will help you learn the program more easily.

As the Command window aids you with messages, the cursor also gives you clues about what to do. Figure 2.7 illustrates the various modes of the cursor and gives a brief description of the role of each mode. Take a moment to study this figure.

FIGURE 2.7

The drawing cursor's modes

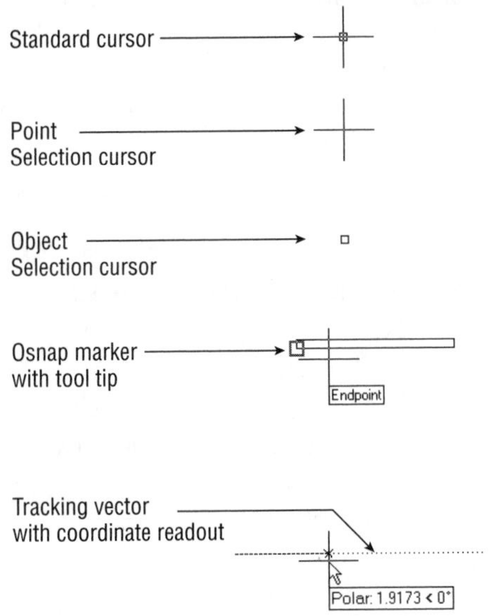

The Standard cursor tells you that AutoCAD is waiting for instructions. You can also edit objects using grips when you see this cursor. Grips are squares that appear at endpoints and its midpoint of objects when they are selected. (You may know them as *workpoints* from other graphics programs.)

The Point Selection cursor appears whenever AutoCAD expects point input. It can also appear in conjunction with a rubber-banding line. You can either click a point or enter a coordinate through the keyboard. The Object Selection cursor tells you that you must select objects—either by clicking them or by using any of the object selection options available. The *Osnap (object snap)* marker appears along with the Point Selection cursor when you invoke an Osnap. Osnaps let you accurately select specific points on an object, such as endpoints or midpoints. The tracking vector appears when you use the Polar Tracking or Object Snap Tracking feature. Polar Tracking aids you in drawing orthogonal lines, and Object Snap Tracking helps you align point in space relative to the geometry of existing objects. Object Snap Tracking works in conjunction with Osnap. You'll learn more about the tracking vector in Chapters 3 and 4.

TIP *If you are an experienced AutoCAD user, you might prefer to use the old-style crosshair cursor that crosses the entire screen. Choose Tools ➢ Options to open the Options dialog box, and then click the Display tab. Set the Crosshair Size option near the bottom left of the dialog box to 100. The cursor then appears as it did in previous versions of AutoCAD. As the option name implies, you can set the crosshair size to any percentage of the screen you want. The default is 5 percent.*

Choosing Command Options

Many commands in AutoCAD offer several options, which are often presented to you in the Command window in the form of a prompt. This section uses the Arc command to illustrate the format of AutoCAD's prompts.

Usually, in a floor-plan drawing in the United States, an arc is drawn to indicate the direction of a door swing. Figure 2.8 shows some of the other standard symbols used in architectural style drawings. This is a small sampling of the symbols available on the CD included with this book. See Appendix A for more information.

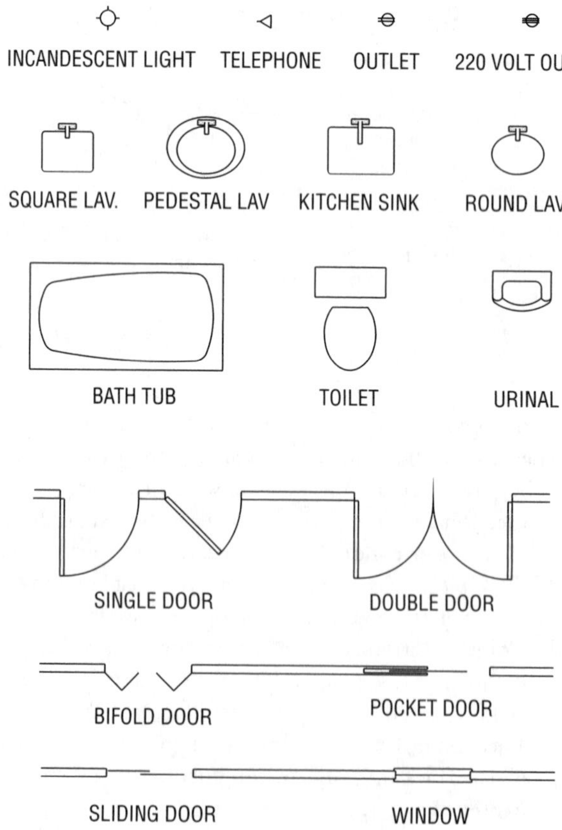

FIGURE 2.8

Samples of standard symbols used in architectural drawings

Next, you'll draw the arc for the door you started in the previous exercise.

1. Click the Arc tool in the Draw toolbar. The prompt `Specify start point of arc or [Center]:` appears, and the cursor changes to Point Selection mode.

Let's examine this `Specify start point of arc or [Center]:` prompt. The start point contains two options. The default option is the one stated in the main part of the prompt. In this case, the default option is to specify the start point of the arc. If other options are available, they will appear within brackets. In the Arc command, you see the word `Center` within brackets telling you that if you prefer, you can also start your arc by selecting a center point instead of a start point. If multiple options are available, they appear within the brackets and are separated by slashes (/). The default is the option AutoCAD assumes you intend to use unless you tell it otherwise.

2. Type **C**↵ to select the Center option. The prompt `Specify center point of arc:` appears. Notice that you only had type in the **C** and not the entire word **Center**.

TIP *When you see a set of options in the Command window, note their capitalization. If you choose to respond to prompts using the keyboard, these capitalized letters are all you need to enter to select that option. In some cases, the first two letters are capitalized to differentiate two options that begin with the same letter, such as* `LAyer` *and* `LType`.

3. Now pick a point representing the center of the arc near the upper-left corner of the door (see the first image in Figure 2.9). The prompt `Specify start point of arc:` appears.
4. Type **@3<0**. Metric users should type **@9<0**. The prompt `Specify end point of arc or [Angle/chord Length]:` appears.
5. Move the mouse and a temporary arc appears, originating from a point 3 units to the right of the center point you selected and rotating about that center, as in the middle image in Figure 2.9. (Metric users will see the temporary arc originating 9 units to the right of the center point.)

As the prompt indicates, you now have three options. You can enter an angle, a chord length, or the endpoint of the arc. The prompt default, to specify the endpoint of the arc, picks the arc's endpoint. Again, the cursor is in a point selection mode, telling you it is waiting for point input. To select this default option, you only need to pick a point on the screen indicating where you want the endpoint.

6. Move the cursor so that it points in a vertical direction from the center of the arc. You'll see the Polar Tracking vector snap to a vertical position.

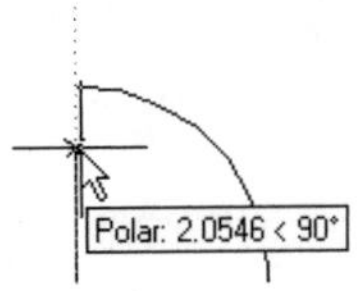

7. Click any location with the Polar Tracking vector in the vertical position. The arc is now fixed in place, as in the bottom image in Figure 2.9.

FIGURE 2.9

Using the Arc command

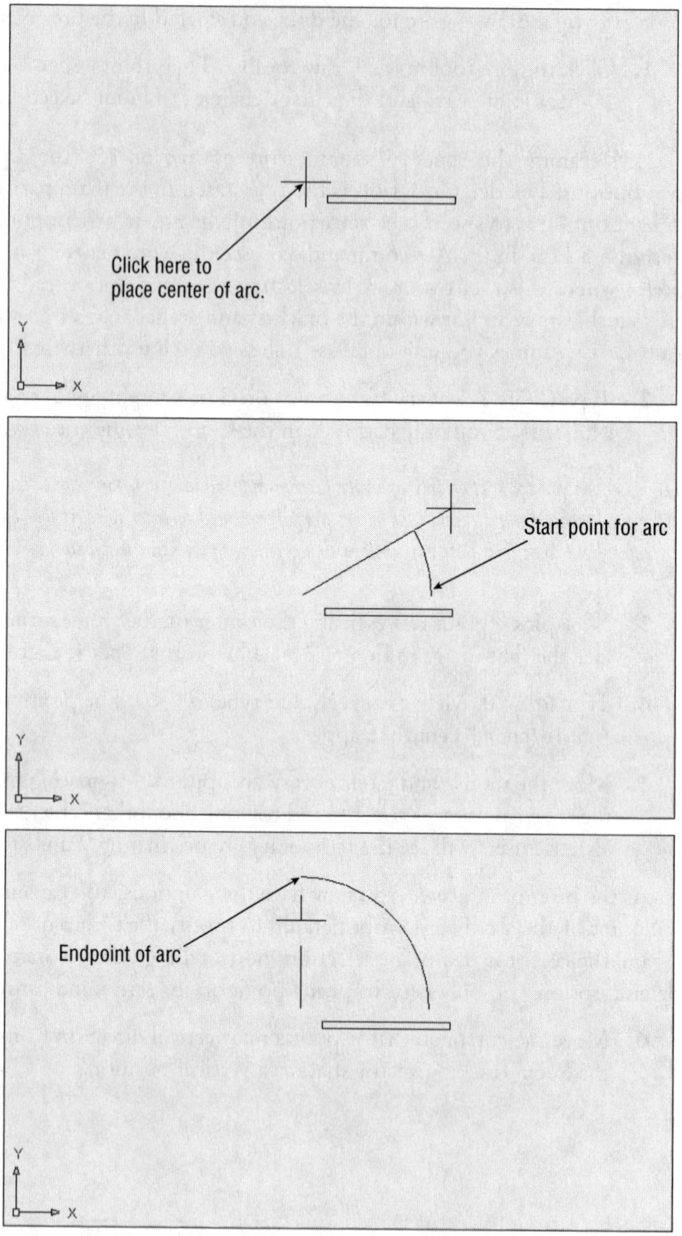

This exercise has given you some practice working with AutoCAD's Command window prompts and entering keyboard commands—skills you will need when you start to use some of the more advanced AutoCAD functions.

As you can see, AutoCAD has a distinct structure in its prompt messages. You first issue a command, which in turn offers options in the form of a prompt. Depending on the option you select, you get another set of options or you are prompted to take some action, such as picking a point, selecting objects, or entering a value.

As shown in Figure 2.10, the sequence is something like a tree. As you work through the exercises, you will become intimately familiar with this routine. Once you understand the workings of the toolbars, the Command window prompts, and the dialog boxes, you can almost teach yourself the rest of the program!

FIGURE 2.10

A typical command structure, using the Arc command as an example. The messages you see depend on the options you choose as you progress through the command. This figure shows the various pathways to creating an arc.

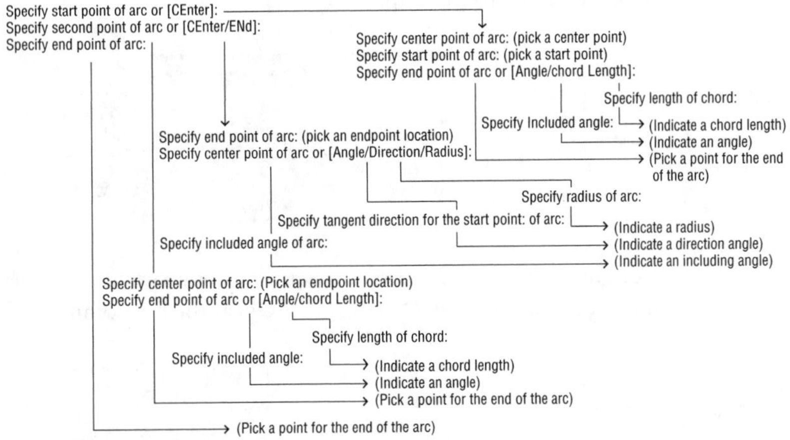

SELECTING OPTIONS FROM A SHORTCUT MENU

Now you know that you can select command options by typing them. You can also right-click at any time during a command to open a shortcut menu containing those same options. For example, in step 2 in the previous exercise, you typed C↵ to tell AutoCAD that you wanted to select the center of the arc. Instead of typing, you can also right-click the mouse to open a menu of options applicable to the Arc command at that time.

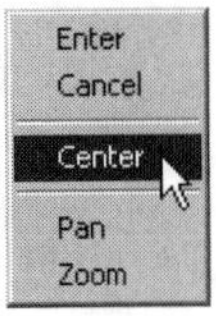

Notice that in addition to the options shown in the command prompt, the shortcut menu also shows you a few more options, namely Enter, Cancel, Pan, and Zoom. The Enter option is the same as pressing ↵. Cancel cancels the current command. Pan and Zoom allow you to make adjustments to your view as you are working through the current command.

As you work with AutoCAD, you'll find that you can right-click at any time to display a shortcut menu. This menu is context sensitive, so you'll only see options that pertain to the command or activity that is currently in progress. Also, when AutoCAD is expecting a point, an object selection, or a numeric value, right-clicking does not display a shortcut menu. Instead, AutoCAD treats a right-click as ↵.

Be aware that the location of your cursor when you right-click determines the contents of the shortcut list. You've already seen that you can right-click a toolbar to get a list of other toolbars. A right-click in the Command window displays a list of operations you can apply to the command line, such as repeating one of the last several commands you've used or copying the most recent history of command activity to the Clipboard.

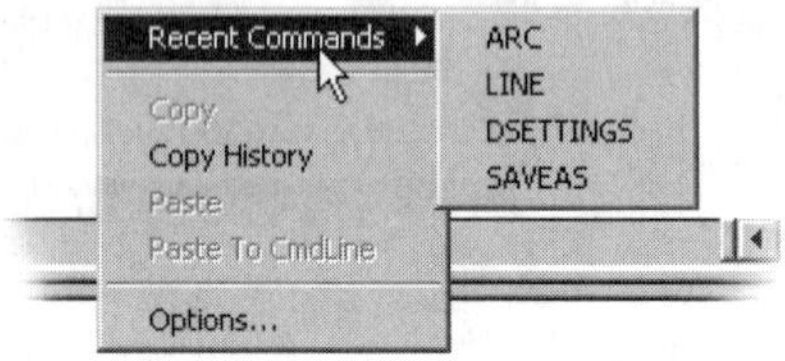

A right-click in the drawing area when no command is active gives you a set of basic options for editing your file, like Cut, Paste, Undo, Repeat the last command, Pan, and Zoom, to name a few.

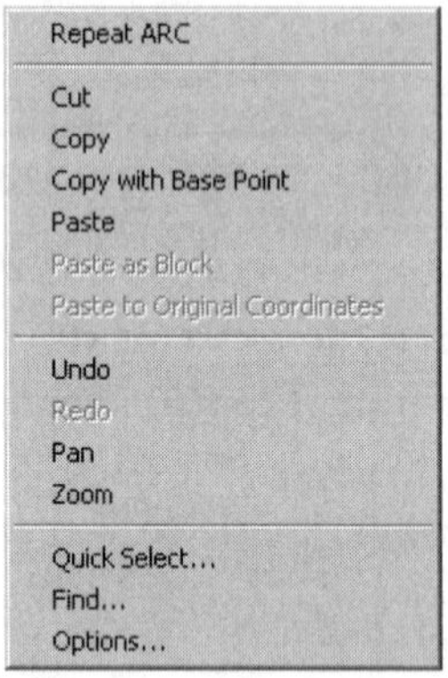

If you're ever in doubt over what to do in AutoCAD, you can right-click to see a list of options. You'll learn more about these options later in this book. For now, let's move on to the topic of selecting objects.

If you're a veteran AutoCAD user, and you prefer to have the right-click issue a ↵ at all times, as in versions prior to AutoCAD 14, instead of opening the shortcut menu, you can configure AutoCAD to do just that. See Appendix B for details on how to set up the mouse's right-click action. Be aware, however, that the tutorials in this book assume that AutoCAD is configured for the shortcut menu.

Selecting Objects

AutoCAD provides many options for selecting objects. This section has two parts: The first part deals with object selection methods unique to AutoCAD, and the second part deals with the more common selection method used in most popular graphic programs, the Noun/Verb method. Because these two methods play a major role in working with AutoCAD, it's a good idea to familiarize yourself with them early on.

TIP *If you need to select objects by their characteristics rather than by their location, see Chapter 13, which describes the Quick Select and Object Selection Filters tools. These tools let you easily select a set of objects based on their properties, including object type, color, layer assignment, and so on.*

Selecting Objects in AutoCAD

Many AutoCAD commands prompt you to `Select objects:`. Along with this prompt, the cursor changes from crosshairs to a small square (look back at Figure 2.7). Whenever you see the `Select objects:` prompt and the square cursor, you have several options while making your selection. Often, as you select objects on the screen, you will change your mind about a selection or accidentally pick an object you do not want. Let's take a look at most of the selection options available in AutoCAD, and learn what to do when you make the wrong selection.

Before you continue, you'll turn off two features that, while extremely useful, can be confusing to new users. These features are called Running Osnaps and Osnap Tracking. You'll get a chance to explore these features in depth later in this book.

1. Check to see if either Running Osnaps or Osnap Tracking is turned on. Look at the Osnap and Otrack buttons in the status bar at the bottom of the AutoCAD window. If they are turned on, they look like they are pressed.

2. To turn off Running Osnap or Osnap Tracking, click the Osnap or Otrack button in the status bar. When turned off, they will look like they are not pressed.

Now let's go ahead and see how to select an object in AutoCAD.

1. Choose Move from the Modify toolbar or type **M↵**.
2. At the `Select objects:` prompt, click each of the two horizontal lines that constitute the door. As you saw in the last chapter, whenever AutoCAD wants you to select objects, the cursor turns into the small square pickbox. This tells you that you are in Object Selection mode. As you pick an object, it is highlighted, as shown in Figure 2.11.

TIP *Highlighting means an object changes from a solid image to one composed of dots. When you see an object highlighted on the screen, you know that you have chosen that object to be acted on by your next or current command.*

3. After making your selections, you may decide to deselect some items. Enter **U↵** from the keyboard. Notice that one line is no longer highlighted. When you type **U↵**, objects are deselected, one at a time, in reverse order of selection.

4. You can deselect objects in another way. Hold down the Shift key and click the remaining highlighted line. It reverts to a solid line, showing you that it is no longer selected for editing.

FIGURE 2.11

Selecting the lines of the door and seeing them highlighted

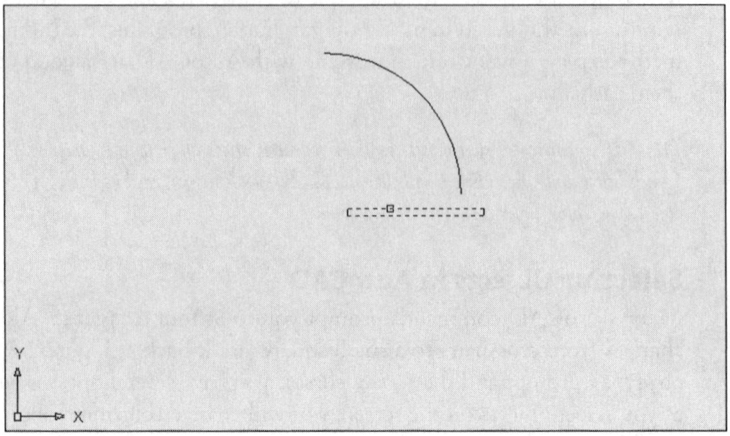

By now you have deselected both lines. Let's try using another method for selecting groups of objects.

5. To window objects, type **W**↵. The cursor changes to a Point Selection cursor, and the prompt changes to

   `Specify First corner:`

6. Click a point below and to the left of the rectangle representing the door. As you move your cursor across the screen, the window appears and stretches across the drawing area.

7. Once the window completely encloses the door but not the arc, click this location to highlight the entire door. This window selects only objects that are completely enclosed by the window, as shown in Figure 2.12.

FIGURE 2.12

Selecting the door within a window

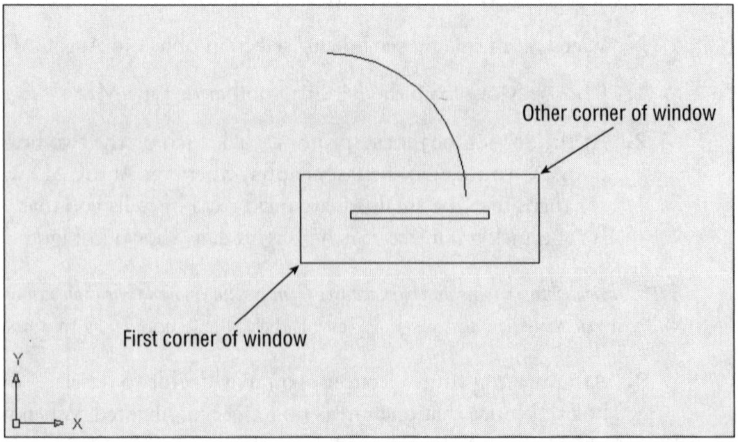

TIP *Don't confuse the selection window you are creating here with the Zoom window you used in Chapter 1, which simply defines an area of the drawing you want to enlarge. Remember that the Window option works differently under the Zoom command than it does for other editing commands.*

WARNING *If you are using a mouse you're not familiar with, it's quite easy to accidentally click the right mouse button when you really wanted to click the left mouse button, and vice versa. If you click the wrong button, you'll get the wrong results. On a two-button mouse, the right button will either act like the ↵ key or open a context-sensitive shortcut menu, depending on your current operation. A ↵ will be issued if you are selecting objects, but otherwise the shortcut menu appears.*

8. Now that you have selected the entire door but not the arc, press ↵. This tells AutoCAD you have finished selecting objects. It is important to remember to press ↵ as soon as you finish selecting the objects you want to edit. A new prompt, `Specify base point or displacement:`, appears. The cursor changes to its Point Selection mode.

Now you have seen how the selection process works in AutoCAD—but you're in the middle of the Move command. The next section discusses the prompt that's now on your screen and describes how to enter base points and displacement distances.

CONTROLLING THE STATUS BAR DISPLAY

To the far right of the status bar, you'll see a downward-pointing arrow, which opens a menu that controls the display of the status bar. You use this menu to turn the items in the status bar on or off. A checkmark by an item indicates that it is currently on. If for some reason you do not see all the buttons mentioned in the previous exercise, check this menu to make sure that all the status bar options are turned on. Note that LT does not have an Otrack option in the status bar.

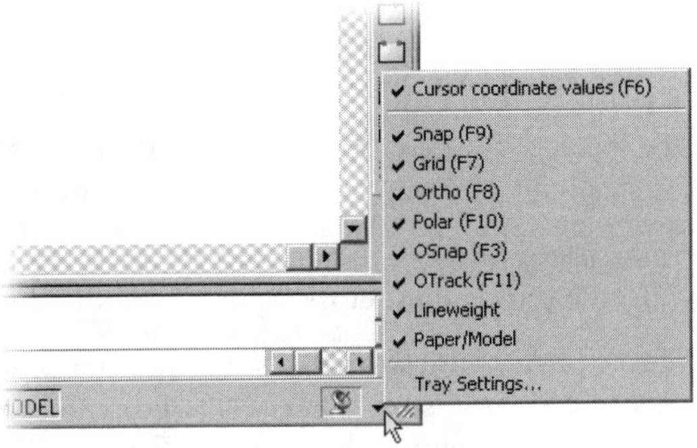

PROVIDING BASE POINTS

When you move or copy objects, AutoCAD prompts you for a base point, which is a difficult concept to grasp. AutoCAD must be told specifically from where and to where the move occurs. The *base point* is the exact location from which you determine the distance and direction of the move. Once the base point is determined, you can tell AutoCAD where to move the object in relation to that point.

1. To select a base point, hold down the Shift key and right-click. A menu appears displaying the Object Snap (Osnap) options.

WARNING *When right-clicking the mouse, make sure the cursor is within the AutoCAD drawing area; otherwise, you will not get the results described in this book.*

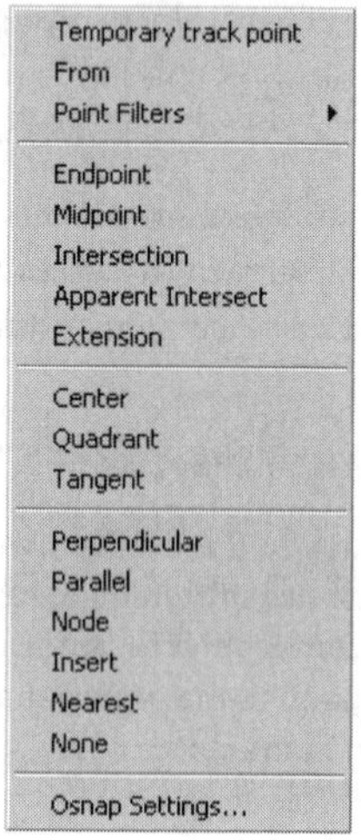

2. Choose Intersection from the Osnap menu. The Osnap menu closes.
3. Move the cursor to the lower-right corner of the door. Notice that as you approach the corner, a small x-shaped graphic appears on the corner. This is called an Osnap marker.
4. After the x-shaped marker appears, hold the mouse motionless for a second or two. A tool tip appears, telling you the current Osnap point AutoCAD has selected.
5. Now click the left mouse button to select the intersection indicated by the Osnap marker. Whenever you see the Osnap marker at the point you want to select, you don't have to point exactly at the location with your cursor. Just left-click the mouse to select the exact Osnap point (see Figure 2.13). In this case, you selected the exact intersection of two lines.
6. At the Specify second point of displacement or <use first point as displacement>: prompt, hold down the Shift key and click the right mouse button again. You'll use the Endpoint Osnap this time, but instead of clicking the option with the mouse, type **E**.

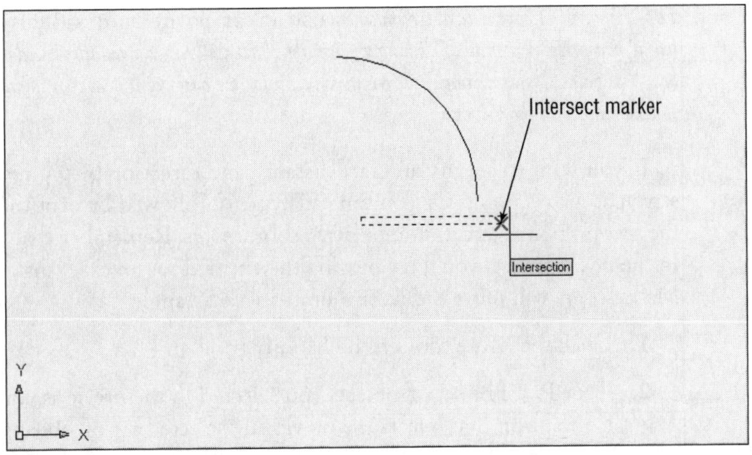

FIGURE 2.13
Using the Osnap cursor

7. Now pick the lower-right end of the arc you drew earlier. (Remember that you only need to move your cursor close to the endpoint until the Osnap marker appears.) The door moves so that the corner of the door connects exactly with the endpoint of the arc (see Figure 2.14).

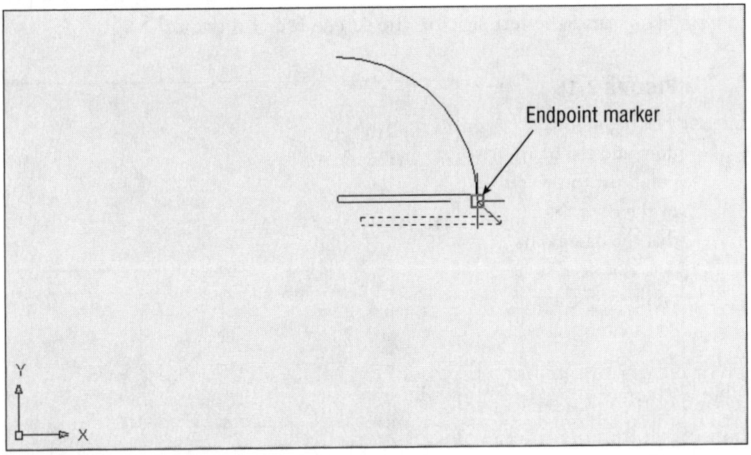

FIGURE 2.14
The rectangle in its new position after using the Endpoint Osnap

As you can see, the Osnap options allow you to select specific points on an object. You used Endpoint and Intersect in this exercise, but other options are available. Chapter 3 discusses some of the other Osnap options. You may have also noticed that the Osnap marker is different for each of the options you used. You'll learn more about Osnaps in Chapter 3. Now let's continue with our look at point selection.

TIP *You might have noticed the statement* `Use first point as displacement` *in the prompt in step 6. This means that if you press ↵ instead of clicking a point, the object will move a distance based on the coordinates of the point you selected as a base point. If, for example, the point you click for the base point is at coordinate 2,4, the object will move 2 units in the x-axis and 4 in the y-axis.*

If you want to specify an exact distance and direction by typing a value, select any point on the screen as a base point. Or you can just type @ followed by ↵ at the base point prompt; then enter the second point's location in relative coordinates. Remember that @ means the last point selected. In the next exercise, you'll try moving the entire door an exact distance of 1 unit in a 45° angle. Metric users will move the door 3 units in a 45° angle.

1. Click the Move tool on the Modify toolbar.
2. Type **P**↵. The set of objects you selected in the previous command is highlighted. **P** is a selection option that selects the previously selected set of objects.
3. You're still in the Object Selection mode, so click the arc to include it in the set of selected objects. Now the entire door, including the arc, is highlighted.
4. Press ↵ to tell AutoCAD that you have finished your selection. The cursor changes to Point Selection mode.
5. At the `Base point or displacement:` prompt, choose a point on the screen between the door and the left side of the screen (see Figure 2.15).

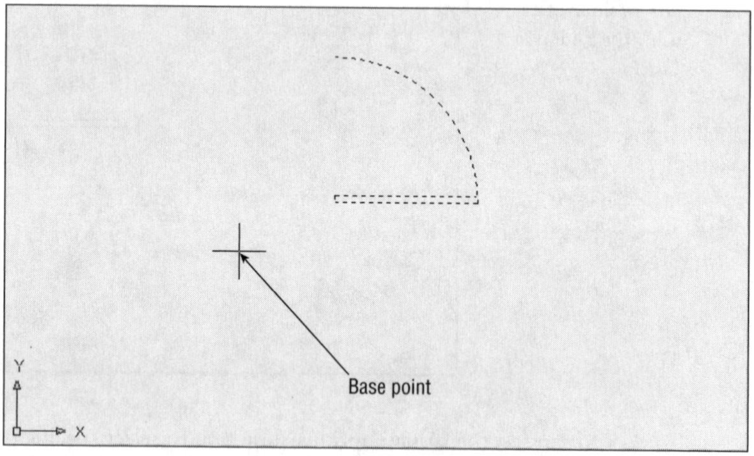

FIGURE 2.15
The highlighted door and the base point just to the left of the door. Note that the base point does not need to be on the object that you are moving.

6. Move the cursor around slowly, and notice that the door moves as if the base point you selected were attached to the door. The door moves with the cursor, at a fixed distance from it. This demonstrates how the base point relates to the objects you select.
7. Now type **@1<45**↵. (Metric users should type **@3<45**↵.) The door moves to a new location on the screen at a distance of 1 unit (or 3 for metric users) from its previous location and at an angle of 45°.

TIP *If AutoCAD is waiting for a command, you can repeat the last command used by pressing the spacebar or by pressing ↵. You can also right-click in the drawing area and select the option at the top of the list. If you right-click the Command window, a shortcut menu offers the most recent commands.*

This exercise illustrates that the base point does not have to be on the object you are manipulating; it can be virtually anywhere on your drawing. You also saw how to reselect a group of objects that were selected previously, without having to duplicate the selection process.

OTHER SELECTION OPTIONS

There are several other selection options you haven't tried yet. You'll see how these options work in exercises later in this book. Or if you are adventurous, try them out now on your own. To use these options, type their keyboard abbreviations (shown in brackets in the following list) at any `Select object:` prompt.

All [all↵] Selects all the objects in a drawing except those in frozen or locked layers. (See Chapter 4 for information on layers.)

Crossing [c↵] Similar to the Select Window option but selects anything that crosses through the window you define.

Crossing Polygon [cp↵] Acts exactly like Window Polygon (see later in this sidebar) but, like the Select Crossing option, selects anything that crosses through a polygon boundary.

Fence [f↵] Selects objects that are crossed over by a temporary line called a fence. This operation is like crossing out the objects you want to select with a line. When you invoke this option, you can then pick points, as when you are drawing a series of line segments. When you finish drawing the fence, press ↵, and then go on to select other objects, or press ↵ again to finish your selection.

Last [l↵] Selects the last object you entered.

Multiple [m↵] Lets you select several objects first, before AutoCAD highlights them. In a very large file, picking objects individually can cause AutoCAD to pause after each pick, while it locates and highlights each object. The Multiple option can speed things up by letting you first pick all the objects quickly and then highlight them all by pressing ↵. This has no menu equivalent.

Previous [p↵] Selects the last object or set of objects that was edited or changed.

Window [w↵] Forces a standard selection window. This option is useful when your drawing area is too crowded to use the Autoselect feature to place a window around a set of objects. (See the Auto entry in this sidebar.) It prevents you from accidentally selecting an object with a single pick when you are placing your window.

Window Polygon [wp↵] Lets you select objects by enclosing them in an irregularly shaped polygon boundary. When you use this option, you see the prompt `First polygon point:`. You then pick points to define the polygon boundary. As you pick points, the prompt `Undo/<Endpoint of line>:` appears. Select as many points as you need to define the boundary. You can undo boundary line segments as you go by clicking the Undo tool on the Standard toolbar or by pressing the U key. With the boundary defined, press ↵. The bounded objects are highlighted and the `Select object` prompt returns, allowing you to use more selection options.

Continued on next page

OTHER SELECTION OPTIONS *(continued)*

The following two selection options are also available, but seldom used. They are intended for use in creating custom menu options or custom toolbar tools.

Auto [au↵] Forces the standard automatic window or crossing window when a point is picked and no object is found (see "Using Autoselect" later in this chapter). A standard window is produced when the two window corners are picked from left to right. A crossing window is produced when the two corners are picked from right to left. Once this option is selected, it remains active for the duration of the current command. Auto is intended for use on systems on which the Automatic Selection feature has been turned off.

Single [si↵] Forces the current command to select only a single object. If you use this option, you can pick a single object; then the current command acts on that object as if you had pressed ↵ immediately after selecting the object. This has no menu equivalent.

Nearly all graphics programs today have tacitly acknowledged the Noun/Verb method for selecting objects. This method requires you to select objects before you issue a command to edit them. The next set of exercises shows you how to use the Noun/Verb method in AutoCAD.

You have seen that when AutoCAD is waiting for a command, it displays the crosshair cursor with the small square. This square is actually a pickbox superimposed on the cursor. It tells you that you can select objects, even while the command prompt appears at the bottom of the screen and no command is currently active. The square momentarily disappears when you are in a command that asks you to select points. From now on, this crosshair cursor with the small box will be referred to as the *Standard cursor*.

TIP *This chapter presents the standard AutoCAD method for object selection. AutoCAD also offers selection methods with which you may be more familiar. See Appendix B to learn how you can control object selection methods. This appendix also describes how you can change the size of the pickbox cursor.*

Now try moving objects by first selecting them and then using the Move command.

1. Press the Esc key twice to make sure AutoCAD isn't in the middle of a command you might have accidentally issued. Then click the arc. The arc is highlighted, and you may also see squares appear at its endpoints and its midpoint. These squares are called *grips*. (You may know them as *workpoints* from other graphics programs.) You'll get a chance to work with them a bit later.
2. Choose Move from the Modify toolbar. The cursor changes to Point Selection mode. Notice that the grips on the arc disappear, but the arc is still selected.
3. At the `Base point:` prompt, pick any point on the screen. The prompt `To point:` appears.
4. Type **@1<0↵**. Metric users should type **@3<0↵**. The arc moves to a new location 1 unit (3 units for metric users) to the right.

WARNING *If you find that this exercise does not work as described here, chances are the Noun/Verb setting has been turned off on your copy of AutoCAD. To turn on Noun/Verb setting, choose Tools ➢ Options to open the Options dialog box, and click the Selection tab. In the Selection Modes group, turn on the Noun/Verb Selection option. Click OK.*

In this exercise, you picked the arc *before* issuing the Move command. Then, when you clicked the Move tool, you didn't see the `Select object:` prompt. Instead, AutoCAD assumed you wanted to move the arc that you selected and went directly to the `Base point:` prompt.

Using Autoselect

Next you will move the rest of the door in the same direction using the Autoselect feature.

1. Pick a point just above and to the left of the rectangle representing the door. Be sure not to pick the door itself. Now a window appears that you can drag across the screen as you move the cursor. If you move the cursor to the left of the last point selected, the window appears dotted (see the first image of Figure 2.16). If you move the cursor to the right of that point, it appears solid (see the second image of Figure 2.16).

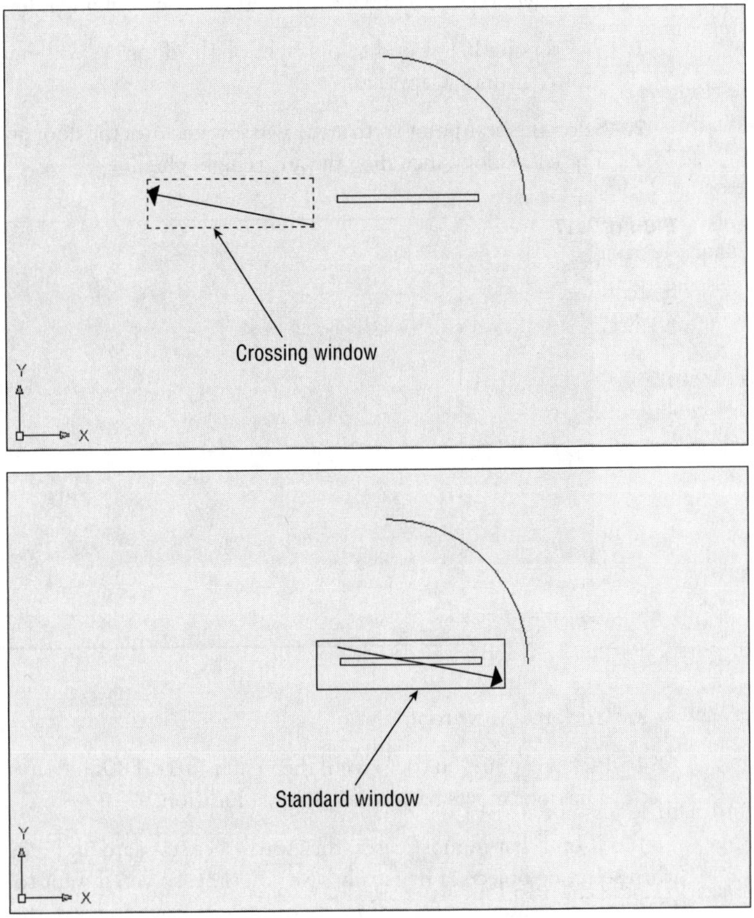

Figure 2.16

The dotted window (first image) indicates a crossing selection; the solid window (second image) indicates a standard selection window.

2. Pick a point below and to the right of the door so that the door is completely enclosed by the window, as shown in the bottom image in Figure 2.16. The door is highlighted (and again, you may see grips appear at the line's endpoints and midpoints).
3. Click the Move tool again. Just as in the last exercise, the `Base point:` prompt appears.
4. Pick any point on the screen; then enter **@1<0↵**. Metric users should enter **@3<0↵**. The door joins with the arc.

The two different windows you have just seen—the solid one and the dotted one—represent a standard window and a crossing window. If you use a standard window, anything that is completely contained within the window is selected. If you use a crossing window, anything that crosses through the window is selected. These two types of windows start automatically when you click any blank portion of the drawing area with a Standard cursor or Point Selection cursor; hence the name Autoselect.

Next, you will select objects with an automatic crossing window.

1. Pick a point below and to the right of the door. As you move the cursor left, the crossing (dotted) window appears.
2. Select the next point so that the window encloses the door and part of the arc (see Figure 2.17). The entire door, including the arc, is highlighted.

FIGURE 2.17

The door enclosed by a crossing window

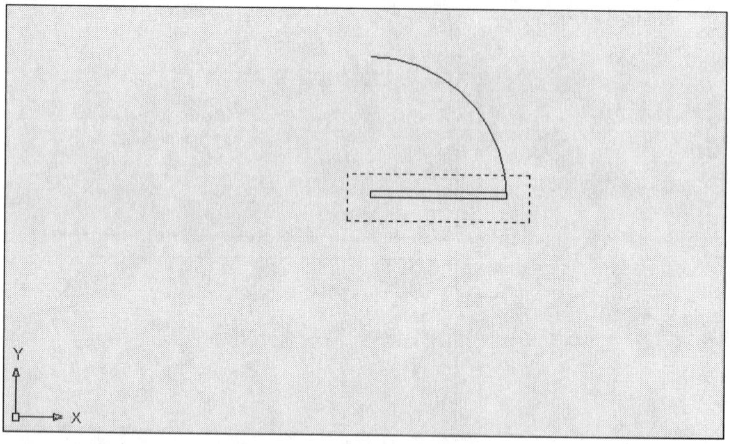

3. Click the Move tool.
4. Pick any point on the screen; then enter **@1<180↵**. Metric users should type **@3<180↵**. The door moves back to its original location.

You'll find that in most cases, the Autoselect standard and crossing windows are all you need when selecting objects. They really save you time, so you'll want to get familiar with these features.

Before continuing, you need to choose File ➢ Save and save the `Door` file. You won't want to save the changes you make in the next section, so saving now stores the current condition of the file on your hard disk for safekeeping.

Restrictions on Noun/Verb Object Selection

If you prefer to work with the Noun/Verb selection feature, you should know that its use is limited to the following subset of AutoCAD commands, listed here in alphabetic order:

Array	Copy	Hatch	Rotate
Block	Dview	List	Scale
Change	Erase	Mirror	Stretch
Chprop	Explode	Move	Wblock

For all other modifying or construction-oriented commands, the Noun/Verb selection method is inappropriate because for those commands you must select more than one set of objects. But you do not need to remember this list. You'll know if a command accepts the Noun/Verb selection method right away. Commands that don't accept the Noun/Verb selection method clear the selection and then display a `Select object:` prompt.

If you want to take a break, now is a good time to do it. If you want, exit AutoCAD and return to this point in the tutorial later. When you return, start AutoCAD and open the `Door` file.

Editing with Grips

Earlier, when you selected the door, grips appeared at the endpoints and midpoints of the lines and arcs. You can use grips to make direct changes to the shape of objects or to quickly move and copy them.

WARNING *If you did not see grips on the door in the previous exercise, your version of AutoCAD may have the Grips feature turned off. To turn them on, refer to the information on grips in Appendix B.*

So far, you have seen how operations in AutoCAD have a discrete beginning and ending. For example, to draw an arc, you first issue the Arc command, and then you go through a series of operations, including answering prompts and picking points. When you are finished, you have an arc, and AutoCAD is ready for the next command.

The Grips feature, on the other hand, plays by a different set of rules. Grips offer a small yet powerful set of editing functions that don't conform to the lockstep command/prompt/input routine you have seen so far. As you work through the following exercises, it is helpful to think of grips as a "subset" of the standard method of operation within AutoCAD.

To practice using the Grips feature, you'll make some temporary modifications to the door drawing.

Stretching Lines Using Grips

In this exercise, you'll stretch one corner of the door by grabbing the grip points of two lines.

1. Press the Esc key to make sure you're not in the middle of a command. Click a point below and to the left of the door to start a selection window.
2. Click above and to the right of the rectangular part of the door to select it.
3. Place the cursor on the lower-left corner grip of the rectangle, *but don't press the pick button yet.* Notice that the cursor jumps to the grip point and the grip changes color.

4. Move the cursor to another grip point. Notice again how the cursor jumps to it. When placed on a grip, the cursor moves to the exact center of the grip point. This means, for example, that if the cursor is placed on an endpoint grip, it is on the exact endpoint of the object.

5. Move the cursor to the upper-left corner grip of the rectangle and click it. The grip becomes a solid color, and is now a *hot grip*. The prompt displays the following message:

```
**STRETCH**
Specify stretch point or [Base point/Copy/Undo/eXit]:
```

This prompt tells you that the Stretch mode is active. Notice the options in the prompt. As you move the cursor, the corner follows, and the lines of the rectangle stretch (see Figure 2.18).

FIGURE 2.18

Stretching lines using hot grips. The first image shows the rectangle's corner being stretched upward. The next image shows the new location of the corner at the top of the arc.

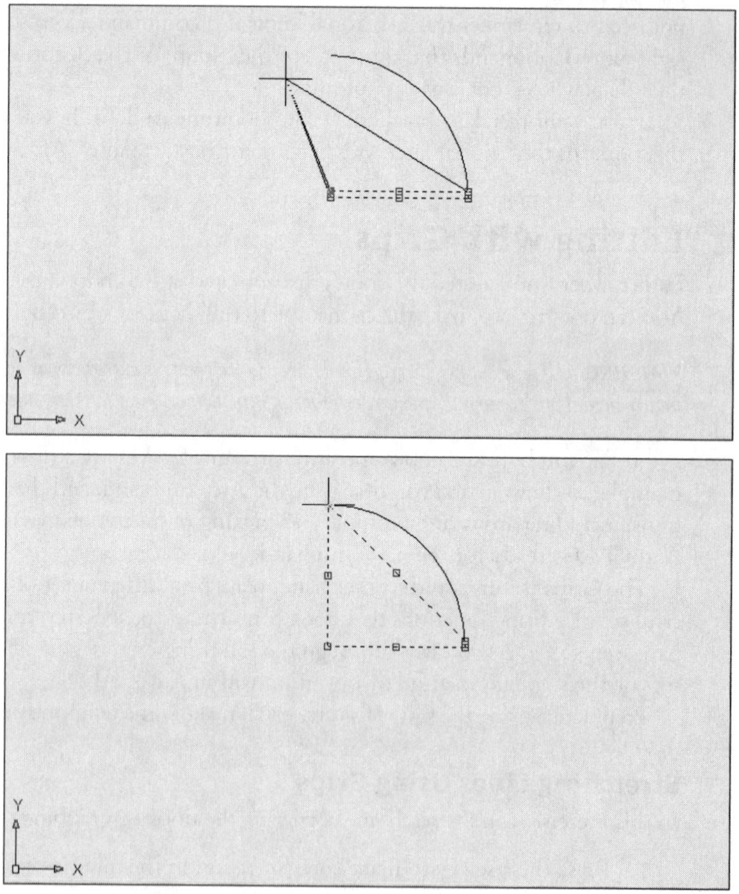

TIP *When you select a grip by clicking it, it turns a solid color (typically red) and is known as a hot grip. You can control the size and color of grips using the Grips dialog box; see Appendix B for the details.*

6. Move the cursor upward toward the top end of the arc and click that point. The rectangle deforms, with the corner placed at your pick point (see Figure 2.18).

TIP *When you click the corner grip point, AutoCAD selects the overlapping grips of two lines. When you stretch the corner away from its original location, the endpoints of both lines follow.*

Here you saw that a command called STRETCH is issued simply by clicking a grip point. As you will see, a handful of other hot grip commands are also available.

1. Notice that the grips are still active. Click the grip point that you moved before to make it a hot grip again.
2. Right-click the mouse to open a shortcut menu that contains a list of grip edit options .

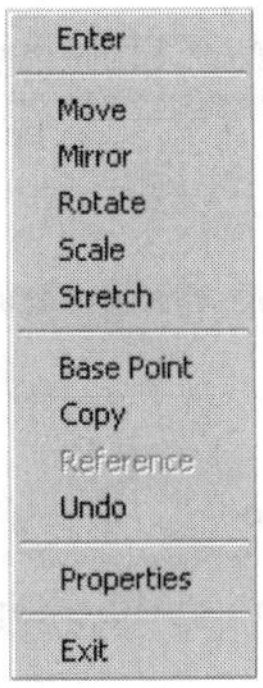

3. Choose Base Point from the list, and then click a point to the right of the hot grip. Now as you move the cursor, the hot grip moves relative to the cursor.
4. Right-click again, choose Copy from the shortcut menu, and enter **@1<-30↵**. (Metric users should enter **@3<-30↵**.) Instead of moving the hot grip and changing the lines, copies of the two lines are made, with their endpoints 1 unit (or 3 units for metric users) below and to the right of the first set of endpoints.
5. Pick another point just below the last. More copies are made.
6. Press ↵ or enter **X↵** to exit the Stretch mode. You can also right-click again and choose Exit from the shortcut menu.

In this exercise, you saw that you can select a base point other than the hot grip. You also saw how you can specify relative coordinates to move or copy a hot grip. Finally, you saw that with grips selected on an object, a right-click of the mouse opens a shortcut menu that contains grip edit options.

Moving and Rotating with Grips

As you've just seen, the Grips feature offers an alternative method for editing your drawings. You've already seen how you can stretch endpoints, but there is much more you can do with grips. The next exercise demonstrates some other options. You will start by undoing the modifications you made in the last exercise.

1. Click the Undo tool in the Standard toolbar, or type **U↵**. The copies of the stretched lines disappear.
2. Press ↵ again. The deformed door snaps back to its original form.

TIP *Pressing ↵ at the command prompt causes AutoCAD to repeat the last command entered—in this case, U.*

3. Select the entire door by first clicking a blank area below and to the right of the door.
4. Move the cursor to a location above and to the left of the rectangular portion of the door, and click. Since you went from right to left, you created a crossing window. Recall that the crossing window selects anything enclosed and crossing through the window.
5. Click the lower-left grip of the rectangle to turn it into a hot grip. Just as before, as you move your cursor, the corner stretches.
6. Right-click and then choose Move from the shortcut menu. The Command window displays the following:

   ```
   **MOVE**
   <Move to point>/Base point/Copy/Undo/eXit:
   ```

   Now as you move the cursor, the entire door moves with it.
7. Position the door near the center of the screen and click. The door moves to the center of the screen. Notice that the command prompt returns, yet the door remains highlighted, telling you that it is still selected for the next operation.
8. Click the lower-left grip again, right-click, and choose Rotate from the shortcut menu. The Command window displays the following:

   ```
   **ROTATE** <Rotation angle>/Base point/copy/Undo/Reference/eXit:
   ```

   As you move the cursor, the door rotates about the grip point.
9. Position the cursor so that the door rotates approximately 180° (see Figure 2.19). Then shift-click the mouse (hold down the shift key and press the left mouse button). A copy of the door appears in the new rotated position, leaving the original door in place.
10. Press ↵ to exit the Grip Edit mode.

TIP *You've seen how the Move command is duplicated in a modified way as a hot grip command. Other hot grip commands (Stretch, Rotate, Scale, and Mirror) also have similar counterparts in the standard set of AutoCAD commands. You'll see how those work in Chapters 9 and 13.*

After you complete any operation using grips, the objects are still highlighted with their grips still active. To clear the grip selection, press the Esc key.

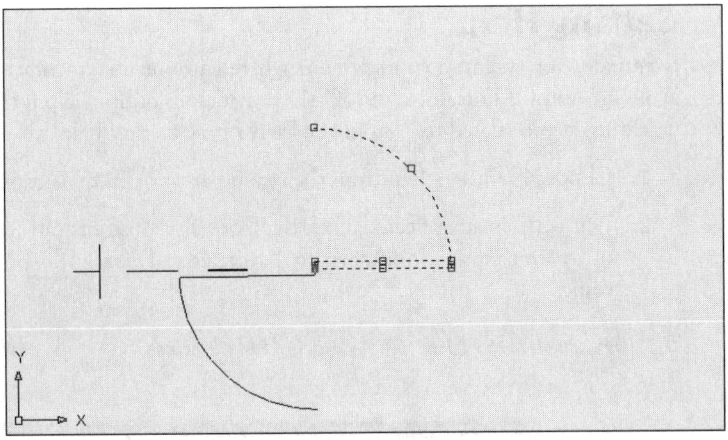

FIGURE 2.19
Rotating and copying the door using a hot grip. Notice that more than one object is being affected by the grip edit, even though only one grip is "hot."

In this exercise, you saw how hot grip options appear in a shortcut menu. Several other options are available in that menu, including Exit, Base Point, Copy, and Undo. You can also adjust an object's properties using the Properties option.

You can access many of these grip edit options by pressing the spacebar or ↵ while a grip is selected. With each press, the next option becomes active. The options then repeat if you continue to press ↵. The Shift key acts as a shortcut to the Copy option. You only have to use it once; then each time you click a point, a copy is made.

A Quick Summary of the Grips Feature

The exercises in this chapter using hot grips include only a few of the grips options. You'll get a chance to use other hot grip options in later chapters. Meanwhile, here is a summary of the grips feature:

- Clicking endpoint grips stretches those endpoints.
- Clicking midpoint grips of lines moves the entire line.
- If two objects meet end to end and you click their overlapping grips, both grips are selected simultaneously.
- You can select multiple grips by holding down the Shift key and clicking the desired grips.
- When a hot grip is selected, the Stretch, Move, Rotate, Scale, and Mirror options are available to you; just right-click the mouse.
- Or you can cycle through the Stretch, Move, Rotate, Scale, and Mirror options by pressing ↵ while a hot grip is selected.
- All the hot grip options allow you to make copies of the selected objects by either using the Copy option or holding down the Shift key while selecting points.
- All the hot grip options allow you to select a base point other than the originally selected hot grip.

Getting Help

Eventually, you will find yourself somewhere without documentation, and you will have a question about an AutoCAD feature. AutoCAD provides an online help facility that gives you information on nearly any topic related to AutoCAD. Here's how to find help:

1. Choose Help ➢ Help from the menu bar to open the AutoCAD 2004 Help window.
2. If it isn't already selected, click the Contents tab. This tab contains a table of contents. The other four tabs— Index, Search, Favorites and Ask Me—provide assistance in finding specific topics.

TIP *You can also press F1 to open the AutoCAD Help window.*

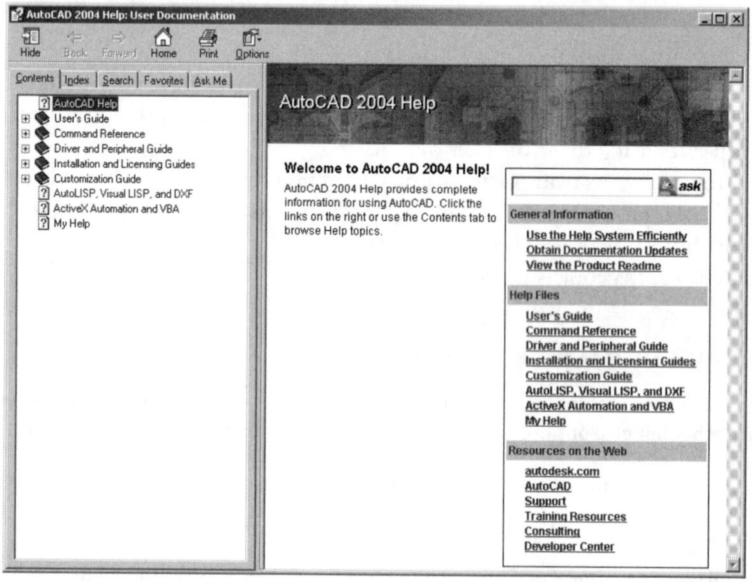

3. Scan down the screen until you see the topic Command References, and double-click it. Both panels of the Help Window change to show more topics.
4. In the panel on the right, click the item labeled C just to the right of the Command listing. The panel expands to display a list of command names that start with the letter C.
5. Look down the list and click the word *Copy*. A description of the Copy command appears in the panel to the right.
6. Click the line that reads Display All Hidden Text On This Page. The panel expands to give more details about the Copy command. You can close the expanded view by scrolling down the panel and selecting Collapse All Hidden Text On This Page.

You also have the Concepts, Procedures, and Reference tabs along the top of the panel on the right. These options offer more detailed information on the use of the selected item. If you want to back up through the steps you have just taken, click the Back button on the toolbar.

Using the Search Tab

If you want to find information on a topic based on a keyword, you can use the Search tab of the Help dialog box.

1. Click the Search tab in the left panel of the Help window. If this is the first time you've selected the Search tab, you may see a message telling you that AutoCAD is setting up an index for searches.
2. Type **Change** in the text box at the top of the Search tab, and then click List Topics or press ↵. The list box displays all the items in the Help system that contain the word *Change*.

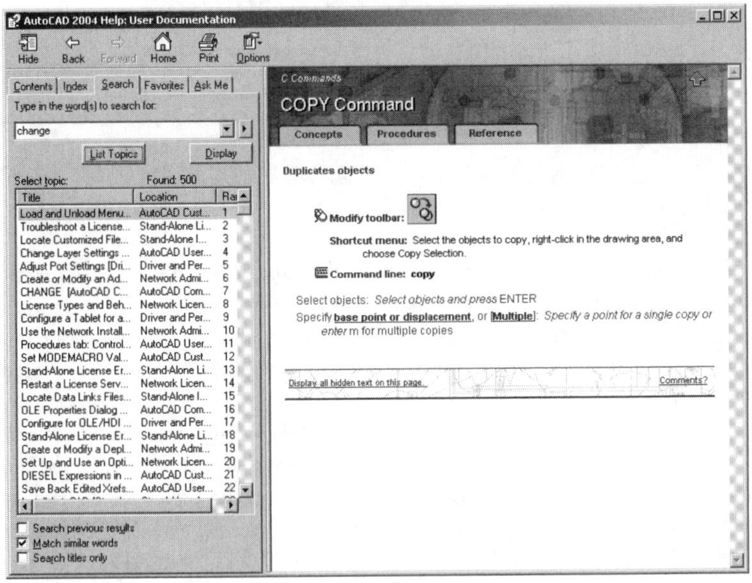

This list is a bit overwhelming. You can use Boolean AND, OR, NEAR, and NOT in conjunction with other keywords to help filter your searches, just as in a typical search engine that you might use in your web browser. Once you've found a topic you want, select it from the Select Topic list and then click the Display button to display information related to the topic in the panel on the right.

Another interesting tool in the Help dialog box is the Ask Me tab. This tab lets you ask "natural language" questions. Try the following steps to see how it works.

1. Click the Ask Me tab.
2. In the top text box, enter **How do I zoom into my view**. The list below the text box changes to show several items that relate to adjusting views in AutoCAD.

3. Click Magnify A View (Zoom). The right panel changes to display a description of how the Zoom command works.

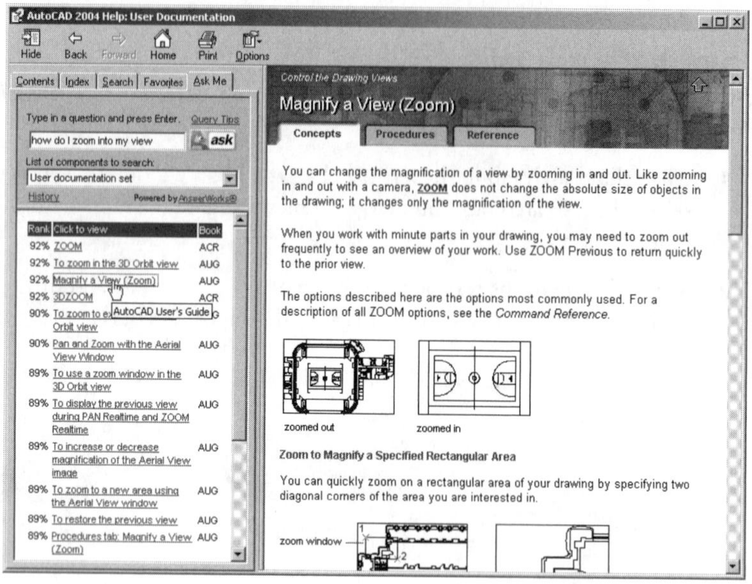

You'll notice a three-letter acronym to the right of each item listed in the Ask Me tab. These tell you the document source for the listed option. For example, the Magnify A View (Zoom) item is listed in the AutoCAD User Guide, or AUG. Other items show ACR for AutoCAD Command Reference. You can also limit the query to specific document sources by selecting a source from the List Of Components To Search list box.

If you scroll down to the bottom of the Ask Me list, you'll find a Search The Web For: option. This does just what it says. If you don't find a satisfactory answer in the AutoCAD help system, you can select this option to open a search web page in the panel on the right. (Make sure you are connected to the Internet if you use this option.)

The Index tab lets you locate specific topics in the AutoCAD Help system by entering a word in a list box. The Favorites tab lets you store locations in the Help system that you refer to frequently.

Using Context-Sensitive Help

AutoCAD also provides *context-sensitive help* to give you information related to the command you are currently using. To see how this works, try the following:

1. Close or minimize the Help window and return to the AutoCAD window.
2. Click the Move tool in the Modify toolbar to start the Move command.
3. Press the F1 function key, or choose Help from the menu bar. to open the Help window. A description of the Move command appears in panel on the right.

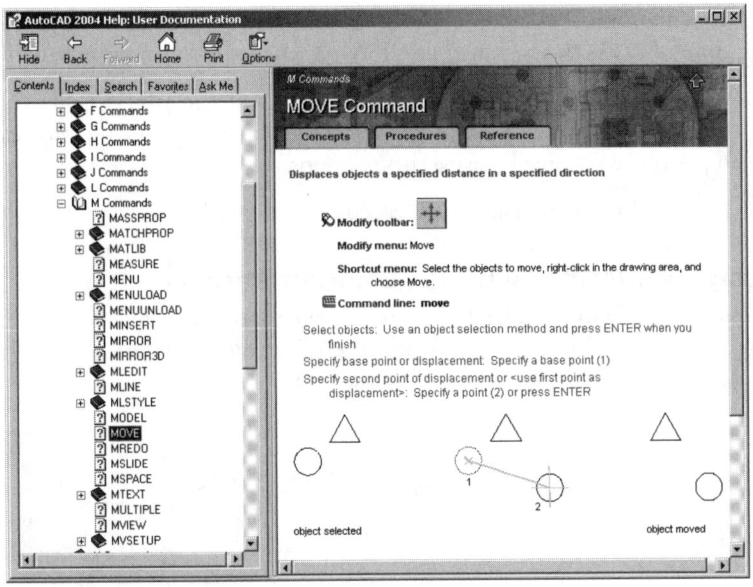

4. Click the Close button or press the Esc key.

5. Press the Esc key to exit the Move command.

If you are already familiar with the basics of AutoCAD, you mgith want to install the AutoCAD Learning Assistant. This tool offers quick tips and brief tutorials on a wide variety of topics, including working in collaborative groups and making the most of the Windows environment. The Learning Assistant is on its own CD as part of the AutoCAD 2004 package.

Additional Sources of Help

The Help Topics tool is the main online source for reference material, but you can also find answers to your questions through the other options found in the Help menu. Here is a brief description of the other Help menu options:

Active Assistance A popup window that offers immediate feedback on the command that you are using. LT users will have the Active Assistance window open by default. If you are a first-time user, this option may be helpful, but some users find it annoying. If you want to turn it off, right-click the Active Assistance icon in the Windows status area (it looks like a question mark) and then choose Exit from the shortcut menu. You can also set up Active Assistance to appear only when opened from the Help menu. Right-click the Active Assistance icon in the status area, and then choose Settings from the shortcut menu to open the Active Assistance Settings dialog box. Turn on the On Demand radio button option, and then click OK.

Developer Help Information specifically for developers. This includes anyone interested in customizing AutoCAD.

New Features Workshop Descriptions and tutorials focused on the new features found in AutoCAD 2004. You can update this unique support tool through the Autodesk website.

Online Resources Offers additional options that start your default web browser and open pages in the Autodesk PointA website. You can find the most up-to-date information regarding AutoCAD support and training by using these options.

About Information about the version of AutoCAD you are using.

Staying Informed with the Communication Center

Another feature that can help you stay informed about the latest news on AutoCAD is the Communication Center. To the far right of the status bar, you'll see the Communication Center icon. You might also see a balloon message pointing to it.

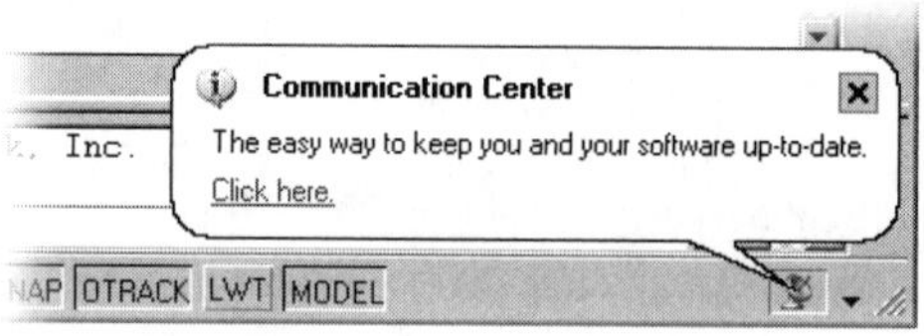

Click the Communication Center icon to open the Communication Center Welcome dialog box.

As the Communication Center welcome dialog box explains, the Communication Center offers a way to stay informed about the latest software updates and support issues for AutoCAD. Click the Settings button to open the Configuration Settings dialog box.

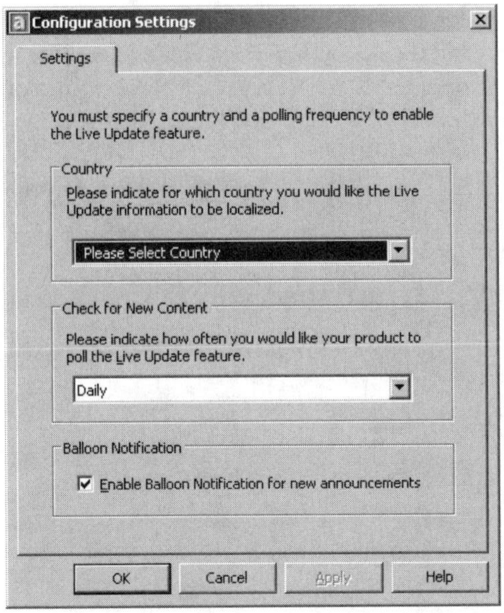

Here you can select your country from the Country drop-down list to ensure that the information is correct for your country. The Check For New Content option lets you select the frequency at which the Communication Center checks for new information. You can choose Daily, Weekly, Monthly, or On Demand. If you want to turn off the balloon message, clear the Enable Balloon Notification For New Announcements check box at the bottom of the dialog box.

Once you've selected a country for the first time, the Communication Center displays the Refresh Content button to the left of the Settings button in the Communication Center dialog box. If you are connected to the Internet, you can click this button at any time to check for updates from Autodesk. If any new information is available, a message alerting you to the new information is displayed in the dialog box.

The Communication Center works best if you use an "always on" Internet connection such as a DSL connection or high-speed cable connection. If you don't have such a connection, you can set the Check For New Contents option to On Demand. You can then check for updates when you connect to the Internet.

Displaying Data in a Text Window

You may have noticed that as you work in AutoCAD, the activity displayed in the Command window scrolls up. Sometimes it is helpful to view information that has scrolled past the view shown in the command window. For example, you can review the command activity from your session to check input values or to recall other data entry information. Try the following exercise to see how the text window works.

1. Choose Tools ➢ Inquiry ➢ List.

2. At the `Select objects:` prompt, click one of the arcs and press ↵. Information about the arc is displayed in the AutoCAD Text Window (see Figure 2.20). Toward the bottom is the list of the arc's properties. Don't worry if the meaning of some listed properties isn't obvious yet. As you work through this book, you'll learn what the properties of an object mean.

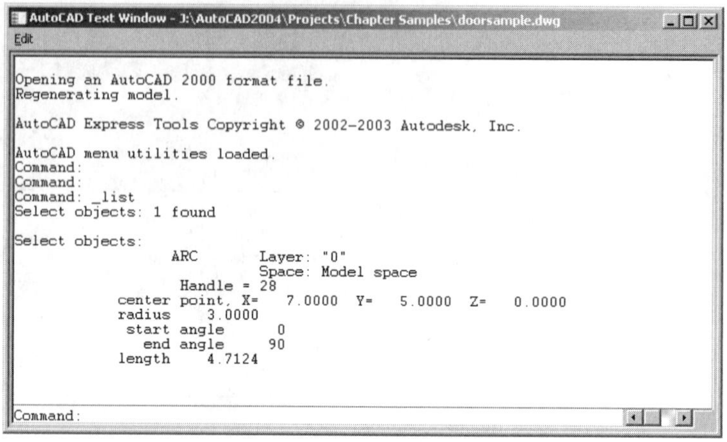

AutoCAD Text Window - J:\AutoCAD2004\Projects\Chapter Samples\doorsample.dwg
Edit
Opening an AutoCAD 2000 format file.
Regenerating model.
AutoCAD Express Tools Copyright © 2002-2003 Autodesk, Inc.
AutoCAD menu utilities loaded.
Command:
Command:
Command: _list
Select objects: 1 found
Select objects:
ARC Layer: "0"
Space: Model space
Handle = 28
center point, X= 7.0000 Y= 5.0000 Z= 0.0000
radius 3.0000
start angle 0
end angle 90
length 4.7124
Command:

FIGURE 2.20
The AutoCAD text screen showing the data displayed by the List tool

3. Press F2 to close the AutoCAD Text window.

TIP *The F2 function key offers a quick way to switch between the drawing editor and the Text Window.*

The scroll bar to the right of the Text Window lets you scroll to earlier events. You can even set the number of lines AutoCAD retains in the Text Window using the Options dialog box, or you can have AutoCAD record the Text Window information in a text file.

When you have more than one document open, the Text Window displays a listing for the drawing that is currently active.

Displaying the Properties of an Object

While we're on the subject of displaying information, you'll want to know about the Properties palette. In the last exercise, you saw how the List command showed some information regarding the properties of an object, such as the location of an arc's center and endpoints. You can also double-click an object to display a Properties palette that shows similar information. (In fact, you might accidentally display the Properties palette from time to time!) To see what this palette is for, try the following exercise.

1. Double-click an arc in the drawing to open the Properties palette, which displays a list of the arc's properties.

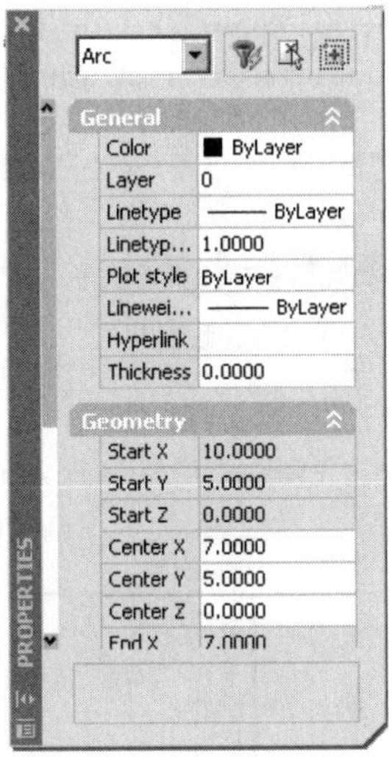

Don't worry if many of the items in this palette are undecipherable. You'll learn more about this palette as you work through the early chapters of this book. For now, just be aware that this palette appears whenever you double-click an object and that it displays the object's properties. It also allows you to modify many of the properties listed.

2. Click the small Auto-Hide box at the bottom left of the Properties palette. It is the icon that looks like a double arrow. The icon changes to a single arrow.

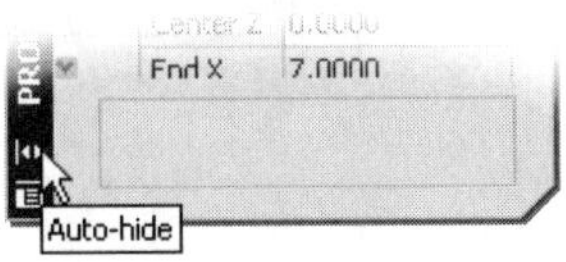

3. Move the cursor away from the Properties palette. The Properties palette collapses so that only the title bar remains.
4. Place the cursor on the Properties palette title bar. The Properties palette opens to reveal all the options again.

The Auto-Hide option in the Properties palette lets you keep the palette open without having it take up too much of the drawing area. This can be useful when you need to edit the properties of many objects.

1. Click the Auto-Hide box again to restore the "always open" mode of the palette.
2. Close the Properties palette by clicking the X in its upper left corner. You can also right-click the title on the left side of the Properties palette, and then choose Close from the shortcut menu.
3. Now you are finished with the door drawing, so choose File ➢ Close.

4. In the Save Changes dialog box, click the No button. (You've already saved this file just as you want it, so you do not need to save it again.)

TIP *You can also open the Properties palette by right-clicking an object and choosing Properties from the shortcut menu.*

If You Want to Experiment...

Try drawing the latch shown in Figure 2.21.

FIGURE 2.21

Try drawing this latch. Dimensions are provided for your reference.

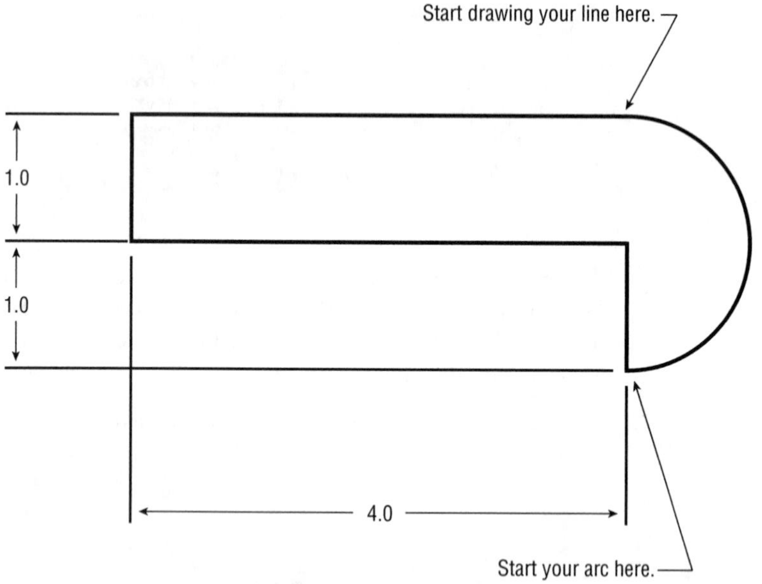
Start drawing your line here.
1.0
1.0
4.0
Start your arc here.

1. Start AutoCAD, open a new file, and name it `Latch`.
2. In the drawing editor, use the Line command to draw the straight portions of the latch. Start a line as indicated in Figure 2.21; then enter relative coordinates from the keyboard. For example, for the first line segment, enter **@4<180↵** to draw a line segment 4 units long from right to left.
3. Click the Arc tool on the Draw toolbar to draw an arc for the curved part.
4. To start your arc, use the Endpoint Osnap to pick the endpoint indicated in Figure 2.21.
5. Type **E↵** to issue the End option of the Arc command.
6. Using the Endpoint Osnap again, click the endpoint above where you started your line. A rubber-banding line and a temporary arc appear.
7. Type **D↵** to issue the Direction option for the Arc command.
8. Position your cursor so the ghosted arc looks like the one Figure 2.21, and then click the mouse button to draw in the arc.

Chapter 3

Learning the Tools of the Trade

CHAPTERS 1 AND 2 covered the basic information you need to understand the workings of AutoCAD. Now you will put this knowledge to work. In this architectural tutorial, which begins here and continues through Chapter 13, you will draw an apartment building composed of studios. The tutorial illustrates how to use AutoCAD commands and gives you a solid understanding of the basic AutoCAD package. With these fundamentals, you can use AutoCAD to its fullest potential, regardless of the kinds of drawings you intend to create or the enhancement products you might use in the future.

In this chapter you will start drawing an apartment's bathroom fixtures. In the process, you will learn how to use AutoCAD's basic tools. You'll also be introduced to the concept of drawing scale and how the size of what you draw is translated into a paper sheet size. Topics include:

- Setting Up a Work Area
- Using the AutoCAD Modes as Drafting Tools
- Exploring the Drawing Process
- Planning and Laying Out a Drawing
- If You Want to Experiment…

Setting Up a Work Area

Before beginning most drawings, you should set up your work area. To do this, determine the *measurement system,* the *drawing sheet size,* and the *scale* you want to use. The default work area is roughly 9" × 16" at full scale, given a decimal measurement system in which 1 unit equals 1 inch. Metric users will find that the default area is roughly 550 mm × 300 mm, in which 1 unit equals 1 mm. If these are appropriate settings for your drawing, you don't have to do any setting up. It is more likely, however, that you will make drawings of various sizes and scales. For example, you might want to create a drawing in a measurement system in which you can specify feet, inches, and fractions of inches at 1" = 1' scale and print the drawing on an 8 1/2" × 11" sheet of paper.

In Chapter 2, you used the Create New Drawing Wizard to set up a drawing file. The Create New Drawing Wizard is a great tool, but it hides many of the drawing setup tools you'll need to know to work with AutoCAD. In this section, you will learn how to set up a drawing exactly the way you want.

USING THE IMPERIAL AND METRIC EXAMPLES

Many of the exercises in this chapter are shown in both the metric and Imperial measurement systems. Please be sure that if you start with the Imperial system, you continue with it throughout this book. Also note that the metric settings described in this book are only approximations of their Imperial equivalents. For example, the drawing scale for the metric example is 1:10, which is close to the 1" = 1'-0" scale used in the Imperial example. In the grid example, you are asked to use a 30-unit grid, which is close to the 1-foot grid of the Imperial example. Dimensions of objects will be similar, but not exact. For example, the Imperial version of the tub will measure 2'8" × 5'0", and the metric version of the tub will be 81 cm × 152 cm. The actual metric equivalent of 2'8" × 5'0" is 81.28 cm × 152.4 cm. Measurements in the tub example are rounded to the nearest centimeter.

Metric users should also be aware that AutoCAD uses a period as a decimal point instead of the comma used in most European nations, South Africa, and elsewhere. Commas are used in AutoCAD to separate the x, y, and z components of a coordinate.

Specifying Units

Start by creating a new file called `Bath`.

1. If you haven't done so already, start up AutoCAD. If AutoCAD is already running, choose File ➢ New.
2. In the Create New Drawing dialog box, select the Start From Scratch option, and then select Imperial from the list just below the button options. Metric users can select Metric. Once you've done this, click OK.

TIP *If you don't see the Create New Drawing dialog box in step 2, but see the Select Template dialog box instead, select Acad.dwt and click Open. Metric users should select Acadiso.dwt then click Open. To set up AutoCAD to display the Create New Drawing dialog box for new drawings, right-click in the drawing area and select Options. In the Options dialog box, select the Systems tab, then select Show Startup Dialog Box from the Startup drop-down list in the General Options group.*

3. Choose File ➢ Save As.
4. In the Save Drawing As dialog box, enter **Bath** for the filename.
5. Check to make sure you are saving the drawing in the `Samples` subdirectory or in the directory you have chosen to store your exercise files, and then click Save.

The first thing you want to tell AutoCAD is the *unit style* you intend to use. So far, you've been using the default, which is decimal inches. In this unit style, whole units represent inches, and decimal units are decimal inches. If you want to be able to enter distances in feet, you must change the unit style to a style that accepts feet as input. You'll do this through the Drawing Units dialog box, shown in Figure 3.1.

FIGURE 3.1

The Drawing Units dialog box

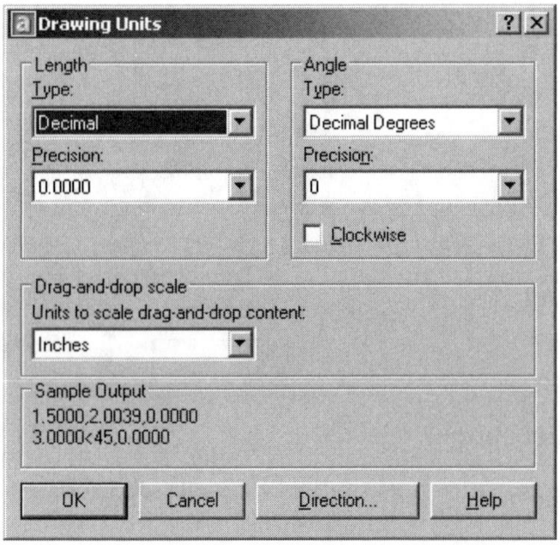

TIP *If you are a civil engineer, you should know that the Engineering unit style allows you to enter feet and decimal feet for distances. For example, the equivalent of 12'-6" is 12.5'. Earlier versions of AutoCAD did not have this feature, so engineers had to resort to using the Decimal unit style and feet as the base unit instead of inches. This caused problems when architectural drawings were combined with civil drawings. The scales of the two drawing types did not match. Even though this feature has existed since Release 12 of AutoCAD, old habits die hard. If you use the Engineering unit style, you will ensure that your drawings conform to the scale of drawings created by your architectural colleagues. And you will have the ability to enter decimal feet.*

1. Choose Formats ➢ Units or type **Un**↵ to open the Drawing Units dialog box. Let's look at a few of the options available.
2. Click the Type drop-down list in the Length button group. Notice the unit styles in the list.
3. Click Architectural. The Sample Output section of the dialog box shows you what the architectural style looks like in AutoCAD. Metric users should keep this setting as Decimal.

TIP *You can also control the Drawing Units settings using several system variables. To set the unit style, you can type* **`'lunits`**↵ *at the command prompt. (The apostrophe lets you enter this command while in the middle of other commands.) At the* `New value for Lunits <2>:` *prompt, enter* **`4`** *for Architectural. See Appendix D for other settings.*

4. Click the Precision drop-down list just below the Type list. Notice the options available. You can set the smallest unit AutoCAD will display in this drawing. For now, leave this setting at its default value of 1/16". Metric users will keep the setting at 0.0000.
5. Press the Esc key to close the drop-down list, and then click the Direction button at the bottom of the dialog box to open the Direction Control dialog box. This dialog box lets you set the direction for the 0° angle and the direction for positive degrees. For now, don't change these settings—you'll read more about them in a moment.

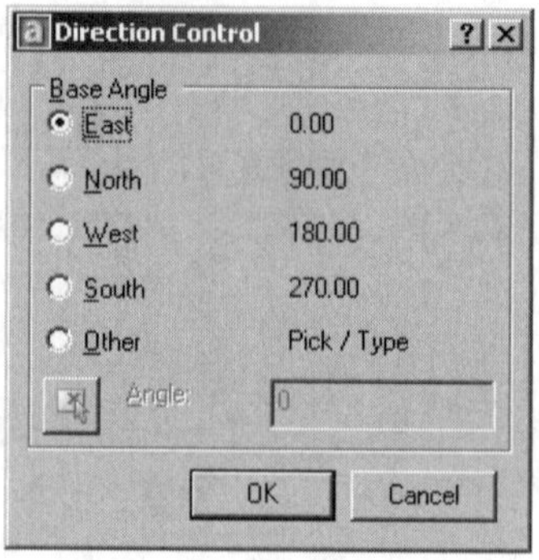

6. Click the Cancel button.
7. Now click the drop-down list in the Drag-and-Drop Scale group. The list shows various units of measure.
8. Click Inches, or if you are a metric user, choose Centimeters. This option allows you to control how AutoCAD translates drawing scales when you import drawings from outside the current drawing. You'll learn more about this feature in Chapter 24.
9. Click OK in the Drawing Units dialog box to return to the drawing.

If you use the Imperial system of measurement, you selected Architectural measurement units for this tutorial, but your own work may require a different unit style. You saw the unit styles available in the Drawing Units dialog box. Table 3.1 shows examples of how the distance 15.5 is entered in each of these styles.

TABLE 3.1: MEASUREMENT SYSTEMS AVAILABLE IN AUTOCAD

MEASUREMENT SYSTEM	AUTOCAD'S DISPLAY OF MEASUREMENT
Scientific	1.55E+01 (inches or metric)
Decimal	15.5000 (inches or metric)
Engineering	1'-3.5" (input as 1'3.5")
Architectural	1'-3 1/2" (input as 1'3-1/2")
Fractional	15 1/2" (input as 15-1/2")

In the previous exercise, you needed to change only two settings. Let's take a look at the other Drawing Units settings in more detail. As you read, you may want to refer to the illustration of the Drawing Units dialog box.

Fine-Tuning the Measurement System

Most of the time, you will be concerned only with the units and angles settings of the Drawing Units dialog box. But as you saw from the last exercise, you can control many other settings related to the input and display of units.

TIP *To measure the distance between two points, choose Tools ➢ Inquiry ➢ Distance from the menu bar, or type Di↵, and then click the two points (Di is the shortcut for entering Dist↵). But if you find that this command doesn't give you an accurate distance measurement, examine the Precision option in the Drawing Units dialog box. If it is set too high, the value returned by the* `Dist` *command may be rounded to a value greater than your tolerances allow, even though the distance is drawn accurately.*

The Precision drop-down list in the Length group lets you specify the smallest unit value that you want AutoCAD to display in the status line and in the prompts. If you choose a measurement system that uses fractions, the Precision list includes fractional units. You can also control this setting with the Luprec system variable.

The Angle group lets you set the style for displaying angles. You have a choice of five angle styles: decimal degrees, degrees/minutes/seconds, grads, radians, and surveyor's units. In the Angle group's Precision drop-down list, you can determine the degree of accuracy you want AutoCAD to display for angles. You can also control these settings with the Aunits and Auprec system variables.

TIP *You can find out more about system variables in Appendix D.*

The Direction Control dialog box lets you set the direction of the 0° base angle. The default base angle (and the one used throughout this book) is a direction from left to right. However, at times you might want to designate another direction as the 0° base angle. You can also tell AutoCAD which direction is positive, either clockwise or counterclockwise. This book uses the default, which is counterclockwise. You can also control these settings with the Angbase and Angdir system variables.

The Drag-and-Drop Scale setting in the Drawing Units dialog box lets you control how blocks from the Tool Palette or DesignCenter are scaled as they are imported into your current drawing. A block is a collection of drawing objects that form a single object. Blocks are frequently used to create standard symbols. You'll learn more about blocks in Chapter 4. The Drag-and-Drop Scale setting lets you compensate for drawings of different scale by offering an automatic scale translation when importing blocks from an external file. The Insunits system variable also controls the Drag-and-Drop Scale setting. You'll learn more about this setting in Chapter 22.

TIP *If you're new to AutoCAD, don't worry about the Drag-and-Drop Scale setting right now. Make a mental note of it. It may come in handy in your work in the future.*

THINGS TO WATCH OUT FOR WHEN ENTERING DISTANCES

When you are using Architectural units, you should be aware of two points:

- Use hyphens only to distinguish fractions from whole inches.
- You cannot use spaces while specifying a dimension. For example, you can specify eight feet, four and one-half inches as 8'4-1/2" or 8'4.5, but not as 8'-4 1/2".

These idiosyncrasies are a source of confusion to many architects and engineers new to AutoCAD because the program often displays architectural dimensions in the standard architectural format but does not allow you to enter dimensions that way.

Continued on next page

THINGS TO WATCH OUT FOR WHEN ENTERING DISTANCES *(continued)*

Here are some tips for entering distances and angles in unusual situations:

- When entering distances in inches and feet, you can omit the inch (") sign. If you are using the Engineering unit style, you can enter decimal feet and forgo the inch sign entirely.
- You can enter fractional distances and angles in any format you like, regardless of the current unit style. For example, you can enter a distance as **@1/2<1.5708r** even if your current unit system is set for decimal units and decimal degrees (**1.5708r** is the radian equivalent of 90°).
- If you have your angle units set to degrees, grads, or radians, you do not need to specify g, r, or d after the angle. You do have to specify g, r, or d, however, if you want to use these units when they are not the current default angle system.
- If your current angle system is set to something other than degrees, but you want to enter angles in degrees, you can use a double less-than symbol (<<) in place of the single less-than symbol (<) to override the current angle system of measure. The << also assumes the base angle of 0° to be a direction from left to right and the positive direction to be counterclockwise.
- If your current angle system uses a different base angle and direction, and you want to specify an angle in the standard base direction, you can use a triple less-than symbol (<<<) to indicate angle.
- You can specify a denominator of any size when specifying fractions. However, be aware that the value you have set for the maximum number of digits to the right of decimal points (under the Precision setting in the Length button group of the Drawing Units dialog box) will restrict the actual fractional value AutoCAD uses. For example, if your units are set for a maximum of two digits of decimals and you give a fractional value of 5/32, AutoCAD rounds this value to 3/16 or 0.16.
- You can enter decimal feet for distances in the Architectural unit style. For example, you can enter 6'-6" as **6.5'**.

Setting Up the Drawing Limits

One of the big advantages in using AutoCAD is that you can draw at full scale; you aren't limited to the edges of a piece of paper the way you are in manual drawing. But you still have to consider what will happen when you want a printout of your drawing. When you start a new drawing, it helps to limit your drawing area to one that can be scaled down to fit on a standard sheet size. Although this is not absolutely necessary with AutoCAD, the limits give you a frame of reference between your work in AutoCAD and the final printed output.

To set up the drawing work area, you need to understand how standard sheet sizes translate into full-scale drawing sizes. Table 3.2 lists widths and heights of drawing areas in inches, according to scales and final printout sizes. The scales are listed in the far-left column; the output sheet sizes are listed across the top.

Let's take an example: To find the area needed in AutoCAD for your bathroom drawing, look across from the scale 1"=1' to the column that reads 8 1/2" × 11" at the top. You'll find the value 102 × 132. This means the drawing area needs to fit within an area 102" × 132" (8.5 feet × 11 feet) in AutoCAD in order to fit a printout of a 1" = 1'-0" scale drawing on an 8 1/2" × 11" sheet of paper. You may want the drawing area to be oriented horizontally, so that the 11 feet will be in the x-axis and the 8.5 feet will be in the y-axis.

TABLE 3.2: WORK AREA IN DRAWING UNITS (INCHES) BY SCALE AND PLOTTED SHEET SIZE

SCALE	81/2"× 11"	11"× 17"	17"× 22"	18"× 24"
3"=1'	34 × 44	44 × 68	68 × 88	72 × 96
11/2"=1'	68 × 88	88 × 136	136 × 176	144 × 192
1"=1'	102 × 132	132 × 204	204 × 264	216 × 288
3/4"=1'	136 × 176	176 × 272	272 × 352	288 × 384
1/2"=1'	204 × 264	264 × 408	408 × 528	432 × 576
1/4"=1'	408 × 528	528 × 816	816 × 1056	864 × 1152
1/8"=1'	816 × 1056	1056 × 1632	1632 × 2112	1728 × 2304
1/16"=1'	1632 × 2112	2112 × 3264	3264 × 4224	3456 × 4608
1/32"=1'	3264 × 4224	4224 × 6528	6528 × 8448	6912 × 9216
1"=10'	1020 × 1320	1320 × 2040	2040 × 2640	2160 × 2880
1"=20'	2040 × 2640	2640 × 4080	4080 × 5280	4320 × 5760
1"=30'	3060 × 3960	3960 × 6120	6120 × 7920	6480 × 8640
1"=40'	4080 × 5280	5280 × 8160	8160 × 10560	8640 × 11520
1"=50'	5100 × 6600	6600 × 10200	10200 × 13200	10800 × 14400
1"=60'	6120 × 7920	7920 × 12240	12240 × 15840	12960 × 17280

TABLE 3.2: WORK AREA IN DRAWING UNITS (INCHES) BY SCALE AND PLOTTED SHEET SIZE (CONTINUED)

SCALE	22"× 34"	24"× 36"	30"× 42"	36"× 48"
3"=1'	88 × 136	96 × 144	120 × 168	144 × 192
11/2"=1'	176 × 272	192 × 288	240 × 336	288 × 384
1"=1'	264 × 408	288 × 432	360 × 504	432 × 576
3/4"=1'	352 × 544	384 × 576	480 × 672	576 × 768
1/2"=1'	528 × 816	576 × 864	720 × 1008	864 × 1152
1/4"=1'	1056 × 1632	1152 × 1728	1440 × 2016	1728 × 2304
1/8"=1'	2112 × 3264	2304 × 3456	2880 × 4032	3456 × 4608
1/16"=1'	4224 × 6528	4608 × 6912	5760 × 8064	6912 × 9216
1/32"=1'	8448 × 13056	9216 × 13824	11520 × 16128	13824 × 18432
1"=10'	2640 × 4080	2880 × 4320	3600 × 5040	4320 × 5760
1"=20'	5280 × 8160	5760 × 8640	7200 × 10080	8640 × 11520
1"=30'	7920 × 12240	8640 × 12960	10800 × 15120	12960 × 17280
1"=40'	10560 × 16320	11520 × 17280	14400 × 20160	17280 × 23040
1"=50'	13200 × 20400	14400 × 21600	18000 × 25200	21600 × 28800
1"=60'	15840 × 24480	17280 × 25920	21600 × 30240	25920 × 34560

If you're a metric user, you'll be drawing the bathroom at a scale of 1 to 10. This scale is close to the 1" = 1'-0" scale used for the Imperial measurements in the exercises. So for an A4 sheet, your work area should be 297 cm × 210 cm. This is the equivalent of an A4 sheet (210 mm × 297 mm) enlarged by a factor of 10.

Now that you know the area you need, you can use the `Limits` command to set up the area.

1. Choose Format ➢ Drawing Limits.
2. At the `Specify lower left corner or [ON/OFF] <0'-0",0'-0">:` prompt, specify the lower-left corner of your work area. Press ↵ to accept the default.
3. At the `Specify upper right corner <1'0",0'9">:` prompt, specify the upper-right corner of your work area. (The default is shown in brackets.) Enter **132,102**. Or if you prefer, you can enter **11',8'6**, since you've set up your drawing for architectural units. Metric users should enter **297,210**.
4. Next, choose View ➢ Zoom ➢ All. You can also select the Zoom All tool from the Zoom Window flyout on the Standard toolbar, or type **Z**↵ **A**↵. Although it appears that nothing has changed, your drawing area is now set to a size that will allow you to draw your bathroom at full scale.

TIP *You can toggle through the Coordinate Readout modes by repeatedly pressing F6 or by clicking the coordinate readout on the status bar. For more on the Coordinate Readout modes, see Chapter 1 and the "Using Grid and Snap Together" section later in this chapter.*

5. Move the cursor to the upper-right corner of the drawing area and watch the coordinate readout. Notice that now the upper-right corner has a Y coordinate of approximately 8'-6" or 300 for metric users. The X coordinate depends on the proportion of your AutoCAD window. The coordinate readout also displays distances in feet and inches.

In step 5, the coordinate readout shows you that your drawing area is larger than before, but no visual clues tell you where you are or what distances you are dealing with. To help you get your bearings, you can turn on the Grid mode, which you will learn about shortly. The Grid mode displays an array of dots that help you visualize distances and the limits of your drawing. Before you get to grids, let's take a closer look at scale factors and how they work.

TIP *The steps you've just taken to set up your drawing are duplicated in the Advanced Setup option of the Create New Drawing Wizard. This section showed you the detailed method of setting up your drawing so you'll understand exactly what is going on, but if you prefer, you can use the Create New Drawing Wizard to set up future drawings. You can then use the Drawing Units dialog box to fine-tune your drawing or make adjustments later.*

Understanding Scale Factors

When you draft manually, you work on the final drawing directly with pen and ink or pencil. With a CAD program, you are a few steps removed from the actual finished product. Because of this, you need a deeper understanding of your drawing scale and how it is derived. In particular, you need to understand scale factors.

For example, one of the more common uses of scale factors is in translating text size in your CAD drawing to the final plotted text size. When you draw manually, you simply draw your notes at the size you want. In a CAD drawing, you need to translate the desired final text size to the drawing scale.

When you start adding text to your drawing (see Chapter 8), you have to specify a text height. The scale factor helps you determine the appropriate text height for a particular drawing scale. For example, you might want your text to appear 1/8" high in your final plot. But if you draw your text to 1/8" in your drawing, it appears as a dot when plotted. The text has to be scaled up to a size that, when scaled back down at plot time, appears 1/8" high. So, for a 1/4" scale drawing, you multiply the 1/8" text height by a scale factor of 48 to get 6". Your text should be 6" high in the CAD drawing in order to appear 1/8" high in the final plot. So where did the number 48 come from?

The scale factor for fractional inch scales is derived by multiplying the denominator of the scale by 12 and then dividing by the numerator. For example, the scale factor for 1/4" = 1'-0" is (4 × 12)/1, or 48/1. For 3/16" = 1'-0" scale, the operation is (16 × 12)/3 or 64. For whole-foot scales such as 1" = 10', multiply the feet side of the equation by 12. Metric scales require simple decimal conversions.

TIP *All the scale factors shown in Table 3.3 were derived by the method described in the previous paragraph.*

All the drawing sizes in Table 3.2 were derived by using scale factors. Table 3.3 shows scale factors as they relate to standard drawing scales. These scale factors are the values by which you multiply the desired final printout size to get the equivalent full-scale size. For example, if you have a sheet size of 11" × 17", and you want to know the equivalent full-scale size for a 1/4"-scale drawing, you multiply the sheet measurements by 48. In this way, 11" becomes 528" (48" × 11") and 17" becomes 816" (48" × 17"). Your work area must be 528" × 816" if you intend to have a final output of 11" × 17" at 1/4" = 1'. You can divide these inch measurements by 12" to get 44' × 68'.

TIP *If you get the message* `**Outside limits`, *you selected a point outside the area defined by the limits of your drawing, and the* `Limits` *command's limits-checking feature is on. (Some third-party programs may use the limits-checking feature.) If you must select a point outside the limits, issue the* `Limits` *command, and then enter* **`off`** *at the* `ON/OFF <Lower left corner>:` *prompt to turn off the limits-checking feature.*

TABLE 3.3: SCALE CONVERSION FACTORS

	SCALE FACTORS FOR ENGINEERING DRAWING SCALES							
1" = n	10'	20'	30'	40'	50'	60'	100'	200'
Scale factor	120	240	360	480	600	720	1200	2400
	SCALE FACTORS FOR ARCHITECTURAL DRAWING SCALES							
n = 1'-0"	1/16"	1/8"	1/4"	1/2"	3/4"	1"	1 1/2"	3"
Scale factor	192	96	48	24	16	12	8	4

If you are using the metric system, you can use the drawing scale directly as the scale factor. For example, a drawing scale of 1:10 has a scale factor of 10; a drawing scale of 1:50 has a scale factor of 50; and so on. Table 3.4 shows drawing areas based on scale and sheet size. The sheet sizes are shown across the top, and the scales are shown in the column to the far left.

TABLE 3.4: WORK AREA IN METRIC UNITS (CENTIMETERS) BY SCALE AND PLOTTED SHEET SIZE. MULTIPLY WORK AREA SIZES BY 10 FOR MILLIMETER EQUIVALENTS.

SCALE	A0 OR F 841MM×1189MM (33.11"×46.81")	A OR D594MM×841MM (23.39"×33.11")
1:5	420 cm × 594 cm	297 cm × 420 cm
1:10	841 cm × 1189 cm	594 cm × 841 cm
1:20	1682 cm × 2378 cm	1188 cm × 1682 cm
1:25	2102.5 cm × 2972.5 cm	1485 cm × 2102.5 cm
1:33 1/3	2803 cm × 3962 cm	1980 cm × 2803 cm
1:40	3360 cm × 4756 cm	2376 cm × 3360 cm
1:50	4200 cm × 5940 cm	2970 cm × 4200 cm
1:75	6307 cm × 8917 cm	4455 cm × 6307 cm
1:10	8410 cm × 11890 cm	5940 cm × 8410 cm
1:125	10512 cm × 14862 cm	7425 cm × 10512 cm

TABLE 3.4: WORK AREA IN METRIC UNITS (CENTIMETERS) BY SCALE AND PLOTTED SHEET SIZE. MULTIPLY WORK AREA SIZES BY 10 FOR MILLIMETER EQUIVALENTS. (CONTINUED)

SCALE	A2 OR C420MM×594MM (16.54"× 23.39")	A3 OR B 297MM×420MM (11.70"×16.54")	A4 OR A 210MM×297MM (8.27"×11.70")
1:5	210 cm × 297 cm	148 cm × 210 cm	105 cm × 148 cm
1:10	420 cm × 594 cm	297 cm × 420 cm	210 cm × 297 cm
1:20	840 cm × 1188 cm	594 cm × 840 cm	420 cm × 594 cm
1:25	1050 cm × 1485 cm	742.5 cm × 1050 cm	5250 cm × 742.5 cm
1:33 1/3	1399 cm × 1980 cm	990 cm × 1399 cm	700 cm × 990 cm
1:40	1680 cm × 2376 cm	1188 cm × 1680 cm	840 cm × 1188 cm
1:50	2100 cm × 2970 cm	1480 cm × 2100 cm	1050 cm × 1480 cm
1:75	3150 cm × 4455 cm	2227 cm × 3150 cm	1575 cm × 2227 cm
1:10	4200 cm × 5940 cm	2970 cm × 4200 cm	2100 cm × 2970 cm
1:125	5250 cm × 7425 cm	3712 cm × 5250 cm	2625 cm × 3712 cm

Metric users need to take special care regarding the base unit. The examples in this book will use centimeters as a base unit, which means that if you enter a distance as 1, you can assume the distance to be 1 cm. If you want to use millimeters as the base unit, multiply the sheet-size values in Table 3.4 by 10.

TIP *Metric users should note that the scale factor depends on whether you are using millimeters, centimeters, or meters as the basis for the final plot size. For example, a drawing that uses millimeters as its base unit of drawing measure (1 drawing unit = 1 millimeter) uses a scale factor of 1 to 500 if the final output is to be at a scale of 1:50 centimeters.*

You will use scale factors to specify text height and dimension settings, so understanding them now will pay off later. Plotting to a particular scale will also be easier with an understanding of scale factors.

Using the AutoCAD Modes as Drafting Tools

After you set up your work area, you can begin the plan of a typical bathroom in your studio. You will use this example to learn about some of AutoCAD's drawing aids. These tools might be compared to a background grid (*Grid mode*), scale (*Coordinate Readout mode*), and a T-square and triangle (*Object Snap Tracking mode* and *Polar Tracking mode*). These drawing modes can be indispensable tools when used properly. The Drafting Settings dialog box helps you visualize the modes in an organized manner and simplifies their management.

Using the Grid Mode as a Background Grid

Using the Grid mode is like having a grid under your drawing to help you with layout. In AutoCAD, the Grid mode lets you see the limits of your drawing because the grid is only displayed within the limits setting of your drawing. The Grid mode also helps you visually determine the distances you are working with in any given view. In this section, you will learn how to control the grid's appearance. The F7 key toggles the Grid mode on and off; you can also click the GRID button in the status bar. Start by setting the grid spacing.

1. Choose Tools ➢ Drafting Settings, or type **Ds**↵ to display the Drafting Settings dialog box, showing all the mode settings.
2. Click the Snap And Grid tab. You see four button groups: Snap, Grid, Polar Spacing, and Snap Type & Style.

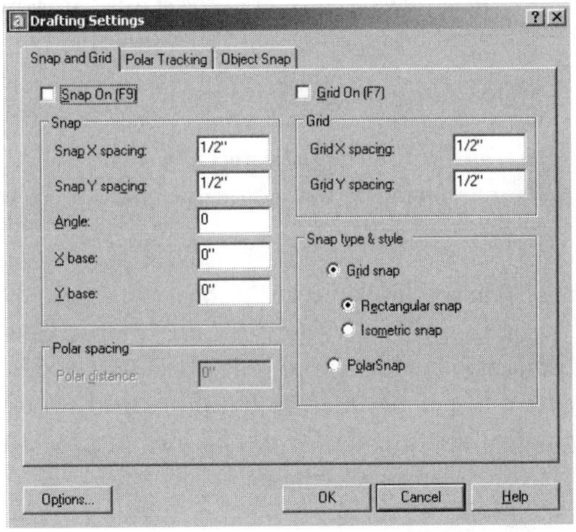

3. Let's start with the Grid group. Notice that the GridX Spacing text box contains a value of 1/2". Metric users see a value of 10.

4. Double-click the GridX Spacing text box to highlight the entry. You can now type a new value for this setting.

TIP *You can use the Gridunit system variable to set the grid spacing. Enter* `'`**`Gridunit`**`↵`, and at the `New value for GRIDUNIT <0'0",0'0">:` *prompt, enter* **`12,12`** *(*__`30,30`__ *for metric users). You must enter the Gridunit value as an XY coordinate.*

5. Type **12** for 12", and then press Tab to move to the GridY Spacing text box. Metric users should type **30**, and then press Tab. Notice that the GridY Spacing text box automatically changes to the same value as the X spacing value you just entered. In the case of the Imperial measurement, the value also changes from 12 to 1'. AutoCAD assumes you want the X and Y grid spacing to be the same, unless you specifically ask for a different Y setting.

TIP *To change an entry in an input text box, you can double-click the text box to highlight the whole entry, and then replace the entry by simply typing a new one. If you just want to change part of an entry, click the text box and then press the cursor keys to move to the exact character you want to change. You can press the Backspace key to delete characters.*

6. Click the Grid On check box to make the grid visible. Also notice the F7 in parentheses. This tells you that the F7 function key also controls the Grid On/Off function.

7. Click OK. The grid now appears as an array of dots with a 12" spacing in your drawing area (30 cm if you are following the metric version of this tutorial). The grid dots will not print or plot with your drawing.

With the grid at a 12-unit spacing (30 cm for metric users), you can see your work area more clearly. It also gives you a visual reference for your drawing. You can see what a 1-foot (or 30-cm) distance looks like in your drawing. Since the grid appears only within the drawing limits, you are better able to see your work area. In the next section, you'll see how the Snap mode works.

1. Press F7, or click the word GRID in the status bar (you can also hold down the Ctrl key and press **G**). The grid disappears.

2. Press F7 again to turn the grid back on.

WARNING *If your view is such that the grid spacing appears quite small, AutoCAD will not display the grid, in order to preserve the readability of the drawing. If this situation occurs, you will see the message* `Grid too dense to display` *in the Command window.*

In this exercise, you set the grid spacing equal to the scale factor of your drawing. This makes the grid spacing equivalent to 1" intervals of the final plotted drawing. For example, if your drawing is 1/4" = 1'-0" scale, you could set your grid spacing to 48. The grid spacing would then reflect the 1-inch spacing for a 1/4" scale drawing. If you're a metric user, you can keep the grid spacing to 10 to display the equivalent distance of 10 cm. This exercise used 30 for the metric grid spacing simply to match the display of the Imperial version.

Using the Snap Modes

The *Snap mode* forces the cursor to move in steps of a specific distance. Snap mode is useful when you know that you will be drawing objects that you want to maintain accuracy while entering distances with the cursor.

Actually, two snap modes are available in AutoCAD: *Grid Snap* and *Polar Snap*. Let's start by looking at the Grid Snap mode.

The F9 key toggles the Grid Snap mode on and off, or you can click the SNAP button in the status bar. Follow these steps to access the Grid Snap mode:

1. Choose Tools ➢ Drafting Settings, or type **Ds**↵ to open the Drafting Settings dialog box.
2. In the Snap group of the dialog box, double-click the SnapX Spacing text box and type **4**. (Metric users should enter **10**.) Then press the Tab key to move to the next option. As with the grid setting, AutoCAD assumes you want the X and Y snap spacing to be the same, unless you specifically ask for a different Y setting.
3. Click the Snap On check box to turn it on.
4. Click OK and start moving the cursor around. Notice how the cursor seems to move in "steps" rather than in a smooth motion. Also notice that the SNAP button in the status bar appears pressed, indicating that the Snap mode is on.
5. Press F9 or click the word SNAP in the status bar (you can also hold down the Ctrl key and press B); then move the cursor slowly around the drawing area. The Snap mode is now off.
6. Press F9 again to turn the Snap mode back on.

TIP *You can use the Snapunit system variable to set the snap spacing. Enter 'Snapunit*↵. Then, at the `New value for SNAPUNIT <0'0",0'0">:` *prompt, enter* **`4,4`** *(***`10,10`** *for metric users). You must enter the Snapunit value as an XY coordinate.*

Take a moment to look at the Drafting Settings dialog box. The other options in the Snap group allow you to set the snap origin point (X Base and Y Base), rotate the cursor to an angle other than its current 0–90° (Angle), and set the horizontal snap spacing to a value different from the vertical spacing (SnapX Spacing and SnapY Spacing).

In the Snap Type & Style group, you can change the snap and grid configuration to aid in creating isometric drawings by choosing the Isometric Snap radio button. The Polar Snap option allows you to set a snap distance for the Polar Snap feature. When you click the Polar Snap radio button, the Polar Distance option at the lower left of the dialog box changes from gray to black and white to allow you to enter a Polar Snap distance. The next exercise discusses these features.

TIP *You can use the Snaptype system variable to set the snap to either the Grid Snap or Polar Snap, and the Snapstyl system variable turns the isometric Grid Snap on and off. The Polardist system variable controls the snap distance for the Polar Snap feature.*

Using Grid and Snap Together

You can set the grid spacing to be the same as the snap setting, allowing you to see every snap point. Let's take a look at how Grid and Snap modes work together.

TIP *You can take a shortcut to the Drafting Settings dialog box by right-clicking the Snap, Grid, Polar, or Otrack button in the status bar and then choosing Settings from the shortcut menu.*

1. Open the Drafting Settings dialog box.
2. Make sure the Snap And Grid tab is selected; then double-click the GridX Spacing text box in the Grid group, and type **0**.
3. Click OK. Now the grid spacing has changed to reflect the 4" (or 10 cm) snap spacing. Move the cursor, and watch it snap to the grid points.
4. Open the Drafting Settings dialog box again.
5. Double-click the SnapX Spacing text box in the Snap group, and type **1** (**3** for metric users).
6. Click OK. The grid automatically changes to conform to the new snap setting.

When the grid spacing is set to 0, the grid then aligns with the snap points. At this density, the grid is overwhelming.

1. Open the Drafting Settings dialog box again.
2. Double-click the GridX Spacing text box in the Grid group, and type **12** (**30** for metric users).
3. Click OK. The grid spacing is now at 12 (or 30) again, which is a more reasonable spacing for the current drawing scale.

With the snap spacing set to 1 (3 for metric users), it is difficult to tell if the Snap mode is turned on based on the behavior of the cursor, but the coordinate readout in the status bar gives you a clue. As you move your cursor, the coordinates appear as whole numbers with no fractional distances. Metric users will notice the coordinate readout displaying values that are multiples of 3.

As you move the cursor over the drawing area, the coordinate readout in the lower-left corner of the AutoCAD window dynamically displays the cursor's position in absolute Cartesian coordinates. This allows you to find a position on your drawing by locating it in reference to the drawing origin—0,0—that is in the lower-left corner of the drawing. You can also set the coordinate readout to display relative coordinates by clicking the readout itself or by pressing the F6 key. Throughout these exercises, coordinates will be provided to enable you to select points using the dynamic coordinate readout. (If you want to review the discussion of AutoCAD's coordinate display, see Chapter 1.)

Next, you'll learn how to use the snap tools as your virtual drawing scale, T-square, and triangle.

Using Polar Tracking and Snap as Your Scale, T-Square, and Triangle

Now you will draw the first item in the bathroom: the toilet. It is composed of a rectangle representing the tank and a truncated ellipse representing the seat. To construct the toilet, you'll use the Polar Tracking and Polar Snap tools. Polar Tracking helps you align your cursor to exact horizontal and vertical angles, much like a T-square and triangle. Polar Snap is similar to Grid Snap in that it forces the cursor to move in exact increments. The main difference is that Polar Snap only works in conjunction with Polar Tracking.

Start by setting up Polar Snap.

1. Open the Drafting Settings dialog box again.

2. Make sure the Snap And Grid tab is selected; then click the Polar Snap radio button in the Snap Type & Style button group.
3. Double-click the Polar Distance setting, and type **.5** for a 1/2-inch Snap setting. Metric users should type **1** for a 1 cm Polar Snap setting.
4. Click OK to close the Drafting Settings dialog box.

You've just set the Polar Snap setting to .5 or one-half (1 cm for metric users). As you move the cursor over the drawing area, notice that the Snap mode seems to be off. When Polar Snap is active, you'll only have the snap in effect when you are actually drawing an object. You can, however, switch between Grid Snap and Polar Snap on the fly. In the next exercise, you'll see how this is done.

1. Click the Line tool on the Draw toolbar, or type **L↵**. You could also select Draw ➢ Line from the menu bar.
2. Right-click the SNAP button in the status bar.
3. Choose Grid Snap On from the shortcut menu to turn on Grid Snap mode.
4. Press F6 until you see the XY coordinates dynamically update as you move the cursor. You can also directly click the coordinate readout to cycle through the static, dynamic, and polar display.

Notice that as you move your cursor, the coordinate readout shows the cursor moving in increments that you set for the Grid Snap.

1. Using your coordinate readout for guidance, start your line at the coordinate 5'-7", 6'-3". Metric users should use 171,189 as the starting coordinate.
2. Right-click the SNAP button again, and then choose Polar Snap in the shortcut menu.
3. Make sure that Polar Tracking is on (the Polar button in the status bar should be in the on position), and then move the cursor directly to the right. The Polar Tracking cursor appears, along with the Polar Tracking readout. Notice that the readout shows distances in 1/2" increments (or 1-unit increments for metric users). It also shows you the angle in the standard AutoCAD distance and angle format. Even though the Grid Snap is set to 1 (3 for metric users), the snap distance changes to the value you set for Polar Snap when Polar Tracking is active and Polar Snap is on.

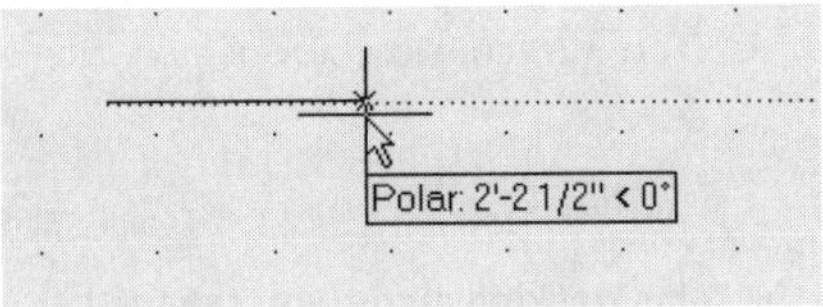

4. Move the cursor until the Polar Snap readout lists 1'-10" < 0° and pick this point. Metric users should use a Polar Tracking readout of 56.0000 < 0°. As in Chapter 2, when you move the cursor around, the rubber-banding line follows it at any angle.
5. Move the cursor downward until the coordinate readout lists 0'- 9" < 270° and click this point. Metric users should use a readout of 23.0000 < 270°.

6. Continue drawing the other two sides of the rectangle by using the Polar Tracking readout. When you've completed the rectangle, press ↵ or the Esc key to exit the Line tool. You should have a drawing that looks like Figure 3.2.

FIGURE 3.2

A plan view of the toilet tank

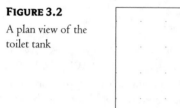

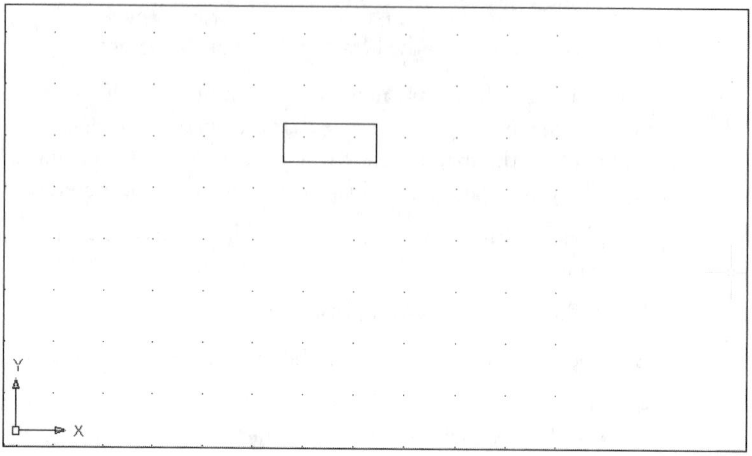

As you can see from the exercise, you can use Polar Tracking to restrain your cursor to horizontal and vertical positions, just like a T-square and triangle. Later, you'll learn how you can set up Polar Tracking to set the angle to any value you want in a way similar to an adjustable triangle.

In some situations, you may find that you do not want Polar Tracking on. You can turn it off by clicking the POLAR button in the status bar. In fact, this is exactly what you did in Chapter 2. You can also press the F10 function key to turn Polar Tracking on or off.

TIP *In step 4, the coordinate readout displayed some extra values. The third coordinate that you see at the end of the coordinate readout listing indicates the z value of the coordinate. This extra coordinate is significant only when you are doing 3D modeling; so for the time being, you can ignore it. If you'd like to know more about the additional z-coordinate listing in the coordinate readout, see Chapter 16.*

Although this exercise tells you to use the Line tool to draw the tank, you can also use the Rectangle tool. The Rectangle tool creates what is known as a *polyline*, which is a set of line or arc segments that acts like a single object. You'll learn more about polylines in Chapter 14.

THE ORTHO MODE

In addition to using the Polar Tracking mode, you can further restrain the cursor to a vertical or horizontal direction by using the Ortho mode. To use the Ortho mode, press F8 or click the word Ortho in the status bar. When you move the cursor around while drawing objects, the rubber-banding line moves only vertically or horizontally. With the Ortho mode turned on, Polar Tracking is automatically turned off.

In versions prior to AutoCAD 2000, the Ortho mode was the only option available for restraining your line work to a vertical or horizontal direction. Polar Tracking is a much more flexible tool for this purpose, though Ortho mode is better suited to a task in many situations. Try them both as you work in AutoCAD on your own.

By using the Snap modes in conjunction with the coordinate readout and Polar Tracking, you can locate coordinates and measure distances as you draw lines. This is similar to the way you draw using a scale. Be aware that the smallest distance the coordinate readout and Polar Tracking readout register depends on the area you have displayed on your screen. For example, if you are displaying an area the size of a football field, the smallest distance you can indicate with your cursor may be 6" or 15 cm. On the other hand, if your view is enlarged to show an area of only one square inch or centimeter, you can indicate distances as small as 1/1000 of an inch or centimeter using your cursor.

Setting the Polar Tracking Angle

You've seen how Polar Tracking lets you draw exact vertical and horizontal lines. You can also set Polar Tracking to draw lines at other angles, such as 30 or 45 degrees. To change the angle Polar Tracking uses, you use the Polar Tracking tab in the Drafting Settings dialog box.

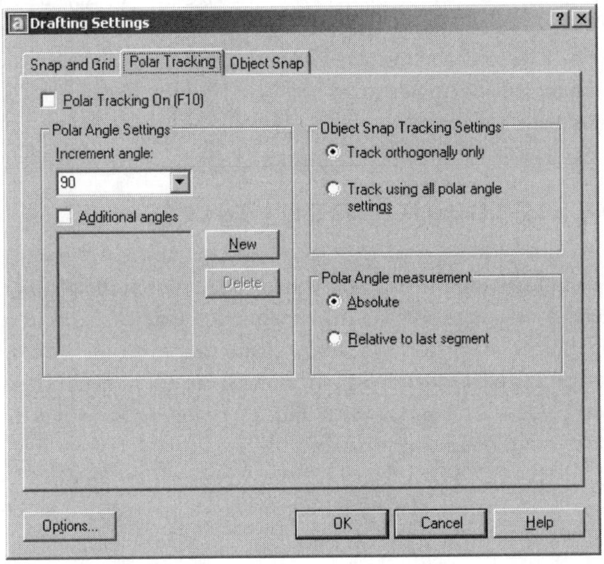

Right-click the POLAR button in the status bar and then schoose Settings from the shortcut menu to open the Drafting Settings dialog box. Or you can choose Tools ➢ Drafting Settings from the menu bar and then click the Polar Tracking tab.

To change the Polar Tracking angle, enter an angle in the Increment Angle text box, or select a predefined angle from the drop-down list. You can do this while drawing a series of line segments, for example, so that you can set angles "on the fly."

Numerous other settings are available in the Polar Tracking tab. Here is a listing of their functions for your reference:

Additional Angles This setting lets you enter a specific angle for Polar Tracking. For example, if you want Polar Tracking to snap to 12 degrees, click the New button next to the Additional Angles list box and enter **12**. The value you enter appears in the list box, and when the Additional Angles check box is checked, Polar Tracking snaps to 12 degrees. To delete a value from the list box, highlight it and click the Delete button.

The Additional Angles option differs from the Increment Angle setting in that the Increment Angle setting causes Polar Tracking to snap to every increment of its setting, while Additional Angles only snaps to the angle specified. You can enter as many angles as you want in the Additional Angles list box.

Object Snap Tracking Settings These settings let you control whether Object Snap Tracking uses strictly orthogonal directions (0, 90, 180, and 270 degrees) or the angles set in the Polar Angle button group of this dialog box. (See the "Aligning Objects Using Object Snap Tracking" section later in this chapter.)

Polar Angle Measurement These radio buttons let you determine the zero angle on which Polar Tracking bases its incremental angles. The Absolute option uses the current AutoCAD setting for the 0° angle. The Relative To Last Segment option uses the last drawn object as the 0° angle. For example, if you draw a line at a 10° angle, and have the Relative To Last Segment option selected with the Increment Angle set to 90, Polar Tracking snaps to 10, 100, 190, and 280 degrees, relative to the actual 0° direction.

Exploring the Drawing Process

This section looks at some of the more common AutoCAD commands and shows you how to use them to complete a simple drawing. As you draw, watch the prompts and notice how your responses affect them. Also notice how you use existing drawing elements as reference points.

While drawing with AutoCAD, you create simple geometric forms to determine the basic shapes of objects, and you can then modify the shapes to fill in detail. This is where the differences between drawing with AutoCAD and manual drafting become more apparent. In essence, you alternately create and edit objects to build your drawing.

AutoCAD offers 14 basic drawing object types: lines, arcs, circles, text, traces, polylines, points, 3D Faces, ellipses, elliptical arcs, spline curves, solids, regions, and multiline text. All drawings are built on these objects. In addition, there are five 3D meshes, which are three-dimensional surfaces composed of 3D Faces. You are familiar with lines and arcs; these, along with circles, are the most commonly used objects. As you progress through the book, you will learn about the other objects and how they are used.

Locating an Object in Reference to Others

To define the toilet seat, you will use an ellipse.

1. Click the Ellipse tool in the Draw toolbar, or type **EL↵**. You can also choose Draw ➤ Ellipse ➤ Axis, End.

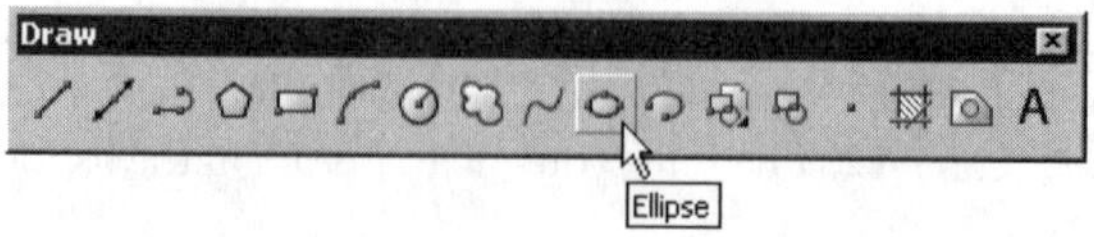

2. At the `Specify axis endpoint of ellipse or [Arc/Center]:` prompt, pick the midpoint of the bottom horizontal line of the rectangle. Do this by opening the Osnap popup menu and selecting Midpoint; then move the cursor toward the bottom line. (Remember, to open the Osnap menu, Shift+click the right mouse button.) When you see the Midpoint Osnap marker on the line, click the left mouse button.

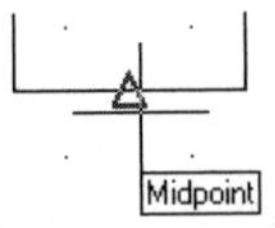

3. At the `Specify other endpoint of axis:` prompt, move the cursor down until the Polar Tracking readout lists 1'-10" < 270°. Metric users should use a readout of 55.0000 < 270°.
4. Pick this as the second axis endpoint.
5. At the `Specify distance to other axis or [Rotation]:` prompt, move the cursor horizontally from the center of the ellipse until the Polar Tracking readout lists 0'-8" < 180°. Metric users should use a readout of 20.0000 < 180°.
6. Pick this as the axis distance defining the width of the ellipse. Your drawing should look like Figure 3.3.

TIP *As you work with AutoCAD, you will eventually run into NURBS. NURBS stands for Non-Uniform Rational B-Splines—a fancy term meaning that curved objects are based on accurate mathematical models. When you trim the ellipse in a later exercise, it becomes a NURBS curve known as a Spline in AutoCAD, not a segmented polyline as in earlier versions of AutoCAD. You'll learn more about polylines and spline curves in Chapter 14.*

FIGURE 3.3

The ellipse added to the tank

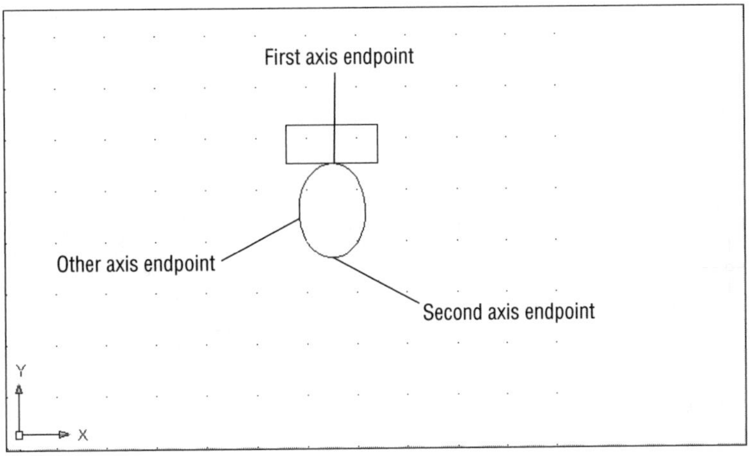

Getting a Closer Look

During the drawing process, you will often want to enlarge areas of a drawing to edit its objects. In Chapter 1, you saw how to use the Zoom capability for this purpose.

1. Click the Zoom Window tool on the Standard toolbar, or type **Z↵ W↵**. You can also choose View ➢ Zoom ➢ Window.

2. At the `First corner:` prompt, pick a point below and to the left of your drawing at or near coordinate 5'-0", 3'-6". Metric users should use the coordinate of 150.0000,102.0000.
3. At the `Other corner:` prompt, pick a point above and to the right of the drawing, at or near coordinate 8'-3", 6'-8" (246.0000,195.0000 for metric users), so that the toilet is completely enclosed by the View window. To obtain this view, use the Zoom Window tool. You can also use the Zoom Realtime tool in conjunction with the Pan Realtime tool. The toilet enlarges to fill more of the screen (see Figure 3.4).

TIP To open the Zoom Realtime tool from the keyboard, type **Z↵**. *If you have a mouse with a scroll wheel, you can place the cursor on the toilet and turn the wheel to zoom into the image.*

FIGURE 3.4

A close-up of the toilet drawing

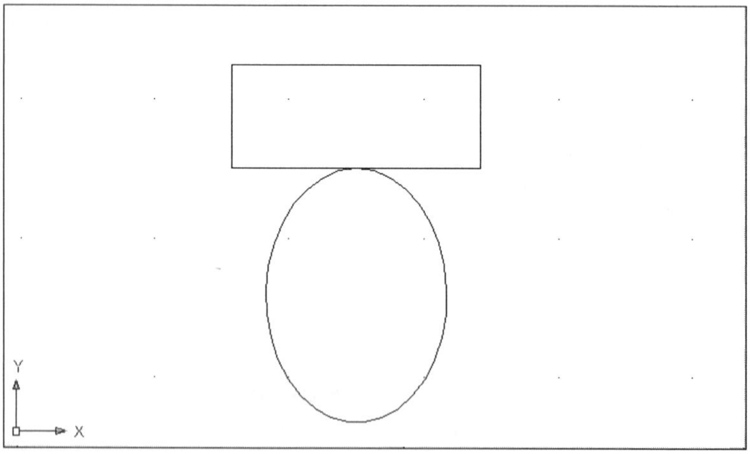

Modifying an Object

Now let's see how editing commands are used to construct an object. To define the back edge of the seat, let's put a copy of the line defining the front of the toilet tank 3" (7 cm for metric users) toward the center of the ellipse.

1. Click the Copy Object tool in the Modify toolbar, or type **co**↵. You can also choose Modify ➢ Copy from the pull-down menu.

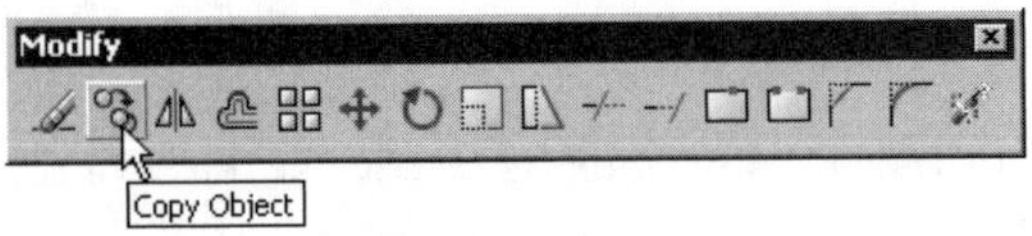

TIP *You can also use the Grip Edit tools to make the copy. See Chapter 2 for more on grip editing.*

2. At the `Select objects:` prompt, pick the horizontal line that touches the top of the ellipse. The line is highlighted. Press ↵ to confirm your selection.
3. At the `Specify base point or displacement, or [Multiple]:` prompt, pick a base point near the line. Then move the cursor down until the Polar Tracking readout lists 0'-3" < 270° or 7.0000 < 270° for metric users.
4. Pick this point. Your drawing should look like Figure 3.5.

FIGURE 3.5
The line copied down

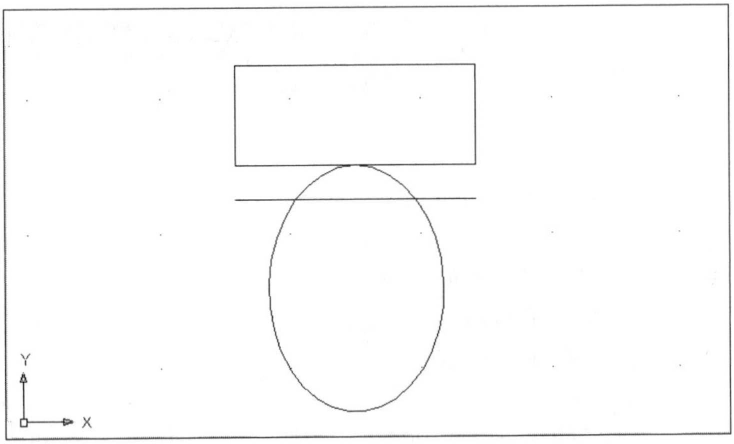

ARCHITECTS AND THEIR SYMBOLS

You may be asking yourself if there is a set of standard architectural measurements for common items, such as the aforementioned toilet tank. Some items, such as doors and kitchen appliances, do have "standard" sizes that architects learn in the course of their professional training. In this particular example, the 3-inch offset is really arbitrary because the toilet symbol is just that, a symbol representing a toilet and not necessarily an exact representation of one. When you see a toilet symbol in an architectural drawing, it's saying "put the toilet here." The actual brand of toilet is specified in the written specs that go with the drawings.

Notice that the `Copy` command acts exactly like the `Move` command you used in Chapter 2, except that `Copy` does not alter the position of the objects you select.

TRIMMING AN OBJECT

Now you must delete the part of the ellipse that is not needed. You will use the `Trim` command to trim off part of the ellipse.

1. First, turn the Snap mode off by pressing F9 or clicking the word SNAP in the status bar. Snap mode may be a hindrance at this point in your editing session because it can keep you from picking the points you want. Snap mode forces the cursor to move to points at a given interval, so you will have difficulty selecting a point that doesn't fall exactly at one of those intervals.
2. Click the Trim tool in the Modify toolbar.

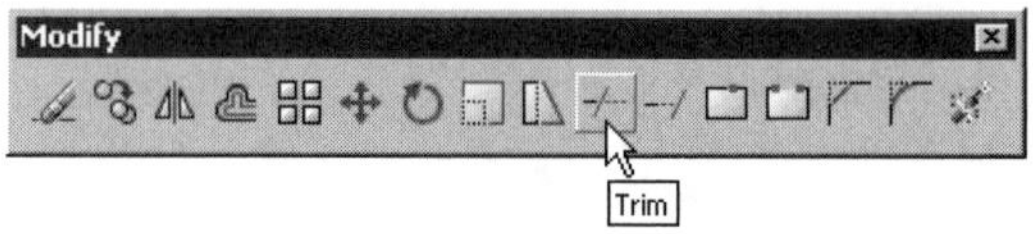

You will see this prompt:

```
Current settings: Projection=UCS Edge=None
Select cutting edges ...
```

3. Click the line you just created—the one that crosses through the ellipse—and press ↵ to finish your selection.
4. At the `Select object to trim or shift-select to extend or [Project/Edge/Undo]:` prompt, pick the topmost portion of the ellipse above the line. This trims the ellipse back to the line.
5. Press ↵ to exit the `Trim` command.

TIP *By holding down the Shift key in step 4, you can change from trimming an object to extending an object. You'll learn about the* `Extend` *command in Chapter 13.*

SELECTING CLOSE OR OVERLAPPING OBJECTS

At times, you will want to select an object that is in close proximity to or lying underneath another object, and AutoCAD won't obey your mouse click. It's frustrating when you click the object you want to select, and AutoCAD selects the one next to it instead. To help you make your selections in these situations, AutoCAD provides Object Selection Cycling. To use it, hold down the Ctrl key while simultaneously clicking the object you want to select. If the wrong object is highlighted, press the left mouse button again (you do not need to hold down the Ctrl key for the second time), and the next object in close proximity is highlighted. If several objects are overlapping or close together, just continue to press the left mouse button until the correct object is highlighted. When the object you want is finally highlighted, press ↵ and continue with further selections.

In step 2 of the preceding exercise, the `Trim` command produces two messages in the prompt. The first prompt, `Select cutting edges:`, tells you that you must first select objects to define *the edge to which you want to trim an object*. In step 4, you are again prompted to select objects, this time to select the *objects to trim*. `Trim` is one of a handful of AutoCAD commands that asks you to select two sets of objects: the first set defines a boundary, and the second is the set of objects you want to edit. The two sets of objects are not mutually exclusive. You can, for example, select the cutting edge objects as objects to trim. The next exercise shows how this works.

First you will undo the trim you just did; then you will use the `Trim` command again in a slightly different way to finish off the toilet.

1. Click the Undo button in the Standard toolbar, or enter **U↵** at the command prompt. The top of the ellipse reappears.
2. Start the Trim tool again by clicking it in the Modify toolbar.
3. At the `Select cutting edges:` prompt, click the ellipse and the line crossing the ellipse (see the first image in Figure 3.6).
4. Press ↵ to finish your selection and move to the next step.

TIP *These Trim options—Project, Edge, and Undo—are described in the section "The Trim Options" later in this chapter.*

5. At the `Select object to trim or [Project/Edge/Undo]:` prompt, click the top portion of the ellipse, as you did in the previous exercise. The ellipse trims back.
6. Click a point near the left end of the trim line, past the ellipse. The line trims back to the ellipse.
7. Click the other end of the line. The right side of the line trims back to meet the ellipse. Your drawing should look like the second image in Figure 3.6.
8. Press ↵ to exit the `Trim` command.
9. Choose File ➢ Save to save the file in its current state. You might want to get in the habit of doing this every 20 minutes.

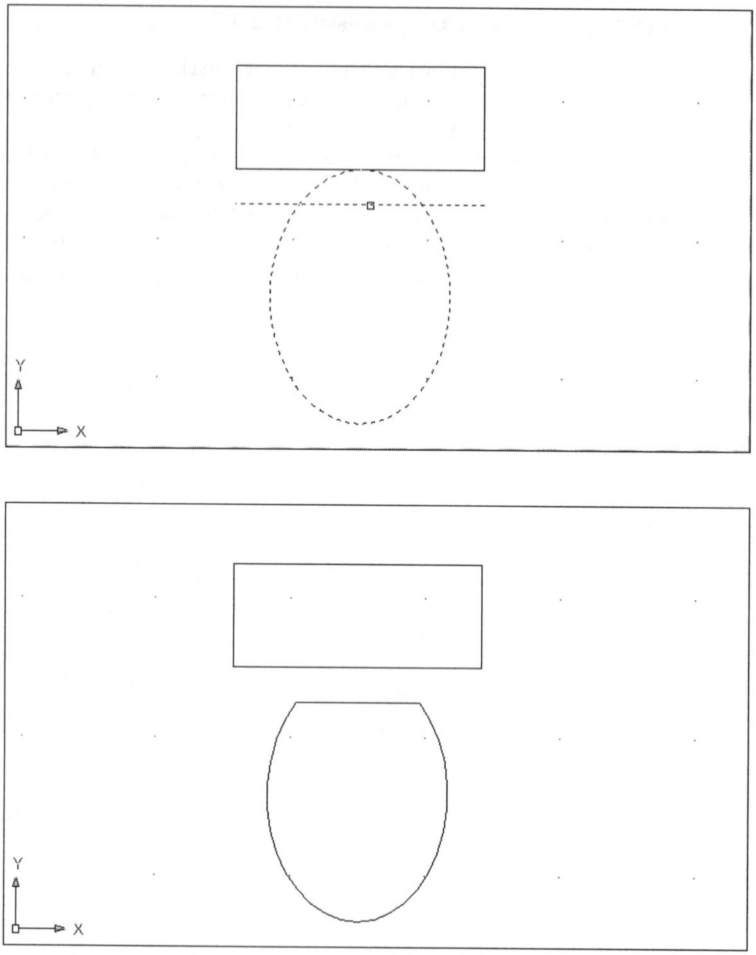

FIGURE 3.6
Trimming the ellipse and the line

Here you saw how the ellipse and the line are both used as trim objects, as well as the objects to be trimmed.

THE TRIM OPTIONS

AutoCAD offers three options for the `Trim` command: Edge, Project, and Undo. As described in the following paragraphs, these options give you a higher degree of control over how objects are trimmed.

Edge [E] Allows you to trim an object to an apparent intersection, even if the cutting-edge object does not intersect the object to be trimmed (see the top of Figure 3.7). Edge offers two options: Extend and No Extend. You can also set these options using the Edgemode system variable.

FIGURE 3.7

The Trim command's options

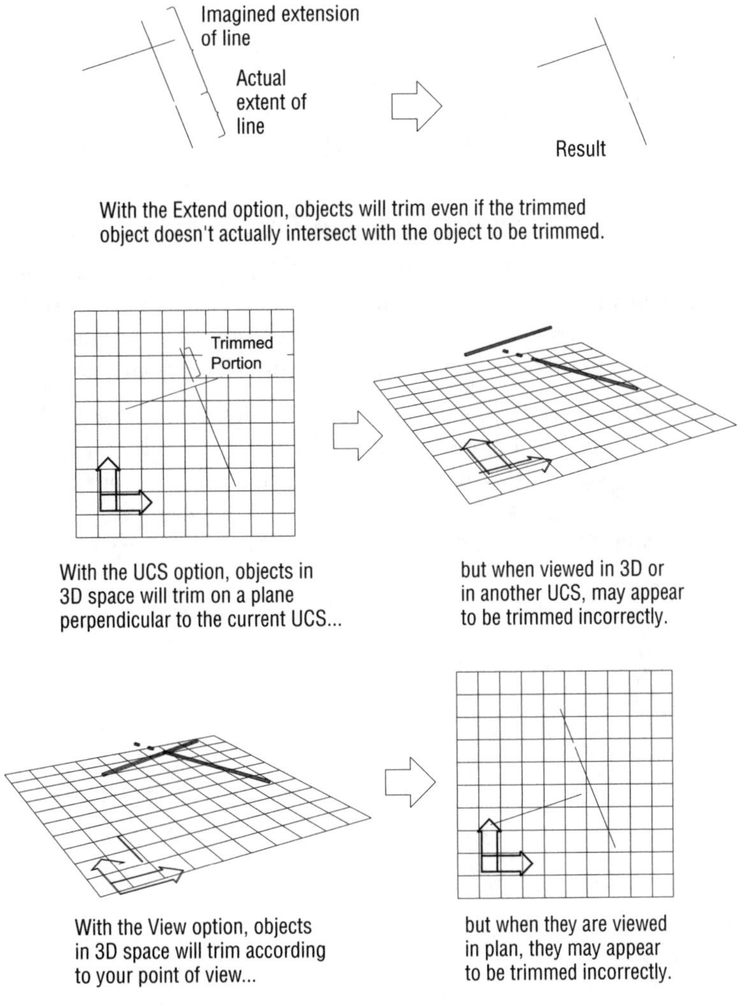

Imagined extension
of line
Actual
extent of
line
Result
With the Extend option, objects will trim even if the trimmed object doesn't actually intersect with the object to be trimmed.
Trimmed
Portion
With the UCS option, objects in 3D space will trim on a plane perpendicular to the current UCS...
but when viewed in 3D or in another UCS, may appear to be trimmed incorrectly.
With the View option, objects in 3D space will trim according to your point of view...
but when they are viewed in plan, they may appear to be trimmed incorrectly.

Project [P] Useful when working on 3D drawings. It controls how AutoCAD trims objects that are not coplanar. Project offers three options: None, UCS, and View. None causes `Trim` to ignore objects that are on different planes so that only coplanar objects will be trimmed. If you choose UCS, the `Trim` command trims objects based on a Plan view of the current UCS and then disregards whether the objects are coplanar (see the middle of Figure 3.7). View is similar to UCS but uses the current view's "line of sight" to determine how non-coplanar objects are trimmed (see the bottom of Figure 3.7).

Undo [U] Causes the last trimmed object to revert to its original length.

You've just seen one way to construct the toilet. However, you can construct objects in many ways. For example, you could have just trimmed the top of the ellipse, as you did in the first Trim exercise, and then used the Grips feature to move the endpoints of the line to meet the endpoints of the ellipse. As you become familiar with AutoCAD, you will start to develop your own ways of working, using the tools best suited to your style.

If you'd like to take a break, now would be a good time. You can exit AutoCAD and then come back to the Bath drawing file when you are ready to proceed.

Planning and Laying Out a Drawing

For the next object, the bathtub, you will use some new commands to lay out parts of the drawing. This will help you get a feel for the kind of planning you must do to use AutoCAD effectively. You'll also get a chance to use some of the keyboard shortcuts built into AutoCAD. First, though, go back to the previous view of your drawing, and arrange some more room to work.

1. Return to your previous view, the one shown in Figure 3.8. A quick way to do this is to click the Zoom Previous tool on the Standard toolbar, or choose View ➢ Zoom ➢ Previous. Your view returns to the one you had before the last `Zoom` command (see Figure 3.8).

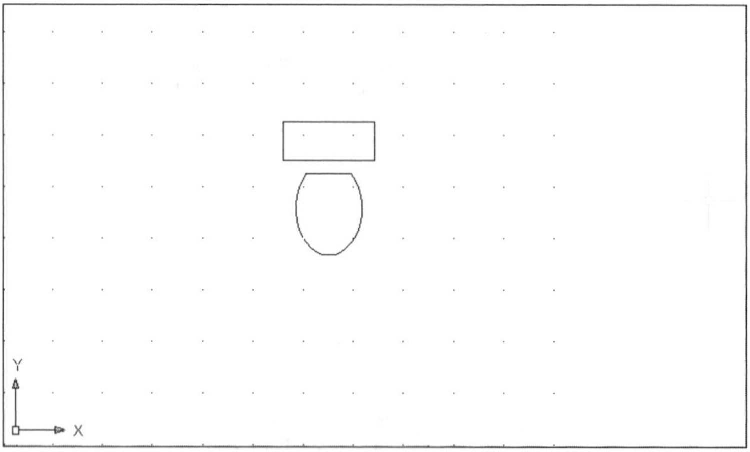

FIGURE 3.8
The view of the finished toilet after using the Zoom Previous tool. You can also obtain this view using the Zoom All tool from the Zoom Window flyout.

You'll begin the bathtub by using the `Line` command to draw a rectangle 2'-8" × 5'-0" (81 cm × 152 cm for metric users) on the left side of the drawing area. For a change this time, you'll use a couple of shortcut methods: the `Line` command's keyboard shortcut and the Direct Distance method for specifying distance and direction.

2. Turn the Grid Snap mode on by right-clicking the SNAP button on the status bar and choosing Grid Snap from the shortcut menu.

3. Type **L**↵ and pick the coordinate location 0'-9",0'-10" at the `Specify first point:` prompt. Metric users use the coordinate 24.0000,27.0000. You can either use the cursor in conjunction with the coordinate readout or enter the coordinate from the keyboard. (Metric users can leave off the zero decimal values while entering coordinates through the keyboard.)

4. Place your cursor to the right of the last point selected so that the rubber-banding line is pointing directly to the right and type **2'8"**; then press ↵ for the first side of the tub. Metric users should enter **81↵**. Notice that the rubber-banding line is now fixed at the length you typed.
5. Now point the rubber-banding line upward toward the top of the screen and type **5'**; then press ↵ for the next side. Metric users should enter **152↵**.
6. Point the rubber-banding line directly to the left of the last point and type **2'8"** (**81** for metric users); then press ↵ for the next side.
7. Type **C↵** to close the rectangle and exit the `Line` command.

TIP *Instead of pressing ↵ during the Direct Distance method, you can press the spacebar or right-click and choose Enter from the shortcut menu.*

Now you have the outline of the tub. Notice that when you enter feet and inches from the keyboard, you must avoid hyphens or spaces. Thus, 2 feet 8 inches is typed as **2'8"**. Also notice that you didn't have to enter the at sign (@) or angle specification. Instead, you used the Direct Distance method for specifying direction and distance. You can use this method for drawing lines or moving and copying objects at right angles. The Direct Distance method is less effective if you want to specify exact angles other than right angles.

Some of the keyboard shortcuts for tools or commands you've used in this chapter are CO (Copy), E (Erase), EL (Ellipse), F (Fillet), M (Move), O (Offset), and TR (Trim). Remember that you can enter keyboard shortcuts, like keyboard commands, only when the command prompt is visible in the Command window.

Making a Preliminary Sketch

The following exercise shows how planning ahead will make your use of AutoCAD more efficient. When drawing a complex object, you will often have to do some layout before you do the actual drawing. This is similar to drawing an accurate pencil sketch using construction lines that you later trace over to produce a finished drawing. The advantage of doing this in AutoCAD is that your drawing doesn't lose any accuracy between the sketch and the final product. Also, AutoCAD allows you to use the geometry of your sketch to aid you in drawing. While planning your drawing, think about what you want to draw, and then decide which drawing elements will help you create that object.

You will use the `Offset` command to establish reference lines to help you draw the inside of the tub. This is where the Osnap overrides are quite useful. (See sidebar "The Osnap Options," later in this chapter.)

Setting Up a Layout

The Offset tool on the Modify toolbar allows you to make parallel copies of a set of objects, such as the lines forming the outside of your tub. Offset is different from the `Copy` command; Offset allows only one object to be copied at a time, but it can remember the distance you specify. The Offset option does not work with all types of objects. Only lines, arcs, circles, and 2D polylines can be offset.

In this exercise, you will use standard lines to lay out your drawing. Standard lines are best suited for the layout of the bathtub in this situation. In Chapter 5 you will learn about two other objects, construction lines (Xlines) and Rays, which are specifically designed to help you lay out a drawing.

1. Click the Offset tool in the Modify toolbar, or type **O**↵. You can also choose Modify ➢ Offset from the pull-down menu.

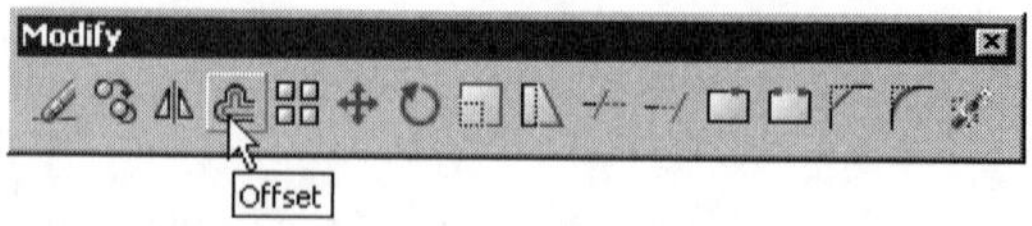

2. At the `Specify offset distance or [Through] <Through>:` prompt, enter **3**↵. This specifies the distance of 3" as the offset distance. Metric users should enter **7** for 7 cm, which is roughly equivalent to 3 inches.
3. At the `Select object to offset or <exit>:` prompt, click the bottom line of the rectangle you just drew.
4. At the `Specify point on side to offset:` prompt, pick a point inside the rectangle. A copy of the line appears. You don't have to be exact about where you pick the side to offset; AutoCAD only wants to know on which side of the line you want to make the offset copy.
5. The prompt `Select object to offset or <exit>:` appears again. Click another side to offset; then click again on a point inside the rectangle.
6. Continue to offset the other two sides; then offset these four new lines inside the rectangle toward the center. You will have a drawing that looks like Figure 3.9.
7. When you are done, exit the `Offset` command by pressing ↵.

FIGURE 3.9

The completed layout

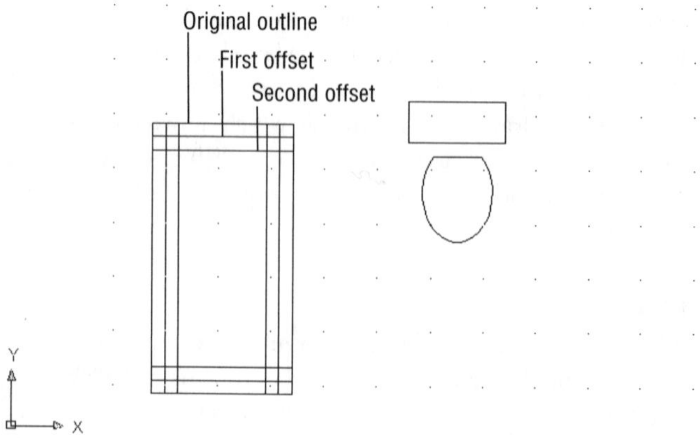

Using the Layout

Now you will begin to draw the inside of the tub, starting with the narrow end. You will use your offset lines as references to construct the arcs that make up the tub. Also in this exercise, you'll set up some of the Osnap tools to be available automatically whenever AutoCAD expects a point selection.

1. Choose Tools ➢ Drafting Settings, and then click the Object Snap tab. You can also type **Ds↵**, or right-click the OSNAP button on the status bar, and then choose Settings from the shortcut menu.
2. Click the Clear All button to turn off any options that might be selected.
3. Click the Endpoint, Midpoint, and Intersection check boxes so that a checkmark appears in the boxes, and make sure the Object Snap On option is checked; then click OK.

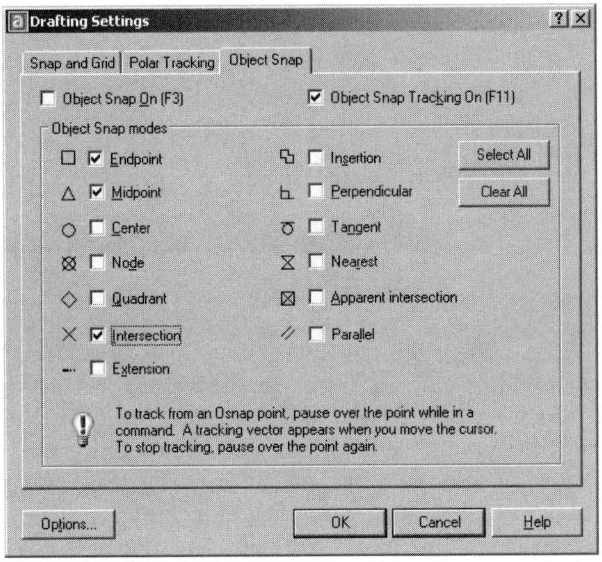

TIP *Take a look at the graphic symbols next to each of the Osnap options in the Object Snap tab. These are the Osnap markers that appear in your drawing as you select Osnap points. Each Osnap option has its own marker symbol. As you work with the Osnaps, you'll become more familiar with how they work.*

MAKING ADJUSTMENTS TO THE AUTOSNAP FEATURE

When you click the Options button in the Object Snap tab of the Drafting Settings dialog box, you'll see the Drafting Settings tab of the Options dialog box. This tab offers a set of options pertaining to the AutoSnap feature. AutoSnap looks at the location of your cursor during Osnap selections and locates the Osnap point nearest your cursor. AutoSnap then displays a graphic called a marker showing you the Osnap point it has found. If it is the one you want, you simply left-click your mouse to select it.

Continued on next page

MAKING ADJUSTMENTS TO THE AUTOSNAP FEATURE *(continued)*

The AutoSnap settings allow you to control its various features:

Marker Turns the graphic marker on or off.

Magnet Causes the Osnap cursor to "jump to" inferred Osnap points.

Display AutoSnap Tooltip Turns the Osnap tool tip on or off.

Display AutoSnap Aperture Box Turns the old-style Osnap cursor box on or off.

AutoSnap Marker Size Controls the size of the graphic marker.

AutoSnap Marker Color Controls the color of the graphic marker.

You've just set up the Endpoint, Midpoint, and Intersection Osnaps to be on by default. This is called a *Running Osnap*; AutoCAD automatically selects the nearest Osnap point without your intervention. Now let's see how a Running Osnap works.

1. In the Draw toolbar, click the Arc tool, or type **a**↵.

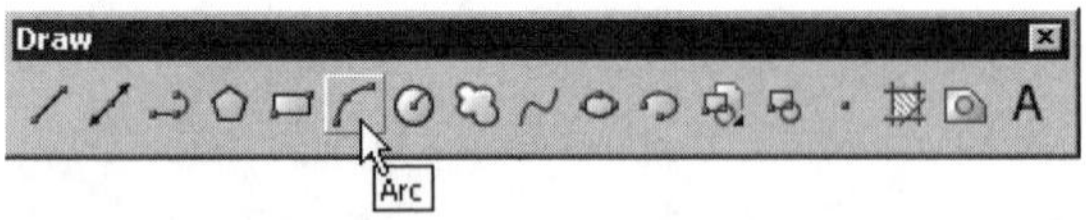

See Figure 3.10 for other Arc options available from the pull-down menu. This illustration shows each pull-down menu option name with a graphic above it depicting the arc and numbers indicating the sequence of points to select. For example, if you want to know how the Draw ➢ Arc ➢ Start, Center, End option works, you can look at the graphic in the bottom-right corner of the figure. It shows the point selection sequence for drawing an arc using that option; 1 for the start point, 2 for the center point, and then 3 for the end of the arc.

2. For the first point of the arc, move the cursor toward the intersection of the two lines as indicated in the first image in Figure 3.11. Notice that the Intersection Osnap marker appears on the intersection.

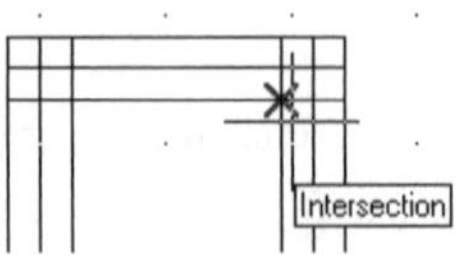

3. With the Intersection Osnap marker on the desired intersection, click the left mouse button.

FIGURE 3.10

If you look at the Draw ➢ Arc cascading menu, you'll see some additional options for drawing arcs. These options provide "canned" responses to the Arc command so that you only have to select the appropriate points as indicated in the pull-down menu option name.

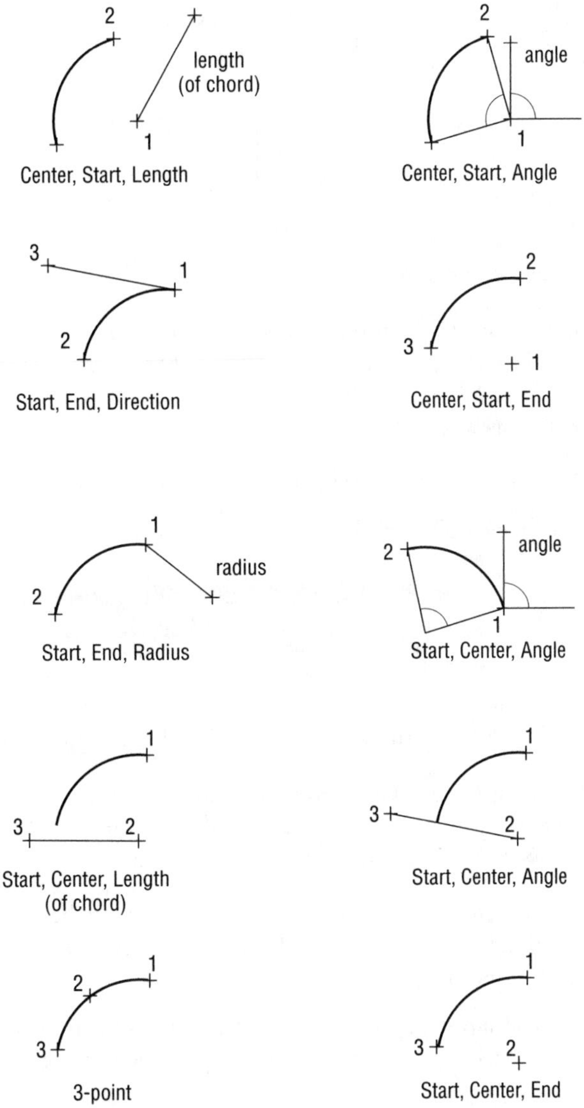

4. Now move the cursor to the midpoint of the second horizontal line near the top. When the Midpoint Osnap marker appears at the midpoint of the line, click the left mouse button.

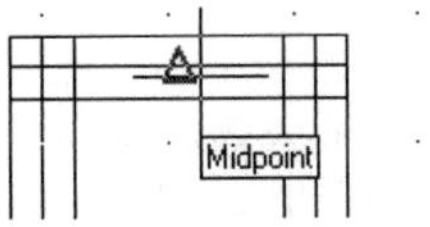

5. Finally, use the Intersection Osnap marker to locate and select the intersection of the two lines at the upper-left side of the bathtub.

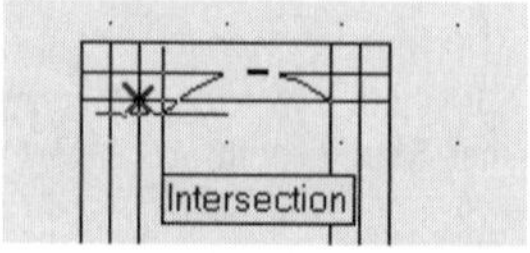

The first image in Figure 3.11 shows the sequence I just described.

TIP *When you see an Osnap marker on an object, you can have AutoCAD move to the next Osnap point on the object by pressing the Tab key. If you have several Running Osnap modes on (Endpoint, Midpoint, and Intersection, for example), pressing the Tab key cycles through those Osnap points on the object. This feature can be especially useful in a crowded area of a drawing.*

Next, you will draw an arc for the left side of the tub.

1. In the Draw toolbar, click the Arc tool again.

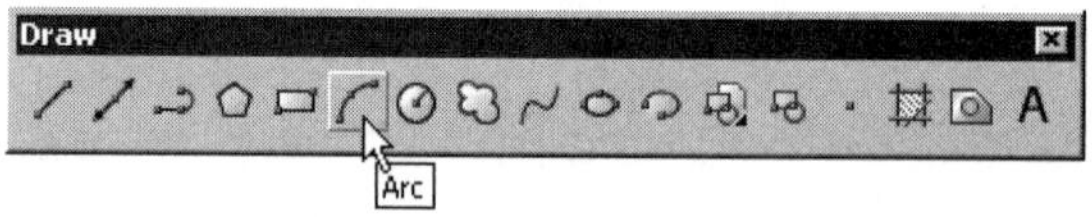

2. Type @↵ to select the last point you picked as the start of the next arc.

WARNING *It's easy for new users to select points inadvertently. If you accidentally select additional points after the last exercise and prior to step 1, you may not get the results described here. If this happens, issue the* `Arc` *command again and then use the Endpoint Osnap and select the endpoint of the last arc.*

3. Type E↵ to tell AutoCAD that you want to specify the other end of the arc, instead of the next point. Or you can right-click anywhere in the drawing area and choose End from the right click menu.
4. At the `End point` prompt, use the Intersection Osnap to pick the intersection of the two lines in the lower-left corner of the tub. See the middle image in Figure 3.11 for the location of this point.

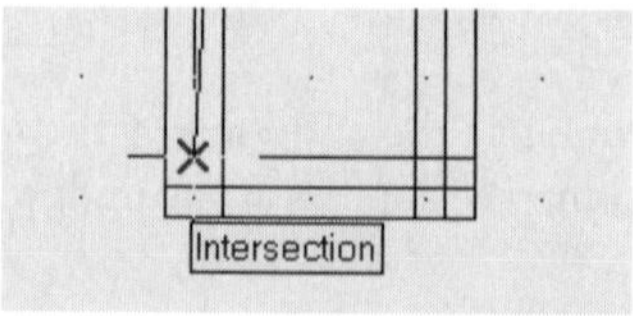

5. Type D↵ to select the Direction option. You can also right-click anywhere in the drawing area and then choose Direction from the right click menu. The arc drags as you move the cursor, along with a rubber-banding line from the starting point of the arc.

6. Move the cursor to the left of the dragging arc until it touches the middle line on the left side of the tub. Then pick that, as shown in the second image in Figure 3.11.

FIGURE 3.11

The top, left side, and bottom of the tub

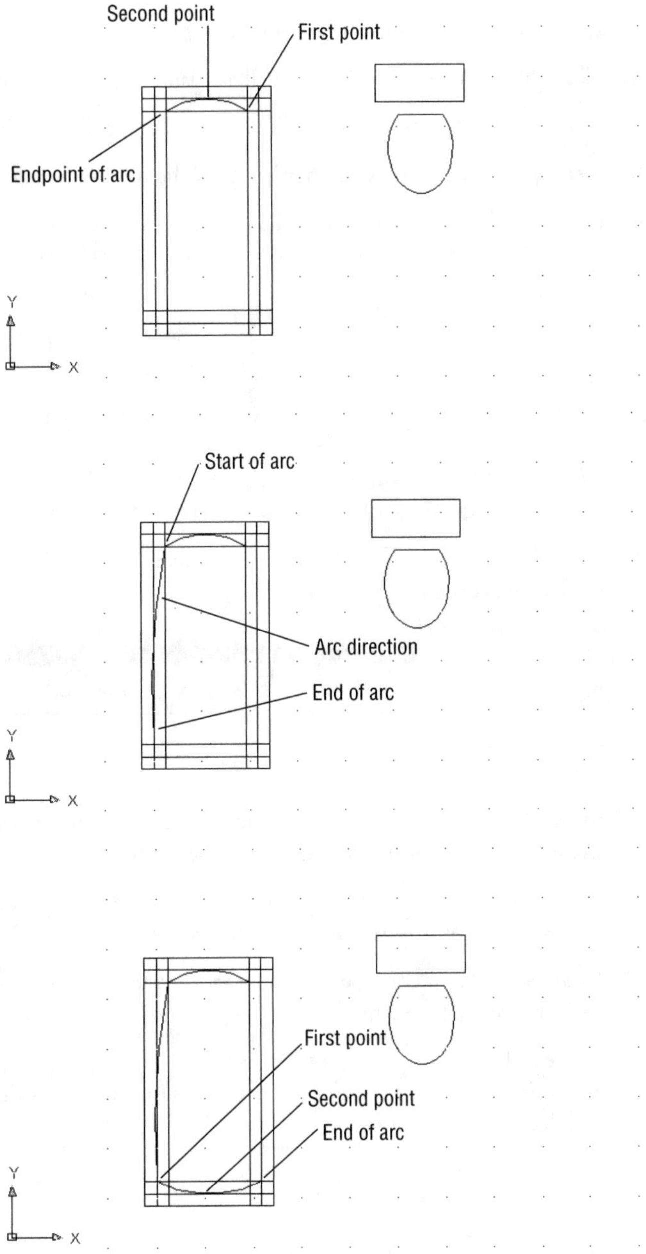

TIP *In step 3, the rubber-banding line indicates the direction of the arc. Be sure Ortho mode is off, because Ortho mode forces the rubber-banding line and the arc in a direction you don't want. Check the status bar; if the Ortho button looks like it's pressed, press F8 or click the Ortho button to turn Ortho mode off.*

Now you will draw the bottom of the tub.

1. Click the Arc tool in the Draw toolbar again. You can also press ↵ to replay the last command.
2. Using the Endpoint Osnap marker, pick the endpoint of the bottom of the arc just drawn.
3. Using the Midpoint Osnap marker, pick the middle horizontal line at the bottom of the tub.
4. Finally, pick the intersection of the two lines in the lower-right corner of the tub (see the third image in Figure 3.11).

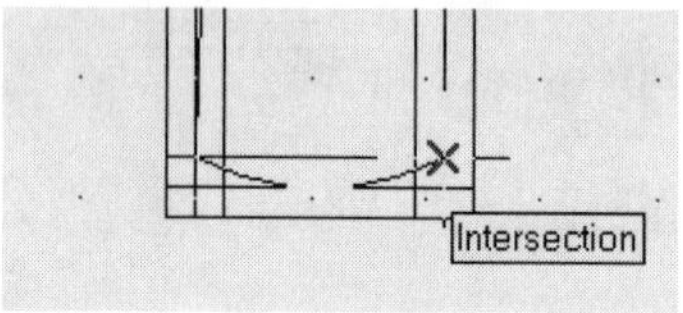

Now create the right side of the tub by mirroring the left side.

1. Click the Mirror tool on the Modify toolbar. You may also choose Modify ➢ Mirror or enter **mi**↵ at the command prompt.

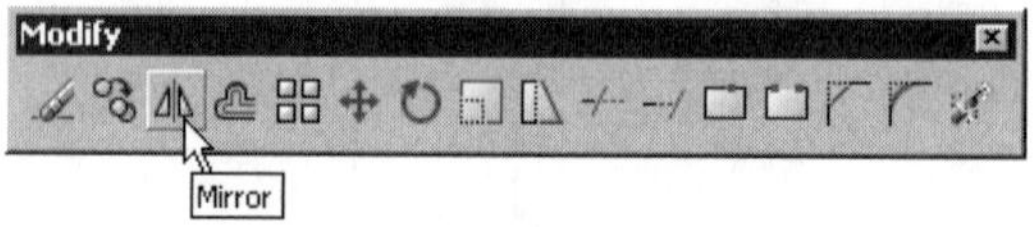

2. At the `Select objects:` prompt, pick the long arc on the left side of the tub to highlight the arc. Press ↵ to indicate that you've finished your selection.
3. At the `Specify first point of mirror line:` prompt, pick the midpoint of the top horizontal line. By now, you should know how to use the automatic Osnap modes you set up earlier.
4. At the `Specify second point of mirror line:` prompt, use the Polar Tracking mode to pick a point directly below the last point selected.
5. At the `Delete source objects? [Yes/No] <N>:` prompt, press ↵ to accept the default, No. A mirror image of the arc you picked appears on the right side of the tub. Your drawing should look like Figure 3.12.

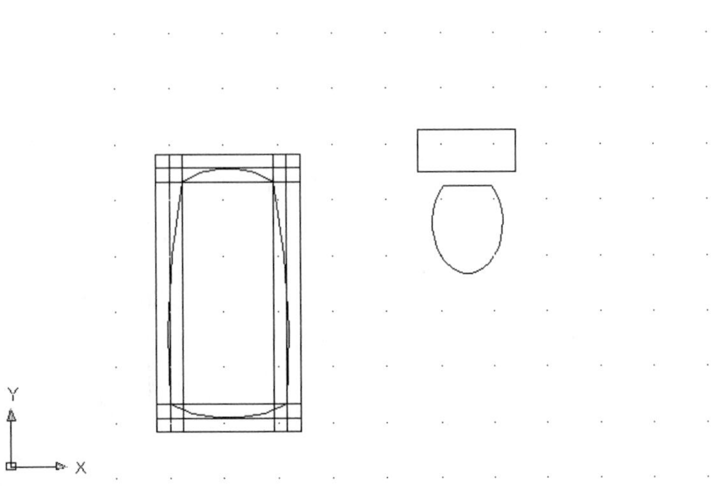

FIGURE 3.12
The inside of the tub completed with the layout lines still in place

In this exercise, you were able to use the Osnaps in a Running Osnap mode. You'll find that you will use the Osnaps nearly all the time as you create your drawings. For this reason, you might want Running Osnaps on all the time. Even so, at times Running Osnaps can get in the way. For example, they may be a nuisance in a crowded drawing when you want to use a Zoom window. The Osnaps can cause you to select an inappropriate window area by automatically selecting Osnap points.

Fortunately, you can turn Running Osnaps on and off quite easily by clicking the OSNAP button in the status bar. This toggles the Running Osnaps on or off. If you don't have any Running Osnaps set, clicking the OSNAP button opens the Object Snap settings in the Drafting Settings dialog box, allowing you to select your Osnaps.

Erasing the Layout Lines

For the next step, you will erase the layout lines you created using the `Offset` command. But this time, you'll try selecting the lines *before* issuing the `Erase` command.

TIP *If the following exercise doesn't work as described, be sure you have the Noun/Verb selection setting turned on. See Appendix B for details.*

1. Click each internal layout line individually.

If you have problems selecting just the lines, try using a window to select single lines. (Remember, a window selects only objects that are completely within the window.) You might also try the Object Selection Cycling option, as explained earlier in this chapter in the "Selecting Close or Overlapping Objects" sidebar.

2. Once all the layout lines are highlighted, enter **E**↵ to use the keyboard shortcut for the `Erase` command, or right-click and choose Erase from the shortcut menu. Your drawing will look like Figure 3.13.

FIGURE 3.13

The drawing after erasing the layout lines

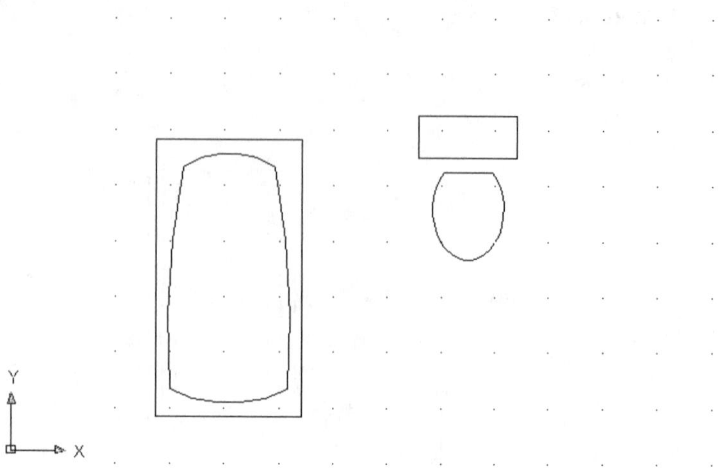

If you right-click to use the shortcut menu in step 2, you'll notice that you have several options besides Erase. You can move, copy, scale, rotate, and mirror the objects you selected. These options act just like the standard Modify toolbar options. Be aware that these commands act somewhat differently from the hot-grip options described in Chapter 2.

TIP *If you need more control over the selection of objects, you will find the Add/Remove Selection Mode setting useful. This setting lets you deselect a set of objects within a set of objects you've already selected. While in Object Selection mode, enter* **R**↵*; then proceed to use a window or other selection tool to remove objects from the selection set. Enter* **A**↵ *to continue to add options to the selection set. Or if you only need to deselect a single object, Shift+click it.*

THE OSNAP OPTIONS

In the previous exercise, you made several of the Osnap settings automatic so that they were available without having to select them from the Osnap popup menu. Another way to invoke the Osnap options is by typing their keyboard equivalents while selecting points or by right-clicking while selecting points to open the Osnap shortcut menu.

Here is a summary of all the available Osnap options, including their keyboard shortcuts. You've already used many of these options in this chapter and in the previous chapter. Pay special attention to those options you haven't yet used in the exercises but might find useful to your style of work. The full name of each option is followed by its keyboard shortcut name in brackets. To use these options, you can enter either the full name or the abbreviation at any point prompt. You can also pick these options from the popup menu obtained by Shift+clicking the right mouse button.

Tip: Sometimes you'll want one or more of these Osnap options available as the default selection. Remember that you can set Running Osnaps to be on at all times. Choose Tools ➢ Drafting Settings from the menu bar, and then click the Object Snap tab. You can also right-click the OSNAP button in the status bar and choose Settings from the shortcut menu.

Continued on next page

THE OSNAP OPTIONS *(continued)*

Available Osnap options:

Apparent Intersection [apint] Selects the apparent intersection of two objects. This is useful when you want to select the intersection of two objects that do not actually intersect. You will be prompted to select the two objects.

Center [cen] Selects the center of an arc or a circle. You must click the arc or circle itself, not its apparent center.

Endpoint [endp] Selects all the endpoints of lines, polylines, arcs, curves, and 3D Face vertices.

Extension [ext] Selects a point that is aligned with an imagined extension of a line. For example, you can pick a point in space that is aligned with an existing line but is not actually on that line. To use that point, type **ext.**↵ during point selection or select Extension from the Osnap popup menu; then move the cursor to the line whose extension you want to use and hold it there until you see a small, cross-shaped marker on the line. The cursor also displays a tool tip with the word *extension* letting you know that the Extension Osnap is active.

From [fro] Selects a point relative to a picked point. For example, you can select a point that is 2 units to the left and 4 units above a circle's center. This option is usually used in conjunction with another Osnap option, such as From Endpoint or From Midpoint.

Insert [ins] Selects the insertion point of text, blocks, Xrefs, and overlays.

Intersection [int] Selects the intersection of objects.

Midpoint [m] Selects the midpoint of a line or arc. In the case of a polyline, it selects the midpoint of the polyline segment.

Nearest [nea] Selects a point on an object nearest the pick point.

Node [nod] Selects a point object.

None [non] Temporarily turns off Running Osnaps.

Parallel [par] Lets you draw a line segment that is parallel to another existing line segment. To use this option, type **par.**↵ during point selection or select Parallel from the Osnap popup menu; then move the cursor to the line you want to be parallel to and hold it there until you see a small, cross-shaped marker on the line. The cursor also displays a tool tip with the word *parallel* letting you know that the Parallel Osnap is active.

Perpendicular [per] Selects a position on an object that is perpendicular to the last point selected. Normally, this option is not valid for the first point selected in a string of points.

Quadpoint [qua] Selects the nearest cardinal (north, south, east, or west) point on an arc or a circle.

Quick [qui] Improves the speed at which AutoCAD selects geometry by sacrificing accuracy. You use Quick in conjunction with one of the other Osnap options. For example, to speed up the selection of an intersection, you enter **QUICK,INT**↵ at a point prompt, and then select the intersection of two objects.

Tangent [tan] Selects a point on an arc or a circle that represents the tangent from the last point selected. Like the Perpendicular option, Tangent is not valid for the first point in a string of points.

TIP *When preparing to erase an object that is close to other objects, you might want to select the object first, using the Noun/Verb selection method. This way you can carefully select objects you want to erase before you actually invoke the* `Erase` *command.*

Putting On the Finishing Touches

The inside of the tub still has some sharp corners. To round out these corners, you can use the versatile `Fillet` command on the Modify toolbar. `Fillet` allows you to join lines and arcs end to end, and it can add a radius where they join, so there is a smooth transition from arc to arc or line to line. `Fillet` can join two lines that do not intersect, and it can trim two crossing lines back to their point of intersection.

1. Click the Fillet tool on the Modify toolbar, or type **f**↵. You can also choose Modify ➢ Fillet from the menu bar.

2. At the prompt

```
Current settings: Mode = TRIM, Radius = 0'-0 1/2"
Select first object or [Polyline/Radius/Trim/mUltiple]:
```

enter R↵ or right-click and choose Radius from the shortcut menu.

3. At the `Specify fillet radius <0'-0 1/2">:` prompt, enter **4**↵. This tells AutoCAD that you want a 4" radius for your fillet. Metric users will see a value of `<10.0000>` for the default radius. Go ahead and keep this value, but keep in mind that you can alter the radius value at this prompt.

4. Pick two adjacent arcs. The fillet arc joins the two larger arcs.

USING AUTOCAD'S AUTOMATIC SAVE FEATURE

As you work with AutoCAD, you may notice that AutoCAD periodically saves your work for you. Your file is saved not as its current filename, but as a file called `Auto.sv$`. The `Auto.sv$` file is an AutoCAD file with the `.sv$` filename extension added to make it distinguishable from other files you may be using. You can find this file in the `c:\Windows\Temp` folder. If you prefer, you can specify another location by modifying the information in the Files tab of the Options dialog box. See Appendix B for details.

In Chapter 1, you used the Options dialog box to change the interval between automatic saves to 20 minutes. You can also change this interval by doing the following:

1. Enter **Savetime**↵ at the command prompt.

2. At the `Enter new value for SAVETIME < 20 >:` prompt, enter the desired interval in minutes. Or, to disable the automatic save feature entirely, enter **0** at the prompt.

5. Press ↵ again and fillet another corner. Repeat until all four corners are filleted. Your drawing should look like Figure 3.14.

FIGURE 3.14
A view of the finished toilet and tub with the tub corners filleted

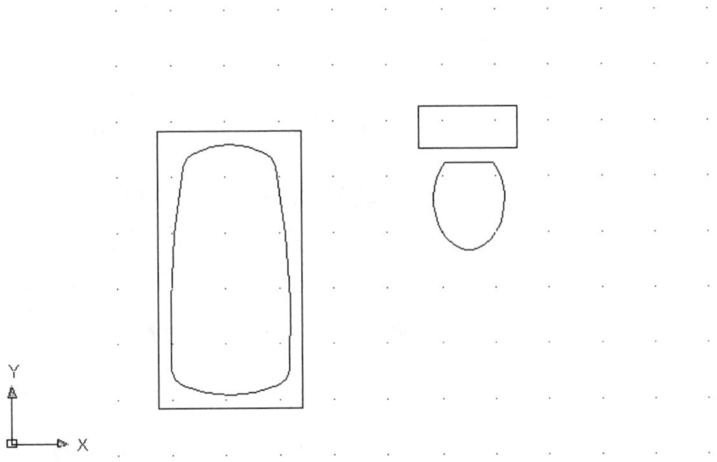

6. Save and close the Bath file.

Aligning Objects Using Object Snap Tracking

ACAD only

You saw how to use lines to construct an object such as the bathtub. In many situations, using these *construction lines* is the most efficient way to draw, but they can also be a bit cumbersome. AutoCAD 2004 offers another tool that helps you align locations in your drawing to existing objects without having to draw intermediate construction lines. The tool is called *Object Snap Tracking* or *Osnap Tracking*.

Osnap Tracking is like an extension of Object Snaps that allows you to *align* a point to the geometry of an object instead of just selecting a point on an object. For example, with Osnap Tracking, you can select a point that is exactly at the center of a rectangle.

In the following set of exercises, you will draw a plan view of a bathroom sink as an introduction to the Osnap Tracking feature. This drawing will be used as a symbol in later chapters.

TIP *If you're a veteran AutoCAD user, think of Object Snap Tracking as an improved version of the XY filter tool. XY filters allow you to selectively filter out the X, Y, or Z coordinate of any point location. Object Snap Tracking allows you to do that and more, in a way that is visually easier to comprehend.*

WARNING *The Object Snap Tracking feature is not available in AutoCAD LT 2004. If you are using LT, follow along with the tutorial until you are asked to draw the ellipse to represent the bowl of the sink. Go ahead and draw an ellipse approximating the shape and size of the one in the tutorial. Later in Chapter 13, you will learn about the Temporary Tracking feature which is available in LT and is similar to the Object Snap Tracking feature.*

A QUICK SETUP

First, as a review, you'll open a new file using the Create New Drawing Wizard. Since this drawing will be used as a symbol for insertion into other CAD drawings, don't worry about setting it up to conform to a sheet size. Chances are, you won't be printing out individual symbols.

1. Choose File ➢ New to create a new drawing for your bathroom sink.
2. Click the Use A Wizard button in the Create New Drawing dialog box, select Quick Setup from the list that appears below the buttons, and then click OK.

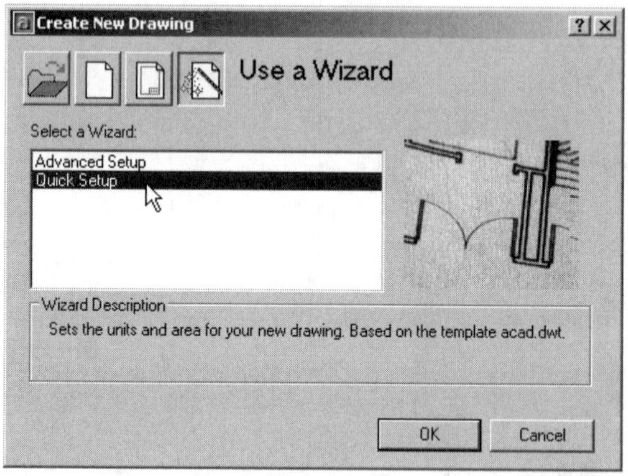

3. In the Units screen, choose Architectural; then click Next. This option performs the same operation as the Drawing Units dialog box you saw earlier in this chapter.

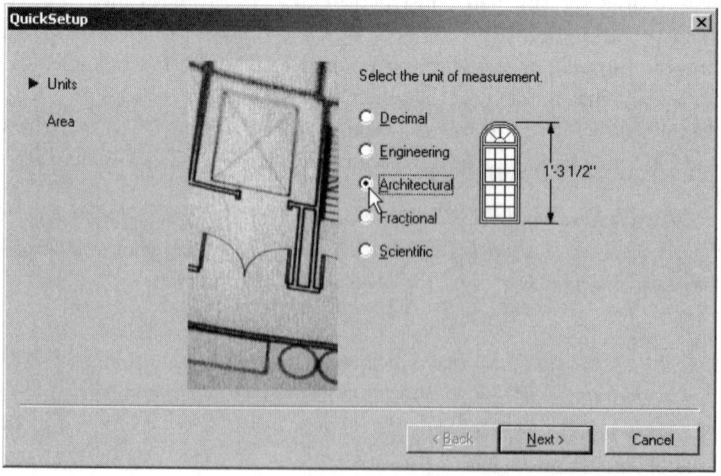

4. In the Area screen, enter **48** for the width and **36** for the length. Metric users should enter **122** for the width and **92** for the length. Click Finish when you've entered the width and length values. This option performs the same operation as choosing Format ➢ Drawing Limits from the menu bar.

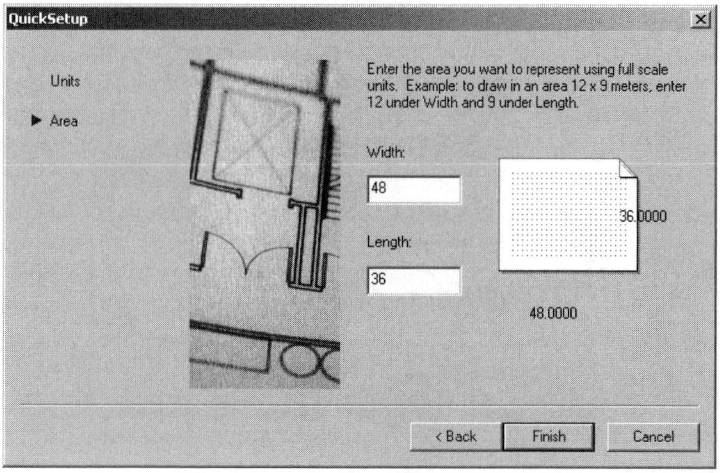

5. Click the GRID button in the status bar, and then choose View ➢ Zoom ➢ All from the menu bar. This allows you to see your entire work area.

6. Choose File ➢ Save As to save the file under the name of Sink.

As you saw in steps 3 and 4, the Create New Drawing Wizard simplifies the drawing setup process by limiting the options you need to work with. Still, it helps to know what the wizard is really doing behind the scenes. Also, the wizard does not translate your work area into a plotted sheet size.

TIP *If you find that you use the same drawing setup over and over, you can create template files that are already set up to your own, customized way of working. Templates are discussed in Chapter 5.*

DRAWING THE SINK

Now you're ready to draw the sink. Start with the outline of the sink countertop.

1. Click the GRID button in the status bar to turn off the grid. It was helpful to let you see the work area, but you don't need it now.

2. Click the Rectangle tool in the Draw toolbar or type **rec↵**.

3. At the prompt

   ```
   Specify first corner point or [Chamfer/Elevation/Fillet/Thickness/Width]:
   ```

   enter **0,0↵**. This places one corner of the rectangle in the origin of the drawing.

4. At the `Specify other corner point or [Dimensions]:` prompt, enter **@2'4,1'6↵**. Metric users should enter **@71,46↵**. This makes the rectangle 2'-4" wide by 1'-6" deep or 71 cm by 46 cm for metric users. Your drawing will look like Figure 3.15.

FIGURE 3.15
The outline of the sink

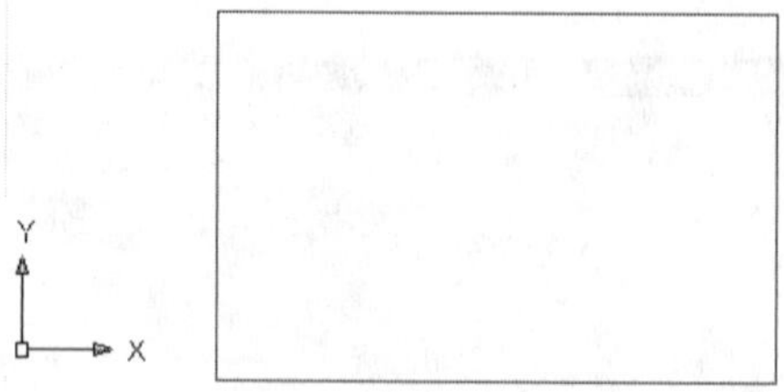

5. Choose View ➢ Zoom ➢ Extents to enlarge the view of the sink outline. Then use the Zoom Realtime tool in the Standard toolbar to adjust your view so it looks similar to the one shown in Figure 3.16.

FIGURE 3.16
The view of the sink after making some adjustments

RECTANGLE OPTIONS

You may have noticed that the Rectangle tool offers a number of options: Chamfer, Elevation, Fillet, Thickness, and Width. Two of these, Chamfer and Fillet, are equivalent to the Chamfer and Fillet tools on the Modify toolbar. They are offered as options in the Rectangle tool as a convenience. Elevation and Thickness are standard properties that all objects possess. You'll learn more about these properties in the chapters that describe how to create 3D drawings. The last option, Width, is a special property of polyline objects. You'll learn about polyline widths in Chapter 14.

Next you'll draw the bowl of the sink. The bowl will be represented by an ellipse. You'll want to place the center of the ellipse at the center of the rectangle you've just drawn. To do this, you will use the midpoint of two adjoining sides of the rectangle as alignment locations. This is where the Osnap Tracking tool will be useful.

First, make sure Running Osnaps are turned on and that they are set to the Midpoint option. Then make sure Osnap Tracking is turned on.

1. Right-click the Otrack button in the status bar and choose Settings from the shortcut menu to open the Drafting Settings dialog box at the Object Snap tab.

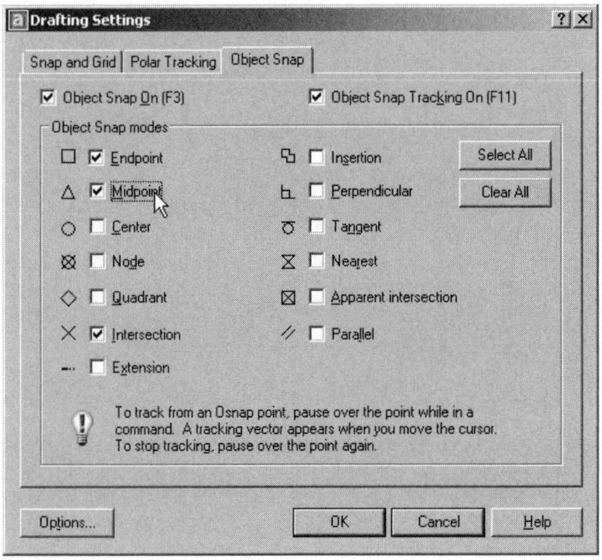

2. Make sure that the Midpoint option in the Object Snap Modes button group is checked.
3. Make sure also that Object Snap On and Object Snap Tracking On are both checked. Click OK.

Finally, you are ready to draw the ellipse.

1. Click the Ellipse tool in the Draw toolbar or enter **El**↵.

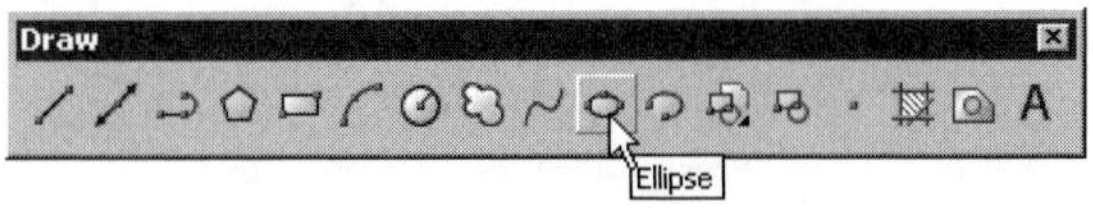

2. At the `Specify axis endpoint of ellipse or [Arc/Center]:` prompt, type C or right-click and choose Center from the shortcut menu.
3. Move your cursor to the top, horizontal edge of the rectangle, until you see the midpoint tool tip.

4. Now move the cursor directly over the Midpoint Osnap marker. Without clicking the mouse, hold the cursor there for a second until you see a small cross appear. Look carefully because the cross is quite small. This is the Osnap Tracking marker.

TIP *You can alternately insert and remove the Osnap Tracking marker by passing the cursor over the Osnap marker.*

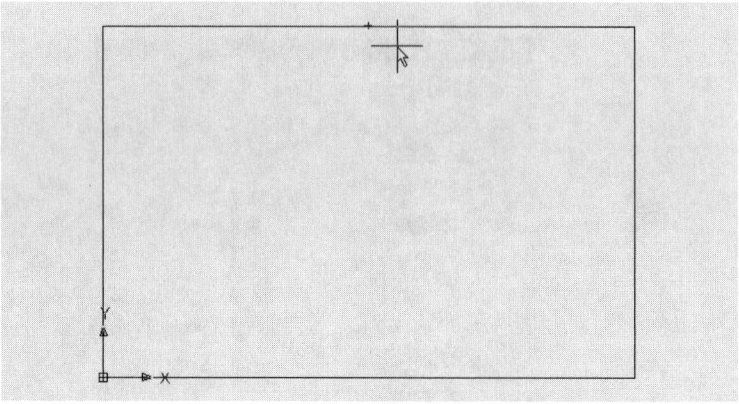

5. Now as you move the cursor downward, a dotted line appears, emanating from the midpoint of the horizontal line.

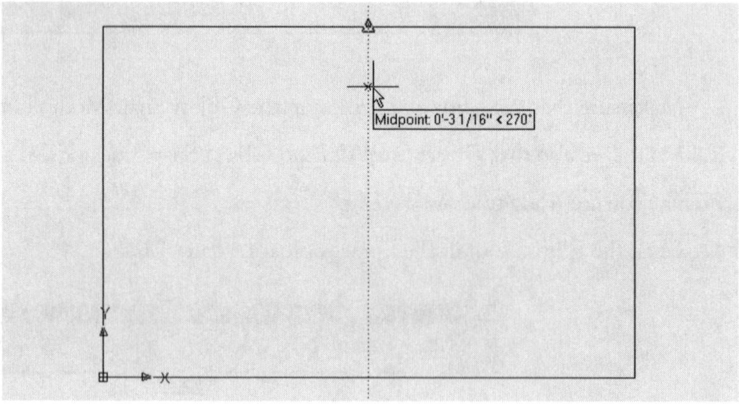

The cursor also shows a small X following the dotted line as you move it.

6. Now move the cursor to the midpoint of the left vertical side of the rectangle. Don't click, but hold it there for a second until you see the small cross. Now as you move the cursor away, a horizontal dotted line appears with an X following the cursor.

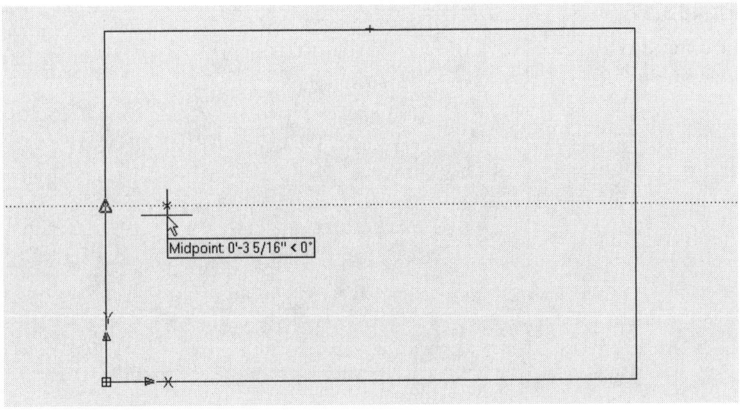

7. Now move the cursor to the center of the rectangle. The two dotted lines appear simultaneously, and a small X appears at their intersection.

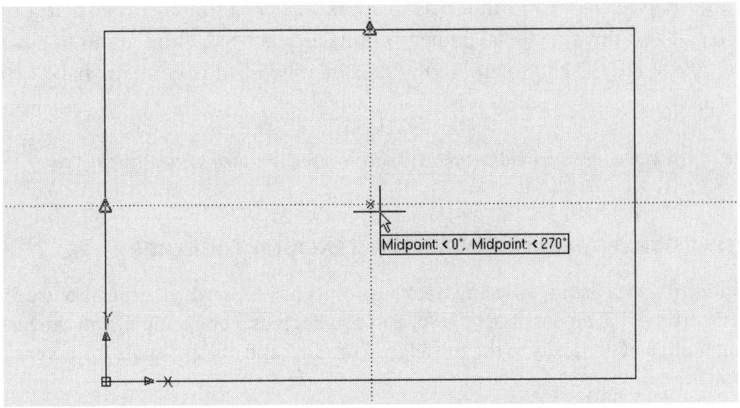

8. With the two dotted lines crossing and the X at their intersection, click the left mouse button to select the exact center of the rectangle.
9. Point the cursor to the right and enter **8↵** to make the width of the bowl 16". Metric users should enter **20↵** for a bowl 20 cm wide.
10. Point the cursor downward and enter **6↵** to make the length of the bowl 12". Metric users should enter **15↵** for a bowl with a length of 15 cm. The basic symbol for the sink is complete (see Figure 3.17).

FIGURE 3.17
The completed bathroom sink

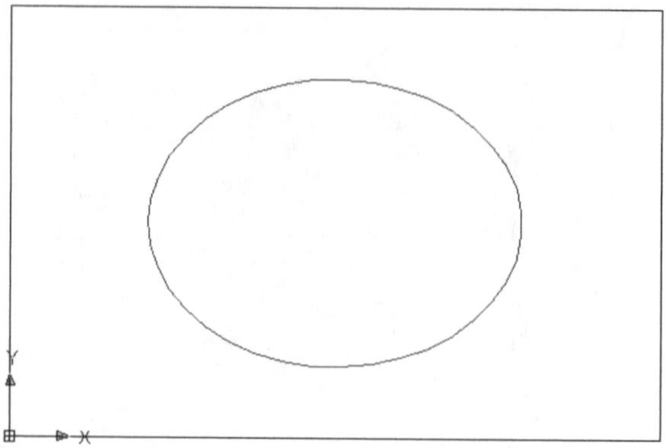

11. Choose File ➢ Save. You can exit AutoCAD now and take a break.

In this exercise, you saw how Osnap Tracking allowed you to align two locations to select a point in space. Although you only used the Midpoint Osnap setting in this exercise, you are not limited to only one Osnap setting. You can use as many as you need to in order to select the appropriate geometry. You can also use as many alignment points as you need, although in this exercise, you only used two. If you like, erase the ellipse and repeat this exercise until you get the hang of using the Osnap Tracking feature.

TIP *As with all the other buttons in the status bar, you can turn Osnap Tracking on or off by clicking the Otrack button.*

USING OSNAP TRACKING AND POLAR TRACKING TOGETHER

In addition to selecting as many tracking points as you need, you can also use different angles besides the basic orthogonal angles of 0, 90, 180, and 270 degrees. For example, you can have AutoCAD locate a point that is aligned vertically to the top edge of the sink and at a 45° angle from a corner.

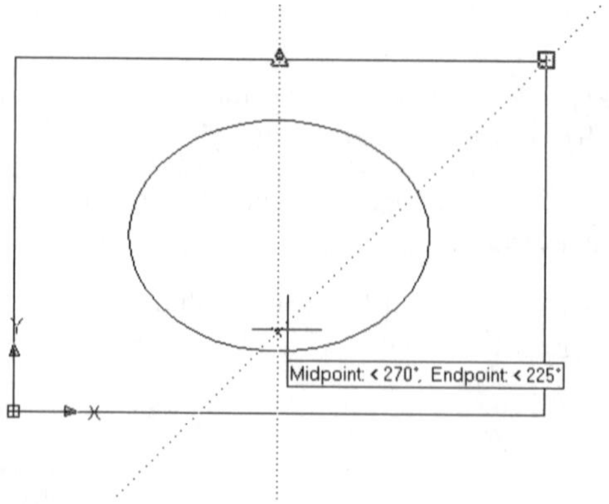

Continued on next page

USING OSNAP TRACKING AND POLAR TRACKING TOGETHER *(continued)*

This can be accomplished by using the settings in the Polar Tracking tab of the Drafting Settings dialog box (see the "Setting the Polar Tracking Angle" section earlier in this chapter). If you set the Increment angle to 45° and turn on the Track Using All Polar Angle Settings option, you will be able to use 45° in addition to the orthogonal directions. You'll see firsthand how this works in Chapter 5.

If You Want to Experiment...

As you draw, you will notice that you are alternately creating objects and then copying and editing them. This is where the difference between hand drafting and CAD really begins to show.

Try drawing the wide flange beam shown in Figure 3.18. The figure shows you what to do, step by step. Notice how you apply the concepts of layout and editing to this drawing.

FIGURE 3.18

Drawing a wide flange beam

1. Draw a box 7 units wide by 8 units high using the Line command.
2. Draw a vertical line through the center of the box.
3. Offset the top and bottom lines of the box a distance of 0.7 units. Offset the center at 0.35 units.
4. Break the sides of the box between the two offset lines.
5. Trim the top and bottom offset lines between the center three vertical lines.
6. Set the fillet radius to 0.4; then fillet the vertical offset lines with the horizontal offset lines.
7. Erase the center vertical line. You have finished the wide flange beam.

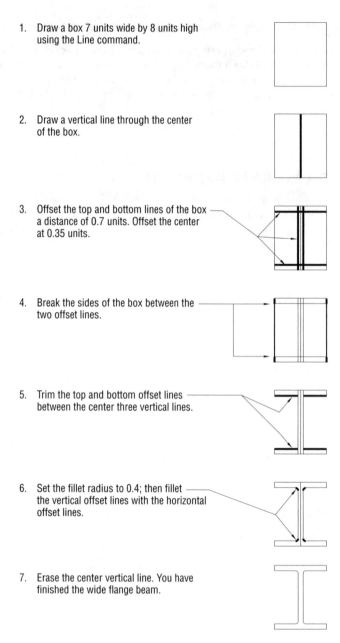

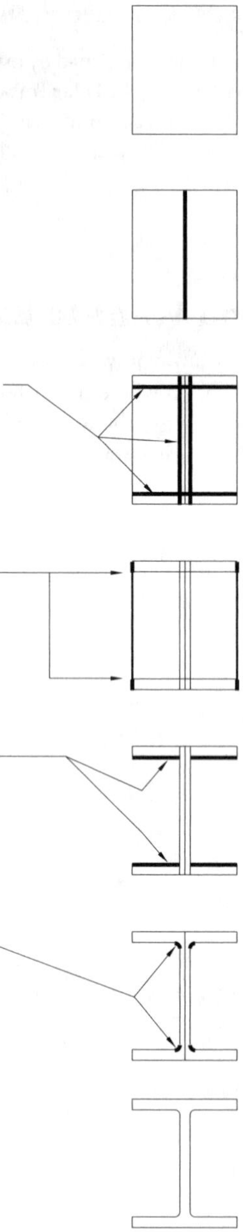

Chapter 4

Organizing Your Work

Drawing the tub and toilet in Chapter 3 may have taken what seemed to you an inordinate amount of time. As you continue to use AutoCAD, however, you will learn to draw objects more quickly. You will also need to draw fewer of them because you can save drawings as symbols to be used like rubber stamps, duplicating drawings instantaneously wherever they are needed. This saves you a lot of time when you're composing drawings.

To make effective use of AutoCAD, you should begin a *symbol library* of drawings you use frequently. A mechanical designer might have a library of symbols for fasteners, cams, valves, or any type of parts for their application. An electrical engineer might have a symbol library of capacitors, resistors, switches, and the like. A circuit designer will have yet another unique set of frequently used symbols. This book's companion CD contains a variety of ready-to-use symbol libraries. Check them out—you're likely to find some you can use.

In Chapter 3, you drew two objects—a bathtub and a toilet—that architects often use. In this chapter, you will see how to create symbols from those drawings. You will also learn about layers and how you can use them to organize information.

This chapter includes the following topics:

- Creating and Inserting a Symbol
- Modifying a Block
- Grouping Objects
- Organizing Information with Layers
- Controlling Line Weights
- Keeping Track of Blocks and Layers
- Finding Files on Your Hard Disk
- Inserting Symbols with Drag and Drop
- If You Want to Experiment...

SYMBOLS FOR PROJECTS LARGE AND SMALL

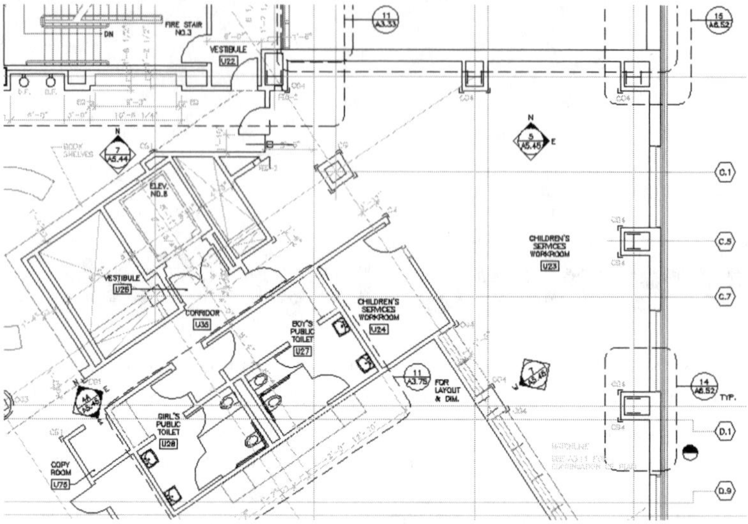

A symbol library was a crucial part of the production of the San Francisco Main Library construction documents. Shown here is a portion of an AutoCAD floor plan of the library in which some typical symbols were used.

Notice the familiar door symbols, such as the door you created in Chapter 2. And, yes, there are even toilets in the lower half of the plan in the public restrooms. The method for drawing the wide flange demonstrated at the end of Chapter 3 is similar to the one that was used to create the I-beam column symbols shown here.

Symbol use isn't restricted to building components. Room number labels, diamond-shaped interior elevation reference symbols, and the hexagonal column grid symbols are all common to an architectural drawing, regardless of the project's size. As you work through this chapter, keep in mind that all the symbols used in the library drawing were created using the tools presented here.

Creating a Symbol

To save a drawing as a symbol, you use the Block tool. In word processors, the term *block* refers to a group of words or sentences selected for moving, saving, or deleting. You can copy a block of text elsewhere within the same file, to other files, or to a separate file on disk for future use. AutoCAD uses blocks in a similar fashion. Within a file, you can turn parts of your drawing into blocks that can be saved and recalled at any time. You can also use entire existing files as blocks.

1. Start AutoCAD, and open the existing `Bath` file. Use the one you created in Chapter 3, or open `04-BATH.dwg` on the companion CD. Metric users can use the `04-bath-metric.dwg` file. The drawing appears just as you left it in the last session.

2. In the Draw toolbar, click the Make Block tool or type **B↵**, the keyboard shortcut for the Make Block tool, to open the Block Definition dialog box. You can also choose Draw ➢ Block ➢ Make.

3. In the Name text box, type **Toilet**.
4. In the Base Point button group, click the Pick Point button. This option enables you to select a base point for the block using your cursor. (The insertion base point of a block is similar to the base point you used as a handle on an object in Chapter 2.) When you've selected this option, the Block Definition dialog box temporarily disappears.

TIP *Notice that the Block Definition dialog box gives you the option to specify the X, Y, and Z coordinates for the base point, instead of selecting a point.*

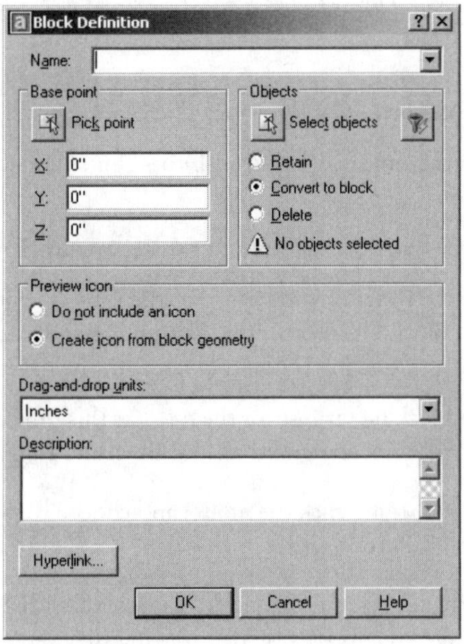

5. Using the Midpoint Osnap, pick the midpoint of the back of the toilet as the base point. Remember that you learned how to set up some Running Osnaps in Chapter 3; all you need to do is point to the midpoint of a line to display the Midpoint Osnap marker and then left-click your mouse.

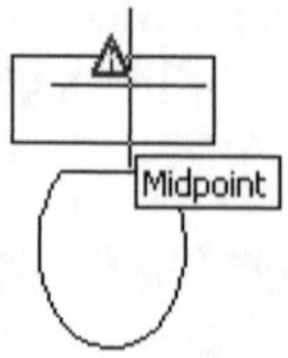

Once you've selected a point, the Block Definition dialog box reappears. Notice that the X, Y, and Z values in the Base Point button group now display the coordinates of the point you picked. For two-dimensional drawings, the Z coordinate should remain at 0.

Next, you need to select the actual objects that you want as part of the block.

1. Click the Select Objects button in the Objects button group. Once again, the dialog box momentarily disappears. You now see the familiar object selection prompt in the Command window, and the cursor becomes an object selection cursor. Click a point below and to the left of the toilet. Then window the entire toilet. The toilet is now highlighted.

WARNING *Make sure you use the Select Objects option in the Block Definition dialog box to select the objects you want to turn into a block. AutoCAD lets you create a block that contains no objects. This can cause some confusion and frustration, even for an experienced user.*

2. Press ↵ to confirm your selection. The Block Definition dialog box appears again.
3. Select Inches from the Drag-And-Drop Units drop-down list. Metric users should select Centimeters.
4. Click the Description list box and enter **Standard Toilet**.
5. Make sure the Retain radio button in the Objects button group is checked and that the Create Icon From Block Geometry radio button is selected in the Preview Icon group, and then click OK. The toilet drawing is now a block with the name Toilet.
6. Repeat the blocking process for the tub, but this time use the upper-left corner of the tub as the insertion base point and give the block the name Tub. Enter **Standard Tub** for the description.

TIP *You can press* ↵ or right-click the mouse and choose Repeat Make Block from the shortcut menu to start the Make Block tool again.

When you turn an object into a block, it is stored within the drawing file, ready to be recalled at any time. The block remains part of the drawing file even when you end the editing session. When you open the file again, the block will be available for your use. In addition, you can access blocks from other drawings using a feature called the AutoCAD DesignCenter and the tool palettes. You'll learn more about the DesignCenter and the tool palettes in Chapter 22.

A block acts like a single object, even though it is really made up of several objects. One unique characteristic of a block is that when you modify a block, all instances of that block are updated to reflect the modifications. For example, you can insert several copies of the toilet into a drawing, and then later, if you decide the toilet needs to be of a different shape, you can edit the Toilet block and all the other copies of the toilet are updated automatically.

You can modify a block in a number of ways once it has been created. In this chapter, you'll learn how to make simple changes to individual blocks by modifying the block's properties. For more detailed changes, you'll learn how to redefine a block after it has been created. Later, in Chapter 6, you'll learn how to use the In Place Xref and Block Edit tool to make changes to blocks.

Restoring Objects That Have Been Removed by the Make Block Tool or the Block Command

Before AutoCAD 2000, Block was the only command available to create blocks. This is a command-line version of the Make Block tool and is still available to those users who are more comfortable entering commands via the keyboard. To use it, you enter the word **Block** preceded by a minus sign at the command prompt, as in **–Block**. When you use the Block command, the objects you turn into a block automatically disappear. AutoCAD's Block tool (Bmake) gives you the option of removing or maintaining the block's source objects by way of the Retain option, shown in step 5 of the preceding exercise.

If you use the Block command, or if for some reason you leave the Retain option unchecked in the Block Definition dialog box, the source objects you select for the block disappear. You can restore the source using the Oops command. You can also use Oops in any situation in which you want to restore an object you accidentally erased. To use it, simply type **Oops**↵ in the Command window. The source objects reappear in their former condition and location, not as a block.

Understanding the Block Definition Dialog Box

The Block Definition dialog box offers several options that can help make the use of blocks easier. If you're interested in these options, take a moment to review the Block Definition dialog box as you read the descriptions of the dialog box options. Or if you prefer, you can continue with the tutorial and come back to this section later.

You've already seen how the Name option of the Block Definition dialog box lets you enter a name for your block. AutoCAD does not let you complete the block creation until you enter a name.

You've also seen how to select a base point for your block. The base point is like the handle of the block. It is the reference point you use when you insert the block back into the drawing. In the exercise, you used the Pick Point option to indicate a base point, but you also have the option to enter X, Y, and Z coordinates just below the Pick Point option. In most cases, however, you will want to use the Pick Point option to indicate a base point that is on or near the set of objects you are converting to a block.

The Objects button group of the Block Definition dialog box lets you select the objects that make up the block. You use the Select Objects button to visually select the objects you want to include in the block you are creating. The Quick Select button to the right of the Select Objects button lets you filter out objects based on their properties. You'll learn more about this tool in Chapter 13.

Other options in the Objects button group allow you to determine what to do with the objects you are selecting for your block. Here is a listing of the options and what they mean:

Retain Keeps the objects you select for your block as they are, unchanged.

Convert To Block Converts the objects you select into the block you are defining. It then acts like a single object once you've completed the Block command.

Delete Deletes the objects you selected for your block. This is what AutoCAD did in earlier versions. You might also notice that a warning message appears at the bottom of the Objects button group. This warning tells you if you've selected objects for the block. Once you've selected objects, this warning changes to tell you how many objects you've selected.

Preview Icon Lets you control whether a preview image is stored with the block or not. This option was added in AutoCAD 2000 and lets you easily locate and identify blocks in a drawing. You can, for example, peek into another drawing file without actually opening the file, and browse through the blocks that are contained in that file.

Insert Units Lets you determine how the object is to be scaled when it is inserted into the drawing. By default, this value will be the same as the current drawing's insert value.

Description Lets you include a brief verbal description or keyword for the block. This option is helpful when you need to find a specific block in a set of drawings. You'll learn more about searching for blocks later in this chapter and in Chapter 22.

Inserting a Symbol

You can recall the Tub and Toilet blocks at any time, as many times as you want. In the following exercise, you'll first draw the interior walls of the bathroom, and then you'll insert the tub and toilet.

1. Delete the original tub and toilet drawings. Click the Erase tool in the Modify toolbar, and then enter **All↵↵** to erase the entire visible contents of the drawing. (Doing so has no effect on the blocks you created previously.)

2. Draw a rectangle 7'-6" × 5'. Metric users should draw a 228 cm × 152 cm rectangle. Orient the rectangle so the long sides go from left to right and the lower-left corner is at coordinate 1'-10",1'-10" (or coordinate 56.0000,56.0000 for metric users). If you draw the rectangle using the Rectangle tool, make sure you explode it using the Explode tool. This is important for later exercises. Your drawing should now look like Figure 4.1.

TIP *The Insert Block tool is also on the Insert toolbar, which you can open using the Toolbars dialog box. To open the Toolbars dialog box, right-click any open toolbar or choose Insert.*

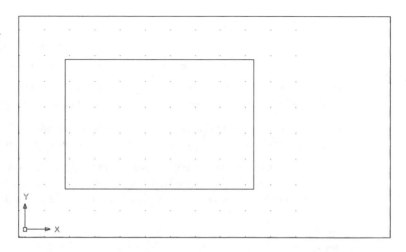

FIGURE 4.1
The interior walls of the bathroom

Now you're ready to place your blocks. Start by placing the tub in the drawing.

1. In the Draw toolbar, click the Insert Block tool or type **I**↵.

The Insert dialog box appears.

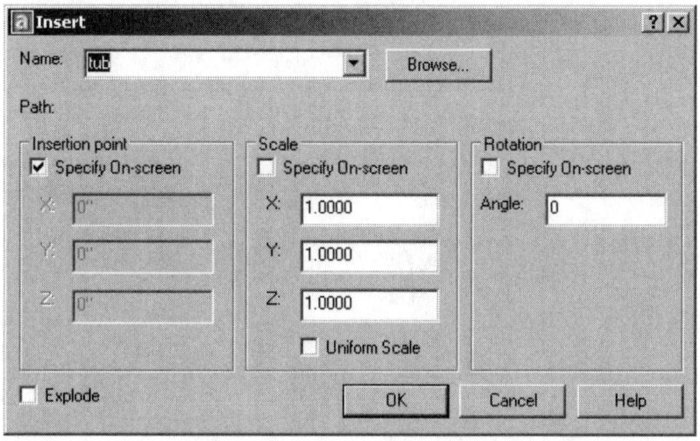

2. Click the Name drop-down list to display a list of the available blocks in the current drawing.

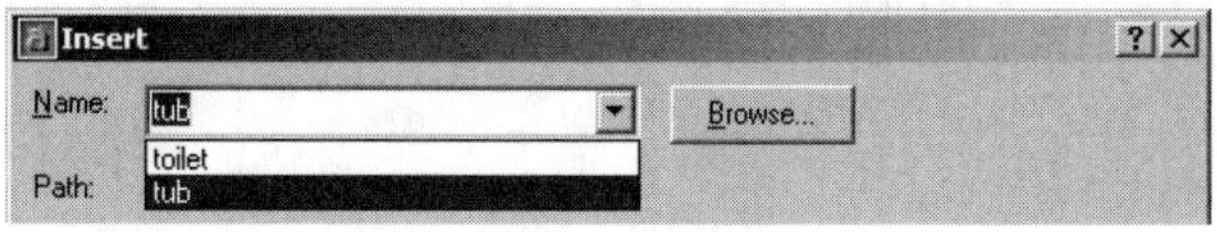

3. Click the block name Tub.
4. In the Rotation button group, click the Specify On-Screen check box. This option allows you to specify the rotation angle of the block graphically as you insert it.
5. Click OK, and you see a preview image of the tub attached to the cursor. The upper-left corner you picked for the tub's base point is now on the cursor intersection.
6. At the `Specify insertion point or [Scale/X/Y/Z/Rotate/Pscale/PX /PY/PZ/PRotate]:` prompt, pick the upper-left intersection of the room as your insertion point.
7. At the `Specify rotation angle <0>:` prompt, notice that you can rotate the block. This lets you visually specify a rotation angle for the block. You won't actually use this feature at this time, so press ↵ to accept the default of 0. You should have a drawing that looks like the top image in Figure 4.2.

FIGURE 4.2

The bathroom, first with the tub and then with the toilet inserted

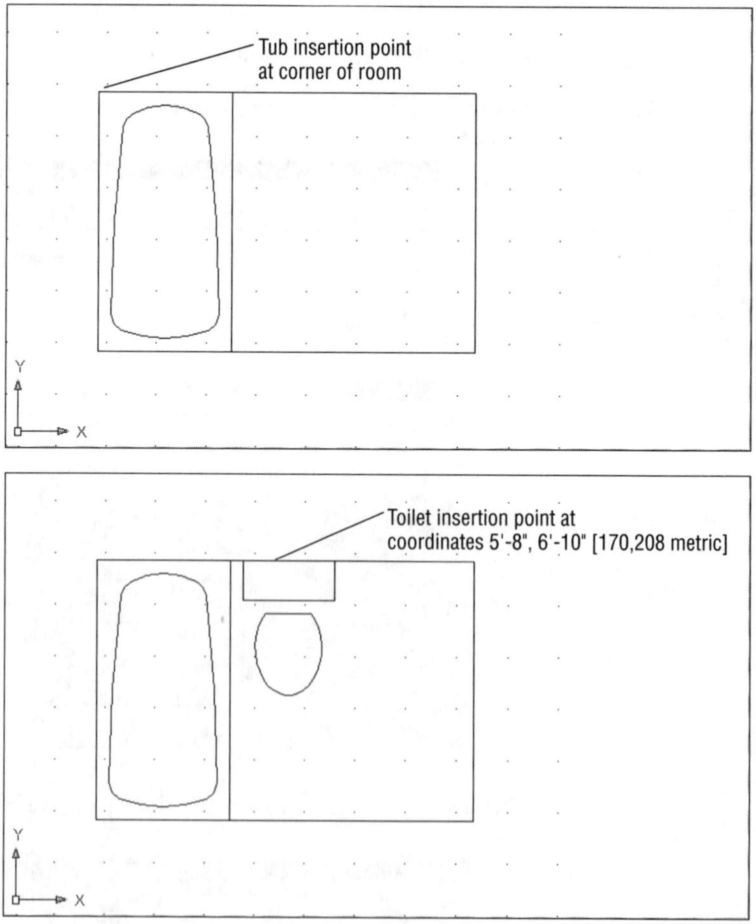

You've got the tub in place. Now place the Toilet block in the drawing.

1. Open the Insert dialog box again, but this time select Toilet in the Name drop-down list.
2. Clear the Specify On-Screen check box in the Rotation button group.
3. Place the toilet at the midpoint of the line along the top of the rectangle representing the bathroom wall as shown in the bottom image in Figure 4.2. Notice that once you select the insertion point, the toilet appears in the drawing; you are not prompted for a rotation angle for the block.

Scaling and Rotating Blocks

In step 7, you can see the tub rotate as you move the cursor. You can pick a point to fix the block in place, or you can enter a rotation value. This is the result of selecting the Specify On-Screen option in the Insert dialog box. You may find that you want the Rotation's Specify On-Screen option turned on most of the time to allow you to adjust the rotation angle of the block while you are placing it in the drawing.

The other options in the Insert dialog box that you did not use are the Scale button group options. These options let you scale the block to a different size. You can scale the block uniformly, or you can distort the block by individually changing its X, Y, or Z scale factor. With the Specify On-Screen option unchecked, you can enter specific values in the X, Y, and Z text boxes to stretch the block in any direction. If you turn on the Specify On-Screen option, you'll be able to visually adjust the X, Y, and Z scale factors in real time. Although these options are not used often, they can be useful in special situations if a block needs to be stretched one way or another to fit in a drawing.

You aren't limited to scaling or rotating a block when it is being inserted into a drawing. You can always use the Scale or Rotate tools or modify an inserted block's properties to stretch it in one direction or another. The next exercise shows you how this is done.

1. Click the Toilet block to select it.
2. Right-click and choose Properties from the shortcut menu to open the Properties palette.

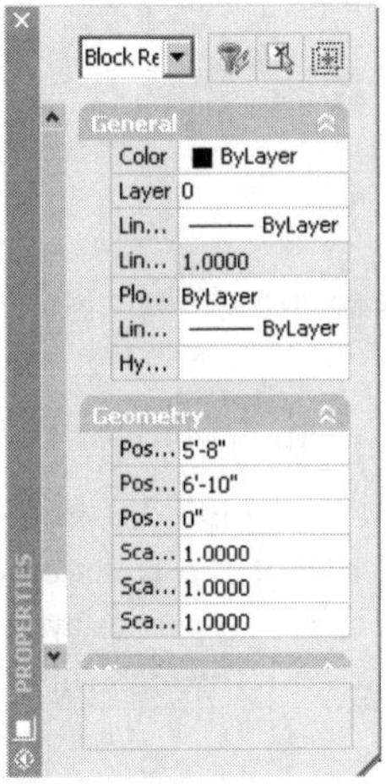

Take a moment to study the Properties palette. Toward the bottom, under the Geometry heading, you'll see a set of labels that show Position and Scale. These labels may appear as Pos… and Sca… if the width of the palette has been adjusted to be too narrow to show the entire label. Remember that you can click and drag the left or right edge of the palette to change its width. Let's take a closer look.

1. Place the cursor on the topmost Position label. A tool tip displays the full wording of the item, which is Position X.

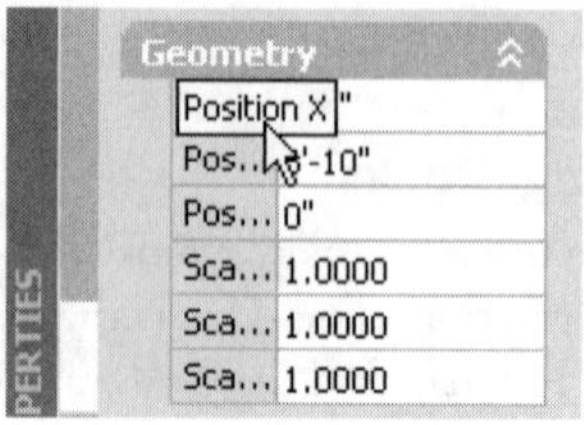

2. Move the cursor down one line to dislay the next tool tip for Position Y.
3. Move the cursor down to the first Scale item to display the tool tip Scale X.

The tool tips display the full title of the listed item. You can also widen the Properties palette by clicking and dragging its left or right border. The columns widen to show the full label of each line.

Now let's try making some changes to the toilet properties.

1. Double-click the Scale X value in the column just to the right of the Scale X label.
2. Enter **1.5**↵. Notice that the toilet changes in width as you do this.

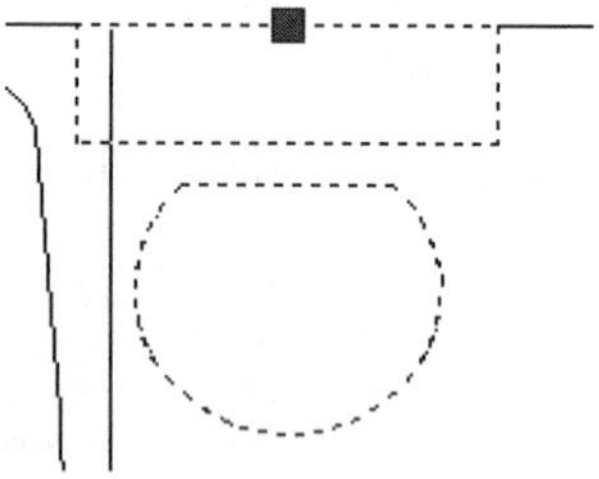

3. You don't really want to change the width of the toilet, so click the Undo tool in the Standard toolbar or enter **U**↵.
4. Close the Properties palette by clicking the X in the upper-left corner.

You've just seen how you can modify the properties of a block using the Properties palette. In the exercise, you changed the X scale of the Toilet block, but you could have just as easily changed the Y value. You may have noticed other properties available in the Properties palette. You'll learn more about those properties as you work through this chapter.

You've seen how you can turn a drawing into a symbol, known as a block in AutoCAD. Now let's see how you can use an existing drawing file as a block.

Using an Existing Drawing as a Symbol

Now you need a door into the bathroom. Since you have already drawn a door and saved it as a file, you can bring the door into this drawing file and use it as a block.

1. In the Draw toolbar, click the Insert Block tool or type **I↵**.
2. In the Insert dialog box, click the Browse button to open the Select Drawing File dialog box.
3. This is a standard Windows file browser window. Locate the `Door` file and double-click it.

TIP *You can also browse your hard disk by looking at thumbnail views of the drawing files in a folder. See the section "Finding Files on Your Hard Disk" later in this chapter.*

4. When you return to the Insert dialog box, make sure the Specify On-Screen options for the Scale and Rotation button groups are checked, and then click OK. As you move the cursor around, notice that the door appears above and to the right of the cursor intersection, as in Figure 4.3.

FIGURE 4.3

The door drawing being inserted in the `Bath` file

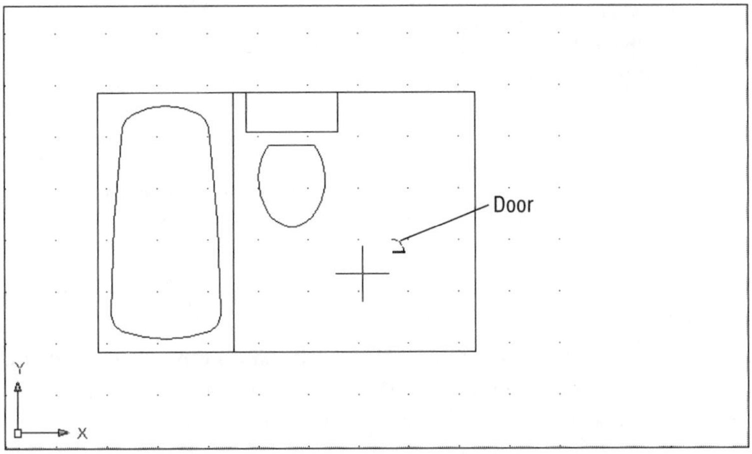

5. At this point, the door looks too small for this bathroom. This is because you drew it 3 units long, which translates to 3". Metric users drew the door 9 cm long. Pick a point near coordinates 7'-2",2'-4", so that the door is placed in the lower-right corner of the room. Metric users should use the coordinate 210,70.
6. If you take the default setting for the X scale of the inserted block, the door will remain 3" long, or 9 cm long for metric users. However, as mentioned earlier, you can specify a smaller

or larger size for an inserted object. In this case, you want a 3' door. Metric users want a 90 cm door. To get that from a 3" door, you need an X scale factor of 12, or 10 for metric users. (You might want to look again at Table 3.3 in Chapter 3 to see how this is determined.)At the `Enter X scale factor, specify opposite corner, or [Corner/XYZ] <1>:` prompt, enter **12↵**. Metric users should enter **10↵**.

7. Press ↵ twice to accept the default Y = X and the rotation angle of 0°.

Now the command prompt appears, but nothing seems to happen to the drawing. This is because when you enlarged the door, you also enlarged the distance between the base point and the object. This brings up another issue to be aware of when you're considering using drawings as symbols: all drawings have base points. The default base point is the absolute coordinate 0,0, otherwise known as the *origin*, which is located in the lower-left corner of any new drawing. When you drew the door in Chapter 2, you didn't specify the base point. So when you try to bring the door into this drawing, AutoCAD uses the origin of the door drawing as its base point (see Figure 4.4).

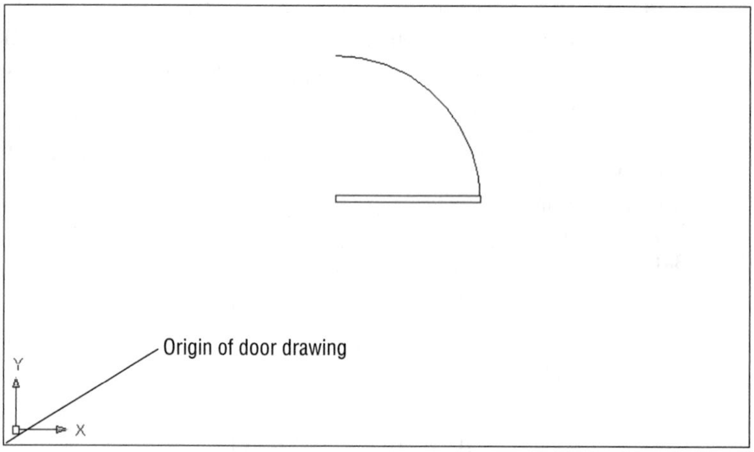

FIGURE 4.4

By default, a drawing's origin is also its insertion point. You can change a drawing's insertion point using the Base command.

Because the door appears outside the bathroom, you must first choose Zoom ➢ All to show more of the drawing and then use the Move command on the Modify toolbar to move the door to the right-side wall of the bathroom. Let's do this now.

1. Choose View ➢ Zoom ➢ All from the menu bar pull-down menu to display the area set by the limits of your drawing (Format ➢ Drawing Limits), plus any other objects that are outside those limits. The view of the room shrinks away, and the door is revealed. Notice that it is now the proper size for your drawing (see Figure 4.5).

FIGURE 4.5

The enlarged door

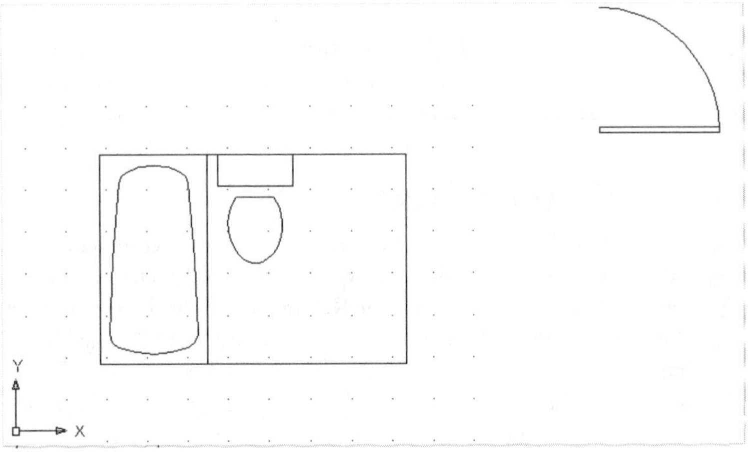

2. Choose Modify ➢ Move, or type **M↵**.
3. To pick the door you just inserted, at the `Select objects:` prompt, click a point anywhere on the door and press ↵. Notice that now the entire door is highlighted. This is because a block is treated like a single object, even though it may be made up of several lines, arcs, and so on.
4. At the `Specify base point or displacement:` prompt, turn the Running Osnaps back on and pick the lower-left corner of the door. Remember that pressing the F3 function key or double-clicking the word `Osnap` in the status bar toggles the Running Osnaps on or off.
5. At the `Specify second point of displacement or <use first point as displacement>:` prompt, use the Nearest Osnap override, and position the door so that your drawing looks like Figure 4.6.

FIGURE 4.6

The door on the right-side wall of the bathroom

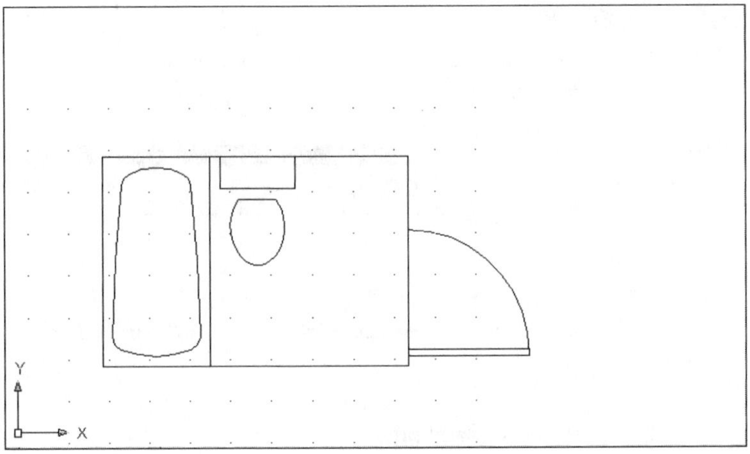

Because the door is an object that you will use often, it should be a common size so you don't have to specify an odd value every time you insert it. It would also be helpful if the door's insertion base point were in a more convenient location—that is, a location that would allow you to place the door accurately within a wall opening. Next, you will modify the Door block to better suit your needs.

Modifying a Block

You can modify a block in two ways. One way is to completely redefine the block. In earlier versions of AutoCAD, this was the only way to make changes to a block. A second way to modify blocks is to use the Reference Edit tool. The Reference Edit tool lets you quickly modify a block in its existing location. Reference Edit offers more flexibility when editing blocks and another type of object called an *Xref*, but it also has a few limitations. In this chapter, you'll learn how to redefine a block by making changes to the door symbol. Later, in Chapter 6, you'll see how the Reference Edit tool allows you to quickly modify a block that will then affect other copies of the block throughout a drawing.

TIP *Double-clicking most objects displays the Properties palette. Double-clicking a block opens the Reference Edit dialog box, which offers another way of editing blocks. The Reference Edit dialog box is not available in AutoCAD LT. You'll learn more about the Reference Edit dialog box in Chapter 6.*

Unblocking and Redefining a Block

One way to modify a block is to break it down into its components, edit them, and then turn them back into a block. This is called *redefining* a block. If you redefine a block that has been inserted in a drawing, each occurrence of that block within the current file changes to reflect the new block definition. You can use this block redefinition feature to make rapid changes to a design.

TIP *If the Regenauto setting is turned off, you have to issue a Regen command to see changes made to redefined blocks. See Chapter 6 for more on Regenauto.*

To separate a block into its components, use the Explode command.

1. Choose Explode from the Modify toolbar. You can also type X↵ to start the Explode command.

TIP *You can simultaneously insert and explode a block by clicking the Explode check box in the lower-left corner of the Insert dialog box.*

2. Click the door and press ↵ to confirm your selection.

Now you can edit the individual objects that make up the door, if you so desire. In this case, you only want to change the door's insertion point because you have already made it a more convenient size. So now you'll turn the door back into a block, this time using the door's lower-left corner for its insertion base point.

1. In the Draw toolbar, select Make Block or type **B↵**. You can also choose Draw ➢ Block ➢ Make.
2. In the Block Definition dialog box, select the name Door from the Name drop-down list.
3. Click the Pick Point button and pick the lower-left corner of the door.
4. Click the Select Objects button and select the components of the door. Press ↵ when you've finished making your selection.
5. Select the Convert To Block option in the Objects button group to automatically convert the selected objects in the drawing into a block.
6. Select Inches from the Insert Units drop-down list, and then enter **Standard door** in the Description list box.
7. Now click OK. You'll see a warning message that reads "Door is already defined. Do you want to re-define it?" You don't want to redefine an existing block accidentally. In this case, you know you want to redefine the door, so click the Yes button to proceed.

TIP *The Select Object and Select Point buttons appear in other dialog boxes. Make note of their appearance, and remember that when you select them, the dialog box temporarily disappears to allow you to select points or objects and otherwise perform operations that require a clear view of the drawing area.*

In step 7, you received a warning message that you were about to redefine the existing door block. But originally, you inserted the door as a file, not as a block. Whenever you insert a drawing file using the Insert Block tool, the inserted drawing automatically becomes a block in the current drawing. When you redefine a block, however, you do not affect the drawing file you imported. AutoCAD changes only the block within the current file.

You've just redefined the door block. Now place the door in the wall of the room.

1. Choose Erase from the Modify toolbar, and then click the door. Notice that the entire door is one object instead of individual lines and an arc. Had you not selected the Convert To Block option in step 5, the components of the block would have remained as individual objects.
2. Now insert the door block again, using the Block button in the Insert dialog box or by choosing Modify ➢ Insert Block. This time, however, use the Nearest Osnap override and pick a point on the right-side wall of the bathroom, near coordinate 9'-4",2'-1". Metric users should insert the door near 284,63.4.
3. Use the Grips feature to mirror the door, using the wall as the mirror axis so that the door is inside the room. Your drawing will look like Figure 4.7.

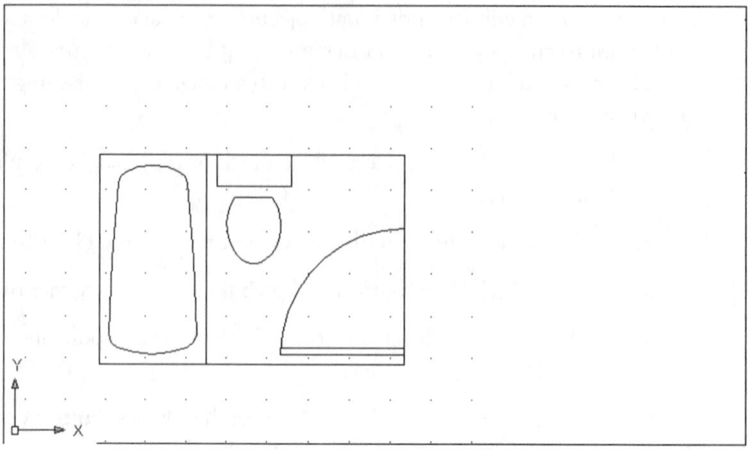

FIGURE 4.7
The bathroom floor plan thus far

TIP *To mirror an object using grips, first be sure that the Grips feature is on (it is usually on by default). Select the objects to mirror, click a grip, and then right-click. Select Mirror from the shortcut menu; then indicate a mirror axis with the cursor.*

Next, you'll see how you can update an external file with a redefined block.

Saving a Block as a Drawing File

You've seen that, with very little effort, you can create a symbol that can be placed anywhere in a file. Suppose you want to use this symbol in other files. When you create a block using the Block command, the block exists within the current file only until you specifically instruct AutoCAD to save it as a drawing file on disk. For an existing drawing that has been brought in and modified, such as the door, the drawing file on disk associated with that door is not automatically updated. To update the `Door` file, you must take an extra step and use the Export option on the File menu. Let's see how this works.

TIP *You can extract blocks that are embedded in other drawings by using a feature called the DesignCenter. See Chapter 22.*

Start by turning the Tub and Toilet blocks into individual files on disk.

1. Choose File ➢ Export to open the Export Data dialog box, which is a simple file dialog box.
2. Open the List Files Of Type drop-down list, and select Block (*.dwg).

TIP *If you prefer, you can skip step 2, and instead, in step 3, enter the full filename, including the .dwg extension, as in* `Tub.dwg`.

3. Double-click the File Name text box and enter **Tub**.
4. Click the Save button to close the Export Data dialog box.

5. At the `[= (block=output file)/* (whole drawing)] <define new drawing>:` prompt, enter the name of the block you want to save to disk as the tub file—in this case, also **Tub**. The Tub block is now saved as a file.

6. Repeat steps 1 through 3 for the Toilet block. Give the file the same name as the block.

TIP *AutoCAD gives you the option to save a block's file under the same name as the original block or with a different name. Usually you will want to use the same name, which you can do by entering an equal sign (=) after the prompt.*

TIP *Normally, AutoCAD saves a preview image with a file. This allows you to preview a drawing file before opening it. Preview images are not included with files that are exported with the File ➢ Export option or the Wblock command, which is discussed in the next section.*

Replacing Existing Files with Blocks

The Wblock command does the same thing as choosing File ➢ Export, but output is limited to AutoCAD *.dwg files. (Veteran AutoCAD users should note that `Wblock` is now incorporated into the File ➢ Export option.) Let's try using the Wblock command this time to save the Door block you modified.

1. Issue the Wblock command by typing **Wblock↵**, or use the keyboard shortcut by typing **w↵** to open the Write Block dialog box.

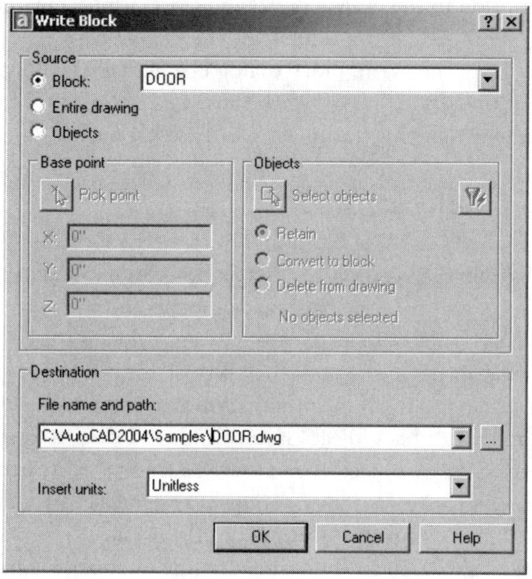

2. In the Source button group, click the Block radio button.

3. Select Door from the drop-down list. Notice that the options under the Destination button group change to reflect the location of the old `Door.dwg` file from which the Door block was originally inserted. You can keep the old name or enter a different name if you prefer.
4. In this case, you want to update the door you drew in Chapter 2, so click OK.
5. You'll see a warning message telling you that the `Door.dwg` file already exists. Go ahead and click Yes to confirm that you want to overwrite the old door drawing with the new door definition.

In this exercise, you typed the Wblock command at the command prompt instead of using File ➢ Export. The results are the same, regardless of which method you use. If you are in a hurry, the File ➢ Export command is a quick way to save part of your drawing as a file. The Wblock option may be easier for new users since it offers options in a dialog box.

Understanding the Write Block Dialog Box Options

The Write Block dialog box offers a way to save parts of your current drawing as a file. As you can see from the dialog box shown in the previous exercise, you have several options to work with.

In that exercise, you used the Block option of the Source button group to select an existing block as the source object to be exported. You can also export a set of objects by choosing the Objects option. If you choose this option, the Base Point and Objects button groups become available. These options work the same way as their counterparts in the Block Definition dialog box that you saw earlier when you created the Tub and Toilet blocks.

The third option in the Source button group, Entire Drawing, lets you export the whole drawing to its own file. This may seem to duplicate the File ➢ Save As option in the menu bar, but saving the entire drawing from the Write Block dialog box actually performs some additional operations, such as stripping out unused blocks or other unused components. This has the effect of reducing file size. You'll learn more about this feature later in this chapter.

Other Uses for Blocks

So far, you have used the Make Block tool to create symbols, and you have used the `Export` and Wblock commands to save those symbols to disk. As you can see, you can create symbols and save them at any time while you are drawing. You have made the tub and toilet symbols into drawing files that you can see when you check the contents of your current folder.

However, creating symbols is not the only use for the Insert Block, Block, Export, and Wblock commands. You can use them in any situation that requires grouping objects (though you might prefer to use the more flexible Object Group command discussed in the next section). You can also use blocks to stretch a set of objects along one axis using the Properties palette. Export and Wblock also allow you to save a part of a drawing to disk. You will see instances of these other uses of the Block, Export, and Wblock commands throughout the book.

Make Block, Export, and Wblock are extremely versatile commands and, if used judiciously, can boost your productivity and simplify your work. If you are not careful, however, you can also get carried away and create more blocks than you can keep track of. Planning your drawings helps you determine which elements will work best as blocks and recognize situations in which other methods of organization are more suitable.

AN ALTERNATIVE TO BLOCKS

Another way to create symbols is by creating shapes. Shapes are special objects made up of lines, arcs, and circles. They can regenerate faster than blocks, and they take up less file space. Unfortunately, shapes are considerably more difficult to create and are less flexible to use than blocks.

You create shapes by using a coding system developed by Autodesk. The codes define the sizes and orientations of lines, arcs, and circles. You first sketch your shape, convert it into the code, and then copy that code into a text file. To learn more about shapes, see your *AutoCAD Customization Manual*.

Another way of using symbols is to use AutoCAD's external reference capabilities. External referenced files, known as Xrefs, are files inserted into a drawing in a way similar to blocks. The difference is that Xrefs do not actually become part of the drawing's database. Instead, they are loaded along with the current file at startup time. It is as if AutoCAD opens several drawings at once: the main file you specify when you start AutoCAD, and the Xrefs associated with the main file.

By keeping the Xrefs independent from the current file, you make sure that any changes made to the Xrefs automatically appear in the current file. You don't have to update each inserted copy of an Xref, as you must for blocks. For example, if you use the External Reference option on the Reference toolbar (discussed in Chapter 13) to insert the Tub drawing, and later you make changes to the tub, the next time you open the `Bath` file, you will see the new version of the tub.

Xrefs are especially useful in workgroup environments, where several people are working on the same project. One person might be updating several files that have been inserted into a variety of other files. Before Xrefs were available, everyone in the workgroup had to be notified of the changes and had to update all the affected blocks in all the drawings that contained them. With Xrefs, the updating is automatic. Many other features are unique to these files, and they are discussed in more detail in Chapters 6 and 13.

Grouping Objects

ACAD only

Blocks are extremely useful tools, but for some situations, they are too restricting. At times, you will want to group objects together so they are connected yet can still be edited individually. For example, consider a space planner who has to place workstations in a floor plan. Though each workstation is basically the same, some slight variations in each station could make the use of blocks unwieldy. For instance, one workstation might need a different configuration to accommodate special equipment, and another workstation might need to be slightly larger than the standard size. Using a block, you would need to create a block for one workstation, and then for each variation, explode the block, edit it, and then create a new block. A better way is to draw a prototype workstation and then turn it into a group. You can copy the group into position and then edit it for each individual situation, without losing its identity as a group. The following exercises demonstrate how this works.

TIP *AutoCAD LT offers a different method for grouping objects. If you are using LT, skip this exercise and continue with the following section "Grouping Objects for LT Users."*

1. Open the drawing named `office1.dwg` from the companion CD.
2. Use the Zoom command to enlarge just the view of the workstation, as shown in the first image in Figure 4.8.

FIGURE 4.8

A workstation in an office plan

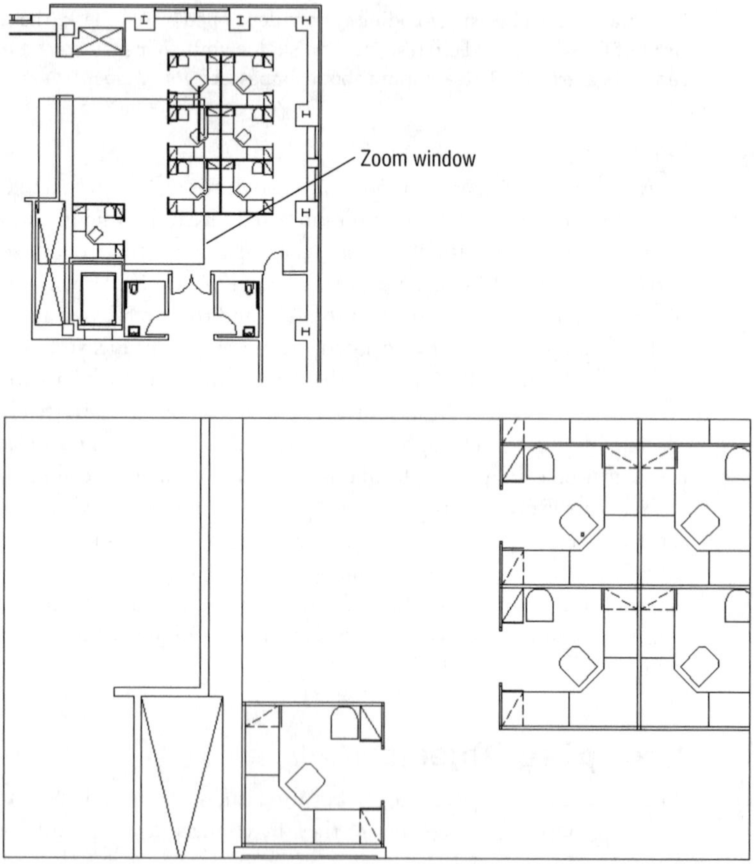

3. Type **G↵** or **Group↵** to open the Object Grouping dialog box.

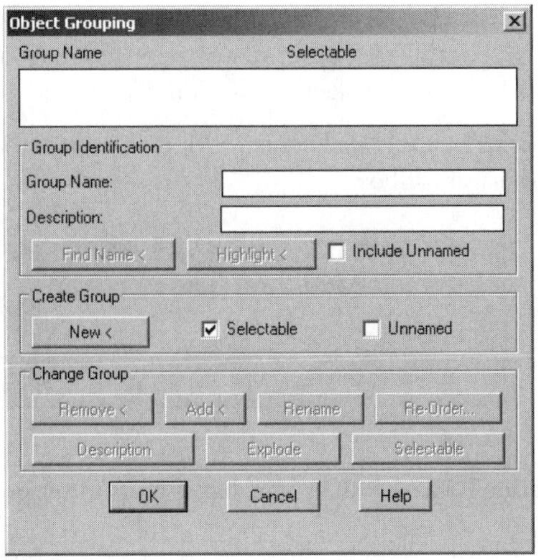

4. Type **Station1**. As you type, your entry appears in the Group Name text box.
5. Click New in the Create Group button group, about midway in the dialog box. The Object Grouping dialog box temporarily disappears to allow you to select objects for your new group.
6. At the `Select objects:` prompt, window the entire workstation in the lower-left corner of the plan and press ↵ to display the Object Grouping dialog box. Notice that the name `STATION1` appears in the Group Name box at the top of the dialog box.
7. Click OK. You have just created a group.

Now, whenever you want to select the workstation, you can click any part of it to select the entire group. At the same time, you can still modify individual parts of the group—the desk, partition, and so on—without losing the grouping of objects.

Grouping Objects for LT Users

LT users will have to use a slightly different method to create a group. If you are using AutoCAD 2004 LT, do the following.

LT only

1. Open the drawing named `office1.dwg` from the companion CD.
2. Use the Zoom command to enlarge just the view of the workstation, as shown in the first image in Figure 4.8.
3. Type **G**↵ or **Group**↵ to open the Group Manager dialog box.

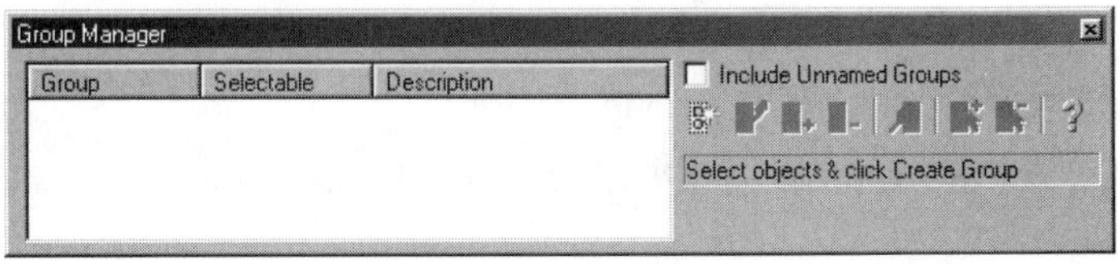

4. Move the dialog box so that you have a clear view of the workstation; then use a selection window to select all the objects of the workstation. You can also click the individual objects of the workstation to make the selection.

5. In the Group Manager dialog box, click the Create Group button. A new listing appears in the Group Manager list box.

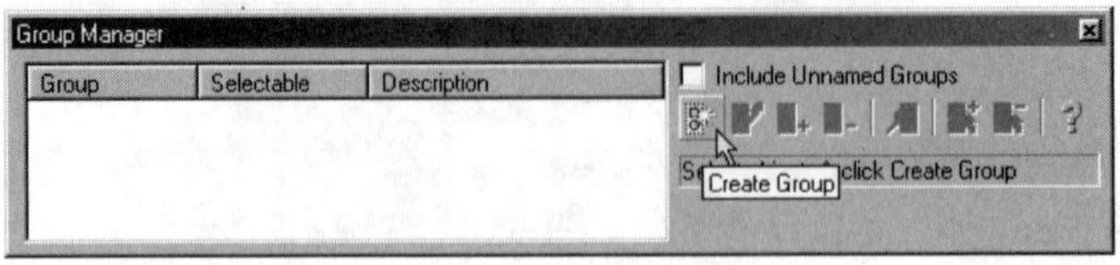

6. Type **Station1↵** in the input box that appears in the group list.

7. Close the Group Manager dialog box.

Now, whenever you want to select the workstation, you can click any part of it to select the entire group. At the same time, you can still modify individual parts of the group—the desk, partition, and so on—without losing the grouping of objects.

Modifying Members of a Group

Next, you will make copies of the original group and modify the copies. Figure 4.9 is a sketch of the proposed layout that uses the new workstations. Look carefully, and you'll see that some of the workstations in the sketch are missing a few of the standard components that exist in the Station1 group. One pair of stations has a partition removed; another station has no desk.

This next exercise shows you how to complete your drawing to reflect the design requirements of the sketch. Start by making a copy of the workstation.

1. Click Copy on the Modify toolbar or type **Co↵**, and click the Station1 group you just created. Notice that you can click any part of the station to select the entire station. If only a single object is selected, press Shift+Ctrl+A and try clicking another part of the group.

2. Press ↵ to finish your selection.

3. At the `Specify base point or displacement, or [Multiple]:` prompt, enter **@↵**. Then enter **@8'2"<90** to copy the workstation 8 feet, 2 inches vertically. Metric users should enter **@249<90**.

TIP *In step 3, you can also use the Direct Distance method by typing* **@↵** *and then pointing the rubber-banding line 90° and typing* **8'2"↵**. *Metric users should type* **249↵**.

4. Issue the Copy command again, but this time click the copy of the workstation you just created. Notice that it, too, is a group.

5. Copy this workstation 8'2" (249 cm for the metric users) vertically, just as you did the original workstation.

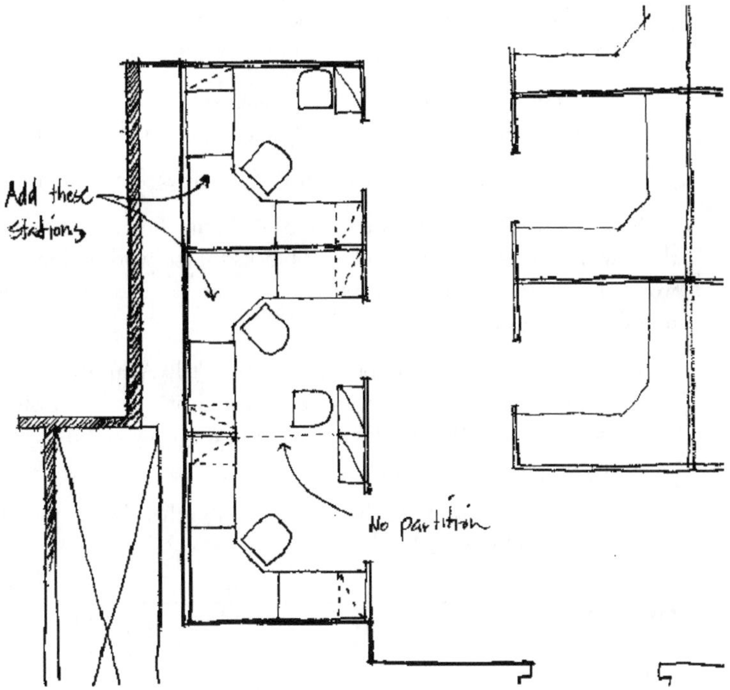

FIGURE 4.9
A sketch of the new office layout

Next, you'll use grips to mirror the first workstation copy.

1. Click the middle workstation to highlight it, and notice that grips appear for all the entities in the group.
2. Click the grip in the middle-left side, as shown in Figure 4.10.

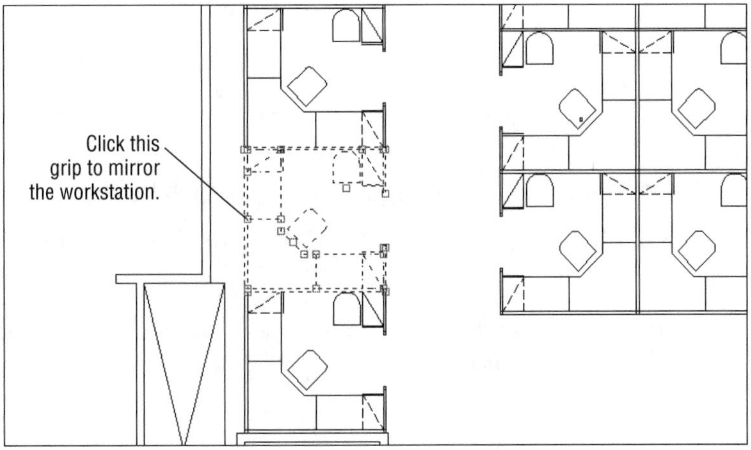

FIGURE 4.10
Mirroring the new group using grips

3. Right-click the mouse and choose Mirror from the shortcut menu. Notice that a temporary mirror image of the workstation follows the movement of your cursor.
4. Turn on the Ortho mode and pick a point directly to the right of the hot grip you picked in step 2. The workstation is mirrored to a new orientation.
5. Press the Esc key twice to clear the grip selection. Also, turn off the Ortho mode.

Now that you've got the workstations laid out, you need to remove some of the partitions between the new workstations. If you had used blocks for the workstations, you would first need to explode the workstations whose partitions you want to edit. Groups, however, let you make changes without undoing their grouping.

1. At the command prompt, press Shift+Ctrl+A. You should see the `<Group off>` message in the command line. If you see the `<Group on>` message instead, press Shift+Ctrl+A until you see `<Group off>`. This turns off groupings so you can select and edit individual objects within a group.
2. Using a window, erase the short partition that divides the two copies of the workstations, as shown in Figure 4.11.

FIGURE 4.11

Remove the partitions between the two workstations.

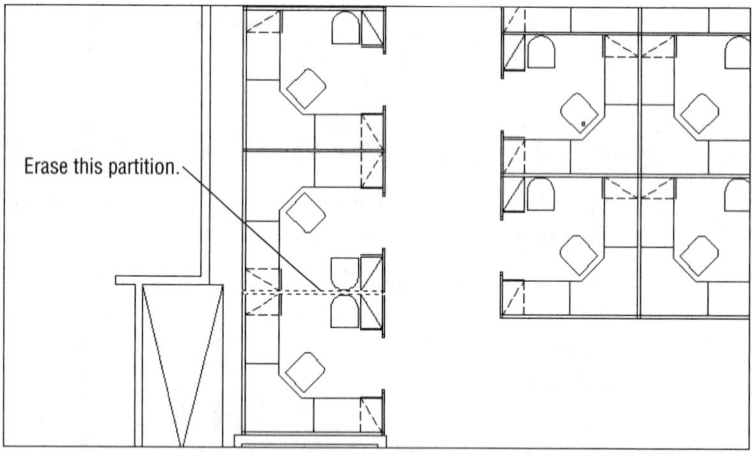
Erase this partition.

3. Press Shift+Ctrl+A again to turn groupings back on.
4. To check your workstations, click one of them to see if all its components are highlighted together.

TIP *Pickstyle is a system variable that controls how groups are selected. See Appendix D for more information about Pickstyle and other system variables.*

Working with the Object Grouping Dialog Box

ACAD only

Each group has a unique name, and you can also attach a brief description of the group in the Object Grouping dialog box. When you copy a group, AutoCAD assigns an arbitrary name to the newly created group. Copies of groups are considered unnamed, but you can still list them in the Object Grouping dialog box by clicking the Unnamed check box. You can click the Rename button in the Object Grouping dialog box to name unnamed groups appropriately.

Objects within a group are not bound solely to that group. One object can be a member of several groups, and you can have nested groups.

Here are the options available in the Object Grouping dialog box.

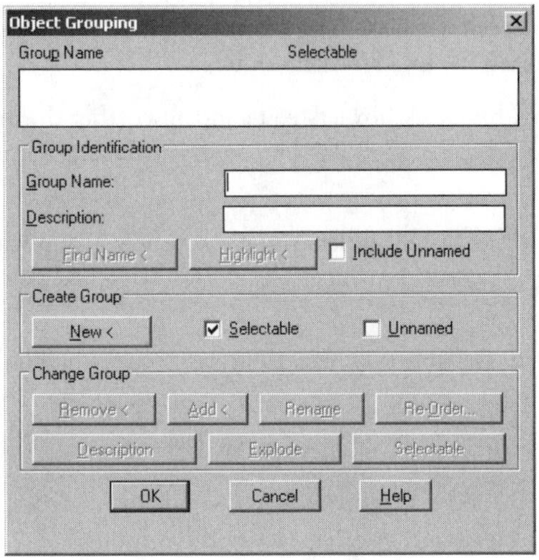

NOTE *AutoCAD LT users have a different set of options. See the "Working with the LT Group Manager" section that follows this section.*

GROUP IDENTIFICATION

Use the Group Identification button group to identify your groups, using unique elements that let you remember what each group is for.

Group Name This text box lets you create a new group by naming it first.

Description This text box lets you include a brief description of the group.

Find Name Click this button to find the name of a group by temporarily closing the Object Grouping dialog box so you can click a group.

Highlight Click this button to highlight a group that has been selected from the group list. This helps you locate a group in a crowded drawing.

Include Unnamed This check box determines whether unnamed groups are included in the Group Name list. Check this box to display the names of copies of groups for processing by this dialog box.

CREATE GROUP

Here's where you control how a group is created.

New Click this button to create a new group. The Object Grouping dialog box closes temporarily so that you can select objects for grouping. To use this button, you must have either entered a group name or checked the Unnamed check box.

Selectable This check box lets you control whether the group you create is selectable or not. See the description of the Selectable button in the Change Group button group in the section that follows.

Unnamed This check box lets you create a new group without naming it.

CHANGE GROUP

These buttons are available only when a group name is highlighted in the Group Name list at the top of the dialog box.

Remove Lets you remove objects from a group.

Add Lets you add objects to a group. While using this option, grouping is temporarily turned off to allow you to select objects from other groups.

Rename Lets you rename a group.

Re-Order Lets you change the order of objects in a group.

Description Lets you modify the description of a group.

Explode Separates a group into its individual components.

Selectable Turns individual groupings on and off. When a group is selectable, it is selectable only as a group. When a group is not selectable, the individual objects in a group can be selected, but not the group.

TIP *If a group is selected, you can remove individual items from the group with a Shift+click. In this way, you can isolate objects within a group for editing or removal without having to temporarily turn off groups.*

LT only

Working with the LT Group Manager

If you are using AutoCAD LT, you use the Group Manager to manage groups. Here is a rundown of the tools that are available in the Group Manager.

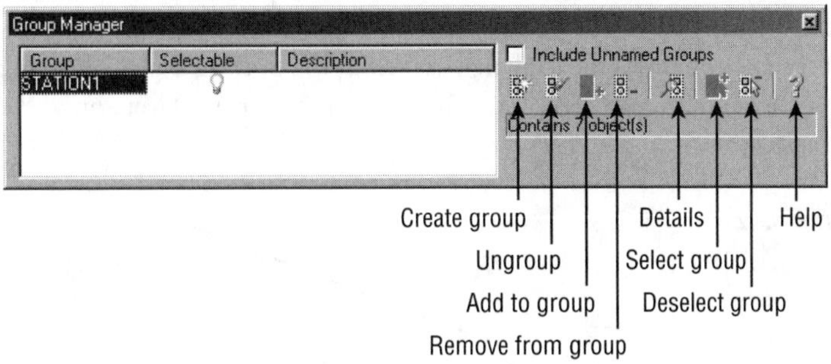

Create Group Lets you convert a set of objects into a group. Select a set of objects, and then click Create Group.

Ungroup Removes the grouping of an existing group. Select the group name from the list, and then select Ungroup.

Add To Group Lets you add an object to a group. At least one group and one additional object must be selected before this option is available.

Remove From Group Lets you remove one or more objects from a group. To isolate individual objects in a group, first select the group, and then Shift+click to remove individual objects from the selection set. After you isolate the object you want to remove, click Remove From Group.

Details Lists detailed information about the group, such as the number of objects in the group and whether it is in model space or a layout. Select the group name from the group list, and then click Details.

Select Group Lets you select a group by name. Highlight the group name in the group list, and then click Select Group.

Deselect Group Removes a group from the current selection set. Hightlight the group name in the group list, and then click Deselect Group.

Help Opens the AutoCAD LT help dialog box and shows you information about the Group Manager.

Other Uses for Groups

You've seen how you can use groups to create an office layout. You can also use groups to help you keep sets of objects temporarily together in a complex drawing. Groups can be especially useful in 3D modeling when you want to organize complex assemblies together for easy selection.

Organizing Information with Layers

Another tool for organization is the *layer*. Layers are like overlays on which you keep various types of information (see Figure 4.12). In a floor plan of a building, for example, you want to keep the walls, ceiling, plumbing fixtures, wiring, and furniture separate so that you can display or plot them individually or combine them in different ways. It's also a good idea to keep notes and reference symbols about each element of the drawing, as well as the drawing's dimensions, on their own layers. As your drawing becomes more complex, you can turn the various layers on and off to allow easier display and modification.

FIGURE 4.12

Placing drawing elements on separate layers

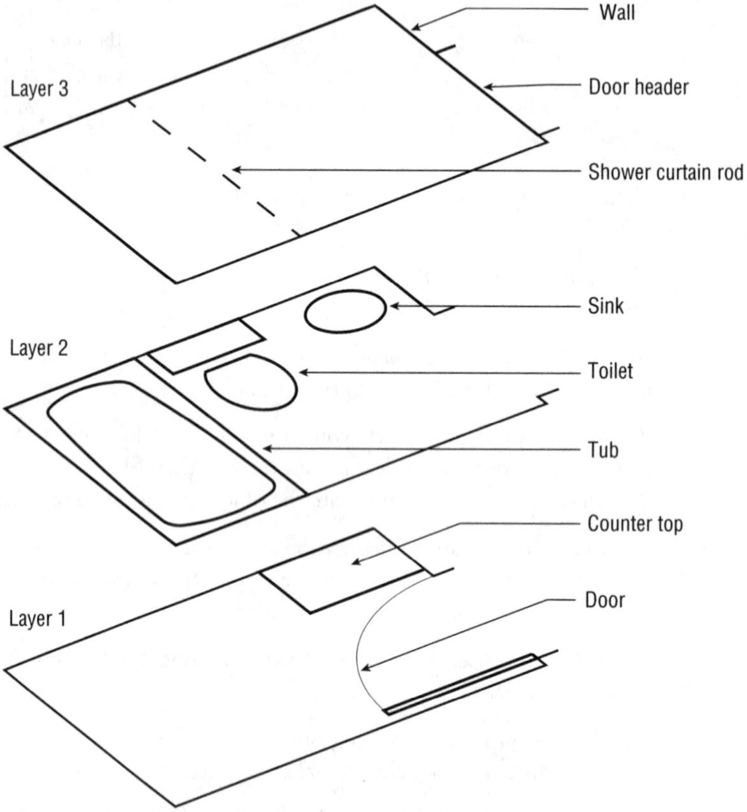

For example, one of your consultants might need a plot of just the dimensions and walls, without all the other information; another consultant might need only a furniture layout. Using manual drafting, you would have to redraw your plan for each consultant or use overlay drafting techniques, which can be cumbersome. With AutoCAD, you can turn off the layers you don't need and plot a drawing containing only the required information. A carefully planned layering scheme helps you produce a document that combines the different types of information needed in each case.

Using layers also enables you to modify your drawings more easily. For example, suppose you have an architectural drawing with separate layers for the walls, the ceiling plan, and the floor plan. If any change occurs in the wall locations, you can turn on the ceiling plan layer to see where the new wall locations will affect the ceiling and then make the proper adjustments.

AutoCAD allows an unlimited number of layers, and you can name each layer anything you want.

Creating and Assigning Layers

To continue with your bathroom, you will create some new layers.

1. Open the `Bath` file you created earlier in this chapter. (If you didn't create one, use the file `04b-bath.dwg` from the companion CD.)

2. To display the Layer Properties Manager dialog box, click the Layer Properties Manager tool in the Properties toolbar, or choose Format ➢ Layer from the pull-down menu. You can also type **LA**↵ to use the keyboard shortcut.

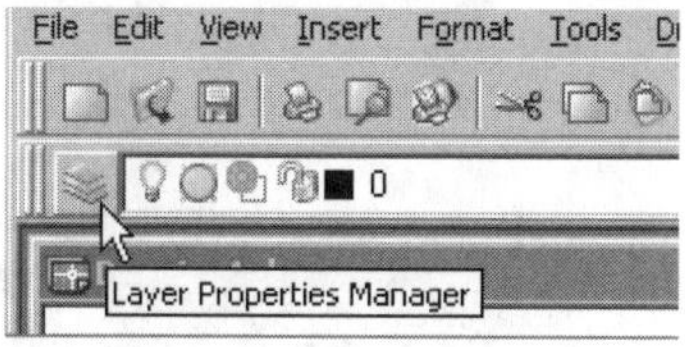

Getting Multiple Uses from a Drawing Using Layers

Layering allows you to use a single AutoCAD drawing for multiple purposes. A single drawing can serve to show both the general layout of the plan and more detailed information such as equipment layout or floor-paving layout.

These two reproductions of the San Francisco Main Library's lower level show how one floor plan file was used for two different purposes. The first view shows the layout of furnishings, and the second view shows a paving layout. In each case, the same floor plan file was used, but in the first panel, the paving information is on a layer that is turned off. Layers also facilitate the use of differing scales in the same drawing. Frequently, a small-scale drawing of an overall plan will contain the same data for an enlarged view of other portions of the plan, such as a stairwell or an elevator core. The detailed information, such as notes and dimensions, may be on a layer that is turned off for the overall plan.

Continued on next page

GETTING MULTIPLE USES FROM A DRAWING USING LAYERS *(continued)*

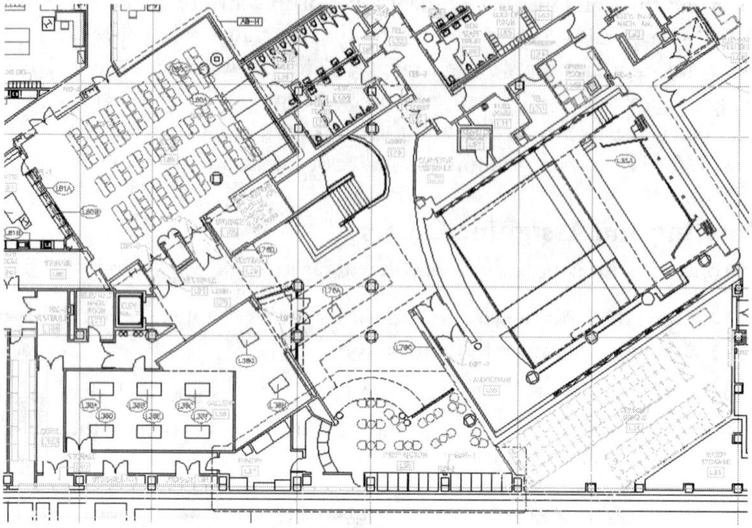

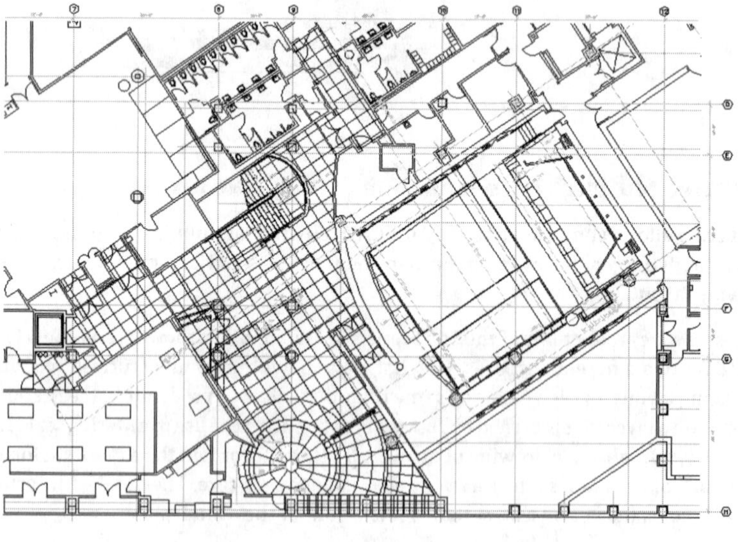

TIP *The Layer Properties Manager dialog box shows you at a glance the status of your layers. Right now, you have only one layer, but as your work expands, so will the number of layers. You will then find this dialog box indispensable.*

3. Click the New button in the upper-right corner of the dialog box. A new layer named Layer1 appears in the list box. Notice that the name is highlighted. This tells you that by typing you can change the default name to something better suited to your needs.

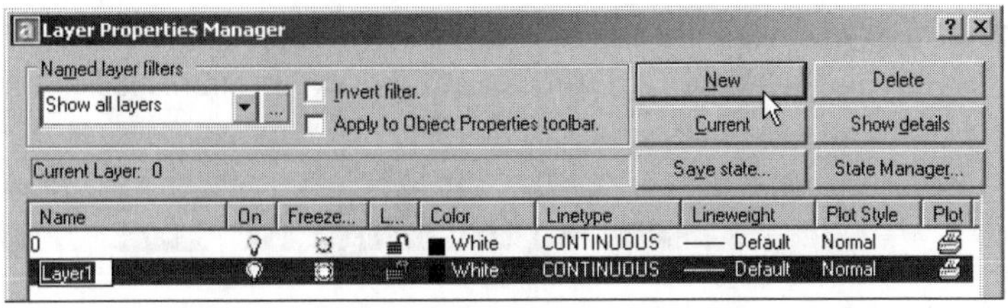

4. Type **Wall**. As you type, your entry replaces the Layer1 name in the list box.
5. Click the Show Details button, also located in the upper-right corner of the dialog box. Additional layer options appear.
6. With the Wall layer name highlighted, click the Color drop-down arrow to display a listing of colors that you can assign to the Wall layer.

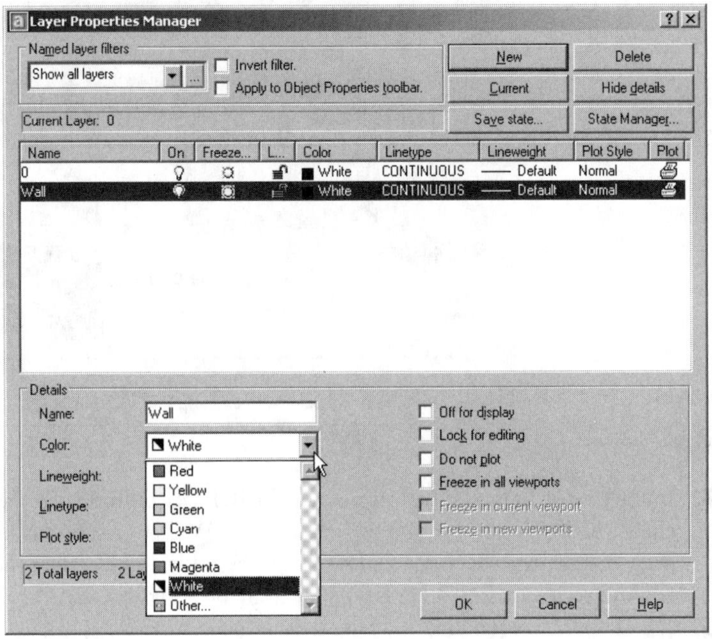

At first glance, this list may seem a bit limited, but you actually have a choice of literally millions of colors. (AutoCAD LT users are still limited to the 256 index colors.)

TIP *Though it isn't readily apparent, all the colors in the Color drop-down list, except for the first seven, are designated by numbers. When you select a color after the seventh color, the color's number rather than its name appears in the Color text box at the bottom of the dialog box.*

7. Click Other from the list, or click the white color swatch (black if your background color is white) in the Wall layer listing, next to the word `Continuous`.

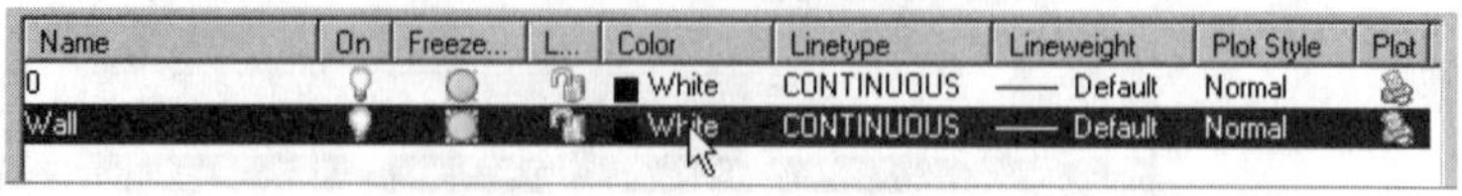

The Select Color dialog box appears.

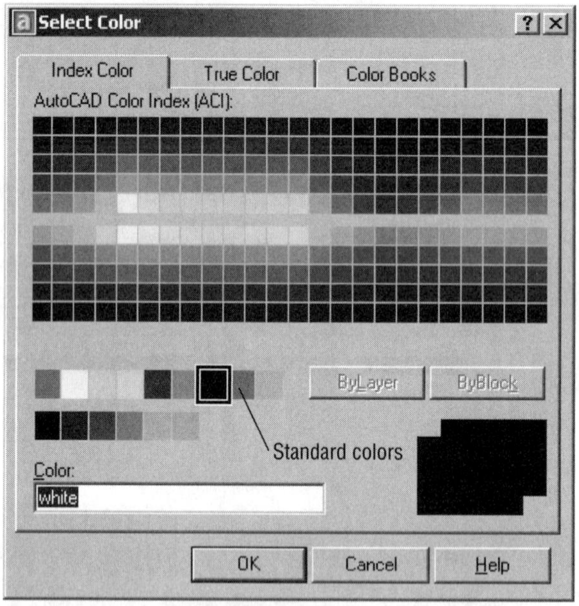

8. In the row of Standard Colors next to the ByLayer button click the green square and then click OK. Notice that the color swatch in the Wall layer listing is now green. (You could have just chosen Green from the Colors drop-down list, but by using the Select Color dialog box you can see that many other colors are available.)

9. When the Layer Properties Manager dialog box returns, click OK to close it.

From this point on, any object assigned to the Wall layer will appear green unless the object is specifically assigned a different color.

Using True or Pantone Colors

ACAD only

In the last exercise, you chose a color from the Index Color tab of the Select Color dialog box. Most of the time, you'll find that the Index Color tab offers enough colors to suit your needs. But if you are creating a presentation drawing in which color selection is important, you can choose colors from either the True Color or the Color Books tab of the Select Color dialog box.

The True Color tab offers a full range of colors through a color palette similar to one found in Adobe Photoshop and other image-editing programs.

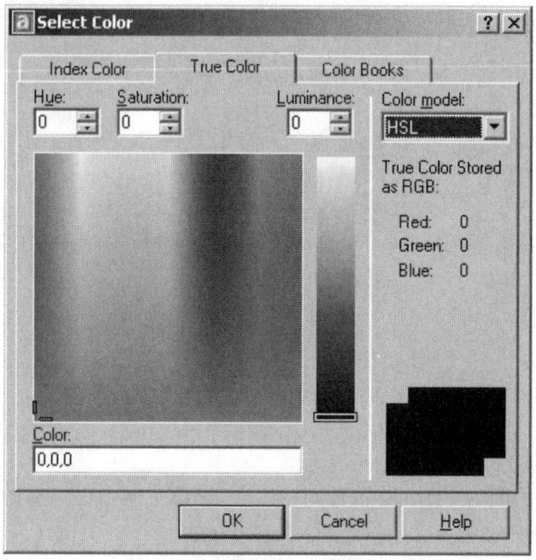

You have the choice of using hue, saturation, and luminance, which is the HSL color model, or you can use the RGB (red, green, blue) color model. You can select HSL or RGB from the Color Model drop-down list in the upper-right corner of the dialog box.

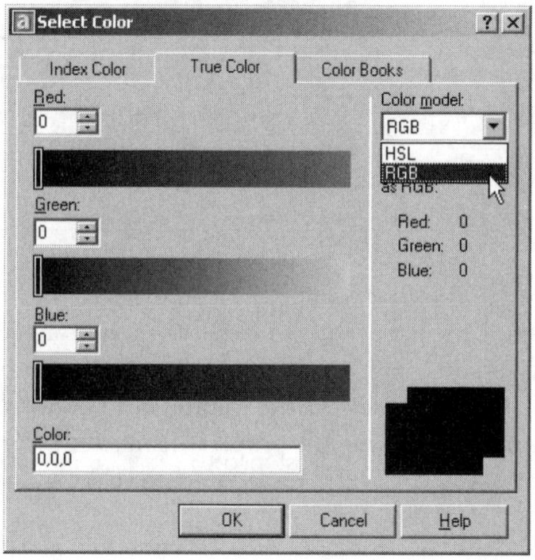

If you installed the PANTONE color option when you installed AutoCAD, you can also select from a PANTONE "color book" using the Color Books tab.

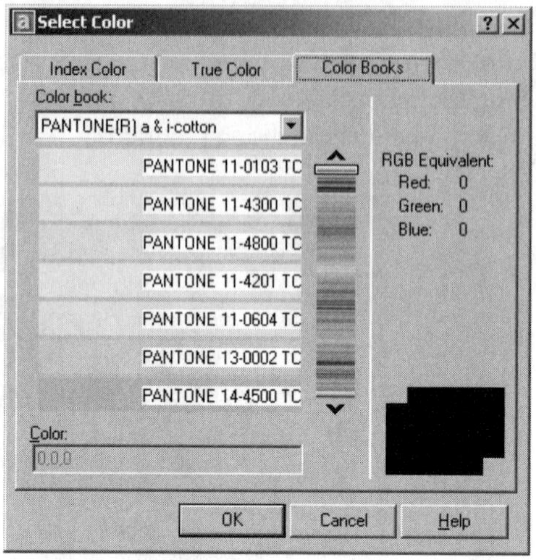

The color book option allows you to match colors to a PANTONE color book for offset printing.

TIP *The Files tab of the Options dialog box (choose Tools ➢ Options) contains the Color Book Location option, which tells AutoCAD where to look for the Color Book settings.*

Now let's continue with our look at layers in AutoCAD.

The Layer Properties Manager Dialog Box

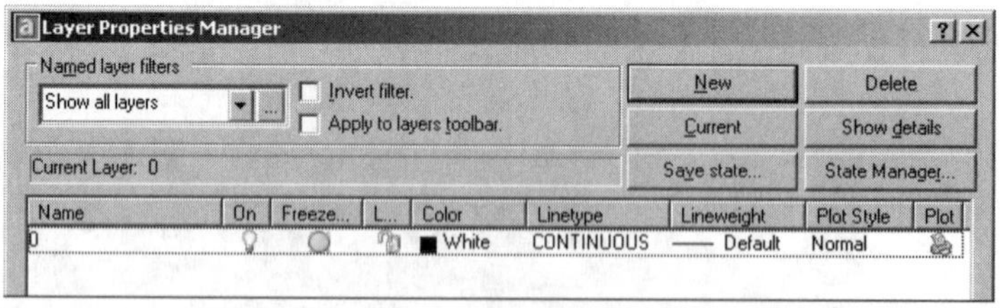

The Layer Properties Manager dialog box conforms to the Windows interface standard. Notice that the bar at the top of the list of layers offers several buttons for the various layer properties. Just as you can adjust Windows Explorer, you can adjust the width of each column in the list of layers by clicking and dragging either side of the column head buttons. You can also sort the layer list based on a property simply by clicking the property name at the top of the list. And, just as with other Windows list boxes, you can Shift+click names to select a block of layer names, or you can Ctrl+click individual names to select multiples that do not appear together. These features will become helpful as your list of layers enlarges.

Controlling Layers through the Layer Command

You have seen how the Layer Properties Manager dialog box makes it easy to view and edit layer information and how you can easily select layer colors from an on-screen toolbar. But you can also control layers through the command prompt.

WARNING *LT users will not see the Pstyle option in the Layer prompt or the Truecolor/Colorbook options in the Color option prompt.*

1. First, press the Esc key to make sure any current command is canceled.
2. At the command prompt, enter **–Layer↵**. Make sure you include the minus sign in front of the word *Layer*. The following prompt appears:

   `[?/Make/Set/New/ON/OFF/Color/Ltype/LWeight/Plot/PStyle/Freeze/Thaw/LOck/Unlock/stAte]:`

   You'll learn about many of the options in this prompt as you work through this chapter.
3. Enter **N↵** to select the New option.
4. At the `Enter name list for new layer(s):` prompt, enter **Wall2↵**. The `[?/Make/Set/New/ON/ OFF/Color/Ltype/LWeight/Plot/PStyle/Freeze/Thaw/LOck/Unlock /stAte]:` prompt appears again.
5. Enter **C↵**.
6. At the `New color [Truecolor/Colorbook] <7 (white)>:` prompt, enter **Yellow↵**. Or you can enter **2↵**, the numeric equivalent of the color yellow in AutoCAD.
7. At the `Enter name list of layer(s) for color 2 (yellow) <0>:` prompt, enter **Wall2↵**. The `[?/Make/Set/New/ON/OFF/Color/Ltype /LWeight/ Plot/Pstyle/Freeze/Thaw/LOck/Unlock/stAte]:` prompt appears again.
8. Press ↵ to exit the Layer command.

Each method of controlling layers has its own advantages. The Layer Properties Manager dialog box offers more information about your layers at a glance. On the other hand, the Layer command offers a quick way to control and create layers if you're in a hurry. Also, if you intend to write custom macros, you will want to know how to use the Layer command as opposed to using the Layer Properties Manager dialog box, because dialog boxes cannot be controlled through custom toolbar buttons or scripts.

TIP *Another advantage of using the keyboard commands is that you can recall previously entered keystrokes by using the Up and Down arrow keys. For example, to recall the layer named Wall2 you entered in step 4 in the previous exercise, press the Up arrow key until Wall2 appears in the prompt. This saves time when you are performing repetitive operations such as creating multiple layers. This feature does not work with tools selected from the toolbars.*

ASSIGNING LAYERS TO OBJECTS

When you create an object, that object is assigned to the current layer. Until now, only one layer has existed—Layer0—which contains all the objects you've drawn so far. Now that you've created some new layers, you can reassign objects to them using the Properties palette.

1. Select the four lines that represent the bathroom walls. If you have problems singling out the wall to the left, use a window to select the wall line.
2. With the cursor in the drawing area, right-click and choose Properties from the shortcut menu to open the Properties palette.

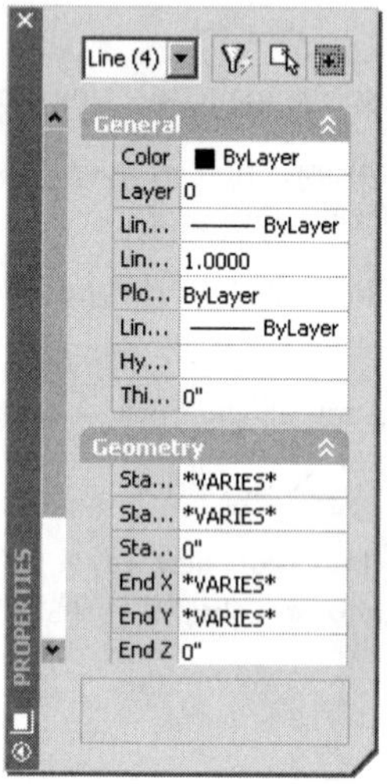

This palette lets you modify the properties of an object or set of objects. (See the "Understanding Object Properties" sidebar later in this chapter for more on the properties of objects.)

4. Click the Layer option from the listing in the Properties palette. Notice that an arrow appears in the layer name to the right of the Layer option.
5. Click the downward-pointing arrow to the far right of the Layer option to display a list of all the available layers.
6. Select the Wall layer from the list. Notice that the wall lines you selected change to a green color. This tells you that that the objects have been assigned to the Wall layer. Remember that you assigned a green color to the Wall layer.
7. Close the Properties palette by clicking the X button in the upper-left corner.

The bathroom walls are now on the new layer, Wall, and the walls are changed to green. Layers are more easily distinguished from one another when you use colors to set them apart.

Understanding Object Properties

It helps to think of the components of an AutoCAD drawing as having properties. For example, a line has geometric properties, such as the length, and coordinates that define its endpoints. An arc has a radius, a center, and beginning and ending coordinates. And even though a layer is not an object you can grasp and manipulate, it can have properties such as color, line types, and line weight.

By default, objects take on the color, line type, and weight of the layer to which they are assigned, but you can also assign these properties directly to individual objects. These general properties can be manipulated through both the Properties palette and the Properties toolbar.

Although many of the options in the Properties palette may seem cryptic to you, don't worry about them at this point. As you work with AutoCAD, these properties will become more familiar. You'll find that you really won't be too concerned with the geometric properties, since you'll be manipulating those through the standard editing tools in the Modify toolbar. The other properties will be explained in the rest of this chapter and in other chapters.

Next, you will practice the commands you learned in this section and try out some new ones by creating some new layers and changing the layer assignments of the rest of the objects in your bathroom.

1. Open the Layer Properties Manager dialog box (choose Format ➢ Layers or click the Layers button in the Properties toolbar). Create a new layer called Fixture, and give it the color blue.

TIP *You can change the name of a layer by clicking it in the Layer Properties Manager dialog box. Once it is highlighted, click it again so that a box surrounds the name. You can then rename the layer. This works in the same way as renaming a file or folder in Windows.*

2. Click the Tub and Toilet blocks, and then right-click and choose Properties from the shortcut menu to open the Properties palette.
3. Click Layer in the list of properties, and then select Fixture from the drop-down layer list to the right of the Layer listing.
4. Click the X in the upper-right corner of the Properties palette to dismiss it, and then press the Esc key to clear your selection.
5. Now create a new layer for the door, name the layer Door, and make it red.

TIP *Within a block, you can change the color assignment and line type of only those objects that are on Layer 0. See the sidebar "Controlling Colors and Line Types of Blocked Objects" later in this chapter.*

6. Just as you have done with the walls and fixtures, use the Properties palette to change the door to the Door layer.
7. Use the Layer Properties Manager dialog box to create three more layers for the ceiling, door jambs, and floor, as shown in Table 4.1. Remember that you can open the Select Color dialog box by clicking the color swatch of the layer listing.

In step 3 of the previous exercise, you used the Properties palette that offered several options for modifying the block. The options displayed in the Properties palette depend on the objects you have selected. With only one object selected, AutoCAD displays options that apply specifically to that object. With several objects selected, you'll see a more limited set of options because AutoCAD can change only those properties that are common to all the objects selected.

TABLE 4.1: CREATE THESE LAYERS AND SET THEIR COLORS AS INDICATED

LAYER NAME	LAYER COLOR (NUMBER)
Ceiling	Magenta (6)
Jamb	Green (3)
Floor	Cyan (4)

CONTROLLING COLORS AND LINE TYPES OF BLOCKED OBJECTS

Layer 0 has special importance to blocks. When objects assigned to Layer 0 are used as parts of a block, and that block is inserted on another layer, those objects take on the characteristics of their new layer. On the other hand, if those objects are on a layer other than Layer 0, they maintain their original layer characteristics even if you insert or change that block to another layer. For example, suppose the tub is drawn on the Door layer, instead of on Layer 0. If you turn the tub into a block and insert it on the Fixture layer, the objects the tub is composed of will maintain their assignment to the Door layer, although the Tub block is assigned to the Fixture layer.

It might help to think of the block function as a clear plastic bag that holds together the objects that make up the tub. The objects inside the bag maintain their assignment to the Door layer even while the bag itself is assigned to the Fixture layer. This may be a bit confusing at first, but it should become clearer after using blocks for a while.

AutoCAD also allows you to have more than one color or line type on a layer. For example, you can use the Color and Linetype buttons in the Change Properties palette (the Object Properties button on the Standard toolbar) to alter the color or line type of an object on Layer 0. That object then maintains its assigned color and line type—no matter what its layer assignment. Likewise, objects specifically assigned a color or line type are not affected by their inclusion into blocks.

Working on Layers

So far you have created layers and then assigned objects to those layers. However, the current layer is still Layer 0, and every new object you draw will be on Layer 0. Here's how to change the current layer.

1. Click the arrow button next to the layer name on the Object Properties toolbar. A drop-down list opens, showing you all the layers available in the drawing.

   Notice the icons that appear next to the layer names; these control the status of the layer. You'll learn how to work with these icons later in this chapter. Also notice the box directly to the left of each layer name. This shows you the color of the layer.

2. Click the Jamb layer name. The drop-down list closes, and the name Jamb appears in the toolbar's layer name box. Jamb is now the current layer.

TIP *You can also use the Layer command to reset the current layer. To do this here, enter* ***–Layer*** *(be sure to include the minus sign) at the command prompt, and at the* `?/Make/Set/New/ON/OFF /Color/Ltype/LWeight/Plot/PStyle/Freeze/Thaw/LOck/Unlock/stAte]:` *prompt, enter S for Set. At the* `Enter layer name to make current or <select object>:`*prompt, enter* ***Jamb*** *and then press* ↵ twice to exit the Layer command.

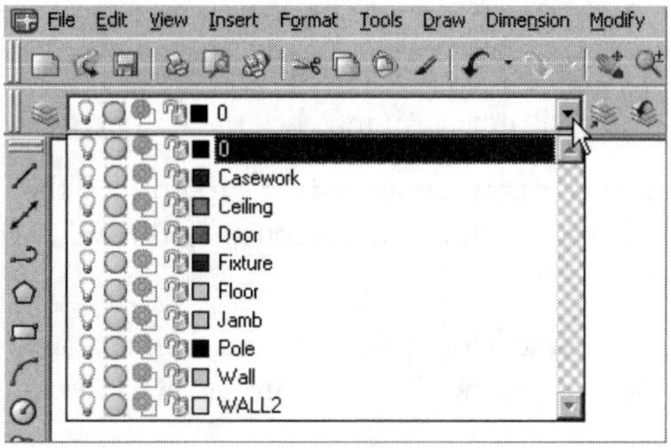

3. Zoom in on the door and draw a 5" line; start at the lower-right corner of the door and draw toward the right. Metric users should draw a 13 cm line.

4. Draw a similar line from the top-right end of the arc. Your drawing should look like Figure 4.13.

FIGURE 4.13

Door at wall with door jamb added

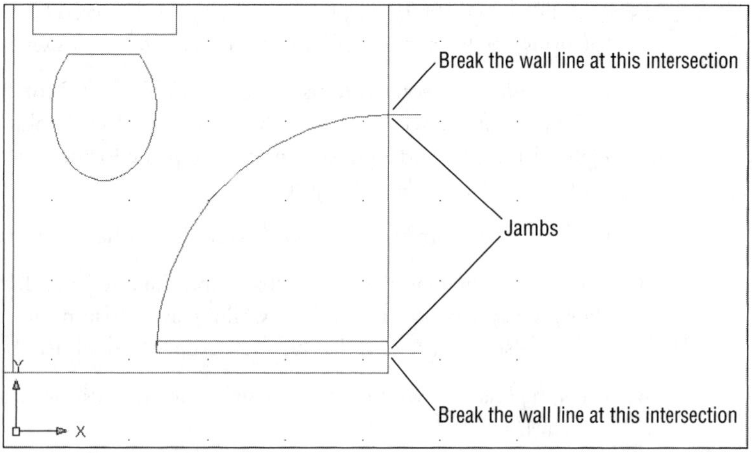

Because you assigned the color green to the Jamb layer, the two lines you just drew to represent the door jambs are green. This gives you immediate feedback about what layer you are on as you draw.

Now you will use the part of the wall between the jambs as a line representing the door header (the part of the wall above the door). To do this, you will have to cut the line into three line segments and then change the layer assignment of the segment between the jambs.

1. In the Modify toolbar, click the Break At Point tool.

2. At the `Select object:` prompt, click the wall between the two jambs.
3. At the `Specify first break point:` prompt, use the Endpoint Osnap override to pick the endpoint of the door's arc that is touching the wall, as shown in Figure 4.13, earlier in this chapter.
4. Click Break on the Modify toolbar, and then repeat steps 2 and 3, this time using the jamb near the door hinge location to locate the break point (see Figure 4.13).

Though it may not be obvious, you've just broken the right-side wall line into three line segments: one at the door opening and two more on either side of the jambs. You can also use the Break tool (next to the Break At Point tool) to produce a gap in a line segment.

TIP *The Break At Point tool will not work on a circle. You can, however, use the Break tool to place a small gap in the circle. If you create a small enough gap, the circle will still appear as a full circle.*

Next, you'll change the Layer property of the line between the two jambs to the Ceiling layer. But instead of using the Properties tool, as you've done in earlier exercises, you'll use a shortcut method.

1. Click the line between the door jambs to highlight it. Notice that the layer listing in the Properties toolbar changes to Wall. Whenever you select an object to expose its grips, the Layer, Color, Linetype, and Line Width listings in the Properties toolbar change to reflect those properties of the selected object.
2. Click the layer name in the Properties toolbar. The Layer drop-down list appears.
3. Click the Ceiling layer. The list closes, and the line you selected changes to the magenta color, showing you that it is now on the Ceiling layer. Also notice that the color list in the Properties toolbar also changes to reflect the new color for the line.
4. Press the Esc key twice to clear the grip selection. Notice that the layer returns to Jamb, the current layer.
5. Click the Zoom Previous tool in the Standard toolbar, or choose View ➢ Zoom ➢ Previous to return to the previous view.

In this exercise, you saw that by selecting an object with no command active, the object's properties are immediately displayed in the Properties toolbar under the Layer, Color, and Linetype boxes.

Using this method, you can also change an object's color, line type, and line width independent of its layer. Just as with the Properties tool, you can select multiple objects and change their layers through the Layer drop-down list. These options in the Properties toolbar offer a quick way to edit some of the properties of objects.

Now you'll finish the bathroom by adding a sink to a layer named Casework.

1. Open the Layer Properties Manager dialog box and create a new layer called Casework.
2. When the Casework layer name appears in the Layer drop-down list, click the Current button at the top of the dialog box.
3. Click the color swatch for the Casework layer, and then select Blue from the Select Color dialog box. Click OK to exit the dialog box.
4. Click OK in the Layer Properties Manager dialog box. Notice that the layer listing in the Properties toolbar indicates that the current layer is Casework.

Now you'll add the sink. As you draw, the objects will appear in blue, the color of the Casework layer.

5. Choose View ➢ Zoom ➢ All.
6. Click the Insert Block tool on the Draw toolbar, and then click the Browse button in the Insert dialog box. This opens the Select Drawing File dialog box.
7. Locate the Sink file and double-click it.
8. In the Insert dialog box, make sure that the Specify On-Screen options in both the Scale and Rotation button groups are not checked; then click OK.
9. Place the sink roughly in the upper-right corner of the bathroom plan, and then use the Move command to place it accurately in the corner, as shown in Figure 4.14.

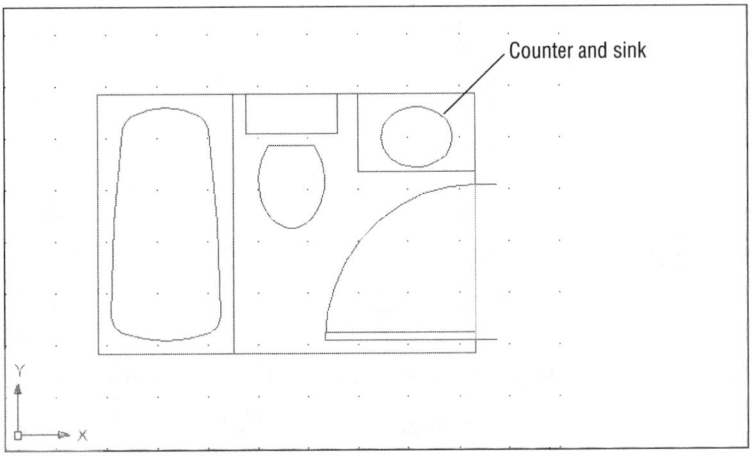

FIGURE 4.14

Bathroom with sink and countertop added

Controlling Layer Visibility

I mentioned earlier that you'll sometimes want to display only certain layers to work with in a drawing. In this bathroom, there is a door header that would normally appear only in a reflected ceiling plan. To turn off a layer so that it becomes invisible, click the Off button in the Layer Properties Manager dialog box.

1. Open the Layer Properties Manager dialog box by clicking the Layers tool in the Properties toolbar.
2. Click the Ceiling layer in the Layer list.
3. Click the lightbulb icon in the Layer list, next to the Ceiling layer name. You can also highlight the Ceiling layer in the Layer Properties Manager dialog box, open the Details group by clicking the Show Details button, and then click the Off For Display check box in the Details group so that no check appears there. In either case, the lightbulb icon changes from yellow to gray to indicate that the layer is off.

TIP *Momentarily placing the cursor on an icon in the Layer drop-down list displays a tool tip that describes the icon's purpose.*

4. Click the OK button to exit the Layer Properties Manager dialog box. When you return to the drawing, the header disappears because you have made it invisible by turning off its layer (see Figure 4.15).

FIGURE 4.15
Bathroom with Ceiling layer turned off

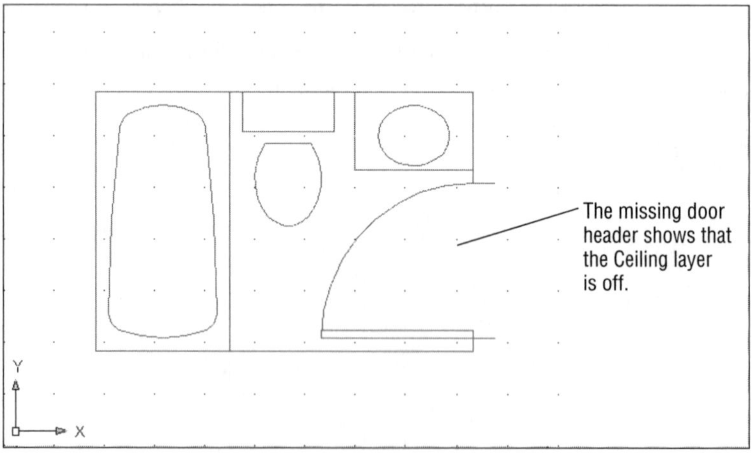

The missing door header shows that the Ceiling layer is off.
Y
X

You can also control layer visibility using the Layer drop-down list on the Object Properties toolbar.

1. On the Object Properties toolbar, click the Layer drop-down list.
2. Find the Ceiling layer, and notice that its lightbulb icon is gray. This tells you that the layer is off and not visible.

3. Click the lightbulb icon to make it yellow.

4. Now click the drawing area to close the Layer drop-down list, and the door header reappears.

Figure 4.16 explains the role of the other icons in the Layer drop-down list.

FIGURE 4.16

The Layer drop-down list icons

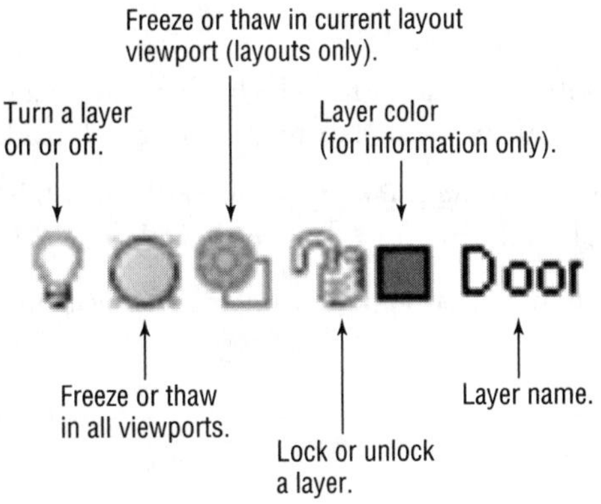
Freeze or thaw in current layout viewport (layouts only).
Turn a layer on or off.
Layer color (for information only).
Door
Freeze or thaw in all viewports.
Lock or unlock a layer.
Layer name.

Finding the Layers You Want

With only a handful of layers, it's fairly easy to find the layer you want to turn off. It becomes much more difficult, however, when the number of layers exceeds 20 or 30. The Layer Properties Manager dialog box offers some useful tools to help you find the layers you want fast.

Now suppose you have several layers whose names begin with C, such as C-lights, C-header, and C-pattern, and you want find those layers quickly. You can click the Name button at the top of the layer list to sort the layer names in alphabetic order. (You can click the Name button again to reverse the order.) To select those layers for processing, click the first layer name that starts with C; then scroll down the list until you find the last layer of the group and Shift+click it. All the layers between those layers will be selected. If you want to deselect some of those layers, hold down the Ctrl key while clicking the layer names you don't want to include in your selection. Or Ctrl+click other layer names you do want selected.

The Color and Linetype buttons at the top of the list let you control which layers appear in the list by virtue of their color or line-type assignments. Other buttons sort the list by virtue of the status: On/Off, Freeze/Thaw, Lock/Unlock, and so forth. (See the "Other Layer Options" sidebar later in this chapter.)

Now try changing the layer settings again, turning off all the layers except Wall and Ceiling and leaving just a simple rectangle. In the exercise, you'll get a chance to experiment with the On/Off options of the Layer Properties Manager dialog box.

1. Click the Layers button in the Object Properties toolbar or choose Format ➢ Layers.

2. Click the topmost layer name in the List box; then Shift+click the bottommost layer name. All the layer names are highlighted.

TIP *Another way to select all the layers at once in the Layer Properties Manager dialog box is to right-click the Layer drop-down list; then choose the Select All option from the shortcut menu. And if you want to clear your selections, right-click the layer list and choose Clear All.*

3. Ctrl+click the Wall and Ceiling layers to deselect them and thus exempt them from your next action.
4. Click the lightbulb icon of any of the highlighted layer names or click the On check box in the Details section of the dialog box to clear the check mark.
5. A message appears warning you that the current layer will be turned off. Click OK in the message box. The lightbulb icons turn gray to show that the selected layers have been turned off.
6. Click OK. The drawing now appears with only the Wall and Ceiling layers displayed (see Figure 4.17).

FIGURE 4.17
The bathroom with all layers except Wall and Ceiling turned off

7. Open the Layer Properties Manager dialog box again and select all the layers as you did in steps 2 and 3, and then click the On button or any of the gray lightbulbs to turn on all the layers at once.
8. Click OK to return to the drawing.

In this exercise, you turned off a set of layers with a single click on a lightbulb icon. You can freeze/thaw, lock/unlock, or change the color of a group of layers in a similar manner by clicking the appropriate layer property. For example, clicking a color swatch of one of the selected layers opens the Select Color dialog box, in which you can set the color for all the selected layers.

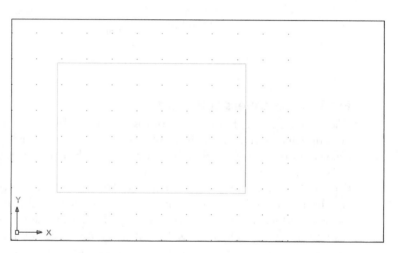

Other Layer Options

You may have noticed the Freeze and Thaw buttons in the Layer Properties Manager dialog box. These options are similar to the On and Off buttons. However, Freeze not only makes layers invisible; it also tells AutoCAD to ignore the contents of those layers when you use the All response to the `Select objects:` prompt. Freezing layers can save time when you issue a command that regenerates a complex drawing. This is because AutoCAD ignores objects on frozen layers during Regen. You will get firsthand experience with Freeze and Thaw in Chapter 6.

Another pair of Layer Properties Manager options, Lock and Unlock, offer a function similar to Freeze and Thaw. If you lock a layer, you can view and snap to objects on that layer, but you can't edit those objects. This feature is useful when you are working on a crowded drawing and you don't want to accidentally edit portions of it. You can lock all the layers except those you intend to edit and then proceed to work without fear of making accidental changes.

Three more options—Lineweight, Plot Style, and Plot—offer control over the appearance of printer or plotter output. Lineweight lets you control the width of lines in a layer. Plot Style lets you assign plotter configurations to specific layers. (You'll learn more about plot styles in Chapter 7.) Plot lets you determine whether a layer gets printed in hard-copy output. This can be useful for setting up layers you might use for layout purposes only.

Finally, you can save layer settings for later recall using the Save State and Restore State buttons in the upper-right corner of the Layer Properties Manager dialog box. This feature is extremely useful when you want to save different layer combinations. The section "Managing Layers" in Chapter 13 shows you how to use this feature. This option is also accessible from the State option in the command-line version of the Layer command.

Taming an Unwieldy List of Layers

Chances are, you will eventually end up with a fairly long list of layers. Managing such a list can become a nightmare, but AutoCAD provides the Layer Filter dialog box to help you locate and isolate only those layers you need to work with.

To use layer filters, click the Show drop-down list near the top of the Layer Properties Manager dialog box. The Show options are described in Table 4.2. See the Chapter 6 for information on Xref-dependent layers.

Table 4.2: The Filter Options

Filter Option	What It Filters
Show all layers	All layers regardless of their status
Show all used layers	All layers that have objects assigned to them
Show all Xref-dependent layers	All layers that contain Xref objects

You can also create your own filter criteria and add it to this drop-down list by clicking the Ellipsis (...) button.

When you click this button, the Named Layer Filters dialog box appears. Here you can create a filter list based on the layer's characteristics.

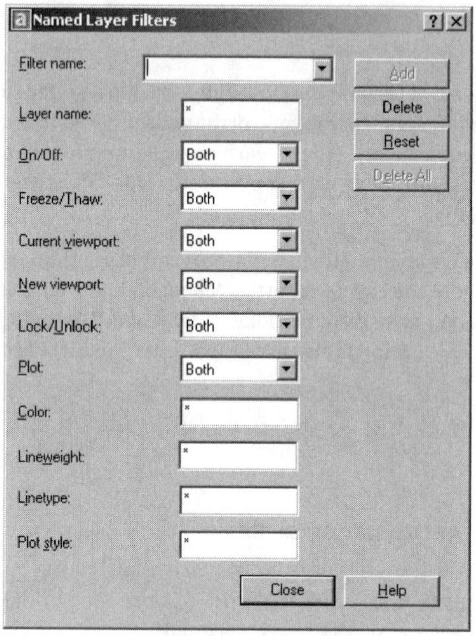

Now suppose you have a drawing whose layer names are set up to help you easily identify floor plan data versus ceiling plan data as in the following list:

A-FP-WALL-JAMB

A-RP-WIND-JAMB

A-FP-WIND-SILL

A-CP-WIND-HEAD

A-CP-DOOR-HEAD

L-FP-CURB

C-FP-ELEV

TIP *These layer examples are loosely based on a layer-naming convention devised by the American Institute of Architects. As you can see from this example, careful naming of layers can help you manage them.*

The first character in the layer name designates the discipline related to that layer: *A* for architectural, *L* for landscape, *C* for civil, and so on. In this example, layers whose names contain the two characters *FP* signify floor plan layers. *CP* designates ceiling information.

If you want to isolate only those layers that have to do with floor plans, regardless of their discipline, enter **??FP*** in the Layer Name text box. You can then give this filter criterion the name Floor Plan by entering **Floor Plan** in the Filter Name text box. Click OK to close the Named Layer Filters dialog box. You can now pick Floor Plan from the Named Layer Filters drop-down list, and only those layers whose names contain the letters *FP* as their third and fourth characters will appear in the list of layers. You can then easily turn all these layers off, change their color assignment, or change other settings quickly, without having to wade through layers you don't want to touch. You can further create other named layer filters to isolate other groups of layers. AutoCAD keeps these filter lists for future use until you delete them using the Delete option in the Named Layer Filters dialog box.

In the ??FP* example, the question marks (??) tell AutoCAD that the first two characters in the layer name can be anything. The *FP* tells AutoCAD that the layer name must contain *F* and *P* in these two places of the name. The asterisk (*) at the end tells AutoCAD that the remaining characters can be anything. The question marks and asterisk are known as *wildcard characters*. They are commonly used filtering tools for both the Unix and Windows operating systems.

The other four text boxes near the bottom—Color, Lineweight, Linetype, and Plot Style—let you control which layers appear in the list according to their settings for these four options. The six popup lists let you filter layers by virtue of the status: On/Off, Freeze/Thaw, Lock/Unlock, and so forth. (See the "Other Layer Options" sidebar earlier in this chapter.)

As the number of layers in a drawing grows, you will find layer filters to be an indispensable tool. But bear in mind that the successful use of the layer filters depends on a careful layer-naming convention. If you are producing architectural plans, you might want to consider the American Institute of Architects (AIA) layering guidelines.

TIP *Check out Chapter 20 for some additional tools that will help you manage layer settings.*

Assigning Line Types to Layers

You will often want to use different line types to show hidden lines, center lines, fence lines, or other noncontinuous lines. You can assign a color and a line type to a layer. AutoCAD comes with several line types, as shown in Figure 4.18. You then see ISO and complex line types, including lines that can be used to illustrate gas and water lines in civil work, or batt insulation in a wall cavity. ISO line types are designed to be used with specific plotted line widths and line-type scales. For example, if you are using a pen width of .5 mm, set the line-type scale of the drawing to .5 as well. (See Chapter 13 for more information on plotting and line-type scale.) The complex line types at the bottom of the figure are industry-specific such as gas and water lines for civil work and a line type that can be used to symbolize batt insulation in a wall cavity. You can also create your own line types (see Chapters 20 and 21).

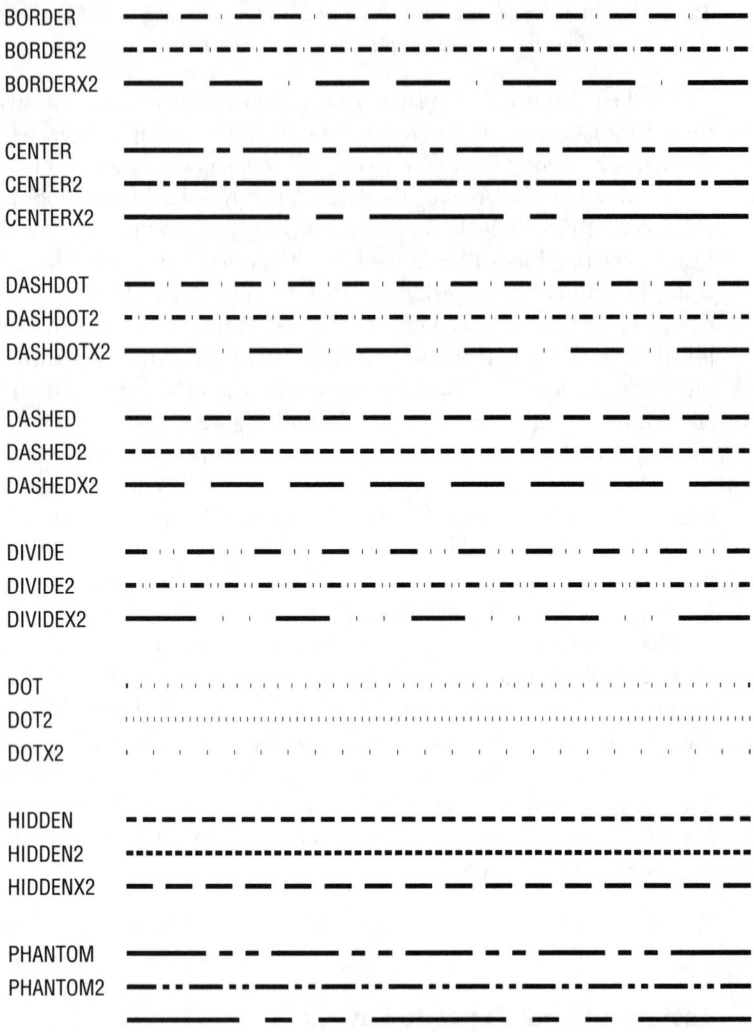

FIGURE 4.18
Standard , ISO, and complex AutoCAD line types

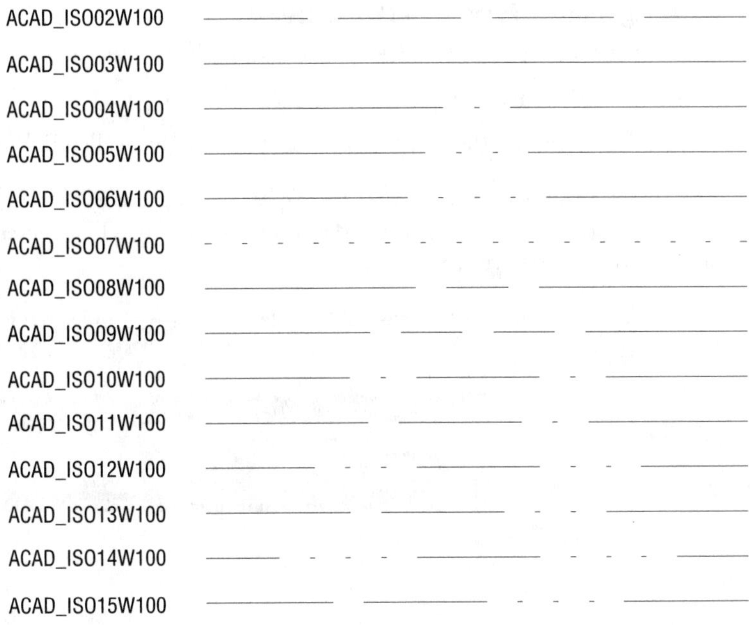

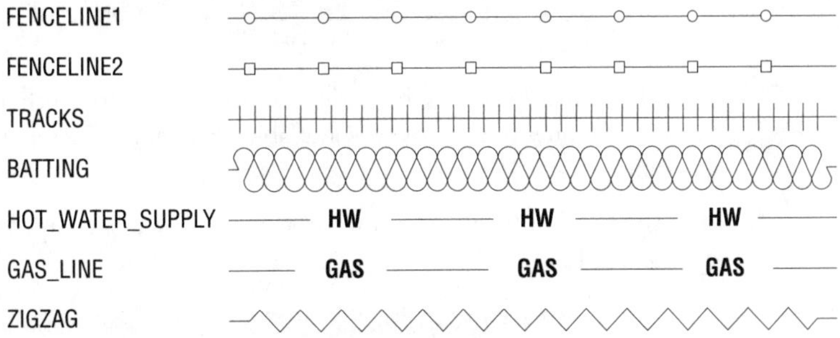

WARNING *Line types that contain text, such as the gas sample, use the current text height and font to determine the size and appearance of the text displayed in the line. A text height of 0 (zero) displays the text properly in most cases. See Chapter 8 for more on text styles.*

AutoCAD stores line-type descriptions in an external file named `Acad.lin` or `Acadiso.lin` for metric users. You can edit this file in a word processor to create new line types or to modify existing ones. You will see how this is done in Chapter 21.

Adding a Line Type to a Drawing

To see how line types work, add a dash-dot line in the bathroom plan to indicate a shower curtain rod.

1. Open the Layers Properties Manager dialog box.
2. Click New and then type **Pole** to create a new layer called Pole.

TIP *If you are in a hurry, you can simultaneously load a line type and assign it to a layer using the Layer command. In this exercise, you would enter* ***–Layer↵*** at the command prompt. Then enter **L↵**, **dashdot↵**, **pole↵**, and press ↵ to exit the Layer command.

3. Click the word `Continuous` in the Pole layer listing (under the Linetype column) to open the Select Linetype dialog box.

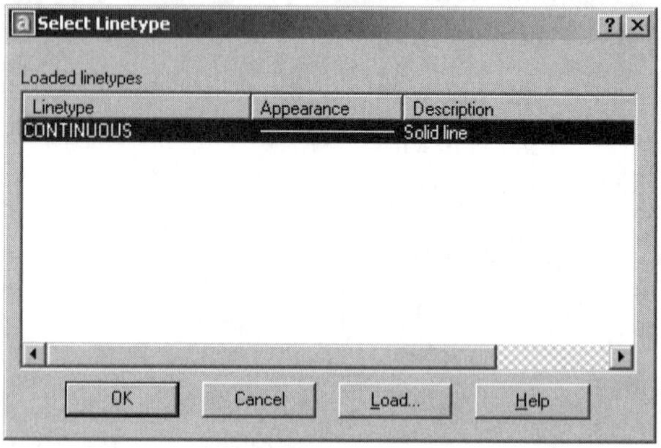

The Select Linetype dialog box offers a list of line types to choose from. In a new file such as the `Bath` file, only one line type is available by default. You must load any additional line type you want to use.

4. Click the Load button at the bottom of the dialog box to open the Load Or Reload Linetypes dialog box.

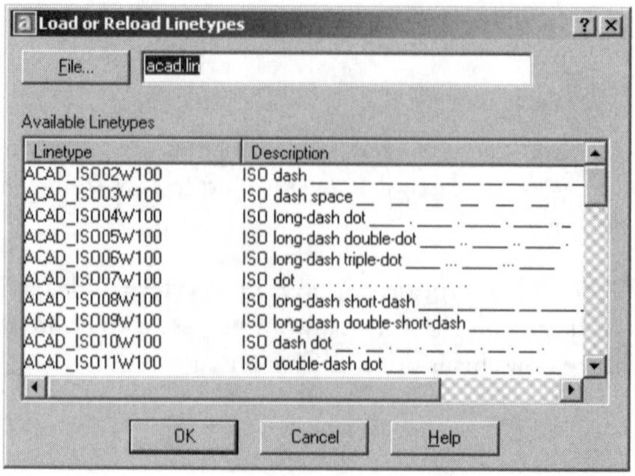

Notice that the list of line-type names is similar to the Layer drop-down list. You can sort the names alphabetically or by description by clicking the Linetype or Description headings at the top of the list.

5. In the Available Linetypes list, scroll down to locate the Dashdot line type, click it, and then click OK.
6. Notice that the Dashdot line type is now added to the line types available in the Select Linetype dialog box.
7. Click Dashdot to highlight it; then click OK. Now Dashdot appears in the Pole layer listing under Linetype.
8. With the Pole layer still highlighted, click the Current button to make the Pole layer current.
9. Click OK to exit the Load Or Reload Linetypes dialog box.
10. Turn off the Running Osnap mode; then draw a line across the opening of the tub area, from coordinate 4'-4",1'-10" to coordinate 4'-4",6'-10". Metric users should draw a line from coordinate 133,56 to 133,208.

CONTROLLING LINE-TYPE SCALE

Although you have designated this as a Dashdot line, it appears solid. Zoom in to a small part of the line, and you'll see that the line is indeed as you specified.

Since you are working at a scale of 1"=1', you must adjust the scale of your line types accordingly. This, too, is accomplished in the Layer Properties Manager dialog box.

1. Choose Format ➢ Linetype from the pull-down menu. You can also select Other from the Linetype drop-down list in the Properties toolbar.

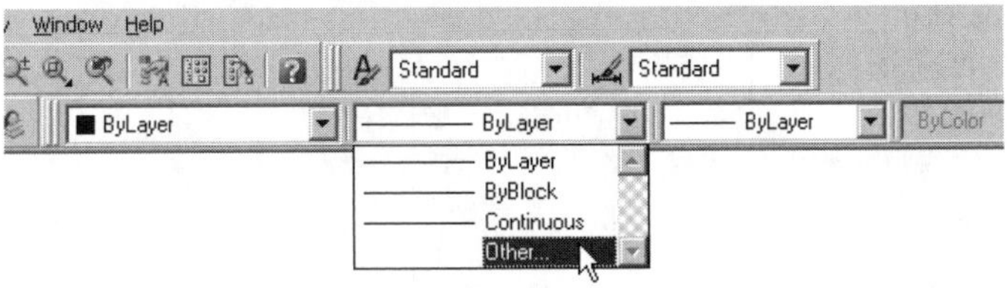

The Linetype Manager dialog box appears.

2. Click the Show Details button in the upper-right corner of the dialog box. You'll see some additional options appear at the bottom.

TIP *You may notice that the Linetype tab of the Layer Properties Manager dialog box also contains the Load and Delete button options that you saw in step 4 of the previous exercise. These offer a way to load or delete a line type directly, without having to go through a particular layer's line-type setting.*

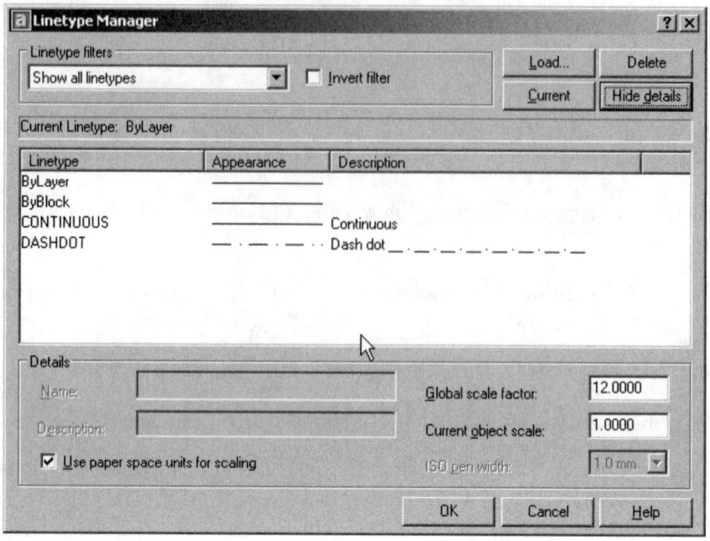

3. Double-click the Global Scale Factor text box, and then type **12** (metric users type **30**). This is the scale conversion factor for a 1"=1' scale (see Chapter 3).
4. Click OK. The drawing regenerates, and the shower curtain rod is displayed in the line type and at the scale you designated.
5. Click the Zoom Previous tool so your drawing looks like Figure 4.19.

FIGURE 4.19

The completed bathroom

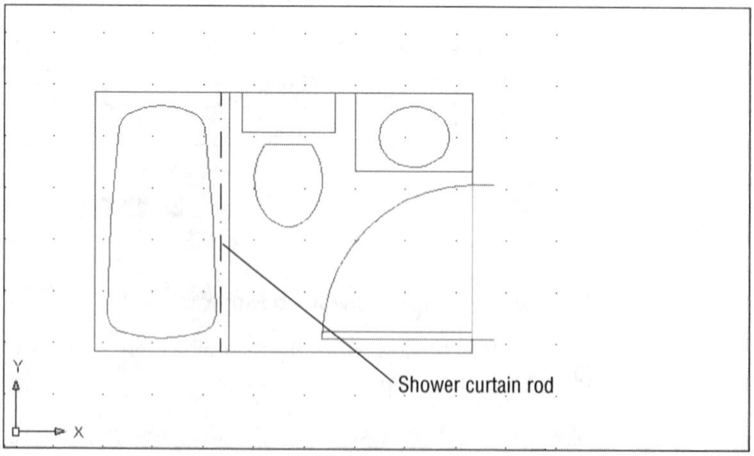

TIP *You can also use the Ltscale system variable to set the line-type scale. Type* ***Ltscale↵****, and at the* `LTSCALE New scale factor <1.0000>:` *prompt, enter* ***12↵****.*

TIP *If you change the line type of a layer or object but the object remains a continuous line, check the Ltscale system variable. It should be set to your drawing scale factor. If this doesn't work, set the Viewres system variable to a higher value (see Chapter 6). (Viewres can also be set by the Arc And Circle Smoothness option in the Display tab of the Options dialog box.) The behavior of line-type scales depends on whether you are in Model Space or in a drawing layout. See Chapter 13 for more on Model Space and layouts.*

Remember that if you assign a line type to a layer, everything you draw on that layer will be of that line type. This includes arcs, polylines, circles, and traces. As explained in the "Setting Individual Colors, Line Types, and Line-Type Scales" sidebar later in this section, you can also assign different colors and line types to individual objects, rather than relying on their layer assignment to define color and line type. However, you might want to avoid assigning colors and line types directly to objects until you have some experience with AutoCAD and a good grasp of your drawing's organization.

In the previous exercise, you changed the global line-type scale setting. This affects all noncontinuous line types within the current drawing. You can also change the line-type scale of individual objects using the Properties button on the Object Properties toolbar. Or you can set the default line-type scale for all new objects, with the Current Object Scale option in the Linetype Manager dialog box.

When individual objects are assigned a line-type scale, they are still affected by the global line-type scale set by the Ltscale system variable. For example, say you assign a line-type scale of 2 to the curtain rod in the previous example. This scale is then multiplied by the global line-type scale of 12, for a final line-type scale of 48.

TIP *You can also set the default Linetype Scale setting for individual objects using the Celtscale system variable. Once it is set, only newly created objects are affected. You must use the Properties tool to change the line-type scale of individual existing objects.*

If the objects you draw appear in a different line type from that of the layer they are on, check the default line type using the Linetype Control drop-down list on the Object Properties toolbar. You can also choose Format ➢ Linetype. Then, in the Linetype Manager dialog box, highlight ByLayer in the Linetype list, and then click the Current button. In addition, check the line-type scale of the object itself, using the Properties palette. A different line-type scale can make a line appear to have an assigned line type that may not be what you expect. (See the sidebar "Setting Individual Colors, Line Types, and Line-Type Scales.")

WARNING *The display of line types also depends on whether you are in Paper Space or drawing layout. If your efforts to control line-type scale have no effect on your line type's visibility, you may be in a drawing layout. See Chapter 13 for more information on how to control line-type scale while in a layout view.*

If you are working through the tutorial, your final task here is to set up an insertion point for the current drawing, to facilitate its insertion into other drawings in the future.

1. Type **Base↵**.

2. At the `Enter base point <0'-0",0'-0",0'-0">:` prompt, pick the upper-left corner of the bathroom. The bathroom drawing is now complete.
3. Choose File ➢ Save to record your work up to now.

SETTING INDIVIDUAL COLORS, LINE TYPES, AND LINE-TYPE SCALES

If you prefer, you can set up AutoCAD to assign specific colors and line types to objects, instead of having objects take on the color and line-type settings of the layer on which they reside. Normally, objects are given a default color and line type called ByLayer, which means each object takes on the color or line type of its assigned layer. (You've probably noticed the word *ByLayer* in the Object Properties toolbar and in various dialog boxes.)

Use the Properties tool on the Object Properties toolbar to change the color or line type of existing objects. This tool opens a dialog box that lets you set the properties of individual objects. For new objects, use the Color tool on the Object Properties toolbar to set the current default color to red (for example), instead of ByLayer. The Color tool opens the Select Color dialog box, in which you select your color from a toolbar. Then everything you draw will be red, regardless of the current layer color.

For line types, you can use the Linetype drop-down list in the Object Properties toolbar to select a default line type for all new objects. The list shows only line types that have already been loaded into the drawing, so you must first load a line type before you can select it.

Another possible color and line-type assignment is ByBlock, which you also set with the Properties button. ByBlock makes everything you draw white, until you turn your drawing into a block and then insert the block on a layer with an assigned color. The objects then take on the color of that layer. This behavior is similar to that of objects drawn on Layer 0. The ByBlock line type works similarly to the ByBlock color.

Finally, if you want to set the line-type scale for each individual object, instead of relying on the global line-type scale (the Ltscale system variable), you can use the Properties button to modify the line-type scale of individual objects. Or you can use the Object Creation Modes dialog box (via the Object Creation button in the Object Properties toolbar) to set the line-type scale to be applied to new objects. In place of using the Properties button, you can set the Celtscale system variable to the line-type scale you want for new objects.

As mentioned earlier, you should stay away from assigning colors and line types to individual objects until you are comfortable with AutoCAD; and even then, use color and line-type assignments carefully. Other users who work on your drawing may have difficulty understanding your drawing's organization if you assign color and line-type properties indiscriminately.

Controlling Line Weights

You may have noticed an option in the Layer Properties Manager dialog box called *Lineweight*. This option lets you control the thickness of your lines by adjusting the Lineweight setting, either through layer assignments or through direct object property assignment. This setting lets you view line weights as they will appear in your final plot.

With the Lineweight option, you have greater control over the look of your drawings. This can save time since you don't have to print your drawing just to check for line weights. You'll be able to see how thick or thin your lines are as you edit your drawing. You'll get a chance to delve into line weights in Chapter 7.

Keeping Track of Blocks and Layers

The Insert and the Layer Properties Manager dialog boxes let you view the blocks and layers available in your drawing, by listing them in a window. The Layer Properties Manager dialog box also includes information about the status of layers. However, you might forget the layer on which an object resides. You've seen how the Properties option on the shortcut menu shows you the properties of an object. The List button on the Object Properties toolbar also allows you to get information about individual objects.

1. Choose Tools ➢ Inquiry ➢ List from the menu bar.

TIP *If you just want to quickly check which layer an object is on, click it. Its layer will appear in the Layer list of the Properties toolbar.*

2. At the `Select objects:` prompt, click the Tub block and then press ↵ to open the AutoCAD Text window.
3. In the Text window, a listing appears that shows not only the layer that the tub is on, but also its space, insertion point, name, rotation angle, and scale.

The information you see in the Text window is duplicated in the Properties palette that you see when you right-click and choose Properties. But having the data in the Text window gives you the flexibility to record the data in a text file, in case you need to store data about parts of your drawing. You can also use the Text window to access and store other types of data regarding your drawings.

TIP *The Space property you see listed for the Tub block designates whether the object resides in Model Space or Layout Space. You'll learn more about these spaces in Chapters 6 and 13.*

Using the Log File Feature

Eventually, you will want a permanent record of block and layer listings. This is especially true if you work on drawing files that are being used by others. Here's a way to get a permanent record of the layers and blocks within a drawing by using the Log File option under the Environment Preferences.

1. Minimize the Text window.
2. Choose Tools ➢ Options, or type **op**↵ to open the Options dialog box. You can also right-click the drawing area and choose Options from the shortcut menu.

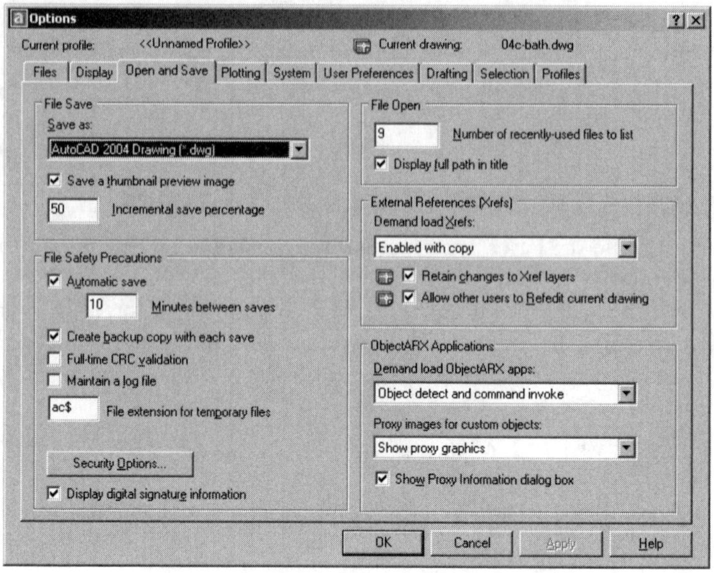

3. Click the Open And Save tab.

4. Click the Maintain A Log File check box in the bottom-left side of the dialog box.

5. Click OK, type **–LAYER**↵ (don't forget the minus sign) at the command prompt, and then type **?**↵. The AutoCAD Text window appears, and a listing of all the layers scrolls into view.

6. Press F2 to return to the AutoCAD drawing screen and then open the Options dialog box again.

7. Click the Open And Save tab, click the Maintain A Log File check box again, and then click OK.

8. Use Windows Notepad to open the AutoCAD log file located in the `C:\Documents and Settings\YourSettings\Local Settings\Application Data\Autodesk\AutoCAD 2004\R16.0\enu\` folder. The name of the log file will start with the name of the current drawing followed by a series of numbers and the .log filename extension, as in `04c-bath-metric_1_1_6500.log`. Notice that the layer listing is recorded there.

WARNING *The location of the* `Acad.log` *file mentioned in step 8 of this exercise is typical for AutoCAD running on Windows XP Professional on a simple workgroup network. The location of the* `Acad.log` *file depends on your operating system, the type of network you are using, and your user profile. If you are using Windows NT or Windows 2000 for example, change* `\Documents and Settings` *to* `\Winnt\Profiles`*. If you have difficulty finding the log file, you can enter* `(getvar "logfilepath")` *at the AutoCAD command prompt to get a listing of the log file location.*

With the Log File feature, you can record virtually anything that appears in the command prompt. You can even record an entire AutoCAD session. The log file can also be helpful in constructing script files to automate tasks. (See Chapter 16 for more information on scripts.) If you want hard copy of the log file, print it from an application such as Windows Notepad or your favorite word processor.

If you want, you can arrange to keep the `Acad.log` file in a folder other than the default AutoCAD subfolder. This setting is also in the Options dialog box under the Files tab. Locate Log File Location in the Search Path, File Names, And File Locations list box. Click the plus sign next to this listing, which expands to show the location for the log file. See Appendix B for more on the AutoCAD Options dialog box settings.

You can double-click the file location listing to open a Browse For Folder dialog box and specify a different location and filename for your log file.

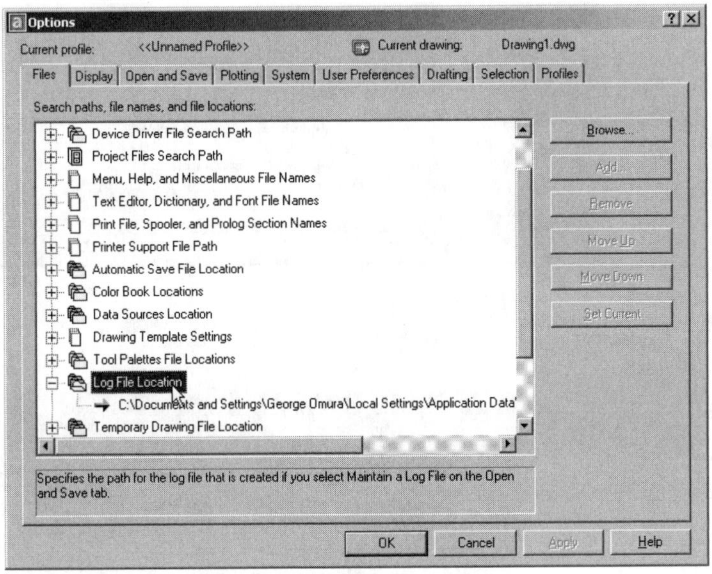

TIP *Once you've settled on a location on disk for the log file, use the Windows Explorer to associate the log file with the Windows Notepad or Wordpad application. Then click and drag the file to the AutoCAD program group. This gives you quick access to your log file by simply double-clicking its icon in the AutoCAD program group.*

Finding Files on Your Hard Disk

As your library of symbols and files grows, you might begin to have difficulty keeping track of them. Fortunately, AutoCAD includes a utility that lets you quickly locate a file anywhere in your computer. The Find utility searches your hard disk for specific files. You can have it search one drive or several, or you can limit the search to one folder. You can limit the search to specific filenames or use wildcard characters to search for files with similar names.

To take a look at the AutoCAD Find dialog box, follow these steps:

1. Choose File ➢ Open to open the Select File dialog box.

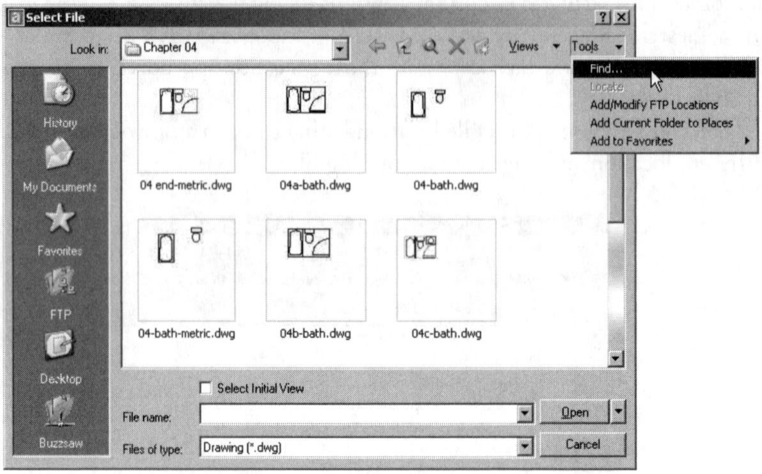

2. Choose Tools ➢ Find to open the Find dialog box.

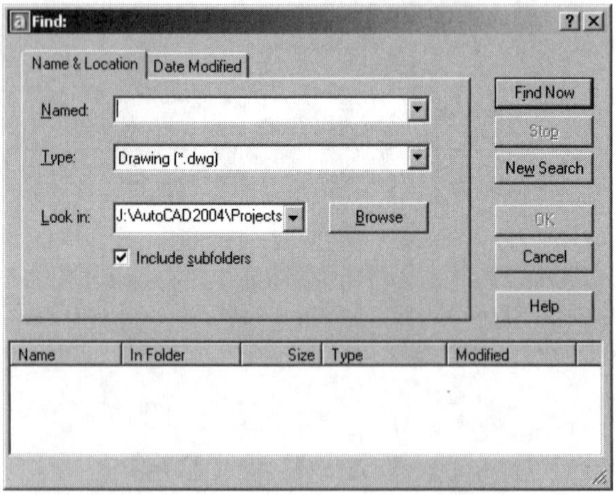

The Find dialog box has two tabs: Name & Location and Date Modified. The Name & Location tab lets you search for a file based on its location on your computer and the file type. It works in a way that is similar to the Windows Search tool . In the Named text box, enter the name of the file for which you want to search. The default is *.dwg, which in the Type drop-down list causes the Find File utility to search for all AutoCAD drawing files. The Look In drop-down list lets you specify the drive and path to be searched.

3. Click the Date Modified tab. Here you find options that let you search based on the date a file was created.

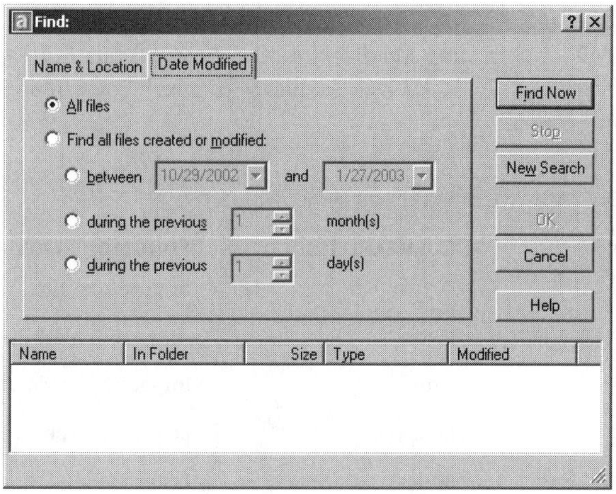

4. When you're ready, click Cancel to exit the Find dialog box, and then click Cancel to exit the Select File dialog box.

MANAGING SYMBOLS AND SETTINGS WITH THE TOOL PALETTE AND THE DESIGNCENTER

One item that has been fairly conspicuous in the AutoCAD window is the Tool palette. The main purpose of the Tool palette is to give you easy access to symbols and patterns that you use frequently. It works by giving you ready access to blocks and other features contained within drawings in your drawing library. Currently, the palette offers blocks from drawings in the Samples folder of the AutoCAD 2004 installation, but you can add your own blocks to the palette using the AutoCAD DesignCenter.

The DesignCenter is a tool that lets you locate and manage AutoCAD drawing files and blocks that reside within drawings. It also allows you to search for and import settings from other drawings, such as layers, line types, text, and dimension styles (you'll learn about text and dimension styles in Chapters 8 and 9) and Xrefs. If your work involves raster images, you can use the DesignCenter to view and import Targa, TIFF, BMP, JPEG, and other image files.

You can learn more about the DesignCenter in Chapter 22, which discusses project management issues. You'll also gain some hands-on experience using the Tool palette in Chapter 22.

Inserting Symbols with Drag and Drop

If you prefer to manage your symbol library using Windows Explorer or to use another third-party file manager for locating and managing your symbols, you'll appreciate AutoCAD's support for drag and drop. With this feature, you can click and drag a file from Windows Explorer into the AutoCAD window. You can also drag and drop from the Windows Search tool. AutoCAD automatically starts the Insert command to insert the file. Drag and drop also works with a variety of other AutoCAD support files.

AutoCAD supports drag and drop for other types of data from applications that support Microsoft's ActiveX technology. Table 4.3 lists the files with which you can use drag and drop and the functions associated with them.

TABLE 4.3: AUTOCAD SUPPORT FOR DRAG AND DROP

FILE TYPE	COMMAND ISSUED	FUNCTION PERFORMED WHEN FILE IS DROPPED
.dxf	Dxfin	Imports .dxf files
.dwg	Insert	Imports or plots drawing files
.txt	Dtext	Imports texts via Dtext
.lin	Linetype	Loads line types
.mnu, .mns, .mnc	Menu	Loads menus
.ps	Psin	Imports PostScript files
.psb, .shp, .shx	Style	Loads fonts or shapes
.scr	Script	Runs script
.lsp	(Load)	Loads AutoLISP routine
.exe, .exp	(Xload)	Loads ADS application

TIP *You can also drag and drop from folder shortcuts placed on your Desktop or even from a website.*

If You Want to Experiment...

If your application is not architecture, you might want to experiment with creating other types of symbols. You might also start thinking about a layering system that suits your particular needs.

Open a new file called `Mytemp`. In it, create layers numbered 1 through 8 and assign each layer the color that corresponds to its number. For example, give Layer 1 the color 1 (red), Layer 2 the color 2 (yellow), and so on. Draw each part shown in Figure 4.20, and turn each part into a file on disk using the Export (choose File ➢ Export) or the Wblock command. When specifying a filename, use the name indicated for each part in the figure. For the insertion point, also use the points indicated in the figure. Use the Osnap modes (see Chapter 2) to select the insertion points. You can use the `Experiment04-1.dwg` sample file as a reference.

FIGURE 4.20

A typical set of symbols

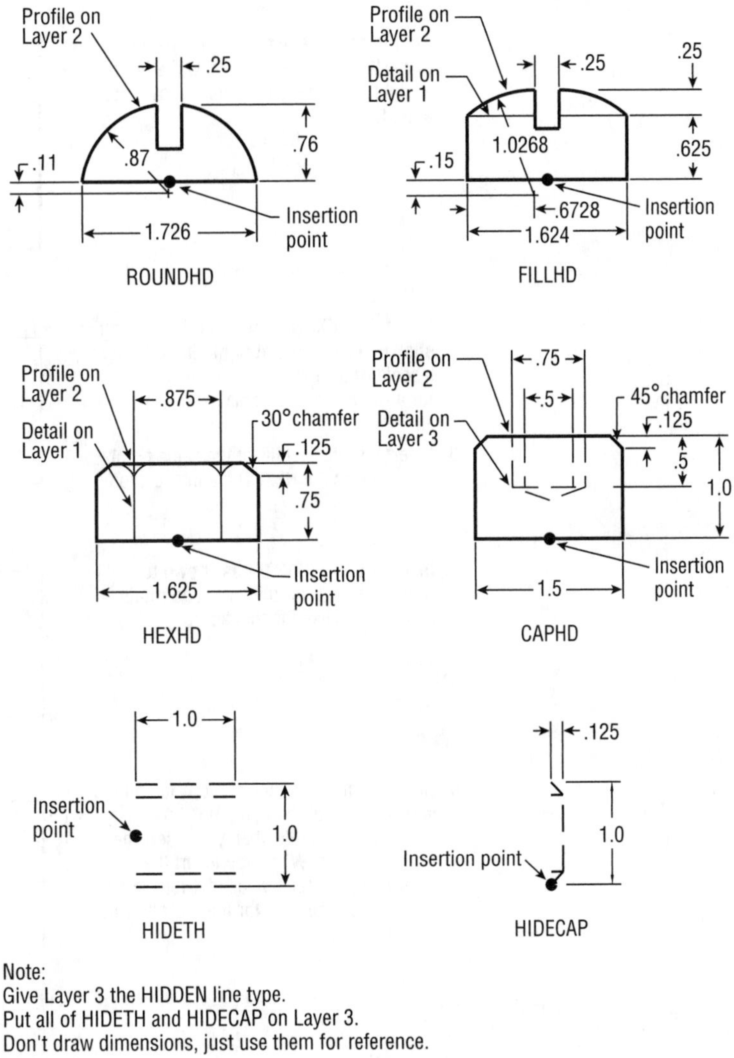

After you create the parts, exit the file by choosing File ➢ Exit, and then open a new file. Set up the drawing as an engineering drawing with a scale of 1/4"=1" on an 11" × 17" sheet. Create the drawing in Figure 4.21, using the Insert Block command to place your newly created parts. You can use the `Experiment04-2.dwg` file as a reference.

FIGURE 4.21

Draw this part using the symbols you create.

1. Set the snap mode to .125 and be sure it is on. Set Ltscale to .25. Draw the figure at right using the dimensions shown as a guide.

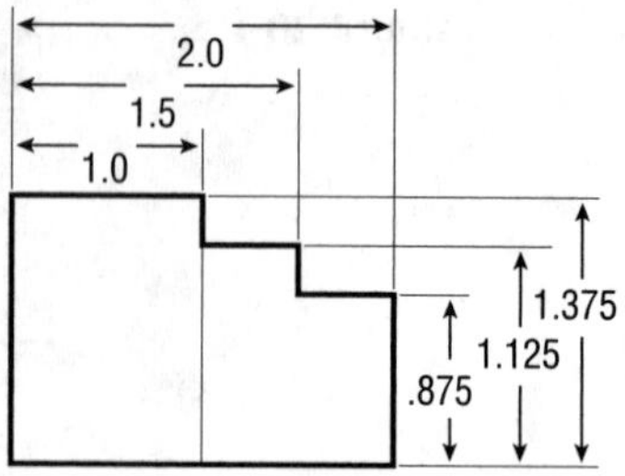

2. Insert the HEXHD drawing at the location shown in the figure at right. Enter .25 for a scale value and when you are asked for a rotation angle, visually orient it as shown.
3. Insert the HIDETH file at the same point and scale as the HEXHD file then explode it.

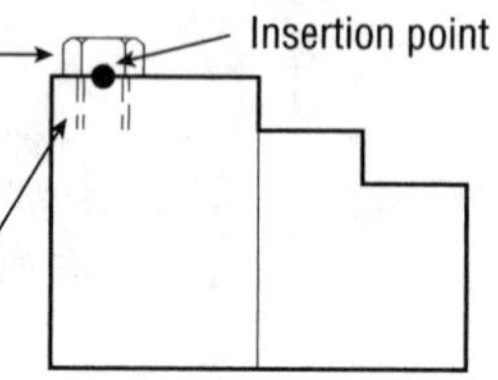

4. Insert the HIDECAP file as shown to the right. Enter .25 for the scale and rotate it so it looks like the this figure.

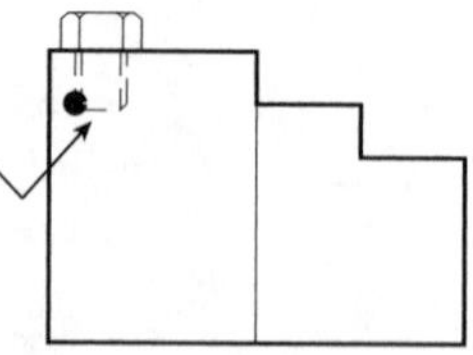

5. Do the same sequence of steps to add the screw shown at the right. This time, use a scale factor of .125 when you insert the ROUNDHD file. When you insert the HIDETH file, enter a value of 1 for the X scale factor and .125 for the Y scale factor.

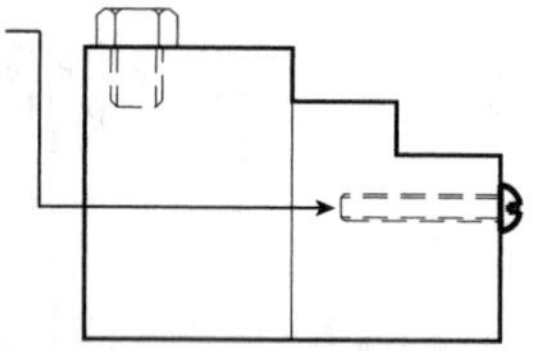

Part 2

Building on the Basics

In this part:

- **Chapter 5: Editing for Productivity**
- **Chapter 6: Enhancing Your Drawing Skills**
- **Chapter 7: Printing and Plotting**
- **Chapter 8: Adding Text to Drawings**
- **Chapter 9: Using Dimensions**

Chapter 5

Editing for Productivity

AT LEAST FIVE AUTOCAD commands are devoted to duplicating objects, ten if you include the Grips options. Why so many? If you're an experienced drafter, you know that you frequently have to draw the same item several times in many drawings. So AutoCAD offers a variety of ways to reuse existing geometry, thereby automating much of the repetitive work usually associated with manual drafting.

In this chapter, as you finish drawing the studio apartment unit, you will explore some of the ways to exploit existing files and objects while constructing your drawing. For example, you will use existing files as prototypes for new files, eliminating the need to set up layers, scales, and sheet sizes for similar drawings. With AutoCAD you can also duplicate objects in multiple arrays. In Chapter 3 you saw how to use the Object snap (Osnap) overrides on objects to locate points for drawing complex forms. This chapter describes other ways of using lines to aid your drawing.

And, because you will begin to use the Zoom command more in the exercises in this chapter, you will review this command as you go along. You'll also discover the Pan command—another tool to help you get around in your drawing.

You're already familiar with many of the commands you will use to draw the apartment unit. So, rather than going through every step of the drawing process, the exercises will sometimes ask you to copy the drawing from a figure, using notes and dimensions as guides and putting objects on the indicated layers. If you have trouble remembering a command you've already learned, just go back and review the appropriate section of the book.

- Creating and Using Templates
- Copying an Object Multiple Times
- Developing Your Drawing
- Drawing Parallel Lines
- Eliminating Blocks, Layers, Line Types, Shapes, and Styles
- If You Want to Experiment...

Creating and Using Templates

Most programs today include what are called *templates*. A template is a file that is already set up for a specific application. For example, in your word processor, you might want to set up letters with a logo, a return address, and a date so you don't have to add these elements each time you create a letter. You might also want to format invoices in a slightly different way. You can set up a template for the needs of each type of document. That way, you don't have to spend time reformatting each new document you create.

Similarly, AutoCAD offers templates, which are drawing files that contain custom settings designed for a particular function. Out of the box, AutoCAD has templates for ISO, ANSI, DIN, GB, and JIS standard drawing formats that include generic title blocks. But you aren't limited to these "canned" templates. You can create your own templates for your particular style and method of drawing.

If you find that you use a particular drawing setup frequently, you can turn one or more of your typical drawings into a template. For example, you might want to create a set of drawings with the same scale and sheet size as an existing drawing. By turning a frequently used drawing into a template, you can save a lot of setup time for subsequent drawings.

Creating a Template

The following exercise guides you through creating and using a template drawing for your studio's kitchenette. Because the kitchenette will use the same layers, settings, scale, and sheet size as the bathroom drawing, you can use the `Bath` file as a prototype.

1. Start AutoCAD in the usual way.
2. Choose File ➢ Open to open the Select File dialog box.
3. Locate the `Bath` file you created in the last chapter. You can also use the file `05-bath.dwg` from the companion CD.
4. Click the Erase button on the Modify toolbar or enter **e** (↵); then type **all**↵ ↵. This erases all the objects that make up the bathroom, but other elements, such as layers, line types, and stored blocks, remain in the drawing.
5. Choose File ➢ Save As to open the Save Drawing As dialog box. Open the File Of Type drop-down list and select AutoCAD Drawing Template (*.dwt). The file list window changes to display the current template files in the `\Template\` folder.

TIP *When you choose the Drawing Template option in the Save Drawing As dialog box, AutoCAD automatically opens the folder containing the template files. The standard AutoCAD installation creates the folder named* `Template` *to contain the template files. If you want to place your templates in a different folder, you can change the default template location using the Options dialog box (choose Tools ➢ Options). Click the Files tab, and then double-click the Template Drawing File Location in the list. Double-click the folder name that appears just below Template Drawing File Location; then select a new location from the Browse For Folder dialog box that appears.*

6. In the File Name text box, enter the name **Arch8x11h**. If you're a metric user, enter the name **A4plan**.

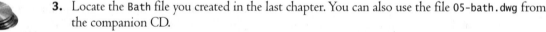

7. Click Save to open the Template Description dialog box.

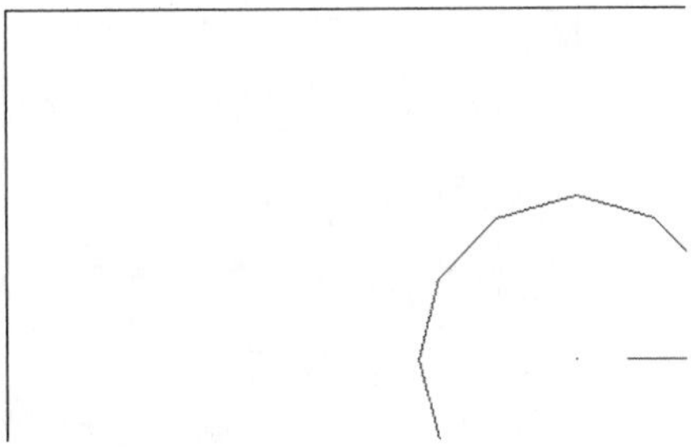

8. Enter the following description: **Architectural One inch scale drawing on 8 1/2 by 11 inch media.** Metric users should enter the description: **Architectural 1:10 scale drawing on A4 media.**

9. Select Imperial or Metric from the Measurement drop-down list, depending on the unit system you're using.

10. Click OK to save your new file and you create a template. Note that the current file has changed to the template file you just saved.

11. Close the template file without saving your changes.

Notice that the current drawing is now the template file you saved in step 10. As with other Windows programs, choosing File ➢ Save As makes the saved file current. This also shows that you can edit template files just as you would regular drawing files.

Using a Template

Now let's see how a template is used. You'll use the template you just created as the basis for a new drawing you will work on in this chapter.

TIP *If the Create New Drawing dialog box does not appear in step 1 of the following exercise, do the following: Choose Tools ➢ Options. Select the System tab. In the General Options group, Choose Show Startup dialog box from the Startup drop down list. Click OK to close the Options dialog box.*

1. Choose File ➢ New to open the Create New Drawing dialog box.

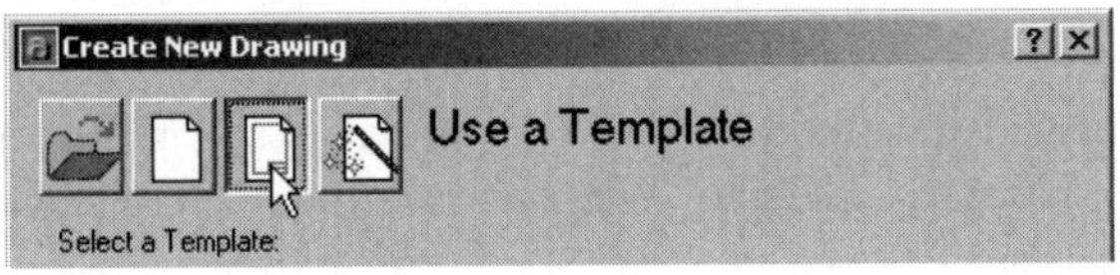

2. Click the Use A Template button to display a list box and a preview window.

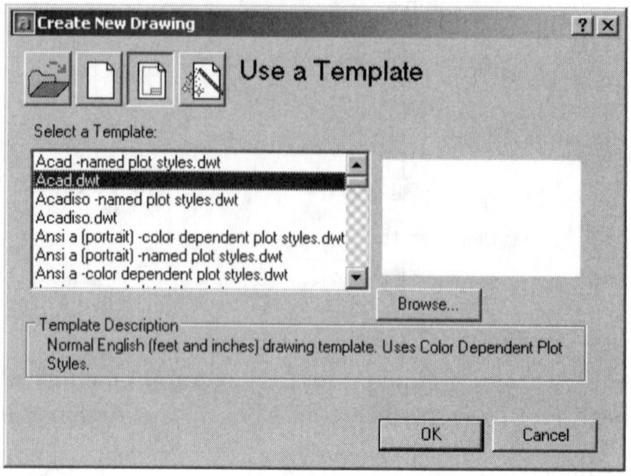

3. In the Select A Template list box, click the filename `Arch8x11h.dwt`. Metric users should click the filename `A4plan.dwt`. Since this file is blank, you won't see anything in the preview window. Notice that the description you entered earlier in the Template Description dialog box appears in the Template Description area below the list.

4. Click OK. It may not be obvious, but your new file is set up with the same architectural units and drawing limits as the bathroom drawing. It also contains the Door, Toilet, and Tub blocks.

5. Now you need to give your new file a name. Choose File ➢ Save to open the Save Drawing As dialog box. (Make sure you choose Save As or you won't get the Save Drawing As dialog box.) Enter **Kitchen** for the filename, and select the appropriate folder in which to save your new kitchen file.

6. Click Save to create the `Kitchen` file and close the dialog box.

TIP *In Chapter 2, you were asked to select the Show Startup Dialog Box option in the General Options of the System tab, found in the Options dialog box. If you decide to turn off the Show Startup Dialog Box option, you can still select a template file when you start a new file. However, instead of the Startup dialog box, you will see the Select Template dialog box, which is a standard AutoCAD file dialog box complete with preview panel. From there, you can select a template file. To create a drawing from scratch using templates, choose the* `Acad.dwt` *template file for imperial units or the* `Acadiso.dwt` *file for metric units.*

You've created and used your own template file. Later, when you have established a comfortable working relationship with AutoCAD, you can create a set of templates that are custom made to your particular needs.

However, you don't need to create a template every time you want to reuse settings from another file. You can use an existing file as the basis or prototype for a new file without creating a template. Open the prototype file, and then choose File ➢ Save As to create a new version of the file under a new name. You can then edit the new version without affecting the original prototype file.

OPENING A FILE AS READ-ONLY

At times you will want to open an important file and view it while ensuring that it is protected from accidental changes. Or you might want to use a file as a starting point for a new project while leaving the original file unchanged. You can protect an open file by using the Open Read-Only option in the Select File dialog box.

Choose File ➢ Open, to open the Select File dialog box. Click the downward pointing arrow to the right of the Open button in the lower-right corner to display a menu that includes the Open Read-Only option.

Choose Open Read-Only to open the selected file. You can still edit the open file any way you please, but if you attempt to choose File ➢ Save, you will get the message "Drawing file is write-protected." You can, however, save your changed file under another name by choosing File ➢ Save As.

The Read-Only option provides a way to protect important files from accidental corruption. It also offers another method for reusing settings and objects from existing files by letting you open a file as a prototype and then save the new file under another name.

Copying an Object Multiple Times

Now let's explore the tools that let you quickly duplicate objects. In the next exercise, you will begin to draw parts to a small kitchen. The first exercise introduces the Array command, which you can use to draw the gas burners of a range top.

As you'll see, an array can be in either a circular pattern, called a *polar array*, or a matrix of columns and rows, called a *rectangular array*.

Making Circular Copies

To start the range top, first set the layer on which you want to draw, and then draw a circle representing the edge of one burner.

1. Set the current layer to Fixture, and turn the Grid Snap mode on by right-clicking the SNAP button in the status bar and selecting Grid Snap On.

TIP *Because you used the* `Bath` *file as a template, Running Osnaps for Endpoint, Midpoint, and Intersection are already turned on and available in this new file.*

2. Click the Circle tool on the Draw toolbar, or type C↵.
3. At the `Specify Center point for circle or [3p/2p/Ttr (tan tan radius)]:` prompt, pick a point at coordinate 4',4'. Metric users should pick a point at coordinate 120,120.
4. At the `Specify radius of circle or [Diameter]:` prompt, enter **3**↵. Metric users should enter **7.6**↵. The circle appears.

Now you're ready to use the Array command to draw the burner grill. You will first draw one line representing part of the grill and then use the Array command to create the copies.

1. Turn off both the Polar Snap and Grid Snap modes by clicking the SNAP button in the status bar, and draw a 4-inch line starting from the coordinate 4'-1", 4'-0" and ending to the right of that point. Metric users should draw a 9 cm line starting at coordinate 122,120 and ending to the right of that point.
2. Zoom into the circle and line to get a better view. Your drawing should look like Figure 5.1.

FIGURE 5.1

A close-up of the circle and line

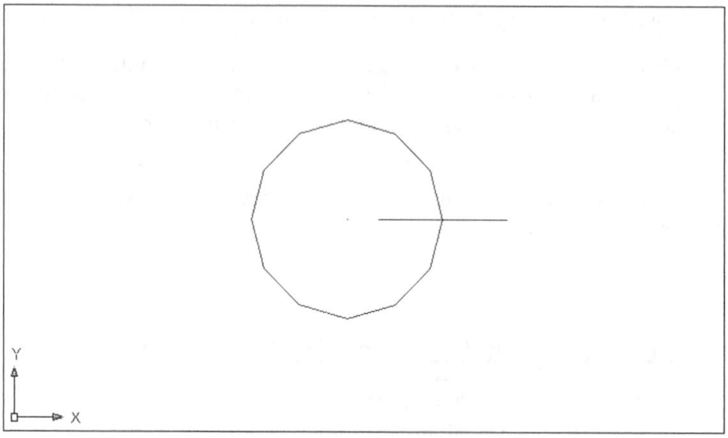

You've got the basic parts needed to create the burner grill. Now you're ready to make multiple copies of the line. For this part, you'll use the Array dialog box.

1. Click Array on the Modify toolbar, or type **AR↵**.

   The Array dialog box appears.

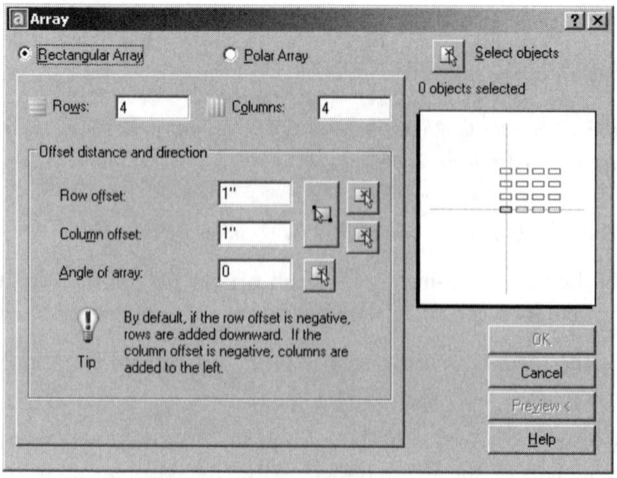

2. Click the Select Objects button. The dialog box temporarily disappears, allowing you to select objects.
3. Type L↵ to select the last object drawn, or click the object you want to array.
4. Next, press ↵ to confirm your selection. The Array dialog reappears.
5. Click the Polar Array radio button at the top of the dialog box to tell AutoCAD you want a circular array. The Array dialog box displays the polar array options.

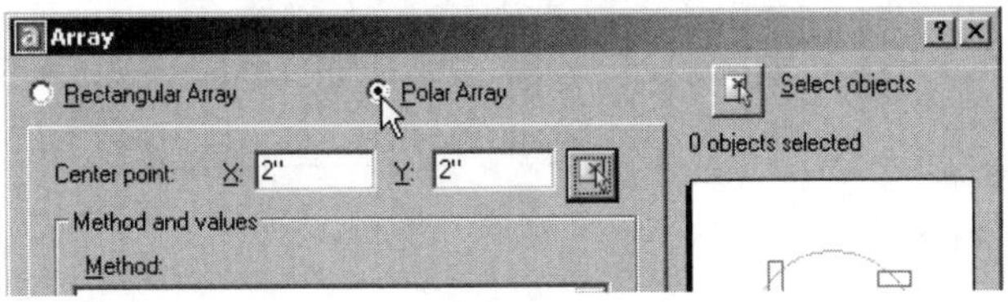

6. Click the Pick Center Point button to temporarily close the Array dialog box.

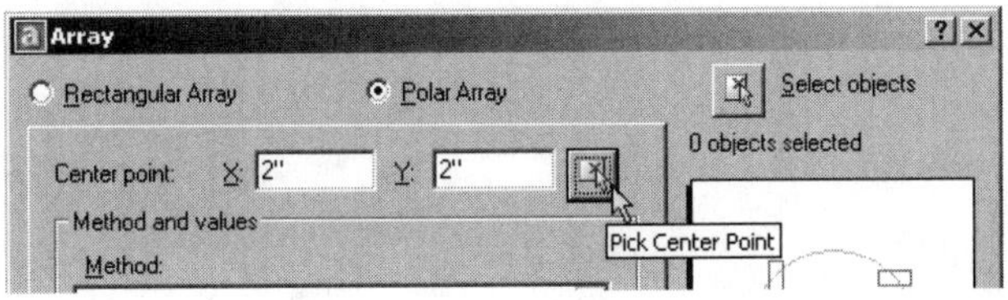

7. Pick the point that represents the center of the circular array. Use Center Osnap to select the center of the circle. Once you've indicated a point, the Array dialog box returns.

TIP *Remember that to access Osnaps other than those set up as Running Osnaps, you Shift+right-click the mouse and then select the Osnap you want to use from the resulting menu.*

WARNING *If you use Center Osnap, you must place the cursor on the circle's circumference, not on the circle's center point.*

At this point, you've selected an object to array, and you've indicated the center location of the array. If you've selected the wrong object or the wrong center point, you can go back and specify these options again.

Now, to complete the process, tell AutoCAD the number of copies in the array and the extent of the array through the circle.

1. In the Array dialog box, enter **8** in the Total Number Of Items text box. This tells AutoCAD to make eight copies including the original.
2. Accept the default of 360 for the Angle To Fill text box. This tells AutoCAD to spread the copies evenly over the full 360 degrees of the circle. Of course, you can enter other values here. For example, if you enter 180, the array will fill half the circle.

TIP *You can click the Pick Angle To Fill button to the right of the Angle To Fill box to graphically select an angle in the drawing.*

3. Make sure the Rotate Items As Copied check box in the lower-left corner of the dialog box is turned on. This ensures that the arrayed object is rotated about the array center. If you turn this option off, the copies will all be oriented in the same direction as the original object.
4. Click the Preview button. AutoCAD shows you the results of your array settings plus a dialog that offers Accept, Modify, and Cancel.
5. Click Accept. The circular array appears in the drawing as shown in Figure 5.2.

FIGURE 5.2
The completed gas burner

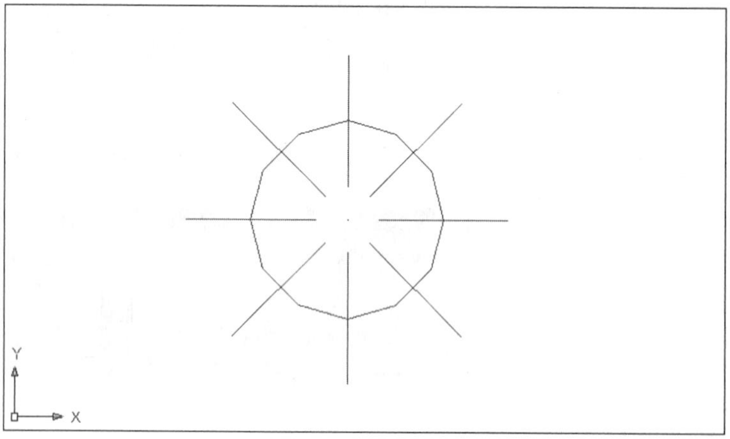

In step 5, you could have selected the Modify option to return to the Array dialog box and change settings before committing to a final array pattern, or you could click Cancel to cancel the whole process. The Array dialog box gives you a lot of leeway in creating your array copies.

TIP *If you're a veteran AutoCAD user and you prefer the command-line version of the Array command, you can type* ***–Array↵*** *or* ***–Ar↵*** *at the command prompt, and then answer the prompts as you would in earlier versions of AutoCAD.*

Making Row and Column Copies

Now you will draw the other three burners of the gas range by creating a rectangular array from the burner you just drew. You will first zoom back a bit to get a view of a larger area. Then you will proceed with the Array command.

1. Choose View ➢ Zoom ➢ Scale, or type **Z↵ S↵**.
2. Enter **.5x↵**. Your drawing will look like Figure 5.3.

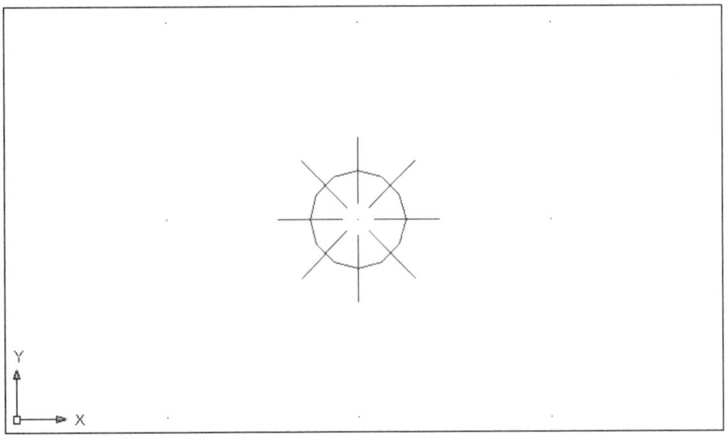

FIGURE 5.3
The preceding view reduced by a factor of 0.5

TIP *If you're not too fussy about the amount you want to zoom out, you can choose View ➢ Zoom ➢ Out to quickly reduce your view, or you can click the Zoom Realtime tool on the Standard toolbar.*

Entering .5x for the Zoom Scale value tells AutoCAD you want a view that reduces the width of the current view to fill half the display area, allowing you to see more of the work area. If you specify a scale value greater than 1 (5, for example), you will magnify your current view. If you leave off the **x**, your new view will be in relation to the drawing limits rather than the current view.

Now you will finish the range top. Here you will get a chance to use the Rectangular Array option to create three additional burners.

1. Click the Array tool on the Modify toolbar again, or type **AR**↵ to open the Array dialog box.
2. Click the Select Objects tool to temporarily close the Array dialog box.
3. Select the entire burner, including the lines and the circle, and then press ↵ to confirm your selection.
4. In the Array dialog box, click the Rectangular Array radio button.
5. Change both the Rows and Columns text boxes to **2**.
6. Change the Row Offset text box value to 1'-2" (35.5 for metric users) and the Column Offset text box value to 1'-4" (or 40.6 for metric users).

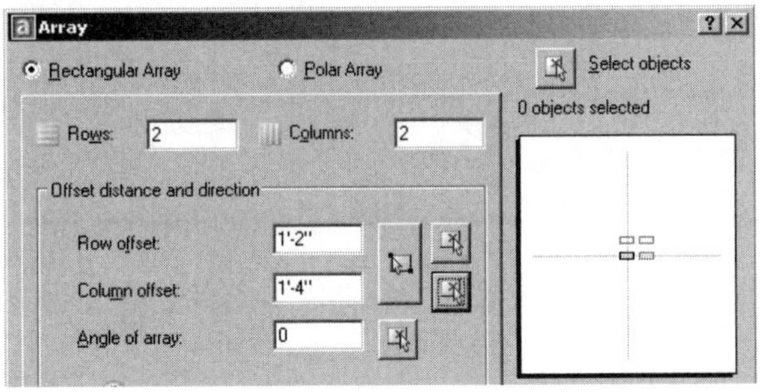

7. Click OK. Your screen will look like Figure 5.4.

FIGURE 5.4
The burners arrayed

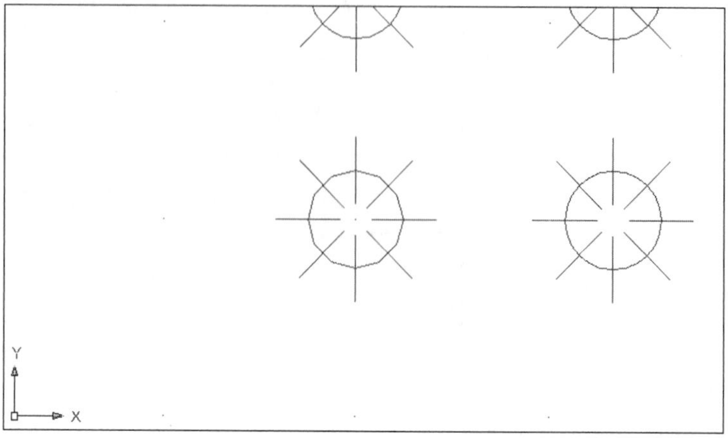

AutoCAD usually draws a rectangular array from bottom to top and from left to right. You can reverse the direction of the array by giving negative values for the distance between columns and rows.

TIP *At times, you might want to do a rectangular array at an angle. To accomplish this, enter the desired angle in the Angle Of Array input box of the Array dialog box. You can also select the angle graphically by clicking the Pick Angle Of Array button just to the right of the Angle Of Array input box.*

If you need to graphically indicate an *array cell*, you can do so using options in the Offset Distance And Direction group of the Array dialog box (see the bottom image in Figure 5.5). An array cell is a rectangle defining the distance between rows and columns (see the top image in Figure 5.5). You might want to use this option when objects are available to use as references from which to determine column and row distances. For example, you might have drawn a crosshatch pattern, as on a calendar, within which you want to array an object. You use the intersections of the hatch lines as references to define the array cell, which is one square in the hatch pattern.

In the Offset Distance And Direction group, the Pick Both Offsets button lets you indicate the row and column distance by placing an array cell graphically in the drawing, as shown in the bottom image in Figure 5.5. You can also indicate a row or column distance graphically using the Pick Row Offset or Pick Column Offset buttons to the right of the Pick Both Offsets button.

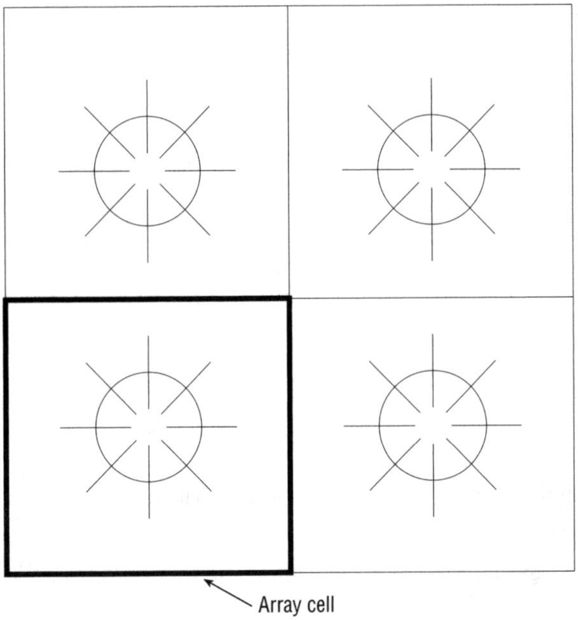

FIGURE 5.5
An array cell and the Array dialog box options that let you graphically indicate array cells

Fine-Tuning Your View

Back in Figure 5.4, you may have noticed that parts of the burners do not appear on the display. To move the view over so you can see all the burners, use the Pan command. Pan is similar to Zoom in that it changes your view of the drawing. However, Pan does not alter the magnification of the view the way Zoom does. Rather, Pan maintains the current magnification while moving your view across the drawing, just as you would pan a camera across a landscape.

To activate the Pan command, follow these steps.

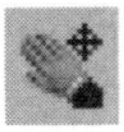

1. Click the Pan Realtime tool on the Standard toolbar, choose View ➢ Pan ➢ Realtime, or type **P**↵. You can also right-click and choose Pan from the shortcut menu.

   A small hand-shaped cursor appears in place of the AutoCAD cursor.

2. Place the hand cursor in the center of the drawing area, and then click and drag it downward and to the left. The view follows the motion of your mouse.
3. Continue to drag the view until it looks similar to Figure 5.6; then release the mouse button.

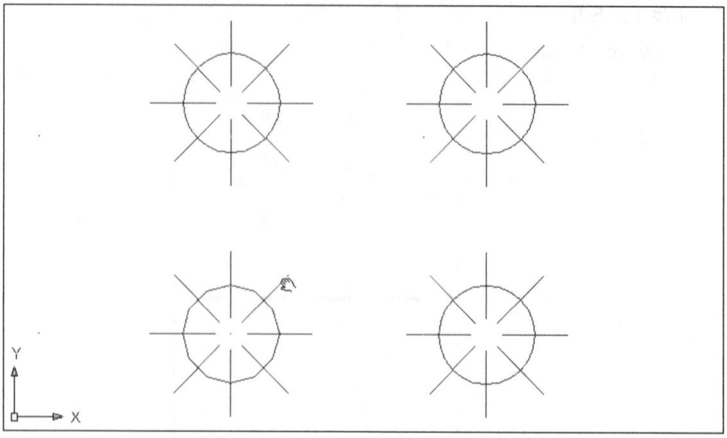

FIGURE 5.6
The panned view of the top range

To finish the kitchen, you will want a view that shows more of the drawing area. Continue with the following steps.

4. Now right-click to open the Zoom/Pan shortcut menu.

TIP *The Zoom/Pan shortcut menu also appears when you right-click during the Zoom Realtime command.*

5. Choose Zoom, and the cursor changes to the Zoom Realtime cursor.
6. Now place the cursor close to the top of the screen, and click and drag the cursor downward to zoom out until your view looks like the top panel of Figure 5.7. You might need to click and drag the zoom cursor a second time to achieve this view.
7. Right-click the mouse again, and choose Exit from the shortcut menu. You're now ready to add more information to the kitchen drawing.

TIP *To exit the Pan Realtime or Zoom Realtime command without opening the shortcut menu, press the Esc key.*

8. Now complete the kitchenette as indicated in the bottom panel of Figure 5.7.

This exercise showed how you can fine-tune your view by easily switching between Pan Realtime and Zoom Realtime. Once you get the hang of these two tools working together, you'll be able to quickly access the best view for your needs. The other options in the shortcut menu—Zoom Window, Zoom Original, and Zoom Extents—perform the same functions as the options in the View pull-down menu.

TIP *The Zoom Window option in the Zoom shortcut menu functions in a slightly different way from the standard Zoom Window option. Instead of clicking two points, you click and drag a window across your view.*

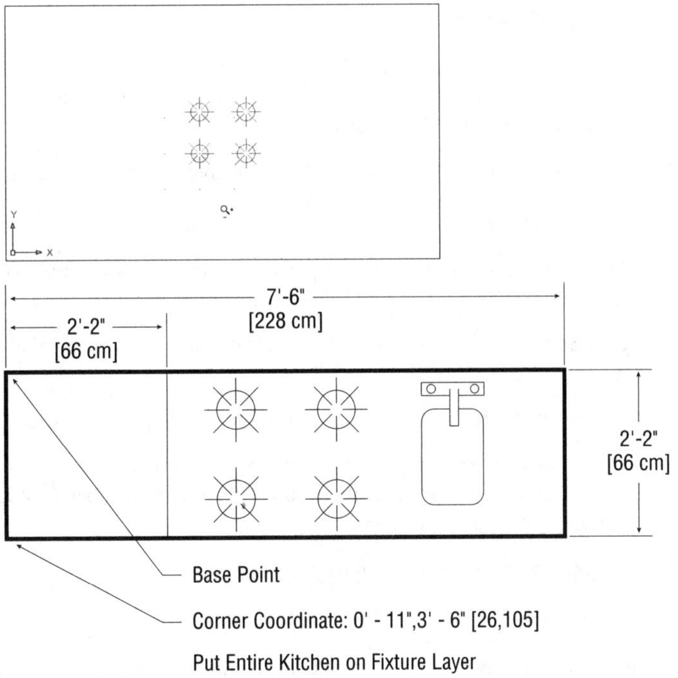

FIGURE 5.7
The final view of the range top burners (top image) and the finished kitchen (bottom image). Metric dimensions are shown in brackets.

While we're on the subject of display tools, don't forget the scroll bars to the right and bottom of the AutoCAD drawing area. They work like any other Windows scroll bars, offering a simple way to move up, down, left, or right in your current view. They also come in handy for quickly panning your view in one direction or another.

TIP *If for some reason the scroll bars do not appear in AutoCAD, or if you prefer to turn them off, open the Options dialog box (choose Tools ➢ Options), click the Display tab, and make sure that Display Scroll Bars in the Drawing Window option is either checked to turn them on or unchecked to turn them off.*

Before you save and close the `Kitchen` file, you need to do one more thing. You will be using this drawing as a symbol and inserting it into the overall plan of the studio apartment unit. To facilitate accurate placement of the kitchen, you will want to change the location of the base point of this drawing to the upper-left corner of the kitchen. This will then be the "handle" of the drawing.

1. Choose Draw ➢ Block ➢ Base from the pull-down menu.
2. At the `Enter base point` prompt, pick the upper-left corner of the kitchen, as indicated in the bottom image of Figure 5.7. The kitchen drawing is complete.
3. Choose File ➢ Save.

MAKING RANDOM MULTIPLE COPIES

Choosing Draw ➢ Array is useful when you want to make multiple copies in a regular pattern. But what if you need to make copies in a random pattern? You can do this in two ways: by using the Copy command's Multiple option and by using the Grips Move option.

To use the Copy command to make random multiple copies, follow these steps:

1. Click Copy Objects on the Modify toolbar, or type **CO**↵.
2. At the Select objects: prompt, select the objects you want to copy and press ↵ to confirm your selections.
3. At the Specify base point or displacement or [Multiple]: prompt, enter **M**↵ to select the Multiple option.
4. At the Specify base point: prompt, select a base point as usual.
5. At the Specify second point or displacement or <use first point as displacement>: prompt, select a point for the copy. You will be prompted again for a second point, allowing you to make yet another copy of your object.
6. Continue to select points for more copies as desired.
7. Press ↵ to exit the Copy command.

When you use the Grips feature to make multiple random copies, you get an added level of functionality because you can also rotate, mirror, and stretch copies by using the shortcut menu (right-click while a grip is selected). Of course, you must have the Grips feature turned on; it is usually on by default, but you might find yourself on a system that has it turned off for some reason.

1. Press the Esc key to make sure you are not in the middle of a command; then select the objects you want to copy.
2. Click a grip point as your base point.
3. Right-click your mouse and select Move.
4. Right-click again and select Copy.
5. Click the location for the copy. Notice that the rubber-banding line persists and that you still see the selected objects follow the cursor.
6. If desired, click other locations for more copies.

Finally, you can make square-arrayed copies using grips by following steps 1 through 3, but instead of step 4, Shift+click a copy location. Continue to hold down the Shift key and select points. The copies snap to the angle and distance you indicate with the first Shift+select point. Release the Shift key to make multiple random copies.

Developing Your Drawing

As mentioned briefly in Chapter 3, when using AutoCAD, you first create the basic forms of your drawing; then you refine them. In this section, you will create two drawings—the studio apartment unit and the lobby—that demonstrate this process in more detail.

First, you will construct a typical studio apartment unit using the drawings you have created thus far. In the process, you will explore the use of lines as reference objects.

You will also further examine how to use existing files as blocks. In Chapter 4, you inserted a file into another file. There is no limit to the size or number of files you can insert. As you might already have guessed, you can also *nest* files and blocks; that is, you can insert blocks or files within other blocks or files. Nesting can help reduce your drawing time by allowing you to build one block out of smaller blocks. For example, you can insert your door drawing into the bathroom plan. In turn, you can insert the bathroom plan into the studio unit plan, which also contains doors. Finally, you can insert the unit plan into the overall floor plan for the studio apartment building.

Importing Settings

In this exercise, you will use the `Bath` file as a prototype for the studio unit plan. However, you must make a few changes to it first. Once the changes are made, you will import the bathroom and thereby import the layers and blocks contained in the bathroom file.

As you go through this exercise, observe how the drawings begin to evolve from simple forms to complex, assembled forms.

1. First, open the `Bath` file. If you skipped drawing the Bath file in Chapter 4, use the file named `04c-bath.dwg` from the companion CD.
2. Use the Base command and select the upper-left corner of the bathroom as the new base point for this drawing, so you can position the `Bath` file more accurately.
3. Save the `Bath` file. If you use the file from the CD, choose File ➢ Save As and save it as **Bath**.
4. Choose File ➢ Close to close the Bath drawing.

Next, you will create a new file. But this time, instead of using the Start From Scratch or Use A Template option in the Create New Drawing dialog box, you'll try out the Use A Wizard option.

1. Choose File ➢ New to open the Create New Drawing dialog box.

2. Click the Use A Wizard button to display two options below the drop-down list: Quick Setup and Advanced Setup.

3. Choose Quick Setup and click OK to open the QuickSetup dialog box.

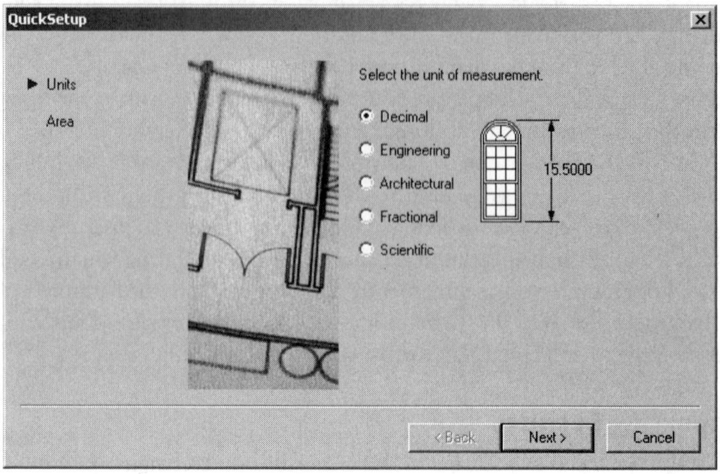

4. Click the Architectural radio button. Metric users should use the default Decimal units.
5. Click Next to display the Area settings.

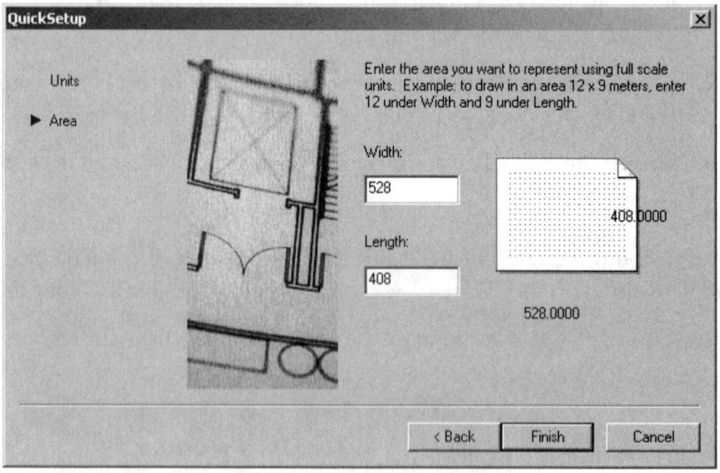

6. Enter **528** in the Width text box and **408** in the Length box. These are the appropriate dimensions for an 8 1/2" × 11" drawing at 1/4"=1'-0" scale. Metric users should enter **1485** for the width and **1050** for the length. This is the work area for a 1:50 scale drawing on an A4 sheet.
7. Click Finish.

8. Choose Tools ➢ Drafting Settings to set the snap spacing to 1" and the grid spacing to 48". The grid spacing setting will change to 4'. This sets the grid spacing to display the equivalent of 1-inch intervals for a 1/4"=1' -0" scale drawing. Metric users should set the snap spacing to 1 and the grid spacing to 120.

TIP *If you need to find out the equivalent drawing area for a given sheet size and scale, see Chapter 3.*

In prior sessions, you opened a blank file and chose Format ➢ Units And Format ➢ Drawing Limits to set up your drawing. This time, you used the QuickSetup Wizard to accomplish the same thing. In fact, the QuickSetup Wizard does nothing more than combine the Format ➢ Units And Format ➢ Drawing Limits options into one dialog box.

Now let's continue by laying out a typical studio unit. You'll also discover how importing a file also imports a variety of drawing items such as layers and line types.

1. Begin the unit by drawing two rectangles, one 14' wide by 24' long, and the other 14' wide by 4' long. Metric users should make the rectangles 426 cm wide by 731 cm long and 427 cm wide by 122 cm long. Place them as shown in Figure 5.8. The large rectangle represents the interior of the apartment unit, and the small rectangle represents the balcony. The size and location of the rectangles are indicated in the figure.

FIGURE 5.8

The apartment unit interior and balcony. Metric locations and dimensions are shown in brackets.

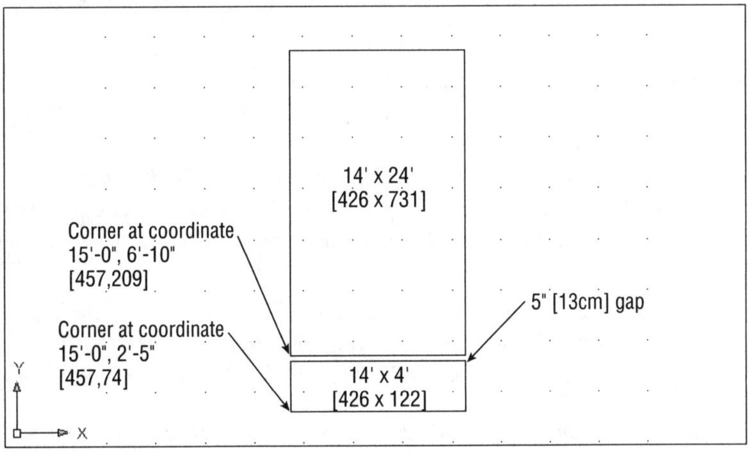

TIP *If you used the Rectangle tool to draw the interior and balcony of the apartment unit, make sure you use the Explode tool on the Modify toolbar to explode the rectangles. The Rectangle tool draws a polyline rectangle instead of simple line segments, so you need to explode the rectangle to reduce it to its component lines. You'll learn more about polylines in Chapter 14.*

2. Click the Insert Block tool on the Draw toolbar to open the Insert dialog box.

3. Click the Browse button, and locate and select the bathroom drawing using the Select Drawing File dialog box. Then click Open.

TIP *If you are using the* `04c-bath.dwg` *file from the CD, do the following: After performing step 3, change the name that appears in the Block text box to Bath instead of* `04c-bath` *before you click OK. This gives the inserted file a block name of Bath, even though its originating filename is* `04c-bath`.

4. Click OK in the Insert dialog box, and then click the upper-left corner of the unit's interior as the insertion point (see Figure 5.9). You can use the Endpoint Osnap to place the bathroom accurately. Use a scale factor of 1.0 and a rotation angle of 0°.

FIGURE 5.9
The unit after the bathroom is inserted

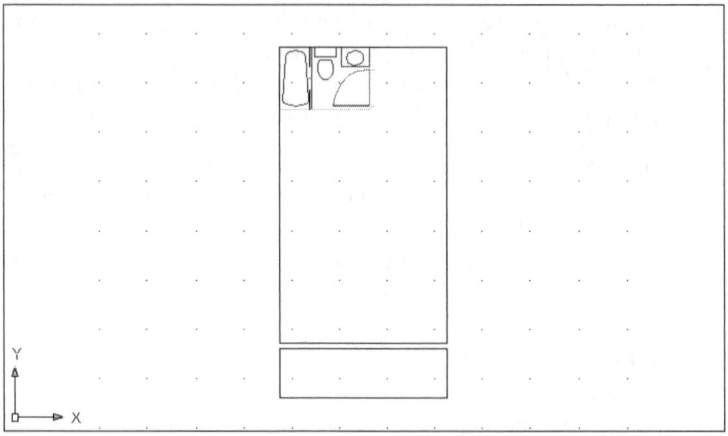

TIP *Because the Running Osnaps have not been set up in this file, you need to use the Osnap shortcut menu (Shift+right-click) to access the Endpoint Osnap. You can set up the Running Osnaps to take advantage of AutoCAD's Auto Snap functions by right-clicking the Osnap box in the status bar. Set the Running Osnaps as described in Chapter 3.*

5. Change the two rectangles that you drew earlier to the Wall layer. To do this, select the two rectangles so they are highlighted, and then open the Layer drop-down list in the Properties toolbar and select Wall. Press the Esc key twice to clear the selection.

TIP *You can also use the Match Properties tool on the Standard toolbar to change layer settings of an object to those of another object in the drawing. See Chapter 6.*

By inserting the bathroom, you imported the layers and blocks contained in the `Bath` file. You were then able to move previously drawn objects to the imported layers. If you are in a hurry, this can be a quick way to duplicate layers that you know exist in another drawing. This method is similar to using an existing drawing as a template, but it allows you to start work on a drawing before deciding which template to use.

WARNING *If two drawings contain the same layers and blocks, and one of these drawings is imported into the other, the layer settings and block definitions of the current file will take priority over those of the imported file. This is important to remember when the layer settings and block definitions are different in the two files.*

Importing Settings from External Reference Files

As explained in Chapter 4, you can use the External Reference (Xref) Attach option to use another file as a background or Xref file. Xref files are similar to blocks except that they do not actually become part of the current drawing's database; nor do the settings from the cross-referenced file automatically become part of the current drawing.

If you want to import layers, line types, text styles, and so forth from an Xref file, you must use the Xbind command, which you will learn more about as you work through this book. Xbind allows you to attach dimension style settings (discussed in Chapter 9 and in Appendix D), layers, line types, or text styles (discussed in Chapter 8) from a cross-referenced file to the current file.

You can also use Xbind to turn a cross-referenced file into an ordinary block, thereby importing all the new settings contained in that file.

See Chapter 13 for a more detailed description of how to use the External References (Xref) and Xbind commands.

Another tool for importing settings is the AutoCAD DesignCenter. You'll learn about the DesignCenter in Chapter 22.

Using Osnap Tracking to Place Objects

You will draw lines in the majority of your work, so it is important to know how to manipulate lines to your best advantage. In this section, you will look at some of the more common ways to use and edit these fundamental drawing objects. The following exercises show you the process of drawing lines, rather than just how individual commands work. While you're building walls and adding doors, you'll get a chance to become more familiar with Polar Tracking and Osnap Tracking.

Roughing In the Line Work

The bathroom you inserted in the last section has only one side of its interior walls drawn. (Walls are usually shown by double lines.) In this next exercise, you will draw the other side. Rather than trying to draw the wall perfectly the first time, you will "sketch" in the line work and then clean it up, in a way similar to manual drafting.

1. Zoom into the bathroom so that the entire bathroom and part of the area around it are displayed, as in Figure 5.10.

TIP *You might notice that some of the arcs in your bathroom drawing are not smooth. Don't be alarmed; this is how AutoCAD displays arcs and circles in enlarged views. The arcs will be smooth when they are plotted. If you want to see them now as they are stored in the file, you can regenerate the drawing by typing* ***Regen↵*** *at the command prompt. Chapter 6 discusses regeneration in more detail.*

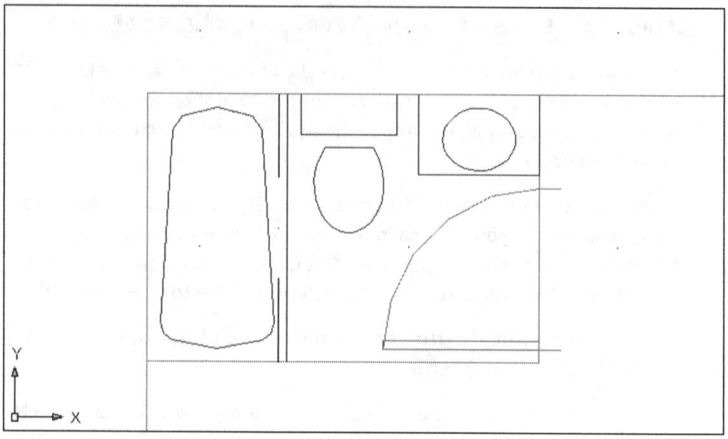

FIGURE 5.10
The enlarged view of the bathroom

2. Select Wall from the Layer drop-down list in the Properties toolbar to make Wall the current layer.
3. Make sure that the Otrack and Osnap buttons on the status bar are pressed, indicating that Osnap Tracking and Object Snap are turned on.

4. Choose Draw ➢ Line, or type L↵.
5. At the `Specify first point:` prompt, move your cursor over the lower-right corner of the bathroom so that the Endpoint Osnap marker appears, but don't click it. As you move the cursor downward, the tracking vector appears. (If the tracking vector doesn't appear at first, move your cursor over the corner again until it does appear.)

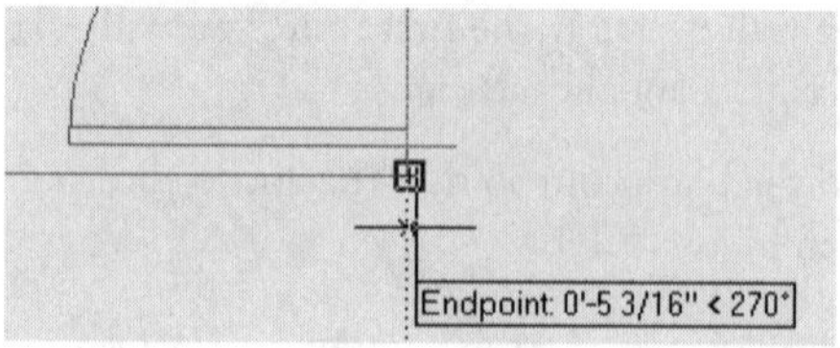

TIP *Remember that a little cross appears at the Osnap location telling you that the Osnap Tracking has "locked on" to that location.*

7. With the tracking vector visible, point the cursor directly downward from the corner, and then type **5↵**. Metric users should type **13↵**. Now a line starts 5" (or 13 cm) below the lower-right corner of the bathroom.

8. Continue the line horizontally to the left to slightly cross the left wall of the apartment unit, as illustrated in the top image in Figure 5.11. Press ↵.

FIGURE 5.11

The first wall line and the wall line by the door

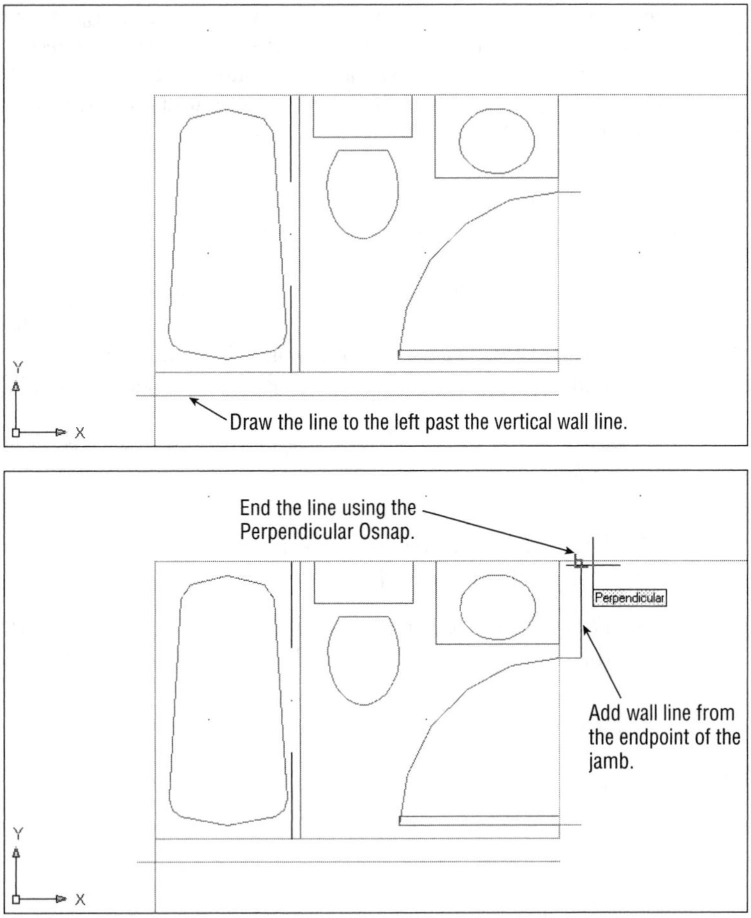

Draw the line to the left past the vertical wall line.
End the line using the Perpendicular Osnap.
Perpendicular
Add wall line from the endpoint of the jamb.

In the previous exercise, Osnap Tracking mode allowed you to specify a starting point of a line at an exact distance from the corner of the bathroom. In step 7, you used the Direct Distance method for specifying distance and direction.

TIP *If you prefer, you can also choose From on the Osnap shortcut menu, and then open the shortcut menu again and select Endpoint. Select the corner and enter a polar coordinate such as @5<-90 to accomplish the same task as this exercise.*

UNDERSTANDING THE OSNAP TRACKING VECTOR

The Osnap Tracking vector only comes into play after you've placed an Osnap marker on a location, in this case, the corner of the bathroom. It won't appear at any other time. If you have both Running Osnaps and Osnap Tracking turned on, you'll get the tracking vector every time the cursor lands on an Osnap location. This can be a bit confusing to novice users, so you might want to use Osnap Tracking sparingly until you become more comfortable with it.

And because Polar Tracking also uses a tracking vector, you can get the two confused. Remember that Polar Tracking lets you point the cursor in a specific direction while selecting points. If you're an experienced AutoCAD user, you can think of it as a more intelligent Ortho mode. On the other hand, Osnap Tracking lets you align points to Osnap locations. Experienced AutoCAD users can think of Osnap Tracking as a more intelligent XYZ filter option.

Now let's continue with the line work.

1. Draw another line upward from the endpoint of the top door jamb to meet the top wall of the unit (see the second image in Figure 5.11). Use the Polar Tracking mode and the Perpendicular Osnap to pick the top wall of the unit. This causes the line to end precisely on the wall line in perpendicular position, as in the bottom image in Figure 5.11.

TIP *You can also use the Perpendicular Osnap override to draw a line perpendicular to a nonorthogonal line—one at a 45° angle, for instance.*

2. Draw a line connecting the two door jambs. Then assign that line to the Ceiling layer (see the first panel in Figure 5.12).
3. Draw a line 6" downward from the endpoint of the door jamb nearest the corner as shown in the second panel in Figure 5.12.

FIGURE 5.12

The corner of the bathroom wall and the filleted wall around the bathroom

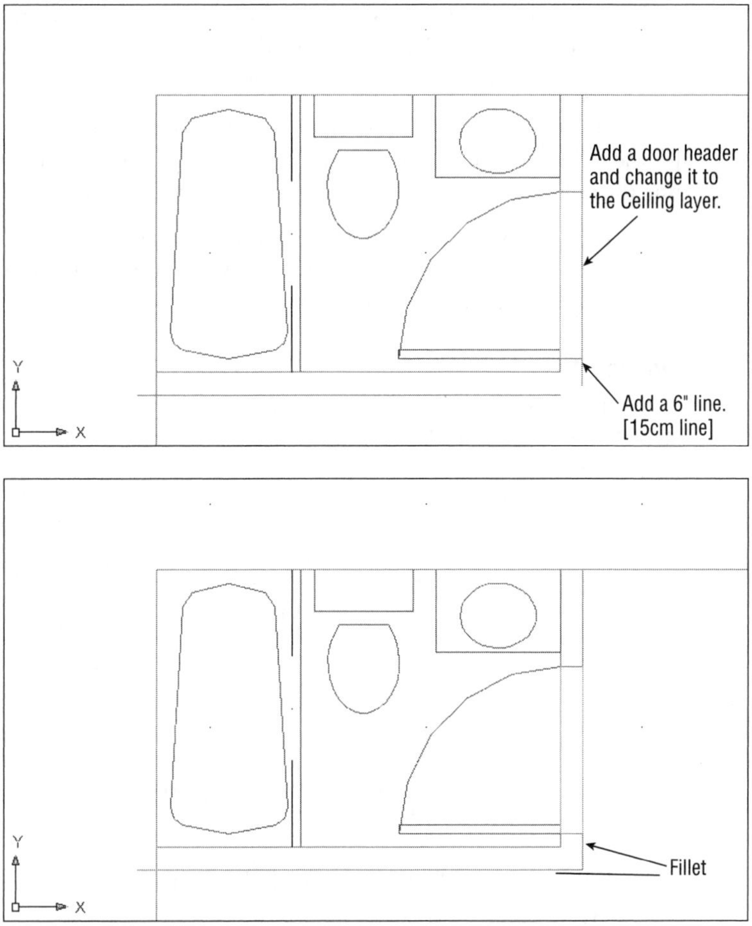
Add a door header
and change it to
the Ceiling layer.
Add a 6" line.
[15cm line]
Fillet

Cleaning Up the Line Work

You've drawn some of the wall lines, approximating their endpoint locations. Next you will use the Fillet command to join lines exactly end to end and then import the Kitchen drawing.

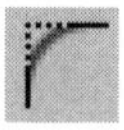

1. Click the Fillet tool on the Modify toolbar.
2. Type **R**↵ **0**↵ to set the fillet radius to 0.

TIP *The Chamfer command performs a similar function to the Fillet command. Unlike Fillet, the Chamfer command allows you to join two lines with an intermediate beveled line rather than an arc. Chamfer can be set to join two lines at a corner in exactly the same manner as Fillet.*

3. Next, fillet the two lines by picking the vertical and horizontal lines, as indicated in the second panel of Figure 5.12. Notice that these points lie on the portion of the line you want to keep. Your drawing will look like the second panel of Figure 5.12.

If you are a veteran AutoCAD user, you should note that since AutoCAD R14, the default value for the Fillet command is now .5 instead of 0. Also note that you no longer have to press ↵ after setting the radius in step 2. The Fillet command now remains active after you set the radius value.

4. Fillet the bottom wall of the bathroom with the left wall of the unit, as shown in Figure 5.13. Make sure the points you pick on the wall lines are on the side of the line you want to keep, not the side you want trimmed.

FIGURE 5.13

The cleaned-up wall intersections

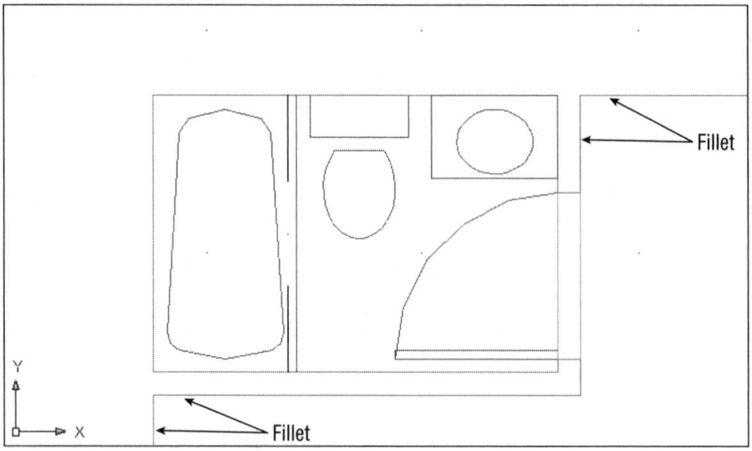

5. Fillet the top wall of the unit with the right-side wall of the bathroom as shown in Figure 5.13.

TIP *You can select two lines at once for the fillet operation by using a Crossing window; type* **C**↵ at the `Select first object:` *prompt. The two endpoints closest to the fillet location are trimmed.*

Where you select the lines affects how the lines are joined. As you select objects for Fillet, the side of the line where you click is the side that remains when the lines are joined. Figure 5.14 illustrates how the Fillet command works and shows what the Fillet options do.

TIP *If you select two parallel lines during the Fillet command, the two lines are joined with an arc.*

FIGURE 5.14

The place where you click the object to select it determines what part of an object gets filleted.

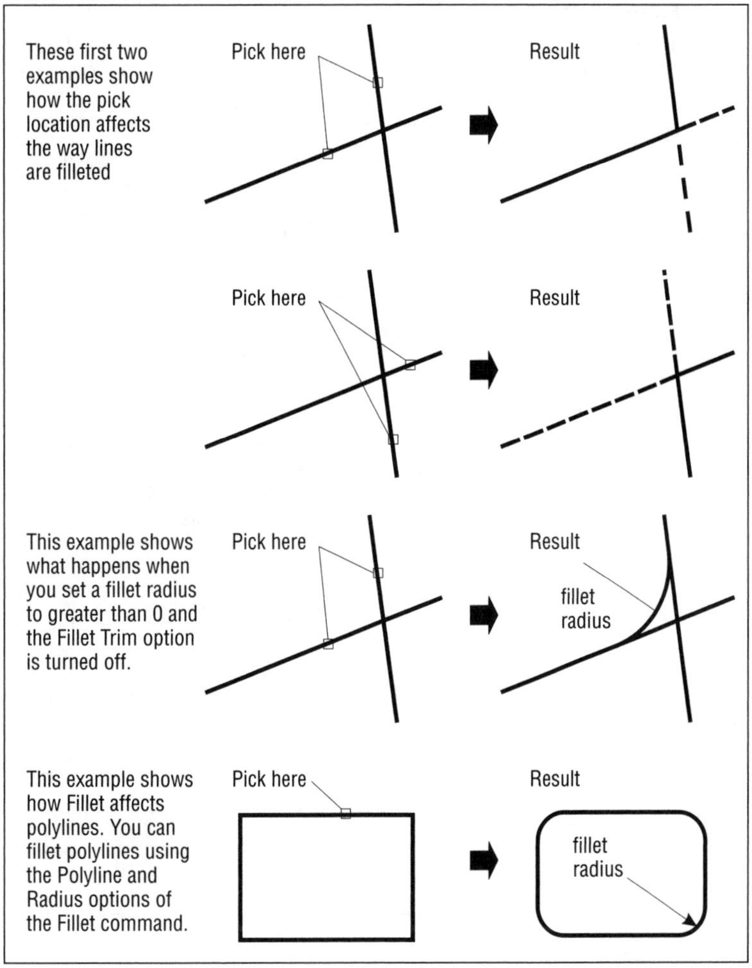

Now import the Kitchen plan you drew earlier in this chapter.

1. Click Insert Block on the Draw toolbar, and then browse to locate the kitchen drawing you created earlier in this chapter. Make sure you leave the Specify On-Screen option unchecked under the Scale and Rotation button groups of the Insert dialog box.
2. Place the kitchen drawing at the wall intersection below the bathtub (see the top image in Figure 5.15).

TIP *If you didn't complete the kitchen earlier in this chapter, you can insert the* `05a-kitchen.dwg` *file from the companion CD.*

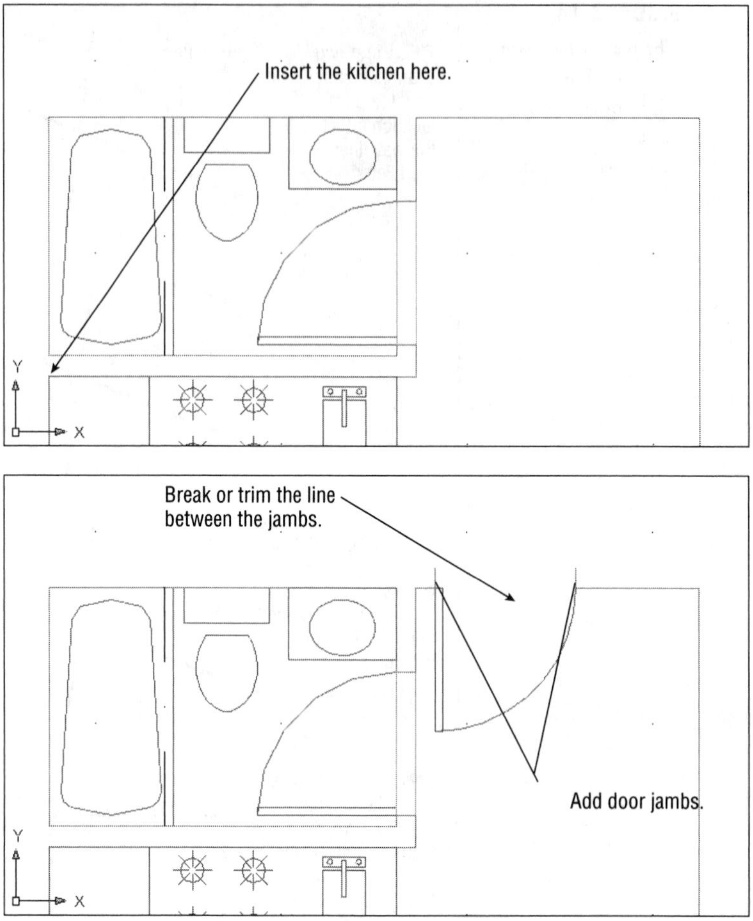

Insert the kitchen here.
Break or trim the line between the jambs.
Add door jambs.

FIGURE 5.15
The view after using Pan, with the door inserted and the jamb and header added

3. Adjust your view with Pan and Zoom so that the upper portion of the apartment unit is centered in the drawing area, as illustrated in the top image in Figure 5.15.

PLACING THE DOOR ACCURATELY

The next step is to add the entry door shown in the bottom image in Figure 5.15. In doing that, you'll use a number of new tools together to streamline the drawing process. You'll practice using the Osnap Tracking feature and the From Osnap option to place the entry door at an exact distance from the upper corner of the floor plan.

1. Right-click the Command window, and choose Recent Commands ➢ Insert from the shortcut menu to open the Insert dialog box.
2. Select Door from the Name drop-down list.

3. Make sure the Specify On-Screen option is checked for the Rotation button group but not in the Scale button group, and then click OK. You'll see the door follow the cursor in the drawing window.
4. Shift+right-click the mouse to open the Osnap shortcut menu, and then choose From.
5. Make sure the Osnap and Otrackbuttons on the status bar are on; then use the Endpoint Running Osnap to pick the corner where the upper horizontal wall line meets the bathroom wall.

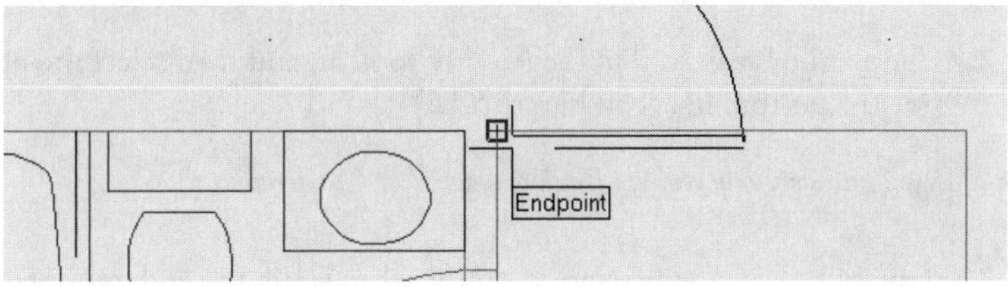

6. Move the cursor over the Osnap marker so that the Osnap Tracking vector appears from the corner. Now as you move the cursor away to the right, you'll see the Osnap Tracking vector extend from the corner.

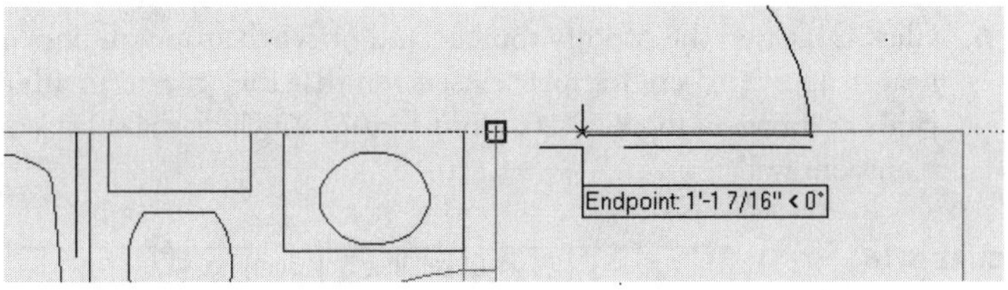

7. Now, move the cursor to the right so that the tracking vector readout shows roughly 6 inches, or 15 cm for metric users.
8. With the cursor in this position, enter **5**↵. Metric users should enter **13**↵. The door is placed exactly 5 (or 13) units to the right of the corner.
9. At the `Specify rotation angle <0>:` prompt, enter **270**↵. Or if you prefer, turn on Polar Tracking to orient the door so that it is swinging *into* the studio. You've now accurately placed the entry door in the studio apartment.

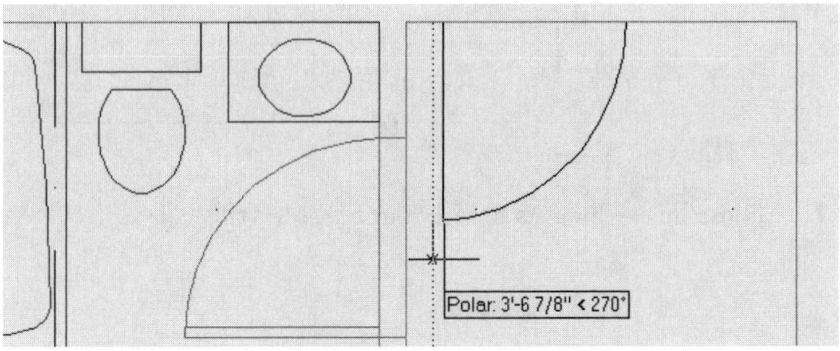

10. Make sure the door is on the Door layer.

TIP *For a shortcut to setting an object's layer, you can select the object or objects, and then select a layer from the Layer drop-down list in the Properties toolbar.*

Now add the finishing touches to the entry door.

1. Add 5" (13 cm for metric users) door jambs and change their Layer property to the Jamb layer, as shown in the bottom image in Figure 5.15.
2. Choose the Break tool in the Modify toolbar, and then select the header over the entry door (see the bottom image in Figure 5.15).

TIP *If you need some help with the Break command, see Chapter 3.*

3. Type F↵ to use the first-point option; then select the endpoint of one of the door jambs.
4. At the `Specify second break point:` prompt, select the endpoint of the other jamb as shown in the bottom image in Figure 5.15.
5. Draw the door header on the Ceiling layer, as shown in Figure 5.16.
6. Click Offset on the Modify toolbar, and offset the top wall lines of the unit and the door header up 5" (13 cm for metric users) so that they connect with the top end of the door jamb, as shown in Figure 5.16. Don't forget to include the short wall line from the door to the bathroom wall.

FIGURE 5.16

The other side of the wall

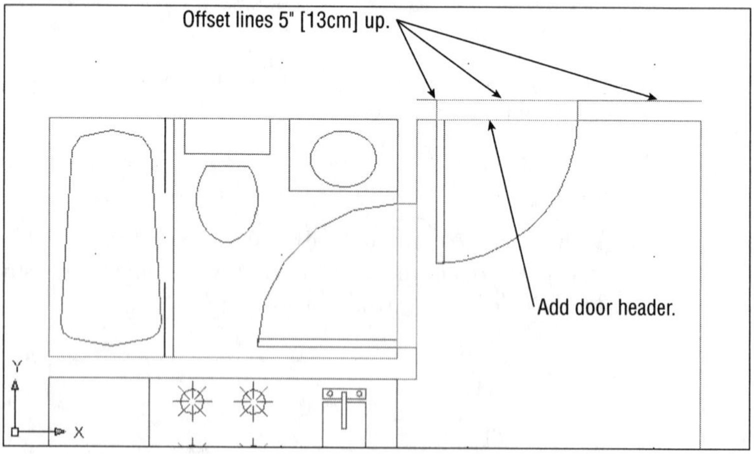

7. Choose File ➢ Save As to save your file as `Unit`.

Other Methods for Using the Break Command

In the exercise for finishing the Unit plan, you used the Break command to accurately place a gap in a line over the entry door. In Chapter 3, you broke a line at a single point to create multiple, contiguous line segments. In both cases you used the F option. You can also break a line without the F option with a little less accuracy. When you don't use the F option, the point at which you select the object is used as the first break point. If you're in a hurry, you can dispense with the F option and simply place a gap in an approximate location. You can then later use other tools to adjust the gap.

In addition, you can use locations on other objects to select the first and second points of a break. For example, you might want to align an opening with another opening some distance away. Once you've selected the line to break, you can then use the F option and select two points on the existing opening to define the first and second break points. The break points will align in an orthogonal direction to the selected points.

Using Polar and Osnap Tracking as a Construction Line Tool

Now you need to extend the upper wall line 5" (13 cm for metric users) beyond the right-side interior wall of the unit. To accomplish this, you will use Polar Tracking to locate the endpoint of the line. Start by changing the Polar Tracking setting to include a 45° angle.

1. Right-click the Polar button in the status bar at the bottom of the AutoCAD window, and choose Settings to open the Drafting Settings dialog box at the Polar Tracking tab.

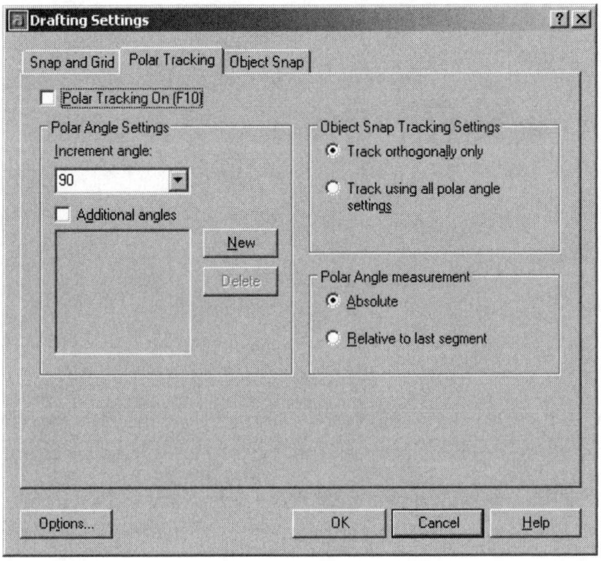

2. Select 45 from the Increment Angle drop-down list in the upper-left corner of the dialog box.

3. In the Object Snap Tracking Settings button group, make sure that the Track Using All Polar Angle Settings option is selected, and click OK.

You're ready to extend the wall line. For this operation, you'll use grip editing.

1. Click the wall line at the top of the plan to the right of the door to select it and expose its grips.

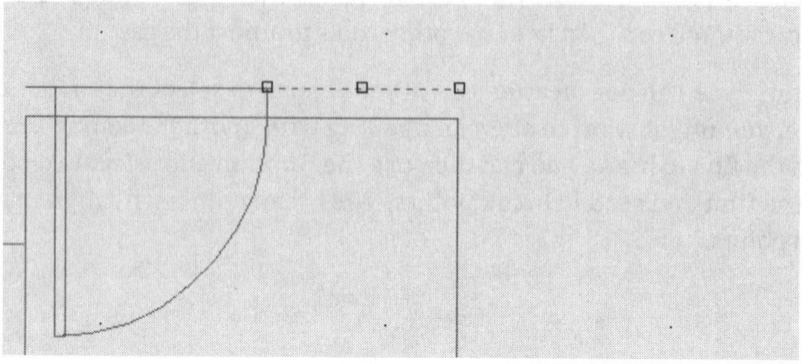

2. Click the Ortho mode button to turn on Ortho mode in the status bar. This keeps the wall line straight as you edit it.
3. Click the rightmost grip of the line to make it "hot."
4. Place the cursor on the upper-right corner of the plan until you see the Endpoint Osnap marker; then move the cursor away from the corner at a 45° angle. The Osnap Tracking vector appears at a 45° angle. Notice the small X that appears at the intersection of the Osnap Tracking vector and the line.

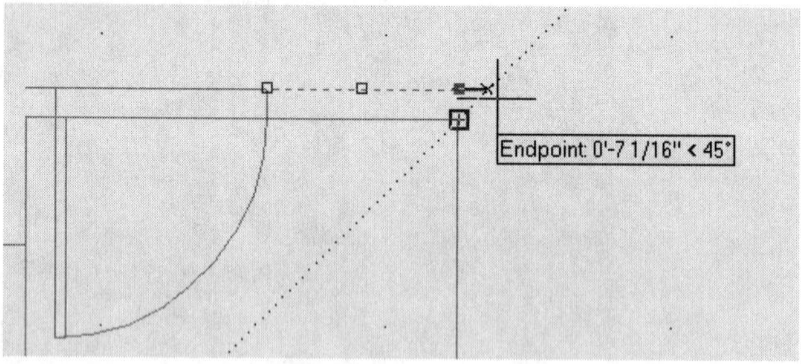

With the Osnap Tracking vector and the line intersecting, click the mouse button. The line changes to extend exactly 5 units beyond the vertical interior wall of the plan.

5. Press the Esc key twice to clear your selection, and then repeat the process for the horizontal wall line to the left of the door to extend that line to the left corner.

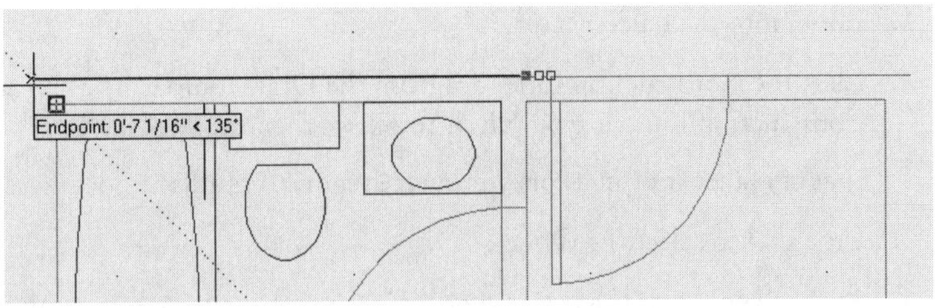

6. Choose View ➢ Zoom ➢ All to view the entire drawing. It will look like Figure 5.17.

TIP *With Polar Tracking set to 45 and Osnap Tracking turned on, you may find that you are selecting points that you don't really want to select in a crowded drawing. Just remember that if a drawing becomes too crowded, you can turn these options off temporarily by clicking the Otrack or Polar buttons in the status bar.*

FIGURE 5.17

The studio unit so far

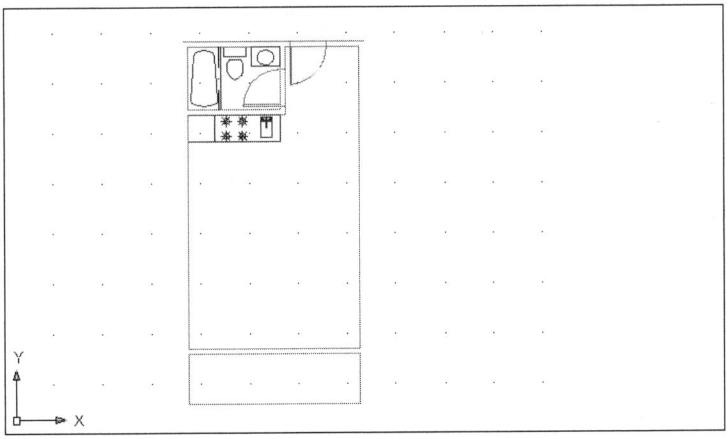

In this exercise, you used Polar Tracking and the Ortho mode to accurately position the two lines used for the exterior walls of the studio unit. This shows how you can take advantage of existing geometry with a combination of tools in the status bar.

TIP *If you prefer to use a standard line instead of a construction line as a construction tool, you can use the ray. A ray is a line that starts from a point you select and continues off to an infinite distance. You specify the start point and angle of the ray. You can place a ray at the corner at a 45° angle and then fillet the ray to the horizontal wall line to shorten or lengthen the line to the appropriate length.*

Now you will finish the balcony by adding a sliding glass door and a rail. This time, you will use lines for construction as well as for parts of the drawing. First, you'll add the door jamb by drawing an Xline. An *Xline* is a line that has an infinite length, but unlike the ray, it extends in both directions. After drawing the Xline, you'll use it to quickly position the door jambs.

1. Zoom into the balcony area.

2. Click the Construction Line tool from the Draw toolbar. You can also choose Draw ➢ Construction Line or type **XL**↵. You'll see this prompt:

   `Specify a point or [Hor/Ver/Ang/Bisect/Offset]:`

3. Type **O**↵ to select the Offset.
4. At the `Specify offset distance or [Through] <0'-5">:` prompt, type **4'**↵. Metric users should type **122**↵.
5. At the `Select a line objects:` prompt, click the wall line at the right of the unit.
6. At the `Specify side to offset:`prompt, click a point to the left of the wall to display the Xline (see the top image of Figure 5.18).

FIGURE 5.18

Drawing the door opening

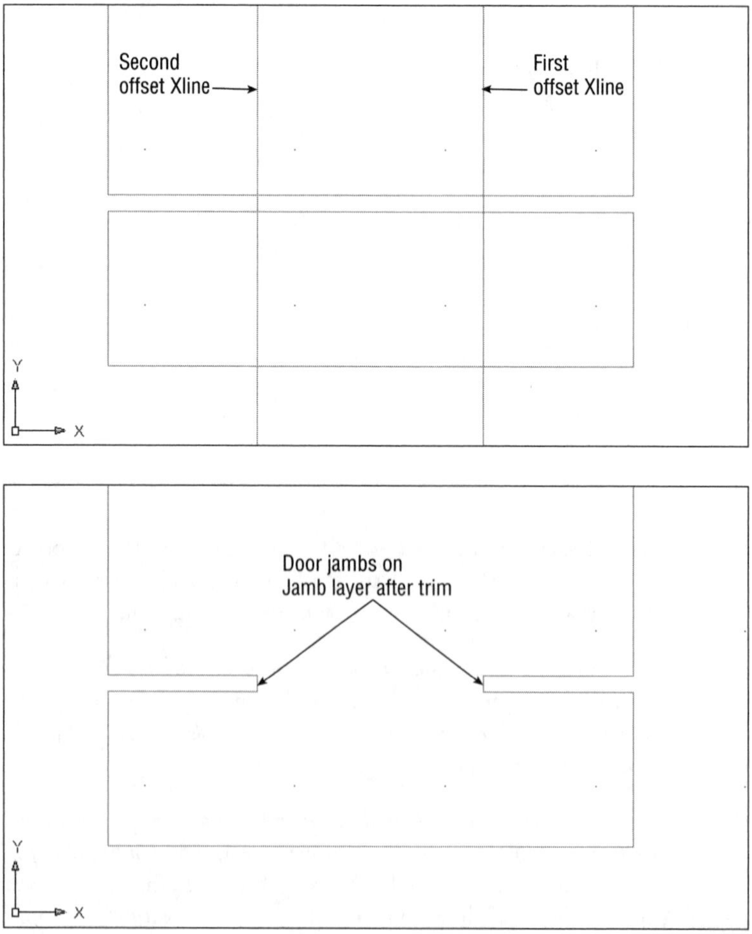

7. At the `Select a line objects:` prompt, click the left wall line, and then click to the right of the selected wall to create another Xline. Your drawing should look like the top image in Figure 5.18.

Next, you'll edit the Xlines to form the jambs.

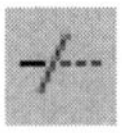

8. Click Trim on the Modify toolbar.
9. Select the Xlines and the two horizontal lines representing the wall between the unit and the balcony, and press ↵. You can either use a crossing window or select each line individually. You have just selected the objects to trim to.

TIP *You can also use the Fence selection option to select the lines to be trimmed. For more information, see Chapter 2 or Chapter 13.*

10. Click the horizontal lines at any point between the two Xlines. Then click the Xlines above and below the horizontal lines to trim them. Your drawing will look like the bottom image in Figure 5.18.
11. Add lines on the Ceiling layer to represent the door header.
12. Now draw lines between the two jambs (on the Door layer) to indicate a sliding glass door (see Figure 5.19).

FIGURE 5.19

Finishing the sliding glass door

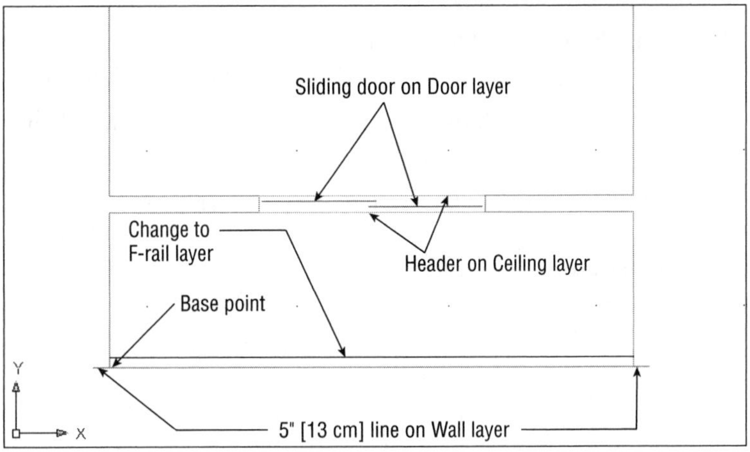

THE XLINE OPTIONS

There is more to the Xline command than you have seen in the exercises of this chapter. Here is a list of the Xline options and their uses:

Hor Draws horizontal Xlines as you click points.

Ver Draws vertical Xlines as you click points.

Angle Draws Xlines at a specified angle as you pick points.

Bisect Draws Xlines bisecting an angle or a location between two points.

Offset Draws Xlines offset at a specified distance.

The wall facing the balcony is now complete. To finish the unit, you need to show a handrail and the corners of the balcony wall.

1. Offset the bottom line of the balcony 3" toward the top of the drawing. Metric users should offset the line 7.6 units.
2. Create a new layer called **F-rail**, and assign this offset line to it.
3. Add a 5" (13 cm for metric users) horizontal line to the lower corners of the balcony, as shown in Figure 5.19.
4. Now choose Draw ➢ Block ➢ Base from the pull-down menu to set the base point at the lower-left corner of the balcony at the location shown in Figure 5.19.
5. Change the lines indicating walls to the Wall layer, and put the sliding glass door on the Door layer (see Figure 5.19).
6. Zoom back to the previous view. Your drawing should now look like Figure 5.20.

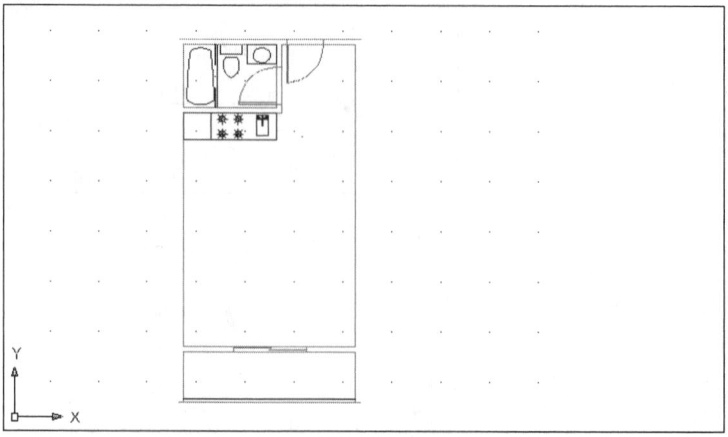

FIGURE 5.20
The completed studio apartment unit

7. Choose File ➢ Save to save the drawing.

Your studio apartment unit plan is now complete. The exercises you've just completed demonstrate a typical set of operations you'll perform while building your drawings. In fact, nearly 80 percent of what you will do in AutoCAD is represented here.

Now, to review the drawing process, and to create a drawing you'll use later, you're going to draw the apartment building's lobby. As you follow the steps, refer to Figure 5.21.

FIGURE 5.21

Drawing the lobby plan. Metric dimensions are shown in brackets.

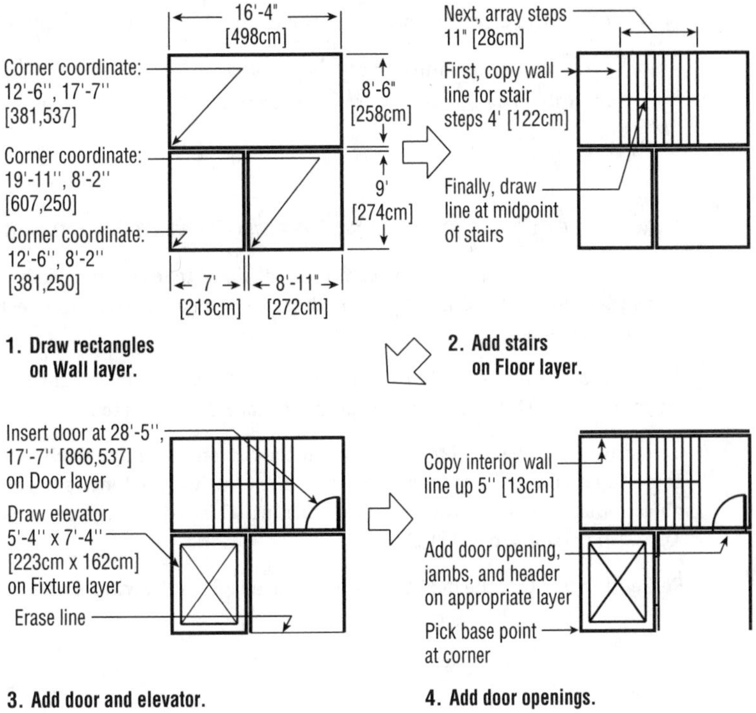

8. As is usual in floor plans, the elevator is indicated by the box with the large X through it, and the stair shaft is indicated by the box with the row of vertical lines through it. If you are in a hurry, use the finished version of this file on the companion CD called `Lobby.dwg` (`Lobby-metric.dwg` for metric users).

To draw the apartment building lobby, follow these steps:

1. Create a new file called Lobby, using the Unit file as a prototype. (Open the Unit file, choose File ➢ Save As, and enter **Lobby** for the new filename.)

2. Erase the entire unit (choose Erase ➢ All).

3. Begin by drawing the three main rectangles that represent the outlines of the stair shaft, the elevator shaft, and the lobby.
4. To draw the stairs, offset the stair shaft's left wall to the right a distance of 4' (122 cm). This creates the first line representing the steps.
5. Array this line in one row of 10 columns, using 11" (28 cm) column spacing.
6. Draw the center line dividing the two flights of stairs.
7. Draw the elevator and insert the door. Practice using Xlines here.
8. Draw the door jambs. Edit the door openings to add the door headers. Your plan should resemble the one in Figure 5.21, step 4.
9. Save the Lobby file.

QUICKLY SETTING THE CURRENT LAYER TO THAT OF AN EXISTING OBJECT

As your list of layers grows, you can find it difficult to locate the exact layer you want quickly. You might know that you want to draw objects on the same layer as an existing object in a drawing, but you are not sure what that layer is.

AutoCAD offers the Make Object's Layer Current tool to help you easily set the current layer. This tool can be found on the Object Properties toolbar next to the Layers tool.

This simple yet powerful tool lets you set the current layer by selecting an object in the drawing instead of selecting its name from a list. To use it, click the Make Object's Layer Current tool, and then click the object whose layer you want to make current. This reduces the three-step or four-step process of earlier AutoCAD versions to one click.

Remember this tool the next time you are faced with a drawing that has a long list of layers.

Finding Distances Along Arcs

You've seen how you can use lines to help locate objects and geometry in your drawing. But if you need to find distances along a curved object such as an arc, lines don't always help. This section describes two ways to find exact distances on arcs. Try these exercises when you're not working through the main tutorial.

FINDING A POINT AT A PARTICULAR DISTANCE FROM ANOTHER POINT

At times you'll need to find the location of a point on an arc that lies at a known straight-line distance from another point on the arc. The distance can be described as a *chord* of the arc, but how do you find the exact chord location? To find a chord along an arc, follow these steps.

1. Click the Circle tool on the Draw toolbar or type **C↵**.
2. Use the Endpoint Osnap to click the endpoint of an arc.

3. At the `Specify radius of circle or [Diameter]:` prompt, enter the length of the chord distance you want to locate along the arc.

The point where the circle intersects the arc is the endpoint of the chord (see Figure 5.22). You can then use the Intersect Osnap override to select the circle and arc intersection.

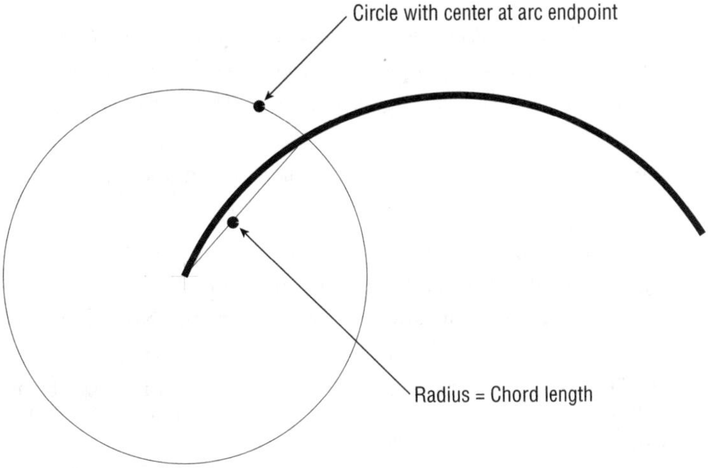

FIGURE 5.22
Finding a chord distance along an arc using a circle

FINDING AN EXACT DISTANCE ALONG AN ARC

To find an exact distance along an arc or curve (nonlinear), or to mark off specific distance increments along an arc or curve, do the following:

1. Choose Format ➢ Point Style from the pull-down menu to open the Point Style dialog box.

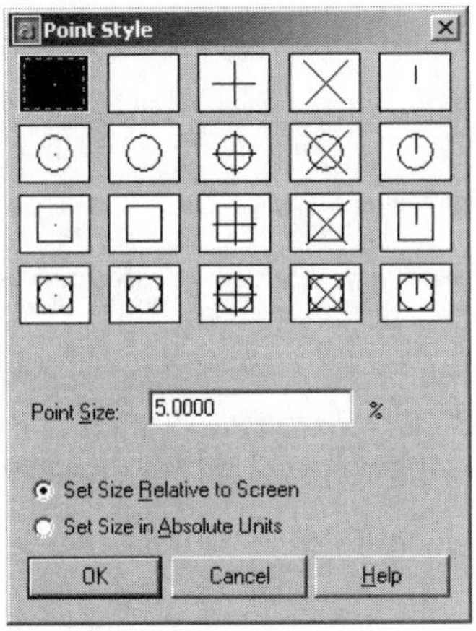

TIP *You can also set the point style by setting the Pdmode system variable to 3. See Appendix D for more on Pdmode.*

2. In the Point Style dialog box, click the X icon in the top row. Also be sure the Set Size Relative To Screen radio button is selected. Then click OK.
3. Choose Draw ➢ Point ➢ Measure from the pull-down menu or type **me**↵.

TIP *The Divide command (choose Draw ➢ Point ➢ Divide) marks off a line, an arc, or a curve into equal divisions, as opposed to divisions of a length you specify. You might use Divide to divide an object into 12 equal segments, for example. Aside from this difference in function, Divide works in exactly the same way as Measure.*

4. At the `Select object to measure:` prompt, click the arc near the end from which you want to find the distance.
5. At the `Specify length of segment or [Block]:` prompt, enter the distance you want. A series of Xs appears on the arc, marking off the specified distance along the arc. You can select the exact location of the Xs using the Node Osnap override (see Figure 5.23).

FIGURE 5.23

Finding an exact distance along an arc using points and the Measure command

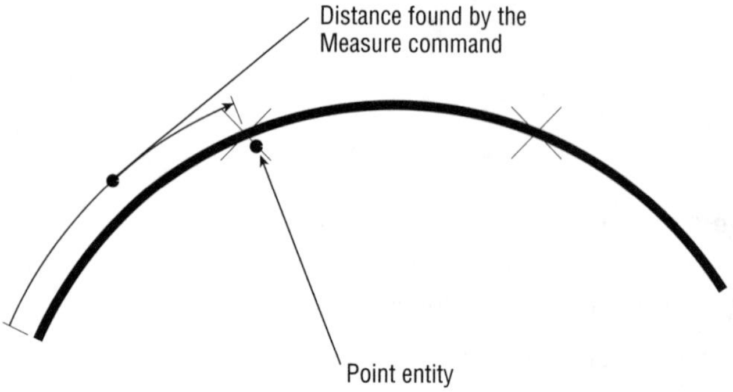

TIP *The Block option of the Measure command allows you to specify a block to be inserted at the specified segment length, in place of the Xs on the arc. You can align the block with the arc as it is inserted. (This is similar to the polar array's Rotate Objects As They Are Copied option.)*

The Measure command also works on Bezier curves. You'll get a more detailed look at the Measure command in Chapter 14.

As you work with AutoCAD, you'll find that constructing temporary geometry such as the circle and points in the two previous examples will help you solve problems in new ways. Don't hesitate to experiment! Remember, you've always got the Save and Undo commands to help you recover from mistakes.

Changing the Length of Objects

Suppose that, after finding the length of an arc, you realize you need to lengthen the arc by a specific amount. Choosing Modify ➢ Lengthen lets you lengthen or shorten arcs, lines, splines, and elliptical arcs. As an example, here's how to lengthen an arc.

1. Choose Modify ➢ Lengthen or type **len**↵.
2. At the `Select an object or [DElta/Percent/Total/DYnamic]:` prompt, type **T**↵.
3. At the `Specify total length or [Angle] <1.0000)>:` prompt, enter the length you want for the arc.
4. At the `Select an object to change or [Undo]:` prompt, click the arc you want to change. Be sure to click at a point nearest the end you want to lengthen. The arc increases in length to the size you specified.

The Lengthen command also shortens an object if it is currently longer than the value you enter.

In this short example, you have learned how to change an object to a specific length. You can use other criteria to change an object's length, using these options available for the Lengthen command:

DElta Lets you lengthen or shorten an object by a specific length. To specify an angle rather than a length, use the Angle suboption.

Percent Lets you increase or decrease the length of an object by a percentage of its current length.

Total Lets you specify the total length or angle of an object.

DYnamic Lets you graphically change the length of an object using your cursor.

Creating a New Drawing Using Parts from Another Drawing

This section explains how to use the Wblock command (which you learned about in Chapter 4), to create a separate stair drawing using the stair you've already drawn for the lobby. Although you haven't turned the existing stair into a block, you can still use Wblock to turn parts of a drawing into a file.

1. If you closed the `Lobby` file, open it now. If you didn't create the Lobby drawing, open the `Lobby.dwg` file from the companion CD.
2. Chose File ➢ Export or type **export**↵ to open the Export Data File dialog box.
3. Enter **stair.dwg** in the File Name text box and click Save. By including the .dwg filename extension, you let AutoCAD know that you want to export to a drawing file and not some other format, such as a .dxf or .wmf file format.
4. At the `Enter name of existing block or [= (block=output file)/* (whole drawing)] <define new drawing>:` prompt, press ↵. When you export to a .dwg format, AutoCAD assumes you want to export a block. Bypassing this prompt by pressing ↵ tells AutoCAD that you want to create a file from part of the drawing, rather than from a block.
5. At the `Specify insertion base point:` prompt, pick the lower-right corner of the stair shaft. This tells AutoCAD the base point for the new drawing.

6. At the `Select objects:` prompt, use a window to select the stair shaft, as shown in Figure 5.24.

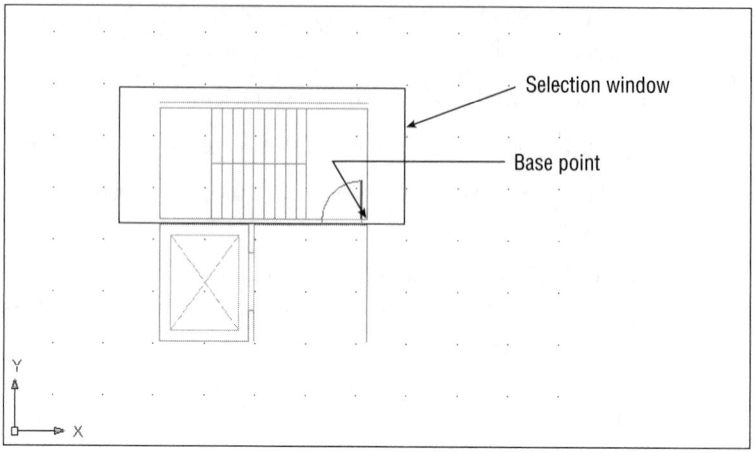

FIGURE 5.24
A selection window enclosing the stair shaft

7. When the stair shaft, including the door, is highlighted, press ↵ to confirm your selection. The stair disappears.
8. Since you want the stair to remain in the lobby drawing, click the Undo button to bring it back. Undo does not affect any files you might export by choosing File ➢ Export, by using Wblock, or by using the Make Block tool.

Drawing Parallel Lines

ACAD only

Frequently, when working on an architectural project, you will first do your schematic layout using simple lines for walls. Then, as the design requirements begin to take shape, you can start to add more detailed information about the walls, for example, indicating wall materials or locations for insulation. AutoCAD provides *multilines* (the Multiline command and its equivalent tool on the Draw toolbar) for this purpose. Multilines are double lines that you can use to represent walls. You can also customize multilines to display solid fills, center lines, and additional line types, as shown in Figure 5.25. You can save your custom multilines as Multiline styles, which are in turn saved in special files for easy access from other drawings.

WARNING *The Multiline command is not available in AutoCAD LT 2004. LT does offer the Dline command which draws simple parallel lines. To use it, enter DL↵ or Dline↵ at the command prompt. Use the Width option to control the distance between the parallel lines.*

TIP *Multilines are especially useful for metric users who need to represent cavity walls.*

The following exercise shows how you might continue to build information into your drawings by using multilines to indicate wall types.

1. Choose Draw ➢ Multiline from the menubar, or type **ML**↵. You'll see two lines in the prompt area:

```
Current settings: Justification = Top, Scale = 1.00, Style = STANDARD
Specify start point or [Justification/Scale/STyle]:
```

FIGURE 5.25

Samples of multiline styles

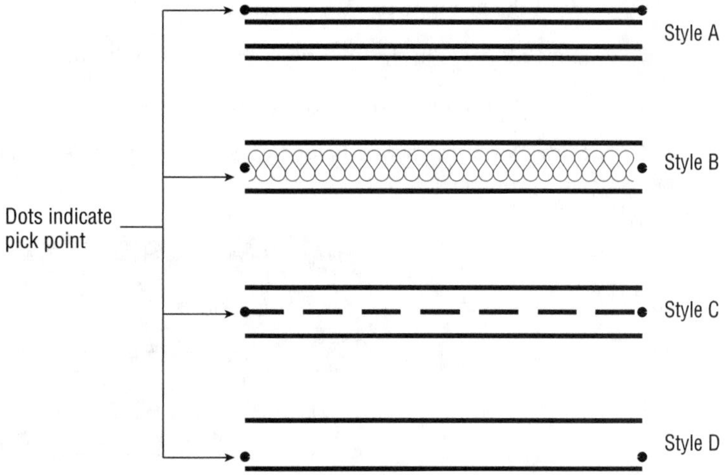

TIP *The first line in the prompt area gives you the current settings for Multiline.*

2. Type **S**↵ (for Scale).
3. At the `Enter mline scale <1.00>:` prompt, type **5**↵.
4. Pick a point to start the double line.
5. Continue to select points to draw more double-line segments, or type **C**↵ to close the series of lines.

Let's take a look at the meaning of the multiline settings included in the prompt you saw in steps 1 and 2.

Justification Controls how far off center the double lines are drawn. The default sets the double lines equidistant from the points you pick. By changing the justification value to be greater than or less than 0, you can have AutoCAD draw double lines off center from the pick points.

Scale Lets you set the width of the double line.

Close Closes a sequence of double lines, much as the Line command's Close option does.

Style Lets you select a style for multilines. You can control the number of lines in the multiline, as well as the line types used for each line in the multiline style, by using the Mledit command.

Customizing Multilines

In Chapter 4 you learned how to make a line appear dashed or dotted using line types. In a similar way, you can control the appearance of multilines using the Multiline Style dialog box. This dialog box allows you to do the following:

- Set the number of lines that appear in the multiline
- Control the color of each multiline
- Control the line type of each multiline
- Apply a fill between the outermost lines of a multiline
- Control if and how ends of multilines are closed

To open the Multiline Styles dialog box, choose Format ➤ Multiline Style , or type **Mlstyle↵** at the command prompt.

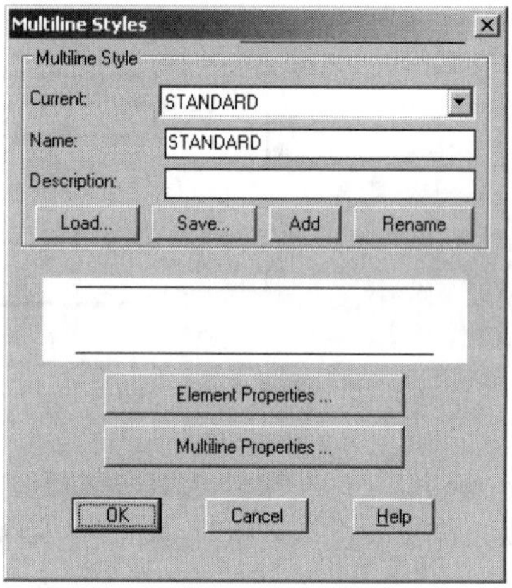

WARNING *Once you have drawn a multiline in a particular style, you cannot modify the style settings for that style in the Element Properties and Multiline Properties dialog boxes described later in this section. The Multiline Styles dialog box only allows you to set up styles before they are used in a drawing.*

At the top of the Multiline Styles dialog box, a group of buttons and text boxes allow you to select the multiline style you want to work with. The Current drop-down list offers a selection of existing styles. In the Name text box, you can name a new style you are creating or rename an existing style. The Description text box lets you attach a description to a multiline style for easy identification. You use the Add and Save buttons to create and save multiline styles as files so they can be accessed by any AutoCAD drawing. With the Load button, you can retrieve a saved style for use in the current drawing. Rename lets you change the name of a multiline style. (The default style in a new drawing is called Standard.)

In the lower half of the Multiline Styles dialog box are two buttons—Element Properties and Multiline Properties—that allow you to make adjustments to the multiline style currently indicated at the top of the dialog box. This multiline is also previewed in the middle of the dialog box.

ELEMENT PROPERTIES

Click the Element Properties button to open the Element Properties dialog box, in which you control the properties of the individual elements of a newly created style, including the number of lines that appear in the multiline, their color, and the distance they appear from your pick points. The Element Properties settings are not available for existing multiline styles.

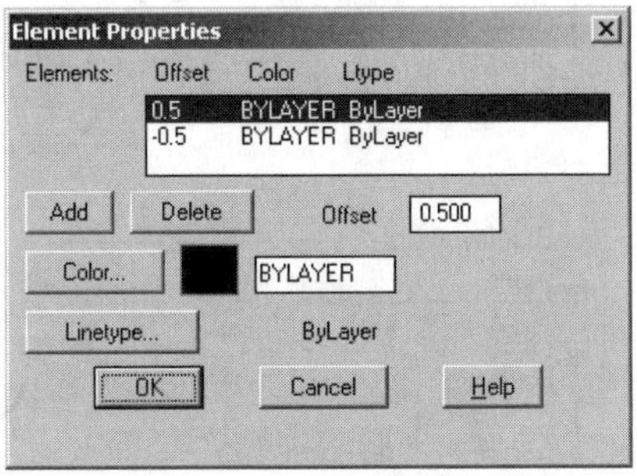

For example, click the Add button to add another line to your multiline. The offset distance of the new line appears in the list box. The default value for new lines is 0.0, which places the line at the center of the standard multiline. To delete a line, highlight its offset value in the list box and click the Delete button. To change the amount of offset, highlight it and enter a new value in the Offset text box.

To change the color and line type of individual lines, use the Color and Linetype buttons, which open the Color and Select Linetype dialog boxes, both of which you have already worked with. Figure 5.26 contains some examples of multilines and their corresponding Element Properties settings.

TIP *You can easily indicate an insulated wall in an architectural drawing by adding a third center line (offset of 0.0) and giving that center line a batting line. This line type draws an S-shaped pattern typically used to represent fiberglass batt insulation in a floor plan. To see how other wall patterns can be created, see Chapter 21.*

FIGURE 5.26

Samples of multiline styles you can create

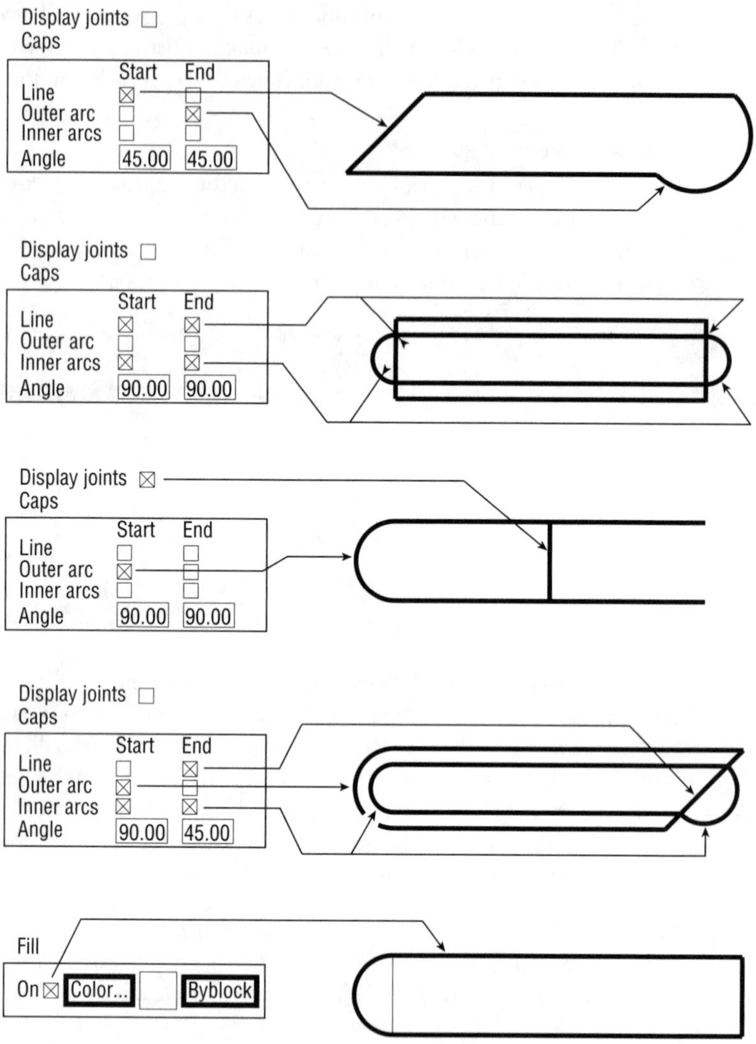

MULTILINE PROPERTIES

Click the Multiline Properties button in the Multiline Styles dialog box to open the Multiline Properties dialog box, which lets you control how the multiline is capped at its ends, as well as whether joints are displayed.

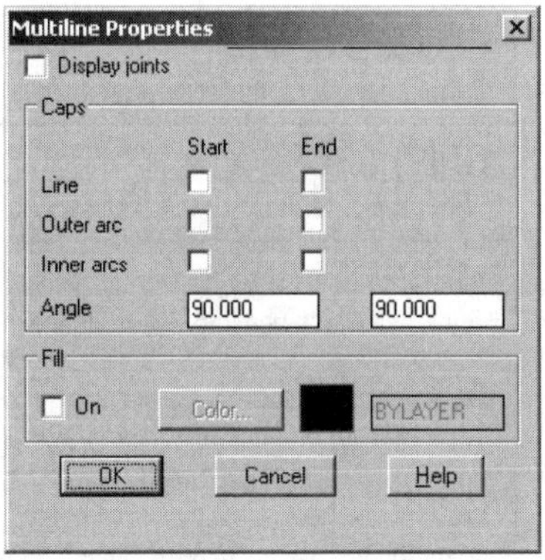

To turn a cap on, click the check box next to the type of cap you want. If you prefer, you can give your multiline style a solid fill by clicking the On check box in the Fill section.

TIP *You can use a solid-filled multiline where you need to fill in a wall with a solid shade (or pouche, to use the drafting term). You can quickly add a pouche by setting one multiline offset to be 0.0 and the other to be the width of the wall. Then trace either the inside or outside of the wall to be pouched, using the multiline style with the Fill option turned on.*

Joining and Editing Multilines

Multilines are unique in their ability to combine several line types and colors into one entity. For this reason, you need special tools to edit them. AutoCAD provides the Modify menu's Object Multiline option and the command line's Mledit command; both have the sole purpose of allowing you to join multilines in a variety of ways, as demonstrated in Figure 5.27.

Here's how to edit multilines.

1. Type **Mledit↵** at the command prompt, or choose Modify ➢ Object ➢ Multiline to open the Multiline Edit Tools dialog box (see Figure 5.28), which provides a variety of ways to edit your multilines.
2. Click the graphic that best matches the edit you want to perform.
3. Select the multilines you want to join or edit.

Another option is to explode multilines and edit them using the editing tools you've used in this and previous chapters. When a multiline is exploded, it is reduced to its component lines. Line-type assignments and layers are maintained for each component.

If you are doing a lot of work with multilines, you can open the Modify II toolbar. It contains the Edit Multiline button that opens the Multiline Edit Tools dialog box. To open the Modify II toolbar, right-click any toolbar and then click the Modify II check box in the Toolbars shortcut menu.

FIGURE 5.27
The Mledit options and their meanings

CLOSED CROSS Trims one of two intersecting multilines so that they appear overlapping.	
OPEN CROSS Trims the outer lines of two intersecting multilines.	
MERGED CROSS Joins two Multilines into one multiline.	
CLOSED TEE Trims the leg of a tee intersection to the first line.	
OPEN TEE Joins the outer lines of a multiline tee intersection.	
MERGED TEE Joins all the lines in a multiline tee intersection	
CORNER JOINT Joins two multilines into a corner joint.	
ADD VERTEX Adds a vertex to a multiline. The vertex can later be moved.	
DELETE VERTEX Deletes a vertex to straighten a multiline.	
CUT SINGLE Creeates an opening in a single line of a multiline.	
CUT ALL Creates a break across all lines in a multiline.	
WELD Closes a break in a multiline.	

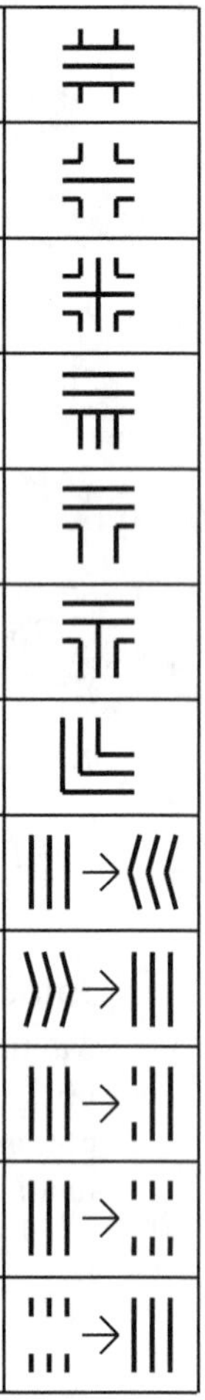

FIGURE 5.28
The Multiline Edit Tools dialog box

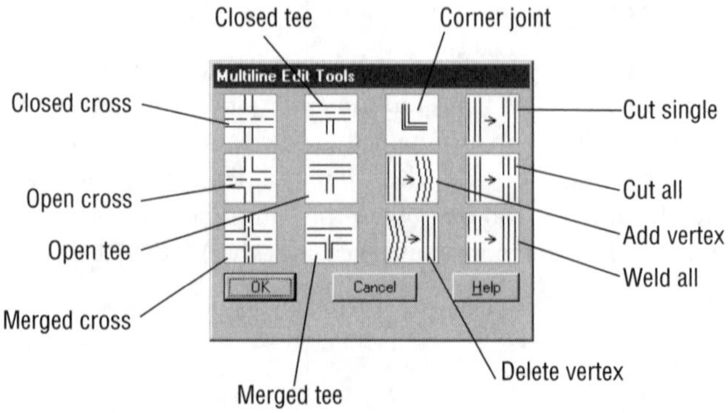

Eliminating Blocks, Layers, Line Types, Shapes, and Styles

A template can contain blocks and layers you don't need in your new file. For example, the lobby you just completed contains the bathroom block because you used the Unit file as a prototype. Even though you erased this block, it remains in the drawing file's database. It is considered "unused" because it doesn't appear as part of the drawing. Such extra blocks can slow you down by increasing the amount of time needed to open the file. They will also increase the size of your file unnecessarily. You can eliminate unused elements from a drawing in two ways: by using the Purge command and by choosing File ➢ Export.

Selectively Removing Unused Elements

You use the Purge command to remove unused individual blocks, layers, line types, shapes, and text styles from a drawing file. To help keep the file size small and to make layer maintenance easier, you will want to purge your drawing of unused elements. Bear in mind, however, that the Purge command does not delete certain primary drawing elements—namely, layer 0, the Continuous line type, and the standard text style.

1. Choose File ➢ Open and open the Lobby file.
2. Choose File ➢ Drawing Utilities ➢ Purge to open the Purge dialog (see Figure 5.29). You'll see a listing of drawing components that can be purged. If the drawing contains any of the types of components listed, you'll see a plus sign to the left of the component name.

FIGURE 5.29
The Purge dialog box

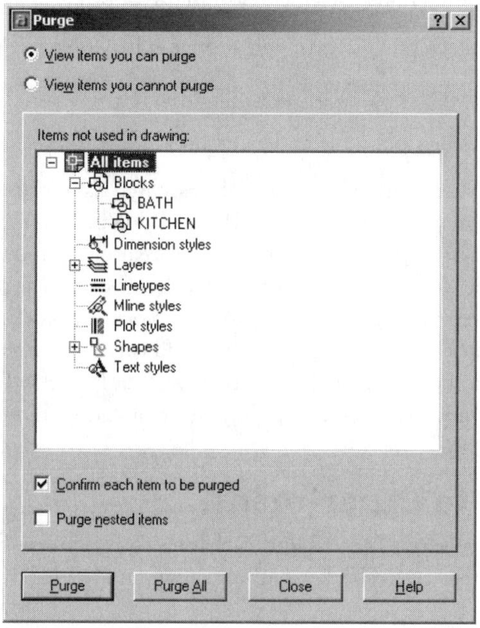

3. Click the plus sign of the component you want to purge. In this exercise, click the plus sign next to the Blocks listing. The list expands to show the names of the items under the component category.
4. Select the name BATH from the expanded list. If you want to select more than one item, you can Ctrl+click individual names or Shift+click to select a group of names.
5. Once the components are selected, click the Purge button in the lower-left corner of the dialog box.

Removing All Unused Elements

In the last exercise, you selected a single block for removal from the Lobby file. If you want to clear all the unused elements from a file at once, you can click the Purge All button at the bottom of the Purge dialog box (see Figure 5.29).

1. Choose File ➢ Drawing Utilities ➢ Purge.
2. Click the Purge Nested Items check box to turn this option on.
3. Click Purge All to open the Confirm Purge dialog box, asking you if you want to purge a block.
4. Click Yes. The Confirm Purge dialog displays the name of another block, asking you to confirm the purge. You can continue to click Yes, and AutoCAD will display the Confirm Purge dialog box for each unused element still in the drawing.
5. Click Yes to All To purge everything at once. The Confirm Purge dialog box closes.
6. At the Purge dialog box, click Close.
7. Close and save the Lobby file and exit AutoCAD.

The Lobby file is now trimmed down to the essential data it needs and nothing else. You might have noticed that when you returned to the Purge dialog box in step 6, the items in the list box no longer showed plus signs. This indicates that there are no longer any unused items in the drawing.

In this last exercise, you used the Purge Nested Items option at the bottom of the dialog box. In the past, the Purge command did not purge nested blocks or blocks that are components of other blocks. You had to either repeat the Purge command over and over until all the nested blocks were removed or employ some arcane operations that were fairly tricky. The Purge Nested Items option automatically purges unused blocks, including those nested within other blocks.

If You Want to Experiment...

Try using the techniques you learned in this chapter to create new files. Use the files you created in Chapter 4 as prototypes to create the symbols shown in Figure 5.30.

Chapter 6

Enhancing Your Drawing Skills

Now that you have created drawings of a typical apartment unit and the apartment building's lobby and stairs, you can assemble them to complete the first floor of the apartment building. In this chapter, you will take full advantage of AutoCAD's features to enhance your drawing skills, as well as to reduce the time it takes to create accurate drawings.

As your drawing becomes larger, you will find that you need to use the Zoom and Pan commands more often. Larger drawings also require some special editing techniques. You will learn how to assemble and view drawings in ways that will save you time and effort as your design progresses. Along the way, you'll see how you can enhance the appearance of your drawings by adding hatch patterns. This chapter includes the following topics:

- Assembling the Parts
- Taking Control of the AutoCAD Display
- Using Hatch Patterns in Your Drawings
- Using External References
- If You Want to Experiment...

Assembling the Parts

Start by creating a new file for the first floor.

1. Create a new file named Plan to contain the drawing of the apartment building's first floor. This is the file you will use to assemble the unit plans into an apartment building. If you want to use a template file, use the `Acad.dwt` template file. Metric users can use the `Acadiso.dwt` template file.
2. Set the Units style to Architectural (choose Format ➢ Units).
3. Set up the drawing for a 1/8"=1'-0" scale on a 24" × 18" drawing area (choose Format ➢ Drawing Limits). If you look at Table 3.2 in Chapter 3, you'll see that such a drawing requires

an area 2304 units wide × 1728 units deep. Metric users should set up a drawing at 1:100 scale on an A2 sheet size. If you look at Table 3.3, you'll see that your drawing area should be 5940 cm × 4200 cm.

4. Create a layer called Plan1 and make it the current layer.
5. In the Drafting Settings dialog box, set the Snap mode to 1, and set the grid to 8', which is the distance required to display 1-inch divisions in a 1/8"=1'-0" scale drawing. Metric users can set the Grid mode to 250.
6. Turn on the grid.
7. Choose View ➢ Zoom ➢ All or type **Z↵ A↵** to get an overall view of the drawing area.

Now you're ready to start building a floor plan of the first floor from the Unit plan. You'll start by creating a mirrored copy of the apartment plan.

1. Make sure Running Osnaps are turned off, and then insert the `Unit.dwg` drawing at coordinate 31'-5",43'-8" (957,1330 for metric users). Accept the default.

TIP *If you prefer, you can specify the insertion point in the Insert dialog box by removing the checkmark from the Specify On-Screen check box. The Input options in the dialog box then become available to receive your input.*

2. Zoom in to the apartment unit plan.
3. Click Mirror on the Modify toolbar, select the Unit plan, and press ↵.
4. At the `Specify first point of the mirror line:` prompt, Shift+right-click the mouse and choose From.
5. Shift+right-click again and choose Endpoint.
6. Select the endpoint of the upper-right corner of the apartment unit, as shown in Figure 6.1.

FIGURE 6.1
The Unit plan mirrored

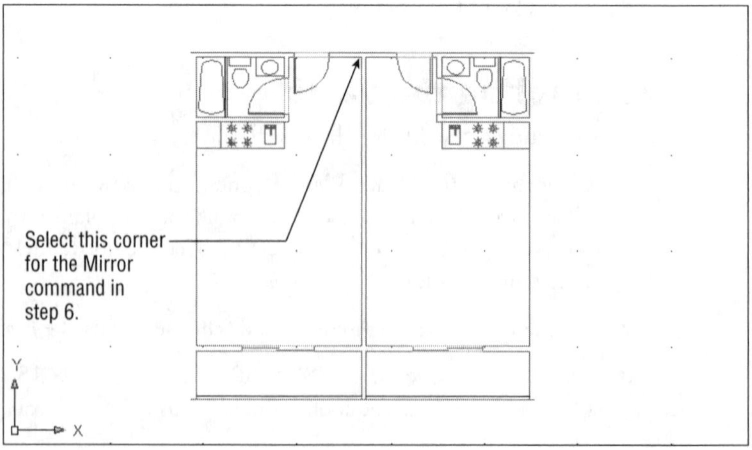

Select this corner for the Mirror command in step 6.
Y
X

7. Enter **@2.5<0↵**. Metric users should enter **@6.5<0↵**. A rubber-banding line appears, indicating the mirror axis.
8. Turn on the Ortho mode and select any point to make the mirror axis point in a vertical orientation.
9. At the `Delete Source Objects? [Yes/No] <N>:` prompt, press ↵. You will get a 5" wall thickness between two studio units. Your drawing should be similar to Figure 6.1.

You now have a mirror image copy of the original plan in the exact location required for the overall plan. Now make some additional copies for the opposite side of the building.

1. Press ↵ to reissue the Mirror command and select both units.
2. Use the From Osnap again, and, using the Endpoint Osnap, select the same corner you selected in step 6.
3. Enter **@24<90** to start a mirror axis 24 inches directly above the selected point. Metric users should enter **@61<90**.
4. With the Ortho mode on, select a point so that the mirror axis is exactly horizontal.
5. Press ↵ to keep the original units and complete the mirror operation.

With the tools you've learned about so far, you've quickly and accurately set up a fairly good portion of the floor plan. Continue with the next few steps to "rough-in" the main components of the floor.

1. Choose View ➢ Zoom ➢ Extents or type **Z↵ E↵** to get a view of the four plans. You can also use the Extents tool on the Zoom Window tool flyout. The Extents option forces the entire drawing to fill the screen at the leftmost side of the display area. Your drawing will look like Figure 6.2.

FIGURE 6.2
The Unit plan, duplicated four times

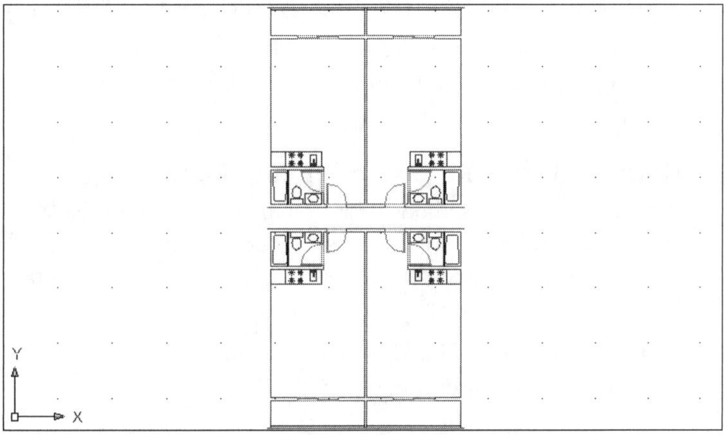

TIP *If you happen to insert a block in the wrong coordinate location, you can use the Properties palette to change the insertion point for the block.*

2. Copy the four units to the right at a distance of 28'-10" (878 cm for metric users), which is the width of two units from centerline to centerline of walls.
3. Insert the lobby at coordinate 89'-1",76'-1" (2713,2318 for metric users).
4. Copy all the unit plans to the right 74'-5" (2267 cm for metric users), the width of four units plus the width of the lobby.
5. Choose View ➢ Zoom ➢ All or type **Z↵ A↵** to view the entire drawing, which should look like Figure 6.3. You can also use the Zoom All tool on the Zoom Window flyout.

FIGURE 6.3

The Plan drawing

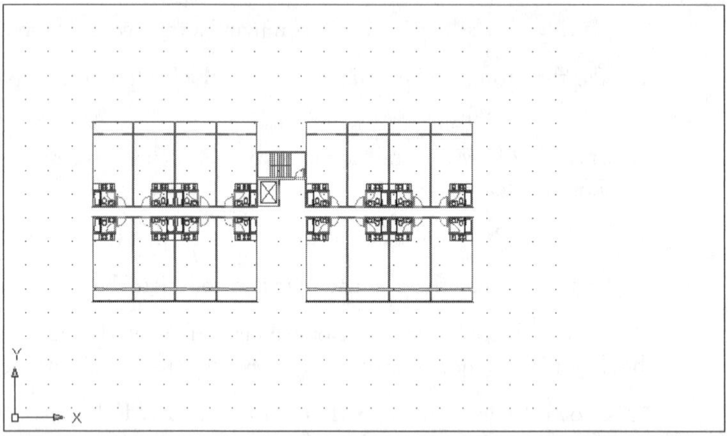

6. Choose File ➢ Save to save this `Plan.dwg` file to disk.

Taking Control of the AutoCAD Display

By now you should be familiar with the Pan and Zoom functions in AutoCAD. Many other tools can also help you get around in your drawing. In this section, you'll get a closer look at the different ways you can view your drawing.

Understanding Regeneration and Redrawing

AutoCAD uses two methods for refreshing your drawing display: the drawing regeneration, or *Regen*, and the *Redraw*. Each method serves a particular purpose, though they may not be clear to a new user.

To better understand the difference between Regen and Redraw, it helps to know that AutoCAD stores drawing data in two ways:

- In a database of highly accurate coordinate information that is part of the properties of objects in your drawing
- In a simplified database used just for the display of the objects in your drawing

As you draw, AutoCAD starts to build an accurate, core database of objects and their properties. At the same time, it creates a simpler database that it uses just to display the drawing quickly. AutoCAD uses this second database to allow quick manipulation of the display of your drawing. For the purposes of this discussion, I'll call this simplified database the "virtual display" because it is like a computer model of the overall display of your drawing. This virtual display is in turn used as the basis for what is shown in the drawing area. When you issue a redraw command, you are telling AutoCAD to reread this virtual display data and display that information in the drawing area. A regen command, on the other hand, causes AutoCAD to rebuild the virtual display based on information from the core drawing database.

As you edit drawings, you may find that some lines in the display disappear or otherwise appear corrupted. Redraw will usually restore such distortions. In earlier versions of AutoCAD, the Blipmode system variable was turned on by default, causing markers called *blips* to appear wherever points were selected. Redraw was, and still is, useful in clearing the screen of these blips.

Regens are used less frequently and are brought to bear when you change settings and options that have a global effect on a drawing, such as a line-type scale, layer color, or text style. (You'll learn more about text styles in Chapter 8.) In fact, in many situations, regens are performed automatically when such changes occur. You usually don't have to issue the Regen command on your own, except in certain situations.

Regens can also occur when you select a view of a drawing that is not currently included as part of the virtual display. The virtual display contains display data for a limited area of a drawing. If you zoom or pan to a view outside that virtual display area, a regen occurs.

TIP *You may notice that the Pan Realtime and Zoom Realtime commands do not work beyond a certain area in the display. When you've reached a point where these commands seem to stop working, you've come to the limits of the virtual display data. To go beyond these limits, AutoCAD must rebuild the virtual display data from the core data; in other words, it must regenerate the drawing.*

In past versions of AutoCAD, regens were to be avoided as much as possible, especially in large files. A regen on a very large file could take several minutes to complete. Today, with faster processors, large amounts of RAM, and a retooled AutoCAD, regens are not the problem they once were. Still, they can be annoying when you're working with large files, particularly if you are using an older Pentium-based computer. For these reasons, it pays to understand the finer points of controlling regens.

In this section, you will discover how to manage regens, thus reducing their impact on complex drawings. You can control how regens impact your work in three ways:

- By taking advantage of AutoCAD's many display-related tools
- By setting up AutoCAD so that regens do not occur automatically
- By freezing layers that do not need to be viewed or edited

This chapter will explore these methods in the upcoming sections.

Exploring Other Ways to Control AutoCAD's Display

Perhaps one of the easiest ways to avoid regens is by making sure you don't cross into an area of your drawing that falls outside the virtual display's area. If you use Pan Realtime and Zoom Realtime, you are automatically kept safely within the bounds of the display list. In this section, you'll be introduced to other tools that will help keep you within those boundaries.

CONTROLLING DISPLAY SMOOTHNESS

You can turn the virtual display on or off using the Viewres command. The Viewres setting is on by default and, for the most part, should remain on. You can turn it off by typing **Viewres↵ No↵** at the command prompt. However, I don't recommend this. With Viewres off, a regen occurs every time you change your view using Pan or Zoom.

The Viewres command also controls the smoothness of line types, arcs, and circles when they appear in an enlarged view. With Viewres turned on, line types sometimes appear as continuous, even when they are supposed to be dotted or dashed. You may have noticed in previous chapters that on-screen arcs appear to be segmented lines, although they are always plotted as smooth curves. You can adjust the Viewres value to control the number of segments an arc appears to have: the lower the value, the fewer the segments and the faster the redraw and regeneration. However, a low Viewres value causes noncontinuous line types, such as dashes or center lines, to appear as continuous, especially in drawings that cover very large areas such as civil site plans.

TIP *The Arc And Circle Smoothness setting in the Display tab of the Options dialog box has the same effect as the Viewres setting.*

Another way to accelerate screen redraw is to keep your drawing limits to a minimum area. If the limits are set unnecessarily high, AutoCAD may slow down noticeably. Also, make sure the drawing origin falls within the drawing limits.

TIP *A good value for the Viewres or Arc And Circle Smoothness setting is 500. At this setting, line types display properly, and arcs and circles have a reasonably smooth appearance. At the same time, redraw speed is not noticeably degraded. However, you might want to keep Viewres lower still if you have a limited amount of RAM. High Viewres settings can adversely affect AutoCAD's overall use of memory.*

USING THE AERIAL VIEW

Let's take a tour of a tool that lets you navigate drawings that represent very large areas. It's called the Aerial view.

1. Choose View ➢ Aerial View on the menu bar to open the Aerial View window, as shown in Figure 6.4.

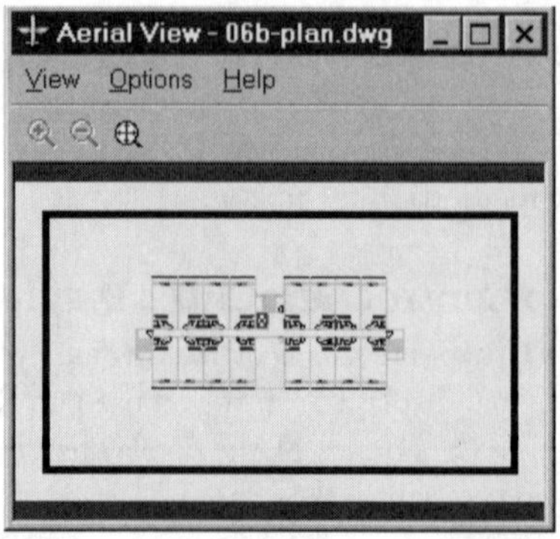

FIGURE 6.4
The Aerial View window and its components

2. Click the Aerial View window. As you move your mouse, notice what happens in the AutoCAD window. Your view pans, following your motion in the Aerial View window. A bold rectangle in the Aerial View window representing your AutoCAD view moves with your cursor.

3. Click the Aerial View window again. Now as you move your cursor from left to right, the view in the AutoCAD window zooms in and out. This is the Zoom mode of the Aerial view. The rectangle in the Aerial View window now shrinks and expands as you move the cursor from left to right, indicating the size of the area being displayed in the AutoCAD window.

4. Move the cursor to the left so that the rectangle representing your AutoCAD view is about half the size of the overall view of the plan, and then right-click. Your AutoCAD view becomes fixed. Also notice that the magnification icon in the Aerial View toolbar becomes available.

As you can see from this exercise, you can cycle through the Pan and Zoom feature of the Aerial view by clicking the mouse. If you simply want to pan the view, you can right-click in step 2 of the previous exercise to fix your view in place. Or you can rapidly alternate between the Pan and Zoom modes by clicking the mouse until you've reached the location and view size you want.

The bold rectangle shows you exactly where you are in the overall drawing at any given time. This feature is especially useful in drawings of large areas that may take several pans to cross.

TIP *Choosing View ➢ Zoom ➢ Dynamic performs a similar function to the Aerial View window, but instead of opening a separate window, the Dynamic option temporarily displays the overall view in the drawing area.*

The Aerial View window is a great tool when you are working on a drawing that requires a lot of magnification in your zoomed-in views. It is also helpful when you need to maintain an overall view of a drawing as you work on closer detail. You may not find it helpful on drawings that don't require lots of magnification, such as the bathroom drawing you worked on in Chapters 3 and 4.

You were able to use the major features of the Aerial view in this exercise. Here are a few more features you can try on your own:

View ➢ Zoom In Zooms in on the view defined by the bold rectangle in the Aerial view.

View ➢ Zoom Out Zooms out of magnified view on the view in the Aerial view.

View ➢ Global Displays an overall view of your drawing in the Aerial View window. Global is like a View ➢ Zoom ➢ Extents option for the Aerial view.

Options ➢ Auto Viewport Controls whether a selected viewport is automatically displayed in the Aerial View window. When this option is checked, the Aerial View window automatically displays the contents of a viewport when it becomes active. (See Chapters 13 and 17 for more on viewports.)

Options ➢ Dynamic Update Controls how AutoCAD updates the Aerial View window. When this setting is on, AutoCAD updates the Aerial view in real time as changes in the drawing occur. When this setting is off, changes in the drawing will not appear in the Aerial view until you click the Aerial View window.

Options ➢ Realtime Zoom Controls whether the AutoCAD display is updated in real time as you zoom and pan in the Aerial View window.

SAVING VIEWS

Another way of controlling your views is by saving them. You might think of saving views as a way of creating a bookmark or a placeholder in your drawing. You'll see how to save views in the following set of exercises.

A few walls in the Plan drawing are not complete. You'll need to zoom in to the areas that need work to add the lines, but these areas are spread out over the drawing. You could use the Aerial View window to view each area. There is, however, another way to edit widely separated areas: First, save views of the areas you want to work on, and then jump from saved view to saved view. This technique is especially helpful when you know you will often want to return to a specific area of your drawing.

1. Close the Aerial View window by clicking the Close button.
2. Choose View ➢ Zoom ➢ All or type **Z↵ A↵** to get an overall view of the plan.
3. Choose View ➢ Named Views or type **V↵** to open the View dialog box.

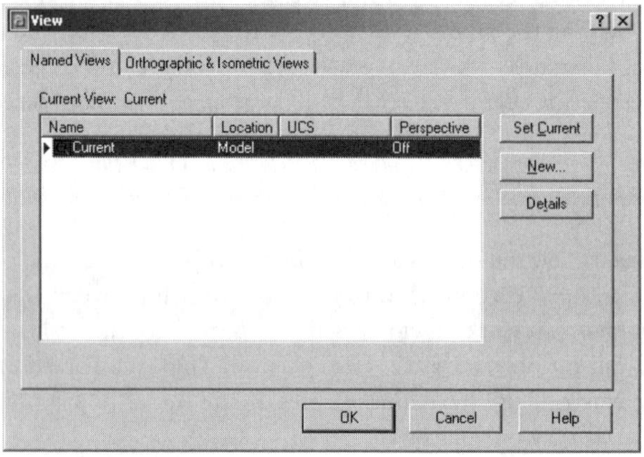

TIP *In the View dialog box, you can call up an existing view (Set Current), create a new view (New), or get detailed information about a view (Details). You can also click the Orthographic & Isometric Views tab to select from a set of predefined views. You'll learn more about these options in Chapter 16.*

4. Make sure the Named Views tab is selected, and then click the New button to open the New View dialog box.

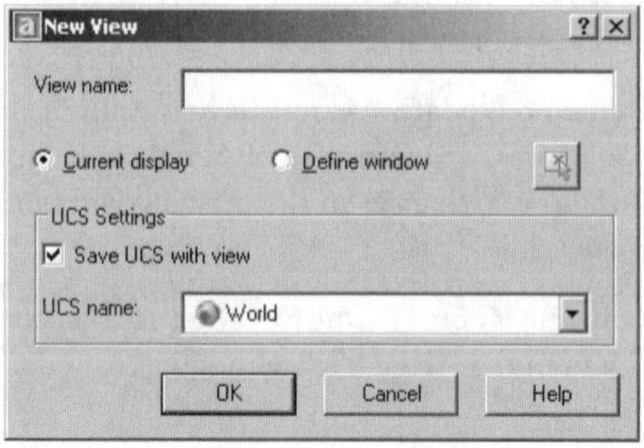

You'll notice some options that deal with the User Coordinate System (UCS). You'll get a chance to look at the UCS in Chapters 16 and 17. For now, you'll concentrate on creating a new view.

5. Click the Define Window radio button. Notice that the grayed button to the right, Define View Window, becomes available.
6. Click the Define View Window button. The dialog boxes momentarily disappear.
7. At the `Specify first corner:` prompt, click near the coordinate 26',40' (1715,1150 for metric users). You don't have to be exact because you are selecting view windows. Also, if you have Running Osnaps turned on, you might want to turn it off while selecting view windows.
8. At the `Specify opposite corner:` prompt, click a location near the coordinate 91',82' (2600,2500 for metric users). The dialog boxes reappear.
9. Click the View Name input box and type **First** for the name of the view you just defined.

WARNING *In previous versions of AutoCAD, view names were converted to all uppercase. Beginning in AutoCAD 2000, view names are recorded as you type them, though they are not case sensitive.*

10. Click the OK button. The New View dialog box closes, and you see First listed in the Name list.
11. Repeat steps 3 through 9 to define five more views, named Second, Third, and so on. Use Figure 6.5 as a guide for where to define the windows. Click OK when you are done.

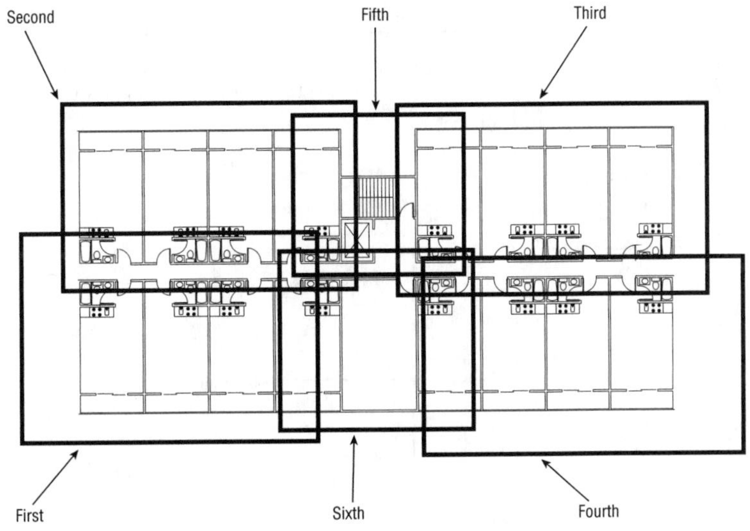

FIGURE 6.5
Save view windows in these locations for the Plan drawing.

Now let's see how to recall these views that you've saved.

1. With the View dialog box open, click First in the list of views.

TIP *A quick way to restore saved views is to type* **–V↵ R↵** and then enter the name of the view you want to restore.

2. Click the Set Current button and then click OK. Your screen displays the first view you selected.

TIP *To set the current view, you can also right-click the view name in the View dialog box. You can then choose Set Current, Delete, Details, or Rename from a shortcut menu.*

3. Set the current layer to Wall, and proceed to add the stairs and exterior walls of the building, as shown in Figure 6.6. (Remember that you exported the stairs from the Lobby drawing in the last chapter. You can also use the `Stair.dwg` file from the companion CD.)

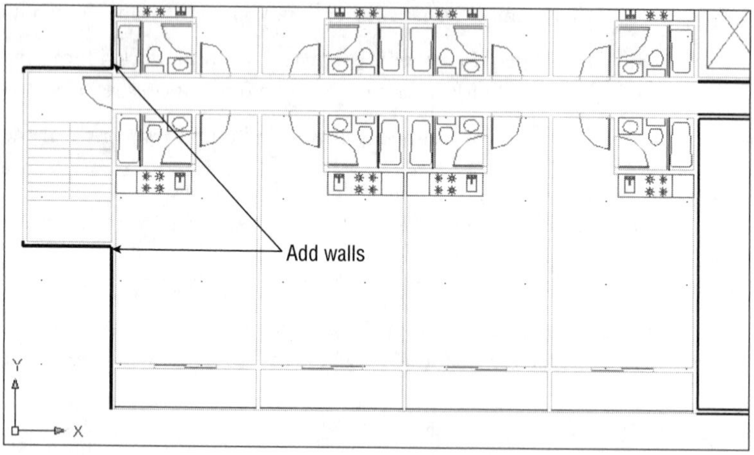

FIGURE 6.6
The stairs added to the restored First view

4. Use the View dialog box again to restore the view named Second. Then add the walls, as shown in Figure 6.7.

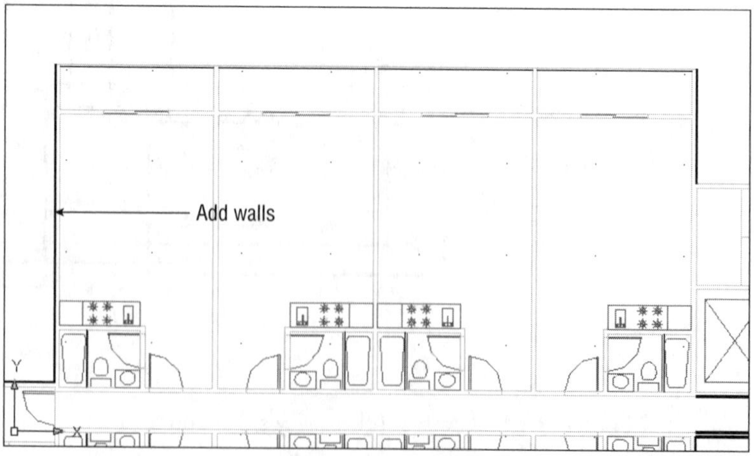

FIGURE 6.7
Walls added to the restored Second view

5. Continue to the other views and add the rest of the exterior walls, as you have done with First and Second. Use the four panels in Figure 6.8 as a guide to completing the views.

FIGURE 6.8

Walls, stairs, and doors added to the other views

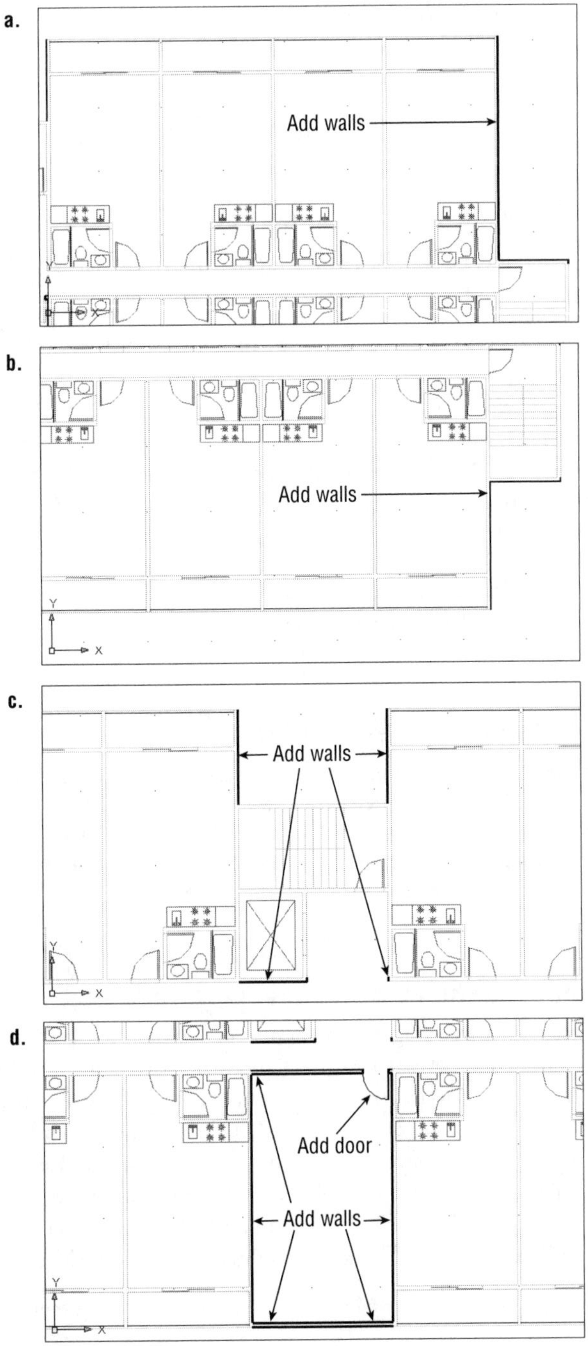

TIP *Remember that when no command is active, you can right-click the Command window and then select Recent Commands to repeat a recently issued command. You can also right-click the drawing area when AutoCAD is idle and repeat the last command.*

If you prefer, you can use the keyboard to invoke the View command and thus avoid all the dialog boxes.

1. Choose View ➢ Zoom ➢ Extents, or type **Z↵ E↵**.
2. Enter **–View↵ s↵** at the command prompt or use the **–V↵ s↵** shortcut. (Don't forget the minus sign in front of **View** or **V**.)
3. At the `Enter view name to save:` prompt, enter **Overall↵**.
4. Save the `Plan` file to disk.

As you can see, this is a quick way to save a view. With the name Overall assigned to this view, you can easily recall the Overall view at any time. (Choosing View ➢ Zoom ➢ All gives you an overall view too, but it may zoom out too far for some purposes, or it may not show what you might consider an overall view.)

TIP *Another useful tool for getting around in your drawing is the Zoom toolbar. It contains the Zoom Window, Dynamic, Scale, Center, In, Out, All, and Extent tools. To open the Zoom toolbar, right-click any toolbar and choose Zoom from the shortcut menu.*

OPENING A FILE TO A PARTICULAR VIEW

The Select File dialog box contains a Select Initial View check box. If you open an existing drawing with this option checked, you are greeted with a Select Initial View dialog box just before the opened file appears on the screen. This dialog box lists any views saved in the file. You can then go directly to a view by double-clicking the view name. If you have saved views and you know the name of the view you want, using Select Initial View saves time when you're opening large files.

Understanding the Frozen Layer Option

As mentioned earlier, you might want to turn certain layers off altogether to plot a drawing containing only selected layers. But even when layers are turned off, AutoCAD still takes the time to redraw and regenerate them. The Layer Properties Manager dialog box offers the Freeze option; this acts like the Off option, except that Freeze causes AutoCAD to ignore frozen layers when redrawing and regenerating a drawing. By freezing layers that are not needed for reference or editing, you can reduce the time AutoCAD takes to perform regens. This can be helpful in very large, multi-megabyte files.

Be aware, however, that the Freeze option affects blocks in an unusual way. Try the following exercise to see firsthand how the Freeze option makes entire blocks invisible.

1. In the Layer Properties Manager dialog box, set the current layer to 0.

TIP *You can freeze and thaw individual layers by clicking the Freeze/Thaw icon (which looks like a sun) in the Layers list in the Object Properties toolbar.*

2. Click the yellow lightbulb icon in the Plan1 layer listing to turn off that layer, and then click OK. Nothing happens to your drawing. Turning off the Plan1 layer, the layer on which the unit blocks were inserted, has no effect.

Now use the Layer Properties Manager dialog box to turn off all the layers.

3. Open the Layer Properties Manager dialog box again, and turn all of the layers back on.

4. Now click the Plan1 layer's Freeze/Thaw icon. (Note that you cannot freeze the current layer.) The yellow sun icon changes to a gray snowflake, indicating that the layer is now frozen.

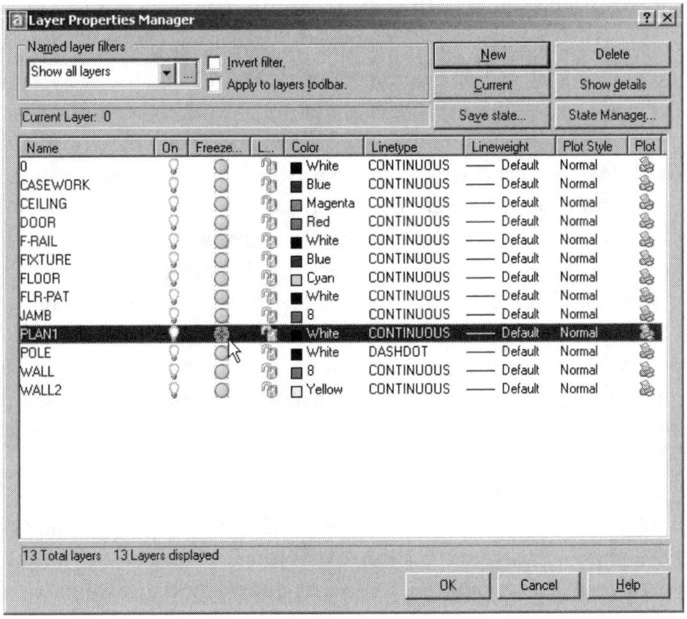

5. Click OK. Now the unit blocks disappear.

Even though none of the objects within the unit blocks were drawn on the Plan1 layer, the entire contents of the blocks assigned to the Plan1 layer are frozen when Plan1 is frozen.

TIP Remember that you can right-click a blank area of the Layer Properties Manager dialog box, and then choose Select All from the shortcut menu to select all the layers at once.

1. Issue the Regen command again and pay attention to the time it takes. The regen is faster this time.

2. Now, thaw layer Plan1 by opening the Layer Properties Manager dialog box and clicking the snowflake icon in the Plan1 layer listing.

3. Turn off the Ceiling layer. Exit the dialog box.

In this relatively small file, the differences between the regen times of the Off and Freeze states are insignificant. But in larger files, the difference can be quite significant. As your drawings become larger, try this exercise again to see how Off affects your regen speed compared with Freeze.

Making Good Use of Freeze and Off

The previous exercise showed the effect that freezing a layer has on blocks. When the layer of a block is frozen, the entire block is made invisible, regardless of the layer assignments of the objects contained in the block.

Keep in mind that when blocks are on layers that are not frozen, the individual objects that are a part of a block are still affected by the status of the layer to which they are assigned.

You can take advantage of this feature by using layers to store parts of a drawing that you might want to plot separately. For example, three floors in your apartment building plan might contain the same information, with some specific variation on each floor. In this case, you can have one layer contain blocks of the objects common to all the floors. Another layer contains the blocks and objects specific to the first floor, and additional layers contain information specific to the second and third floors. When you want to view or plot one floor, you can freeze the layers associated with the other floors. With respect to Freeze/Thaw visibility, external referenced files inserted using the Xref command also act like blocks. For example, you can Xref several drawings on different layers. Then, when you want to view a particular Xref drawing, you can freeze all the layers except the one containing that drawing.

In larger projects, you might not want to combine all your floors into one file, but instead combine different types of data such as electrical, mechanical, interior, site, and lease data. When you want to plot an interior plan, for example, you turn off or freeze layers associated with other disciplines. In fact, this is how the San Francisco Main Library project was organized. However, you can still use common data such as structural grids, columns, elevator core, and stair drawings as part of all your floor plan files.

Using layers and blocks in these ways requires careful planning and record keeping. If used successfully, however, this technique can save substantial time when you're working with drawings that use repetitive objects or that require similar information that can be overlaid.

Taking Control of Regens

If you work with extremely large files and regen times become a problem, you can control regeneration by setting the Regenmode system variable to 0 (zero). You can also use the Regenauto command to accomplish the same thing, by typing **Regenauto↵ Off↵**.

If you then issue a command that normally triggers a regen, AutoCAD will give the message `Regen queued`. For example, when you globally edit attributes, redefine blocks, thaw frozen layers, change the Ltscale setting, or, in some cases, change a text style, you will get the `Regen queued` message. You can "queue up" regens and then, at a time you choose, issue a regen to update all the changes at once by choosing View ➢ Regen or by typing **Re↵**. This way, only one regen occurs instead of several over the course of an editing session.

By taking control of when regens occur, you can reduce the overall time you spend editing large files.

Using Hatch Patterns in Your Drawings

To help communicate your ideas to others, you will want to add graphic elements that represent types of materials, special regions, or textures. AutoCAD provides *hatch patterns* for quickly placing a texture over an area of your drawing. In this section, you will add a hatch pattern to the floor of the studio apartment unit, thereby instantly enhancing the appearance of one drawing. In the process, you'll learn how to quickly update all the units in the overall floor plan to reflect the changes in the unit.

CREATING MULTIPLE VIEWS

So far, you've looked at ways to help you get around in your drawing while using a single view window. You can also set up multiple views of your drawing, called viewports. With viewports, you can display more than one view of your drawing at one time in the AutoCAD drawing area. For example, one viewport can display a close-up of the bathroom, another viewport can display the overall plan view, and yet another can display the unit plan.

When viewports are combined with AutoCAD's Paper Space feature, you can plot multiple views of your drawing. Paper Space is a display mode that allows you to "paste-up" multiple views of a drawing, much like a page layout program. To find out more about viewports and Paper Space, see Chapter 13.

Placing a Hatch Pattern in a Specific Area

It's always a good idea to provide a separate layer for hatch patterns. By doing so, you can turn them off if you need to. For example, in Chapter 3, you saw how the San Francisco Main Library floor plan displayed the floor paving pattern in one drawing, while in another drawing it was turned off so it wouldn't distract from other information.

In the following exercise, you will add a hatch pattern representing floor tile. This will give you the opportunity to learn the different methods of creating and controlling hatch patterns.

1. Open the `Unit` file. Keep in mind that you still have the `Plan` file open as well.
2. Zoom into the bathroom and kitchen area.
3. Create a new layer called Flr-pat.
4. Make Flr-pat the current layer.

Once you've set up the layer for the hatch pattern, you can place the pattern in the drawing.

LT only

WARNING *If you are using LT, you will not see the Gradient tab in the Boundary Hatch dialog box shown in step 1 of the next exercise.*

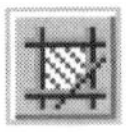

1. Click the Hatch tool on the Draw toolbar or type H↵. Hatch is also located in the Draw pull-down menu.

   The Boundary Hatch And Fill dialog box appears.

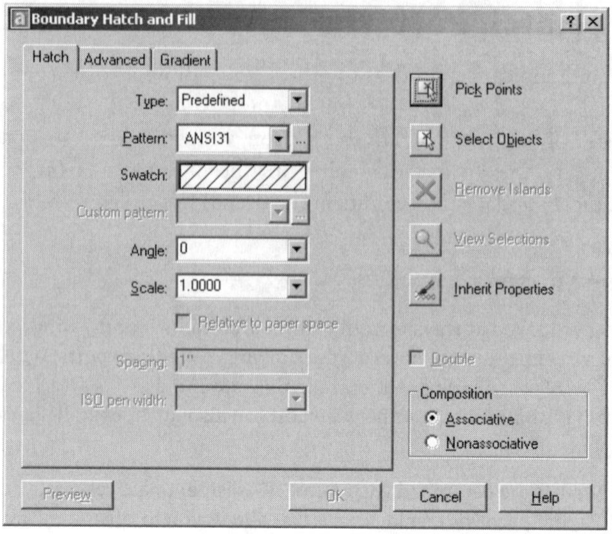

2. In the Type drop-down list box, select User-Defined. The User-Defined option lets you define a simple crosshatch pattern by specifying the line spacing of the hatch and whether it is a single- or double-hatch pattern. The Angle and Spacing input boxes become available, so you can enter values.

3. Double-click the Spacing input box near the bottom and enter **6** (metric users should enter **15**). This tells AutoCAD you want the hatch's line spacing to be 6 inches or 15 cm. Leave the Angle value at 0 because you want the pattern to be aligned with the bathroom.

4. Click the Double check box (just to the right of the Spacing input box). This tells AutoCAD you want the hatch pattern to run both vertically and horizontally. Also notice that the Swatch box display a sample of your hatch pattern.

5. Click the Pick Points button in the upper right corner of the dialog box.

   The dialog box momentarily disappears, allowing you to pick a point inside the area you want hatched.

6. Click a point anywhere inside the bathroom floor area, below the toilet. Notice that a highlighted outline appears in the bathroom. This is the boundary AutoCAD has selected to enclose the hatch pattern. It outlines everything, including the door swing arc.

TIP If you have text in the hatch boundary, AutoCAD will avoid hatching over it, unless the Ignore option is selected in the Boundary Style options of the Advanced Hatch settings. See the section "Using the Advanced Hatch Options" in this chapter for more on the Ignore setting.

7. Press ↵ to return to the Boundary Hatch And Fill dialog box.
8. Click the Preview button in the lower-left corner of the dialog box. The hatch pattern appears everywhere on the floor except where the door swing occurs. You also see the prompt:

   `Pick or press Esc to return to dialog or <Right-click to accept hatch>:`

9. Press Esc or the spacebar to return to the dialog box.
10. Click the Pick Points button again, pick a point inside the door swing, and press ↵.
11. Click Preview again. The hatch pattern now covers the entire floor area.
12. Right-click to place the hatch pattern in the drawing.

The Boundary Hatch And Fill dialog box lets you first define the boundary within which you want to place a hatch pattern. You do this by simply clicking a location inside the boundary area, as in step 6. AutoCAD finds the actual boundary for you. Many options give you control over how a hatch boundary is selected. For details, see the section "Understanding the Boundary Hatch Options" later in this chapter.

TIP *Say you want to add a hatch pattern that you have previously inserted in another part of the drawing. You might think that you have to guess at its scale and rotation angle. But with the Inherit Properties option in the Boundary Hatch And Fill dialog box, you can select a previously inserted hatch pattern as a prototype for the current hatch pattern. However, this feature does not work with exploded hatch patterns.*

Positioning Hatch Patterns Accurately

In the previous exercise, we placed the hatch pattern in the bathroom without regard for the location of the lines that make up the pattern. In most cases, however, you will want accurate control over where the lines of the pattern are placed.

TIP *You can also click the Swatch button to browse through a graphical representation of the predefined hatch patterns.*

Hatch patterns use the same origin as the snap origin (see Chapter 3 for more information about the snap origin). By default, this origin is the same as the drawing origin, 0,0. You can change the snap origin (and thus the hatch pattern origin) by using the Snapbase system variable. The following exercise guides you through the process of placing a hatch pattern accurately, using the example of adding floor tile to the kitchenette.

1. Pan your view so that you can see the area below the kitchenette, and using the Rectangle tool in the Draw toolbar, draw the 3'0" × 8'0" outline of the floor tile area, as shown in Figure 6.9. Metric users should create a rectangle that is 91 cm × 228 cm. You can also use a closed polyline.

TIP *If you know the coordinates of the new snap origin, you can enter them in the Drawing Aids dialog box under the X Base and Y Base input boxes instead of using the Snapbase system variable.*

FIGURE 6.9

The area below the kitchen showing the outline of the floor tile area

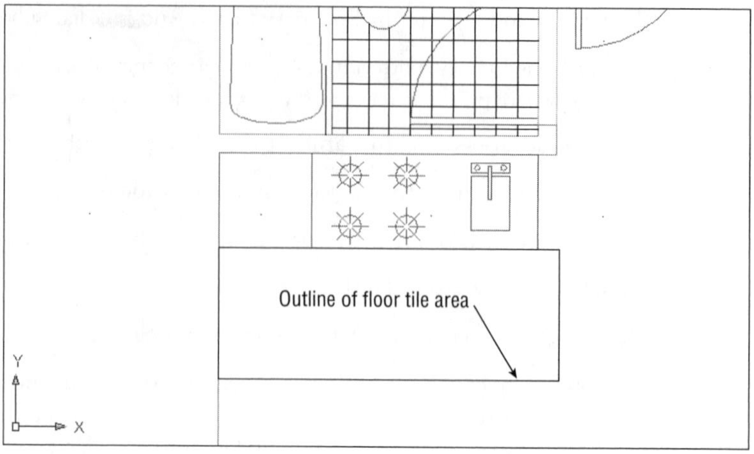

2. At the command prompt, type **Snapbase**↵.
3. At the `Enter new value for Snapbase <0'-0",0'-0">:` prompt, use the Endpoint Osnap and click the lower-left corner of the area you just defined (see Figure 6.9).
4. Click the Hatch tool in the Draw toolbar.
5. In the Boundary Hatch And Fill dialog box, make sure that Predefined is selected in the Type drop-down list box.
6. Click the button labeled with the ellipses (...) just to the right of the Pattern drop-down list.

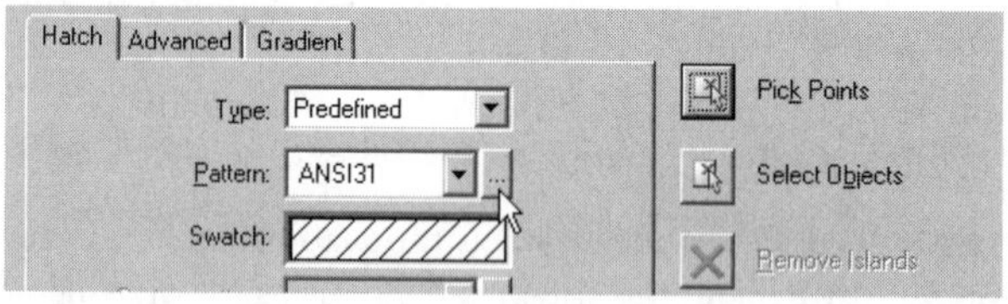

The Hatch Pattern Palette dialog box appears. This dialog box lets you select a predefined pattern from a graphic that shows what the pattern looks like.

TIP *If you know the name of the pattern you want, you can select it from the Pattern drop-down list in the Boundary Hatch And Fill dialog box.*

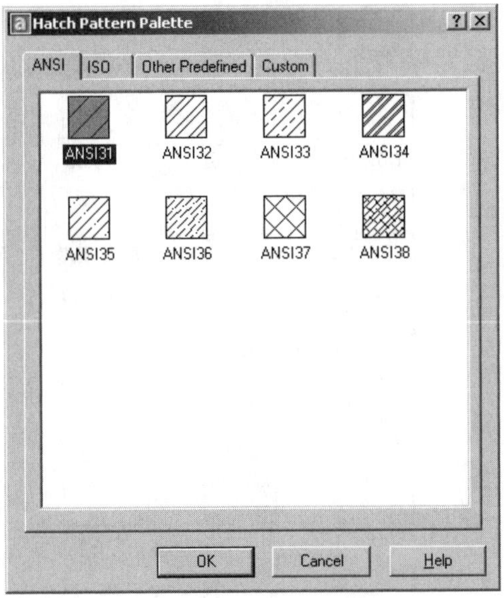

7. Click the Other Predefined tab, and then locate and click AR-PARQ1.
8. Click OK to exit the dialog box.
9. Click the Pick Points button.
10. Click the interior of the area to be tiled, and press ↵. Metric users should double-click the Scale input box and enter **2.54** to scale this pattern appropriately to match the proportions of the English measurement example.
11. Click OK. A parquet-style tile pattern appears in the defined area.
12. Save the `Unit` file, but keep it open.

TIP *You can use the Solid predefined hatch pattern at the top of the list to create solid fills. And don't forget that you can drag and drop solid fills and hatch patterns from the Tool Palettes you saw in Chapter 1.*

Notice that each tile is shown whole; none of the tiles is cut off as in the bathroom example. This is because you first used the Snapbase system variable to set the origin for the hatch pattern. You can now move the Snapbase setting back to the 0,0 setting and not affect the hatch pattern.

In the previous exercise, you got a chance to use a predefined hatch pattern. Figure 6.10 shows you all the patterns available. You can also create your own custom patterns, as described in Chapter 20.

FIGURE 6.10
Predefined hatch patterns available in AutoCAD

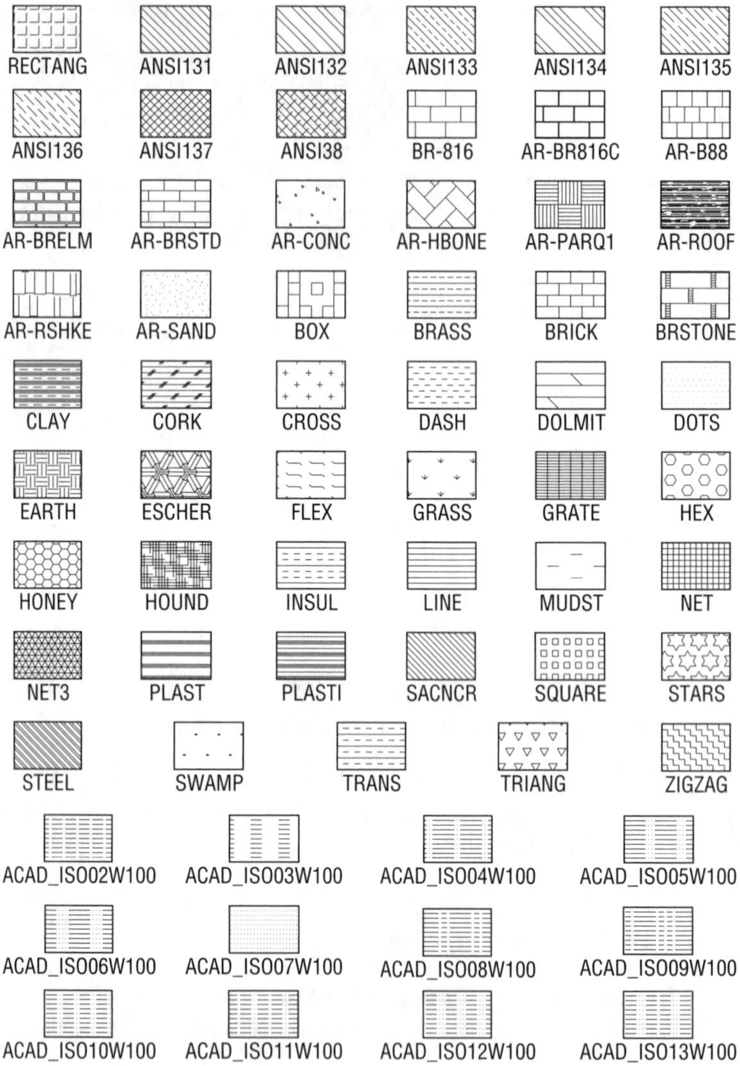

In the next exercise, you'll use this updated Unit file to update all the units in the Plan file.

TIP *The predefined patterns with the AR prefix are architectural patterns that are drawn to full scale. In general, you will want to leave their scale settings at 1. You can adjust the scale after you place the hatch pattern using the Properties palette, as described later in this chapter.*

TIP *If you are a veteran AutoCAD user, you might hesitate to use many hatch patterns in an already crowded drawing. In the past, hatch patterns were memory hogs. If you are upgrading from AutoCAD 14, you'll be happy to know that hatch patterns are much more memory efficient. Memory efficient solid fill hatch patterns are also available.*

Updating Blocks in the Plan File

As you progress through a design project, you make countless revisions. With traditional drafting methods, revising a drawing such as the studio apartment floor plan takes a good deal of time. If you change the bathroom layout, for example, you have to erase every occurrence of the bathroom and redraw it 16 times. With AutoCAD, on the other hand, revising this drawing can be a quick operation. You can update the studio unit you just modified throughout the overall plan drawing by replacing the current Unit block with the updated Unit file. AutoCAD can update all occurrences of the Unit block. The following exercise will show you how this is accomplished.

1. Make sure you've saved the `Unit` file with the changes, and then return to the `Plan` file that is still open. Choose Window ➢ *directory path*\Plan.dwg. Note that your full path to the `Plan.dwg` file will be shown in the Windows menu.

WARNING *This method does not update exploded blocks. If you plan to use this method to update parts of a drawing, do not explode the blocks you plan to update. See Chapter 4.*

2. Click the Insert Block tool on the Draw toolbar.
3. Click the Browse button, and from the Select Drawing File dialog box, double-click the Unit filename.
4. Click OK. A warning message tells you that a block already exists with the same name as the file. You can cancel the operation or redefine the block in the current drawing.
5. Click Yes. The drawing regenerates (unless you have Regenauto turned off).
6. At the `Insertion point:` prompt, press the Esc key. You do this because you really don't want to insert a Unit plan into your drawing, but rather are just using the Insert feature to update an existing block. The Insert dialog box returns.
7. Click Cancel to return to the drawing.
8. If Regenauto is turned off, type **Regen**↵ to view the results of the Insert dialog box.

WARNING *If Regenauto is turned off, you must use the Regen command to force a regeneration of the drawing before the updated Unit block appears on the display.*

9. Now zoom in to one of the units. You will see that the floor tile appears in all the units as you drew it in the Unit file (see Figure 6.11).

Nested blocks must be updated independently of the parent block. For example, if you modified the Toilet block while editing the Unit file and then updated the Unit drawing in the `Plan` file, the old Toilet block would not have been updated. Even though the toilet is part of the `Unit` file, it is still a unique, independent block in the `Plan` file, and AutoCAD will not modify it unless specifically instructed to do so. In this situation, you must edit the original Toilet block and then update it in both the `Plan` and `Unit` files.

FIGURE 6.11

The Plan drawing with the tile pattern

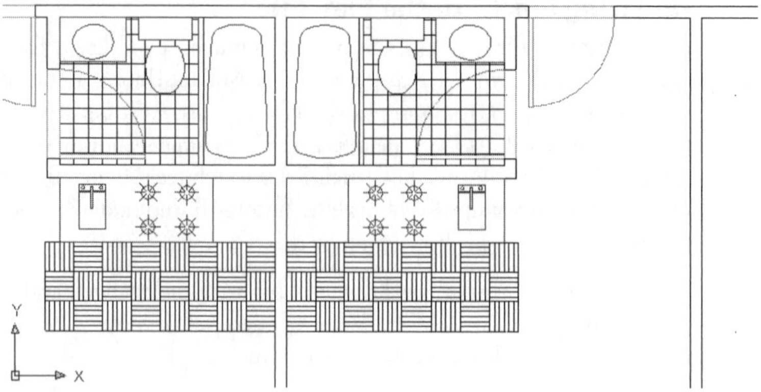

TIP *If you want to substitute one block for another within the current file, type* ***–Insert↵****. (Don't forget the minus sign in front of the word* ***Insert****). At the* `Block name` *prompt, enter the block name followed by an equal sign (=), and then enter the name of the new block or the filename. Do not include spaces between the names and the equal sign.*

Also, block references and layer settings of the current file take priority over those of the imported file. For example, if a file to be imported has layers of the same name as the current file, but those layers have color and line-type assignments that are different from the current file's, the current file's layer color and line-type assignments will determine those of the imported file. This does not mean, however, that the actual imported file on disk is changed; only the inserted drawing is affected.

SUBSTITUTING BLOCKS

In the preceding example, you updated a block in your `Plan` file using the Browse option in the Insert dialog box. In that exercise, the block name and the filename were the same. You can also replace a block with another block or file of a different name. Here's how to do this.

1. Open the Insert dialog box.
2. Click the Browse button, locate and select the file you want to use as a substitute, and then click Open to open the Insert dialog box.
3. Change the name in the Block input box to the name of the block you want replaced.
4. Click OK. A warning message appears, telling you that a block with this name already exists. Click OK to proceed with the block substitution.

You can use this method of replacing blocks if you would like to see how changing one element of your project can change your design. You might, for example, draw three different apartment unit plans and give each plan a unique name. You could then generate and plot three apartment building designs in a fraction of the time it would take you to do it by hand.

Continued on next page

SUBSTITUTING BLOCKS *(continued)*

Block substitution can also reduce a drawing's complexity and accelerate regenerations. To substitute blocks, you temporarily replace large, complex blocks with schematic versions of those blocks. For example, you might replace the Unit block in the Plan drawing with another drawing that contains just a single-line representation of the walls and bathroom fixtures. You would still have the wall lines for reference when inserting other symbols or adding mechanical or electrical information, but the drawing would regenerate much faster. When doing the final plot, you reinsert the original Unit block showing every detail.

Changing the Hatch Area

You might have noticed the Associative option in the Boundary Hatch And Fill dialog box. When this option is checked, AutoCAD creates an associative hatch pattern. Associative hatches adjust their shapes to any changes in their associated boundary, hence the name. The following exercise demonstrates how this works.

Suppose you want to enlarge the tiled area of the kitchen by one tile. Here's how it's done.

1. Return to the `Unit` file (choose Window ➢ *directory path*\\Unit.dwg); then click the outline border of the hatch pattern you created earlier. Notice the grips that appear around the hatch pattern area.

TIP *You might need to zoom in closer to the pattern area or use the object selection cycling feature to select the hatch boundary. For more on selection cycling, see Chapter 13.*

2. Shift+click the grip in the lower-left corner of the hatch area.

TIP *If the boundary of the hatch pattern consists of line segments, you can use a crossing window or polygon-crossing window to select the corner grips of the hatch pattern.*

3. With the lower-left grip highlighted, Shift+click the lower-right grip.
4. Now click the lower-right grip again, but don't Shift+click this time.
5. Enter **@12<–90** (**@30<–90** for metric users) to widen the hatch pattern by 1 foot. The hatch pattern adjusts to the new size of the hatch boundary.
6. Press the Esc key twice to clear any grip selections.
7. Save the `Unit` file to disk and exit the file.
8. Return to the `Plan` file (choose Window ➢ *directory path*\\Plan.dwg) and repeat the steps in the exercise in the "Updating Blocks in the Plan File" section, earlier in this chapter, to update the units again.

The Associative feature of hatch patterns can save time when you need to modify your drawing, but you need to be aware of its limitations. A hatch pattern can lose its associativity when you do any of the following:

- Erase or explode a hatch boundary
- Erase or explode a block that forms part of the boundary
- Move a hatch pattern away from its boundary

These situations frequently arise when you edit an unfamiliar drawing. Often, boundary objects are placed on a layer that is off or frozen, so the boundary objects are not visible. Or the hatch pattern may be on a layer that is turned off, and you proceed to edit the file, not knowing that a hatch pattern exists. When you encounter such a file, take a moment to check for hatch boundaries so you can deal with them properly.

Modifying a Hatch Pattern

Like everything else in a project, a hatch pattern may eventually need to be changed in some way. Hatch patterns are like blocks in that they act like single objects. You can explode a hatch pattern to edit its individual lines. The Properties tool in the Object Properties toolbar offers most of the settings you'll need to make changes to your hatch patterns.

1. Return to the Unit drawing by choosing Window ➢ *directory path*\\Unit.dwg.
2. Press the Esc key to clear any grip selections that may be active from earlier exercises.
3. Double-click the hatch pattern in the kitchen to open the Hatch Edit dialog box. It is the same as the Boundary Hatch And Fill dialog box with a few options grayed out.

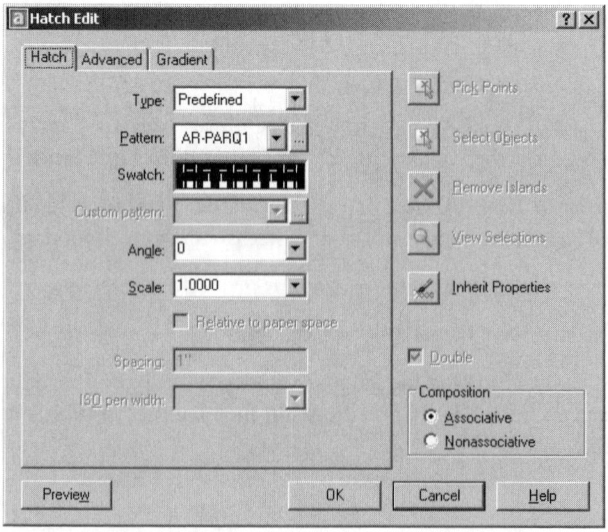

TIP *When you double-click a hatch pattern, you don't get the typical Properties palette. Double-clicking complex objects such as text, blocks, attributes, and hatch patterns opens a dialog box that allows you to edit the object in a more direct way. You can still access the Properties palette for any object by right-clicking the object and choosing Properties from the shortcut menu.*

4. Click the ellipsis button to the right of the Pattern drop-down list to open the Hatch Pattern Palette dialog box at the Other Predefined tab.

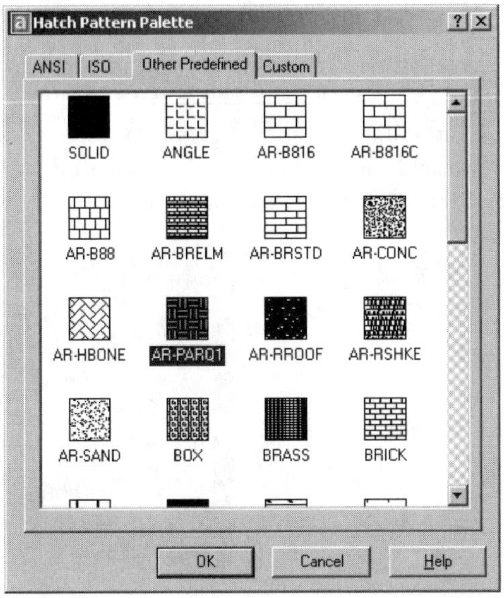

5. Locate and double-click the pattern named AR-BRSTD. It's the pattern that looks like a brick wall. The Hatch Pattern Palette dialog box disappears, and you see the AR-BRSTD hatch pattern in the Pattern drop-down list.
6. Click OK to accept the change to the hatch pattern. The AR-BRSTD pattern appears in place of the original parquet pattern.
7. You want to keep the old pattern in your drawing, so at this point, exit the `Unit` file without saving it.

In this exercise, you were able to change the hatch just by double-clicking it. Although you only changed the pattern type, other options are available to you. You can, for example, modify a predefined pattern to a user-defined one by selecting User Defined from the Type listing in the Hatch Edit dialog box.

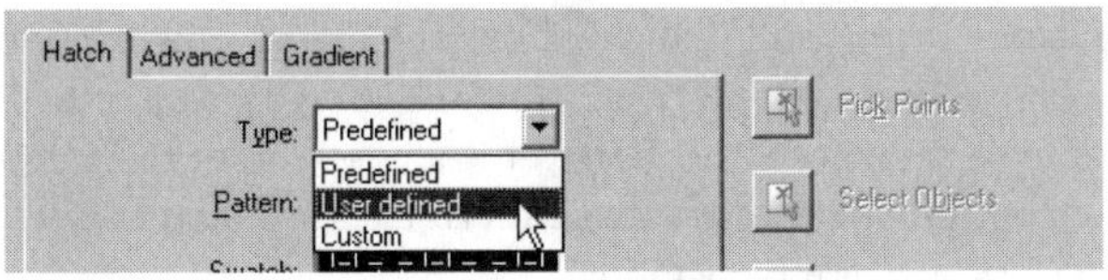

You can then enter angle and spacing values for your hatch pattern in the spaces provided in the Hatch Edit dialog box.

The other items in the Hatch Edit dialog box duplicate some of the options in the Boundary Hatch And Fill dialog box. They let you modify the individual properties of the selected hatch pattern. The section "Understanding the Boundary Hatch Options" describes these other properties in detail.

If you create and edit hatch patterns frequently, you will find the Modify II toolbar useful. It contains an Edit Hatch tool that gives you ready access to the Hatch Edit dialog box. To open the Modify II toolbar, right-click any toolbar, and then click the Modify II check box in the Toolbars dialog box that opens.

EDITING HATCH PATTERNS FROM THE PROPERTIES PALETTE

If you prefer, you can still use the older method to edit a hatch pattern. To open the Properties palette, right-click a pattern, and choose Properties from the shortcut menu. The Properties palette displays a Pattern category, which offers a Pattern Name option.

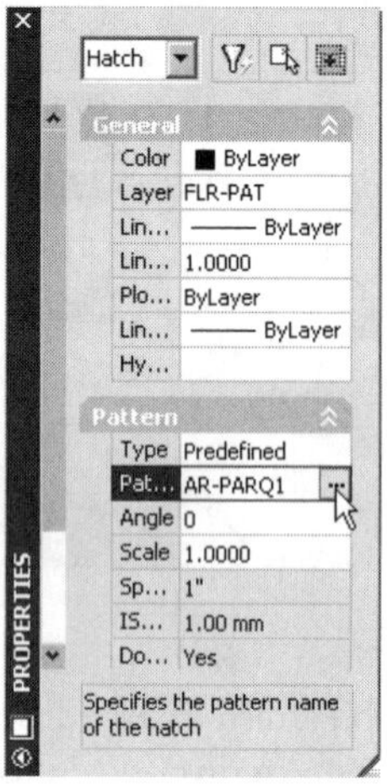

When you click this option, an ellipsis button appears, allowing you to open the Hatch Pattern Palette, just as in step 4 of the previous exercise. You can then select a new pattern from the dialog box. The Type option in the Properties palette lets you change the type of hatch pattern from Predefined to User Defined.

TIP *If you're working through the tutorial in this chapter, this would be a good place to take a break or stop. You can pick up the next exercise, which is in the "Attaching a Drawing as an External Reference" section, at another time.*

Understanding the Boundary Hatch Options

The Boundary Hatch And Fill dialog box offers many other options that you didn't explore in the previous exercises. For example, instead of selecting the area to be hatched by clicking a point, you can select the actual objects that bound the area you want to hatch using the Select Objects button. The Swatch button opens the Hatch Pattern Palette dialog box, which lets you select a predefined hatch pattern from a graphic window.

The Hatch Pattern Palette dialog box has several tabs that further divide the types of hatch patterns into four categories: ANSI, ISO, Other Predefined, and Custom. The Custom tab is empty until you create your own set of custom hatch patterns. See Chapter 20 for details on how to create custom hatch patterns.

Other options in the right column of the Boundary Hatch And Fill dialog box include Remove Islands, View Selections, and Inherit Properties.

Remove Islands Lets you remove an area within a hatch pattern boundary that has been removed from the hatch pattern. An example of this is the toilet seat in the bathroom. This option is only available when you select a hatch area using the Pick Points option and an island has been detected.

View Selections Temporarily closes the dialog box and then highlights the objects that have been selected as the hatch boundary by AutoCAD.

Inherit Properties Lets you select a hatch pattern from an existing one in the drawing. This is helpful when you want to apply a hatch pattern that is already used, but you do not know its name or its scale, rotation, or other properties.

At the very bottom of the column of options is the Composition button group. This option lets you determine whether the hatch pattern being inserted is associative or nonassociative. As discussed earlier, an associative hatch pattern automatically changes to fill its boundary whenever that boundary is stretched or edited.

Using the Advanced Hatch Options

AutoCAD's Boundary Hatch command has a fair amount of intelligence. As you saw in an earlier exercise, it was able to detect not only the outline of the floor area, but also the outline of the toilet seat that represents an island within the pattern area. If you prefer, you can control how AutoCAD treats these island conditions and other situations by selecting options available when you click the Advanced tab in the Boundary Hatch And Fill dialog box.

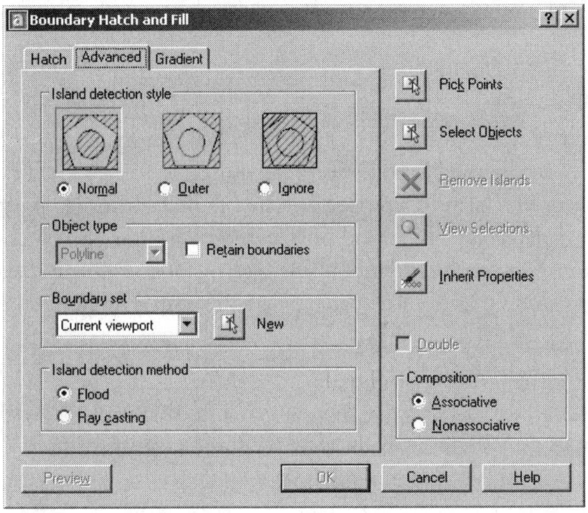

In addition to controlling the Island Detection feature of hatch patterns, the Advanced tab lets you fine-tune other aspects of hatch pattern creation.

ISLAND DETECTION STYLE

The Island Detection Style button group at the top of the dialog box controls how nested boundaries affect the hatch pattern. The graphics in this button group show examples of the effect of the selected option. The Island Detection Style options include the following:

Normal Causes the hatch pattern to alternate between nested boundaries. The outer boundary is hatched; if there is a closed object within the boundary, it is not hatched. If another closed object *is* inside the first closed object, *that* object is hatched. This is the default setting.

Outer Applies the hatch pattern to an area defined by the outermost boundary and by any boundaries nested within the outermost boundary. Any boundaries nested within the nested boundaries are ignored.

Ignore Supplies the hatch pattern to the entire area within the outermost boundary, ignoring any nested boundaries.

OBJECT TYPE

The Boundary Hatch command can also create an outline of the hatch area using one of two objects: 2D regions, which are like 2D planes, or polyline outlines. Boundary Hatch actually creates such a polyline boundary temporarily, to establish the hatch area. These boundaries are automatically removed after the hatch pattern is inserted. If you want to retain the boundaries in the drawing, make sure the Retain Boundaries check box is checked. Retaining the boundary can be useful if you know you will be hatching the area more than once or if you are hatching a fairly complex area.

TIP *Retaining a hatch boundary is useful if you want to know the hatched area's dimensions in square inches or feet, because you can find the area of a closed polyline using the List command. The Boundary command creates a polyline outline or region within a selected area. It works much like the Boundary Hatch command but does not add a hatch pattern.*

ISLAND DETECTION

You might have noticed that the Boundary Hatch command did not place a hatch pattern on the toilet seat. This is because the Island Detection feature was turned on. The toilet seat is like an island within the hatch area. The Island Detection Method radio buttons let you control whether islands such as the toilet seat are detected. The Flood option detects islands and hatches around them. The Ray Casting option determines the boundary outline by first looking for the nearest object to your pick point and then tracing along that object in a counterclockwise direction.

BOUNDARY SET OPTIONS

The Boundary Hatch feature is view-dependent; that is, it locates boundaries based on what is visible in the current view. If the current view contains a lot of graphic data, AutoCAD can have difficulty finding a boundary, or it can be slow in finding a boundary. If you run into this problem, or if you want to single out a specific object for a point selection boundary, you can further limit the area that AutoCAD uses to locate hatch boundaries by using the Boundary Set options.

New Lets you select the objects from which you want AutoCAD to determine the hatch boundary, instead of searching the entire view. The screen clears and lets you select objects. This option discards previous boundary sets. It is useful for hatching areas in a drawing that contain many objects that you do not want to include in the hatch boundary.

Current Viewport Tells you that AutoCAD will use the current view to determine the hatch boundary. Once you select a set of objects using the New button, you also see Existing Set as an option in this drop-down list. You can then use this drop-down list to choose the entire view or the objects you select for the hatch boundary.

The Boundary Set options are designed to give you more control over the way a point selection boundary is created. These options have no effect when you use the Select Objects button to select specific objects for the hatch boundary.

Using Gradient Shading

ACAD only

You might have noticed that one of the hatch patterns offered is a solid. The solid hatch pattern lets you apply a solid color to a bounded area instead of a pattern. AutoCAD also offers a set of gradient patterns that let you apply a color gradient to an area.

You can apply a gradient to an area using the same method you used to apply a hatch pattern, but instead of using the Hatch tab of the Boundary Hatch And Fill dialog box, you use the Gradient tab to select a gradient pattern.

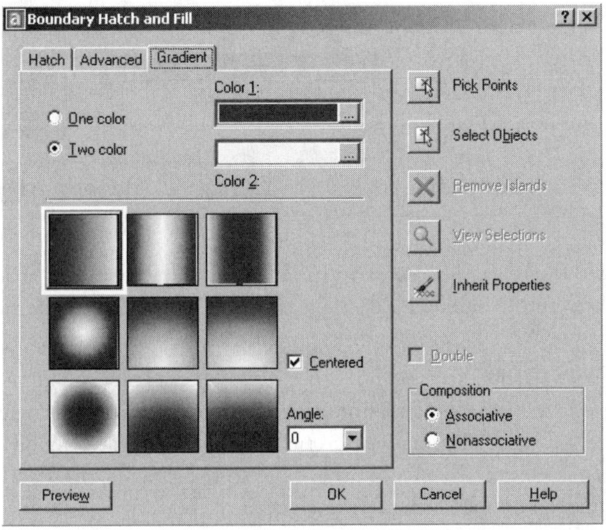

CHOOSING A GRADIENT COLOR

Instead of offering hatch patterns, the Gradient tab offers a variety of gradient patterns. It also lets you control the color of the gradient. For example, if you want to set the gradient between different shades of blue, you can click the One Color radio button and then double-click the blue color swatch at the top of the dialog box.

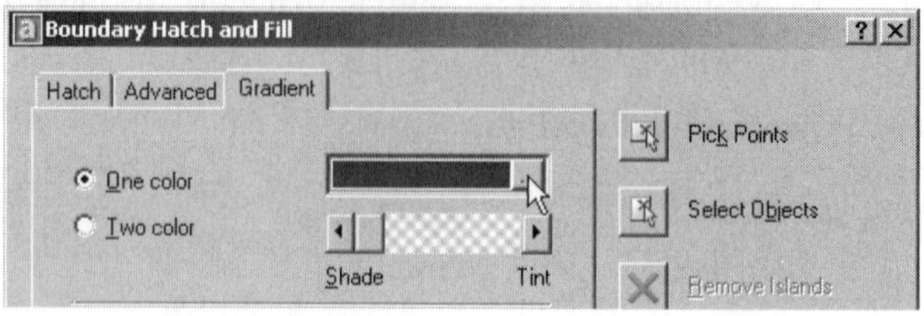

When you double-click the color swatch, the Select Color dialog box appears, offering a palette of true color options.

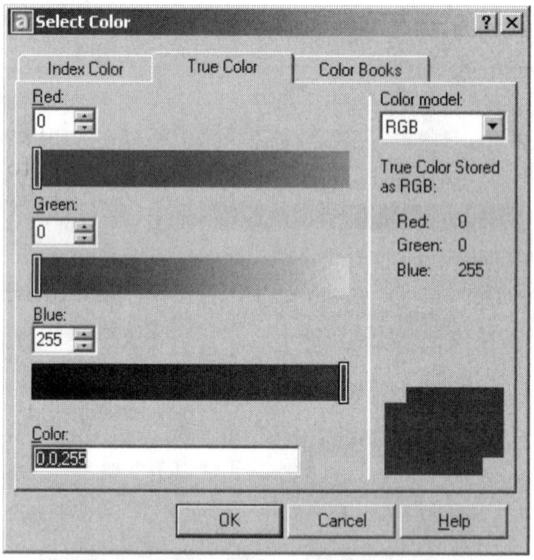

You can then select the color you want for the gradient. The Shade/Tint slider just below the color swatch in the Gradient tab lets you control the shade of the single color gradient.

USING TWO COLORS

You can choose a gradient that transitions between shades of a single color using the One Color radio button, or you can transition between two entirely different colors by selecting the Two Color radio button. When you select Two Color, the slider to the right of the Two Color option changes to a color swatch. You can double-click the swatch or click the ellipses button to the right of the swatch to open the Select Color dialog box.

SELECTING GRADIENT PATTERNS

Just below the One Color and Two Color options are the gradient pattern options. You can choose from nine patterns, plus you can select an angle for the pattern from the Angle drop-down list box. The Center option places the center of the gradient at the center of the area selected for the pattern.

To place a gradient pattern, select a set of objects or a point within a bounded area, just as you would for a hatch pattern. You can then click the Preview button to preview your hatch pattern, or you can click OK to apply the gradient to the drawing.

Tips for Using the Boundary Hatch

Here are a few tips on using the Boundary Hatch feature:

- Watch out for boundary areas that are part of a very large block. AutoCAD examines the entire block when defining boundaries. This can take time if the block is quite large. Use the Boundary Set option to "focus in" on the set of objects you want AutoCAD to use for your hatch boundary.
- The Boundary Hatch feature is view-dependent; that is, it locates boundaries based on what is visible in the current view. To ensure that AutoCAD finds every detail, zoom in to the area to be hatched.
- If the area to be hatched will be very large yet will require fine detail, first outline the hatch area using a polyline. (See Chapter 14 for more on polylines.) Then use the Select Objects option in the Boundary Hatch And Fill dialog box to select the polyline boundary manually, instead of depending on Boundary Hatch to find the boundary for you.
- Consider turning off layers that might interfere with AutoCAD's ability to find a boundary. For example, in the previous exercise, you could turn off the Door layer and then use Pick Points to locate the boundary of the hatch pattern.
- Boundary Hatch works on nested blocks as long as the nested block entities are parallel to the current UCS and are uniformly scaled in the x- and y-axes.

HOW TO QUICKLY MATCH A HATCH PATTERN AND OTHER PROPERTIES

Another tool to help you edit hatch patterns is Match Properties, which is similar to Format Painter in the Microsoft Office suite. This tool lets you change an existing hatch pattern to match another existing hatch pattern. Here's how to use it.

1. Click the Match Properties tool in the Standard toolbar.
2. Click the source hatch pattern you want to copy.
3. Click the target hatch pattern you want to change.

The target pattern changes to match the source pattern.

The Match Properties tool transfers other properties as well, such as layer, color, and line-type settings. You can select the properties that are transferred by opening the Property Settings dialog box.

Continued on next page

HOW TO QUICKLY MATCH A HATCH PATTERN AND OTHER PROPERTIES *(continued)*

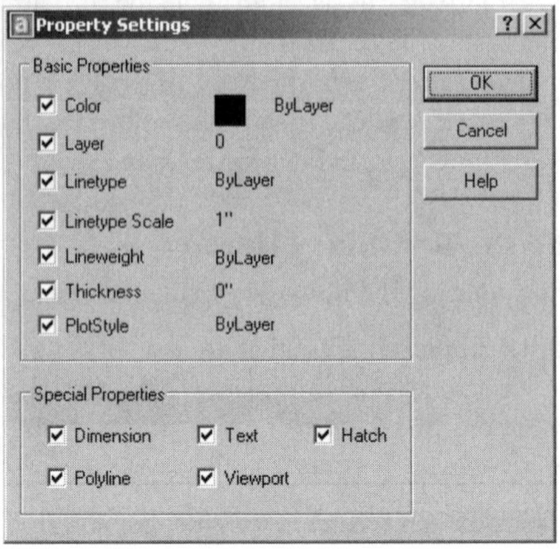

To open this dialog box, type **S**↵ after selecting the object in step 2, or right-click and choose Settings from the shortcut menu. You can then select the properties you want to transfer from the options shown. All the properties are selected by default. Note that text and dimension style settings can also be transferred. You'll learn more about text and dimension styles in Chapters 8 and 9.

Space Planning and Hatch Patterns

Suppose you are working on a plan within which you are constantly repositioning equipment and furniture, or you are in the process of designing the floor covering. You might be a little hesitant to place a hatch pattern on the floor because you don't want to have to rehatch the area each time you move a piece of equipment or change the flooring. You have two options in this situation: You can use the Boundary Hatch's associative capabilities to include the furnishings in the boundary set, or you can use the Display Order feature.

USING ASSOCIATIVE HATCH

Associative Hatch is the most straightforward method. Make sure the Associative option is checked in the Boundary Hatch And Fill dialog box and include your equipment or furniture in the boundary set. You can do this by using the Select Objects option in the dialog box.

Once the pattern is in place, the hatch pattern automatically adjusts to its new location when you move the furnishings in your drawing. One drawback, however, is that AutoCAD attempts to hatch the interior of your furnishings if they cross over the outer boundary of the hatch pattern. Also, if any boundary objects are erased or exploded, the hatch pattern no longer follows the location of your furnishings. To avoid these problems, you can use the method described in the next section.

OVERLAPPING OBJECTS WITH DISPLAY ORDER

The Display Order feature lets you determine how objects overlap each other. In the space-planning example, you can create furniture using a solid hatch to indicate horizontal surfaces (see Figure 6.12).

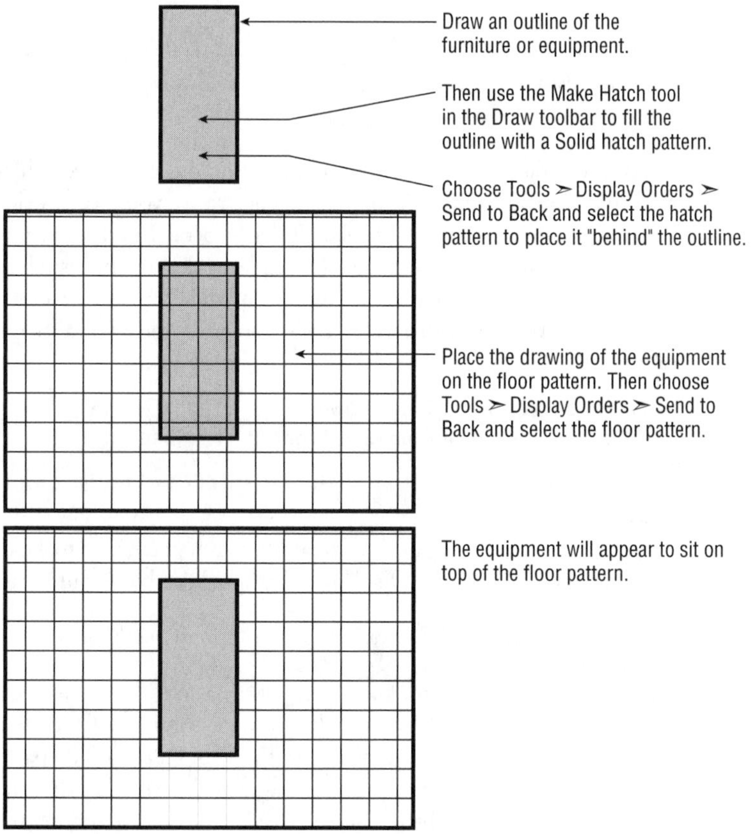

Draw an outline of the furniture or equipment.
Then use the Make Hatch tool in the Draw toolbar to fill the outline with a Solid hatch pattern.
Choose Tools ➢ Display Orders ➢ Send to Back and select the hatch pattern to place it "behind" the outline.
Place the drawing of the equipment on the floor pattern. Then choose Tools ➢ Display Orders ➢ Send to Back and select the floor pattern.
The equipment will appear to sit on top of the floor pattern.

FIGURE 6.12
Using Display Order to create an overlapping effect over a hatch pattern

You can then place the furniture "on top" of the floor-covering pattern, and the pattern will be covered and hidden by the furniture. Here's how to do that. (These steps are not part of the regular exercises of this chapter. They are shown here as general guidelines when you need to use the Display Order feature.)

1. Draw the equipment outline, and make sure the outline is a closed polygon.
2. Use the Hatch tool described earlier in this chapter to place a Solid hatch pattern inside the equipment outline.
3. Choose Tools ➢ Display Order ➢ Send To Back.
4. At the `Select Object` prompt, select the solid hatch pattern, and then press ↵ to confirm your selection.

5. Turn the outline and solid hatch into a block, or use the Group command to group them together.

6. Choose Tools ➢ Display Order ➢ Bring To Front, and select the equipment. When you are done, the equipment will "cover" the floor hatch pattern (see the bottom panel in Figure 6.12).

WARNING *When you use the Display Order options, all the Object Sort Method options in the User Preferences tab of the Options dialog box are turned on. This can increase regeneration and redraw times. See Appendix B for more on User Preferences and the Object Sort Method options.*

After you take these steps, you can place the equipment over a hatched floor pattern, and the equipment will appear to rest on top of the pattern. If you create a floor pattern *after* you create the equipment, choose Tools ➢ Display Order ➢ Send To Back to move the pattern to the back of the display order. You can also change the display order of objects relative to other objects.

The Display Order options are all part of the Draworder command. As an alternative to the dialog box, you can type **Draworder↵** at the command prompt and then enter an option at the Draworder prompt:

```
Enter object ordering option
[Above object/Under object/Front/Back] <Back>:
```

For example, the equivalent of choosing Tools ➢ Display Order ➢ Send To Back is entering **Draworder↵ B↵**.

If you need to "white out" an area of a hatch pattern to make text more readable, you can use a solid hatch along with the Display Order option to block out areas behind text.

TIP *In AutoCAD 2004, Draworder now supports Xref and Block Draworder settings.*

You've had a detailed look at hatch patterns and fills in this section. Remember that you can also make use of the Tool Palettes to help organize and simplify access to your favorite hatch patterns, or just use the patterns already available in the Tool Palettes. The patterns found in the Tool Palettes can be edited and manipulated in the same way as described in this chapter. If you want to know how to make full use of the Tool Palettes, check out the discussion on the AutoCAD DesignCenter in Chapter 22.

Using External References

This chapter's discussion about freezing layers mentioned that you can insert drawing files as external references, in a way similar to inserting blocks. To accomplish this, choose Insert ➢ External Reference (Xref). Chapter 4 briefly introduced external references. As discussed there, the difference between Xref files and blocks is that Xref files do not actually become part of the drawing's database. Instead, they are "loaded" along with the current file at startup time. It is as if AutoCAD were opening several drawings at once: the currently active file you specify when you start AutoCAD and any file inserted as an Xref.

If you keep Xref files independent from the current file, any changes you make to the Xref automatically appear in the current file. You don't have to update the Xref file manually as you do blocks. For example, if you used Xref to insert the `Unit` file into the `Plan` file, and you later made changes to the `Unit` file, you would see the new version of the `Unit` file in place of the old the next time you opened the `Plan` file.

TIP *You cannot Xref a file if the file has the same name as a block in the current drawing. If this situation occurs, but you still need to use the file as an Xref, you can rename the block of the same name using the Rename command. You can also use Rename to change the name of various objects and named elements. See Chapter 8.*

Another advantage of Xref files is that since they do not actually become part of a drawing's database, drawing size is kept to a minimum. This results in more efficient use of your hard disk space.

TIP *Xref files, like blocks, cannot be edited. You can, however, use Osnaps to snap to a location in an Xref file, or you can freeze or turn off the Xref file's insertion layer to make it invisible.*

Attaching a Drawing as an External Reference

The next exercise shows how to use an Xref in place of an inserted block to construct the studio apartment building. You'll start with creating a new `Unit` file by copying the old one. Then you bring a new toolbar, the External Reference toolbar, to the screen.

1. Return to the Unit file; choose File ➢ Save As to save it under the name `Unitxref.dwg`, and then exit the `Unitxref.dwg` file. This will make a copy of the `Unit.dwg` file for the following steps. Or if you prefer, you can use the `Unitxref.dwg` file from the companion CD for the following steps.
2. Return to the `Plan` file, choose Save As, and save the file under the name `Planxref`. The current file is now `Planxref.dwg`.
3. Erase all the objects (enter **E↵ All↵↵**) and purge the Unit, Stair, and Lobby blocks. (By doing steps 2 and 3, you save yourself from having to set up a new file.)
4. Choose File ➢ Drawing Utilities ➢ Purge to open the Purge dialog box, and then click the Purge All button to open the Confirm Purge dialog box.
5. Click Yes to All.

Now you're ready to use the Xref Manager.

ACAD only

WARNING *The Open option in the Xref Manager is not available in LT.*

1. Choose Insert ➢ Xref Manager or type **XR↵** to open the Xref Manager dialog box (see Figure 6.13). (You can go directly to this dialog box by choosing Insert ➢ External Reference, but it's useful to know where to find the Xref Manager.)
2. Click the Attach button to open the Select Reference File dialog box. This is a typical AutoCAD file dialog box complete with a preview window.

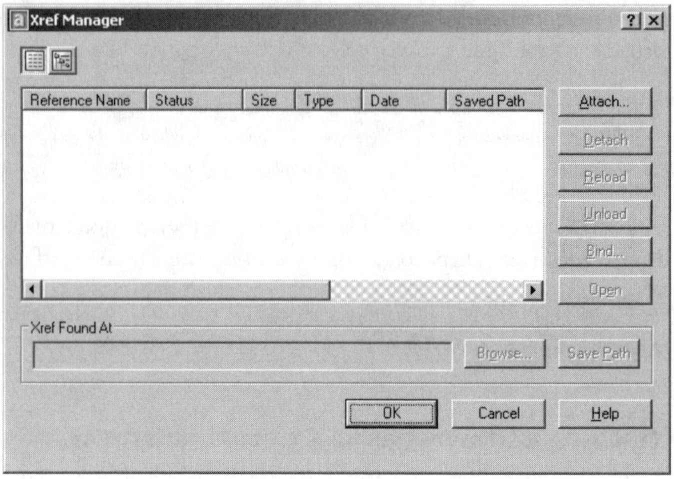

FIGURE 6.13
The Xref Manager dialog box

3. Locate and select the `Unitxref.dwg` file, and then click Open to open the External Reference dialog box (see Figure 6.14). Notice that this dialog box looks similar to the Insert dialog box. It offers the same options for insertion point, scale, and rotation.

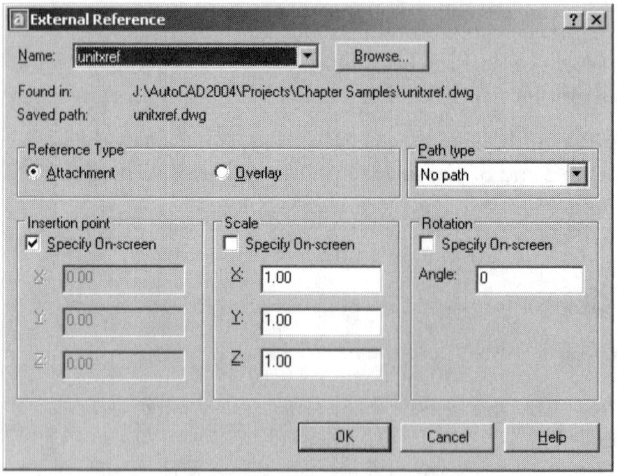

FIGURE 6.14
The External Reference dialog box

4. You'll get a description of the options presented in this dialog box. For now, click OK.
5. Enter **31'–5",43'–8"** (metric users enter **957,1330**) for the insertion point.
6. After the `Unitxref.dwg` file is inserted, re-create the same layout of the floor plan you created in the first section of this chapter by copying and mirroring the `Unitxref.dwg` external reference.

7. Save the `Planxref` file.

You now have a drawing that looks like the `Plan.dwg` file you created earlier in this chapter, but instead of using blocks that are detached from their source file, you have a drawing composed of Xrefs. These Xrefs are the actual `Unitxref.dwg` file, and they are loaded into AutoCAD at the same time that you open the `Planxref.dwg` file. An icon in the lower-right corner of the AutoCAD window tells you that the current drawing contains Xrefs.

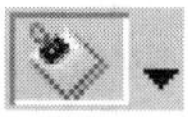

This icon not only alerts you to xrefs, but it also allows you to open the Xref manager as you'll see in the next exercise.

Next, you'll modify the `Unitxref.dwg` file and see the results in the `Planxref.dwg` file.

LT only

WARNING *Xopen and the Open Xref option in the shortcut menu are not available in LT. If you are using LT, choose File ➢ Open, and use the Select File dialog box to open the* `Unitxref.dwg` *file.*

1. To open the `Unitxref.dwg` file, in the current `Planxref` file, right-click the Unit, and then choose Open Xref from the shortcut menu. You can also enter **Xopen↵** at the command prompt, and then select the Unit plan Xref.
2. Erase the hatch pattern and kitchen outline for the floors, and save the `Unitxref.dwg` file.
3. Choose Window ➢ Planxref.dwg to return to the `Planxref.dwg` file. Click the Xref icon in the lower-right corner of the AutoCAD window to open the Xref Manager dialog box.
4. Select the Unitxref name in the list box, click Reload, and then click OK. Notice that the units in the Planxref drawing have been updated to include the changes you made to the `Unitxref` file.

In this exercise, you used Xopen to open an Xref. You can open multiple Xrefs at once by selecting more than one Xref while using the Xopen command.

TIP *The Open button in the Xref Manager dialog box performs the same function as the Xopen command or the Open Xref option in the shortcut menu. To use this option, select the Xref files from the list box in the Xref Manager dialog box, and then click Open.*

You will want to be aware that when an Xref has been modified, the Xref icon in the lower-right of the AutoCAD window changes to show an exclamation mark. This alerts you to changes in an Xref in the current drawing.

Click the Xref icon to open the Xref Manager dialog box. The Xref that has been changed is indicated by a message in the Status column of the list box..

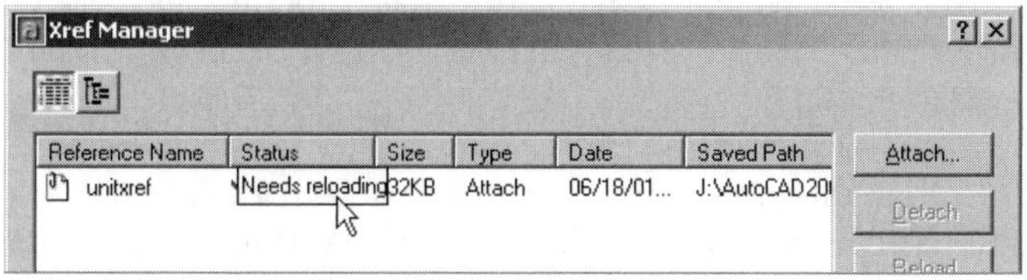

You can then select the Xref that needs to be updated and click the Reload button. You can also right-click the Xref icon and choose the Reload Xref option from the shortcut menu to reload all Xrefs in the drawing without having to open the Xref Manager dialog box.

Importing Blocks, Layers, and Other Named Elements from External Files

You can use the Xbind command to import blocks and other drawing components from another file. First, use External Reference Attach to cross-reference a file; type **Xbind** at the command prompt. In the Xbind dialog box, click the plus sign next to the Xref filename, and then select Block. Locate the name of the block you want to import, click the Add button, and click OK. Finally, open the Xref Manager dialog box, select the Xref filename from the list, and click Detach to remove the Xref file. The imported block remains as part of the current file. (See Chapter 13 for details on importing drawing components.) You can also use the AutoCAD DesignCenter to import items from external files. DesignCenter is described in Chapter 22.

The Tool Palettes give you access to frequently used blocks and hatch patterns that reside in other drawings. You can open the Tool Palettes by clicking the Tool Palettes icon in the Standard toolbar.

In the standard AutoCAD installations, the Tool Palettes are configured with sample blocks and hatch patterns that you can drag and drop into your current drawing. Just select a tab for the Tool Palettes that contain the block or pattern you want, then click and drag the item into your drawing. In the case of hatch patterns, click and drag the pattern into an area that is bounded on all sides by objects. When you are ready to customize the Tool Palettes, you do so using the DesignCenter.

Here you saw how an Xref file is updated in a different way from blocks. Since Xrefs are loaded along with the drawing file that contains them, the containing file, which in this case was the `Plan` file, automatically displays any changes made to the Xref when it is opened. Also, you avoid having to update nested blocks, because AutoCAD updates nested Xrefs, as well as non-nested Xrefs. When an Xref is modified while you are editing a file, you are alerted to the change through the Xref icon located in the lower-right corner of the AutoCAD window.

Editing Xrefs and the Files That Contain Them at the Same Time

In the exercise in the "Attaching a Drawing as an External Reference" section, you closed the `Planxref.dwg` file, edited the `Unitxref.dwg` file, and then reopened the `Planxref.dwg` file. This demonstrates that the Xref is automatically updated when you open the `Planxref.dwg` file. You could also keep the `Planxref.dwg` file open while editing the `Unitxref.dwg` file and then refresh the `Unitxref.dwg` Xref from the Xref Manager dialog box.

To refresh an Xref, open the Xref Manager dialog box while in the `Planxref.dwg` file. Highlight the Unitxref name in the list box, click the Reload button, and click OK. Since both the Xref file and the containing file are open, you'll get the message you saw in step 3 of the previous exercise:

```
File is open for editing. Unable to Demand load, Perform a full read instead?
```

Click OK at this message to update the Xref. By the way, you'll get the same message if someone else is working on the `Unitxref` file over a network while you're attempting to update the Xref in the

`Planxref.dwg` file. The warning message tells you that an Xref file is currently being edited. See the section "Controlling Xref Settings in the Options Dialog Box" later in this chapter for more information on the Demand Load feature.

TIP *If you find that you use Xrefs frequently, you might want to place the Insert toolbar permanently in your AutoCAD window. It contains tools for inserting both blocks and Xrefs. To open the Insert toolbar, right-click any toolbar, and then click the Insert check box in the Toolbar dialog box.*

Other Differences between External References and Blocks

Here are a few other differences between external references (Xrefs) and inserted blocks that you will want to keep in mind:

- Any new layers, text styles, or line types brought in with cross-referenced files do not become part of the current file. If you want to import any of these items, you can use the Xbind command (described in Chapter 13).
- If you make changes to the layers of a cross-referenced file, those changes are not retained when the file is saved, unless you checked the Retain Changes To Xref Layers option in the Open And Save tab of the Options dialog box. This option can be found in the External References (Xrefs) button group. This option instructs AutoCAD to remember any layer color or visibility settings from one editing session to the next. In the standard AutoCAD settings, this option is on by default.

TIP *Another way to ensure that layer settings for Xrefs are retained is to enter* ***Visretain↵*** *at the command prompt. At the* `New value for VISRETAIN <0>:` *prompt, enter* ***1***.

- To segregate layers in Xref files from layers in the current drawing, the Xref file's layers are prefixed with their file's name. A vertical bar separates the filename prefix and the layer name when you view a list of layers in the Layer drop-down list or the Layer Properties Manager dialog box (as in Unitxref | wall).
- You cannot explode Xrefs. You can, however, convert an Xref into a block and then explode it. To do this, click the Bind button in the External Reference dialog box to open another dialog box that offers two ways of converting an Xref into a block. See the section "The External Reference Dialog Box" later in this chapter for more information on this dialog box.
- If an Xref is renamed or moved to another location on your hard disk, AutoCAD won't be able to find that file when it opens other files to which the Xref is attached. If this happens, you must use the Browse option in the External Reference dialog box to tell AutoCAD where to find the cross-reference file.

WARNING *Take care when relocating an Xref file with the Browse button. The Browse button can assign a file of a different name to an existing Xref as a substitution.*

Xref files are especially useful in workgroup environments in which several people are working on the same project. For example, one person might be updating several files that are inserted into a variety of other files. Using blocks, everyone in the workgroup would have to be notified of the changes and would have to update all the affected blocks in all the drawings that contained them. With cross-referenced files, however, the updating is automatic; so you avoid confusion about which files need their blocks updated.

External References in the San Francisco Main Library Project

Although these exercises demonstrate how Xrefs work, you aren't limited to using them in the way shown here. Perhaps one of the more common ways of using Xrefs is to combine a single floor plan with different title block drawings, each with its own layer settings and title block information. In this way, single-drawing files can be reused in several drawing sheets of a final construction document set. This helps keep data consistent across drawings and reduces the number of overall drawings needed.

This is exactly how Xrefs were used in the San Francisco Main Library drawings. One floor plan file contained most of the main information for that floor. The floor plan was then used as an Xref in another file that contained the title block, as well as additional information such as furnishings or floor finish reference symbols. Layer visibility was controlled in each title block drawing so only the data related to that drawing appeared.

Multiple Xref files were also used by segregating the structural column grid layout drawings from the floor plan files. In other cases, portions of plans from different floors were combined into a single drawing using Xrefs, as shown here.

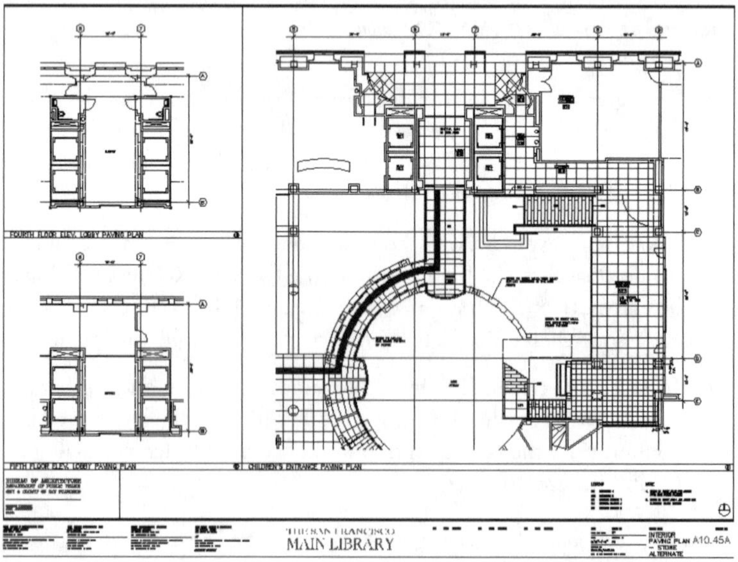

Other External Reference Options

There are many other features unique to external reference files. Let's briefly look at some of the other options in the Xref Manager dialog box.

Options in the Xref Manager Dialog Box

The following options are found in the main Xref Manager dialog box, shown in Figure 6.13 earlier in this chapter. All but the Attach option are available only when an Xref is present in the current drawing and its name is selected from the list of Xrefs shown in the main part of the dialog box.

Attach Opens the Select Reference dialog box, in which you can select a file to attach and set the parameters for the attachment.

Detach Detaches an Xref from the current file. The file is then completely disassociated from the current file.

Reload Restores an unloaded Xref.

Unload Similar to Detach but maintains a link to the Xref file so that it can be quickly reattached. This has an effect similar to freezing a layer and can reduce redraw, regeneration, and file-loading times.

Bind Converts an Xref into a block. Bind offers two options: Bind (again) and Insert. Bind's Bind option maintains the Xref's named elements (layers, line types, and text and dimension styles) by creating new layers in the current file with the Xref's filename prefix (see Chapter 13). The Insert option does not attempt to maintain the Xref's named elements but merges them with named elements of the same name in the current file. For example, if both the Xref and the current file have layers of the same name, the objects in the Xref are placed in the layers of the same name in the current file.

ACAD only

Open Lets you open an Xref. Select the Xref from the list, and then click Open. The Xref opens in a new window when you close the Xref Manager dialog box.

Browse Opens the Select New Path dialog box from which you can select a new file or a location for a selected Xref.

Save Path Saves the file path displayed in the Xref Found At input box.

List View/Tree View These two buttons are in the upper-left corner of the Xref Manager dialog box. They let you switch between a List view of your Xrefs and a hierarchical Tree view. The Tree view can be helpful in determining how Xrefs are nested. The Xref list works like other Windows lists and can be sorted by name, status, size, type, date, or path. To sort by name, for example, click the Reference Name button at the top of the list.

The External Reference Dialog Box

The External Reference dialog box, shown in Figure 6.14 earlier in this chapter, offers these options:

Browse Opens the Select Reference File dialog box to allow you to change the file you are importing as an Xref.

Attachment Causes AutoCAD to include other Xref attachments that are nested in the selected file.

Overlay Causes AutoCAD to ignore other Xref attachments that are nested in the selected file. This avoids multiple attachments of other files and eliminates the possibility of circular references (referencing the current file into itself through another file).

Path Type Xref files can be located anywhere on your system, including network servers. For this reason, links to Xrefs can be easily lost either by moving them or rearranging file locations. To help you manage Xrefs, the Path Type option offers three options for locating xrefs: Full Path, Relative Path, and No Path. Full Path retains the current full path. Relative Path maintains paths in relation to the current drawing. The current drawing must be saved before using the Relative Path option. The No Path option is for drawings in which Xrefs are located in the same folder as the current drawing or in the Support file search path that is specified in the Files tab of the Options dialog box (choose Tools ➢ Options).

Specify On-Screen Appears in three places. It gives you the option to enter insertion point, scale factors, and rotation angles within the dialog box or in the Command window, in a way similar to inserting blocks. If you clear this option for any of the corresponding parameters, the parameters change to allow input. If they are checked, you are prompted for those parameters after you click OK to close the dialog box. With all three Specify On-Screen check boxes cleared, the Xref is inserted in the drawing using the settings indicated in the dialog box.

Clipping Xref Views and Improving Performance

Xrefs are frequently used to import large drawings for reference or backgrounds. Multiple Xrefs, such as a floor plan, column grid layout, and site plan drawing, might be combined into one file. One drawback to multiple Xrefs in earlier versions of AutoCAD is that the entire Xref is loaded into memory, even if only a small portion of the Xref is used for the final plotted output. For computers with limited resources, multiple Xrefs could slow the system to a crawl.

AutoCAD 2004 offers two tools that help make display and memory use more efficient when using Xrefs: the Xclip command and the Demand Load option in the Options dialog box.

Clipping Views

The Xclip command allows you to clip the display of an Xref or a block to any shape you want, as shown in Figure 6.15. For example, you might want to display only an L-shaped portion of a floor plan to be part of your current drawing. Xclip lets you define such a view. To access the command, choose Modify ➢ Clip ➢ Xref.

You can clip blocks and multiple Xrefs as well. And you can specify a front and back clipping distance so that visibility of objects in 3D space can be controlled. You can define a clip area using polylines or spline curves, although curve-fitted polylines will revert to decurved polylines. (See Chapter 14 for more on polylines and spline curves.)

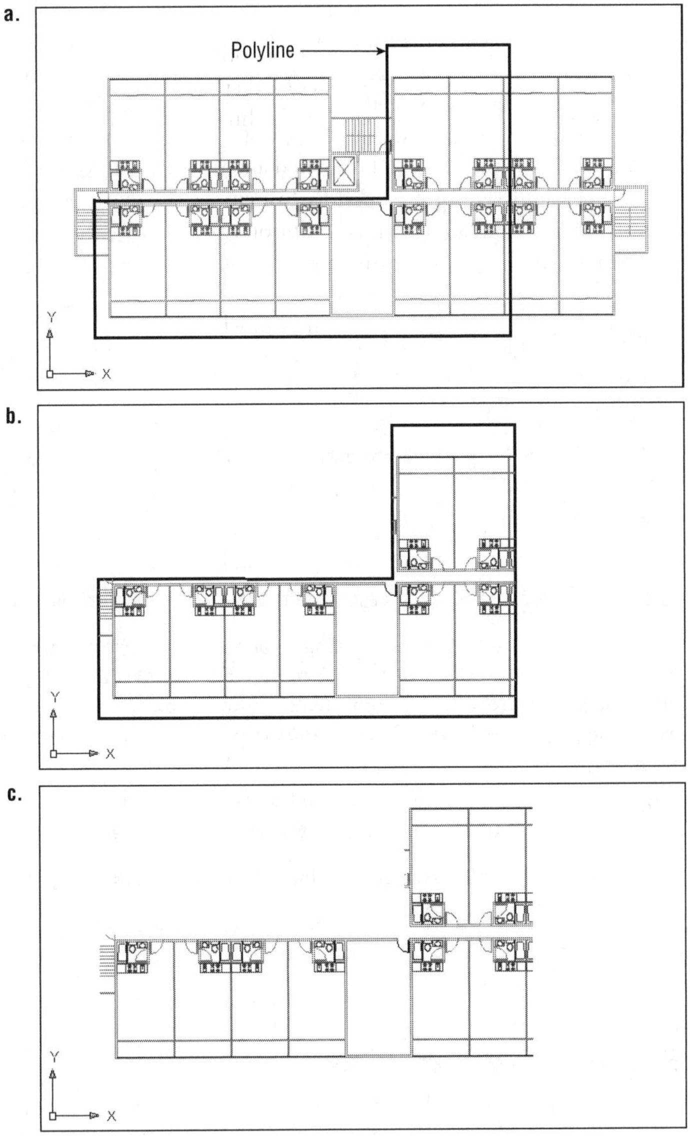

FIGURE 6.15

The first panel shows a polyline outline of the area to be isolated with Xclip. The second panel shows how the Xref appears after Xclip is applied. The last panel shows a view of the plan with the polyline's layer turned off.

CONTROLLING XREF SETTINGS IN THE OPTIONS DIALOG BOX

The External Reference button group in the Open and Save tab of the Options dialog box offers some tools to help you manage memory use and other features related to Xrefs. If you're working on large projects with others in a workgroup, you'll want to be aware of these settings and what they do.

The Demand Load Xref drop-down list offers three settings: Disabled, Enabled, and Enabled With Copy. Demand Load is enabled by default in the standard AutoCAD drawing setup. Besides reducing the amount of memory an Xref consumes, Demand Load also prevents other users from editing the Xref while it is being viewed as part of your current drawing. This is done to help aid drawing version control and drawing management. The Enabled With Copy option creates a copy of the source Xref file and then uses the copy, thereby allowing other AutoCAD users to edit the source Xref file.

Demand loading improves performance by loading only the parts of the referenced drawing that are needed to regenerate the current drawing. You can set the location for the Xref copy in the Files tab of the Options dialog box under Temporary External Reference File Location.

Two other options are also available in the Options dialog box.

Retain Changes To Xref-Layers Instructs AutoCAD to remember any layer color or visibility settings of Xrefs from one editing session to the next. In the standard AutoCAD settings, this option is on by default.

Allow Other Users To Refedit Current Drawing Lets others edit the current drawing using the Modify ➢ In-Place Xref And Block Edit ➢ Edit Reference command (Refedit). You'll learn about this command in the next section.

Special Save As Options That Affect Demand Loading

AutoCAD offers a few additional settings that boost the performance of the Demand Load feature. When you choose File ➢ Save As to save a file in the standard .dwg format, you see the Options button. Clicking the Options button opens the Export Options dialog box. Using the options on the Index Type drop-down list can help improve the speed of demand loading. The index options are as follows:

None No index is created.

Layer AutoCAD loads only layers that are both turned on and thawed.

Spacial AutoCAD loads only portions of an Xref or raster image within a clipped boundary.

Layer & Spacial Turns on both the Layer and Spacial options.

Editing Xrefs in Place

ACAD only

You've seen different methods for editing blocks and Xrefs as external files. There is another way to edit a block or an Xref directly within a file, without having to edit an external file. You use the In-Place Xref And Block Edit option in the Modify pull-down menu. This option issues the Refedit command. The following exercise demonstrates how Refedit works.

1. If it isn't already open, open the `Planxref.dwg` file. Also make sure that you have closed the `Unitxref.dwg` file.

2. Zoom into the Unit plan in the lower-left corner of the drawing so you see a view similar to Figure 6.16.

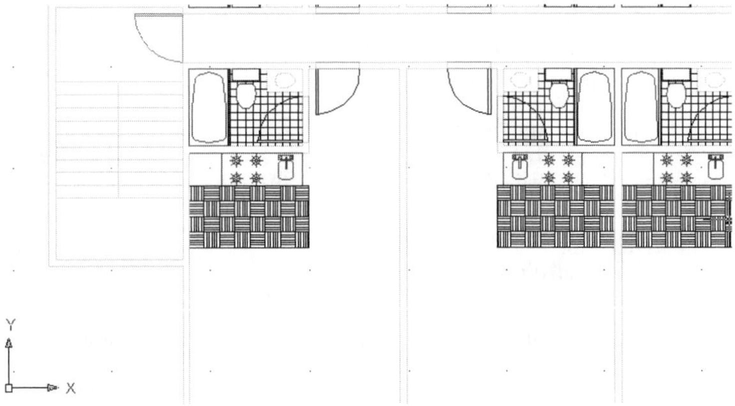

FIGURE 6.16

The enlarged view of the Unit Xref in the `Planxref` file

3. Double-click the kitchenette in the corner of the unit. You can also choose Modify ➢ In-Place Xref and Block Edit ➢ Edit Reference from the menu bar. Then, at the `Select reference:` prompt, click the kitchenette in the corner unit to open the Reference Edit dialog box.

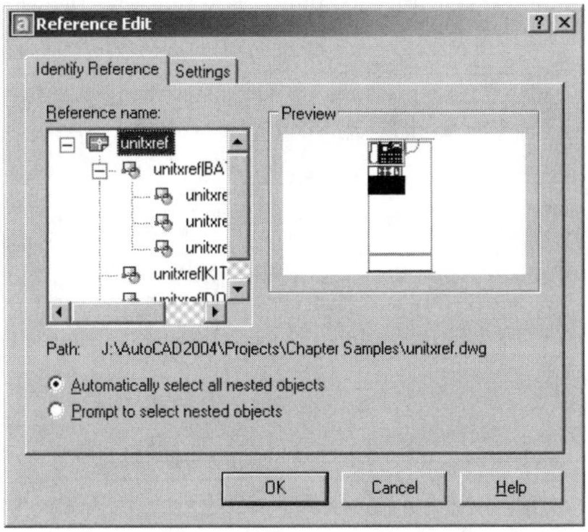

4. The Reference Edit dialog box contains two panels. The right panel shows the entire Xref that you are editing. The left panel shows a listing of the specific item you selected in the Xref. Notice that the listing shows the hierarchical relationship of the kitchenette block in relation to the Unitxref Xref.

5. In the left panel, click the Kitchen listing, and then click OK. The Reference Edit dialog box disappears, and the Refedit toolbar appears.

6. Use a selection window to select the entire lower-left corner unit. Notice that only the kitchenette is highlighted; all other objects become gray. This shows you that only the kitchen is available for editing.

7. Press the Escape key to clear your selection.

TIP *You can open the Refedit toolbar so that it stays on the screen by right-clicking any toolbar and choosing Refedit from the shortcut menu.*

The Refedit command isolates the objects you select in step 5 for editing. You cannot edit anything else in the Xref until you exit the Refedit command and start over.

At this point, you can edit a block within an Xref. Now let's continue editing the kitchenette.

1. Zoom in on the kitchenette, and then move the four burners to the right 8 inches (20 cm for metric users).

2. Erase the sink.

3. Click the Save Back Changes To Reference button on the Refedit toolbar or choose Modify ➢ In-Place Xref And Block Edit ➢ Save Reference Edit.

4. A warning message appears, telling you that the changes you've made to the Xref will be saved to disk. Click OK.

5. Zoom back to your previous view. Notice that the other units now reflect the changes you made to the Unitxref Xref (see Figure 6.17).

FIGURE 6.17

The Xrefs after being edited

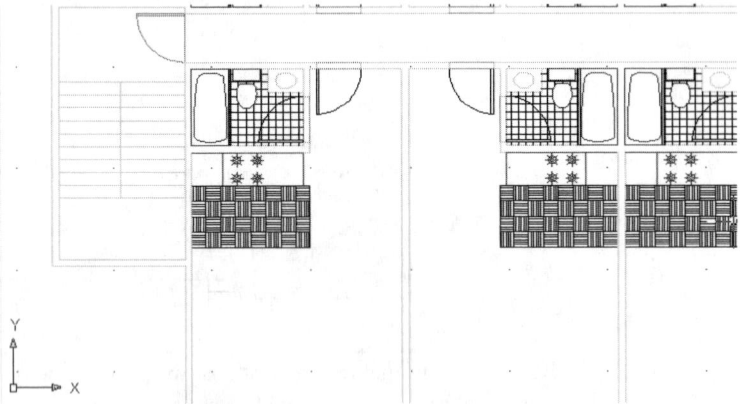

6. Open the `Unitxref.dwg` file. Notice that the kitchen now reflects the changes you made to the Xref of the unit in the `Planxref` file. This shows you that by choosing to save the reference edit in step 3, you actually save the changes back to the Xref's source file.

As you saw from these two exercises, it's possible to edit a specific block within an Xref, but to do that you must select the block name in the Refedit dialog box. .

In these exercises, you edited a block contained within an Xref, but you could have just as easily edited a block within the current drawing. You can also edit nested blocks using the Refedit command. Changes in blocks in the current file will not affect other files since blocks are not linked to external files. The changes to blocks remain within the current file until you explicitly export the changed block to a file, as you saw in earlier exercises.

Adding and Removing Objects from Blocks and Xrefs

ACAD only

In the previous exercises, you removed objects from the Kitchen block simply by using the Erase command. You can also move objects from a block or an Xref into the current drawing without erasing it. To do this, choose Modify ➢ In-Place Xref And Block Edit ➢ Remove From Working Set. This removes the object from the block or Xref without erasing it. Likewise, you can add new objects to the block or Xref by choosing Modify ➢ In-Place Xref And Block Edit ➢ Add To Working Set. Both of these menu options invoke the Refset command, with different options applied. To see how Refset works, try the following exercise.

1. Close the `Unitxref.dwg` file.
2. In the `Planxref` file, zoom into the kitchenette to get a view similar to Figure 6.18.

FIGURE 6.18

Moving the burners out of the Kitchen block and the rectangle in

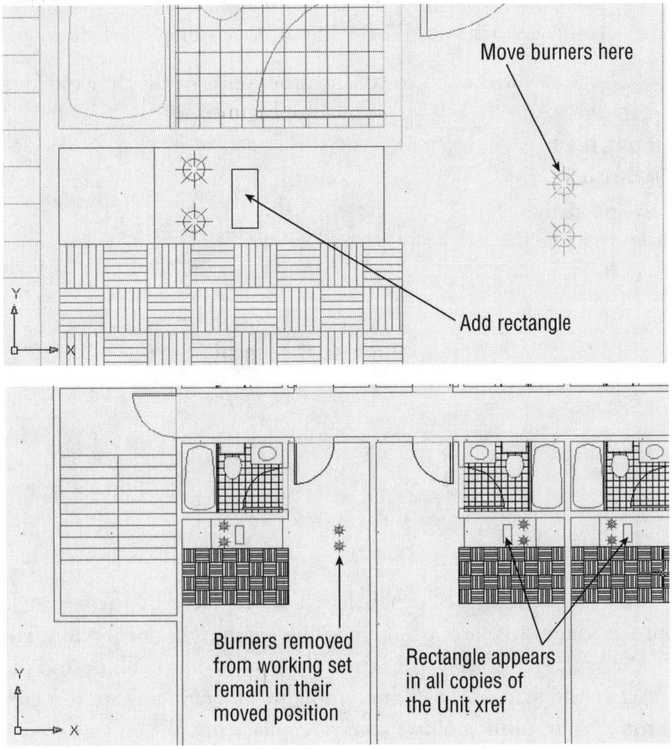

3. Double-click the Unit plan drawing. You can also choose Modify ➢ In-Place Xref And Block Edit ➢ Edit Reference and then click the Unit plan.
4. Click the Kitchen listing in the Reference Edit dialog box, and then click OK.
5. Use the Move tool to move the two burners on the right just to the right of the kitchenette, as shown in Figure 6.18.

6. Click the Remove Objects From Working Set tool in the Refedit toolbar, or choose Modify ➢ In-Place Xref And Block Edit ➢ Remove From Working Set.
7. Select the two burners you just moved, and then press ↵.

Notice that the burners become grayer to show that they are now removed from the working set. They remain as part of the Planxref drawing, but they are no longer part of the Kitchen block.

Now add a rectangle to the Kitchen block in place of the burners.

1. Draw a 7" × 16" (18 cm × 40 cm) rectangle in place of the moved burners, as shown in Figure 6.18.
2. Select the rectangle you drew in place of the moved burners and press ↵.
3. Click Save Back Changes To Reference Tool on the Refedit toolbar or choose Modify ➢ In-Place Xref And Block Edit ➢ Save Reference Edits.
4. Zoom out enough to see the other units in the drawing (see Figure 6.19).

FIGURE 6.19

The Planxref drawing with the changes made to the Unitxref Xref

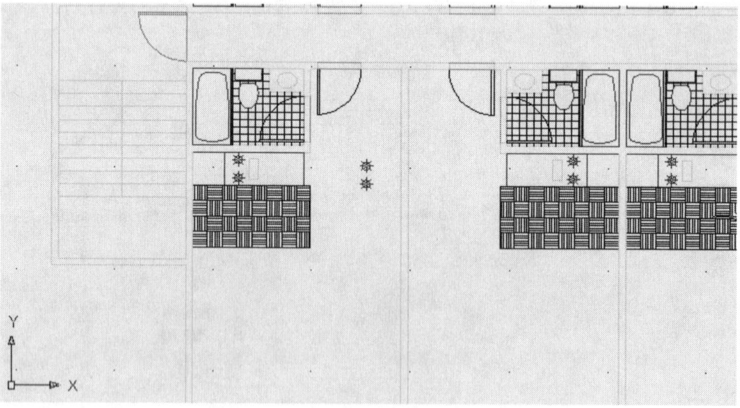

You can see that the burners have been replaced by the rectangle in all the other Xref units. The burners you moved are still there in the lower-right corner unit, but they have been removed from all the Xrefs. It is as if you had extracted them from the block and placed them in the Plan drawing.

Once you start the Refedit command, any new objects you create are added to the working set automatically, until you save your reference edits. When you drew the rectangle in step 1, for example, it was automatically included in the working set, which is the set of objects included in the block or Xref you are currently working on. You didn't have to specifically add it to the working set.

If you want to include existing objects in the working set, choose Modify ➢ In-Place Xref And Block Edit ➢ Add To Working Set option, or choose Add Objects To Working Set from the Refedit toolbar.

You've completed the exercises in this chapter so you can exit AutoCAD without saving these changes.

Understanding Reference Edit Dialog Box Options

ACAD only

The Reference Edit dialog box offers you the option to isolate specific blocks within the Xref by selecting them from the hierarchy list. You might have also noticed the two radio button options: Automatically Select All Nested Objects and Prompt To Select Nested Objects. The default option, Automatically Select All Nested Objects, lets you select any object contained within the selected object in the hierarchy listing. If you select the Prompt To Select Nested Objects option, you are prompted to select objects on the screen before the Reference Edit toolbar appears.

In addition to the options you used in the exercises, the Reference Edit dialog box also offers the Settings tab with some additional options.

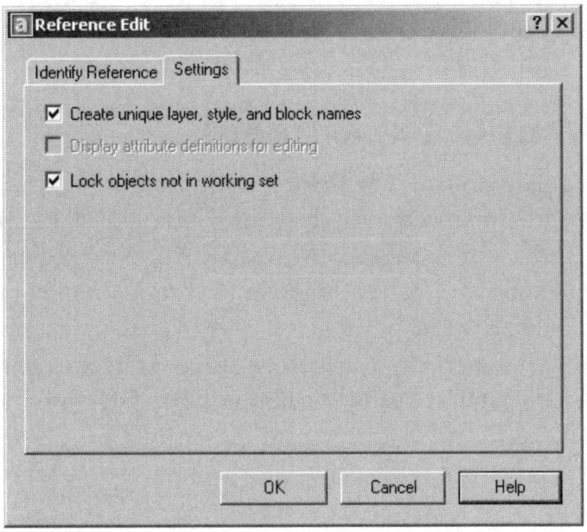

Create Unique Layer, Style, and Block Names

When you use the Refedit command with the Automatically Select All Nested Objects option turned on, you can import nested blocks into the current drawing. For example, if you selected the Bath block in the hierarchy list in the previous exercise, you would have access to the Tub and Toilet blocks in the Bath block. You can then copy either of those blocks into the current file. When you make a copy of a block from an Xref, AutoCAD needs to assign that block a name. The Create Unique Layer, Style, And Block Names option tells AutoCAD to use the original block name and append a $#$ prefix to the name (# is a numeric value starting with zero). If you were to import the Bath block, for example, it would become 0bath in the current drawing. This ensures that the block will maintain a unique name when it is imported even if there is a block with the same name in the current drawing. If you turn off the Create Unique layer, Style, And Block Name option, the original name will be maintained. If the current drawing contains a block of the same name, the imported block will use the current file's definition of that block.

DISPLAY ATTRIBUTE DEFINITIONS FOR EDITING

If your drawing contains attributes (see Chapter 10 for more on attributes), this option is offered. If you turn on this option, you can then edit attribute definitions using the Refedit command. While using the Refedit command, if you select a block that contains an attribute definition, the attribute definition will be exposed allowing you to make changes. Changes to attribute definitions affect only new attribute insertions. Except for the attribute of the edited block, existing attributes are not affected. If you want to update existing attributes to a newly edited definition, use the Sync option of the Block Attribute Manager (choose Modify ➢ Object ➢ Attribute ➢ Block Attribute Manager).

LOCK OBJECTS NOT IN WORKING SET

In the Refedit exercises, you saw that objects that are not selected in the Reference Edit dialog box are grayed out and are not selectable. The Lock Objects Not In Working Set option controls this feature and is turned on by default.

If You Want to Experiment...

If you'd like to see firsthand how block substitution works, try doing the exercise in Figure 6.20. It shows how quickly you can change the configuration of a drawing by careful use of block substitution. As you work through the exercise, keep in mind that some planning is required to use blocks in this way. If you know that you will have to try various configurations in a drawing, plan to set up files to accommodate them.

You might also want to try the exercise using Xrefs instead of inserting files as blocks. Once you've attached the Xref, try substituting the Tab1 Xref with the Tab2 Xref by using the Browse button in the External Reference dialog box. Highlight Tab1 in the list of Xrefs, and then click Browse and select Tab2. The current file still calls the Xref Tab1 by its original name, but instead loads Tab2 in its place.

TIP *You can substitute Xrefs in a way similar to blocks as shown in this example.*

By now, you might be anxious to see how your drawings look on paper. In the next chapter, you will explore the use of AutoCAD's printing and plotting commands.

FIGURE 6.20

An exercise in block substitution

1. Open a file called PART1 and draw the object shown at right.

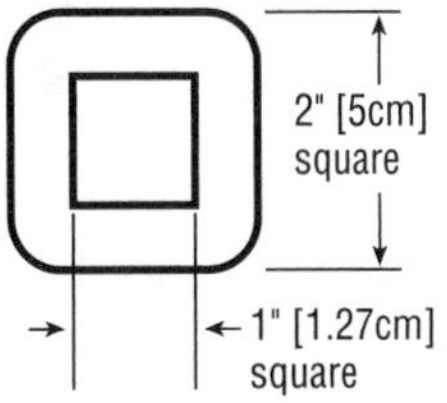

2. Next to that object, draw the object shown at right. Use the Wblock command and turn it into a file called TAB1.
(Note the insertion point location.)

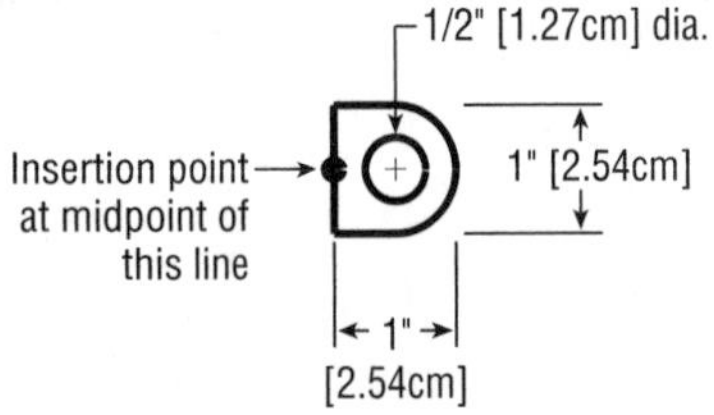

3. Draw the object shown at right and turn it into a file called TAB2.

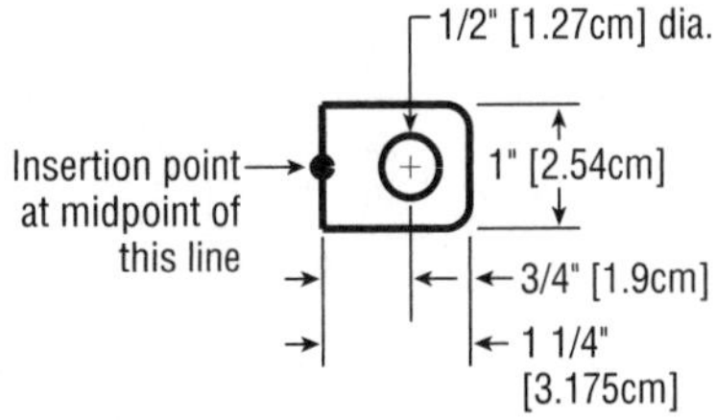

4. Insert TAB1 into the drawing in four places as shown in here. You can insert one then use the Polar option under the Array command for the other three tabs.

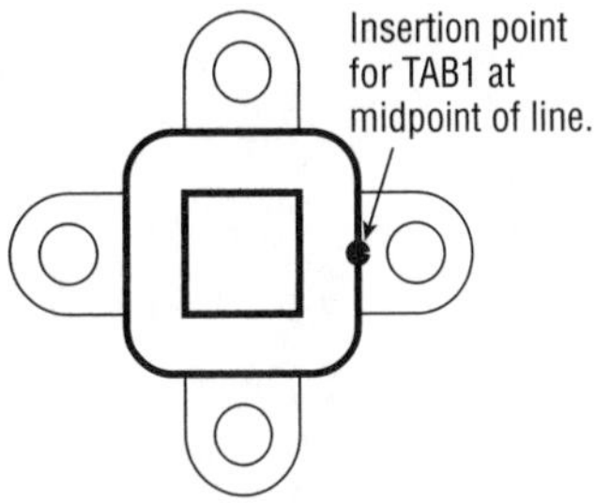

5. Start the Insert command again but at the prompt

```
Block name (or ?):
```

enter `TAB1=TAB2`. The drawing regenerates and an alternative version of the part appears with TAB2 replacing TAB1.
Cancel the Insert command.

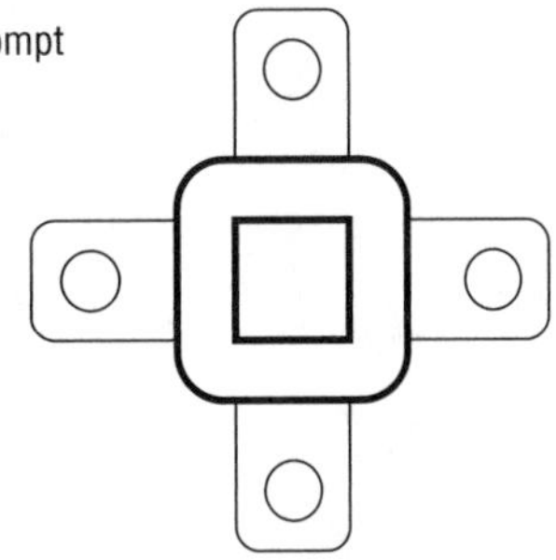

Chapter 7

Printing, Plotting, and Layouts

GETTING HARD-COPY OUTPUT FROM AutoCAD is something of an art. You'll need to be intimately familiar with both your output device and the settings available in AutoCAD. You will probably spend a good deal of time experimenting with AutoCAD's plotter settings and with your printer or plotter to get your equipment set up just the way you want.

With the huge array of output options available, this chapter can provide only a general discussion of plotting. It's up to you to work out the details and fine-tune the way you and AutoCAD together work with your plotter. This chapter describes the features available in AutoCAD and discusses some general rules and guidelines to follow when setting up your plots.

I'll start with an overview of the plotting features in AutoCAD and then delve into the finer details of setting up your drawing and controlling your plotter.

- Plotting the Plan
- Understanding the Plotter Settings
- Using Plot Styles
- Batch Plotting
- If You Want to Experiment…

Plotting the Plan

To see firsthand how the Plot command works, you'll plot the `Plan` file using the default settings on your system. Start by getting a preview of your plot, before you commit to actually printing your drawing. As an introduction, you'll plot from the Model tab of an AutoCAD drawing, but be aware that typically you will want to plot from a Layout tab. The Layout tabs give you a greater degree of control over how your output will look. You'll be introduced to the Layout tab later in this chapter. Now let's get started!

1. Be sure your printer or plotter is connected to your computer and is turned on.
2. Start AutoCAD and open the `Plan` file.
3. Choose View ➢ Zoom ➢ All to display the entire drawing.

4. Choose File ➢ Plot to open the Plot dialog box. You can also right click the Model tab at the bottom of the AutoCAD Window and choose Plot.

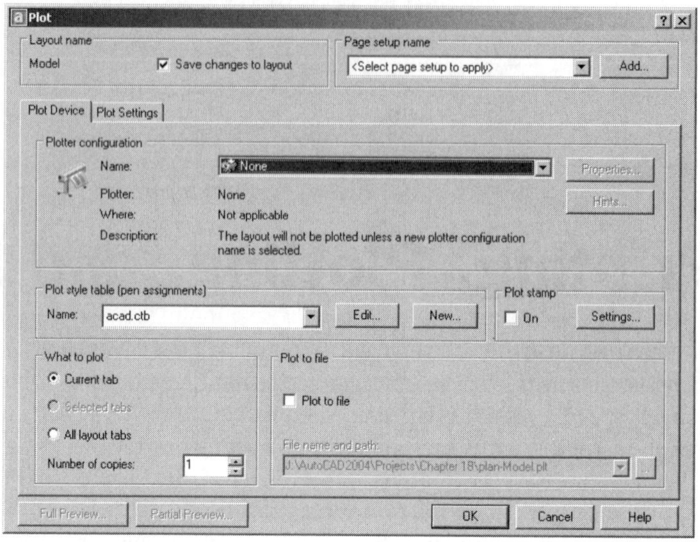

5. Make sure the Plot Device tab is selected. If the Plotter Configuration group's Name field shows None, click the drop-down arrow and select your current Windows system printer.

6. Click the Plot Settings tab, and click the Display radio button in the Plot Area button group. This tells AutoCAD to plot the drawing as it looks in the drawing window.

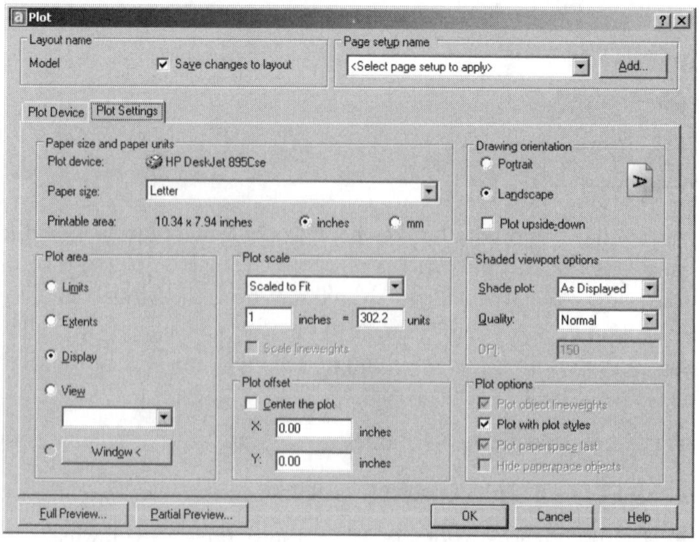

7. Make sure the Scaled To Fit option is selected in the Plot Scale button group.
8. Click the Full Preview button in the lower-left corner of the dialog box. AutoCAD works for a moment and then displays a sample view of how your drawing will appear on your printer output.

TIP *The appearance of the print preview depends on the type of output device you chose when you installed AutoCAD or when you last selected a Plotter Device option (described in the section "WYSIWYG Plotting Using Layout Tabs" later in this chapter). The print preview is also affected by other settings in the Plot Settings tab in the Plot dialog box, such as those in the Drawing Orientation, Plot Offset, and Plot Area group. This example shows a typical preview view using the Windows default system printer in portrait mode. Also note that the preview image displays the paper in its orientation as it leaves the printer. This may be a bit confusing if you are printing in landscape mode. The image appears sideways, which is the proper orientation for the landscape image in relation to the paper, even though the paper appears in a portrait orientation.*

Notice that the view also shows the Zoom Realtime cursor. You can use the Zoom/Pan Realtime tool to get a close-up of your print preview. Now go ahead and plot the file.

9. Right-click and choose Plot from the shortcut menu. AutoCAD sends the drawing to your printer.
10. Your plotter or printer prints the plan to no particular scale.

You've just done your first plot to see how the drawing looks on paper. You used the minimal settings to ensure that the complete drawing appears on the paper. Next, try plotting your drawing to an exact scale.

WARNING *It is important to make sure you use the appropriate unit settings in this chapter. If you've been using the metric measurements for previous exercises, make sure you use the metric settings in the exercises of this chapter; otherwise, your results will not coincide.*

1. Choose File ➢ Plot again to open the Plot dialog box.
2. If your last printout was not oriented on the paper correctly, select the Landscape option in the Drawing Orientation button group.
3. Open the drop-down list in the Plot Scale group, and select 1/16" = 1'-0". Metric users should select 1:20. As you can see, you have several choices for the scale of your output.
4. In the Paper Size And Paper Units button group, click the Inches radio button and then select Letter (8.5 × 11 in.). Metric users should click the MM radio button and select A4 (210 × 297 mm). The options available in this drop-down list depend on your Windows system printer or the output device you configured for AutoCAD.
5. In the Plot Area button group, click the Limits option. This tells AutoCAD to use the limits of your drawing to determine which part of your drawing to plot.
6. Click Full Preview again to get a preview of your plot.
7. Right-click and choose Plot from the shortcut menu. This time, your printout is to scale.

Here, you were asked to specify a few more settings in the Plot dialog box. A number of settings work together to produce a drawing that is to scale and that fits properly on your paper. This is where it pays to understand the relationship between your drawing scale and your paper's size, discussed in Chapter 3.

TIP *The next section is lengthy but doesn't contain any exercises. If you prefer to continue with the exercises in this chapter, skip to the section "WYSIWYG Plotting Using Layout Tabs." Be sure to come back and read the following section while the previous exercises are still fresh in your mind.*

Understanding the Plotter Settings

In this section, you'll explore all the settings in the Plot Settings tab of the Plot dialog box. These settings give you control over the size and orientation of your image on the paper. They also let you control which part of your drawing gets printed. All these settings work together to give you control over how your drawing will fit on your printed output.

WARNING *If you're a veteran AutoCAD user, be aware that AutoCAD 2004 relies mainly on the Windows system printer configuration instead of its own plotter drivers. This gives you more flexibility and control over your output, but it can also create some confusion if you're used to the previous method that AutoCAD used to set up plots. Just be aware that you'll need to understand the Windows system printer settings, in addition to those offered by AutoCAD.*

Paper Size and Paper Units

You use the options in this group to select the paper size and the measurement system you are using. You can select a paper size from the Paper Size drop-down list.

These sizes are derived from the sizes available from your currently selected system printer. You'll find out how to select a different printer later in this chapter.

The Printable Area radio buttons offer Inches and MM. When you select one of these options, the Printable Area listing changes to show you the area in the units you selected. Options in the Plot Scale button group also change to reflect the measurement system choice.

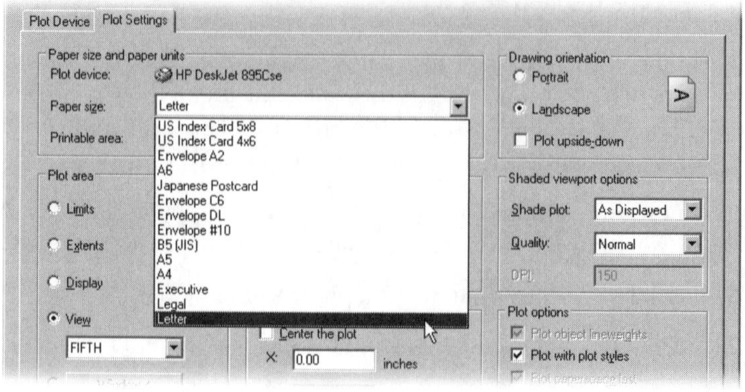

Drawing Orientation

When you used the Full Preview option in the first exercise in this chapter, you saw your drawing as it would be placed on the paper. In that example, it was placed in what is called a *landscape orientation*, which places the image on the paper so that the width of the paper is greater than its height. You can rotate the image on the paper 90 degrees into what is called a *portrait orientation* by selecting the Portrait radio button in the Drawing Orientation button group. A third option, Plot Upside-Down, lets you change the orientation further by turning the landscape or portrait orientation upside down. These three settings let you print the image in any one of four orientations on the sheet.

In AutoCAD, the preview displays the paper in the orientation that it leaves the printer. So for most small-format printers, if you're printing in the portrait orientation, the image appears in the same orientation as you see it when you are editing the drawing. If you're using the landscape orientation, the preview image is turned sideways. For large-format plotters, the preview may be oriented in the opposite direction.

The Plot Area

The Radio buttons on the lower-left side of the Plot dialog box let you specify which part of your drawing you want to plot. You might notice some similarities between these settings and the Zoom command options.

The Limits Option

The Limits printing option (available in Model Space only) uses the limits of the drawing to determine what to print (see Figure 7.1). If you let AutoCAD fit the drawing onto the sheet (by selecting Scaled To Fit from the Scale drop-down list), the plot displays exactly the same thing that you would see on the screen had you selected View ➢ Zoom ➢ All.

The Layout Option

The Layout option (available in Layout tabs only) replaces the Limits option when you plot from a Layout tab (see the section "WYSIWYG Plotting Using Layout Tabs" later in this chapter). This option plots everything displayed within the paper margins shown in the Layout tab view.

The Extents Option

The Extents option draws the entire drawing, eliminating any space that borders the drawing (see Figure 7.2). If you let AutoCAD fit the drawing onto the sheet (that is, you select Scaled To Fit from the Scale drop-down list), the plot displays exactly the same thing that you would see on the screen if you choose View ➢ Zoom ➢ Extents.

FIGURE 7.1

The screen display and the printed output when Limits is chosen

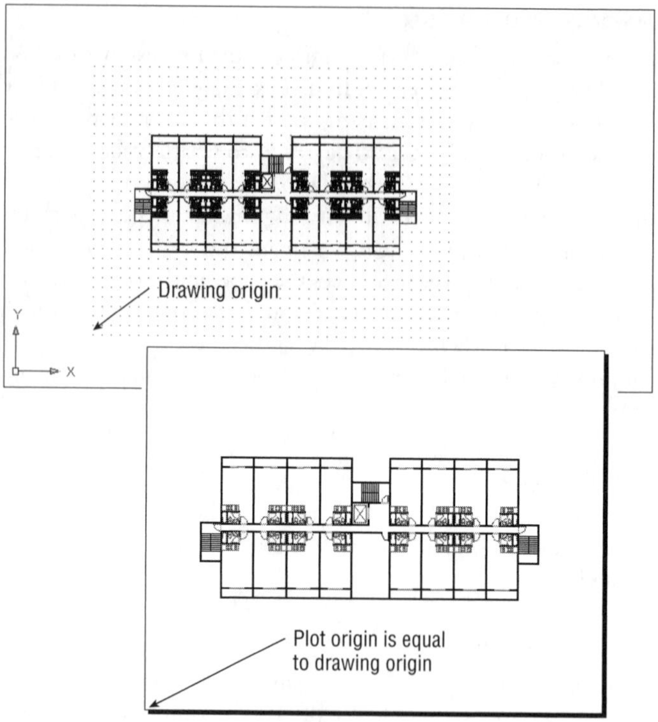

FIGURE 7.2

The printed output when Extents is chosen

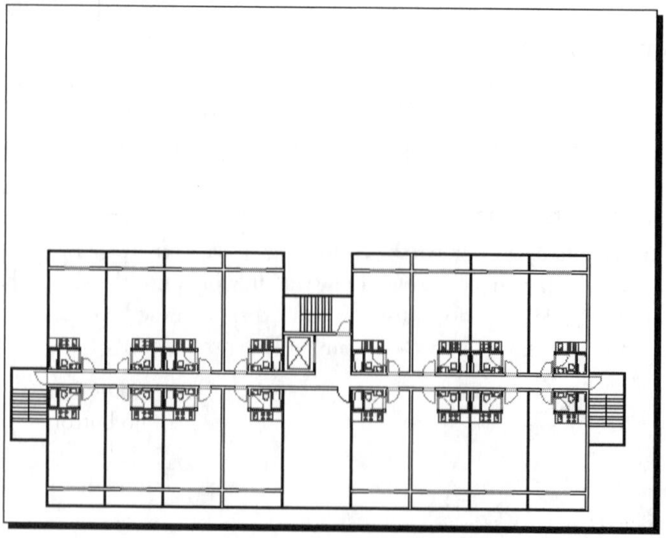

THE DISPLAY OPTION

Display is the default option; it tells AutoCAD to plot what is currently displayed on the screen (see the top panel in Figure 7.3). If you let AutoCAD fit the drawing onto the sheet (that is, you select the Scaled To Fit option from the Scale drop-down list), the plot is exactly the same as what you see on your screen (see the bottom panel in Figure 7.3).

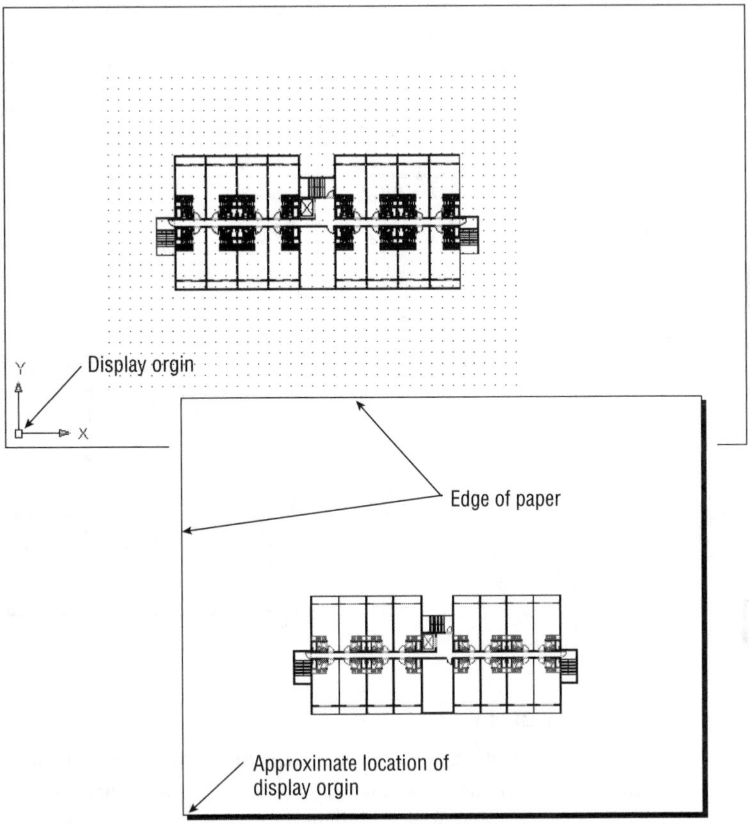

FIGURE 7.3
The screen display and the printed output when Display is chosen and no Scale is used. (The drawing is scaled to fit the sheet.)

THE VIEW OPTION

The View printing option uses a previously saved view to determine what to print (see Figure 7.4). To use this option, create a view, and click the View Radio button. You can then select a view from the drop-down list, just to the right of the View Radio button.

If you let AutoCAD fit the drawing onto the sheet (by selecting Scaled To Fit from the Scale drop-down list), the plot displays exactly the same thing that you would see on the screen if you had recalled the view you are plotting.

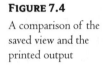

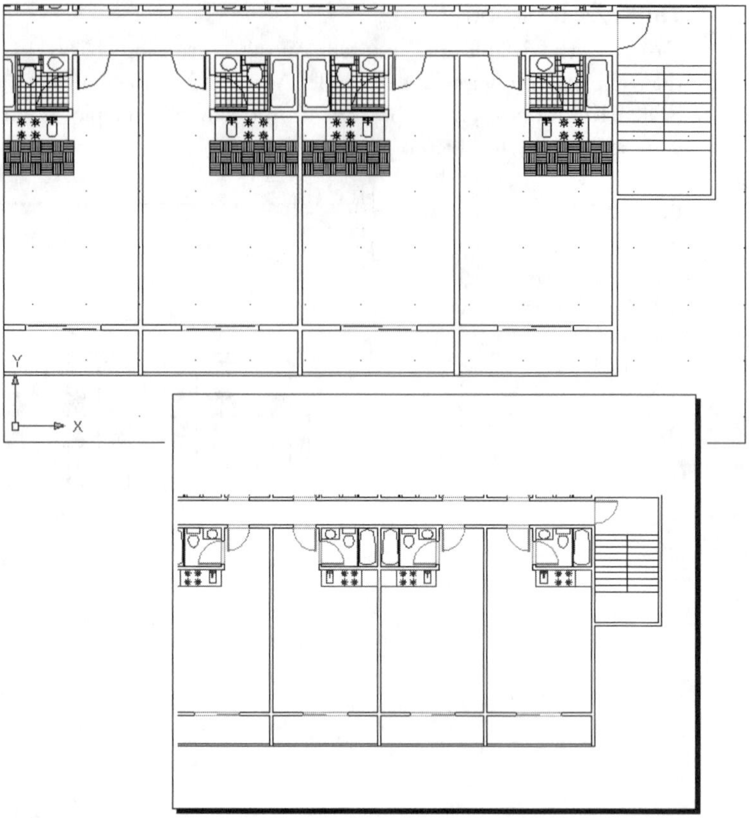

FIGURE 7.4

A comparison of the saved view and the printed output

THE WINDOW OPTION

The Window option allows you to use a window to indicate the area you want to plot (see Figure 7.5). Nothing outside the window prints. To use this option, click the Window button, and then indicate a window in the drawing area. The dialog box temporarily closes to allow you to select points. When you're done, click OK.

If you let AutoCAD fit the drawing onto the sheet using the Scaled To Fit option in the Scale drop-down list, the plot displays exactly the same thing that you enclose within the window.

TIP *Do you get a blank printout, even though you selected Extents or Display? Chances are the Scaled To Fit option is not selected, or the Plotted Inches = Drawing Units setting is inappropriate for the sheet size and scale of your drawing. If you don't care about the scale of the drawing, make sure the Scaled To Fit option is selected. Otherwise, make sure the Plot Scale settings are set correctly. The next section describes how to set the scale for your plots.*

FIGURE 7.5

A selected window and the resulting printout

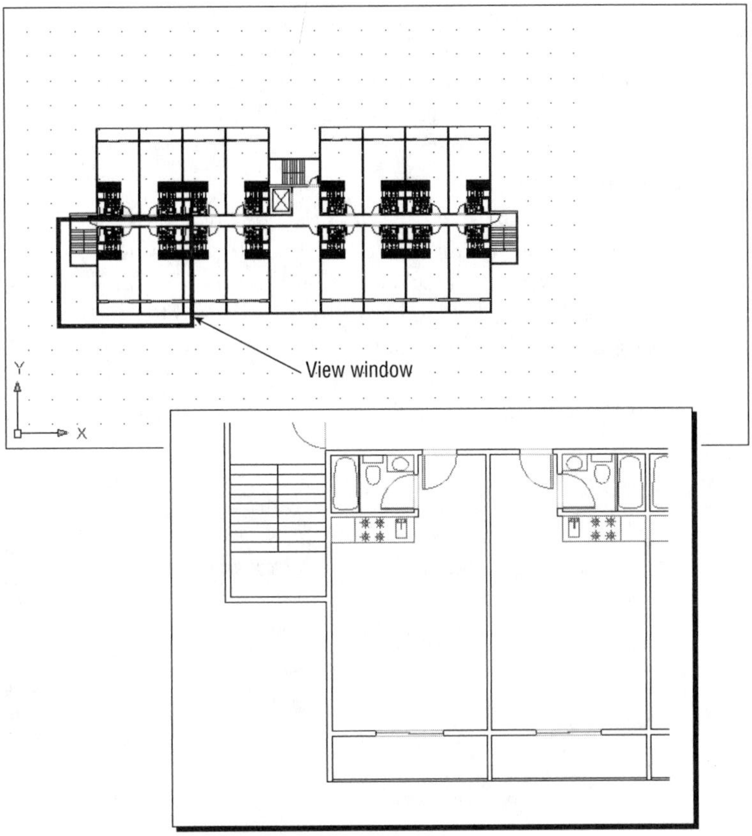

Plot Scale

In the previous section, the descriptions of several Plot Area options indicate that the Scaled To Fit option must be selected. Bear in mind that when you apply a scale factor to your plot, it changes the results of the Plot Area settings, and some problems can arise. This is usually where most new users have difficulty.

For example, the apartment plan drawing fits nicely on the paper when you use Scaled To Fit. But if you try to plot the drawing at a scale of 1"=1', you will probably get a blank piece of paper because, at that scale, hardly any of the drawing fits on your paper. AutoCAD will tell you that it is plotting and then tell you that the plot is finished. You won't have a clue as to why your sheet is blank.

TIP *Remember that the* `Plan1.dwg` *file was set up for an 18" × 24" (A2 or 594 mm × 420 mm for metric users) sheet at a scale of 1/8" = 1'-0" (1:10 for metric users). If you select these settings from the Plot Settings tab of the Plot dialog box (provided your printer or plotter supports 18" × 24" or A2 paper) and you also select Limits for your plot area, your drawing will fit on the paper and will be at the appropriate scale.*

If an image is too large to fit on a sheet of paper because of improper scaling, the plot image will be placed on the paper differently, depending on whether the plotter uses the center of the image or the lower-left corner for its origin (see Figure 7.1 earlier in this chapter). Keep this in mind as you specify scale factors in this area of the dialog box.

DRAWING SCALE

You can select a drawing scale from a set of predefined scales in the Scale drop-down list. These options cover the most common scales you'll need to use.

You've already seen how one option from this drop-down list, Scaled To Fit, allows you to avoid giving a scale altogether and forces the drawing to fit on the sheet. This works fine if you are doing illustrations that are not to scale. If you select another option such as 1/8" = 1'-0", you'll see the Custom input boxes change to reflect this scale. The Inches input box changes to 1, and the Drawing Units input box changes to 96, the scale factor for a 1/8" scale drawing.

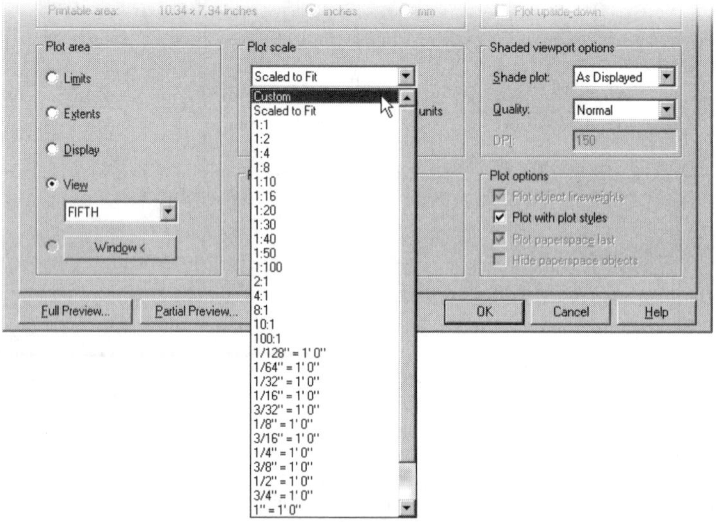

CUSTOM SCALE

If you can't find the scale you want in the Scale drop-down list, you can use the two Custom input boxes in the Plot Scale button group: Inches (or MM if you select MM in the Paper Size And Paper Units button group) and Drawing Units.

Through these input boxes, you can indicate how the drawing units within your drawing relate to the final plotted distance in inches or millimeters. For example, if your drawing is of a scale factor of 96, follow these steps.

1. Double-click the Inches input box, enter **1**, and press the Tab key.
2. Double-click the Drawing Units input box, enter **96**, and press the Tab key.

Metric users who want to plot to a scale of 1:10 should enter **1** in the MM input box and **10** in the Drawing Units input box.

If you are more used to the Architectural unit style in the Imperial measurement system, you can enter a scale as a fraction. For example, for a 1/8" scale drawing:

1. Double-click the Inches input box, enter **1/8**, and press the Tab key.
2. Double-click the Drawing Units input box, enter **12**, and press the Tab key.

If you specify a different scale from the one you chose while setting up your drawing, AutoCAD will plot your drawing to that scale. You are not restricted in any way as to scale, but entering the correct scale is important: if it is too large, AutoCAD will think your drawing is too large to fit on the sheet, although it will attempt to plot your drawing anyway. See Chapter 3 for a discussion of unit styles and scale factors.

TIP *If you plot to a scale that is different from the scale you originally intended, objects and text will appear smaller or larger than would be appropriate for your plot. You'll need to edit your text size to match the new scale. You can do so using the Properties palette. Select the text whose height you want to change, click the Properties tool on the Standard toolbar, and then change the Height setting in the Properties palette.*

SCALE LINEWEIGHTS

AutoCAD offers the option to assign line weights to objects either by their layer assignments or by directly assigning a line weight to individual objects. The line weight option, however, doesn't have any meaning until you specify a scale for your drawing. Once you do specify a scale, the Scale Lineweights option is available. Check this box if you want the line weight assigned to layers and objects to appear correctly in your plots. You'll get a closer look at line weights and plotting later in this chapter.

Shaded Viewport Options

ACAD only

Most of your plotting will probably involve 2D technical line drawings, but occasionally you might need to plot a shaded or rendered 3D view. You might need to include such 3D views combined with 2D or 3D Wireframe views. AutoCAD offers the Shaded Viewport Options that enable you to plot shaded or rendered 3D views of your AutoCAD drawing. These options give you control over the quality or your rendered output.

The Shaded Viewport Options group offers three options:

- The Shade Plot drop-down list
- The Quality drop-down list
- The DPI (dots per inch) input box

The Shade Plot drop down list lets you control how a Model Space view will be plotted. You can choose from As Displayed, Wireframe, Hidden, or Rendered. (LT users will not have the Rendered option.) As Displayed plots the Model Space view as it appears on your screen. Hidden plots your Model Space view with hidden lines removed. Rendered renders your Model Space view before plotting. The Shade Plot options are not available if you are plotting from a Layout tab. You can control the way each individual layout viewport is plotted through the viewport's Properties settings. You'll learn more about layout viewport properties later in this chapter.

The Quality drop-down list offers options to control the print quality of your shaded or rendered view. Each option detemines the DPI (dots per inch) setting for your output. The Draft option plots 3D views as wireframe. The Preview option offers 150 dpi resolution. The Normal option offers 300 dpi resolution. The Presentation option offers 600 dpi resolution, and the Maximum option defers dpi resolution to the current output devices settings. The Custom option lets you set a custom dpi setting. When Custom is selected, the DPI input box is made available for your input.

TIP *If you are a bit confused by some of the terms discussed for the Shaded Viewport Options, don't be alarmed. You'll learn about 3D Shaded and Rendered views in Part IV of this book. And when you start to explore 3D modeling in AutoCAD, come back and review the Shaded Viewport Options.*

Plot Offset

Frequently, your first plot of a drawing shows the drawing positioned incorrectly on the paper. You can fine-tune the location of the drawing on the paper using the Plot Offset settings. To adjust the position of your drawing on the paper, you enter the location of the view origin in relation to the plotter origin in x- and y-coordinates (see Figure 7.6).

FIGURE 7.6

Adjusting the image location on a sheet

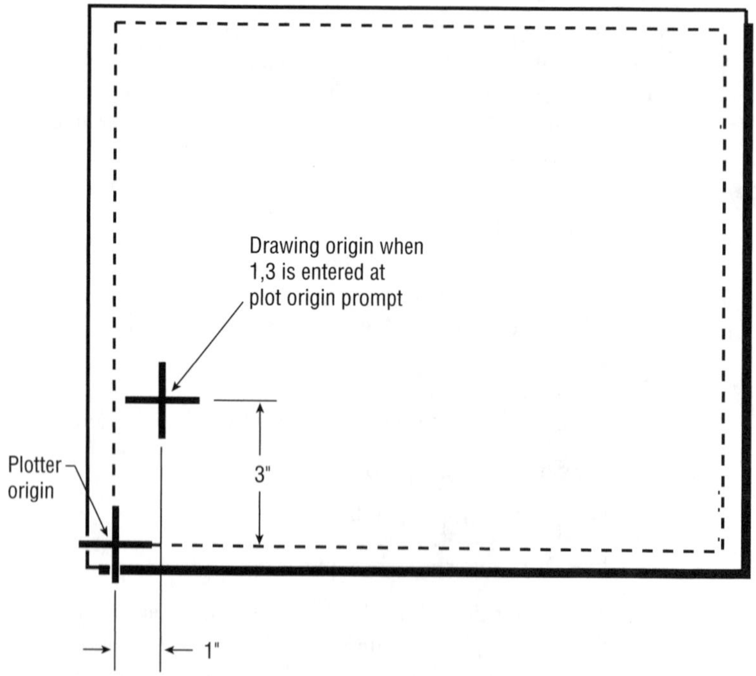

For example, suppose you plot a drawing, and then realize that it needs to be moved 1" to the right and 3" up on the sheet. You can replot the drawing by making the following changes.

1. Double-click the X input box, type **1**, and press the Tab key.
2. Double-click the Y input box, type **3**, and press the Tab key.

Now proceed with the rest of the plot configuration. With the above settings, when the plot is done, the image is shifted on the paper exactly 1" to the right and 3" up.

Plot Options

The options in the Plot Options button group offer a greater amount of control over your output and require some detailed instruction. Here is a brief description of these options. You'll learn more about them in the next section.

Plot Object Lineweights

As mentioned earlier, AutoCAD now lets you assign line weights to objects either through their layer assignment or by directly assigning a line weight to the object itself. If you use this feature in your drawing, this option lets you turn line weights on or off in your output.

Plot with Plot Styles

Plot styles give you a high degree of control over your drawing output. You can control whether your output is in color or black and white, and you can control whether filled areas are drawn in a solid color or a pattern. You can even control the way lines are joined at corners. You'll learn more about these options and how they affect your work in the next section.

Plot Paperspace Last

When you are using a Layout tab, otherwise known as Paper Space, this option determines whether objects in Paper Space are drawn before or after objects in Model Space. You'll learn more about Model Space and Paper Space later in this chapter.

Hide Paperspace Objects

This option pertains to 3D models in AutoCAD. When you draw in 3D, you see your drawing as a *wireframe view*. In a wireframe view, your drawing looks like it's transparent even though it is made up of "solid" surfaces. Using hidden line removal, you can view and plot your 3D drawings so that solid surfaces are opaque. To view a 3D drawing in the editor with hidden lines removed, use the Hide command. To plot a 3D drawing with hidden lines removed, use the Hide Objects option.

WARNING *Hide Paperspace Objects does not work for views in the Layout tab viewport described in the next section. Instead, you need to set the viewport's Hideplot property to On. (Click the viewport, right-click, and choose Hideplot ➢ On from the shortcut menu.)*

WYSIWYG Plotting Using Layout Tabs

You've probably noticed the tabs at the bottom of the drawing area labeled Model, Layout 1, and Layout 2. So far, you've done all your work in the Model tab, also known as Model Space. The other two tabs open views to your drawing that are specifically geared toward printing and plotting. The Layout views allow you to control drawing scale, add title blocks, and even set up different layer settings from those in the Model tab. You can think of the Layout tabs as page layout spaces that act like a desktop-publishing program.

You can have as many Layout tabs as you like, each set up for a different type of output. You can, for example, have two or three Layout tabs, each set up for a different scale drawing or with different layer configurations for reflected ceiling plans, floor plans, or equipment plans. You can even set up multiple views of your drawing at different scales within a single Layout tab. In addition, you can draw and add text and dimensions in Layout tabs just as you would in Model Space.

TIP *When you create a new file, you see two Layout tabs. If you open a pre-AutoCAD 2000 file, you only see one Layout tab.*

To get familiar with the Layout tabs, try the following exercise.

1. With the `Plan` file open, click the Layout 1 tab to open the Page Setup dialog box.

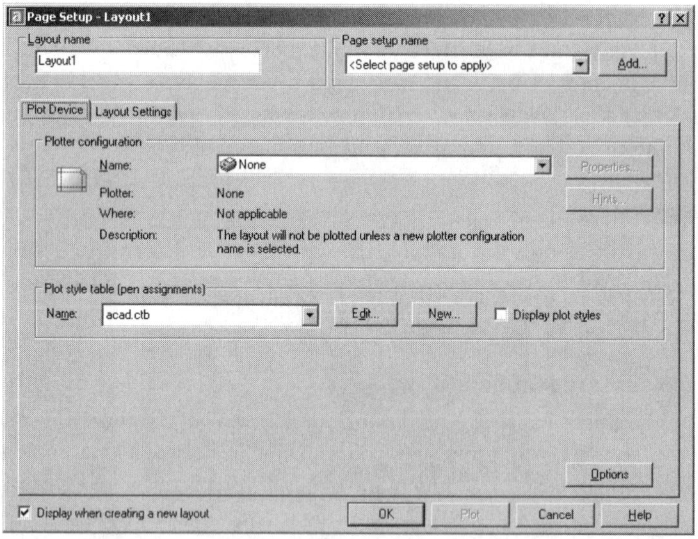

TIP *If the Page Setup dialog box does not appear, you need to turn on the Show Page Setup Dialog For New Layouts option in the Display tab of the Options dialog box (choose Tools ➢ Options).*

2. From the Name drop-down list, select your current default Windows system printer. Next, click the Layout Settings tab, and select Letter (8.5 × 11 in.) from the Paper Size drop-down

list. Metric users should choose A4 (210 × 297 mm). Notice that the Page Setup dialog box is identical to the Plot dialog box.

3. Click OK. A view of your drawing appears on a gray background as shown in Figure 7.7. This is a view of your drawing as it will appear when plotted on your current default printer or plotter. The white area represents the printer or plotter paper.

4. Try zooming in and out using the Realtime Zoom tool. Notice that the entire image zooms in and out, including the area representing the paper.

FIGURE 7.7

A view of the Layout 1 tab

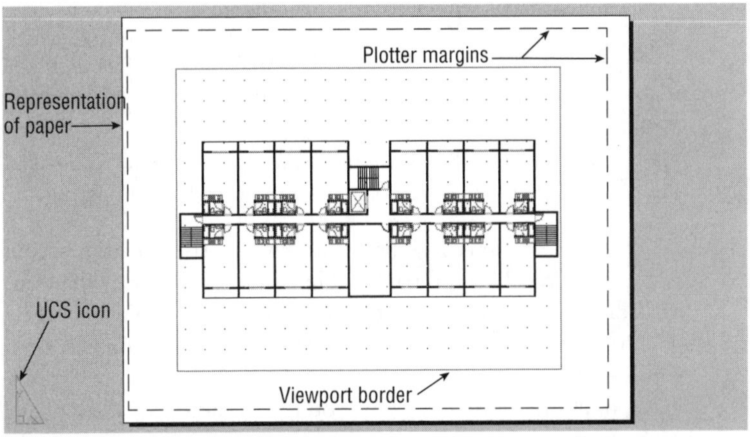

Let's take a moment to look at the elements in the Layout 1 tab. As mentioned previously, the white background represents the paper on which your drawing will be printed. The dashed line immediately inside the edge of the white area represents the limits of your printer's margins. Finally, the solid rectangle that surrounds your drawing is the outline of the Layout viewport. A viewport is an AutoCAD object that works like a window into your drawing from the Layout tab. You might also notice the triangular symbol in the lower-left corner of the view. This is the UCS icon for the Layout tab. It tells you that you are currently in the Layout tab space. You'll see the significance of this icon in the following exercise.

1. Try selecting part of your drawing by clicking in the lobby area. Nothing is selected.

2. Click the viewport border, which is the solid rectangle surrounding the drawing, as shown in Figure 7.7. This is the viewport into the Model tab. Notice that you can select it.

3. Right-click, and choose Properties from the shortcut menu. You can see from the Properties palette that the viewport is just like any other AutoCAD object with layer, line-type, and color assignments. You can even hide the viewport outline by turning off its layer.

4. Close the Properties palette.

5. With the viewport still selected, click the Erase tool in the Modify toolbar. The view of your drawing disappears with the erasure of the viewport. Remember that the viewport is like a

window into the drawing you created in the Model tab. Once the viewport is erased, the drawing view goes with it.

6. Type **U**↵ or click the Undo button in the Standard toolbar to restore the viewport.
7. Double-click anywhere within the viewport's boundary. Notice that the UCS icon you're used to seeing appears in the lower-left corner of the viewport. The Layout UCS icon disappears.
8. Click the lobby of your drawing. You can now select parts of your drawing.
9. Try zooming and panning your view. Changes in your view only take place within the boundary of the viewport.
10. Choose View ➢ Zoom ➢ All or type **Z**↵ **A**↵ to display the entire drawing in the viewport.
11. To return to Paper Space, double-click an area outside the viewport.

TIP *You can also type* ***PS***↵ *to return to Paper Space and* ***MS***↵ *to access the space within the viewport. Or click the Paper/Model button in the status bar at the bottom of the AutoCAD window.*

This exercise shows you the unique characteristics of the Layout tab. The objects within the viewport are inaccessible until you double-click the interior of the viewport. You can then move about and edit your drawing within the viewport, just as you would while in the Model tab.

The Layout tabs can contain as many viewports as you like, and each viewport can hold a different view of your drawing. You can size and arrange each viewport in any way you like, or you can even create multiple viewports, giving you the freedom to lay out your drawing as you would a page in a desktop-publishing program. You can also draw in the Layout tab or import Xrefs and blocks for title blocks and borders.

Plot Scale in the Layout Tab Viewports

In the first part of this chapter, you plotted your drawing from the Model tab. You learned that to get the plot to fit onto your paper, you either had to use the Scaled To Fit option in the Plot Settings tab of the Plot dialog box or indicate a specific drawing scale, plot area, and drawing orientation.

The Layout tab works in a different way: it is designed to allow you to plot your drawing at a 1-to-1 scale. Instead of specifying the drawing scale in the Plot dialog box, as you did when you plotted from the Model tab, you let the size of your view in the Layout tab viewport determine the drawing scale. You can set the viewport view to an exact scale by making changes to the properties of the viewport.

To set the scale of a viewport in a Layout tab, try the following exercise.

1. Press the Esc key to clear any selections. Then double-click the viewport border. You can also select the viewport, right-click, and choose Properties from the shortcut menu. Either way, the Properties palette for the viewport appears.
2. Scroll down the Properties palette using the scroll bar on the left side, and then locate the Standard Scale option under the Misc category. Click this option. The item to its right turns into a list box.

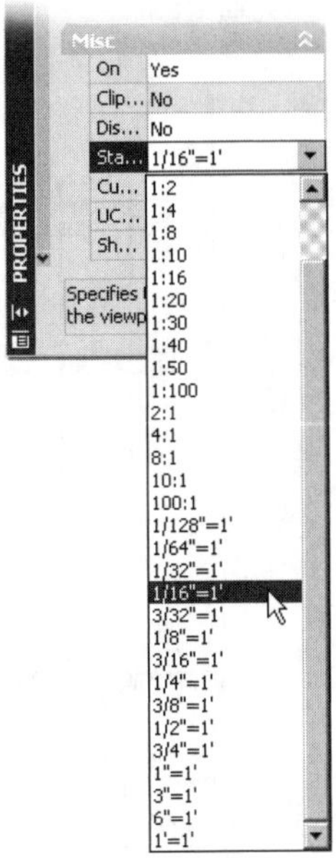

3. Open the list box and select 1/16" = 1' (metric users should select 1:20). The view in the drawing window changes to reflect the new scale for the viewport. Now most of the drawing fits into the viewport, and it is to scale.

TIP *The scale of 1/16" = 1' is similar to the metric 1:200 scale, but since you used centimeters instead of millimeters as the base unit for the metric version of the* `Plan` *file, you drop the second 0 in 200. The metric scale becomes 1:20.*

4. Close the Properties palette.
5. Use the viewport grips to enlarge the viewport enough to display all the drawing as shown in Figure 7.8. You only need to move a single corner grip. As you move a corner grip, notice that the viewport maintains a rectangular shape.
6. Choose File ➢ Plot, and, in the Plot dialog box, make sure the Scale option in the Plot Settings tab is set to 1:1; then click OK. Your drawing is plotted as it appears in the Layout tab, and it is plotted to scale.
7. After reviewing your plot, close the drawing without saving it.

In step 4, you saw that you can select a scale for a viewport by selecting it from the Properties palette. If you look just below the Standard Scale option, you'll see the Custom Scale option. Both options work like their counterpart, the Plot scale group, in the Plot Settings tab of the Plot dialog box.

TIP *Veteran AutoCAD users can still choose View ➢ Zoom ➢ Scale to control the scale of the viewport view.*

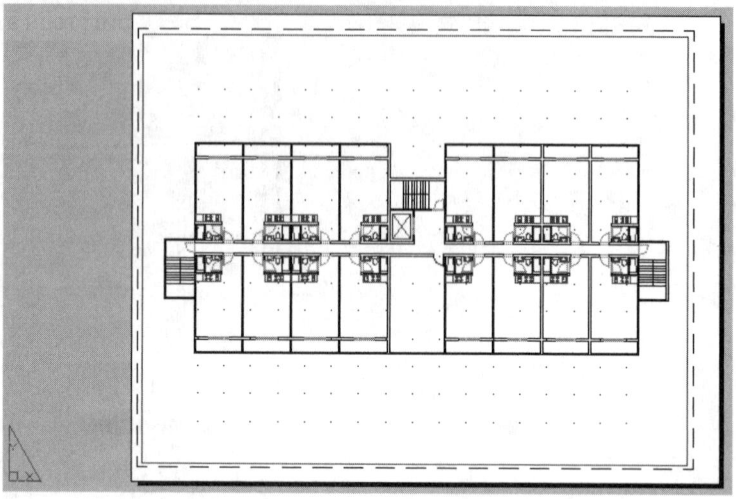

FIGURE 7.8
The enlarged viewport

Layout tabs and viewports work in conjunction with your plotter settings to give you a better idea of how your plots will look. In fact, there are numerous plotter settings that can dramatically change the appearance of your Layout tab view and your plots. In the next section, you'll learn how some of the plotter settings can enhance the appearance of your drawings. You'll also learn how Layout tabs can display those settings, letting you see on your computer screen exactly what will appear on your paper output.

CONTROLLING THE APPEARANCE OF THE LAYOUT TABS

The Options dialog box offers a set of controls dedicated to the Layout tabs. If you don't like some of the graphics in the Layout tab, you can turn them off. Open the Options dialog box, and click the Display tab to see a set of options in the Layout Elements group.

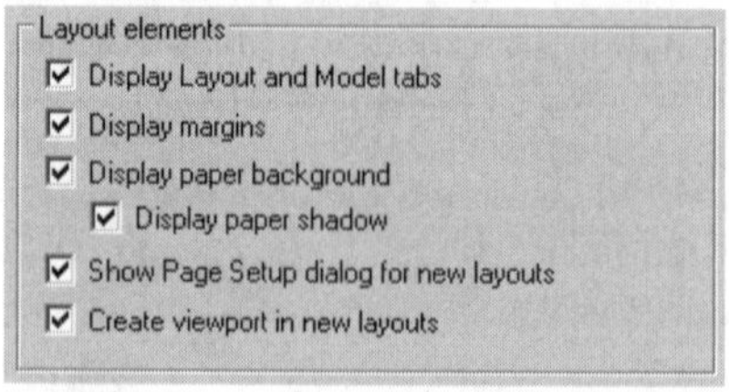

As you can see, you can control the display of the tabs themselves, the margins, the paper background, and the paper shadow. In addition, you can specify whether AutoCAD automatically creates a viewport or opens the Page Setup dialog box when you open a Layout tab for the first time.

Setting Color, Line Corner Styles, and Shading Patterns with Plot Styles

To gain full control over the appearance of your output, you'll want to know about *plot style tables.* With plot style tables, you can control how colors are translated into line weight and how area fills are converted into shades of gray or screened colors, as well as many other output options. You can also control how the plotter treats each individual object in a drawing.

If you don't use plot style tables, your plotter will produce output as close as possible to what you see in the drawing editor, including colors. You can, however, force your plotter to plot all colors in black, for example. You can also assign a fill pattern or a screen to a color. This can be useful for charts and maps that require area fills of different gradations. You can create multiple plot style tables to produce different looking output from a drawing depending on your output requirements.

The following set of exercises will show you firsthand how you can use plot style tables to enhance your plotter output. You'll look at how you can adjust the line weight of the walls in the `Plan` file and make color changes to your plotter output.

Choosing between Color and Named Plot Style Tables

AutoCAD offers two types of plot style tables: color and named. Color plot style tables allow you to assign plotting properties to the AutoCAD colors. For example, you can assign a 0.50 mm pen width to the color red so that anything that is red in your drawing is plotted with a line width of 0.50 mm. You can, in addition, set the pen color to black so that everything that is red in your drawing is plotted in black.

Named plot style tables let you assign plotting properties directly to objects in your drawing, instead of relying on their color property. They also allow you to assign plotter properties directly to layers. For example, with named plot styles, you can assign a black pen color and a 0.50 mm pen width to a single circle in a drawing, regardless of its color.

Named plot styles are more flexible than color plot styles, but if you already have a library of AutoCAD drawings set up for a specific set of plotter settings, the color plot styles would be a better choice when opening files that were created in AutoCAD 14 and earlier. This is because color plot styles are more similar to the older method of assigning AutoCAD colors to plotter pens. You might also want to use color plot style tables with files that you intend to share with an individual or office that is still using earlier versions of AutoCAD.

The type of plot style table assigned to a drawing depends on the settings in the Plotting tab of the Options dialog box at the time the file is created. In the case of drawings created in earlier versions of AutoCAD, the type of plot style table used depends on the settings of the Output tab in the Options dialog box the first time the file is opened in AutoCAD 2004.

TIP *You can change the type of plot style table assigned to a drawing. See the sidebar "Converting a Drawing from Color Plot Styles to Named Plot Styles" later in this chapter for more information on plot style conversions.*

Here's how to set up the plot style type for new and pre-AutoCAD 2000 files.

1. Open the Options dialog box and click the Plotting tab.
2. In the Default Plot Style Behavior button group, click Use The Color Dependent Plot Styles radio button. In a later exercise, you'll use the Use Named Plot Styles option.
3. Click OK to return to the drawing.

Once you've set up AutoCAD for color plot style tables, any new drawings you create are only allowed to use color plot style tables. You can change this setting at any time for new files, but once a file is saved, the type of plot style that is current when the file is created is the only type of plot style available to that file. If you find that you need to change a color plot style to a named plot style drawing, see the sidebar "Converting a Drawing from Color Plot Styles to Named Plot Styles" later in this chapter.

Next, you'll set up a custom color plot style table. Plot style tables are stored as files with the .ctb or .stb filename extension. The tables that end with .ctb are color plot style tables. The table files that end with .stb are named plot style tables.

TIP *Veteran AutoCAD users who use Hewlett-Packard InkJet plotters may be familiar with many of the settings in the plot style table options. These are similar to the settings offered by the Hpconfig command from versions prior to AutoCAD 2000.*

Creating a Color Plot Style Table

You can have several plot style table files on hand to quickly apply plot styles to any given plot or Layout tab. You can set up each plot style table to create a different look for your drawing. These files are stored in the Plot Styles folder off the main AutoCAD folder. Take the following steps to create a new plot style table. You'll use an existing file that was created in Release 14 as an example to demonstrate the plot style features.

TIP *If you change your mind about a selection you make while using a wizard, you can move forward or backward by clicking the Next and Back buttons.*

1. Open the sample file from the companion CD called `Plan-color.dwg`; then click the Layout 1 tab.
2. In the Page Setup dialog box, click the Plot Device tab. Notice that the Page Setup dialog box is similar to the Plot dialog box. The main difference is that the Page Setup dialog box has an extra button at the bottom labeled Plot.

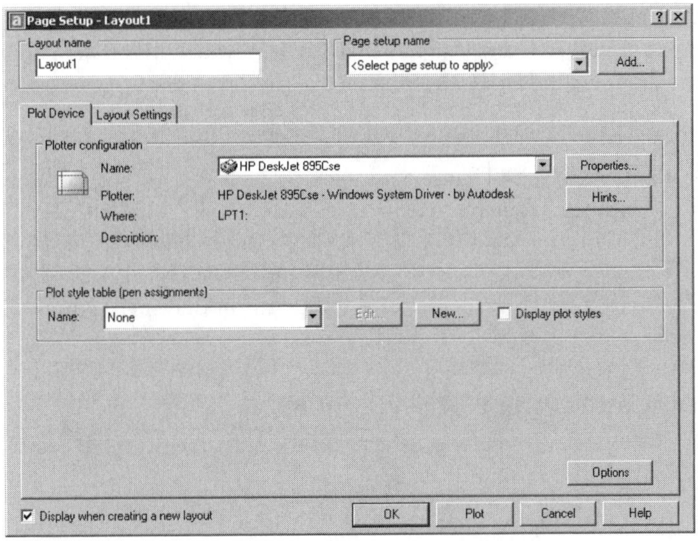

3. In the Plot Style Table button group, click the New button to start the Add Color-Dependent Plot Style Table Wizard.

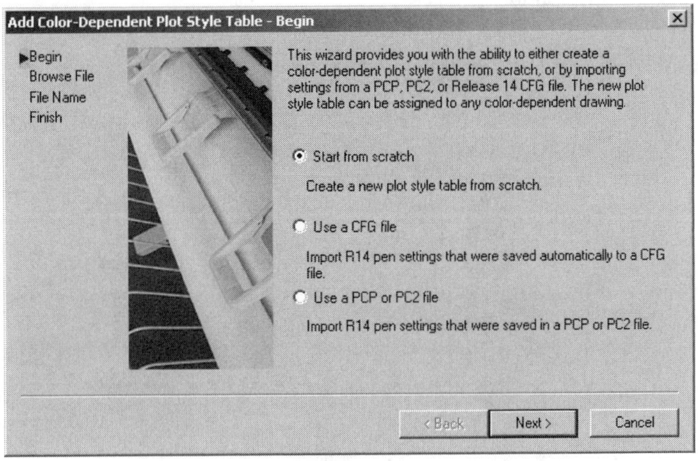

4. Click the Start From Scratch radio button, and then click Next. The next screen of the wizard asks for a filename. You can also specify whether this new plot style table you are creating will be the default for all drawings from now on or whether you want to apply this plot style table just to the current drawing.

5. Enter **Mystyle** for the filename and click Next. The next screen of the wizard lets you edit your plot style and assign the plot style to your current, new, or old drawings. You'll learn about editing plot styles a bit later.
6. Click Finish to return to the Page Setup dialog box.

With the Add Color-Dependent Plot Style Table Wizard, you can create a new plot style table from scratch, or you can create one based on an AutoCAD R14 CFG, PCP, or PC2 file. You can also access the Add Color-Dependent Plot Style Table Wizard by choosing File ➢ Plot Style Manager and then double-clicking the Add Color-Dependent Plot Style Table Wizard icon.

The steps shown here are the same whether your drawing is set up for color plot styles or named plot styles.

Editing and Using Plot Style Tables

You now have your own plot style table. In the next exercise, you'll edit the plot style and see firsthand how plot styles affect your drawing.

1. In the Page Setup dialog box, click the Plot Device tab.
2. The filename `Mystyle.ctb` should appear in the Name field of the Plot Style Table group. If not, open the Name drop-down list to select it.
3. Click the Edit button to open the Plot Style Table Editor. Click the Form View tab, which is shown in Figure 7.9.

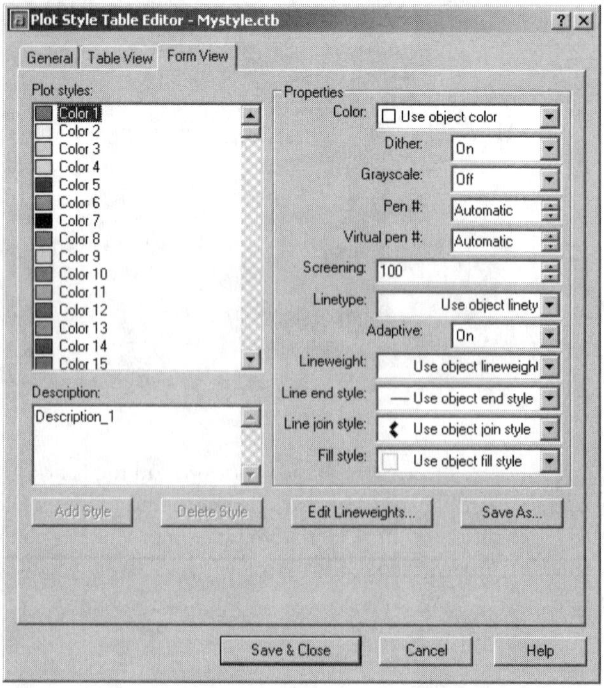

FIGURE 7.9

The Plot Style Table Editor dialog box, open at the Form View tab

TIP *You can also open and edit existing plot style tables by choosing File ➢ Plot Style Manager to open the Plot Styles dialog box. You can then double-click the plot style you want to edit. A third option is to double-click the Plot Style Table file in the Plot Style subfolder of the* `\AutoCAD2004\` *main folder.*

The Plot Style Table Editor dialog box has three tabs that give you control over how each color in AutoCAD is plotted. The Form View tab lets you select a color from a list box and then set the properties of that color using the options on the right side of the tab.

TIP *The Table View tab displays each color as a column of properties. Each column is called a plot style. The property names are listed in a column to the far left. While the layout is different, both the Table View tab and the Form View tab offer the same functions.*

Next, you'll continue by changing the line width property of the color 3 (green) plot style. Remember that green is the color assigned to the Wall layer of your Plan drawing.

4. Click the Color 3 listing in the Plot Styles list box.
5. Click the Lineweight drop-down list and select 0.5000 mm.

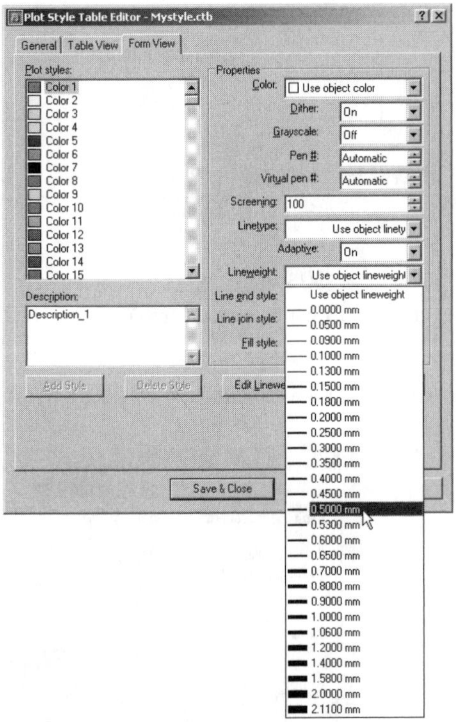

6. Click Save & Close to return to the Page Setup dialog box.

7. Click the Display Plot Styles check box in the Plot Style Table group; then click OK.

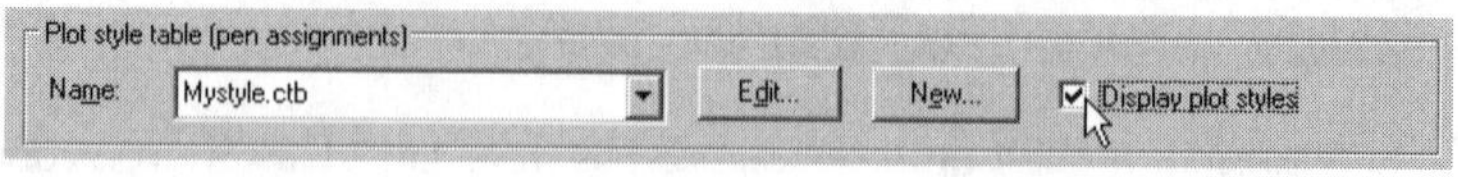

8. Zoom into the plan to enlarge the view of a unit bathroom and entrance.

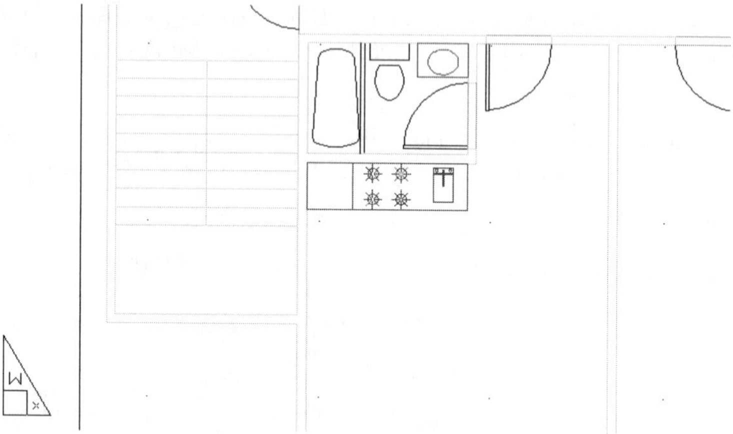

WARNING *If your view does not reflect the Plot Style settings, make sure you have the Display Plot Styles option turned on in step 7.*

MAKING YOUR PLOT STYLES VISIBLE

You won't see any changes in your drawing yet. You'll need to make one more change to your drawing options.

1. Choose Format ➢ Lineweight to open the Lineweight Settings dialog box.

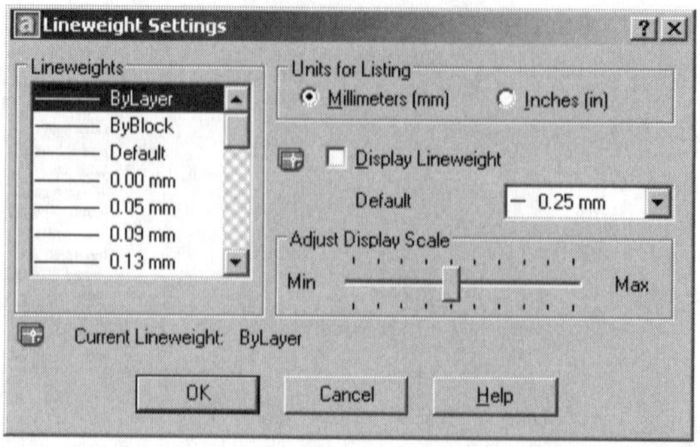

TIP *You can also click the User Preferences tab in the Options dialog box and then click the Lineweight Settings button to open the Lineweight Settings dialog box.*

The Lineweight Settings dialog box lets you control the appearances of line weights in the drawing editor. If line weights are not showing up, this is the place to look to make them viewable. You can find out more about the Lineweight Settings dialog box in Chapter 12.

2. Click the Display Lineweight check box to turn on this option.
3. Just below the Display Lineweight option, click the Default drop-down list and select 0.09 mm. This will make any unassigned or default line weight a very fine line.
4. Click OK.

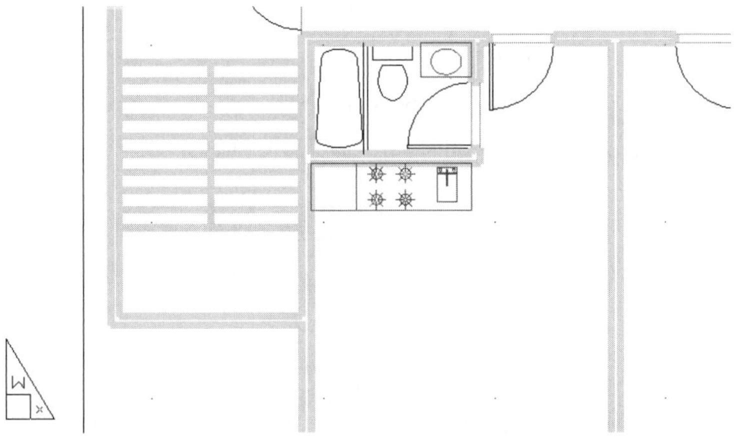

WARNING *If your view does not reflect the Plot Style settings, make sure you have the Display Plot Styles option selected in the Plot Device tab of the Page Setup dialog box.*

LINEWEIGHTS PAST AND PRESENT

In the "Editing and Using Plot Style Tables" section, you learned how you can assign a line weight to an AutoCAD color. In fact, this is the method used in earlier versions of AutoCAD for controlling line weight. But prior to AutoCAD 2000, there was no way to view the effects of line weight settings until you produced a printout, nor was there a tool such as the Plot Style Manager to help you take control over how AutoCAD colors are plotted. The plot style table not only gives you a greater degree of control over the translation of AutoCAD colors to final plot, but it adds some additional features. And the Layout tabs let you "proof" your color settings before you commit your drawing to paper.

With AutoCAD 2004, you can also assign line weights through the Layer Properties Manager dialog box. You may recall from Chapter 3 that layers have a line-weight property that can be set inside the Layer Properties Manager dialog box. You can also assign line weights directly to objects through the Properties palette. If you assign line weights through layers or object properties, you can use the Use Object Lineweight option in the Plot Style Table Editor to display and plot the line weights as you intend them.

Remember that if you want to view any line-weight setting, be sure to turn on the Display Lineweight option as described in the "Making Your Plot Styles Visible" section.

MAKING CHANGES TO MULTIPLE PLOT STYLES

Chances are, you'll want to plot your drawing in black and white for most of your work. You can edit your color plot style table to plot one or all of your AutoCAD colors as black instead of the AutoCAD colors.

You saw how you can open the Plot Style Table Editor from the Page Setup dialog box to edit your color plot style table. In this exercise, you'll try a different route.

1. Choose File ➢ Plot Style Manager to open the Plot Styles window. This is a view to the Plot Styles folder under the `\AutoCAD2004\` folder.
2. Locate the file `Mystyle.ctb` and double-click it to open the Plot Style Table Editor dialog box.
3. Click the Form View tab.
4. Click Color 3 in the Plot Styles list box.
5. Click the Color drop-down list and select Black.

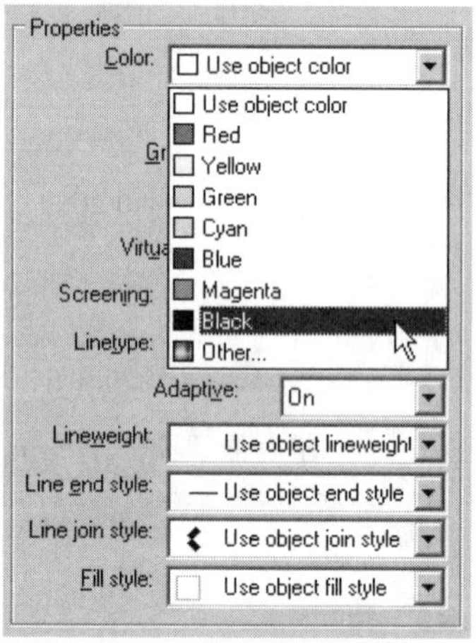

6. Click Save & Close; then close the Plot Styles window.
7. Choose View ➢ Regen All to view your drawing. Now the green objects appear black in the Layout tab.
8. Click the Model tab to view your drawing in Model Space. Notice that the objects are still in their original colors. This shows you that you haven't actually changed the colors of your objects or layers. You've only changed the color of the plotted output.

Next try changing all the output colors to black.

1. Repeat steps 1 and 2 of the previous exercise to open the `Mystyle.ctb` file.
2. Click the Form View tab; then click Color 1 in the Plot Styles list box.

3. Shift+click Color 9 in the Plot Styles list box to select all the plot styles from Color 1 to Color 9.

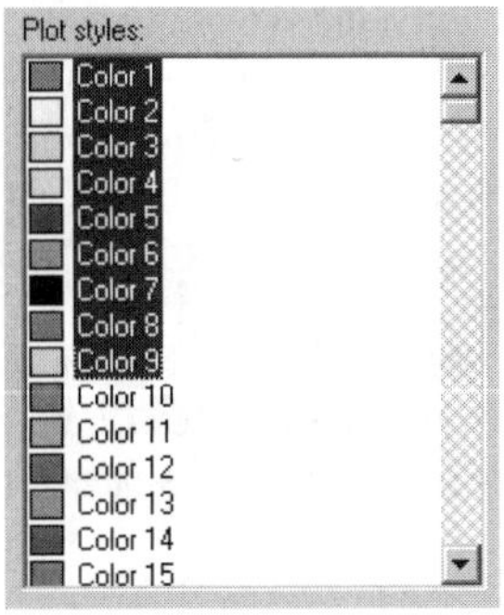

4. Click the Color drop-down list and select Black.
5. Click Save & Close, and close the Plot Style window.
6. Choose View ➢ Regen All. Now all the colors have changed to black.

Now when you plot your drawing, you will get a plot that is composed entirely of black lines.

These exercises have shown that the Plot Style Table Editor lets you set the color of your printed output to be different from the colors you see in Model Space. In the exercises, you set the pen colors to black, but if you look down the Color drop-down list, you'll see that you can choose from any number of colors. The Other option in the Color drop-down list lets you select colors from the Select Color dialog box.

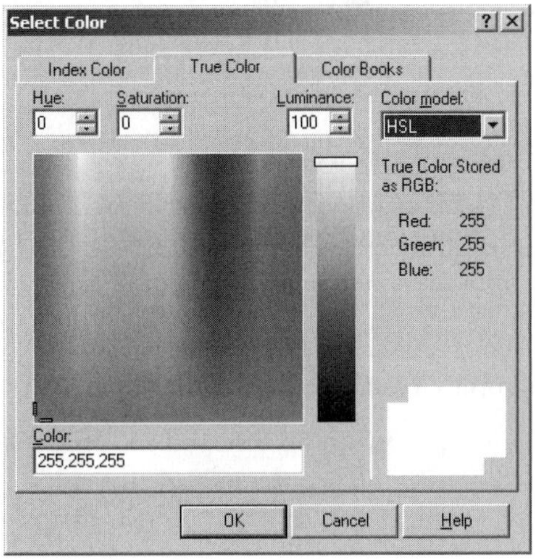

NOTE *To get the view shown here, make sure the True Color tab is selected and the HSL option is selected in the Color Model group of the True Color tab. LT users will not see a Color Books tab.*

ACAD only

In Chapter 4, you were introduced to the Select Color dialog box in the context of selecting colors for layers. Here, you can use it to assign colors to plot styles. The same three tabs are available: Index Color, True Color, and Color Books. (LT users will not see the Color Books tab.) The Index Color tab lets you select from the standard AutoCAD 256 index colors. The True Color tab lets you to choose virtually any color you want. The Color Books tab lets you use PANTONE colors.

WARNING *If you open the Plot Style Table Editor from the AutoCAD File menu, you might not see the PANTONE options of the Color Books tab. If you encounter this problem, open the Plot Style Table Editor from within the AutoCAD Plot or Page Setup dialog box, and make sure you installed the PANTONE colors from the AutoCAD installation disk.*

SETTING UP LINE CORNER STYLES

You might notice that the corners of the wall lines appear to be notched instead of having a crisp, sharp corner.

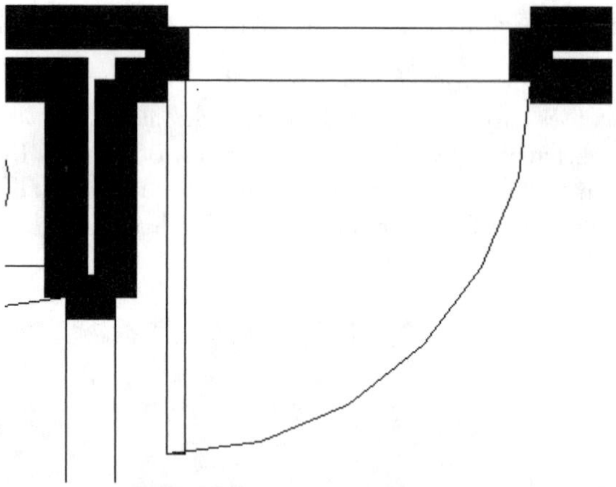

You can adjust the way AutoCAD draws these corners at plot time through the Plot Style Table Editor.

1. Open the `Mystyle.ctb` plot style table, as you did in the previous exercise.
2. Click the Form View tab, and then click Color 3 in the Plot Styles list box.
3. Click the Line End Style drop-down list and select Square.

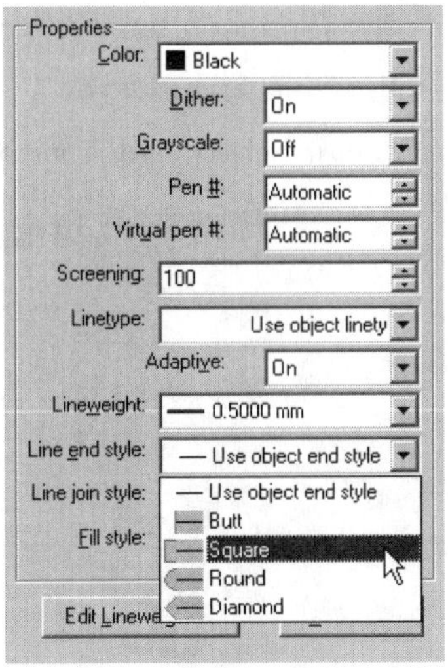

4. Click Save & Close; then click OK to close the Page Setup dialog box.
5. Choose View ➢ Regen All to view your changes. Notice that now the corners meet in a sharp angle.

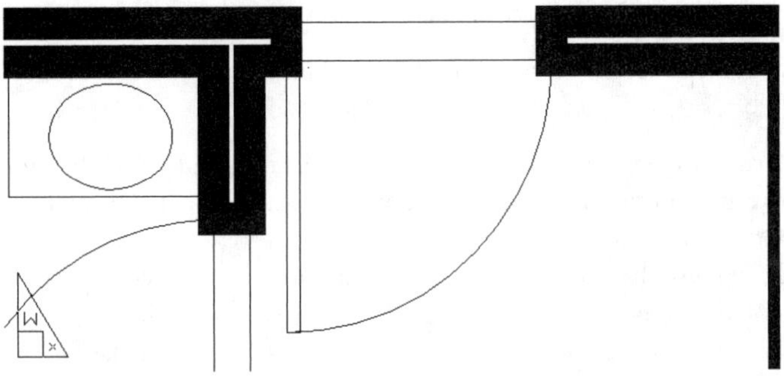

The Square option in the Line End Style drop-down list extends the endpoints of contiguous lines so that their corners meet in a clean corner instead of a notch. The Line Join Style drop-down list offers a similar set of settings for polylines. For example, you can round the corner of polyline corners using the Round option in the Line Join Style drop-down list.

Setting Up Screen Values for Solid Areas

The last option you'll look at is how to change a color into a screened area. Frequently, you'll want to add a gray or colored background to an area of your drawing to emphasize that area graphically, as in a focus area in a map or to designate functions in a floor plan. The setting you're about to use will allow you to create shaded backgrounds.

1. Open the Page Setup dialog box again, and then open the Plot Style Table Editor.
2. Select Color 3 from the Plot Styles list box.
3. In the Screening list box, double-click the number 100 to select it.

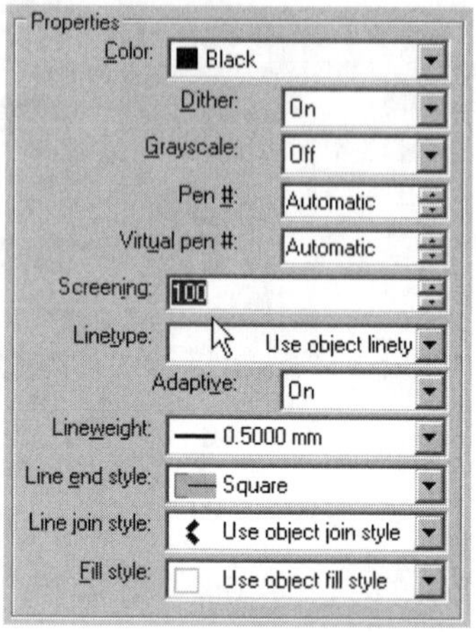

4. Type **50**↵.
5. Click Save & Close; then click OK in the Page Setup dialog box.
6. Choose View ➢ Regen All. Notice that now the walls are a shade of gray instead of solid black.

As you can see from these exercises, you turned a wide black line into a gray one. In this example, the Screening option lets you "tone down" the chosen color from a solid color to a color that has 50 percent of its full intensity.

You can use the Screening option in combination with color to obtain a variety of tones. If you need to cover large areas with color, you can use the Solid hatch pattern to fill those areas, and then use the Screening option in the Plot Style Table Editor to make fine adjustments to the area's color.

Controlling the Visibility of Overlapping Objects

You'll also want to know about the Draworder command in conjunction with solid filled areas. This command lets you control how objects hide or overlap when displayed or plotted. If you find that your solid hatches are hiding text or other graphics, you need to learn about Draworder. See Chapter 12 for more information. Some output devices offer a Merge Control option that determines how overlapping graphics are plotted. For more information, see Appendix A.

Colors and Line Weights in the San Francisco Main Library

Technical drawings can have a beauty of their own, but they can also be deadly boring. What really sets a good technical drawing apart from a poor one is the control of line weights. Knowing how to vary and control line weights in both manual and CAD drawings can make a huge difference in the readability of the drawing.

In the San Francisco Main Library project, the designers at SMWM Associates were especially concerned with line weights in the reflected ceiling plan. The following graphic shows a portion of the reflected ceiling plan from the library drawings.

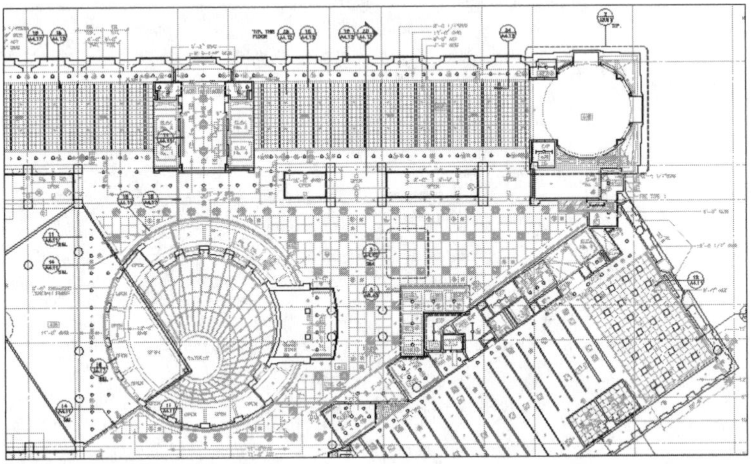

As you can see, it contains a good deal of graphical information, which, without careful line-weight control, could become confusing. (Although you can't see it in the black-and-white print, a multitude of colors were used to vary line weight.) When the electronic drawings were plotted, colors were converted into lines of varying thickness. Bolder lines were used to create emphasis in components such as walls and ceiling openings, and fine lines were used to indicate ceiling tile patterns.

By emphasizing certain lines over others, visual monotony is avoided, and the various components of the drawing can be seen more easily.

Other Options in the Plot Style Table Editor

You've seen a lot of the plot style options so far, but there are many others that you might want to use in the future. This section describes those options that were not covered in the previous exercises.

TIP *The options in the Plot Style Table Editor are the same regardless of whether you are editing a color plot style table or a named plot style table.*

The General Tab

You didn't really look at the General tab of the Plot Style Table Editor in the exercise presented earlier. The General tab offers information regarding the plot style you are currently editing. You can enter a description of the style in the Description box. This can be useful if you plan to include the plot style with a drawing you are sending to someone else for plotting.

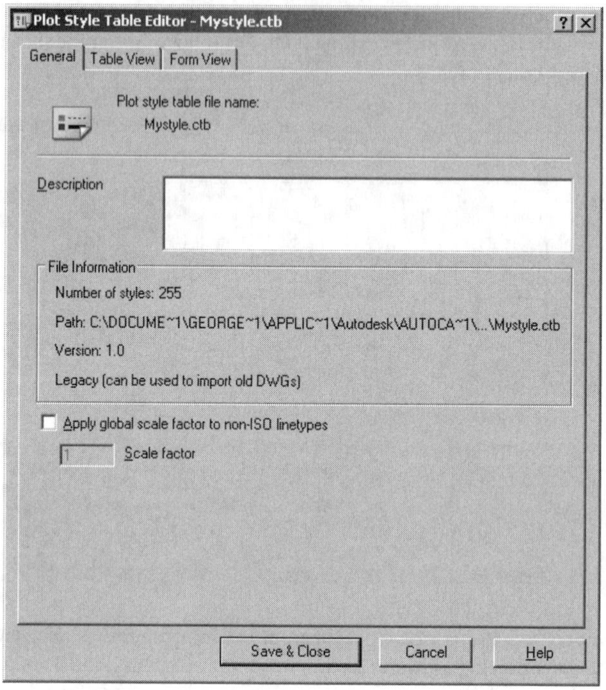

The File Information group gives you the basic information on the file location and name, as well as the number of color styles included in the plot style table.

The Apply Global Scale Factor To Non-ISO Linetypes check box lets you determine whether ISO line-type scale factors are applied to all line types. When this item is checked, the Scale Factor input box becomes active, allowing you to enter a scale factor.

ISO Pen Widths

You may have noticed a setting called ISO Pen Width in the Linetype Manager dialog box discussed in Chapter 4 (choose Format ➢ Linetype). This setting is in the form of a pull-down list. When you select a pen width from that list, the line-type scale is updated to conform to the ISO standard for that width. However, this setting has no effect on the actual plotter output. If you are using ISO standard widths, it is up to you to match the color of the lines to their corresponding widths in the Plot Style Table Editor.

THE FORM VIEW TAB

You've already seen and worked with the Form View tab, shown in Figure 7.9 earlier in this chapter. This tab contains the same settings as the Table View tab but in a different format. Instead of displaying each color as a column of properties, the properties are listed as options along the right side, and the colors are listed in a list box.

To modify the properties of a color, you select the color from the list and then edit the values in the Properties button group in the right side of the dialog box. So to change the screen value of the Color 3 style, highlight Color 3 in the Plot Styles list, and then double-click the Screening input box and enter a new value.

You've already seen what the Screening, Color, Lineweight, and Line Join Style options do. Here's a description of the other style properties.

TIP *The names of the properties in the Table View tab are slightly different from those in the Form View tab. The Table View property names are enclosed in brackets in this listing.*

Description This option allows you to enter a description for each individual color.

Dither [Enable Dithering] Dithering is a method that enables your plotter to simulate colors beyond the basic 256 colors available in AutoCAD. Although this option is desirable when you want to create a wider range of colors in your plots, it can also create some distortions, including broken, fine lines and false colors. For this reason, dithering is usually turned off. This option is not available in all plotters.

[Convert to] Grayscale This option converts colors to grayscale.

[Use Assigned] Pen # This option lets you specify what pen number is assigned to each color in your drawing. This option only applies to pen plotters.

Virtual Pen # Many inkjet and laser plotters offer "virtual pens" to simulate the processes of the old-style pen plotters. Frequently, such plotters offer as many as 255 virtual pens. Plotters with virtual pens often let you assign AutoCAD colors to a virtual pen number. This is significant if the virtual pens of your plotter can be assigned screening width, end style, and joint styles. You can then use the virtual pen settings instead of using the settings in the Plot Style Table Editor. This option is most beneficial for users who already have a library of drawings that are set up for plotters with virtual pen settings.

You can set up your inkjet printer for virtual pens under the Vector Graphics listing of the Device And Documents Setting tab of the Plotter Configuration Editor. See Appendix A for more on setting up your printer or plotter configuration.

Linetype If you prefer, you can use this setting to control line types in AutoCAD based on the color of the object. By default, this option is set to Use Object Linetype. I recommend that you leave this option at its default.

Adaptive [Adjustment] This option controls how non-continuous line types begin and end. This option is on by default, which forces line types to begin and end in a line segment. With the option turned off, the same line type is drawn without regard for its ending. In some cases, this may produce a line that appears incomplete. For more on adaptive adjustment, see Chapter 21.

Line End Style This option lets you specify the shape of the end of simple lines that have a line weight greater than zero.

Line Join Style This option lets you determine the shape of the corners of polylines.

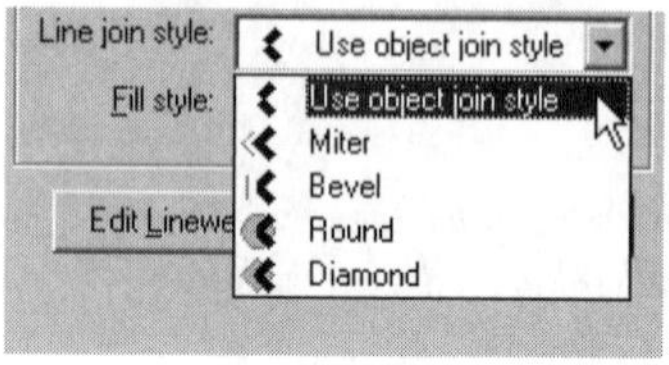

Fill Style This option lets you set up a color to be drawn as a pattern when used in a solid filled area. The patterns appear as follows:

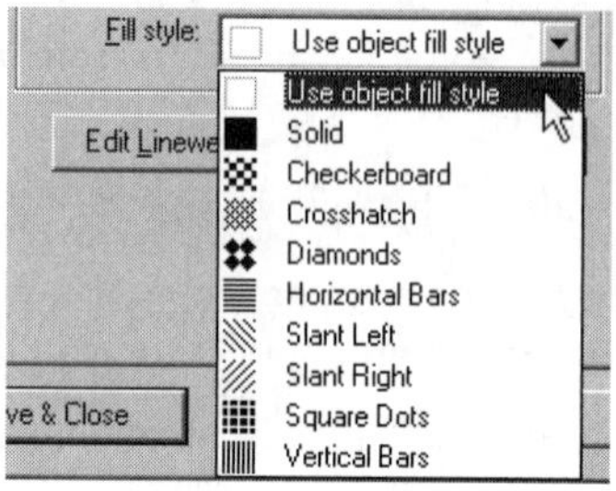

Add Style Clicking this button lets you add more plot styles or colors.

Delete Style Clicking this button deletes the selected style.

Save As Clicking this button lets you save the current plot style table.

THE TABLE VIEW TAB

The Table View tab offers the same settings as the Form View tab, only in a different format. Each plot style is shown as a column with the properties of each plot style listed along the left side of the tab. To change a property, click the property in the column.

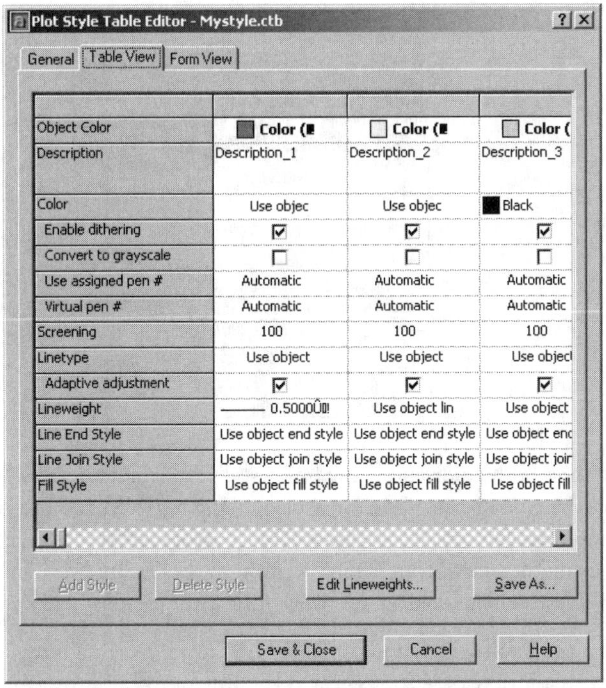

To apply the same setting to all plot styles at once, right-click a setting you want to use from a single plot style, and choose Copy from the shortcut menu. Right-click the setting again, and then choose Apply To All Styles from the shortcut menu.

Click the Edit Lineweights button to open the Edit Lineweights dialog box, which lets you adjust the lineweight settings for the plot styles.

Assigning Plot Styles Directly to Layers and Objects

So far, you've learned that you can control how AutoCAD translates drawing colors into plotter output. You have been using a color plot style table, which assigns a plot style to each color in AutoCAD. You can also assign plot styles directly to objects or layers. To do this, you need to employ what is called a *named plot style table*. Named plot style tables allow you to create plot styles that have names, rather than being assigned directly to colors in AutoCAD. You can then assign a plot style by name to objects or layers in your drawing. In this section you'll learn how to set up AutoCAD with a named plot style table to assign plot styles to objects; then you'll create a new plot style table.

Using Named Plot Style Tables

Out of the box, AutoCAD uses the color-dependent plot style table for all new drawings. You can create a new drawing that uses named plot style tables in two ways. The simpler way is to use any of the named plot style template files when you first create a new drawing. You'll see these templates under the Template option in the Create New Drawing dialog box or in the Select Template dialog box.

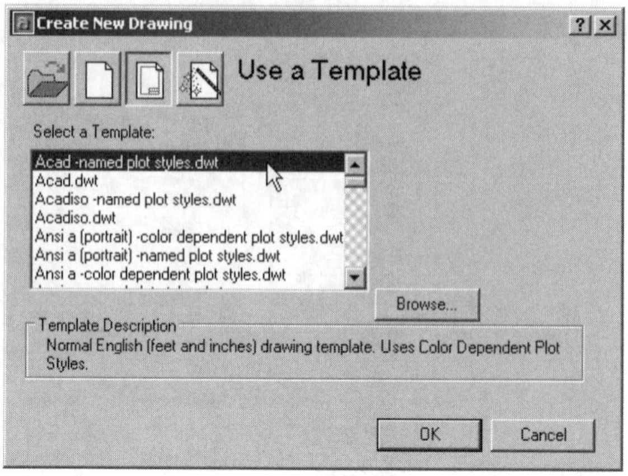

By offering both color and named plot style drawing templates, AutoCAD makes it easy to create and select the type of plot style for your drawing regardless of the current default style.

If you prefer, you can set up AutoCAD to use a named plot style by default when you create a drawing using the Start From Scratch option in the Create New Drawing dialog box. To set up the default plot style table for new drawings, follow these steps:

1. Choose Tools ➢ Options to open the Options dialog box, and click the Plotting tab. This tab offers a variety of settings geared toward your plotter or printer.
2. In the upper-right corner of the dialog box, click the Use Named Plot Styles radio button.
3. Click OK to close the Options dialog box.

To create and try out a new named plot style, you can open an existing file from an earlier version of AutoCAD. In the next few exercises, you'll use the `Plan-named.dwg` file from the companion CD. This is a Release 14 file that will be assigned the type of plot style table that is currently the default as determined by the Use Named Plot Styles option you just set in the previous exercise.

1. Open the `Plan-name.dwg` file from the companion CD.
2. Choose File ➢ Plot Style Manager to open a window to the Plot Styles folder.
3. Double-click the Add-A-Plot Style Table Wizard icon to start the Plot Style Table Wizard.
4. Click Next to open the Begin screen, choose Start From Scratch, and then click Next to open the Pick Plot Style Table screen.
5. Click the Named Plot Style Table radio button, and then click Next to open the File Name screen.
6. Enter **Mynamedstyle1** in the File Name input box, and click Next to open the Finish screen. Here you can exit, or you can edit the new plot style table. This time you'll edit the table from the wizard.
7. Click the Plot Style Table Editor button to open the Plot Style Table Editor dialog box.

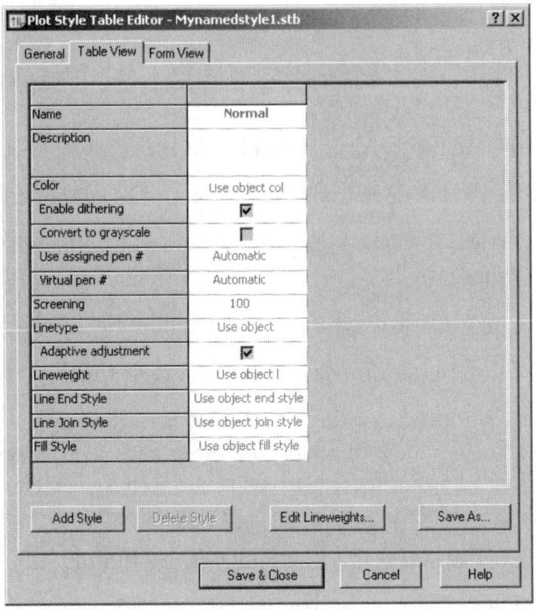

Notice that you only have one style named. Unlike the color plot style tables, you aren't assigning a style to each AutoCAD color; so you don't need a style for each of the 255 colors. Instead, you can create a limited set of styles, giving each style the characteristics you want to apply to objects or layers. Continue by adding some additional plot styles.

1. Click the Add Style button to display a new Style 1 column.

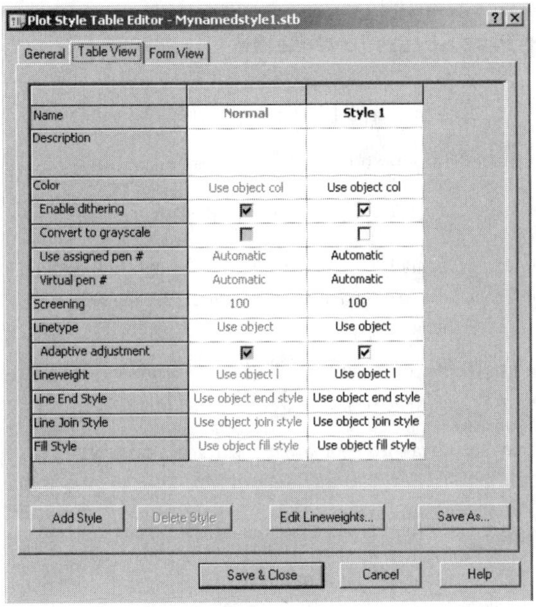

The name is highlighted. If you choose, you can give the style a different name at this point simply by typing it.

2. Click the Form View tab, and then select Style 1 from the Plot Styles list.
3. Click the Lineweight drop-down list and select 0.5000 mm.
4. Click the Add Style button, and then click OK in the Add Plot Style dialog box.
5. Select Style 2 from the Plot Styles list; then click the Lineweight drop-down list and select 0.7000 mm.
6. Click Save & Close to return to the Add Plot Style Table Wizard.
7. Click Finish to exit the wizard, and then close the Plot Styles window.

You may have noticed that the Add A Plot Style Table Wizard works in a slightly different way when you start it from the Plot Styles window. It adds an extra option (in step 5 of the exercise before the last one) that lets you choose between a color plot style table and a named plot style table.

You've just created a named plot style. Next, make `Mynamedstyle.stb` the default plot style.

1. Open the Options dialog box, and click the Plotting tab.
2. In the Default Plot Style Behavior For New Drawings button group, click the Use Named Plot Styles radio button.
3. Click the Default Plot Style Table drop-down list and select the plot style you just created, `Mynamedstyle1.stb`.
4. Click OK to exit the Options dialog box.

Now you're ready to start assigning plot styles to the objects in your drawing.

Assigning Plot Styles to Objects

Once you've set up AutoCAD to use named plot styles, you can begin to assign plot styles to objects through the Properties palette. Here are the steps to take to assign plot styles to objects.

1. Back in the `Plan-named.dwg` file, click the Layout1 tab.
2. If the Page Setup dialog box does not appear, choose File ➢ Page Setup.

TIP *If you clear the Display When Creating A New Layout check box in the Page Setup dialog box, AutoCAD does not display the Page Setup dialog box the first time you select a Layout tab.*

3. In the Page Setup dialog box, click the Plot Device tab and select `Mynamedstyle1.stb` from the Name drop-down list in the Plot Style Table group.
4. You may see a warning message asking if you want to assign this plot style to all Layout tabs. Click No.
5. Make sure the Display Plot Styles check box is checked.
6. Click OK to close the dialog box.

You've assigned a named plot style table to Layout 1. Note that you can assign different named plot styles to different Layouts.

Next make sure the plot styles will be displayed in the drawing.

1. Choose Format ➢ Lineweight, make sure there is a check in the Display Lineweight check box, and click OK.
2. Set up your view so you see a close-up of the lower-left corner unit.
3. Select the line representing the outer wall of the unit at the bottom-left side of the plan; then right-click, and choose Properties from the shortcut menu.

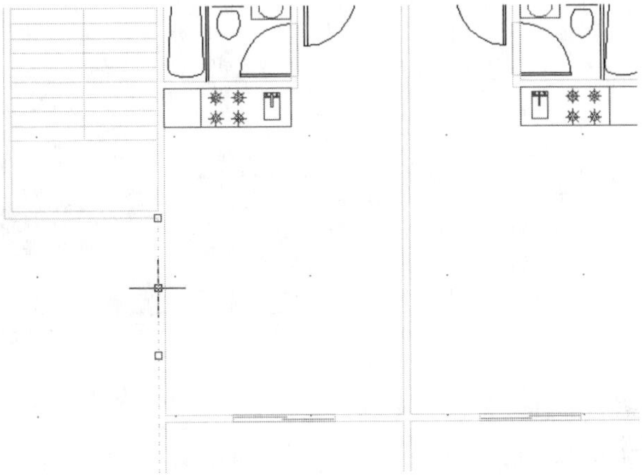

4. In the Properties palette, click the Plot Style option. The option turns into a drop-down list with a downward pointing arrow to the far right.

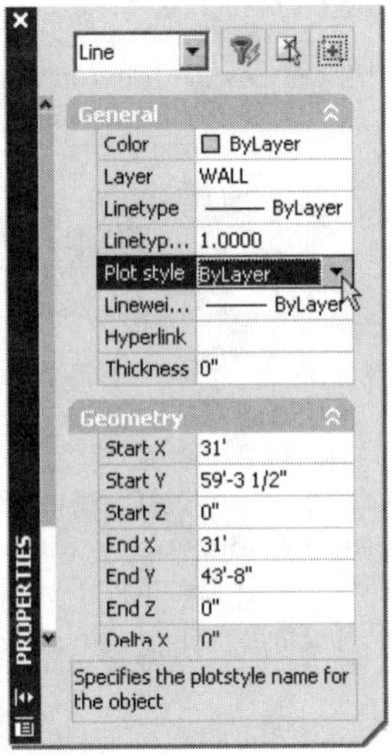

5. Click the downward-pointing arrow, and then select Other from the list to open the Select Plot Style dialog box.

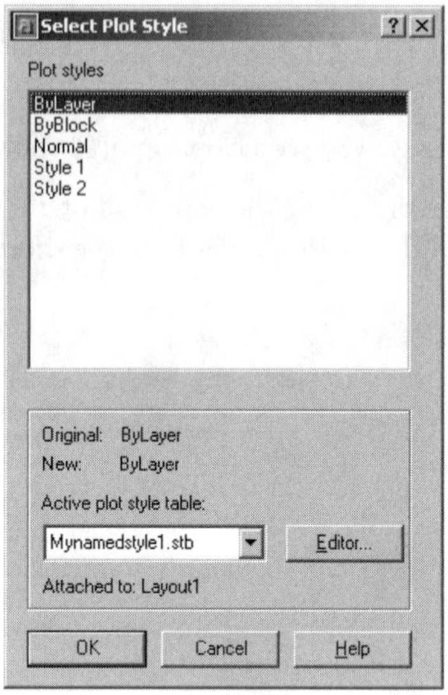

6. Select Style 1 and click OK.

7. Click the Plot Style list box again and make sure that Style 1 shows up as the value for the Plot Style in the Properties palette.

8. Close the Properties palette.

9. Choose View ➢ Regen All. If you have the line-weight visibility turned on, you'll see the results in the drawing editor.

Another way to assign plot styles to individual objects is through the Plot Style Control drop-down list.

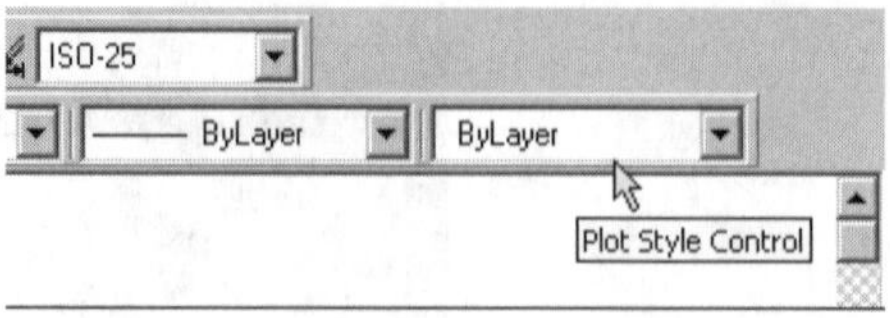

This allows you to select a plot style in a manner similar to the Layer & Linetype drop-down list. You can assign plot styles to individual objects by selecting the objects and then selecting a plot style from the Plot Style Control drop-down list. If you are using a color plot style table like the one you created in earlier exercises, the Plot Style Control drop-down list is unavailable.

Assigning Plot Style Tables to Layers

You can also assign named plot style tables to layers. This has a similar effect to using the color plot style tables. The main difference is that with named plot style tables, you assign the plot style tables directly to the layer instead of assigning a plot style to the color of a layer. Here's how to assign a plot style table to a layer.

1. In the Properties toolbar, click the Layer tool to open the Layer Properties Manager dialog box.
2. Select the Wall layer.
3. Click the Plot Style column of the Wall layer listing.

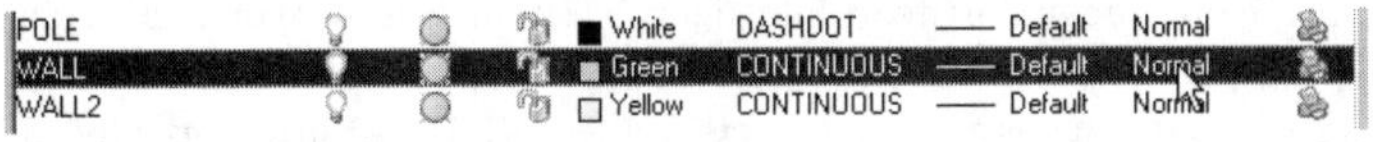

The Select Plot Style dialog box appears.

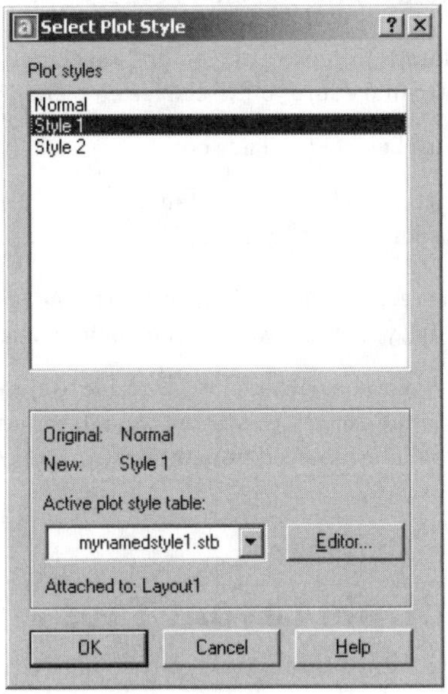

4. Select Style 1 from the Plot Styles list.
5. Click OK. The Layer Properties Manager appears again, this time showing the Plot Style property for the Wall layer listed as Style 1.
6. Close the Layer Properties Manager dialog box; then choose View ➢ Regen All. Your view of the plan changes to reflect the new plot style assignment to the Wall layer.

CONVERTING A DRAWING FROM COLOR PLOT STYLES TO NAMED PLOT STYLES

If you need to convert a color plot style drawing to a named plot style drawing, you can use the Convertctb and Convertpstyles commands. The conversion is a two-part process. In the first stage, which is needed only the first time you perform the conversion, you convert a color plot style table file into a named plot style table file. Then you actually convert the drawing file.

1. Start AutoCAD and, at the command prompt, enter **Convertctb↵**. This command lets you convert a color plot style table file into a named plot style table file. A Select File dialog box opens to allow you to select a color plot style table file; these files have the filename extension .ctb. For this example, you can choose the `Acad.ctb` file.
2. Click Open to open the Create File dialog box, which allows you to provide a name for the converted file. If you opened the `Acad.ctb` file in step 1, you might want to give the new file the name `AcadConvert` so you know that it is a converted .ctb file. AutoCAD will automatically add the .stb filename extension.
3. Once you click Save, AutoCAD creates a new Named Plot Style Table file, with the .stb filename extension, from the .ctb file you selected in step 1.

The next part is to actually convert the drawing file.

1. Open the file you want to convert and enter **Convertpstyles↵** at the command prompt. You will see a warning message to make sure you've converted a .ctb file to a .stb file.
2. Click OK to open the Select File dialog box.
3. Select the converted .stb file you created using the Convertctb command. The current drawing is converted to use a named plot style table.

In the process shown here, I've suggested converting the `Acad.ctb` file but if you have some custom settings saved in another .ctb file, you might want to convert your custom .ctb file instead.

To convert a drawing that uses a named plot style table to one that uses a color plot style table, just open the file in question and use the Convertpstyles command. You will see a warning message telling you that all the named plot styles will be removed from the drawing. Click OK to convert the drawing.

Plotting Multiple Layout Tabs

When you first open a Layout tab, you see the Page Setup dialog box. Since Layout tabs show you the layout of your drawing as it will appear when it is plotted, layouts need to be linked to a sheet size. You also need to link a layout to a plot style table. This allows you to produce two completely different-looking plots from the same drawing file. You've already seen that you can set up several layouts, each with its own layer settings and title block information. With the ability to attach different plot style tables to each Layout tab, you can also use one drawing to plot presentation-style drawings or construction documents.

Once you've got your Layout tabs set up, the Plot dialog box offers a set of options that will allow you to plot multiple tabs at once. The What To Plot button group in the Plot Device tab of the Plot dialog box offers four options: Current Tab, Selected Tabs, All Layout Tabs, and Number Of Copies.

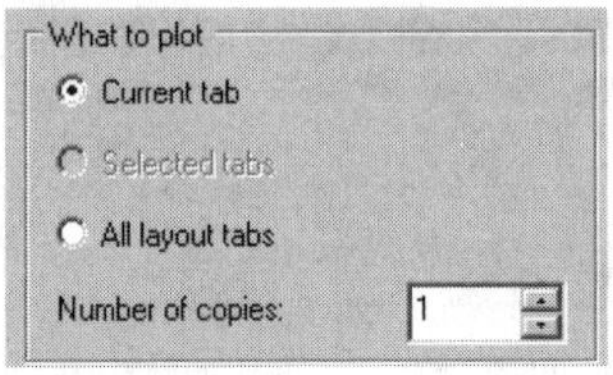

The functions of these options are mostly clear, although one option needs a bit of explaining. If you want to selectively plot certain tabs in your drawing, you can Shift+click the tabs just before you plot. You can then choose the Selected Tabs radio button in the Plot Device tab of the Plot dialog box to plot the selected Layout tabs.

The Plot To File button group lets you save your plots to a file on your hard drive. This can be helpful if you have multiple plotters and printers. You can save your plot files and send them to the different printers or plotters at a later time. This can be helpful if you are on a network and want to send plots to a network plotter. Or you can send your plot file over the Internet for plotting at a remote location.

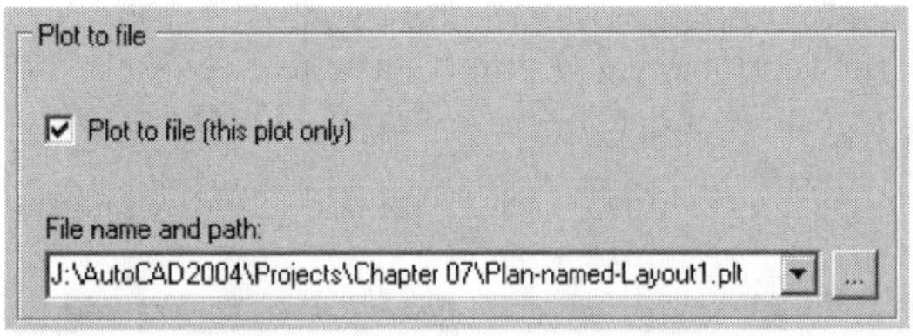

Adding an Output Device

This chapter mentioned that you can set up AutoCAD for more than one output device. You can do this even if you have only one printer or plotter connected to your computer. You might want multiple printer configurations in AutoCAD for many reasons. You might want to set up your system so that you can print to a remote location over a network or the Internet. Some printer configurations are strictly file-oriented, such as the AutoCAD DWF format for Internet Web pages or raster file output. (See Chapter 22 for more on .dwf files.)

AutoCAD works best with printers and plotters configured as Windows system devices. Although you can add devices through the AutoCAD Plot Manager, Autodesk recommends that you set up your plotters and printers as Windows devices and then use the System Printer option in AutoCAD to select your output device. You can use the Add-A-Plotter Wizard to create predefined settings for your system printer so that you can quickly choose a printer or plotter setup.

You can also configure additional printers through the AutoCAD Plot Manager. Here's how it's done.

1. Choose File ➢ Plotter Manager to open the Plotters window. Your view of the Plotters window may look a little different depending on your operating system, but the same basic information is there.

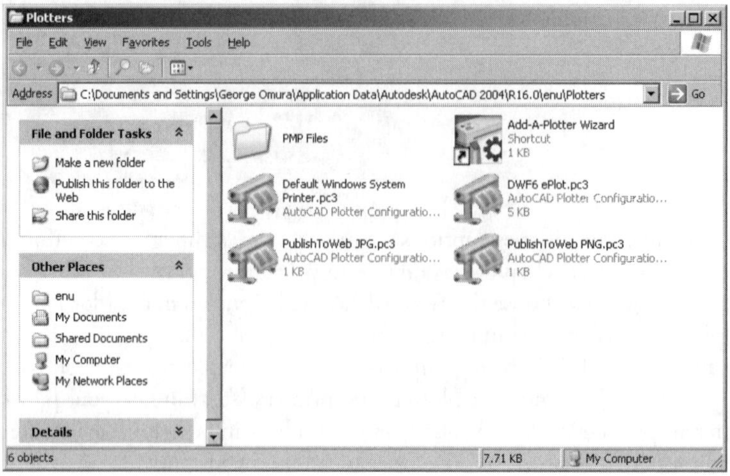

You can also open this window by clicking the Add Or Configure Plotter button in the Output tab of the Options dialog box. It's just an Explorer window showing you the contents of the `Plotters` folder under the main AutoCAD folder.

2. Double-click the Add-A-Plotter Wizard icon to start the AddPlotter Wizard.

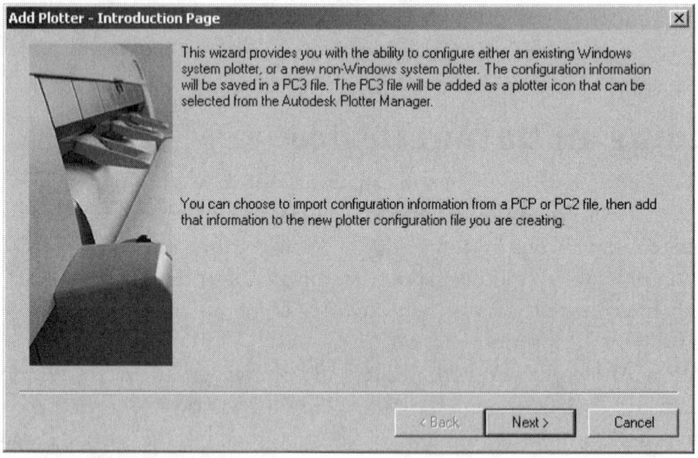

3. Click Next. The next screen of the wizard lets you select the type of setup you want.

Here you are offered three options: My Computer, Network Plotter Server, and System Printer. The My Computer and the Network Plotter Server options offer plotter options based on AutoCAD-specific drivers. The main difference between these two options is that the Network Plotter option asks you for a network server name. Otherwise, they both offer the same set of options.

4. If you click the My Computer radio button and then click Next, you see a listing of plotter models that are supported by AutoCAD directly through AutoCAD's own drivers.

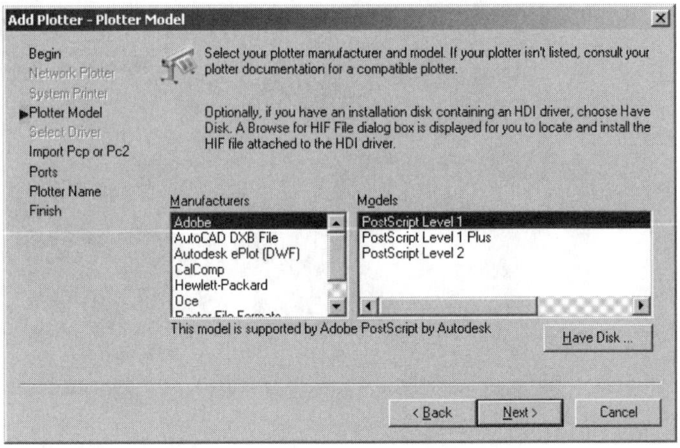

If you use a PostScript device, or if you want to convert drawings to raster formats, this is the place to select those options.

5. Once you've made a selection, click Next. You are then asked if you want to use an existing PCP or PC2 configuration file for the selected plotter. PCP and PC2 configurations files are plotter configuration files from earlier releases of AutoCAD.

6. Click Next on the Import PCP Or PC2 screen. If you selected My Computer in step 4, the Ports screen opens.

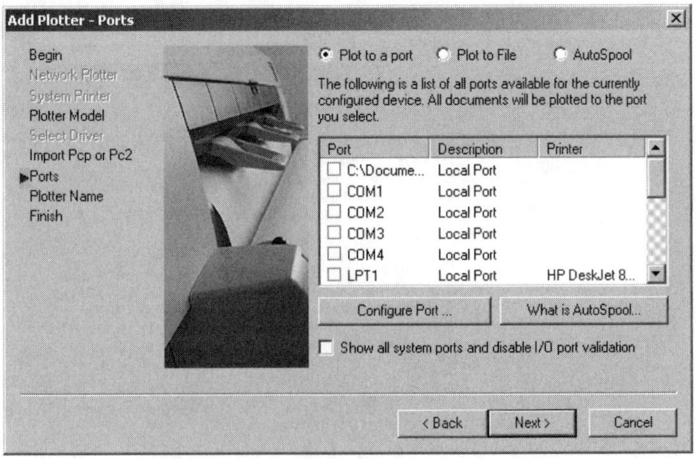

If you selected a different option in step 4, skip this option, and the Plotter Name screen opens.

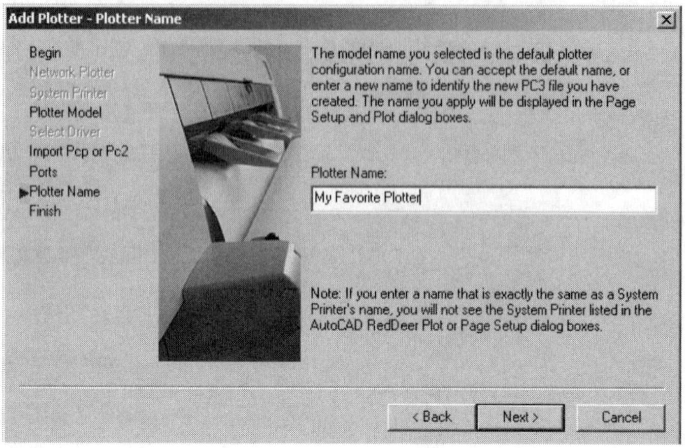

7. Enter a name for this configuration in the space provided; then click Next to open the Finish screen.
8. This screen gives you the option to make adjustments to the configuration you've just created by clicking the Edit Plotter Configuration button. Click Finish to exit the AddPlotter wizard. Your new configuration appears in the Plotters window.

In step 8, you can further adjust the plotter settings by clicking the Edit Plotter Configuration button to open the Plotter Configuration Editor dialog box.

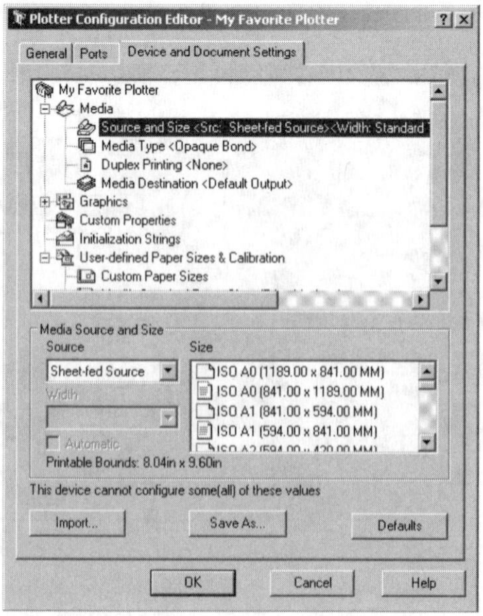

This editor lets you fine-tune your plotter settings. For example, you can calibrate your plotter for more accurate scaling of your plots, or if you're creating a raster file output configuration, you can create a custom page setting for extremely high resolution raster images.

Once you've set up a plotter, the plotter information is stored as a file with the .pc3 filename extension in the `Plotters` subfolder of the main AutoCAD folder.

Plotting Image Files and Converting 3D to 2D

If your work involves producing manuals, reports, or similar documents, you might want to add the Raster File Export option to your list of plotter configurations. The Raster File Export option lets you plot your drawings to a wide range of raster file formats including CALS, JPEG, PCX, Targa, Tiff, and BMP. You can then import your drawings into documents that accept bitmap images. Images can be up to 8000 × 8000 pixels (set through the Plotter Configuration Editor) and can contain as many colors as the file format allows. If you need several different raster formats, you can use multiple instances of this or any plotter configuration.

If you want to convert your 3D wireframe models into 2D line drawings, add the AutoCAD DXB File output format. This format lets you plot a 3D image to a file. You can then import the resulting .dxb file by choosing Insert ➢ Drawing Exchange Binary.

Yet another option is to add an HPGL output device to your AutoCAD setup and then plot your 3D model to an HPGL file. You can then use the Convert PLT to DWG (choose Express ➢ File Tools ➢ Convert PLT To DWG) Express tool described in Chapter 20 to import an HPGL plot file into an AutoCAD drawing.

Editing a Plotter Configuration

In step 7 of the previous exercise, you exited the AddPlotter Wizard without editing the newly created plotter configuration. You can always go back and edit the configuration by opening the Plotters window (choose File ➢ Plotter Manager) and double-clicking the configuration you want to edit. You can also double-click the .pc3 file of the configuration you want to edit.

Many users will use their Windows system printer or plotter for other applications besides AutoCAD, and frequently the AutoCAD settings for that printer will be different from the settings used for other applications. You can set up AutoCAD to automatically use its own settings so you don't have to reconfigure your Windows system printer every time you switch applications. To do so, take the following steps.

1. Choose File ➢ Page Setup to open the Page Setup dialog box.
2. Click the Plot Device tab.
3. Select the printer that you want to configure in the Name drop-down list of the Plotter Configuration group.
4. Click the Properties button to open the Plotter Configuration Editor dialog box.

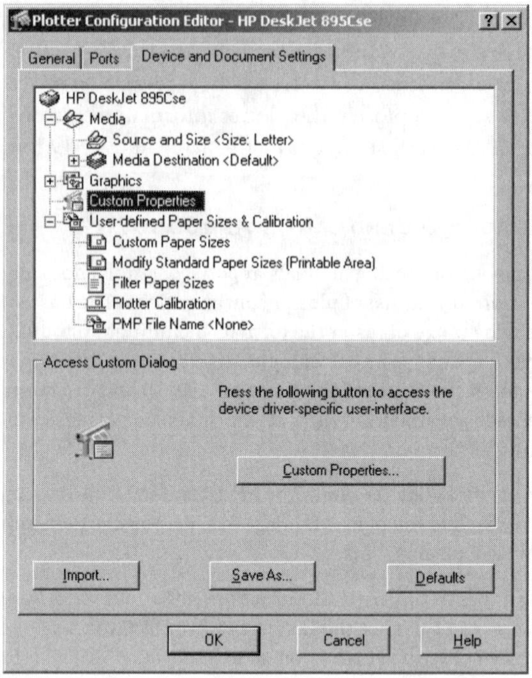

A list box displays all the properties of the printer or plotter. Not all these properties are editable, however. Each time you click a property in the list box, the lower half of the dialog box displays the options associated with that property.

5. Click the Custom Properties item in the list box. The lower half of the dialog box displays the Custom Properties button.
6. Click the Custom Properties button. You'll see the Windows system printer options. These are the same options you see when you edit the properties of your printer by choosing Start ➢ Settings ➢ Printers.
7. Adjust these settings the way you want them when you plot from AutoCAD and click OK.
8. Back in the Plotter Configuration Editor dialog box, click the Save As button. A standard file dialog box appears.
9. Enter the name of the plot configuration you've set up, or accept the default name, which is usually the name of the Windows printer or plotter, and click OK.
10. Click OK in the Plotter Configuration Editor dialog box; then click OK in the Page Setup dialog box.

The Plotter Configuration Editor offers a wide variety of options that are fairly technical in nature. If you want to know more about the Plotter Configuration Editor, see Appendix A.

Storing a Page Setup

Unlike most other programs, AutoCAD offers hundreds of page setup options. It can be quite a chore keeping track of and maintaining all these options. But as you settle into using AutoCAD, you'll probably find that you will set up a few plotter configurations and stick to them. AutoCAD 2004 lets you save a page setup under a name to help you store and manage those settings you use the most.

The Page Setup Name option in the upper-right corner of the Plot or Page Setup dialog box lets you store the settings from these dialog boxes under a name. Click the Add button to open the User Defined Page Setups dialog box.

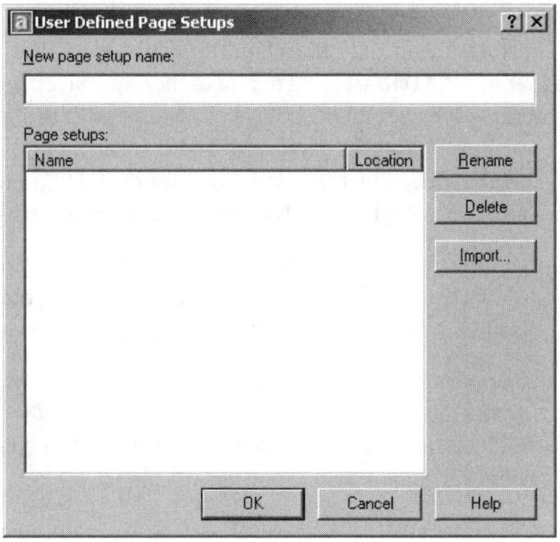

To save the current page setup, enter a name in the New Page Setup Name input box and click OK. The name you enter appears in the Page Setup Name drop-down list of the Plot or Page Setup dialog box. You can also import other user-defined page setups by clicking the Import button. Since page setups are stored in the drawing, the Import button opens a standard file dialog box that displays drawing files.

UNDERSTANDING THE PLOTTING TAB IN THE OPTIONS DIALOG BOX

You've worked with the Plotting tab in the Options dialog box on a few occasions in this chapter. This tab contains several options related to plotting. Here's a summary of those options and their purpose.

Continued on next page

UNDERSTANDING THE PLOTTING TAB IN THE OPTIONS DIALOG BOX *(continued)*

DEFAULT PLOT SETTINGS FOR NEW DRAWINGS

The settings in this group let you control the default plot settings for new drawings and for drawings from earlier versions of AutoCAD that are opened for the first time in AutoCAD 2004. The Use As Default Output Device radio button and drop-down list let you select the default plotter or printer to be used with new drawings. When selected, the Use Last Successful Plot Settings radio button uses the last successful plotter settings for subsequent plots. This is how earlier versions of AutoCAD worked. The Add Or Configure Plotters option opens the Plotters window. This is the same as choosing Files ➢ Plot Manager from the AutoCAD menu bar. From the Plotters window, you can launch the AddPlotter Wizard to add new plotter configurations. You can also edit existing plotter configurations.

GENERAL PLOT OPTIONS

These options control some of the general plotter parameters. The Keep The Layout Paper Size If Possible radio button causes AutoCAD to attempt to plot to the paper size specified in the Plot Settings tab of the Plot dialog box, regardless of the actual paper size in the plotter. If the specified size is larger than the capacity of the plotter, a warning message is displayed. The Use The Plot Device Paper Size option causes AutoCAD to use the paper size specified by the system printer or the PC3 plot configuration file currently in use. Both settings are also controlled by the Paperupdate system variable.

The System Printer Spool Alert drop-down list offers control over printer spooling alert messages. The OLE Plot Quality drop-down list offers control over the quality of OLE objects embedded or linked to a drawing. This setting can also be controlled through the Olequality system variable.

When the Use OLE Application When Plotting OLE Objects check box is checked, AutoCAD will launch any application that is associated with an OLE object embedded or linked to the AutoCAD drawing that is currently being plotted. This helps improve the plot quality of OLE objects. This option can also be set through the Olestartup system variable.

DEFAULT PLOT STYLE BEHAVIOR FOR NEWER DRAWINGS

You've used two of these options in exercises in this chapter. These options control the type of plot styles used in AutoCAD. In the case of named plot styles, you can also select a default plot style for Layer 0 and a default plot style for objects. Note that the Use Color Dependent Plot Styles and Use Named Plot Styles radio buttons do not have an effect on the current drawing; they affect only new drawings and pre-AutoCAD 2000 drawings being opened for the first time. The Default Plot Style Table drop-down list lets you select a default plot style table for new and pre-AutoCAD 2000 drawings. These settings are also controlled by the Pstylepolicy system variable.

The Add Or Edit Plot Style Tables button opens the Plot Styles dialog box. From there, you can double-click an existing plot style table file or start the Add A Plot Style Table Wizard to create a new plot style.

Plotter and Printer Hardware Considerations

Positioning an AutoCAD drawing on the printer output is something of an art. Before you face a deadline with hundreds of plots to produce, you might want to create some test plots and carefully refine your plotter settings so that you'll have AutoCAD set up properly for those rush jobs.

Part of the setup process will be to understand how your particular printer or plotter works. Each device has its own special characteristics, so a detailed description of printer hardware setup is beyond the scope of this section. However, here are a few guidelines that will make the process easier.

Understanding Your Plotter's Limits

If you're familiar with a word-processing or desktop-publishing program, you know that you can set the margins of a page, thereby telling the program exactly how far from each edge of the paper you want the text to appear. With AutoCAD, you don't have that luxury. To accurately place a plot on your paper, you must know the plotter's *hard clip limits*. The hard clip limits are like built-in margins, beyond which the plotter will not plot. These limits vary from plotter to plotter (see Figure 7.10).

FIGURE 7.10

The hard clip limits of a plotter

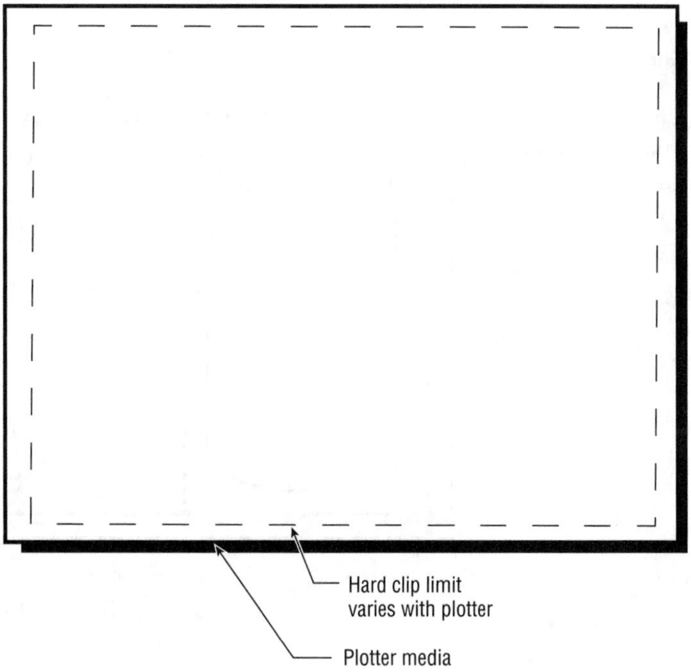

It's crucial that you know your printer's or plotter's hard clip limits in order to place your drawings accurately on the sheet. Take some time to study your plotter manual and find out exactly what these limits are. Then make a record of them and store it somewhere, in case you or someone else needs to format a sheet in a special way.

Hard clip limits for printers often depend on the software that drives them. You might need to consult your printer manual or use the trial-and-error method of plotting several samples to see how they come out.

Once you've established the limits of your plotter or printer, you'll be better equipped to fit your drawing within those limits. You can then establish some standard drawing limits based on your plotter's limits. You'll also need to know the dimensions of those hard clip limits to define custom sheet sizes. Although AutoCAD offers standard sheet sizes in the Paper Size And Orientation button group of the Plot Configuration dialog box, these sizes do not take into account the hard clip limits.

Knowing Your Plotter's Origins

Another important consideration is the location of your plotter's origin. For example, on some plotters, the lower-left corner of the plot area is used as the origin. Other plotters use the center of the plot area as the origin. When you plot a drawing that is too large to fit the sheet on a plotter that uses a corner for the origin, the image is pushed toward the top and to the right of the sheet (see Figure 7.11). When you plot a drawing that is too large to fit on a plotter that uses the center of the paper as the origin, the image is pushed outward in all directions from the center of the sheet.

FIGURE 7.11

Plotting an oversized image on a plotter that uses the lower-left corner for its origin

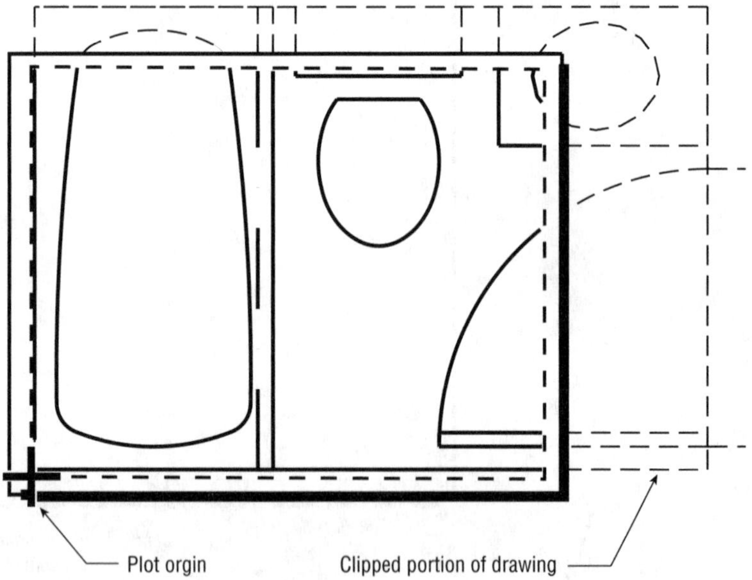

In each situation, the origin determines a point of reference from which you can relate your drawing in the computer to the physical output. Once you understand this, you're better equipped to accurately place your electronic drawing on the physical media.

Batch Plotting

AutoCAD 2004 includes a tool that enables you to plot several unattended drawings at once. This can be helpful when you've finished a set of drawings and want to plot them during a break or overnight. Here's how to use the Batch Plot utility.

1. From the Windows Desktop, choose Start ➢ Programs ➢ Autodesk ➢ AutoCAD 2004 ➢ Batch Plot Utility. The Batch Plot Utility window opens, along with an AutoCAD session.

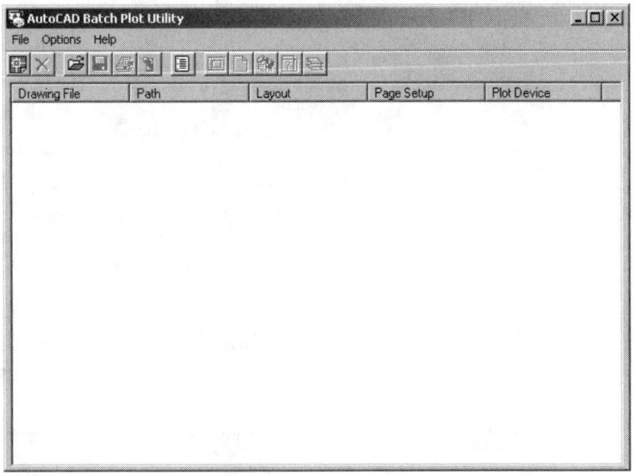

2. Click the Add Drawing button to open the Add Drawing dialog box. This is a typical Windows file dialog box.
3. Locate and select a file you want to plot. The name of the file you select appears in the list box of the Batch Plot Utility window.
4. Repeat steps 2 and 3 until you've included all the drawings you want to plot in your list.
5. Choose File ➢ Plot to plot the list of files.

Once you've compiled a list of files for plotting, you can save the list by choosing File ➢ Save List. To later open a saved list, choose File ➢ Open List. The filename will have the .bp3 file extension.

If you have special requirements for each file, such as a special plotter or layout you want to use, you can establish those settings and save them along with the list. To find these options, click a drawing name and then select the option from the Options pull-down menu, or right-click a listed file. Here is a description of those options.

Layouts Opens a dialog box that lets you select the Layout tabs for a file for plotting.

Page Setups Opens a dialog box that lets you import the Page Setup settings from an existing drawing.

Plot Devices Opens a dialog box that lets you select a plot configuration file for the listed file.

Plot Settings Opens the Plot Settings dialog box at the Plot Settings tab, in which you can select the plot area and the scale and specify whether you want to plot to a file.

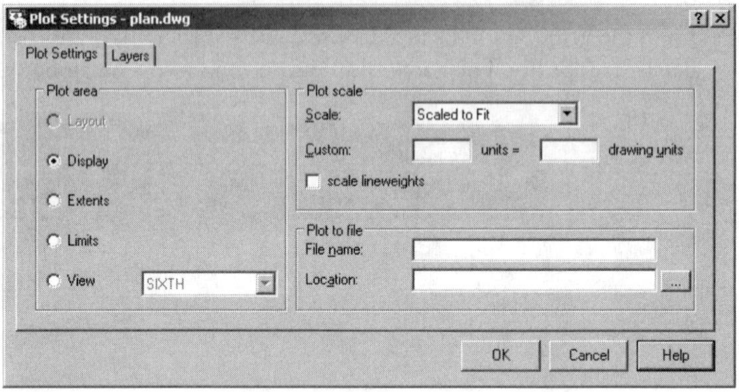

Layers Opens the Plot Settings dialog box at the Layers tab. The Layers tab lets you control which layers get plotted for a particular file.

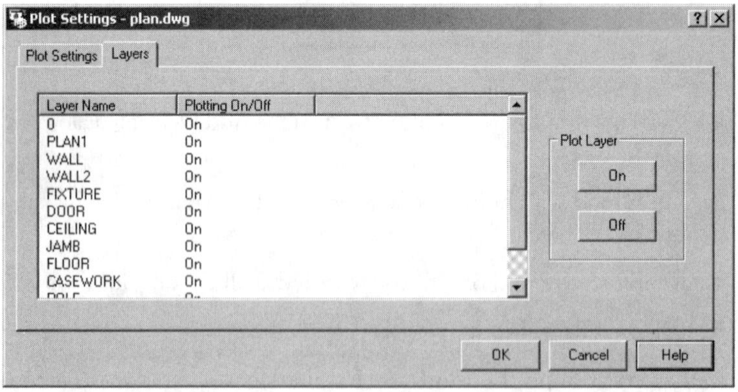

If you want to maintain a log of the plots you create with the Batch Plot Utility, choose File ➢ Logging to open the Logging dialog box, in which you can select the log file location and see a description for the log.

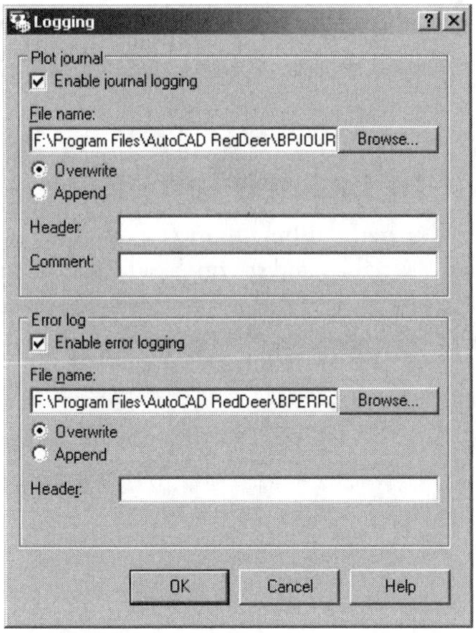

A log file can be useful if you intend to send plot files to a remote site. You can also create an error log to store error messages. This can be helpful for unattended plots when you might otherwise miss error messages that occur during a plot.

Another useful tool is Plot Test (choose File ➢ Plot Test). Plot Test checks to make sure that the resources for each drawing are available. The resources include Xref files, fonts, and custom line-type and hatch patterns that are required to open or plot a file.

TIP *If you have already set up a system using scripts for accessing the Plot command, you can restore the command-line version of the Plot command by changing the Plotlegacy system variable to 1. You can also turn on this system variable selecting the Plot With Legacy Command Line Prompts option in the Output tab of the Options dialog box. Bear in mind that, due to minor changes in the way that command-line plotting works, you may need to make changes to your plot script. See Chapter 16 for more information about scripts.*

Sending Your Drawings to a Service Bureau

Using a plotting service can be a good alternative to purchasing your own plotter. Or you might consider using a low-cost plotter for check plots and then sending the files to a service bureau for your final product. Most reprographic services, such as blueprinters, offer plotting in conjunction with their other services. Quite often you can send files over a high-speed connection, eliminating the need for using courier services or regular mail.

If you foresee the need for service bureaus, consider establishing a relationship with one or two service bureaus fairly early. Send them some sample plot files to make sure that they will produce the results you want. One of the greatest difficulties is miscommunication between what you want and what the service provides in the way of plotter output.

You might be able to use the PC3 and other plotter setting files as part of your relationship with a service bureau. Plot configuration files and plot style table files can help communicate exactly what you're expecting.

If You Want to Experiment...

At this point, since you aren't rushing to meet a deadline, you might want to experiment with some of the plotter and printer variables and see firsthand what each one does. Try plotting the `Plan-color.dwg` and `Plan-named.dwg` files using the plot style tables you created earlier in this chapter. Also, try changing other plot style table options to see the results on paper.

Chapter 8

Adding Text to Drawings

ONE OF THE MORE tedious drafting tasks is applying notes to your drawing. Anyone who has had to manually draft a large drawing containing a lot of notes knows the true meaning of writer's cramp. AutoCAD not only makes this job go faster by allowing you to type your notes right into the same document as the corresponding drawing, but it also helps you to create more professional-looking notes by using a variety of fonts, type sizes, and type styles.

In this chapter, you will add notes to your apartment building plan. In the process, you will explore some of AutoCAD's text creation and editing features. You will learn how to control the size, slant, type style, and orientation of text and how to import text files. Topics include the following:

- Adding Text to a Drawing
- Understanding Text Formatting in AutoCAD
- Organizing Text by Styles
- What Do the Fonts Look Like?
- Adding Special Characters and Simple Text Objects
- Checking Spelling and Substituting Fonts
- Finding and Replacing Text
- Accelerating Zooms and Regens with Qtext
- If You Want to Experiment…

Adding Text to a Drawing

In this first section, you will add some simple labels to your Unit drawing to identify the general design elements: the bathroom, the kitchen, and the living room. Start by setting up a drawing to which you can apply some text.

1. Start AutoCAD and open the `Unit` file. If you haven't created the Unit file, you can use the file called `08a-unit.dwg` from the companion CD. Once open, choose File ➢ Save As to save the Unit drawing to a file called `Unit.dwg`.

2. Create a layer called Notes and make it the current layer. Notes is the layer on which you will keep all your text information.
3. Turn off the Flr-pat layer. Otherwise, the floor pattern you added previously will obscure the text you enter during the exercises in this chapter.

TIP *It's a good idea to keep your notes on a separate layer, so you can plot drawings containing only the graphics information or freeze the Notes layer to save redraw/regeneration time.*

4. Set up your view so it looks similar to the top image in Figure 8.1.

FIGURE 8.1

The top image shows the points to pick to place the text boundary window. The bottom image shows the completed text.

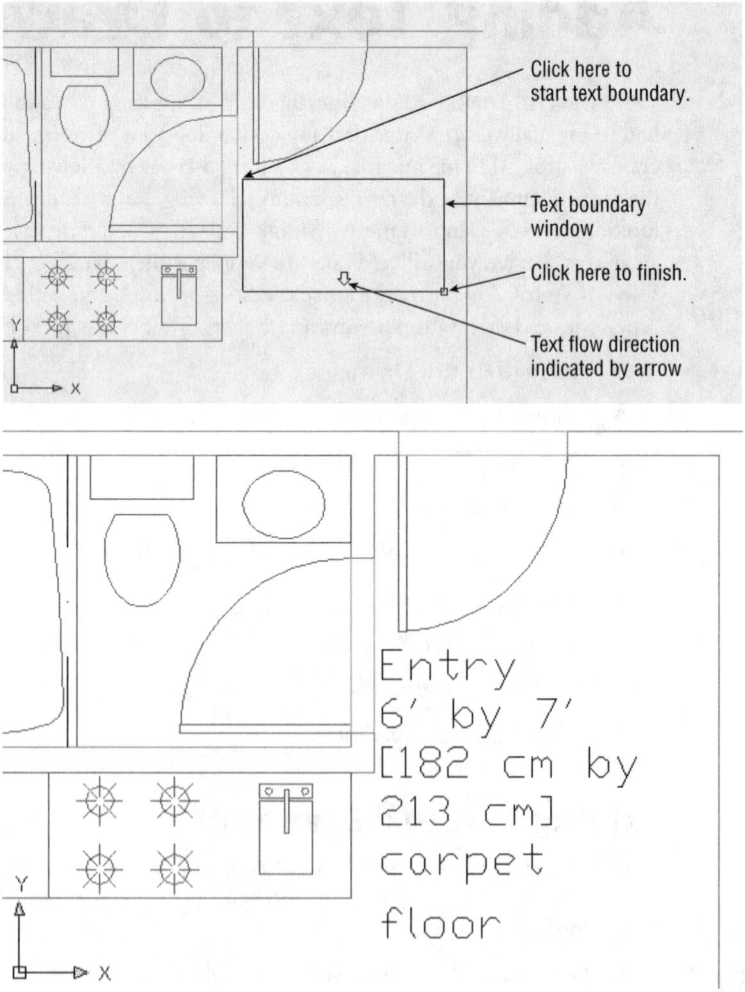

You've got the drawing ready. Now add some text.

1. Choose the Draw ➢ Text ➢ Multiline Text from the menubar, or type **MT**↵. You can also select the Multiline Text tool from the Draw toolbar.
2. Click the first point indicated in the top image in Figure 8.1 to start the text boundary window. This boundary window indicates the area in which to place the text. Notice the arrow near the bottom of the window. It indicates the direction of the text flow.

TIP *You don't have to be too precise about where you select the points for the boundary because you can adjust the location and size later.*

3. Click the second point indicated in the top image in Figure 8.1. The Text Formatting toolbar appears with the Multiline Text Editor superimposed over the area you just selected.

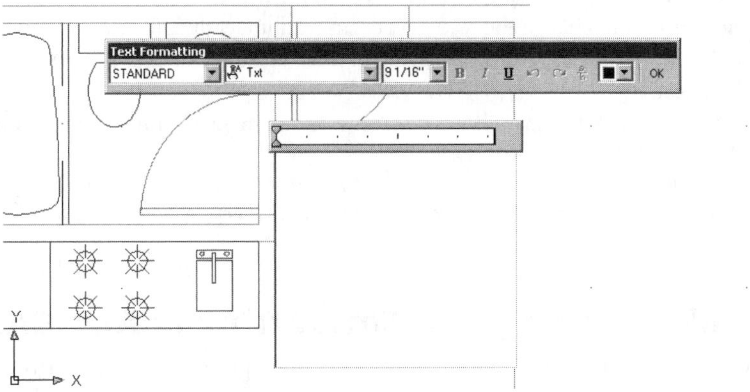

4. You could start typing the text for the room label, but first you need to select a size. Point to the Text Height drop-down list and click it. The default font size highlights.

5. Enter **6** to make the default height 6 inches. Metric users should enter **15** for a text height of 15 cm.

TIP *Why make the text so high? Remember that you are drawing at full scale, and anything you draw will be reduced in the plotted drawing. Text height is discussed in more detail later in this chapter.*

6. Click the text panel and type the word **Entry**. As you type, the word appears in the text panel, just as it will appear in your drawing. As you will see later, the text also appears in the same font as the final text.

TIP *The default font is a native AutoCAD font called* `Txt.shx`*. As you will see later, you can also use TrueType fonts and PostScript fonts.*

7. Press ↵ to advance one line; then enter **6' by 7'**.
8. Press ↵ to advance another line and enter **[182 cm by 213 cm]**.
9. Press ↵ again to advance another line and enter **carpet floor**.
10. Click OK in the Text Formatting toolbar. The text appears in the drawing just as it did in the text editor (see the bottom image in Figure 8.1).

The Text Formatting toolbar and text editor work like any text editor, so if you make a typing error, you can highlight the error and then retype the letter or word. You can also perform other word processing functions such as search and replace, you can import text, and you can make font changes.

You also saw how the text editor shows you how your text will appear in the location you selected in step 3. If your view of the drawing is such that the text is too small to be legible, the Text Formatting toolbar will enlarge the text so you can read it clearly. Likewise, if you are zoomed in too close to see the entire text, the Text Formatting toolbar will adjust the text in its text editor to enable you to see all the text.

In the next section, you'll look at some of the many options you have available for formatting text.

TIP *If text is included in an area where a hatch pattern is to be placed, AutoCAD automatically avoids hatching over the text. If you add text over a hatched area, you must rehatch the area to include the text in the hatch boundary.*

Understanding Text Formatting in AutoCAD

AutoCAD offers a wide range of text formatting options. You can control fonts, text height, justification, line spacing, and width. You can even include special characters such as degree symbols or stacked fractions. In a departure from the somewhat clumsy text implementation of earlier AutoCAD versions, you now have a much wider range of controls over your text.

Adjusting the Text Height and Font

Let's continue our look at AutoCAD text by adding a label for the living room of the studio apartment. You'll use the Multiline Text tool again, but this time you'll get to try out some of its other features. In this first exercise, you'll see how you can adjust the size of text in the editor:

1. Pan your view so that the kitchen is just at the top of the drawing, as shown in the first image in Figure 8.2.

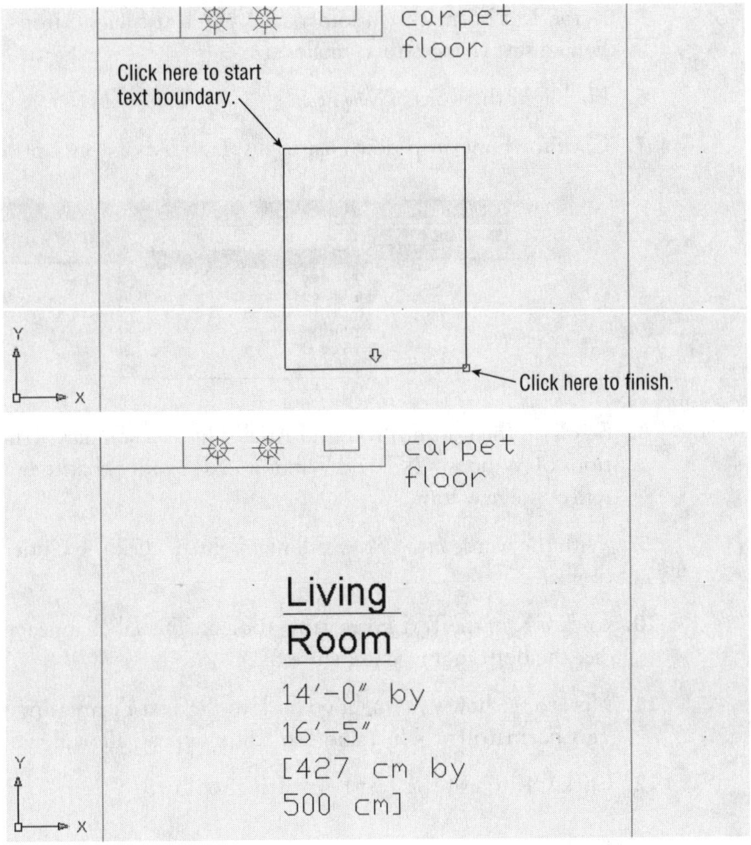

FIGURE 8.2
Placing the text boundary window for the living room label and the final label

2. Click the Multiline Text tool again; then select a text boundary window, as shown in the first image in Figure 8.2.
3. In the text editor, start typing the following text:

```
Living Room
14'-0" by 16'-5"
[427 cm by 500 cm]
```

   As you type, notice that the words *Living* and *Room* become two separate lines even though you did not press ↵ between them. AutoCAD uses word wrap to fit the text inside the text boundary area.
4. Highlight the text 14'-0" by 16'-5" [427 cm by 500 cm] as you would in any word processor. For example, you can click the end of the line to place the cursor there; then Shift+click the beginning of the line to highlight the whole line.

5. In the Text Formatting toolbar, click the Text Height drop-down list and select 6. The highlighted text changes to a smaller size.
6. Highlight the words *Living Room*.
7. Click the Font drop-down list to display a list of font options.

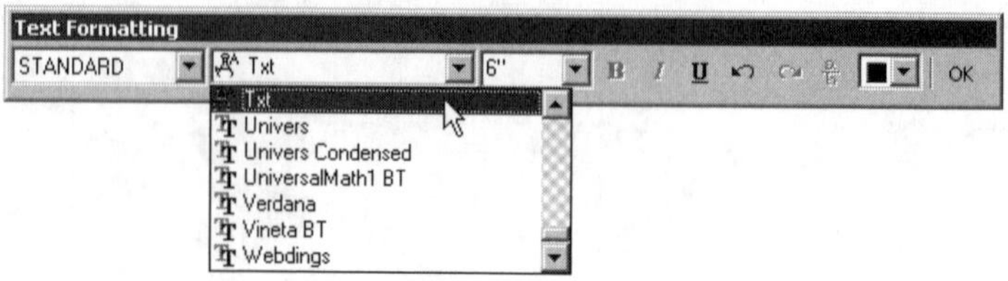

8. Scroll up the list until you find Arial. This is a standard TrueType font available in all installations of Windows NT and Windows XP. Notice that the text in the text editor changes to reflect the new font.

9. With the words *Living Room* still highlighted, click the Underline button in the Text Formatting toolbar.
10. Click OK in the Text Formatting toolbar. The label appears in the area you indicated in step 2 (see the bottom image in Figure 8.2).
11. Now to see how you might go back to the Text Formatting toolbar, double-click the text. The Text Formatting toolbar and text editor appear, allowing you to make changes to the text.
12. Click OK to exit the Text Formatting toolbar.

USING POSTSCRIPT FONTS

If you have PostScript fonts that you would like to use in AutoCAD, you need to compile them into AutoCAD's native font format. To do so, follow these steps:

1. Type **Compile**↵ to open the Compile Shape Or Font File dialog box.
2. Select PostScript Font (*.pfb) from the File Of Type drop-down list, and then browse to find the font you want to convert.
3. Double-click the PostScript font you want to convert into the AutoCAD format. AutoCAD will work for a moment; then you'll see this message:

```
"Compiling shape/font description file"
Compilation successful. Output file Program Files\AutoCAD2004\ FONTS\fontname.shx
contains 59578 bytes.
```

When AutoCAD is finished, you have a file with the same name as the PostScript font file but with the .shx filename extension. If you place your newly compiled font in AutoCAD's Fonts folder, it will be available in the Style dialog box.

Continued on next page

USING POSTSCRIPT FONTS *(continued)*

When you work with AutoCAD's .shx font files, it is important to remember the following:

- License restrictions still apply to the AutoCAD-compiled version of the PostScript font.
- Like other fonts, compiled PostScript fonts can use up substantial disk space, so compile only the fonts you need.

While using the Multiline Text tool, you might have noticed the `[Height/Justify/Line spacing/Rotation/Style/Width]` prompt immediately after you picked the first point of the text boundary. You can use any of these options to make on-the-fly modifications to the height, justification, line spacing, rotation style, or width of the multiline text.

For example, right after clicking the first point for the text boundary, you can type **R**↵ and then specify a rotation angle for the text window, either graphically with a rubber-banding line or by entering an angle value. Once you've entered a rotation angle, you can resume selecting the text boundary.

Scaling Multiple Text Objects in a Hurry

Another way to quickly change the size of text is to use the Scaletext command. Choose Modify ➢ Object ➢ Text ➢ Scale, or type **Scaletext** at the command prompt, and then select the text you want to scale. You can select multiple text objects. Press ↵ when you've completed your selection. You see the prompt:

```
[Existing/Left/Center/Middle/Right/TL/TC/TR/ML/MC/MR/BL/BC/BR/]<TL>:
```

Enter the letters corresponding to the location to which you want to scale the text. (See the section "Justifying Single-Line Text Objects" later in this chapter for a description of these options.) Once you've entered an option, you see the next prompt:

```
Specify new height or [Match object/Scale factor] <Current height>:
```

At this prompt you have three options. You can enter a new height; you can type **M**↵ and then select another text object whose height you want to match; or you can type **S**↵ and then enter a scale factor to scale the text to a specific ratio.

Adding Color, Stacked Fractions, and Special Symbols

In the previous exercise, you were able to adjust the text height and font, just as you would in any word processor. You saw how you can easily underline portions of your text using the tool buttons in the editor. Other tools allow you to set the color for individual characters or words in the text, create stacked fractions, or insert special characters. Here's a brief description of how these tools work:

- To change the color of text, highlight it and then select the color from the Text Color drop-down list.

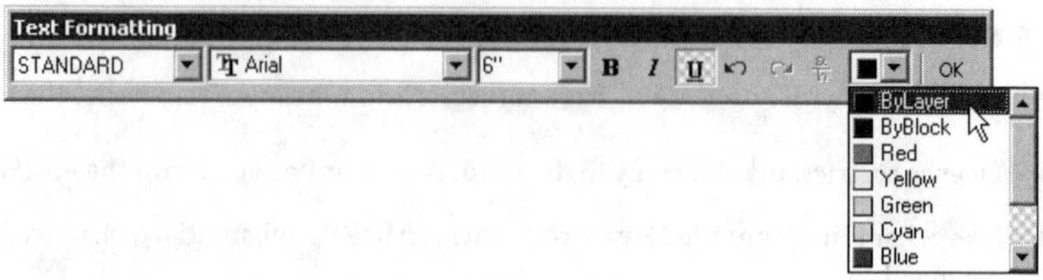

- To turn a fraction into a stacked fraction, highlight the fraction and then click the Stack/Unstack tool.

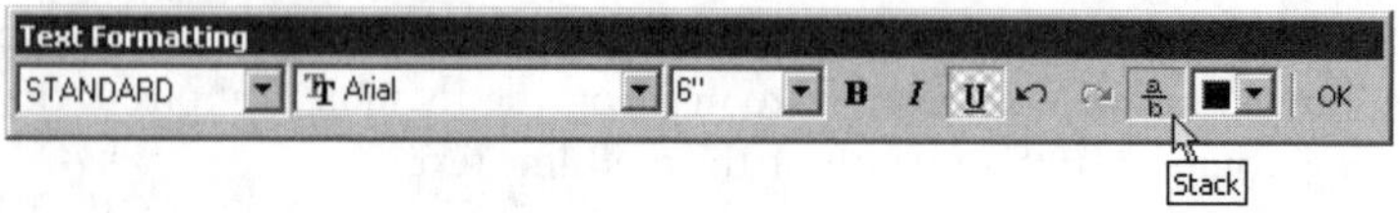

- To add a special character, place the cursor at the location of the character, right-click, and then choose an option for special characters from the shortcut menu.

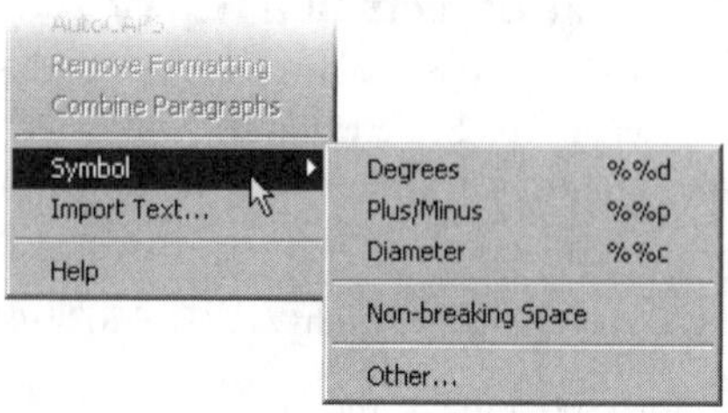

The Symbol tool offers three standard options that are typical for most technical drawings: the Degrees, Plus/Minus, and Diameter signs. When you select these options, AutoCAD inserts the proper AutoCAD text code in the text that corresponds to these symbols. You'll get a more detailed look at special symbols later in this chapter.

Adjusting the Width of the Text Boundary Window

Although the font and height of your text are formatted correctly, the text appears stacked in a way that is too tall and narrow. The following steps will show you how to change the boundary to fit the text:

1. Click any part of the text you just entered to highlight it.
2. Click the upper-right grip.
3. Drag the grip to the right to the location shown in Figure 8.3; then click that point.
4. Click any grip, and then right-click the mouse and choose Move.
5. Move the text to a location that is more centered in the room.

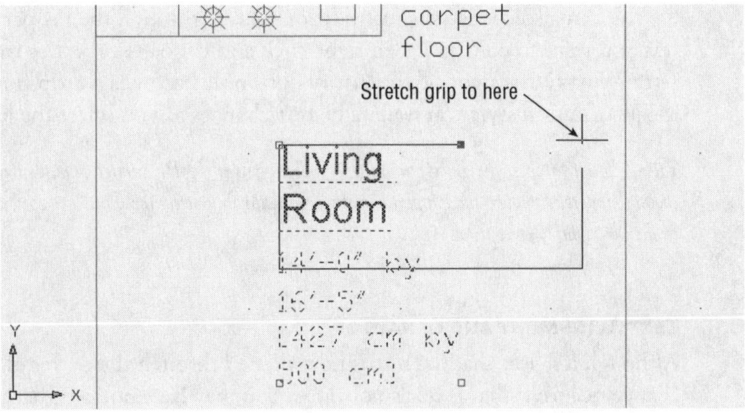

FIGURE 8.3

Adjusting the text boundary window

AutoCAD's word-wrap feature automatically adjusts the text formatting to fit the text boundary. This feature is especially useful to AutoCAD users because other drawing objects often impact the placement of text. As your drawing changes, you will need to adjust the location and boundary of your notes and labels.

Adjusting the Text Alignment

ACAD only

The text is currently aligned on the left side of the text boundary. For a label such as the one in the living room, it is more appropriate to center the text. Here's how you can make changes to the text alignment:

1. Double-click the text to display the Text Formatting toolbar. You can also right-click the text after selecting it and then select Mtext Edit from the shortcut menu. Or, from the menu bar, choose Modify ➢ Object ➢ Text ➢ Edit.

4. Right-click the text, and then choose Justification ➢ Top Center from the shortcut menu. The living room label moves to a centered position above the second line.

5. Click OK. The text changes to align through the center of the text, as shown in Figure 8.4.

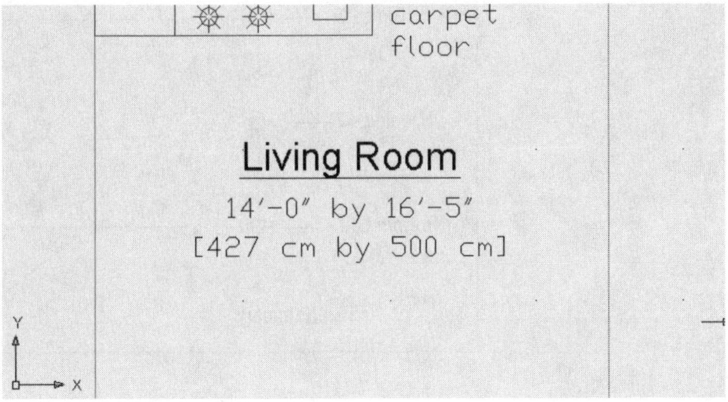

FIGURE 8.4

The text aligned using the Top Center alignment option

You can also change the justification of text through the Properties palette. Select the multiline text you want to edit, and then right-click and choose Properties from the shortcut menu. Click the setting just to the right of the Justify option. It becomes a drop-down list. Open the list and select the justification style you want. The text changes as you select the justification style.

TIP *You can open the Text Formatting toolbar from the Properties palette. Right-click the text after selecting it; then choose Properties to open the Properties palette. You can then select the Contents option and click the ellipsis button that appears to the far right of the option.*

TEXT ALIGNMENT AND OSNAPS

Although it's clear that the text is now aligned through the center of the text boundary, one important change occurred that is not so obvious. You may have noticed that the object alignment list offered three centered options: Top Center, Middle Center, and Bottom Center. All three of these options have the same effect on the text's appearance, but they each have a different effect on how Osnaps act upon the text. Figure 8.5 shows where the Osnap point occurs on a text boundary, depending on which alignment option is selected. A multiline text object has only one insertion point on its boundary that you can access with the Insert Osnap.

FIGURE 8.5

The location of the Insert Osnap points on a text boundary based on its alignment setting

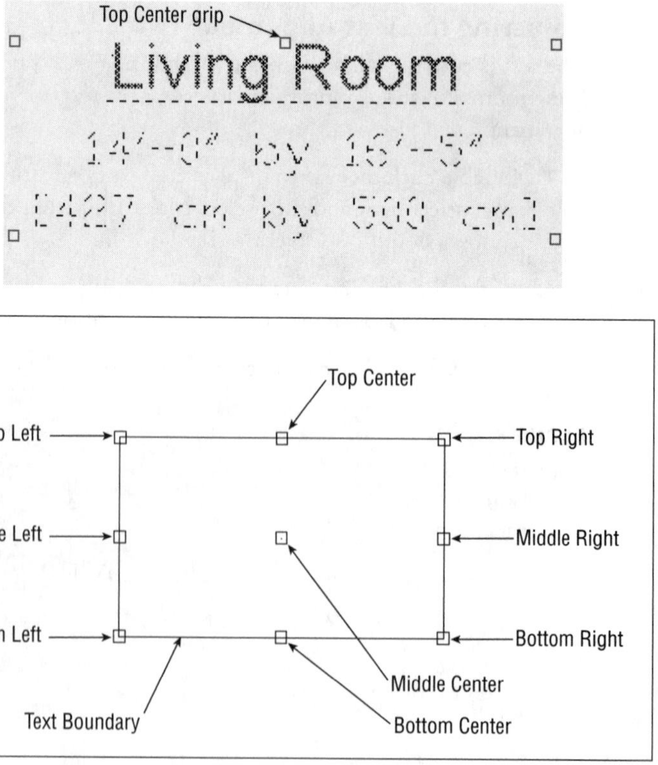

The Osnap point also appears as an extra grip point on the text boundary when you click the text. If you click the text you just entered, you will see that a grip point now appears at the top center of the text boundary.

Knowing where the Osnap points occur can be helpful when you want to align the text with other objects in your drawing. In most cases, you can use the grips to align your text boundary, but the Top Center and Middle Center alignment options allow you to use the center and middle portions of your text to align the text with other objects.

Changing Justification of Multiple Text Objects

You've seen how you can change the justification of an individual text object, but you will often find that you need to change the justification of several text objects at one time. AutoCAD offers the Justifytext command for this purpose. To use it, choose Modify ➢ Object ➢ Text ➢ Justify, or type **Justifytext**↵ at the command prompt. At the `Select object:` prompt, select the text you want to change, and then press ↵ to confirm your selection. You'll see the following prompt in the command line:

```
[Left/Align/Fit/Center/Middle/Right/TL/TC/TR/ML/MC/MR/BL/BC/BR] <BC>:
```

Enter the letters corresponding to the type of justification you want to use for the text. (See the section "Justifying Single-Line Text Objects" later in this chapter for a description of these options.) Once you've entered an option, the selected text will change to conform to the selected justification option.

Setting Indents and Tabs

You'll also want to know about the indent and tab features of the Text Formatting toolbar's text window. You may have noticed the ruler at the top of the text editor. Figure 8.6 shows that ruler, including tab and indent markers.

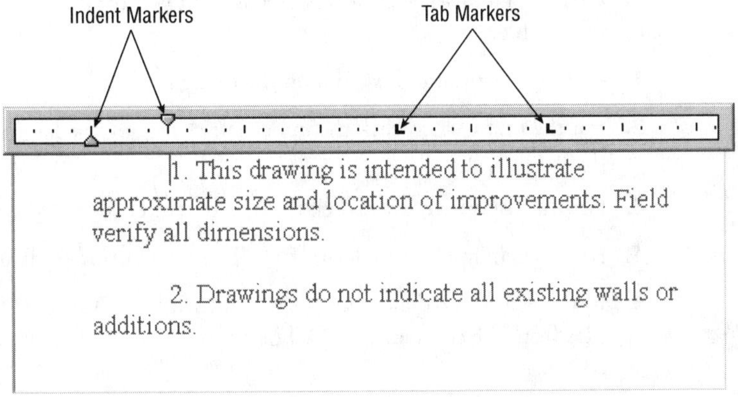

FIGURE 8.6

The ruler at the top of the text editor lets you quickly set tabs and indents for text.

The indent markers let you control the indention of the first line and the rest of the paragraph. The tab markers give you control over tab spacing. For new text, the tab markers don't appear until you add them by clicking the ruler. The following exercises will demonstrate the use of these markers more clearly.

Start by practicing with the indent markers.

1. Open the `Indents.dwg` file from the companion CD. This file contains some text that you will experiment with.
2. Double-click the text at the top of the drawing to open the Text Formatting toolbar.
3. Press Ctrl+A to highlight all the text in the text editor. This is necessary to indicate the group of text to be affected by your indent settings.
4. Click and drag the top indent marker two spaces to the left. Notice that the indent of the first line moves with the marker. A note appears above the ruler showing you how much indent you are applying. Also notice that the text at the first tab remains at its starting location.

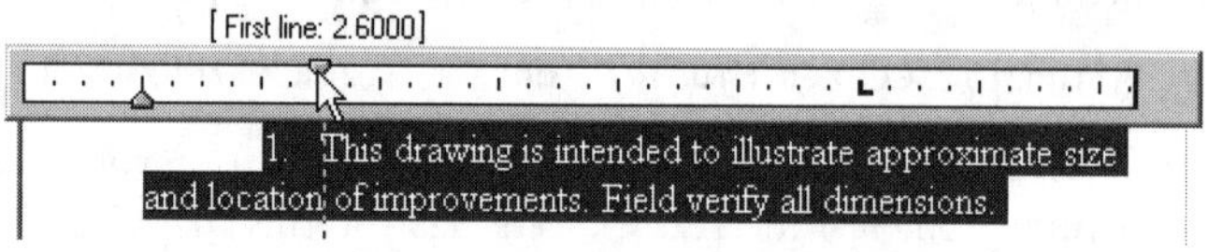

5. Click and drag the bottom indent marker two spaces to the left. Notice that the rest of the paragraphs moves with the marker. Again, you see a note by the ruler showing you how much indent you are applying.

Here you see how you can control the indents of the selected text with the indent markers. You can set different paragraphs of a single Mtext object differently, giving you a wide range of indent formatting possibilities. Just select the text you want to set, and then adjust the indent markers.

Now try the tab markers. For this exercise you will try the text import feature to import a tab-delimited text file.

1. Click the Multiline Text tool on the Draw toolbar.
2. For the first corner, click the upper-left corner of the large rectangle in the drawing just below the paragraph.
3. For the opposite corner, click the lower-right corner of the rectangle.
4. Right-click in the text editor of the Text Formatting toolbar and select Import Text.
5. In the Select File dialog box, locate and select the `Tabtest.txt` file from the Chapter 8 sample files from the companion CD. The contents of the `Tabtest.txt` file are displayed in the text editor.

The file you just imported was generated from the Attribute Extraction feature of AutoCAD. You'll learn more about this feature in Chapter 10. The important thing to note is that this file contains tabs to align the columns of the information. You can adjust those tabs in the Text Formatting toolbar, as you'll see in the next set of steps.

Now use the tab markers to adjust the tab spacing of the columns of text.

1. Press Ctrl+A to select all the text.
2. Click the ruler at a point that is at the 12th mark from the left. An L-shaped marker appears, and the first tab column of text moves to this position.

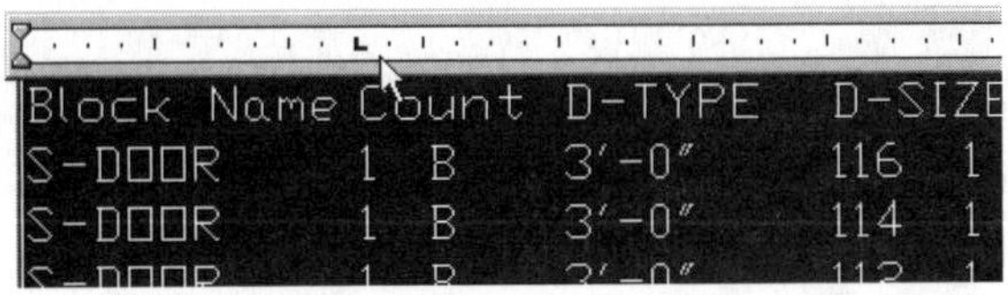

3. Click the ruler again at the 20th mark. The second column aligns to this position.

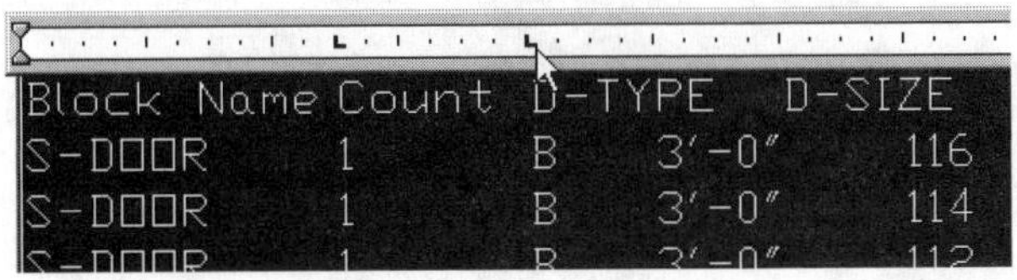

4. Continue to click the ruler to add more tab markers so that the text looks similar to Figure 8.7. Don't worry about being exact. This is just for practice. Once you've placed a marker, you can click and drag it to make adjustments.

FIGURE 8.7

Add tab markers so that your text looks similar to this figure.

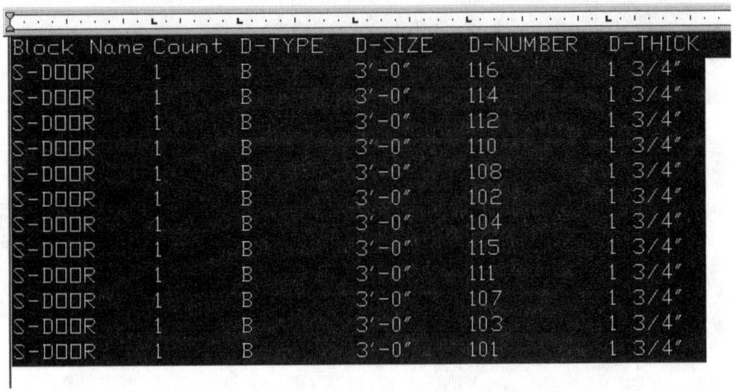

5. Click Close on the Text Formatting toolbar. The text appears in the drawing as a door schedule.

Here you saw how you can create a table or a schedule from an imported text file. You can also create a schedule from scratch by composing it directly in the text editor of the Text Formatting toolbar. A third option is to cut and paste text from a text-based program into the text window. The point is, you can fine-tune the column spacing of your schedule using the tab markers.

Besides using the indent and tab markers on the ruler, you can also control indents and tabs through the Indents And Tabs dialog box. Do the following to get a first-hand look.

1. Double-click the text at the top of the drawing (the one you edited in the first part of this section) and then press Ctrl+A to select all the text.
2. Right-click the ruler above the text editor, and then click Indents And Tabs.

The Indents And Tabs dialog box appears.

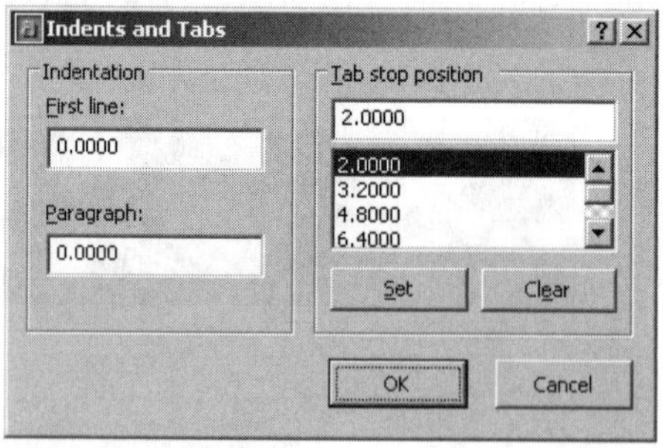

3. Change the value in the Paragraph input box to 2.2.
4. Double-click the Tab Stop Position input box in the upper-right corner, enter **2.2↵**. You can also click the Set button instead of pressing ↵.
5. Click OK. Notice that the text now appears with the text indented from the numbers.

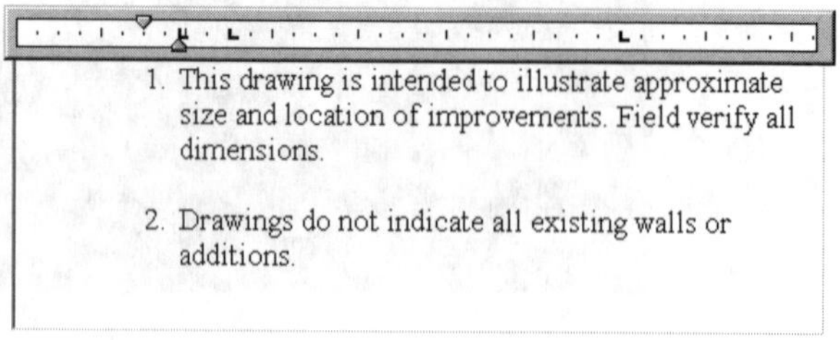

6. Close the Text Formatting toolbar. Notice how the text in the drawing is now formatted as it appeared in the text editor of the Text Formatting toolbar.
7. Exit the `Indents.dwg` file.

In this exercise, you used the Indents And Tabs dialog box to set the paragraph indent and the first tab marker to be the same value. This causes the text portion of the list to be aligned at a distance of 2.2 drawing units from the left text boundary, leaving the list number extended farther to the left. This gives the list a more professional appearance.

The Indents And Tabs dialog box gives you fine control over the formatting of your text. It lets you delete tabs by highlighting the tab in the list and clicking the Clear button. You can also add tabs at specific distances from the left margin of the text boundary by entering new tab locations in the Tab Stop Position input box and clicking the Set button.

You specify distances in drawing units. If your drawing is set up to use Architectural units, for example, you can enter values in feet and inches or just inches. The First Line and Paragraph input boxes let you enter a numeric value for paragraph indents. As you have just seen, you can use the First Line and Paragraph input boxes to create a numbered list by setting the Paragraph input box value to be the same as the first tab stop position.

TIP *You might nave noticed the Set Mtext Width right-click option in step 2 of the exercise. This option opens a simple dialog box that allows you to enter a width for the text boundary. You can also click and drag the right inside edge of the ruler to change the text boundary width.*

Adjusting Line Spacing

Another text-editing feature that is related to text indents and tabs is the Line Spacing option. You can adjust line spacing between the range of 0.5 and 4 times the height of the text. Here's how it works:

1. Go back to the Unit drawing, select the words *Living Room,* and then right-click.
2. Choose Properties from the shortcut menu to open the Properties palette.
3. Use the scroll bar at the left of the Properties palette to scroll down until you see all the Text group of the palette.
4. Double-click the Line Space Factor value in the Text group.

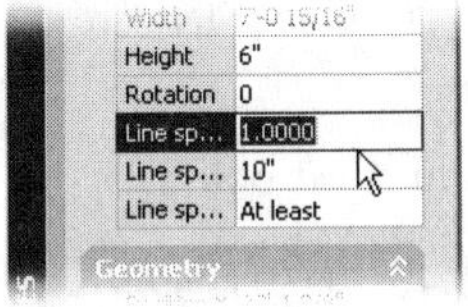

5. Enter **4**↵. The value changes to reflect the spacing of the text at 4 times the height of the text.
6. Close the Properties palette. You see that the line spacing of the selected text has changed.
7. Type **U**↵ or click the Undo button in the Standard toolbar. You don't need to save this change to the text.

In step 5 you entered **4** to indicate that you want a line-spacing value that is 4 times the text height. Just below the Line Space Factor option in the Properties palette, you will see the Line Space Style option. This allows you to choose between an approximate spacing and an exact spacing.

Editing Text Content

It is helpful to think of text in AutoCAD as a collection of text documents. Each text boundary window you place is like a separate document. You've already seen how to change the formatting of text using the Text Formatting toolbar. Now try changing the contents. This time, you'll try out the Ddedit command, which works in a slightly different way from the usual double-click method:

1. Choose Modify ➢ Object ➢ Text ➢ Edit, or type **Ddedit↵** at the command prompt.
2. Click the words *Living Room* to display the Text Formatting toolbar along with the text editor.
3. Place and click the text cursor on the end of the line that reads *Living Room*, and then type **↵230 square feet.**
4. Click OK. The text appears in the drawing with the additional line.
5. The Ddedit command is still active, so press ↵ to exit Ddedit.

In step 5, the Ddedit command remains active so that you can continue to edit other text objects. You can select another text object to make changes, or you can press ↵ to exit the Ddedit command.

As with the prior exercise, you can change the formatting of the existing or new text while in the text editor of the Text Formatting toolbar. Notice that the formatting of the new text is the same as the text that preceded it. Just as in Microsoft Word, the formatting of text depends on the paragraph or word to which it is added. If you had added the text after the last line, it would appear in the AutoCAD Txt font and in the same 6-inch height.

TIP *You can highlight text in the text window, then click and drag to move it or Ctrl-click and drag to copy.*

There is an AutoCAPS option in the Text Editor shortcut menu that allows you to turn on Caps Lock. This can be handy when you import text that needs to be in all uppercase letters.

Converting Text to Lowercase or Uppercase

If you find that you need to change the case of existing text, you can do so with the shortcut menu while in the Text Formatting toolbar. Here are the steps. (You don't need to apply these steps to your drawing exercises.)

1. Double-click a multiline text object.
2. Highlight the text you want to change.
3. Right-click, and then choose Change Case ➢ Uppercase or choose Change Case ➢ Lowercase, depending on which option you want.
4. Click Close to exit the Text Formatting toolbar.

Understanding Text and Scale

In the first few exercises of this chapter, you were asked to make the text height 6 inches. This is necessary to give the text the proper scale for the drawing. But where did we come up with the number 6?

Why not 4 or 10? The 6-inch height was derived by carefully considering the desired final height of the text in relation to the designated scale of the drawing. Just as in Chapter 3 where you applied a scale factor to a drawing's final sheet size to accommodate a full-scale drawing, you need to make a scale conversion for your text size to make the text conform to the drawing's intended scale.

Text-scale conversion is a concept many people have difficulty grasping. As you discovered in previous chapters, AutoCAD allows you to draw at full scale, that is, to represent distances as values equivalent to the actual size of the object. When you later plot the drawing, you tell AutoCAD at what scale you want to plot, and the program reduces the drawing accordingly. This allows you the freedom to enter measurements at full scale and not worry about converting them to various scales every time you enter a distance. Unfortunately, this feature can also create problems when you enter text and dimensions. Just as you had to convert the plotted sheet size to an enlarged size equivalent at full scale in the drawing editor, you must convert your text size to its equivalent at full scale.

To illustrate this point, imagine you are drawing the Unit plan at full size on a very large sheet of paper. When you are finished with this drawing, it will be reduced to a scale that allows it to fit on an 8.5" × 11" sheet of paper. So you have to make your text quite large to keep it legible once it is reduced. This means that if you want text to appear 1/8" high when the drawing is plotted, you must convert it to a considerably larger size when you draw it. To do this, you multiply the desired height of the final plotted text by a scale conversion factor.

If your drawing is at 1/8"=1'-0" scale, you multiply the desired text height, 1/8", by the scale conversion factor of 96 to get a height of 12". This is the height you must make your text to get 1/8"-high text in the final plot. (Chapter 3 shows scale factors as they relate to standard drawing scales.) Table 8.1 shows you some other examples of text height to scale.

TABLE 8.1: 1/8"-HIGH TEXT CONVERTED TO SIZE FOR VARIOUS DRAWING SCALES

DRAWING SCALE	SCALE FACTOR	AUTOCAD DRAWING HEIGHT FOR 1/8"-HIGH TEXT
1/16" = 1'-0"	192	24.0"
1/8" = 1'-0"	96	12.0"
1/4" = 1'-0"	48	6.0"
1/2" = 1'-0"	24	3.0"
3/4" = 1'-0"	16	2.0"
1" = 1'-0"	12	1.5"
1 1/2" = 1'-0"	8	1.0"
3" = 1'-0"	4	0.5"

Organizing Text by Styles

If you understand the Text Formatting toolbar and text scale, you know all you need to know to start labeling your drawings. As you expand your drawing skills and your drawings become larger, you will want to start organizing your text into *styles*. You can think of text styles as a way to store your most common text formatting. Styles will store text height and font information, so you don't have to reset these options every time you enter text. But styles also include some settings not available in the Multiline Text Editor.

Creating a Style

In the prior examples, you entered text using the AutoCAD default settings for text. Whether you knew it or not, you were also using a text style: AutoCAD's default style called Standard. The Standard style uses the AutoCAD Txt font and numerous other settings that you will learn about in this section. These other settings include width factor, oblique angle, and default height.

TIP *If you don't like the way the AutoCAD default style is set up, open the* `Acad.dwt` *template file and change the Standard text style settings to your liking. You can also add other styles that you use frequently. Remember that the AutoCAD files that use the .dwt filename extension are just AutoCAD .dwg files with a slightly different extension to set them apart.*

The previous exercises in this chapter demonstrate that you can modify the formatting of a style as you enter the text. But for the most part, once you've set up a few styles, you won't need to adjust settings such as fonts and text height each time you enter text. You'll be able to select from a list of styles you've previously created and just start typing.

To create a style, choose Format ➢ Text Style and then select from the available fonts. This next exercise will show you how to create a style:

1. Choose Format ➢ Text Style or type **St**↵ to open the Text Style dialog box.

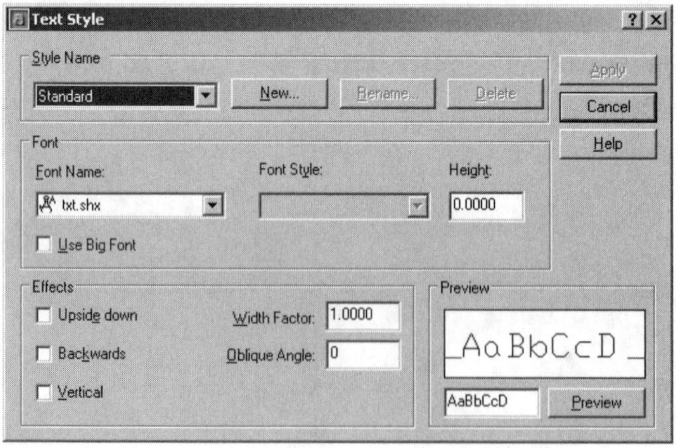

2. Click the New button in the Style Name group to open the New Text Style dialog box.
3. Enter **Note1 (Note one)** for the name of your new style; then click OK.
4. Now select a font for your style. Click the Font Name drop-down list in the Font group.

5. Locate the Courier New TrueType font and select it.

6. In the Height input box, enter **6**.

7. Click Apply, and then click Close.

Using a Type Style

Now let's see how your new text style looks by adding more text to the `Unit.dwg` drawing:

1. Pan your view so that the balcony is centered in the AutoCAD drawing area, as shown in Figure 8.8.

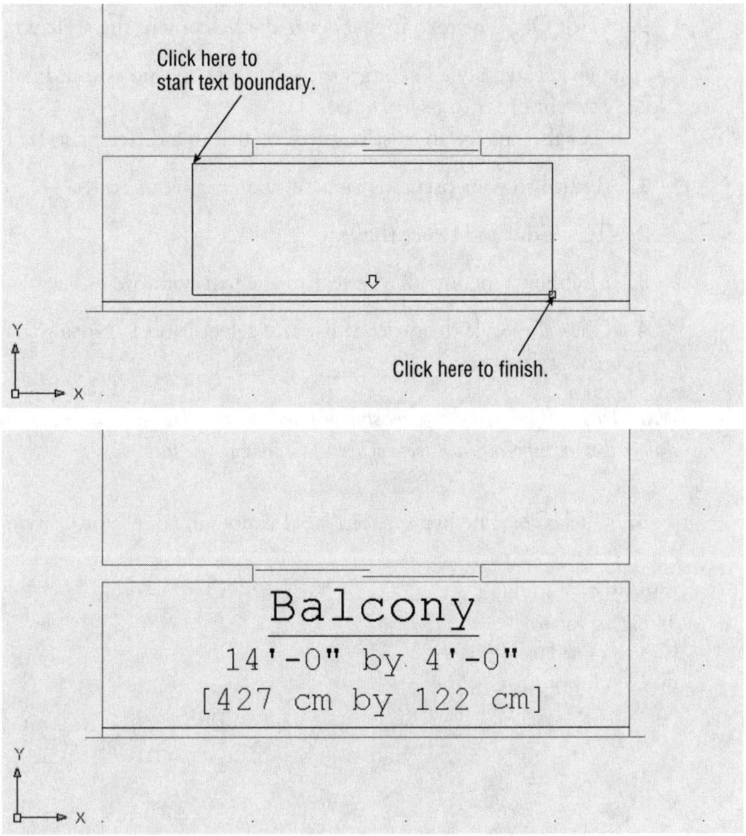

FIGURE 8.8

Adding the balcony label using the Note1 text style

2. Click the Multiline Text tool on the Draw toolbar.

3. Place the text boundary as shown in the top image in Figure 8.8. Notice that the font and height settings reflect the Note1 style you created earlier.

4. Enter the following text:

```
Balcony ↵
14'-0" by 4'-0"↵
[427 cm by 122 cm]
```

5. Highlight the word *Balcony*, and then click the Underline button.
6. With *Balcony* still highlighted, click the Text Height drop-down list and enter **9**↵.
7. Highlight all of the text.
8. Right-click, then select Justification ➢ Top Center.
9. Click OK. The text appears over the balcony in the style you selected.

A newly created style becomes the default style, and you didn't have to explicitly select your new Note1 style in order to use it.

You can also change an existing piece of text to a different style. The following steps show you how:

1. Return to your previous view of the *Living Room* text.
2. Type **Ed**↵ and select the text.
3. Highlight one line of the text in the text window.
4. Click the Style drop-down list and select Note1. Notice that all the text is converted to the new style.

WARNING *When you change the style of a text object, it loses any custom formatting it may have, such as font or height changes that are different from those of the text's default style settings.*

5. Click OK. The living room label is now in your Note1 style (see Figure 8.9).

FIGURE 8.9

The living room label converted to the Note1 style

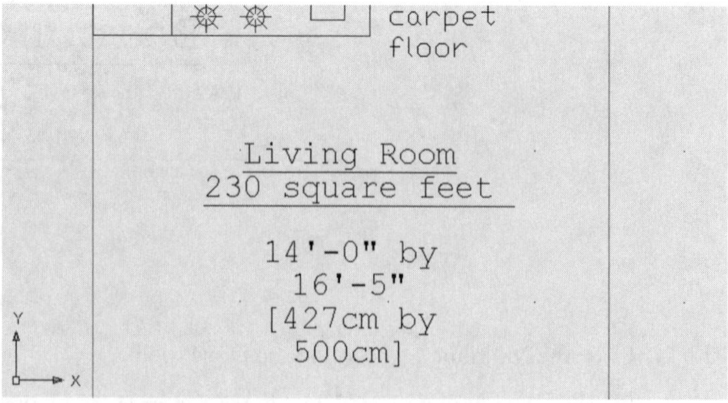

WARNING *The Style input box in the Text Formatting toolbar allows you to select a new style for a text object. This option does not affect the style of text if the text has other custom format changes, such as a font and size change from its default settings.*

Setting the Current Default Style

The previous exercise showed you how you can change the style of existing text. But suppose you want all the new text you create to be of a different style than the current default style. You can change the current style by using the Text Style dialog box. Here's how it's done:

1. Choose Format ➢ Text Style, or type **St**↵ to open the Text Style dialog box.
2. Select a style name from the Style Name drop-down list. For this exercise, choose Standard to return to the Standard style.
3. Click Close.

Or, you can quickly select a style from the Styles toolbar, which is just to the right of the standard toolbar.

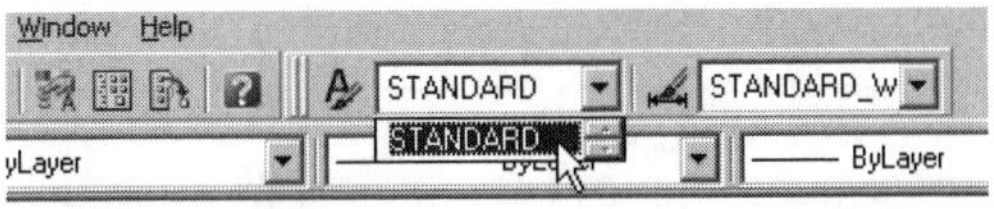

Once you've done this, the selected style will be the default until you select a different style. AutoCAD records the current default style with the drawing data when you issue a File ➢ Save command, so that the next time you work on the file you will still have the same default style.

Understanding the Text Style Dialog Box Options

Now you know how to create a new style. As mentioned, there are other settings in the Text Style dialog box that you didn't apply in an exercise. Here is a listing of those settings and their purposes. Some of them, like the Width Factor, can be quite useful. Others, like the Backwards and Vertical options, are rarely used.

STYLE NAME

In the Style Name section, you have the following options.

New Lets you create a new text style.

Rename Lets you rename an existing style. This option is not available for the Standard style.

Delete Deletes a style. This option is not available for the Standard style.

FONT

In the Font section, you have the following options:

Font Name Lets you select a font from a list of available fonts. The list is derived from the font resources available to Windows NT or Windows 95/98, plus the standard AutoCAD fonts.

Font Style Offers variations of a font, such as italic or bold, when they are available.

Height Lets you enter a font size. A 0 height has special meaning when entering text using the Dtext command, described later in this chapter.

EFFECTS

In the Effects section, you have the following options:

Upside Down Prints the text upside down.

Backwards Prints the text backward.

Width Factor Adjusts the width and spacing of the characters in the text. A value of 1 keeps the text at its normal width. Values greater than 1 expand the text, and values less than 1 compress the text.

This is the Simplex font expanded by 1.4
This is the simplex font using a width factor of 1
This is the simplex font compressed by .6

Oblique Angle Skews the text at an angle. When this option is set to a value greater than 0, the text appears to be italicized. A value of less than 0 (–12, for example) causes the text to "lean" to the left.

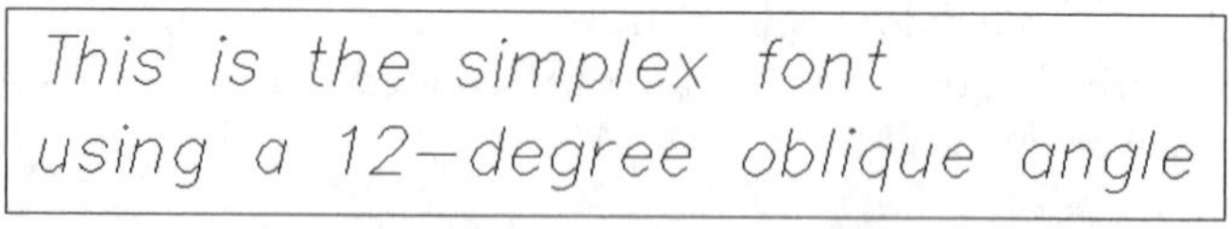

This is the simplex font
using a 12–degree oblique angle

Renaming a Text Style

You can use the Rename option in the Text Style dialog box to rename a style. An alternate method is to use the Ddrename command. This is a command that allows you to rename a variety of AutoCAD settings. Here's how to use it:

TIP *This exercise is not part of the main tutorial. If you are working through the tutorial, make note of it and then try it out later.*

1. Choose Format ➢ Rename or enter **Ren**↵ at the command prompt to open the Rename dialog box.

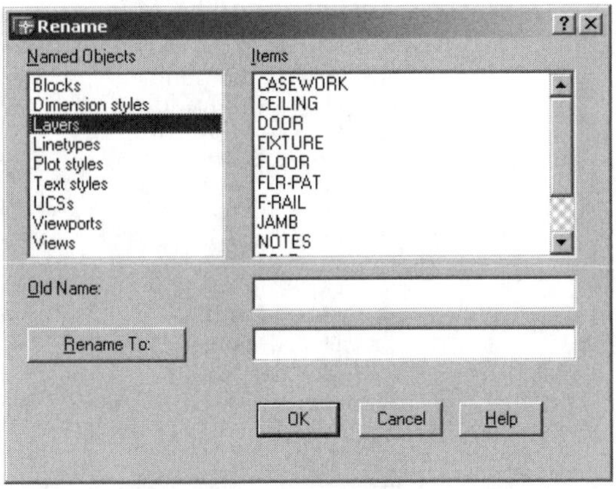

TIP *The Ddrename command allows you to rename blocks, dimension styles, layers, line types, user coordinate systems, viewports, and views, as well as text styles.*

2. In the Named Objects list box, choose Text Styles.
3. Click the name of the style you want to change from the list on the right; the name appears in the Old Name input box below the list.
4. In the input box next to the Rename To button, enter the new name. Click the Rename To button, and click OK.

TIP *If you are an experienced AutoCAD user and accustomed to entering the Rename command at the command prompt, you still can. Then answer the prompts that appear.*

TIP *If you need to change the style of one text object to match that of another, you can use the Match Properties tool. See Chapter 6 for details on how to use this tool.*

What Do the Fonts Look Like?

You've already seen a few of the fonts available in AutoCAD. Chances are, you are familiar with the TrueType fonts available in Windows. You have some additional AutoCAD fonts from which to choose. In fact, you might want to stick with the AutoCAD fonts for all but your presentation drawings, as other fonts can consume more memory.

Figure 8.10 shows the basic AutoCAD text fonts. The Roman font is perhaps the most widely used because it offers a reasonable appearance while consuming little memory. Figure 8.11 lists the symbols and Greek fonts.

FIGURE 8.10
The standard AutoCAD text fonts

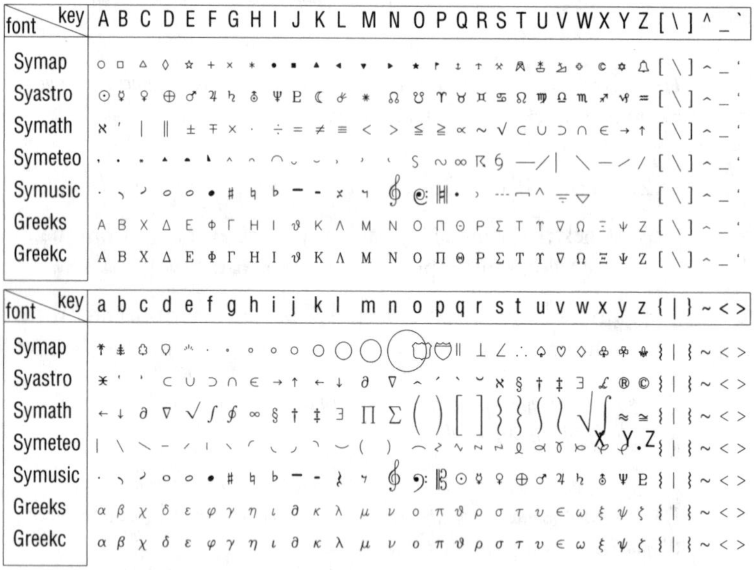

FIGURE 8.11
The AutoCAD symbols and Greek fonts

THE TEXTFILL SYSTEM VARIABLE

Unlike the standard sticklike AutoCAD fonts, TrueType and PostScript fonts have filled areas. These filled areas take more time to generate; so if you have a lot of text in these fonts, your redraw and regen times will increase. To help reduce redraw and regen times, you can set AutoCAD to display and plot these fonts as outline fonts, even though they are filled in their true appearance.

To change its setting, type **Textfill**.↵ and then type **0**.↵. This turns off text fill for PostScript and TrueType fonts. For plots, you can remove the check mark on the Text Fill option. (This is the same as setting the Textfill system variable to 0.)

This section showed you samples of the AutoCAD fonts. You can see samples of all the fonts, including TrueType fonts, in the preview window of the Text Style dialog box. If you use a word processor, you're probably familiar with at least some of the TrueType fonts available in Windows and AutoCAD.

Adding Special Characters

Earlier in this chapter, you saw that you can add special characters using the Symbol option from the text editor's shortcut menu. For example, you use the Degrees symbol to designate angles and the Plus/Minus symbol to show tolerance information. The Diameter characters are already available as special characters. AutoCAD also offers a nonbreaking space. You can use the nonbreaking space when you have a space between two words but you do not want the two words to be separated by a line break.

WARNING *The Character Map dialog box is a Windows accessory. If it does not appear when you choose Symbol ➢ Other from the Text Formatting toolbar's shortcut menu, you may need to install the Character Map from your Windows installation CD.*

By clicking the Other option in the Symbol shortcut menu, you can also add other special characters from the Windows Character Map dialog box. Characters such as the trademark (™) and copyright (©) symbols are often available. The contents of the Symbol drop-down list will depend on the font currently selected.

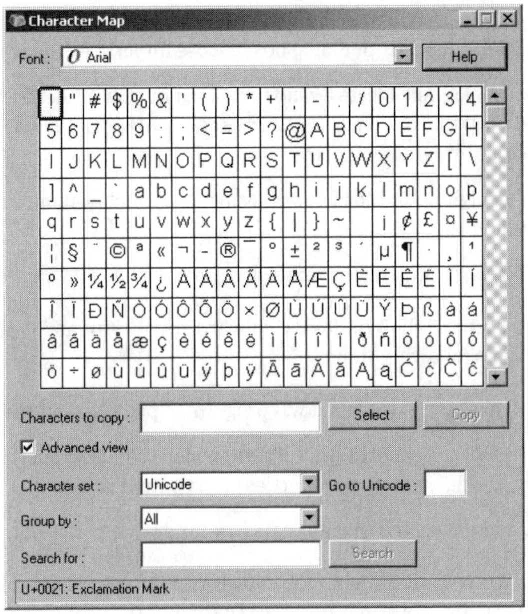

To use the characters from this dialog box, proceed with the following steps:

TIP *This is not part of the regular tutorial in this chapter, but you can experiment with these steps on your own.*

1. To open the Text Formatting toolbar, double-click a multiline text object, right-click in the text editor, and then choose Symbol ➢ Other from the shortcut menu.
2. Highlight the character you want in the Character Map dialog box.
3. Either double-click the character or click the Select button. The character appears in the box at the upper-right corner of the dialog box.
4. Click Copy to copy the character to the Clipboard.
5. Close the Character Map dialog box.
6. In the text editor, place the cursor where you want the special character to appear.
7. Press Ctrl+V to paste the character into your text. You can also right-click the mouse and choose Paste from the shortcut menu.

IMPORTING TEXT FILES

With multiline text objects, AutoCAD allows you to import ASCII text or Rich Text Format (RTF) files. Here's how you import text files:

1. In the Multiline Text Editor dialog box, choose Import Text.
2. In the Open dialog box, locate a valid text file. It must be either a file in a raw text (ASCII) format, such as a Notepad (.txt) file, or a Rich Text Format (.rtf) file. RTF files can store formatting information, such as boldface and varying point sizes.
3. Once you've highlighted the file you want, double-click it or click Open. The text appears in the Edit Mtext window.
4. You can then click OK, and the text will appear in your drawing.

In addition, you can use the Windows Clipboard and the Cut and Paste functions to add text to a drawing. To do this, take the following steps:

1. Choose Cut or Copy in any Windows program to place text on the Windows Clipboard.
2. Open AutoCAD, and choose Edit ➢ Paste to open the OLE Properties dialog box, in which you can adjust the height, width, and other properties of the pasted object.
3. Click OK, and the pasted text appears in your drawing. It is not, however, editable within AutoCAD.

Because AutoCAD is an OLE client, you can also attach other types of documents to an AutoCAD drawing file. See Chapter 15 for more on AutoCAD's OLE support.

Adding Simple Text Objects

You may find that you are entering a lot of single words or simple labels that don't require all the bells and whistles of the Multiline Text Editor. AutoCAD offers the *single-line text object* that is simpler to use and can speed text entry if you are adding only small pieces of text.

Continue the tutorial on the `Unit.dwg` file by trying the following exercise:

1. Adjust your view so it looks like Figure 8.12.

FIGURE 8.12

Adding simple labels to the kitchen and bath using the Dtext command

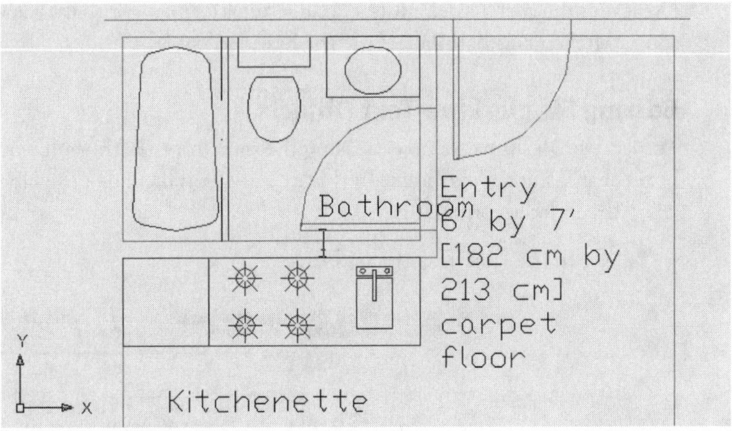

2. Enter **Dt↵**, or choose Draw ➢ Text ➢ Single Line Text. This issues the Dtext command.
3. At the `Specify start point of text or [Justify/Style]:` prompt, pick the starting point for the text you are about to enter, just below the kitchen at coordinate 16'-2",21'-8" (490,664 for metric users). Note that the prompt offers the Justify and Style options.
4. At the `Specify height:` prompt, enter **6"** (**15** for metric users) to indicate the text height.
5. At the `Specify rotation angle of text <0>:` prompt, press ↵ to accept the default, 0°. You can specify any angle other than horizontal (for example, if you want your text to be aligned with a rotated object). You'll see a text I-beam cursor at the point you picked in step 3.
6. At the `Enter text:` prompt, enter the word **Kitchenette**. As you type, the word appears in the drawing as well as in the Command window.

TIP *If you make a typing error, use the Right and Left arrow keys to move the text cursor in the Command window to the error; then use the Backspace key to correct the error. You can also paste text from the Clipboard into the cursor location using the Ctrl+V keyboard shortcut or by right-clicking in the Command window to access the shortcut menu.*

7. Press ↵ to move the cursor down to start a new line.
8. This time you want to label the bathroom. Pick a point to the right of the door swing at coordinate 19'-11",26'-5" (610,805 for metric users). The text cursor moves to that point.

9. Type **Bathroom↵**. Figure 8.12 shows how your drawing should look now.
10. Press ↵ again to exit the Dtext command.

TIP *If for some reason you need to stop entering single-line text objects to do something else in AutoCAD, you can continue the text where you left off by pressing ↵ at the* `Start point:` *prompt of the Dtext command. The text continues immediately below the last line of text entered.*

Here you were able to add two single lines of text in different parts of your drawing fairly quickly. Dtext uses the current default text style settings (remember that earlier you set the text style to Standard), so the kitchen and bath labels use the Standard style.

Editing Single-Line Text Objects

You edit single-line text objects using the same tools as those for multiline text, although the dialog boxes that result are different. In this exercise, you'll change the labels in both the kitchen and bath using the Ddedit command:

1. Open the Edit Text dialog box.

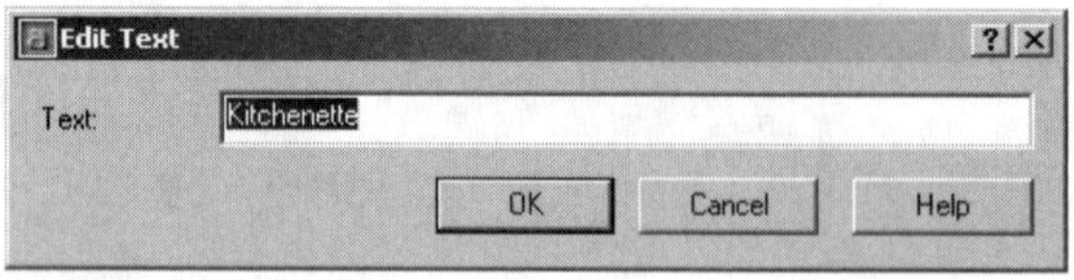

   Choose Modify ➢ Object ➢ Text ➢ Edit and then select the Kitchenette label, or select and right-click the label and choose Text Edit.
2. Using the cursor, highlight *ette* in *Kitchenette* and delete it.
3. Click OK. (Notice that Ddedit is still active.)
4. Click the Bathroom label.
5. In the Edit Text dialog box that appears, highlight *room* in *Bathroom* and delete it.
6. Click OK and then press ↵ to exit the Ddedit command.

As you can see, even the editing is simplified. You are limited to editing the text only. This can be an advantage, however, when you need to edit several pieces of text. You don't have other options to get in the way of your editing.

You can change other properties of single-line text using the Properties palette. For example, suppose you want to change the bath label to a height of 9 inches.

1. Click the Bath text, and then right-click and choose Properties to open the Properties palette.
2. Select the Height value in the Properties palette and change it to **9"**.
3. Press ↵ and the text in the drawing increases in size to 9 inches high.
4. Click the Undo tool on the menu bar to undo the change in text height.

5. Choose File ➢ Save to save the changes you've made thus far.

6. Close the Properties palette.

The Properties palette lets you change the Height, Rotation, Width Factor, Obliquing, Justification, and Style of a single-line text object. You can also modify the text content.

Justifying Single-Line Text Objects

Justifying single-line text objects works in a slightly different way from justifying multiline text. For example, if you change the justification setting to Center, the text moves so the center of the text is placed at the text insertion point. In other words, the insertion point stays in place while the text location adjusts to the new justification setting. Figure 8.13 shows the relationship between single-line text and the insertion point based on different justification settings.

FIGURE 8.13

Text inserted using the various justification options

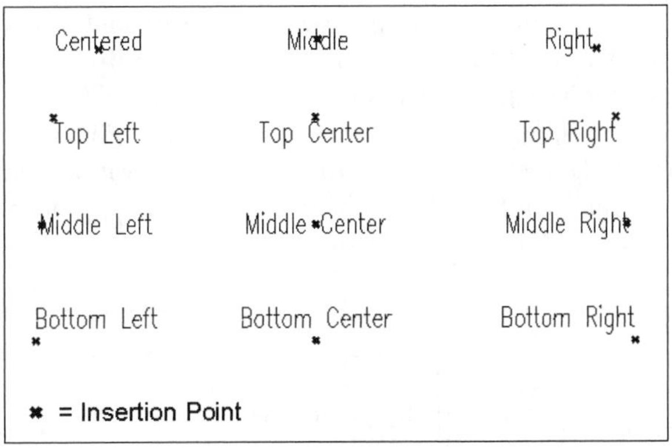

To set the justification of text as you enter it, you must enter **J**↵ at the `Specify start point of text or [Justify/Style]:` prompt after issuing the Dtext command.

TIP *You can also change the current default style by entering* **S**↵ and then the name of the style at the `Specify start point of text or [Justify/Style]:` *prompt.*

Once you've issued the Dtext's Justify option, you get the following prompt:

```
Enter an option
[Align/Fit/Center/Middle/Right/TL/TC/TR/ML/MC/MR/BL/BC/BR]:
```

Here are descriptions of each of these options. (I've left Fit and Align until last, because these options require a bit more explanation.)

Center Centers the text on the start point, with the baseline on the start point.

Middle Centers the text on the start point, with the baseline slightly below the start point.

Right Justifies the text to the right of the start point, with the baseline on the start point.

TL, TC, and TR TL, TC, and TR stand for Top Left, Top Center, and Top Right. Text using these justification styles appears entirely below the start point, justified left, center, or right, depending on which option you choose.

ML, MC, and MR ML, MC, and MR stand for Middle Left, Middle Center, and Middle Right. These styles are similar to TL, TC, and TR, except that the start point determines a location midway between the baseline and the top of the lowercase letters of the text.

BL, BC, and BR BL, BC, and BR stand for Bottom Left, Bottom Center, and Bottom Right. These styles, too, are similar to TL, TC, and TR, but here the start point determines the bottom-most location of the letters of the text (the bottom of letters that have descenders, such as *p*, *q*, and *g*).

Align and Fit With the Align and Fit justification options, you must specify a dimension within which the text is to fit. For example, suppose you want the word *Refrigerator* to fit within the 26"-wide box representing the refrigerator. You can use either the Fit or the Align option to accomplish this. With Fit, AutoCAD prompts you to select start and end points and then stretches or compresses the letters to fit within the two points you specify. You use this option when the text must be a consistent height throughout the drawing and you don't care about distorting the font. Align works like Fit, but instead of maintaining the current text style height, the Align option adjusts the text height to keep it proportional to the text width, without distorting the font. Use this option when it is important to maintain the font's shape and proportion. Figure 8.14 demonstrates how Fit and Align work.

FIGURE 8.14

The word *Refrigerator* as it appears normally and with the Fit and Align options selected

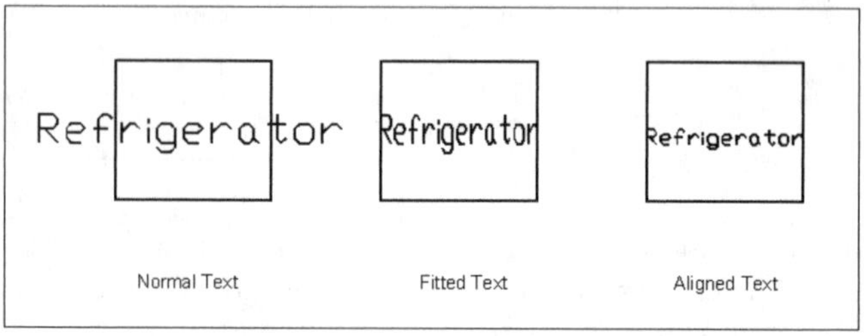

You can change the justification of single-line text using the Properties palette, but the text will move from its original location while maintaining its insertion point. If you want to change the justification of text without moving the text, you can use the Justifytext command. Choose Modify ➢ Object ➢ Text ➢ Justify or type **Justifytext** at the command prompt; then select the text you want to change. Justifytext works on both multiline and single-line text.

Using Special Characters with Single-Line Text Objects

Just as with multiline text, you can add a limited set of special characters to single-line text objects. For example, you can place the degree symbol (°) after a number, or you can *underscore* (underline) text. To accomplish this, you use double percent (%%) signs in conjunction with a special code. For example, to underscore text, you enclose that text with %% followed by the letter *u*, which is the underscore code. So, to get this text, "This is underscored text." you enter the following at the prompt:

This is %%uunderscored%%u text.

Overscoring (putting a line above the text) operates in the same manner. To insert codes for symbols, you just place the codes in the correct positions for the symbols they represent. For example, to enter 100.5°, you type **100.5%%d**.

Here is a list of the codes you can use:

Code	What It Does
%%o	Toggles overscore on and off.
%%u	Toggles underscore on and off.
%%d	Places a degree sign (°) where the code occurs.
%%p	Places a plus-minus sign where the code occurs.
%%%	Forces a single percent sign; useful when you want a double percent sign to appear or when you want a percent sign in conjunction with another code.
%%*nnn*	Allows the use of extended characters when these characters are used in a text-definition file; *nnn* is the three-digit value representing the character.

USING THE CHARACTER MAP DIALOG BOX TO ADD SPECIAL CHARACTERS

You can add special characters to a single line of text in the same way you add special characters to multiline text. You may recall that to access special characters, you use the Character Map dialog box.

To open the Character Map dialog box, choose Start ➢ All Programs ➢ Accessories ➢ System Tools ➢ Character Map. You can then use the procedure discussed in the "Adding Special Characters" section earlier in this chapter to cut and paste a character from the Character Map dialog box. If you find that you use the Character Map dialog box often, create a shortcut for it and place the shortcut in your Start menu or Desktop.

KEEPING TEXT FROM MIRRORING

At times you will want to mirror a group of objects that contain some text. This operation causes the mirrored text to appear backward. You can change a setting in AutoCAD to make the text read normally, even when it is mirrored:

1. At the command prompt, enter **Mirrtext**↵.
2. At the `New value for MIRRTEXT <1>:` prompt, enter **0**↵.

Now, any mirrored text that is not in a block will read normally. The text's position, however, will still be mirrored, as shown in the following graphic. Mirrtext is set to 0 by default.

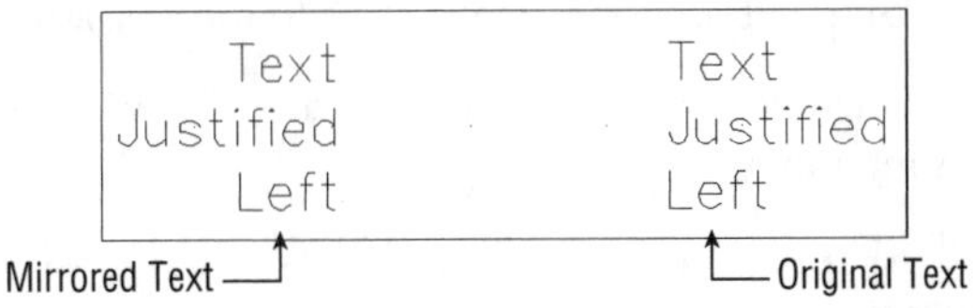

Using the Check Spelling Feature

Although AutoCAD is primarily a drawing program, you will find that some of your drawings contain more text than graphics. Autodesk has recognized this and included a spelling checker starting in AutoCAD Release 14. If you've ever used the spelling checker in a typical word processor, such as Microsoft Word, the AutoCAD spelling checker's operation will be familiar to you. These steps show you how it works:

1. Choose Tools ➢ Spelling from the pull-down menu, or type **Sp**↵.
2. At the `Select objects:` prompt, select any text object you want to check. You can select a mixture of multiline and single-line text. When the spelling checker finds a word it does not recognize, the Check Spelling dialog box appears.

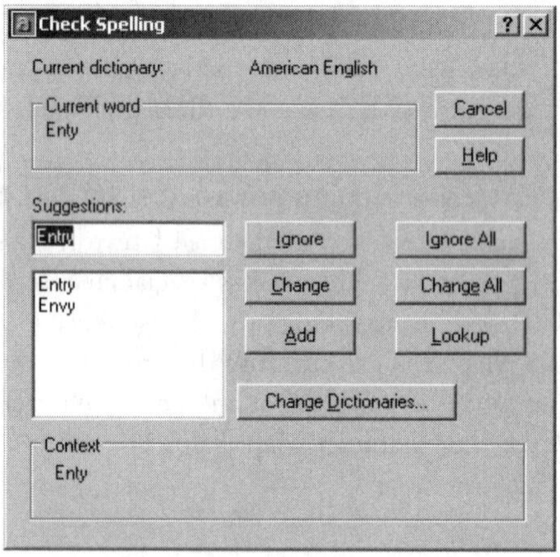

In the Check Spelling dialog box, you'll see the word in question, along with the spelling checker's suggested alternate word in the Suggestions input box. If the spelling checker finds more than one suggestion, a list of suggested alternate words appears below the input box. You can then highlight the desired replacement and click the Change button to change the misspelled word, or you can click Change All to change all occurrences of the word in the selected text. If the suggested word is inappropriate, choose another word from the replacement list (if any), or enter your own spelling in the Suggestions input box. Then choose Change or Change All.

Here is a list of the options available in the Check Spelling dialog box:

Ignore Skips the word.

Ignore All Skips all occurrences of the word in the selected text.

Change Changes the word in question to the word you have selected (or entered) from the Suggestions input box.

Change All Changes all occurrences of the current word when there are multiple instances of the misspelling.

Add Adds the word in question to the current dictionary.

Lookup Checks the spelling of the word in question. This option is for the times when you want to find another word that doesn't appear in the Suggestions input box.

Change Dictionaries Lets you use a different dictionary to check spelling. This option opens the Change Dictionaries dialog box, described in the upcoming section.

The Check Spelling feature includes types of notation that are more likely to be found in technical drawings. It will also check the spelling of text that is included in block definitions.

Choosing a Dictionary

Clicking the Change Dictionaries button in the Check Spelling dialog box opens the Change Dictionaries dialog box, where you can select a particular main dictionary for foreign languages or create or choose a custom dictionary. Main dictionary files have the .dct extension. The main dictionary for the U.S. version of AutoCAD is `Enu.dct`.

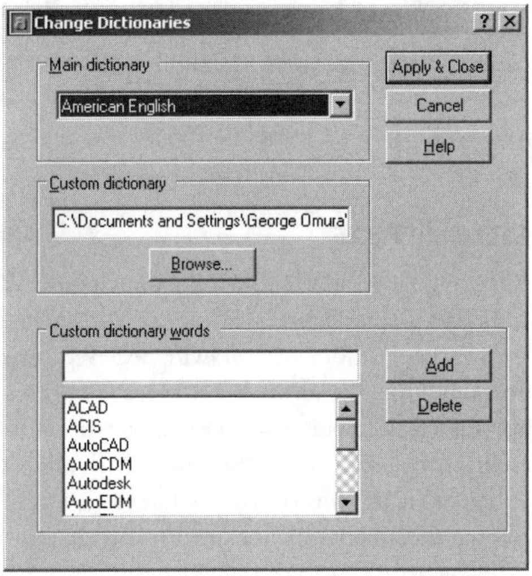

In the Change Dictionaries dialog box, you can also add or delete words from a custom dictionary. Custom dictionary files are ASCII files with the .cus extension. Because they are ASCII files, you can edit them outside AutoCAD. Click the Browse button to view a list of existing custom dictionaries.

If you prefer, you can also select a main or custom dictionary using the Dctust and Dctmain system variables. See Appendix D for more on these system variables.

You can also select a dictionary is in the Files tab of the Options dialog box (choose Tools ➢ Options). You can find the dictionary listing under Text Editor, Dictionary, And Font File Names. Click the plus sign next to this listing, and then click the plus sign next to the Main Dictionary listing to expose the dictionary options.

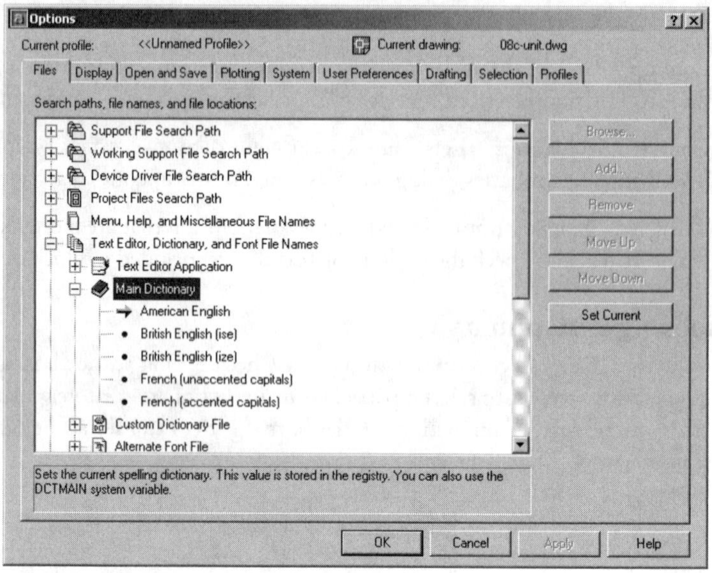

From here, you can double-click the dictionary you prefer.

Substituting Fonts

At times you'll want to change all the fonts in a drawing quickly. For instance, you might want to convert TrueType fonts into a simple `Txt.shx` font to help shorten redraw times while you are editing. Or you might need to convert the font of a drawing received from another office to a font that conforms to your own office standards. In AutoCAD 2004, the Fontmap system variable works in conjunction with a font-mapping table, allowing you to easily substitute fonts in a drawing.

The font-mapping table is an ASCII file called `Acad.fmp`. You can also use a file you create yourself. You can give this file any name you choose, as long as it has the .fmp extension.

This font-mapping table contains one line for each font substitution you want AutoCAD to make. A typical line in this file would read as follows:

```
romant; C:\ProgramFiles\Acad 2004\Font\Txt.shx
```

In this example, AutoCAD is directed to use the `Txt.shx` font in place of the `Romant.shx` font. To execute this substitution, you type

`Fontmap` ↵ ***`Fontmap_filename`***

`Fontmap_filename` is the font-mapping table you've created. This tells AutoCAD where to look for the font-mapping information. Then you issue the Regen command to view the font changes. To disable the font-mapping table, you type

`Fontmap` ↵ **.**↵

You can also specify a font-mapping file in the Files tab of the Options dialog box. Look for the Text Editor, Dictionary, And Font File Names listing. Click the plus sign next to this listing, and then click the plus sign next to the Font Mapping File listing to expose the current default font-mapping filename. If you hold the cursor over the name, AutoCAD displays the full location of the file.

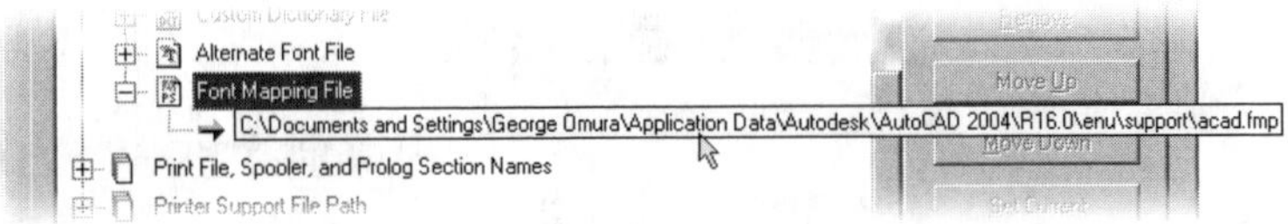

You can double-click this filename to open the Select A File dialog box. From there, you can select a different font-mapping file.

See Appendix D for more on the Fontmap system variable and other system variables.

MAKING SUBSTITUTIONS FOR MISSING FONTS

When text styles are created, the associated fonts do not become part of the drawing file. Instead, AutoCAD loads the needed font file at the same time that the drawing is loaded. So if a text style in a drawing requires a particular font, AutoCAD looks for the font in the AutoCAD search path; if the font is there, it is loaded. Usually this isn't a problem if the drawing file uses the standard fonts that come with AutoCAD or Windows. But occasionally you will encounter a file that uses a custom font.

In earlier versions of AutoCAD, you saw an error message when you attempted to open such a file. This missing-font message would often send the new AutoCAD user into a panic.

Fortunately, AutoCAD automatically substitutes an existing font for the missing font in a drawing. By default, AutoCAD substitutes the `Simplex.shx` font, but you can specify another font using the Fontalt system variable. Type **Fontalt**↵ at the command prompt and then enter the name of the font you want to use as the substitute.

You can also select an alternate font through the Files tab of the Options dialog box. Locate the Text Editor, Dictionary, And Font File Names listing, and then click the plus sign at the left. Locate the Alternate Font File listing, and click the plus sign at the left. The current alternate is listed. You can double-click the font name to select a different font through a Standard File dialog box.

Be aware that the text in your drawing will change in appearance, sometimes radically, when you use a substitute font. If the text in the drawing must retain its appearance, substitute a font that is as similar in appearance to the original font as possible.

Finding and Replacing Text

One of the most time-consuming tasks in drafting is replacing text that appears repeatedly throughout a drawing. Fortunately, you have a Find And Replace tool to help make this task a simple one.

AutoCAD's Find And Replace works like any other find-and-replace tool in a word processing program. There are a few options that work specifically with AutoCAD. Here's how it works.

1. Choose Edit ➢ Find from the menu bar or enter **Find**↵ at the command prompt to open the Find And Replace dialog box.

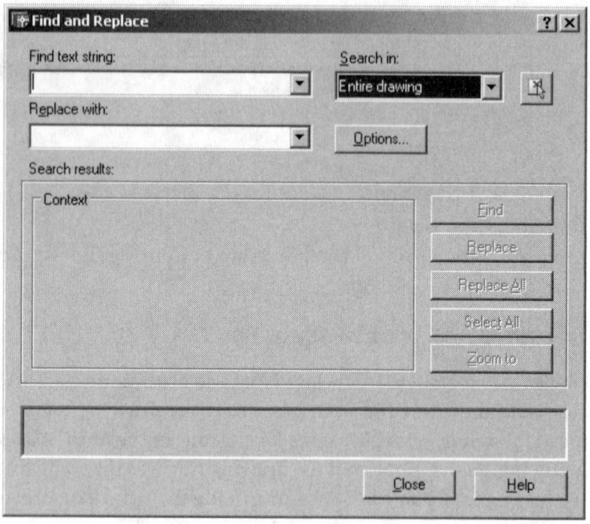

2. Enter the text you want to locate in the Find Text String input box.
3. Enter the replacement text in the Replace With input box.
4. Click Find. When AutoCAD finds the word, it appears in the Context window, along with any other text next to the word.
5. If you have any doubts, click the Zoom To button to display the text in the AutoCAD drawing area.
6. Finally, when you've made certain that this is the text you want to change, click Replace.

If you want to replace all occurrences of a word in the drawing, click Replace All. You can also limit your find-and-replace operation to a specific area of your drawing by clicking the Select Objects button in the upper-right corner of the Find And Replace dialog box.

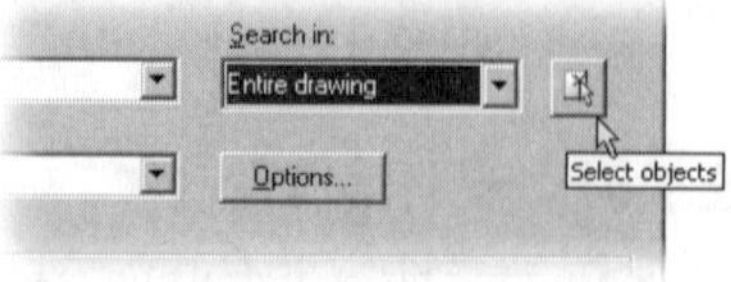

When you click the Select Objects button, the Find And Replace dialog box disappears temporarily to allow you to select a set of objects or a region of your drawing. Find And Replace will then limit its search to those objects or the region you select.

You can further control the types of objects that Find And Replace looks for by clicking the Options button to open the Find And Replace Options dialog box.

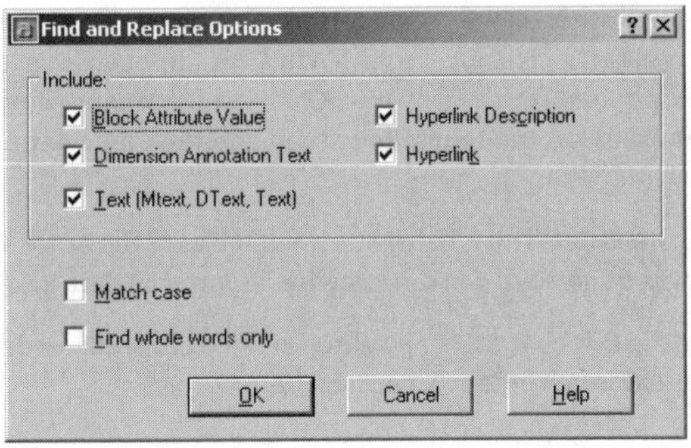

With this dialog box, you can refine your search by limiting it to blocks, dimension text, standard text, or hyperlink text. You can also determine whether to match case or find whole words only.

Accelerating Zooms and Regens with Qtext

If you need to edit a drawing that contains a lot of text, but you don't need to edit the text, you can use the Qtext command to help accelerate redraws and regenerations when you are working on the drawing. Qtext turns lines of text into rectangular boxes, saving AutoCAD from having to form every letter. This allows you to see the note locations so you don't accidentally draw over them.

TIP *Selecting a large set of text objects for editing can be annoyingly slow. To improve the speed of text selection (and object selection in general), turn off the Highlight and Dragmode system variables. This disables certain convenience features but may improve overall performance, especially on large drawings. See Appendix D for more information on these system variables.*

The following steps tell you how to turn on Qtext:

1. Enter **Qtext↵** at the command prompt.
2. At the `ON/OFF <OFF>:` prompt, enter **ON↵**.
3. To display the results of Qtext, issue the Regen command from the prompt.

TIP *You can also open the Options dialog box (choose Tools ➢ Options), click the Display tab, and then click the Show Text Boundary Frame Only option to display text as rectangular regions.*

When Qtext is off, text is generated normally. When Qtext is on, rectangles show the approximate size and length of text.

MANIPULATING TEXT BEYOND LABELS

This chapter concentrates on methods for adding labels to your drawing, but you also use text in other ways with AutoCAD. Many of the inquiry tools in AutoCAD, such as Dist and List, produce text data. You can use the Windows Clipboard to manipulate such data to your benefit.

For example, you can duplicate the exact length of a line by first using the List command to get a listing of its properties. Once you have the property list in the AutoCAD Text window, you can highlight its length listing and then press Ctrl+C to copy it to the Windows Clipboard. Next, you can start the Line command and then pick the start point for the new line. Click the Command window and press Ctrl+V to paste the line length data into the Command window; then add the angle data or use the Direct Distance method to draw the line.

You can copy any text data from dialog box input boxes or the AutoCAD Text window to the Clipboard using the Ctrl+C keyboard shortcut. You can likewise import that data into any part of AutoCAD that accepts text.

Consider using the Clipboard the next time you need to transfer data within AutoCAD or even when you need to import text from some other application.

If You Want to Experiment...

At this point, you might want to try adding some notes to drawings you have created in other "If You Want to Experiment..." sections of this book. Also, try the exercise shown in Figure 8.15. In addition, you might try importing a finish or door schedule from a word processor in the Monotxt font, to see how that works. If your application is mechanical, you might try importing a parts list.

FIGURE 8.15

The sample mechanical drawing with notes added

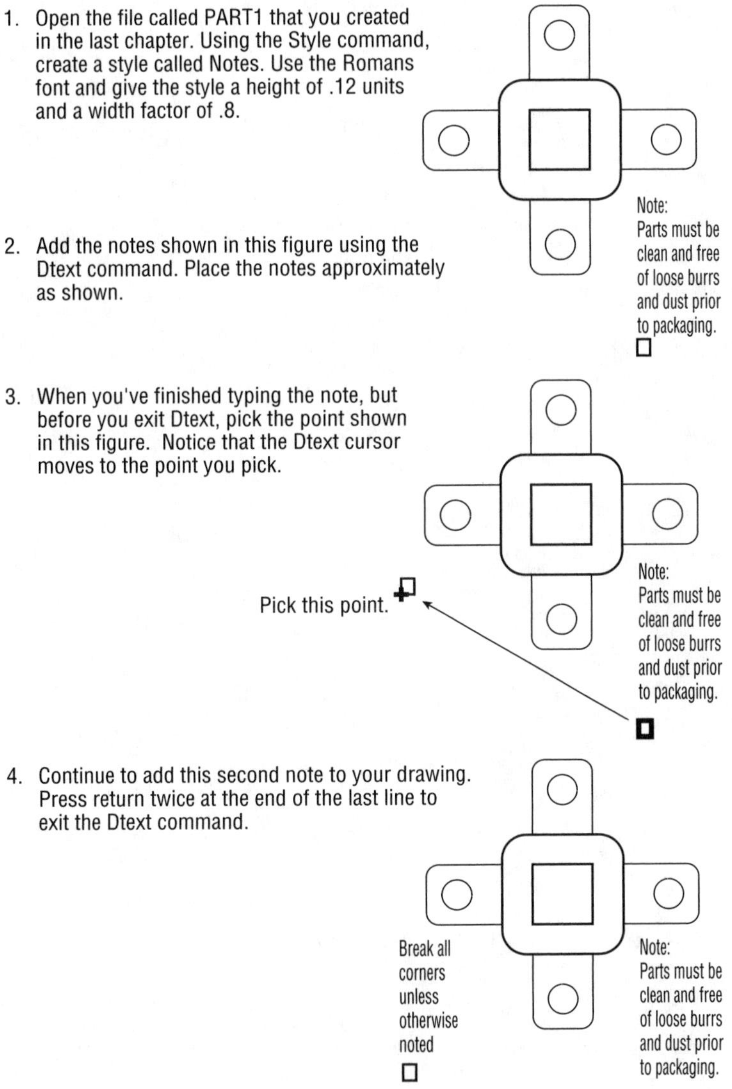
1. Open the file called PART1 that you created in the last chapter. Using the Style command, create a style called Notes. Use the Romans font and give the style a height of .12 units and a width factor of .8.
2. Add the notes shown in this figure using the Dtext command. Place the notes approximately as shown.
Note:
Parts must be
clean and free
of loose burrs
and dust prior
to packaging.
3. When you've finished typing the note, but before you exit Dtext, pick the point shown in this figure. Notice that the Dtext cursor moves to the point you pick.
Pick this point.
Note:
Parts must be
clean and free
of loose burrs
and dust prior
to packaging.
4. Continue to add this second note to your drawing. Press return twice at the end of the last line to exit the Dtext command.
Break all
corners
unless
otherwise
noted
Note:
Parts must be
clean and free
of loose burrs
and dust prior
to packaging.

Chapter 9

Using Dimensions

BEFORE YOU DETERMINE THE dimensions of a project, your design is in flux, and many questions may be unanswered. Once you begin dimensioning, you will begin to see if things fit or work together. Dimensioning can be crucial to how well a design works and how quickly it develops. The dimensions answer questions about code conformance if you are an architect; they answer questions about tolerances, fit, and interference if you are involved in mechanical applications. Once you and your design team reach a design on a schematic level, communicating even tentative dimensions to others on the team can accelerate design development. Dimensions represent a point from which you can further develop your ideas.

With AutoCAD, you can easily add tentative or final dimensions to any drawing. AutoCAD gives you an accurate dimension without your having to take measurements. You simply pick the two points to be dimensioned and the dimension line location, and AutoCAD does the rest. AutoCAD's *associative dimensioning* capability automatically updates dimensions whenever the size or shape of the dimensioned object changes. These dimensioning features can save you valuable time and reduce the number of dimensional errors in your drawings.

- Understanding the Components of a Dimension
- Creating a Dimension Style
- Dimensioning Nonorthogonal Objects
- Skewing Dimension Lines
- Applying Ordinate Dimensions
- Adding Tolerance Notation
- If You Want to Experiment…

Understanding the Components of a Dimension

Before you get started with the exercises in this chapter, it will help you to know the names of the parts of a dimension. Figure 9.1 shows a sample of a dimension with the parts labeled. The *dimension line* is the line that represents the distance being dimensioned. It is the line with the arrows on either end. The *extension lines* are the lines that originate from the object being dimensioned. They show you the exact location from which the dimension is taken. The *dimension text* is the actual dimension value, usually shown inside or above the dimension line.

FIGURE 9.1

The components of a dimension

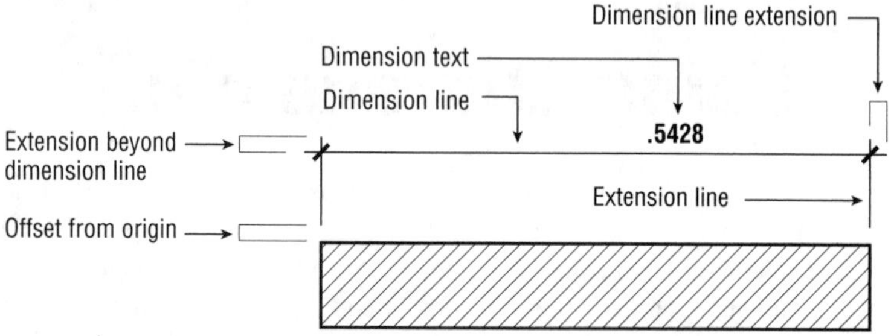

Another component of a dimension line is the *dimension line extension*. This is the part of the dimension line that extends beyond the extension line. Dimension line extensions are usually used only on architectural dimensions. The extension lines usually extend beyond the dimension lines in all types of dimensions. The extension line *offset from origin* is the distance from the beginning of the extension line to the object being dimensioned.

You can control each of these components by creating or editing *dimension styles*. Dimension styles are the settings that determine the look of your dimensions. You can store multiple styles within a single drawing. The first exercise in this chapter will show you how to create a dimension style.

Creating a Dimension Style

Dimension styles are similar to text styles. They determine the look of your dimensions as well as the size of dimensioning features, such as the dimension text and arrows. You might set up a dimension style to have special types of arrows, for instance, or to position the dimension text above or in line with the dimension line. Dimension styles also make your work easier by allowing you to store and duplicate your most common dimension settings.

AutoCAD gives you one of two default dimension styles called *ISO-25* or *Standard*, depending on whether you use the metric or Imperial measurement system. You will probably add many other styles to suit the type of drawings you are creating. You can also create variations of a general style for those situations that call for only minor changes in the dimension's appearance.

In this first section you'll learn how to set up your own dimension style based on the Standard dimension style (see Figure 9.2). For metric users, the settings will be different, but the overall methods will be the same.

FIGURE 9.2
AutoCAD's Standard dimension style compared with an architectural-style dimension

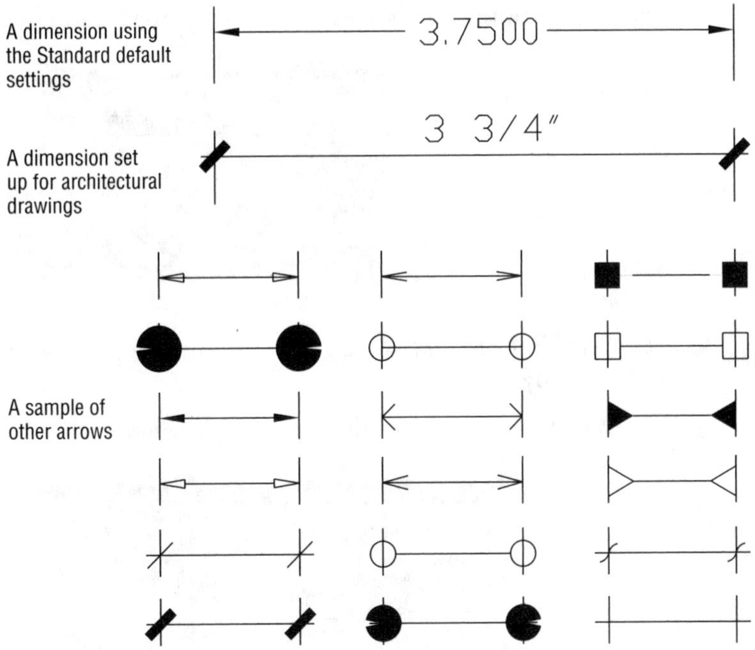

1. Open the `Unit` file you edited in the last chapter. If you didn't create one, use the `09a-unit.dwg` file on the companion CD and rename it `Unit.dwg`.
2. Issue Zoom All to display the entire floor plan.
3. Choose Format ➢ Dimension ➢ Style or type **D↵** at the command prompt to open the Dimension Style Manager dialog box.
4. Select Standard from the Styles list box. Metric users should select ISO-25.

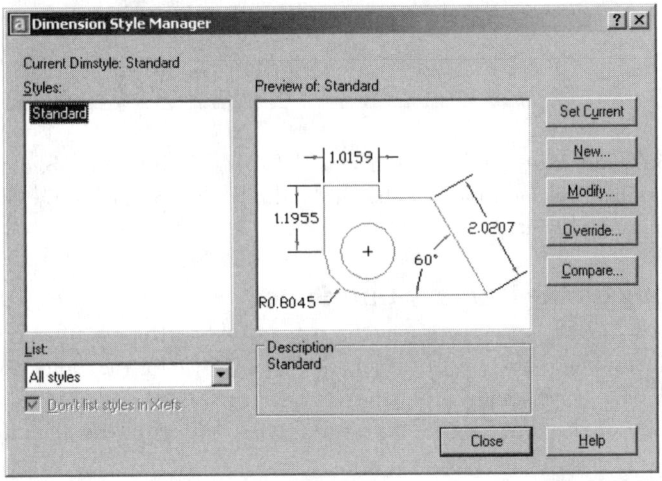

5. Click New to open the Create New Dimension Style dialog box.

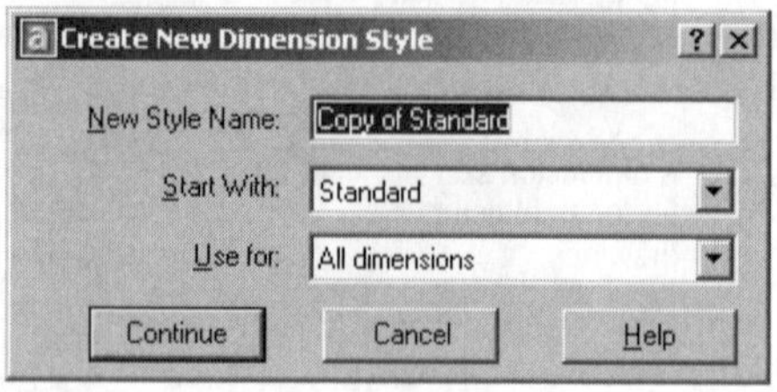

6. With the Copy Of Standard or ISO-25 name highlighted in the New Style Name input box, enter **My Architectural**.

7. Click Continue to open the detailed New Dimension Style dialog box.

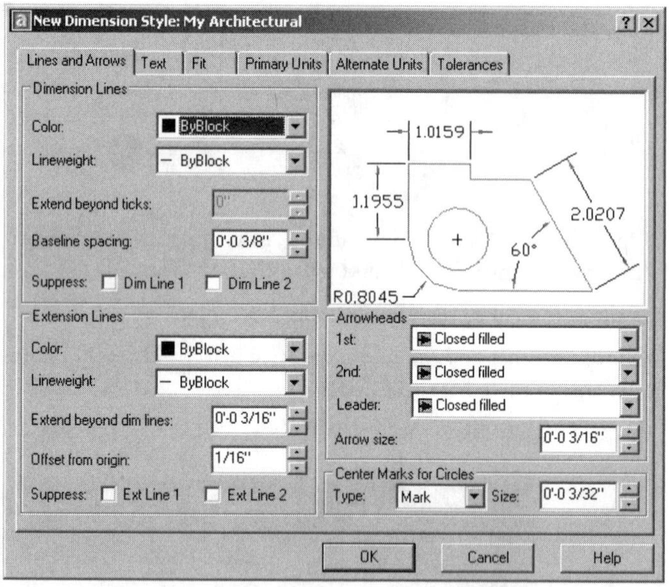

You've just created a dimension style called My Architectural, but at this point it is identical to the Standard style on which it is based. Nothing has happened to the Standard style; it is still available if you need to use it.

Setting Up the Primary Unit Style

Now you need to set up your new dimension style so that it conforms to the U.S. architectural style of dimensioning. Let's start by changing the unit style for the dimension text. Just as you changed the overall unit style of AutoCAD to a feet-and-inches style for your toilet and tub drawing in Chapter 3, you must do the same for your dimension styles. Setting the overall unit style does not automatically set the dimension unit style.

1. In the New Dimension Style dialog box, click the Primary Units tab.

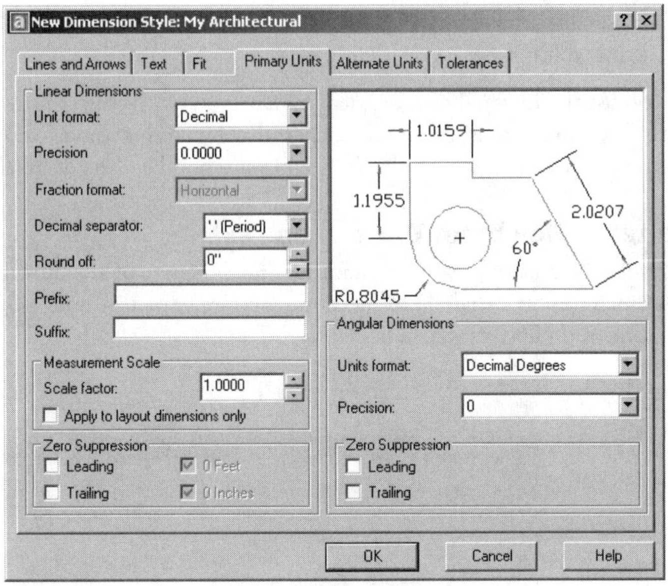

2. In the Linear Dimensions button group, open the Unit Format drop-down list and choose Architectural. Notice that this drop-down list contains the same unit styles as the main Units dialog box (choose Format ➢ Units). Metric users can skip this option.

TIP *You might notice the Decimal Separator option a few settings below the Unit Format option. The Decimal Separator option lets you choose between a period and a comma for decimal points. Metric users often use the comma for a decimal point, and U.S. users will use a period. This option doesn't have any meaning for feet-and-inch measurements, so it is dimmed when the Architectural unit format is selected.*

3. Select 0'-0 1/4" from the Precision drop-down list, just below the Unit Format list. Metric users should select 0.00. The Precision option allows you to set the level of precision that is displayed in the dimension text. It doesn't limit the precision of AutoCAD's drawing database. This value is only used to limit the display of dimension text values.

TIP *Every dimension style setting has an equivalent system variable. See Appendix D for more on system variables that are directly associated with dimensions.*

4. Just below the Precision drop-down list, open the Fraction Format drop-down list and select Diagonal. Notice what happens to the graphic . The fractional dimensions change to show you how your dimension text will look. Metric users can skip this step, since it isn't available when the Decimal unit format is selected.

5. In the Zero Suppression group in the lower-left corner, click 0 Inches to turn off this check box. If you leave it turned on, indications of 0 inches will be omitted from the dimension text. (In architectural drawings, 0 inches are shown as in this dimension: 12'-0".) Metric users can ignore this option.

If you use the Imperial measurement system, you have set up My Architectural's dimension unit style to show dimensions in feet and inches, the standard method for U.S. construction documents. Metric users have just changed the Precision value and kept the decimal unit system.

Setting the Height for Dimension Text

Along with the unit style, you will want to adjust the size of the dimension text. The Text tab of the New Dimension Style dialog box lets you set a variety of text options, including text location relative to the dimension line, style, and height.

1. Click the Text tab to display the text options.

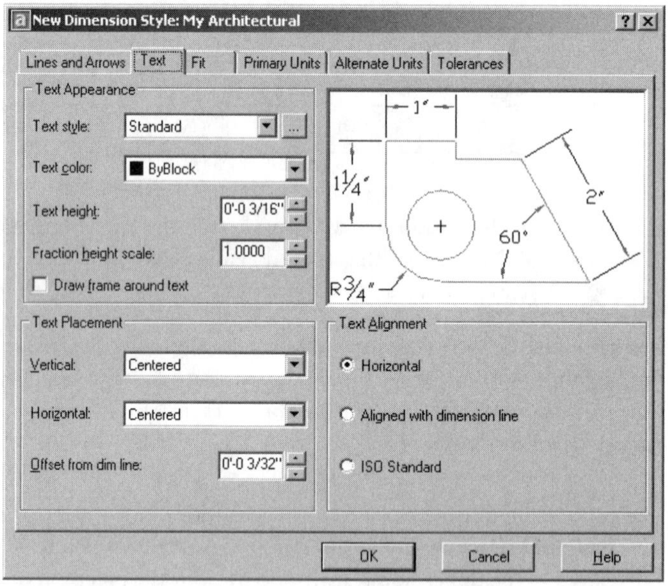

2. Highlight the contents of the Text Height input box.

3. Type **1/8**↵ to make the text height 1/8" high. Metric users should enter **0.3**↵ for the text height.

Unlike the text you created in Chapter 8, you specify the text height by its final plot size. You then specify an overall dimension scale factor that affects the sizing of all the dimensioning settings such as text and arrows.

If you want to use a specific text style for your dimensions, select a text style in the Text Style drop-down list in the Text tab. If the style you select happens to have a height specification greater than 0, that height will override any text height settings you enter in the Text tab.

Setting the Location and Orientation of Dimension Text

AutoCAD's default setting for the placement of dimension text puts the text in line with the dimension line, as shown in the example at the top of Figure 9.2, earlier in this chapter. However, you want the new Architectural style to put the text above the dimension line, as is done in the center of Figure 9.2. To do that, you will use the Text Placement and Text Alignment options in the Text tab of the New Dimension Style dialog box.

1. In the Text Alignment group in the lower-right corner of the dialog box, click the Aligned With Dimension Line radio button.
2. In the Text Placement group, open the Vertical drop-down list and select Above. Notice how the appearance of the sample image changes to show you how your new settings will look.
3. Again in the Text Placement group, change the Offset From Dim Line value to 1/16. This setting controls the size of the gap between the dimension line and the dimension text.

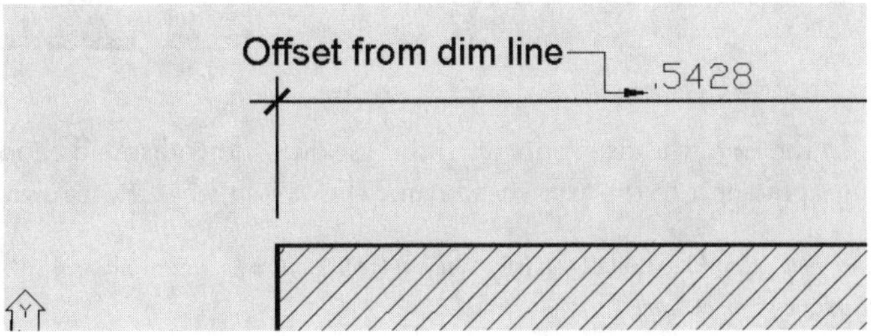

Each time you change a setting, you get immediate feedback on how your changes will affect your dimension style by watching the graphic.

TIP *Metric users may not need to change these settings, depending on your preference for dimension styles.*

Choosing an Arrow Style and Setting the Dimension Scale

Next, you want to specify a different type of arrow for your new dimension style. For linear dimension in architectural drawings, a diagonal line or "tick" mark is typically used, rather than an arrow.

In addition, you want to set the scale for the graphical components of the dimension, such as the arrows and text. Recall from Chapter 8 that text must be scaled up in size in order to appear at the proper size in the final output of the drawing. Dimensions, too, must be scaled so they look correct when the drawing is plotted. The arrows are controlled by settings in the Lines And Arrows tab, and the overall scale of the dimension style is set in the Fit tab.

1. Click the Lines And Arrows tab to display the options for controlling the arrow style and dimension line extensions.

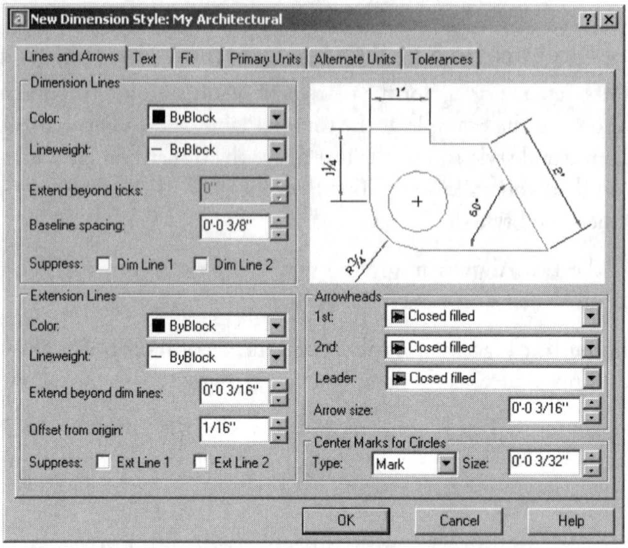

2. In the Arrowheads group, open the 1st drop-down list and choose Architectural Tick. The graphic next to the arrowhead name shows you what the arrowhead looks like.

TIP *See Appendix D for details on how you can create your own arrowheads. Also, AutoCAD 2004 lets you set up a separate arrow style for leaders.*

3. In the Arrowheads group, change the Arrow Size setting to **1/8**. Metric users should enter **.3**.
4. In the Dimension Lines group, highlight the value in the Extend Beyond Ticks input box, and then enter **1/16**. (Metric users should enter **0.15**.) This causes the dimension lines to extend past the tick arrows. This is a standard graphic practice used for dimensioning linear dimensions in architectural plans.

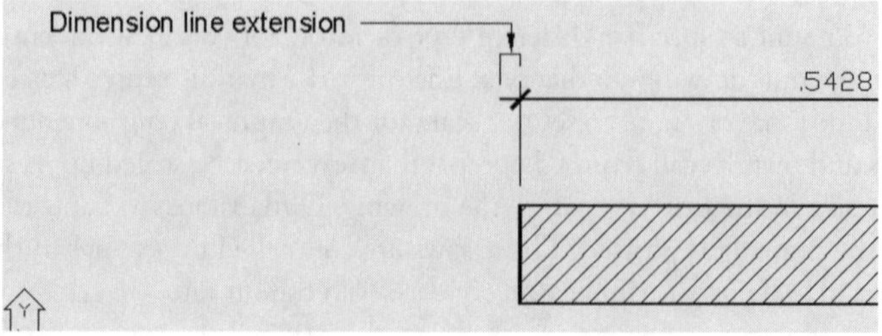

5. In the Extension Lines group, change the Extend Beyond Dim Lines setting to **1/8**. Metric users should change this to **.3**. This setting determines the distance that the extension line extends past the dimension line.

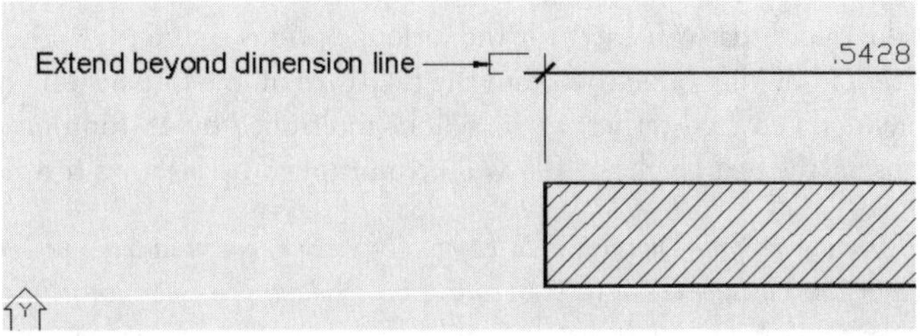

6. Again in the Extension Lines group, change the Offset From Origin setting to **1/8**. Metric users should change this to **.3**. This sets the distance from the point being dimensioned to the beginning of the dimension extension line.

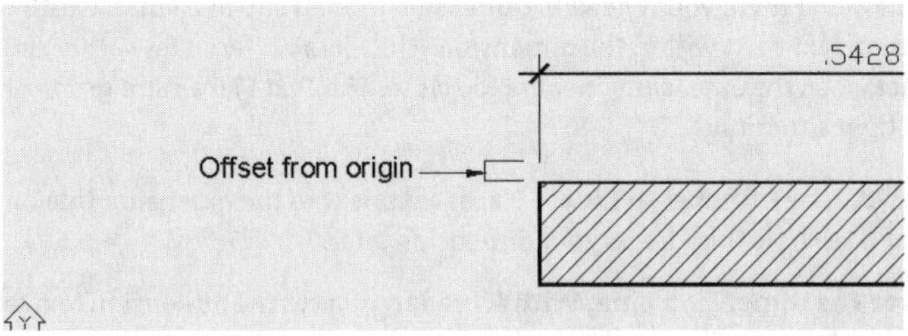

7. Click the Fit tab of the New Dimension Style dialog box to display the options for overall dimension scale and miscellaneous settings.

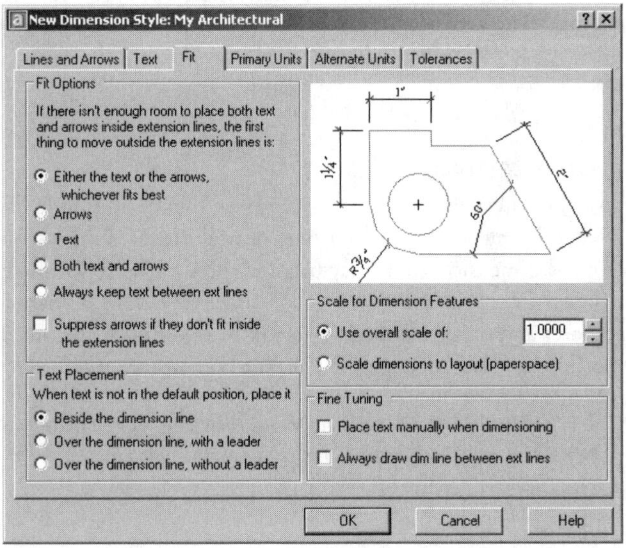

8. In the Scale For Dimension Features group, select the Use Overall Scale Of radio button.
9. Double-click the list box just to the right of the Use Overall Scale Of radio button, and then enter **48**. This is the scale factor for a 1/4" scale drawing. Metric users should enter **50**.

All the values that you enter for the various options in the New Dimension Style dialog box will be multiplied by this value to obtain the final size of the dimension components. For example, the text height you entered earlier, 1/4", will be multiplied by 48 for a dimension text height of 6". For metric users, the text height of 0.3 will be multiplied by 50 for a text height of 15 cm.

TIP *If you use the Scale Dimensions To Layout (Paperspace) option in the Scale For Dimension Features group of the Fit tab, AutoCAD uses the layout viewport scale to size the dimension components. See Chapter 7 for more information on viewport scale settings. This can be useful if you have a drawing that you want to print at multiple scales.*

FITTING TEXT AND ARROWS IN TIGHT PLACES

Every now and then, you'll need to dimension a small gap or a small width of an object that won't allow a dimension text to fit within the dimension. The Fit tab offers a few other settings that control how dimensions act when the extension lines are too close. The Text Placement group offers three options to place the text in tight situations:

Beside The Dimension Line Places text next to the extension line but close to the dimension line. You'll see how this affects your dimension later.

Over The Dimension Line, With A Leader Places the dimension text farther from the dimension line and includes an arrow or leader from the dimension line to the text.

Over The Dimension Line, Without A Leader Does the same as the previous setting, but does not include the leader.

The options in the Fit Options group let you control how text and arrows are placed when there isn't enough room for both of them between the extension lines.

Setting Up Alternate Units

You can use the Alternate Units tab of the New Dimension Style dialog box to set up AutoCAD to display a second dimension in centimeters or millimeters. Likewise, if you are a metric user, you can set up a second dimension to display feet and inches. The following exercise shows you how to set up alternate dimensions. You don't have to do this exercise now. It's here for your information. If you like, come back later and try it out to see how it affects your dimensions. For now, pick up the tutorial in the next section entitled "Setting the Current Dimension Style".

TIP *If you decide later that you do not want the alternate units to be displayed, you can turn them off by returning to this dialog box and removing the checkmark in the Display Alternate Units check box.*

1. In the New Dimension Style dialog box, click the Alternate Units tab.

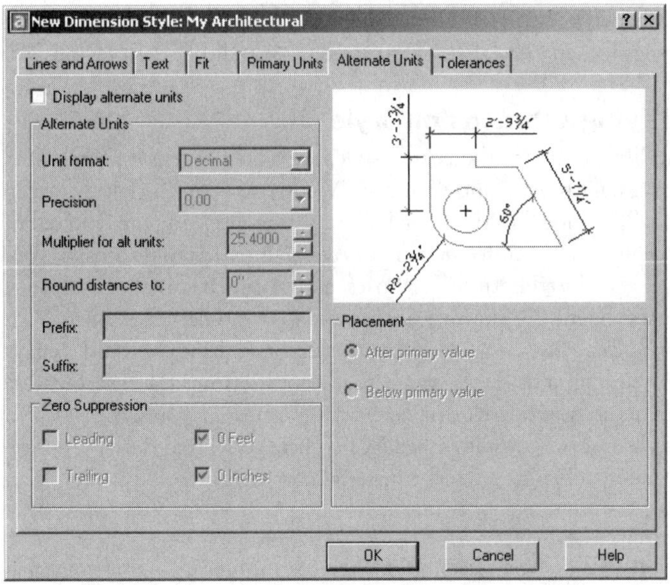

2. Click the Display Alternate Units check box. The options in the tab become available for your input.
3. Select the appropriate option from the Unit Format drop-down list. U.S. users should select Decimal to show metric alternate units. Metric users should select Architectural.
4. Select an appropriate precision value from the Precision drop-down list.
5. Enter a scale factor for your alternate dimension in the Multiplier For Alt Units input box. For U.S. users, the default value is 25.4. This value converts feet-and-inch dimensions to millimeters. In our metric examples, you've been using centimeters, so change this setting to **2.54**. Metric users should enter **0.3937** to convert centimeters to feet and inches.
6. In the Placement group, select where you would like the alternate dimension to appear in relation to the main dimension.
7. Click OK to close the New Dimension Style dialog box. The Dimension Style Manager dialog box reappears.

Setting the Current Dimension Style

Before you can begin to use your new dimension style, you must make it the current default.

1. Click My Architectural in the Styles list box in the Dimension Style Manager dialog box.
2. Click the Set Current button in the far-right side of the dialog box.
3. Click Close to exit the Dimension Style Manager dialog box.

You're now ready to use your new dimension style.

In the next set of exercises, you will be using the My Architectural style you just created. To switch to another style, open the Dimension Style Manager dialog box again, select the style you want from the Styles list, and click Set Current, just as you did in the previous exercise.

Modifying a Dimension Style

To modify an existing dimension style, open the Dimension Style Manager dialog box, highlight the style you want to edit, and then click Modify to open the Modify Dimension Style dialog box, which is virtually identical to the New Dimension Style dialog box you've been working with. You can then make changes to the different components of the selected dimension style. When you've finished making changes and closed both dialog boxes, all the dimensions associated with the edited style will update automatically in your drawing. For example, if you decide you need to change the dimension scale of a style, you can open the Modify Dimension Style dialog box and change the Scale value in the Fit tab.

This section introduces you to the various settings that let you set the appearance of a dimension style. This section doesn't discuss every option, so if you want to learn more about the other dimension style options, consult Appendix D. There you'll find descriptions of all the items in the Dimension Style dialog box, plus reference material covering the system variables associated with each option.

TIP *If your application is strictly architectural, you might want to make these same dimension style changes to the* `Acad.dwt` *template file or create a set of template files specifically for architectural drawings of differing scales.*

USING GRIDS IN ARCHITECTURAL DIMENSIONS

Common, if not essential, elements in architectural drawings are the building grids. These are the center lines of the main structural components, which are usually the columns and structural walls of the building. Grids are labeled similarly to map grids, with numeric labels going horizontally and alphabetic labels going vertically. A circle or hexagon is used at the end of the grid to label it. The grids are the first items dimensioned, and all other building components are dimensioned from the grid lines. The San Francisco Main Library made ample use of grids, incorporating both major and minor grid systems. There, a hexagon was used to label the grids.

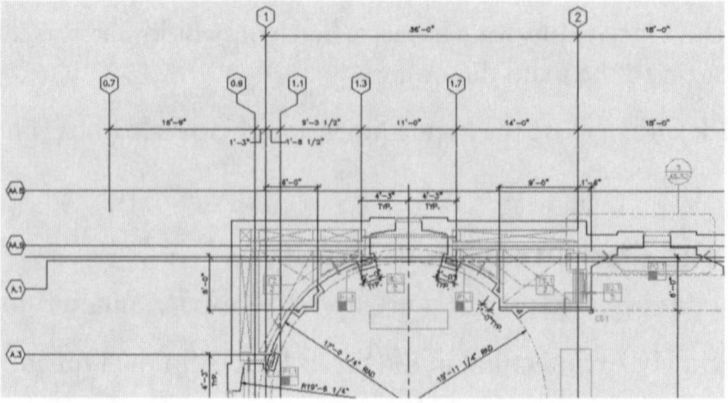

Continued on next page

USING GRIDS IN ARCHITECTURAL DIMENSIONS *(continued)*

Since the structural components of a building are usually the first parts that are put in place, they play a crucial role in locating other components of the building during the construction process. When producing floor plans, the grid is usually the first thing an architect draws, mimicking to some degree the construction process. All other elements of the plan are then drawn in relation to that grid.

While working in AutoCAD, you can use a grid to start building your drawing. Once the grid is in place, you can use the Offset tool to locate walls or other building components. Using AutoCAD's tracking feature, you can easily align drawing elements to grid lines.

Drawing Linear Dimensions

The most common type of dimension you'll be using is the *linear dimension.* The linear dimension is an orthogonal dimension measuring the width and length of an object. AutoCAD offers three dimensioning tools for this purpose: Linear (Dimlinear), Continue (Dimcont), and Baseline (Dimbase). These options are readily accessible from the Dimension toolbar or the Dimension pull-down menu.

WARNING *In the following set of exercises, you'll see figures displaying dimensions in both Imperial and metric units. I've included both measurements so that both Imperial and metric users can more easily follow the tutorial. But in your own drawing you will only see one dimension value displayed above the dimension line.*

Finding the Dimension Toolbar

Before you apply any dimension, you'll want to open the Dimension toolbar. This toolbar contains nearly all the commands necessary to draw and edit your dimensions.

To open the Dimension toolbar, right-click any toolbar, and choose Dimension from the shortcut menu.

The Dimension commands are also available from the Dimension pull-down menu. Now you're ready to begin dimensioning.

TIP *To help keep your screen organized, you might want to dock the Dimension toolbar on the right side of the AutoCAD window. Note that you will lose the Style drop-down list if you dock the toolbar on either side of the AutoCAD window. The drop-down list remains in place if you dock the toolbar at the top or bottom. See Chapter 1 for more on docking toolbars.*

Placing Horizontal and Vertical Dimensions

Let's start by looking at the basic dimensioning tool, Linear Dimension. The Linear Dimension button (the Dimlinear command) on the Dimension toolbar accommodates both the horizontal and vertical dimensions.

In this exercise, you'll add a vertical dimension to the right side of the Unit plan.

1. To start either a vertical or horizontal dimension, click Linear Dimension on the Dimension toolbar, or enter **Dli**↵ at the command prompt. You can also choose Dimension ➢ Linear from the pull-down menu.
2. The Specify first extension line origin or <select object>: prompt is asking you for the first point of the distance to be dimensioned. An extension line is the line that connects the object being dimensioned to the dimension line. Use the Endpoint Osnap override and pick the upper-right corner of the entry, as shown in Figure 9.3.

FIGURE 9.3

The dimension line added to the Unit drawing

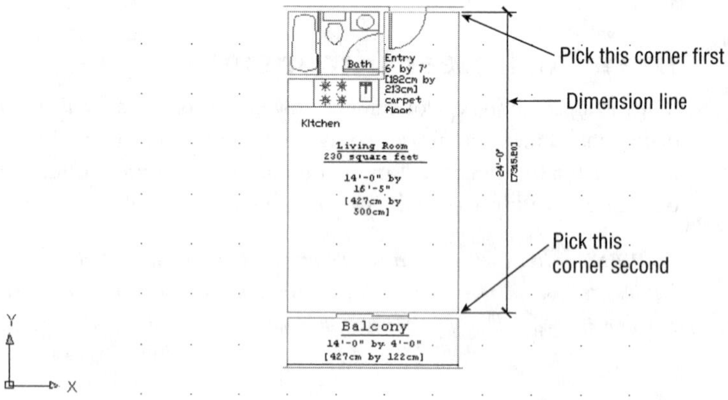

TIP *Notice that the prompt in step 2 gives you the option of pressing ↵ to select an object. If you do this, you are prompted to pick the object you want to dimension, rather than the actual distance to be dimensioned. This method is discussed later in this chapter.*

3. At the Specify second extension line origin: prompt, pick the lower-right corner of the living room, as shown in Figure 9.3.
4. In the next prompt, Specify dimension line location or [Mtext/Text/ Angle/Horizontal/ Vertical/Rotated]:, the dimension line is the line indicating the direction of the dimension and containing the arrows or tick marks. Move your cursor from left to right to display a temporary dimension. This allows you to visually select a dimension line location.

TIP *In step 4, you can append information to the dimension's text or change the dimension text altogether. You'll see how later in this chapter.*

5. Enter **@4'<0**↵ to tell AutoCAD you want the dimension line to be 4' to the right of the last point you selected. Metric users should enter **@122<0**↵. (You could pick a point using your cursor, but this doesn't let you place the dimension line as accurately.) After you've done this, the dimension is placed in the drawing, as shown in Figure 9.3.

Continuing a Dimension

You will often want to enter a group of dimensions strung together in a line. For example, you might want to continue dimensioning the balcony and align the continued dimension with the dimension you just entered. To do this, use the Continue option found in both the Dimension toolbar and the Dimension pull-down menu.

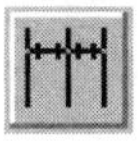

1. Click the Continue Dimension option on the Dimension toolbar, or enter **Dco↵**. You can also choose Dimension ➢ Continue from the pull-down menu.
2. At the `Specify a second extension line origin or [Undo/Select] <Select>:` prompt, pick the upper-right corner of the balcony (see the top image in Figure 9.4).

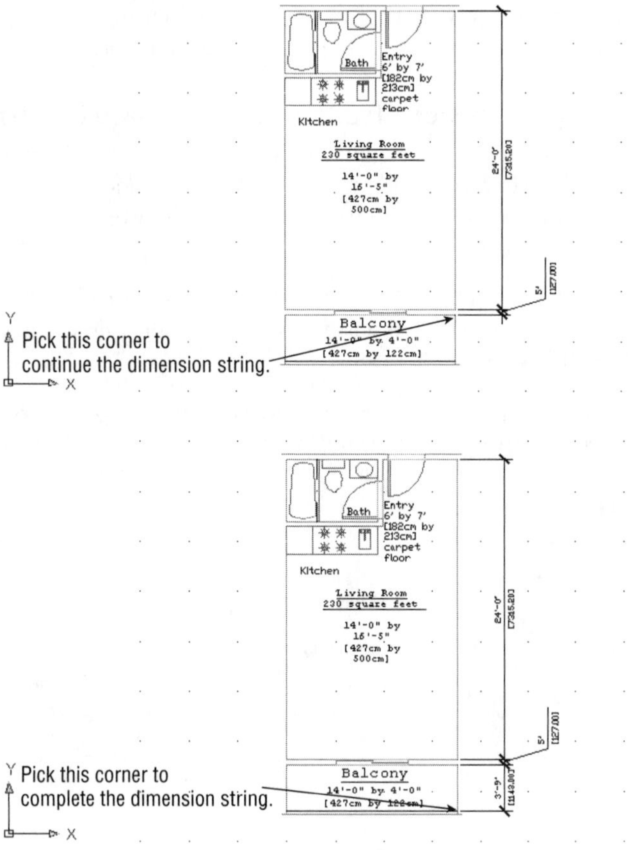

FIGURE 9.4

The dimension string continued and completed

3. Pick the right end of the rail on the balcony. See the bottom image of Figure 9.4 for the results.
4. Press ↵ twice to exit the command.

TIP *If you find that you've selected the wrong location for a continued dimension, you can click the Undo tool or press U↵ to back up your dimension.*

The Continue Dimension option adds a dimension from where you left off. The last drawn extension line is used as the first extension line for the continued dimension. AutoCAD keeps adding dimensions as you continue to pick points, until you press ↵.

You probably noticed that the 5" dimension is placed away from the dimension line with a leader line pointing to it. This is the result of the 5" dimension's not having enough space to fit between the dimension extension lines. You'll learn about dimension style settings that can remedy this problem. For now, let's continue with adding dimensions to the plan.

CONTINUING A DIMENSION FROM A PREVIOUS DIMENSION

If you need to continue a string of dimensions from an older linear dimension, instead of the most recently added one, press ↵ at the `Specify a second extension line origin or (<select>/Undo):` prompt you saw in step 2 of the previous exercise. Then, at the `Select continued dimension:` prompt, click the extension line from which you want to continue.

Drawing Dimensions from a Common Base Extension Line

Another method for dimensioning objects is to have several dimensions originate from the same extension line. To accommodate this, AutoCAD provides the Baseline option on the Dimension toolbar or Dimension pull-down menu. To see how this works, you will start another dimension—this time a horizontal one—across the top of the plan.

1. Click Linear Dimension on the Dimension toolbar. Or, just as you did for the vertical dimension, you can type **Dli**↵ to start the horizontal dimension. This option is also on the Dimension pull-down menu.

2. At the `Specify first extension line origin or <select object>:` prompt, use the Endpoint Osnap to pick the upper-left corner of the bathroom, as shown in Figure 9.5.

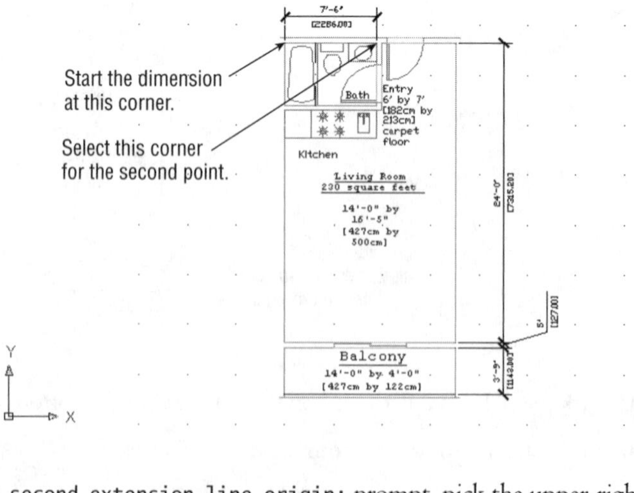

FIGURE 9.5
The bathroom with horizontal dimensions

3. At the `Specify second extension line origin:` prompt, pick the upper-right corner of the bathroom, as shown in Figure 9.5.

4. At the `Specify dimension line location or [Mtext/Text/Angle/ Horizontal/Vertical/ Rotated]:` prompt, pick a point above the Unit plan, as shown in Figure 9.5. If you need to, pan your view downward to fit the dimension in.

TIP *Since you usually pick exact locations on your drawing as you dimension, you might want to turn on Running Osnaps to avoid the extra step of selecting Osnaps from the Osnap shortcut menu.*

Now you're all set to draw another dimension continuing from the first extension line of the dimension you just drew.

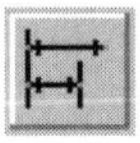

5. Click the Baseline Dimension option on the Dimension toolbar. Or you can type **Dba**↵ at the command prompt to start a baseline dimension.

6. At the `Specify second extension line origin or [Undo/Select] <Select>:` prompt, click the upper-right corner of the entry, as shown in Figure 9.6.

FIGURE 9.6

The overall width dimension

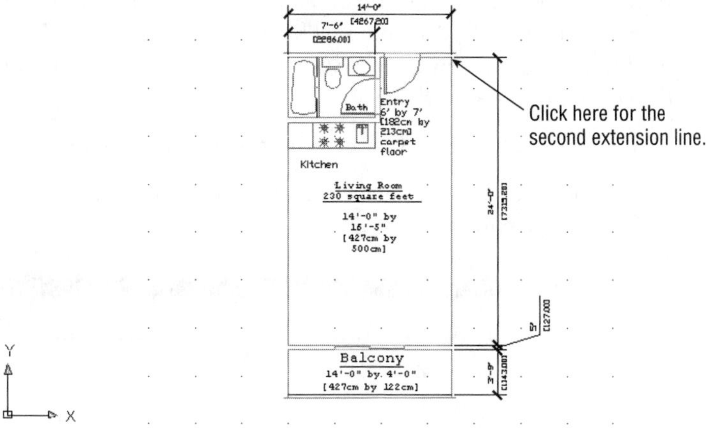

7. Press ↵ twice to exit the Baseline Dimension command.

8. Pan your view down so it looks similar to Figure 9.6.

In this example, you see that the Baseline Dimension option is similar to the Continue Dimension option, except that the Baseline Dimension option allows you to use the first extension line of the previous dimension as the base for a second dimension.The distance between the two horizontal dimension lines is controlled by the Baseline Spacing setting in the Lines and Arrows tab of the Dimension Style dialog box.

CONTINUING FROM AN OLDER DIMENSION

You might have noticed in step 7 that you had to press ↵ twice to exit the command. As with the Continue Dimension, you can draw the baseline dimension from an older dimension by pressing ↵ at the `Specify a second extension line origin [Undo/Select] <select>:` prompt. You then get the `Select base dimension:` prompt, at which you can either select another dimension or press ↵ again to exit the command.

Editing Dimensions

As you begin to add more dimensions to your drawings, you will find that AutoCAD will occasionally place a dimension text or line in an inappropriate location, or you may need to modify the dimension text. In this section, you'll take an in-depth look at how you can modify dimensions to suit those special circumstances that always crop up.

Appending Data to Dimension Text

So far in this chapter, you've been accepting the default dimension text. You can append information to the default dimension value or change it entirely if you need to. At the point when you see the temporary dimension dragging with your cursor, enter **T↵**. Then, by using the less than (<) and greater than (>) symbols, you can add text either before or after the default dimension or replace the symbols entirely to replace the default text. The Properties button on the Object Properties toolbar lets you modify the existing dimension text in a similar way. Let's see how this works by changing an existing dimension's text in your drawing.

1. Choose Modify ➢ Object ➢ Text ➢ Edit or type **ED↵**.
2. Click the last horizontal dimension you added to the drawing at the top of the screen to open the Text Formatting toolbar.

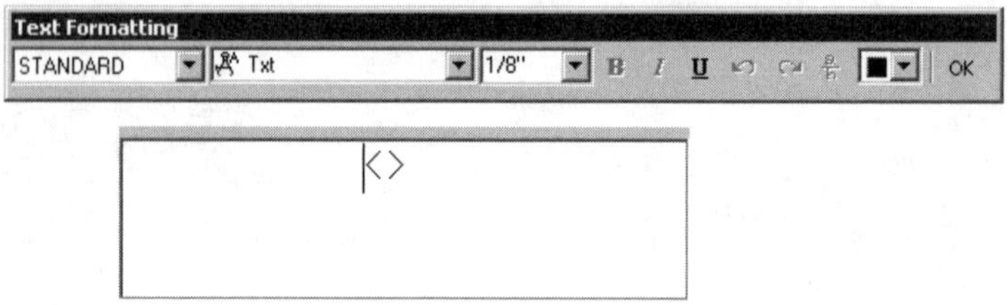

3. Click the text editor, move the cursor behind the <> sign, and then type **to face of stud.**
4. Click OK on the Text Formatting toolbar. The dimension changes to read `14'-0" to face of stud`. The text you entered is appended below the dimension text.
5. Because you don't really need the new appended text for the tutorial, click the Undo button in the Standard toolbar to remove the appended text.

TIP *Place your appended text in front of the <> symbols if you want to add text to the beginning of the dimension text. You can also replace the dimension text entirely by replacing the <> sign in the Contents input box with new text. If you want to restore a dimension that has been modified, delete everything in the Contents input box, including space. Or include a space to leave the dimension text blank.*

TIP *In this exercise, you were able to edit only a single dimension. To append text to several dimensions at once, you need to use the Dimension Edit tool. See the "Making Changes to Multiple Dimensions" sidebar in this chapter for more on this command.*

You can also have AutoCAD automatically add a dimension suffix or prefix to all dimensions, instead of just a chosen few, by using the Suffix or Prefix option in the Primary Units tab of the Dimension Style dialog box. See Appendix D for more on this feature.

MAKING CHANGES TO MULTIPLE DIMENSIONS

You can use the Dimension Edit tool to quickly edit existing dimensions. It gives you the ability to edit more than one dimension's text at one time. One common use for the Dimension Edit tool might be to change a string of dimensions to read "Equal," instead of showing the actual dimensioned distance. The following example shows an alternative to the Properties palette for appending text to a dimension:

1. Click the Dimension Edit tool in the Dimension toolbar, or type **Ded**↵.
2. At this prompt

   ```
   Enter type of dimension Edit [Home/New/Rotate/Oblique]<Home>:
   ```

   type **N**↵ to use the New option. The Multiline Text Editor appears showing the <> brackets in the text box.
3. Click the space behind or in front of the <> brackets, and then enter the text you want to append to the dimension. Or you can replace the brackets entirely to replace the dimension with your text.
4. Click OK.
5. At the `Select objects:` prompt, pick the dimensions you want to edit. The `Select objects:` prompt remains, allowing you to select several dimensions.
6. Press ↵ to finish your selection. The dimension changes to include your new text or to replace the existing dimension text.

The Dimension Edit tool is useful in editing dimension text, but you can also use this command to make graphical changes to the text. Here is a listing of the other Dimension Edit tool options:

Home Moves the dimension text to its standard default position and angle.

Rotate Allows you to rotate the dimension text to a new angle.

Oblique Skews the dimension extension lines to a new angle. (See the "Skewing Dimension Lines" section later in this chapter.)

AutoCAD provides the associative dimensioning capability to automatically update dimension text when a drawing is edited. Objects called *definition points* are used to determine how edited dimensions are updated.

The definition points are located at the same points you pick when you determine the dimension location. For example, the definition points for linear dimensions are the extension line origin and the intersection of the extension line/dimension line. The definition points for a circle diameter are the points used to pick the circle and the opposite side of the circle. The definition points for a radius are the points used to pick the circle, plus the center of the circle.

Definition points are actually point objects. They are difficult to see because they are usually covered by the feature that they define. You can, however, see them indirectly by using grips. The definition points of a dimension are the same as the dimension's grip points. You can see them simply by clicking a dimension. Try the following:

1. Make sure the Grips feature is turned on. (See Chapter 2 to refresh your memory on the Grips feature.)
2. Click the longest of the three vertical dimensions you drew in the earlier exercise. You will see the grips of the dimension, as shown in Figure 9.7.

FIGURE 9.7

The grip points are the same as the definition points on a dimension.

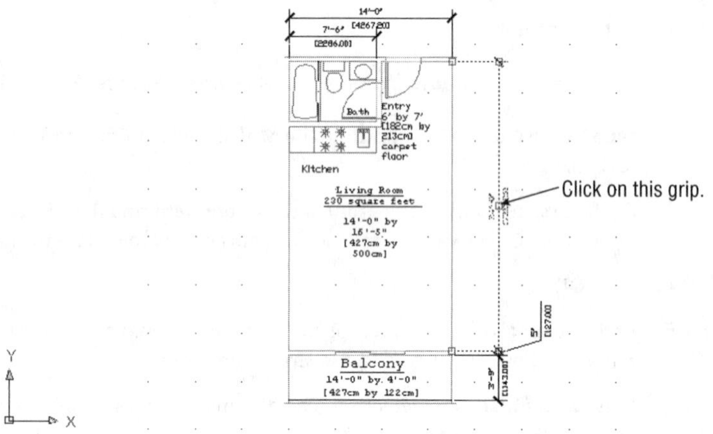

TIP *AutoCAD 2004 treats dimensions as fully associative. This means that dimensions are updated automatically whenever an object associated with the dimension is modified. See the section "Using True Associative Dimensions" later in this chapter.*

Making Minor Adjustments to Dimensions Using Grips

The definition points, whose location you can see through their grips, are located on their own unique layer called *Defpoints*. Definition points are displayed regardless of whether the Defpoints layer is on or off. To give you an idea of how these definition points work, try the following exercises, which show you how to directly manipulate the definition points.

1. With the grips visible, click the grip near the dimension text.

TIP *Since the Defpoints layer has the unique feature of being visible even when turned off, you can use it as a layer for laying out your drawing. While Defpoints is turned off, you can still see objects assigned to it, but the objects won't plot.*

2. Move the cursor around. Notice that when you move the cursor vertically, the text moves along the dimension line. When you move the cursor horizontally, the dimension line and text move together, keeping their parallel orientation to the dimensioned floor plan.

TIP *Here the entire dimension line, including the text, moves. In a later exercise, you'll see how you can move the dimension text independently of the dimension line.*

3. Enter **@9'<0↵**. Metric users should enter **@275<0↵**. The dimension line, text, and the dimension extensions move to the new location to the right of the text (see Figure 9.8).

TIP *If you need to move several dimension lines at once, select them all at the command prompt; then Shift+click one set of dimension-line grips from each dimension. Once you've selected the grips, click one of the hot grips again. You can then move all the dimension lines at once.*

FIGURE 9.8

Moving the dimension line using its grip

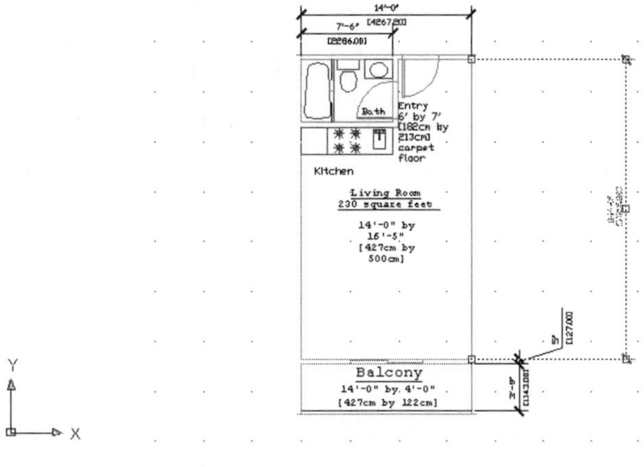

In step 3 of the previous exercise, you saw that you can specify an exact distance for the dimension line's new location by entering a relative polar coordinate. Cartesian coordinates work just as well. You can even use object snaps to relocate dimension lines. Next, try moving the dimension line back using the Perpendicular Osnap:

1. Click the grip at the bottom of the dimension line you just edited.
2. Shift+click the right mouse button and choose Perpendicular from the Osnap shortcut menu.
3. Place the cursor on the vertical dimension line that dimensions the balcony and click it.

The selected dimension line moves to align with the other vertical dimension, back to its original location.

Changing Style Settings of Individual Dimensions

In some cases, you will have to make changes to an individual dimension's style setting in order to edit that dimension. For example, if you try to move the text of a typical linear dimension, you may find that the text and dimension lines are inseparable. You need to make a change to the dimension style setting that controls how AutoCAD locates dimension text in relation to the dimension line. This section describes how you can make changes to the style settings of individual dimensions to facilitate changes in the dimension.

TIP *If you need to change the dimension style of a dimension to match that of another, you can use the Match Properties tool. See Chapter 6 for details on how to use this tool.*

MOVING A FIXED DIMENSION TEXT

Earlier in this chapter, you saw how a dimension text is attached to the dimension line so that when the text is moved, the dimension line follows. You might encounter situations in which you want to move the text independently of the dimension line. The following exercise shows you how you can separate dimension text from its dimension line. In the process, you'll learn how you can make a change to a single dimension's style settings. Then you'll use grips to move the dimension text away from the dimension line.

1. Press the Esc key twice to cancel the grip selection from the previous exercise.
2. Zoom in to the 24' dimension so you have a view similar to Figure 9.9.

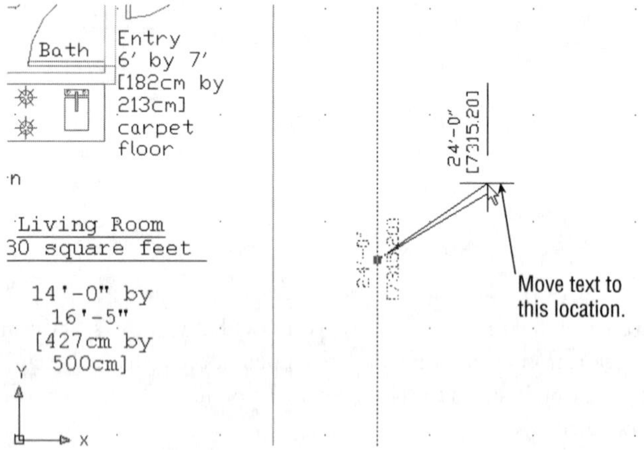

FIGURE 9.9
Selecting and then moving the 24-foot dimension

3. Click the 24'-0" dimension to expose its grips.
4. Right-click and choose Properties from the shortcut menu to open the Properties palette.
5. Scroll down the list of properties until you see the Fit option. If you do not see a list of options under Fit, click the downward pointing arrow to the right to display a new set of options.

6. Scroll down the list farther until you see the Keep Dim Line With Text option to the right of the Text Movement listing, and then click this option.
7. Click the arrow that appears next to the Text Movement listing to open the drop-down list; then select the Move Text, Add Leader option.

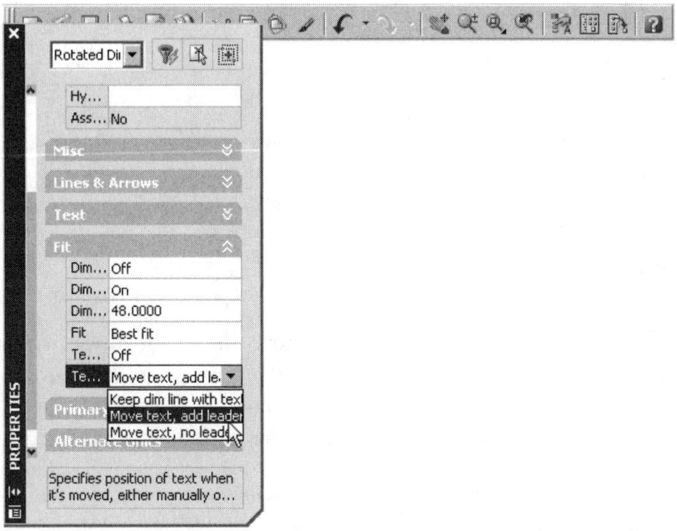

8. Close the Properties palette.

Let's see the effect of the changes you just made.

1. Click the grip of the 24'-0" dimension text and move it up and to the right, and click again to place the text in a new location, as shown in Figure 9.9.
2. Review the changes that you made, and then click the Undo button to return to the state before you moved the dimension text.

Moving the text in step 1 demonstrates that the text is no longer tied to the dimension line. In the Properties palette, the Move Text, Add Leader option in the Fit options lets you move the dimension text independently of the dimension line. It also draws a leader from the dimension line to the text. Another option, Move Text, No Leader, does the same thing but doesn't include a leader. You can also set these options for a dimension style using the Text Placement options in the Fit tab of the Dimension Style dialog box.

As you can see from this exercise, the Properties palette gives you access to many of the settings that you saw for setting up dimension styles. The main difference here is that the Properties palette affects only the dimensions that you have selected.

In the previous exercise, you changed the format setting of a single dimension *after* it was placed. These settings can be made a standard part of your Architectural dimension style by using the Modify button in the Dimension Style Manager dialog box.

You need to make one more change to the drawing's dimension to set up for the next exercise.

1. Pan your view downward so you can see the 5" dimension clearly, and then click the 5" dimension and move it into a position in line with the dimension text.

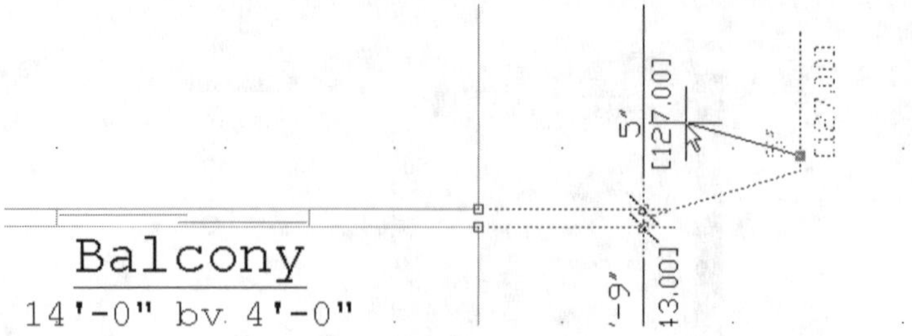

2. Choose View ➢ Zoom All, and then choose File ➢ Save to save this file in its current state.

In this short exercise, you were able to move the 5" dimension without making any changes to its properties. AutoCAD automatically selects the appropriate Text Movement setting if the text is too large to fit between the dimension extension lines. In the case of the 5" dimension text, AutoCAD automatically chose the Move Text, Add Leader setting when the dimension was placed in the drawing.

TIP *If you have multiple dimension styles and you want to change an existing dimension to the current dimension style, use the Dimension Update tool. Click the Dimension Update tool on the Dimension toolbar, or choose Dimension Update from the pull-down menu. Then select the dimensions you want to change. Press ↵ when you've finished selecting dimensions. The selected dimensions will be converted to the current style.*

ROTATING A DIMENSION TEXT

Once in a while, a dimension text works better if it is kept in a horizontal orientation, even if the dimension itself is not horizontal. If you find you need to rotate dimension text, here's the way to do it:

1. Click the Undo button twice in the toolbar or type **U↵** to return the 5" dimension to its original location.

2. Click the Dimension Edit tool in the Dimension toolbar.
3. At the `Enter type of dimension editing [Home/New/Rotate/Oblique] <Home>:` prompt, enter **R↵**.
4. At the `Enter text angle:` prompt, type **45↵** to rotate the text to a 45° angle.
5. At the `Select objects:` prompt, click the 5" dimension text again. Press ↵.
6. Click the Undo button to undo the text rotation. You won't want to save this change to your drawing.

TIP You can also choose Dimension ➢ Align Text ➢ Angle, select the dimension text, and then enter an angle. A 0°angle will cause the dimension text to return to its default angle.

The Dimension Text Edit tool (Dimtedit command) also allows you to align the dimension text to either the left or right side of the dimension line. This is similar to the Alignment option in the Multiline Text Editor that controls text justification.

As you have seen in this section, the Grips feature is especially well suited to editing dimensions. With grips, you can stretch, move, copy, rotate, mirror, and scale dimensions.

MODIFYING THE DIMENSION STYLE SETTINGS USING OVERRIDE

In the "Moving a Fixed Dimension Text" section, you used the Properties button on the toolbar to facilitate the moving of the dimension text. You can also choose Dimension ➢ Override (Dimoverride command) to accomplish the same thing. The Override option allows you to change an individual dimension's style settings. Here's an example showing how you can use the Override option in place of the Properties button in the first exercise of the "Moving a Fixed Dimension Text" section.

1. Press the Esc key twice to make sure you are not in the middle of a command. Then choose Dimension ➢ Override from the pull-down menu.
2. At the next prompt

   ```
   Enter dimension variable name to override or [Clear overrides]:
   ```

   type **Dimfit**↵.
3. At the `Current value <3>:` prompt, enter **4**↵. This has the same effect as selecting Move Text, Add Leader from the Fit option of the Properties palette.
4. The `Enter dimension variable to override...` prompt appears again, allowing you to enter another dimension variable. Press ↵ to move to the next step.
5. At the `Select objects:` prompt, select the dimension you want to change. You can select a group of dimensions if you want to change several dimensions at once. Press ↵ when you have finished with your selection. The dimension settings will change for the selected dimensions.

As you can see from this example, the Dimoverride command requires that you know exactly which dimension variable to edit in order to make the desired modification. In this case, setting the Dimfit variable to 4 lets you move the dimension text independently of the dimension line. If you find the Dimoverride command useful, consult Appendix D to find which system variable corresponds to the Dimension Style dialog box settings.

UNDERSTANDING THE DIMENSION TEXT EDIT TOOL

One dimension text-editing tool you haven't used yet is the Dimension Text Edit tool.

Although it may sound as though this tool allows you to edit dimension text, its purpose is to allow you to quickly position dimension text to the left, right, or center of the dimension line. To use it, choose Dimension Text Edit from the toolbar, and then click the dimension text you want to move. You'll see the prompt:

```
Click on a dimension and the Select dimension: Specify new location for
 dimension text or [Left/Right/Center/Home/Angle]:
```

You can then enter the letter of the option you want. For example, if you enter L↵, the dimension text moves to the left side of the dimension line.

Editing Dimensions and Other Objects Together

Certainly it's helpful to be able to edit a dimension directly using its grips. But the key feature of AutoCAD's dimensions is their ability to *automatically* adjust themselves to changes in the drawing. As long as you include the dimension's definition points when you select objects to edit, the dimensions themselves will automatically update to reflect the change in your drawing.

To see how this works, try moving the living room closer to the bathroom wall. You can move a group of lines and vertices using the Stretch command and the Crossing option:

1. Click the Stretch tool in the Modify palette, or type S↵ and then C↵. You will see the following prompt:

   ```
   At the Select objects to stretch by crossing-window or -polygon...
   Select objects: C
   Specify first corner:
   ```

2. Pick a crossing window, as illustrated in Figure 9.10, and then press ↵ to confirm your selection.

FIGURE 9.10

The Stretch crossing window

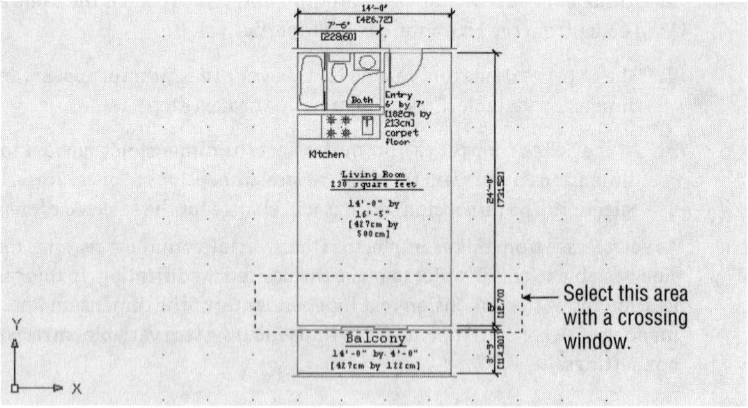

3. At the `Specify base point or displacement:` prompt, pick any point on the screen.

4. At the `Specify second point of displacement:` prompt, enter @2'<90 to move the wall 2' in a 90° direction. The wall moves, and the dimension text changes to reflect the new dimension, as shown in Figure 9.11.

TIP In some situations, you may find that a crossing window selects objects other than those you want to stretch. This frequently occurs when many objects are close together at the location of a vertex you want to stretch. To be more selective about the vertices you move and their corresponding objects, use a standard window instead of a crossing window to select the vertices. Then pick the individual objects whose vertices you want to move.

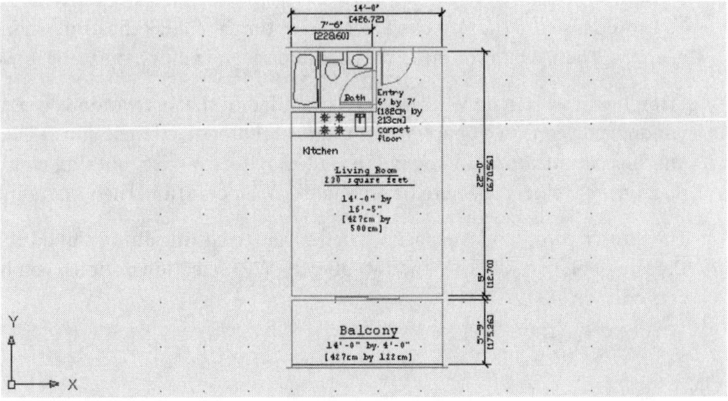

FIGURE 9.11
The moved wall, with the updated dimensions

When you selected the crossing window corners, you included the definition points of both vertical dimensions. This allowed you to move the dimension extension lines along with the wall, thereby updating the dimensions automatically.

UNDERSTANDING THE STRETCH COMMAND

The tool you used for moving the wall and the dimension line extensions is the Stretch command. This is one of the most useful, yet least understood, AutoCAD commands. Think of the Stretch command as a vertex mover: its sole purpose is to move the vertices (or endpoints) of objects.

The Stretch command actually requires you to do two things: select the objects you want to edit, and then select the vertices you want to move. The crossing window and the Cpolygon window are convenient ways to kill two birds with one stone because they select objects and vertices in one operation. But when you want to be more selective, you can click objects and window vertices instead. For example, consider the exercise in this chapter in which you moved a wall with the Stretch command. To move the walls but not the dimension-line extensions, take the following steps:

1. Click the Stretch tool on the Modify toolbar or click Stretch on the Modify pull-down menu. You can also type **S**↵.
2. At the `Select objects:` prompt, enter **W**↵ (Window) or **WP**↵ (Window Polygon).
3. Window the vertices you want to move. Since the Window and Window Polygon selection options select objects completely enclosed within the window, most of the items you want to stretch will already be selected.

Continued on next page

UNDERSTANDING THE STRETCH COMMAND *(continued)*

4. Click the vertical walls to include them in the set of objects to be edited.
5. Press ↵ to finish your selection.
6. Indicate the base point and second point for the stretch.

You could also use the Remove Selection option and click the dimensions to deselect them in the previous exercise. Then, when you enter the base and second points, the walls move but the dimensions stay in place.

Stretch will stretch only the vertices included in the last window, crossing window, crossing polygon, or window polygon. (See Chapter 2 for more on these selection options.) Thus, if you had attempted to window another part of your drawing in the wall-moving exercise, nothing would have moved. Before Stretch will do anything, objects need to be highlighted (selected) and their endpoints windowed.

The Stretch command is especially well suited to editing dimensioned objects, and when you use it with the Crossing Polygon (CP) or Window Polygon (WP) selection options, you have substantial control over what gets edited.

You can also use the Mirror, Rotate, and Stretch commands with dimensions. The polar arrays also work, and you can use Extend and Trim with linear dimensions.

When editing dimensioned objects, be sure to select the dimension associated with the object being edited. As you select objects, using the Crossing (C) or Crossing Polygon (CP) selection option helps you include the dimensions. For more on these selection options, see Chapter 2.

TIP *If a hatch pattern or solid fill completely covers a dimension, you can use the Draworder command to have AutoCAD draw the dimension over the hatch or solid fill. See Chapter 13 for more on the Draworder command.*

Using True Associative Dimensions

You've seen how you can edit dimensions by manipulating their definition points. For versions prior to 2002, if you want to edit dimensions together with the objects, you need to use a crossing window because the dimension is not fully associated with the object it is dimensioning. AutoCAD uses the dimension's definition point to simulate what is known as *associative dimensioning*. If you prefer, you can also fully associate a dimension with an object so that you need only change the object and the dimension will follow.

To use this feature, called *True Associative Dimensioning*, you'll need to turn it on in the Options dialog box. Here's how it's done:

1. Choose Tools ➢ Options to open the Options dialog box, and then click the User Preferences tab.
2. In the Associative Dimensioning group, turn on the Make New Dimensions Associative option
3. Click OK.

From now on, any dimension you place will be associated with the object you are dimensioning. Try the following exercise to see how it works:

1. Choose File ➢ New and create a new blank file from the `Acad.dwt` template.
2. Click the Rectangle tool from the Draw toolbar; then draw a rectangle roughly 12 units wide by 1 unit high.
3. Use the Zoom Window tool in the Standard toolbar to get a good view of your drawing so far.
4. Choose Dimension ➢ Linear, turn on the Object Snap mode, and then dimension the top of the rectangle.

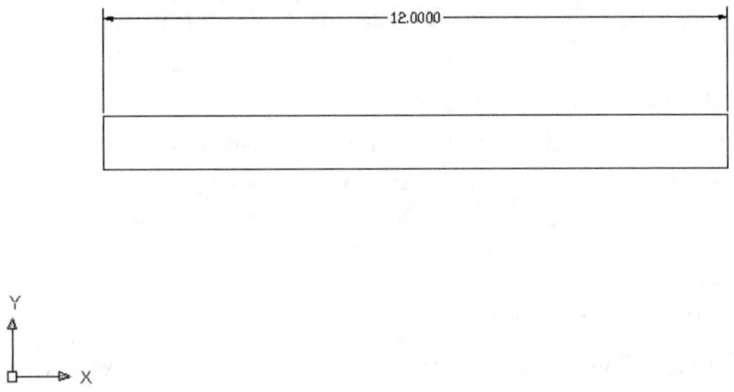

5. Click the rectangle to select it; then click the grip in the upper-right corner of the rectangle.
6. Move the grip to the right and upward and then click. The rectangle corner moves and the dimension moves with it.

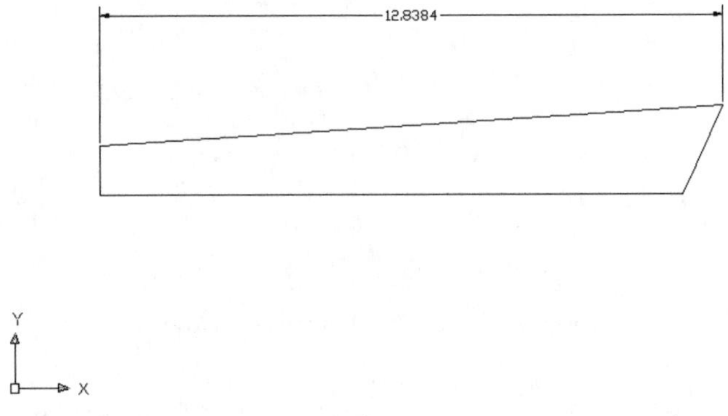

In this case, you only had to change the shape of the rectangle, and the dimension followed the change. The dimension in this example is fully associated with the rectangle.

Associative Dimensioning also works with external references (see Chapter 13 for more on external references, or Xrefs) and blocks. This means that you can dimension an Xref, edit the source Xref file, and have the dimensions update in the current file. Such changes are not completely automatic; you need to issue the Dimregen command to update dimensions to the new Xref configuration.

You can use Associative Dimensioning on objects within blocks, and if the block is edited, those dimensions will update automatically. But be aware that non-uniform scaling of a block—that is, scaling along one axis and not the other—will not affect an associative dimension.

In AutoCAD 2004, you can dimension a Model Space object in Paper Space, and the Paper Space dimension will be associated with the Model Space object. This means that even though the Paper Space dimension will not be visible in Model Space, the Paper Space dimension will reflect changes made to objects in Model Space. In some instances, you may need to use the Dimregen command to "refresh" Paper Space dimensions. See Chapter 13 for more on these features.

ASSOCIATING DIMENSIONS WITH OBJECTS

Now suppose you have a drawing from an older version of AutoCAD, and you want to create an association between an existing dimension and an object. The next exercise will show you how this is done. You'll use the Unit plan to associate one of the dimensions you've already created with a line representing a wall.

1. Close the rectangle drawing file. You don't have to save it.
2. Back in the Unit drawing, zoom in to the balcony area so your view looks similar to Figure 9.12.

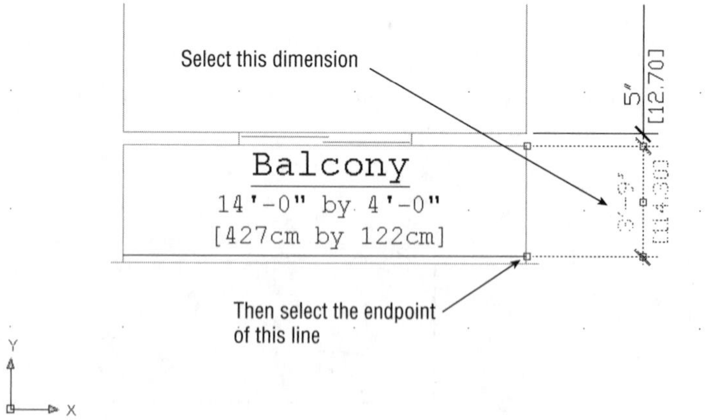

FIGURE 9.12

Reassociating a dimension to an object

3. Choose Dimension ➢ Reassociate Dimensions. You can also type **Dimreassociate↵** at the command prompt.
4. At the `Select dimension to reassociate… Select Object:` prompt, select the vertical dimension that dimensions the balcony (see Figure 9.12), and then press ↵.

5. At the Specify first `extension line origin or [Select object] <next>:` prompt, you'll see an X at the top definition point of the dimension.

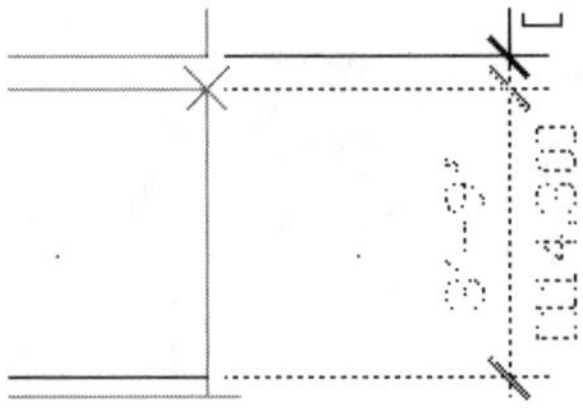

6. Press ↵. This tells AutoCAD to go to the next extension line origin. You'll see an X at the bottom definition point of the dimension.

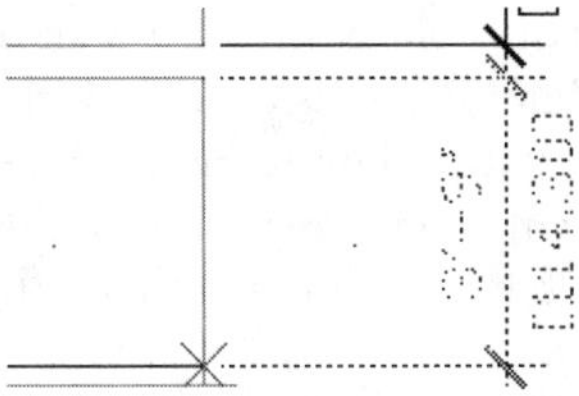

7. Use the Endpoint Osnap and click the end of the line representing the rail of the unit (see Figure 9.12).

You now have the dimension associated with the endpoint of the line representing the rail of the balcony. Try moving the rail to see what happens.

8. Use the Move tool in the Modify toolbar to move the balcony rail downward, as shown in Figure 9.13. The dimension follows the line.

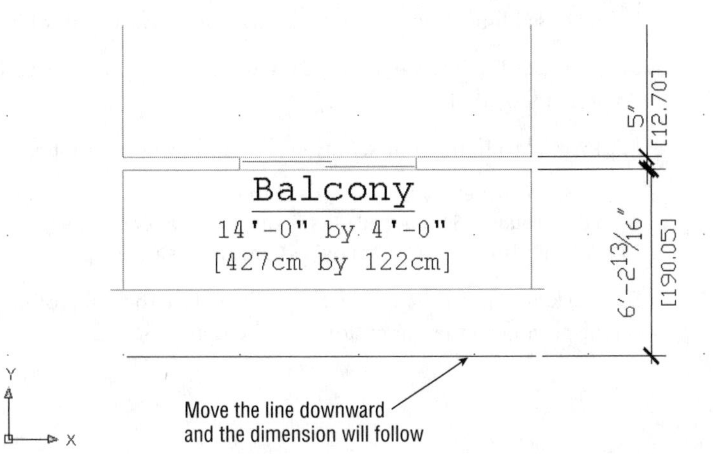

FIGURE 9.13
The reassociated dimension follows the rail as it is moved.

In step 5, you saw an X appear at the location of a dimension definition point. If the definition point is already associated with an object, the X will appear with a box around it.

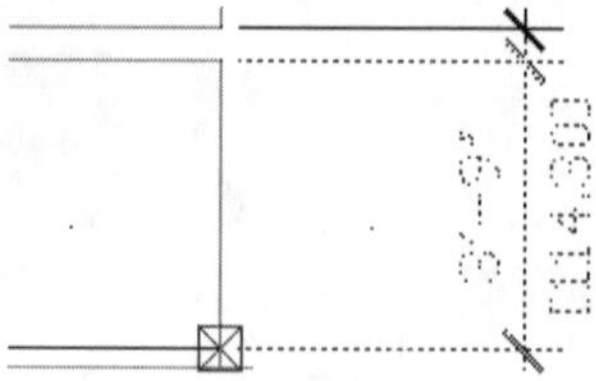

The box is a reminder that the definition point is already associated with an object and that you will be changing its association.

Also in step 5, you have the option to select an object. This option allows you to associate the dimension with an entire object instead of with just one endpoint. If you type S↵ at that prompt in step 5, you can then select the object that you want to associate with the dimension. The dimension will change so that its definition points coincide with the endpoints of the object. The dimension will remain in its original orientation. For example, a vertical dimension will remain vertical even if you associate the dimension with a horizontal line. In this situation, the dimension dutifully dimensions the endpoints of the line but will show a distance of zero.

TIP *You can remove a dimension's association with an object by using the Dimdisassociate command. Type* ***Dimdisassociate↵*** *at the command prompt, select the dimension(s), and then press ↵.*

Adding a String of Dimensions with a Single Operation

AutoCAD 2004 provides a method for creating a string of dimensions using a single operation. The Qdim command lets you select a set of objects instead of having to select points. The following exercise demonstrates how the Qdim command works.

1. If you haven't done so already, zoom out so you have an overall view of the Unit floor plan.

2. Choose Dimension ➤ Quick Dimension or click Quick Dimension on the Dimension toolbar.
3. At the `Select geometry to dimension:` prompt, place a selection window around the entire left-side wall of the unit.
4. Press ↵ to finish your selection. The following prompt appears:

```
Specify dimension line position, or
[Continuous/Staggered/Baseline/Ordinate/Radius/Diameter/
datumPoint/Edit/seTtings] <Continuous>:
```

5. Click a point to the left of the wall to place the dimension. A string of dimensions appears, displaying all the dimensions for the wall.

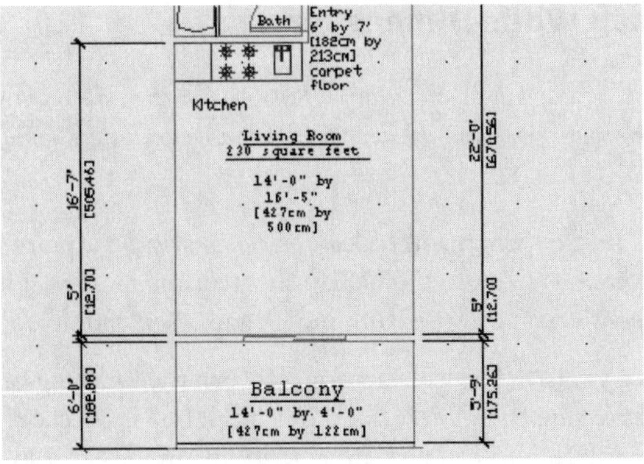

6. When you have finished reviewing the results of this exercise, exit the file without saving it.

The prompt in step 4 indicates several types of dimensions you can choose from. For example, if you want the dimensions to originate from a single baseline, you can enter **B↵** in step 5 to select the Baseline option.

The Qdim command can be a time-saver when you want to dimension a wall quickly. It may not work in all situations, but if the object you're dimensioning is fairly simple, it can be all you need.

TIP *In this exercise, you used a simple window to select the wall. For more complex shapes, try using a crossing polygon selection window. See Chapter 2 for more on crossing polygons.*

Removing the Alternate Dimensions

In the beginning of this chapter, you set up the My Architectural dimension style to include an alternate dimension. You can remove those alternate dimensions by turning off the alternate dimension features. Here's how it's done:

1. Choose Dimension ➢ Style or enter **D↵** to open the Dimension Style Manager dialog box.
2. Select the style that uses the alternate units. In the Styles list box, choose Modify.
3. Click the Alternate Units tab.
4. Click the Display Alternate Units check box to remove the checkmark.
5. Click OK, and then click Close to close the Dimension Style Manager dialog box.

The dimensions that use the style you just edited change to remove the alternate dimensions. You can also perform the reverse operation and add alternate dimensions to an existing set of dimensions. Follow the steps shown here, but instead of removing the checkmark in step 4, add the checkmark and make the appropriate setting changes to the rest of the Alternate Units tab.

Using Osnap While Dimensioning

WARNING *There is a drawback to setting a Running Osnap mode: When your drawing gets crowded, you can end up picking the wrong point by accident. However, you can easily toggle the Running Osnap mode off by clicking Osnap in the status bar.*

You may find that when you pick intersections and endpoints frequently, as during dimensioning, it is a bit inconvenient to use the Osnap shortcut menu. If you know you will be using certain Osnaps frequently, you can use Running Osnaps. You can do so in the following two ways:

- Choose Tools ➢ Drafting Settings to open the Drafting Settings dialog box. In the Object Snap tab, make sure the Object Snap On check box is checked, and then select the desired default Osnap mode. You can pick more than one mode—for example, Intersection, Endpoint, and Midpoint—so that whichever geometry you happen to be nearest will be the point selected.
- Another way to accomplish this is to type **–osnap**↵ at the command prompt and then enter the name of the Osnap modes you want to use. If you want to use more than one mode, enter their names separated by commas; for example:

  ```
  endpoint,midpoint,intersect
  ```

Once you've designated your Running Osnaps, the next time you are prompted to select a point, the selected Osnap modes are automatically activated. You can still override the default settings using the Osnap shortcut menu (Shift+click the right mouse button). You can toggle the Running Osnaps on or off by clicking the Osnap label in the status bar or by pressing F3. The toggle feature is especially helpful in crowded drawings where you can accidentally select an Osnap location while panning, zooming, or selecting points for other operations.

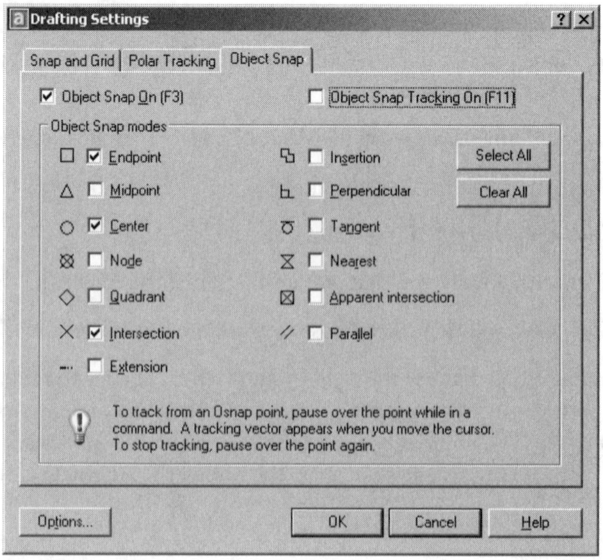

Dimensioning Nonorthogonal Objects

So far, you've been reading about how to work with linear dimensions. You can also dimension nonorthogonal objects, such as circles, arcs, triangles, and trapezoids. In this section, you will practice dimensioning nonorthogonal objects by drawing an elevation of a window in the set of plans for your studio apartment building. You'll start by setting up the drawing, and then you'll draw the window itself:

1. Create a new file called `Window`.
2. In the Create New Drawing Wizard, click the Start From Scratch icon at the top, and then click the Imperial radio button if you are using feet and inches or click the Metric radio button. This is important because, depending on which option you select, AutoCAD will set up the drawing with different dimension style defaults. AutoCAD will create a style called ISO-25 as the default style for metric users.
3. Set the file up as an architectural drawing at a scale of 3"=1"-0" on an 8 1/2" × 11" sheet. Metric users set up an A4 sheet at a scale of 1:4. Consult Chapter 3 for drawing areas.
4. If you are using the Imperial measurement system, start by setting the dimension scale to 4. Normally, you would use the Dimension Style Manager dialog box to set the dimension scale. A shortcut is to type **Dimscale↵ 4↵**. This changes the scale factor of the current dimension style to 4. Metric users can use the default setting.
5. Imperial system users should specify two more settings. Enter **Dimtih↵ 0↵**. This turns off the setting that forces the dimension text to be horizontal. Next type **Dimtad↵ 1↵**. This turns on the text-above-dimension feature. You'll want these two settings on to match the appearance of text in the metric ISO-25 style. Again, metric users do not have to change these settings.

Now you are ready to start drawing the window.

WARNING *In the figures shown for the following exercises, you'll see both Imperial and metric dimensions for the benefit of users of both systems. Your view will contain only the measurement in the system you've chosen in the previous exercise.*

1. Click Polygon on the Draw toolbar, or type **Pol↵**.
2. At the `Enter number of sides:` prompt, enter **6↵**.
3. At the `Specify center of polygon or [Edge]:` prompt, pick the center of the polygon at coordinate 22,18. Metric users use 59,42 for the center coordinate.

TIP *You can turn on the Snap mode to help you locate points for this exercise.*

4. Enter **C↵** at the `Enter an option [Inscribe in circle/circumscribe about circle] <I>:` prompt to select the Circumscribe option. This tells AutoCAD to place the polygon outside the temporary circle used to define the polygon.
5. At the `Specify radius of circle:` prompt, you will see the hexagon drag along with the cursor. You can pick a point with your mouse to determine its size.

6. Enter **8↵** to get an exact size for the hexagon. Metric users enter **20.32↵**.
7. Draw a circle with a radius of 7" using 22,18 as its center. Metric users draw a circle with a radius of 17.78 using 59.42 for the center location. Your drawing will look like Figure 9.14.

FIGURE 9.14
The window frame

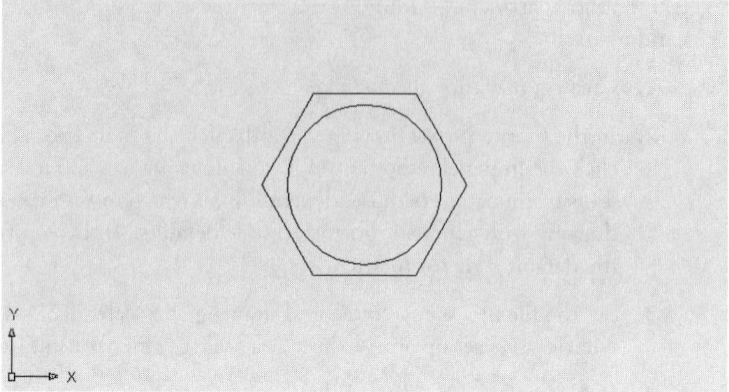

Dimensioning Nonorthogonal Linear Distances

Now you will dimension the window. The unusual shape of the window prevents you from using the horizontal or vertical dimensions you've used already. However, choosing Dimension ➢ Aligned allows you to dimension at an angle:

1. Click the Aligned Dimension tool on the Dimension toolbar. You can also enter **Dal↵** to start the aligned dimension or choose Dimension ➢ Aligned.
2. At the `Specify first extension line origin or <select object>:` prompt, press ↵. You could have picked extension line origins as you did in earlier examples, but using the ↵ shows you firsthand how the Select option works.
3. At the `Select object to dimension:` prompt, pick the upper-right face of the hexagon near coordinate 2'-5",1'-10" (75,55 for metric users). As the prompt indicates, you can also pick an arc or circle for this type of dimension.
4. At the `Specify` dimension line location or `[Mtext/Text/Angle]:` prompt, pick a point near coordinate 34,26 (90,60 for metric users). The dimension appears in the drawing as shown in Figure 9.15.

TIP *Just as with linear dimensions, you can enter* ***T↵*** at step 4 to enter alternate text for the dimension.

FIGURE 9.15

The aligned dimension of a nonorthogonal line

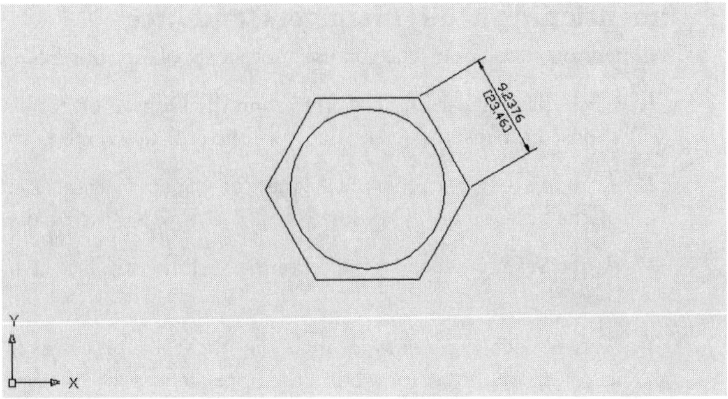

Next, you will dimension a face of the hexagon. Instead of its actual length, however, you will dimension a distance at a specified angle—the distance from the center of the face:

1. Click the Linear Dimension tool on the Dimension toolbar.
2. At the `Specify first extension line origin or <select> object:` prompt, press ↵.
3. At the `Select object to dimension:` prompt, pick the lower-right face of the hexagon near coordinate 30,16 (77,33 for metric users).
4. At the `Specify dimension line location or [Mtext/Text/Angle/Horizontal/Vertical/Rotated]:` prompt, type R↵ to select the rotated option.
5. At the `Specify angle of dimension line angle <0>:` prompt, enter **30**↵.
6. At the `Specify dimension line location or [Mtext/Text/Angle/Horizontal/Vertical/Rotated]:` prompt, pick a point near coordinate 35,8 (88,12 for metric users). Your drawing will look like Figure 9.16.

FIGURE 9.16

A linear dimension using the Rotated option

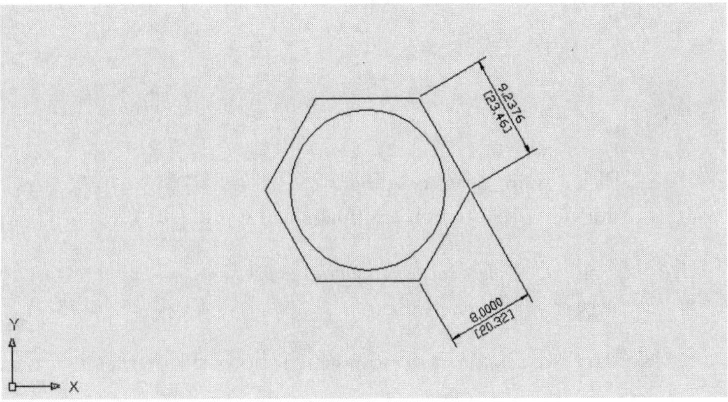

Dimensioning Radii, Diameters, and Arcs

To dimension circular objects, you use another set of options from the Draw ➢ Dimensioning menu:

1. Click the Angular Dimension tool on the Dimension toolbar. Or you can enter **Dan↵** or choose Dimension ➢ Angular from the pull-down menu to start the angular dimension.
2. At the `Select arc, circle, line, or <Specify vertex>:` prompt, pick the upper-left face of the hexagon near coordinate 15,22 (44,57 for metric users).
3. At the `Select second line:` prompt, pick the top face at coordinate 21,26 (54,62 for metric users).
4. At the `Specify dimension arc line location or [Mtext/Text/Angle]:` prompt, notice that as you move the cursor around the upper-left corner of the hexagon, the dimension changes, as shown in the top images of Figure 9.17.

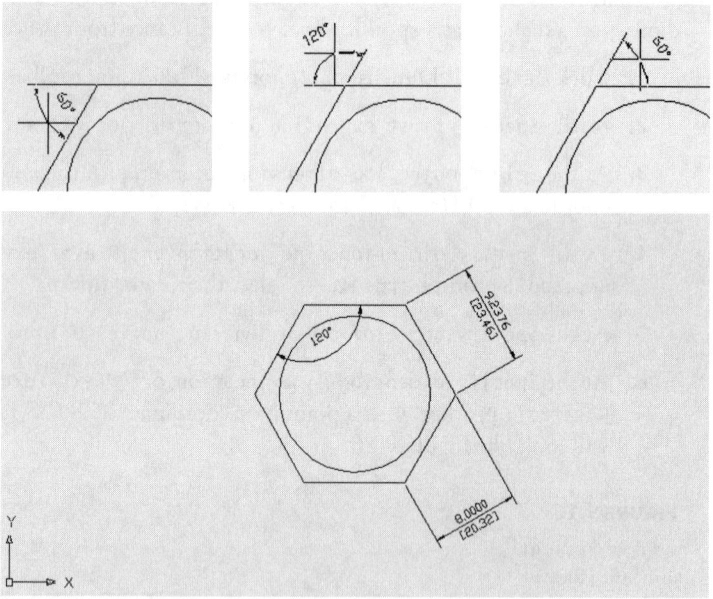

FIGURE 9.17

The angular dimension added to the window frame

5. Pick a point near coordinate 21,23 (49,50 for metric users). The dimension is fixed in the drawing (see the bottom image of Figure 9.17).

TIP *If you need to make subtle adjustments to the dimension line or text location, you can do so using grips, after you place the angular dimension.*

Now try the Diameter option, which shows the diameter of a circle:

1. Click the Diameter Dimension tool on the Dimension toolbar. Or you can enter **Ddi↵** at the command prompt.
2. At the `Select arc or circle:` prompt, pick the circle.
3. At the `Specify dimension line location or [Mtext/Text/Angle]:` prompt, you will see the diameter dimension drag along the circle as you move the cursor. If you move the cursor outside the circle, the dimension will change to display the dimension on the outside. (See the top image in Figure 9.18.)

FIGURE 9.18

Dimension showing the diameter of a circle

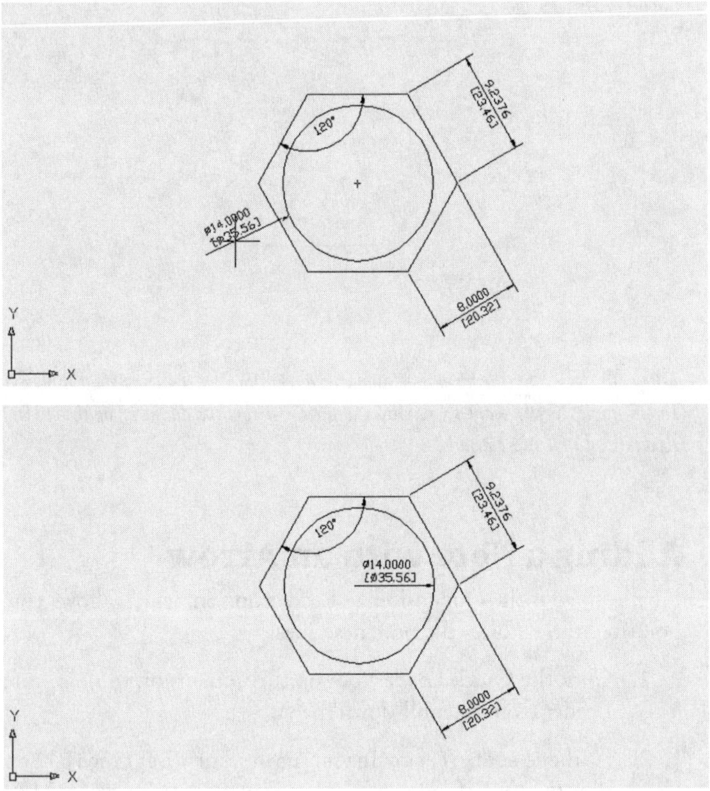

TIP *If the dimension text can't fit within the circle, AutoCAD gives you the option to place the dimension text outside the circle as you drag the temporary dimension to a horizontal position.*

4. Place the cursor inside the circle so that the dimension arrow points in a horizontal direction, as shown in the bottom image of Figure 9.18.
5. With the text centered, click the mouse.

The Radius Dimension tool on the Dimension toolbar gives you a radius dimension just as the diameter dimension provides a circle's diameter.

Figure 9.19 shows a radius dimension on the outside of the circle, but you can place it inside in a manner similar to the diameter dimension. The Center Mark tool on the Dimension toolbar just places a cross mark in the center of the selected arc or circle.

FIGURE 9.19

A radius dimension shown on the outside of the circle

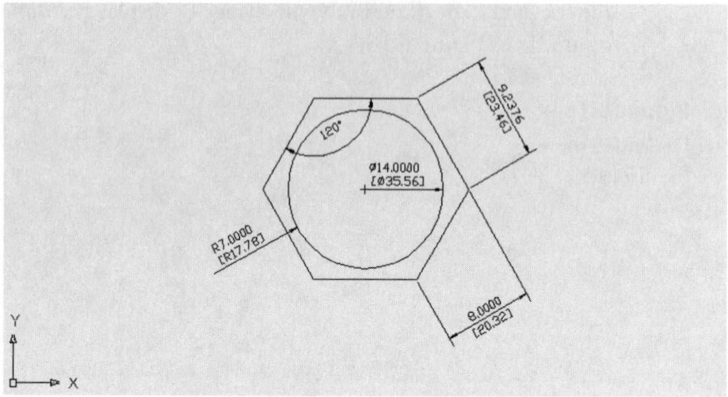

TIP *You can alter the format of diameter dimensions by changing the Dimtix and Dimtofl dimension variable settings. For example, if you want two arrows to appear across the diameter of the circle, turn on both Dimtix and Dimtofl. See Appendix D for more details.*

Adding a Note with an Arrow

Finally, there is the Dimension ➢ Leader option, which allows you to add a note with an arrow pointing to the object the note describes:

1. Click the Quick Leader tool on the Dimension toolbar, enter **Le**↵, or choose Dimension ➢ Leader from the pull-down menu.

2. At the `Specify first leader point, or [Settings] <Settings>:` prompt, pick a point near the top-left edge of the hexagon at coordinate 16,24 (45,59 for metric users).

3. At the `Specify next point:` prompt, enter **@6<110**↵. Metric users should enter **@15<110**↵.

4. At the `Specify next point:` prompt, you can continue to pick points just as you would draw lines. For this exercise, however, press ↵ to finish drawing leader lines.

TIP *You can also add multiline text at the leader. See the next section, "Exploring the Leader Options."*

5. At the `Specify text width <0">:` prompt, press ↵.

6. At the `Enter first line of annotation text <Mtext>:` prompt, type **Window Frame↵** as the label for this leader.
7. At the `Enter next line of annotation text:` prompt, press ↵ to finish the leader. Your drawing will look like Figure 9.20.

FIGURE 9.20

The leader with a note added

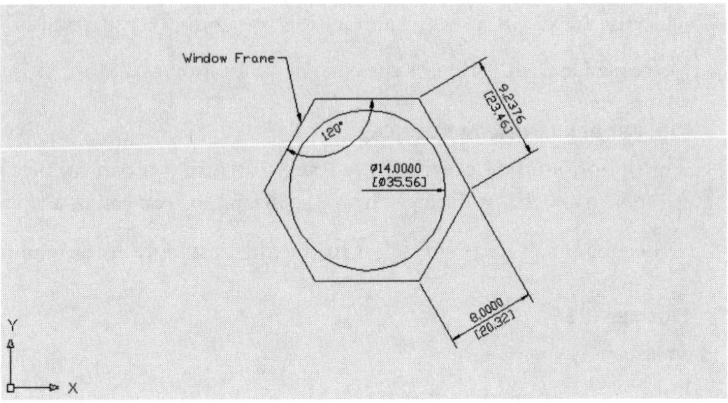

Exploring the Leader Options

The Leader tool is a deceptively simple tool with numerous options. In step 2 of the previous exercise, after choosing Dimension ➢ Leader from the menu bar, you can enter **S↵** to open the Leader Settings dialog box.

From here, you can have the Leader tool perform any number of functions, depending on the type of leader you want.

THE ANNOTATION TAB

The options in the Annotation tab let you control the type of annotation that is attached to the leader. AutoCAD uses the MText option by default, which places a multiline text object at the end of the leader.

In the Annotation Type button group are the following options:

Copy An Object Prompts you to select text, tolerance, or blocks to be copied to the endpoint of the leader.

Tolerance Opens the Tolerance dialog box when you've finished drawing the leader lines. See the section "Adding Tolerance Notation" later in this chapter.

Block Reference Lets you insert a block at the end of the leader.

None Ends the leader without adding a note.

In the MText Options button group are the following options:

Prompt For Width Asks you to select a width for multiline text.

Always Left Justify Left justifies multiline text.

Frame Text Draws a frame around the text.

In the Annotation Reuse button group are the following options:

None Always prompts you for annotation.

Reuse Next Reuses the annotation you enter for the next leader.

Reuse Current Reuses the current annotation text.

THE LEADER LINE & ARROW TAB

The options in the Leader Line & Arrow tab give you control over the leader line and arrow. You can select an arrow that is different from the default, or you can constrain the lines to follow a specific angle.

Leader Line Lets you select from either a straight line or spline for your lines. (see Figure 9.21).

FIGURE 9.21

Straight and spline leader lines

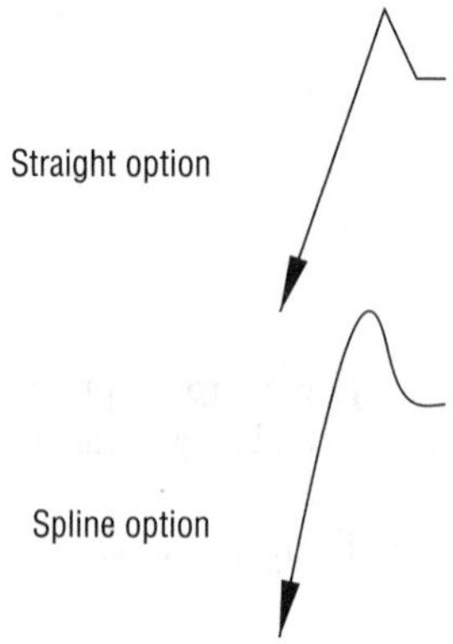

Number Of Points Lets you constrain the number of points you select before the command prompts you for the annotation.

Arrowhead Lets you select an arrowhead from a list similar to the one in the Dimension Style dialog box.

Angle Constraints Lets you constrain the angle at which the leader line extends from the arrow and the second point.

THE ATTACHMENT TAB

The options in the Attachment tab (see Figure 9.22) let you control how the leader connects to MText annotation, depending on which side of the leader the annotation appears. The location of the leader endpoint in relation to the note is frequently a focus of drafting standards. These options let you customize your leader to produce results that conform to the standards you work with.

TIP *Just as with other dimensions, and objects in general, you can modify some of the properties of a leader using the Properties dialog box. You can, for example, change a straight leader into a spline leader.*

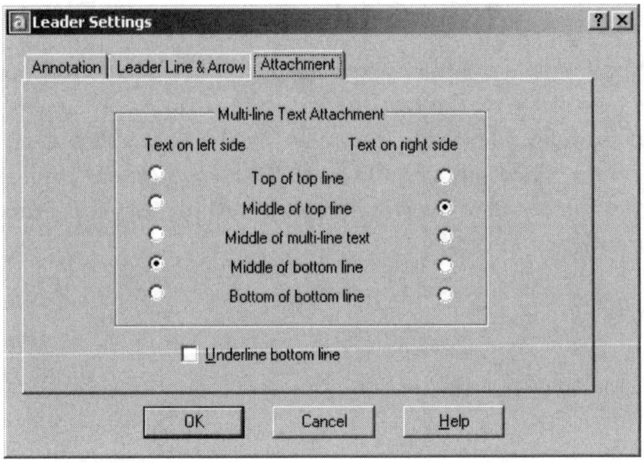

FIGURE 9.22
The Leader Settings dialog box, open at the Attachment tab

Skewing Dimension Lines

At times, you may find it necessary to force the extension lines to take on an angle other than 90° to the dimension line. This is a common requirement of isometric drawings, in which most lines are at 30° or 60° angles instead of 90°. To facilitate nonorthogonal dimensions like these, AutoCAD offers the Oblique option:

1. Choose Dimension ➢ Oblique, or type **Ded**↵ **O**↵. You can also select the Dimension Edit tool from the Dimension toolbar, and then type **O**↵.
2. At the `Select objects:` prompt, pick the aligned dimension at the upper-right of the drawing and press ↵ to confirm your selection.
3. At the `Enter obliquing angle (Press enter for none):` prompt, enter **60** for 60 degrees. The dimension will skew so that the extension lines are at 60°, as shown in Figure 9.23.

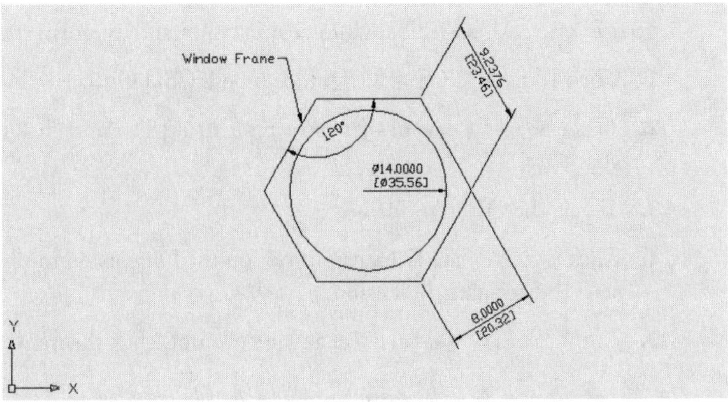

FIGURE 9.23
A dimension using the Oblique option

4. Exit AutoCAD.

Applying Ordinate Dimensions

In mechanical drafting, *ordinate dimensions* are used to maintain the accuracy of machined parts by establishing an origin on the part. All major dimensions are described as X coordinates or Y coordinates of that origin. The origin is usually an easily locatable feature of the part, such as a machined bore or two machined surfaces. Figure 9.24 shows a typical application of ordinate dimensions. In the lower-left corner, note the two dimensions whose leaders are jogged. Also note the origin location in the upper-right corner.

FIGURE 9.24

A drawing using ordinate dimensions

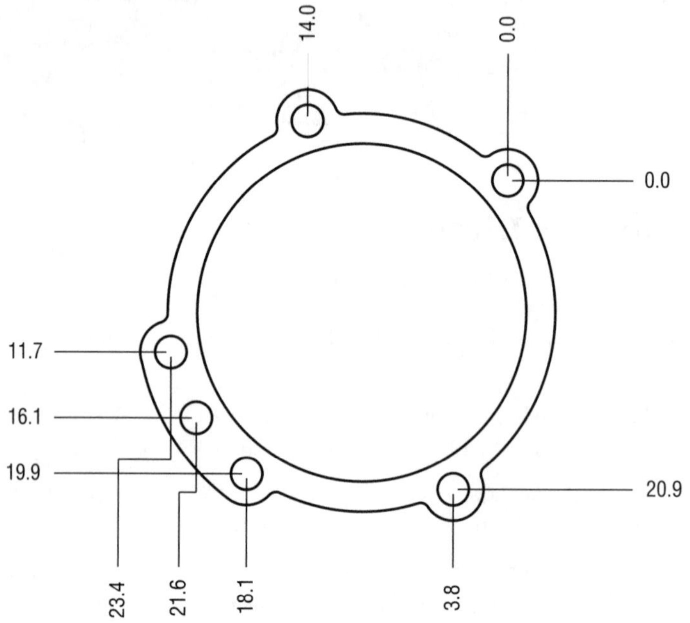

To use AutoCAD's Ordinate Dimension command, perform the following steps.

1. Click Tools ➢ UCS ➢ Origin, or type **UCS↵ Or↵**.
2. At the `Specify new origin point <0,0,0>:` prompt, click the exact location of the origin of your part.
3. Toggle the Ortho mode on.
4. 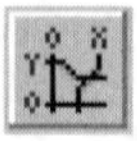 Click the Ordinate Dimension tool on the Dimension toolbar. You can also enter **Dor↵** to start the ordinate dimension.
5. At the `Specify feature location:` prompt, click the item you want to dimension.

TIP *The direction of the leader determines whether the dimension will be of the Xdatum or the Ydatum.*

6. At the `Specify leader endpoint or [Xdatum/Ydatum/Mtext/Text/Angle]:` prompt, indicate the length and direction of the leader. Do this by positioning the rubber-banding leader perpendicular to the coordinate direction you want to dimension and then clicking that point.

In steps 1 and 2, you used the UCS feature to establish a second origin in the drawing. The Ordinate Dimension tool then uses that origin to determine the ordinate dimensions. You will get a chance to work with the UCS feature in Chapter 17.

You may have noticed options in the Command window for the Ordinate Dimension tool. The Xdatum and Ydatum options force the dimension to be of the X or Y coordinate no matter what direction the leader takes. The MText option opens the Multiline Text Editor, allowing you to append or replace the ordinate dimension text. The Text option lets you enter a replacement text directly through the Command window.

TIP *As with all other dimensions, you can use grips to adjust the location of ordinate dimensions.*

If you turn Ortho mode off, the dimension leader will be drawn with a jog to maintain the orthogonal (look back at Figure 9.24).

Adding Tolerance Notation

In mechanical drafting, *tolerances* are a key part of a drawing's notation. They specify the allowable variation in size and shape that a mechanical part can have. To help facilitate tolerance notation, AutoCAD provides the Tolerance command, which offers common ISO tolerance symbols together with a quick way to build a standard *feature control* symbol. Feature control symbols are industry-standard symbols used to specify tolerances. If you are a mechanical engineer or drafter, AutoCAD's tolerance notation options will be a valuable tool. However, a full discussion of tolerances requires a basic understanding of mechanical design and drafting and is beyond the scope of this book.

To use the Tolerance command, choose Tolerance from the Dimension toolbar, type **Tol**↵ at the command prompt, or choose Dimension ➢ Tolerance from the drop-down menu.

The Geometric Tolerance dialog box appears.

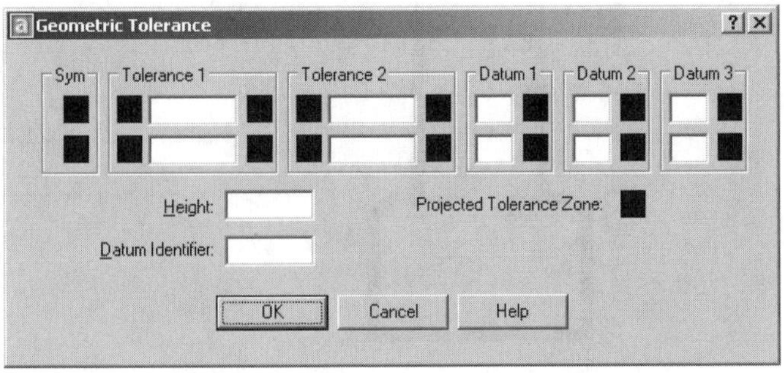

This is where you enter tolerance and datum values for the feature control symbol. You can enter two tolerance values and three datum values. In addition, you can stack values in a two-tiered fashion.

Click a box in the Sym group, to open the Symbol dialog box.

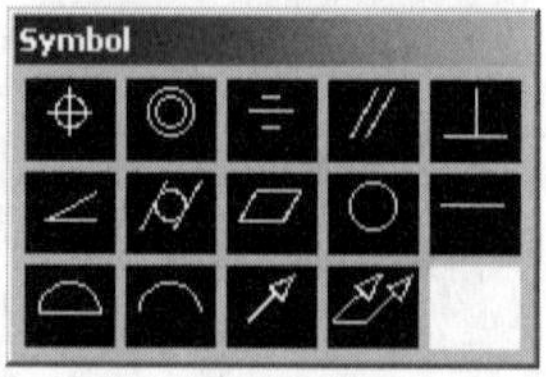

The top image in Figure 9.25 shows what each symbol in the Symbol dialog box represents. The bottom image shows a sample drawing with a feature symbol used on a cylindrical object.

FIGURE 9.25

The tolerance symbols

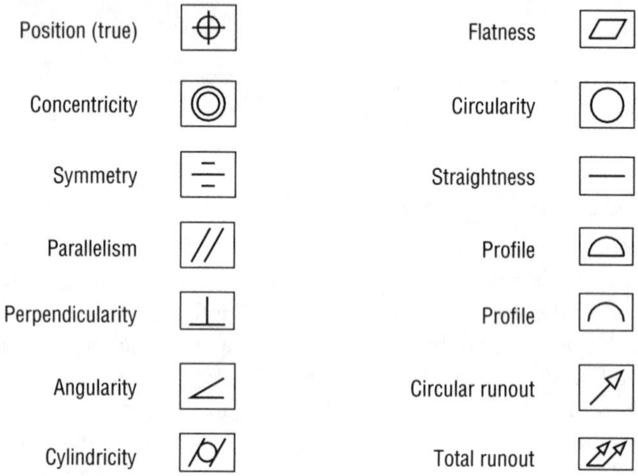

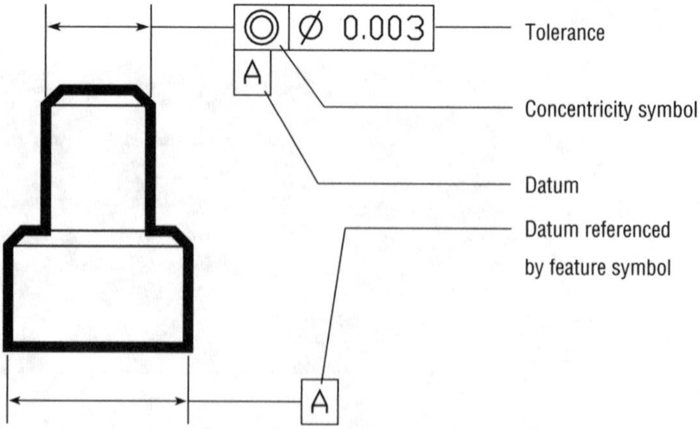

In the Geometric Tolerance dialog box, you can click a box in any of the Datum groups or a box in the right side of the Tolerance groups to open the Material Condition dialog box.

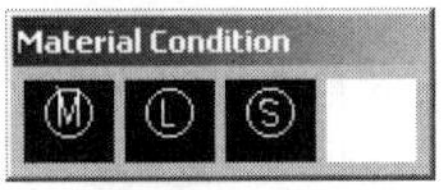

Understanding the Power of the Properties Palette

In both this and the previous chapter, you made frequent use of the Properties palette. By now, you may have recognized that the Properties palette is a gateway to editing virtually any object. It allows you to edit the general properties of layer, color, and line type assignments. When used with individual objects, it allows you to edit properties that are unique to the selected object. For example, through this tool, you can change a spline leader with an arrow into one with straight-line segments and no arrow.

If the Properties palette does not provide specific options to edit the object, it provides a button to open a palette that will. If you edit a multiline text object with the Properties palette, for example, you can open the Multiline Text Editor. The same is true for dimension text.

Beginning with AutoCAD 2000, Autodesk has made a clear effort to make AutoCAD's interface more consistent. The text-editing tools now edit text of all types—single-line, multiline, and dimension text—so you don't have to remember which command or tool you need for a particular object. Likewise, using the Properties palette is a powerful way to edit all types of objects in your drawing.

As you continue with the rest of this tutorial, you might want to experiment with the Properties palette with new objects you learn about. In addition to allowing you to edit properties, the Properties palette can show you the status of an object, much like the List tool.

If You Want to Experiment...

At this point, you might want to experiment with the settings described in this chapter to identify the ones that are most useful for your work. You can then establish these settings as defaults in a prototype file or the `Acad.dwt` file.

It's a good idea to experiment even with the settings you don't think you will need often—chances are you will have to alter them from time to time.

As an added exercise, try the steps shown in Figure 9.26. This exercise will give you a chance to see how you can update dimensions on a drawing that has been scaled down.

FIGURE 9.26

A sample mechanical drawing with dimensions

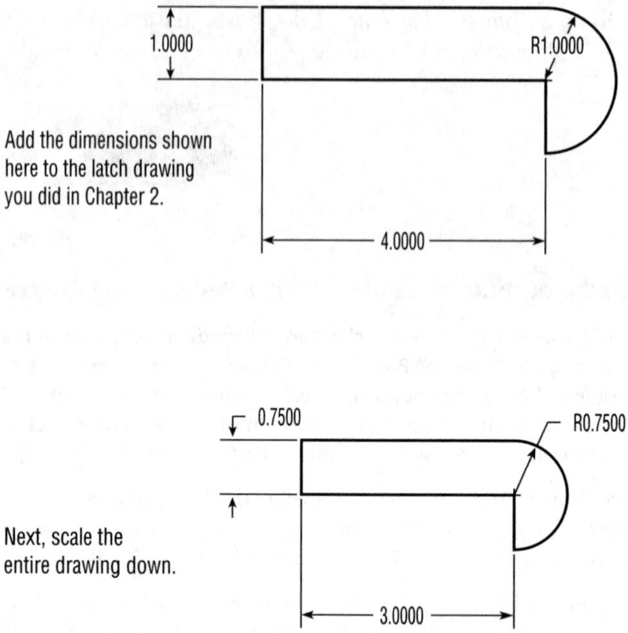

Part 3

Becoming an Expert

In this part:

Chapter 10

Attributes—Storing Data with Graphics

ATTRIBUTES ARE UNIQUE TO computer-aided design and drafting; nothing quite like them exists in traditional drafting. Because of this, they are often poorly understood. Attributes enable you to store information as text that you can later extract to use in database managers, spreadsheet programs, and word processors. By using attributes, you can keep track of virtually any object in a drawing or maintain textual information within the drawing that can be queried.

Keeping track of objects is just one way to use attributes. You can also use them in place of text objects when you must enter the same text, with minor modifications, in many places in your drawing. For example, if you are drawing a schedule that contains several columns of information, you can use attributes to help simplify your data entry.

In this chapter you will use attributes for one of their more common functions: maintaining lists of parts. In this case, the parts are doors. This chapter will also describe how to import these attributes into a database management program. As you go through these exercises, think about the ways attributes can help you in your particular application.

This chapter covers the following topics:

- Creating Attributes
- Editing Attributes
- Extracting and Exporting Attribute Information
- If You Want to Experiment…

Creating Attributes

Attributes depend on blocks. You might think of an attribute as a tag attached to a block; the tag contains information about the block. For example, you could include an attribute definition with the door drawing you created in Chapter 2. Then, every time you subsequently insert the door, you would be prompted for a value associated with that door. The value can be a number, a height or width value, a name, or any type of text information you want. When you insert the block, you are prompted for an attribute value. Once you enter a value, it is stored as part of the block within the drawing database. This value can be displayed as text attached to the door, or it can be invisible. You can change the value at any time. You can even specify the text for the prompts.

However, suppose you don't have the attribute information when you design the door. As an alternative, you can add the attribute to a *symbol* that is later placed by the door when you know enough about the design to specify what type of door goes where. The standard door type symbol suits this purpose nicely because it is an object that you can set up and use as a block independent of the actual door block.

TIP *A door type symbol is a graphic code that indicates special characteristics of the associated door. The code refers to a note on another drawing or in a set of written specifications.*

In the following exercises, you will create a door type symbol with attributes for the values normally assigned to doors, namely size, thickness, fire rating, material, and construction.

Adding Attributes to Blocks

In this exercise, you will create a door type symbol, which is commonly used to describe the size, thickness, and other characteristics of any given door in an architectural drawing. The symbol is usually a circle, a hexagon, or a diamond with a number in it. The number is usually cross-referenced to a schedule that lists all the door types and their characteristics.

Although in this exercise you will create a new file containing attribute definitions, you can also include such definitions in blocks you create using the Make Block tool (the Block command) or in files you create using the Wblock command. Just create the attribute definitions as shown here, and then include them with the Block or Wblock selections.

1. Create a new file and call it `S-door` (for symbol-door). The symbol will fit in the default limits of the drawing, so you don't have to change the limits setting.

TIP *Since this is a new drawing, the circle is automatically placed on Layer 0. Remember that objects in a block that are on Layer 0 take on the color and line-type assignment of the layer on which the block is inserted.*

2. Draw a circle with a radius of 0.125 (0.3 for metric users) and with its center at coordinate 7,5.
3. Next, zoom in to the circle so it is about the same size as that shown in Figure 10.1.

FIGURE 10.1
The attribute inserted in the circle and the second attribute added

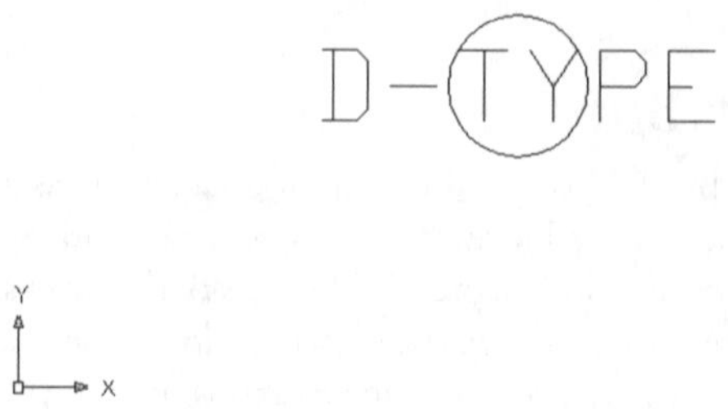

4. If the circle looks like an octagon, choose View ➢ Regen or type **Re↵** to regenerate your drawing.

5. Choose Draw ➢ Block ➢ Define Attributes or type **Att↵** to open the Attribute Definition dialog box.

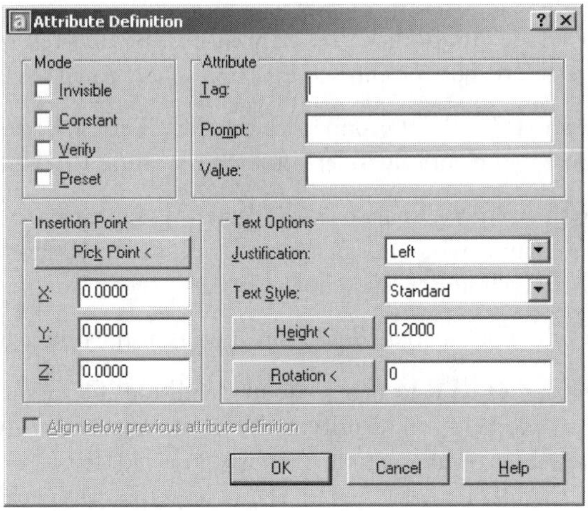

6. In the Attribute group, click the Tag input box, and enter **d-type**.

TIP *The attribute tag is equivalent to a field name in a database; it can be a maximum of 31 characters but cannot contain spaces. If you plan to use the attribute data in a database program, check that program's documentation for other restrictions on field names.*

7. Press the Tab key or click the Prompt input box, and enter **Door type**. This is the text for the prompt that will appear when you insert the block containing this attribute. Often the prompt is the same as the tag, but it can be anything you like. Unlike the tag, the prompt can include spaces.

TIP *Use a prompt that gives explicit instructions so the user will know exactly what is expected. Consider including an example within the prompt. (Enclose the example in angle brackets to imitate the way AutoCAD prompts often display defaults.)*

8. Click the Value input box, and enter a hyphen. This is the default value for the door type prompt.

TIP *If an attribute is to contain a number that will later be used for sorting in a database, use a default value such as 000 to indicate the number of digits required. The zeros can also serve to remind the user that values less than 100 must be preceded by a leading zero, as in 099.*

9. Click the Justification drop-down list, and select Middle. This allows you to center the attribute on the circle's center. You might notice several other options in the Text Options group. Since attributes appear as text, you can apply the same settings to them as you would to single-line text.
10. Double-click the input box next to the Height < button, and enter **0.125**. (Metric users should enter **0.3**.) This makes the attribute text 0.125 inches (0.3 cm) high.
11. In the Mode group, click the Verify check box. This tells AutoCAD to verify any answers you give to the attribute prompts at insertion time. (You'll see later in this chapter how Verify works.)
12. In the Insertion Point group, click the Pick Point < button. The Attribute Definition dialog box closes momentarily to let you pick a location for the attribute.
13. Using the Center Osnap, pick the center of the circle. You need to place the cursor on the circle's circumference, not in the circle's center, to obtain the center using the Osnap. The Attribute Definition dialog box reappears.
14. Click OK. The attribute definition appears at the center of the circle (see Figure 10.1).

You have just created your first attribute definition. The attribute definition displays its tag in all uppercase letters to help you identify it. When you later insert this file into another drawing, the tag turns into the value you assign to it when it is inserted. If you only want one attribute, you can stop here and save the file. The next section shows how you can quickly add several more attributes to your drawing.

Adding Attribute Specifications

Next, you will add a few more attribute definitions, but instead of using the Attribute Definition dialog box, you will make an arrayed copy of the first attribute and then edit the attribute definition copies. This method can save you time when you want to create several attribute definitions that have similar characteristics. By making copies and editing them, you'll also get a chance to see firsthand how to change an attribute definition.

1. Click Array on the Modify toolbar or type **Ar**↵ to open the Array dialog box.
2. Click the Rectangular Array radio button in the upper-left corner.

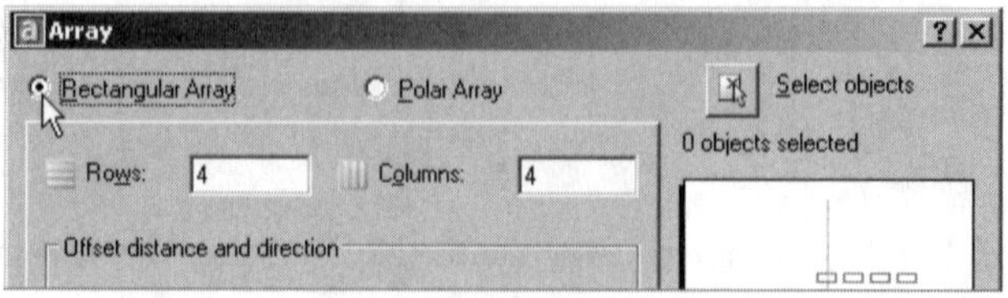

3. Click the Select Objects button, and select the attribute definition you just created. Press ↵ to confirm your selection.

4. In the Rows input box, enter **7** and in the Columns input box, enter **1**.
5. Enter **–0.18** in the Row Offset input box (**–0.432** for metric users) and **0** in the Column Offset input box. The Row Offset value is approximately 1.5 times the height of the attribute text height. The minus sign in the Row Offset value causes the array to be drawn downward.
6. Click the OK button.
7. Issue a Zoom Extents command or click the Zoom Realtime tool to view all the attributes.

Now you are ready to modify the copies of the attribute definitions.

1. Press the Esc key to clear any selections or commands, and click the attribute definition just below the original.
2. Right-click, and choose Properties from the shortcut menu to open the Properties palette.

TIP *You can double-click an attribute definition to change its Tag, Prompt, or Default value in the Edit Attribute Definition dialog box. However, this dialog box doesn't let you change an attribute definition's visibility mode.*

3. Scroll down the list of properties until you see the Invisible option in the Misc category.
4. Select Yes from the Invisible option drop-down list.

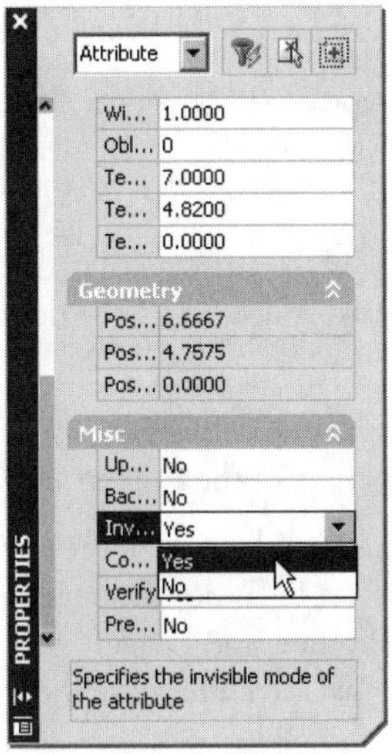

5. Scroll back up the list of properties and locate the Tag option in the Text category.

6. Highlight the Tag value to the right, and type **D-SIZE**↵. The attribute changes to reflect the change in the tag value.

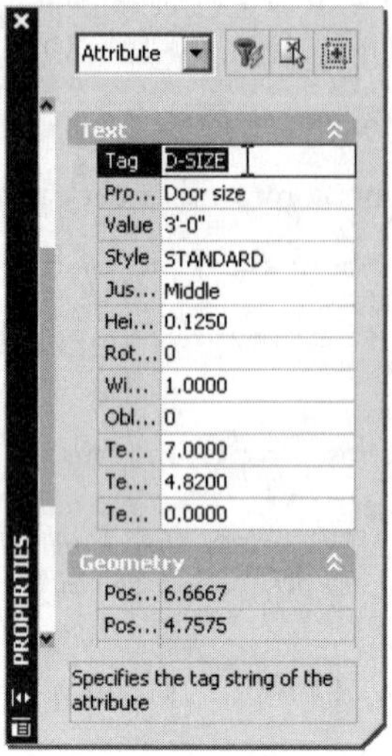

7. While still in the Text category, highlight the Prompt value and type **Door size**↵.
8. In the Value field, type **3'-0"**↵. Metric users should type **90**↵.

TIP *Make sure you press ↵ after entering a new value for the properties in the Properties palette. Pressing ↵ confirms your new entry.*

You've just learned how to edit an attribute definition. Now go ahead and make changes to the other attribute definitions.

1. Press the Esc key so that no attribute is selected, and then click the next attribute down so you can display its properties in the Properties palette.
2. Continue to edit this and the rest of the attribute definition properties using the attribute settings listed in Table 10.1. To do this, repeat steps 4 through 9 for each attribute definition, replacing the Tag, Prompt, and Default values with those shown in Table 10.1. Also, make sure all but the original attributes have the Invisible option turned on.
3. When you've finished editing the attribute definition properties, close the Properties palette.
4. After you modify all the attributes, choose Draw ➢ Block ➢ Base to change the base point of this drawing to the center of the circle. Use the Center Osnap to get the exact center.
5. Now you have finished creating your door type symbol with attributes. Save the `S-door` file.

TABLE 10.1 ATTRIBUTES FOR THE DOOR TYPE SYMBOL

TAG	PROMPT	DEFAULT VALUE
D-NUMBER	Door number	-
D-THICK	Door thickness	-
D-RATE	Fire rating	-
D-MATRL	Door material	-
D-CONST	Door construction	-

Make sure the Invisible option is checked.

When you later insert a file or a block containing attributes, the attribute prompts will appear in the order that their associated definitions were created. If the order of the prompts at insertion time is important, you can control it by editing the attribute definitions so their creation order corresponds to the desired prompt order. You can also control the order using the Block Attribute Manager, which you'll look at later.

UNDERSTANDING ATTRIBUTE DEFINITION MODES

In the Attribute Definition dialog box, you saw several choices in the Mode group, and you've used two of these modes to see what they do. You won't use any of the other modes in this tutorial, so here is a list describing all the modes for your reference.

Invisible Controls whether the attribute is shown as part of the drawing.

Constant Creates an attribute that does not prompt you to enter a value. Instead, the attribute simply has a constant, or fixed, value you give it during creation. The Constant mode is used when you know you will assign a fixed value to an object. Once constant values are set in a block, you cannot change them using the standard set of attribute editing commands.

Verify Causes AutoCAD to review the attribute values you enter at insertion time and ask you if they are correct.

Preset Causes AutoCAD to assign the default value to an attribute automatically when its block is inserted. This saves time because a preset attribute will not prompt you for a value. Unlike the Constant mode, a Preset attribute can be edited.

You can have all four modes on, all four off, or any combination of on and off. With the exception of the Invisible mode, none of these modes can be altered once the attribute becomes part of a block. Later in this chapter, I'll show you how to make an invisible attribute visible.

Inserting Blocks Containing Attributes

In the last section, you created a door type symbol at the desired size for the actual plotted symbol. This means that whenever you insert that symbol, you have to specify an x and y scale factor appropriate to the scale of your drawing. This allows you to use the same symbol in any drawing, regardless of its scale.

(You could have several door type symbols, one for each scale you anticipate using, but this would be inefficient.)

1. Open the `Plan` file you created in earlier exercises. Or you can use the `10a-plan.dwg` file from the companion CD. Metric users can use the file named `06b-plan-metric.dwg` (from the CD's `Chapter 6` folder).
2. Turn on the Attribute Dialog mode by entering **Attdia↵ 1↵** at the command prompt. This allows you to enter attribute values through a dialog box in the next exercise.
3. Choose View ➢ Named Views to restore the view named First.
4. Be sure the Ceiling and Flr-Pat layers are off. Normally in a floor plan, the door headers are not visible, and they will interfere with the placement of the door reference symbol.
5. Click the Insert Block tool or type **I↵** to open the Insert dialog box.
6. Click the Browse button.
7. Locate the `S-DOOR` file in the file list and double-click it.
8. In the Scale button group, make sure the Uniform Scale check box is selected; then enter **96** in the X input box. Metric users should enter **100** in the X input box.
9. In the Rotation group, make sure that the Specify On Screen option is turned off, then Click OK.

You created the `S-DOOR` file at the actual plotted size, so in step 7, you needed to scale it up by the drawing scale factor to make it the appropriate size for this drawing. Now you're ready to place the file in your drawing and enter the attribute values for the symbol.

1. AutoCAD is waiting for you to select a location for the symbol. To place the symbol, click in the doorway of the lower-left unit, near coordinate 41'-3",72'-4". Metric users should use coordinate 1256,2202. When you click the location, the Enter Attributes dialog box opens.

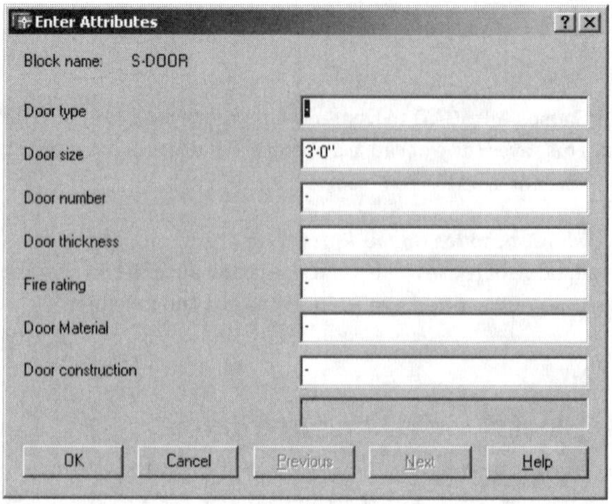

2. In the Door Type input box, enter **A**↵. Note that this prompt is the prompt you created. Note also that the default value is the hyphen you specified.

TIP *Attribute data is case sensitive, so any text you enter in all capital letters will be stored in all capital letters.*

3. In the Door Number input box, change the hyphen to **116**. Continue to change the values for each input box, as shown in Table 10.2.

4. When you are finished changing values, click OK and the symbol appears. The only attribute you can see is the one you selected to be visible: the door type.

TIP *If the symbol does not appear, go back to the* `s-door.dwg` *file and make sure you have set the base point to the center of the circle.*

5. Add the rest of the door type symbols for the apartment entry doors by copying or arraying the door symbol you just inserted. You can use the previously saved views to help you get around the drawing quickly. Don't worry that the attribute values won't be appropriate for each unit. You'll see how to edit the attributes in the next section.

TABLE 10.2 ATTRIBUTE VALUES FOR THE TYPICAL STUDIO ENTRY DOOR

PROMPT	VALUE
Door type	A
Door number	(Will be same as room number)
Door thickness	1 3/4"
Fire rating	20 min.
Door material	Wood
Door construction	Solid core

As a review exercise, you'll now create another file for the apartment number symbol (shown in Figure 10.2). This will be a rectangular box with the room number that you will place in each studio apartment.

1. Save the `Plan` file and then open a new file called `S-apart` (for the apartment number symbol).

2. Create an attribute definition and give it the tag name **R-number**, the prompt **Room number**, a default value of **000**, and a text height of **0.125** inches.

3. Use the Base command (choose Draw ➢ Block ➢ Base) to set the base point of this drawing in the lower-left corner of the rectangle.

4. Save and close `S-apart`.

FIGURE 10.2

The apartment number symbol

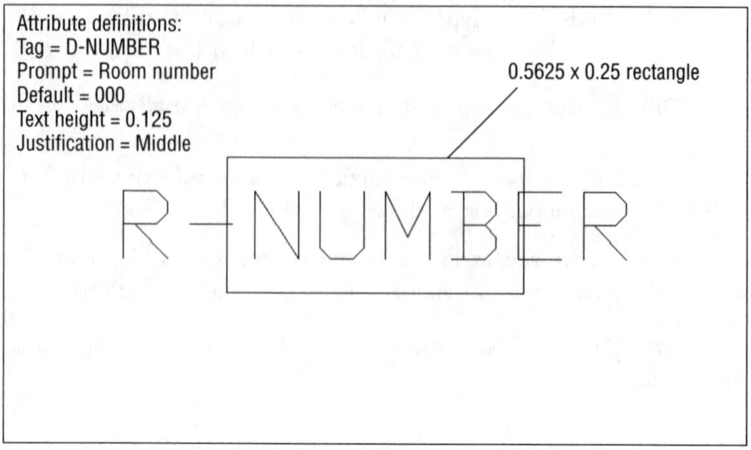

5. Open the `Plan` file again and insert the S-apart drawing you just created (using an x-scale factor of 96) into the lower-left unit. Give this attribute the value **116**.
6. Copy or array the room number symbol so that there is one symbol in each of the units. You'll learn how to modify the attributes to reflect their proper values in the following section, "Editing Attributes." Figure 10.3 shows what the view should look like once you've entered the door symbols and the apartment numbers.

FIGURE 10.3

An overall view of the plan with door symbols and apartment numbers added

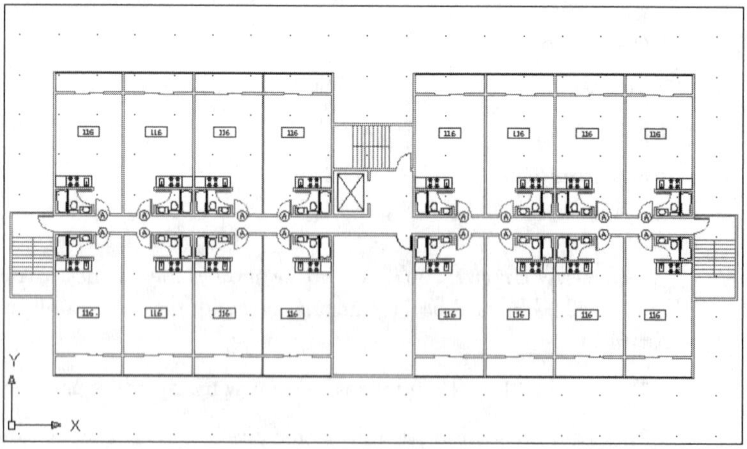

Editing Attributes

Because drawings are usually in flux even after actual construction or manufacturing begins, you will eventually have to edit previously entered attributes. In the example of the apartment building, many things can change before the final set of drawings is completed.

Attributes can be edited individually or *globally*—you can edit several occurrences of a particular attribute tag all at one time. In this section you will make changes to the attributes you have entered so far, using both individual and global editing techniques, and you will practice editing invisible attributes.

TIP *If you prefer to access editing windows using a toolbar, the Modify II toolbar in AutoCAD 2004 offers tools for the Enhanced Attribute Editor and the Block Attribute Manager discussed in this section.*

Editing Attribute Values One at a Time

AutoCAD offers an easy way to edit attributes one at a time through a dialog box. The following exercise demonstrates this feature.

1. Choose View ➢ Named View to restore the First view.
2. Double-click the apartment number attribute in the unit just to the right of the first unit in the lower-left corner to open the Enhanced Attribute Editor. You can also choose Modify ➢ Object ➢ Attribute ➢ Single, and then select the attribute.

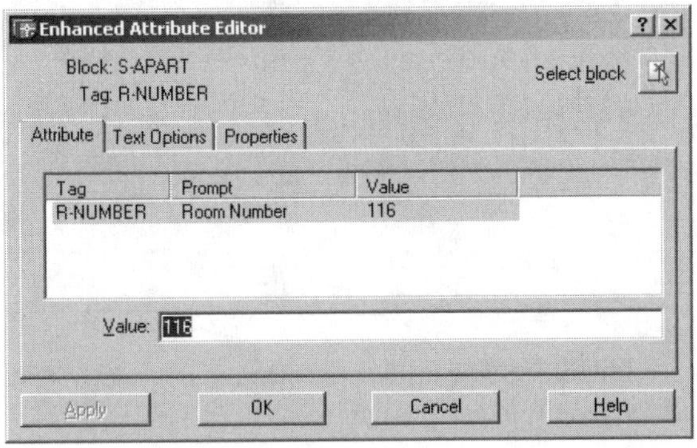

WARNING *LT users will see the Edit Attributes dialog box which lists the attributes in a single column.*

3. Change the value in the Value input box to **112** and then click OK to make the change.
4. Do this for each room number, using Figure 10.4 to assign room numbers.

TIP *If you're a veteran AutoCAD user, you can still use the Ddatte (**Ate**↵ shortcut) command to open the Edit Attributes dialog box. This dialog box is useful for reviewing attributes as well as editing them because both visible and invisible attributes are displayed in the dialog box.*

FIGURE 10.4

Apartment numbers for one floor of the studio apartment building

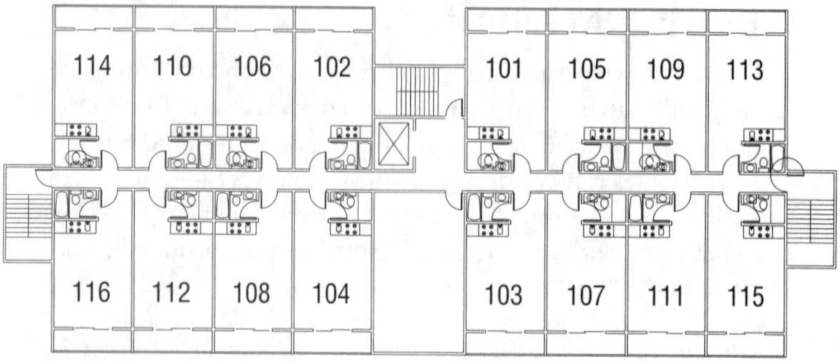

ACAD only

Editing Attribute Text Formats and Properties

You may have noticed that the Enhanced Attribute Editor in the last exercise has three tabs: Attribute, Text Options, and Properties. When you double-click a block containing an attribute, the Enhanced Attribute Editor dialog box opens at the Attribute tab. You can use the other two tabs to control the size, font, color, and other properties of the selected attribute.

The Text Options tab lets you alter the attribute text style, justification, height, rotation, width factor, and oblique angle. (See Chapter 8 for more on these text options.)

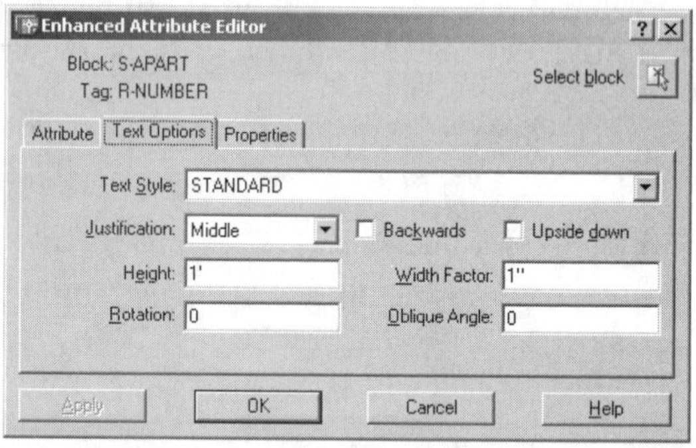

The Properties tab lets you alter the attribute's layer, line type, color, line weight (effective only on AutoCAD fonts), and plot style assignments.

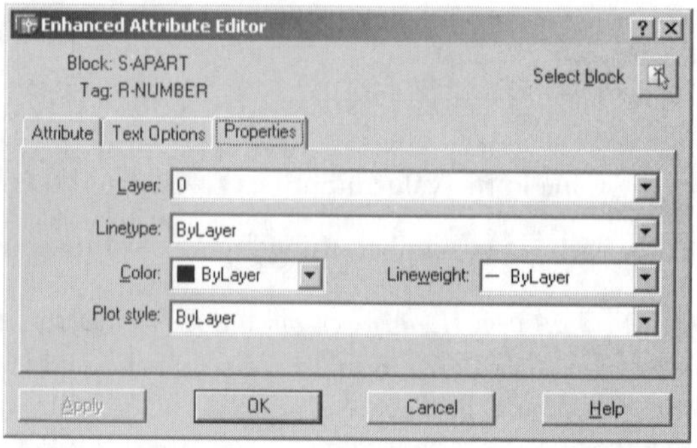

In the previous exercise, you edited a block containing just a single attribute. Double-clicking a block that contains multiple attributes, such as the S-DOOR block, opens the Enhanced Attribute Editor dialog box at the Attribute tab, which displays all the attributes, regardless of whether they are visible, as shown in Figure 10.5. You can then edit the value, formats, and properties of the individual attributes by highlighting the attribute in the Attribute tab and then using the other tabs to make changes. The changes you make will affect only the attribute you've highlighted in the Attribute tab.

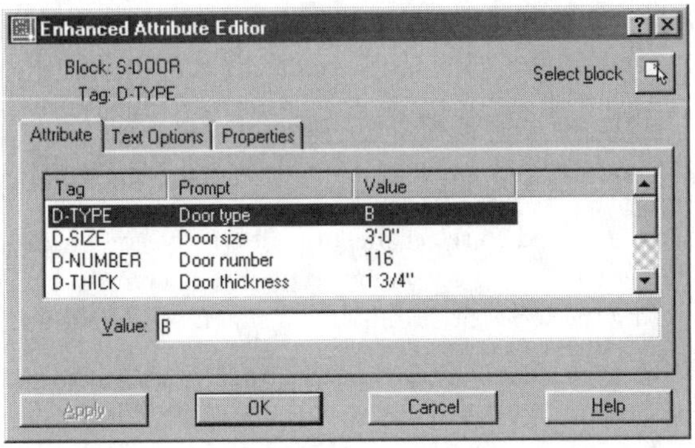

FIGURE 10.5

The Enhanced Attribute Editor showing the contents of a block that contains several attributes

TIP *If you want to change the location of individual attributes in a block, you can move attributes using grips. Click the block to expose the grips and then click the grip connected to the attribute. Or if you've selected several blocks, Shift+click the attribute grips; then move the attributes to their new location. They will still be attached to their associated blocks.*

The Enhanced Attribute Editor lets you change attribute values, formats, and properties one block at a time, but, as you'll see in the next section, you can also make changes to several attributes at once.

Making Global Changes to Attribute Values

At times you'll want to change the value of several attributes in a file to be the same value. You can use the Edit Attribute Globally option to make any global changes to attribute values.

Suppose you decide you want to change all the entry doors to a type designated as B, rather than A. Perhaps door type A was an input error, or type B happens to be better suited for an entry door. The following exercise demonstrates how this is done.

1. Choose View ➢ Named View to open the View Control dialog box, and to restore the view named Fourth. Pan your view down so you can see the door reference symbol for all the rooms in this view of the drawing.
2. Choose Modify ➢ Object ➢ Attribute ➢ Global, or type **Attedit↵** at the command prompt.
3. At the `Edit Attributes one at a time? [Yes/No] <Y>:` prompt, enter **N↵** for No. You will see the message `Performing global editing of attribute values.` This tells you that you are in the Global Edit mode.
4. At the `Edit only attributes visible on screen? [Yes/No] <Y>:` prompt, press ↵. As you can see from this prompt, you have the option to edit all attributes, including those out of the view area. You'll get a chance to work with this option later in the chapter.

5. At the `Enter block name specification <*>:` prompt, press ↵. Optionally, you can enter a block name to narrow the selection to specific blocks.
6. At the `Enter attribute tag specification <*>:` prompt, press ↵. Optionally, you can enter an attribute tag name to narrow your selection to specific tags.
7. At the `Enter attribute value specification <*>:` prompt, press ↵. Optionally, you can narrow your selection to attributes containing specific values.
8. At the `Select Attributes:` prompt, select the door type symbols for units 103 to 115. You can use a window to select the attributes if you prefer.
9. At the `Enter string to change:` prompt, enter **A**↵.
10. At the `Enter new String:` prompt, enter **B**↵. The door type symbols all change to the new value.

In step 8, you are asked to select the attributes to be edited. AutoCAD limits the changes to those attributes you select. If you know you need to change every single attribute in your drawing, you can do so by answering the series of prompts in a slightly different way, as in the following exercise.

1. Try the same procedure again, but this time enter **N** at the `Edit only attributes visible on screen:` prompt (step 4 in the previous exercise). The message `Drawing must be regenerated afterwards` appears. The AutoCAD text window appears.
2. Once again, you are prompted for the block name, the tag, and the value (steps 5, 6, and 7 in the previous exercise). Respond to these prompts as you did before. Once you have done that, you get the message `128 attributes selected`. This tells you the number of attributes that fit the specifications you just entered.
3. At the `Enter string to change:` prompt, enter **A**↵ to indicate you want to change the rest of the A attribute values.
4. At the `Enter new string:` prompt, enter **B**↵. A series of Bs appears, indicating the number of strings that were replaced.

WARNING *If the Regenauto command is off, you must regenerate the drawing to see the change.*

You may have noticed in the previous exercise that the `Select Attribute:` prompt is skipped and you go directly to the `String to change:` prompt. AutoCAD assumes that you want it to edit every attribute in the drawing, so it doesn't bother asking you to select specific attributes.

USING SPACES IN ATTRIBUTE VALUES

At times, you may want the default value to begin with a blank space. This enables you to specify text strings more easily when you edit the attribute. For example, you might have an attribute value that reads 3334333. If you want to change the first 3 in this string of numbers, you have to specify 3334 when prompted for the string to change. If you start with a space, as in _3334333 (I'm only using an underline here to represent the space; it doesn't mean you type an underline character), you can isolate the first 3 from the rest by specifying _3 as the string to change (again, type a space instead of the underline).

You must enter a backslash character (\) before the space in the default value to tell AutoCAD to interpret the space literally, rather than as a press of the spacebar (which is equivalent to pressing ↵).

Making Invisible Attributes Visible

You can edit invisible attributes, such as those in the door reference symbol, globally using the tools just described. You might, however, want to be a bit more selective about which invisible attribute you want to modify. Or you might simply want to make them temporarily visible for other editing purposes. This section describes how you can make invisible attributes visible.

1. Enter **Attdisp↵**.

TIP *You can also use the View menu to change the display characteristics of attributes. Choose View ➢ Display ➢ Attribute Display, and then click the desired option on the cascading menu.*

2. At the `Enter attribute visibility setting [Normal/ON/OFF] <Normal>:`prompt, enter **ON↵**. Your drawing will look like Figure 10.6. If Regenauto is turned off, you might have to issue the Regen command. At this point, you could edit the invisible attributes individually, as in the first attribute-editing exercise. For now, set the attribute display back to normal.

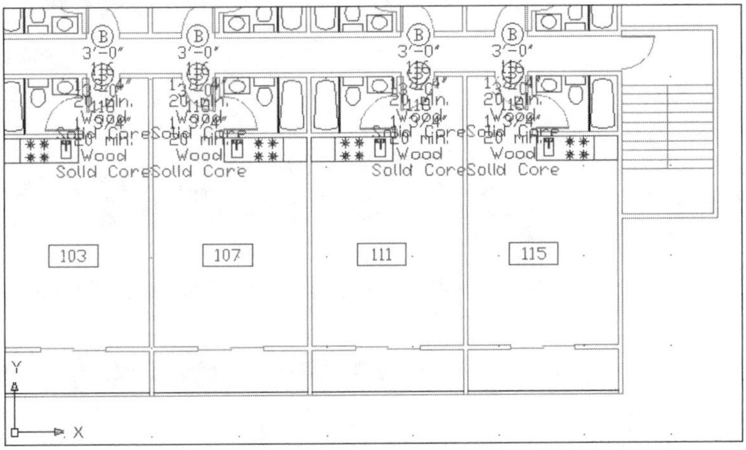

FIGURE 10.6
The drawing with all the attributes visible. (Door type symbols are so close together that they overlap.)

3. Enter **Attdisp↵** again; then at the `Enter attribute visibility setting [Normal/ON/OFF] <ON>:` prompt, enter **N↵** for normal.

TIP *You've seen the results of the On and Normal options. The Off option makes all attributes invisible, regardless of the mode used when they were created.*

Because the attributes were not intended to be visible, they appear to overlap and cover other parts of the drawing when they are made visible. Just remember to turn them back off when you are done reviewing them.

ACAD only

Making Global Format and Property Changes to Attributes

While we're on the subject of global editing, you'll want to know how to make global changes to the format and properties of attributes. Earlier in this section, you saw how you can make format changes to individual attributes using the Enhanced Attribute Editor dialog box. You can also use the Enhanced Attribute Editor dialog box to make global changes, as the following exercise demonstrates.

TIP *While LT does not support the Edit Attribute dialog box, you can use the command-line version of the Attedit command to edit some of the format and property values of attributes. Enter* ***-attedit*** ↵ *at the command line and follow the prompts.*

1. Choose Modify ➢ Object ➢ Attribute ➢ Block Attribute Manager to open the Block Attribute Manager dialog box.
2. Select S-APART from the Block drop-down list at the top of the dialog box. This list displays all the blocks that contain attributes. The only attribute you've defined for the selected block is displayed in the list box below it.

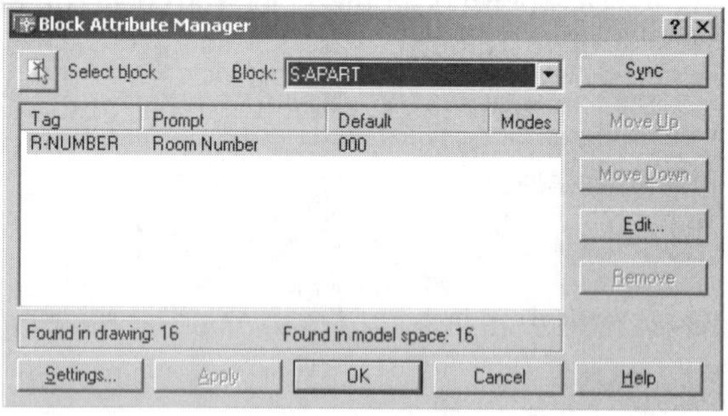

3. Click the attribute value in the list and click the Edit button to open the Edit Attribute dialog box.

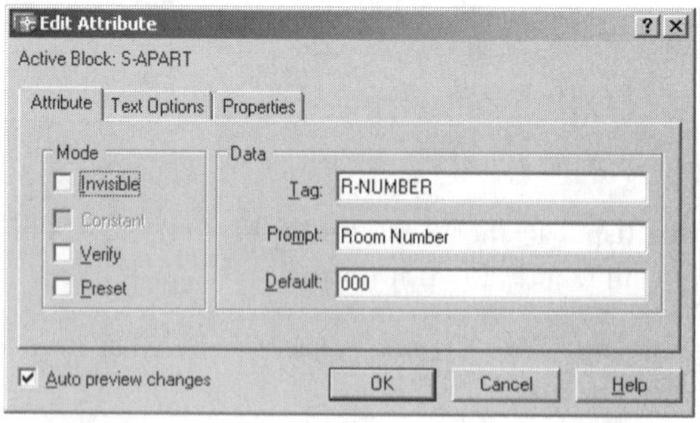

TIP *If there is only one attribute in the attribute list box, you don't have to select it before clicking the Edit button.*

The Edit Attribute dialog box is nearly identical to the Enhanced Attribute Editor you saw earlier in this section.

4. Click the Properties tab, select Red from the Color drop-down list, and click OK.
5. Click OK to exit the dialog box.

The Edit Attribute dialog box you saw in the previous exercise offers a slightly different set of options from those in the Enhanced Attribute Editor dialog box. In the Attribute tab of the Edit Attribute dialog box, you have the option to change some of the mode settings for the attribute, such as visibility and the Verify and Preset modes. You can also change the Tag, Prompt, and Default values.

You may recall that the Attribute tab in the Enhanced Attribute Editor dialog box allows you to change the attribute value but none of the other attribute properties.

Other Block Attribute Manager Options

There are a few other options in the Block Attribute Manager dialog box that weren't covered in the exercises. Here's a rundown of the Settings, Move Up, Move Down, and Remove buttons.

Settings Click this button to open the Settings dialog box, which lets you control which attribute properties are displayed in the list box of the Block Attribute Manager dialog box.

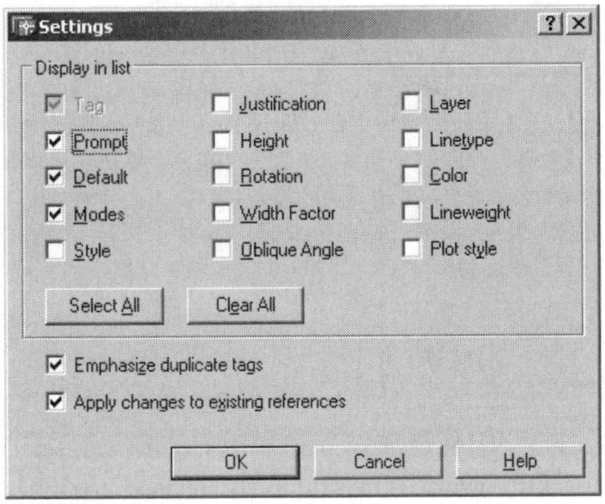

You can then select the properties to be displayed. The Emphasize Duplicate Tags option highlights duplicate tag names by showing them in red. The Apply Changes To Existing References option forces any changes you make to the attribute properties to be applied to existing attributes. If this setting is turned off, you have to use the Sync button to update existing attributes, and the changes you make to attribute properties are applied only to new attributes added after the change. You can also enter **Attsync↵** at the command prompt to synchronize older attributes.

Move Up And Move Down Clicking this button moves a selected attribute up and down the list of attributes in the list box. If you move an item down the list, the item will change its position when viewed using the Ddatte command or when viewing the attribute's properties in the Enhanced Attribute Editor dialog box. Of course, this only has an effect on blocks containing multiple attributes.

Remove Clicking this button removes the selected attribute from the block, so make sure you really mean it when you click this button.

ACAD only

Redefining Blocks Containing Attributes

Finally, you should be aware that attributes act differently from other objects when included in redefined blocks. Normally, blocks that have been redefined change their configuration to reflect the new block definition. But if a redefined block contains attributes, the attributes will maintain their old properties, including their position in relation to other objects in the block. This means that the old attribute position, style, and so on do not change even though you may have changed them in the new definition.

Fortunately, AutoCAD offers a tool specifically designed to let you update blocks with attributes. The following steps describe how to update attribute blocks.

1. Before you use the command to redefine an attribute block, you must first create the objects and attribute definitions that are going to make up the new replacement attribute block. The simplest way to do this is to explode a copy of the attribute block you want to update. This ensures that you have the same attribute definitions in the updated block.
2. Make your changes to the exploded attribute block.

WARNING *Before you explode the attribute block copy, be sure that it is at a 1-to-1 scale. This is important, because if you don't use the original size of the block, you could end up with all your new attribute blocks at the wrong size. Also be sure you use some marker device, such as a line, to locate the insertion point of the attribute block before you explode it. This will help you locate and maintain the original insertion point for the redefined block.*

3. Type **Attredef↵**.
4. At the `Enter name of block you wish to redefine:` prompt, enter the appropriate name.
5. At the `Select objects for new block:` prompt, select all the objects, including the attribute definitions, you want to include in the revised attribute block.
6. At the `Insertion base point of new block:` prompt, pick the same location used for the original block.

Once you pick the insertion point, AutoCAD takes a few seconds to update the blocks. The amount of time depends on the complexity of the block and the number of times the block occurs in the drawing. If you include a new attribute definition with your new block, it too will be added to all the updated blocks, with its default value. Attribute definitions that are deleted from your new definition will be removed from all the updated blocks.

TIP *You can also use the Refedit command (choose Modify ➢ Xref and Block Editing ➢ Edit Reference In-Place) to modify Attribute definitions. Once edited, you must use the Sync option in the Attribute Block Manager to update all instances of the modified block.*

COMMON USES FOR ATTRIBUTES

Using attributes is an easy way to combine editable text with graphic symbols without resorting to groups or separate text and graphic elements. One of the more common uses of attributes is in column grid symbols. Attributes are well suited for this purpose because they maintain their location in relation to the circle or hexagon shape usually used for grid symbols, and they can be easily edited.

Here is a portion of the San Francisco Main Library with a typical set of grid symbols. Each symbol contains an attribute similar to the one you created earlier for the room numbers. Other symbols in the figure, such as cut lines and detail bubbles, are also blocks with attributes for text.

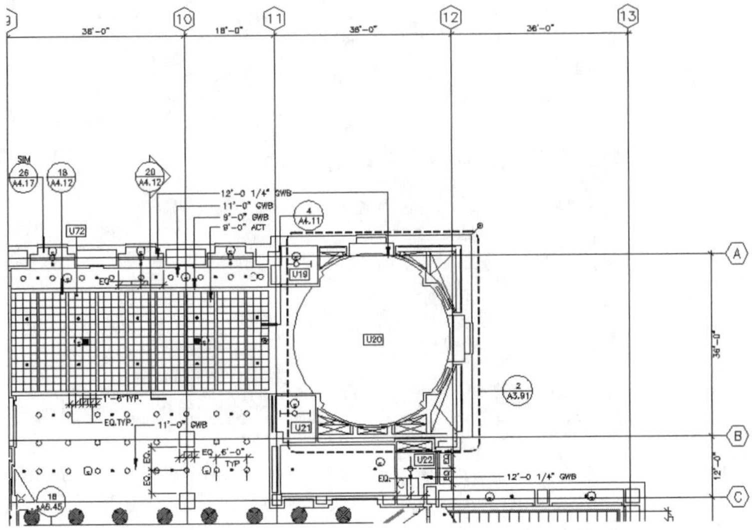

Extracting and Exporting Attribute Information

After you enter the attributes in your drawing, you can extract the information contained in the attributes and use it to generate reports or to analyze the attribute data in other programs. You might, for example, want to keep track of the number and type of doors in your drawing through a database manager. This is especially useful if you have a project such as a large hotel that contains thousands of doors.

When you extract attribute data, AutoCAD creates a text file. You can choose to export the file in either comma-delimited or tab-delimited format. If you have Microsoft Excel or Access installed, you can also export the attribute data in a format compatible with these programs.

Performing the Extraction

ACAD only

In the past, extracting the attribute data from a drawing was an error-prone task involving the creation of a template file. This template file had to contain a series of codes that described the data you wanted to extract.

AutoCAD 2004 has a greatly improved system for attribute data extraction, in the form of the Attribute Extraction Wizard. The following exercise will walk you through a sample extraction.

NOTE *LT does not offer the Attribute Extraction Wizard. Instead, you see the more simplified Attribute Extraction dialog box that offers the file format options (comma or space delimited or DXF output), the output filename, and template file options. For LT, the template file is used as an option to filter the attributes.*

1. Go back to the Plan file and choose Tools ➢ Attribute Extraction to start the Attribute Extraction Wizard.

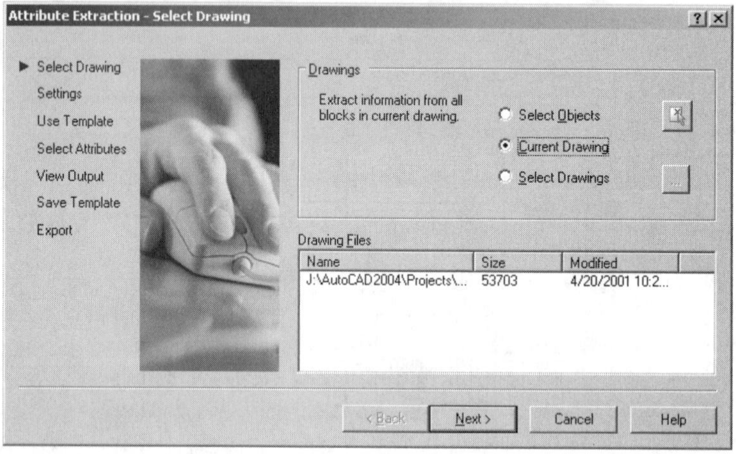

In the Select Drawing scree, you have can select specific blocks for the attribute data extraction. You can also select drawings other than the current drawing. The default is to select the entire current drawing. The name of the selected drawing files appears in the list box at the bottom of the dialog box.

2. Click Next to open the Settings screen. Here you can choose to extract attribute data from Xrefs and nested blocks.

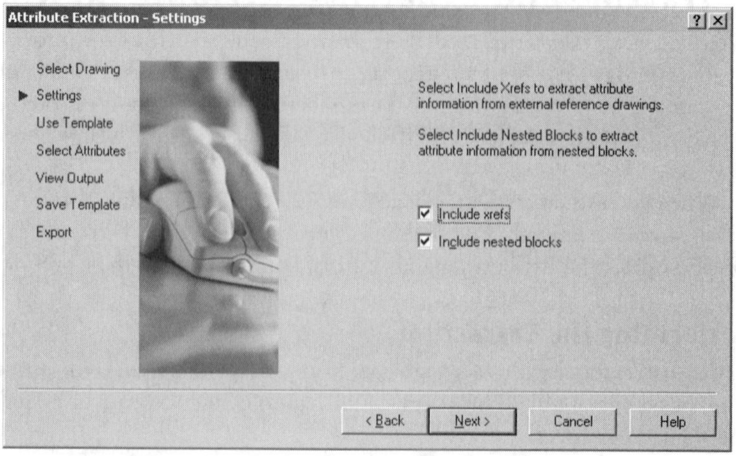

3. Click Next to open the Use Template screen.

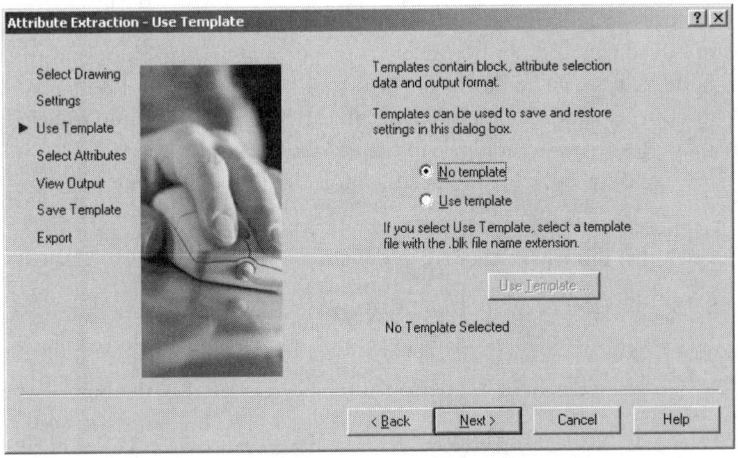

This screen allows you to import settings from an external file. Right now, it's not likely that you have any saved settings available, but in a later screen of the Attribute Extraction Wizard, you will have a chance to save the options you select as a template file that you can import in later Attribute Extraction sessions.

4. Click Next to open the Select Attributes screen.

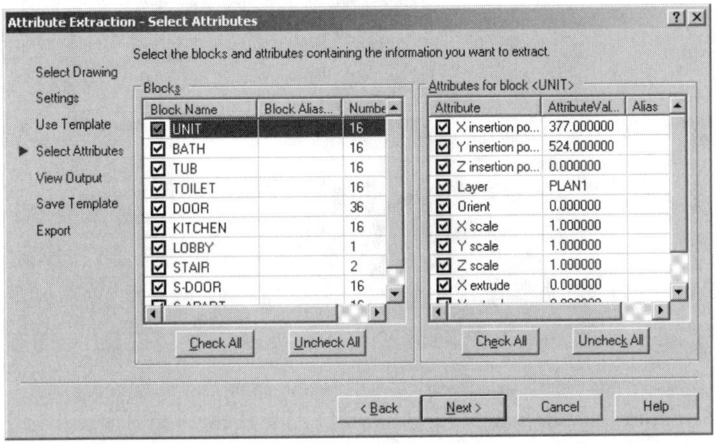

Selecting What to Extract

Take a moment to study the Select Attributes screen. It is the heart of the extraction process. Here you select the blocks that contain attributes as well as the specific attributes you want to extract.

Notice that in the left list box, all the blocks in the drawing are displayed—not just those that contain attributes. The Attribute For Block list box to the right displays attribute and block properties.

You can obtain some helpful information about your drawing just by looking at this screen. For example, you can find out how many copies of a particular block occur in the drawing by looking at the right column of the Blocks list box.

You can also add an alternate name in the Block Alias column to help better describe the block. An Alias option is also available in the Attribute For Block list box.

Let's continue by selecting specific information for the extraction.

1. Click the Uncheck All button at the bottom of the Blocks list to clear the boxes to the left of the list box.
2. Scroll down to the bottom of the Blocks list box and check the S-DOOR block name. Notice that the attribute list changes to show values for the selected block.
3. Click the Uncheck All button at the bottom of the Attributes For Block list.
4. Scroll down to the bottom of the Attributes For Block list and check all the attribute names. Remember that the attribute names are all prefixed with *D-*.
5. Click Next to open the View Output screen, which displays a listing of the attribute data that you selected in the previous screen. You see each attribute in order as you scroll down the list.

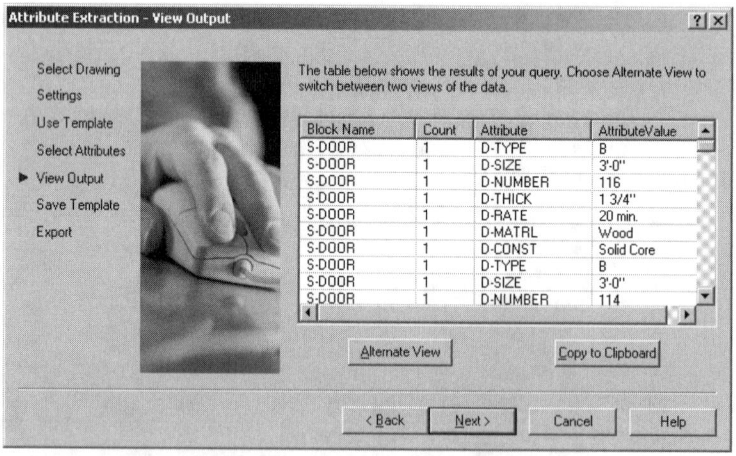

6. Click the Alternate View button. The list changes so that the attribute values are shown in a row and column matrix with each block listed as a row and the attributes of the block listed in columns. You can use the horizontal scroll bar at the bottom of the list to view all the columns.

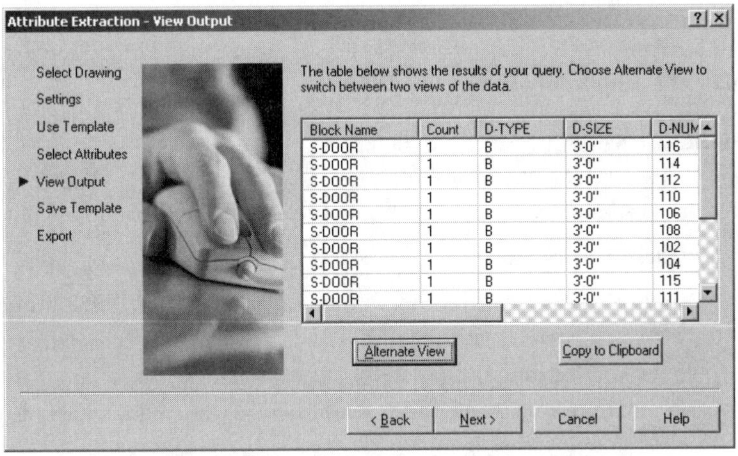

This alternate offers a clearer view of the data. Notice that every door is listed. When any attribute data differs in each block, the Attribute Extraction Wizard dutifully shows the data for each occurrence of the block. But suppose all the attribute data is the same for each block? The Attribute Extraction Wizard will then consolidate the data into a more compact form. Try the following to see how this works.

1. Click the Back button to return to the Select Attributes screen.
2. Go to the bottom of the Attributes For Block list and remove the check next to the D-NUMBER attribute. This is the only attribute that changes for each instance of the S-DOOR block, and you are no longer extracting it.
3. Click Next to return to the View Output screen. Now you see only a single listing for the S-DOOR block. But this time, a new column called *Count* has been added.

Because all the data is the same for each selected attribute, the Attribute Extraction Wizard lists the block name once and then tells you the number of times the block appears in the drawing under the Count column.

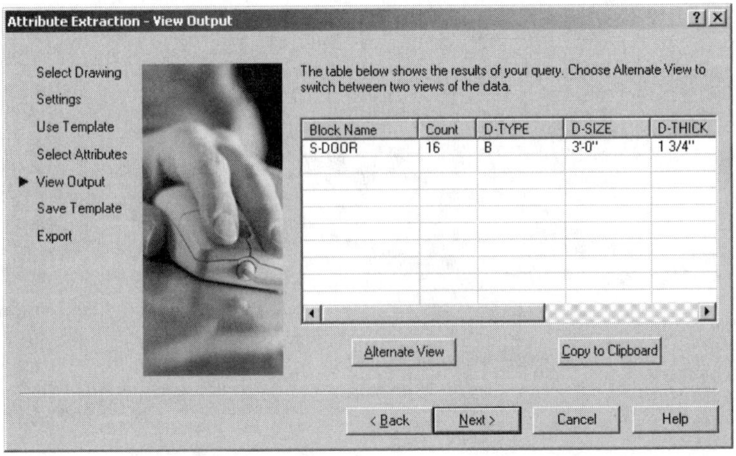

As you can see from the exercises so far, you can use the Attribute Extraction Wizard to quickly view attribute and block data without performing the entire extraction process. You can also copy the data to the Clipboard to save the data "on the fly."

SAVING THE ATTRIBUTE DATA TO A FILE

Now let's go ahead and complete the extraction process. First go back and restore the D-NUMBER attribute so you can get a complete listing of the S-DOOR data.

1. Click the Back button.
2. In the Attributes For Block list, make sure the D-NUMBER attribute is checked, and click Next to open the View Ouput screen.
3. Click Next again to open the Save Template screen. You may recall that earlier you had the option to recall a template file. This is where you can save a template file for subsequent recall.

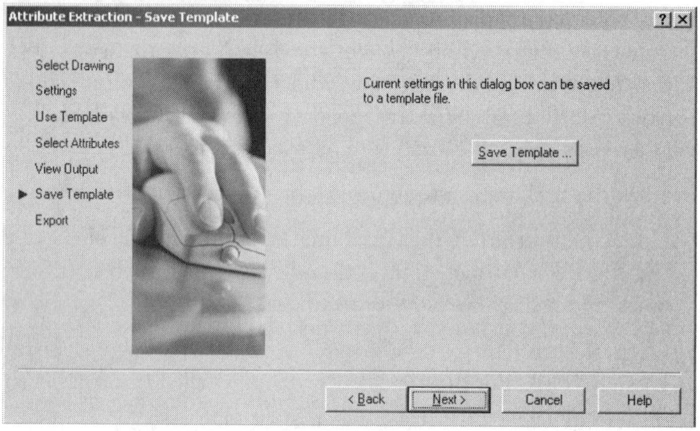

4. Click Next to open the Export screen. This is where you specify the filename and type of file you want to extract.

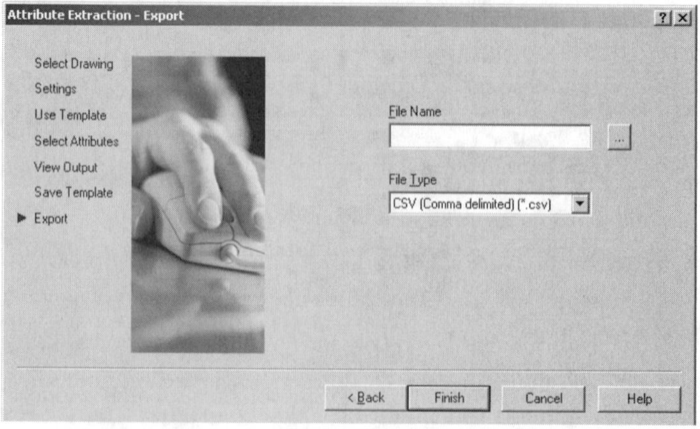

5. Click the File Type drop-down list and select Tab Delimited File (*.txt).
6. Click the ellipsis (...) button to the right of the File Name input box to open the Save As dialog box. Enter **Planattribute.**
7. Using the Save In drop-down list, locate the folder where you are storing your sample files for the exercises in this book, and click Save.
8. Back in the Export screen, click Finish to return to your drawing.

You now have a file called `Planattribute.txt` that contains the data you saw earlier in the View Output screen of the Attribute Extraction Wizard. You can import that data into any program that will accept a tab-delimited data file, including database, spreadsheet, and word-processing programs.

Using Extracted Attribute Data with Other Programs

In step 6 of the previous exercise, you also had the option to save the file in a CSV or comma-delimited format. This format is common to many Microsoft Office products. If you have Microsoft Excel or Access, you can also export files to the native formats of these programs.

USING A TEMPLATE FILE

If you prefer the older method of using a template file to determine which attributes to extract, you may do so using the command-line version of the Attext command. Enter **-Attext**↵ then follow the prompts. Make sure you have a template file ready.

A template file is a simple TXT file that contains the tag name of the attribute you wish to extract, followed by a code that determines the type of value being extracted and the spaces required. For example, a template file containing D-NUMBER C005000 tells AutoCAD to extract the D-NUMBER attribute. The code C005000 tells AutoCAD that D-NUMBER is a character value (C) that needs 5 spaces (005). The three zeros at the end are required place holders. If the value is numeric, the code would be N005001 where N denotes a numeric value, 005 denotes the number of spaces and 001 denotes the number of decimal places required. Each attribute entry requires a line in the template file.

If You Want to Experiment...

You can use attributes to help automate data entry into drawings. To demonstrate this, try the following exercise.

1. Create a drawing file called `Record` with the attribute definitions shown in Figure 10.7. Note the size and placement of the attribute definitions as well as the new base point for the drawing.
2. Save and exit the file, and then create a new drawing called `Schedule` containing the schedule shown in Figure 10.8.
3. Use the Insert command and insert the `Record` file into the schedule at the point indicated.

Note that you are prompted for each entry of the record. Enter any value you like for each prompt. When you are done, the information for one record is entered into the schedule.

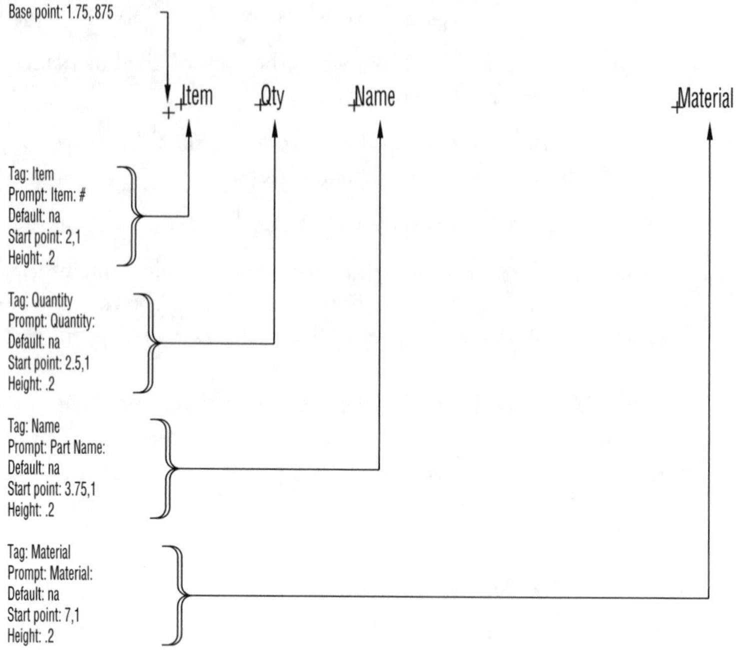

FIGURE 10.7
The Record file with attribute definitions

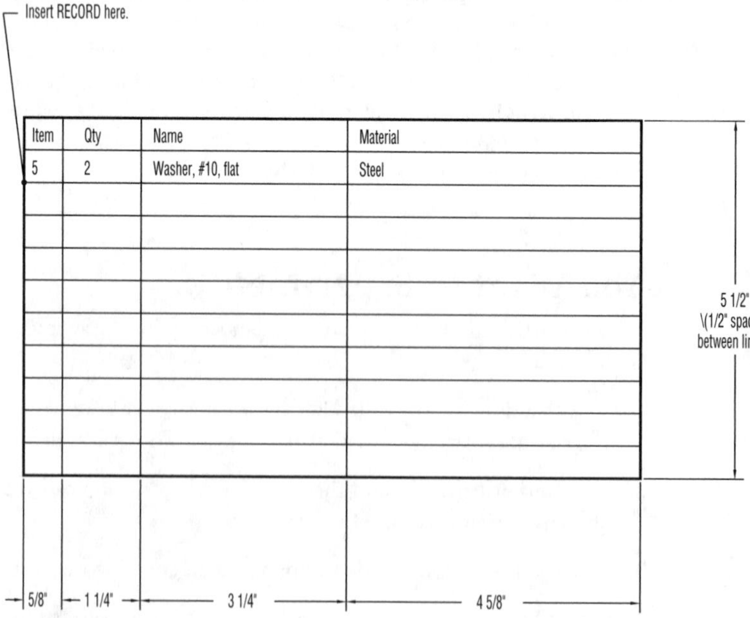

FIGURE 10.8
The Schedule drawing with Record inserted

Chapter 11

Working with External Databases

In Chapter 10, you worked with attributes, which offer a way to store data within an AutoCAD drawing. But you may find that you need a way to work with database information that is externally linked to your AutoCAD drawing. By doing so, you can use more sophisticated software tools to analyze the nongraphic data you need to work with in your design projects. For example, a facilities manager for a hospital might want to track equipment data using a database manager and, at the same time, use an AutoCAD drawing to help locate equipment in a floor plan. A mechanical engineer might want to link a parts list with a schematic drawing of a mechanical assembly. In this chapter, you'll look at the AutoCAD dbConnect Manager, which offers a way to link database files to AutoCAD drawings.

NOTE *The dbConnect feature is not available in AutoCAD LT 2004. If you are using LT, you can skip this chapter, or you can review the material presented here if you plan to upgrade to AutoCAD 2004.*

This chapter covers the following topics:

- Accessing External Databases
- Setting Up Your System for Database Access
- Opening a Database from AutoCAD
- Linking Objects to a Database
- Adding Labels with Links to a Database
- If You Want to Experiment...

Accessing External Databases

You can access an external database from within AutoCAD through the dbConnect Manager, a tool that lets you read and manipulate data from external database files. You can also use dbConnect Manager to *link* parts of your drawing to an external database.

There are numerous reasons for doing this. The most obvious is to keep inventory on parts of your drawing. If you are an interior designer doing office planning, you can link inventory data from a database to your drawing, with a resulting decrease in the size of your drawing file. If you are a facilities manager, you can track the movement of people and facilities using AutoCAD linked to a database file.

This section will avoid the more complex programming issues of database management systems, and it does not discuss the SQL language, which can be used to query and edit your database files through the dbConnect Manager. Still, you should be able to make good use of the dbConnect Manager with the information provided here. You'll also be departing from the studio apartment example to make use of an office plan example that has already been created by Autodesk.

AUTOCAD AND YOUR DATABASE

These exercises assume that you are somewhat familiar with databases. For example, these exercises will refer frequently to something called a table. A *table* is an SQL term referring to the row-and-column data structure of a typical database file. Other terms I'll use are *rows*, which are the records in a database, and *columns*, which refer to the database fields. Finally, it is important that you follow the instructions in these beginning exercises carefully. If you miss anything in the beginning, later exercises will not work properly. AutoCAD uses Windows Open Database Connectivity (ODBC) and OLE DB to help link drawings to databases. ODBC and OLE DB are software interfaces that let diverse programs connect to a variety of different types of databases. They serve as translators between the program, which in this case is AutoCAD, and the database file you want your program to "talk to." Before ODBC and OLE DB can do their translating, you need to install a driver that allows these interface tools to communicate with the particular database type you want to work with.

Due to the diverse methods used to connect to database files, you should consult with the documentation of your database program before attempting to link your particular set of data files to AutoCAD. In the examples in this chapter, you'll use an OLE DB interface to link to a sample Microsoft Access file.

Setting Up Your System for Database Access

The dbConnect Manager doesn't create new database files. You must use existing files or create them in the database program yourself before you use this tool. In addition, you will need to set up a Data Link file that will direct AutoCAD to the database file you want to work with. You can create a Data Link file through AutoCAD's dbConnect Manager. Once you've created and set up a Data Link file, you can begin to access and link databases to AutoCAD drawings.

In the first set of exercises, you'll learn how to create a new Data Link file that tells AutoCAD where to look for database information. Then for the rest of the tutorial, you will use a Microsoft Access file from the CD included with this book. The file, called `db-Mastersample.mdb`, is installed when you install the sample figures from the CD. Look for it among those files.

The `db-mastersample.mdb` file contains three tables: Computer, Employee, and Inventory. The contents of the Employee table are shown in Figure 11.1.

FIGURE 11.1

The contents of the Employee table from the `db-mastersample.mdb` file

EMP_ID	LAST_NAME	FIRST_NAME	DEPT	TITLE	ROOM	EXT
1000	Meredith	Dave	Sales	V.P.	101	8600
1001	Williams	Janice	Sales	Western Region Mgr.	102	8601
1003	Smith	Jill	Sales	Central Region Mgr.	104	8603
1004	Nelson	Kirk	Sales	Canadian Sales Mgr.	109	8640
1005	Clark	Karl	Sales	Educational Sales Mgr.	106	8605
1006	Wilson	Cindy	Accounting	Accountant	109	8606
1007	Ortega	Emilio	Accounting	Accountant	109	8607
1008	Benson	Adam	Accounting	Accountant	109	8608
1009	Rogers	Kevin	Accounting	Accountant	109	8609
1011	Thompson	Frank	Engineering	Mechanical Engineer	123	8611
1012	Simpson	Paul	Engineering	Mechanical Engineer	124	8612
1013	Debrine	Todd	Engineering	Design Engineer	125	8613
1014	Frazier	Heather	Engineering	Application Engineer	126	8614
1016	Taylor	Patrick	Engineering	Software Engineer	128	8616
1017	Chang	Yuan	Engineering	Software Engineer	129	8617
1018	Dempsy	Phil	Engineering	Application Engineer	112	8618
1019	Kahn	Jenny	Engineering	Programmer	113	8619
1020	Moore	George	Engineering	Programmer	114	8620
1021	Price	Mark	Engineering	Software Engineer	115	8621
1022	Quinn	Scott	Engineering	Software Engineer	116	8622
1023	Sanchez	Maria	Engineering	Mechanical Engineer	117	8623
1024	Ross	Ted	Engineering	Application Engineer	118	8624
1025	Saunders	Terry	Engineering	Software Engineer	119	8625
1026	Fong	Albert	Engineering	Programmer	120	8626

Creating a Data Link File

A Data Link file is like a switchboard that connects applications to database files. The application can be anything that requires Data Link files for database connections, not just AutoCAD. You can have as many Data Link files as you need for your application, and as you'll see, you can access all of them from the AutoCAD dbConnect Manager.

1. Open the `dbSample.dwg` file from the `\Program Files\AutoCAD2004\Projects` folder. This is the folder where the sample files from the Mastering AutoCAD CD are stored.

2. Choose Tools ➢ dbConnect, type **dbc**↵, or press Crtl+6 to open the dbConnect Manager palette.

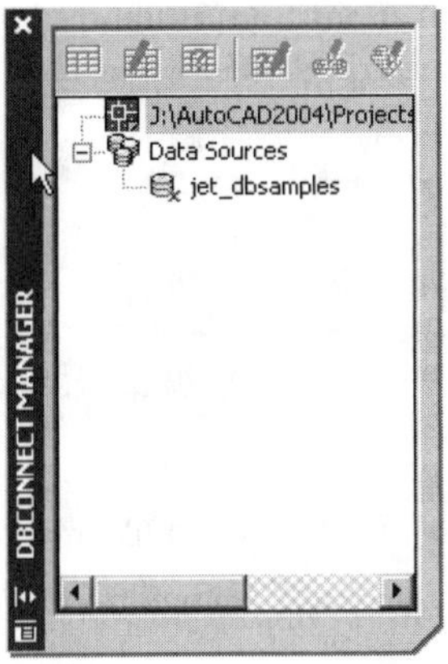

3. Right-click the Data Sources listing, and choose Configure Data Source to open the Configure A Data Source dialog box. You can also choose dbConnect ➢ Data Sources ➢ Configure.

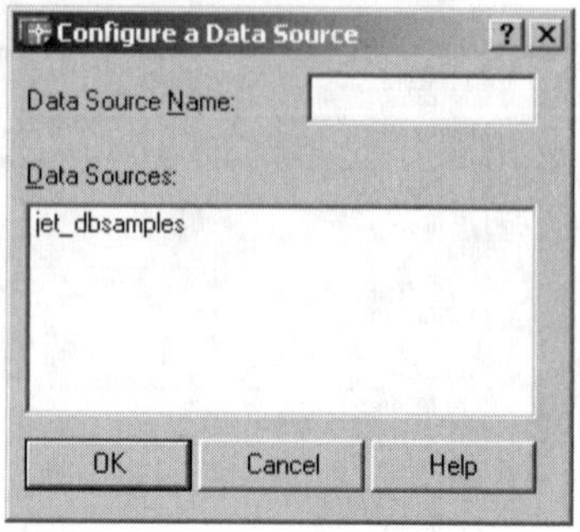

4. In the Data Source Name input box, enter **My Acad Data Link**, and then click OK to open the Data Link Properties dialog box.

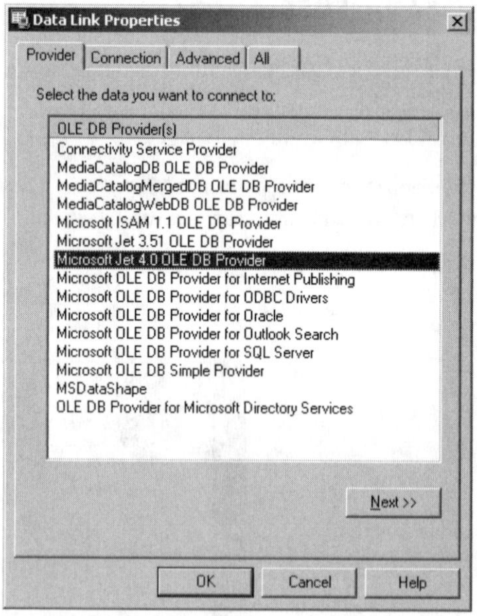

5. Select the Microsoft Jet 4.0 OLE DB Provider listing, and then click Next. The Connection tab opens to display a different set of options.

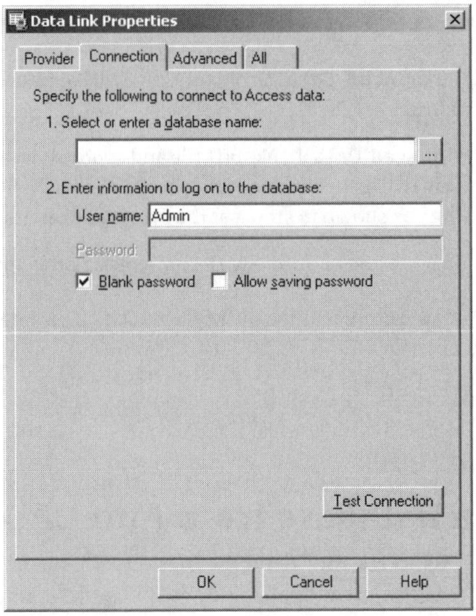

6. To the right of the Select Or Enter Database Name input box, click the ellipses button to open the Select Access Database dialog box. This is a typical file dialog box.

7. Select the `db_mastersample.mdb` file that is in the Chapter 10 folder of the sample files installed from the companion CD.
8. Click the Test Connection button to check the connection to the database file.
9. Click OK. You'll see the My Acad Data Link data source name listed in the dbConnect Manager.

You've just created a Data Link (UDL) file. You can find the UDL files in the `C:\Documents and Settings\`*`Your Name`*`\Application Data\Autodesk\AutoCAD 2004\R16\enu\Data Links` folder. *`Your Name`* is the name you use to log in to Windows. If you are uncertain of the data link file location, open the Files tab of the Options dialog box (Tools ➢ Options) and look under the Data Source Location listing to find its exact location.

Creating a Data Link File in Windows

You can also create a new Data Link File outside AutoCAD using Windows Explorer.

1. In Windows Explorer, locate the Data Links folder. Typically, this is in `C:\Documents and Settings\`*`Your Name`*`\Application Data\Autodesk\AutoCAD 2004\R16\enu\Data Links`.
2. Right-click a blank area in the folder listing, and choose New ➢ Text Document. A new file appears, called `New Text Document.txt`.

Continued on next page

CREATING A DATA LINK FILE IN WINDOWS *(continued)*

3. Rename this file `My Acad Data Link.udl`. You will see a warning message that the file may become unusable. Click Yes.
4. Right-click the `My Acad Data Link.udl` file and choose Properties from the shortcut menu to open the My Acad Data Link.UDL Properties dialog box. This dialog box is basically the same as the Data Link Properties dialog box shown in step 4 of the previous exercise.
5. Click the Provider tab and continue with step 5 of the previous exercise.

Once you take these steps, you will see the My Acad Data Link data source listed in the dbConnect Manager the next time you open it.

Opening a Database from AutoCAD

Now you're ready to access your database files directly from AutoCAD. You've done the work of establishing a connection to a database. Now all you have to do is open the database using the dbConnect Manager.

1. In the dbConnect Manager, right-click the `My Acad Data Link`, and choose Connect from the shortcut menu to display the listing of the tables in the Access database file below `My Acad Data Link`.

2. Click the Employee listing, then click the Edit Table tool in the dbConnect Manager palette, or right-click the Employee listing and choose Edit Table to open the Data View dialog box. (You can also double-click the Employee listing.) Your view of the data may be wider than the one shown here.

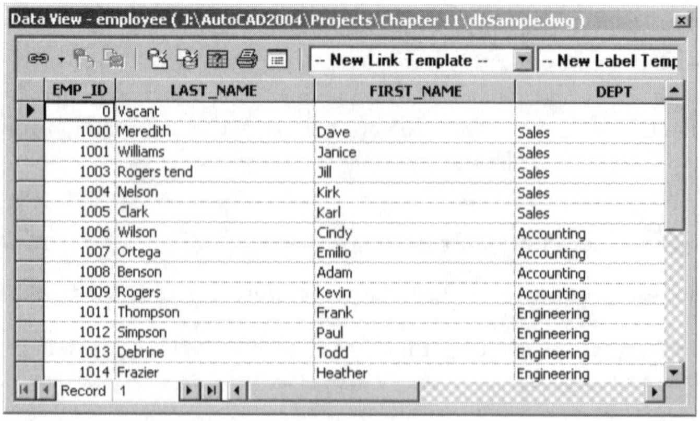

Data View - employee (J:\AutoCAD2004\Projects\Chapter 11\dbSample.dwg)
-- New Link Template --
-- New Label Temp
EMP_ID
LAST_NAME
FIRST_NAME
DEPT
0 Vacant
1000 Meredith Dave Sales
1001 Williams Janice Sales
1003 Rogers tend Jill Sales
1004 Nelson Kirk Sales
1005 Clark Karl Sales
1006 Wilson Cindy Accounting
1007 Ortega Emilio Accounting
1008 Benson Adam Accounting
1009 Rogers Kevin Accounting
1011 Thompson Frank Engineering
1012 Simpson Paul Engineering
1013 Debrine Todd Engineering
1014 Frazier Heather Engineering
Record 1

TIP *If you right-click the label at the top of each field in the Data View dialog box, a shortcut menu lets you sort the table by values in the field, control alignment of the field values, and perform simple find or replace functions. You can also resize the column widths by clicking and dragging the borders between the column headings.*

You are now connected to the Employee table of the `db-Mastersample.mdb` database.

Take a moment to look at the dbConnect Manager palette. (You might need to move the Data View dialog box out of the way to do so.) At the top is a set of buttons that duplicate the options you saw in step 4 in the shortcut menu. Also notice that you now have two more options in the menu bar: dbConnect and Data View. Most of the options in these two pull-down menus are duplicated in other parts of the dbConnect Manager palette and the Data View dialog box.

You've already seen that dbConnect's Edit Table tool opens the Data View dialog box to allow you to edit a database table. The View tool opens a view of the database, without allowing you to edit anything. You'll learn about the functions of the New Link and New Label template options later in this tutorial.

Finding a Record in the Database

Now that you are connected to the database, suppose you want to find the record for a specific individual. You might already know that the individual you're looking for is in the Accounting department.

1. Click the Query icon in the Data View toolbar to open the New Query dialog box.

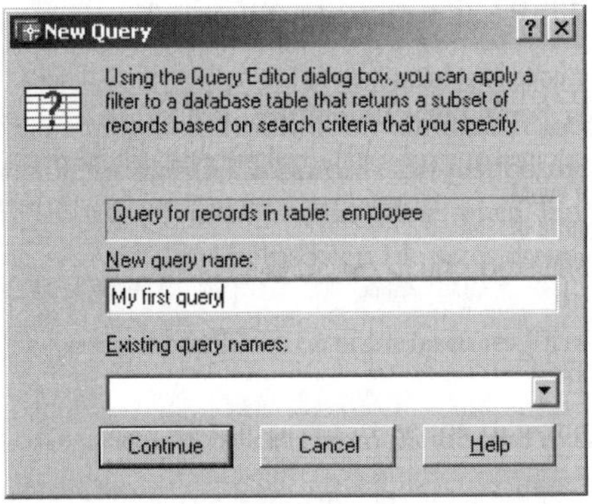

2. In the New Query Name input box, type **My first query**. You can save queries under different names in case you need to repeat a query later.
3. Click Continue to open the Query Editor dialog box.

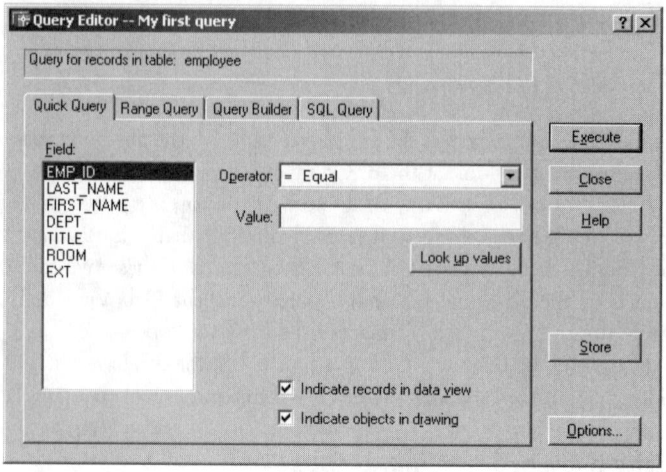

The Query Editor dialog box lets you set the criteria for your query. As you can see from the numerous tabs, you can use several methods to query the database. Try using the Quick Query method, which is the tab already selected.

4. Highlight DEPT in the Field list box.
5. Click the Look Up Values button to display a listing of the DEPT categories.

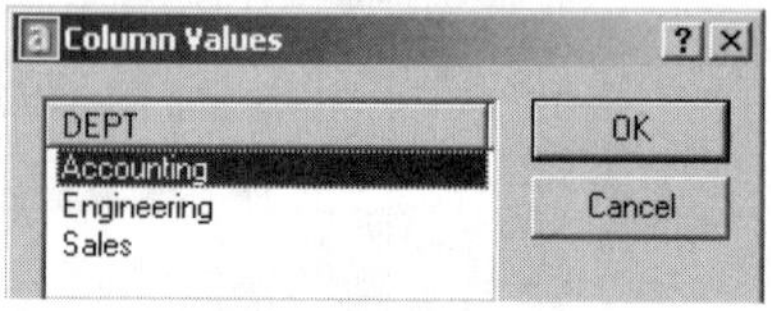

6. Select Accounting from the list and click OK.
7. Click Store. This saves the current query under the name that you entered in the New Query dialog box. The name *My first query* appears in the dbConnect Manager palette, just under the drawing name.
8. Click Execute. The Data View dialog box changes to show only the Accounting department records.

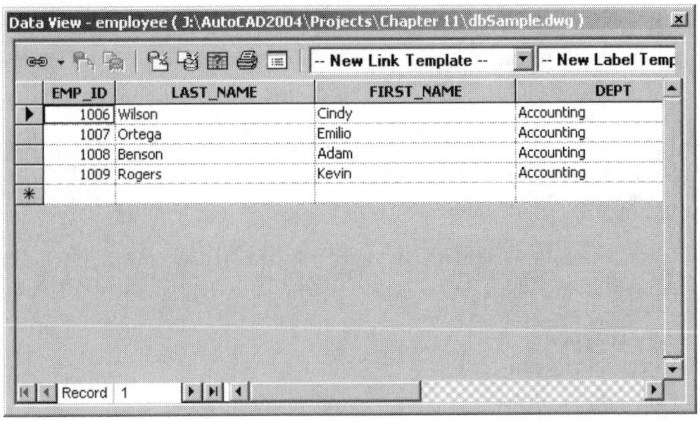

9. After reviewing the results of this exercise, right-click the Employee listing in the dbConnect Manager palette and choose Edit Table from the shortcut menu to restore the view of the entire table.

You've just seen how you can locate and view a set of records in a database. If you want to edit any of those records, you only need to highlight the field of a record you want to change and then enter a new value. If you open the Data View dialog box using the View option in the dbConnect Manager palette, you are locked out of making changes to your database. In some cases, the View option is the only option available to access a database. You might be limited to the View option if the database is locked or if the OLE DB provider for a database does not allow editing.

You used the Store option to store your query. Once you've stored a query, you can quickly re-execute it from the dbConnect Manager palette. Right-click the query name and choose Execute from the shortcut menu. You can also modify a stored query. Right-click the query name in the dbConnect Manager palette and choose Edit Query from the shortcut menu to open the Query Editor dialog box, in which you can make changes and re-execute your query. Other options in the shortcut menu allow you to rename the query or delete it altogether.

TIP *You can also launch a new query from the dbConnect Manager palette. Right-click the database filename and choose New Query to open the New Query dialog box. You can then proceed with your query, just as you did in this exercise.*

The ability to access databases in this way can help you connect AutoCAD graphic data with database information. For example, you might want to keep track of tenant information in your studio apartment building. As you will see later, you can actually link graphics to database records so you can quickly access data regarding a particular tenant. Another application might be generating a bill of materials for a mechanical project, in which records in the database relate to parts in a mechanical assembly.

Adding a Row to a Database Table

Now let's get back to our office example. Suppose you have a new employee who needs to be set up in an office. The first thing you need to do is add their name to the database. Here's how it's done.

1. In the Data View dialog box, right-click any button to the far left of the table and choose New Record from the shortcut menu. A blank row appears, and the cursor appears in the first field of the row for entering data.
2. Enter the following data in the blank row. To add an item, click the appropriate field, and then enter the new data. After you type the new data, press the Tab key to move to the next field.

   `EMP_ID` **`2000`**
   `LAST_NAME` **`Ryan`**
   `FIRST_NAME` **`Roma`**
   `DEPT` **`Creative Resources`**
   `TITLE` **`Producer/Lyricist`**
   `ROOM` **`122`**
   `EXT` **`8888`**

3. Press ↵ after entering the last entry. You've just added a new record to the database.

KEEPING YOUR WINDOWS ORGANIZED

If you plan to work with a database for an extended period of time, you will find it easier to work with the dbConnect Manager palette and the Data View dialog box by docking them in your AutoCAD windows.

First, maximize the AutoCAD window to fill your entire screen. Next, right-click the title bar of either the palette or the dialog box and make sure that Allow Docking is checked in the shortcut menu. Move both the palette and the dialog box into the AutoCAD window. You can place the dbConnect Manager palette on either side of the window and Data View at the bottom. Although this reduces the size of your AutoCAD drawing window, it will help you keep the dbConnect Manager palette and the Data View dialog box out of your way and in a place that is accessible.

Linking Objects to a Database

So far, you've looked at ways you can access and edit an external database file. You can also *link* specific drawing objects to elements in a database. This can be useful as a means to quickly obtain data about a specific object in a drawing.

Before you can link your drawing to data, you must create a *link template*. Link templates let you set up different sets of links to a database. For example, you can set up a link template that associates all the phones in your AutoCAD drawing with specific records in your database file. Another link template can link the room numbers in your drawing to the LAST_NAME records in your database file.

This section will show you how to create a link to the database by linking your new employee to one of the vacant rooms.

Creating a Link

In the following set of exercises, you will link an AutoCAD object to the record you just added to the Employee database table. The first step is to set up a link template.

1. Close the Data View dialog box.

2. Highlight the Employee table listing in the dbConnect Manager palette, and then click the New Link Template tool in the dbConnect toolbar to open the NewLink Template dialog box. You can also right-click the Employee listing and select New Link Template from the shortcut menu.

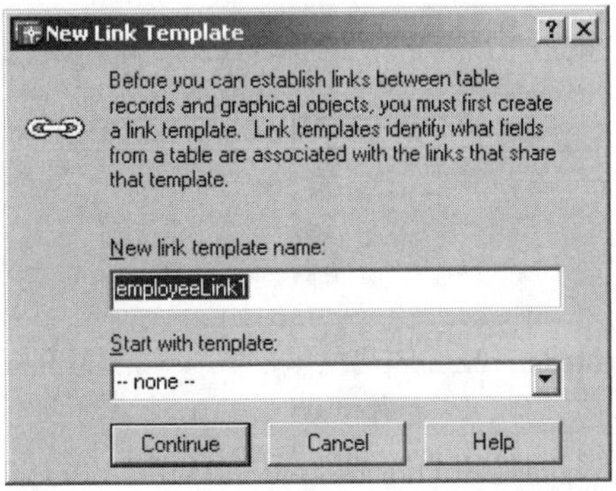

Notice that the format of the NewLink Template dialog box is similar to that of the New Query dialog box. You can enter a name for your link template in the New Link Template Name input box.

3. Enter **Room Number** for the name and click Continue to open the Link Template dialog box.

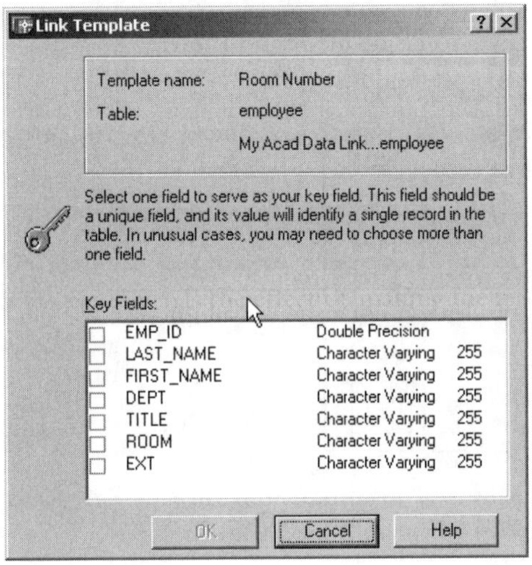

The Link Template dialog box lets you select a field to act as your key field. You can select more than one field for your key field.

TIP A key field is any field whose values uniquely identify that table. For example, the set of values of the Employee ID field is unique to this table. You can further improve uniqueness by including another field, such as the room numbers. The choice of fields is somewhat arbitrary, but you will want to select fields that will not change frequently.

4. Click LAST_NAME and ROOM; then click OK. Now the Room Number template appears in the dbConnect Manager palette.

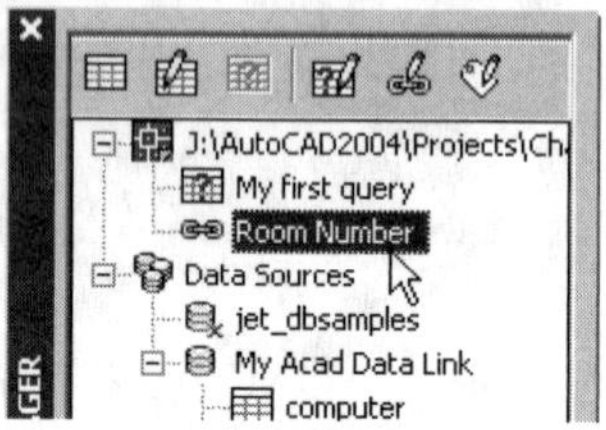

You've just created a link template. You'll see your link template listed in the dbConnect Manager palette under the drawing name. If you need to edit this link template, you can do so by right-clicking its name and choosing Edit or by double-clicking the template. Right now, you'll continue to add a link between your drawing and the database.

You are ready to add a link to room 122. The first step is to set up your AutoCAD drawing so you can easily access the rooms you will be linking to. You will then locate the record that is associated with room 122 in the Data View dialog box.

1. Zoom in to the set of rooms in the lower-right corner of the plan so your view looks like Figure 11.2.

FIGURE 11.2
The view of the drawing showing the rooms to the right of 122

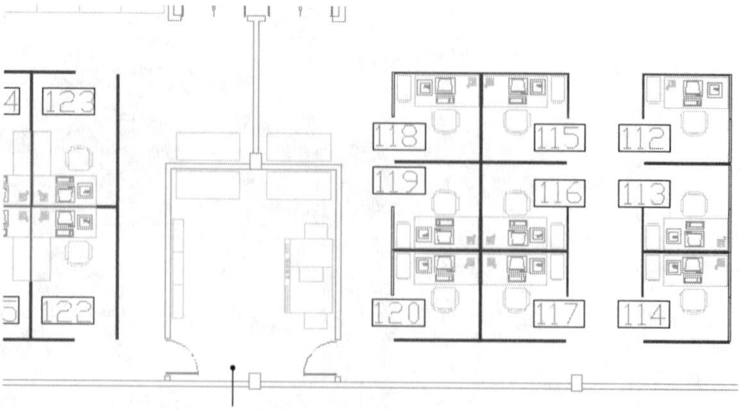

2. Click the Employee listing in the dbConnect Manager palette, and click the Edit Table tool in the dbConnect Manager palette toolbar to open the Data View dialog box. Notice that *Room Number* appears in the list box in the toolbar. This tells you which link template you are using. If you have more than one link template, you can select the link template you want to use from this list box.

3. Scroll down the records to locate the record you added in the previous exercise. You can also use the New Query option to isolate the record, or you can quickly go to the end of the records by clicking the end-of-table navigation arrow at the bottom of the dialog box.

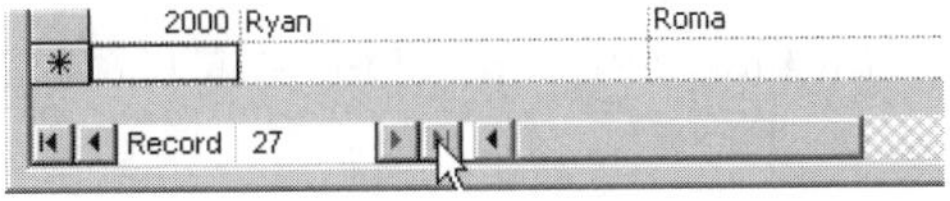

4. Once you've found the record, click any field of the record.

5. Click the Link And Label Settings tool in the toolbar and make sure that the Create Links option is selected. This option determines what type of link AutoCAD will create.

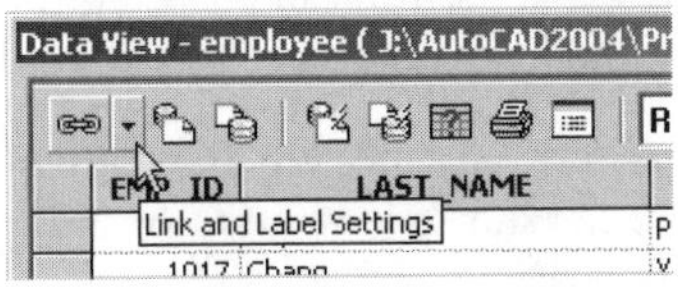

6. Click the Link tool in the left end of the toolbar. The Data View dialog box closes, and you see the selection cursor in the AutoCAD window.

7. Click the room number 122 and the phone in the upper-left corner of the room. If you accidentally select a different object, you can Shift+click the object to remove it from the selection.

8. Press ↵ to finish your selection. The Data View dialog box returns. Now you see that the record is highlighted in yellow, indicating that it is linked to an object in the current drawing.

9. In the Data View dialog box, link the records for rooms 116 and 114 to the same room numbers in the drawing. Remember to first select the record you want to link, click the Link tool, and then select the room number you want to link to. Room 116 is assigned to employee number 1022, and room number 114 is assigned to employee 1020.

Now you have a link established between the records for rooms 122, 116, and 114 in the database and their room numbers in your drawing. Next you'll learn how you can use those links to locate objects in the drawing or records in your database.

Locating Database Records through Drawing Objects

Now that you've got database links established, you can begin to make use of them. In the following exercise, you'll see how you can locate a database record by selecting an object in your drawing.

1. Go to the top of the table by clicking the first-record button at the bottom-left corner of the Data View dialog box.

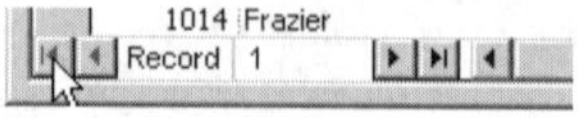

2. Click the View Linked Records In Data View button in the Data View toolbar to close the dialog box.
3. Click the telephone in the upper-left corner of room 122, and then click room numbers 114 and 116.
4. Press ↵ when you've completed your selections. The Data View dialog box appears again with the records for employees 1020, 1022, and 2000.

As you can see from step 3, you can select several objects. AutoCAD isolates all the records that are linked to the selected objects. You can go a step further and have AutoCAD display only the records associated with the linked objects.

1. Right-click the Room Number link template in the dbConnect Manager palette, and choose Link Select from the shortcut menu to open the Link Select dialog box.

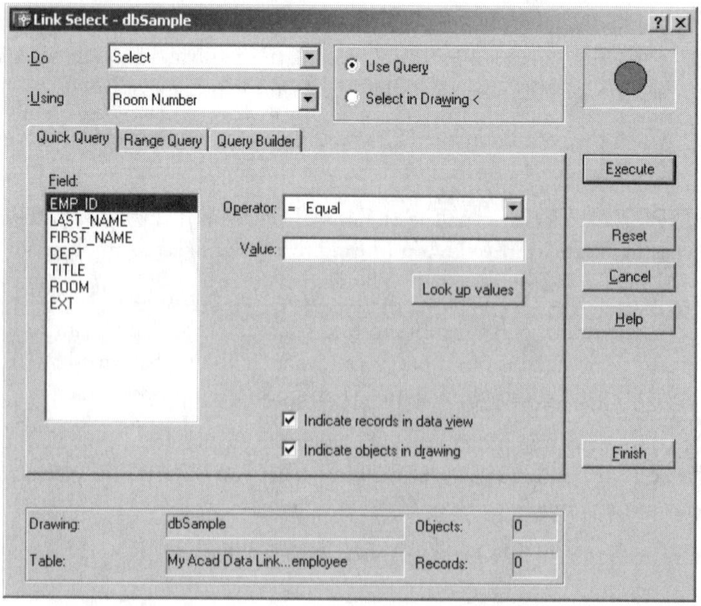

2. Click the Select In Drawing < radio button. Notice that the Execute button changes into a Select button.
3. Click the Select button. The dialog box disappears to allow you to select objects in the drawing.
4. Select room number 116 and press ↵. The Link Select dialog box reappears.
5. Click Finish. The Data View dialog box now displays only the record linked to the room number you selected.

The Link Select dialog box offers many more features that allow you to locate data either within your drawing or in your database.

Finding and Selecting Graphics through the Database

You've just seen how you can use links to locate records in a database. Links can also help you find and select objects in a drawing that are linked to a database. The next exercise shows, in a simplified way, how this works.

1. Click the Employee listing in the dbConnect Manager palette, and then click the Edit Table tool to open the entire table. You can also just double-click the Employee listing.

2. In the Data View dialog box, select the record for employee 2000. You can click the last-record button at the bottom-left of the Data View dialog box to take you there.

3. Click the View Linked Objects In Drawing tool in the Data View toolbar.
4. Move the Data View dialog box out of the way temporarily so you can view your drawing. Notice that the room number 122 and the telephone are highlighted and their grips are exposed. These are the objects in the drawing that are linked to employee 2000 in the data view dialog box.

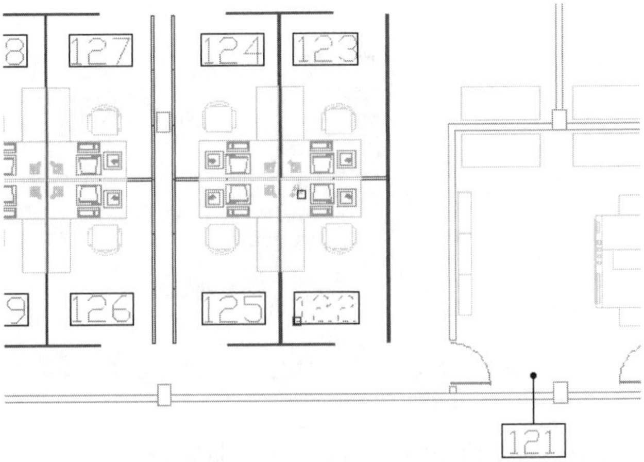

After you take these steps, you can use the Previous Object Selection option to select those objects that were highlighted in step 3.

In this example, you only selected objects in one office. However, you can create a record called Vacant and then link all the vacant offices to this one record. When a new employee is hired, you can then quickly locate all the vacant rooms in the floor plan to place the new employee. If you continue to link each database record with rooms in the drawing, you can then later locate a person's room through the same process.

Adding Labels with Links to a Database

Database links can help you add labels to a drawing by using the data from a database table for the label text. The following exercise will show how you can add the employee name and telephone extension number to the sample drawing.

1. In the Data View dialog box, click the Link And Label Settings tool in the toolbar and make sure that the Create Freestanding Labels option is selected. When you do this, the tool to the left changes to the Create Freestanding Label tool.

2. Click the button to the left of employee number 2000 to select that record.
3. Click the Create Freestanding Label tool in the toolbar to open the New Label Template dialog box.

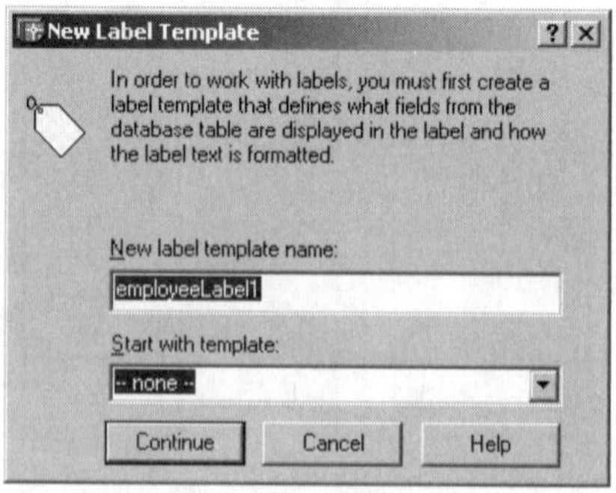

4. Enter the name **Employee Names**, and click Continue to open the Label Template dialog box. Notice that it looks quite similar to the Text Formatting dialog box.

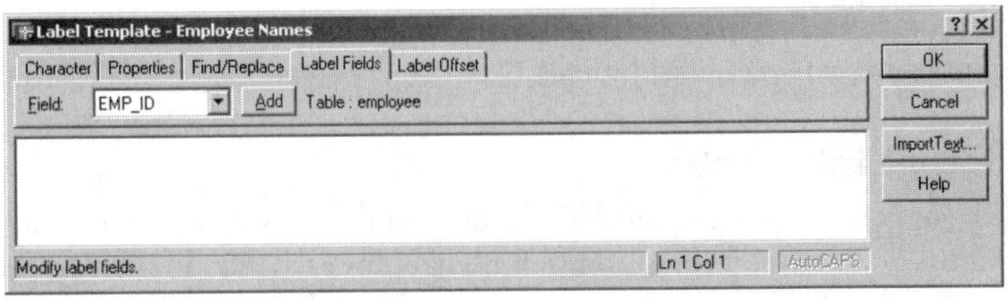

5. Click the Character tab.
6. Click the Text Height drop-down list and enter **6**↵.
7. Click the Label Fields tab.
8. Select Last Name from the Field drop-down list, and click Add. The LAST_NAME entry appears in the text box.
9. Select Title from the Field drop-down list, and click Add again. The TITLE entry appears in the text box.
10. Click OK. The dialog box closes, and the point selection cursor appears in the AutoCAD window.
11. Click a clear location in room 122. The last name and title of employee 2000 appear as text in the drawing. Notice that these are the actual field values from the record you selected in step 2 and the fields you selected in steps 5 and 6.

Notice that now you have a listing in the dbConnect Manager palette called Employee Names. This is the Label template you created in steps 4 through 10. Next, you'll add a few more employee name labels to the floor plan. First, you'll turn on the AutoView Linked Objects In Drawing tool so you can pan to the selected room number automatically. Then you'll proceed to add the new labels.

1. In the Data View dialog box, click the AutoView Linked Objects In Drawing tool to open the Data View dialog box.
2. Click the button to the far left of the record for employee number 1020. Your view of the drawing pans to the link in room 114 that is already established in the drawing.
3. Click the Create Freestanding Label tool.
4. In the drawing, click a clear space in room 114 to place the label.
5. In the Data View dialog box, select the record for employee number 1022, and then click the Create Freestanding Label tool.
6. In the drawing, click a free space in room 116 to place a label there.

Each label you add is linked to its corresponding record in the database. Notice that the label template appears just below the link template in the dbConnect Manager palette. This tells you that the label template is dependent on the link template.

If you want to create labels based on different field data, you can create other label templates that include different sets of field values.

Adding Linked Labels

Now suppose you want to label all the links in the drawing automatically. For example, suppose you want to show the telephone extension number for each link. In the next exercise, you'll create a new label template for the telephone extension field of the database table.

1. In the dbConnect Manager palette, highlight the Employee listing; then click the New Label Template tool or right-click and select New Label Template from the shortcut menu to open the New Label Template dialog box.
2. Enter **Extension** in the input box, and then click Continue to open the Label Template dialog box.
3. Select the Character tab.
4. Highlight the value in the Font Height drop-down list and enter **8↵**.
5. Click the Label Fields tab and select Ext from the Field drop-down list.
6. Click Add and then OK to exit the dialog box.

You now have a label template for the telephone extension numbers. This label template is also dependent on the link template you created earlier in this set of exercises. You can use this template to automatically add phone extension labels to the drawing.

1. In the Data View dialog box, make sure the Extension label template appears in the Label Template drop-down list.
2. Click the Link And Label Settings tool, and select Create Attached Labels.
3. Select the record for employee number 1020, and click the Create Attached Label tool. Telephone extension number labels appear on each item that is linked to the record. The labels are placed on top of the object they are linked to.
4. Click the telephone extension label that is on top of the employee name; then use its grip to move it away from the name. This shows you that the labels can be adjusted to a new position once they are placed.
5. Repeat steps 3 and 4 for employee numbers 1022 and 2000.

Each label you add with the Create Attached Label tool is linked to its associated record in the database.

UPGRADING DATA LINKS FROM OLDER AUTOCAD VERSIONS

If you have some pre–AutoCAD 2000 drawings that contain data links, you will need to update those links before you can use them. The dbConnect feature offers the Link Conversion dialog box to facilitate the update. To open the Link Conversion dialog box, open the dbConnect Manager palette (choose Tools ➢ dbConnect), and then choose dbConnect ➢ Link Conversion.

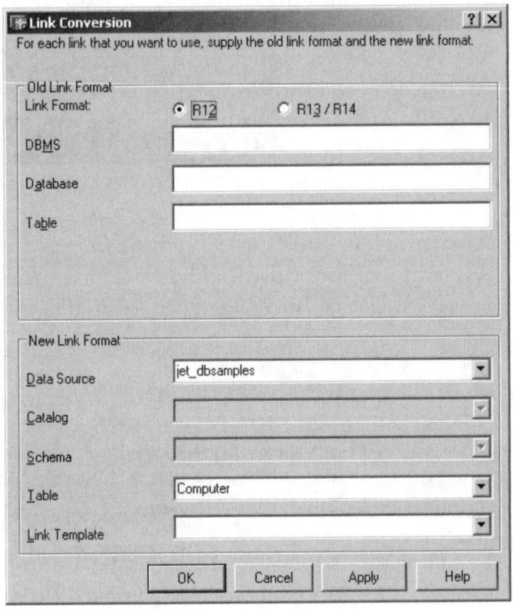

Select the version of the original AutoCAD file from the Link Format radio buttons, and then fill in the input boxes.

Hiding Labels

You can edit the label in your drawing as you would any other multiline text object. Another characteristic of database labels is that you can control their visibility.

1. Right-click the Extension label template listed in the dbConnect Manager palette and choose Hide Labels. The labels associated with the extension label template disappear.
2. Right-click the link template again and click Show Labels. The label reappears.

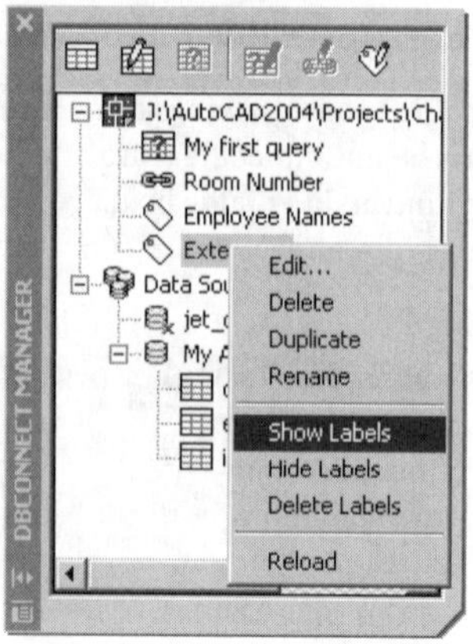

If you want to delete all the labels associated with a label template, right-click the label template's name in the dbConnect Manager palette and choose Delete Labels from the shortcut menu. Once you've done this, you can delete the label template as well by right-clicking the label template name and choosing Delete.

Editing Links

People and databases are always changing, so you need a way to update the links between your database and objects in your drawing. AutoCAD offers the Link Manager for this purpose.

Suppose you want to delete the link between the room number 116 in your drawing and the record for employee 1022.

1. Press Escape to clear any active selection, and then click room number 116 to select it.
2. Right-click and choose Links ➢ Link Manager to open the Link Manager dialog box.

3. Click the Delete button.
4. Click OK. The link is removed and the linked label disappears.

You can also delete all the links associated with a link table. Select the link table name in the dbConnect Manager palette, right-click, and then choose Delete Links from the shortcut menu.

If You Want to Experiment...

You've explored most of the dbConnect features in AutoCAD. One fairly simple feature you haven't used is the Sort dialog box. The Sort dialog box lets you arrange the order in which the data appears. It functions in a way similar to the column header in Microsoft Excel or Access. Try the following to see how it works.

1. In the Data View dialog box, right-click any of the column header labels (see Figure 11.3).

FIGURE 11.3

The column header labels

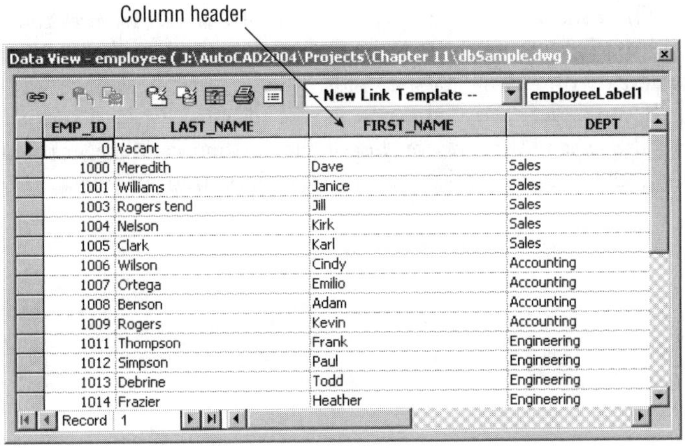

2. Choose Sort from the shortcut menu to open the Sort dialog box.

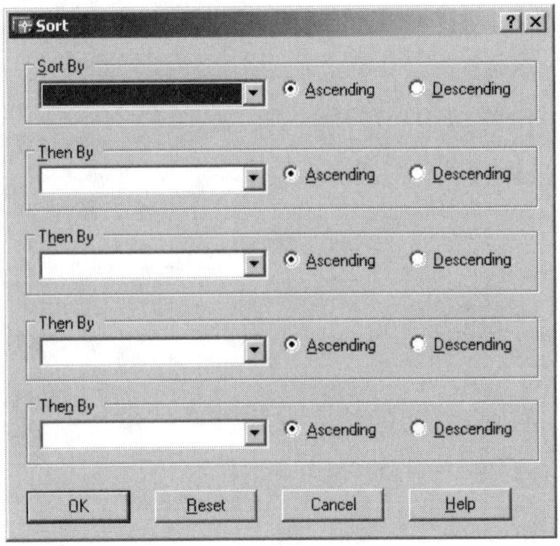

3. In the Sort By group at the top of the dialog box, select LAST_NAME and make sure the Ascending radio button is selected.

4. Click OK. The data now appears in alphabetic order according to the LAST_NAME column.

You can see from the Sort dialog box that you can add additional sort criteria to refine the sort order.

In step 1, when you right-click the column header, you see a few other options that allow you to control the column formatting. You can hide or freeze a column. The Freeze option moves the column to the far left. Once you hide or freeze a column, you can unhide or unfreeze using the Unhide All or Unfreeze All options. Unfreeze All moves a frozen column back to its original location. The Align options let you specify the justification style of text in the column. You also have Find and Replace options that work in a similar way to Find and Replace in word processors. Finally, if you want to adjust the width of a column, just click and drag the column header label borders.

This concludes our exploration of the dbConnect feature. You've seen how you can access a database and link your drawing to it. This brief tutorial can help you find the information you will need to develop your own database needs.

If you understand SQL, you can take advantage of it to perform more sophisticated searches. You can also expand the functionality of the dbConnect Manager palette. For more detailed information about dbConnect and SQL, refer to the *AutoCAD SQL Extension* reference manual.

Chapter 12

Copying Pre-existing Drawings into AutoCAD

AT TIMES YOU WILL want to turn a hand-drafted drawing into an AutoCAD drawing file. It may be that you are modifying a design you created before you started using AutoCAD or that you are converting your entire library of drawings for future AutoCAD use. Or perhaps you want to convert a sketch into a formal drawing. This chapter discusses three ways to enter a hand-drafted drawing: tracing, scaling, and scanning. Each of these methods of drawing input has its advantages and disadvantages.

This chapter covers the following topics:

- Tracing, Scaling, and Scanning Drawings
- Tracing a Drawing
- Importing and Tracing Raster Images
- If You Want to Experiment...

Tracing, Scaling, and Scanning Drawings

Tracing with a digitizing tablet is the easiest way to enter a hand-drafted drawing into AutoCAD, but a traced drawing usually requires some cleaning up and reorganization. If dimensional accuracy is not too important, tracing is the best way to enter existing drawings into AutoCAD. It is especially useful for drawings that contain irregular curves, such as the contour lines of a topographical map.

TIP *Even if you don't plan to trace drawings into AutoCAD, read the following section on tracing because some of the information presented here will help you with everyday editing tasks.*

Scaling a drawing is the most flexible method because you don't need a tablet to do it and, generally, you are faced with less cleanup afterward. Scaling also facilitates the most accurate input of orthogonal lines because you can read dimensions directly from the drawing and enter them into

AutoCAD. The main drawback with scaling is that if the drawing does not contain complete dimensional information, you must constantly look at the hand-drafted drawing and measure distances with a scale. Also, irregular curves are difficult to scale accurately.

ACAD only

Scanning offers some unique opportunities with AutoCAD 2004, especially if you have a lot of RAM and a fast hard drive. Potentially, you can scan a drawing, save it on your computer as an image file, import the image into AutoCAD, and then trace over it. You still need to perform some cleanup work on the traced drawing, but because you can see your tracing directly on your screen, you have better control, and you won't have quite as much cleaning up to do as you do when tracing from a digitizer.

Vectorizing programs automatically convert an image file into a vector file of lines and arcs. These programs might offer some help, but they require the most cleaning up of the options presented here. Like tracing, scanning is best used for drawings that are difficult to scale, such as complex topographical maps containing more contours than are practical to trace on a digitizer, or nontechnical line art, such as letterhead and logos.

Tracing a Drawing

The most common way to enter a hand-drafted drawing into AutoCAD is tracing with a digitizer. If you are working with a large drawing and you have a small tablet, you might have to cut the drawing into pieces that your tablet can manage, trace each piece, and then assemble the completed pieces into the large drawing. However, the best solution is a large tablet.

The following exercises are designed for a 4" × 5" (10 cm × 12.7 cm) or larger tablet. The sample drawings are small enough to fit completely on this size tablet. You can use either a stylus or a puck to trace them, but the stylus provides the most natural feel because it is shaped like a pen. A puck has crosshairs that you have to center on the line you want to trace, and this requires a bit more dexterity.

TIP *If you don't have a digitizing tablet, you can use scaling to enter the utility room drawing used in this section's tracing exercise. (You will insert the utility room into your apartment building plan in Chapter 13.)*

Reconfiguring the Tablet for Tracing

When you first installed AutoCAD, you configured the tablet to use most of its active drawing area for AutoCAD's menu template (see Appendix B for more information). Because you will need the tablet's entire drawing area to trace this drawing, you now need to reconfigure the tablet to eliminate the menu. Otherwise, you won't be able to pick points on the drawing outside the 4" × 3" (10 cm × 7.6 cm) screen pointing area AutoCAD normally uses (see Figure 12.1).

TIP *You can save several different AutoCAD configurations that can be easily set using the Options dialog box (see Appendix B).*

Here are the steps to follow:

1. Start AutoCAD and create a new file called `Utility`.
2. Set up the file as a 1/4"=1'-scale architectural drawing on an 8 1/2" × 11" sheet (limits set to 0,0 for the lower-left corner and 528,408 for the upper-right corner). Metric users should

set up their drawing at a 1:50 scale on an A4 size sheet. (Limits for metric users should be 0,0 for the lower-left corner and 1480,1050 for the upper-right corner.)

3. Choose Tools ➢ Tablet ➢ Configure, or type **Ta↵ CFG↵**.
4. At the `Enter number of tablet menus desired (0-4):` prompt, enter **0↵**.

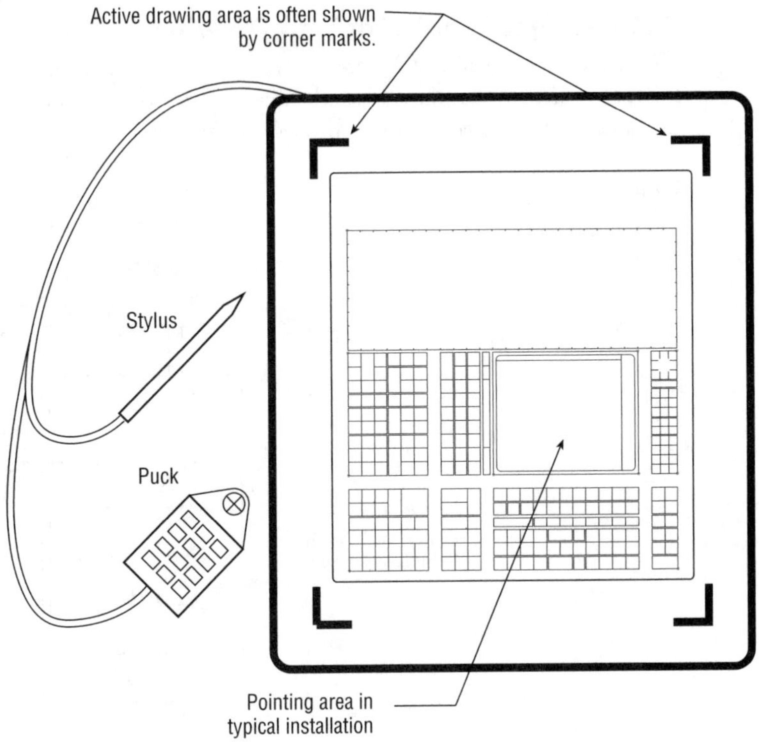
Active drawing area is often shown by corner marks.
Stylus
Puck
Pointing area in typical installation

FIGURE 12.1
The tablet's active drawing area

WARNING *When selecting points on the tablet, take care not to accidentally press the pick button twice, as this will give you erroneous results. Many tablets have sensitive pick buttons that can cause problems when you are selecting points.*

5. At the `Do you want to respecify the Fixed Screen Pointing Area?:` prompt, enter **Y↵**.
6. At the `Digitize lower left corner of screen pointing area:` prompt, pick the lower-left corner of the tablet's active drawing area.

TIP *On some tablets, a light shows you the active area; other tablets use a permanent mark, such as a corner mark. AutoCAD won't do anything until you have picked a point, so you don't have to worry about picking a point outside this area.*

7. At the `Digitize upper right corner of screen pointing area:` prompt, pick the upper-right corner.

8. At the `Do you want to specify the Floating Screen pointing area <N>:` prompt, press ↵.

Now as you move your stylus or puck, you'll notice a difference in the relationship between your hand movement and the screen cursor. The cursor moves more slowly and is active over more of the tablet surface.

Calibrating the Tablet for Your Drawing

Now make a photocopy of Figure 12.2, which represents a hand-drafted drawing of a utility room for your apartment building. Place the photocopied drawing on your tablet so that it is aligned with the tablet and completely within the tablet's active drawing area (see Figure 12.3).

FIGURE 12.2
The utility room drawing

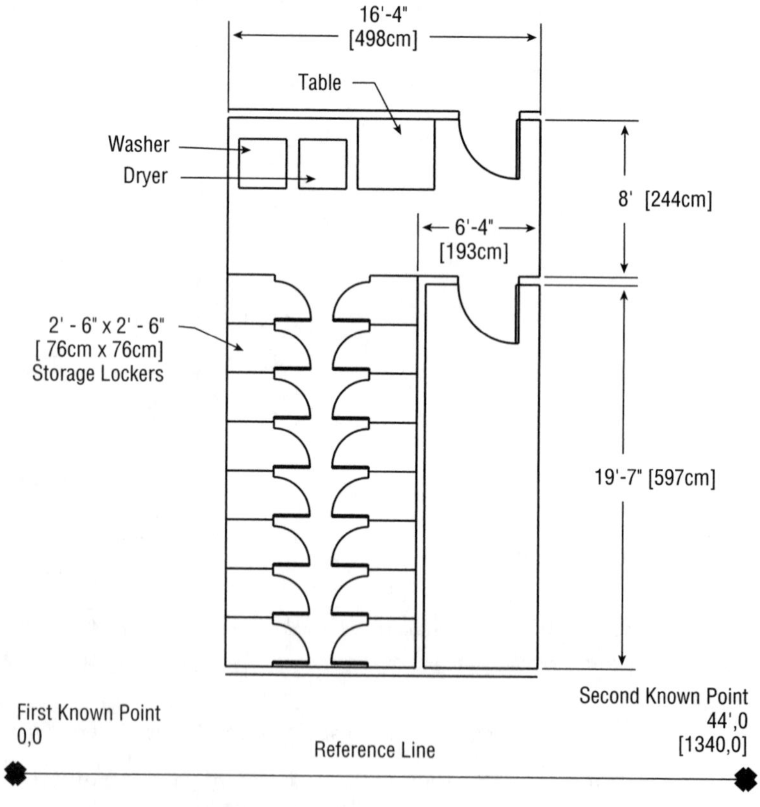

Before you can trace anything into your computer, you must calibrate your tablet. This means you must give some points of reference so AutoCAD can know how distances on the tablet relate to distances in the drawing editor. For example, you might want to trace a drawing that was created at a scale of 1/8"=1'-0". You will have to show AutoCAD two specific points on this drawing, as well as where those two points should appear in the drawing editor. To do this, use the Tablet command's Cal option.

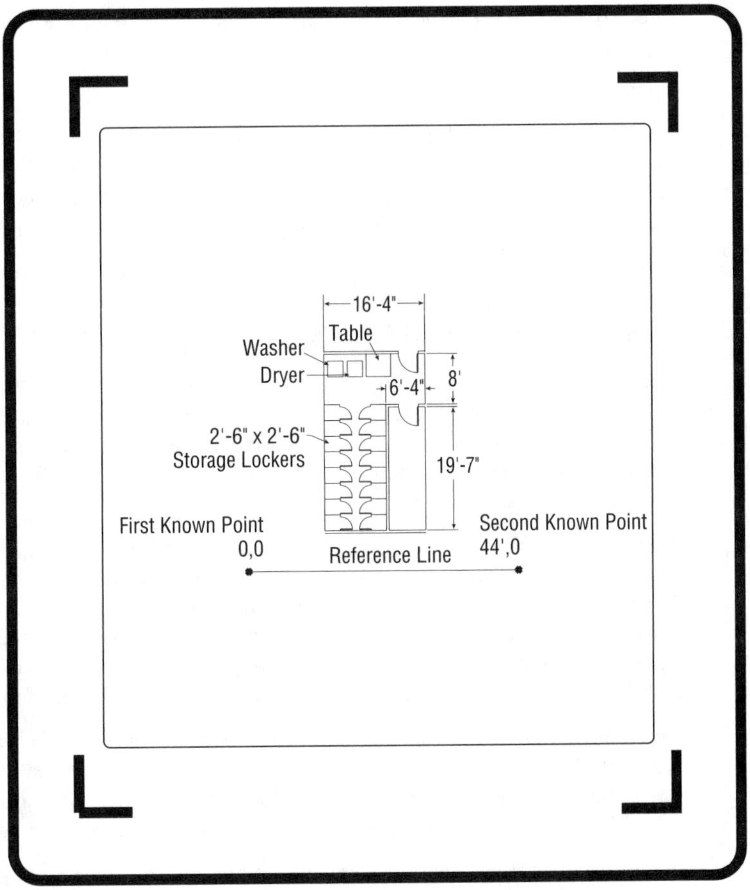

FIGURE 12.3
The drawing placed on the tablet

TIP *When you calibrate a tablet, you are setting ratios for AutoCAD; for example, 2 inches on your tablet equals 16 feet in the drawing editor.*

In Figure 12.2, we have already determined the coordinates for two points on a reference line.

1. Choose Tools ➢ Tablet ➢ Calibrate, or enter **Tablet↵ Cal↵** at the command prompt.
2. The prompt `Digitize point #1:` appears, asking you to pick the first point for which you know the absolute coordinates. Pick the X on the left end of the reference line.
3. At the `Enter coordinates for point #1:` prompt, enter **0,0↵**. This tells AutoCAD that the point you just picked is equivalent to the coordinate 0,0 in your drawing editor.
4. Next, the `Digitize point #2:` prompt asks you to pick another point for which you know the coordinates. Pick the X on the right end of the reference line.
5. At the `Enter coordinates for point #2:` prompt, enter **44',0↵**. Metric users should enter **1340,0↵**.

6. At the `Digitize point #3 (or RETURN to end):` prompt, press ↵. The tablet is now calibrated.

The word TABLET appears on the status bar to tell you that you are in Tablet mode. In this mode, you can trace the drawing, but you cannot access the menus in Windows with some digitizers. (Check your digitizer manual for further information.) If you want to choose a menu item, you must toggle the Tablet mode off by pressing the F4 function key. Or you can enter commands through the keyboard. (If you need some reminders of the keyboard commands, type **Help**↵, and click Commands in the Help dialog box to get a list.)

Calibrating More Than Two Points

In step 6 of the previous exercise, you bypassed the prompt that offered you the chance to calibrate a third point. In fact, you can calibrate as many as 31 points. Why would anyone want to calibrate so many points? Often the drawing or photograph you are trying to trace will be distorted in one direction or another. For example, blueline prints are usually stretched in one direction because of the way prints are rolled through a print machine.

You can compensate for distortions by specifying several known points during your calibration. For example, we could include a vertical distance on the utility room drawing to indicate a distance in the y-axis. You could then pick that distance and calibrate its point. AutoCAD would then have a point of reference for the y distance as well as the x distance. If you calibrate only two points, as you did in the previous exercise, AutoCAD will scale x and y distances equally. Calibrating three points causes AutoCAD to scale x and y distances separately, making adjustments for each axis based on their respective calibration points.

Now suppose you want to trace a perspective view of a building, but you want to "flatten" the perspective so that all the lines are parallel. You can calibrate the four corners of the buildings facade to stretch out the narrow end of the perspective view to be parallel with the wide end. This is a limited form of what cartographers call rubber-sheeting, in which various areas of the tablet are stretched by specific scale factors.

When you select more than two points for calibration, you will get a message similar to that shown here. Let's take a look at the parts of this message.

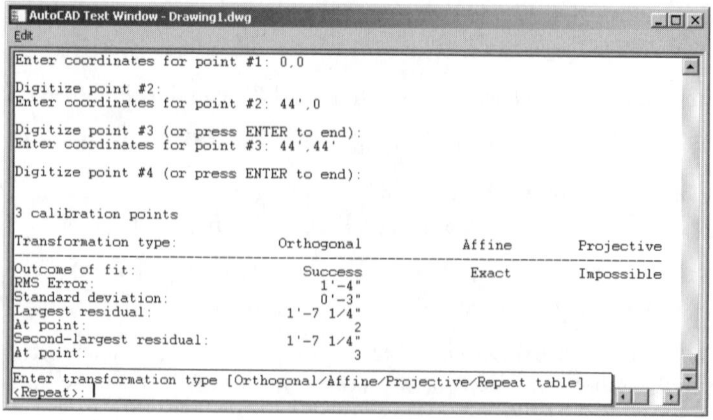

Continued on next page

CALIBRATING MORE THAN TWO POINTS *(continued)*

In the text window, you see the labels Orthogonal, Affine, and Projective. These are the three major types of calibrations or transformations. The orthogonal transformation scales the x-axis and y-axis using the same values. Affine transformation scales the x-axis and y-axis separately and requires at least three points. How the projective transformation stretches the tablet coordinates depends on where you are on the tablet. It requires at least four calibration points.

For each transformation type you will see the Outcome of fit; either Success, Exact, or Impossible. This tells you whether any of these transformation types are available to you. Because this example shows what you see when you pick three points, you get Impossible for the projective transformation.

The far-left column tells you what is shown in each of the other three columns.

Finally, the prompt at the bottom of the screen lets you select which transformation type to use. If you calibrate four or more points, the projective transformation is added to the prompt. The Repeat Table option simply refreshes the table.

Take care when you calibrate points on your tablet. Here are some tips:

- Use only known calibration points.
- Try to locate calibration points that cover a large area of your image.
- Don't get carried away. Try to limit calibration points to those necessary to get the job done.

Tracing Lines from a Drawing

Now you are ready to trace the utility room. If you don't have a digitizer, you can skip this exercise. A traced file is included on the companion CD that you can use for later exercises.

1. Make sure the Orthos and Polar buttons are off in the status bar.
2. Click the Line tool on the Draw toolbar, or type **L↵**.
3. Trace the outline of all the walls except the storage lockers.
4. Add the doors by inserting the `Door` file at the appropriate points and then mirroring them. The doors may not fit exactly, but you'll get a chance to make adjustments later.
5. Trace the washer, and, because the washer and dryer are the same size, copy the washer over to the position of the dryer.

TIP *Once a tablet has been calibrated, you can trace your drawing from the tablet, even if the area you are tracing is not displayed in the drawing editor.*

At this point, your drawing should look something like the first image of Figure 12.4—a close facsimile of the original drawing, but not as exact as you might like. Zoom in to one of the doors. Now you can see the inaccuracies of tracing. Some of the lines are crooked, and others don't meet at the right points. These inaccuracies are caused by the limited resolution of your tablet, coupled with the lack of steadiness in the human hand. The best digitizing tablets have an accuracy of 0.001 inch, which is actually not very good when you are dealing with tablet distances of 1/8" and smaller. In the following section, you will clean up your drawing. (The raggedness of the door arc is the result of the way AutoCAD displays arcs when you use the Zoom command. See Chapter 6 for further explanation.)

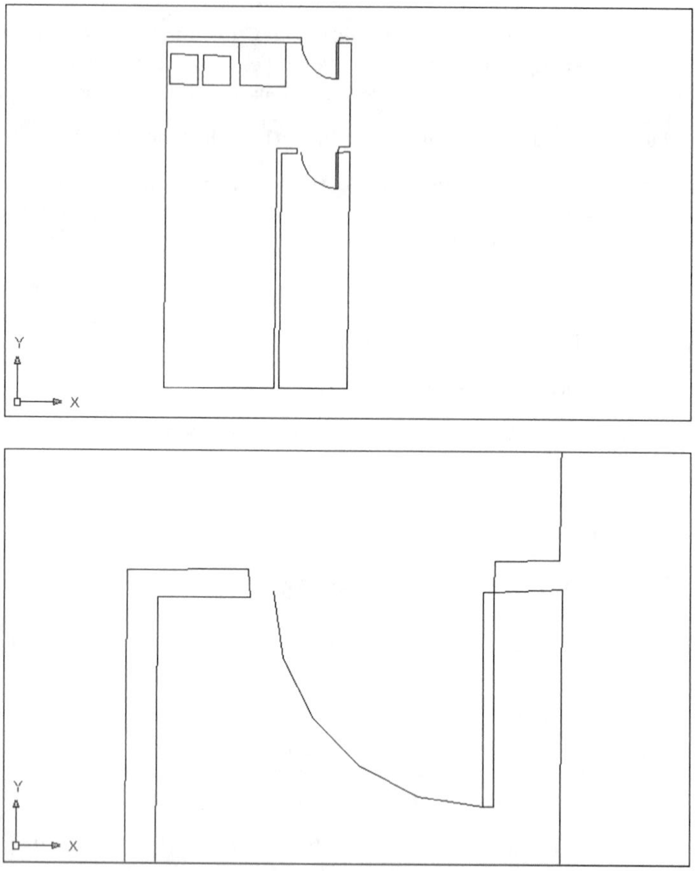

FIGURE 12.4
The traced drawing and a close-up of the door

Cleaning Up a Traced Drawing

In this section, you'll reposition a door jamb, straighten some lines, adjust a dimension, and add the storage lockers to the utility room. If you didn't have a chance to digitize your own `Utility` file, use the file `12a-util.dwg` from the companion CD to do the following exercises.

MOVING THE END OF A WALL

In Figure 12.4, one of the door jambs is not in the right position (the second image gives you the best look). In this next exercise, you will fix this by repositioning a group of objects while keeping their vertices intact, using the Grips feature.

1. Enlarge your view so it looks similar to the second image in Figure 12.4.
2. Pick a crossing window enclosing the door jamb to be moved (see the top image in Figure 12.5).

FIGURE 12.5

A window crossing the door jamb, and the door jamb being stretched

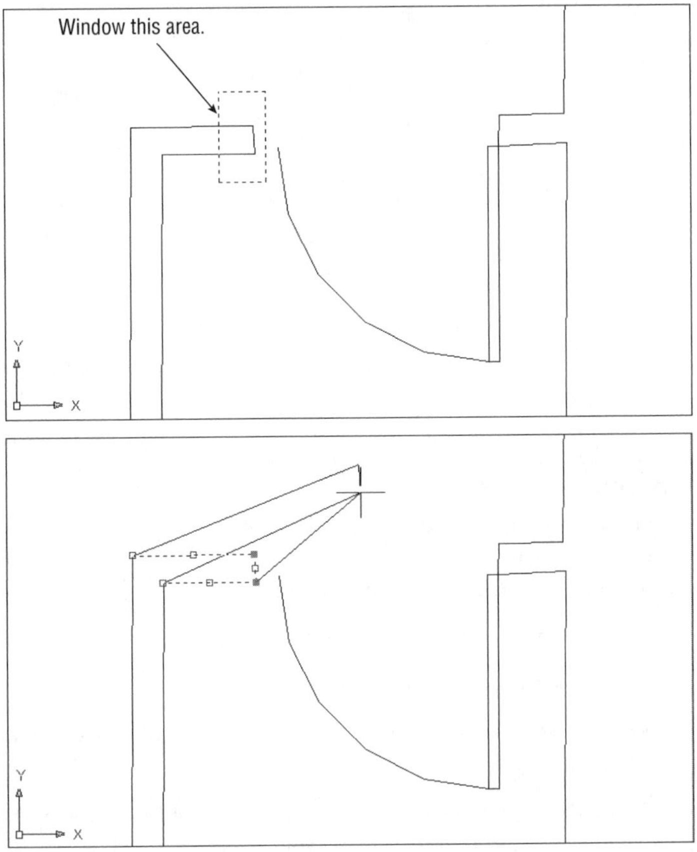
Window this area.
Y
X
Y
X

3. Click one of the grips at the end of the wall, and then Shift+click the other grip. You should have two hot grips at the door jamb.
4. Click the lower of the two hot grips, and drag the corner away to see what happens (see the bottom image in Figure 12.5).

5. Use the Endpoint Osnap to pick the endpoint of the arc. The jamb repositions itself, and all the lines follow (see Figure 12.6).

FIGURE 12.6
The Repositioned door jamb.

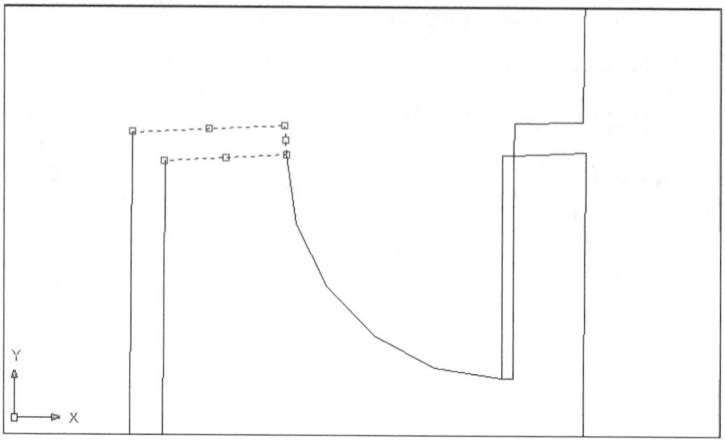

TIP If AutoCAD doesn't respond in the way described in this section, make sure the Noun/Verb selection setting and the Grips feature are both turned on.

STRAIGHTENING LINES

Another problem in this drawing is that some of the lines are not orthogonal. To straighten them, you use the Change command, together with the Ortho mode. In the following exercise, you'll use the Change command keyboard shortcut.

1. Press the Esc key to clear any active grip selections.
2. Toggle the Ortho mode on.
3. Type **–Ch↵** at the command prompt to start this operation. Make sure you include the minus sign.
4. At the `Object selection:` prompt, pick the four lines representing the walls just left of the door, and press ↵ to confirm your selection.
5. At the `Specify change point or [Properties]:` prompt, click the corner where the two walls meet. The four lines straighten out, as shown in Figure 12.7.

FIGURE 12.7
The lines after using the Change Point option of the Change command

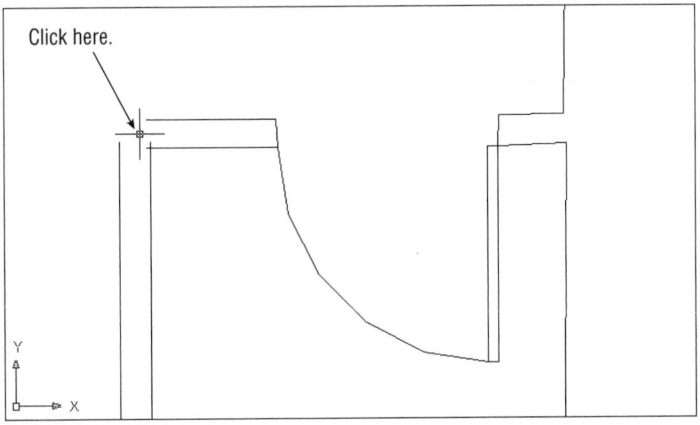

6. Once the lines have been straightened, use the Fillet tool in the Modify toolbar to join the corners. You can also choose Modify Fillet ➢ Fillet.

WARNING *The Change command's Change Point option changes the location of the endpoint closest to the new point location. This can cause erroneous results when you are trying to modify groups of lines.*

As you have just seen, you can use the Change command to quickly straighten a set of lines. When used carefully, this command can be a real time-saver.

WARNING *Be aware that the Change command moves the nearest endpoints of selected lines to the new location. This can cause unpredictable results in some situations (see Figure 12.9 later in this chapter). Note that the Change command does not affect polyline line segments.*

In addition to straightening lines, you can use the Change command to align a set of lines to another line. For example, when you combine Change with the Perpendicular Osnap, you can align several lines at a perpendicular angle to another line. However, this works only with the Ortho mode on.

You also can extend several lines to be perpendicular to a nonorthogonal line. To do so, you must rotate the cursor to that line's angle (see the top image in Figure 12.8), using the Snapang system variable. (You can also use the Snap Angle input box in the Drawing Aids dialog box (choose Tools ➢ Drawing Aids) to rotate the cursor.) Then use the process just described to extend or shorten the other lines (see the bottom image in Figure 12.8).

FIGURE 12.8
You can use the Change command to quickly straighten a set of nonparallel lines and to align their endpoints to another reference line.

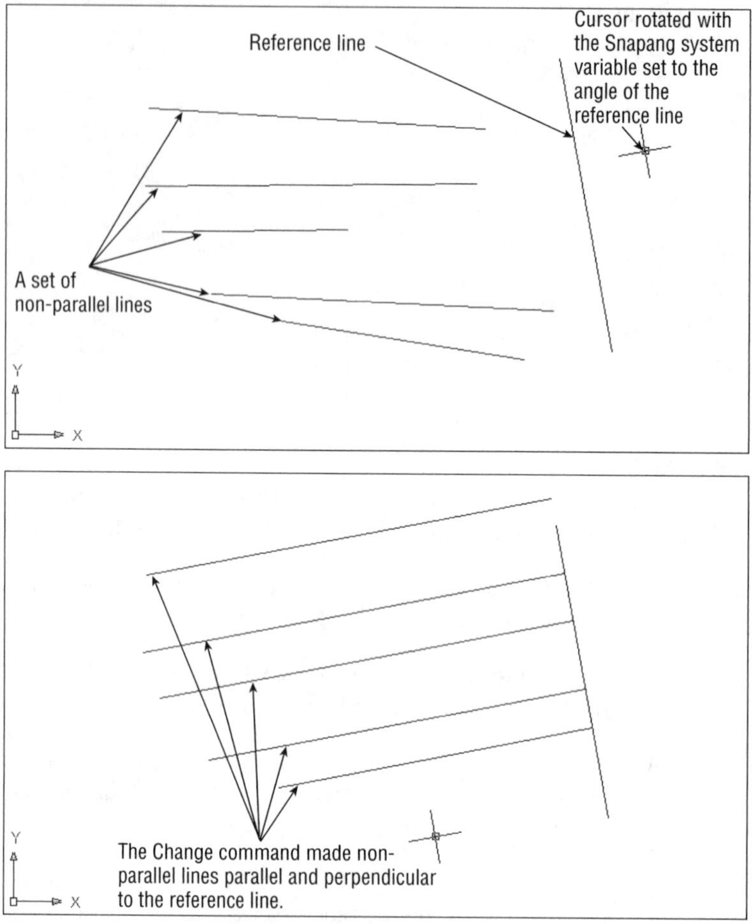

When changing several lines to be perpendicular to another line, you must carefully choose the new endpoint location. Figure 12.9 shows what happens to the same line shown in the top image in Figure 12.8 when a perpendicular reference is placed in the middle of the set of lines. Some lines are straightened to a perpendicular orientation, while others have the wrong endpoints aligned with the reference line.

Before moving on to the next section, use the Change command to straighten the other lines in your drawing. Start by straightening the corner to the right of the door in Figure 12.7, earlier in this chapter.

1. Issue the Change command again.
2. Select the four lines that represent the walls to the right of the door, and then press ↵.
3. Click a point near the corner.
4. Chances are, the two vertical lines are not aligned. Move the top line so that it aligns with the lower one. You can use the Perpendicular Osnap to help with the alignment.

5. Use the Change command on each of the other corners until all the walls have been straightened. You can also use Change in a similar way to straighten the door jambs.

6. Once you've straightened the lines, use the Fillet tool on the Modify toolbar to join the corners end to end.

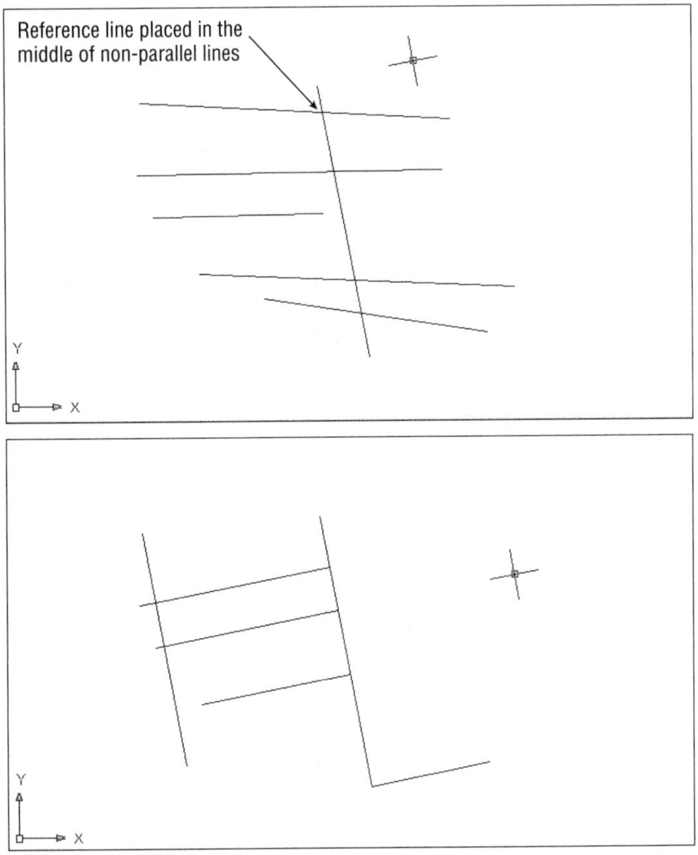

FIGURE 12.9

The results of the Change command can be unpredictable if the endpoint location is too close to the lines being changed.

TIP *When you confirm your selection to the Change command in step 4, you have the option to press* **P↵** *for the Properties option. This option lets you change the color, elevation, layer, line type, line-type scale, line weight, and thickness of the selected object. It can be especially helpful in 3D work when you want to set the elevation of several objects to the same elevation.*

TIP *When using the Fillet tool to join lines, you can issue the Fillet command, type* **C↵**, *and enclose the two lines you want to fillet with a crossing window.*

ADJUSTING THE ROOM SIZE

The overall interior dimension of the original utility room drawing is 16'-4" × 28'-0". Chances are that the dimensions of the drawing you traced will vary somewhat from these. You will need to adjust your drawing to fit these dimensions.

1. Draw a horizontal line 16'-4" long (498 cm for metric users) from the left wall; then draw a vertical line 28' long (856.6 cm for metric users) from the bottom wall line, as shown in Figure 12.10.

FIGURE 12.10

The walls stretched to the proper dimensions

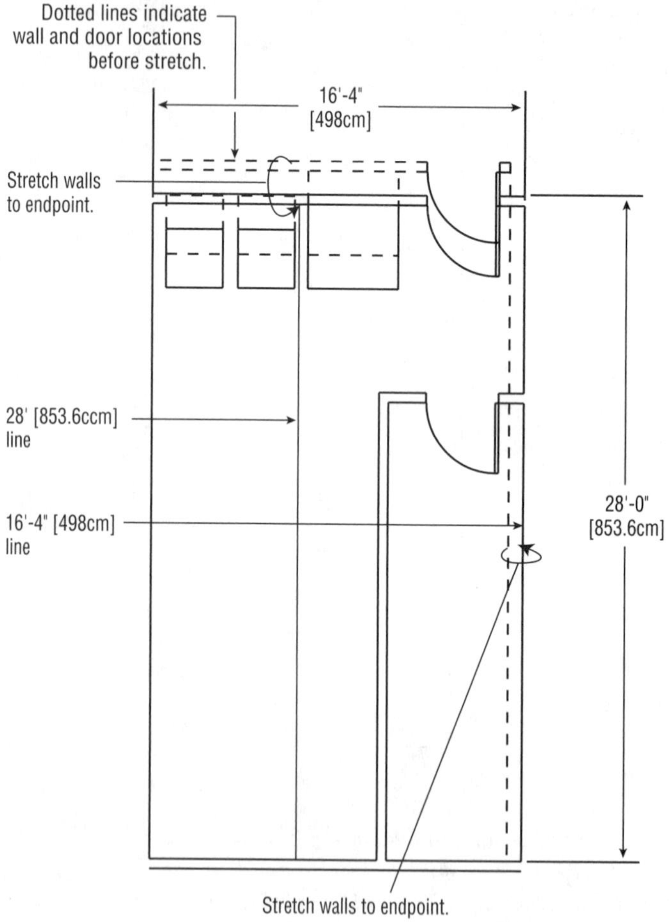

2. Use the two lines you drew in step 1 to adjust the walls to their proper positions (see Figure 12.10). You can either use the Grips feature or click Stretch on the Modify toolbar.
3. Choose Draw ➢ Block ➢ Base, or type **Base**. Then make the upper-left corner of the utility room the base point.
4. To add the storage lockers, begin by drawing one 30" × 30" (76 cm × 76 cm for metric users) locker accurately.

5. Use the Mirror and Array commands to create the other lockers. Both commands are available on the Modify toolbar. (For entering objects repeatedly, this is actually a faster and more accurate method than tracing. If you traced each locker, you would also have to clean up each one.)

Finally, you might want to add the dimensions and labels shown earlier in Figure 12.2.

1. Create a layer called Notes to contain the dimensions and labels.
2. Set the Dimscale dimension setting to **48** (**50** for metric users) before you start dimensioning. To do this, choose Dimension Style from the Dimension toolbar. Make sure the Standard dimension style is selected; then click Modify. In the Modify Dimension Style dialog box, click the Fit tab and click the Use Overall Scale Of radio button. Next, enter **48** (**50** for metric users) in the input box to the right of the Use Overall Scale Of radio button. (See Chapter 9 for details on this process.)

TIP *You can also set the Dimscale setting by typing* ***Dimscale↵*** and then entering the desired scale of **48**.

3. Click the Text tab and set the text height to 1/8" (0.3 for metric users).
4. When you are done, click OK. Then click Close, save the file, and exit AutoCAD.

TIP *Make sure that the text style you are using with your dimension style is set to a height of 0 if you want the dimension style text height to take effect.*

Working Smarter with Digitizers

In the first exercise in this chapter, you traced most of a drawing and used Mirror and Array to speed up the drawing re-creation. However, you could have just traced the major lines with the Ortho mode on, and then used the Offset command to draw the wall thickness. The Fillet and Trim commands (see Chapter 5) could then be used to clean up the drawing where lines cross or where they don't meet.

If you are a civil engineer, you will probably take a different approach. In laying out a road, for instance, you might first trace the center lines and then use the Offset option on the Modify toolbar to place the curb and gutter. You could trace curved features using arcs (just to see what the radius of the curve is) and then redraw the arc accurately, joining straight-line segments. The digitizer can be a great tool if it is used with care and a touch of creativity.

SCANNING A DRAWING

No discussion of drawing input can be complete without mentioning scanners. Imagine how easy it would be to convert an existing library of drawings into AutoCAD drawing files by simply running them through a scanning device. Unfortunately, scanning drawings is not quite that simple.

In scanning, the drawing size can be a problem. Desktop scanners are generally limited to an 8 1/2" × 14" or 26 cm × 37 cm sheet size. Some low-cost handheld scanners will scan a 22" × 14" or 56 cm × 37 cm area. Larger format scanners are available but more expensive.

Once the drawing is scanned and saved as a file, you have two paths to importing it into AutoCAD. One path is to convert the scanned image into AutoCAD objects such as lines, arcs, and circles. This requires special software and is usually a fairly time-consuming process. Finally, the drawing usually requires some cleanup, which can take even longer than cleaning up a traced drawing. The poorer the condition of the original drawing, the more cleanup you'll have to do.

Another path is to import a scanned image directly into AutoCAD and then use all or part of the scanned image in combination with AutoCAD objects. You can trace over the scanned image using the standard AutoCAD tools and then discard the image when you are done, or you can use the scanned image as part of your AutoCAD file. With AutoCAD's ability to import raster images, you can, for example, import a scanned image of an existing paper drawing and then mask off the area you want to edit. You can then draw over the masked portions to make the required changes.

Whether a scanner can help you depends on your application. If you have drawings that would be difficult to trace—large, complex topographical maps, for example—a scanner might well be worth a look. You don't necessarily have to buy one; some scanning services offer excellent value. And if you can accept the quality of a scanned drawing before it is cleaned up, you can save a lot of time. On the other hand, a drawing composed mostly of orthogonal lines and notes might be more easily traced by hand with a large tablet or entered directly by using the drawing's dimensions.

Scanning can be an excellent document management tool for your existing paper drawings. You might consider scanning your existing paper drawings for archiving purposes. Some blueprint companies even offer free large document scanning as an incentive to other digital reproduction services.

You can then use portions or all of your scanned drawings later, without committing to a full-scale, paper-to-AutoCAD scan conversion.

Importing and Tracing Raster Images

ACAD only

If you have a scanner and you would like to use it to import drawings and other images into AutoCAD, you can use AutoCAD's raster image import capabilities. There are many reasons for wanting to import a scanned image. In architectural plans, a vicinity map is frequently used to show the location of a project. With the permission of its creator, you can scan a map into AutoCAD and incorporate it into a cover sheet. That cover sheet can also contain other images, such as photographs of the site, computer renderings and elevations of the project, and company logos.

WARNING *LT users cannot import raster images, however, images placed in drawings can be viewed, moved and scaled in LT, and their frames can be turned on or off.*

Another reason for importing scanned images is to use the image as a reference to trace over. You can trace a drawing with greater accuracy using a scanned image as opposed to a digitizing tablet. With the price of scanners falling to less than $100, a scanner is a cost-effective tool for tracing a wide variety of graphic material. In this section, you'll learn firsthand how you can import an image as a background for tracing.

Choose Insert ➢ Image Manager to open the Image Manager dialog box, which lets you import a full range of raster image files.

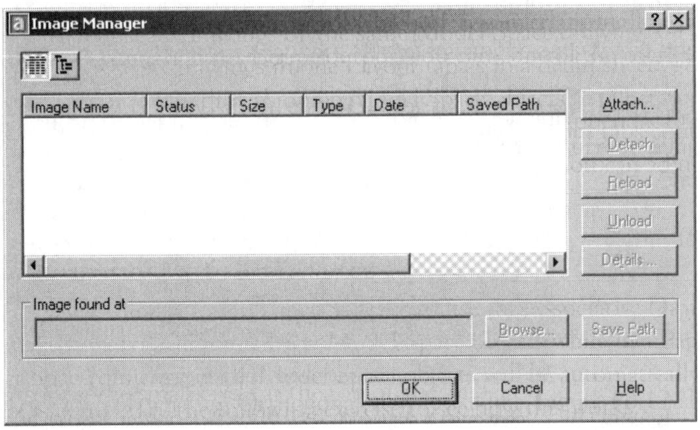

If you've read Chapter 6, this dialog box should look familiar. It looks and works just like the External Reference dialog box. The similarities are more than just cosmetic. Just like external references (Xrefs), raster images are loaded when the current file is open, but they are not stored as part of the current file when the file is saved. This helps keep file sizes down, but it also means that you need to keep track of inserted raster files. You will need to make sure that they are kept together with the AutoCAD files in which they are inserted. For example, you might want to keep image files in the same folder as the drawing file to which they are attached.

Tips for Importing Raster Images

When you scan a document into your computer, you get a raster image file. Unlike AutoCAD files, raster image files are made up of a matrix of colors that form a picture. Vector files, like those produced by AutoCAD, are made up of lines, arcs, curves, and circles. The two formats, raster and vector, are so different that it is difficult to accurately convert one format to the other. It is easier to trace a raster file in AutoCAD than it is to try to have some computer program make the conversion for you.

But even tracing a raster image file can be difficult if the image is of poor quality. Here are a few points you should consider if you plan to use raster import for tracing drawings:

- Scan in your drawing using a grayscale or color scanner, or convert your black-and-white scanned image to grayscale using your scanner software.

Continued on next page

TIPS FOR IMPORTING RASTER IMAGES *(continued)*

- Use a paint program or your scanner software to clean up unwanted gray or spotted areas in the file before importing it into AutoCAD.
- If your scanner software or paint program has a "de-speckle" or "de-spot" feature, use it. It can help clean up your image and ultimately reduce the raster image file size.
- Scan at a reasonable resolution. Remember that the human hand is usually not more accurate than a few thousandths of an inch, so scanning at 150 to 200 dpi may be more than adequate.
- If you plan to make heavy use of raster import, upgrade your computer to the fastest processor you can afford and don't spare the memory.

The raster import commands can incorporate paper maps or plans into 3D AutoCAD drawings for presentations. I know of one architectural firm that produces some impressive presentations with little effort by combining 2D scanned images with 3D massing models for urban design studies. (A *massing model* is a model that shows only the rough outline of buildings without giving too much detail. Massing models show the general scale of a project without being too fussy.) Raster images do not, however, appear in perspective views.

TIP *AutoCAD offers a utility called eTransmit that will collect AutoCAD files and their related support files, such as raster images, external references, and fonts, into any folder or drive that you specify. See Chapter 22 for details.*

Another similarity between Xrefs and imported raster images is that you can clip a raster image so that only a portion of the image is displayed in your drawing. Portions of a raster file that are clipped are not stored in memory, so your system won't get bogged down, even if the raster file is huge.

The following exercise gives you step-by-step instructions for importing a raster file. It also gives you a chance to see how scanned resolution translates into an image in AutoCAD. This is important for those of you interested in scanning drawings for the purpose of tracing over them.

1. Create a new file called `Rastertrace`.
2. Set up the file as a 1/4"=1'-scale architectural drawing on an 8 1/2" × 11" sheet (limits set to 0,0 for the lower-left corner and 528,408 for the upper-right corner). Make sure that the drawing units type is set to Architectural. Metric users should set up their drawing at a 1:50 scale on an A4 size sheet. (Limits for metric users should be 0,0 for the lower-left corner and 1480,1050 for the upper-right corner).
3. Choose View ➢ Zoom ➢ All to make sure the entire drawing limits are displayed on the screen.
4. Draw a line across the screen from coordinates 0,20' to 64',20'. Metric users should draw the line from 0,600 to 1820,600. You will use this line in a later exercise.
5. Click the line you just drew, and then select red from the color drop-down list in the Properties toolbar. This will help make the line more visible.
6. Choose Insert ➢ Image Manager or type **Im**↵ to open the Image Manager dialog box.

7. Click the Attach button in the upper-right corner to open the Select File To Attach dialog box. This is a typical AutoCAD file dialog box complete with a preview window.

8. Locate and select the `Raster1.jpg` file from the companion CD. Notice that you can see a preview of the file in the right side of the dialog box.

9. Click Open to open the Image dialog box. Click OK.

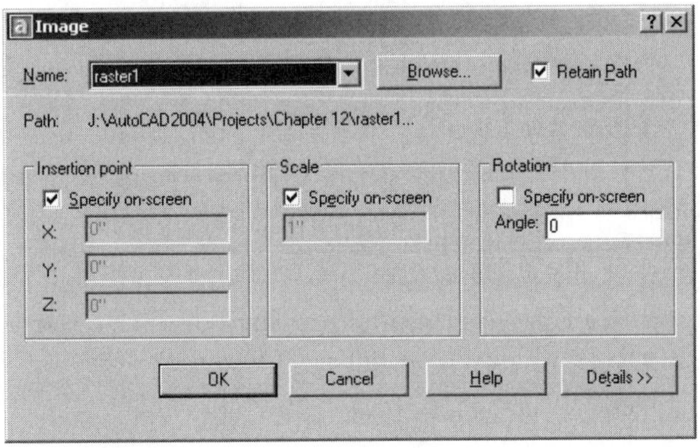

10. Press ↵ at the `Insertion Point:` prompt to accept the 0,0 coordinates.

11. At the `Specify Scale Factor <1>:` prompt, use the cursor to scale the image so it fills about half the screen, as shown in Figure 12.11.

TIP *You can bypass the Image dialog box and go directly to the Attach Image dialog box by entering* ***Iat↵*** *at the command prompt.*

FIGURE 12.11
Manually scaling the raster image

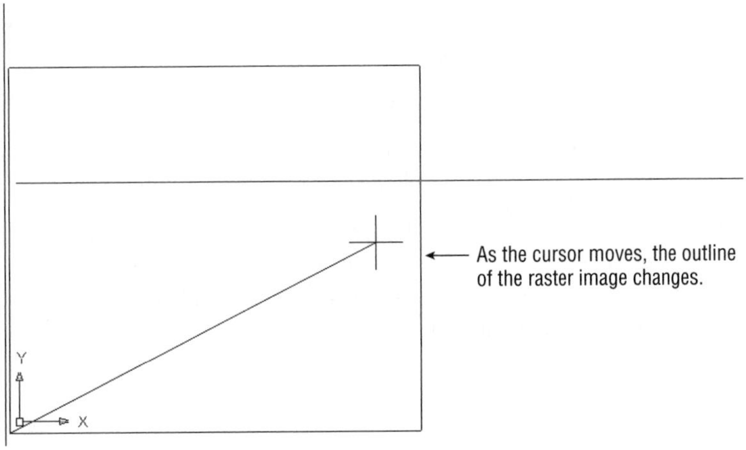

Y
X
As the cursor moves, the outline of the raster image changes.

THE IMAGE MANAGER BOX OPTIONS

The Image Manager dialog box you saw in step 6 of the previous exercise helps you manage your imported image files. It is especially helpful when you have a large number of images in your drawing. Its options are similar to the Xref Manager dialog box; you can temporarily unload images (to help speed up the editing of AutoCAD objects), reload, detach, and relocate raster image files. See Chapter 6 for a detailed description of these options.

Scaling a Raster Image

The `Raster1.jpg` file from the companion CD is a scanned image of Figure 12.2 that you saw earlier in this chapter. It was scanned as a grayscale image at 100 dpi. This shows that you can get a reasonable amount of detail at a fairly low scan resolution.

Now suppose you want to trace over this image to start an AutoCAD drawing. The first thing you'll want to do is to scale the image to the appropriate size. You can scale an image file to full size. Try the following steps to see how you might begin the process.

1. Choose View ➢ Zoom ➢ Extents.
2. Click Scale on the Modify toolbar.

3. Click the edge of the raster image to select it.
4. Press ↵ to finish your selection.
5. At the `Specify base point:` prompt, click the X in the lower-left corner of the image—the one you used in the first exercise to calibrate your digitizing tablet.
6. At the Specify `scale factor or [Reference]:` prompt, enter **R**↵ to use the Reference option.
7. At the Specify `reference length <1>:` prompt, type **@**↵. This tells AutoCAD that you want to use the last point selected as one end of the reference length. Once you enter the @ symbol, you'll see a rubber-banding line emanating from the X.
8. At the `Specify second point:` prompt, click the X at the lower-right corner of the image.
9. At the `Specify new length:` prompt, enter **44'**↵. Metric users should enter **1341**↵. The image enlarges. Remember that this reference line is 44 feet or 1341 cm in length.

The image is now scaled properly for the plan it portrays. You can proceed to trace over the image. You can also place the image on its own layer and turn it off from time to time to check your trace work. Even if you don't trace the scanned floor plan line for line, you can read the dimensions of the plan from your computer monitor, instead of having to go back and forth between measuring the paper drawing and drawing the plan on the computer.

Controlling Object Visibility and Overlap with Raster Images

With the introduction of raster image support, AutoCAD inherits a problem fairly common to programs that use them. Raster images will obscure other objects that were placed before the raster image. The image you imported in the previous exercise, for example, obscures the line you drew when you first opened the file. In most cases, this overlap may not be a problem, but in some situations you will want AutoCAD vector objects to overlap an imported raster image. An example of this is a civil engineering drawing showing an AutoCAD drawing of a new road superimposed over an aerial view of the location for the road.

Paint and page-layout programs usually offer a "to front/to back" tool to control the overlap of objects and images. AutoCAD offers the Draworder command. Here's how it works.

1. Choose View ➢ Zoom ➢ Extents to get an overall view of the image.
2. Choose Tools ➢ Display Order ➢ Bring Above Object.
3. At the `Select objects:` prompt, select the horizontal line you drew when you first opened the file.
4. You could go on to select other objects. Press ↵ to finish your selection.
5. At the `Select Reference Object:` prompt, click the edge of the raster image of the Utility room.

The drawing regenerates, and the entire line appears, no longer obscured by the raster image.

TIP *You can mask out areas of an imported raster image by creating a solid hatch area and using the Draworder command to place the solid hatch "on top" of the raster image. Such masks can be helpful as backgrounds for text that must be placed over a raster image.*

The Display Order command you just used actually offers four options:

Tools➢ Display Order ➢ Bring To Front Places an object or a set of objects at the top of the draw order for the entire drawing. The effect is that the objects are completely visible.

Tools➢ Display Order ➢ Send To Back Places an object or a set of objects at the bottom of the draw order for the entire drawing. The effect is that other objects in the drawing may obscure those objects.

Tools➢ Display Order ➢ Bring Above Object Places an object or a set of objects above another object in the draw order. This has the effect of making the first set of objects appear above the second selected object.

Tools➢ Display Order ➢ Bring Under Object Places an object or a set of objects below another object in the draw order. This has the effect of making the first set of objects appear underneath the second selected object.

You can also use the **Dr** keyboard shortcut to issue the Display Order command. If you do this, you see these prompts:

```
Select objects:
Enter object ordering option [Above object/Under object/Front/Back]<Back>:
```

You must then select the option by typing the capitalized letter of the option.

Although this section discussed the display order tools in relation to raster images, they can also be invaluable in controlling visibility of line work in conjunction with hatch patterns and solid fills. See Chapter 14 for a detailed discussion of the display order tools and solid fills.

TIP *Under certain conditions, the draw order of external reference files may not appear properly. If you encounter this problem, open the Xref file and make sure the draw order is correct. Then use the Wblock command to export all its objects to a new file. Use the new file for the external reference instead of the original external reference.*

Clipping a Raster Image

ACAD only

In Chapter 6, you saw how you can clip an external reference object so that only a portion of it appears in the drawing. You can also clip imported raster images in the same way. Just as with Xrefs, you can create a closed outline of the area you want to clip, or you can specify a simple rectangular area. In the following exercise, you'll try out the Imageclip command to control the display of the raster image.

1. Choose Modify ➢ Clip ➢ Image, or type **Icl**↵.
2. At the `Select image to clip:` prompt, click the edge of the raster image.
3. At the `Enter image clipping option [ON/OFF/Delete/New boundary]<New>:` prompt, press ↵ to create a new boundary.
4. At the `Enter clipping type [Polygonal/Rectangular]<Rectangular>:` prompt, enter **P**↵ to draw a polygonal boundary.
5. Select the points shown in the top image in Figure 12.12 and then press ↵. The raster image is clipped to the boundary you created, as shown in the second image in Figure 12.12.

As the prompt in step 3 indicates, you can turn the clipping off or on, or you can delete an existing clipping boundary through the Clip Image option.

Once you have clipped a raster image, you can adjust the clipping boundary using its grips.

1. Click the boundary edge of the raster image to expose its grips.
2. Click a grip in the upper-right corner, as shown in the final image in Figure 12.12.
3. Drag the grip up and to the right, and then click a point. The image adjusts to the new boundary.

In addition to hiding portions of a raster image that are unimportant to you, clipping an image file reduces the amount of RAM the raster image uses during your editing session. AutoCAD loads only the visible portion of the image into RAM and ignores the rest.

FIGURE 12.12

Adjusting the boundary of a clipped image

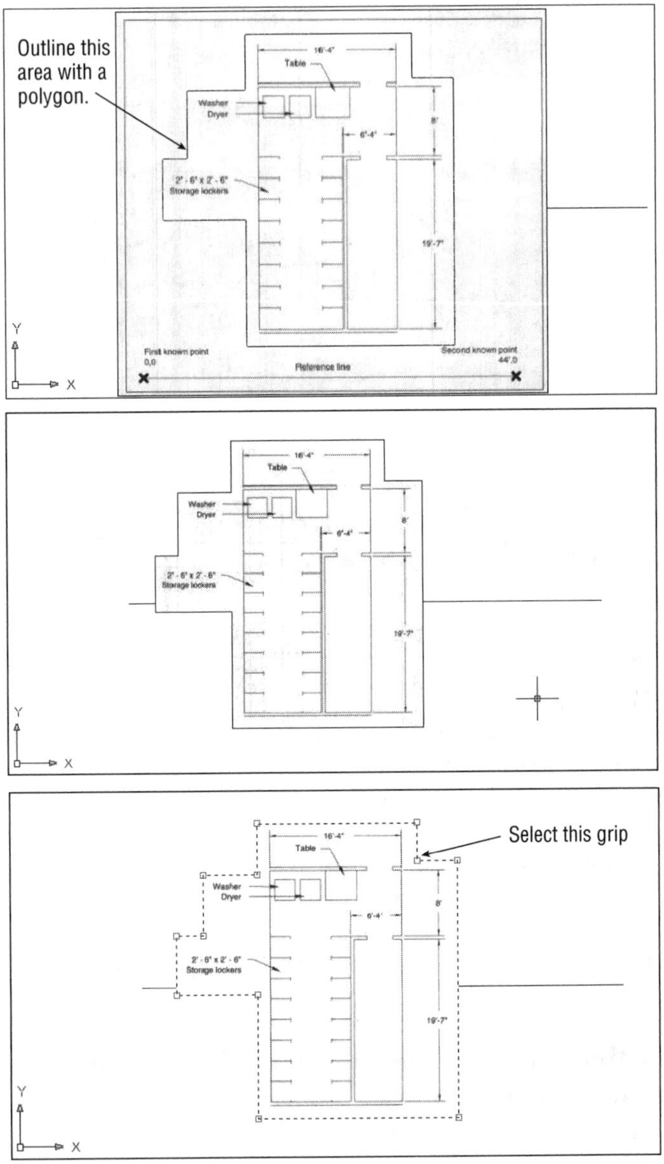

Adjusting Brightness, Contrast, and Strength

ACAD only

AutoCAD offers a tool that allows you to adjust the brightness, contrast, and strength of a raster image. Try making some adjustments to the raster image of the utility room in the following exercise.

1. Choose Modify ➢ Object ➢ Image ➢ Adjust, or type **Iad**↵.

2. At the `Select Image(s):` prompt, click the edge of the raster image and press ↵ to open the Image Adjust dialog box.

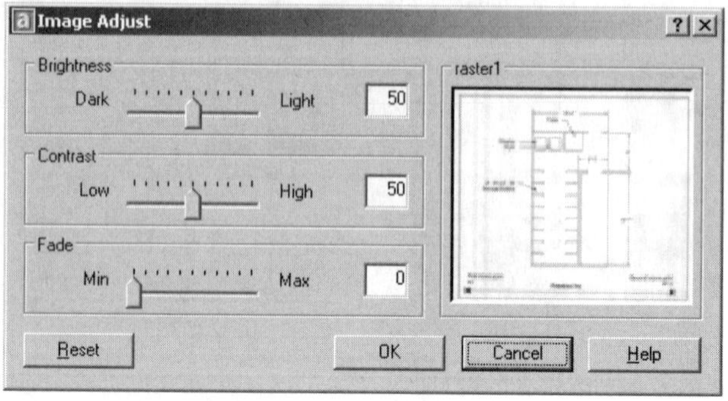

3. Click and drag the Fade slider to the right so that it is near the middle of the slider scale. Or enter **50** in the Fade input box that is just to the right of the slider. Notice how the sample image fades to the AutoCAD background color as you move the slider.
4. Click OK. The raster image appears faded.
5. Save the file as `Rasterimport.dwg`.

You can adjust the brightness and contrast using the other two sliders in the Image Adjust dialog box. Clicking the Reset button resets all the settings to their default value.

By using the Image Adjust option in conjunction with image clipping, you can create special effects. Figure 12.13 shows an aerial view of downtown San Francisco. This view consists of two copies of the same raster image. One copy serves as a background, which was lightened using the same method demonstrated in the previous exercise. The second copy is the darker area of the image with a roughly triangular clip boundary applied. You might use this technique to bring focus to a particular area of a drawing you are preparing for a presentation.

If the draw order of objects is incorrect after opening a file or performing a Pan or Zoom, issue a Regen to recover the correct draw order view.

Turning Off the Frame, Adjusting Overall Quality, and Controlling Transparency

You can make three other adjustments to your raster image: *frame visibility*, *image quality*, and *image transparency*.

By default, a raster image displays an outline or a frame. In many instances, this frame can detract from your drawing. You can globally turn off image frames by choosing Modify ➢ Object ➢ Image ➢ Frame (LT users should choose Modify ➢ Object ➢ Image Frame) and then entering **On** or **Off**, depending on whether you want the frame visible or invisible (see Figure 12.14). You can also type **Imageframe**↵ **Off**↵.

FIGURE 12.13

Two copies of the same image can be combined to create emphasis on a portion of the drawing.

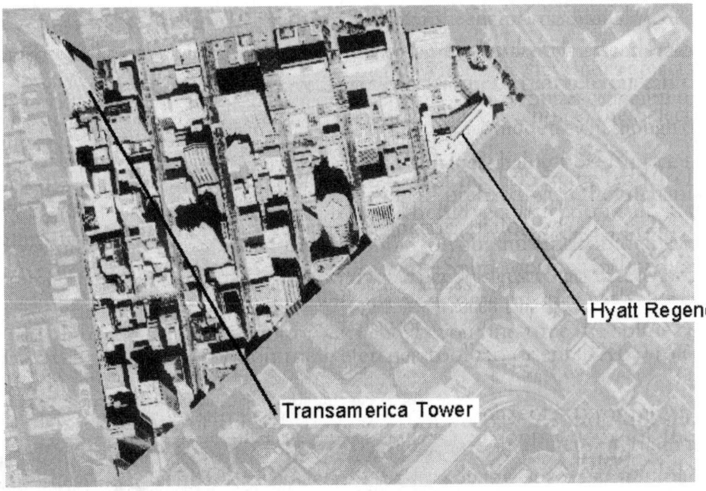

FIGURE 12.14

A raster image with the frame on (top) and off (bottom)

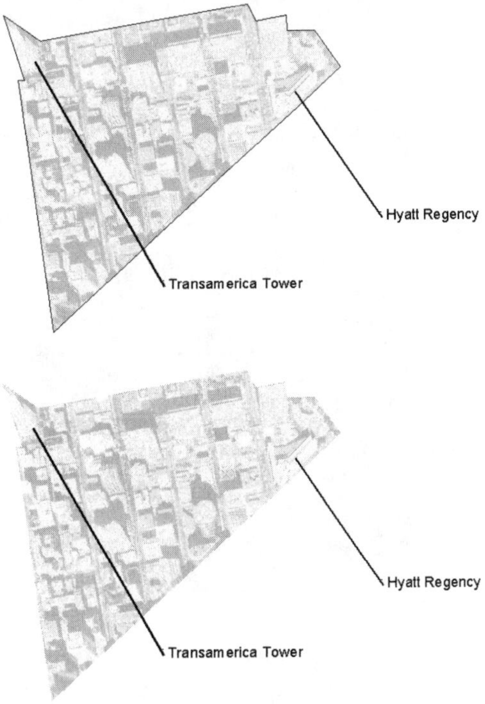

WARNING *If you turn off the frame of a raster image, you will not be able to select the image for editing. You can use this to your advantage if you don't want a raster image to be moved or otherwise edited. To make a raster image selectable, turn on the image frame setting.*

ACAD only

If your drawing doesn't require the highest quality image, you can set the image quality to Draft mode. You might use Draft mode when you are tracing an image or when the image is already of a high quality. To set the image quality, choose Modify ➢ Object ➢ Image ➢ Quality, and then enter **H** for high quality or **D** for Draft mode. In Draft mode, your drawing will regenerate faster.

The High mode softens the pixels of the raster image, giving the image a smoother appearance. The Draft mode displays the image in a "raw," pixelated state. If you look carefully at the regions between the truck and the background in the second image in Figure 12.15, you will see that it appears a bit jagged. The first image in Figure 12.15 uses the High setting to soften the edges of the truck. You may need to look closely to see the difference.

FIGURE 12.15

A close-up of a raster image with quality set to High (top) and Draft (bottom)

Finally, you can control the transparency of raster image files that allow transparent pixels. Some file formats, such as the CompuServe GIF 89a format, allow you to set a color in the image to be transparent (usually the background color). Most image-editing programs support this format because it is a popular one used on web pages.

When you turn on the Transparency setting, objects normally obscured by the background of a raster image may show through. Choose Modify ➢ Object ➢ Image ➢ Transparency, and then select the raster image that you want to make transparent. Enter **On** or **Off**, depending on whether you want the image to be transparent or not. Unlike the Frame and Quality options, Transparency works on individual objects rather than globally.

TIP *The Properties tool in the Object Properties toolbar offers many of the same adjustments described in this section, and you can use it for quick access to the Transparency setting and other raster image settings. You can access the Image Adjust dialog box, hide or display clipped areas, or hide the entire raster image.*

WARNING *In earlier versions of AutoCAD, you had the option to import PostScript files. AutoCAD 2004 no longer supports this function. If you need to import a PostScript file, you will have to convert the file into a format that AutoCAD will accept. Most programs that generate PostScript files will also produce DXF files or Windows Metafile files (WMF). Either of these formats can be imported to AutoCAD using the Insert menu.*

If You Want to Experiment...

You've seen how you can import a scanned image of an existing drawing and scale it to full scale. Try tracing over that scanned image in the next exercise.

1. If you have closed the `Rasterimport.dwg` file, open it again.
2. Use the Line tool and trace over the outline of the floor plan. As you draw, use the dimensions shown in the scanned image to determine the lengths of the lines. Use the Direct Distance method described in Chapter 2 to place the lines. You might also want to use the Ortho mode or the Polar Tracking mode to keep your lines straight.
3. Create a layer called Image, and change the layer assignment of the raster image to the Image layer.
4. Turn the Image layer off to view your floor plan.

Chapter 13

Power Editing

BECAUSE YOU MAY NOT know all of a project's requirements when it begins, you usually base the first draft of a design on projected needs. As the plan goes forward, you make adjustments for new requirements as they arise. As more people enter the project, additional design restrictions come into play, and the design is further modified. This process continues throughout the project, from the first draft to the end product.

In this chapter, you will review much of what you've already learned. Throughout the process, you will look at some techniques for setting up drawings to help manage the continual changes a project undergoes. You will also be introduced to tools and techniques you can use to minimize duplication of work. AutoCAD can be a powerful timesaving tool if used properly. This chapter examines ways to harness that power.

This chapter includes the following topics:

- Editing More Efficiently
- Using External References (Xrefs)
- Using the Layout Tabs and Paper Space
- Understanding Line Weights, Line Types, and Dimensions in Paper Space
- Managing Layers
- Advanced Tools: Quick Select, Selection Filters, and the Calculator
- If You Want to Experiment...

Editing More Efficiently

The apartment building plan you've been working on is currently incomplete. For example, you need to add the utility room you created in Chapter 12. In the real world, this building plan would also undergo numerous changes as the project developed. Wall and door locations would change, and more notes and dimensions would be added. However, in the space of this book's tutorials, we can't develop these drawings to full completion. But we can give you a sample of what is in store while using AutoCAD on such a project.

In this section, you will add a closet to the Unit plan. (You will update the `Plan` file later in this chapter.) In the editing you've already done, you've probably found that you use the following commands frequently: Move, Offset, Fillet, Trim, Grips, and the Osnap overrides. Now you will learn some ways to shorten your editing time by using them more efficiently.

QUICK ACCESS TO YOUR FAVORITE COMMANDS

As you continue to work with AutoCAD, you'll find that you use a handful of commands 90 percent of the time. You can collect your favorite commands into a single toolbar using AutoCAD's toolbar customization feature. This way, you can have ready access to your most frequently used commands. Chapter 21 gives you all the information you need to create your own custom toolbars.

Editing an Existing Drawing

First, let's look at how you can add a closet to the Unit plan. You'll begin by copying existing objects to provide the basis for the closet:

1. Open the `Unit` file.
2. Make Wall the current layer by trying the following: click the Make Object's Layer Current tool on the Object Properties toolbar, and then click a wall line.
3. Make sure the Notes and Flr-pat layers are frozen. This will keep your drawing clear of objects you won't be editing.

TIP *If you didn't create a Unit plan, you can use* `13a-unit.dwg` *from the companion CD.*

4. If they are not already on, turn on Noun/Verb Selection and the Grips feature. Also turn off Running Osnaps and Polar Tracking for now. They may get in the way of point selection in these exercises.
5. Click the right-side wall, and then click its midpoint grip.
6. Enter **C↵** to start the Copy mode; then enter **@2'<180↵**. Metric users should enter **@60<180↵** (see Figure 13.1).
7. Press the Esc key to exit the Grip mode.
8. Zoom in to the entry area shown in Figure 13.2.
9. Click Offset on the Modify toolbar, or type **O↵**.
10. At the `Offset distance or through:` prompt, use the Nearest Osnap and pick the outside wall of the bathroom near the door, as shown in Figure 13.2.
11. At the `Second point:` prompt, use the Perpendicular Osnap override and pick the other side of that wall (see Figure 13.2).

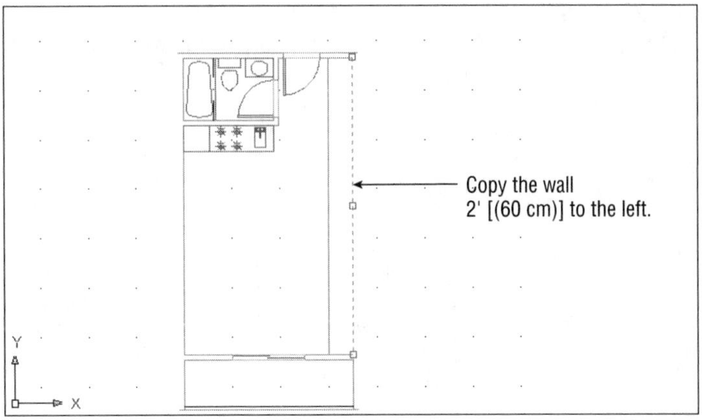
Copy the wall
2' [(60 cm)] to the left.
Y
X

FIGURE 13.1

Copying the wall to start the closet

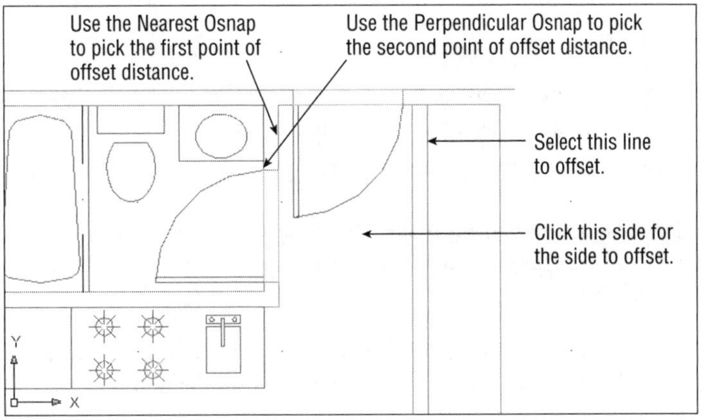
Use the Nearest Osnap to pick the first point of offset distance.
Use the Perpendicular Osnap to pick the second point of offset distance.
Select this line to offset.
Click this side for the side to offset.
Y
X

FIGURE 13.2

Using an existing wall as a distance reference for copying

12. Click the copy of the wall line you just created, and then click a point to the left of it.

13. Press ↵ to exit the Offset command.

In steps 9 and 10 of the previous exercise, you determined the offset distance by selecting existing geometry. If you know you want to duplicate a distance but don't know what that distance is, you can often use existing objects as references.

Next, use the same idea to copy a few more lines for the other side of the closet:

1. Click to highlight the two horizontal lines that make up the wall at the top of your view.

2. Shift+click the midpoint grips of these lines (see Figure 13.3).

FIGURE 13.3
Adding the second closet wall

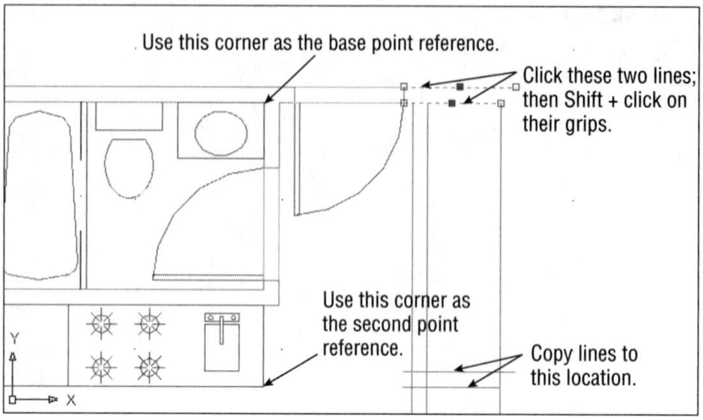

3. Click again one of the midpoint grips, and then enter **C**↵ to select the Copy option.
4. Enter **B**↵ to select a base point option.
5. Use the upper-right corner of the bathroom for the base point and the lower-right corner of the kitchen as the second point.
6. Press the Esc key twice to clear the grip selection.

TIP In these exercises, you are asked to enter the grip options through the keyboard. This can be a quicker method to access the Copy and Base grip options. You can also right-click your mouse and select the Copy and Base options from the shortcut menu.

Now you have the general layout of the closet. The next step is to clean up the corners. First, you'll have to do a bit of prep work and break the wall lines near the wall intersections, as shown in Figure 13.4.

FIGURE 13.4
Breaking the wall lines

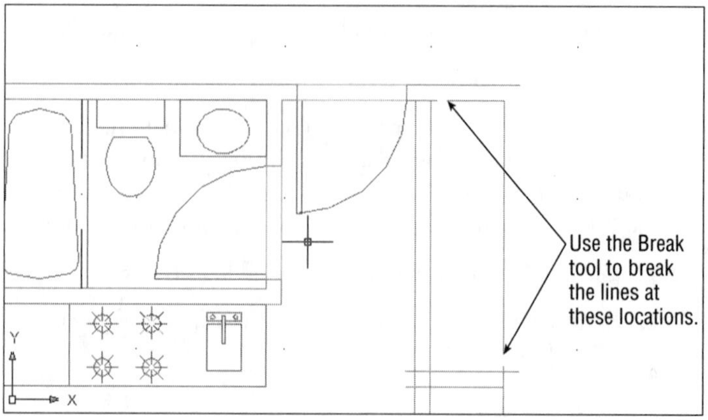

1. Click Break on the Modify toolbar. This tool creates a gap in a line, an arc, or a circle.
2. Click the vertical wall to the far right at a point near the location of the new wall (see Figure 13.4).
3. Click the vertical line again near the point you selected in step 2 to create a small gap, as shown in Figure 13.4.
4. Use the Break tool again to create a gap in the horizontal line at the top of the unit, near the door, as shown in Figure 13.4.

5. Click Fillet on the Modify toolbar, or type **F↵**, and join the corners of the wall, as shown in Figure 13.5.

FIGURE 13.5

Filleting the corners

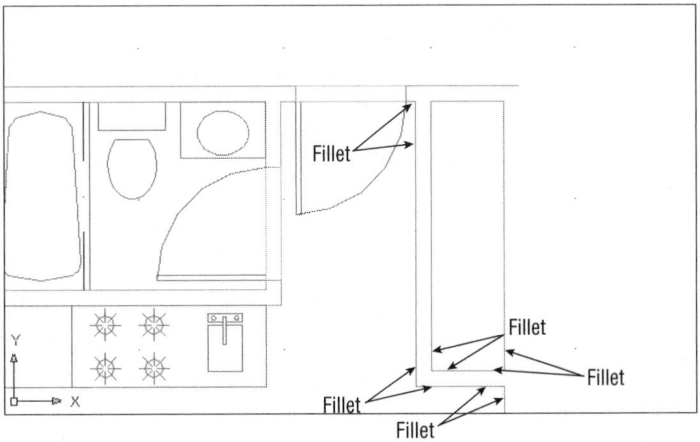

TIP If Fillet is not trimming lines, type ***Trimmode↵ 1↵****. This sets the Trimmode system variable to 1, which causes the Fillet and Chamfer tools to "trim" objects back to their intersection points.*

In steps 2 and 3, you didn't have to be too exact about where to pick the break points because choosing Construct ➢ Fillet takes care of joining the wall lines exactly. Now you are ready to add the finishing touches:

1. At the closet door location, draw a line from the midpoint of the interior closet wall to the exterior (see the top image in Figure 13.6). Make sure this line is on the Jamb layer.
2. Offset the new line 3' in both directions (90 cm for metric users). These new lines are the closet door jambs.
3. Erase the first line you drew at the midpoint of the closet wall.

4. Click Trim on the Modify toolbar, or type **Tr↵**.
5. Click the two jambs, and then press ↵.

FIGURE 13.6
Constructing the closet door jambs

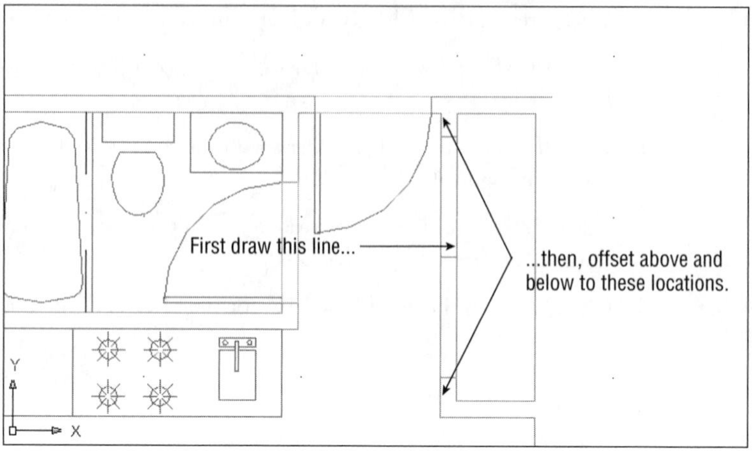

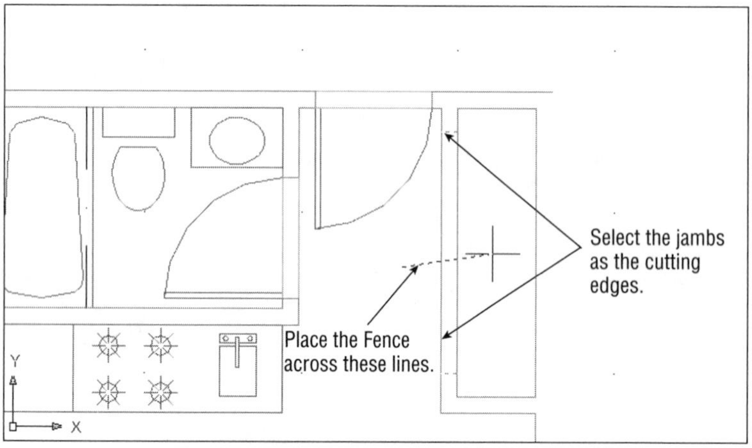

6. Type F↵ to invoke the Fence selection option; then click a point to the left of the wall, as shown in the bottom image in Figure 13.6.
7. As you move the cursor, you see a rubber-banding line from the last point you picked. Click a point to the right of the closet wall so that the rubber-banding line crosses over the two wall lines, as shown in Figure 13.6.
8. Press ↵ to finish your fence selection. The wall lines trim back to the jambs.
9. Press ↵ again to exit the Trim command.
10. As shown in Figure 13.7, add the door headers and the sliding doors and assign these objects to their appropriate layers.
11. Choose File ➢ Save to save the file. If you used the file from the companion CD, choose File ➢ Save As and save the file under the name `Unit`.

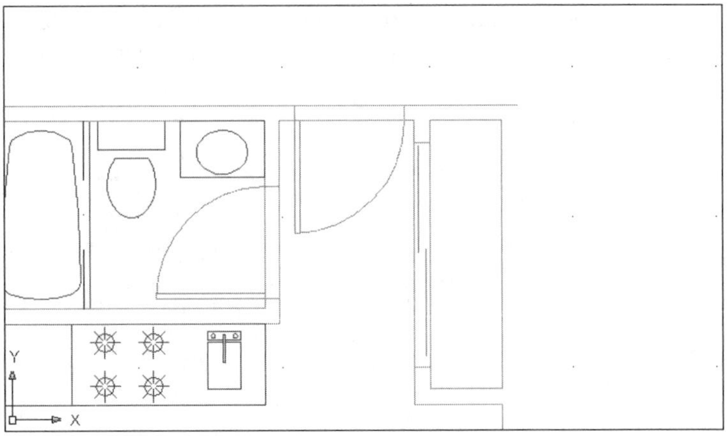

FIGURE 13.7
The finished closet

TIP *You can use the Match Properties tool to make a set of objects match the layer of another object. Click Match Properties on the Standard toolbar, select the objects whose layer you want to match, and then select the objects you want to assign to the objects layer. See Chapter 6 for more on the Match Properties tool.*

In this exercise, you used the Fence selection option to select the objects you wanted to trim. You could have selected each line individually by clicking it, but the Fence selection option offered you a quick way to select a set of objects without having to be too precise about where they are selected. You'll get a closer look at the Fence selection option a bit later in this chapter.

This exercise also showed that it's easier to trim lines back and then draw them back in than to try to break them precisely at each jamb location. At first this may seem counterproductive, but trimming the lines and then drawing in headers actually takes fewer steps and is a less-tedious operation than some other routes. And the end result is a door that is exactly centered on the closet space.

Building on Previously Drawn Objects

Suppose your client decides that your apartment building design needs a few one-bedroom units. In this exercise, you will use the studio unit drawing as a basis for the one-bedroom unit. To do so, you will double the studio's size, add a bedroom, move the kitchen, rearrange and add closets, and move the entry doors. In the process of editing this new drawing, you will see how you can build on previously drawn objects.

Start by setting up the new file. As you work through this exercise, you'll be using commands that you've seen in previous exercises, so I won't bother describing every detail. But do pay attention to the process taking place, as shown in Figures 13.8 through 13.12.

1. You've already saved the current `Unit` file. Now choose File ➢ Save As to save this file under the name of `Unit2.dwg`. This way, you can use the current file as the basis for the new one-bedroom unit.
2. Turn on the Notes layer and type Z↵ A↵ to get an overall view of the drawing.

3. Move the dimension string at the right of the unit, 14'-5" (439 cm) farther to the right, and copy the unit the same distance to the right. Your drawing should look like Figure 13.8.

FIGURE 13.8

The copied unit

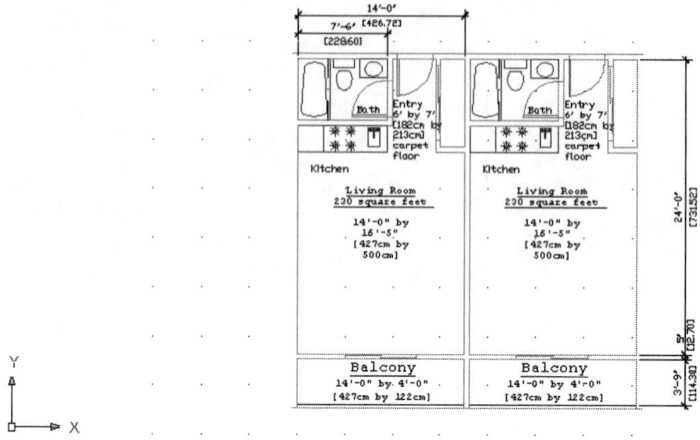

4. Now erase the bathroom, kitchen, door, closet, room labels, and wall lines, as shown in Figure 13.9.

TIP *Although you could be more selective in step 4 about the objects you erase and then add line segments where there are gaps in walls, this is considered bad form. When editing files, it's wise to keep lines continuous rather than fragmented. Adding line segments increases the size of the drawing database and slows down editing operations.*

FIGURE 13.9

Objects to be erased

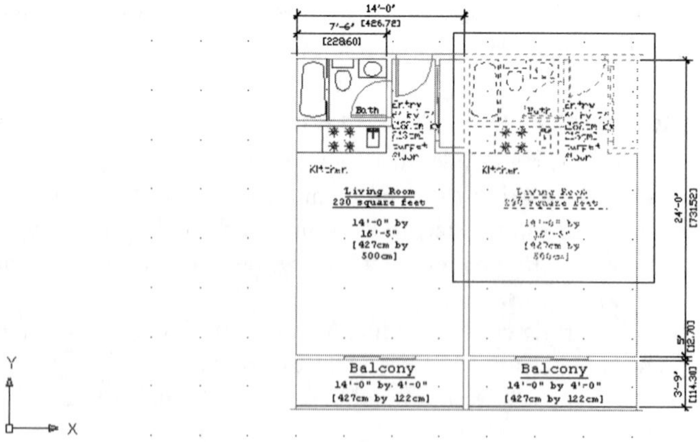

USING THE TEMPORARY TRACKING POINT FEATURE

The living room of this one-bedroom unit will be on the right side. You will want to move the Living Room label from the left half to the right half. Normally, you would probably just move the label without worrying about accuracy, but I'll take this opportunity to show how the Temporary Tracking Point feature works. In the next exercise, you will place the Living Room label in the center of the living room area:

1. Make sure the Osnap and Polar buttons are off in the status bar; then click the Living Room label in the unit to the left.
2. Click the top-center grip in the label, as shown in the first image in Figure 13.10.

FIGURE 13.10

Using the Tracking feature to move the Living Room label to the center of the new living room

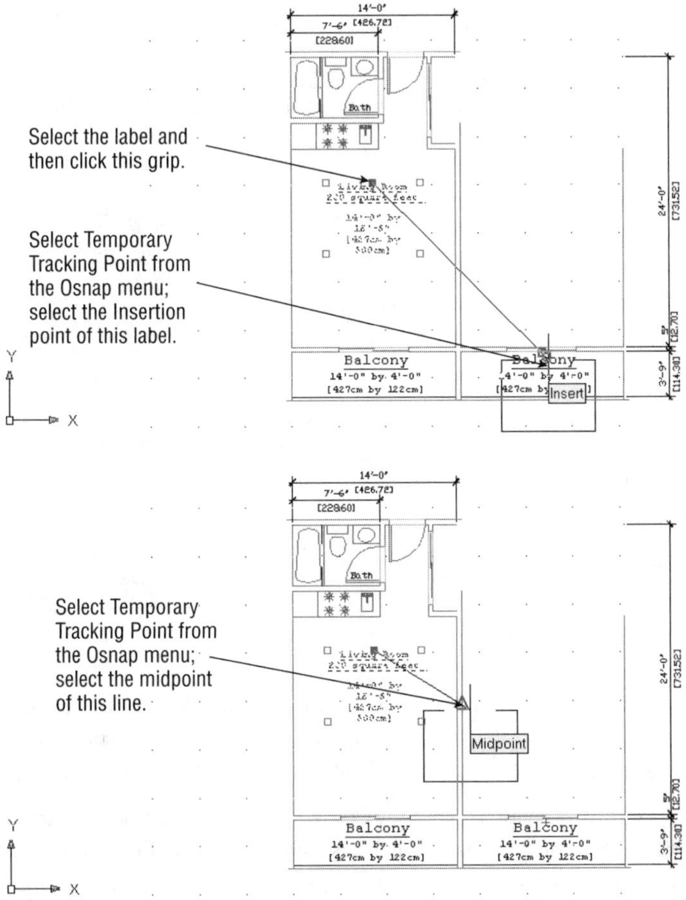

Select the label and then click this grip.
Select Temporary Tracking Point from the Osnap menu; select the Insertion point of this label.
Insert
Balcony
Select Temporary Tracking Point from the Osnap menu; select the midpoint of this line.
Midpoint

3. Shift+right-click the mouse to open the Osnap menu.
4. Choose Temporary Tracking Point. LT users should select Tracking.
5. Shift+right-click again, and then choose Insert from the Osnap menu.

6. Click the insertion point of the Balcony label of the unit to the right, as shown in the first image in Figure 13.10. Notice a tracking vector emanating from the selected insertion point, as shown in the second image in Figure 13.10.
7. Shift+right-click and select Temporary Tracking Point. LT users should select Tracking.
8. Shift+right-click again and select Midpoint.
9. This time, click the midpoint of the vertical wall between the two units, as shown in the second image in Figure 13.10. Notice that a tracking vector now emanates from a point that represents the intersection of the text insertion point and the midpoint of the wall.
10. Move the text to the middle of the room to the right, as shown in Figure 13.11. Notice that two tracking vectors appear and converge in the middle of the room (LT users will not see the tracking vectors).

FIGURE 13.11

The tracking vectors intersect in the middle of the room.

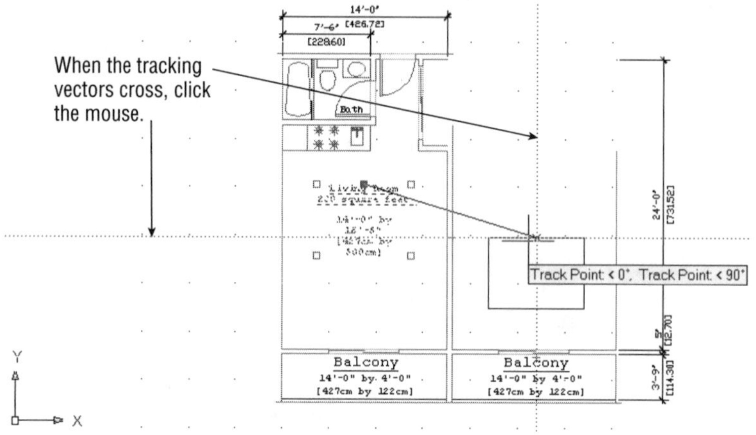

11. With the tracking vectors crossing and the text in the approximate location shown in Figure 13.11, click the mouse. (LT users can just press ↵ without clicking the mouse). The text moves to the middle of the unit to the right.

In earlier chapters, you saw how to use the Object Snap Tracking feature with Running Osnaps. Here, you used Object Snap Tracking in a slightly different way through the Temporary Tracking Point feature (or Tracking in LT). The Temporary Tracking Point feature works by allowing you to select points that are aligned orthogonally, like the insertion point of the balcony text and the midpoint of the wall in the previous exercise. But unlike Object Snap Tracking with Running Osnaps, the Temporary Tracking Point feature lets you focus on specific object snap points.

The following exercise shows how you can use Temporary Tracking Point in conjunction with the Polar Tracking tool to move the endpoint of a line to align with the endpoint of another line.

1. Click the line at the top-right side of the unit to expose its grips, as shown in the top image in Figure 13.12.

FIGURE 13.12

Stretching a line using the Tracking function

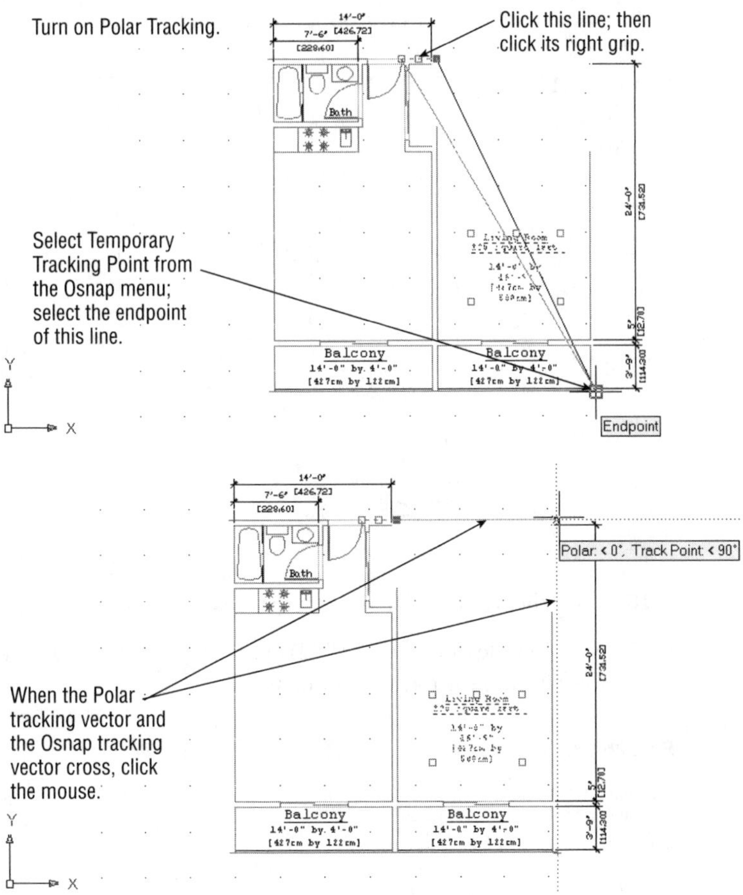

2. Click the grip at the right end of the line.
3. As in the previous exercise, choose Temporary Tracking Point from the Osnap menu.
4. Open the Osnap menu again and choose Endpoint.
5. Click the Polar button in the status bar to turn it on.
6. Select the rightmost endpoint of the short line at the bottom-right corner of the unit, as shown in the top image in Figure 13.12.
7. Move the cursor so that the Polar Tracking vector crosses the Osnap Tracking vector in the upper-right corner of the drawing, as shown in the bottom image in Figure 13.12; then click that point.
8. Press the Esc key twice to clear the grip selection.

9. Move the kitchen to the opposite corner of the unit, as shown in Figure 13.13.

FIGURE 13.13
Moving the closet and kitchen

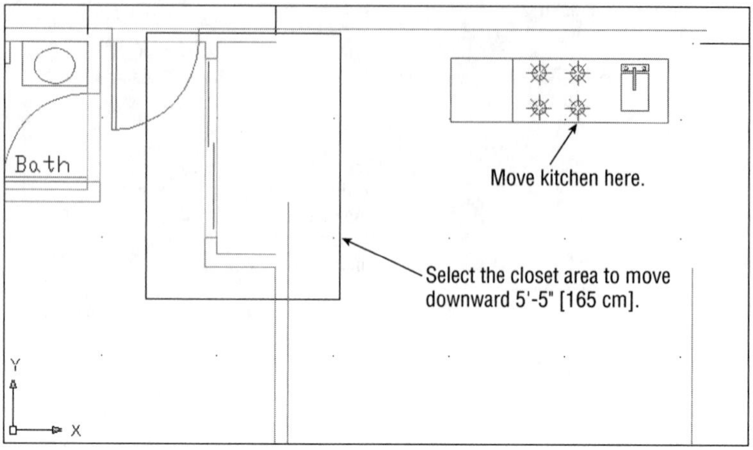

10. Click the Move tool and select the closet area, as shown in Figure 13.13.
11. Move the closet down 5'-5" (165 cm), as shown in Figure 13.14. You can use the corners of the bathroom as reference points.

FIGURE 13.14
Using an existing door to create a door opening

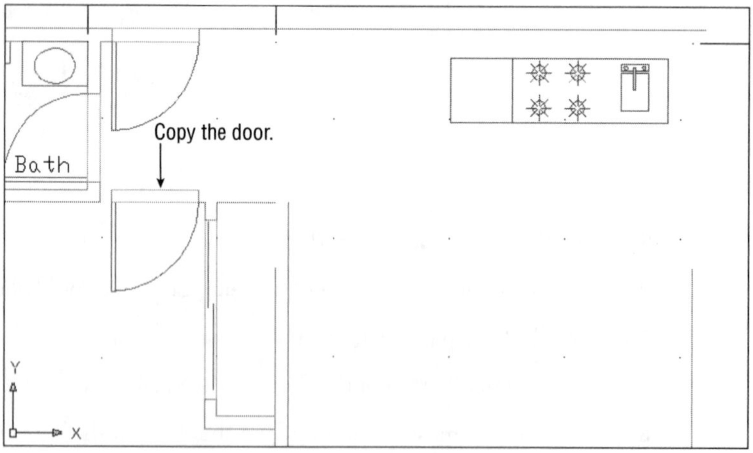

When a drawing gets crowded, you may find that Running Osnaps gets in the way of your work. The Temporary Tracking Point feature lets you access the Osnap Tracking vector without having to turn on Running Osnaps.

The Temporary Tracking Point feature and the other tools that use tracking vectors take a little practice to use, but once you understand how they work, they are an indispensable aid in your drawing.

WORKING WITH THE FENCE SELECTION OPTION

Next, you'll work on finishing the new bedroom door and entry. Once again, you will get a chance to work with the Fence selection option. Fence is a great tool for selecting locations on objects that would otherwise be difficult to select. With Fence, you can select objects by crossing over them with a rubber-banding line. It's like selecting objects by crossing them out. In addition, the point at which the rubber-banding line crosses the object is equivalent to a pick point. This is important when using commands that respond differently depending on where objects are selected. The following exercise shows how the Fence selection option can be helpful in selecting objects in tight spaces.

1. Copy the existing entry door downward, including header and jambs (see Figure 13.14). Use the Endpoint override to locate the door accurately.
2. Clean up the walls by adding new lines and filleting others, as shown in Figure 13.15.

TIP *Use the midpoint of the door header as the first axis endpoint.*

FIGURE 13.15

Cleaning up the wall

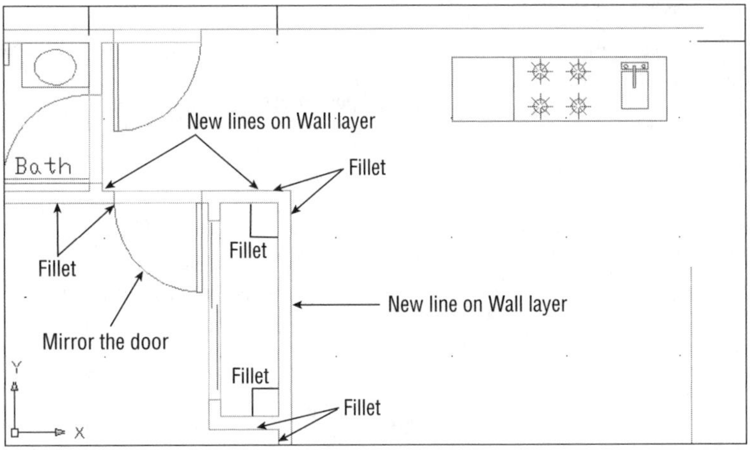

3. Mirror the door you just copied so it swings in the opposite direction.
4. Use Stretch (click Stretch on the Modify toolbar) to move the entry door a distance of 8' (244 cm) to the right, as shown in Figure 13.16. Remember to use a crossing window to select the objects and endpoints you want to stretch.
5. Once you've moved the entry door, mirror it in the same way you mirrored the other door.

In this exercise, you once again used parts of a previous drawing instead of creating new parts. In only a few instances are you adding new objects. Next, you'll use the Fence selection option to add a new closet wall.

1. Set the view of your drawing so it looks similar to the first image in Figure 13.17, and turn off Polar Tracking and Running Osnaps, if they are on.

FIGURE 13.16

Moving the door

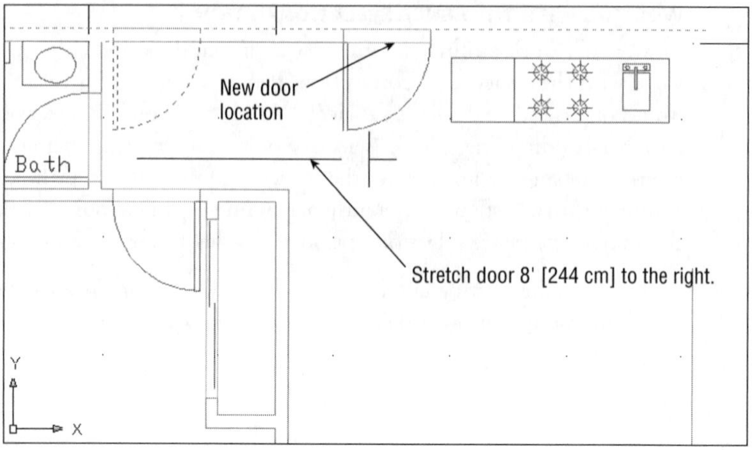

FIGURE 13.17

Adding walls for a second closet

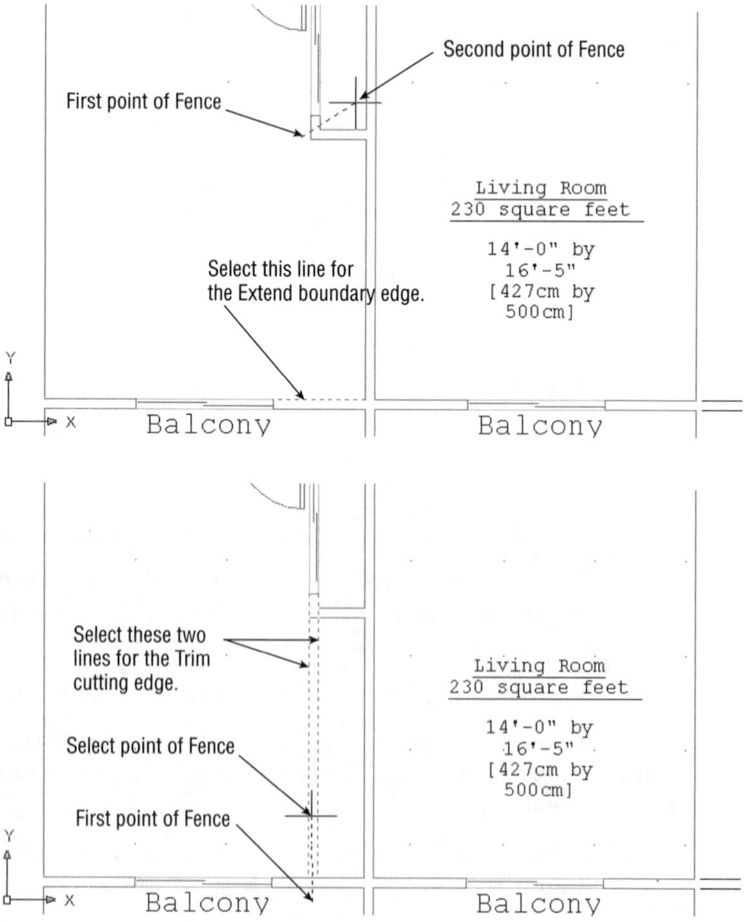

2. Click Extend on the Modify toolbar, or type **Ex↵** at the command prompt.
3. At the `Select boundary edge(s)... Select objects:` prompt, pick the wall at the bottom of the screen, as shown in Figure 13.17, and press ↵. Just as with Trim, the Extend command requires that you first select a set of objects to define the boundary of the extension and then select the objects you want to extend.
4. At the `Select object to extend or shift-select to trim or [Project/ Edge/Undo]:` prompt, you need to pick the two lines just below the closet door. To do this, first enter **F↵** to use the Fence selection option.
5. At the `First Fence point:` prompt, pick a point just to the left of the lines you want to extend.
6. Make sure the Ortho mode is off. Then at the `Undo/<Endpoint of line>:` prompt, pick a point to the right of the two lines so that the fence crosses over them (see the first image in Figure 13.17).
7. Press ↵. The two lines extend to the wall.
8. Press ↵ again to exit the Extend command.

You've extended the wall to form another closet space. The next step is to clean up the wall connections at the balcony.

1. Click Trim, and then select the two lines you just extended.
2. Press ↵ to finish your selection.
3. Type **F↵**, and then pick two points to place a fence between the endpoints of the two selected lines (see the second image in Figure 13.17).
4. Use a combination of Trim and Fillet to clean up the other walls.
5. Add another closet door on the right side of the new closet space you just created. Your drawing should look like Figure 13.18.

FIGURE 13.18

The second closet

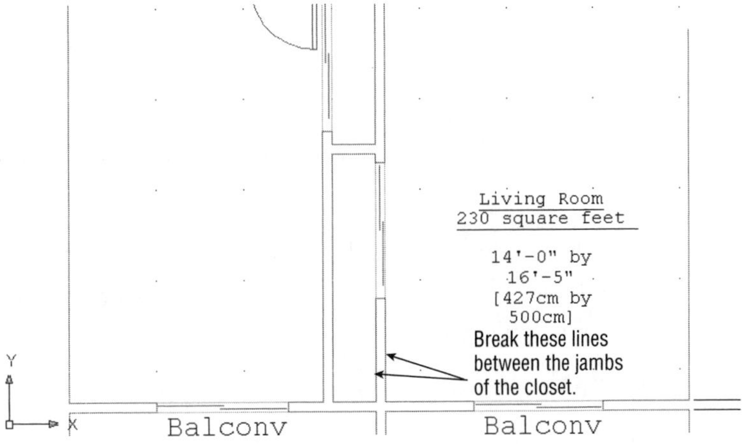

The Extend tool works just like the Trim tool: First you select the boundary objects, and then you select the objects you want to modify. Here again, you used the Fence selection option to select the object to extend. In this situation, the Fence option is crucial because it may be more difficult to select the lines individually.

TIP *At times you need to trim and extend in a single operation. You can do so by using the Shift key with the Trim or Extend command. When you hold down the Shift key in the Extend command while selecting objects to extend, the Extend command trims the objects. Likewise, when you hold down the Shift key while selecting objects to trim in the Trim command, AutoCAD extends the objects.*

Using Grips to Simplify Editing

Throughout this book, I've shown you ways of using the Grips feature to edit drawings. When and how you use grips will really depend on your preference, but in some situations editing with grips makes more sense than editing without them. Here you'll explore some basic situations in which grips can be useful.

Now, suppose you want to change the location and orientation of the kitchen. In this exercise, you will use the Grips feature to do just that.

1. Set up a view similar to the one in Figure 13.19 and turn on Polar Tracking.

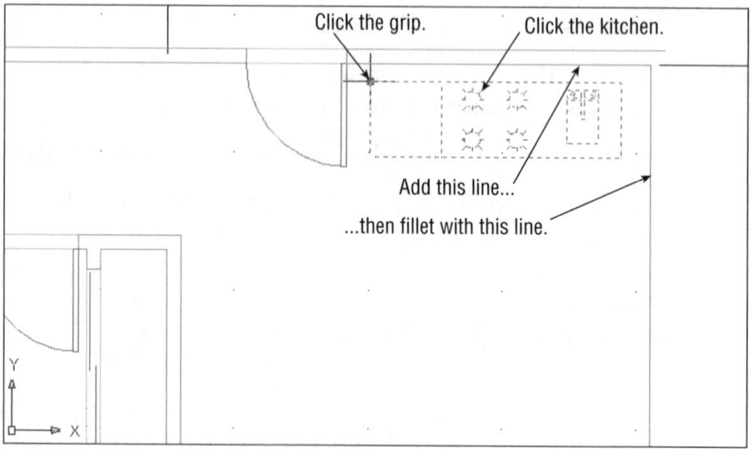

FIGURE 13.19
Finishing the kitchen wall and selecting the kitchen rotation base point

2. Add the horizontal line at the top of the kitchen, as shown in Figure 13.19.
3. Fillet the new line with the vertical wall line to the right of the unit.
4. Click the kitchen.
5. Click the grip in the upper-left corner to make it a hot grip. The grip changes from hollow to solid.

6. Right-click the mouse and then choose Rotate from the shortcut menu. (You can also press ↵ two times until you see the `*** ROTATE ***` message at the prompt.)

TIP *Remember that the spacebar acts the same as the* ↵ key for most commands, including the Grips modes.

7. Enter **–90** or rotate the kitchen by pointing the cursor downward until the tracking vector appears, and then click the mouse.
8. Click the kitchen grip again; then, using the Endpoint Osnap, click the upper-right corner of the room.
9. Press the Esc key twice to clear the grip selection. Your drawing should look like Figure 13.20.

FIGURE 13.20
The revised kitchen

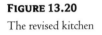

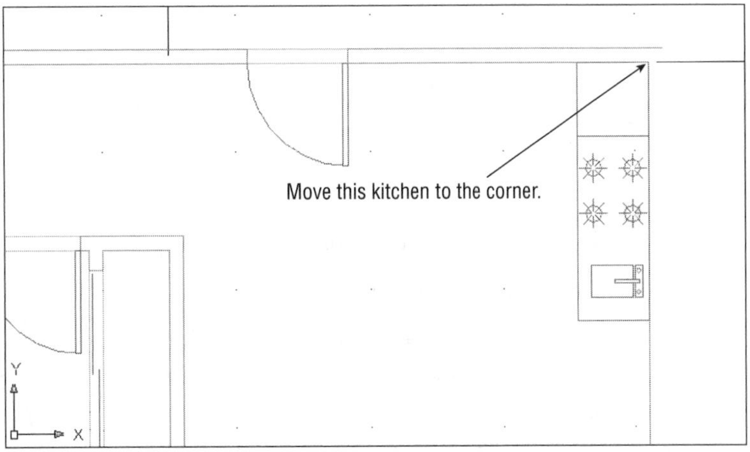
Move this kitchen to the corner.
Y
X

Because the kitchen is a block, its grip point is the same as its insertion point. This makes the kitchen block—as are all blocks—a great candidate for grip editing. Remember that the door, too, is a block.

DISPLAYING GRIPS OF OBJECTS WITHIN A BLOCK

You can set up AutoCAD to display the grips on all the entities within a block. This allows you to use those grips as handles for any of the grip operations such as Move, Rotate, or Scale. However, you cannot edit individual objects within the block.

To display all the grips within a block, type **Gripblock**↵ **1**↵. You can also turn on the Enable Grips Within A Block option in the Grips dialog box (choose Tools ➢ Grips).

Now suppose you want to widen the entrance door from 36" to 42" (90 cm to 105 cm for metric users). Try the following exercise involving a door and its surrounding wall.

1. Use a crossing window to select the door jamb to the left of the entry door, as shown in Figure 13.21.

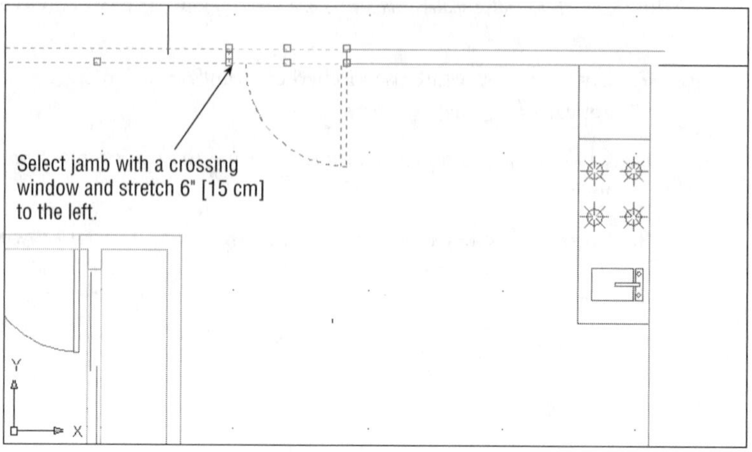

Select jamb with a crossing window and stretch 6" [15 cm] to the left.
Y
X

FIGURE 13.21
The widened door opening

2. Shift+click both of the door jamb's corner grips.
3. Click the bottom corner grip again. It is now a hot grip.
4. At the `** Stretch **` prompt, enter **@6<180** (metric users should enter **@15<180**). The door should now look like Figure 13.21. You can also use the Direct Distance method: With Polar Tracking on, point the cursor to the left and then type **6**↵.

TIP *The Stretch hot grip command will ignore a block as long as you do not include its insertion point in the stretch window.*

Notice that in step 4 you didn't have to specify a base point to stretch the grips. AutoCAD assumes the base to be the original location of the selected hot grip (the grip selected in step 3).

Now you can enlarge the door using the Grip command's Scale option. Scale allows you to change the size of an object or a group of objects. You can change the size visually by entering a scale value or by using an object for reference. In this exercise, you will use the current door width as a reference.

1. Press the Esc key twice to clear your selection set.
2. Click the door, and then click the door's grip point at the hinge side.
3. Right-click the mouse and choose Scale.
4. At the `Specify scale factor or [Base point/Copy/Undo/Reference /eXit]:` prompt, enter **R**↵ to select the Reference option.
5. At the `Specify reference length <0'-1">:` prompt, type **@**↵ to indicate that you want to use the door insertion point as the first point of the reference length.

6. At the `Specify second point:` prompt, click the grip at the endpoint of the door's arc at the wall line (see the first image in Figure 13.22). Now as you move the cursor, the door changes in size relative to the distance between the grip and the end of the arc.

FIGURE 13.22
The enlarged door

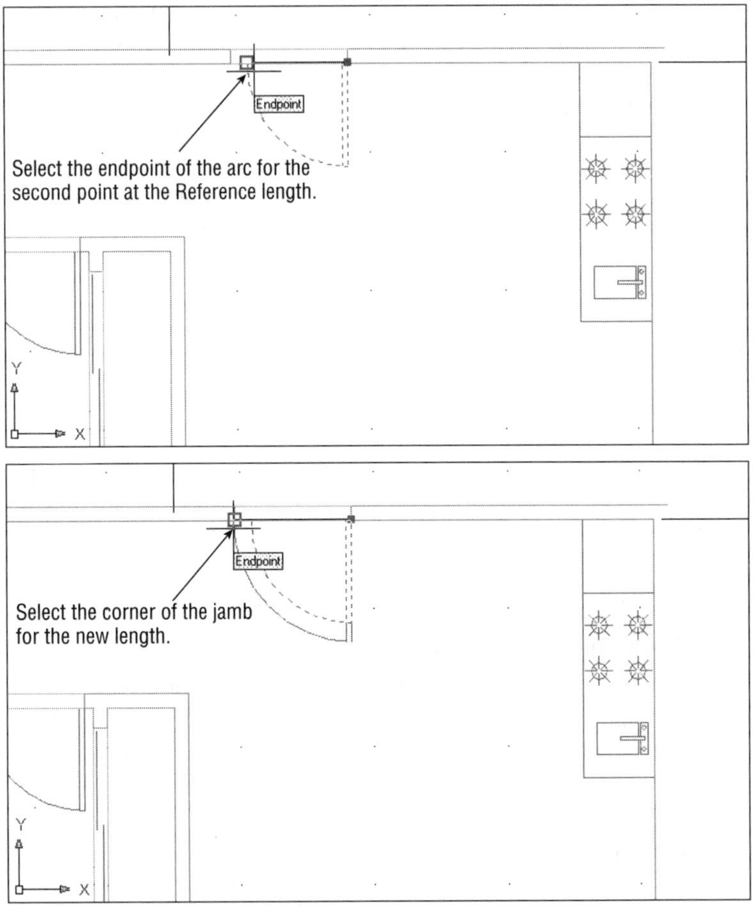
Endpoint
Select the endpoint of the arc for the second point at the Reference length.
Y
X
Endpoint
Select the corner of the jamb for the new length.
Y
X

7. At the `Specify new length or [Base point/Copy/Undo/Reference/ eXit]:` prompt, use the Endpoint Osnap again and click the door jamb directly to the left of the arc endpoint. The door enlarges to fit the new door opening (see the second image in Figure 13.22).

8. To finish this floor plan, zoom out to get the overall view of the unit, turn on the Flr-pat layer, and then erase the floor pattern in the bedroom area just below the bathroom.

9. Save the file.

You could have used the Modify ➢ Scale option to accomplish the operation performed in the this exercise with the Scale hot grip command. The advantage to using grips is that you don't need to use the Osnap to select exact grip locations, thereby reducing the number of steps you must take to accomplish this task.

In the next section, you will update the `Plan` file to include the revised studio apartment and the one-bedroom unit you have just created (see Figure 13.23). You will be making changes such as these throughout the later stages of your design project. As you have seen, AutoCAD's ability to make changes easily and quickly can ease your work and help you test your design ideas more accurately.

FIGURE 13.23

The finished one-bedroom unit

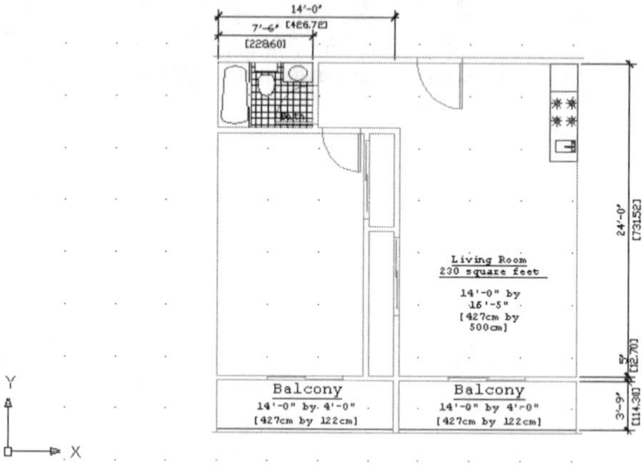

Singling Out Proximate Objects

Chapter 3 mentioned that you will encounter situations in which you need to select an object that is overlapping or very close to another object. Often in this situation, you end up selecting the wrong object. To help you select the exact object you want, AutoCAD offers the Selection Cycling tool and the Object Selection Settings dialog box.

SELECTION CYCLING

Selection cycling lets you cycle through objects that overlap until you select the one you want. To use this feature, hold down the Ctrl key and click the object you want to select. If the first object highlighted is not the one you want, click again, but this time don't hold down the Ctrl key. When several objects are overlapping, just keep clicking until the right object is highlighted and selected. When the object you want is highlighted, press ↵, and then go on to select other objects or press ↵ to finish the selection process. You might want to practice using selection cycling a few times to get the hang of it. It can be a bit confusing at first, but once you've gotten accustomed to how it works, the Selection Cycling tool can be invaluable.

OBJECT SORTING

If you are a veteran AutoCAD user, you may have grown accustomed to selecting the most recently created object of two overlapping objects by simply clicking it. In later versions of AutoCAD, you don't always get to the most recently drawn object when you click overlapping objects. But AutoCAD offers user-definable controls that set the method of selecting overlapping objects. These controls change the way AutoCAD selects overlapping objects.

If you prefer, you can set up AutoCAD to offer the most recently drawn object. Choose Tools ➢ Options to open the Options dialog box, and then click the User Preferences tab. The Object Sorting Methods button group of this tab lets you set the sort method for a variety of operations. If you enable any of the operations listed, AutoCAD sorts objects based on the order that they were added to the drawing. You will probably not want to change the sort method for Object Snap or Regens. But by checking Object Selection, you can control which of two overlapping lines is selected when you click them. For plotting and for PostScript output, you can control the overlay of screened or hatched areas.

These settings can also be controlled through system variables. See Appendix D for details.

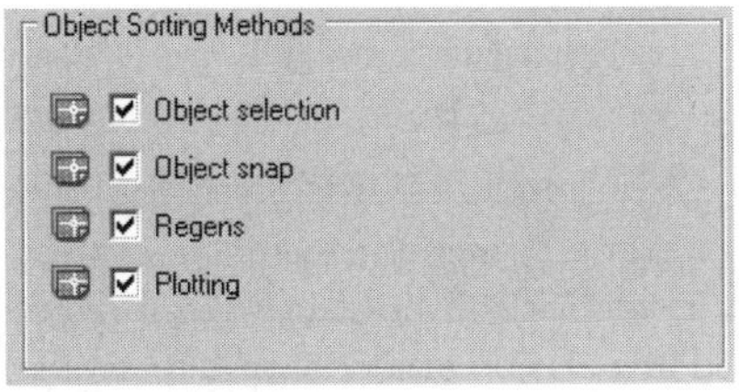

TIP *When you use the Draworder command (the Tools ➢ Display Order options), all the options in the Object Sorting Methods button group of the User Preferences tab of the Options dialog box are turned on.*

Using External References (Xrefs)

Chapter 6 mentioned that careful use of blocks, external references (Xrefs), and layers can help you improve your productivity. In this section you will see firsthand how to use these features to help reduce design errors and speed up delivery of an accurate set of drawings. You do this by controlling layers in conjunction with blocks and external referenced files to create a common drawing database for several drawings.

Preparing Existing Drawings for Cross-Referencing

Chapter 6 discussed how you can use Xrefs to assemble one floor of the apartment. In this section you will explore the creation and use of Xrefs to build multiple floors, each containing slightly different sets of drawing information. By doing so, you will learn how Xrefs allow you to use a single file in multiple drawings to save time and reduce redundancy. You'll see that by sharing common data in multiple files, you can reduce your work and keep the drawing information consistent.

You'll start by creating the files that you will use later as Xrefs:

1. Open the `Plan` file. If you didn't create the `Plan` file, you can use the `12a-plan.dwg` file from the companion CD (see Figure 13.24).

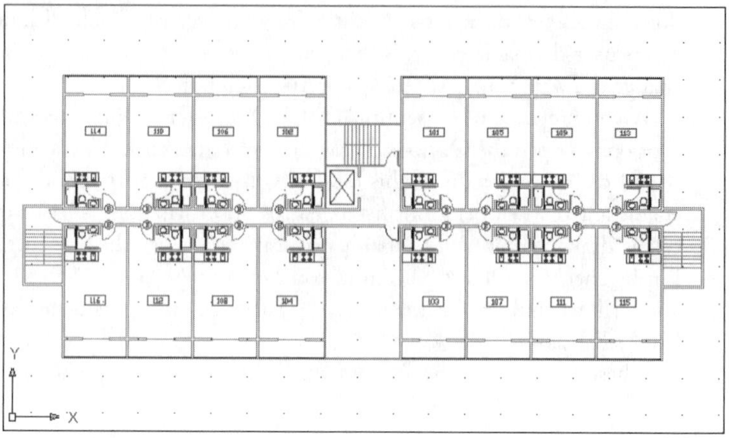

FIGURE 13.24
The overall plan

2. Turn off the Ceiling and Flr-pat layers to get a clear, uncluttered view of the individual unit plans.
3. Use the Wblock command (enter **W↵** at the command prompt) and write the eight units in the corners of your plan to a file called `Floor1.dwg` (see Figure 13.25). When you select objects for the Wblock, be sure to include the door symbols for those units. Use 0,0 for the Wblock insertion base point. Also make sure that the Delete From Drawing option is checked in the Write Block dialog box before you click OK.

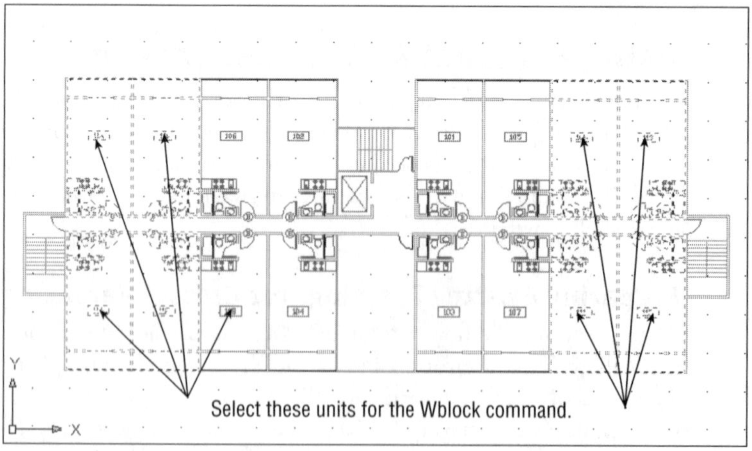

Select these units for the Wblock command.

FIGURE 13.25
Units to be exported to the `Floor1` file

4. Using Figure 13.26 as a guide, insert Unit2 into the corners where the other eight units were previously.

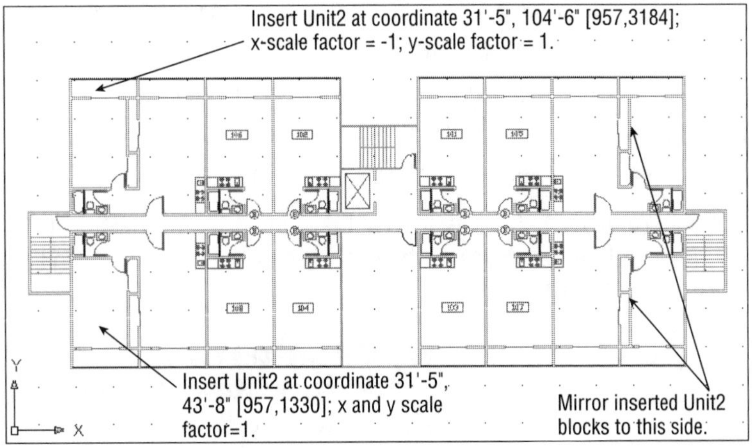
Insert Unit2 at coordinate 31'-5", 104'-6" [957,3184]; x-scale factor = -1; y-scale factor = 1.
Insert Unit2 at coordinate 31'-5", 43'-8" [957,1330]; x and y scale factor=1.
Mirror inserted Unit2 blocks to this side.
Y
X

FIGURE 13.26
Insertion information for Unit2. Metric coordinates are shown in brackets.

TIP *If you didn't create the* `Unit2` *file earlier in this chapter, use the* `12cUnit2.dwg` *file from the companion CD.*

5. Once you've accurately placed the corner units, use the Wblock command to write these corner units to a file called `Floor2.dwg`. Again, use the 0,0 coordinate as the insertion base point for the Wblock.

6. Choose File ➢ Save As to turn the remaining set of unit plans into a file called `Common.dwg`.

You've just created three files: `Floor1`, `Floor2`, and `Common`. Each of these files contains unique information about the building. Next, you'll use the Xref command to recombine these files for the different floor plans in your building.

Assembling External References to Build a Drawing

You will now create composite files for each floor, using external references of only the files needed for the individual floors. You will use the Attach option of the Xref command to insert all the files you exported from the Plan file.

1. Close the `Common.dwg` file, open a new file, and call it **`Xref-1`**.

2. Set up this file as an architectural drawing 8 1/2" × 11" with a scale of 1/16"=1'. The upper-right corner limits for such a drawing are 2112, 1632. Metric users should set up a drawing at 1:200 scale on an A4 sheet size. If you look at Table 3.4 in Chapter 3, you'll see that your drawing area should be 4200 cm by 5940 cm.

TIP *You are asked to use a small paper size since it is the most common size available to readers. Normally, you would specify a larger size and scale for architectural drawings.*

3. Set the Ltscale value to **192**. Metric users should set it to **200**.

4. Open the Reference toolbar by right-clicking a toolbar and then selecting Reference from the shortcut menu.

5. Click External Reference Attach on the Reference toolbar, or type **Xa↵** to open the Select Reference File dialog box.
6. Locate and select the `Common.dwg` file.
7. In the External Reference dialog box, make sure the Specify On-Screen check box in the Insertion Point group is not checked. Then make sure the X, Y, and Z values in the Insertion Point group are all 0.

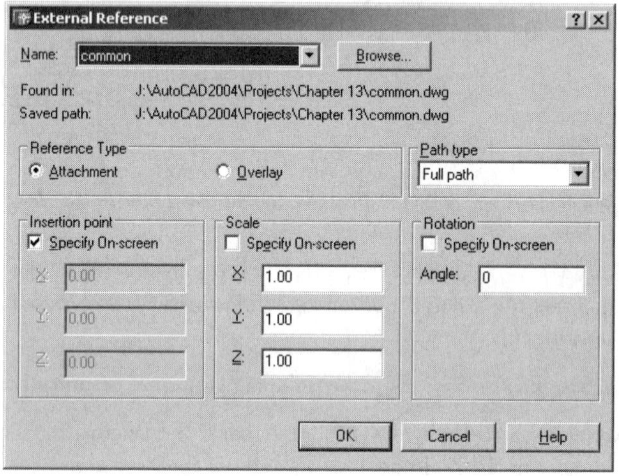

TIP *Because the insertion points of all the files are the same, namely 0,0, they will fit together perfectly when they are inserted into the new files.*

8. Click OK. The `Common.dwg` file appears in the drawing.
9. Click the External Reference Attach tool on the Reference toolbar again, and then click the Browse button to locate, select, and insert the `Floor1` file.

10. Repeat step 9 to insert the `Col-grid.dwg` file as an Xref. The `Col-grid.dwg` file can be found on the companion CD. You now have the plan for the first floor.
11. Save this file.

Now use the current file to create another file representing a different floor.

1. Choose File ➢ Save As to save this file as `Xref-2.dwg`.

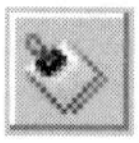

2. Click the External Reference tool in the Reference toolbar or type **Xr↵**.

3. In the Xref Manager dialog box, highlight Floor1 in the list of Xrefs, and then click Detach.

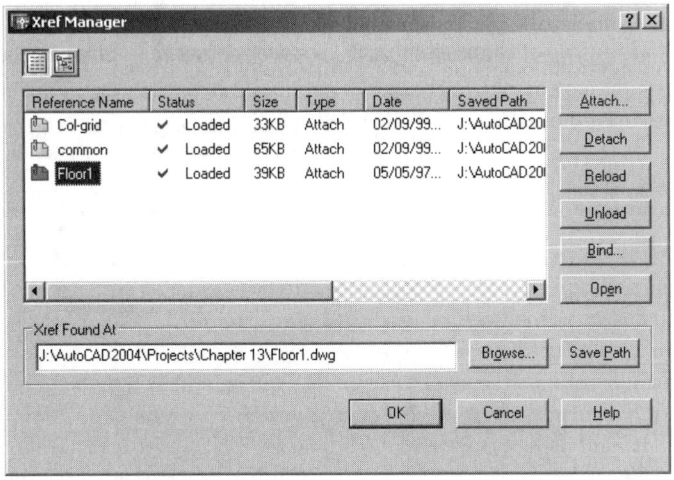

4. Click Attach.
5. Locate and select `Floor2.dwg`.
6. In the External Reference dialog box, make sure that the X, Y, and Z values in the Insertion Point group are all set to 0.
7. Click OK. The Floor2 drawing appears in place of Floor1.

WARNING *If you move an external reference file after you insert it into a drawing, AutoCAD may not be able to find it later when you attempt to open the drawing. If this happens, you can click the Browse button in the External Reference dialog box to tell AutoCAD the new location of the external reference file.*

Now when you need to make changes to `Xref-1` or `Xref-2`, you can edit the individual external reference files that they comprise. Then, the next time you open either `Xref-1` or `Xref-2`, the updated Xrefs will automatically appear in their most recent forms.

External references do not need to be permanent. As you saw in the previous exercise, you can attach and detach them easily at any time. This means, if you need to get information from another file—to see how well an elevator core aligns, for example—you can temporarily attach as an external reference the other file to quickly check alignments and then detach it when you are finished.

Think of these composite files as final plot files that are used only for plotting and reviewing. You can then edit the smaller, more manageable external reference files. Figure 13.27 illustrates the relationship of these files.

The combinations of external references are limited only by your imagination, but you should avoid multiple external references of the same file in one drawing.

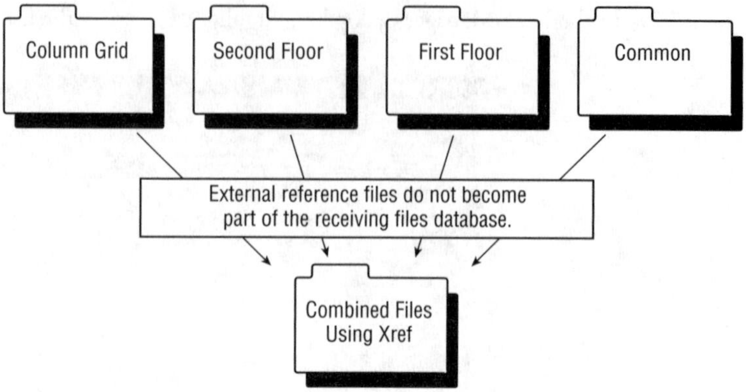

FIGURE 13.27
A diagram of external reference file relationships

TIP *Because Xref files do not become part of the file they are referenced into, you must take care to keep Xref files in a location where AutoCAD can find them when the referencing file is opened. This can be a minor annoyance when you need to send files to others outside your office. To help you keep track of external references, choose File ➢ eTransmit. See Chapter 22 for details.*

UPDATING BLOCKS IN EXTERNAL REFERENCES

Several advantages are associated with using external reference files. Because the Xrefs don't become part of the drawing file's database, the referencing files remain quite small. Also, because Xref files are easily updated, work can be split up among several people in a workgroup environment or on a network. For example, in our hypothetical apartment building, one person can be editing the `Common` file while another works on `Floor1`, and so on. The next time the composite `Xref-1.dwg` or `Xref-2.dwg` file is opened, it automatically reflects any new changes made in the external reference files. Now let's see how to set this up.

1. Close the `Xref-2` file and then open the `Common.dwg` file.

2. Update the Unit plan you edited earlier in this chapter. Click Insert Block on the Draw toolbar.
3. In the Insert dialog box, click the File button, and then locate and select `Unit.dwg`. Then click Open here, and again in the Insert dialog box.
4. At the warning message, click OK.
5. At the `Insertion point:` prompt, press the Esc key.
6. Enter RE↵ to regenerate the drawing. You will see the new Unit plan in place of the old one (see Figure 13.28). You might also see all the dimensions and notes for each unit.
7. If the Notes layer is on, use the Layer & Linetype Properties dialog box or the Layer drop-down list to turn it off.

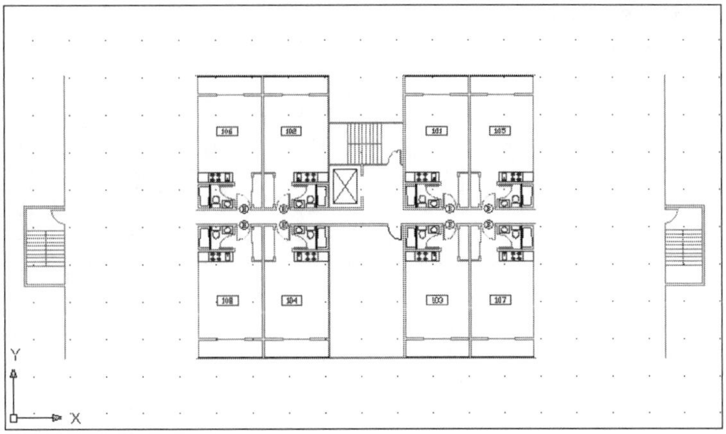

FIGURE 13.28
The `Common` file with the revised Unit plan

8. Using the Insert Block tool on the Draw toolbar again, replace the empty room across the hall from the lobby with the utility room you created in Chapter 11 (see Figure 13.29). If you didn't create the utility room drawing, use the `Utility.dwg` file from the companion CD.

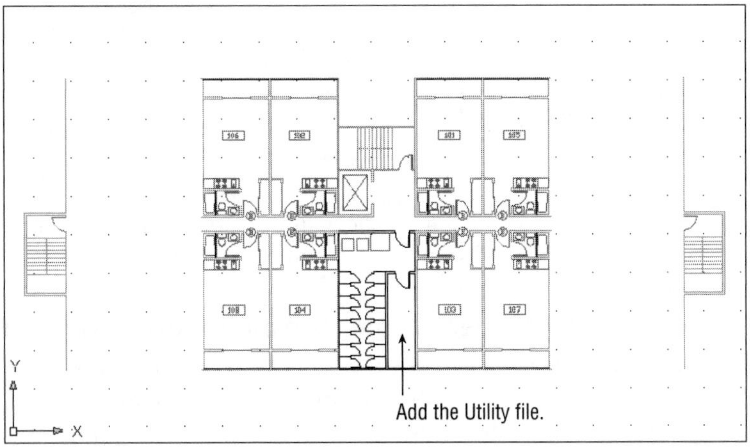
Add the Utility file.

FIGURE 13.29
The utility room installed

9. Save the `Common` file.

10. Now open the `Xref-1` file. You will see the utility room and the typical units in their new form. Your drawing should look like the top image in Figure 13.30.

11. Open `Xref-2`. You see that the utility room and typical units are updated in this file as well (see the bottom image in Figure 13.30).

FIGURE 13.30
The Xref-1 file with the units updated

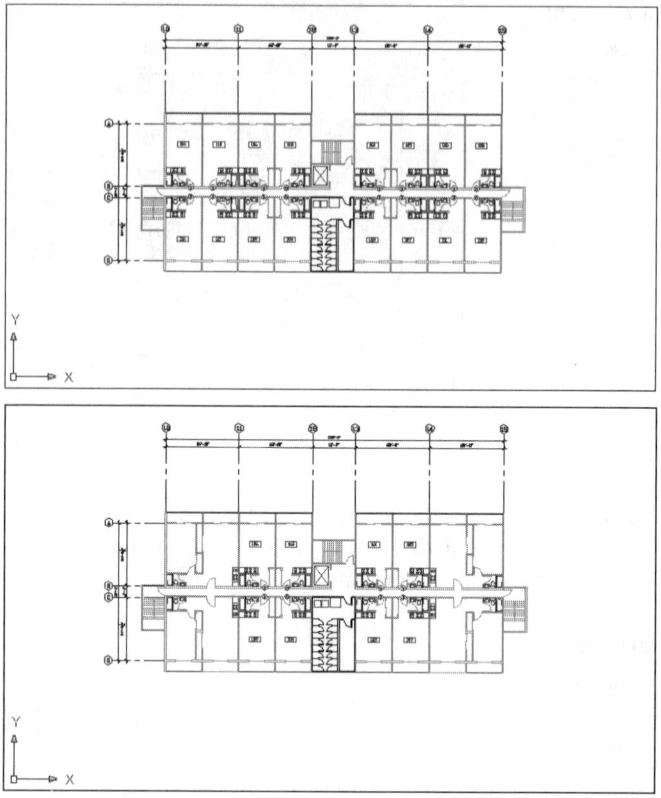

If this were a typical manually drafted project, someone would have had to make changes to both plans shown in Figure 13.30, duplicating a great deal of work.

Importing Named Elements from External References

Chapter 5 discussed how layers, blocks, line types, and text styles—called *named elements*—are imported along with a file that is inserted into another file. External reference files, on the other hand, do not import named elements. You can, however, review their names and use a special command to import the ones you want to use in the current file.

TIP *You can set the Visretain system variable to 1 to force AutoCAD to remember layer settings of external reference files. Or turn on the Retain Changes To Xref Layers option in the Open And Save tab of the Options dialog box. You can also use the Save and Restore State options in the Layer Properties Manager dialog box to save layer settings for later recall. The Save and Restore State options are described in detail later in this chapter.*

AutoCAD renames named elements from Xref files by giving them the prefix of the filename from which they come. For example, the Wall layer in the Floor1 file will be called Floor1 | WALL in the Xref-1 file; the Toilet block will be called Floor1 | TOILET. You cannot draw on the layer

Floor | WALL, nor can you insert Floor1 | TOILET; but you can view external reference layers in the Layer Control dialog box, and you can view external reference blocks using the Insert dialog box.

Next, you'll look at how AutoCAD identifies layers and blocks in external reference files, and you'll get a chance to import a layer from an Xref.

1. With the `Xref-1` file open, open the Layer Properties Manager dialog box. Notice that the names of the layers from the external reference files are all prefixed with the filename and the vertical bar (|) character. Exit the Layer Manager Properties dialog box.

TIP *You can also open the Layer Control shortcut menu to view the layer names.*

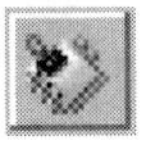

2. Click the External Reference Bind tool on the Reference toolbar, or enter **Xb**↵ to open the Xbind dialog box.

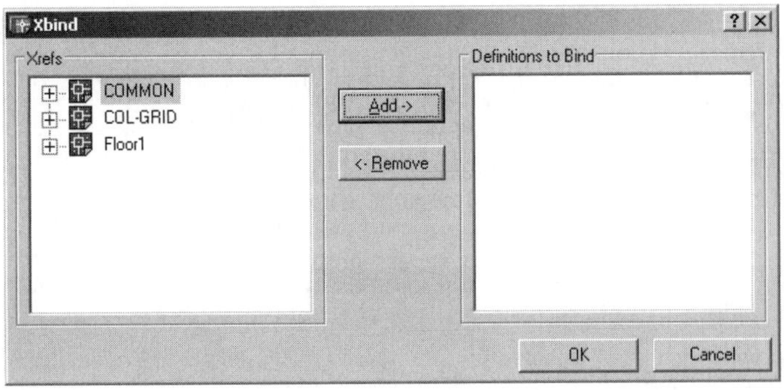

You see a listing of the current Xrefs. Each listing shows a plus sign to the left. This list box follows the Microsoft Windows format for expandable lists, much like the tree view in Windows Explorer.

3. Click the plus sign next to the Floor1 Xref listing. The list expands to show the types of elements available to bind.

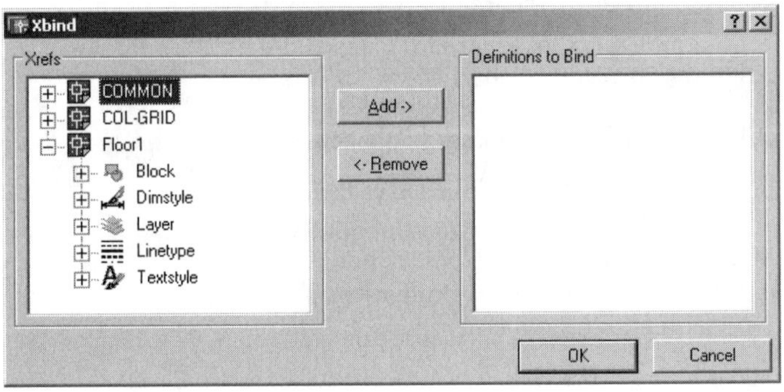

4. Now click the plus sign next to the Layer listing. The list expands further to show the layers available for binding.

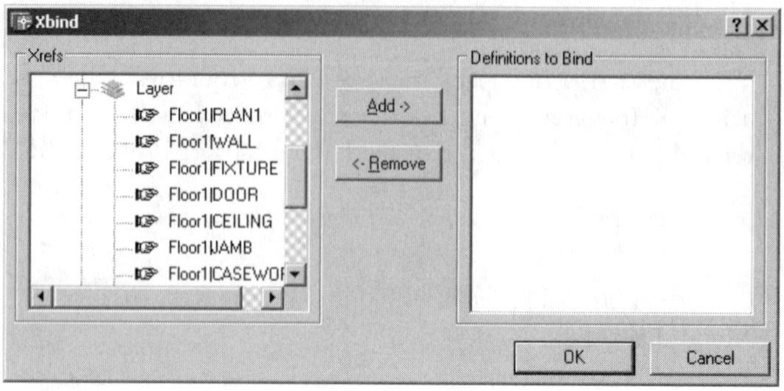

5. Locate Floor1 | WALL in the listing, click it, and then click the Add button. Floor1 | WALL is added to the list to the right: Definitions To Bind.
6. Click OK to bind the Floor1 | WALL layer.
7. Now open the Layer & Linetype Properties dialog box.
8. Scroll down the list and look for the Floor1 | WALL layer. You will not find it. In its place is a layer called Floor1$0$wall.

TIP *The AutoCAD DesignCenter lets you import settings and other drawing components from any drawing, not just Xref drawings. You'll learn more about the AutoCAD DesignCenter in Chapter 22.*

As you can see, when you use Xbind to import a named item, such as the Floor1 | WALL layer, the vertical bar (|) is replaced by two dollar signs surrounding a number, which is usually zero. (If for some reason the imported layer name Floor1$0$wall already exists, the zero in that name is changed to 1, as in Floor1$1$wall.) Other named items are also renamed in the same way, using the 0 replacement for the vertical bar.

You can also use the Xbind dialog box to bind multiple layers, as well as other items from Xrefs attached to the current drawing.

TIP *You can bind an entire Xref to a drawing, converting it to a simple block. By doing so, you have the opportunity to maintain unique layer names of the Xref being bound or merge the Xref's similarly named layers with those of the current file. See Chapter 6 for details.*

NESTING EXTERNAL REFERENCES AND USING OVERLAYS

External references can be nested. For example, if the Common.dwg file created in this chapter used the Unit.dwg file as an external reference rather than an inserted block, you would still get the same result in the Xref-1.dwg file. That is, you would see the entire floor plan, including the unit plans, when you open Xref-1.dwg. In this situation, Unit.dwg is nested in the Common.dwg file, which is in turn external referenced in the Xref-1.dwg file.

Though nested Xrefs can be helpful, take care in using external references in this way. For example, you might create an external reference using the Common.dwg file in the Floor1.dwg file as a means of referencing walls and other features of the Common.dwg file. You might also reference the Common.dwg file into the Floor2.dwg file for the same reason. Once you do this, however, you will have three versions of the Common plan in the Xref-1.dwg file, because each Xref now has Common.dwg attached to it. And because AutoCAD would dutifully load Common.dwg three times, Xref-1.dwg would occupy substantial computer memory, slowing your computer down when you edit the Xref-1.dwg file.

To avoid this problem, use the Overlay option in the External Reference dialog box. An overlayed external reference cannot be nested. For example, if you use the Overlay option when inserting the Common.dwg file into the Floor1.dwg and Floor2.dwg files, the nested Common.dwg files are ignored when you open the Xref-1.dwg file, thereby eliminating the redundant occurrence of Common.dwg. In another example, if you use the Overlay option to import the Unit.dwg file into the Common.dwg file and then attach the Common .dwg into Xref-1.dwg as an Xref, you do not see the Unit plan in Xref-1.dwg. The nested Unit.dwg drawing is ignored.

Controlling the Xref Search Path

One problem AutoCAD users have encountered in the past is a lost or broken link to an Xref. This occurs when an Xref is moved from its original location or when you receive a set of drawings that includes Xrefs. The Xref links are broken because AutoCAD doesn't know where to look. AutoCAD 2004 gives you better control over how AutoCAD looks for Xref files.

When you insert an Xref, the External Reference dialog box opens, offering you options for insertion point, scale, and rotation. This dialog box also offers the Path Type option, which allows you to select a method for locating Xrefs. You have three path type options to choose from:

Full Path Lets you specify the exact filename and path for an Xref, including disk drive or network location. Use this option when you want AutoCAD to look in a specific location for the Xref.

Relative Path Lets you specify a file location relative to the location of the current or host drawing. For example, if the host drawing is located in a folder called c:\mycadfiles and the xrefs are located in a folder called c:\mycadfiles\xrefs, you can specify .\xrefs for the location of the Xref file. This option is useful when you know you will maintain the folder structure of the host and Xref files when moving or exchanging these files. Note that since this is a relative path, this option is only valid for files that reside on the same local hard drive.

No Path Perhaps the most flexible option, this tells AutoCAD to use its own search criteria to find Xrefs. When No Path is selected, AutoCAD first looks in the same folder of the host drawing; then it looks in the project search path that is defined in the Files tab of the Options dialog box.

(See Appendix B for more on the Options dialog box.) Last, AutoCAD looks in the `Support` search path, also defined in the Files tab of the Options dialog box. If you plan to send your files to a client or a consultant, you might want to use this option.

Using the Layout Tabs and Paper Space

Your set of drawings for this studio apartment building would probably include a larger scale, more detailed drawing of the typical Unit plan. You already have the beginnings of this drawing in the form of the `Unit` file.

As you have seen, the notes and dimensions you entered into the `Unit` file can be turned off or frozen in the `Plan` file so they don't interfere with the graphics of the drawing. The `Unit` file can be part of another drawing file that contains more detailed information on the typical unit plan at a larger scale. To this new drawing you can add other notes, symbols, and dimensions. Whenever the `Unit` file is altered, you update its occurrence in the large-scale drawing of the typical unit as well as in the `Plan` file (see Figure 13.31). The units are thus quickly updated, and good correspondence is ensured among all the drawings for your project.

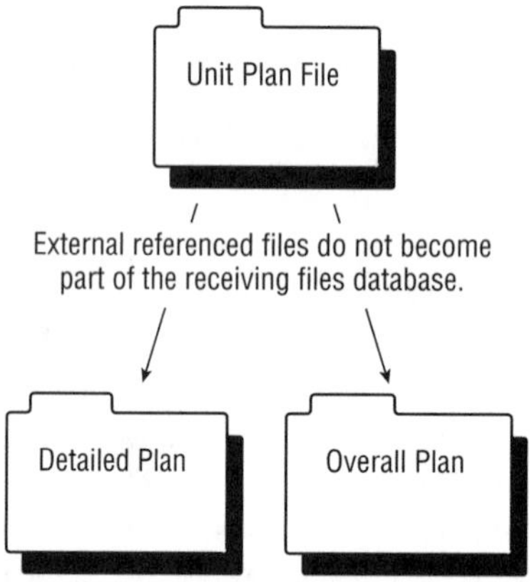

FIGURE 13.31
The relationship of drawing files in a project

Now suppose that you want to combine drawings having different scales in the same drawing file—for example, the overall plan of one floor plus an enlarged view of one typical unit. You can do so using the Layout tabs and a feature called Paper Space.

Understanding Model Space and Paper Space

So far, you've looked at ways to help you get around in your drawing while using a single view. This single view representation of your AutoCAD drawing is called the *Model Space* display mode. You can also set up multiple views of your drawing, called *floating viewports*. You create floating viewports using the Layout tabs to work in *Paper Space* display mode.

To get a clear understanding of the Model Space and Paper Space modes, imagine that your drawing is actually a full-size replica or model of the object you are drawing. Your computer screen is your window into a "room" where this model is being constructed, and the keyboard and mouse are your means of access to this room. You can control your window's position in relation to the object through the use of Pan, Zoom, View, and other display-related commands. You can also construct or modify the model by using drawing and editing commands. Think of this room as your Model Space.

So far, you have been working on your drawings by looking through a single "window" into Model Space. Now suppose you have the ability to step back and add windows with different views looking into your Model Space. The effect is as if you have several video cameras in your Model Space "room," each connected to a different monitor. You can view all your windows at once on your computer screen or enlarge a single window to fill the entire screen. Further, you can control the shape of your windows and easily switch from one window to another. This is what Paper Space is like.

Paper Space lets you create and display multiple views of Model Space. Each view window, called a *viewport,* acts like an individual virtual screen. One viewport can have an overall view of your drawing, while another can be a close-up. You can also control layer visibility individually for each viewport and display different versions of the same area of your drawing. You can move, copy, and stretch viewports and even overlap them.

TIP *Another type of viewport called the Tiled viewport can be set up in Model Space. Chapter 17 discusses this type of viewport.*

Perhaps one of the more powerful features of Paper Space is that you can plot several views of the same drawing on one sheet of paper. You can also include graphic objects such as borders and notes that appear only in Paper Space. In this function, Paper Space acts much like a page-layout program such as Quark or Adobe PageMaker. You can "paste up" different views of your drawing and then add borders, title blocks, general notes, and other types of graphic and textural data. Figure 13.32 shows the Plan drawing set up in Paper Space mode to display several views.

FIGURE 13.32

Different views of the same drawing in Paper Space

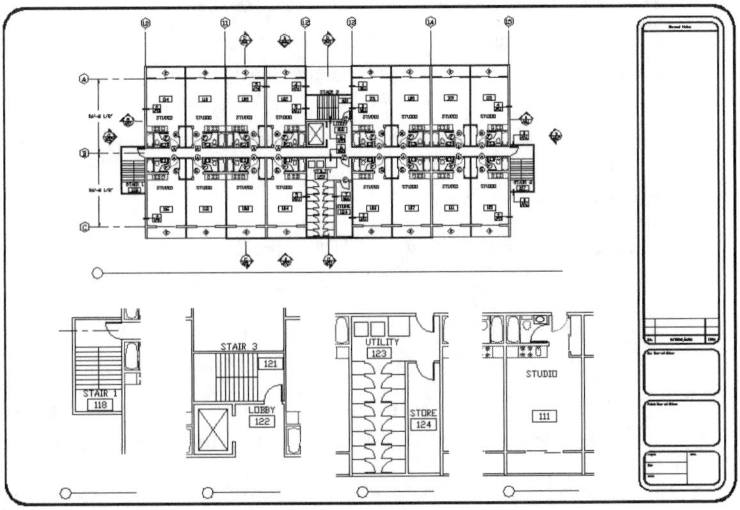

CREATING A PAPER SPACE LAYOUT

Your gateway to Paper Space is the Layout tab at the bottom of the AutoCAD window. When the Model tab is selected, you are in Model Space. When you select a Layout tab, you are in Paper Space.

TIP *You can also use a system variable to switch between tabs. When Tilemode is set to 1 (On), the default setting, you are in Model Space. When it is set to 0 (Off), you are in Paper Space.*

Let's start with the basics of entering Paper Space:

1. If it isn't already open, open the `Xref-1` file, making sure your display shows all of the drawing.
2. Click the Layout1 tab or click Model on the status bar to open the Page Setup dialog box, which allows you to set up your plotter or printer for this Layout tab.
3. Make sure that the Layout Settings tab is selected; then select the Letter (8.5" × 11") paper size option from the Paper Size drop-down list. Metric users should select A4 (210 mm × 297 mm). The paper size you select here determines the shape and margin of the Paper Space layout area.
4. Click OK to display the drawing in your Paper Space view. Note that the word PAPER replaces the word MODEL in the status bar; this tells you at a glance that you are in Paper Space.

In step 3, AutoCAD stops to ask you what paper size you want. AutoCAD bases the Paper Space work area on the paper size that you specify. Once you've opened a Layout tab for the first time and specified a sheet size, the area shown in Paper Space reflects the area of the paper size you select in step 3. From then on, you won't see the Page Setup dialog box again. If for some reason you need to change the paper size, you can do so by clicking the Layout tab you want to change and then choosing File ➢ Page Setup to open the Page Setup dialog box.

Creating New Paper Space Viewports

As you saw in Chapter 7, the different look of the Layout tab tells you that you are in Paper Space. You also learned that a viewport is automatically created when you first open a Layout tab Paper Space view. The viewport displays an overall view of your drawing to no particular scale.

In this section, you will work with multiple viewports in Paper Space, instead of just the default single viewport you get when you open the Layout tab. This first exercise shows you how to create three new viewports at once:

1. Right-click the Draw or Modify toolbar, and choose Viewports to open the Viewports toolbar. You'll use this toolbar a bit later in this exercise.
2. Click the viewport border to select it. The viewport border is the solid rectangle surrounding your drawing, just inside the dashed rectangle.
3. Click the Erase tool to erase the viewport. Your drawing disappears. Don't panic; remember that the viewport is like a window to Model Space. The objects in Model Space are still there.
4. Click Display Viewports Dialog in the Viewports toolbar to open the Viewports dialog box. You can also choose View ➢ Viewports ➢ New Viewports. This dialog box contains a set of predefined viewport layouts.

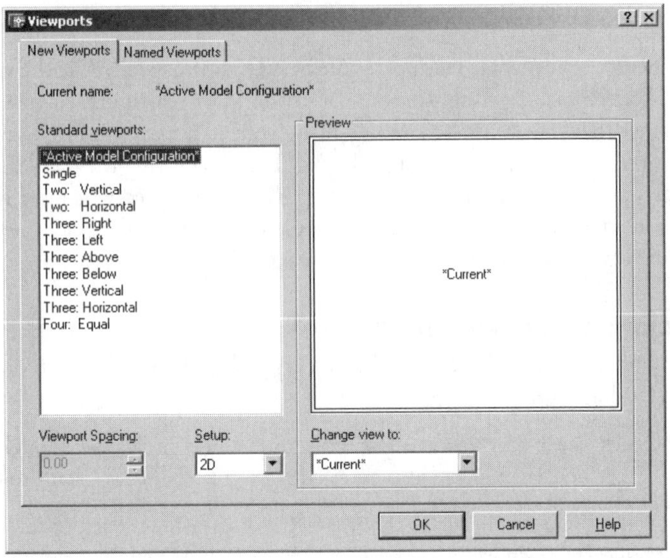

TIP *You'll learn more about the Viewports dialog box and its options in Chapter 17.*

5. Click the Three: Above option in the Standard Viewports list box. The box to the right shows a sample view of the Three: Above layout you selected.
6. Click OK. The `Specify first corner or [Fit] <Fit>:` prompt appears.
7. Press ↵ to accept the default Fit option. The Fit option fits the viewport layout to the maximum area allowed in your Paper Space view. Three rectangles appear in the formation shown in Figure 13.33. Each of these is a viewport to your Model Space. The viewport at the top fills the whole width of the drawing area; the bottom half of the screen is divided into two viewports.

FIGURE 13.33

The newly created viewports

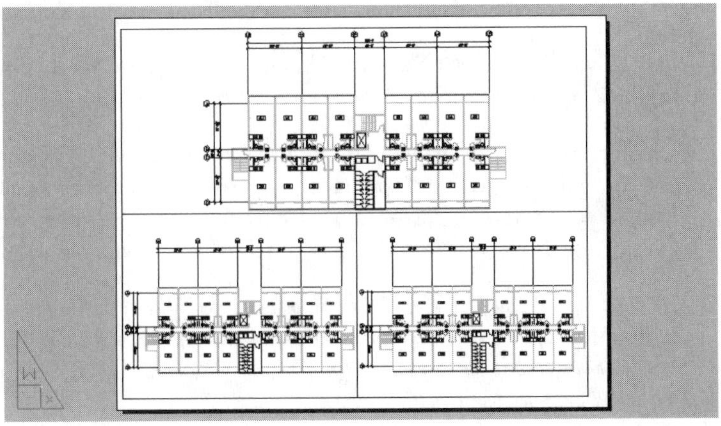

8. Press ↵.

When you create new viewports, AutoCAD automatically fills the viewport with the extents of your Model Space drawing. You can specify an exact scale for each viewport, as you'll see later.

Notice that the dashed line representing your paper margin has disappeared. That's because the viewports are pushed to the margin limits, thereby covering the dashed line.

You could have kept the original viewport that appeared when you first opened the Layout1 tab and then added two new viewports. Completely replacing the single viewport is a bit simpler since it fits the viewports in the allowed space for you.

Reaching Inside Viewports

Now suppose you need access to the objects within the viewports in order to adjust their display and edit your drawing.

1. Click Paper on the status bar. This gives you control over Model Space even though you are in Paper Space. (You can also enter **MS↵** as a keyboard shortcut to entering Model Space mode.)

The first thing you notice is that the UCS icon changes back to its L-shaped arrow form. It also appears in each viewport, as if you had three AutoCAD windows instead of just one.

2. Move your cursor over each viewport. Notice that in one of the viewports the cursor appears as the AutoCAD crosshair cursor, while in the other viewports it appears as an arrow pointer. The viewport that shows the AutoCAD cursor is the active one; you can pan and zoom, as well as edit objects in the active viewport.

TIP *If your drawing disappears from a viewport, you can usually retrieve it by choosing View ➢ Zoom ➢ Extents (Zoom↵ E↵).*

3. Click the lower-left viewport to activate it.
4. Choose View ➢ Zoom ➢ Window and window the elevator area.
5. Click the lower-right viewport and choose View ➢ Zoom ➢ Window to enlarge your view of a typical unit. You can also use the Pan Realtime and Zoom Realtime tools.

TIP *If you don't see the UCS icon, it has been turned off. Type* ***UCSicon↵ On↵*** to turn it on. See Chapter 17 for more on the UCS icon.

When you click the Paper button on the status bar, the UCS icon again changes shape—instead of one triangular-shaped icon, you have three arrow-shaped ones, one for each viewport on the screen. Also, as you move your cursor into the currently active viewport, the cursor changes from an arrow into the usual crosshair. Another way to tell which viewport is the active one is by its bold border.

TIP *You can also switch between Model Space and Paper Space by double-clicking an area in either region. For example, to go to Model Space from Paper Space, double-click inside a viewport. To get back to Paper Space, double-click the area outside the viewport. If you have an enlarged view of a viewport and no portion of the Paper Space area is available to click, click the Paper button on the status bar.*

You can move from viewport to viewport even while you are in the middle of most commands. For example, you can issue the Line command, pick the start point in one viewport, go to a different viewport to pick the next point, and so on. To activate a different viewport, you simply click it (see Figure 13.34).

TIP *You may find it difficult to access the contents of overlapping viewports, especially if the viewports are the same size or if one is enclosed by another. In this situation, you can move between viewports by pressing Ctrl+R repeatedly until you get to the viewport you want.*

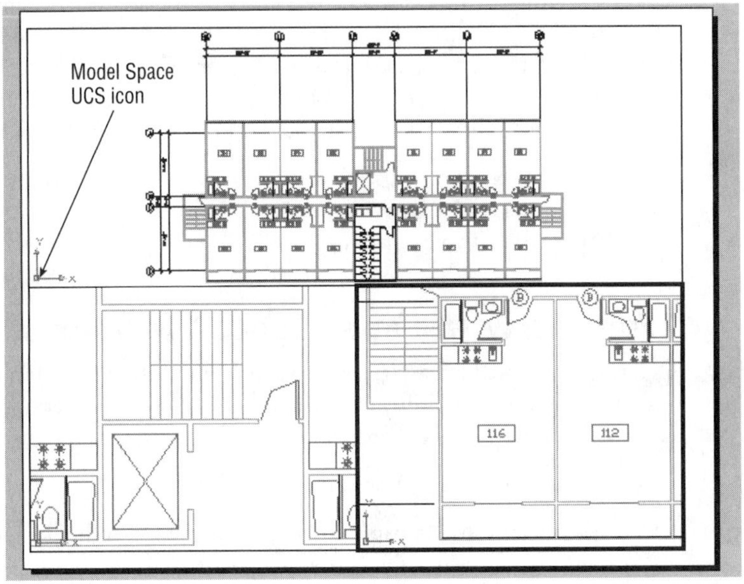

FIGURE 13.34

The three viewports, each with a different view of the plan

You've seen how you can zoom into a viewport view, but what happens when you use the Zoom command while in Paper Space? Try the following exercise to find out:

1. Click the Model button on the status bar or double-click an area outside the viewports to return to Paper Space.
2. Click the Realtime Zoom tool in the Standard toolbar, and then zoom in to the Paper Space view. The entire view enlarges, including the views in the viewports.
3. Choose View ➢ Zoom ➢ All or enter **Z**↵ **A**↵ to return to the overall view of Paper Space.

This brief exercise shows that you can use the Zoom tool in Paper Space just as you would in Model Space. All the display-related commands are available, including the Pan Realtime command.

Getting Back to Full-Screen Model Space

Once you've created viewports, you can then re-enter Model Space through the viewport using the Model/Paper button on the status bar. This button performs two functions: It shows you which space you are in, and it allows you to switch between the two spaces. But what if you want to quickly get back into the old, familiar, full-screen Model Space you were in before you entered Paper Space? The following exercise demonstrates how this is done:

1. Click the Model tab at the bottom of the drawing area, or enter **Tm↵ 1↵**. Your drawing returns to the original full-screen Model Space view—everything is back to normal.
2. Click the Layout1 tab, or enter **Tm↵ 0↵**. You are back in Paper Space. Notice that all the viewports are still there when you return to Paper Space. Once you've set up Paper Space, it remains part of the drawing until you delete all the viewports. Also notice that you didn't see the Page Setup dialog box this time. Once you've chosen a sheet size, AutoCAD assumes that you will continue to use that sheet size and other page setup information until you tell it otherwise.

You may prefer doing most of your drawing in Model Space, using Paper Space for setting up views for plotting. Since viewport layouts are retained, you won't lose anything when you go back to Model Space to edit your drawing.

Working with Paper Space Viewports

Paper Space is intended as a page-layout or composition tool. You can manipulate viewports' sizes, scale their view independently of one another, and even set layering and line-type scales independently. Let's try manipulating the shape and location of viewports using the Modify toolbar options.

1. Turn off Running Osnaps if it is on.
2. Make sure you're in paper space (the Paper button should appear to the right of the status bar buttons), then click the bottom edge of the lower-left viewport to expose its grips (see the top image in Figure 13.35).
3. Click the upper-right grip, and then drag it to the location shown in the top image in Figure 13.35.
4. Press the Esc key and then erase the lower-right viewport by clicking Erase in the Modify toolbar. Then click the bottom edge of the viewport.
5. Move the lower-left viewport so it is centered in the bottom half of the window, as shown in the bottom image in Figure 13.35.

In this exercise, you clicked the viewport edge to select it for editing. If, while in Paper Space, you attempt to click the image within the viewport, you will not select anything. Later you will see, however, that you can use the Osnap modes to snap to parts of the drawing image within a viewport.

FIGURE 13.35

Stretching, erasing, and moving viewports

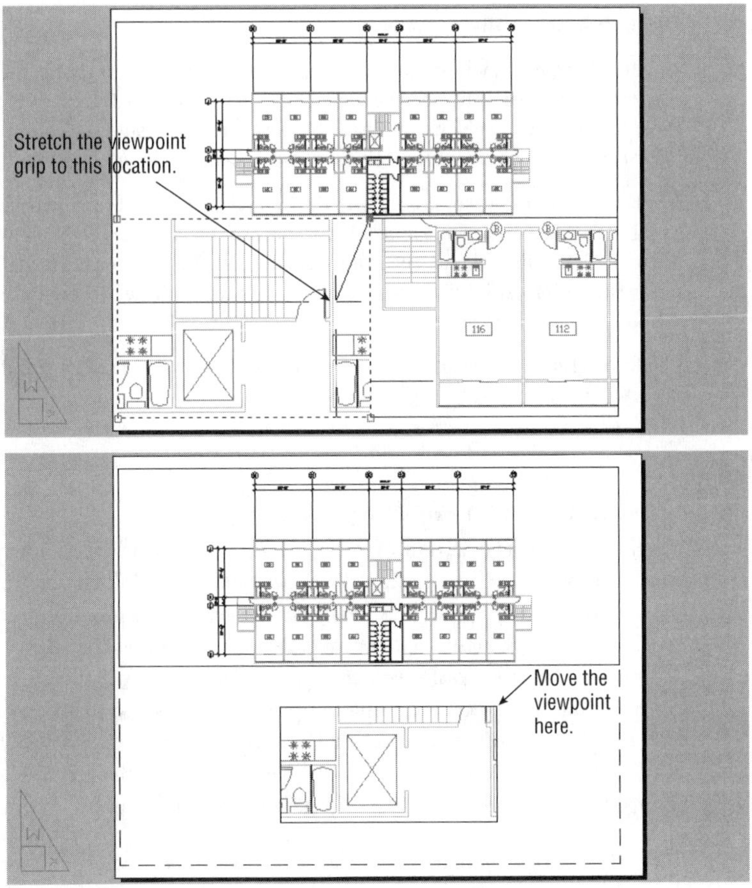

Because viewports are recognized as AutoCAD objects, you can manipulate them using all the editing commands, just as you would manipulate any other object. In the previous exercise you moved, stretched, and erased viewports. Next, you'll see how layers affect viewports.

1. Create a new layer called Vport.
2. In the Properties Palette, change the viewport borders to the Vport layer.
3. Finally, turn off the Vport layer. The viewport borders disappear.
4. After reviewing the results of step 3, turn the Vport layer back on.

You can assign a viewport's border a layer, a color, a line type, and even a line weight. If you put the viewport's border on a layer that has been turned off or frozen, that border becomes invisible, just like any other object on such a layer. Making the borders invisible is helpful when you want to compose a final sheet for plotting. Even when turned off, the active viewport has a heavy border around it when you switch to the floating model, and all the viewports still display their views.

DISAPPEARING VIEWPORTS

As you add more viewports to a drawing, you might discover that some of them blank out, even though you know you haven't turned them off. Don't panic. AutoCAD limits the number of viewports that display their contents at any given time to 64. (A viewport that displays its contents is said to be active.) This limit is provided because too many active viewports can bog down a system.

If you are using a slow computer with limited resources, you can lower this limit to two or three viewports to gain some performance. Then only two or three viewports will display their contents. (All viewports that are turned on will still plot, regardless of whether their contents are visible.) Zooming in to a blank viewport restores its visibility, thereby allowing you to continue to work with enlarged Paper Space views containing only a few viewports.

The Maxactvp system variable controls this value. Type **Maxactvp** and then enter the number of viewports you want active at any given time.

Scaling Views in Paper Space

Paper Space has its own unit of measure. You have already seen how you are required to specify a paper size when opening a Layout tab to a Paper Space view. When you first enter Paper Space, regardless of the area your drawing occupies in Model Space, you are given limits that are set by the paper size you specify in the Page Setup dialog box. If you keep in mind that Paper Space is like a paste-up area that is dependent on the printer you configured for AutoCAD, this difference of scale becomes easier to comprehend. Just as you might paste up photographs and maps representing several square miles onto an 11" × 17" board, so can you use Paper Space to paste up views of scale drawings representing city blocks or houses on an 8 1/2" × 11" sheet of paper. But in AutoCAD, you have the freedom to change the scale and size of the objects you are pasting up.

TIP *While in Paper Space, you can edit objects in a Model Space viewport, but to do so, you must use Floating Model Space. You can then click a viewport and edit within that viewport. While in this mode, objects that were created in Paper Space cannot be edited. Choosing View ➢ Paper Space brings you back to the Paper Space environment.*

If you want to be able to print your drawing at a specific scale, you must carefully consider scale factors when composing your Paper Space paste-up. Let's see how to put together a sheet in Paper Space and still maintain accuracy of scale.

1. Make sure you're in Paper Space. Check to see if the Paper appears on the status bar. If Model appears there, click that button to change it to Paper.
2. Click the topmost viewport's border to select it.
3. Right-click and then choose Properties from the shortcut menu to open the Properties palette.
4. Scroll down the list of properties until you see the Standard Scale listing.
5. Click the Custom setting next to the Standard Scale listing; then click the downward-pointing arrow that appears next to Custom to open the list.
6. Select 1/32"=1' from the drop-down list. Notice how the view in the top viewport changes.

7. Press the Esc key twice to clear the selection of the viewport.
8. Click the lower viewport border. The information in the Properties palette changes to reflect the properties of the newly selected viewport.
9. Click the Standard Scale Custom listing and open the drop-down list as you did in step 5.
10. Select 3/16"=1' from the list. Notice that the view in the viewport changes to reflect the new scale (see Figure 13.36).

FIGURE 13.36

Paper Space viewport views scaled to 1/32"=1' and 3/16"=1'

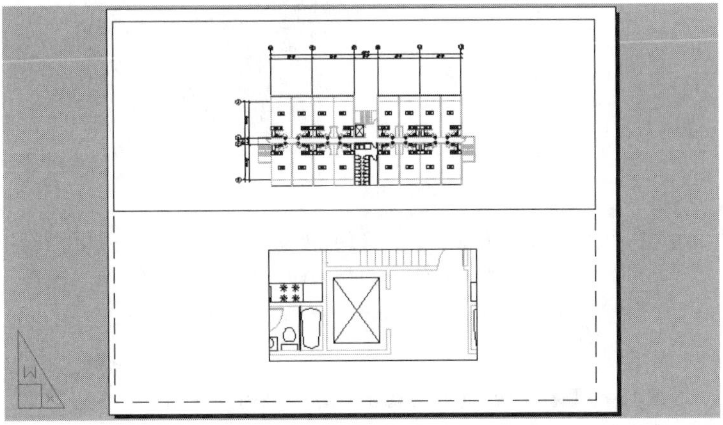

It's easy to adjust the width, height, and location of the viewports so that they display only the parts of the unit you want to see. While in Paper Space, use the Stretch, Move, or Scale command to edit any viewport border, or just use the viewport's grips to edit its size. The view within the viewport itself remains at the same scale and location, while the viewport changes in size. You can move and stretch viewports with no effect on the size and location of the objects within the view.

If you need to overlay one drawing on top of another, you can overlap viewports. Use the Osnap overrides to select geometry within each viewport, even while in Paper Space. This allows you to align one viewport on top of another at exact locations.

You can also add a title block in Paper Space at a 1:1 scale to frame your viewports and then plot this drawing from Paper Space at a scale of 1:1. Your plot appears just as it does in Paper Space, at the appropriate scale. Paper Space displays a dashed line to show you where the nonprintable areas occur near the edge of the paper.

While working in Paper Space, pay close attention to whether you are in Paper Space or Floating Model Space mode. It is easy to accidentally perform a pan or zoom within a Floating Model Space viewport when you intend to pan or zoom your Paper Space view. This can cause you to lose your viewport scaling or alignment with other parts of the drawing. It's a good idea to save viewport views by choosing View ➢ Named Views in case you happen to accidentally change a viewport view.

Another way to prevent your viewport view from being accidentally altered is to turn on View Lock. To do this, while in Paper Space, click a viewport border. Right-click to open the shortcut menu, and then choose Display Locked ➢ Yes. Once the view is locked, you cannot pan or zoom a viewport view. You also cannot change the size of the viewport. This setting is also available in the viewport's Properties palette.

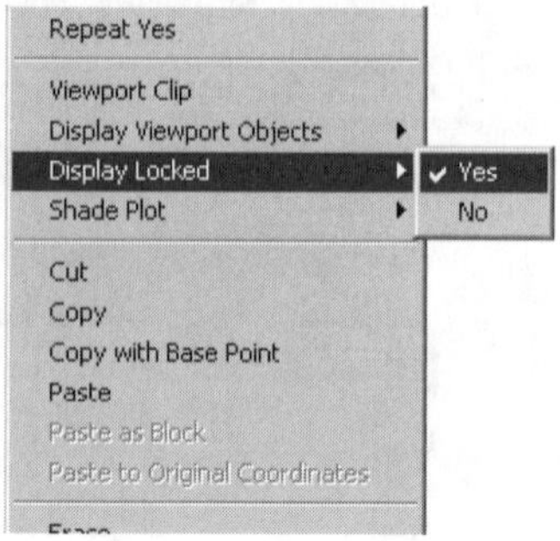

TIP If you find that your viewport views are automatically zooming to extents when you enter them, the Ucsfollow system variable has been changed from its default setting of 0 (zero). Change Ucsfollow back to 0 by typing ***Ucsfollow↵*** ***0↵****. You can also use the UCS dialog box to change this setting. Choose Tools ➢ Named UCS. In the UCS dialog box, click the Settings tab, and then make sure that the Update View To Plan When UCS Is Changed option is turned off.*

Setting Layers in Individual Viewports

Another unique feature of Paper Space viewports is their ability to freeze layers independently. You could, for example, display the usual plan information in the overall view of a floor but show only the walls in the enlarged view of one unit.

You control viewport layer visibility through the Layer Properties Manager dialog box. You may have noticed that there are three sun icons for each layer listing.

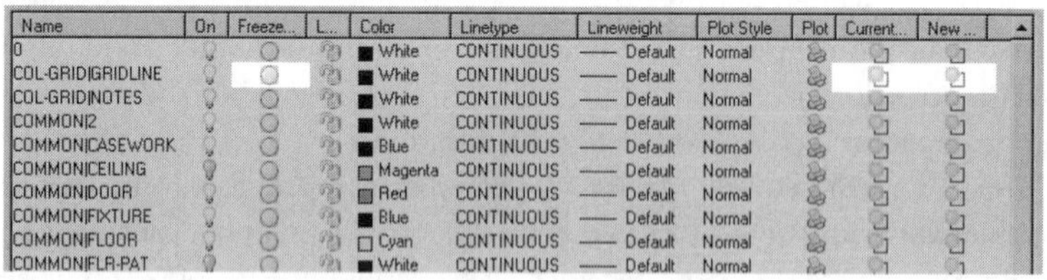

TIP You might need to widen the Layer Properties Manager dialog box to view all the columns. Simply click and drag the right border of the dialog box to the right.

You're already familiar with the sun icon farthest to the left. This is the Freeze/Thaw icon that controls the freezing and thawing of layers globally. Several columns to the right of that icon is a sun icon with a transparent rectangle. This icon controls the freezing and thawing of layers in individual viewports. The next exercise shows you firsthand how it works.

1. Click the Paper button on the status bar to go to Floating Model Space.

2. Activate the lower viewport.
3. Open the Layer Properties Manager dialog box.

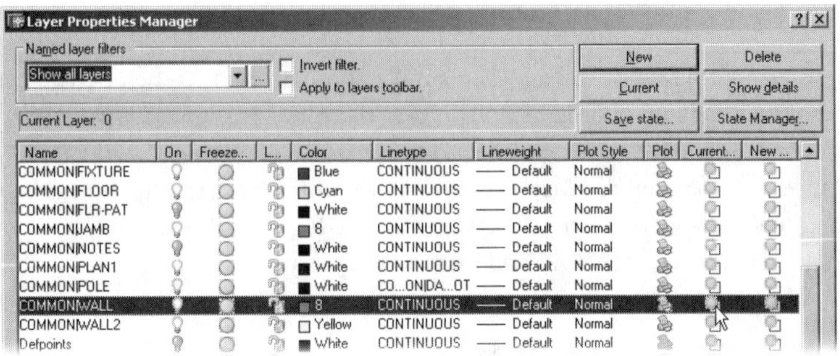

4. Locate the COMMON | WALL layer; then click its name to help you isolate this layer.

WARNING *You cannot use the Cur VP and New VP options in the Layer Properties Manager dialog box while you are in tiled Model Space.*

5. Click the column labeled Current VP Freeze for the selected layer. You may need to widen the Layer Properties Manager dialog box to do this. The Current VP Freeze column is the second column from the right side of the dialog box. The icon looks like a transparent rectangle over a sun. Once you've clicked the icon, the sun changes to a snowflake, telling you that the layer is now frozen for the current viewport.
6. Click OK. The active viewport regenerates, with the Wall layer of the Common Xref made invisible in the current viewport. However, the walls remain visible in the other viewport (see Figure 13.37).

FIGURE 13.37

The drawing editor with the Wall layer turned off in the active viewport

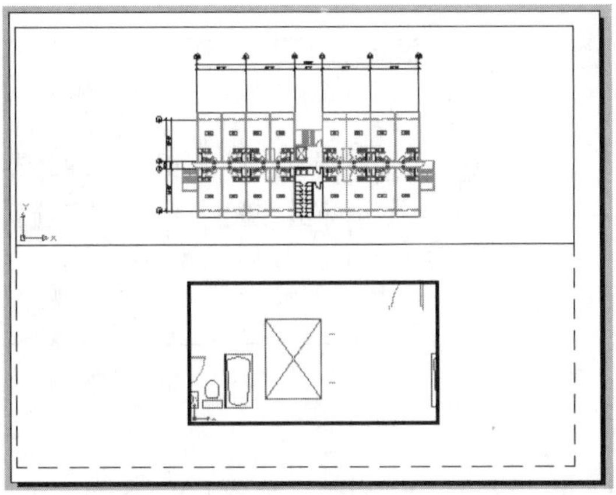

7. After reviewing the effects of the Current VP Freeze setting, go back to the Layer Properties Manager and thaw the COMMON | WALL layer by clicking its Current VP Freeze icon again so it turns back into a sun.

8. Click OK to exit the dialog box.

You might have noticed another, similar sun icon next to the one you used in the previous exercise. This icon shows an opaque rectangle over the sun. This icon controls layer visibility in any new viewports you might create next, rather than controlling existing viewports.

If you prefer, you can also use the Layer Control shortcut menu in the toolbar to freeze layers in individual viewports. Select the layer from the list, and then click the same sun icon with the small rectangle below it. Now save and exit the `Xref-1` file.

MASKING OUT PARTS OF A DRAWING

Chapter 6 described a method for using AutoCAD's Display Order feature to hide floor patterns under equipment or furniture in a floor layout. You can use a similar method to hide irregularly shaped areas in a Paper Space viewport. This would be desirable for plotting site plans, civil plans, or floor plans that require portions of the drawing to be masked out. Or you might want to mask part of a plan that is overlapped by another to expose dimension or text data.

This section concludes the apartment building tutorial. Although you haven't drawn the complete building, you've already learned all the commands and techniques you need to do so. Figure 13.38 shows you a completed plan of the first floor; to complete your floor plans and get some practice using AutoCAD, you might want to add the symbols shown in this figure to your `Plan` file.

FIGURE 13.38

A completed floor of the apartment building

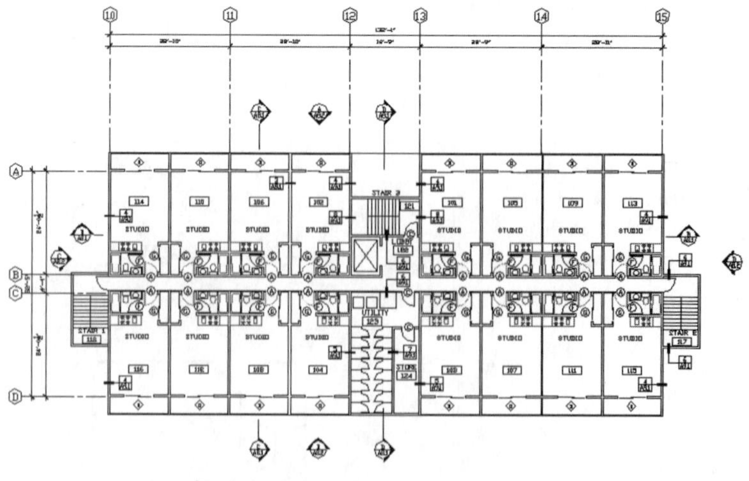

Since buildings like this one often have the same plans for several floors, the plan for the second floor can also represent the third floor. Combined with the first floor, this gives you a three-level apartment building. This project might also have a ground-level garage, which would be a separate file. You can use the `Col-grid.dwg` file from the companion CD in the garage file as a reference for dimensions. The other symbols can be blocks stored as files that can be retrieved in other files.

PAPER SPACE AND THE SAN FRANCISCO MAIN LIBRARY PROJECT

The San Francisco Main Library project made extensive use of Paper Space. As you've seen in earlier chapters, the library project used multiple instances of the same file to show different types of information. Paper Space was instrumental in enabling the CAD specialists to manage large amounts of drawing data. One floor plan drawing served as the basis for several sheets, including floor plans, reflected ceiling plans, equipment plans, exit plans, and others.

The following image shows a Paper Space view of a drawing from the San Francisco Main Library construction document set. This particular sheet shows the floor pattern layout of some of the main circulation areas.

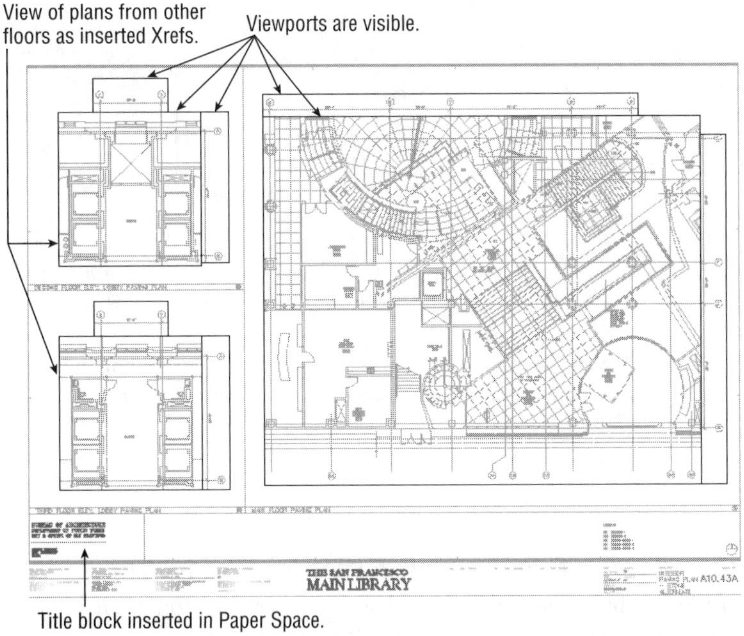
View of plans from other floors as inserted Xrefs.
Viewports are visible.
THE SAN FRANCISCO
MAIN LIBRARY
Title block inserted in Paper Space.

The title block is inserted in Paper Space as a block, rather than as an Xref. This was done because each drawing has unique drawing title information that is kept as attribute data in the title block. The attributes can be easily updated from a dialog box.

The plan drawings are Xrefs inserted into Model Space, with Paper Space viewports displaying selected areas. The viewport borders are turned on in this view to show how they are arranged. These borders are turned off when the drawing is plotted.

Continued on next page

PAPER SPACE AND THE SAN FRANCISCO MAIN LIBRARY PROJECT *(continued)*

Notice that the grid reference symbols are in their own viewport adjacent to the main enlarged floor plan. These adjacent grid viewports display portions of the drawing that are actually some distance away from the floor plan shown in the main viewport. The following image shows the overall floor plan with the viewport areas outlined. Here you can see that the column grid symbols are actually at the edge of the drawing.

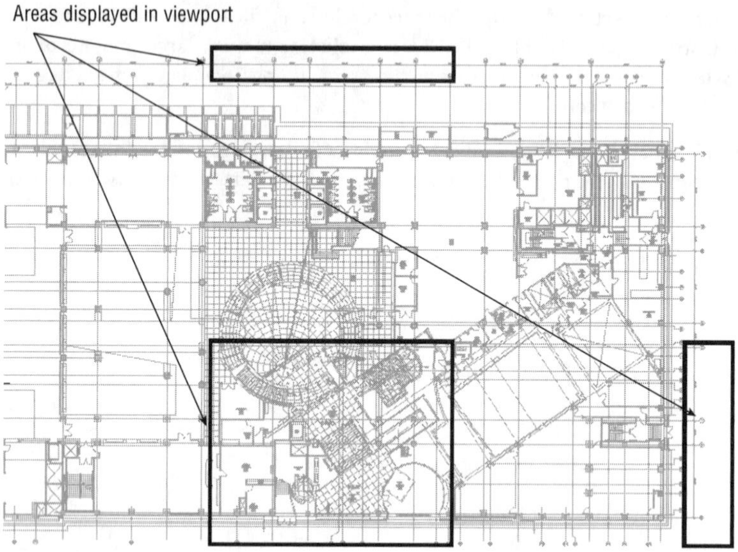

This example shows how viewports helped the creator of this drawing reuse existing data. If a change is made to the overall plan, including the column grids, the enlarged plan of the entry is automatically updated.

Creating and Using Multiple Paper Space Layouts

You're not limited to just one or two Paper Space layouts. You can have as many Paper Space layouts as you want, with each layout set up for a different sheet size containing different views of your drawing. You can use this feature to set up multiple drawing sheets based on a single AutoCAD drawing file. For example, a client requires full sets of plans in both 1/8"=1' scale and 1/16"=1" scale. You can set up two Layout tabs, each with a different sheet size and viewport scale.

You can also set up different Paper Space layouts for the different types of drawings. In the San Francisco Main Library project, a single drawing contained the data for mechanical layout, equipment and furnishing, floor plans, and reflected ceiling plans. Although that project used multiple files to set the layers for each plan, a single file with multiple Layout tabs can serve the same purpose in AutoCAD 2004.

To create new Layout tabs, do the following:

1. Right-click any tab.
2. Choose New Layout from the shortcut menu to add a new tab to those that already exist.
3. Click the new tab to open the Page Setup dialog box.
4. Click OK. The new tab appears with its single default viewport.

When you click a new tab, the Page Setup dialog box appears just as it did in the first exercise of this section. The Layout tab shortcut menu also include the From Template option. The From Template option lets you create a Paper Space layout based on an AutoCAD template file. AutoCAD offers several standard layouts that include title blocks based on common sheet sizes.

The Layout tab shortcut menu also includes options that allow you to delete, rename, move, copy, or select all the tabs. If you find that there are more tabs than can fit in the space provided, you can navigate the tabs using the arrows just to the left of the tabs.

ACAD only

Creating Odd-Shaped Viewports

In many situations, a rectangular viewport will not provide a view appropriate for what you want to accomplish. For example, you might want to isolate part of a floor plan that is L-shaped or even circular. You can create viewports from virtually any shape you need, as the following exercise demonstrates.

Now suppose you want to set up this Layout tab to show only the lower apartment units and the elevators and stairs.

1. Click the Clip Existing Viewport tool in the Viewports toolbar. You can also choose Modify ➢ Clip ➢ Viewport.
2. At the `Select viewport to clip:` prompt, click the viewport border.
3. At the `Select clipping object or [Polygonal] <Polygonal>:` prompt, press ↵.
4. Turn off Running Osnaps and draw the outline shown in the top portion of Figure 13.39.
5. When you finish selecting points, press ↵. The viewport changes to conform to the new shape.
6. Click the viewport border to expose its grips.
7. Click a grip and move it to a new location. Notice that the viewport view conforms to the new shape, as shown in the bottom view of Figure 13.39.

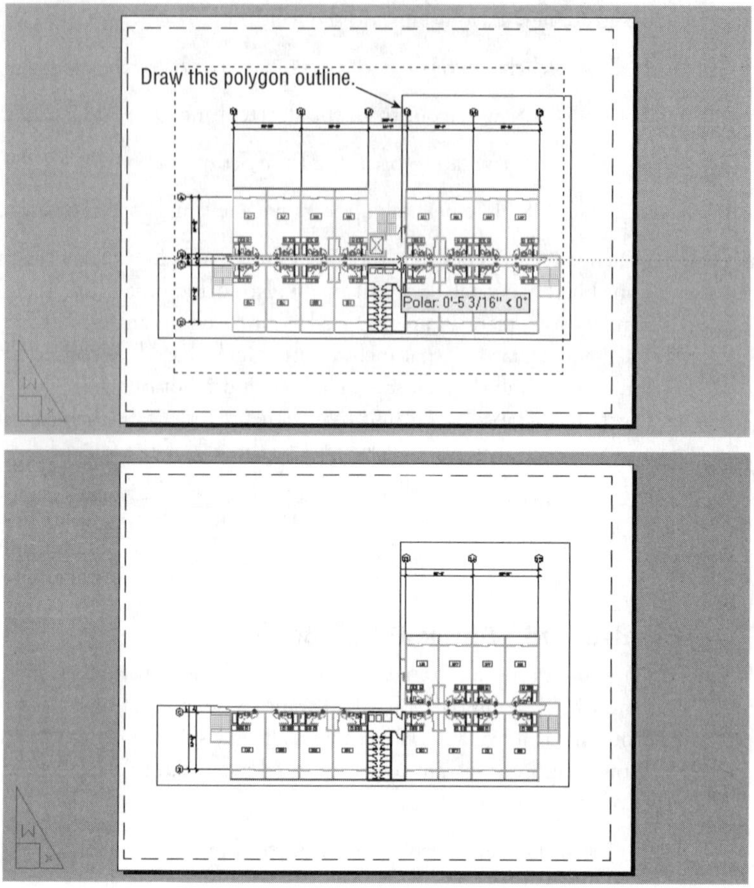

FIGURE 13.39
Drawing a polygon outline for a viewport

The new viewport shape gives you more flexibility in isolating portions of a drawing. This can be especially useful if you have a large project that is divided into smaller sheets. You can set up several Layout tabs, each displaying a different portion of the plan.

What if you want a viewport that is not rectilinear? The next exercise shows you how to create a circular viewport.

1. Erase the viewport you just modified.
2. Draw a circle that roughly fills the Paper Space area.
3. Click the Convert Object To Viewport option on the Viewports toolbar or choose View ➢ Viewports ➢ Object.
4. Click the circle. The plan appears inside the circle, as shown in Figure 13.40.

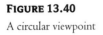

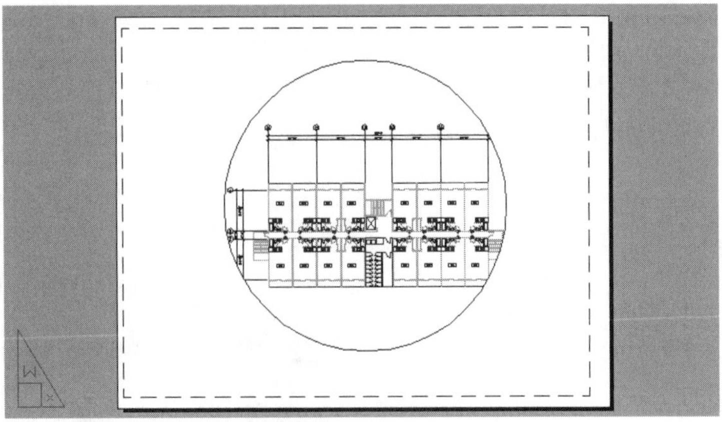

FIGURE 13.40
A circular viewpoint

To simplify this exercise, you were asked to draw a circle to use as the basis for a new viewport. You are not limited to circles; you can use any closed polyline or spline of any shape (see Chapter 14 for a detailed discussion on polylines and splines). You can also use the Polygon tool in the Draw toolbar to create a shape and then turn it into a viewport.

If you look carefully at the series of prompts [for the previous exercise, you'll notice that the Convert Object To Viewport option invokes a command-line version of the Vports command (**–vports**). The command-line version of Vports offers some options that the standard Vports command does not. The following options are available with the command-line version of Vports:

```
-vports
[ON/OFF/Fit/Shadeplot/Lock/Object/Polygonal/Restore/2/3/4] <Fit>:
```

You used two of the options in the two previous exercises, the Polygonal option and the Object option. If you're an experienced AutoCAD user, you may notice that this command-line version of Vports is the same as the Mview command of earlier releases. You can still use the Mview command if you prefer.

Understanding Line Weights, Line Types, and Dimensions in Paper Space

The behavior of a number of AutoCAD features depends on whether you are in Paper Space or Model Space. The most visible of these features are line weights, line types, and dimensions. In this section, you'll take a closer look at these features, and you'll see how to use them in conjunction with Paper Space.

Controlling and Viewing Line Weights in Paper Space

Line weights can greatly improve the readability of technical drawings. You can make important features stand out with bold line weights while keeping the "noise" of smaller details from overpowering a drawing. In architectural floor plans, walls are traditionally drawn with heavier lines so that the outline of a plan can be easily read. Other features exist in a drawing for reference only, so they are drawn in a lighter weight than normal.

In Chapter 7, you saw how to control line weights in AutoCAD using plot style tables. You can apply either a named plot style table or a color plot style table to a drawing. If you already have a library of AutoCAD drawings, you might want to use color plot style tables for backward compatibility. AutoCAD 2004 also allows you to assign line weights directly to layers or objects and view the results of your line-weight settings in Paper Space. Here's an exercise that demonstrates this feature.

1. Click the Layout1 tab; then open the Layer Properties Manager dialog box.
2. Right-click the Layer list; then choose Select All.
3. Click the Lineweight column to open the Lineweight dialog box.

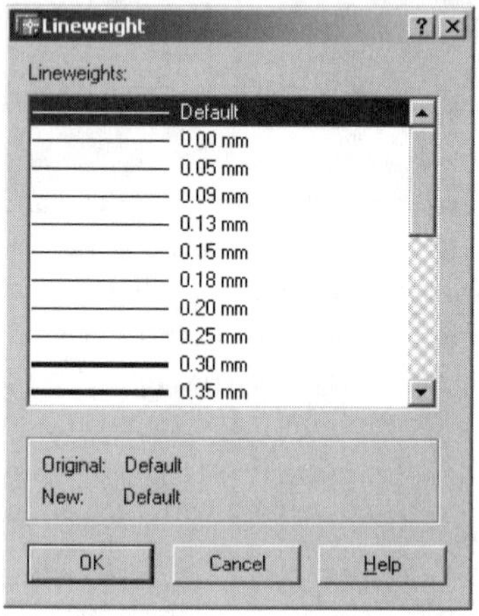

4. Select 0.13 mm from the list and then click OK. You've just assigned the 0.13 mm line weight to all layers.
5. Right-click the Layer list again and choose Clear All.
6. Ctrl+click the layers COMMON | WALL and Floor1 | WALL to select them.
7. Click the Lineweight column for either of the two selected layers to open the Lineweight dialog box again.
8. Select 0.4 mm from the dialog box; then click OK. You've just assigned the 0.4 mm line weight to the two selected layers.
9. Click OK in the Layer Properties Manager dialog box.

Although you set the line weights for the layers in the drawing, you need to make a few more changes to the file settings before they are visible in Paper Space.

1. Choose Format ➢ Lineweight to open the Lineweight Settings dialog box.

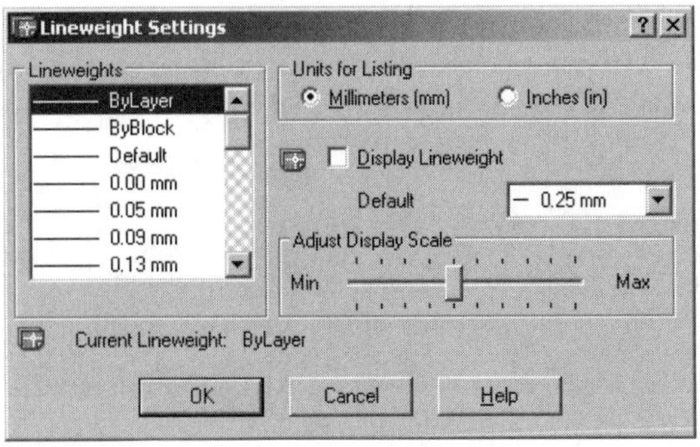

2. Click the Display Lineweight check box, and then click OK.
3. Make sure you are in Paper Space, and then zoom in to the drawing.
4. Choose View ➢ Regen All. You'll see the lines representing the walls appear with thickness, as shown in Figure 13.41.

FIGURE 13.41

An enlarged view of the plan with line weights displayed

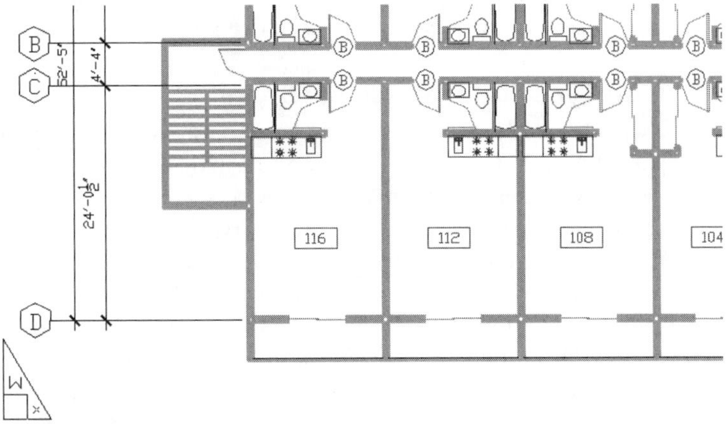

With the ability to display line weights in Paper Space, you have better control over your output. Instead of using a trial-and-error method to print your drawing and then checking your printout to see if the line weights are correct, AutoCAD 2004 lets you see the line weights right on your screen.

This exercise showed you how to set line weights so that they appear in Paper Space as they will when you plot your drawing. If you normally plot your drawings in black, you can go one step further and set all your layer colors to black to really see how your plots will look. But you'll need to save your layer settings so you can restore the layers to their original colors. You'll learn more about saving and restoring layer settings later in this chapter. Another way to view your drawing in black and white without affecting your layer settings is to use the color plot style table described in Chapter 7.

TIP *When line weight display is turned on, you'll see line weights in Model Space as well as in Paper Space. Line weights can be distracting while you work on your drawing in Model Space, but you can quickly turn them off by entering* ***Lwdisplay↵ 0↵*** *at the command prompt. Entering* ***Lwdisplay↵ 1↵*** *turns the line weight display back on.*

The Lineweight Settings Dialog Box

There were a number of other settings in the Lineweight Settings dialog box that you didn't use in the previous exercise. Here is a description of those settings for your reference.

Units For Listing You can choose between millimeters and inches for the unit of measure for line weights. The default is millimeters.

Adjust Display Scale This setting lets you control just how thick line weights appear in the drawing. Move the slider to the right for thicker lines and to the left for thinner lines. This setting affects only the display on your monitor. As you move the slider, you can see a sample of the results in the Lineweights list box.

Default drop-down list This drop-down list lets you select the default line weight that you see in the Layer Properties Manager dialog box. It is set to 0.01" (0.25 mm) by default. You might want to lower the default line weight to .005" (.13 mm) just as a matter of course, since most printers these days can print lines to that size and even smaller.

Line-Type Scales and Paper Space

As you have seen in previous exercises, you must carefully control drawing scales when creating viewports. Fortunately, this is easily done through the Properties palette. Although Paper Space offers the flexibility of combining different scale images in one display, it also adds to the complexity of your task in controlling that display. Your drawing's line-type scale, in particular, needs careful attention.

In Chapter 4, you saw that you had to set the line-type scale to the scale factor of the drawing in order to make the line type visible. If you intend to plot that same drawing from Paper Space, you will have to set the line-type scale back to 1 to get the line types to appear correctly. This is because AutoCAD faithfully scales line types to the current unit system. Remember that Paper Space units differ from Model Space units. When you scale a Model Space image down to fit within the smaller Paper Space area, the line types remain scaled to the increased line-type scale settings. In the Chapter 4 example, line types are scaled up by a factor of 48. This causes noncontinuous lines to appear as continuous in Paper Space because you see only a small portion of a greatly enlarged noncontinuous line type.

The Psltscale system variable allows you to determine how line-type scales are applied to Paper Space views. You can set Psltscale so that the line types will appear the same, regardless of whether you view them directly in tiled Model Space or through a viewport in Paper Space. By default, this system variable is set to 1. This causes AutoCAD to scale all the line types uniformly across all the viewports in Paper Space. You can set Psltscale to 0 to force the viewports to display line types exactly as they appear in Model Space.

You can also control this setting in the Linetype Manager dialog box (choose Format ➢ Linetype). When you click the Show Details button, you see a setting called Use Paper Space Units For Scaling in the lower-right corner. When this is checked, Psltscale is set to 1. When it is unchecked, Psltscale is set to 0.

Dimensioning in Paper Space Layouts

At times, you may find it more convenient to add dimensions to your drawing in Paper Space rather than directly on your objects in Model Space. This can be helpful when you are using different Layout tabs to produce different scale drawings of the same Model Space drawing. Or you might want to combine several different scale drawings in one Layout tab as in a detail sheet.

You have two basic options when dimensioning Model Space objects in Paper Space. The Associative Dimensioning feature can make quick work of dimensions for Layout tabs containing different scale drawings. Or, if you prefer not to use Associative Dimensioning, you can adjust settings for individual dimension styles.

Using Associative Dimensioning in Paper Space

Perhaps the simplest way to dimension in Paper Space is to use the Associative Dimensioning feature. With this feature turned on, you can dimension Model Space objects while in a Paper Space layout. Furthermore, Paper Space dimensions of Model Space objects will be automatically updated if the Model Space object is edited. Try the following exercise to see how this works.

1. Choose File ➢ New and use the Start From Scratch option to create a new blank file.
2. Draw a rectangle 12 units wide by 4 units high. If you're using a metric file, make the rectangle 480 units wide by 160 units high.
3. Click the Layout1 tab, and then in the Page Setup dialog box, choose the Letter paper size in the Layout Settings tab and click OK.
4. Right-click in the drawing area, and then choose Options from the shortcut menu.
5. In the Options dialog box, click the User Preferences tab and make sure the Make New Dimensions Associative option in the Associative Dimensioning group is turned on. Click OK to exit the dialog box.

Next, you'll use the rectangle you drew in Model Space to test the Associative Dimensioning feature in a the Layout1 tab.

1. Choose Dimension ➢ Linear, and then using the Endpoint Osnaps, dimension the bottom edge of the rectangle you drew in Model Space. The dimension shows 12.0000 (480 for metric drawings), the actual size of the rectangle.

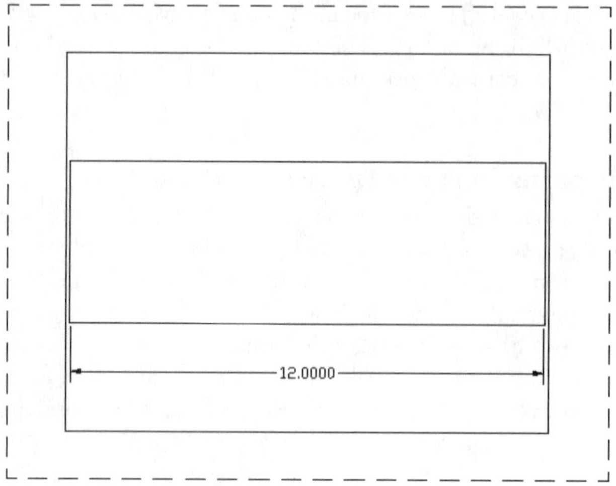

2. Double-click inside the viewport, and then use the Zoom tool to zoom out a bit so that the rectangle appears smaller in the viewport. Once you exit the Zoom tool, the dimension follows the new view of the rectangle.

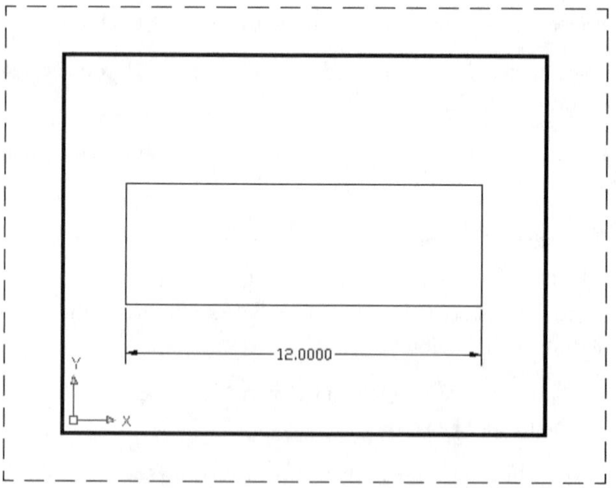

3. While you're in Floating Model Space, click the rectangle, and then click the grip in the lower-left corner and drag it upward and to the right.

4. Click again to place the corner of the rectangle in a new location. The dimension changes to conform to the new shape.

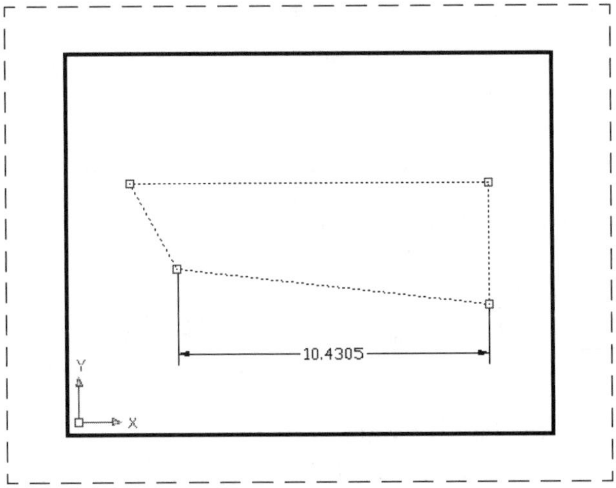

5. Go ahead and close the rectangle file without saving it. You won't need it in the future.

You've just seen how you can dimension an object in Model Space while in Paper Space. You can also dimension Model Space Xrefs in Paper Space in much the same way. The only difference is that changes made to the Xref file will not automatically update dimensions made in Paper Space. You'll need to employ the Dimregen command to refresh Paper Space dimensions of Xref objects.

Updating Associative Dimensions

If you use a wheel mouse to pan and zoom in a Floating Model Space viewport, you might need to use the Dimregen command to refresh an associative dimension. Simply type **Dimregen↵** at the command prompt. You can also use Dimregen to refresh dimensions from drawings that have been edited in earlier versions of AutoCAD or, as mentioned already, to refresh dimensions of objects contained in external references.

Paper Space Dimensioning without Associative Dimensioning

In some situations, you might not want to use Associative Dimensioning, but you still want to dimension Model Space objects in Paper Space. For example, you might be in an office that has different versions of AutoCAD, or you might be sharing your drawings with other offices that are not using AutoCAD 2004, and the use of Associative Dimensioning creates some confusion.

To dimension Model Space objects in Paper Space without Associative Dimensioning, you need to have AutoCAD adjust the dimension text to the scale of the viewport from which you are dimensioning. You can have AutoCAD scale dimension values in Paper Space so they correspond to a viewport zoom-scale factor. The following steps show you how this setting is made.

1. Open the Dimension Style Manager dialog box.

2. Select the dimension style you want to edit and click Modify.

3. Click the Primary Units tab.
4. In the Measurement Scale button group, enter the scale factor of the viewport you intend to dimension in the Scale Factor input box. For example, if the viewport is scaled to a 1/2"=1'-0" scale, enter **24**.
5. Click the Apply To Layout Dimensions Only check box.
6. Click OK, and then click Close in the Dimension Style Manager dialog box. You are ready to dimension in Paper Space.

Remember that you can snap to objects in a floating viewport so you can add dimensions as you normally would in Model Space. If you are dimensioning objects in viewports of different scales, you'll need to set up multiple dimension styles, one for each viewport scale.

Other Uses for Paper Space

The exercises in this section should give you a sense of how you work in Paper Space. I've given examples that reflect the more common uses of Paper Space. Remember that Paper Space is like a page-layout portion of AutoCAD—separate yet connected to Model Space through viewports.

You needn't limit your applications to floor plans. Interior and exterior elevations, 3D models, and detail sheets can all take advantage of Paper Space. When used in conjunction with AutoCAD raster import capabilities, Paper Space can be a powerful tool for creating large-format presentations.

Managing Layers

In a survey of AutoCAD users, Autodesk discovered that one of the most frequently used features in AutoCAD was the Layer command. You'll find that you are turning layers on and off to display and edit the many different levels of information contained in your AutoCAD files. As your files become more complex, the control of layer visibility becomes more difficult. Fortunately, AutoCAD offers the Layer Manager to make your work a little easier.

Saving and Recalling Layer Settings

The Layer Manager lets you save layer settings. This can be crucial when you are editing a file that serves multiple uses, such as a floor plan and reflected ceiling plan. You can, for example, turn layers on and off to set up the drawing for a reflected ceiling plan view and then save the layer settings. Later, when you need to modify the ceiling information, you can recall the layer setting to view the ceiling data. The following steps show you how the Layer Manager works.

1. In AutoCAD, open the `13b-unit.dwg` file. Open the Layer Properties Manager dialog box and turn on all the layers except the Notes and Flr-pat layers. Your drawing should look similar to the top image in Figure 13.42.

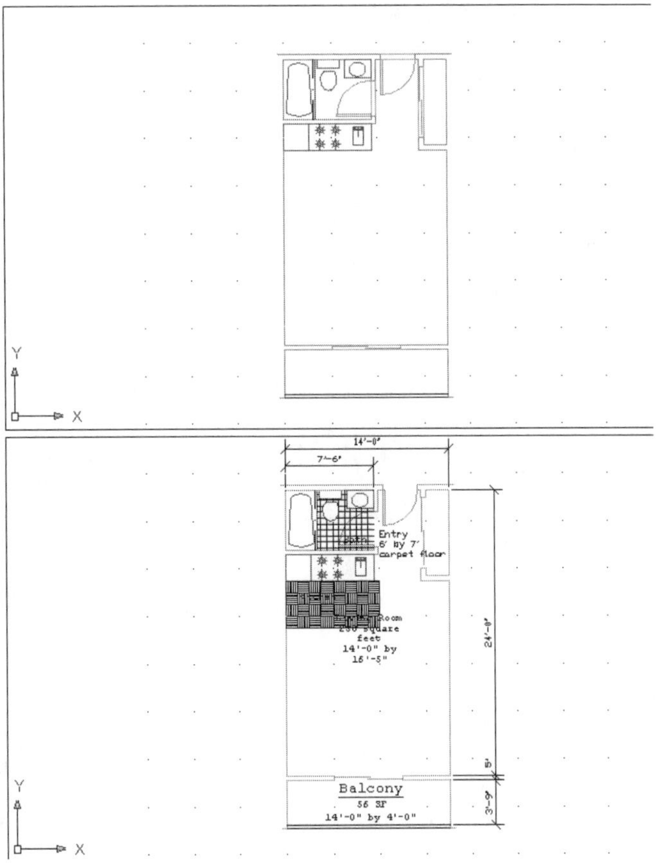

FIGURE 13.42

The view of the `Unit.dwg` file, before and after changing layer settings

2. Open the Layer Properties Manager dialog box again, and click the Save State button to open the Save Layer States dialog box.

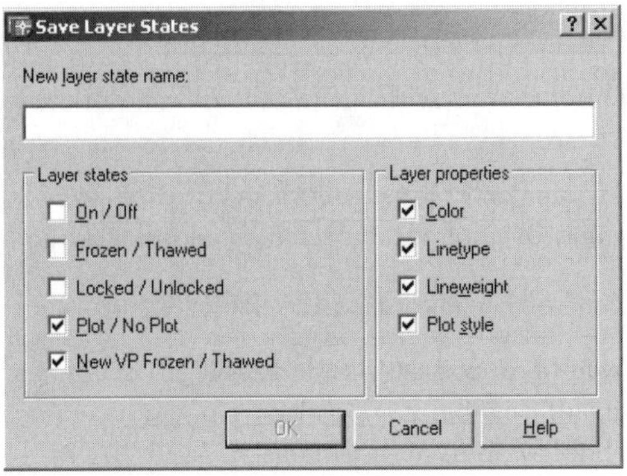

Take a moment to look at the options in this dialog box. This is where you enter a layer state name. You can also specify which layer settings you want saved with this layer state.

Save the current layer state by taking the following steps:

1. Enter **blank floor plan** in the New Layer State Name input box, turn on the On/Off option in the Layer States group, and then click OK.
2. In the Layer Properties Manager dialog box, turn on the Flr-pat and Notes layers and turn off the Ceiling layer.
3. Click OK. Your drawing will look like the bottom image in Figure 13.42.
4. Reopen the Layer Properties Manager dialog box.
5. Click the State Manager button to open the Layer State Manager dialog box.

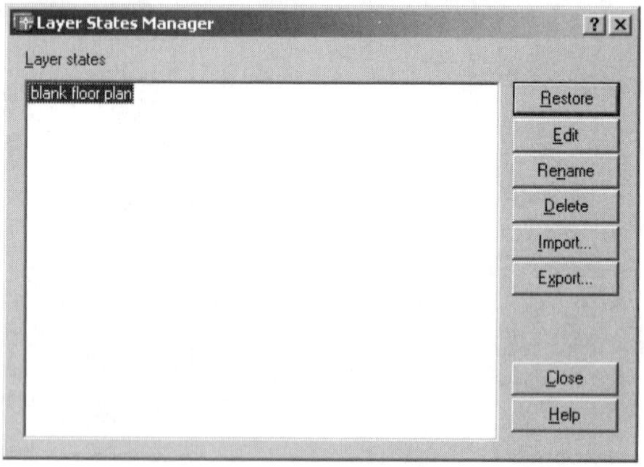

6. Select BLANK FLOOR PLAN from the list, and then click Restore. You return to the Layer Properties Manager dialog box. Notice that the layer settings have changed back to the settings you saved.
7. Click OK. Your drawing reverts to the previous view with the Notes and Flr-pat layers turned off and the Ceiling layer on.

The layer states are saved with the file so you can retrieve them at a later date. As you can see from the Layer State Manager dialog box, you have a few other options.

Edit Opens the Layer Properties Manager dialog box to let you edit the settings for a layer state. Highlight the layer state in the list, and then choose Edit.

Rename Lets you rename an existing layer setting.

Delete Deletes a layer state from the list.

Import Imports a set of layer states that have been exported using the Export option of this dialog box.

Export Saves a set of layer states as a file. By default, the file is given the name of the current file with the .lay filename extension. You can import the layer state file into other files.

In addition to saving layer states by name, you can quickly revert to a previous layer state by clicking the Layer Previous tool in the left side of the Layers toolbar.

This tool allows you to quickly revert to the previous layer settings without affecting other settings in AutoCAD. Note that the Layer Previous mode does not restore renamed or deleted layers, nor does it remove new layers.

Once you become familiar with these layer state tools, you'll find yourself using them frequently in your editing sessions.

TIP The Layerpmode command controls the tracking of layer states. It is normally turned on, but if it is turned off, the Layer Previous tool will not work. To turn it on, enter ***Layerpmode↵*** **On↵**.

Advanced Tools: Quick Select, Selection Filters, and the Calculator

Two other tools are extremely useful in your day-to-day work with AutoCAD: selection filters and the Calculator. I have saved the discussion of these tools until the end of this chapter because you don't really need them until you've become accustomed to the way AutoCAD works. Chances are you've already experimented with some of the AutoCAD menu options not yet discussed in the tutorial. Many of the pull-down menu options and their functions are self-explanatory. Selection filters and the Calculator, however, do not appear in any of the menus and require some further explanation.

Let's start with selection filters. There are actually two selection-filtering tools in AutoCAD. The Quick Select tool offers a quick way to locate objects based on their properties. The Filter tool lets you select objects based on a more complex set of criteria.

Filtering Selections

Suppose you need to isolate just the walls of your drawing in a separate file. One way to do this is to turn off all the layers except the Wall layer. You can then use the Wblock command and select the remaining walls, using a window to write the wall information to a file. Filters can simplify this operation by allowing you to select groups of objects based on their properties.

1. Open the `Unit` file.
2. Type **w↵** to start the Wblock command. Then, in the Write Block dialog box, enter **Unitwall** in the File Name input box.
3. Make sure the Object radio button is selected in the top of the dialog box, and then click the Select Objects button in the Objects group. The dialog box disappears to allow you to select objects.

4. At the `Object Selection:` prompt, type **'Filter↵** to open the Object Selection Filters dialog box.

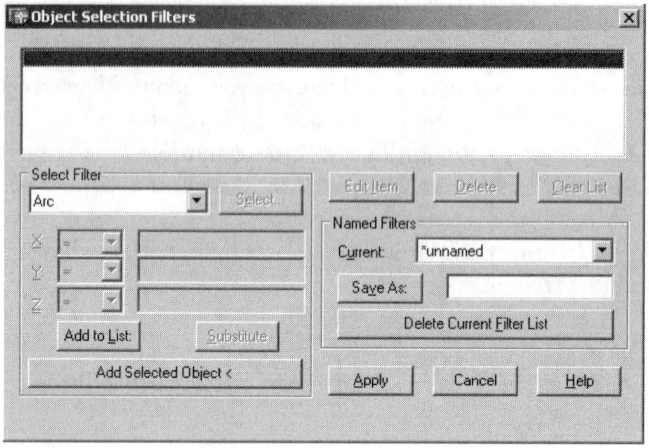

5. Open the drop-down list in the Select Filter button group.
6. Scroll down the list, and find and highlight the Layer option.
7. Click the Select button next to the drop-down list to display a list of layers, highlight Wall, and then click OK.
8. In the Object Selection Filters dialog box, click the Add To List button toward the bottom of the Select Filter button group to add Layer = Wall to the list box.
9. Click Apply to close the Object Selection Filters dialog box.
10. Type **all↵** to select everything in the drawing. Only the objects assigned to the Wall layer are selected. You'll see a message in the Command window indicating how many objects were found and how many were filtered out.
11. Press ↵ and you'll see the message `Exiting Filtered selection. 14 found.`
12. Press ↵ again to complete the Wblock command. All the walls are written out to a file called `Unitwall`.
13. After reviewing the results of the exercise, type **U↵** or click the Undo button in the Standard toolbar to undo the Wblock command.

In this exercise, you filtered out a layer using the Wblock command. Once a filter is designated, you then select the group of objects you want AutoCAD to filter through. AutoCAD finds the objects that match the filter requirements and passes those objects to the current command.

As you've seen from the previous exercise, you can choose from many options in this utility. Let's take a closer look.

WORKING WITH THE OBJECT SELECTION FILTERS DIALOG BOX

To use the Object Selection Filters dialog box, first select the criteria for filtering from the pull-down list. If the criterion you select is a named item (layer, line type, color, or block), you can then click the Select button to choose specific items from a list. If there is only one choice, the Select button is dimmed.

Once you've determined what to filter, you must add it to the list by clicking the Add To List button. The filter criterion then appears in the list box at the top of the Object Selection Filters dialog box. Once you have something in the list box, you can then apply it to your current command or to a later command. AutoCAD remembers your filter settings, so if you need to reselect a filtered selection set, you don't have to redefine your filter criteria.

SAVING FILTER CRITERIA

If you prefer, you can preselect filter criteria. Then, at any `Select objects:` prompt, you can click Selection Filters on the toolbar (or type **'Filter↵**), highlight the appropriate filter criteria in the list box, and click Apply. The specifications in the Object Selection Filters dialog box remain in place for the duration of the current editing session.

You can also save a set of criteria by entering a name in the input box next to the Save As button and then clicking the button. The criteria list data is saved in a file called `Filter.nfl`. You can then access the criteria list at any time by opening the Current drop-down list and choosing the name of the saved criteria list.

FILTERING OBJECTS BY LOCATION

Notice the X, Y, and Z drop-down lists just below the main Select Filter drop-down list in the Object Selection Filters dialog box. These lists become accessible when you select a criterion that describes a geometry or a coordinate (such as an arc's radius or center point). You can use these lists to define filter selections even more specifically, using greater than (>), less than (<), equal to (=), or not equal to (!=) comparisons (called *relational operators*).

For example, suppose you want to grab all the circles whose radii are greater than 4.0 units. To do this, choose Circle Radius from the Select Filter drop-down list. Then in the X list, select >. Enter **4.0** in the input box to the right of the X list, and click Add To List. You see the item

```
Circle Radius > 4.0000
```

added to the list box at the top of the dialog box. You used the > operator to indicate a circle radius greater than 4.0 units.

CREATING COMPLEX SELECTION SETS

At times you'll want to create a specific filter list. For instance, say you need to filter out all the door blocks on the layer Floor2 *and* all arcs with a radius equal to 1. To do this, you use the *grouping operators* found at the bottom of the Select Filter drop-down list. You'll need to build a list as follows:

```
** Begin OR
** Begin AND
Entity = Block
Layer = Floor2
```

```
** End AND
** Begin AND
Entity = Arc
Arc Radius = 1.0000
** End AND
** End OR
```

Notice that the `Begin` and `End` operators are balanced; that is, for every `Begin OR` or `Begin AND`, there is an `End OR` or `End AND`.

This list may look rather simple, but it can get confusing—mostly because of the way you normally think of the terms `AND` and `OR`. If criteria are bounded by the `AND` grouping operators, the objects must fulfill *both* criteria before they are selected. If criteria are bounded by the `OR` grouping operators, the objects fulfilling *either* criteria will be selected.

Here are the steps to build the previous list:

1. In the Select Filter drop-down list, choose `**Begin OR`, and click Add To List. Then do the same for `**Begin AND`.
2. Click Block in the Select Filter drop-down list, and then click Add To List.
3. For the layer, click Layer from the Select Filter drop-down list. Then click Select, choose the layer name, and click Add To List.
4. In the Select Filter drop-down list, choose `**End AND` and click Add To List. Then do the same for `**Begin AND`.
5. Select Arc from the Select Filter drop-down list and click Add To List.
6. Select Arc Radius from the Select Filter list, and enter **1.0** in the input box next to the X drop-down list. Be sure the equal sign (=) shows in the X drop-down list, and then click Add To List.
7. Choose `**End AND` and click Add To List. Then do the same for `**End OR`.

If you make an error in any step, simply highlight the item, select an item to replace it, and click the Substitute button instead of the Add To List button. If you only need to change a value, click Edit Item near the center of the dialog box.

Quick Select

The Filter command offers a lot of power in isolating specific types of objects, but in many situations, you may not need such an elaborate tool. The Qselect command can filter your selection based on the object properties, which are more common filter criteria. To access the Qselect command, choose Tools ➢ Quick Select or right-click the drawing area when no command is active and choose Quick Select from the shortcut menu to open the Quick Select dialog box.

Quick Select is also offered as an option on a few dialog boxes. Try using the Wblock command again, this time using the Quick Select option offered in its dialog box.

1. With the `Unit` file open, type **W↵** to start the Wblock command, and then in the Write Block dialog box, enter **Unitwall2** in the File Name input box.

2. Make sure the Object radio button is selected in the top of the dialog box. Then click the Quick Select button to the right of the Select Objects button in the Objects group to open the Quick Select dialog box.

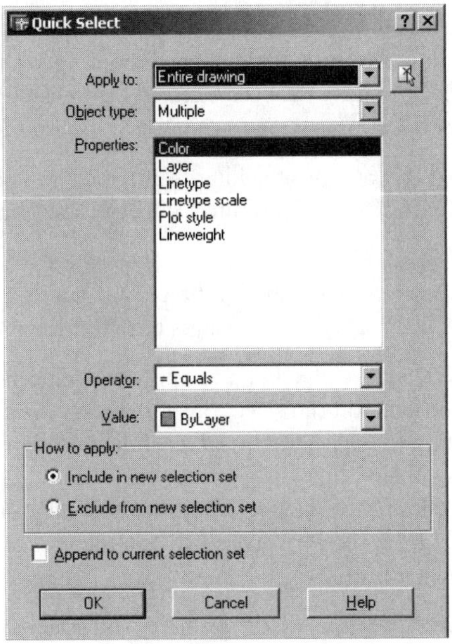

3. Select Layer from the Properties list.
4. Select Wall from the Value drop-down list near the bottom of the dialog box.
5. Click the Select Objects button in the upper-right corner of the dialog box. The dialog box disappears to allow you to select objects.
6. Select the entire drawing using a window, and then press ↵ to finish your selection. The Quick Select dialog box returns.
7. Click OK, and then click OK in the Write Block dialog box. The walls disappear, indicating that they have been written to a file.

The Qselect command selects objects based on the object's properties, as shown in the Properties list box. You can apply the selection criteria based on the entire drawing, or you can use the Select Objects button in the upper-right corner of the dialog box to isolate a set of objects to which you want to apply the selection criteria.

In the previous exercise, you used Quick Select from within another dialog box. As mentioned earlier, you can also use Quick Select by choosing Tools ➢ Quick Select or by right-clicking the drawing area when no command is active and choosing Quick Select from the shortcut menu. Quick Select then makes use of the Noun/Verb selection method so you select objects using Quick Select first, and then you apply editing commands to the selected objects.

TIP *If you want to use Quick Select with a command that does not allow the Noun/Verb selection method, you can select objects using Quick Select, start the command you want to use, and then use the Previous Selection option.*

Here is a description of the Quick Select dialog box options:

Apply To Lets you determine the set of objects to which you want to apply the Quick Select filters. The default is the entire drawing, but you can use the Select Objects button to select a set of objects. If a set of objects has been selected before issuing the Quick Select command, you also see the Current Selection option in the Apply To drop-down list.

Object Type Lets you limit the filter to specific types of objects such as lines, arcs, circles, and so on. The Multiple option lets you filter your selection from all the objects in the drawing regardless of its type.

Properties Once you select an object type, you can then select the property of the object type you want to filter. The Properties list changes to reflect the properties that are available to be filtered.

Operator Offers a set of criteria to apply to the property you select in the Properties list to make your selection. You can select objects that are *equal to* or *not equal to* the criteria you select in the Object Type and Properties lists. Depending on the property you select, you also may have the option to select objects that are *greater than* or *less than* a given property value. For example, you can select all lines whose X coordinate is less than 5 by choosing Line from the Object Type drop-down list and Start X from the Properties list. You then select < Less Than from the Operator drop-down list and enter **5** in the Value input box.

Value Displays the values of the property you select in the Properties list. For example, if you select Layer from the Properties list, the Value option lists all the layers available.

How To Apply Lets you determine whether to include or exclude the filtered objects in a new selection set.

Append To Current Selection Set Lets you append the filtered objects to an existing selection set or create an entirely new selection set.

ACAD only

Finding Geometry with the Calculator

Another useful AutoCAD tool is the Geometry Calculator. Like most calculators, it adds, subtracts, divides, and multiplies. If you enter an arithmetic expression such as 1 + 2, the calculator returns 3. This is useful for doing math on the fly, but the Calculator does much more than arithmetic, as you will see in the next examples.

FINDING THE MIDPOINT BETWEEN TWO POINTS

One of the most common questions heard from AutoCAD users is, How can I locate a point midway between two objects? You can draw a construction line between the two objects and then use the Midpoint override to select the midpoint of the construction line. The Calculator offers another method that doesn't require drawing additional objects.

In the following exercise, you start a line midway between the center of an arc and the endpoint of a line. Draw a line and an arc and try this.

1. Start the Line command, and at the `Specify first point:` prompt, type **'Cal↵**.
2. At the >> `Expression:` prompt, enter **(end + cen)/2↵**.
3. At the >> `Select entity for END snap:` prompt, the cursor turns into a square. Place the square on the endpoint of a line and click it.
4. At the >> `Select entity for CEN snap:` prompt, click an arc. The line starts midway between the arc's center and the endpoint of the line.

TIP *Typing the Calculator expressions may seem a bit too cumbersome to do on a regular basis, but if you find that you could use some of its features, you can create a toolbar macro to simplify the Calculator's use. See Chapter 21 for more on customizing toolbars.*

Using Osnap Modes in Calculator Expressions

In the previous exercise, you used Osnap modes as part of arithmetic expressions. The Calculator treats them as temporary placeholders for point coordinates until you actually pick the points (at the prompts shown in steps 3 and 4).

The expression

```
(end + cen)/2
```

finds the average of two values. In this case, the values are coordinates, so the average is the midpoint between the two coordinates. You can take this one step further and find the centroid of a triangle using this expression:

```
(end + end + end)/3
```

Note that only the first three letters of the Osnap mode are entered in Calculator expressions. Table 13.1 shows what to enter in an expression for Osnap modes.

TABLE 13.1: The Geometry Calculator's Osnap Modes

Calculator Osnap	Meaning
End	Endpoint
Ins	Insert
Int	Intersection
Mid	Midpoint
Cen	Center
Nea	Nearest
Nod	Node

Continued on next page

TABLE 13.1: THE GEOMETRY CALCULATOR'S OSNAP MODES *(continued)*

CALCULATOR OSNAP	MEANING
Qua	Quadrant
Per	Perpendicular
Tan	Tangent
Rad	Radius of object
Cur	Cursor pick

Table 13.1 includes two items that are not really Osnap modes, although they work similarly when they are used in an expression. The first is Rad. When you include Rad in an expression, you get the following prompt:

```
Select circle, arc or polyline segment for RAD function:
```

You can then select an arc, a polyline arc segment, or a circle, and its radius is used in place of Rad in the expression.

The other item, Cur, prompts you for a point. Instead of looking for specific geometry on an object, it just locates a point. You could have used Cur in the previous exercise in place of the End and Cen modes to create a more general-purpose midpoint locator, as in the following form:

```
(cur + cur)/2
```

Since AutoCAD does not provide a specific tool to select a point midway between two other points, the form shown here would be useful as a custom toolbar macro. You'll learn how to create macros in Chapter 21.

FINDING A POINT RELATIVE TO ANOTHER POINT

Another common task in AutoCAD is starting a line at a relative distance from another line. The following steps describe how to use the Calculator to start a line from a point that is 2.5" in the x-axis and 5.0" in the y-axis from the endpoint of another line:

1. Start the Line command. At the `First point:` prompt, enter **'Cal↵**.
2. At the >> `Expression:` prompt, enter **end + [2.5,5.0]↵**.
3. At the >> `Select entity for END snap:` prompt, pick the endpoint. The line starts from the desired location.

In this example, you used the Endpoint Osnap mode to indicate a point of reference. This is added to Cartesian coordinates in square brackets, describing the distance and direction from the reference point. You could have entered any coordinate value within the square brackets. You could also have entered a polar coordinate in place of the Cartesian coordinate, as in the following: **end + [5.59<63]**.

You don't have to include an @, because the Calculator assumes you want to add the coordinate to the one indicated by the Endpoint Osnap mode. Also, it's not necessary to include every coordinate in the square brackets. For example, to indicate a displacement in only one axis, you can leave out a value for the other two coordinates, as in the following examples:

```
[4,5] = [4,5,0] [,1] = [0,1,0]
[,,2] = [0,0,2]
```

Adding Feet and Inch Distances on the Fly

If you use feet and inches, one of the more frustrating situations you may have run across is having to stop in the middle of a command to find the sum of two or more distances. Say you start the Move command, select your objects, and pick a base point. You then realize you don't know the distance for the move, but you do know that the distance is the sum of two values—unfortunately, one value is in feet and the other is in inches. Usually in this situation you would have to reach for pen and paper (or, if you have one, a feet-and-inches calculator), figure out the distance, and then return to your computer to finish the task. AutoCAD's Geometry Calculator puts an end to this runaround.

The following steps show you what to do if you want to move a set of objects a distance that is the sum of 12' 6-5/8" and 115-3/4".

1. Issue the Move command, select objects, and pick a base point.
2. At the `Second point:` prompt, start the Calculator.
3. At the >> `Expression:` prompt, enter **[@12'6-5/8" + 115-3/4" < 45]**. Then press ↵, and the objects move into place at the proper distance.

WARNING *You must always enter an inch symbol (") when indicating inches in the Calculator.*

In this example, you are mixing inches and feet, which under normal circumstances is a time-consuming calculation. Notice that the feet-and-inches format follows the standard AutoCAD syntax (no space between the feet and inch values). The coordinate value in square brackets can have any number of operators and values, as in the following:

```
[@4 * (22 + 15) - (23.3 / 12) + 1 < 13 + 17]
```

This expression demonstrates that you can also apply operators to angle values.

Guidelines for Working with the Calculator

You may be noticing some patterns in the way expressions are formatted for the Calculator. Here are some guidelines to remember:

- Coordinates are enclosed in square brackets.
- Nested or grouped expressions are enclosed in parentheses.
- Operators are placed between values, as in simple math equations.
- Object snaps can be used in place of coordinate values.

Table 13.2 lists all the operators and functions available in the Calculator. You might want to experiment with these other functions on your own.

TABLE 13.2: THE GEOMETRY CALCULATOR'S FUNCTIONS

OPERATOR/FUNCTION	WHAT IT DOES	EXAMPLE
+ or –	Add or subtract numbers or vectors	2 – 1 = 1 [a,b,c] + [x,y,z] = [a+x, b+y, c+z]
* or /	Multiply or divide numbers or vectors	2 * 4.2 = 8.4 a*[x,y,z] = [a*x, a*y, a*z]
^	Exponentiation of a number	3^2 = 9
sin	Sine of angle	sin (45) = 0.707107
cos	Cosine of angle	cos (30) = 0.866025
tang	Tangent of angle	tang (30) = 0.57735
asin	Arcsine of a real number	asin (0.707107) = 45.0
acos	Arccosine of a real number	acos (0.866025) = 30.0
atan	Arctangent of a real number	atan (0.57735) = 30.0
ln	Natural log	ln (2) = 0.693147
log	Base-10 log	log (2) = 0.30103
exp	Natural exponent	exp (2) = 7.38906
exp10	Base-10 exponent	exp10 (2) = 100
sqr	Square of number	sqr (9) = 81.0
abs	Absolute value	abs (–3.4) = 3.4
round	Round to nearest integer	round (3.6) = 4
trunc	Drop decimal portion of real number	trunc (3.6) = 3
r2d	Convert radians to degrees	r2d (1.5708) = 90.0002
d2r	Convert degrees to radians	d2r (90) = 1.5708
pi	The constant pi	3.14159

The Geometry Calculator is capable of much more than the typical uses you've seen here. A description of its full capabilities extends beyond the scope of this text. Still, the processes described in this section will be helpful as you use AutoCAD. If you want to know more about the Calculator, consult the AutoCAD Help User Documentation (choose Help ➢ Help).

If You Want to Experiment...

You may want to experiment further with Paper Space to become more familiar with it. Try the following exercise. In it you will add two more viewports using the View ➢ Viewports (Floating) options (Mview and Copy commands). In the process, you'll find that editing Paper Space views requires frequent shifts from Model Space to Paper Space and back:

1. Open the `13-xref1` file you used for the earlier Paper Space exercise.
2. If you aren't already in Paper Space, click the Layout1 tab and make sure that Paper appears in the status bar.
3. Stretch the lower viewport so that it occupies the lower-right third of the screen (see the first image in Figure 13.43).

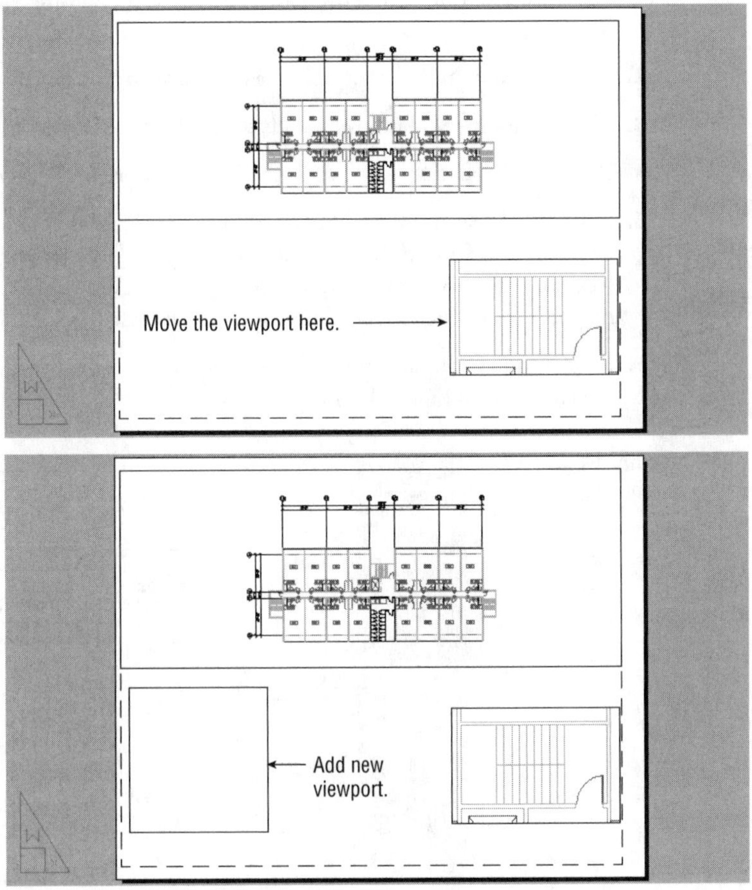

FIGURE 13.43
Creating new viewports in Paper Space

4. Switch to Floating Model Space and click the lower viewport.
5. Pan the view so the entire stair is displayed.
6. Return to Paper Space to create a new viewport.
7. Choose View ➢ Viewports ➢ New Viewport, or type **vports**↵.
8. In the Viewports dialog box, make sure the New Viewports tab is selected and select Single from the list.
9. Click OK, and then click the lower-left corner of the screen.
10. At the `Other corner:` prompt, size the viewport so that it is similar to the viewport on the right, as shown in the bottom image in Figure 13.43.
11. Click the Paper button in the status bar to go to Floating Model Space; then click the lower-left viewport.
12. Type **Regen**↵. Notice that only the current viewport regenerates.
13. Use the Zoom and Pan commands to display the stairway at the far left of the floor plan.
14. Return to Paper Space and copy the new viewport to the right.
15. Return to Floating Model Space and use the Realtime Pan tool to pan the view in the new viewport to display the stairway to the far right of the floor plan. Notice that when you use the Realtime Pan tool, you can pan across the entire AutoCAD window; you're not limited to panning just inside the viewport area. You can also use the scroll bar to pan the active viewport.
16. Return to Paper Space to resize the viewports to display only the stairs in the lower half of the layout, as in Figure 13.44.

FIGURE 13.44
Creating new viewports in Paper Space

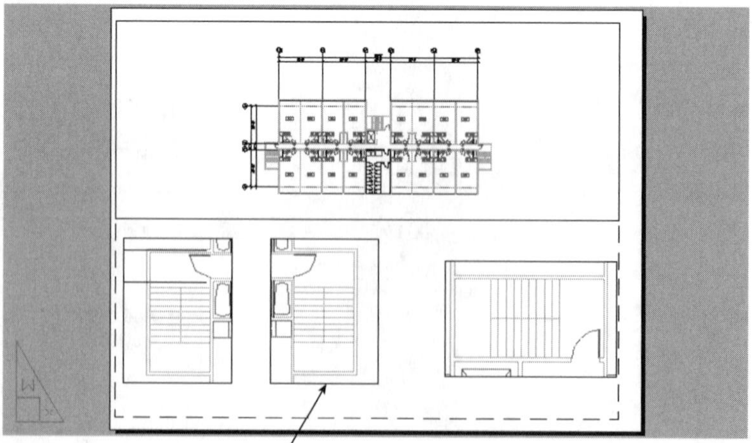

Copy viewport and change view to show other stair.

Chapter 14

Drawing Curves and Solid Fills

So far in this book, you've been using basic lines, arcs, and circles to create your drawings. Now it's time to add polylines and spline curves to your repertoire. Polylines offer many options for creating forms, including solid fills. Spline curves are perfect for drawing smooth, nonlinear objects. The splines are true *NURBS* curves. NURBS stands for Non-Uniform Rational B-Splines.

- Introducing Polylines
- Editing Polylines
- Creating a Polyline Spline Curve
- Using True Spline Curves
- Marking Divisions on Curves
- Sketching with AutoCAD
- Filling In Solid Areas
- If You Want to Experiment…

Introducing Polylines

Polylines are like composite line segments and arcs. A polyline may look like a series of line segments, but it acts like a single object. This characteristic makes polylines useful for a variety of applications, as you'll see in the upcoming exercises.

Drawing a Polyline

First, to introduce you to the polyline, you will begin a drawing of the top view of the joint in Figure 14.1.

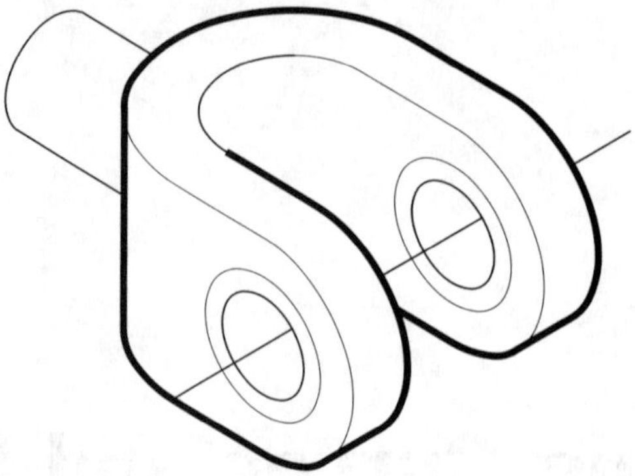

FIGURE 14.1
A sketch of a metal joint

1. Open a new file and save it as `Joint2d`. Don't bother to make special setting changes, because you will create this drawing with the default settings.
2. Set the limits to **0,0** for the lower-left corner and **12,9** for the upper-right corner, and then choose View ➢ Zoom ➢ All or type **Z↵ A↵**.
3. Click the Polyline tool on the Draw toolbar or type **Pl↵**.
4. At the `Specify start point:` prompt, enter a point at coordinate 3,3 to start your polyline.
5. At the `Specify next point or [Arc/Halfwidth/Length/Undo/Width]:` prompt, enter **@3<0↵** to draw a horizontal line of the joint.

TIP *You can draw polylines just as you do with the Line command. Or you can use the other Pline options to enter a polyline arc, specify the polyline thickness, or add a polyline segment in the same direction as the previously drawn line.*

6. At the prompt

   `Specify next point or [Arc/Close/Halfwidth/Length/Undo/Width]:`

   enter **A↵** to continue your polyline with an arc.

TIP *The Arc option allows you to draw an arc that starts from the last point you selected. Once selected, the Arc option offers additional options. The default Save option is the endpoint of the arc. As you move your cursor, an arc follows it in a tangential direction from the first line segment you drew.*

7. At the prompt

   ```
   Specify endpoint of arc or
   [Angle/CEnter/CLose/Direction/Halfwidth/Line/Radius/Second pt/Undo/Width]:
   ```

   enter **@4<90↵** to draw a 180° arc from the last point you entered. Your drawing should now look like Figure 14.2.

FIGURE 14.2

A polyline line and arc

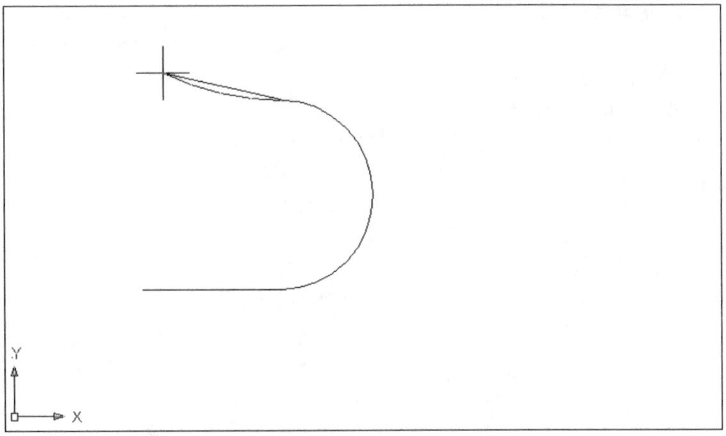

8. To continue the polyline with another line segment, enter **L↵**.
9. At the prompt

   `Specify next point or [Arc/Close/Halfwidth/Length/Undo/Width]:`

   enter **@3<180↵**. Another line segment continues from the end of the arc.
10. Press ↵ to exit Pline.

You now have a sideways, U-shaped polyline that you will use in the next exercise to complete the top view of your joint.

Polyline Options

Let's pause from the tutorial to look at some of the Polyline options you didn't use:

Close Draws a line segment from the last endpoint of a sequence of lines to the first point picked in that sequence. This works exactly like the Close option for the Line command.

Length Enables you to specify the length of a line that will be drawn at the same angle as the last line entered.

Halfwidth Creates a tapered line segment or an arc by specifying half its beginning and ending widths (see Figure 14.3).

Width Creates a tapered line segment or an arc by specifying the full width of the segment's beginning and ending points.

Undo Deletes the last line segment drawn.

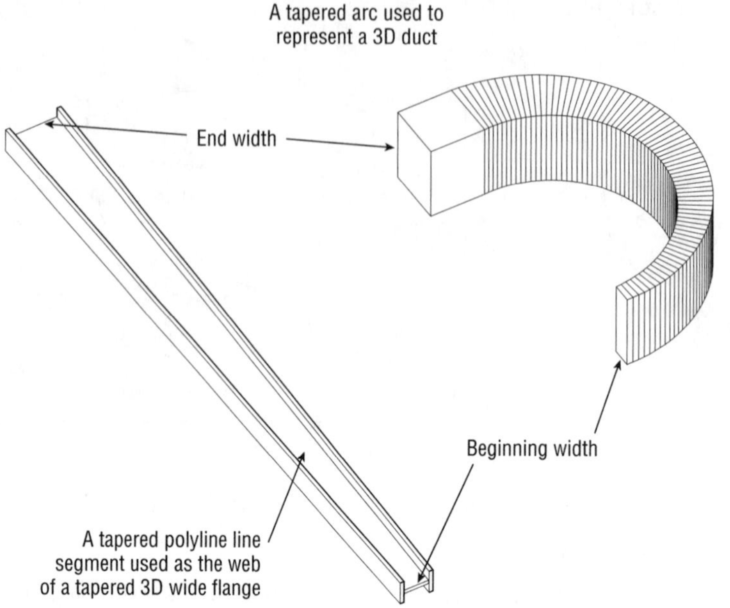

FIGURE 14.3
A tapered line segment and an arc created with Halfwidth

If you want to break down a polyline into simple lines and arcs, you can use the Explode option on the Modify toolbar, just as you would with blocks. Once a polyline is exploded, it becomes a set of individual line segments or arcs.

To turn off the filling of solid polylines, open the Options dialog box and click the Display tab. Clear the Apply Solid Fill check box in the Display Performance group. (The options in the Display Performance group are explained in detail later in this chapter in the section on solid fills.)

TIP *You can use the Fillet tool on the Modify toolbar to fillet all the vertices of a polyline composed of straight-line segments. Click Fillet, and then set your fillet radius. Click Fillet again, type* ***P↵*** *to select the Polyline option, and then pick the polyline you want to fillet.*

Editing Polylines

You can edit polylines with many of the standard editing commands. To change the properties of a polyline, double-click the polyline to open the Properties palette. You can use the Stretch command on the Modify toolbar to displace vertices of a polyline, and the Trim, Extend, and Break commands on the Modify toolbar also work with polylines.

In addition, many editing capabilities are offered only for polylines. For instance, later in this chapter you will see how to smooth out a polyline using the Curve Fit option in the Pedit command and the Modify Polyline dialog box. In the next exercise, you'll use the Offset command on the Modify toolbar to add the inside portion of the joint:

1. Click the Offset tool in the Modify toolbar, or type **O↵**.

2. At the `Specify offset distance or [Through] <1.0000>:` prompt, enter **1**.
3. At the `Select object to offset or <exit>:` prompt, pick the U-shaped polyline you just drew.
4. At the `Specify point on side to offset:` prompt, pick a point toward the inside of the U. A concentric copy of the polyline appears (see Figure 14.4).

FIGURE 14.4

The offset polyline

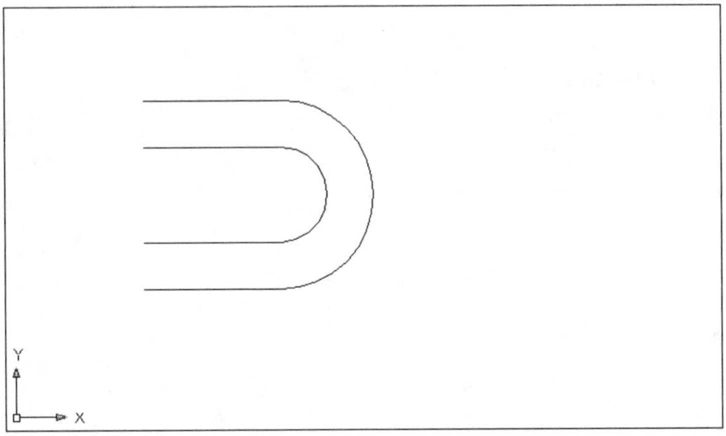
Y
X

5. Press ↵ to exit the Offset command.

The concentric copy of a polyline made with Modify ➢ Offset can be useful when you need to draw complex parallel curves like the ones in Figure 14.5.

FIGURE 14.5

Sample complex curves drawn by using offset polylines

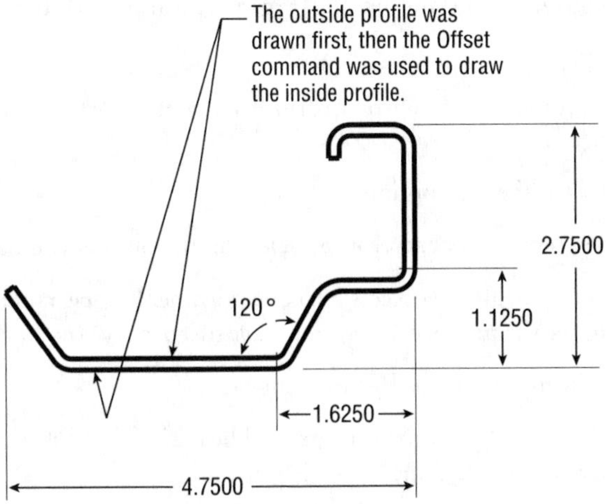
The outside profile was drawn first, then the Offset command was used to draw the inside profile.
120°
2.7500
1.1250
1.6250
4.7500

Next, complete the top view of the joint:

1. Connect the ends of the polylines with two short line segments (see Figure 14.6).

WARNING *If the objects to be joined don't touch the existing polyline exactly endpoint to endpoint, they will not join. To ensure that you place the endpoints of the lines exactly on the endpoints of the polylines, use the Endpoint Osnap override to select each polyline endpoint.*

FIGURE 14.6
The joined polyline

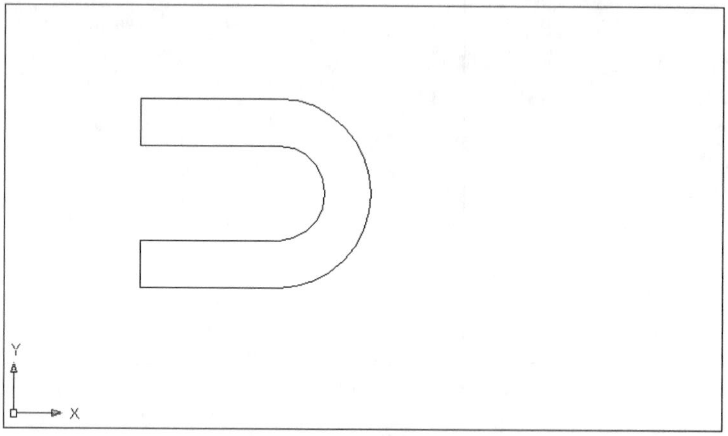

2. Choose Modify ➢ Object ➢ Polyline, or type **Pe**↵. You can also choose Edit Polyline from the Modify II toolbar.
3. At the `Select polyline or [Multiple]:` prompt, pick the outermost polyline.
4. At the prompt

   ```
   Enter option [Close/Join/Width/Edit vertex/Fit/Spline/Decurve/Ltype
   gen/Undo]:
   ```

   enter **J**↵ for the Join option.
5. At the `Select objects:` prompt, select all the objects you have drawn so far.
6. Press ↵ to join all the objects into one polyline. It appears that nothing has happened, although you will see the message `5 segments added to polyline` in the Command window.
7. Press ↵ again to exit the Pedit command.
8. Click the drawing to expose its grips. The entire object is highlighted, telling you that all the lines have been joined into a single polyline.

By using the Width option under Edit Polyline, you can change the thickness of a polyline. Let's change the width of your polyline, to give some thickness to the outline of the joint.

1. Type **Pe↵** or click the Edit Polyline tool on Modify II toolbar again.
2. Click the polyline.
3. At the prompt

   `[Close/Join/Width/Edit vertex/Fit/Spline/Decurve/Ltype gen/Undo]:`

   enter **W↵** for the Width option.
4. At the `Enter new width for all segments:` prompt, enter **.03↵** for the new width of the polyline. The line changes to the new width (see Figure 14.7), and you now have a top view of your joint.

FIGURE 14.7

The polyline with a new thickness

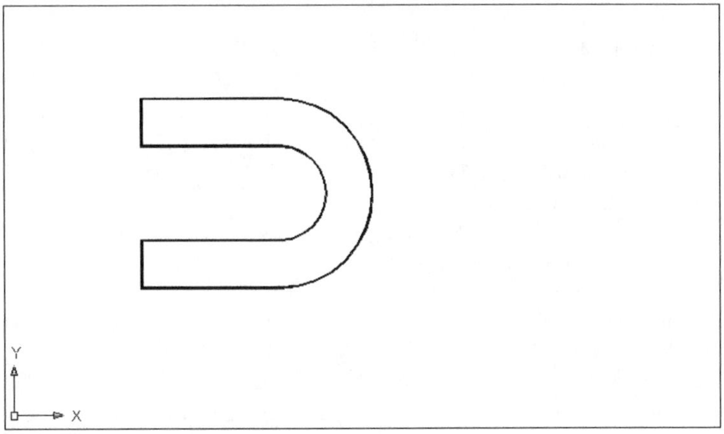

5. Press ↵ to exit the Pedit command.
6. Save this file.

Now here's a brief look at a few of the Pedit options you didn't try firsthand:

Close Connects the two endpoints of a polyline with a line segment. If the polyline you selected to be edited is already closed, this option changes to Open.

Open Removes the last segment added to a closed polyline.

Spline/Decurve Smooths a polyline into a spline curve (discussed in detail later in this chapter).

Edit Vertex Lets you edit each vertex of a polyline individually (discussed in detail in the next section).

Fit Turns polyline segments into a series of arcs.

Ltype Gen Controls the way non-continuous line types pass through the vertices of a polyline. If you have a fitted or spline curve with a non-continuous line type, turn on this option .

TIP You can change the thickness of regular lines and arcs by using Pedit to change them into polylines and then using the Width option to change their width.

Smoothing Polylines

You can create a curve in AutoCAD in many ways. If you don't need the representation of a curve to be accurate, you can use a polyline curve. In the following exercise, you will draw a polyline curve to represent a contour on a topographical map.

1. Open the `Topo.dwg` drawing that is included on the CD that comes with this book. The first image in Figure 14.8 contains the drawing of survey data. Some of the contours have already been drawn in between the data points.

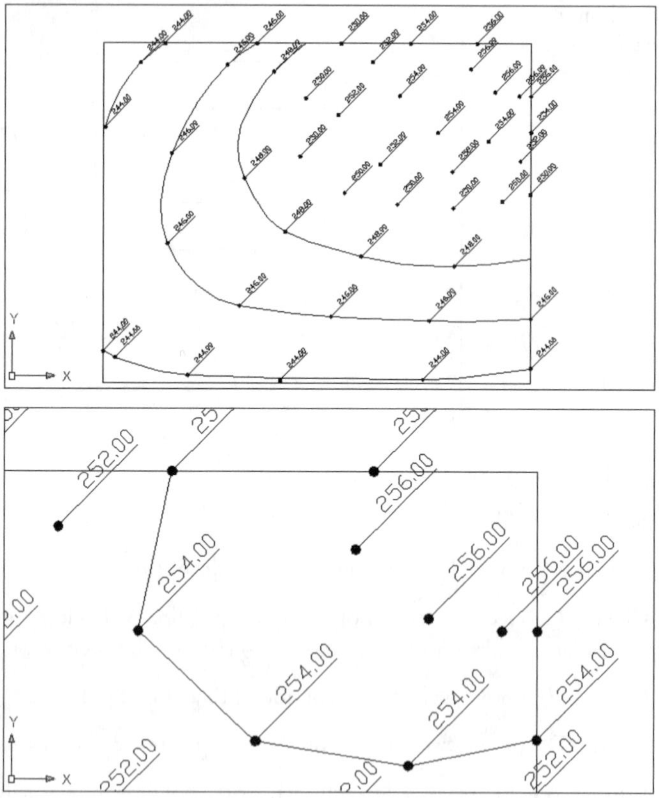

FIGURE 14.8
The `Topo.dwg` drawing shows survey data portrayed in an AutoCAD drawing. Notice the dots indicating where elevations were taken. The actual elevation value is shown with a diagonal line from the point.

2. Zoom in to the upper-right corner of the drawing, so your screen displays the area shown in the second image in Figure 14.8.

3. Click the Polyline tool in the Draw toolbar. Using the Center Osnap, draw a polyline that connects the points labeled "254.00." Your drawing should look like the second image in Figure 14.8.
4. Press ↵.

TIP *If Running Osnaps are not set, you can choose Tools ➢ Drafting Settings or type* ***Os↵*** *to open the Osnap Settings dialog box. From there, you can select Center to open the Center Running Osnaps dialog box. See Chapter 3 for more on this dialog box.*

Next, you will convert the polyline you just drew into a smooth contour line.

1. Choose Modify ➢ Object ➢ Polyline, or type **Pe↵**.
2. At the `PEDIT Select polyline or [Multiple]:` prompt, pick the contour line you just drew.
3. At the prompt

   `Enter an option [close/Join/Width/Edit vertex/Fit/Spline/Decurve/Ltype gen/Undo]:`

   press **F↵** to select the Fit option. This causes the polyline to smooth out into a series of connected arcs that pass through the data points.
4. Press ↵ to end the Pedit command.

Your contour is now complete. The Fit Curve option under the Pedit command causes AutoCAD to convert the straight-line segments of the polyline into arcs. The endpoints of the arcs pass through the endpoints of the line segments, and the curve of each arc depends on the direction of the adjacent arc. This gives the effect of a smooth curve. Next, you'll use this polyline curve to experiment with some of the editing options unique to the Pedit command.

TURNING OBJECTS INTO POLYLINES AND POLYLINES INTO SPLINES

At times you will want to convert regular lines, arcs, or even circles into polylines. You might want to change the width of lines or join lines to form a single object such as a boundary. Here are the steps to take to convert lines, arcs, and circles into polylines.

1. Choose Modify ➢ Object ➢ Polyline. You can also type **Pe↵** at the command prompt.
2. At the `Select polyline or [Multiple]:` prompt, pick the object you want to convert. If you want to convert a circle to a polyline, first break the circle (using the Break option on the Modify toolbar) so that it becomes an arc of approximately 359°.
3. At the prompt

   `Object selected is not a polyline. Do you want to turn it into one? <Y>:`

   press ↵ twice. The object is converted into a polyline.

Continued on next page

TURNING OBJECTS INTO POLYLINES AND POLYLINES INTO SPLINES *(continued)*

If you have several objects that you want to convert to polylines, type **M**↵ at the `Select polyline or [Multiple]` prompt; then select the objects you want to convert. You will then see the `Convert Lines and Arcs to polylines [Yes/No]?:` prompt. Type **Y**↵, and all the selected objects will be converted to polylines. You can then go on to use other Pedit options on the selected objects.

To turn a polyline into a true spline curve, do the following:

1. Choose Modify ➢ Object ➢ Polyline, or type **Pe**↵. Select the polyline you want to convert.
2. Type **S**↵ to turn it into a polyline spline; then press ↵ to exit the Pedit command.
3. Click the Spline tool in the Draw Toolbar or type **Spl**↵. You can also choose Draw ➢ Spline from the pull-down menu.
4. At the `Specify first point or [Object]:` prompt, type **O**↵ for the Object option.
5. At the `Select objects:` prompt, click the polyline spline. Though it may not be apparent at first, the polyline is converted into a true spline.

You can also use the Spline Edit tool (choose Modify ➢ Spline or enter **Spe**↵) on a polyline spline. If you do, the polyline spline is automatically converted into a true spline.

Editing Vertices

One of the Pedit options that I haven't yet been discussed, Edit Vertex, is almost like a command within a command. Edit Vertex has numerous suboptions that allow you to fine-tune your polyline by giving you control over its individual vertices. This section discusses the Edit Vertex option in depth.

To access the Edit Vertex options, follow these steps:

1. First, turn off the Data and Border layers to hide the data points and border.
2. Issue the Pedit command again, and then select the polyline you just drew.
3. Type E↵ to enter the Edit Vertex mode. An X appears at the beginning of the polyline, indicating the vertex that will be affected by the Edit Vertex options.

WARNING *When using Edit Vertex, you must be careful about selecting the vertex to be edited. Edit Vertex has six options, and you often have to exit the Edit Vertex operation and use Pedit's Fit option to see the effect of Edit Vertex's options on a curved polyline.*

EDIT VERTEX SUBOPTIONS

Once you've entered the Edit Vertex mode of the Pedit command, you have the option to perform the following functions:

- Break the polyline between two vertices

- Insert a new vertex
- Move an existing vertex
- Straighten a polyline between two vertices
- Change the tangential direction of a vertex
- Change the width of the polyline at a vertex

These functions are presented in the form of the following prompt:

`[Next/Previous/Break/Insert/Move/Regen/Straighten/Tangent/Width/eXit] <N>:`

This section examines each of the options presented in this prompt, starting with the Next and Previous options.

The Next and Previous Options

These options let you select a vertex for editing. When you start the Edit Vertex option, an X appears on the selected polyline to designate its beginning. As you select Next or Previous, the X moves from vertex to vertex to show which one is being edited. Let's try this.

1. Press ↵ a couple of times to move the X along the polyline. (Because Next is the default option, you only need to press ↵ to move the X.)
2. Type **P**↵ for Previous. The X moves in the opposite direction. Notice that now the default option becomes P.

TIP *To determine the direction of a polyline, note in which direction the X moves when you use the Next option. Knowing the direction of a polyline is important for some of the other Edit Vertex options.*

The Break Option

The Break option breaks the polyline between two vertices:

1. Position the X on one end of the segment you want to break.
2. Enter **B**↵ at the command prompt.
3. At the `Enter an option [Next/Previous/Go/eXit] <N>:` prompt, use Next or Previous to move the X to the other end of the segment to be broken.
4. When the X is in the proper position, choose Edit Vertex ➢ Go or enter **G**↵ to break the polyline (see Figure 14.9).

TIP *You can also use the Break and Trim options on the Modify toolbar to break a polyline anywhere, as you did when you drew the toilet seat in Chapter 3.*

FIGURE 14.9

How the Break option works

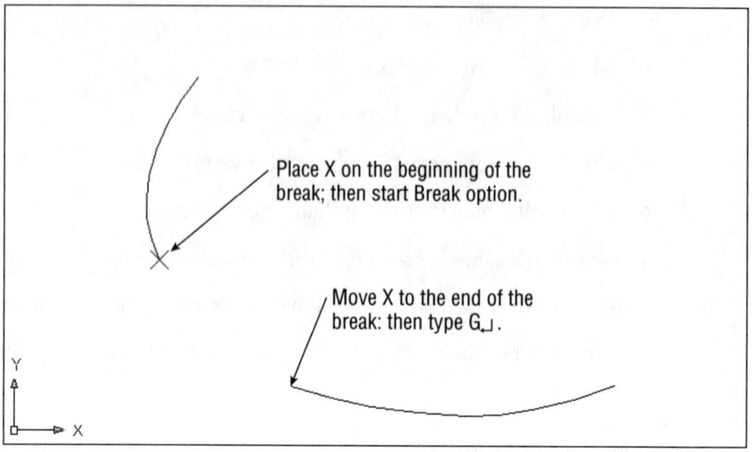

The Insert Option

Next, try the Insert option, which inserts a new vertex.

1. Type X↵ to temporarily exit the Edit Vertex option. Then type U↵ to undo the break.
2. Type E↵ to return to the Edit Vertex option, and position the X before the new vertex.
3. Press ↵ to advance the X marker to the next point.
4. Enter I↵ to select the Insert option.
5. When the prompt `Specify location for new vertex:` appears, along with a rubber-banding line originating from the current X position (see Figure 14.10), pick a point indicating the new vertex location. The polyline is redrawn with the new vertex.

FIGURE 14.10

The new vertex location

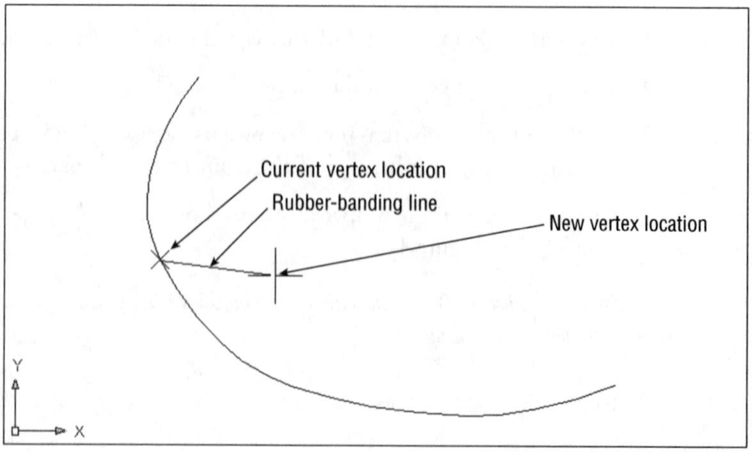

Notice that the inserted vertex appears between the currently marked vertex and the *next* vertex, so the Insert option is sensitive to the direction of the polyline. If the polyline is curved, the new vertex will not immediately be shown as curved (see the first image in Figure 14.11). You must smooth it out by exiting the Edit Vertex option and then using the Fit option, as you did to edit the site plan (see the second image in Figure 14.11). You can also use the Stretch command (on the Modify toolbar) to move a polyline vertex.

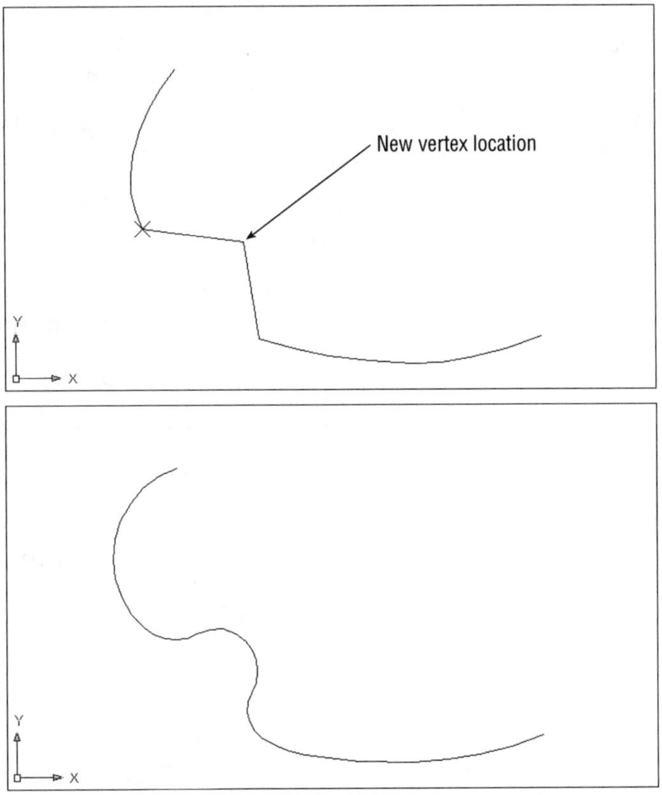

FIGURE 14.11
The polyline before and after the curve is fitted

The Move Option

In this brief exercise, you'll use the Move option to move a vertex.

1. Undo the inserted vertex by exiting the Edit Vertex option (enter **X↵**) and typing **U↵**.
2. Restart the Edit Vertex option, and use the Next or Previous option to place the X on the vertex you want to move.
3. Enter **M↵** for the Move option.

4. When the `Specify new location for marked vertex:` prompt appears, along with a rubber-banding line originating from the X (see the first image in Figure 14.12), pick the new vertex. The polyline is redrawn (see the second image in Figure 14.12). Again, if the line is curved, the new vertex appears as a sharp angle until you use the Fit option (see the final image in Figure 14.12).

TIP *You can also move a polyline vertex using its grip.*

FIGURE 14.12

Picking a new location for a vertex, with the polyline before and after the curve is fitted

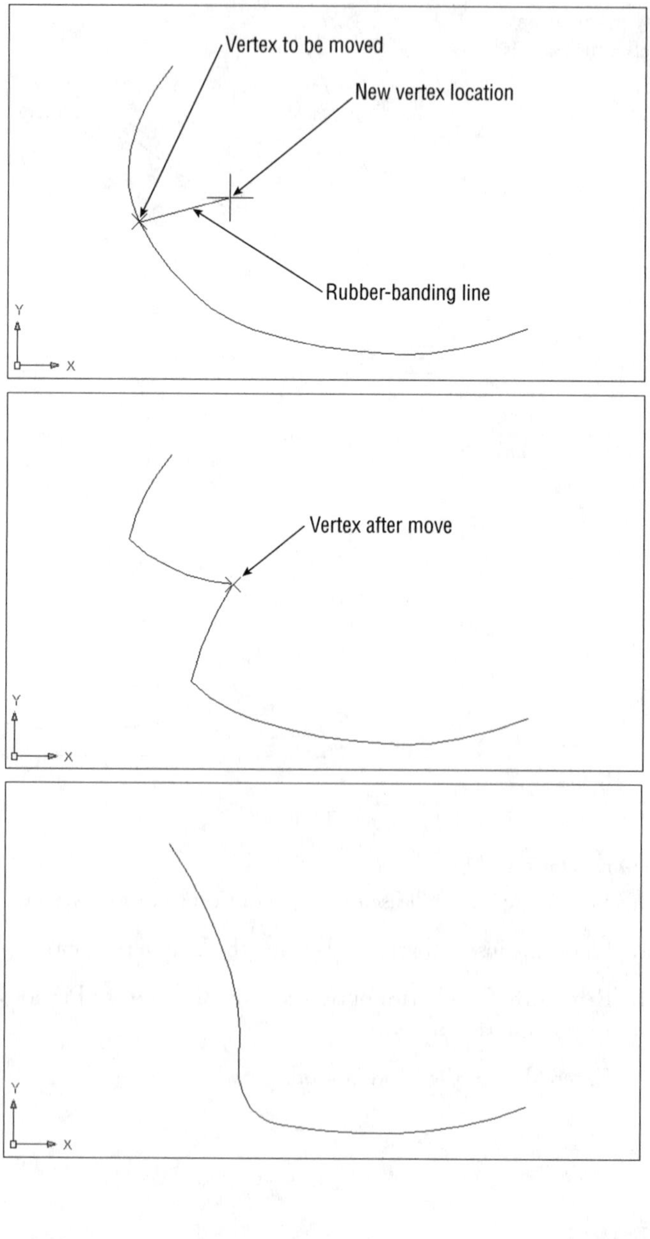

The Straighten Option

The Straighten option straightens all the vertices between two selected vertices, as shown in the following exercise.

1. Undo the moved vertex (from the previous exercise).
2. Start the Edit Vertex option again, and select the starting vertex for the straight line.
3. Enter **S↵** for the Straighten option.
4. At the `Enter option [Next/Previous/Go/eXit] <N>:` prompt, move the X to the location for the other end of the straight-line segment.
5. Once the X is in the proper position, enter **G↵** for the Go option. The polyline straightens between the two selected vertices (see Figure 14.13).

TIP *Using the Straighten option is a quick way to delete vertices from a polyline.*

FIGURE 14.13
A polyline after straightening

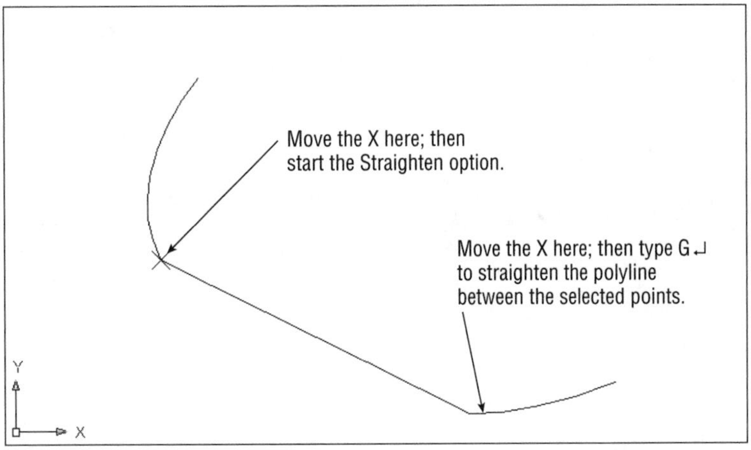

The Tangent Option

The Tangent option alters the direction of a curve on a curve-fitted polyline.

1. Undo the straightened segment from the previous exercise.
2. Restart the Edit Vertex option, and position the X on the vertex you want to alter.
3. Enter **T↵** for the Tangent option. A rubber-banding line appears (see the top image in Figure 14.14).

FIGURE 14.14

Picking a new tangent direction

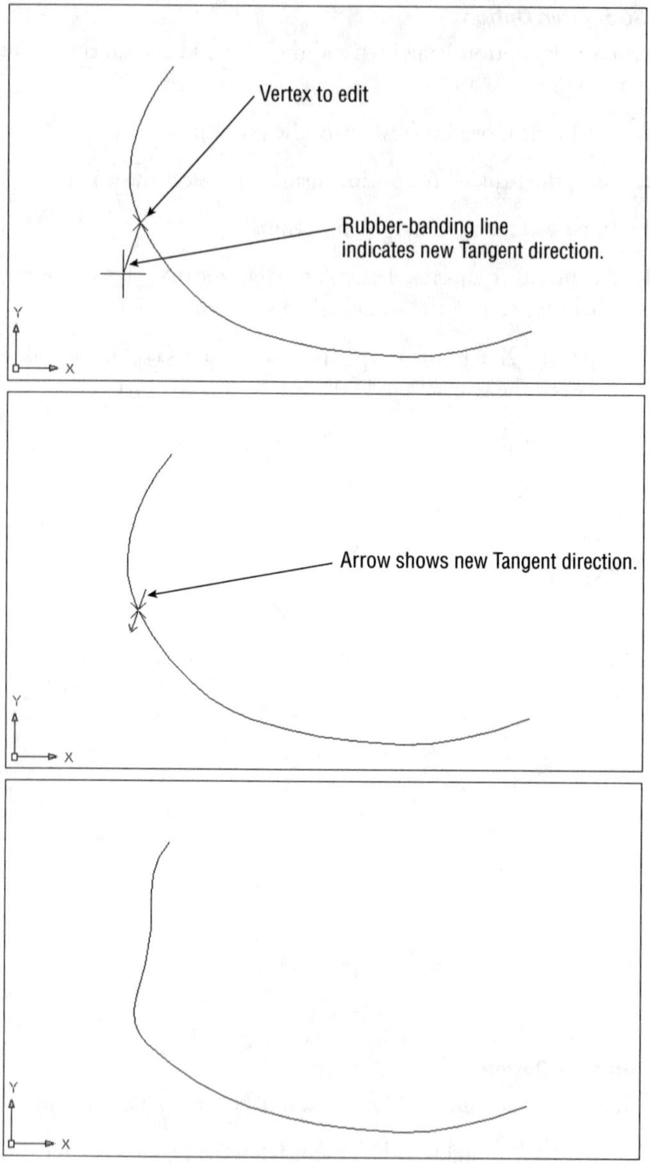

4. Point the rubber-banding line in the direction for the new tangent, and click the mouse. An arrow appears, indicating the new tangent direction (see the second image in Figure 14.14).

Don't worry if the polyline shape does not change. You must use Fit to see the effect of Tangent (see the final image in Figure 14.14).

The Width Option

Finally, try out the Width option. Unlike the Pedit command's Width option, the Edit Vertex/Width option enables you to alter the width of the polyline at any vertex. Thus, you can taper or otherwise vary polyline thickness.

1. Undo the tangent arc from the previous exercise.
2. Return to the Edit Vertex option, and place the X at the beginning vertex of a polyline segment you want to change.
3. Type **W**↵ to issue the Width option.
4. At the `Specify starting width for next segment <0.0000>:` prompt, enter a value, **12** for example, indicating the polyline width desired at this vertex.
5. At the `Specify ending width for next segment <12.0000>:` prompt, enter the width, **24** for example, for the next vertex.

Again (as with Tangent), don't be alarmed if nothing happens after you enter this Width value. To see the result, you must exit the Edit Vertex command (see Figure 14.15).

TIP *The Width option is useful when you want to create an irregular or curved area in your drawing that is to be filled in solid. This is another option that is sensitive to the polyline direction.*

FIGURE 14.15

A polyline with the width of one segment increased

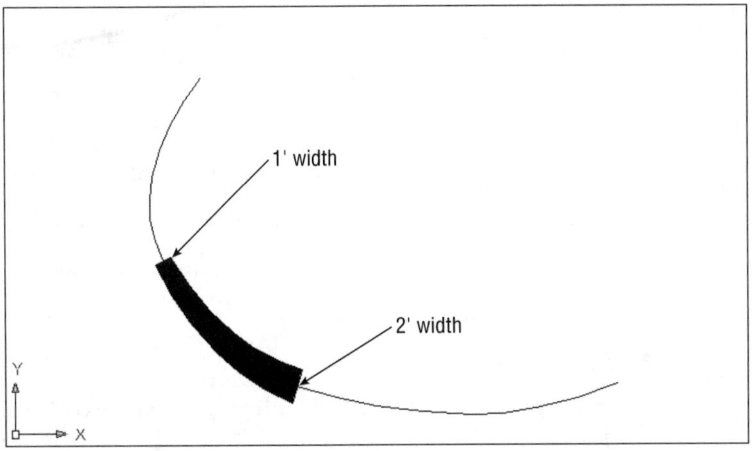

As you have seen throughout these exercises, you can use the Undo option to reverse the last Edit Vertex option used. And you can use the eXit option to leave Edit Vertex at any time. Just enter **X**↵ to display the Pedit prompt:

```
Enter an option [Close/Join/Width/Edit vertex/Fit/Spline/Decurve/Ltype
gen/Undo]:
```

Creating a Polyline Spline Curve

The Pedit command's Spline option (named after the spline tool used in manual drafting) offers you a way to draw smoother and more controllable curves than those produced by the Fit option. A polyline spline does not pass through the vertex points as a fitted curve does. Instead, the vertex points act as weights pulling the curve in their direction. The polyline spline touches only its beginning and end vertices. Figure 14.16 illustrates this concept.

TIP *A polyline spline curve does not represent a mathematically true curve. See the section "Using True Spline Curves" later in this chapter to learn how to draw a more accurate spline curve.*

FIGURE 14.16

The polyline spline curve pulled toward its vertices

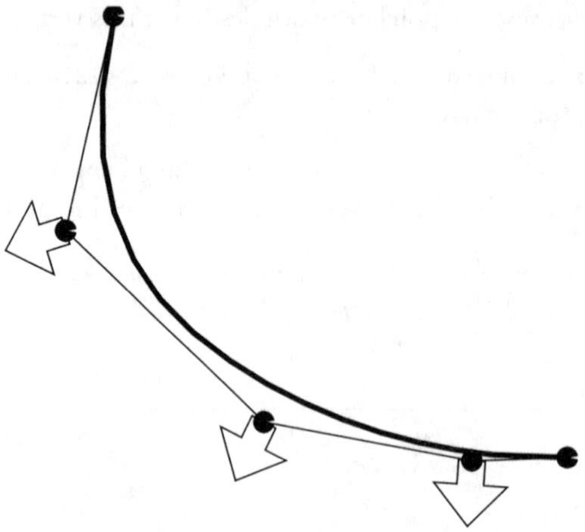

Let's see how using a polyline spline curve might influence the way you edit a curve.

1. Undo the width changes you made in the previous exercise.
2. To change the contour into a polyline spline curve, choose Modify ➢ Object ➢ Polyline.
3. Pick the polyline to be curved.
4. At the prompt

   ```
   Enter an option [Close/Join/Width/Edit vertex/Fit/Spline/Decurve/Ltype
   gen/Undo]:
   ```

   enter S↵. Your curve changes to look like Figure 14.17.
5. Press ↵ to exit Edit Polyline.

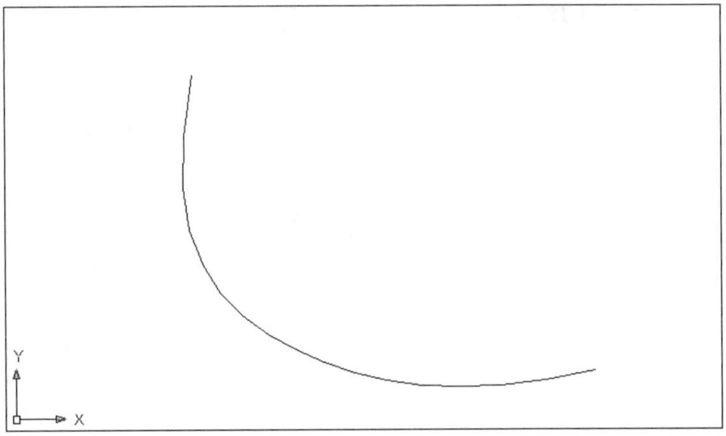

FIGURE 14.17
A spline curve

The curve takes on a smoother, more graceful appearance. It no longer passes through the points you used to define it. To see where the points went and to find out how spline curves act, do the following:

1. Make sure the Noun/Verb Selection mode and the Grips feature are turned on.
2. Click the curve. You'll see the original vertices appear as grips (see the first image in Figure 14.18).
3. Click the grip that is second from the top of the curve, as shown in the second image in Figure 14.18, and move the grip around. Notice how the curve follows, giving you immediate feedback on how the curve will look.
4. Pick a point as shown in the third image in Figure 14.18. The curve is fixed in its new position.

TIP *You can set up AutoCAD to display both the curved and the straight segments defining the curve by turning on the Splframe system variable. Enter* ***splframe*↵ 1↵** *and then issue a Regen command. You'll see a frame that connects the grips of the curve. To turn off the display of the straight segments, enter* ***splframe*↵ 0↵**.

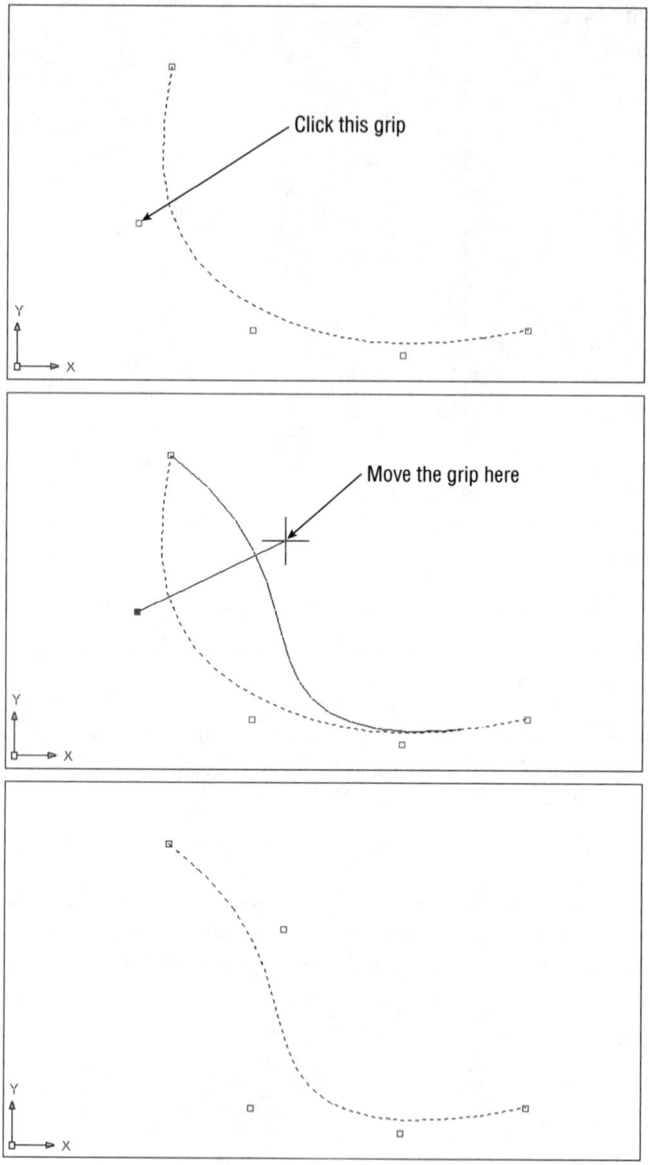
Click this grip
Move the grip here
Y
X

FIGURE 14.18
The fitted curve changed to a spline curve, with the location of the second vertex and the new curve

Using True Spline Curves

So far, you've been working with polylines to generate spline curves. The advantage to using polylines for curves is that they can be enhanced in other ways. You can modify their width, for instance, or join several curves together. But at times you will need a more exact representation of a curve. The

Spline object, created by choosing Draw ➢ Spline, produces a more accurate model of a spline curve, as well as giving you more control over its shape.

Drawing a Spline

The following exercise shows you how to create a spline curve.

1. Undo the changes made in the previous two exercises.
2. Turn the Data layer on so you can view the data points.
3. Adjust your view so you can see all the data points with the elevation of 250.00 (see Figure 14.19).

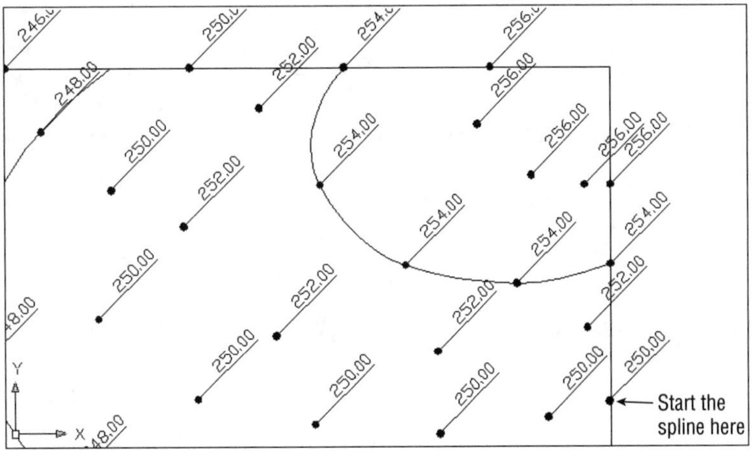

FIGURE 14.19
Starting the spline curve at the first data point

4. Choose Draw ➢ Spline, or type **Spl↵**.
5. At the `Specify first point or [Object]:` prompt, use the Center Osnap to start the curve on the first data point in the lower-right corner (see Figure 14.19). The prompt changes to `Specify next point:`.
6. Continue to select the 250.00 data points until you reach the last one. Notice that as you pick points, a curve appears, and it bends and flows as you move your cursor.
7. Once you've selected the last point, press ↵. Notice that the prompt changes to `Specify start tangent:`. Also, a rubber-banding line appears from the first point of the curve to the cursor. As you move the cursor, the curve adjusts to the direction of the rubber-banding line. Here, you can set the tangency of the first point of the curve (see the first image in Figure 14.20).
8. Press ↵. This causes AutoCAD to determine the first point's tangency based on the current shape of the curve. A rubber-banding line appears from the last point of the curve. As with the first point, you can indicate a tangent direction for the last point of the curve (see the second image in Figure 14.20).

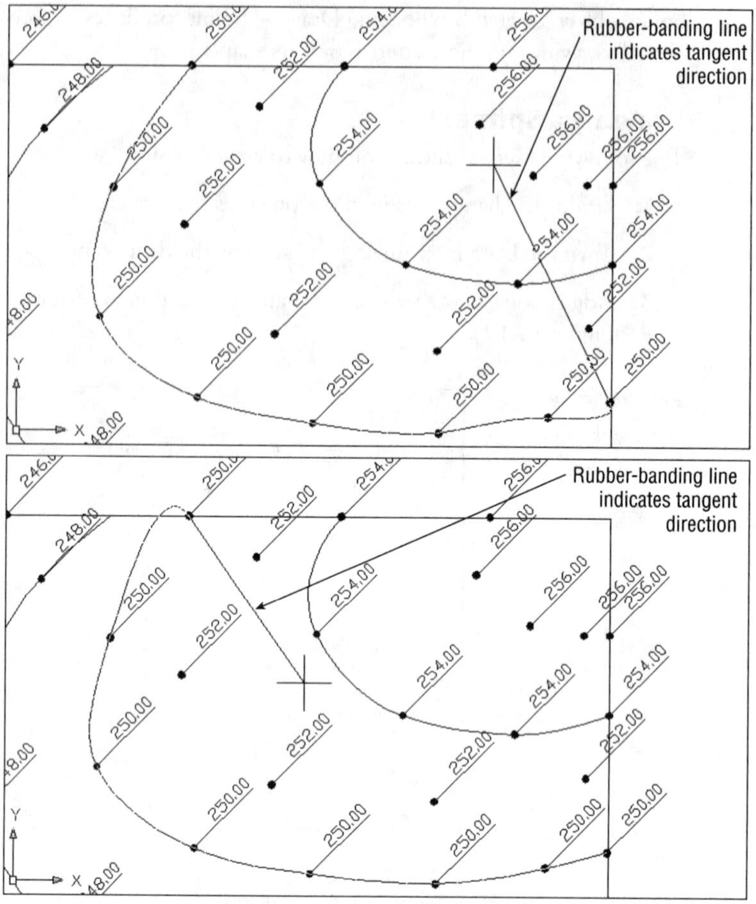

FIGURE 14.20
The last two prompts of the Spline command let you determine the tangent direction of the spline.

9. Press ↵ to exit the Spline command without changing the endpoint tangent direction.

You now have a smooth curve that passes through the points you selected. These points are called the *control points*. If you click the curve, you'll see the grips appear at the location of these control points, and you can adjust the curve simply by clicking the grip points and moving them. (You may need to turn off the Data layer to see the grips clearly.)

TIP *See Chapter 2 for more detailed information on grip editing.*

You might have noticed two other options—Fit Tolerance and Close—as you were selecting points for the spline in the previous exercise. Here is a description of these options:

Fit Tolerance Lets you change the curve so that it doesn't actually pass through the points you pick. When you select this option, you get the prompt `Enter Fit Tolerance <0.0000>`. Any value greater than 0 causes the curve to pass close to, but not through, the points. A value of 0 causes the curve to pass through the points. (You'll see how this works in a later exercise.)

Close Lets you close the curve into a loop. If you choose this option, you are prompted to indicate a tangent direction for the closing point.

Fine-Tuning Spline Curves

Spline curves are different from other types of objects, and many of the standard editing commands won't work on splines. AutoCAD offers the Modify ➢ Object ➢ Spline option (Splinedit command) for making changes to splines. The following exercise will give you some practice with this command. You'll start by focusing on Splinedit's Fit Data option, which lets you fine-tune the spline curve.

CONTROLLING THE FIT DATA OF A SPLINE

The following exercise demonstrates how the Fit Data option lets you control some of the general characteristics of the curve.

1. Choose Modify ➢ Object ➢ Spline, or type **Spe↵** at the command prompt.
2. At the `Select Spline:` prompt, select the spline you drew in the previous exercise.
3. At the prompt

   ```
   Enter an option [Fit data/Close/Move vertex/Refine/rEverse/Undo]:
   ```

   type **F↵** to select the Fit Data option.

TIP *The Fit Data option is similar to the Edit Vertex option of the Pedit command in that Fit Data offers a subset of options that let you edit certain properties of the spline.*

Controlling Tangency at the Beginning Points and Endpoints

Next, let's see how you can adjust the tangency of the first and last points of a spline.

1. At the prompt

   ```
   [Add/Close/Delete/Move/Purge/Tangents/toLerance/eXit] <eXit>:
   ```

   type **T↵** to select the Tangents option. Move the cursor, and notice that the curve changes tangency through the first point, just as it did when you first created the spline (see Figure 14.20).
2. Press ↵. You can now edit the other endpoint tangency.
3. Press ↵ again. You return to the prompt

   ```
   [Add/Close/Delete/Move/Purge/Tangents/toLerance/eXit] <eXit>:
   ```

Adding New Control Points

Now add another control point to the spline curve.

1. At the prompt

   `[Add/Close/Delete/Move/Purge/Tangents/toLerance/eXit] <eXit>:`

   type A↵ to access the Add option.

2. At the `Specify control point <exit>:` prompt, click the third grip point from the bottom end of the spline (see the top image in Figure 14.21). A rubber-banding line appears from the point you selected. That point and the next point are highlighted. The two highlighted points tell you that the next point you select will fall between these two points. You also see the `Specify new point <exit>:` prompt.

FIGURE 14.21

Adding a new control point to a spline

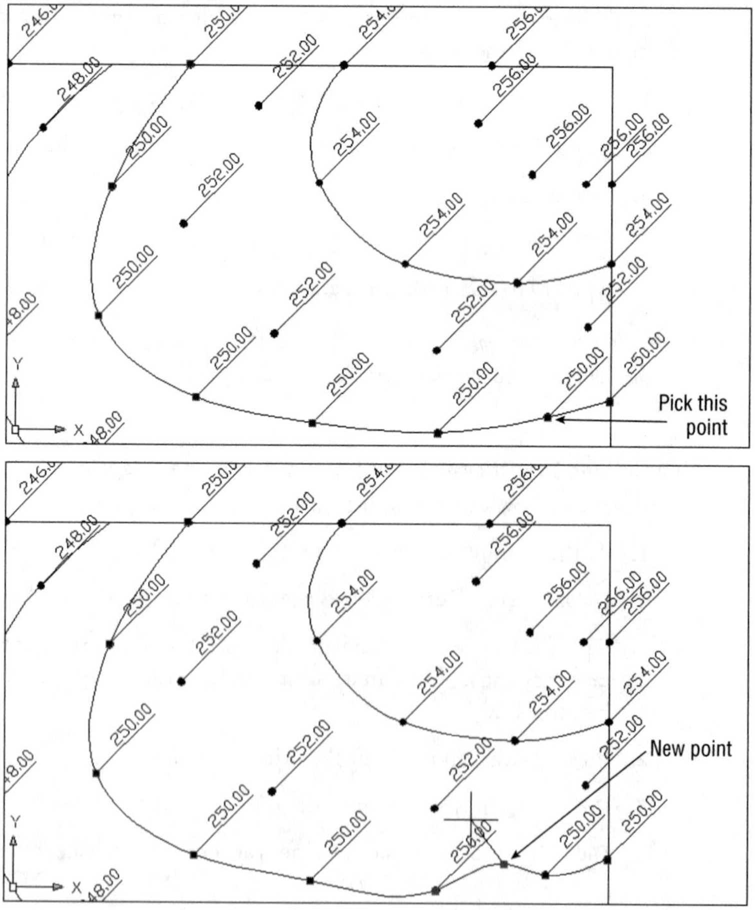

3. Click a new point. The curve changes to include that point. In addition, the new point becomes the highlighted point, indicating that you can continue to add more points between it and the other highlighted point (see the bottom image in Figure 14.21).
4. Press ↵. The `Specify control point <exit>:` prompt appears, allowing you to select another point if you so desire.
5. Press ↵ again to return to the prompt

   `[Add/Close/Delete/Move/Purge/Tangents/toLerance/eXit] <eXit>:`

   Type **X**↵ to exit.

Adjusting the Spline Tolerance Setting

Before ending the description of the Fit Data options, let's look at how Tolerance works.

1. At the prompt

   `[Add/Close/Delete/Move/Purge/Tangents/toLerance/eXit] <eXit>:`

   type **L**↵ to select the Tolerance option. This option sets the tolerance between the control point and the curve.
2. At the `Enter fit tolerance <0.0000>:` prompt, type **30**↵. Notice how the curve no longer passes through the control points, except for the beginning and endpoints (see Figure 14.22). The fit tolerance value you enter determines the maximum distance away from any control point the spline can be.
3. Type **X**↵ to exit the Fit Data option.

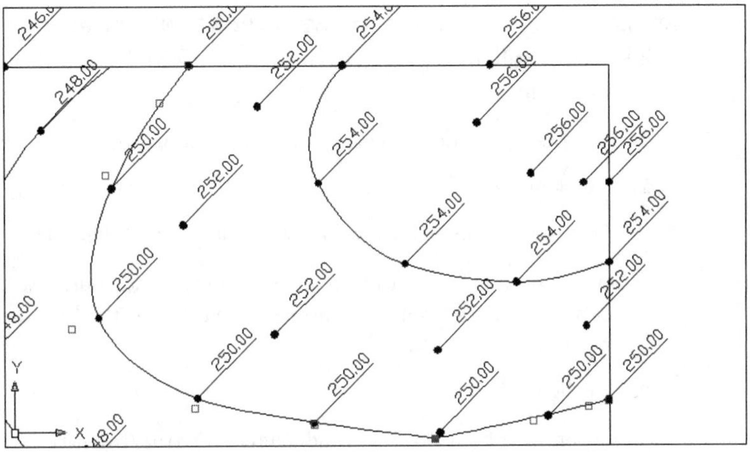

FIGURE 14.22
The spline after setting the control point tolerance to 30

You've seen how you can control many of the shape properties of a spline through the Fit Data option. Here are descriptions of the other Fit Data options you didn't try in these exercises:

Delete Removes a control point in the spline.

Close Lets you close the spline into a loop.

Move Lets you move a control point.

Purge Deletes the fit data of the spline, thereby eliminating the Fit Data option for the purged spline.

When Can't You Use Fit Data?

The Fit Data option of the Splinedit command offers many ways to edit a spline; however, this option is not available to all spline curves. When you invoke certain of the other Splinedit options, a spline curve will lose its fit data, thereby disabling the Fit Data option. These operations are as follows:

- Fitting a spline to a tolerance (Spline/Fit Tolerance) and moving its control vertices
- Fitting a spline to a tolerance (Spline/Fit Tolerance) and opening or closing it
- Refining the spline
- Purging the spline of its fit data using the Purge option of the Splinedit command (choose Modify ➢ Object ➢ Spline or enter **Splinedit↵**, and then select the spline and enter **F↵ P↵**)

Also, note that the Fit Data option is not available when you edit spline curves that have been created from polyline splines. See the "Turning Objects into Polylines and Polylines into Splines" sidebar earlier in this chapter.

ADJUSTING THE CONTROL POINTS WITH THE REFINE OPTION

While you are still in the Splinedit command, let's look at another of its options, Refine, with which you can fine-tune the curve.

1. Type **U↵** to undo the changes you made in the previous exercise.
2. At the prompt

   `[Fit data/Close/Move vertex/Refine/rEverse/Undo]:`

   type **R↵**. The Refine option lets you control the "pull" exerted on a spline by an individual control point. This isn't quite the same effect as the Fit Tolerance option you used in the previous exercise.
3. At the prompt

   `Enter a refine option [Add control point/Elevate order/Weight/eXit] <eXit>:`

   type **W↵**. The first control point is highlighted.

4. At the next prompt

   `Enter new weight (current = 1.000) or [Next/Previous/Select Point/eXit] <N>:`

   press ↵ three times to move the highlight to the fourth control point.

5. Type **25**↵. The curve not only moves closer to the control point, it also bends around the control point in a tighter arc (see Figure 14.23).

FIGURE 14.23

The spline after increasing the Weight value of a control point

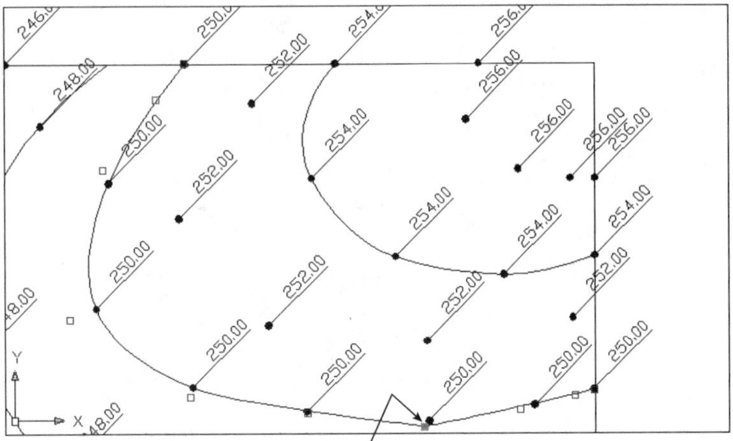
Spline is closer and tighter

You can use the Weight value of Splinedit's Refine option to pull the spine in tighter. Think of it as a way to increase the "gravity" of the control point, causing the curve to be pulled closer and tighter to the control point.

Continue your look at the Splinedit command by adding more control points—without actually changing the shape of the curve. You do this using Refine's Add Control Point and Elevate Order options.

1. Type **1**↵ to return the spline to its former shape.
2. Type **X**↵ to exit the Weight option; then type **A**↵ to select the Add Control Point option.
3. At the `Specify a point on the spline <exit>:` prompt, click the second-to-last control point toward the top end of the spline (see the top image in Figure 14.24). The point you select disappears and is replaced by two control points roughly equidistant from the one you selected (see the bottom image in Figure 14.24). The curve remains unchanged. Two new control points now replace the one control point you selected.

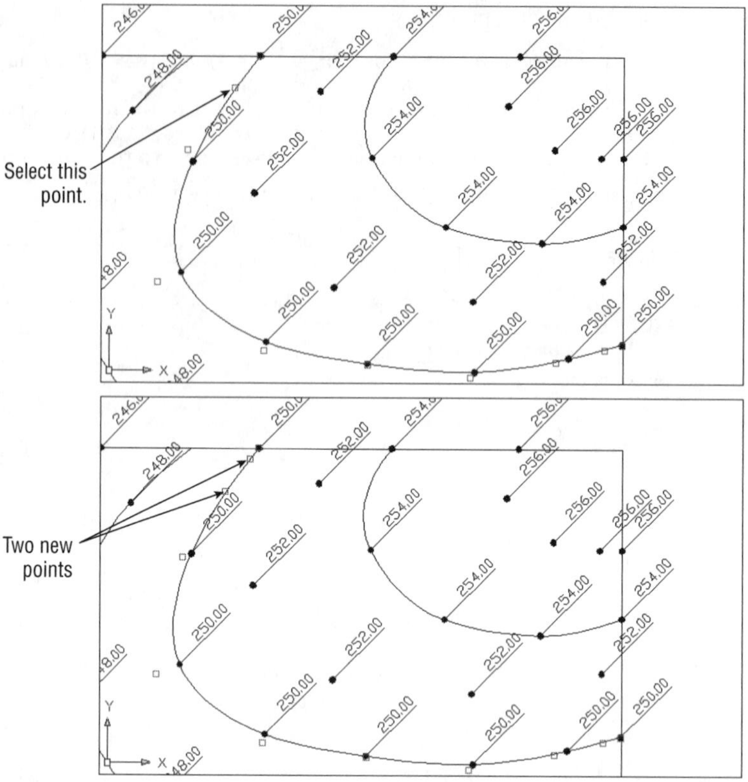

FIGURE 14.24
Adding a single control point using the Refine option

4. Press ↵ to exit the Add Control Point option.
5. Now type **E**↵ to select the Elevate Order option.
6. At the `Enter new order <4>:` prompt, type **6**↵. The number of control points increases, leaving the curve itself untouched.
7. Type **X**↵ twice to exit the Refine option and then the Splinedit command.

You will probably never edit the contour lines of a topographical map in quite the way these exercises have shown. But by following this tutorial, you have explored all the potential of AutoCAD's spline object. Aside from its usefulness for drawing contours, it can be a great tool for drawing free-form illustrations. It is also an excellent tool for mechanical applications, in which precise, non-uniform curves are required, such as drawings of cams or sheet metal work.

Marking Divisions on Curves

Perhaps one of the most difficult things to do in manual drafting is to mark regular intervals on a curve. AutoCAD offers the Divide and Measure commands to help you perform this task with speed and accuracy.

TIP *The Divide and Measure commands are discussed here in conjunction with polylines, but you can use these commands on any object except blocks and text.*

Dividing Objects into Segments of Equal Length

You use the Divide command to divide an object into a specific number of equal segments. For example, suppose you need to mark off the contour you've been working on in this chapter into nine equal segments. One way to do this is to first find the length of the contour by using the List command and then sit down with a pencil and paper to figure out the exact distances between the marks. But there is another, easier way.

The Divide command places a set of point objects on a line, an arc, a circle, or a polyline, marking off exact divisions. This following exercise shows how it works.

1. Open the `13a-divd.dwg` file from the companion CD. This file is similar to the one you have been working with in the previous exercises.
2. Choose Draw ➢ Point ➢ Divide, or type **Div**↵.
3. At the `Select object to divide:` prompt, pick the spline contour line.
4. The `Enter number of segments or [Block]:` prompt that appears next is asking for the number of divisions you want on the selected object. Enter **9**↵.

The command prompt now returns, and it appears that nothing has happened. But AutoCAD has placed several points on the contour that indicate the locations of the nine divisions you requested. To see these points more clearly, follow these steps:

5. Choose Format ➢ Point Style to open the Point Style dialog box.

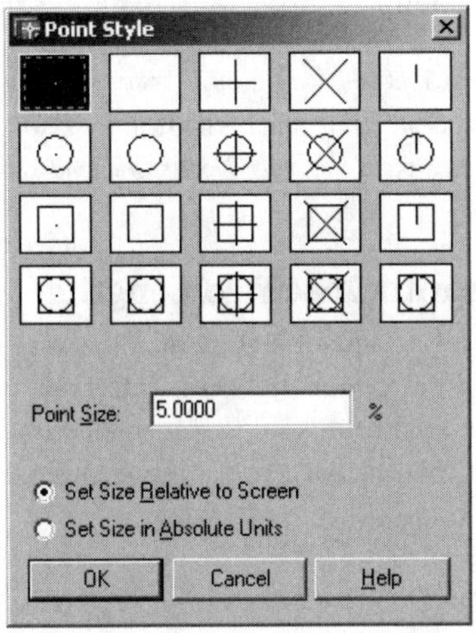

6. Click the X point style in the upper-right side of the dialog box, click the Set Size Relative To Screen radio button, and then click OK.

7. If the Xs don't appear, choose View ➢ Regen or enter **Re**↵. A set of Xs appears, showing the nine divisions (see Figure 14.25).

FIGURE 14.25
Using the Divide command on a polyline

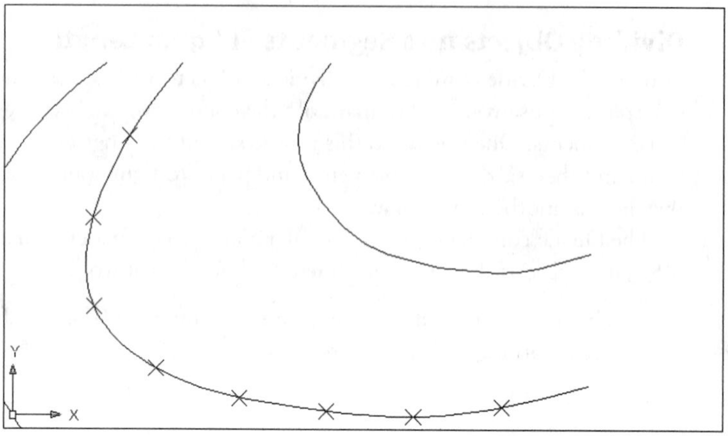

TIP *You can also change the point style by changing the Pdmode system variable. When Pdmode is set to 3, the point appears as an X. See Appendix D for more information on Pdmode.*

The Divide command uses *point* objects to indicate the division points. You create point objects by using the Point command; they usually appear as dots. Unfortunately, such points are nearly invisible when placed on top of other objects. But, as you have seen, you can alter their shape using the Point Style dialog box. You can use these X points to place objects or references to break the object being divided. (The Divide command does not actually cut the object into smaller divisions.)

TIP *If you are in a hurry, and you don't want to bother changing the shape of the point objects, you can do the following: Set the Running Osnaps to Node. Then, when you are in the Point Selection mode, move the cursor over the divided curve. When the cursor gets close to a point object, the Node Osnap marker appears.*

Dividing Objects into Specified Lengths

The Measure command acts just like Divide; however, instead of dividing an object into segments of equal length, the Measure command marks intervals of a specified distance along an object. For example, suppose you need to mark some segments exactly 5' apart along the contour. Try the following exercise to see how the Measure command is used to accomplish this task.

1. Erase the X-shaped point objects.
2. Choose Draw ➢ Point ➢ Measure or type **Me**↵.
3. At the `Select object to measure:` prompt, pick the contour at a point closest to its lower endpoint. I'll explain shortly why this is important.

4. At the `Specify length of segment or [Block]:` prompt, enter **60**↵. The X points appear at the specified distance.

5. Exit this file.

TIP *The Measure command is AutoCAD's equivalent of the divider tool in manual drafting. A divider is a V-shaped instrument, similar to a compass, used to mark off regular intervals along a curve or line.*

Bear in mind that the point you pick on the object to be measured determines where the Measure command begins measuring. In the previous exercise, for example, you picked the contour near its bottom endpoint. If you picked the top of the contour, the results would be different because the measurement would start at the top, not the bottom.

MARKING OFF INTERVALS USING BLOCKS INSTEAD OF POINTS

You can also use the Block option under the Divide and Measure commands to place blocks at regular intervals along a line, a polyline, or an arc. Here's how to use blocks as markers:

1. Be sure the block you want to use is part of the current drawing file.

2. Start either the Divide or Measure command.

3. At the `Specify length of segment or [Block]:` prompt, enter **B**↵.

4. At the `Enter name of block to insert:` prompt, enter the name of a block.

5. At the `Align Block with Object? [Yes/No]:` prompt, press ↵ if you want the blocks to follow the alignment of the selected object. (Entering **N**↵ inserts each block to at a 0° angle.)

6. At the `Enter the number of Segments:` prompt, enter the number of segments. The blocks appear at regular intervals on the selected object.

One example of using Divide's or Measure's Block option is to place a row of sinks equally spaced along a wall. Or you might use this technique to make multiple copies of an object along an irregular path defined by a polyline. In civil projects, you can indicate a fence line using Divide or Measure to place Xs along a polyline.

Sketching with AutoCAD

No discussion of polylines would be complete without mentioning the Sketch command. Though AutoCAD isn't a sketch program, you *can* draw "freehand" using the Sketch command. With Sketch, you can rough in ideas in a free-form way and later overlay a more formal drawing using the usual lines, arcs, and circles. You can use Sketch with a mouse, but it makes more sense to use this command with a digitizing tablet that has a stylus. The stylus affords a more natural way of sketching.

Freehand Sketching with AutoCAD

Here's a step-by-step description of how to use Sketch.

1. Make sure the Ortho and Snap modes are turned off. Then type **Skpoly**↵ **1**↵. This sets the Sketch command to draw using polylines.

2. Type **Sketch**↵ at the command prompt.

3. At the `Record increment <0.1000>:` prompt, enter a value that represents the smallest line segment you will want Sketch to draw. This command approximates a sketch line by drawing a series of short line segments. So the value you enter here determines the length of those line segments.

4. At the `Sketch. Pen eXit Quit Record Erase Connect.` prompt, click the Pick button and then start your sketch line. Notice that the message `<Pen down>` appears, telling you that AutoCAD is recording your cursor's motion.

TIP *You can also start and stop the sketch line by pressing the P key.*

5. Click the Pick button to stop drawing. The message `<Pen up>` tells you that AutoCAD has stopped recording your cursor motion. As you draw, notice that the line is green. This indicates that you have drawn a temporary sketch line and have not committed the line to the drawing.

6. A line drawn with Sketch is temporary until you use Record to save it, so turn the sketch line into a polyline now by typing **R**.

7. Type **X**↵ to exit the Sketch command.

Here are some of the other Sketch options:

Connect Allows you to continue a line from the end of the last temporary line drawn. Type **C** and then move the cursor to the endpoint of the temporary line. AutoCAD automatically starts the line, and you just continue to draw. This works only in the `<Pen up>` mode.

Period (.) Allows you to draw a single straight-line segment by moving the cursor to the desired position and then pressing the period key. This works only in the `<Pen up>` mode.

Record, Erase, Quit, and Exit Control the recording of lines and exiting from the Sketch command. Record is used to save a temporary sketched line; once a line has been recorded, you must edit it as you would any other line. With Erase, you can erase temporary lines before you record them. Quit ends the Sketch command without saving unrecorded lines. On the other hand, the Exit option on the Sketch menu automatically saves all lines you have drawn and then exits the Sketch command.

Filling In Solid Areas

You have learned how to create a solid area by increasing the width of a polyline segment. But suppose you want to create a simple solid shape or a very thick line. AutoCAD provides the Solid, Trace, and Donut commands to help you draw simple filled areas. The Trace command acts just like the Line command (with the added feature of drawing wide line segments), so only the Solid and Donut commands are discussed here.

TIP *You can create free-form, solid-filled areas using the Solid hatch pattern. Create an enclosed area using any set of objects, and then use the Hatch tool to apply a solid hatch pattern to the area. See Chapter 6 for details on using the Hatch tool.*

Drawing Solid Filled Areas

If you've ever played with a paint program, you know how to do a solid fill. It's usually accomplished with a paint bucket tool. This tool always looks like a paint bucket, and it seems to be universal among paint programs. In AutoCAD, doing solid fills is not quite so obvious. It's actually one of many hatch patterns offered with the Boundary Hatch tool. Here is a short exercise to demonstrate how to use the Boundary Hatch tool to do a solid fill.

1. Open the file `14a-htch.dwg` from the companion CD.
2. Click the Hatch tool on the Draw toolbar.
3. In the Boundary Hatch and Fill dialog box, click the Pick Points button.
4. Click the area bounded by the border and contour line in the upper-right corner of the drawing, as shown in the first image in Figure 14.26. Then press ↵. You have the option here to click more areas if you so desire.

FIGURE 14.26

Locating the area to fill, and the final result of the solid hatch

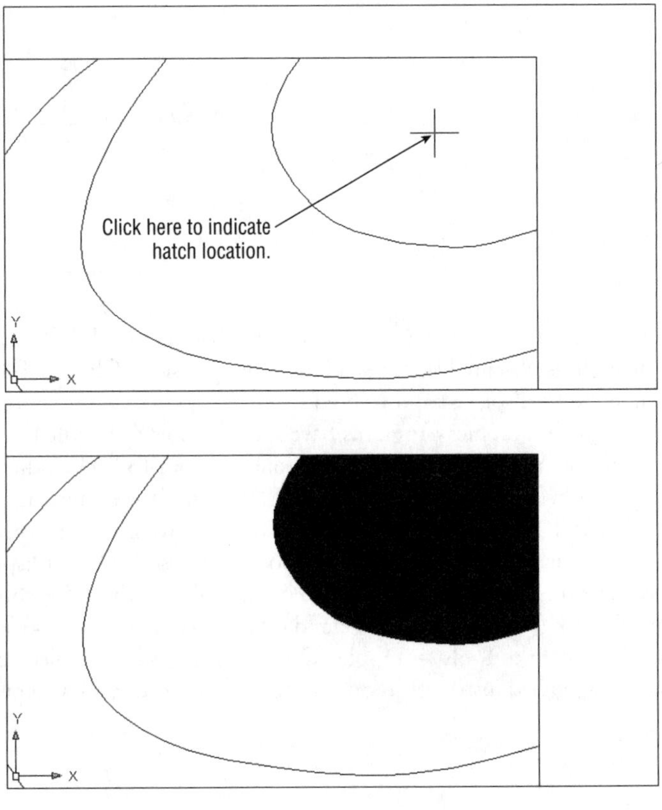
Click here to indicate
hatch location.
Y
X
Y
X

5. Back in the Boundary Hatch and Fill dialog box, click the Ellipsis button to the left of the Pattern combo box.
6. In the Hatch Pattern Palette dialog box, select the solid box in the Other Predefined tab.
7. Click OK, and then click OK. A solid fill is applied to the selected area, as shown in the second image in Figure 14.26.

Overlapping Solid Lines and Shaded Fills

If you use an ink-jet plotter, a raster plotter, or a laser printer that can convert solid areas into screened or gray-shaded areas, you might encounter the problem of shading areas overlapping lines and hiding them. This problem may not be apparent until you actually plot the drawing; it frequently occurs when a gray-shaded area is bounded by lines (see Figure 14.27).

FIGURE 14.27

Problems that occur with overlapping lines and gray areas

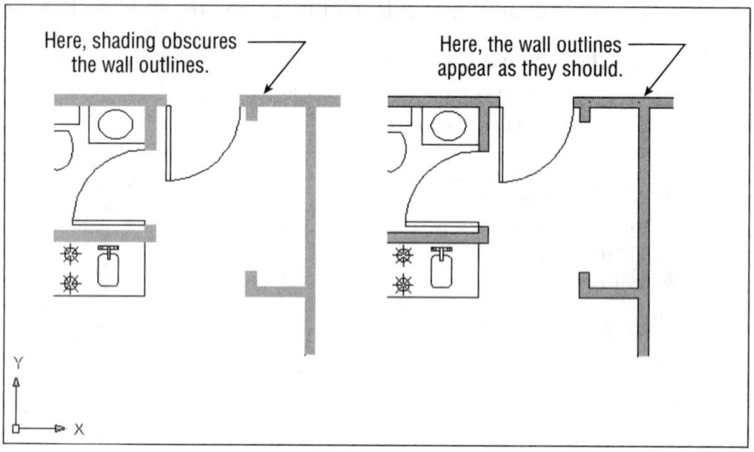

The left side of Figure 14.27 shows how shading or solid fills can cover line work. The outline of the walls is obscured by the shading. The right side of Figure 14.27 shows how the drawing was intended to be displayed and printed.

Most other graphics programs have specific tools to handle this overlapping difficulty. These tools are commonly named Move To Front or Move To Back, indicating that you move an object in front of or behind another object. AutoCAD offers the Draworder command to perform the same function as the Move To Back and Move To Front tools of other programs.

To force an object to appear above another, choose Tools ➢ Display Order ➢ Bring To Front, and then select the object that you want to overlap all the others. Or choose Tools ➢ Display Order ➢ Send To Back to place an object behind other objects. You can also select specific objects to overlay or underlay using the Tools ➢ Display Order ➢ Bring Above Object and Send Under Object options. For more detailed instructions on how to use Draworder, see Chapter 12.

Drawing Filled Circles

If you need to draw a thick circle, such as an inner tube, or a solid filled circle, follow these steps:

1. Choose Draw ➢ Donut, or type **Do**↵ at the command prompt.
2. At the `Specify inside diameter of donut <0'-1/2">:` prompt, enter the desired diameter of the donut "hole." This value determines the opening at the center of your circle.
3. At the `Specify outside diameter of donut <0'-1">:` prompt, enter the overall diameter of the circle.
4. At the `Specify center of doughnut or <exit>:` prompt, click the desired location for the filled circle. You can continue to select points to place multiple donuts (see Figure 14.28).
5. Press ↵ to exit this process.

FIGURE 14.28

Drawing wide circles using the Donut command

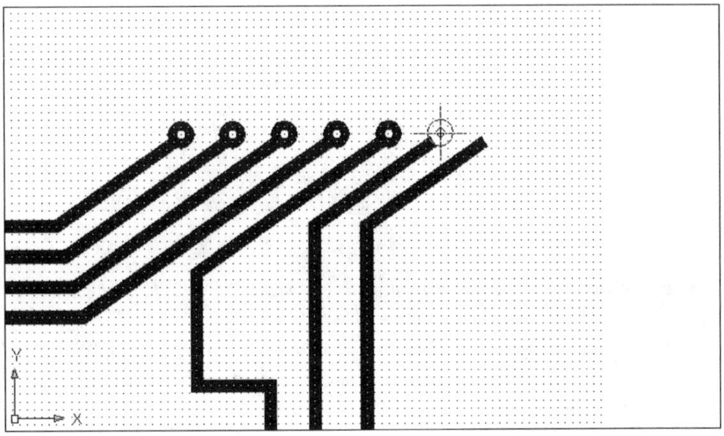

If you need to fill only a part of a circle, such as a pie slice, you can use the Donut command to draw a full, filled circle. Then use the Trim or Break option on the Modify toolbar to cut out the portion of the donut you don't need.

Toggling Solid Fills On and Off

Once you have drawn a solid area with the Pline, Solid, Trace, or Donut command, you can control whether the solid area is actually displayed as filled in. Open the Options dialog box (choose Tools ➢ Options), and then click the Display tab. Locate the Display Performance group in the lower-right corner of the dialog box. The Apply Solid Fill option controls whether solid areas are displayed. If the Solid Fill check box does not show a checkmark, thick polylines, solids, traces, and donuts appear as outlines of the solid areas (see Figure 14.29).

TIP *You can shorten regeneration and plotting time if solids are not filled in.*

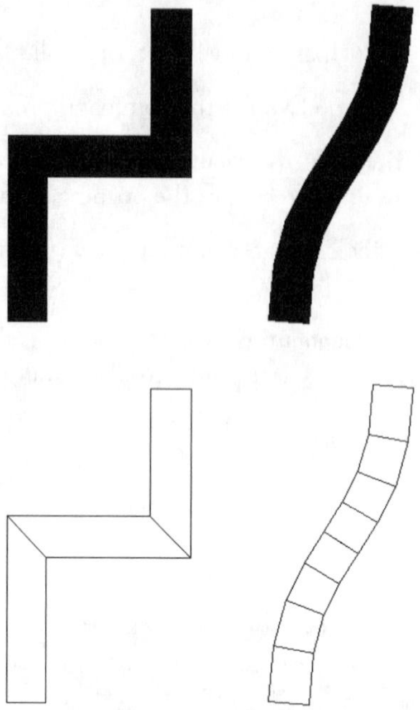

FIGURE 14.29
Two polylines with the Fill option turned on (top) and turned off (bottom)

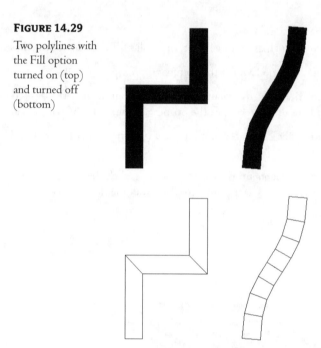

WARNING *If Regenauto is turned off, you have to issue the Regen command to display the effects of the Fill command.*

The Drawing Aids Solid Fill option is an easy-to-remember way to control the display of solid fills. Or you can enter **Fill↵** at the command prompt; then, at the `ON/OFF <ON>:` prompt, enter your choice of **on** or **off**.

If You Want to Experiment...

There are many valuable uses for polylines beyond those covered in this chapter. I encourage you to become familiar with this unique object so you can take full advantage of AutoCAD.

To further explore the use of polylines, try the following exercise, illustrated in Figure 14.30. It will give you an opportunity to try out some of the options discussed in this chapter that weren't included in exercises:

1. Open a new file called `PART14`. Set the Snap mode to .25, and be sure that Snap mode is on. Use the Pline command to draw the object shown in step 1 of Figure 14.30. Draw it in the direction indicated by the arrows and start at the upper-left corner. Use the Close option to add the last line segment.
2. Start the Pedit command, select the polyline, and then type **E↵** to issue the Edit Vertex option. At the prompt

   `[Next/Previous/Break/Insert/Move/Regen/Straighten/Tangent/ Width/eXit] <N>:`

press ↵ until the X mark moves to the first corner, shown in Figure 14.30. Enter **S↵** for the Straighten option.

FIGURE 14.30

Drawing a simple plate with curved edges

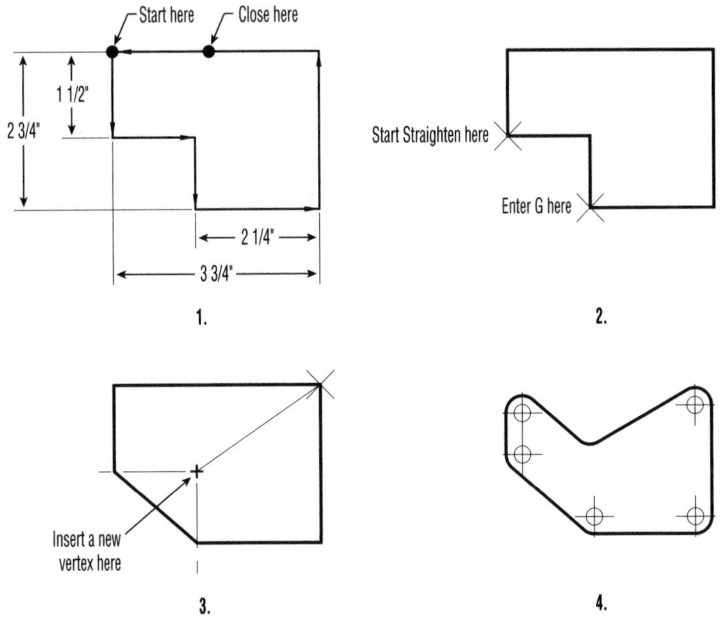

3. At the prompt

   `Enter an option [Next/Previous/Go/eXit] <N>:`

   press ↵ twice to move the X to the other corner shown in Figure 14.30. Press **G↵** for Go to straighten the polyline between the two selected corners.

4. Press ↵ twice to move the X to the upper-right corner, and then enter **I↵** for Insert. Pick a point as shown in Figure 14.30. The polyline changes to reflect the new vertex. Enter **X↵** to exit the Edit Vertex option, and then press ↵ to exit the Pedit command.

5. Start the Fillet command and use the Radius option to set the fillet radius to .30. Press ↵ to start the Fillet command again, but this time use the Polyline option and pick the polyline you just edited. All the corners fillet to the .30 radius. Add the .15 radius circles as shown in Figure 14.30 and exit the file with the End command.

Chapter 15

Getting and Exchanging Data from Drawings

AutoCAD drawings contain a wealth of data. In them, you can find graphic information such as distances and angles between objects, as well as precise areas and the properties of objects. But as you become more involved with AutoCAD, you will find that you also need data of a different nature. For example, as you begin to work in groups, the various settings in a drawing become important. You will need statistics on the amount of time you spend on a drawing when you are billing computer time. As your projects become more complex, file maintenance requires a greater degree of attention. To take full advantage of AutoCAD, you will want to exchange much of this data with other people and other programs.

In this chapter, you will explore the ways in which all types of data can be extracted from AutoCAD and made available to you, your coworkers, and other programs. First, you will discover how to get specific data on your drawings. Then you will look at ways to exchange data with other programs—such as word processors, desktop-publishing software, and even other CAD programs.

This chapter covers the following topics:

- Finding the Area of Closed Boundaries
- Exchanging CAD Data with Other Programs
- Using AutoCAD Drawings in Desktop Publishing
- Combining Data from Different Sources
- Using DesignXML for Internet Data Exchange
- If You Want to Experiment…

Finding the Area of Closed Boundaries

One of the most frequently sought pieces of data you can extract from an AutoCAD drawing is the area of a closed boundary. In architecture, you want to find the area of a room or the footprint of a building. In civil engineering, you want to determine the area covered by the boundary of a property line or the area of cut for a roadway. In this section, you'll learn how you can use AutoCAD to obtain exact area information from your drawings.

TIP *To find absolute coordinates in a drawing, use the ID command. Choose Tools ➢ Inquiry ➢ ID Point, or type ID↵.* At the `ID Point:` *prompt, use the Osnap overrides to pick a point, and its X, Y, and X coordinates are displayed on the prompt line.*

Finding the Area or Location of an Object

Architects, engineers, and facilities planners often need to know the square footage of a room or a section of a building. A structural engineer might want to find the cross-sectional area of a beam. In this section, you will practice determining the areas of both regular and irregular objects.

First, you will find out the square-foot area of the living room and entry of your studio unit plan.

1. Start AutoCAD and open the `Unit` file you created earlier, or use the `15a-unit.dwg` file from the companion CD.
2. Enter **Blipmode↵ on↵**. This turns on a marking feature that displays a tiny cross called a *blip* whenever you click in the drawing area. Blips do not print and can be cleared from the screen with a redraw. You'll use them to help keep track of your point selections in this exercise.
3. Zoom into the living room and entry area so you have a view similar to Figure 15.1.
4. Choose Tools ➢ Inquiry ➢ Area, or type **Area↵** at the command prompt.

TIP *You can also select the Area command from the Inquiry toolbar. Right-click any toolbar and choose Inquiry from the shortcut menu.*

5. Using the Endpoint Osnap, start with the lower-left corner of the living room and select the points shown in Figure 15.1. You are indicating the boundary.
6. When you have come full circle to the eighth point shown in Figure 15.1, press ↵. You get the following message:

   ```
   Area = 39570.00 square in. (274.7917 square ft), Perimeter = 76'-0"
   ```

7. Now turn off Blipmode by typing **Blipmode↵ off↵**. Then choose View ➢ Redraw to clear the blips from the screen.

There is no limit to the number of points you can pick to define an area, so you can obtain the areas of very complex shapes. Use the Blipmode feature to keep track of the points you select so you know when you come to the beginning of the point selections.

FIGURE 15.1

Selecting the points to determine the area of the living room and entry

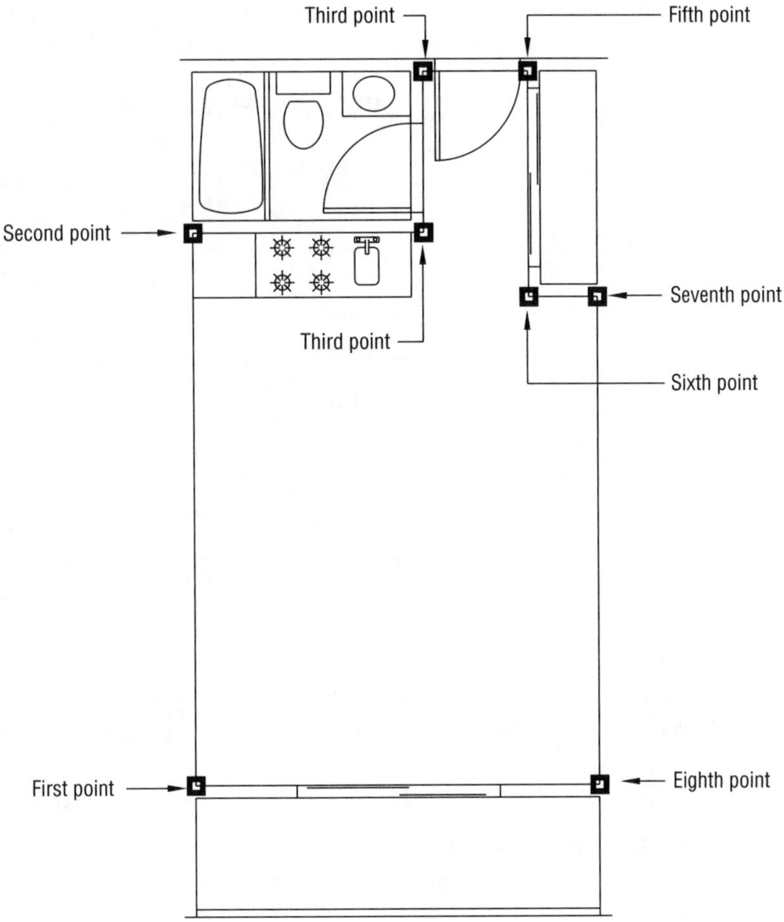

USING BOUNDARY

Using the Object option of the Area command, you can also select circles and polylines for area calculations. Using this option in conjunction with another AutoCAD utility called Boundary, you can quickly get the area of a bounded space. Recall from the discussion on hatch patterns in Chapter 6 that when you use the Hatch function, you draw a region polyline; Boundary works similarly. Whereas Hatch generates a hatch pattern that conforms to the outline of a boundary, Boundary generates a polyline outline without adding the hatch. The following steps show you how to use it.

1. Set the current layer to Floor.
2. Turn off the Door and Fixture layers. Also make sure the Ceiling layer is turned on. You want the boundary to follow the interior wall outline, so you need to turn off any objects that will affect the outline, such as the door and kitchen.

3. Choose Draw ➢ Boundary or type **bo**↵ to open the Boundary Creation dialog box. Notice that it is actually the Boundary Hatch dialog box with several of the options dimmed.

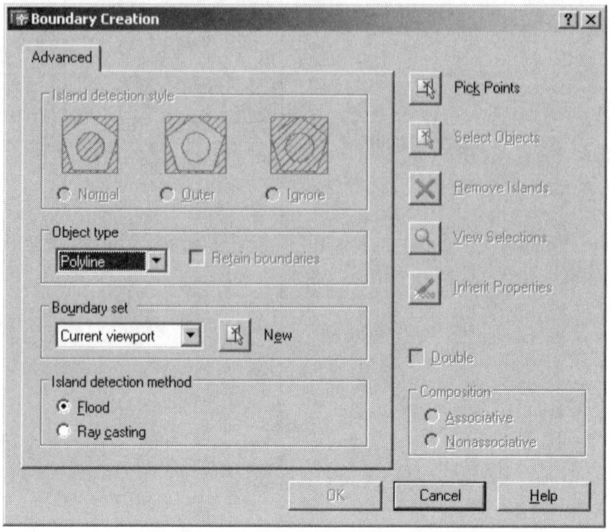

WARNING *There is one caveat to using Boundary: You must be sure that the area you are trying to define has a continuous border. If there are any gaps, no matter how small, Boundary will give you an error message.*

4. Click the Pick Points button. The Boundary Creation dialog box closes.
5. At the `Select internal point:` prompt, click in the interior of the Unit plan. The outline of the interior is highlighted (see Figure 15.2).

FIGURE 15.2

Once you select a point on the interior of the plan using Boundary, an outline of the area is highlighted and surrounded by a dotted line.

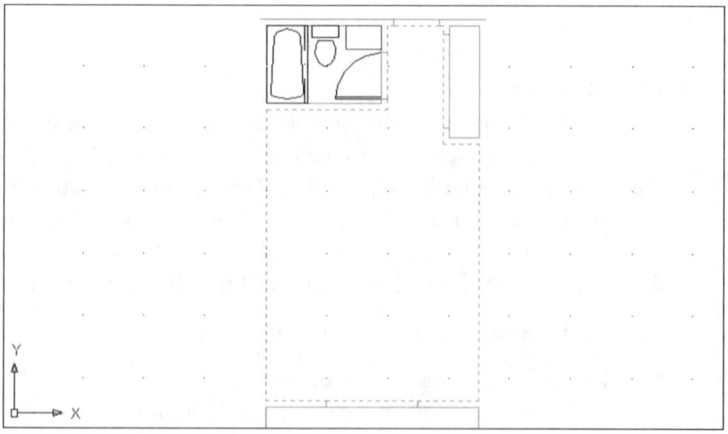

6. Press ↵. Boundary draws an outline of the floor area using a polyline. Since the current layer is Floor, the boundary is drawn on the Floor layer and given the default cyan color of the layer.

7. Choose Tools ➢ Inquiry ➢ Area again, or type **Area↵** at the command prompt. Then enter **O↵** for the Object option.

8. Click the boundary; when it is highlighted, press ↵. Again you get the following message:

```
Area = 39570.00 square in. (274.7917 square ft), Perimeter = 76'-0"
```

Tip   If you need to recall the last area calculation value you received, enter ***'Setvar↵ Area↵****. The area is displayed in the prompt. Enter* ***'Perimeter↵*** *to get the last perimeter calculated.*

The Boundary command creates a polyline that conforms to the boundary of an area. This feature, combined with the ability of the Area command to find the area of a polyline, makes short work of area calculations. As you saw in step 3, Boundary uses the same dialog box as Boundary Hatch. See Chapter 6 for the options available in the Boundary Hatch dialog box.

Finding the Area of Complex Shapes

The Boundary command works fine as long as the area does not contain *islands* that you do not want included in the area calculation. An island is a closed area within a larger area within which you are attempting to hatch or create a boundary. In the case of the flange part, the islands are the two circles at the lower end.

For areas that do contain islands, you must enlist the aid of the other Area command options: Object, Add, and Subtract. Using Add and Subtract, you can maintain a running total of several separate areas being calculated. This gives you flexibility in finding areas of complex shapes.

The exercise in this section guides you through the use of these options. First, you'll look at how you can keep a running tally of areas. For this exercise, you will use a flange shape that contains circles. This shape is composed of simple arcs, lines, and circles.

1. Exit the `Unit` file and open the file named `Flange.dwg` from the companion CD (see Figure 15.3). Don't bother to save changes in the `Unit` file.

2. Choose Draw ➢ Boundary to open the Boundary dialog box.

3. Click Pick Points.

4. Click in the interior of the flange shape. Notice that the entire shape is highlighted, including the circle islands.

5. Press ↵.

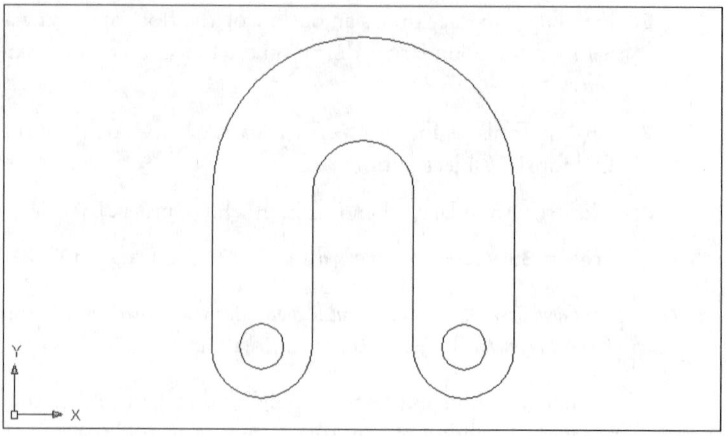

FIGURE 15.3

A flange to a mechanical device

You now have a polyline outline of the shape. As you saw in the previous exercise, the polyline aids you in quickly obtaining the area. Now let's continue by using the Area command's Add and Subtract options.

1. Choose Tools ➢ Inquiry ➢ Area.
2. Type **A**↵ to enter the Add mode, and then type **O**↵ to select an object.
3. Click the outline of the flange. You see the following message:

   ```
   Area = 27.7080, Perimeter = 30.8496
   Total area = 27.7080
   ```

4. Press ↵ to exit the Add mode.
5. Type **S**↵ to enter the Subtract mode, and then type **O**↵ to select an object.
6. Click one of the circles. You see the following message:

   ```
   Area = 0.6070, Perimeter = 2.7618
   Total area = 27.1010
   ```

   This shows you the area and perimeter of the selected object and a running count of the total area of the flange outline minus the circle.

7. Click the other circle. You see the following message:

   ```
   Area = 0.6070, Perimeter = 2.7618
   Total area = 26.4940
   ```

   Again, you see a listing of the area and perimeter of the selected object along with a running count of the total area, which now shows a value of 26.4940. This last value is the true area of the flange.

8. Press ↵ twice to exit the Area command.

In this exercise, you first selected the main object outline and then subtracted the island objects. You don't have to follow this order; you can start by subtracting areas to get negative area values and then add other areas to come up with a total. You can also alternate between Add and Subtract modes, in case you forget to add or subtract areas.

You may have noticed that the Area command prompt offered `Specify first corner point or [Object/Add/Subtract]:` as the default option for both the Add and Subtract modes. Instead of using the Object option to pick the circles, you can start selecting points to indicate a rectangular area, as you did in the first exercise of this chapter.

Whenever you press ↵ while selecting points for an area calculation, AutoCAD automatically connects the first and last points and returns the calculated area. If you are in the Add or Subtract mode, you can then continue to select points, but the additional areas are calculated from the *next* point you pick.

As you can see from these exercises, it is simpler to first outline an area with a polyline, wherever possible, and then use the Object option to add and subtract area values of polylines.

In this example, you obtained the area of a mechanical object. However, the same process works for any type of area you want to calculate. It can be the area of a piece of property on a topographical map or the area of a floor plan. For example, you can use the Object option to find an irregular area such as the one shown in Figure 15.4, as long as it is a polyline.

FIGURE 15.4
The site plan with an area to be calculated

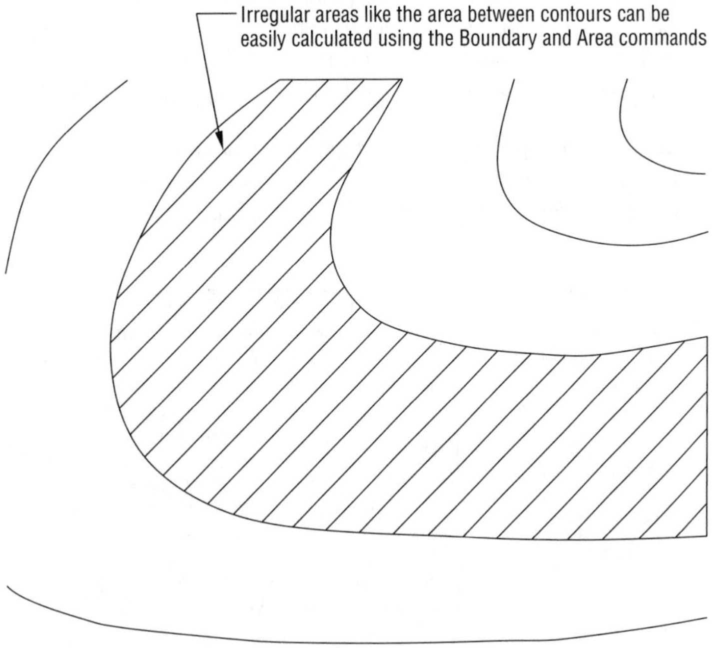

Irregular areas like the area between contours can be easily calculated using the Boundary and Area commands

RECORDING AREA DATA IN A DRAWING FILE

Once you find the area of an object, you'll often need to record it somewhere. You can write it down in a project logbook, but this is easy to overlook. A more dependable way to store area information is to use *attributes*.

Consider the following example. In a building project, you can create a block that contains attributes for the room number, room area, and the date when the room area was last taken. You might make the area and date attributes invisible, so only the room number appears. You can then insert this block into every room. Once you find the area, you can easily add it to your block attribute with the Ddatte command. In fact, you can use such a block with any drawing in which you want to store area data. See Chapter 10 for more on attributes.

Getting General Information

So far in this book, you've seen how to get data about the geometry of your drawings. AutoCAD also includes a set of tools that you can use to access the general state of your drawings. You can gather information about the time at which a drawing was created and last edited or the status of current settings in a file. In this section, you will practice extracting this type of information from your drawing, using the tools found in the Tools ➢ Inquiry option's cascading menu.

Determining the Drawing's Status

When you work with a group of people on a large project, keeping track of a drawing's setup becomes crucial. You can use the Status command to obtain some general information about the drawing you are working on, such as the base point, current mode settings, and workspace or computer memory use. The Status command is especially helpful when you are editing a drawing someone else has worked on, because you might want to identify and change settings for your own style of working. Choosing Tools ➢ Inquiry ➢ Status displays a list like the one shown in Figure 15.5.

TIP *If you have problems editing a file created by someone else, the difficulty can often be attributed to a new or different setting you are not used to working with. If you find that AutoCAD is acting in an unusual way, use the Status command to get a quick glimpse of the file settings before you start calling for help.*

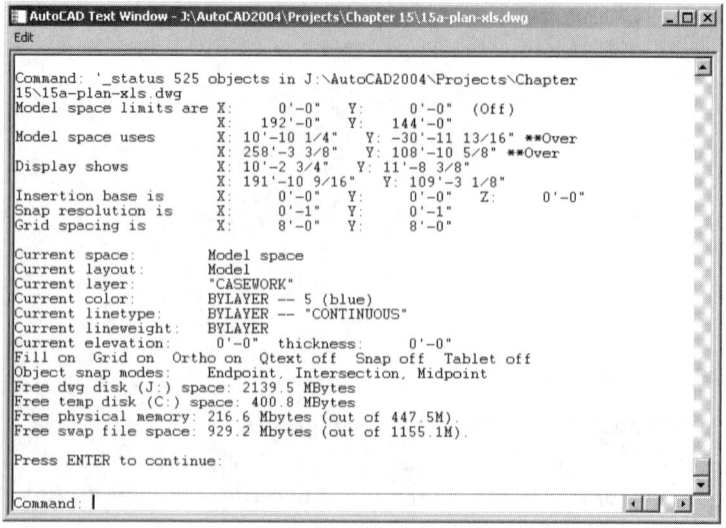

FIGURE 15.5
The Status screen of the AutoCAD Text Window

Here is a brief description of each item on the Status screen. Note that some of the items you see listed on the screen will vary somewhat from what I've shown here, but the information applies to virtually all situations except where noted.

(Number)* Objects In D:*Folder**Subfolder The number of entities or objects in the drawing.

Model Space Limits Are The coordinates of the Model Space limits. (See Chapter 3 for more details on limits.)

Model Space Uses The area the drawing occupies; equivalent to the extents of the drawing.

****Over:** If present, this item means that part of the drawing is outside the limit boundary.

Display Shows The area covered by the current view.

Insertion Base Is, Snap Resolution Is, and Grid Spacing Is The current default values for these mode settings.

Current Space Model Space or Paper Space.

Current Layout The current tab.

Current Layer The current default layer.

Current Color The color assigned to new objects.

Current Linetype The line type assigned to new objects.

Current Lineweight The current default Lineweight setting.

Current Elevation/Thickness The current default Z coordinate for new objects, plus the default thickness of objects; these are both 3D-related settings. (See Chapter 16 for details.)

Fill, Grid, Ortho, Qtext, Snap, and Tablet The status of these options.

Object Snap Modes The current default Osnap setting.

Free Dwg Disk (*Drive:*) Space The amount of space available to store drawing-specific temporary files.

Free Temp Disk (*Drive:*) Space The amount of space you have left on your hard drive for AutoCAD's resource temporary files.

Free Physical Memory The amount of free RAM available.

Free Swap File Space The amount of Windows swap file space available.

TIP *When you are in Paper Space, the Status command displays information regarding the Paper Space limits. See Chapter 13 for more on Model Space and Paper Space.*

In addition to being useful in understanding a drawing file, the Status command is an invaluable tool for troubleshooting. Frequently, a technical support person can isolate problems using the information provided by the Status command.

TIP *For more information on memory use, see Appendix C.*

Keeping Track of Time

The Time command allows you to keep track of the time spent on a drawing, for billing or analysis purposes. You can also use the Time command to check the current time and find out when the drawing was created and most recently edited. Because the AutoCAD timer uses your computer's time, be sure the time is set correctly in Windows.

To access the Time command, enter **Time.⏎** at the command prompt, or choose Tools ➤ Inquiry ➤ Time. You get a message like the one in Figure 15.6.

FIGURE 15.6

The Time screen in the AutoCAD Text Window

```
AutoCAD Text Window - J:\AutoCAD2004\Projects\Chapter 15\15a-plan-xds.dwg          _|□|×|
Edit

Current time:              Thursday, December 05, 2002 at 12:06:58:186 PM
Times for this drawing:
  Created:                 Monday, April 07, 1997 at 1:00:25:790 PM
  Last updated:            Sunday, May 18, 1997 at 5:23:27:040 PM
  Total editing time:      0 days 06:02:15.551
  Elapsed timer (on):      0 days 06:02:15.567
  Next automatic save in:  0 days 01:57:11.860

Enter option [Display/ON/OFF/Reset]: |
```

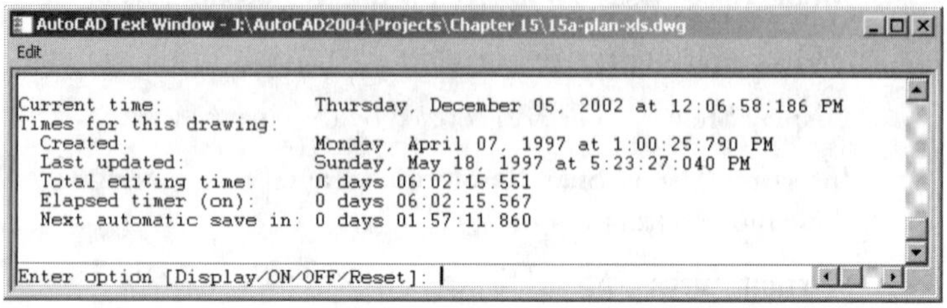

The first three lines of this message tell you the current date and time, the date and time the drawing was created, and the last time the drawing was saved or ended.

The fourth line shows the total time spent on the drawing from the point at which the file was opened. This elapsed timer lets you time a particular activity, such as changing the width of all the walls in a floor plan or redesigning a piece of machinery. You can turn the elapsed timer on or off or reset it by entering **ON, OFF,** or **Reset** at the prompt shown as the last line of the message. Or press ⏎ to exit the Time command. The last line tells you when the next automatic save will be.

Getting Information from System Variables

If you've been working through this book's ongoing studio apartment building tutorial, you'll have noticed occasional mentions of a *system variable* in conjunction with a command. You can check the status or change the setting of any system variable while you are in the middle of another command. To do this, you simply type an apostrophe ('), followed by the name of the system variable, at the command prompt.

For example, if you start to draw a line and suddenly decide you need to rotate your cursor 45°, you can do the following:

1. At the Specify next point or [Undo]: prompt, enter **'snapang**.

2. At the Enter new value for SNAPANG <0>: prompt, enter a new cursor angle. Once you have entered an angle value, you are returned to the Line command with the cursor in its new orientation.

You can also recall information such as the last area or distance calculated by AutoCAD. Because the Area system variable duplicates the name of the Area command, you need to choose Tools ➤ Inquiry ➤ Set Variables, and then type **Area⏎** to read the last area calculation. You can also type **'Setvar.⏎. Area.⏎.** The Tools ➤ Inquiry ➤ Set Variables option also lets you list all the system variables and their status, as well as access each system variable individually by entering a question mark (**?**).

Many of the system variables give you direct access to detailed information about your drawing. They also let you fine-tune your drawing and editing activities. In Appendix D you'll find all the information you need to familiarize yourself with the system variables available. Don't feel that you have to memorize them all at once; just be aware that they are available.

TIP *Many of the dialog box options you have been using throughout this book, such as the options in the Options dialog box, are actually system variable settings.*

Keeping a Log of Your Activity

At times you may find it helpful to keep a log of your activity in an AutoCAD session. A log is a text file containing a record of your activities in AutoCAD. It can also contain notes to yourself or others about how a drawing is set up. Such a log can help you determine how frequently you use a particular command, or it can help you construct a macro for a commonly used sequence of commands.

The following exercise demonstrates how you can save and view a detailed record of an AutoCAD session using the Log feature.

1. Choose Tools ➢ Options to open the Options dialog box. Click the Open And Save tab. A new set of options appears.

TIP *As a shortcut, you can quickly turn the Maintain A Log File feature on and off by typing* ***Logfileon↵*** *and* ***Logfileoff↵*** *at the command prompt.*

2. In the File Safety Precautions group, Click the Maintain A Log File check box and then click OK.
3. Choose Tools ➢ Inquiry ➢ Status.
4. Return to the Open And Save tab of the Options dialog box, and turn off the Maintain A Log File option.
5. Click OK to exit the dialog box.
6. Switch to Windows and start the Notepad application or any text editor.
7. With the text editor, open the log file whose name starts with `15a-unit` in the folder listed here:

   `C:\Documents and Settings\`*`User Name`*`\Local Settings\Application Data\Autodesk\AutoCAD 2004\R16.0\enu\`

   This file stores the text data from the command prompt whenever the Log File option is turned on. You must turn off the Log File option before you can actually view this file in AutoCAD.

As you can see in step 7, the log file is given the name of the drawing file from which the log is derived, with some additional numeric values. Since the `15a-unit` log file is a standard text file, you can easily send it to other members of your workgroup or print it for a permanent record.

TIP *If you cannot find the log file for the current drawing, you can enter* ***)(setvar "logfilename")***↵ *at the command prompt, and AutoCAD will display the filename including the full path. If you want to change the default location for the log file, open the Options dialog box and click the Files tab. Click the plus sign to the left of the Log File Location option in the list box. A listing appears showing you where the drawing logfile is stored. You can then modify this setting to indicate a new location. LT users enter* ***Modemacro***↵, *then* ***$(getvar, logfilepath)***.

Capturing and Saving Text Data from the AutoCAD Text Window

If you are working in groups, it is often quite helpful to have a record of the status, editing time, and system variables for particular files readily available to other group members. It is also convenient to keep records of block and layer information, so you can see if a specific block is included in a drawing or what layers are normally on or off.

You can use the Windows Clipboard to capture and save such data from the AutoCAD text window. The following steps show you how it's done.

1. Move the arrow cursor to the command prompt at the bottom of the AutoCAD window.
2. Right-click and choose Copy History from the shortcut menu to copy the contents of the text window to the Clipboard.

By default, the text window stores 400 lines of text. You can change this number by changing the options in the Text Window group in the Display tab of the Options dialog box.

If you want to copy only a portion of the text window to the Clipboard, perform the following steps:

1. Press the F2 function key to open the Text Window.
2. Using the I-beam text cursor, highlight the text you want to copy to the Clipboard.
3. Right-click and then choose Copy from the shortcut menu. You can also choose Edit ➢ Copy from the Text Window's menu bar. The highlighted text is copied to the Clipboard.
4. Open Notepad or another word-processing application and paste the information.

Although you used the Text Window to copy text in this exercise, you can also copy from the docked command line at the bottom of the AutoCAD window.

You may notice four other options on the shortcut menu: Recent Commands, Paste, Paste To CmdLine, and Options. Choosing Recent Commands displays a list of the most recent commands. You'll find that for most activities, you use a handful of commands repeatedly. The Recent Commands option can save you time by giving you a shortcut to those commands you use the most. The Paste options paste the first line of the contents of the Clipboard into the command line or input box of a dialog box. This can be useful for entering repetitive text or for storing and retrieving a frequently used command. Choosing Options opens the Options dialog box.

TIP *Items copied to the Clipboard from the AutoCAD Text Window can be pasted into dialog box input boxes. This can be a quick way to transfer layers, line types, or other named items from the Text Window into dialog boxes. You can even paste text into the drawing area.*

Storing Searchable Information in AutoCAD Files

As you start to build a library of AutoCAD files, you'll have to start thinking about how to manage those files. Keeping track of AutoCAD files can be a daunting task. Most AutoCAD users start to name files by their job number to keep things organized. But even the best organization schemes don't help if you need to find that one special file among thousands of files in your library. In this section, you'll learn how to include information in an AutoCAD file that you can use later to locate the file using the Windows Find utility.

TIP *AutoCAD 2004 includes the DesignCenter, a tool that can help you locate a file more easily based on a keyword or description. Chapter 22 contains a complete discussion of the DesignCenter.*

To add general information about your drawing file that is searchable, use the Drawing Properties dialog box. Choose File ➢ Drawing Properties to open the Drawing Properties dialog box. Here's a description of the four tabs in this dialog box.

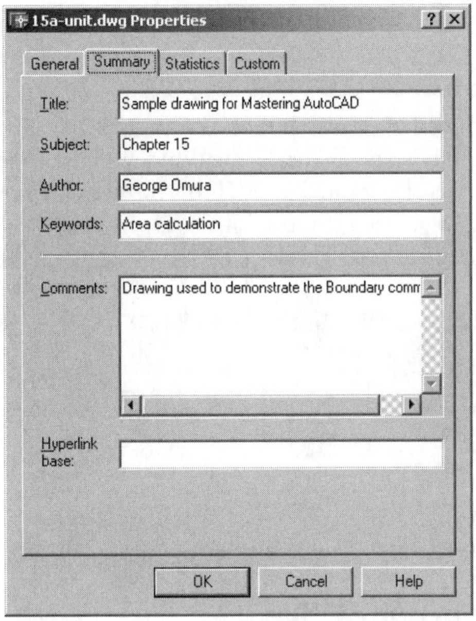

THE GENERAL TAB

The General tab gives you general information about the file. This information is similar to what you would see if you use the Properties options in Windows Explorer to view the properties of a file.

THE SUMMARY TAB

In the Summary tab, enter any text in the Title, Subject, Author, and Keywords fields that is appropriate to the drawing. The information you enter here is stored with the drawing and can be used to locate the file through the AutoCAD DesignCenter or the Windows Find Files Or Folders utility (choose Start ➢ Search).

In addition, you can enter a base location for hyperlink links that are applied to objects in your drawing. This base location can be a folder on your computer or network or an Internet web address. See Chapter 22 for more information on hyperlinks.

THE STATISTICS TAB

The Statistics tab contains the Windows user name of the person who last edited the drawing, as well as the time spent on the file. This is the login name at the beginning of the Windows session.

THE CUSTOM TAB

The Custom tab contains two columns of input boxes. This tab lets you store additional custom data with the drawing that is also searchable. For example, you might enter **Job Number** in the Name column and then enter **9901** in the Value column. You might also include information such as project manager names, consultants, or revision numbers. You can then locate the file using the AutoCAD DesignCenter or the Windows Find utility by doing a search for those keywords from the Name and Value columns.

Searching for AutoCAD Files

Once you've included information in the Properties dialog box of a file, you can use the AutoCAD DesignCenter, the File dialog box, or the Windows Find functions to locate your file.

A Find option is also located in the Tools menu in the upper-right corner of the AutoCAD Select File dialog box. To get to it, choose File ➢ Open, and then in the Select File dialog box, choose Tools ➢ Find in the upper-right corner.

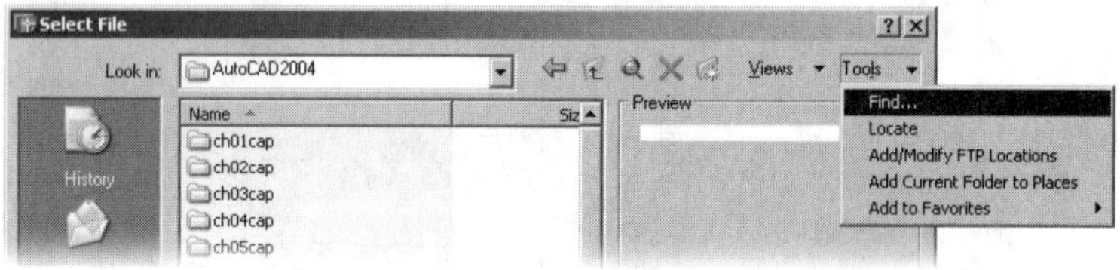

This option opens a Find dialog box that works just like the Windows XP Search dialog box.

Recovering Corrupted Files

No system is perfect. Eventually, you will encounter a file that is corrupted in some way. AutoCAD offers two tools that can frequently salvage a corrupted file: Audit and Recover. Audit allows you to check a file that you are able to open but you suspect has some problem. Recover allows you to open a file that is so badly corrupted that AutoCAD is unable to open it in a normal way. You can access these tools from the File ➢ Drawing Utilities cascading menu. The functions of these options are as follows:

Audit Checks the currently opened file for any errors and displays the results in the Text Window.

Recover Lets you check an unopened AutoCAD file for errors. A File dialog box appears, allowing you to select a file for recovery. Once you select a file, it is opened and checked for errors.

More often than not, these tools will do the job, although they aren't a panacea for all file-corruption problems. In the event that you cannot recover a file even with these tools, make sure your computer is running smoothly and that other systems are not faulty.

Exchanging CAD Data with Other Programs

AutoCAD offers many ways to share data with other programs. Perhaps the most common type of data exchange is simply to share drawing data with other CAD programs. In this section, you'll see how you can export and import CAD drawings using the .dxf file format. You'll also see how you can use bitmap graphics, both to and from AutoCAD, through the Windows Clipboard.

Other types of data exchange involve text, spreadsheets, and databases. Chapter 11 covers database links, but this section describes how you can include text, spreadsheet, and database files in a drawing or include AutoCAD drawings in other program files using a Windows feature called Object Linking and Embedding (OLE).

Using the .dxf File Format

A *.dxf file* is a plain text file that contains all the information needed to reconstruct a drawing. It is often used to exchange drawings created with other programs. Many CAD and technical drawing programs, including some 3D perspective programs, can generate or read files in .dxf format. You might want to use a 3D program to view your drawing in a Perspective view, or you might have a consultant who uses a different CAD program that accepts .dxf files.

Be aware that not all programs that read .dxf files will accept all the data stored therein. Many programs that claim to read .dxf files will "throw away" much of the .dxf file's information. Attributes are perhaps the most commonly ignored objects, followed by many of the 3D objects, such as meshes and 3D Faces. But .dxf files, though not the perfect medium for translating data, have become something of a standard.

TIP *AutoCAD no longer supports the IGES (Initial Graphics Exchange Specification) standard for CAD data translation.*

EXPORTING .DXF FILES

To export your current drawing as a .dxf file, follow these steps:

1. Choose File ➢ Save As to open the Save Drawing As dialog box.
2. Click the Files Of Type drop-down list. You can export your drawing under a number of formats, including four.dxf formats.

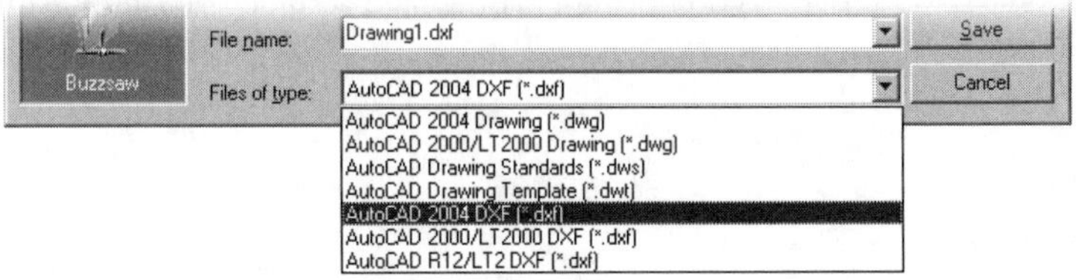

3. Select the appropriate .dxf format, and then enter a name for your file. You do not have to include the .dxf filename extension.
4. Select a folder for the file, and then click Save.

In step 2, you can select from the following .dxf file formats:

- AutoCAD 2004 DXF
- AutoCAD 2000/LT 2000 DXF
- AutoCAD R12/LT2 DXF

Choose the format appropriate to the program you are exporting to. In most cases, the safest choice is AutoCAD R12/LT2 DXF if you are exporting to another CAD program, though AutoCAD will not maintain the complete functionality of AutoCAD 2004 for such files.

Once you've selected a .dxf format from the Files Of Type drop-down list, you can set more detailed specifications by choosing Tools ➢ Options in the upper-right corner of the Save Drawing As dialog box. Doing so opens the Saveas Options dialog box. For DXF files, select the DXF Options tab:

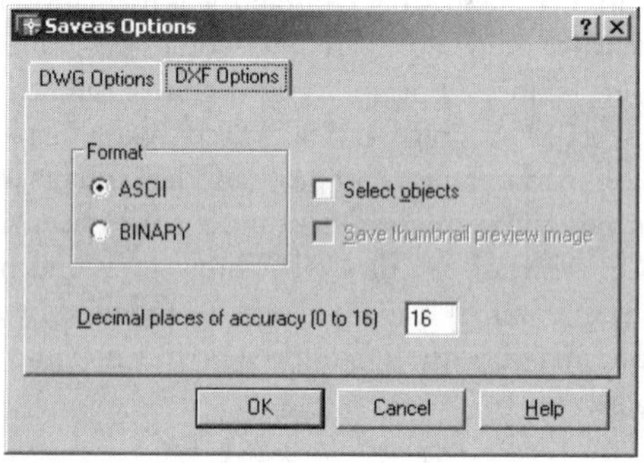

The DXF Options tab contains the following options:

Format Lets you choose between ASCII (plain text) or binary file formats. Most other programs accept ASCII, so it is the safest choice. Some programs accept binary .dxf files, which have the advantage of being more compact than the ASCII format.

Select Objects Lets you select specific objects within the drawing for export. You can select objects after you close the Export Options dialog box and choose Save from the Export Data dialog box.

Decimal Places Of Accuracy Allows you to determine the accuracy of the exported file. Keeping this value low helps reduce the size of the export file, particularly if it is to be in ASCII format. Some CAD programs do not support the high accuracy of AutoCAD, so using a high value here may have no significance.

*TIP You can also type **Dxfout↵** at the command prompt to open the Create DXF File dialog box. This is a standard Windows file dialog box that includes the Options button described here. This dialog box displays only .dxf file formats in the Save As Type drop-down list.*

OPENING OR IMPORTING .DXF FILES

Some offices have standardized their CAD drawings on the .dxf file format. This is most commonly seen in offices that use a variety of CAD software besides AutoCAD. AutoCAD 2004 can be set up to read and write DXF files by default, instead of the standard .dwg file format. Here's how it's done:

1. Choose Tools ➢ Options to open the Options dialog box.
2. Select the Open And Save tab.
3. In the File Save group, select any of the .dfx formats from the Save As drop-down list.
4. Click OK.

Once you do this, all your drawings are automatically saved in the .dxf format of your choice.

You can also set the default AutoCAD file type by clicking the Options button in the Save Drawing As dialog box. As you saw in an earlier section, the Saveas Options dialog box includes the DWG Options tab. You can select a default file type from the Save All Drawings As drop-down list.

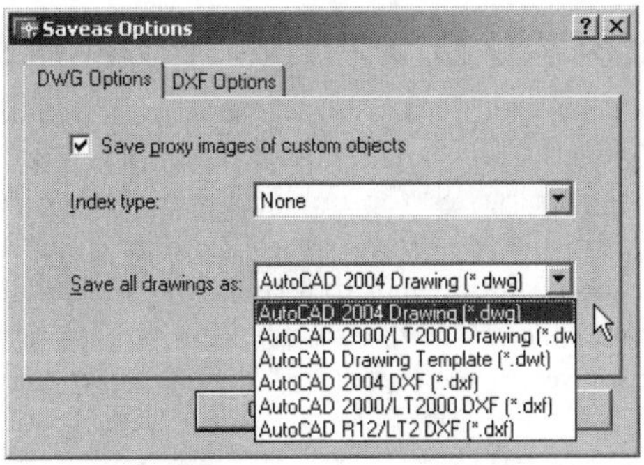

If you just need to open a DXF file once in a while, you can do so by selecting DXF from the Files Of Type drop-down list in the Select File dialog box. This is the dialog box you see when you choose File ➢ Open. You can also import DXF files into the current open file, provided that the DXF file does not contain blocks or other named elements that do not exist in the current file.

1. Type **Dxfin↵** at the command prompt to open the Select .DXF File dialog box.
2. Locate and select the DXF file you want to import.
3. Double-click the filename to begin importing it.

If the drawing is large, the import may take several minutes.

EXCHANGING FILES WITH EARLIER RELEASES

One persistent dilemma that has plagued AutoCAD users is how to exchange files between earlier versions of the program. In the past, if you upgraded AutoCAD, you were locked out from exchanging your drawings with people using earlier versions. Release 12 alleviated this difficulty by making Release 12 files compatible with Release 11 files.

With Release 13, the file structure was radically different from earlier versions of AutoCAD. Then AutoCAD 14 made it possible to freely exchange files between Release 13 and 14.

AutoCAD 2002 uses the AutoCAD 2000 file format, which has some features, such as multiple layouts and searchable properties, that do not translate to earlier versions. AutoCAD 2004 has some new features that make it incompatible with AutoCAD 2000 and 2002.

If compatibility with earlier versions is more important than the new features of AutoCAD 2004, you can set up AutoCAD 2004 to read and write to AutoCAD 2000 or release 12 files. Or if you're willing to work with DXF files, you can set up AutoCAD 2004 to automatically write AutoCAD 12 DXF files.

To set up AutoCAD to automatically write earlier versions, use the Options dialog box to set the default file type as described in the "Opening or Importing .dxf Files" section, but instead of selecting a DXF file type, select the DWG file type you want to use.

Using AutoCAD Drawings in Desktop Publishing

As you probably know, AutoCAD is a natural for creating line art, and because of its popularity, most desktop-publishing programs are designed to import AutoCAD drawings in one form or another. Those of you who employ desktop-publishing software to generate user manuals or other technical documents will probably want to use AutoCAD drawings in your work. This section will examine ways to output AutoCAD drawings to formats that most desktop-publishing programs can accept.

You can exporting AutoCAD files to desktop-publishing formats in two ways: by using raster export and by using vector file export.

Exporting Raster Files

In some cases, you may need only a rough image of your AutoCAD drawing. You can export your drawing as a raster file that can be read in virtually any desktop-publishing and word-processing program. To do this, you must create a new plotter configuration that plots to an image file instead of an output device. (Chapter 7 describes how to use the Add-A-Plotter Wizard to add a plotter configuration to AutoCAD.) Here is some additional information on how to use that wizard to set up AutoCAD for raster file output.

1. On the Begin screen of the Add-A-Plotter Wizard, choose My Computer.
2. On the Plotter Model screen, select Raster File Formats from the Manufacturers list, and then select the type of raster file you want to use from the Models list. For example, you can choose Independent JPEG Group JFIF (JPEG Compression). This is one of the more universal file types.

3. Skip over the Import PCP or PC2 screen and the Ports screen.
4. Enter a name for your raster output settings on the Plotter Name screen.
5. On the Finish screen, click the Enter Plotter Configuration button to open the Plotter Configuration Editor dialog box.

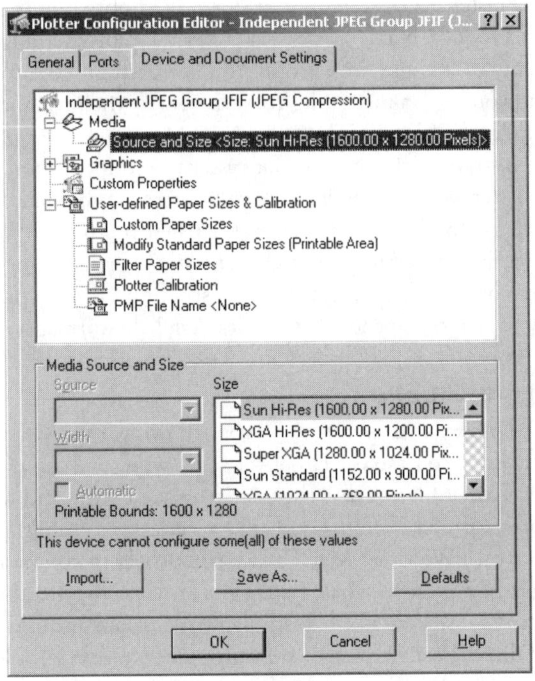

6. Click the Source And Size listing that appears in the large list box in the top of the dialog box. A list of options appears in the Size list box in the lower-right corner of the dialog box.
7. Click Custom Paper Sizes from the large list box at the top of the dialog box. The options change in the lower half of the dialog box.
8. Click the Add button to start the Custom Paper Size Wizard.
9. Click the Start From Scratch radio button, and then click Next to open the Media Bounds screen.
10. Enter a height and width in pixels for your image file, and then click Next to open the Paper Size Name screen. Enter a name that best describes the size of the image file, and then click Next to open the File Name screen.
11. Enter a name for the Plotter Model Parameters file. This file stores specific setting information about the plotter. Click Next when you are finished.

12. On the Finish screen, click Finish. The Plotter Configuration Editor dialog box reappears. Click OK, and then click Finish in the Add-A-Plotter Wizard.

Once you've finished creating a plotter configuration, it appears as a file in the `Plotter` subfolder of the `AutoCAD2004` folder. You can access this file through Windows Explorer or from AutoCAD by choosing File ➢ Plotter Manager.

To create a raster file version of your drawing, choose File ➢ Plot, and then in the Plot dialog box, click the Plot Device tab and select your raster file plotter configuration from the Name drop-down list of the Plotter Configuration group. You can then proceed to plot your drawing, but instead of paper output, you'll get a raster file. You can specify the filename in the Plot Device tab of the Plot dialog box under the Plot To File group.

If you need to make changes to your raster file configuration, choose File ➢ Plotter Manager, and then in the Plotter window, double-click your raster file configuration file. You will see the same Plotter Configuration Editor you used to set up the raster plotter configuration.

You can set up a different plotter configuration for each type of raster file you use. You can also set up plotter configurations for different resolutions, if you choose. To learn more about plotting in general, see Chapter 7. Appendix C provides detailed information on the Plotter Configuration Editor.

Exporting Vector Files

If you need to preserve the accuracy of your drawing, or if you want to take advantage of TrueType or PostScript fonts, you can use either the .dxf, .wmf, or PostScript vector formats.

For vector format files, .dxf is the easiest to work with, and with TrueType support, .dxf can preserve font information between AutoCAD and desktop-publishing programs that support the .dxf format. The .wmf (Windows MetaFile) format is also a commonly accepted file format for vector information, and it preserves TrueType fonts and line weights that are used in your drawings.

PostScript is a raster/vector hybrid file format that AutoCAD supports; unfortunately, AutoCAD has dropped direct PostScript font support since Release 14. However, you can still use substitute fonts to stand in for PostScript fonts. These substitute fonts are converted to true PostScript fonts when AutoCAD exports the drawing. You won't see the true results of your PostScript output until you actually print your drawing on a PostScript printer.

The .dxf file export was covered in the "Using the .dxf File Format" section of this chapter, so this section will concentrate on the .wmf and PostScript file formats.

TIP *If you are a circuit board designer or drafter, you might want to use the PostScript Out option to send your layout to PostScript typesetting devices. This saves time and reduces file size since the PostScript Out option converts AutoCAD entities into true PostScript descriptions.*

WMF OUTPUT

The Windows MetaFile (WMF) file type is one of the more popular vector file formats in Windows. It can be opened and edited by most illustration programs, including CorelDraw and Adobe Illustrator. Most word-processing, database, and spreadsheet programs can also import WMF files. It's a great option for AutoCAD file export because it preserves TrueType fonts, and now that AutoCAD offers line-weight settings, you can export WMF files that preserve line weights as well.

To export WMF files, do the following:

1. Choose File ➢ Export to open the Export Data dialog box.
2. The default file type in this dialog box happens to be WMF, so all you need to do is enter a name and location for your WMF file and then click OK. The dialog box closes, and you are prompted to select objects.
3. Select the objects you want to export to the WMF file and press ↵. The objects are saved to your WMF file.

PostScript Output

AutoCAD can export to the Encapsulated PostScript file format (.eps). If you are using AutoCAD 2004, you can actually obtain PostScript output in two ways. You can use the File ➢ Export option on the menu bar, or you can install a PostScript printer driver and plot your drawing to an EPS file. LT users cannot export to EPS using the File ➢ Export option. To set up AutoCAD to plot your drawing to an EPS file, follow the same steps described in the previous "Exporting Raster Files" section, but in step 2, select Adobe from the Manufacturers list and then select the appropriate PostScript level from the Models list.

WARNING *AutoCAD does not preserve font information when creating EPS files from the printer option. It also produces larger files, especially if your drawing contains a lot of area fills and filled fonts.*

ACAD only

PostScript Font Substitution

I mentioned earlier that AutoCAD substitutes its own fonts with PostScript fonts when a file is exported to an EPS file using the Export Data dialog box. If your work involves PostScript output, you will want to know these font names in order to make the appropriate substitution. Table 15.1 shows a list of AutoCAD font names and their equivalent PostScript names.

To take advantage of AutoCAD's ability to translate fonts, you need to create AutoCAD fonts that have the names listed in the first column of Table 15.1. You then need to use those fonts when creating text styles in AutoCAD. AutoCAD then converts the AutoCAD fonts into the corresponding PostScript fonts.

Creating the AutoCAD fonts can be simply a matter of copying and renaming existing fonts to those listed in Table 15.1. For example, you can make a copy of the `Romans.shx` font and name it `Agd.shx`. Better yet, if you have the PostScript PFB file of the font, you can compile it into an AutoCAD font file and rename the compiled file appropriately. By compiling the PFB file, you get a close approximation of its appearance in AutoCAD. See Chapter 8 for a description of how to compile PostScript fonts.

TABLE 15.1: A PARTIAL LIST OF AUTOCAD FONT FILENAMES AND THEIR CORRESPONDING POSTSCRIPT FONTS

AutoCAD Font Name	PostScript Font Name	AutoCAD Font Name	PostScript Font Name
agd	AvantGarde-Demi	agdo	AvantGarde-DemiOblique
agw	AvantGarde-Book	agwo	AvantGarde-BookOblique
bdps	Bodoni-Poster	bkd	Bookman-Demi
bkdi	Bookman-DemiItalic	bkl	Bookman-Light
bkli	Bookman-LightItalic	c	Cottonwood
cibt	CityBlueprint	cob	Courier-Bold
cobo	Courier-BoldOblique	cobt	CountryBlueprint
com	Courier	coo	Courier-Oblique
eur	EuroRoman	euro	EuroRoman-Oblique
fs	FreestyleScript	ho	Hobo
hv	Helvetica	hvb	Helvetica-Bold
hvbo	Helvetica-BoldOblique	hvn	Helvetica-Narrow
hvnb	Helvetica-Narrow-Bold	hvnbo	Helvetica-Narrow-BoldOblique
hvno	Helvetica-Narrow-Oblique	hvo	Helvetica-Oblique
lx	Linotext	ncb	NewCenturySchlbk-Bold
ncbi	NewCenturySchlbk-BoldItalic	nci	NewCenturySchlbk-Italic
ncr	NewCenturySchlbk-Roman	par	PanRoman
pob	Palatino-Bold	pobi	Palatino-BoldItalic
poi	Palatino-Italic	por	Palatino-Roman
rom	Romantic	romb	Romantic-Bold
romi	Romantic-Italic	sas	SansSerif
sasb	SansSerif-Bold	sasbo	SansSerif-BoldOblique
saso	SansSerif-Oblique	suf	SuperFrench
sy	Symbol	te	Technic
teb	Technic-Bold	tel	Technic-Light
tib	Times-Bold	tibi	Times-BoldItalic
tii	Times-Italic	tir	Times-Roman
tjrg	Trajan-Regular	vrb	VAGRounded-Bold
zcmi	ZapfChancery-MediumItalic	zd	ZapfDingbats

If you are using PostScript fonts not listed in Table 15.1, you can add your own AutoCAD-to-PostScript substitution by editing the `Acad.psf` file. This is a plain-text file that contains the font substitution information as well as other PostScript translation data.

TIP *The HPGL plot file format is another vector format you can use to export your AutoCAD drawings. Use the method described earlier in the section "Exporting Raster Files" to add the HPGL plotter driver to your printer/plotter configuration.*

Combining Data from Different Sources

Imagine being able to import and display spreadsheet data in an AutoCAD drawing. Further imagine that you can easily update that spreadsheet data, either directly from within the drawing or remotely by editing the source spreadsheet document. With a little help from a Windows feature called Object Linking and Embedding (OLE), such a scenario is within your grasp. The data is not limited to spreadsheets; it can be a word-processed document, a database report, or even a sound or video clip.

To import data from other applications, you use the Cut and Paste features found in virtually all Windows programs. You cut the data from the source document and then paste it into AutoCAD.

When you paste data into your AutoCAD file, you can *link* it to the source file or you can *embed* it. If you link it to the source file, the pasted data is updated whenever the source file is modified. This is similar to an AutoCAD cross-referenced file. (See Chapter 13 for more on cross-referenced files.)

You can also paste data into AutoCAD without linking it; then it is considered an embedded object. You can still open the application associated with the data by double-clicking it, but the data is no longer associated with the source file. This is similar to a drawing inserted as a block; changes in the source drawing file have no effect on the inserted block.

Let's see firsthand how OLE works. The following exercise shows how to link an Excel spreadsheet to AutoCAD. You will need a copy of Microsoft Excel 2002 or later, but if you have another application that supports OLE, you can follow along.

1. Open the file called `15a-plan-xls.dwg` from the companion CD. This is a copy of the plan you may have created in earlier exercises.
2. Open the Excel worksheet called `15a-plan.xls`, also from the companion CD.
3. In Excel, highlight the door data, as shown in Figure 15.7, by clicking cell A1 and dragging to cell G17.
4. Choose Edit ➢ Copy to place a copy of the selected data into the Windows Clipboard.
5. Switch to AutoCAD, either by clicking a visible portion of the AutoCAD window or by clicking the AutoCAD button in the Taskbar at the bottom of the Windows Desktop.

FIGURE 15.7

The Excel worksheet

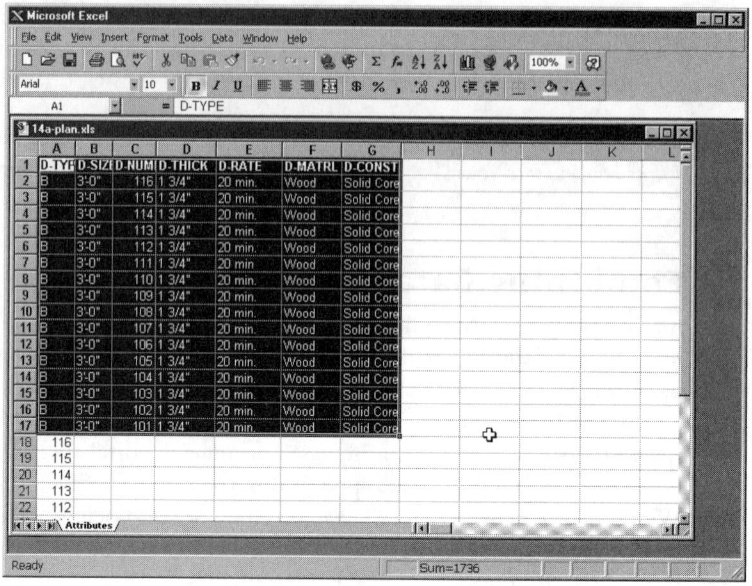

6. Choose Edit ➢ Paste Special to open the Paste Special dialog box.

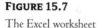

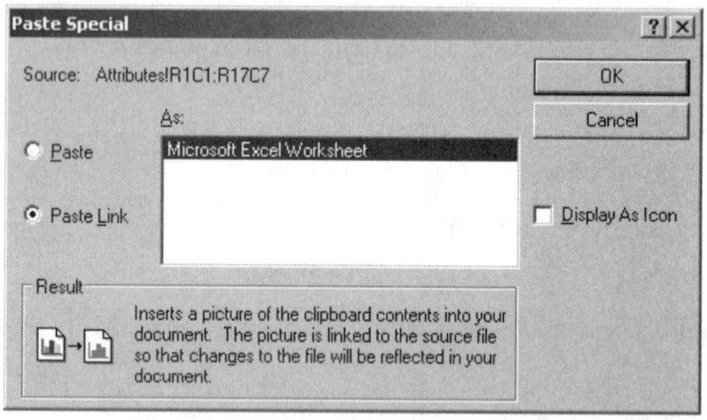

7. Click the Paste Link radio button to tell AutoCAD that you want this paste to be a link. Notice that the list of source types changes to show only one option: Microsoft Excel Worksheet.
8. Click OK. The worksheet data appears in the drawing (see Figure 15.8).
9. Place the cursor on the upper-left corner of the worksheet so that a double-headed diagonal arrow appears, and then click and drag the corner downward and to the right to make the worksheet the size shown in Figure 15.9.

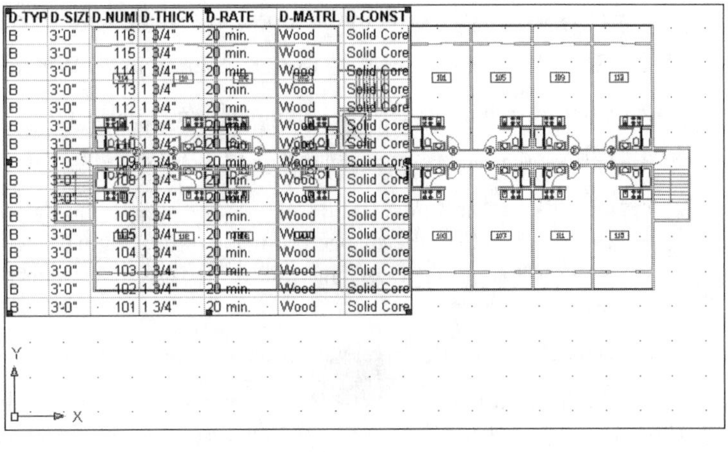

FIGURE 15.8

The AutoCAD drawing with the worksheet pasted in

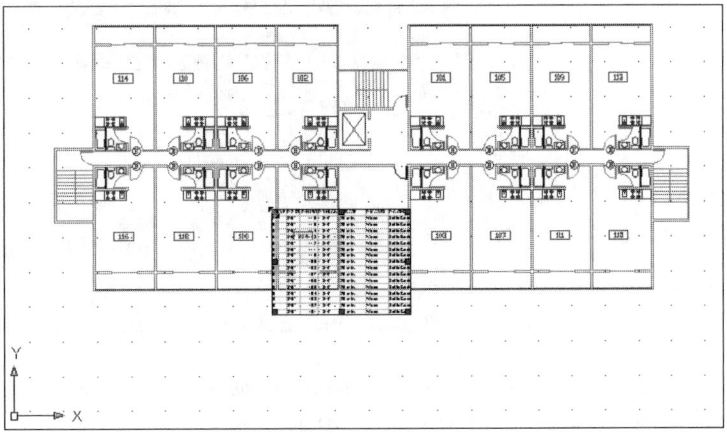

FIGURE 15.9

Resizing the worksheet within AutoCAD

10. Place the cursor over the worksheet data so that the cursor looks like a cross, and then click and drag the worksheet to the lower-right corner of the drawing.

11. Zoom into the worksheet so you can read its contents clearly.

As you saw in steps 8 and 9, you can resize a pasted object using the corner or side grips. The corner grips maintain the original proportion of the inserted object.

You now have a linked object inserted into the AutoCAD drawing. You can save this file and send it off to someone else, along with the pasted document, `15a-plan.xls`. The other person will be able to open the AutoCAD file and view the drawing with the spreadsheet.

WARNING *Objects that are pasted into AutoCAD are maintained within AutoCAD until you use the Erase command to delete them. They act like other AutoCAD objects where layers are concerned. One limitation to pasted objects is that they do not appear in prints or plots unless you use the Windows system printer or plotter.*

Now let's see how the Link feature works by making some changes to the worksheet data.

1. Go back to Excel by clicking the Excel button in the Windows toolbar.
2. Click the cell just below the column heading D-RATE.
3. Change the cell's contents by typing **No Rating**↵.
4. Go back to AutoCAD, and notice that the corresponding cell in the inserted worksheet has changed to reflect the change you made to the original document. Since you inserted the worksheet as a linked document, OLE updates the pasted copy whenever the original source document changes.
5. Now close both the Excel worksheet and the AutoCAD drawing.

In addition to using the Edit ➢ Paste Special option, you can also import an OLE object by choosing Insert ➢ OLE Object to open the Insert Object dialog box:

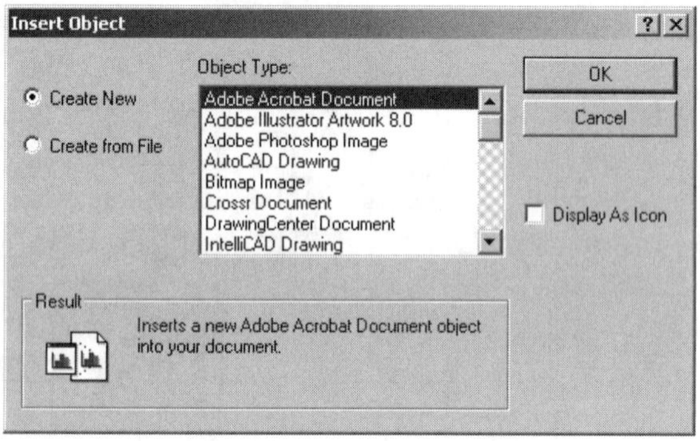

You can then select the type of object you want to import from the list box. Two radio buttons to the left of the list box let you import an existing object or create a new object of the type listed in the list box. If you choose the Create New radio button, the application associated with the object type will start and open a new file. If you choose the Create From File radio button, the dialog box changes to show a filename and a Browse button.

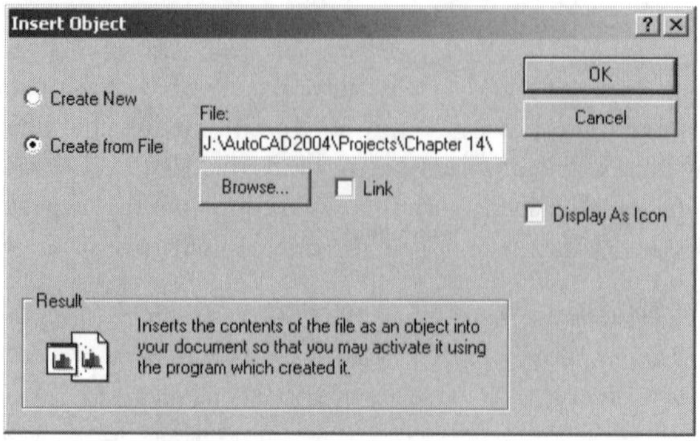

You can then browse for an existing file to import. The Link check box lets you specify whether the imported file is to be linked. If you choose Insert ➢ OLE Object to import an Excel worksheet, the entire worksheet is imported.

TIP *In prior versions of AutoCAD, you could not insert OLE objects beyond a certain size limit. The good news is, AutoCAD 2004 no longer limits the OLE insert size. However, you must use Windows XP and the XP version of Microsoft's Office Suite.*

Editing Links

Once you've pasted an object with links, you can control the links by choosing Edit ➢ OLE Links (Olelinks). If there are no linked objects in the drawing, this option does nothing; otherwise it opens the Links dialog box.

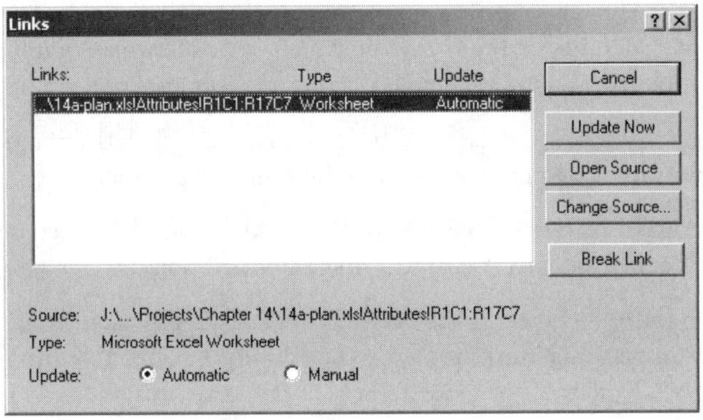

The options available in the Links dialog box are as follows:

Cancel Does just that. It cancels the link between a pasted object and its source file. Once this option is used, changes in the source file have no effect on the pasted object. This is similar to using the Bind option in the Xref command.

Update Now Updates an object's link when the Manual option is selected.

Open Source Opens the application associated with the object and lets you edit it.

Change Source Lets you change the object's link to a different file. When you select this option, AutoCAD opens the Change Link dialog box, which lets you select another file of the same type. For example, if you are editing the link to a sound file, the Change Link dialog box will display files with the .wav file extension.

Automatic and Manual Radio buttons control whether linked objects are updated automatically or manually.

Break Link Disconnects the link between the inserted data and the source document. The inserted data then becomes embedded, rather than linked.

ADDING SOUND, MOTION, AND PHOTOS TO YOUR DRAWINGS

You've already seen how you can include scanned images in AutoCAD drawings through the Raster Image tools. Through OLE, you can also include sound files, video clips, and animation. Imagine how you might be able to enhance your AutoCAD files with these types of data. You can include voice annotation or, if the file is to go to a client, an animated walk-through of your building or mechanical design. The potential for this feature is enormous.

Options for Embedding Data

If you don't need to link the imported data to its source, the Paste Special dialog box lets you convert the imported data to a number of other formats. Here is a brief description of each format that is available:

Picture (Metafile) Imports the data as vector or bitmap graphics, whichever is appropriate. If applicable, text is also maintained as text, though you cannot edit it within AutoCAD.

Bitmap Imports the data as a bitmap image, closely reflecting the appearance of the data as it appears on your computer screen in the source application.

AutoCAD Entities Converts the data into AutoCAD objects such as lines, arcs, and circles. Text is converted into AutoCAD single-line text objects.

Image Entity Converts the data into an AutoCAD raster image. You can then edit it using the raster image-related tools found in the Modify ➢ Object ➢ Image cascading menu of the menu bar. See Chapter 12 for more on how to use raster images.

Text Converts the data into AutoCAD multiline text objects.

The options you see in the Paste Special dialog box depend on the type of data being imported. You saw how the Microsoft Excel Worksheet option maintains the imported data as an Excel worksheet. If the contents of the Clipboard come from another program, you are offered that program as a choice in place of Excel.

TIP *Choosing Edit ➢ Paste embeds OLE data objects into AutoCAD, as does the Paste From Clipboard tool in the Standard toolbar.*

Using the Clipboard to Export AutoCAD Drawings

Just as you can cut and paste data into AutoCAD from applications that support OLE, you can also cut and paste AutoCAD images to other applications. This can be useful as a way of including AutoCAD images in word-processed documents, worksheets, or desktop-publishing documents. It can also be useful in creating background images for visualization programs such as 3D Studio or paint programs such as Fractal Painter.

TIP *If you cut and paste an AutoCAD drawing to another file using OLE and then send the file to someone using another computer, they must also have AutoCAD installed before they can edit the pasted AutoCAD drawing.*

The receiving application does not need to support OLE, but if it does, the exported drawing can be edited with AutoCAD and will maintain its accuracy as a CAD drawing. Otherwise, the AutoCAD image will be converted to a bitmap graphic.

To use the Clipboard to export an object or a set of objects from an AutoCAD drawing, choose Edit ➢ Copy. You are then prompted to select the objects you want to export. If you want to simultaneously export and erase objects from AutoCAD, choose Edit ➢ Cut.

If you want the AutoCAD image to be linked to AutoCAD, choose Edit ➢ Copy Link. You won't be prompted to select objects. The current visible portion of your drawing will be exported. If you want to export the entire drawing, choose View ➢ Zoom ➢ Extents before using the Copy Link option. Otherwise, set up AutoCAD to display the portion of your drawing you want to export, before using Copy Link.

In the receiving application, choose Edit ➢ Paste Special. You'll see a dialog box similar to AutoCAD's Paste Special dialog box. Select the method for pasting your AutoCAD image, and then click OK. If the receiving application does not have a Paste Special option, choose Edit ➢ Paste. The receiving application converts the image into a format it can accept.

TIP *You can copy multiple viewport views from Paper Space into the Clipboard using the Edit ➢ Copy Link option.*

If You Want to Experiment...

With a little help from a Visual Basic macro and OLE, you can have Excel extract attribute data from a drawing and then display that data in a worksheet imported into AutoCAD. The following exercise uses a Visual Basic macro embedded in the `15a-plan.xls` file you used in an earlier exercise.

1. Open the `15a-plan-xls.dwg` file in AutoCAD again.
2. Open the `15a-plan.xls` file in Excel.
3. Repeat the exercise in the "Combining Data from Different Sources" section of this chapter, but stop before exiting the two files.
4. In AutoCAD, choose Modify ➢ Attribute ➢ Single, and then click the door symbol in room 115.
5. Change the Fire Rating Attribute value to 1 hour, and then click OK.
6. Go to Excel, and then choose Tools ➢ Macro ➢ Macros.
7. In the Macros dialog box, highlight the Extract macro, and then click Run. Excel takes a moment to extract the attribute data from the open file; then it displays the data in the worksheet.
8. Return to AutoCAD and check the Fire Rating Value for room 115 in the imported worksheet. It reflects the change you made in the attribute in step 4.
9. Close both files.

The macro you used in the Excel file is a small sample of what can be done using AutoCAD's implementation of Visual Basic Automation. You can learn more about VBA in the Bonus chapter on the CD entitled "Exploring VBA".

In this chapter, you have seen how AutoCAD allows you to access information ranging from the areas of objects to information from other programs. You may never use some of these features, but knowing they are there may, at some point, help you to solve a production problem.

You've just completed Part III of our tutorial. If you've followed the tutorial from the beginning, this is where you get a diploma. You have reached Expert status in 2D drawing and have the tools to tackle any drawing project thrown at you. You only need to log in some time on a few real projects to round out your experience.

From now on, you won't need to follow the book's chapters in order. If you're interested in 3D, go ahead and continue to Part IV, where you'll get thorough instructions on 3D drawing and imaging with AutoCAD. Otherwise, you can skip to Part V to become a full-fledged AutoCAD power user.

Also, don't miss the appendices and the CD—they are packed with information that will answer many of your specific questions or problems. Of course, the entire book is a ready reference to answer questions as they arise or to refresh your memory about specific commands.

Good luck!

Part 4

3D Modeling and Imaging

In this part:

Chapter 16

Introducing 3D

VIEWING AN OBJECT IN three dimensions gives you a sense of its true shape and form. It also helps you conceptualize the design, which results in better design decisions. Finally, using three-dimensional objects helps you communicate your ideas to those who may not be familiar with the plans, sections, and side views of your design.

A further advantage to drawing in three dimensions is that you can derive 2D drawings from your 3D model, which might otherwise take considerably more time with standard 2D drawing methods. For example, you can model a mechanical part in 3D and then quickly derive its top, front, and right-side views using the techniques discussed in this chapter.

AutoCAD offers two methods for creating 3D models: *surface modeling* and *solid modeling*. This chapter will introduce you to surface modeling. You'll get a chance to explore solid modeling in Chapter 19.

With surface modeling, you use two types of objects. One is called a *3D Face*, which you will learn about later in this chapter. The other is the standard AutoCAD set of objects you've been using all along, but with a slight twist. By changing the thickness property of objects, you can create 3D surfaces. These surfaces, along with some 3D editing tools, let you create virtually any 3D form you might need.

In this chapter, you will use AutoCAD's 3D capabilities to see what your studio apartment looks like from various angles. Topics include the following:

- Creating a 3D drawing
- Viewing a 3D drawing
- Visualizing your 3D model
- Getting the 3D results you want
- Drawing 3D surfaces
- Creating and using slides
- If you want to experiment…

Creating a 3D Drawing

By now, you are aware that AutoCAD objects have properties that you can manipulate to set color, line type, line weight, and layer assignments. Another property called *thickness* lets you turn two-dimensional objects into 3D forms. For example, to draw a cube, you first draw a square, and then you change the thickness property of the square to the length of one side (see Figure 16.1). This thickness property is a value given as a Z coordinate. Imagine that your screen's drawing area is the drawing surface. A Z coordinate of 0 is on that surface. A A coordinate greater than 0 is a position closer to you and above that surface. Figure 16.2 illustrates this concept.

TIP *When you change the thickness property of a 2D shape by assigning a Z coordinate greater than 0, you are said to be extruding the shape.*

FIGURE 16.1

Creating a cube by changing a square's line thickness

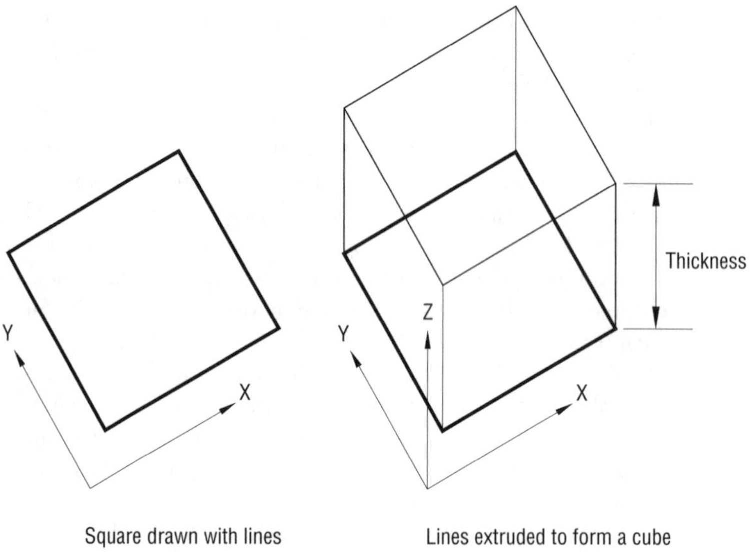

When you draw an object with thickness, you don't see the thickness until you view the drawing from a different angle. This is because normally your view is perpendicular to the imagined drawing surface. At that angle, you cannot see the thickness of an object because it projects toward you—just as a sheet of paper looks like a line when viewed from one end. Thus, to view an object's thickness, you must change the angle at which you view your drawing.

Another object property related to 3D is *elevation*. You can set AutoCAD so that everything you draw has an *elevation*. By default, objects have a zero elevation. This means that objects are drawn on the imagined 2D plane of Model Space, but you can set the Z coordinate for your objects so that whatever you draw is above or below that surface. An object with an elevation value other than 0 rests not *on* the imagined drawing surface but *above* it (or *below* it if the Z coordinate is a negative value). Figure 16.3 illustrates this concept.

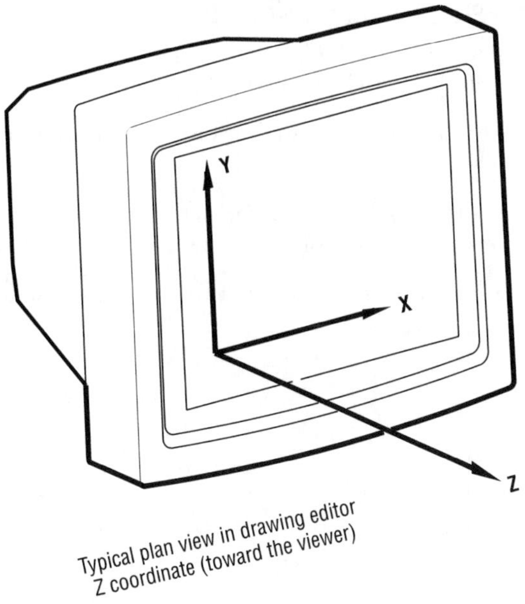

FIGURE 16.2
The Z coordinate in relation to the X coordinate and Y coordinate

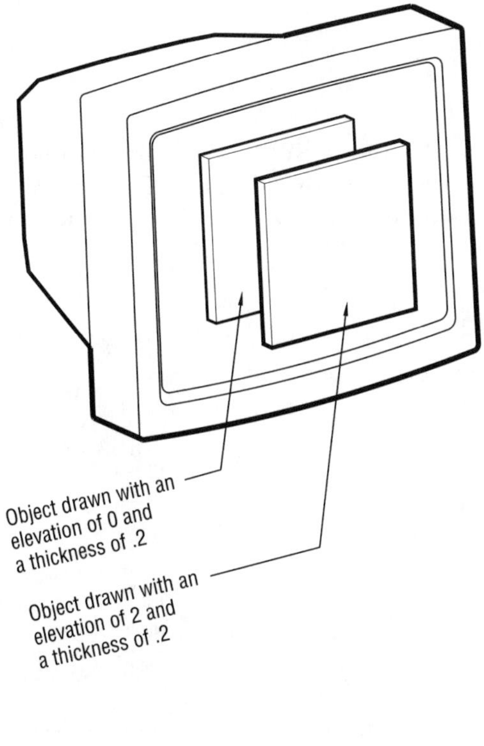

FIGURE 16.3
Two identical objects at different elevations

Changing a 2D Plan into a 3D Model

In this exercise, you will turn the 2D Unit drawing into a 3D drawing by changing the properties of the wall lines. You will also learn how to view the 3D image.

1. Start AutoCAD and open the `Unit` file or use `16a-unit.dwg` from the companion CD; then choose View ➢ Zoom ➢ All.
2. Set the current layer to Wall, and freeze all the other layers except Jamb. Remember that Freeze is the option just to the right of the lightbulb in the Layer Properties Manager dialog box.
3. Turn on the grid (if it isn't on already). Your screen should look like Figure 16.4.

FIGURE 16.4
The Plan view of the walls and door jambs

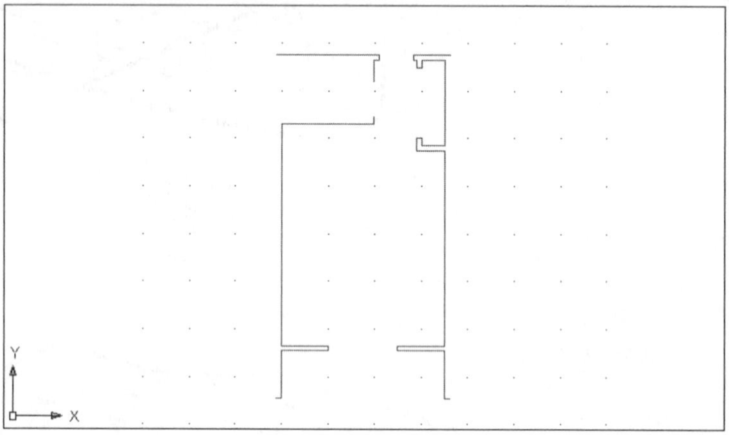

4. Choose View ➢ 3D Views ➢ SW Isometric. Your view now looks as if you are standing above and to the left of your drawing, rather than directly above it (see Figure 16.5). The UCS icon helps you get a sense of your new orientation. The grid also shows you the angle of the drawing surface.

FIGURE 16.5
A 3D view of the floor plan

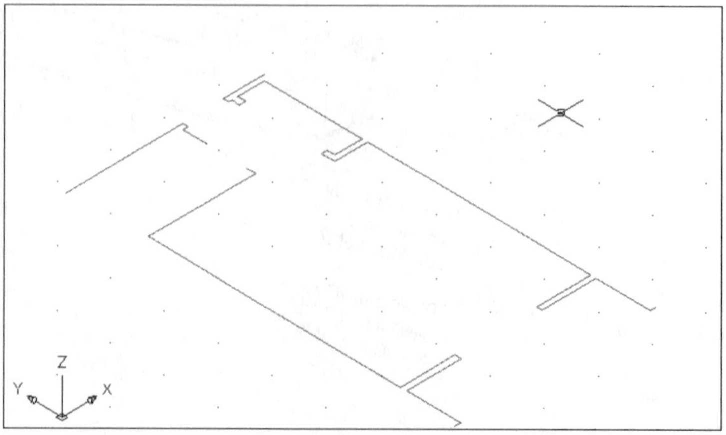

TIP *The interior walls of the bathroom are not visible because the layer on which the bathroom block was inserted was frozen. For the purpose of this exercise, you can ignore the interior bathroom wall. Since the bathroom is a block, you cannot change the thickness property of the wall without using the In-Place Xref And Block Edit tool.*

5. Select all the objects in the drawing.
6. Click the Properties tool on the Standard toolbar, or right-click and choose Properties from the shortcut menu.
7. In the Properties palette, locate the Thickness option, and click its 0 value.
8. Enter **8'**↵ (metric users should enter **244**↵). The walls and jambs now appear to be 8' (244 cm) high.
9. Close the Properties palette and then press the Esc key to exit the selection.

Figure 16.6 shows the extruded wall lines. You can see through the walls because this is a *Wireframe view*. A Wireframe view shows the volumes of a 3D object by showing the lines representing the intersections of surfaces. Later in this chapter, I'll discuss how to make an object's surfaces opaque in order to facilitate a particular point of view for a drawing.

FIGURE 16.6
The wall lines, extruded (Wireframe view)

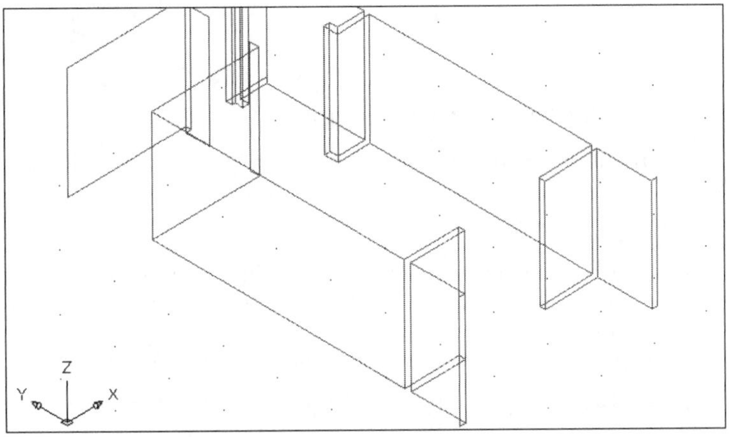

In step 4, you were able to quickly obtain a 3D view from a set of 3D View options. You'll learn more about these options as you progress through this chapter.

TIP *Notice that when you extruded the walls, the interior bathroom walls did not change with the others. This is because those walls are part of a block. You must redefine the block to change the thickness of the objects it contains.*

Next you will change the elevation of the door headers by moving them in the z-axis using grips.

1. First, zoom out a bit to get all the drawing in view, as shown in Figure 16.7. You can use the Pan and Zoom tools in this 3D view as you would in a 2D view.

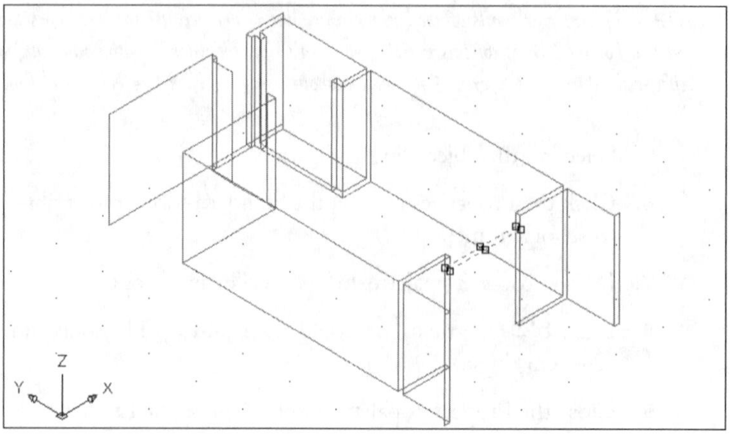

FIGURE 16.7
The header lines at the new elevation

2. Thaw on the Ceiling layer. The door headers appear as lines on the floor where the door openings are located.
3. Click the two magenta lines representing the header over the balcony door. As you do so, notice that your cursor's shape conforms to the 3D view.
4. Shift+click the midpoint grips of these two lines.
5. Click one of the hot grips again.
6. At the `** STRETCH **` prompt, enter **@0,0,7'↵** (metric users should enter **@0,0,214↵**). Don't forget to indicate feet for the 7. The lines move to a new position 7' (214 cm) above the floor (see Figure 16.7).
7. Click the Properties button on the Standard toolbar and change the thickness of the header to 1' (30 cm) using the Thickness setting in the Properties palette. Click OK.
8. Click the four lines representing the door header for the closet and entry.
9. Repeat steps 3 through 7. Your drawing will look like Figure 16.8.
10. Use the View Control dialog box (choose View ➢ Named Views) to create a new view under the name of 3D. See Chapter 6 if you need help saving views.

You could have used the Move command to move the lines to their new elevation, entering the same **@0,0,7'** at the `Specify second point of displacement or <use first point as displacement>:` prompt for Move. However, because you must select objects to edit them using grips, with the Move command, you save a step by not having to select the lines a second time for the Properties tool.

FIGURE 16.8
The headers with the new thickness

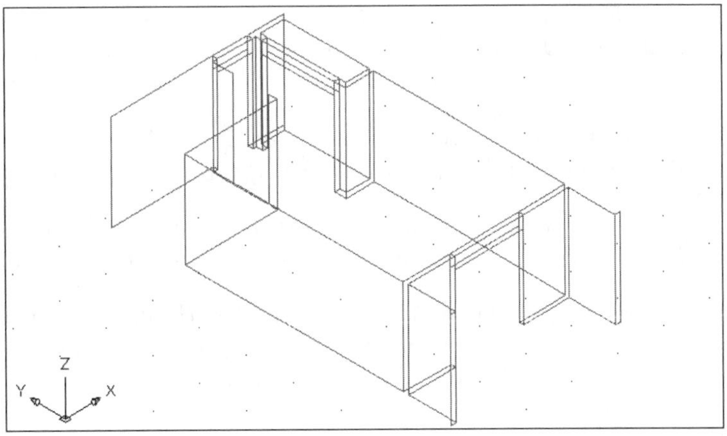

Creating a 3D Object

Though you may visualize a design in 3D, you will often start sketching it in 2D and later generate the 3D views. When you know from the start what the thickness and height of an object will be, you can set these values so that you don't have to extrude the object later. The following exercise shows you how to set elevation and thickness before you start drawing.

1. Choose Format ➢ Thickness.
2. Enter **12"↵** at the `Enter new value for THICKNESS <0.0000>:` prompt. Metric users should enter **30↵**. Now as you draw objects, they will appear 12" (30 cm) thick.
3. Draw a circle representing a planter at one side of the balcony (see Figure 16.9). Make it 18" (45 cm for metric users) in diameter. The planter appears as a 3D object with the current thickness and elevation settings.

FIGURE 16.9
The planter

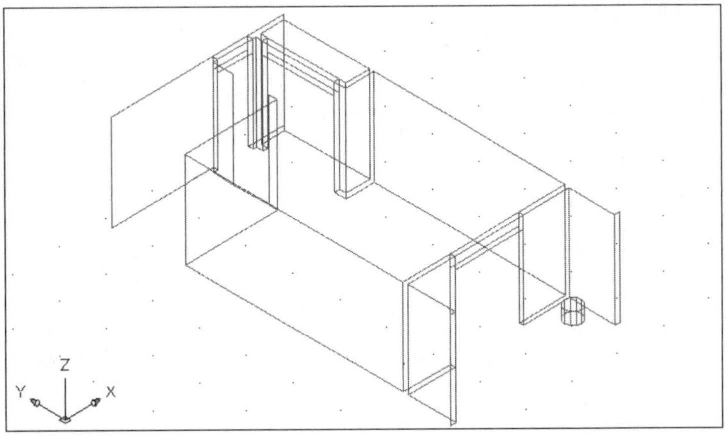

TIP *If you use the same thickness and elevation often, you can create a template file with these settings so they are readily available when you start your drawings. The command for setting thickness and elevation is Elev. You can also use the Elevation and Thickness system variables to set the default elevation and thickness of new objects.*

Now that you have set the thickness setting to 12" (30 cm), everything you draw will have a thickness of 12 inches (30 cm) until you change it back to 0 or some other setting.

TIP *You can also change the default elevation from 0 to some other positive or negative value. To do this, you type* ***Elev↵*** *and then enter the elevation you want. You are then prompted for a thickness as well.*

Giving objects thickness and modifying their elevation is a simple process, as you have seen. With these two properties, you can create nearly any three-dimensional form you need. Next, you will discover how to control your view of your drawing.

Viewing a 3D Drawing

Your first 3D view of a drawing is a Wireframe view. It appears as if it were an open model made of wire; none of the sides appear solid. This section describes how to manipulate the Wireframe view so you can see your drawing from any angle. This section will also describe how, once you have selected your view, you can view the 3D drawing as a solid object with the hidden lines removed. You will also learn how to save views for later recall.

Finding Isometric and Orthogonal Views

First, let's start by looking at some of the viewing options available. You used one option already to get the current 3D view. Choosing View ➢ 3D Views ➢ SW Isometric displays an Isometric view from a southwest direction; north is the same direction as the y-axis. Figure 16.10 illustrates the three other Isometric View options: SE Isometric, NE Isometric, and NW Isometric. The cameras represent the different viewpoint locations. You can get an idea of their location in reference to the grid and UCS icon.

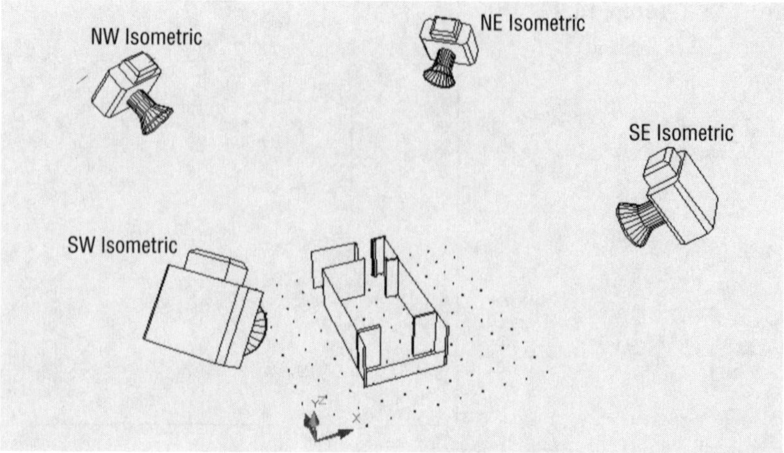

FIGURE 16.10

This diagram shows the isometric viewpoints for the four Isometric views available from the View ➢ 3D Views cascading menu.

The View ➢ 3D Views cascading menu offers another set of options: Top, Bottom, Left, Right, Front, and Back. These are Orthogonal views that show the sides, top, and bottom of the model, as illustrated in Figure 16.11. In this figure, the cameras once again show the points of view.

FIGURE 16.11
This diagram shows the six viewpoints of the Orthogonal view options on the View ➢ 3D Views cascading menu.

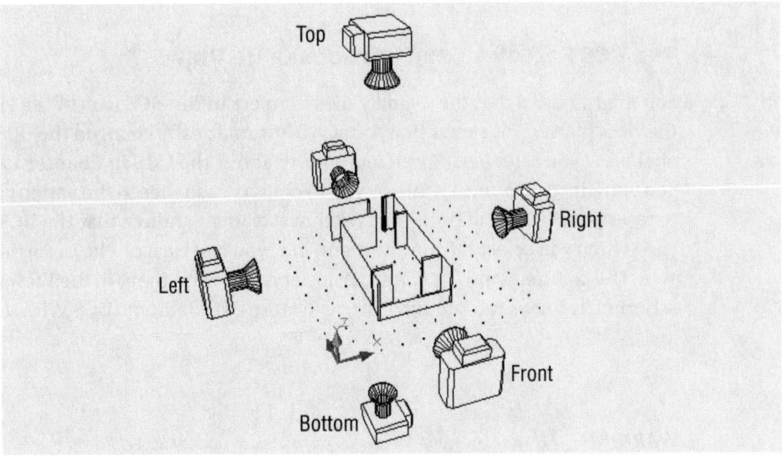

To give you a better idea of what an Orthogonal view looks like, Figure 16.12 shows the view that you see when you choose View ➢ 3D Views ➢ Right. It is a side view of the unit.

FIGURE 16.12
The view of the unit model you see when you choose View ➢ 3D Views ➢ Right.

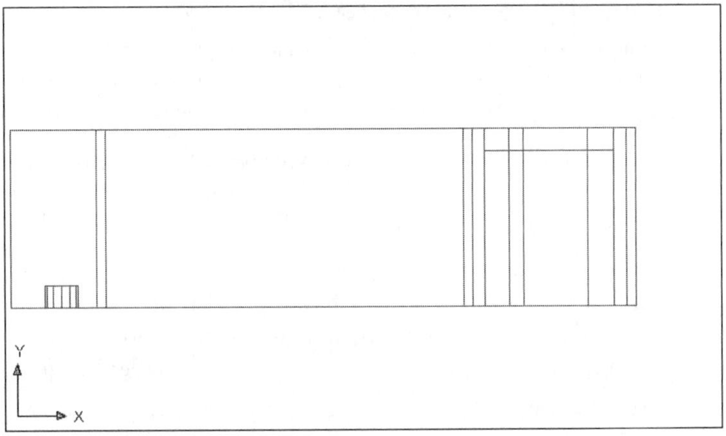

When you use any of the View options described here, AutoCAD attempts to display the extents of the drawing. You can then use the Pan and Zoom tools to adjust your view.

If you find you use these View options frequently, you might want to open the View toolbar.

WARNING *LT users will not see the Camera tool at the far right of the View toolbar.*

This toolbar offers quick, single-click access to all the options discussed in this section. To open it, right-click any toolbar, and then click View from the shortcut menu.

THE UCS FOLLOWS YOUR ORTHOGRAPHIC VIEWS

You might notice that the x- and y-axis markers in the UCS icon of the view in Figure 16.12 are oriented to the view plane. This shows that AutoCAD automatically changed the UCS so that it is normal to the orthogonal view you selected. (You'll learn more about the UCS in Chapter 17.) This feature comes in handy as you work in 3D, because it allows you to construct shapes in the various orthogonal planes without having to reset your UCS each time you switch views. If you notice that the UCS is not following your Orthogonal view when you select it from the menu bar, you can turn on the Ucsortho system variable by typing **UCS↵ 1↵** at the command prompt. You can also type ***V↵*** and then, in the View dialog box, click the Orthographic & Isometric Views tab and turn on the Restore Orthographic UCS With View option.

WARNING *If you tried out the Orthographic view options described in this section, make sure you set the UCS back to the world coordinate system before you continue to the next exercise. You can do this by typing **UCS↵ W↵** at the command prompt. You can also choose Tools ➢ New UCS ➢ World from the menu bar.*

Using a Dialog Box to Select 3D Views

You now know that you can select from a variety of "canned" viewpoints to view your 3D model. You can also fine-tune your view by indicating an angle from the drawing's x-axis and from the floor plane using the Viewpoint Presets dialog box. The following steps show you how it works.

1. Choose View ➢ 3D Views ➢ Viewpoint Presets or type **Vp↵** to open the Viewpoint Presets dialog box (see Figure 16.13). The square dial to the left lets you select a viewpoint location in degrees relative to the x-axis. The semicircle to the right lets you select an elevation for your viewpoint.
2. Click the area labeled 135 in the upper left of the square dial. Then click the area labeled 60 in the semicircle on the right. Notice that the pointer moves to the angle you've selected and the input boxes below the graphic change to reflect the new settings.
3. Click OK. Your view changes according to the new settings you just made.

Other settings in this dialog box let you determine whether the selected view angles are relative to the World Coordinate System or to the current User Coordinate System. You can also go directly to a Plan view by clicking the Set To Plan View button.

A few features of the Viewpoint Presets dialog box are not readily apparent. First, you can select the exact angle indicated by the label of either graphic by clicking anywhere inside the outlined regions around the pointer (see Figure 16.13). For example, in the graphic to the left, click anywhere in the region labeled 90 to set the pointer to 90° exactly.

You can also set the pointers to smaller degree increments by clicking within the pointer area. For example, if you click in the area just below the 90 region in the left graphic, the pointer moves to that location. The angle will be slightly greater or less than 90°.

If you want to enter an exact value from the x-axis or x-y plane, you can do so by entering an angle value in the input boxes. You can obtain virtually any view you want using the options in the Viewpoint Presets dialog box.

FIGURE 16.13

The Viewpoint Presets dialog box

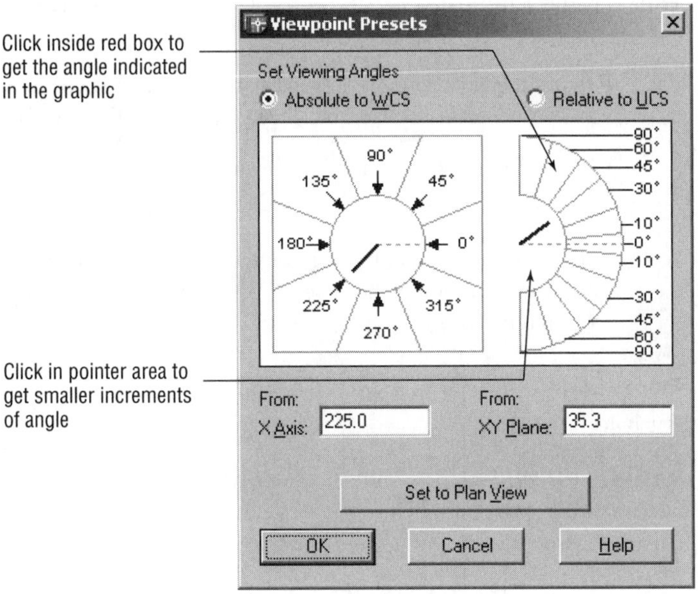

TIP *Another tool, called 3D Orbit, can help you visualize your model. Like 3D orbiting tools found in other 3D programs, 3D Orbit lets you pan around a 3D object. You'll get a detailed look at 3D Orbit in Chapter 17.*

Visualizing Your 3D Model

As you work with your 3D model, you will want to get an idea of how it looks with hidden lines removed. Frequently, object intersections and shapes are not readily apparent until you can see which objects lie in front of others.

AutoCAD provides two helpful viewing commands for this situation. First, the Hide command allows you to quickly view your drawing with the hidden lines removed. You can then assess where surfaces are and get a better feel for the model. Hide is also an option at plot time, allowing you to create printed line drawings of a 3D model. You can then render the hard copy using manual techniques if you want.

The second command, Shademode, lets you work with your 3D model as if it were composed of opaque surfaces instead of lines. Shademode also has a variety of options for controlling how colors are applied. You can't plot views as they appear when Shademode is turned on. It is intended only as a visualization aid for constructing 3D models.

Let's begin by looking at the Hide command, and then I'll discuss the Shademode command.

Removing Hidden Lines

Hide is perhaps the easiest of all the AutoCAD 3D viewing commands to use. Try the following to see a hidden-line view of your model.

1. Restore the view you saved earlier with the name 3D using the View dialog box. This shows you that you can store and recall 3D views as well as 2D views.
2. Choose View ➢ Hide, or enter **Hi↵** at the command prompt. AutoCAD displays this message:

   ```
   Regenerating Model
   ```

   If the drawing is complex, a graphic bar appears in the status bar showing the progress of the hidden-line removal. When AutoCAD is done, the image appears with the hidden lines removed (see Figure 16.14).

FIGURE 16.14

A unit in the apartment building drawing with hidden lines removed

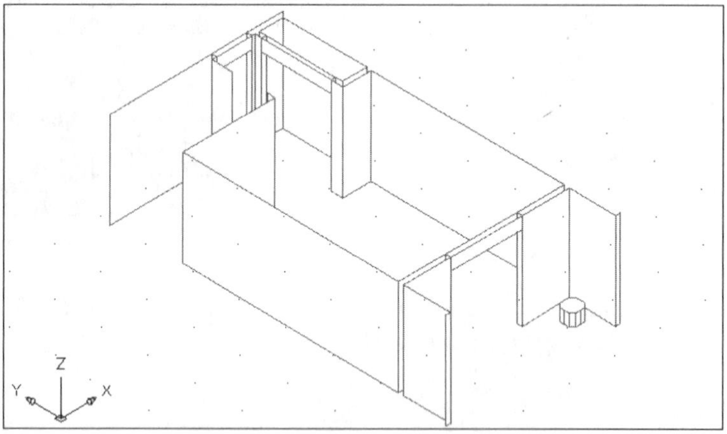

3. After you review the results of the View ➢ Hide, choose View ➢ Regen or type **Re↵** to return to your Wireframe view.

TIP *You can also plot a view with hidden lines removed by checking the Hide Objects check box in the Plot Configuration dialog box before you start your plot. Using the Hide Objects option generally adds only a few minutes to your plot time. If you're plotting a Layout tab, you need to turn on the Hideplot property of the viewport containing the 3D view.*

This hidden-line view remains until your drawing is regenerated. Note that you cannot use the View command to save a hidden-line view. You can, however, save this view as a slide.

TIP *In earlier versions of AutoCAD, text would not hide when using the Hide command. AutoCAD 2004 offers the Hidetext system variable that controls whether text is hidden when using the Hide command. See Appendix D for more on System Variables.*

Although it did not take much time to perform a hidden-line removal on this drawing, the more complex the 3D drawing, the longer the Hide command takes. But even the most complex model you create does not take much more than several minutes.

WARNING *If you want to use the Zoom Realtime tool after you use the Hide command, you must choose View ➢ Regen.*

Showing Hidden Lines as Dashed

In most architectural 3D drawings, you don't want to show the hidden lines in your final views. In mechanical applications, however, you might want to show hidden lines as dashed to help better visualize the form of an object. AutoCAD offers two system variables, Obscuredltype and Obscuredcolor, that will allow you to control how hidden lines are displayed when the Hide command is used.

Obscuredltype gives you control over the line type of hidden lines. Normally, Obscuredltype is set to 0 so that hidden lines are invisible. If Obscuredltype is set to 1, hidden lines are made visible even when Hide is used. If it is set to 2, hidden lines are shown as dashed lines, as in a mechanical drawing.

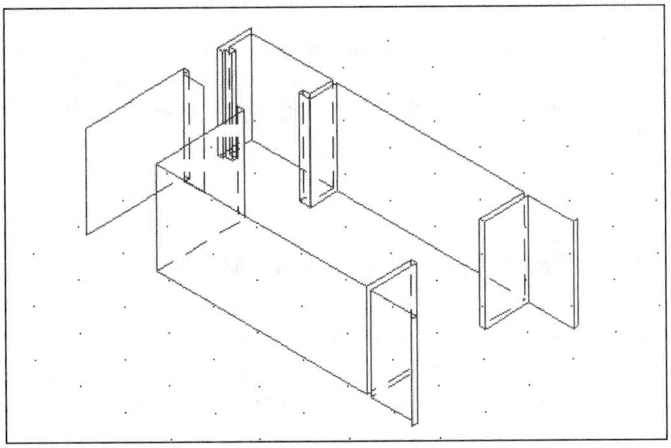

Obscuredltype offers the 11 line-type settings shown here with their corresponding numeric values.

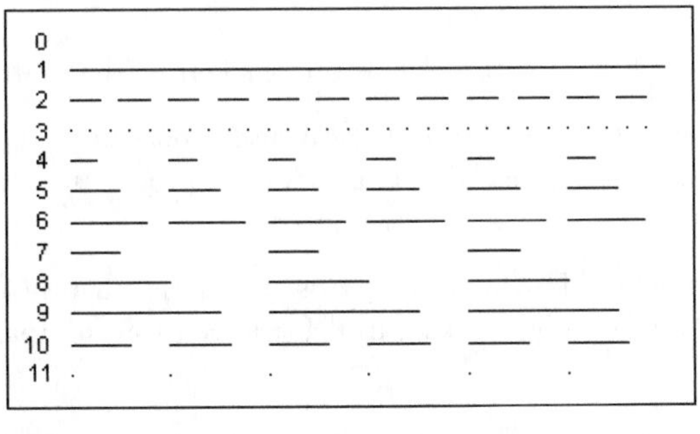

Obscuredcolor gives you control over the color of hidden lines. This system variable has no effect unless Obscuredltype is set to a value other than 0. Obscuredcolor can be set to any value from 0 to 255; the numeric value corresponds to the 255 AutoCAD colors. You can make use of the Obscuredcolor setting in combination with color plot style tables to alter the appearance of hidden lines in print or plotter output.

To use either of these system variables, enter the variable name at the command prompt; then enter the numeric value that corresponds to the desired effect.

OBSCUREDCOLOR AND OBSCUREDLTYPE TIPS

When you plot a hidden-line drawing from Model Space, and you have Obscuredltype set to a value other than 0, you will get a plot that looks like your hidden line view in the AutoCAD Model Space work area. (Make sure you select Hide Objects in the Layout Settings tab of the Plot dialog box.) However, if you plot from a Layout tab with the Hideplot setting turned on for the viewport, the Obscureltype line-type setting will not appear in your printer or plotter output; the output will look like a normal plot showing the hidden lines as solid lines.

To get around this limitation, you can use Obscuredcolor in conjunction with a color plot style to create a plot with dashed hidden lines when plotting from a Layout tab. You may need to convert your drawing to one that uses color plot style tables. See Chapter 7 for more on color plot styles and plot style conversions.

Also note that the Ltscale system variable has no effect on the line type generated by Obscuredltype. Finally, if you prefer, you can control Obscuredcolor and Obscuredltype settings through the Obscured Lines group of the Hidden Line Settings dialog box. To open the Hidden Lines Settings dialog box, enter Hlsettings↵ at the command prompt.

Using a Shaded Mode with Your 3D Model

ACAD only

If you're used to working with wireframe 3D images, the Hide command is usually good enough to give you an idea of how your model looks from time to time as you work on it. But when you want to get an even better visualization of the form your model is taking on, it's time for the Shademode command. To see how Shademode works, try the following exercise.

TIP *The Shademode command is set up as a toolbar with several tools. Each tool issues the Shademode command and applies a different option. If you prefer, you can enter the Shademode command at the command prompt and enter the appropriate options to get the same results as the toolbar tools. Shademode in LT only offers the option of 2D wireframe and Hidden.*

1. Right-click any toolbar and choose Shade from the shortcut menu to open the Shade toolbar.

2. Click the Flat Shaded tool. You can also choose View ➢ Shade ➢ Flat Shaded. Notice that a ground plane appears. This is an aid to help you better visualize the model; it isn't part of your drawing.
3. Click the Grid button in the status bar. Notice that the 3D grid turns off. Click the button again to turn the grid back on. The grid you see with the shaded view does not reflect the grid

spacing you set in the Drafting Settings dialog box. It's only there to help you visualize the plane represented by the x-y axes at 0 elevation. It also shows you the limits of your drawing, just like the standard grid.

4. In the Shade toolbar, click the Flat Shaded, Edges On tool, or choose View ➢ Shade ➢ Flat Shaded, Edges On from the menu bar. Notice that this time, the edge of each surface is highlighted for visibility (see Figure 16.15).

FIGURE 16.15

The Unit plan shaded using the Flat Shaded, Edges On option

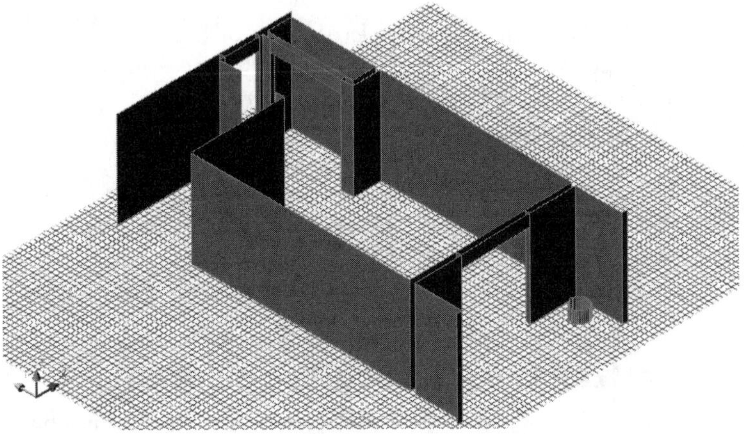

5. Click the Hidden tool or choose View ➢ Shade ➢ Hidden. Your drawing changes to look as it did when you used the View ➢ Hide option. But there is a difference in this option.
6. Choose View ➢ Regen. The view doesn't change. AutoCAD remains in a Shaded view mode until you click 2D Wireframe on the Shade toolbar or choose View ➢ Shade ➢ 2D Wireframe.

7. Click the 2D Wireframe tool in the Shade toolbar. Your drawing returns to the Wireframe view you started with. Remember this tool when you want to return to the standard 2D Wireframe view of your drawing.

The Hidden Shade mode makes it easier to visualize your 3D drawing. Depending on the type of model and its complexity, you can even work on it with the Hidden Shade mode turned on. You can always go back to the Wireframe view using the 2D Wireframe option. In fact, at times you might want to "see through" a wall or other object while you're editing your 3D model. That's when the 2D Wireframe view will be more helpful.

Before you continue editing the Unit plan, you might want to know the functions of the other options on the Shade toolbar. The 3D Wireframe option displays a view similar to the 2D Wireframe view, with the addition of the ground plane you first saw in step 2. The other two options are Gouraud Shaded and Gouraud Shaded, Edges On. Both are used to get a smooth shade effect on curved surfaces as shown in Figure 16.16. These Gouraud options don't have an effect on flat surface models like the walls of the Unit plan. You can see the effect of the Gouraud options in the planter of the Unit plan.

FIGURE 16.16

A sphere shaded using different shade modes

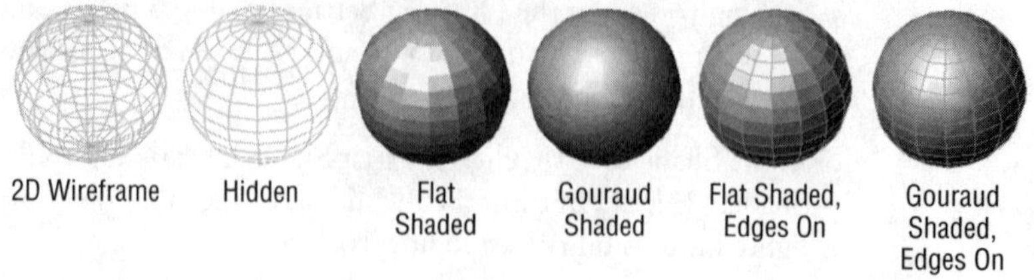

The Edges On options display the edge of flat surfaces. The spheres in Figure 16.16 are made up of flat surfaces, which can be seen in the Hidden example. The Gouraud Shaded options smooth out the facets of the sphere. The Gouraud Shaded, Edges On option shows the edges of the facets even though the smoothing effect is on.

A third method for visualizing your model lets you place varying light sources in your drawing. The AutoCAD rendering functions on the Render toolbar let you adjust light reflectance of surfaces, smooth out faceted surfaces such as spheres and cylinders, and place light sources accurately. You'll get a chance to work with the rendering functions in Chapter 18. For now, let's look at some other factors that affect how a 3D model will look when it is shaded or when hidden lines are removed.

Getting the 3D Results You Want

You've seen how you can make an opaque vertical surface just by changing the thickness property of an object. To make a horizontal surface appear opaque, you can draw it with a wide polyline, a solid hatch, or a 3D Face. For example, consider a table. You might represent the tabletop with a rectangle and give it the appropriate thickness, but the top appears to be transparent when the lines are hidden. Only the sides of the tabletop become opaque. To make the entire tabletop opaque if the tabletop is an irregular shape, you can use a solid hatch or an object called a *region*. Chapter 19 discusses regions. When the lines are hidden, the tabletop appears to be opaque (see Figure 16.17).

FIGURE 16.17

One table using lines for the top, and another using a solid fill

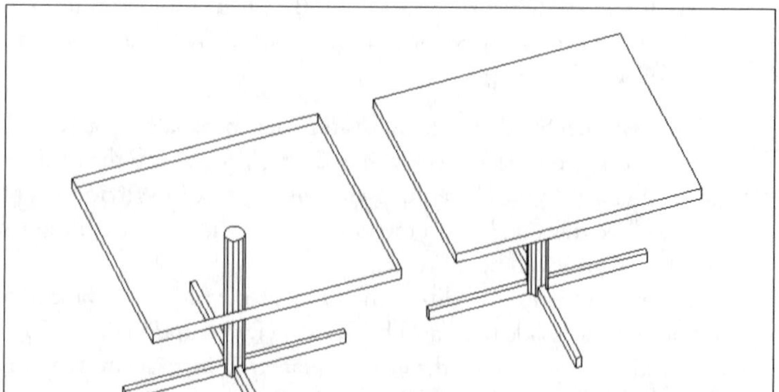

SETTING LAYERS AND HIDDEN LINES CAREFULLY

Bear in mind that the Hide command that you used first to hide the Wireframe view hides objects that are obscured by other objects on layers that are turned off. For example, if a couch in the corner of the studio unit is on a layer that is off when you use Hide, the lines behind the couch are hidden even though the couch does not appear in the view, as shown here.

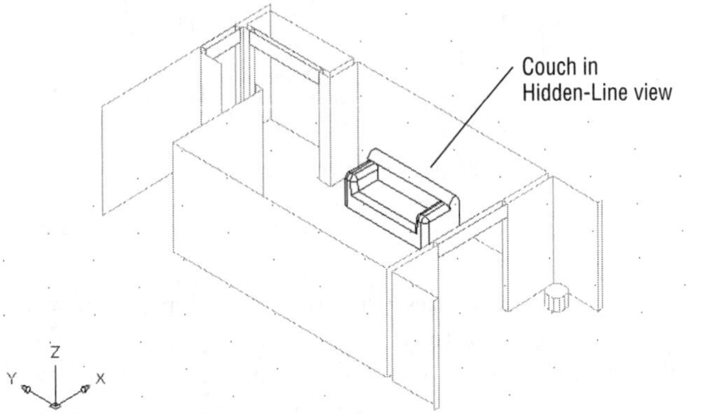

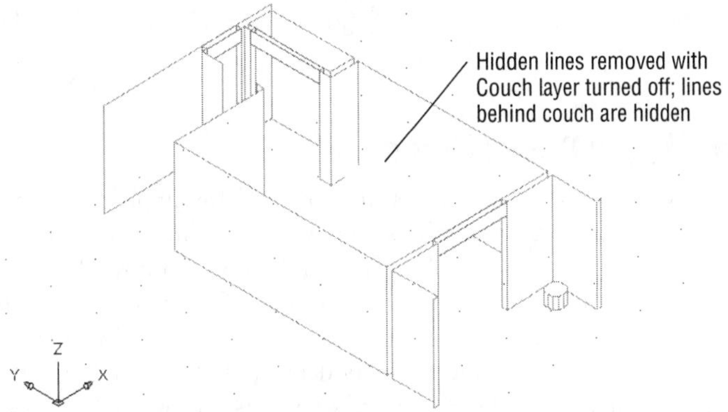

You can, however, freeze any layer containing objects that you do not want affected by the hidden-line removal process. This is important to be aware of since the Hide command reproduces what you see when you plot your drawing. In fact, you can use the Hide command to test your 3D model before you print.

You may notice that AutoCAD does not always display the intersection of 3D surfaces properly. You can set up AutoCAD to always display surface intersections by turning on the Display intersections option in the Hidden Line Settings dialog box. To open the Hidden Lines Settings dialog box, enter Hlsettings↵ at the command prompt. You may also enter Intersectiondisplay↵ 1↵ to turn on this feature.

When a circle is used as an extruded form, the top surface appears opaque when you use the Hide command. Where you want to show an opening at the top of a circular volume, as in a circular chimney, you can use two 180° arcs (see Figure 16.18).

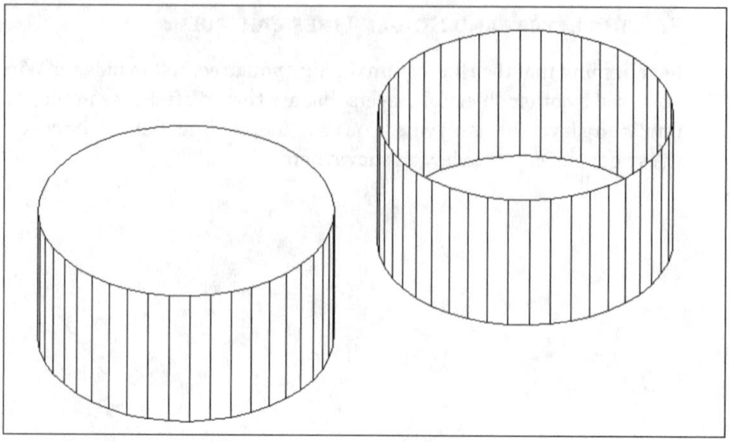

FIGURE 16.18
A circle and two joined arcs

For complex horizontal surfaces, you can use a combination of wide polylines, solids, and 3D Faces. For example, a sidewalk on a street corner would use a donut for the rounded corner and would use solids or 3D Faces at either side for the straight portion of the sidewalk. It's okay to overlap surfaces to achieve the effect you want. Polylines are useful for creating window mullions or other shapes that might be formed by a straight extrusion in the real world. (You'll learn how to create a curved extruded shape in Chapter 19).

Drawing 3D Surfaces

In your work with 3D so far in this chapter, you have simply extruded existing forms, or you have set AutoCAD to draw extruded objects. But extruded forms have their limitations. Using just extruded forms, it's hard to draw diagonal surfaces in the z-axis. AutoCAD provides the 3D Face object to give you more flexibility in drawing surfaces in three-dimensional space. The 3D Face produces a 3D surface on which each corner can be given an *x*, *y*, and *z* value. By using 3D Faces in conjunction with extruded objects, you can create a 3D model of just about anything. When you view these 3D objects in a 2D Plan view, you will see them as 2D objects showing only the *x* and *y* positions of their corners or endpoints.

Using Point Filters

Before you start working with 3D surfaces, you should have a good idea of what the Z coordinate values are for your model. The simplest way to construct surfaces in 3D space is to first create some layout lines to help you place the endpoints of 3D Faces.

AutoCAD offers a method for 3D point selection, called *filtering*, that simplifies the selection of Z coordinates. Filtering allows you to enter an *x*, *y*, or *z* value by picking a point on the screen and telling AutoCAD to use only the *x*, *y*, or *z* value of that point or any combination of those values. If you don't specify a Z coordinate, the current elevation setting is assumed.

In the following exercises, let's imagine you decide to add a new two-story unit to your apartment design. You will add a stair rail to the studio apartment to access that second floor. In doing this, you will practice using 3D Faces and filters. You'll start by doing some setup, so you can work on a copy of the `Unit` file and keep the old Unit plan for future reference.

1. Save the `Unit` file, and then choose File ➢ Save As to create a drawing called `Unitloft` from the current file. (You can also use the `Unitloft.dwg` file supplied on the companion CD.)
2. Choose Format ➢ Thickness and set the Thickness to 0.
3. Set the current layer to Wall.

Now you are ready to lay out your stair rail.

1. Click the Line tool on the Draw toolbar.
2. At the `Specify first Point:` prompt, Shift+right-click to display the Osnap menu; then choose Point Filters ➢ .XY. As an alternative, you can enter **.xy↵** instead of using the Osnap menu. By doing this, you are telling AutoCAD that you are going to first specify the X coordinate and Y coordinate for this beginning point, and then later indicate the Z coordinate.

TIP *Notice the .X, .Y, and .Z options on the Object Snap menu (Shift+right-click). These are the 3D filters. By choosing one of these options as you select points in a 3D command, you can filter an x, y, or z value, or any combination of values, from that selected point. You can also enter filters through the keyboard.*

3. At the `Specify first Point: .xy of:` prompt, pick a point that is 2'-7" (79 cm for metric users) from the corner of the bathroom near coordinate 25'-6",25'-5". (Metric users use the coordinate 777,775.) This will be the first line at the bottom of the stair rail. (You don't need to be too exact because we are just practicing.)
4. At the `(need Z):` prompt, enter **9'↵** (the Z coordinate). Metric users enter **274↵**.
5. At the `Specify next point or [Undo]:` prompt, choose .XY again from the Osnap menu, or enter **.xy↵**.
6. Enter **@12' <270↵**. Metric users enter **@365<270↵**. This locates the X coordinate and Y coordinate for the other end of the stair rail.
7. At the `(need Z):` prompt, enter **0↵**.
8. Press ↵ to end the Line command. Your drawing should look like Figure 16.19.

TIP *You can also use filters in a 2D drawing to select an x or y component of an object to which you want to align a point.*

Now you will copy the line vertically to draw the top of the stair rail.

1. Click the Copy Object button on the Modify toolbar.
2. Select the 3D line you just drew, and press ↵.

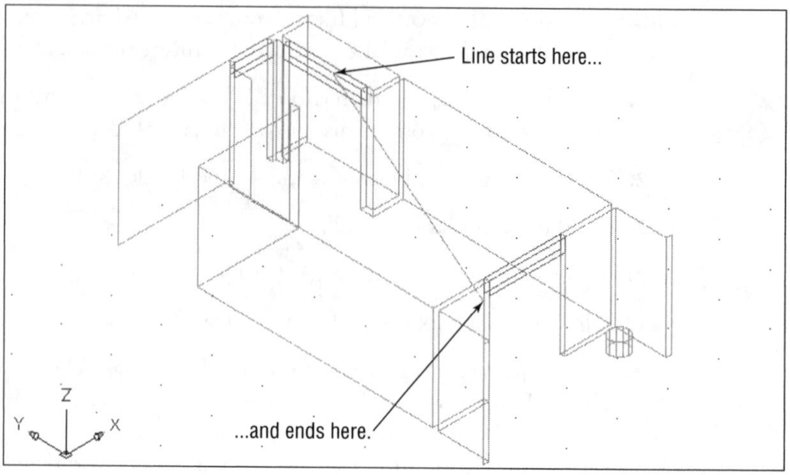

FIGURE 16.19
A 3D view of the stair rail

3. At the `Specify base point or displacement, or [Multiple]:` prompt, pick any point on the screen.

4. At the prompt

   `Specify second point of displacement or <use first point as displacement>:`

   enter **.xy**↵, and then enter **@**↵. This tells AutoCAD that your second point will maintain the X coordinate and Y coordinate of the first point.

5. At the `(need Z)` prompt, enter **3'6"**↵ to place the copy 3'-6" on the z-axis. Metric users should enter **106**↵ to place the copy 106 cm on the z-axis. A copy of the 3D line appears 3'-6" (106 cm) above the original.

In step 4 you specified that the second point use the same X coordinate and Y coordinate of the base point, so you only needed to enter the *z* value for the second point. In the earlier exercise, you used a relative coordinate to move door headers to a position 7' higher than their original location. You could have used the same method here to copy the line vertically, but in this exercise you got a chance to see how the point filter works.

Creating Irregular 3D Surfaces

Sometimes you will want to draw a solid surface so that when you remove hidden lines, objects will appear as surfaces rather than as wireframes. If you were to continue drawing the side of the stair rail using lines, the side of the stair rail would appear transparent. So the next step is to fill in the side using 3D Faces.

TIP *It generally makes life easier to first draw a wireframe of your object using lines and then use their endpoints to fill in the surfaces.*

ACAD only

Loading the Surfaces Toolbar

The 3dface command and AutoCAD's 3D shapes are located in the Surfaces toolbar. Right-click any toolbar, and then choose Surfaces from the shortcut menu.

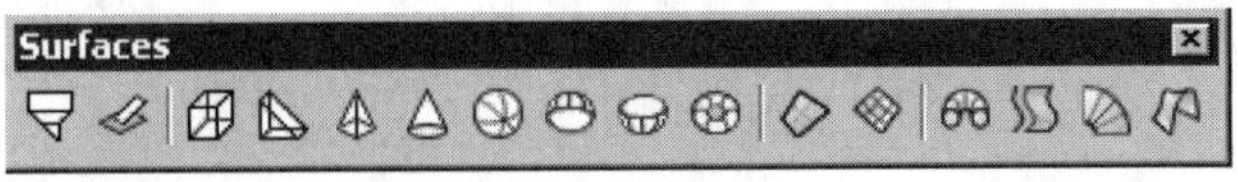

WARNING *LT users do not have the 3D surface modeling tools described here. In many instances, however, you can use Regions in place of 3D Faces. See Chapter 19 for more on Regions.*

ACAD only

Adding a 3D Face

Now that you've opened the Surfaces toolbar, you can begin to draw 3D Faces.

1. Zoom in to the two lines you just created, so you have a view similar to Figure 16.20.

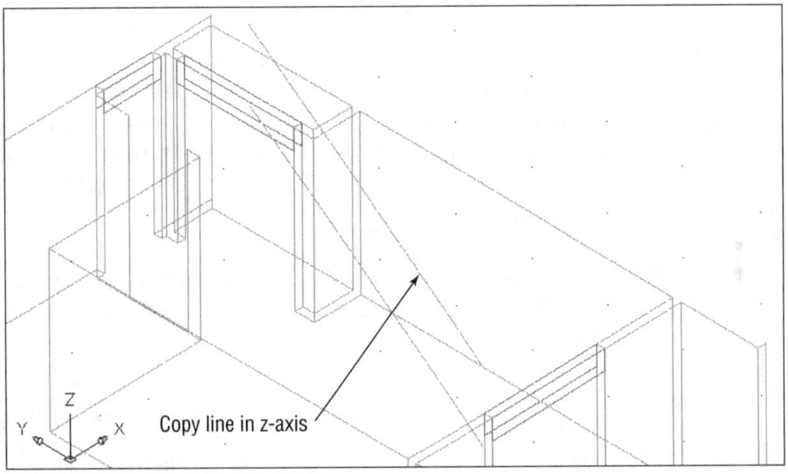

FIGURE 16.20
Zooming in to the stair rail lines

2. Click the 3D Face button on the Surfaces toolbar, or type **3f↵**. You can also choose Draw ➢ Surfaces ➢ 3D Face.
3. At the `Specify first point or [Invisible]:` prompt, use the Osnap overrides to pick the first of the four endpoints of the 3D lines you drew. Be sure the Ortho mode is off.

TIP *The Running Osnap mode can help you select endpoints quickly in this exercise. See Chapter 3 if you need help remembering how to set up the Running Osnap mode.*

4. As you continue to pick the endpoints, you are prompted for the second, third, and fourth points.

With the 3DFace command, you pick four points in a circular fashion, as shown in Figure 16.21. Once you've drawn one 3D Face, you can continue to add more by selecting more points.

FIGURE 16.21

The 3D Face

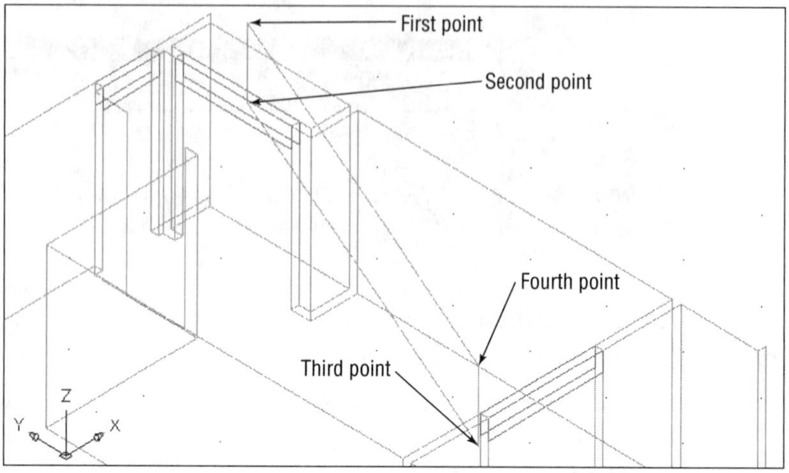

5. When the `Specify third point or [Invisible] <exit>:` prompt appears again, press ↵ to end the 3DFace command. A 3D Face appears between the two 3D lines. It is difficult to tell if they are actually there until you use the Hide command, but you should see vertical lines connecting the endpoints of the 3D lines. These vertical lines are the edges of the 3D Face (see Figure 16.21).

TIP *When the* `Specify third point or [Invisible] <exit>:` *prompt reappears, you can draw more 3D Faces if you like. The next 3D Face will use the last two points selected as the first two of its four corners—hence, the prompt for a third point.*

6. Copy the 3D Face you just drew 5" horizontally in the 0-angle direction.
7. Use the 3DFace command to put a surface on the top and front side of the rail, as demonstrated in the top and middle images in Figure 16.22.
8. Use the Intersection Osnap override to snap to the corners of the 3D Faces.
9. Use the Hide command to get a view that looks like the bottom image in Figure 16.22.
10. Copy the three 3D Faces you just created 3' horizontally in the 0-angle direction.
11. Now you can save the `Unitloft.dwg` file.

FIGURE 16.22

The top and front faces of the stair rail, and the stair rail with the hidden lines removed

Start the 3Dface command. Then using the Endpoint Osnap override, pick the four points shown here.

Continue to pick two more endpoints as shown here. When you have picked the last point, press ↵ to exit the 3Dface command.

Issue the Hide command to see the results of adding the 3D faces.

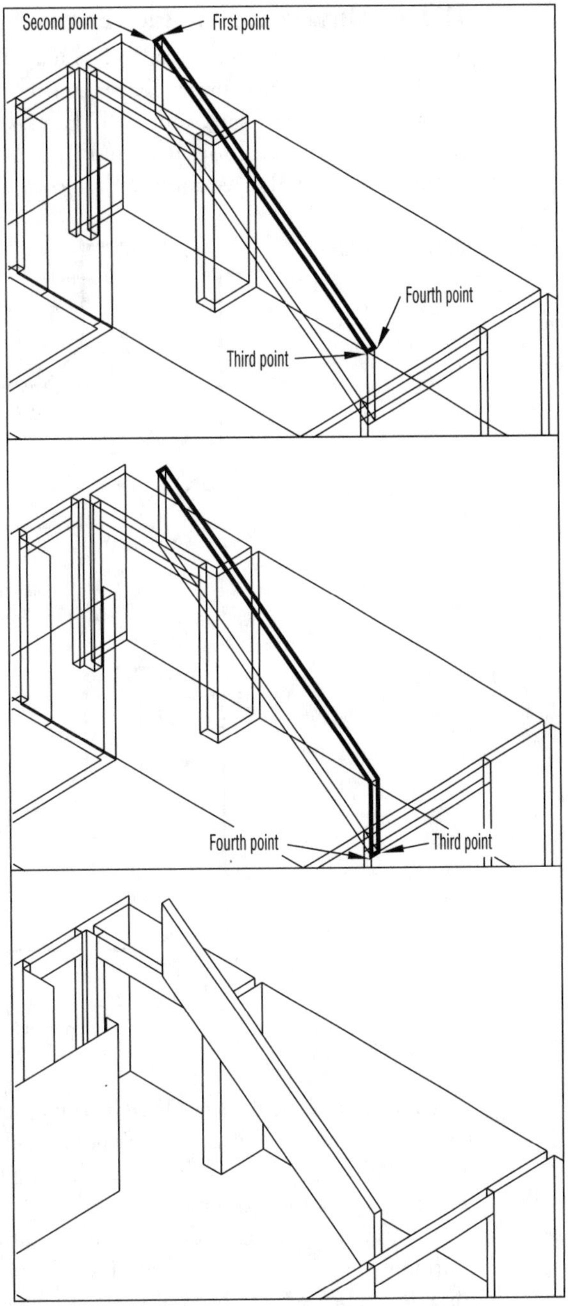

Hiding Unwanted Surface Edges

When using the 3DFace command, you are limited to drawing surfaces with four sides. You can, however, create more complex shapes by simply joining several 3D Faces. Figure 16.23 shows an odd shape constructed of three joined 3D Faces. Unfortunately, you are left with extra lines that cross the surface as shown in the top image in Figure 16.23; but you can hide those lines by using the Invisible option under the 3DFace command, in conjunction with the Splframe variable.

FIGURE 16.23

Hiding the joined edge of multiple 3D Faces

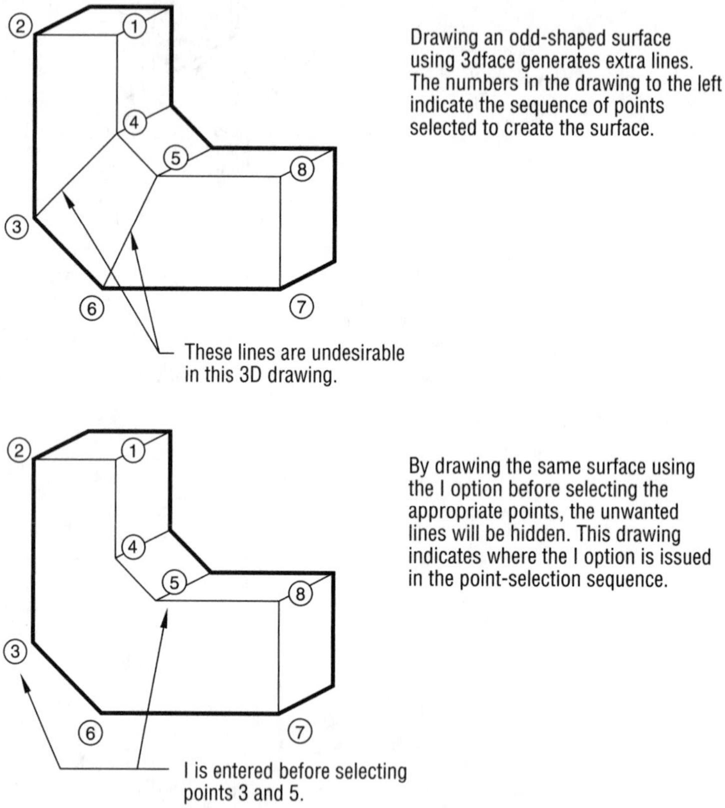

1
2
3
4
5
6
7
8
Drawing an odd-shaped surface using 3dface generates extra lines. The numbers in the drawing to the left indicate the sequence of points selected to create the surface.
These lines are undesirable in this 3D drawing.
1
2
3
4
5
6
7
8
By drawing the same surface using the I option before selecting the appropriate points, the unwanted lines will be hidden. This drawing indicates where the I option is issued in the point-selection sequence.
I is entered before selecting points 3 and 5.

To make an edge of a 3D Face invisible, start the 3DFace command as usual. While selecting points, just before you pick the first point of the edge to be hidden, enter **I**↵ as shown in the bottom image in Figure 16.23. When you are drawing two 3D Faces sequentially, only one edge needs to be invisible to hide their joining edge.

You can make invisible edges visible for editing by setting the Splframe system variable to 1. Setting Splframe to 0 causes AutoCAD to hide the invisible edges. Bear in mind that the Splframe system variable can be useful in both 3D and 2D drawings.

TIP *The Edge option on the Surfaces toolbar lets you change an existing visible 3D Face edge to an invisible one. Click the Edge button and then select the 3D Face edge to be hidden.*

Using Predefined 3D Surface Shapes

You may have noticed that the Surfaces toolbar offers several 3D surface objects, such as cones, spheres, and torus (donut-shaped). All are made up of 3D Faces. To use them, click the appropriate button on the Surfaces toolbar. When you select an object, AutoCAD prompts you for the points and dimensions that define that 3D object; then AutoCAD draws the object. This provides quick access to shapes that would otherwise take substantial time to create.

Things to Watch Out for When Editing 3D Objects

You have seen how you can use the Copy command on 3D lines and 3D Faces. You can also use the Move and Stretch commands on 3D lines, 3D Faces, and 3D shapes to modify their Z coordinate values—but you have to be careful with these commands when editing in 3D. Here are a few tips to keep in mind:

- The Scale command will scale an object's Z coordinate value, as well as the standard X coordinate and Y coordinate. Suppose you have an object with an elevation of 2 units. If you use the Scale command to enlarge that object by a factor of 4, the object will have a new elevation of 2 units times 4, or 8 units. If, on the other hand, that object has an elevation of 0, its elevation will not change, because 0 times 4 is still 0.
- You can also use Array, Mirror, and Rotate (on the Modify toolbar) on 3D lines, 3D Faces, and 3D shapes, but these commands won't affect their Z coordinate values. Z coordinates can be specified for base and insertion points, so take care when using these commands with 3D models.
- Using the Move, Stretch, and Copy commands (on the Modify toolbar) with object snaps can produce some unpredictable and unwanted results. As a rule, it is best to use point filters when selecting points with Osnap overrides. For example, to move an object from the endpoint of one object to the endpoint of another on the same Z coordinate, invoke the .XY point filter at the `Specify base Point…` and `Specify second Point…` prompts before issuing the endpoint override. Proceed to pick the endpoint of the object you want; then enter the Z coordinate, or just pick any point to use the current default Z coordinate.
- When you create a block, the block will use the UCS that is active at the time the block is created to determine its own local coordinate system. When that block is later inserted, it will orient its own coordinate system with the current UCS. (The UCS is discussed in more detail in Chapter 17.)

Turning a 3D View into a 2D AutoCAD Drawing

Many architectural firms use AutoCAD 3D models to study their designs. Once a specific part of a design is modeled and approved, they convert the model into 2D elevations, ready to plug in to their elevation drawing.

If you need to convert your 3D models into 2D line drawings, configure the AutoCAD Plotter for an ADI Plotter. Set it up to plot a .dxb file. Your plots then generate .dxb files, which you can import by choosing Insert ➢ Drawing Exchange Binary. This opens the Select DXB File dialog box from which you can select the appropriate .dxb file.

Creating and Using Slides

Three-dimensional graphics are often handy for presentations, and 3D AutoCAD images are frequently used for that purpose, as well as for producing drafted 2D drawings. You might want to show off some of your 3D work directly from the computer screen. However, if your drawings are complicated, your audience might get impatient waiting for the hidden lines to be removed. Fortunately, AutoCAD provides two commands that let you save a view from your screen in a form that will display quickly.

The Mslide and Vslide commands both save a view as a file on disk. Such a view is called a *slide*. You can display a slide any time you are in the AutoCAD drawing editor. Slides display at redraw speed, no matter how complex they are. This means you can save a slide of a hidden-line view of your 3D drawing and recall that view quickly at any time.

Slides can also be used for reference during editing sessions, instead of panning, zooming, or viewing. A slide cannot be edited, however; nor will it be updated when you edit the drawing.

Creating Slides

In the following exercise, you will make a few slides of the `Unit` file.

1. Open the `Unit` file and click the Hide button on the Render toolbar to get a hidden-line view of the unit.
2. Type **Mslide**↵ at the command prompt.
3. In the File dialog box, click Save to accept the default filename, `Unit.sld`. (The default slide name is the same name as the current drawing, with the extension .sld.) The actual drawing file is not affected.
4. Zoom in to the bathroom, and use Mslide to save another view called `Unitbath`, this time without the hidden lines removed.
5. In the File dialog box, highlight the File input box at the bottom of the dialog box, enter **Unitbath**↵, and click OK.

Viewing Slides

Now that you've saved two views, let's see how to view them.

1. Zoom back to the previous view and then type **Vslide**↵.
2. In the File dialog box, locate and select `Unitbath.dwg` and click Open to open the slide of the bathroom. You can move the cursor around the view and start commands in the normal way, but you cannot edit or obtain information from this slide.
3. Start Vslide again.
4. This time, click Open in the dialog box to accept the default slide filename, `Unit`. The 3D view of the unit appears with its hidden lines removed. Because slides display at redraw speed, you don't have to wait to view the unit without its hidden lines.

TIP *Any command that performs a redraw also returns you to the current drawing.*

5. Choose View ➢ Redraw to return to the drawing being edited.
6. Open the `Plan` file and use the Vslide command to view the Unitbath slide again. As you can see, you can call up the slide from any file, not just the one you were in when you created the slide.
7. Now create a slide of the Plan file and call it `Plan1`.

Next, you'll get to see how you might automate a slide presentation using the slides you just created.

Automating a Slide Presentation

As mentioned in Chapter 7, you can use Script (choose Tools ➢ Run Script) to run a sequence of commands automatically. Let's create a script file to automatically show the slides you made in the last exercise.

A script file is really nothing more than a list of "canned" AutoCAD commands and responses. In this example, you'll add the Delay command, whose sole function is to pause a script for a specific length of time.

1. Use a text editor such as Windows Notepad to create a file called `Show.scr`, and enter the following lines into this file, pressing ↵ at the end of each line:

```
vslide
unit
delay 3000
vslide
unitbath
delay 3000
vslide
Plan1
```

These lines are a sequence of predetermined instructions to AutoCAD that can be played back later. Save this file in the same folder as your slide files. When you play this script file, each line is entered at the AutoCAD command prompt, just as you would enter it through the keyboard. Notice that the Vslide command is executed before each slide, which is then followed by the line `delay 3000`, which tells AutoCAD to pause roughly 3000 milliseconds after each Vslide command is issued (you can substitute another value if you like). If you don't specify a delay, the next slide displays as soon as the previous slide is completed.

You can also have the slides repeat continuously by adding the Rscript command at the very end of the `Show.scr` file. You might want to do this in a presentation intended for casual viewing, such as an exhibit in a display area with people passing through. To stop a repeating script, press the Backspace key.

Now try playing the script.

2. Return to AutoCAD, and then choose Tools ➢ Run Script, or enter **Script↵**.
3. In the Select Script File dialog box, highlight and pick the file you just created (`Show.scr`) from the file list, and then click OK.

The slides you saved will appear on the screen in the sequence in which you entered them in the `Show.scr` file.

Creating a Slide Library

You can group slide files together into one file to help keep your slides organized—for example, by project or by drawing type. Slide libraries also save disk space, since they often require less space than the total consumed by the individual slide files.

Slide files are also used to create custom dialog boxes that show sample views of objects. An example of such a dialog box is the 3D Objects dialog box, which is displayed when you choose Draw ➢ Surfaces ➢ 3D Surfaces.

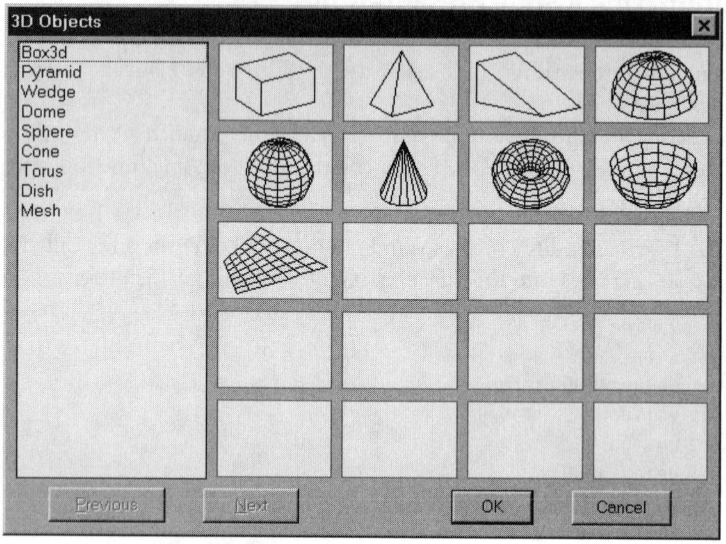

The tool you use to create a slide library is the `Slidelib.exe` utility that comes with AutoCAD. This utility can be found in the AutoCAD 2004 folder. To create a slide library, follow these steps:

1. In a word processor, make a list of the slides you want to include in the library. For the slides you created earlier, this list would look like the following:

   ```
   unit
   unitbath
   plan1
   ```

   Notice that you do not have to include the .sld extension in the filenames in your list.

2. Save this list as a plain text file, with an appropriate name. For this example, call it `Slide1.lst`. Be sure it is saved in the same folder as your slide files.

3. Locate the `Slidelib.exe` program; you should find it in the `AutoCAD 2004` folder. Be sure your `Slidelib.exe` file is in the same folder as your slide list file and slide files.

4. Open a Windows command prompt window and go to your `AutoCAD 2004` folder. You can open a Windows command prompt by selecting Start ➢ All Programs ➢ Accessories ➢ Command Prompt.

5. At the Windows command prompt, enter **slidelib Myslides < slide1.lst↵** to create a file named `Myslides.slb`. The library name can be any legal DOS filename, but don't use filenames of more than eight characters, such as those allowed by Windows 95 and later versions. Also do not include the filename extension; the Slidelib utility program automatically adds the file extension .slb. For example, if you use Plans as the library name, a slide library file called `Plans.slb` is created.

ACAD only

WARNING *LT users do not have access to Autolisp so the method for viewing slide libraries described here will not work. You must instead use a script file.*

Now let's test your slide library. To view a slide from a slide library, you'll need to employ some Autolisp commmands. But don't worry, you just need to enter the Vslide command in a certain way at the command prompt.

1. At the AutoCAD command prompt, enter `(command "vslide")`↵. This is just a way of issuing the Vslide command through Autolisp. Enter it just as it is shown here complete with parentheses and quotation marks.
2. At the Enter Name of Slide File to View <C:\Program Files\AutoCAD2004\Support\Acad.slb >: prompt, enter `Myslides(plan1)`↵. (You may see a different filename and path listed between the angle brackets of the prompt.) Notice that the slide library name is specified followed by the individual slide name in parentheses. The slide appears in the drawing area.

The reason you issued the Vslide command through Autolisp is because it forces the Vslide command into a text-only mode. Otherwise you would see the Vslide dialog box which does not allow you to specify a slide from a slide library.

WARNING *If you placed the slide library file in a folder other than the current one, be sure to enter the folder name before the slide library name in step 2.*

To use slide libraries from a script, you use the slide library and slide name following the Vslide command, as in the following example:

```
vslide
myslides(unit)
delay 3000
vlside
myslides(unitbath)
delay 3000
vslide
myslides(plan1)
delay 3000
rscript
```

You've seen how you can save and display 3D views quickly and how you can automate a presentation of slides using scripts. With these tools, you can create an impressive, fast-paced presentation.

If You Want to Experiment...

Architects traditionally use 3D models made from cardboard or *chipboard* to help others visualize their ideas. And if you've ever taken a class in architectural design, chances are you've had to make such a model yourself. 3D modeling on a computer is faster and a lot more fun than creating a physical chipboard model, and in some cases it can show you things that a physical model cannot.

The following exercise is really just for fun. It shows you how to do a limited form of animation, using View ➢ 3D Viewpoint, the Mslide command, and scripts.

1. Open the Unit plan.
2. Do a hidden-line removal; then use Mslide to create a slide called V1.
3. Click and drag the Inquiry button on the Object Properties toolbar, and then select Locate Point on the flyout. Pick a point in the center of the floor plan. This marks the view center for the next step.
4. Enter **Vpoint↵** R↵ at the command prompt.
5. At the `Enter angle at XY plane:` prompt, enter **235↵**; at the next prompt, press ↵.
6. Do another hidden-line removal, and use Mslide again to create a slide called **V2**.
7. Repeat steps 4 through 6, but this time increase by 10 the angle value you entered in step 5 (to **245**). In step 6, increase the slide name by 1 (to **V3**).
8. Keep repeating steps 4 through 6, increasing the angle value by 10 each time and increasing the slide filename by 1. Repeat these steps at least five more times.
9. Use a text editor to create a script file called `Animate.scr`, containing the following lines, pressing ↵ at the end of each line:

```
Vslide v1
Vslide v2
Vslide v3
Vslide v4
Vslide v5
Vslide v6
Vslide v7
Vslide v8
Rscript
```

10. Return to AutoCAD. At the command prompt, enter **Script↵** and click Animate in the File dialog box. Then click OK and watch the show.
11. Press the Esc key or Backspace to end the show.

You might also want to try creating an animation that moves you completely around the Unit plan.

Here's another suggestion for experimenting: To practice drawing in 3D, turn the kitchen of your 3D Unit drawing into a 3D object. Make the cooking top 30" high and add some cabinet doors.

Have fun!

Chapter 17

Using Advanced 3D Features

AutoCAD's extended set of tools for working with 3D drawings lets you create 3D objects with few limitations on shape and orientation. This chapter focuses on the use of these tools, which help you easily generate 3D forms and view them in both the Perspective and Orthogonal modes. Topics include the following:

- Mastering the User Coordinate System
- Creating Complex 3D Surfaces
- Other Surface-Drawing Tools
- Editing a Mesh
- Moving Objects in 3D Space
- Viewing Your Model in Perspective
- If You Want to Experiment…

Mastering the User Coordinate System

The User Coordinate System (UCS) allows you to define a custom coordinate system in 2D and 3D space. In fact, you've been using a default UCS, called the *World Coordinate System (WCS)*, all along. By now you are familiar with the L-shaped icon in the lower-left corner of the AutoCAD screen, containing a small square and the letters X and Y. The square indicates that you are currently in the WCS; the X and Y indicate the positive directions of the x- and y-axes. WCS is a global system of reference from which you can define other User Coordinate Systems.

It may help to think of these AutoCAD User Coordinate Systems as different drawing surfaces, or two-dimensional planes. You can have several User Coordinate Systems at any given time. By setting up these different UCSs, you can draw as you would in the WCS in 2D, yet draw a 3D image. Suppose you want to draw a house in 3D with doors and windows on each of its sides. You can set up a UCS for each of the sides; then you can move from UCS to UCS to add your doors and windows (see Figure 17.1). Within each UCS, you draw your doors and windows as you would in a typical 2D drawing. You can even insert elevation views of doors and windows that you created in other drawings.

FIGURE 17.1

Different User Coordinate Systems in a 3D drawing

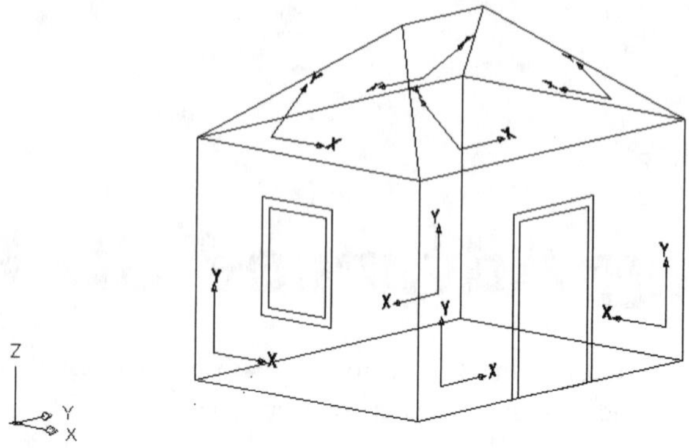

In this chapter you will be experimenting with a number of different views and UCSs. All the commands you will use are available both at the command line and via the menu bar. In addition, you can access a number of the UCS commands from the UCS toolbar.

Defining a UCS

In the first set of exercises, you will draw a chair that you can later add to your 3D Unit drawing. In drawing this chair, you will be exposed to the use of the UCS, as well as to some of the other 3D capabilities available in AutoCAD.

Begin the chair by drawing the seat and seat back.

1. Start AutoCAD and create a new file called `Barcelon`.
2. Set up your drawing as an architectural drawing with a scale of 1"=1'-0" on an 8 1/2" × 11" sheet. You will want to set the upper-right corner of the limits to 132 × 102. If you're a metric user, you'll be drawing the chair at a scale of 1:10 on an A4 sheet. Your work area should be 297 × 210, which is the equivalent of a 297 cm by 210 cm area.

TIP *If you are a metric user and you prefer to work in millimeters, you can set the upper-right corner of the limits to 2970,2100. Then, when the book specifies a length or coordinate, multiply the specified value by 10. For example, 50 cm becomes 500 mm. Coordinate 50,50 becomes 500,500. Your scale factor would also change to 100.*

3. Choose View ➢ Zoom ➢ All or type Z↵ A↵.
4. To draw the seat of the chair, click the Rectangle tool on the Draw toolbar. Draw a rectangle measuring 20" in the x-axis and 30" in the y-axis. Position the rectangle so the lower-left corner is at the coordinate 2'-0",2'-0" (see the top image in Figure 17.2). Metric users should draw a rectangle that is 50 cm by 76 cm with its lower-left corner at coordinate 50,50.

FIGURE 17.2

The chair seat (top) and back (bottom) in the Plan and Isometric views

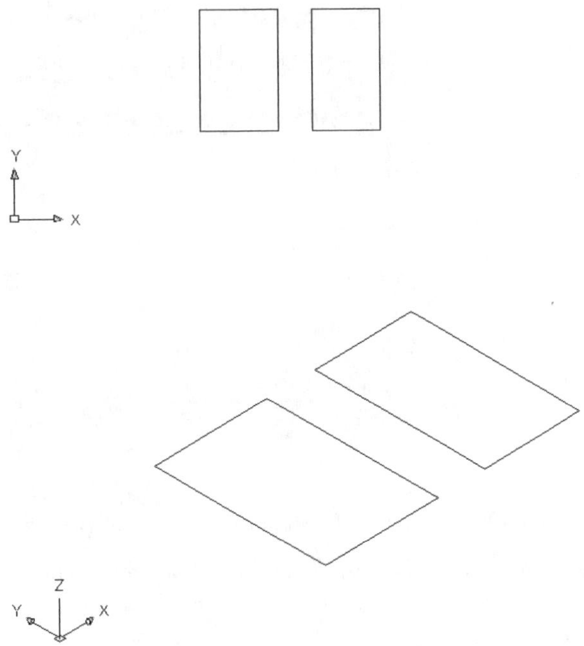

5. To draw the back of the chair, draw another rectangle 17" in the x-axis and 30" in the y-axis, just to the right of the previous rectangle (see the top image in Figure 17.2). Metric users should make this rectangle 43 cm by 76 cm.
6. Choose View ➢ 3D Views ➢ SW Isometric. This gives you a 3D view from the lower-left of the rectangles, as shown in the bottom image in Figure 17.2.
7. Select the two rectangles, and then click the Properties tool on the Standard toolbar.
8. In the Properties palette, enter **3** in the Thickness setting and click OK. This gives the seat and back a thickness of 3". Metric users should make the thickness 7.6 cm.
9. Close the Properties palette.
10. Zoom out a bit and give yourself some room to work.

Notice that the UCS icon appears in the same plane as the current coordinate system. The icon will help you keep track of which coordinate system you are in. Now you can see the chair components as 3D objects.

Next, you will define a UCS that is aligned with one side of the seat.

1. Right-click any toolbar, and choose UCS from the shortcut menu to open the UCS toolbar.

2. Click the Display UCS Dialog tool in the UCS toolbar to open the UCS dialog box. You may also choose Tools ➢ Named UCS from the toolbar.

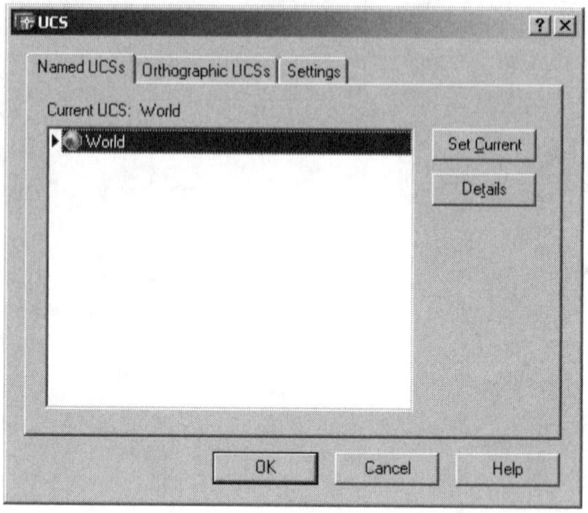

3. Select the Orthographic UCSs tab to view a set of predefined UCSs.
4. Select Front in the list box. Figure 17.3 shows the orientation of the Front UCS.

FIGURE 17.3

The six predefined UCS orientations

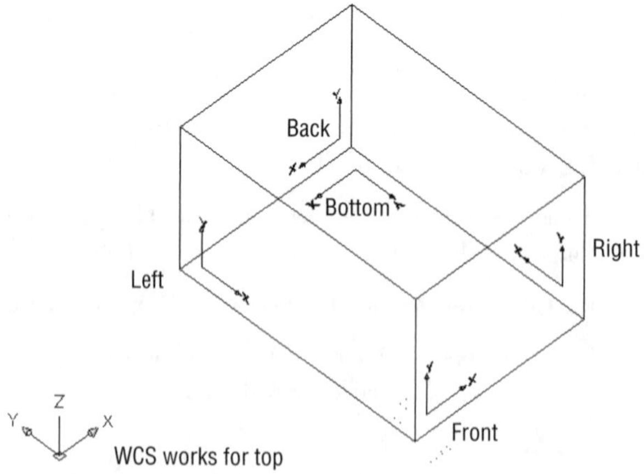

5. Click the Set Current button to make the Front UCS current.
6. Click OK to close the dialog box.

The Orthographic UCSs tab offers a set of predefined UCSs for each of the six standard orthographic projection planes. Figure 17.3 shows these UCSs in relation to the World Coordinate System. You can also access these orthographic UCSs from the Tools ➢ Orthographic UCS cascading menu or from the UCS dialog box.

Since a good part of 3D work involves drawing in these orthographic planes, AutoCAD supplies these ready-made UCS orientations for quick access. But you aren't limited to these six orientations by any means. If you're familiar with mechanical drafting, you'll see that the orthographic UCSs correspond to the typical orthographic projection used in mechanical drafting. If you're an architect, the Front, Left, Back, and Right UCSs correspond to the south, west, north, and east elevations of a building. Before you continue building the chair model, you'll want to move the UCS to the surface on which you will be working. Right now, the UCS has its origin located in the same place as the WCS origin. You can move a UCS so that its origin is anywhere in the drawing where it's needed.

1. Click the Origin UCS tool in the UCS toolbar. You can also choose Tools ➢ New UCS ➢ Origin from the menubar.
2. Use the Endpoint Osnap and click the bottom-front corner of the chair seat, as shown in Figure 17.4. The UCS icon moves to indicate its new origin's location.

FIGURE 17.4
Setting up a UCS

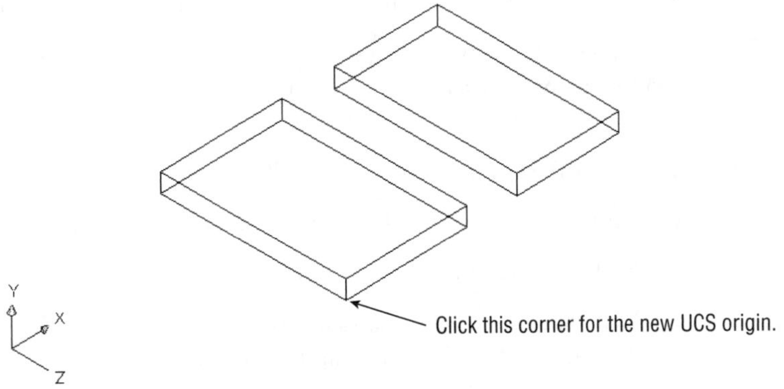
Y
X
Z
Click this corner for the new UCS origin.

The operation you just performed created a new UCS based on the Front UCS you selected from the UCS dialog box. Now as you move your cursor, you'll see that the origin of the UCS icon corresponds to a 0,0 coordinate. Although you've got a new UCS, the World Coordinate System still exists, and you can always return to it when you need to.

Saving a UCS

Once you've gone through the work of creating a UCS, you might want to save it, especially if you think you'll want to come back to it later. Here's how to save a UCS.

1. Click the Display UCS Dialog tool on the UCS toolbar to open the UCS dialog box. You can also choose Tools ➢ Named UCS.

2. Make sure the Named UCS tab is selected, and then highlight the Unnamed option in the Current UCS list box.
3. Right-click Unnamed, and then choose Rename from the shortcut menu. The item changes to allow editing.
4. Type **3DSW**↵ for the name of your new UCS.
5. Click OK to exit the dialog box.

Your UCS is now saved under the name of 3DSW. You'll be able to recall it from the UCS dialog box or by using other methods that you'll learn about later in this chapter.

Working in a UCS

Next, you will want to arrange the seat and back and draw the legs of the chair. Your UCS is oriented so that you can easily adjust the orientation of the chair components. As you work through the next exercise, notice that while you are manipulating 3D objects, you are really using the same tools you've used to edit 2D objects.

1. Click the seat back to expose its grips.
2. Click the bottom grip, as shown in the first image in Figure 17.5.
3. Right-click the mouse to open the Grip Edit shortcut menu.
4. Choose Rotate from the menu. Notice how the seat back now rotates with the movement of the cursor. Take a moment to play with this rotation, as it may take a while to grow accustomed to it. Since this is an Isometric view, you can get an optical illusion effect.
5. Type **80**↵ to rotate the seat back 80°. Your view will look like the second image in Figure 17.5.
6. Click the bottom grip shown in the second image in Figure 17.5.
7. Right-click the mouse again and choose Move.
8. Using the Endpoint Osnap, click the top corner of the chair seat, as shown in the second image in Figure 17.5, to join the chair back to the seat.
9. Click both the chair seat and back; then click the bottom-corner grip of the seat, as shown in the third image in Figure 17.5.
10. Right-click the mouse, and then choose Rotate from the Grip Edit shortcut menu.
11. Enter **–10**↵ to rotate both the seat and back a minus 10 degrees. Press the Esc key twice to clear the grips. Your chair will look like Figure 17.6.

FIGURE 17.5

Moving the components of the chair into place

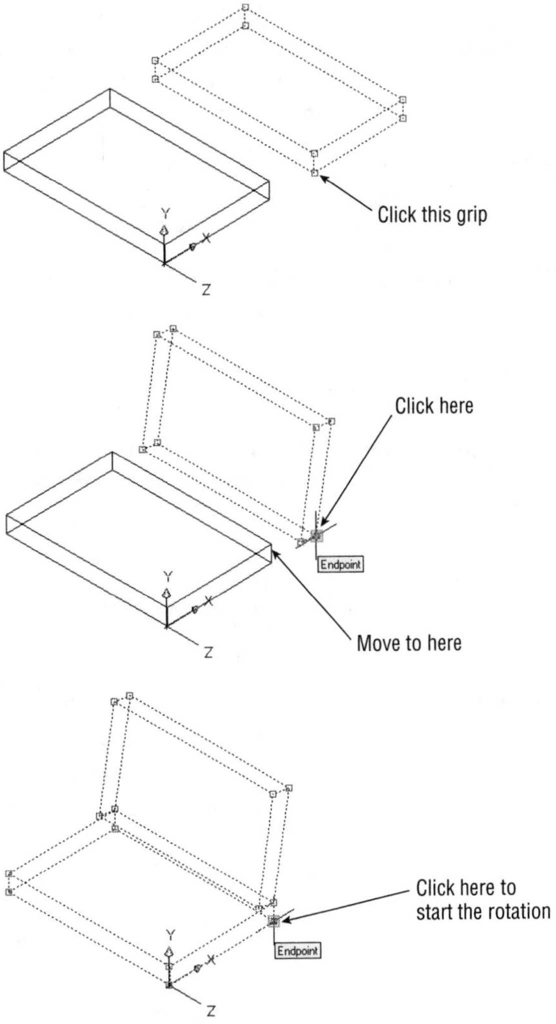

FIGURE 17.6

The chair after rotating and moving the components into place

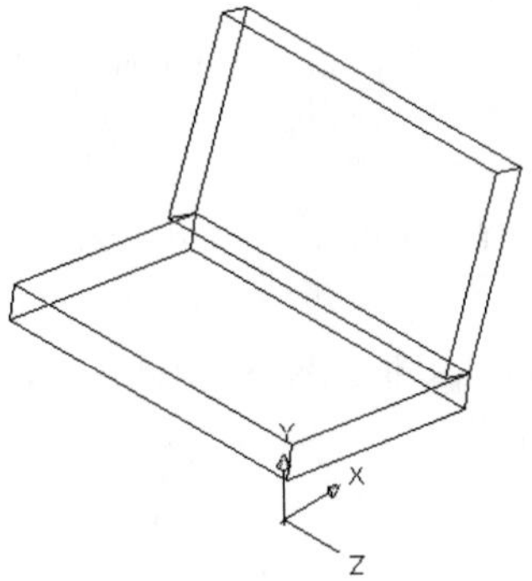

The new UCS orientation enabled you to use the grips to adjust the chair seat and back. All the grip rotation in the previous exercise was confined to the plane of the new UCS. Mirroring and scaling will also occur in relation to the current UCS.

Now, to finish the chair seat and back, add 3D Faces to their top and bottom surfaces.

ACAD only

1. To help you visualize what's going on as you add the 3D Faces, turn on the Hidden Shade mode by choosing View ➢ Shade ➢ Hidden. Or, if you have the Shade toolbar open, you can click the Hidden tool. LT users enter **Shademode↵ H↵**.

TIP *LT does not have the 3D Face tool. If you are using LT, skip to the end of the exercise to find out how you can create the additional surfaces to the chair seat and back.*

2. Click the 3D Face button on the Surfaces toolbar or choose Draw ➢ Surfaces ➢ 3D Face to draw surfaces over the top sides of the chair seat and back. For the chair seat, start the 3D Face in the leftmost corner and work in a counterclockwise fashion, as shown in Figure 17.7. For the chair back, you can start at any corner as long as you select points sequentially around the edge.

FIGURE 17.7

The 3D view of your drawing so far, showing where to pick points for the 3D Faces

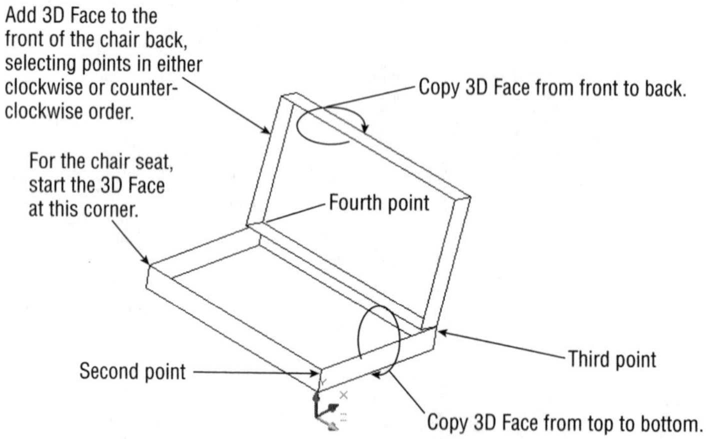
Add 3D Face to the front of the chair back, selecting points in either clockwise or counter-clockwise order.
Copy 3D Face from front to back.
For the chair seat, start the 3D Face at this corner.
Fourth point
Second point
Third point
Copy 3D Face from top to bottom.

TIP *To display the Surfaces toolbar, right-click any toolbar and choose Surfaces from the Toolbars dialog box. If you need help with the 3dface command, see Chapter 16.*

3. Copy the 3D Faces to the bottom of the chair seat and to the reverse of the chair back, as shown in Figure 17.7.

4. When you've finished adding the 3D Faces, turn off the Hidden Shade mode. Choose View ➢ Shade ➢ 2D Wireframe.

Normally, when you're picking points for 3D Faces, it doesn't matter where you start. But for the purpose of this tutorial, you selected points for the seat's 3D Face starting at the leftmost corner and working in a counterclockwise fashion. The way you create the chair seat will influence the action of some UCS command options, which you'll use later in this chapter.

Since LT users do not have the 3D Face available, you'll need to employ a slightly different method for adding the surfaces.

1. Type **UCS↵ ob↵**, then click the rectangle representing the seat.
2. Select the Rectangle tool from the Draw toolbar and using endpoint osnaps place a rectangle on the top surface of the seat. The rectangle may blend in with the seat so you won't see it right away.
3. Click the Region tool in the Draw toolbar and select the rectangle you just drew. Press ↵ to complete your selection.
4. Repeat the steps, only this time in step 1, click the rectangle representing the back of the seat.
5. To go back to a wireframe view, enter **Shademode↵** ↵.

Now you need to return to the UCS you created earlier in order to get back in sync with the rest of the tutorial.

1. Choose Tools ➢ Named UCS.
2. Select **3DSW** from the list box, then click Set Current.
3. Click OK to exit the dialog box.

You used the command line version of the UCS commands Object option. You'll learn more about this option later in this chapter. You also used the Region tool, which you'll learn more about in Chapter 19. Basically, the Region tool converts a closed polyline into a special kind of flat surface.

Controlling the UCS Icon

If the UCS icon is not behaving as described in the exercises of this chapter, chances are that its settings have been altered. You can control the behavior of the UCS icon through the UCS dialog box. To open the UCS dialog box, choose Tools ➢ Named UCS. You can also click the Display UCS Dialog tool on the UCS II or UCS toolbar. Once you've opened the dialog box, click the Settings tab.

The settings in the UCS Icon Settings group affect the way the UCS icon behaves. Normally, the On and Display At UCS Origin Point check boxes are checked. If On is not checked, you won't see the UCS icon at all. If the Display At UCS Origin Point box is not checked, the UCS icon will remain in the lower-left corner of the drawing window, no matter where its origin is placed in the drawing.

If you have multiple viewports set up in a drawing, you can set these two options independently for each viewport. The third option, Apply To All Active Viewports, forces the first two settings to apply in all viewports.

Continued on next page

CONTROLLING THE UCS ICON *(continued)*

Two more options appear in the UCS settings group. If you have multiple viewports open, the Save UCS With Viewport option allows AutoCAD to maintain a separate UCS for each viewport. The Update View To Plan When UCS Is Changed option forces the display to show a plan view of the current UCS. This means that if you change a UCS orientation, AutoCAD will automatically show a plan view of the new UCS orientation. This option also forces viewport views to show the extents of plan views; so if you find that your views are automatically zooming to extents when you don't want them to, turn this setting off.

Another tool for controlling the UCS icon is the UCS Icon dialog box. To open it, enter **Ucsicon**↵ P↵.

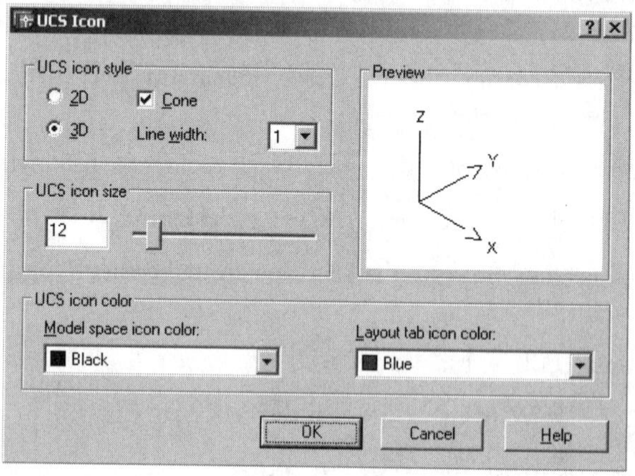

With this dialog box, you can fine-tune the appearance of the UCS icon, including size and color. The 2D radio button in the UCS Icon Style group changes the UCS icon to the old style UCS icon used in earlier versions of AutoCAD.

Using Viewports to Aid in 3D Drawing

In Chapters 7 and 13, you were introduced to AutoCAD's floating viewports in Paper Space. In this section, you will use *tiled* viewports to see your 3D model from several sides at the same time. This is helpful in both creating and editing 3D drawings because it allows you to refer to different portions of the drawing without having to change views. Tiled viewports are created directly in Model Space.

1. Choose View ➢ Viewports ➢ Named Viewports to open the Viewports dialog box.

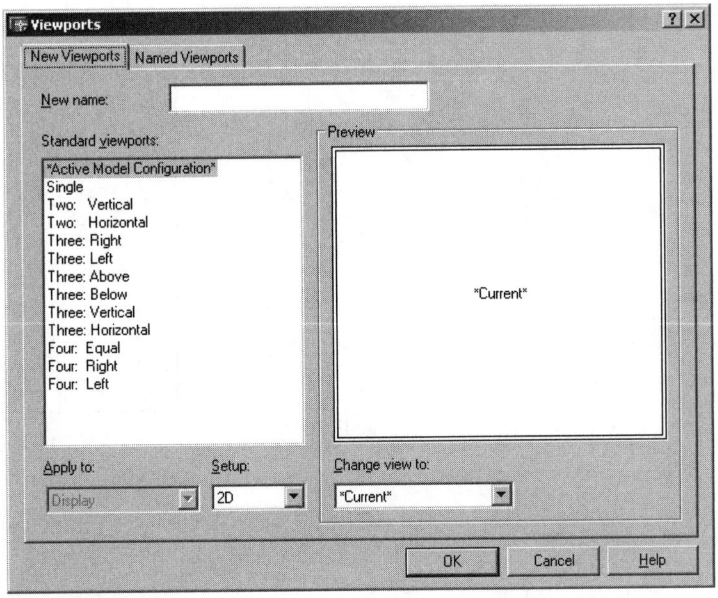

2. Make sure the New Viewports tab is selected, and then select Three: Right from the Standard Viewports list on the left. The window on the right changes to display a sample of the viewport configuration. It shows three rectangles, which represent the viewports, arranged with two on the left and one larger one to the right. Notice that each rectangle is labeled as Current. This tells you that the current view will be placed in each viewport.

3. Open the Setup drop-down list at the bottom of the dialog box and select 3D. Now notice that the labels in the viewport sample change to indicate Top, Front, and SE Isometric. This is close to the arrangement that you'll want, but you need to make one more adjustment. The viewport to the right, SE Isometric, shows the back side of the chair. You want an SW Isometric view in this window.

4. Click the SE Isometric viewport sample. Notice that the sample viewport border thickens to indicate that it is selected.

5. Open the Change View To drop-down list just below the sample viewports and select SW Isometric. The label in the selected viewport changes to let you know that the view will now contain the SW Isometric view. Notice that the Change View To list contains the standard four isometric views and the six orthogonal views. By clicking a sample viewport and selecting an option from the Change View To drop-down list, you can arrange your viewport views in nearly any way you want.

6. To keep this viewport arrangement, enter **My Viewport Setup** in the New Name input box.

7. Now click OK. Your display changes to show three viewports arranged as they were indicated in the Viewports dialog box (see Figure 17.8).

FIGURE 17.8
Three viewports, each displaying a different view

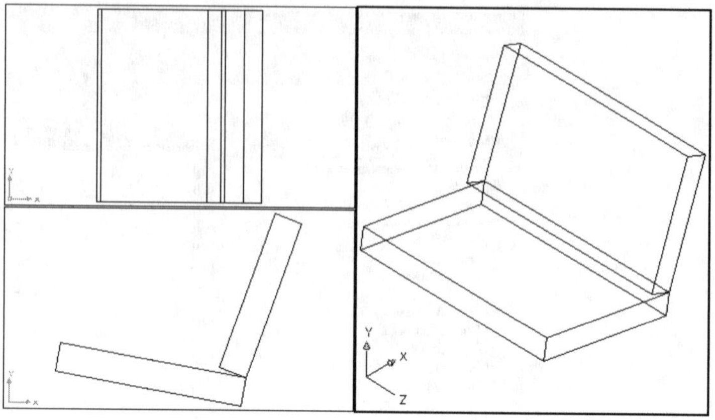

You've set up your viewport. Let's check to see that your viewport arrangement was saved.

1. Choose View ➢ Viewports ➢ Named Viewports to open the Viewports dialog box again.
2. Click the Named Viewports tab. My Viewport Setup is listed in the Named Viewports list box. If you click it, a sample view of your viewport arrangement appears on the right.
3. After you've reviewed the addition to the Named Viewports list, close the dialog box.

Now take a close look at your viewport setup. Notice that the UCS icon in each of the two orthogonal views in the two left viewports are oriented to the plane of the view. AutoCAD allows you to set up a different UCS for each viewport. The top view uses the WCS since it is in the same plane as the WCS. The side view has its own UCS, which is parallel to its view. The isometric view to the right retains the UCS you saved—namely the 3DSW UCS.

WARNING *LT users will see the UCS icon oriented to the current UCS and not aligned with the orthogonal viewport views.*

Another Viewports dialog box option you haven't tried yet is the Apply To drop-down list in the New Viewports tab.

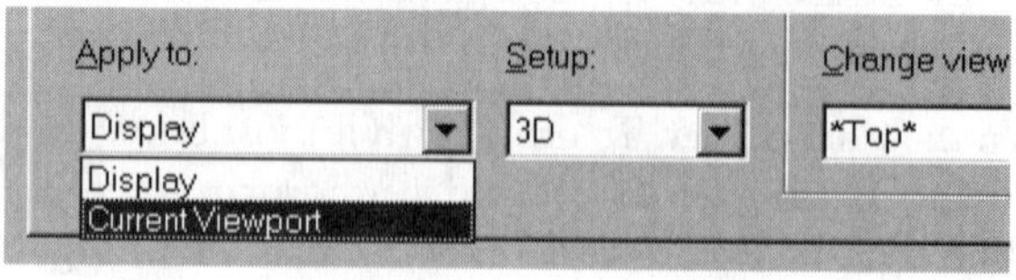

This list shows two options: Display and Current Viewport. When Display is selected, the option you choose from the Standard Viewports list applies to the overall display. When Current Viewport is selected, the option you select applies to the selected viewport in the sample view in the right side of the dialog box. You can use the Current Viewport option to build multiple viewports in custom arrangements.

ADDING THE LEGS

The next items you will add to your chair are the legs. Before you do that, you'll want to set up the 3DSW UCS in the side view of your chair.

1. Click the lower-left viewport to make it active.
2. Click the Display UCS Dialog tool on the UCS toolbar.
3. Click the Named UCSs tab, and then select 3DSW from the list of UCSs.
4. Click the Set Current button. The triangular marker to the left of the UCS names moves to 3DSW.
5. Click OK.

Now you're ready to draw the legs using the coordinate information shown in Figure 17.9.

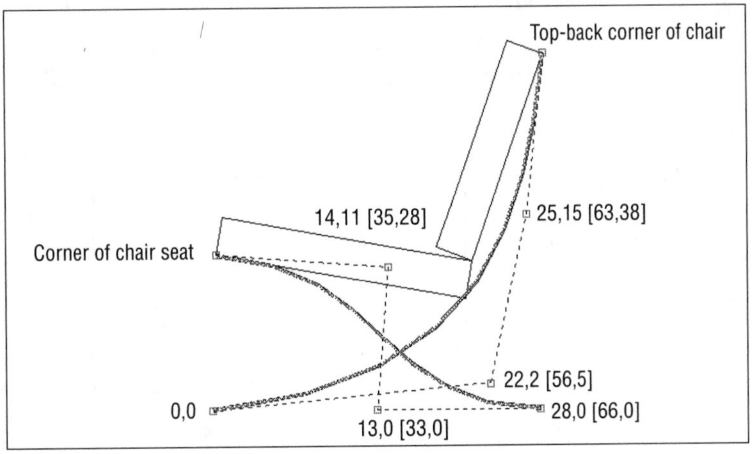

FIGURE 17.9
Drawing the legs of the chair. Metric coordinates are shown in brackets.

1. Go to the side view of the chair, and move the chair seat and back vertically in the y-axis 8.5" or 21.6 cm for metric users. Make sure you select all the lines and 3D Faces for the move. You may have to pan the view down so that the entire chair is displayed.

TIP *If you anticipate moving a group of 3D objects frequently, use the Group command to group objects together. The Group command is especially useful in 3D work, since you can group sets of objects together for easy manipulation, yet you can still edit the individual objects within a group.*

2. Next, draw two curved polylines, as shown in Figure 17.9. You may have to adjust your view so that you can draw the legs more easily. You don't have to be absolutely perfect about placing or shaping these lines.
3. Use the grips of the polylines to adjust their curve, if necessary.
4. Choose Modify ➢ Object ➢ Polyline to give the polylines a width of 0.5" (1.27 cm for metric users).

5. Use the Properties palette to give the polylines a thickness of –2" (minus 2 inches). Metric users should make the thickness –5 cm. Notice that as you draw and edit a polyline, it appears in both the Plan and 3D views.

6. Close the Properties palette when you are done changing the thickness property.

TIP *Polylines are the best objects to use for 3D, because you can generate complex shapes easily by giving the polylines thickness and width.*

You've got the legs for one side. The next step is to make a mirrored copy of those legs for the other side.

1. Click the top view of the chair in the upper-left viewport.
2. Turn the Ortho mode on, and then click the Mirror tool on the Modify toolbar.
3. In the upper-left viewport, click the two polylines representing the chair legs, and then press ↵.
4. At the `Specify first point of mirror line:` prompt, use the Midpoint Osnap and select the midpoint of the chair seat, as shown in Figure 17.10.

FIGURE 17.10

Mirroring the legs from one side to another

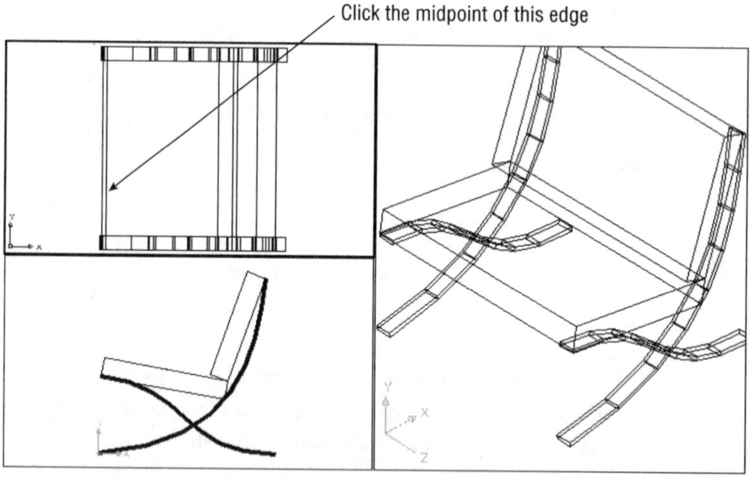
Click the midpoint of this edge

5. At the `Specify second point of mirror line prompt`, pick any location to the right of the point you selected so that the rubber-banding line is exactly horizontal.
6. Press ↵ at the `Delete source objects?` prompt. The legs are mirrored to the opposite side of the chair. Your screen should look similar to Figure 17.10.

Notice that the broken-pencil UCS icon has shifted to the viewport in the lower-left corner. This icon tells you that the current UCS is perpendicular to the plane of that view.

Your chair is now complete. Let's finish by getting a better look at it.

1. Click the viewport to the right showing the isometric view.

2. Open the Viewport dialog box and click the New Viewport tab.
3. Select Single from the Standard Viewports list, and then click OK.
4. Use the Zoom tool to adjust your view so that it looks similar to Figure 17.11.
5. Choose View ➢ Hide to get a view of your chair with the lines hidden, as shown in Figure 17.11.

FIGURE 17.11
The chair in 3D with hidden lines removed

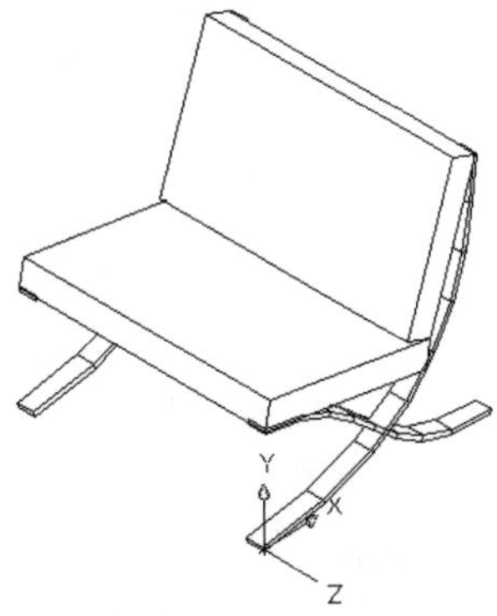

Controlling the UCS

You've seen how you can select a UCS from a set of predefined UCSs. You can frequently use these preset UCSs and make minor adjustments to them to get the exact UCS you want.

You can define a UCS in a number of other ways. You can, for example, use the 3D Face of your chair seat as the definition for a UCS. In the following set of exercises, you will get some practice moving your UCS around. Learning how to move effortlessly between UCSs is crucial to mastering the creation of 3D models, so you'll want to pay special attention to the command options shown in these procedures. These options are accessible from either the Tools ➢ UCS cascading menu or the UCS toolbar.

UCS BASED ON OBJECT ORIENTATION

You can define a UCS based on the orientation of an object. This is helpful when you want to work on a predefined object to fill in details on its surface plane.

1. Click the Object UCS tool on the UCS toolbar, or choose Tools ➢ New UCS ➢ Object. You can also type **UCS↵ OB↵**.
2. At the `Select object to align UCS:` prompt, pick the 3D Face used to define the top surface of the chair seat. Because the 3D Face and the polyline outline of the seat share a common edge, you might need to use the Selection Cycling feature to pick the 3D Face. The UCS icon shifts to reflect the new coordinate system's orientation (see Figure 17.12).

TIP *If you have a Hidden-Line view, selection cycling will not work for picking 3D Faces. Issue a Regen to return to a wireframe view.*

FIGURE 17.12
Using the Object option of the UCS command to locate a UCS

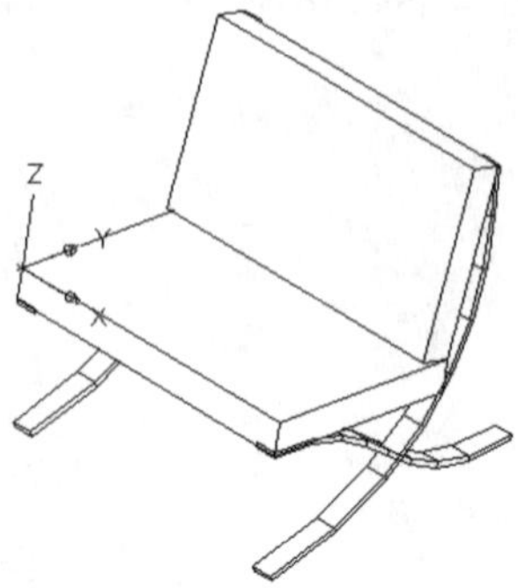

Orientation of the UCS Origin

Remember earlier in the chapter when you drew the 3D Face for the seat in a specific way? Well, the location of the UCS origin and its orientation depend on how that 3D Face was created. If you had drawn it other than as instructed, the UCS you defined using the Object option in the previous exercise would not have been generated as described.

Table 17.1 describes how an object can determine the orientation of a UCS.

TABLE 17.1: EFFECTS OF OBJECTS ON THE ORIENTATION OF A UCS

OBJECT TYPE	UCS ORIENTATION
Arc	The center of the arc establishes the UCS origin. The x-axis of the UCS passes through the pick point on the arc.
Circle	The center of the circle establishes the UCS origin. The x-axis of the UCS passes through the pick point on the circle.
Dimension	The midpoint of the dimension text establishes the origin of the UCS origin. The x-axis of the UCS is parallel to the x-axis that was active when the dimension was drawn.
Line	The endpoint nearest the pick point establishes the origin of the UCS, and the x-z plane of the UCS contains the line.
Point	The point location establishes the UCS origin. The UCS orientation is arbitrary.
2D Polyline	The starting point of the polyline establishes the UCS origin. The x-axis is determined by the direction from the first point to the next vertex.

Continued on next page

TABLE 17.1: EFFECTS OF OBJECTS ON THE ORIENTATION OF A UCS *(continued)*

OBJECT TYPE	UCS ORIENTATION
Solid	The first point of the solid establishes the origin of the UCS. The second point of the solid establishes the x-axis.
Trace	The direction of the trace establishes the x-axis of the UCS, and the beginning point sets the origin.
3D Face	The first point of the 3D Face establishes the origin. The first and second points establish the x-axis. The plane defined by the 3D Face determines the orientation of the UCS.
Shapes, Text, Blocks, Attributes, and Attribute Definitions	The insertion point establishes the origin of the UCS. The object's rotation angle establishes the x-axis.

UCS BASED ON OFFSET ORIENTATION

At times you might want to work in a UCS that has the same orientation as the current UCS but is offset. For example, you might be drawing a building that has several parallel walls offset with a saw-tooth effect (see Figure 17.13). You can easily hop from one UCS to a parallel UCS by using the Origin option.

FIGURE 17.13
Using the Origin option to shift the UCS

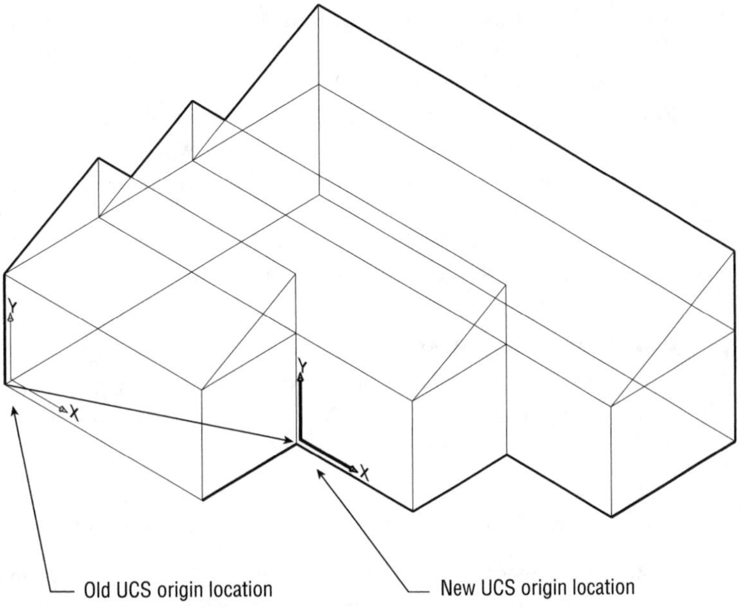

1. Click the Origin UCS tool on the UCS toolbar, or choose Tools ➢ New UCS ➢ Origin. You can also type **UCS↵ O↵**.

2. At the `Specify new origin point <0,0,0>:` prompt, pick the bottom end of the chair leg, just below the current UCS origin. The UCS icon shifts to the end of the leg, with its origin at the point you picked (see Figure 17.14).

FIGURE 17.14
Moving the origin of the UCS

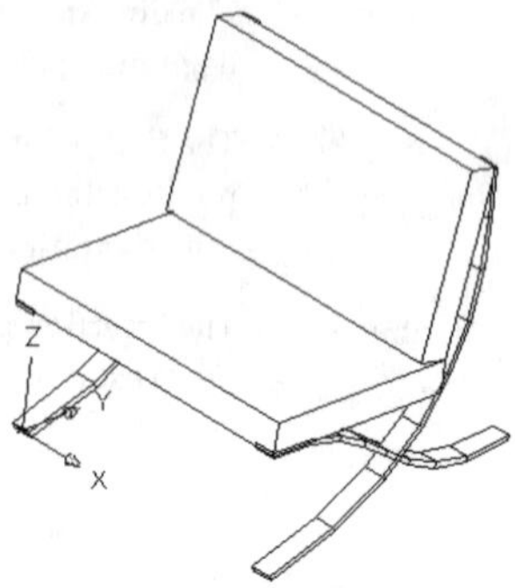

MOVING VERSUS CREATING A UCS ORIGIN

The Origin UCS tool creates a new UCS that you can save under its own name. A similar option is Move UCS on the Tools pull-down menu. At first glance, they seem to do the same thing; that is, they create a new UCS by moving an existing UCS's origin. There is a subtle difference between the two, however. The Tools ➢ Move UCS option is intended to move an existing named UCS to a new location. It doesn't actually create a new one. For example, if you use Move UCS to move the 3DSW UCS you created earlier in this chapter, 3DSW will appear in its new location when you recall it. On the other hand, if you use the Origin UCS tool to change the origin of the 3DSW UCS, AutoCAD creates an entirely different UCS and maintains the original location of 3DSW.

The Tools ➢ Move UCS option can also be found on the UCS II toolbar. You'll get a chance to work with the UCS II toolbar in the next section.

UCS ROTATED AROUND AN AXIS

Now suppose you want to change the orientation of the x-, y-, or z-axis of a UCS. You can accomplish this by using the X, Y, or X Axis Rotate UCS options on the UCS toolbar. Let's try rotating the UCS about the z-axis to see how this works.

1. Click the Z Axis Rotate UCS tool on the UCS toolbar, or choose Tools ➢ New UCS ➢ Z. You can also type **UCS↵ Z↵**. This will allow you to rotate the current UCS around the z-axis.

2. At the `Specify rotation angle about Z axis <90>:` prompt, press ↵ to accept the default of 90°. The UCS icon rotates to reflect the new orientation of the current UCS (see Figure 17.15).

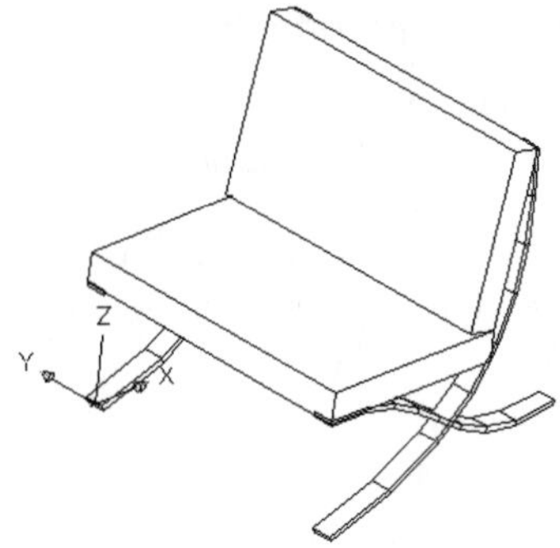

FIGURE 17.15
Rotating the UCS about the z-axis

Similarly, the X and Y Axis Rotate UCS options allow you to rotate the UCS about the current x- and y-axis, respectively, just as you did for the z-axis earlier. The X and Y Axis Rotate UCS tools are helpful in orienting a UCS to an inclined plane. For example, if you want to work on the plane of a sloped roof of a building, you can first use the Origin UCS tool to align the UCS to the edge of a roof and then use the X Axis Rotate UCS tool to rotate the UCS to the angle of the roof slope, as shown in Figure 17.16. Note that the default is 90°, so you only have to press ↵ to rotate the UCS 90°, but you can also enter a value at the `Specify another rotation angle` prompt.

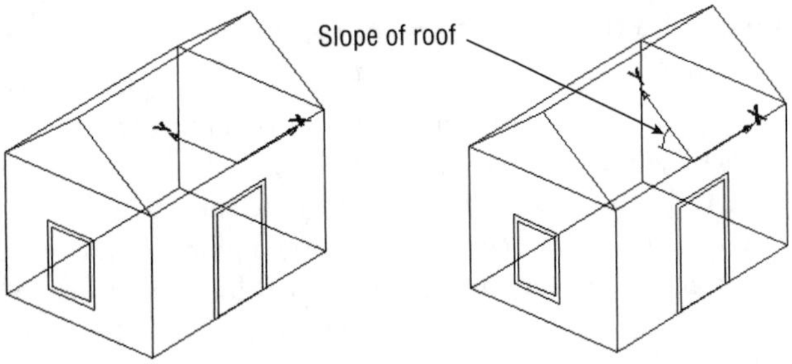

FIGURE 17.16
Moving a UCS to the plane of a sloping roof

Finally, you can skew the UCS using the Z Axis Vector option. This is useful when you need to define a UCS based on a z-axis determined by two objects.

1. Click the Z Axis Vector UCS tool on the UCS toolbar, or choose Tools ➢ UCS ➢ Z Axis Vector. You can also type **UCS↵ ZA↵**.
2. At the `Specify new origin point <0,0,0>:` prompt, press ↵ to accept the default, which is the current UCS origin. You can shift the origin point at this prompt if you like.

3. At the next prompt:

   `Specify point on positive portion of Z-axis <0'-0", 0'- 0", 0'-1">:`

   use the Endpoint Osnap override and pick the other chair leg end, as shown in Figure 17.17. The UCS twists to reflect the new z-axis of the UCS.

WARNING *Because your cursor location is in the plane of the current UCS, it is best to pick a point on an object using either the Osnap overrides or the coordinate filters.*

FIGURE 17.17

Picking points for the Z Axis Vector option

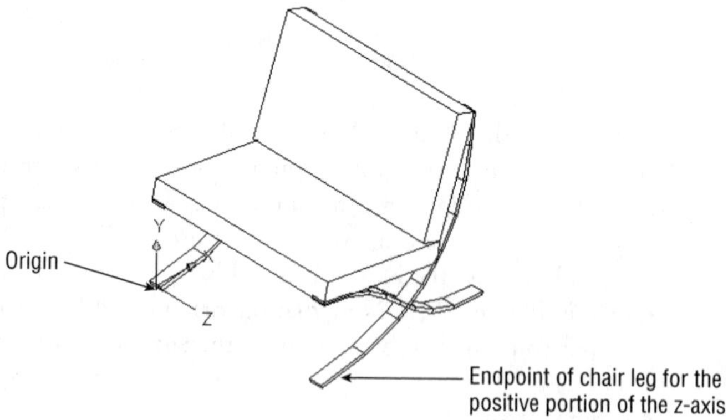

ORIENTING A UCS IN THE VIEW PLANE

Finally, you can define a UCS in the current view plane. This is useful if you want to switch quickly to the current view plane for editing or for adding text to a 3D view.

Click the View UCS tool on the UCS toolbar, or choose Tools ➢ New UCS ➢ View. You can also type **UCS**↵ V↵. The UCS icon changes to show that the UCS is aligned with the current view.

AutoCAD uses the current UCS origin point for the origin of the new UCS. By defining a view as a UCS, you can enter text to label your drawing, just as you would in a technical illustration. Text entered in a plane created in this way appears normal.

Now you've finished your tour of the UCS command. Set the UCS back to the World Coordinate System and save the `Barcelon.dwg` file.

You've explored nearly every option in creating a UCS, except for one. In the next section, you'll learn about the 3 Point option for creating a UCS. This is the most versatile method for creating a UCS, but it is a bit more involved than some of the other UCS options.

SAVING A UCS WITH A VIEW

AutoCAD 2000 introduced the ability to save a UCS with a view. Choose View ➢ Named Views to open the Views dialog box, and then click the Named Views tab . Click the New button to open the

New View dialog box. Enter a name for your new view; then make sure the Save UCS With View option is checked. By default, AutoCAD saves the current UCS with the view. You can also choose a UCS to save with a new view using the UCS Name drop-down list.

Creating Complex 3D Surfaces

In the previous example, you drew a chair composed of objects that were mostly straight lines or curves with a thickness. All the forms in that chair were defined in planes perpendicular to each other. For a 3D model such as this, you can get by using the Orthographic UCSs. At times, however, you will want to draw objects that do not fit so easily into perpendicular or parallel planes. The following exercise demonstrates how you can create more complex forms using some of AutoCAD's other 3D commands.

TIP *Most of the operations in this tutorial are available in LT except for the mesh surfaces.*

Laying Out a 3D Form

In this next group of exercises, you will draw a butterfly chair. This chair has no perpendicular or parallel planes to work with, so you will start by setting up some points that you will use for reference only. This is similar in concept to laying out a 2D drawing. As you progress through the drawing construction, notice how the reference points are established to help create the chair. You will also construct some temporary 3D lines to use for reference. These temporary lines will be your layout. These points will define the major UCSs needed to construct the drawing.

1. If it isn't open already, open the `Barcelon` drawing, and then choose File ➢ Save As to save the file under the name `Btrfly`.
2. Choose View ➢ 3D Views ➢ Plan View ➢ World UCS. Then choose View ➢ Zoom ➢ All to display the overall area of the drawing.

TIP *You will draw the butterfly chair almost entirely while viewing it in 3D. This approach is useful when you are creating complex shapes.*

3. Erase the entire contents of the drawing, and then make sure you are in the WCS by choosing Tools ➢ New UCS ➢ World.
4. Click Rectangle on the Draw toolbar. Draw a square 20" square with its first corner at coordinate 36,36. Metric users should draw a square 51 cm square, with its first corner at coordinate 81,81.
5. Use the Offset tool to offset the square 4" out, so you have two concentric squares with the outer square measuring 28". Metric users should offset 10 cm for an outer square measuring 71 cm.
6. Move the larger of the two squares, the 28" square, to the left 2". Metric users should move the larger square 5 cm to the left. Your screen should look similar to Figure 17.18.

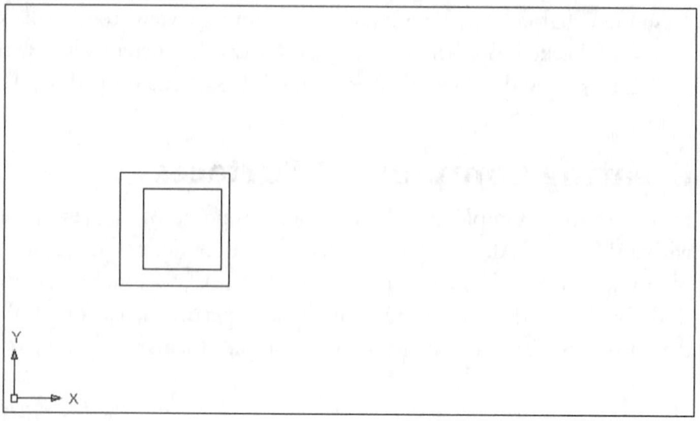

FIGURE 17.18
Setting up a layout for a butterfly chair

7. Choose View ➢ 3D Views ➢ SW Isometric. This will give you a view from the lower-left side of the rectangles.
8. Zoom out so the rectangles occupy about a third of the drawing area window.

Now you need to move the outer rectangle in the z-axis so that its elevation is 30" (76 cm for metric users).

1. Click the outer rectangle, and then click one of its grips.
2. Right-click to open the Grip Edit shortcut menu.
3. Choose Move, and then enter **@0,0,30↵**. Metric users should enter **@0,0,76↵**. This tells AutoCAD to move the rectangle a 0 distance in both the x- and y-axes, and 30" (or 76 cm) in the z-axis.
4. Pan your view downward so it looks similar to Figure 17.19.

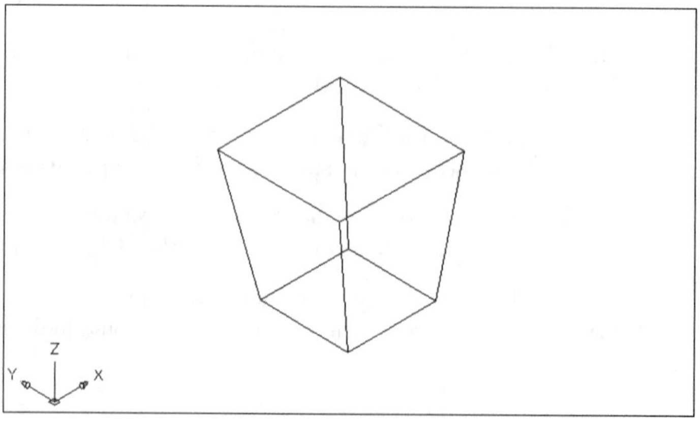

FIGURE 17.19
The finished chair layout

5. Use the Line tool to draw lines from the corners of the outer square to the corners of the inner square. Use the Endpoint Osnap to select the exact corners of the squares. This is the layout for your chair—not yet the finished product.

SPHERICAL AND CYLINDRICAL COORDINATE FORMATS

In the previous exercise, you used relative Cartesian coordinates to locate the second point for the Move command. For commands that accept 3D input, you can also specify displacements by using the *Spherical* and *Cylindrical Coordinate* formats.

The Spherical Coordinate format lets you specify a distance in 3D space while specifying the angle in terms of degrees from the x-axis of the current UCS and degrees from the x-y plane of the current UCS (see the top image in Figure 17.20). For example, to specify a distance of 4.5" (11.43 cm) at a 30° angle from the x-axis and 45° from the x-y plane, enter **@4.5<30<45** (**@11.43<30<45** for metric users). This refers to the direct distance, followed by a < symbol; then the angle from the x-axis of the current UCS followed by another < symbol; then the angle from the x-y plane of the current UCS. To use the spherical coordinate format to move the rectangle in the exercise, enter **@30<0<90** at the `Second point:` prompt or **@76<0<90** for metric users.

The Cylindrical Coordinate format, on the other hand, lets you specify a location in terms of a distance in the plane of the current UCS and a distance in the z-axis. You also specify an angle from the x-axis of the current UCS (see the bottom image in Figure 17.20). For example, to locate a point that is a distance of 4.5" (11.43 cm) in the plane of the current UCS, at an angle of 30° from the x-axis, and a distance of 3.3" (8.38 cm) in the z-axis, enter **@4.5<30,3.3** (**@11.43<30,8.38** for metric users). This refers to the distance of the displacement from the plane of the current UCS, followed by the < symbol; then the angle from the x-axis, followed by a comma; then the distance in the z-axis. Using the cylindrical format to move the rectangle, you enter **@0<0,30** at the `Second point:` prompt or **@0<0,76** for metric users.

Using a 3D Polyline

Now you will draw the legs for the butterfly chair using a 3D polyline. This is a polyline that can be drawn in 3D space.

1. Choose Draw ➢ 3D Polyline, or type **3p**↵.
2. At the `Specify start point of polyline:` prompt, pick a series of points, as shown in Figure 17.21, using the Endpoint and Midpoint Osnap.

TIP *This would be a good place to use the Running Osnaps feature.*

3. Draw another 3D polyline in the mirror image of the first (see Figure 17.21).
4. Erase the rectangles and connecting lines that make up the frame.

All objects, with the exception of lines, 3D Faces, 3D Meshes, and 3D polylines, are restricted to the plane of your current UCS. The Pline command can only be used to draw polylines in one plane, but the 3dpoly command allows you to create a polyline in three dimensions. Three-dimensional polylines cannot, however, be given thickness or width.

FIGURE 17.20
The Spherical and Cylindrical Coordinate formats

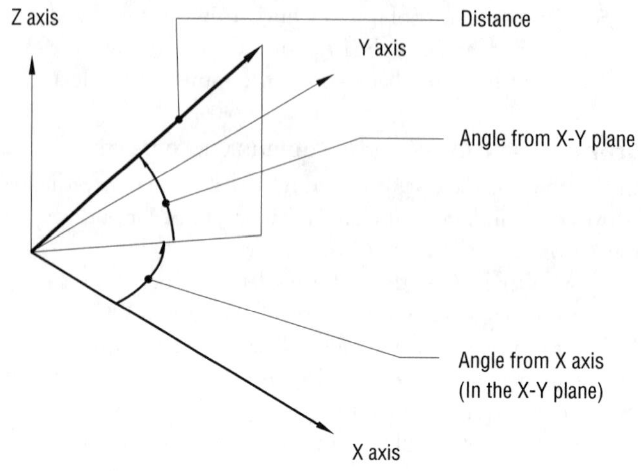

[Distance] < [Angle from X axis] < [Angle from X-Y plane]

The Spherical Coordinate Format

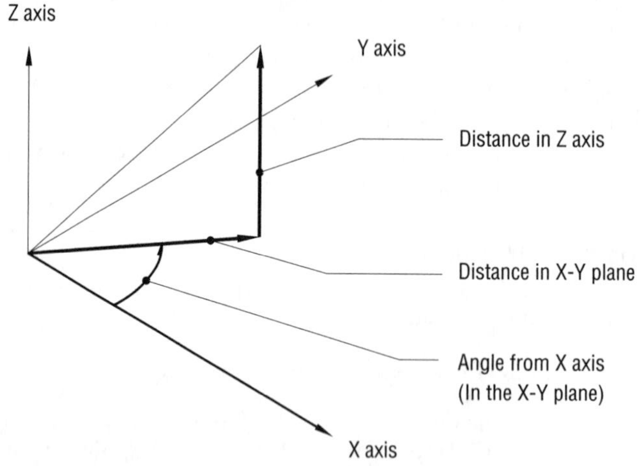

[Distance in X-Y plane] < [Angle from X axis] , [Distance in Z axis]

The Cylindrical Coordinate Format

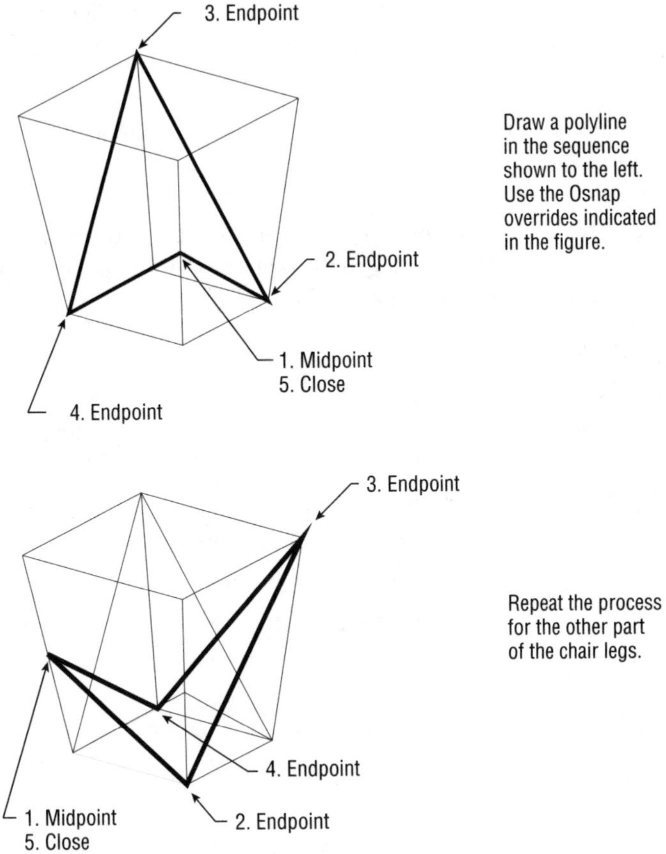
3. Endpoint
2. Endpoint
1. Midpoint
5. Close
4. Endpoint
Draw a polyline in the sequence shown to the left. Use the Osnap overrides indicated in the figure.
3. Endpoint
4. Endpoint
1. Midpoint
5. Close
2. Endpoint
Repeat the process for the other part of the chair legs.

FIGURE 17.21
Using 3D polylines to draw the legs of the butterfly chair

Creating a Curved 3D Surface

Next, you will draw the seat of the chair. The seat of a butterfly chair is usually made of canvas and drapes from the four corners of the chair legs. You will first define the perimeter of the seat using arcs, and then you'll use the Edge Surface tool on the Surfaces toolbar to form the shape of the draped canvas. The Edge Surface tool creates a surface based on four objects defining the edges of that surface. In this example, you will use arcs to define the edges of the seat.

To draw the arcs defining the seat edge, you must first establish the UCSs in the planes of those edges. In the previous example you created a UCS for the side of the chair before you could draw the legs. In the same way, you must create a UCS defining the planes that contain the edges of the seat.

Since the UCS you want to define is not orthogonal, you will need to use the three-point method. This lets you define the plane of the UCS based on three points.

1. Click the 3 Point UCS tool on the UCS toolbar. You can also choose Tools ➢ New UCS ➢ 3 Point, or type **UCS**↵ **3**↵. This option allows you to define a UCS based on three points that you select.

TIP *Remember, it helps to think of a UCS as a drawing surface situated on the surface of the object you want to draw or edit.*

2. At the `Specify new origin point <0,0,0>:` prompt, use the Endpoint Osnap to pick the bottom of the chair leg to the far left, as shown in the top panel of Figure 17.22. This is the origin point of your new UCS.

FIGURE 17.22

Defining and saving three UCSs

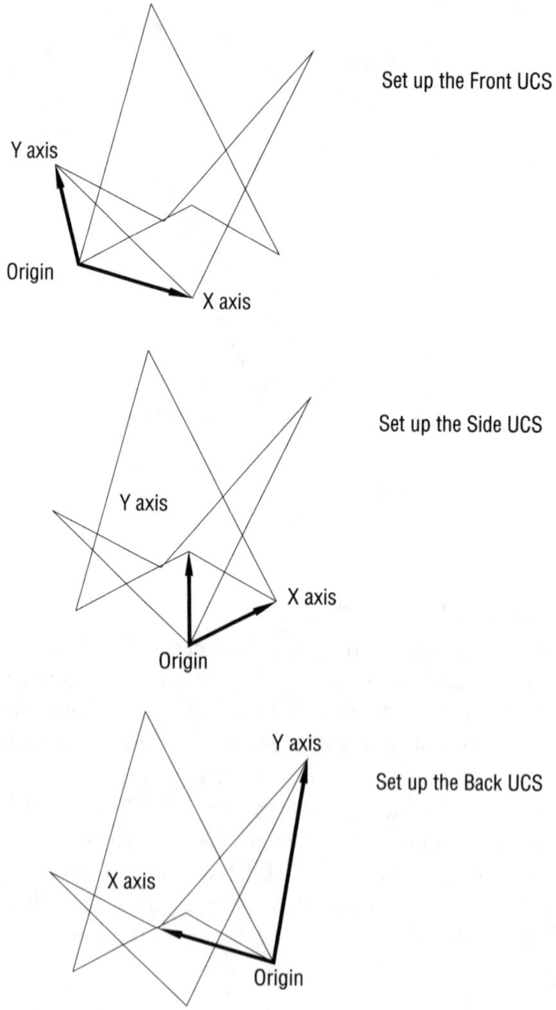

3. At the `Specify point on positive portion of X-axis:` prompt, use the Endpoint Osnap to pick the bottom of the next leg to the right of the first one, as shown in the top panel in Figure 17.22.
4. At the `Specify point on positive - Y portion of the UCS XY plane:` prompt, pick the top corner of the butterfly chair seat, as shown in the top panel in Figure 17.22. The UCS icon changes to indicate your new UCS.

5. Now that you have defined a UCS, you need to save it so that you can return to it later. Click Display UCS Dialog on the UCS toolbar, or choose Tools ➢ UCS ➢ Named UCS to open the UCS dialog box. You can also type **UC↵**.
6. With the Named UCSs tab selected, right-click the Unnamed item in the list box and choose Rename from the shortcut menu.
7. Enter **Front Side↵**.
8. Click OK to exit the UCS dialog box.

WARNING *Don't skip step 4. If you do, you will not get the results you want when you start picking the arc's endpoints in step 5. AutoCAD draws arcs only in the current UCS. Remember: Only lines, 3D polylines, and other 3D objects can be drawn in three-dimensional space. All other objects can be drawn only in the current UCS.*

You've defined and saved a UCS for the front side of the chair. As you can see from the UCS icon, this UCS is at a nonorthogonal angle to the WCS. Continue by creating UCSs for the other four sides of the butterfly chair.

1. Define a UCS for the side of the chair as shown in the middle image in Figure 17.23. Use the UCS Control dialog box to rename this UCS Left Side, just as you did for Front Side in steps 5 through 8. Remember that you renamed the Unnamed UCS.
2. Repeat these steps again for a UCS for the back of the chair, named Back. Use the bottom image in Figure 17.23 for reference.
3. Open the UCS dialog box again, and in the Named UCSs tab, highlight Front Side.
4. Click the Current button, and then click OK. This activates Front Side as the current UCS.
5. Choose Draw ➢ Arc ➢ Start, End, Direction.
6. Draw the arc defining the front edge of the chair (see Figure 17.23). Use the Endpoint Osnap override to pick the top endpoints of the chair legs as the endpoints of the arc. (If you need help with the Arc command, refer to Chapter 3.)
7. Repeat steps 3 through 6 for the UCS named Side, and then again for the UCS named Back—each time using the top endpoints of the legs for the endpoints of the arc.

FIGURE 17.23
Drawing the seat edge using arcs

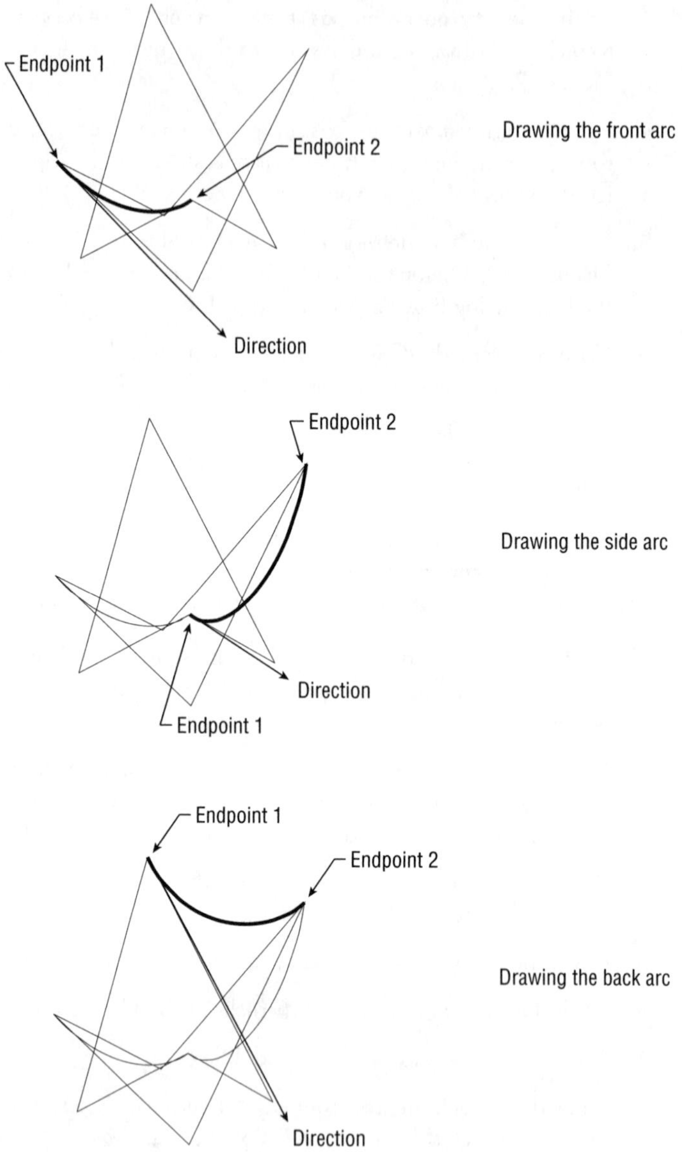

Next, you will mirror the side-edge arc to the opposite side. This will save you from having to define a UCS for that side.

1. Click World UCS on the UCS toolbar to restore the WCS. The reason for doing this is that you want to mirror the arc along an axis that is parallel to the plane of the WCS. Remember that you must go to the coordinate system that defines the plane in which you want to work.

2. Click the arc you drew for the side of the chair (the one drawn on the Side UCS).
3. Click the midpoint grip of the arc in the Side UCS; then right-click and choose Mirror from the shortcut menu.
4. Enter C↵ to select the Copy option.
5. Enter B↵ to select a new base point for the mirror axis.
6. At the `Base point:` prompt, use the Intersect Osnap to pick the intersection of the two lines in the Front plane.
7. Next, use the Intersection override to pick the intersection of the two legs in the Back plane. Refer to Figure 17.24 for help. The arc should mirror to the opposite side, and your chair should look like Figure 17.25.
8. Press the Esc key twice to clear the grips.

FIGURE 17.24

Mirroring the arc that defines the side of the chair seat

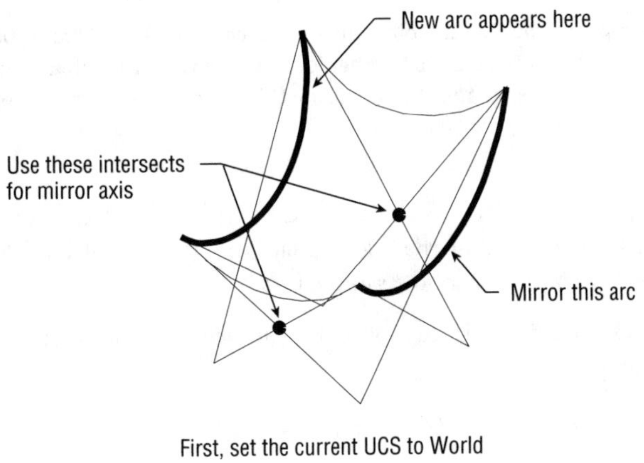
New arc appears here
Use these intersects for mirror axis
Mirror this arc
First, set the current UCS to World

FIGURE 17.25

Your butterfly chair so far

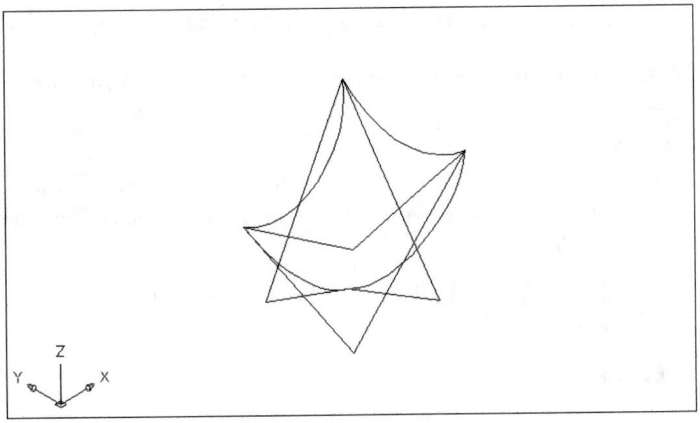
Z
Y
X

QUICK HOPS TO YOUR UCSS

If you find you're jumping from one saved UCS to another, you'll want to know about the UCS II toolbar. The UCS II toolbar offers a drop-down list that contains all the saved UCSs in a drawing. You can use this list as a quick way to move between UCSs that you've set up or even between the predefined orthogonal UCSs.

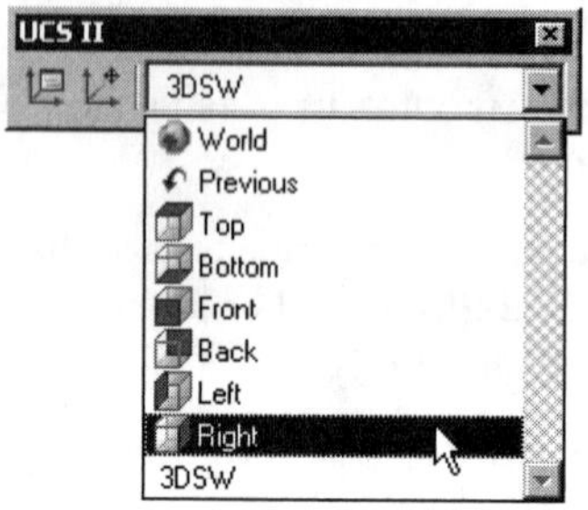

Two other tools on the UCS II toolbar give you access to the UCS dialog box and the Move UCS origin tool, which moves an existing UCS to another location. As with all toolbars, you can open the UCS II toolbar by right-clicking any toolbar and then choosing UCS II from the shortcut menu.

ACAD only

Finally, let's finish off this chair by adding the mesh representing the chair seat. LT users will have to skip this exercise because the Edge Surface tool is not available. You can view the results by opening the `Butterfly.dwg` file from the sample files.

1. Click the Edge Surface tool on the Surfaces toolbar, or enter Edgesurf↵ at the command prompt.

TIP *To display the Surfaces toolbar, choose Tools ➢ Toolbars ➢ Surfaces.*

2. At the `Select object 1 for surface edge:` prompt, pick the arc on the Front UCS.
3. At the `Select object 2 for surface edge:` prompt, pick the next arc on the Side UCS.

WARNING *For the command to work properly, the arcs (or any set of objects) used with the Edge Surface option to define the boundary of a mesh must be connected exactly end-to-end.*

4. Continue to pick the other two arcs in succession. (The arcs must be picked in a circular fashion, not crosswise.) A mesh appears, filling the space between the four arcs. Your chair is now complete.
5. Choose View ➢ Hide to get a better view of the butterfly chair. You should have a view similar to Figure 17.26.
6. Save this file.

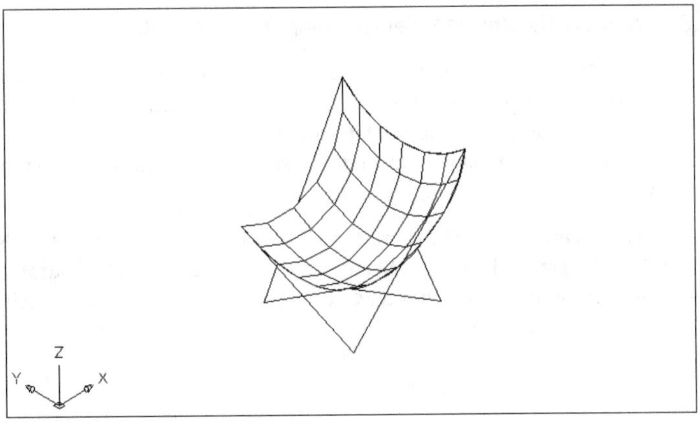

FIGURE 17.26
The completed butterfly chair

At this point, you've been introduced to a few of the options on the Surfaces toolbar. You'll get a chance to use these later in this chapter. Next, you'll learn how to edit mesh objects such as the butterfly chair's seat.

ACAD only

Adjusting the Settings That Control Meshes

As you can see, the seat in our butterfly chair is made up of rectangular segments. If you want to increase the number of segments in the mesh, you can change the Surftab1 and Surftab2 system variables. Surftab1 controls the number of segments along edge 1, the first edge you pick in the sequence; and Surftab2 controls the number of segments along edge 2. AutoCAD refers to the direction of edge 1 as *m* and the direction of edge 2 as *n*. These two directions can be loosely described as the x- and y-axes of the mesh, with *m* being the x-axis and *n* being the y-axis.

TIP *See Chapter 15 and Appendix D for more information on system variables.*

In Figure 17.27, the setting for Surftab1 is 24, and for Surftab2 the setting is 12. The default value for both settings is 6. To try different Surftab settings on the chair mesh, you'll need to erase the existing mesh, change the Surftab settings, and then use the Edge Surface tool again to define the mesh.

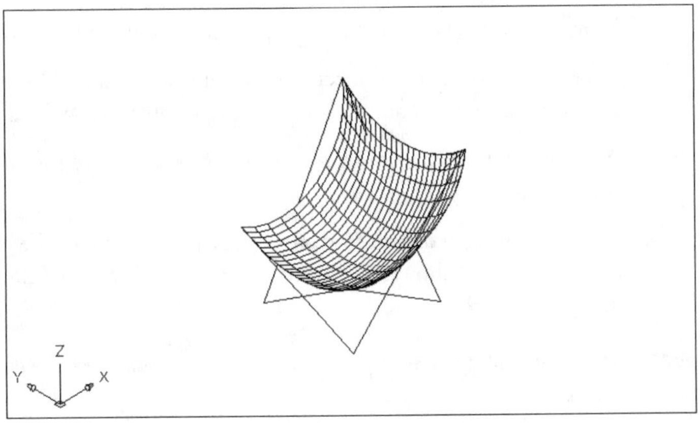

FIGURE 17.27
The butterfly chair with different Surftab settings

CREATING A 3D MESH BY SPECIFYING COORDINATES

If you need to draw a mesh like the one in the previous example, but you want to give exact coordinates for each vertex in the mesh grid, you can use the 3DMesh command. Suppose you have data from a survey of a piece of land; you can use 3DMesh to convert your data into a graphic representation of its topography. Another use of the 3DMesh command is to plot mathematical data to get a graphic representation of a formula.

Because you must enter the coordinate for each vertex in the mesh, 3DMesh is better suited in scripts or AutoLISP programs, in which a list of coordinates can be applied automatically to the 3DMesh command in a sequential order. See Chapter 20 and the *ABCs of AutoLISP*, which is on the companion CD, for more information on AutoLISP.

Other Surface-Drawing Tools

In the previous example, you used the Edge Surface tool to create a 3D surface. You can also use several other 3D surface commands to generate complex surface shapes easily.

TIP *All the objects described in this section, along with the meshes described earlier, are actually composites of 3D Faces. This means that you can explode these 3D objects into their component 3D Faces, which in turn can be edited individually.*

Using Two Objects to Define a Surface

The Ruled Surface tool on the Surfaces toolbar draws a surface between two 2D objects, such as a line and an arc or a polyline and an arc. This command is useful for creating extruded forms that transform from one shape to another along a straight path. Let's see firsthand how the Ruled Surface tool works.

1. Open the file called `Rulesurf.dwg` from the companion CD. It looks like the first image on Figure 17.28. This drawing is of a simple half-circle, drawn using a line and an arc. Ignore the diagonal blue line for now.
2. Move the line between the arc endpoints 10 units in the z-axis.

3. Now you are ready to connect the two objects with a 3D surface. Click the Ruled Surface tool on the Surfaces toolbar, or choose Draw ➢ Surfaces ➢ Ruled Surface.
4. At the `Select first defining curve:` prompt, place the cursor toward the right end of the arc and click.
5. At the `Select second defining curve:` prompt, move the cursor toward the right end of the line and click, as shown in the second image in Figure 17.28. The surface will appear as shown in Figure 17.29.

WARNING *The position you use to pick the second object will determine how the surface is generated.*

FIGURE 17.28
Drawing two edges for the Ruled Surface option

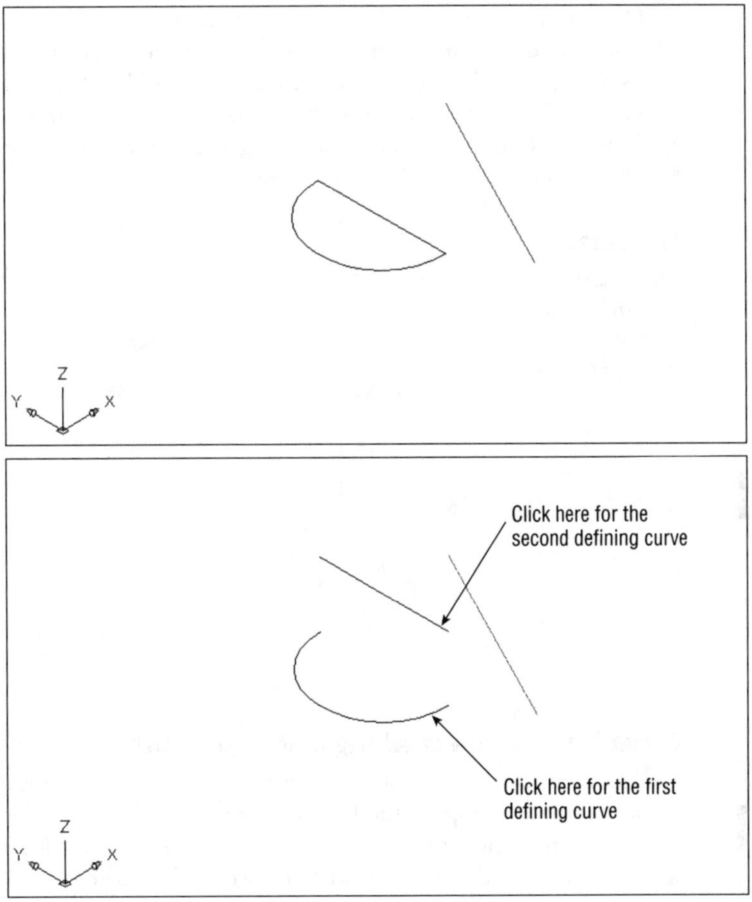
Z
Y
X
Click here for the second defining curve
Click here for the first defining curve
Z
Y
X

FIGURE 17.29
The Rulesurf surface

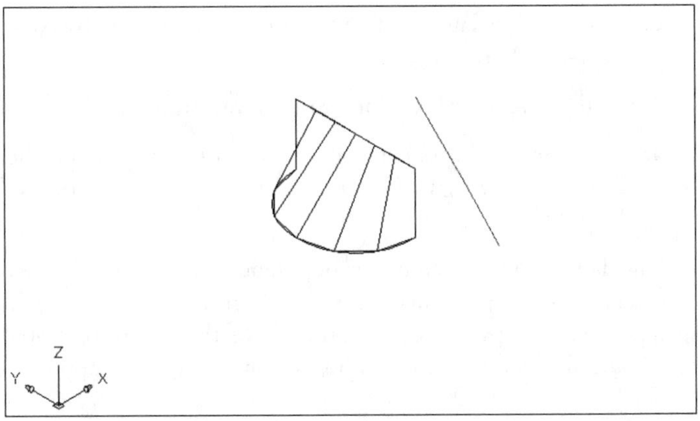
Z
Y
X

The location you use to select the two objects for the ruled surface is important. You selected specific locations on the arc and line so that the ruled surface is generated properly. Had you selected the opposite end of the line, for example, your result would look more like Figure 17.30. Notice that the segments defining the surface cross each other. Picking the defining objects near opposite endpoints causes this crossing effect. The arc was picked near its lower end, and the line was picked toward the top end. At times, you may want this effect.

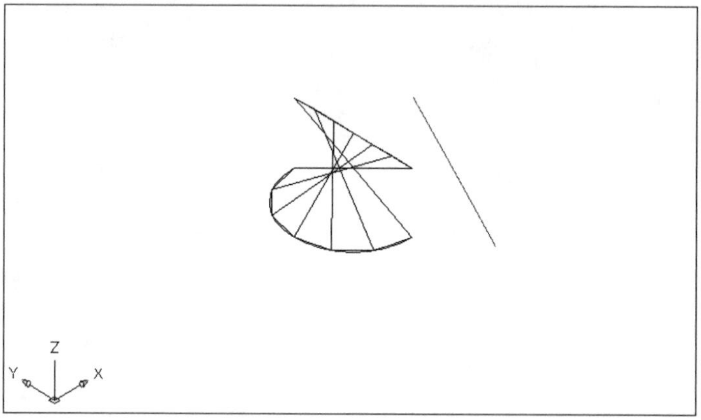

FIGURE 17.30
The ruled surface redrawn by using different points to select the objects

Extruding an Object Along a Straight Line

The Tabulated Surface tool also uses two objects to draw a 3D surface, but instead of drawing the surface between the objects, the Tabulated Surface tool extrudes one object in a direction defined by a direction vector. The net result is an extruded shape that is the length and direction of the direction vector. To see what this means firsthand, try the following exercise.

1. While still in the Rulesurf drawing, click the Undo button in the Standard toolbar to undo the ruled surface from the previous exercise.

2. Click the Tabulated Surface tool on the Surface toolbar, or choose Draw ➢ Surfaces ➢ Tabulated Surfaces.
3. At the `Select object for path curve:` prompt, click the arc.
4. At the `Select object for direction vector:` prompt, click the lower end of the blue line farthest to the right. The arc is extruded in the direction of the blue line, as shown in Figure 17.31.

The direction vector can be any object, but AutoCAD will only consider the object's two endpoints when extruding the path curve. Just as with the Ruled Surface tool, the point at which you select the direction vector object affects the outcome of the extrusion. If you had selected a location near the top of the blue line, the extrusion would have gone in the opposite direction from the exercise.

FIGURE 17.31

Extruding an arc using a line to indicate the extrusion direction

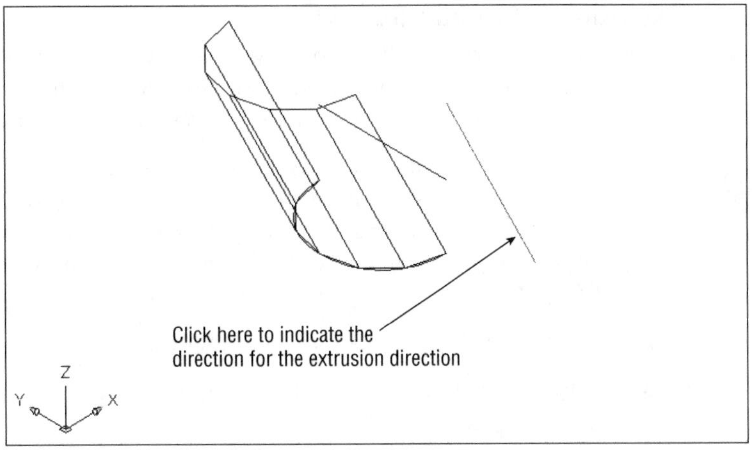
Click here to indicate the direction for the extrusion direction
Z
Y
X

Since the direction vector can point in any direction, the Tabulated Surface tool allows you to create an extruded shape that is not restricted to a direction perpendicular to the object being extruded.

The path curve defining the shape of the extrusion can be an arc, a circle, a line, or a polyline. You can use a curve-fitted polyline or a spline polyline to create more complex shapes, as shown in Figure 17.32. There you see a set of objects in the upper left that were created using the Ruled Surface tool. The Tabulated Surface tool and the line in the lower right were used to create the forms in the right side of the figure.

FIGURE 17.32

Samples of shapes created using the Ruled Surface and Tabulated Surface tools

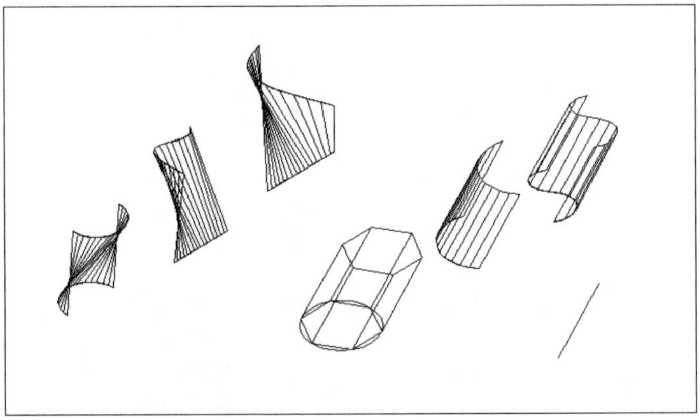

To increase the number of facets in either the Ruled Surface or Tabulated Surface tools, set the Surftab1 system variable to the number of facets you want.

Extruding a Circular Surface

The Revolved Surface tool allows you to generate circular extrusions quickly. Typical examples are vases or teacups. The following exercise illustrates how you can use the Revolved Surface tool to draw a pitcher. You'll use an existing drawing that has a profile of the pitcher already drawn.

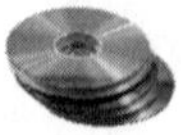

1. Open the `Pitcher.dwg` file from the companion CD. This file contains a polyline profile of a pitcher as well as a single line representing the center of the pitcher (see the top image in Figure 17.34 later in this chapter). The profile and line have already been rotated to a position that is perpendicular to the WCS. The grid is turned on so you can better visualize the plane of the WCS.

2. Click the Revolved Surface tool on the Surfaces toolbar.
3. At the `Select object to revolve:` prompt, click the polyline profile, as shown in the first image in Figure 17.33.

FIGURE 17.33

Drawing a pitcher using the Revolved Surface tool

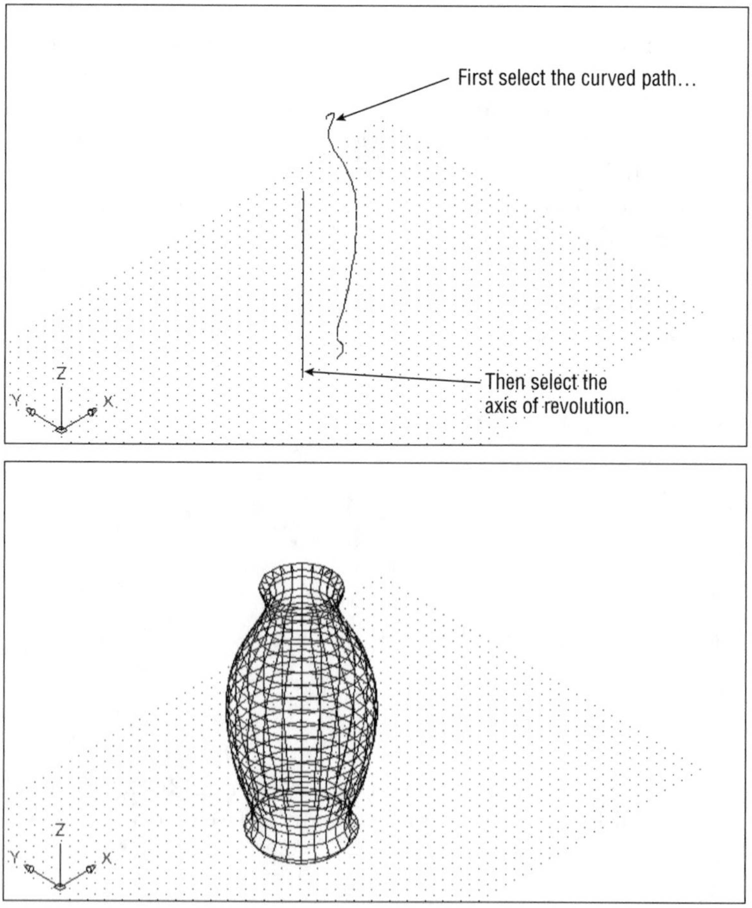
First select the curved path...
Then select the axis of revolution.
Z
Y
X
Z
Y
X

4. At the `Select object that defines the axis of Revolution:` prompt, click near the bottom of the vertical line representing the center of the vase, as shown in the first image in Figure 17.33.
5. At the `Specify start angle <0>:` prompt, press ↵ to accept the 0 start angle.
6. At the `Specify included angle (+=ccw, -=cw) <360>:` prompt, press ↵ to accept the Full Circle default. The pitcher appears, as shown in the second image in Figure 17.33.

Notice that the pitcher is made up of a faceted mesh, like the mesh that is created by the Edge Surface tool. Just as with the Edge Surface tool, you can set the number of facets in each direction using the Surftab1 and Surftab2 system variable settings. Both Surftab1 and Surftab2 were already set to 24 in the `Pitcher.dwg` file, so the pitcher shape should appear fairly smooth.

You may have noticed that in steps 5 and 6 of the previous exercise you have a few options. In step 5, you can specify a start angle. In this case, you accepted the 0 default. Had you entered a different value, 90 for example, the extrusion would have started in the 90° position relative to the current WCS. In step 6, you have the option of specifying the angle of the extrusion. Had you entered 180, for example, your result would have been half the pitcher. You can also specify the direction of the extrusion by specifying a negative or positive angle.

Editing a Mesh

Once you've created a mesh surface with either the Edge Surface or Revolved Surface tool, you can modify it. For example, suppose you want to add a spout to the pitcher you created in the previous exercise. You can use grips to adjust the individual points on the mesh to reshape the object. Here, you must take care how you select points. The UCS will become useful for editing meshes, as shown in the following exercise.

1. Zoom into the area shown in the first image in Figure 17.34.
2. Click the pitcher mesh to expose its grips.
3. Shift+click the grips shown in the second image in Figure 17.34.
4. Click the grip shown in the third image in Figure 17.34 and slowly drag the cursor to the left. As you move the cursor, notice how the lip of the pitcher deforms.
5. When you have the shape of a spout, select that point. The spout is fixed in the new position.

You can refine the shape of the spout by carefully adjusting the position of other grip points around the edge of the pitcher. Later, when you render the pitcher, you can apply a smooth shading value so that the sharp edges of the spout are smoothed out.

This exercise shows how easy it is to make changes to a mesh by moving individual grip locations. When you move mesh grips manually, however (as opposed to entering coordinates), their motion is restricted to a plane that is perpendicular to the current UCS. You can use this restriction to your advantage. For example, if you want to move the spout downward at a 30° angle, rotate the UCS so it is tipped at a 30° angle in relation to the top of the pitcher. Then edit the mesh grips as you did in the previous exercise.

FIGURE 17.34

Adding a spout to the pitcher mesh

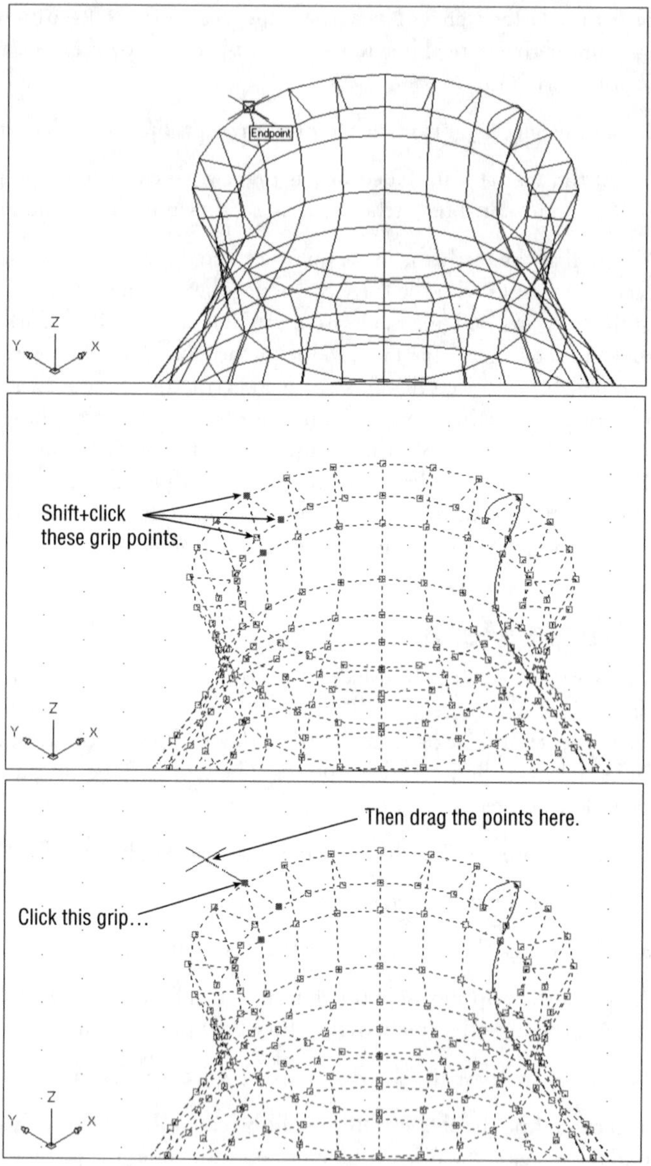

Another option is to specify a *relative* coordinate as opposed to selecting a point. By specifying a coordinate, such as **@.5<50**, you do not have to move the UCS. Using this method, however, removes you from the spontaneity of being able to select a point visually.

Other Mesh-Editing Options

You can choose Modify ➢ Object ➢ Polyline to edit meshes in a way similar to editing polylines. When you choose this option and pick a mesh, you get the following prompt:

```
Enter an option [Edit vertex/Smooth surface/Desmooth/Mclose/Nclose/Undo]:
```

Here are the descriptions of these options:

`Edit vertex` Allows you to relocate individual vertices in the mesh.

`Smooth surface` This option is similar to the Spline option for polylines. Rather than having the mesh's shape determined by the vertex points, the Smooth Surface option adjusts the mesh so that mesh vertices act as control points that pull the mesh—much as a spline frame pulls a spline curve.

TIP *You can adjust the amount of pull the vertex points exert on a mesh by using the* `Smooth surface` *option in conjunction with the Surftype system variable.*

`Desmooth` Reverses the effects of the `Smooth surface` option.

`Mclose` and `Nclose` Allow you to close the mesh in either the *m* or *n* direction. When either of these options is used, the prompt line changes, replacing `Mclose` or `Nclose` with `Mopen` or `Nopen` and allows you to open a closed mesh.

The Edit Polyline tool on the Modify II toolbar performs the same function as choosing Modify ➢ Object ➢ Polyline.

ACAD only

Moving Objects in 3D Space

AutoCAD provides two tools for moving objects in 3D space: Align and 3D Rotate. Both commands are found on the Modify ➢ 3D Operations menu. They help you perform some of the more common moves associated with 3D editing.

Aligning Objects in 3D Space

In mechanical drawing, you often create the parts in 3D and then show an assembly of the parts. The Align command can greatly simplify the assembly process. The following exercise describes how Align works.

1. Choose Modify ➢ 3D Operation ➢ Align, or type **Al**↵.
2. At the `Select objects:` prompt, select the 3D source object you want to align to another part. (The *source object* is the object you want to move.)
3. At the `Specify first source point:` prompt, pick a point on the source object that is the first point of an alignment axis, such as the center of a hole or the corner of a surface.
4. At the `Specify first destination point:` prompt, pick a point on the destination object to which you want the first source point to move. (The *destination object* is the object with which you want the source object to align.)

5. At the Specify second source point: prompt, pick a point on the source object that is the second point of an alignment axis, such as another center point or other corner of a surface.
6. At the Specify second destination point: prompt, pick a point on the destination object indicating how the first and second source points are to align in relation to the destination object.
7. At the Specify third source point or <continue/>: prompt, you can press ↵ if two points are adequate to describe the alignment. Otherwise, pick a third point on the source object that, along with the first two points, best describes the surface plane you want aligned with the destination object.
8. If you pick a third source point in step 7, you'll be prompted for a third destination point. Pick a point on the destination object that, along with the previous two destination points, describes the plane with which you want the source object to be aligned. The source object will move into alignment with the destination object.
9. If you press ↵ at step 7, you see the Scale objects based on alignment points? [Yes/No] <N>: prompt. If you press ↵ to accept the default, the selected object(s) will move into alignment with the destination points without changing size. If you enter **Y**↵, the selected object(s) will be scaled up or down to align exactly with the two destination points.

Figure 17.35 shows some examples of how the Align tool works.

FIGURE 17.35

Aligning two 3D objects

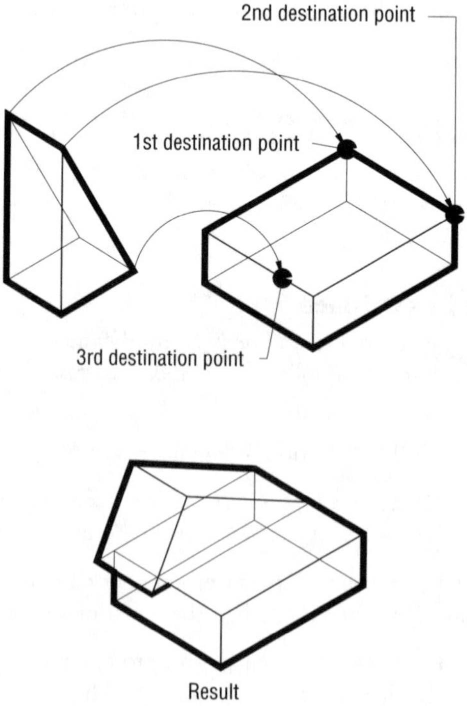

Rotating an Object in 3D

If you just want to rotate an object in 3D space, the Modify ➢ 3D Operation ➢ Rotate 3D option on the menu bar can simplify the operation. Once you've selected this option and selected the objects you want to rotate, you get the following prompt:

```
Axis by Object/Last/View/Xaxis/Yaxis/Zaxis/<2points>:
```

This prompt is asking you to describe the axis of rotation. Here are descriptions of the options in the prompt:

`Object` Allows you to indicate an axis by clicking an object. When you select this option, you are prompted to pick a line, a circle, an arc, or a 2D polyline segment. If you click a line or polyline segment, the line is used as the axis of rotation. If you click a circle, an arc, or a polyline arc segment, AutoCAD uses the line passing through the center of the circle or arc and perpendicular to its plane as the axis.

`Last` Uses the last axis that was used for a 3D rotation. If no previous axis exists, you are returned to the `Axis by Object/Last/View/Xaxis/YAxis/Zaxis/<2points>:` prompt.

`View` Uses the current view direction as the direction of the rotation axis. You are then prompted to select a point on the view direction axis to specify the exact location of the rotation axis.

`Xaxis/Yaxis/Zaxis` Uses the standard x-, y-, or z-axis as the direction for the rotation axis. You are then prompted to select points on the x-, y-, or z-axis to locate the rotation axis.

`2points` Uses two points you provide as the endpoints of the rotation axis.

So far, you have had a chance to practice creating and editing 3D objects using nearly every type of object available in AutoCAD. You might want to experiment on your own with the predefined 3D shapes on the Surfaces toolbar. In the next section, you'll discover how you can generate perspective views.

Viewing Your Model in Perspective

So far, your views of 3D drawings have been in *parallel projection*. This means that parallel lines appear parallel on your screen. Although this type of view is helpful while constructing your drawing, you will want to view your drawing in true perspective from time to time, to get a better feel for what your 3D model actually looks like.

AutoCAD provides the 3D Orbit tool to help you get the 3D view you want. You can use the 3D Orbit tool to refine your parallel projection views, but it is also the gateway to perspective views of your model. 3D Orbit has a lot of features and settings. With this in mind, you might want to begin these exercises when you know you have an hour or so to complete them all at one sitting.

TIP *LT users do not have the 3D Orbit tool, but many of the functions of 3D Orbit are duplicated in the Dview command, which is available in LT. Consult the* AutoCAD 2004 Instant Reference *on the companion CD or the AutoCAD LT help system for more information on the Dview command.*

If you are ready now, let's begin!

1. Open the `Setting.dwg` file from the companion CD. You'll use this file to practice using the 3D Orbit tool. This file contains a simple 3D model of some chairs, a table, and a lamp.

2. Right-click any toolbar and then choose 3D Orbit from the from the shortcut menu. Open the View toolbar as well.

3. Click the Camera tool on the View toolbar.
4. At the `Specify new camera position:` prompt, click the lower-left corner of the drawing, as shown in Figure 17.36.

FIGURE 17.36
Selecting the camera and target points

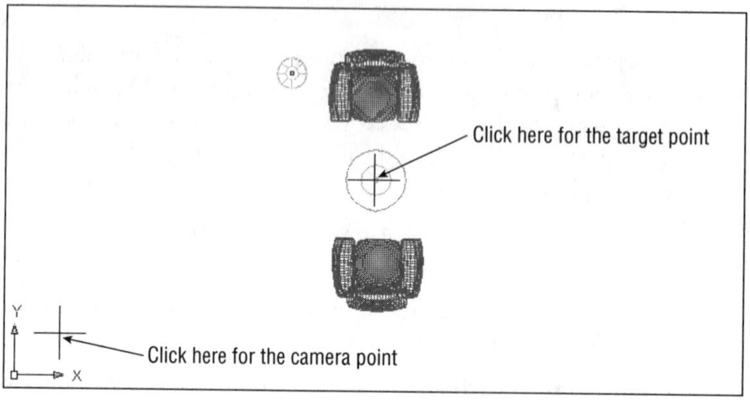
Click here for the target point
Click here for the camera point
Y
X

5. At the `Specify new camera target:` prompt, click the center of the circle that appears in the middle of the drawing, as shown in Figure 17.36. Your view changes to a side view of the chairs, as shown in Figure 17.37.

FIGURE 17.37
The side view of the chairs

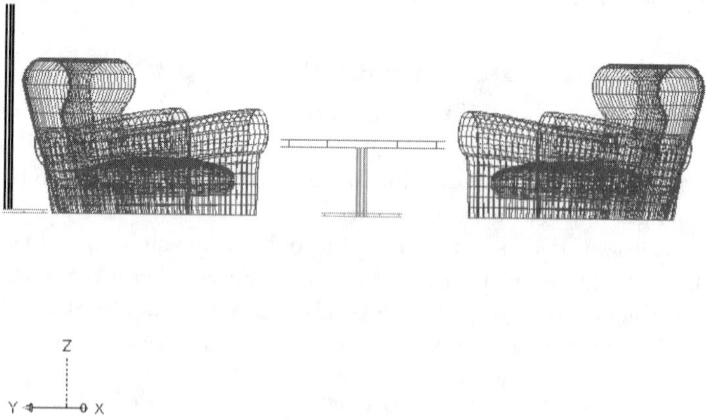
Z
Y
X

This new view is from the camera point that you specified in step 4. The view's center is the target point you selected in step 5. Now you're ready to use the 3D Orbit tool. The camera and target points you selected are at the 0 coordinate on the z-axis, so your view is aimed at the bottom of the chairs. That's why the view is oriented toward the top of the screen.

1. Click the 3D Orbit tool on the 3D Orbit toolbar. You can also choose View ➢ 3D Orbit. You see a circle with four smaller circles at its cardinal points. This circle is called an *arcball.* It helps you control your view, along with the cursor. In addition, the UCS icon changes to appear shaded.

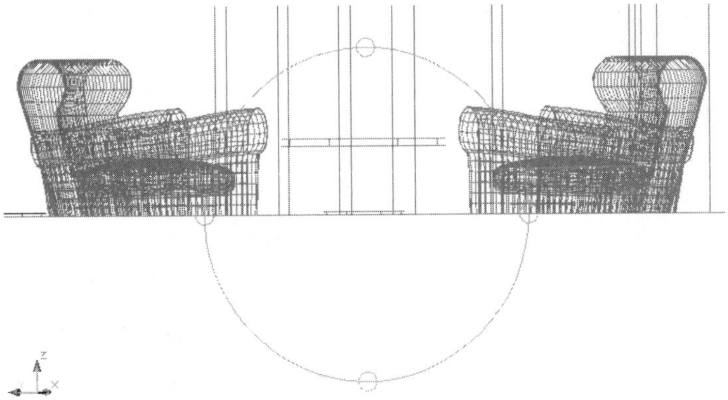

2. Place the cursor on the small circle at the top of the arcball. The cursor changes its appearance to a vertically elongated ellipse.
3. Click and drag the cursor downward from the top circle of the arcball, but don't let go yet. The view follows your cursor, and the motion is restrained to be vertical. When you've got a view similar to Figure 17.38, release the mouse button.

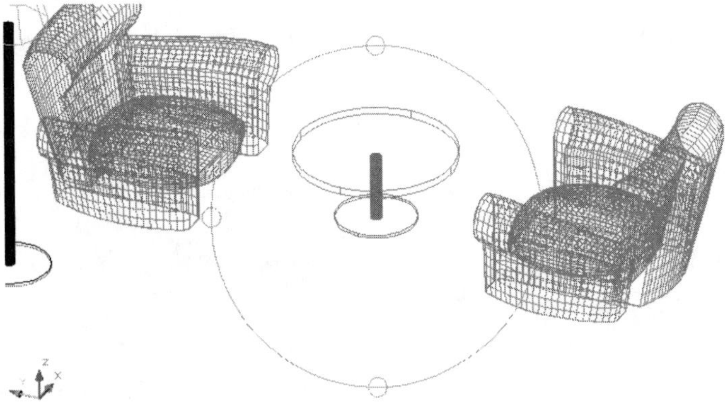

FIGURE 17.38
The view after clicking and dragging the top arcball circle

When you click and drag the circle at the top or bottom of the arcball, your view rotates about the target point you selected in step 5 of the first exercise in this section. You can relocate the rotation point by using the Camera tool to select a new target point.

Now let's continue by rotating the view sideways.

1. Place the cursor on the circle on the left side of the arcball. Notice that this time the cursor changes to look like an ellipse that is elongated horizontally.
2. Click and drag the cursor to the left from this circle on the arcball, but don't let go. The view now rotates about the target point from left to right.
3. Position your view so it looks like Figure 17.39 and release the mouse.

FIGURE 17.39

The view after clicking and dragging the left arcball circle

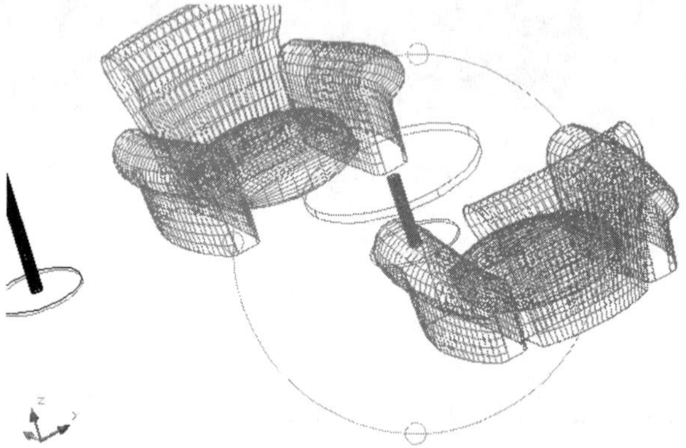

By now, you should have a feel for the way the arcball works. You click and drag until you get the view you want. But right now, the view is not exactly right. You'll want to rotate the view to straighten it out.

1. Move the cursor to the outside of the arcball. Notice that it now looks like a circle.
2. With the cursor outside the arcball, click and drag downward. The view rotates in the direction that you move the cursor.
3. Adjust the view until it looks similar to the one in Figure 17.40.

FIGURE 17.40

The view straightened out

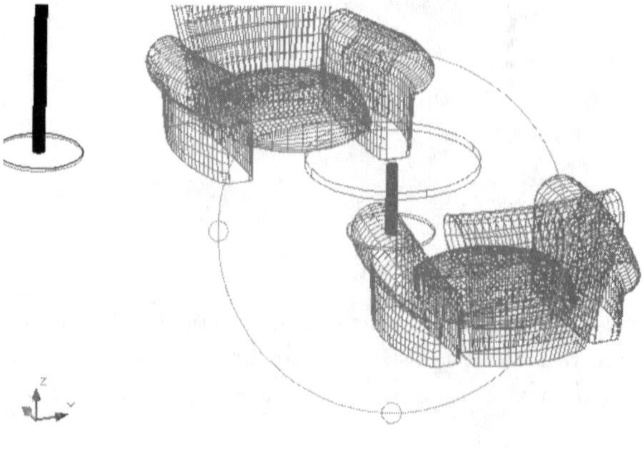

When the cursor appears as a circle, you can rotate the view in the view plane. This allows you to "straighten" your view once you've moved your viewpoint or camera location.

You've tried nearly all the arcball options. There's one more option that is a combination of the top and side circles.

1. Place the cursor inside the arcball. The cursor now looks like two superimposed ellipses.
2. Click and drag the cursor and move it in a slight circular motion. Notice how the view pivots in all directions about the target point.
3. Return the view to the one shown in Figure 17.40.

This last option gives you a bit more freedom to move the view, though it can be a bit unwieldy.

Tip You can change the target point, and therefore the point around which your 3D Orbit view rotates, by using the Camera tool on the View toolbar. Click the Camera tool; then press ↵ when you are prompted for a camera location. Select the new target location. You can use an object in your drawing as a selection point.

Turning on a Perspective View

The view is still a bit high in the AutoCAD window. You will want to move it downward to include more of the lamp and the chair at the top. You're also still viewing your drawing in a parallel projection mode. In the next exercise, you'll switch to a perspective view, and then use the Pan tool to center your view.

1. Right-click and choose Projection ➢ Perspective from the shortcut menu. Your view changes to a perspective one. The view is a bit high, so you'll want to use the 3D Orbit Pan tool to center your view.

2. Right-click and choose Pan from the shortcut menu. You can also select 3D Pan from the 3D Orbit toolbar. The arcball disappears, and the cursor turns into the familiar Pan cursor.
3. Click and drag the view downward to center the table top in the view. Your view should look like Figure 17.41.

FIGURE 17.41
The perspective view after panning downward

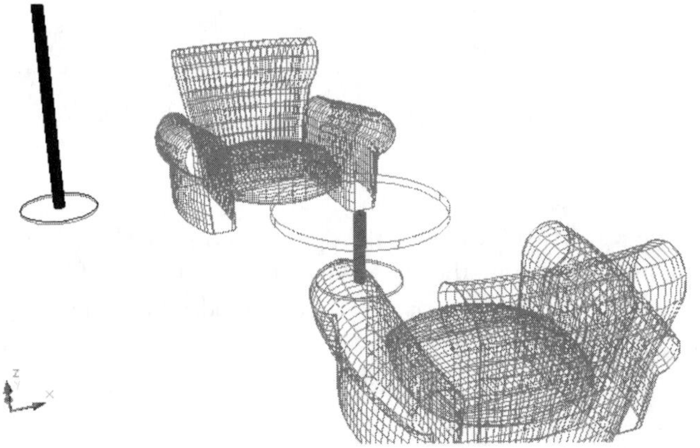

You saw several things happen in this brief exercise. First, you saw how easy it is to obtain a perspective view. You were also introduced to the 3D Orbit shortcut menu. This menu offers a few options that don't appear on the 3D Orbit toolbar.

You also used the Pan tool on the 3D Orbit toolbar. This tool works just like the standard Pan tool you've been using all along, but there is a difference. You may have noticed that when you panned your view, the perspective changed as you panned. The effect is similar to that of looking out a car's side window as you move down the highway. When you pan your view using the 3D Pan tool on the 3D Orbit toolbar, you are moving both the camera viewpoint and the target point together. This maintains your camera and target orientation while moving the overall scene.

Using Some Visual Aids

You're still in 3D Orbit mode, even though you no longer see the arcball. This can be a bit confusing. You can use a visual aid to remind yourself that 3D Orbit is still active.

1. Right-click and then choose Visual Aids ➢ Compass from the shortcut menu. The 3D Orbit Compass appears.
2. Right-click again and choose Visual Aids ➢ Grid. A grid appears at the zero Z coordinate.
3. To help visualize the forms of the objects in this scene, turn on the Shade mode. Right-click and then choose Shading Modes ➢ Hidden. You've already seen both the Grid and the Hidden Shade mode in Chapter 16. Figure 17.42 shows how your view will look after turning on the Compass, Grid, and Hidden Shade modes.

FIGURE 17.42
The view with the Compass, Grid, and Hidden shade modes turned on

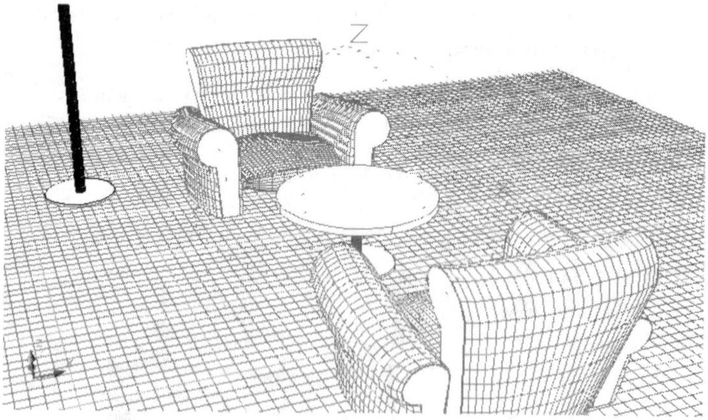

You may have noticed that the options under the Shading Modes cascading menu were the same options available from the Shade Mode toolbar. They're offered in the 3D Orbit menu for easy access, in case you want to view your model with hidden lines removed.

Adjusting the Camera

The 3D Orbit arcball lets you rotate your camera location about the target. You've also seen how the Pan option moves both the target and the camera to view a different part of your 3D model. All these tools maintain the distance between the target and the camera. In the following set of exercises, you learn how to use the tools that allow you to fine-tune your camera location and characteristics.

Start by changing the distance between the camera and the target.

1. Right-click and then choose More ➢ Adjust distance from the shortcut menu. You can also select the 3D Adjust Distance tool from the 3D Orbit toolbar. The cursor turns into a double-headed arrow in a perspective view.
2. Click and drag the mouse downward. As you do, the view recedes as if you were backing away from the scene. You are moving the camera away from the target location.
3. Adjust your view so that it looks like Figure 17.43.

FIGURE 17.43

The view after using the 3D Adjust Distance tool

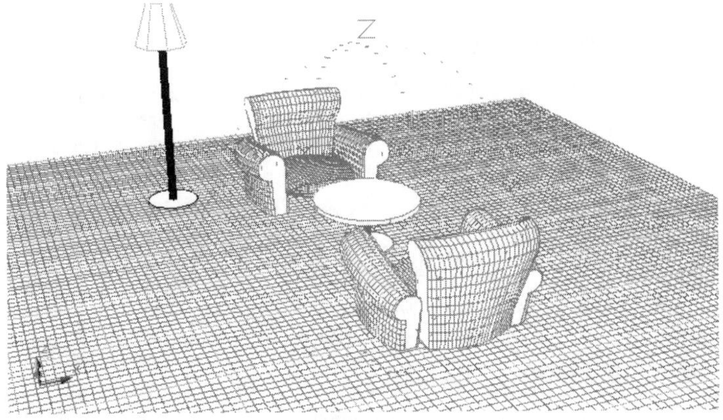

You can adjust the camera distance from the target by clicking and dragging up or down. An upward motion brings the camera closer to the target. A downward motion moves the camera away.

At first glance, the Zoom option on the 3D Orbit toolbar appears to do the same thing as the 3D Adjust Distance option. However, the Zoom option actually has a very different effect on the display. Although it enlarges or reduces the size of the image, it does so by changing the field of view of the camera. This is like using a telephoto lens on a camera. You can zoom in on a scene without actually changing your position relative to the scene.

A telephoto lens does its work by changing its focal length. By increasing its focal length, you get a closer view. By decreasing the focal length, you see more of the scene. If you shorten the focal length too much, the image begins to distort, like the image in a fish-eye lens. The Zoom option of the 3D Orbit tool works in the same way. Try the following exercise to see firsthand.

1. Right-click and choose Orbit from the shortcut menu. The arcball returns.
2. Click the circle on the right side of the arcball, and drag the view to the right so you get a side view of both the chairs.

3. Use the arcball to adjust your view so it looks like Figure 17.44.

FIGURE 17.44
The side view of the chairs after rotating the view horizontally

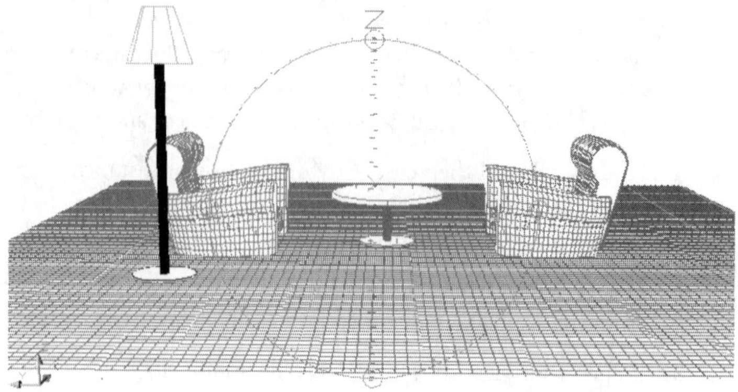

Next, you'll temporarily leave the 3D Orbit tool to turn on a layer.

1. Right-click and then choose Exit from the shortcut menu to exit the 3D Orbit tool.
2. Use the Layer drop-down list to locate and turn on the Wall layer. You'll see some walls appear in the foreground.

3. Choose View ➢ 3D Orbit and then right-click and choose Zoom. You can also select the 3D Zoom tool from the 3D Orbit toolbar.
4. Click and drag the mouse slowly downward. As your view moves slowly away, it also begins to distort. The vertical walls start to splay outward more and more as you zoom out, as shown in the first image in Figure 17.45. You also see that the 3D Orbit compass distorts.
5. Bring your view back to normal by clicking and dragging the mouse upward until you have a view similar to the second image in Figure 17.45.

In this exercise, you turned on the walls of the room and then used the Zoom option to see the effects. As you zoomed back, you were actually changing the field of view, or focal length of the camera, to that of a wide-angle lens. You can control the focal length in a more precise way by using another command outside the 3D Orbit tool—the Dview command. The following exercise will show you how you can precisely set the focal length of the camera.

1. Right-click and then choose Exit from the shortcut menu.
2. Enter **Dv**↵↵ **Z**↵. Your display changes to show a crude house. This is a visual aid for the Dview command; your drawing hasn't changed.
3. You see the `Specify lens length:` prompt, with the current lens focal length shown in brackets as a default.
4. Type **35**↵ for a 35-mm lens focal length. Your view changes to offer a wider view of the room as shown in Figure 17.46.

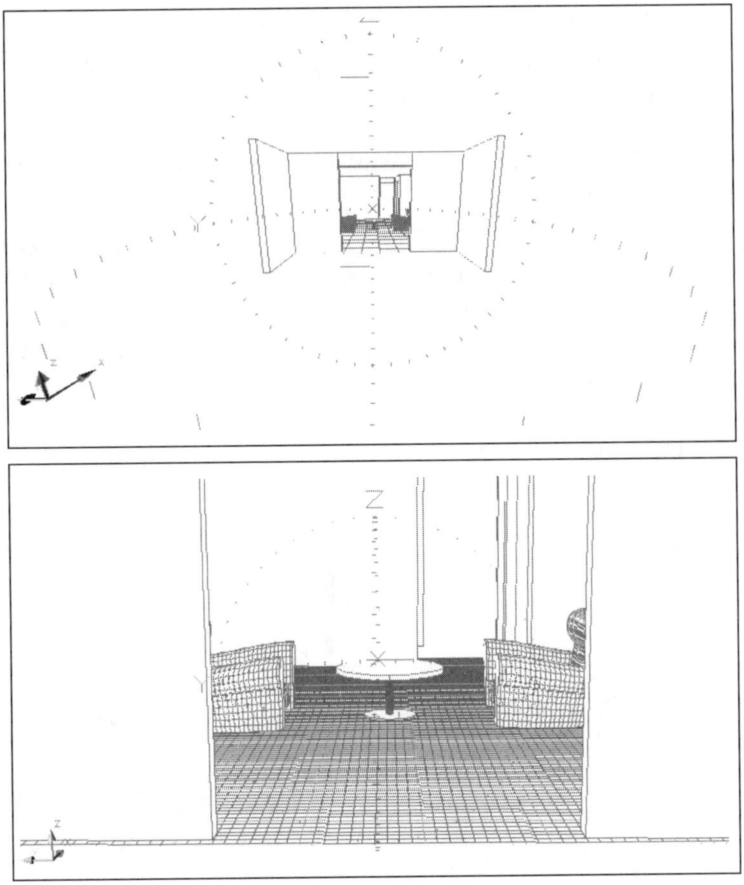

FIGURE 17.45
A view of the walls begins to distort when zooming out

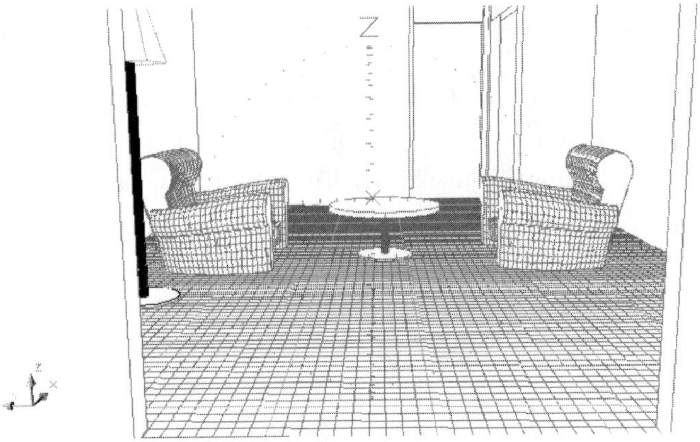

FIGURE 17.46
The view of the room after setting the camera focal length to 35mm

5. Press ↵ again to exit the Dview command.

The Dview command offers the same functions as the 3D Orbit tool, but it is much more difficult to use. However, it does offer the ability to set the camera focal length precisely. This feature can be of great use when setting up views of interior spaces in an architectural model.

Now, suppose you want to move the target of your view upward slightly to encompass more of the back of the room. You can accomplish this by rotating the camera. Here's how it's done.

1. Choose ➢ View 3D Orbit from the menubar. Then right-click and choose More ➢ Swivel Camera. You can also click the 3D Swivel tool in the 3D Orbit toolbar. The cursor changes to a camera icon with a curved arrow.
2. Click and drag the mouse upward to view more of the back wall of the room so that it looks similar to Figure 17.47.

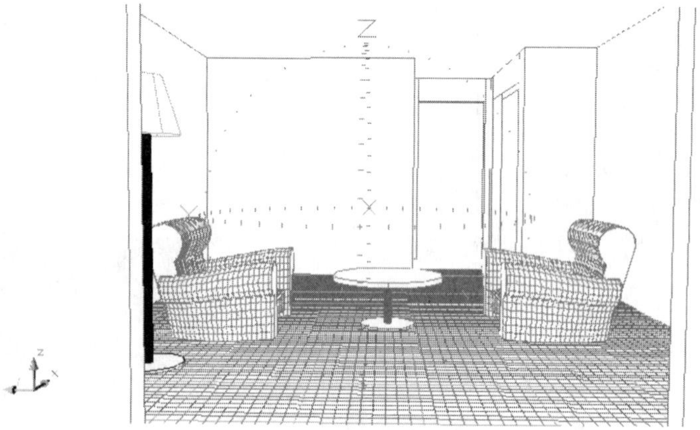

FIGURE 17.47
The room after swiveling the camera upward

Using Clipping Planes to Hide Parts of Your View

The walls in the foreground obscure the current view of the interior of the room. Although this may be an accurate view of your model, you might want to remove parts of your model that obstruct your view in the foreground. To do this, you can use clipping planes.

1. In the 3D Orbit mode, right-click, and then choose More ➢ Adjust Clipping Planes to open the Adjust Clipping Planes dialog box. It shows your model as though you were looking at it from above.

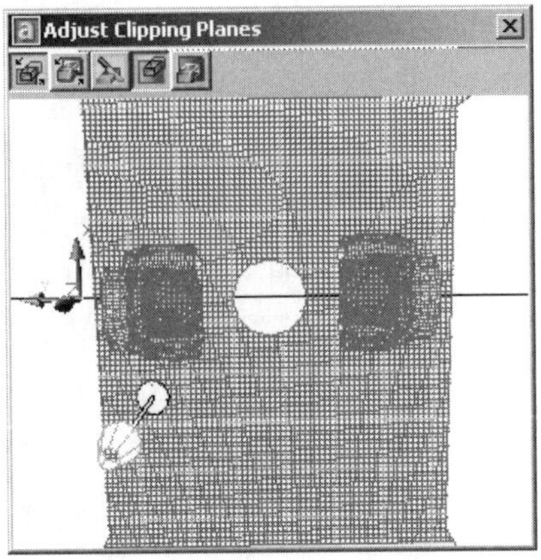

Also notice that the view of the room in the AutoCAD window changes. You see more of the room, and the chairs appear to be sliced in half.

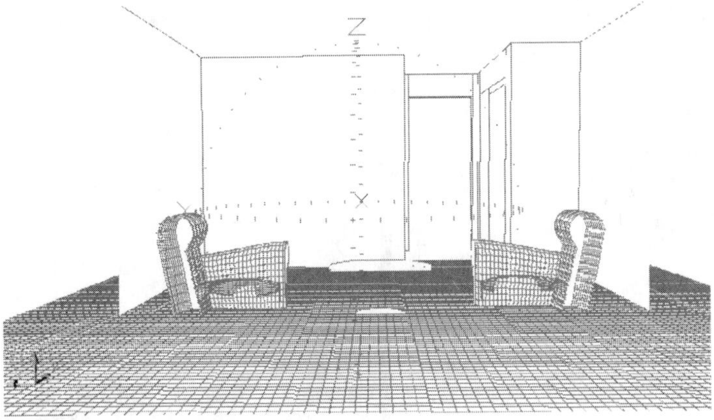

2. Right-click in the Adjust Clipping Planes dialog box to open the shortcut menu, which contains several options.

3. Make sure the Adjust Front Clipping option shows a checkmark next to it; then click the screen to close the shortcut menu. This allows you to adjust the front clipping plane. You can also click the Adjust Front Clipping button on the dialog box toolbar.

4. Place the cursor over the horizontal line in the middle of the dialog box; then click and drag downward. The line moves downward. This line represents the location of the front clipping plane in relation to the objects in the drawing. Notice what happens to your view in the main part of the AutoCAD window as you move the clipping plane. The chairs become whole again, and the lamp appears. Move the cursor up and down to see the effect.

5. Move the clipping plane downward until it is just past the lamp toward the bottom of the dialog box.

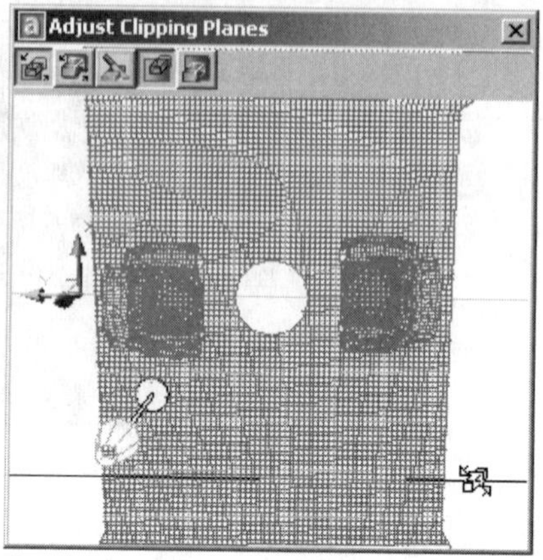

6. Close the Adjust Clipping Planes dialog box. Your view should now show more of the room, as shown in Figure 17.48.

FIGURE 17.48

The interior view of the room with the front clipping plane turned on

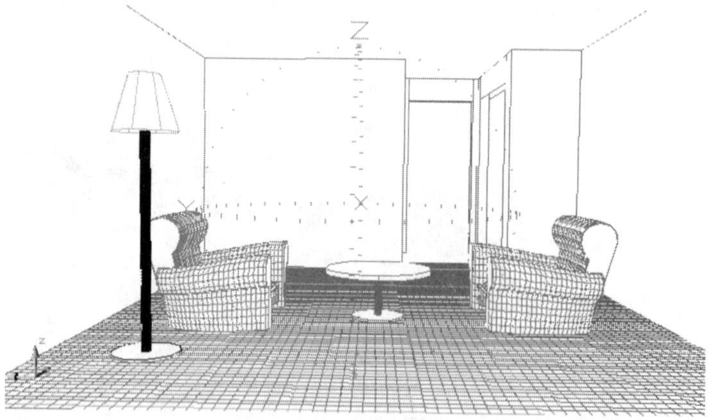

The front clipping plane is turned on as soon as you open the Adjust Clipping Planes dialog box. You can then adjust the clipping plane by moving in the dialog box. In addition, you can turn on and adjust a back clipping plane to hide objects in the back of your scene, as shown in Figure 17.49. To do this, you turn on the back clipping plane; then adjust it just as you did the front clipping plane. Two buttons control these functions in the Adjust Clipping Planes dialog box:

The Adjust Back Clipping button lets you adjust the location of the back clipping plane, and the Back Clipping On/Off button turns the back clipping plane on or off.

FIGURE 17.49
The effects of the clipping planes

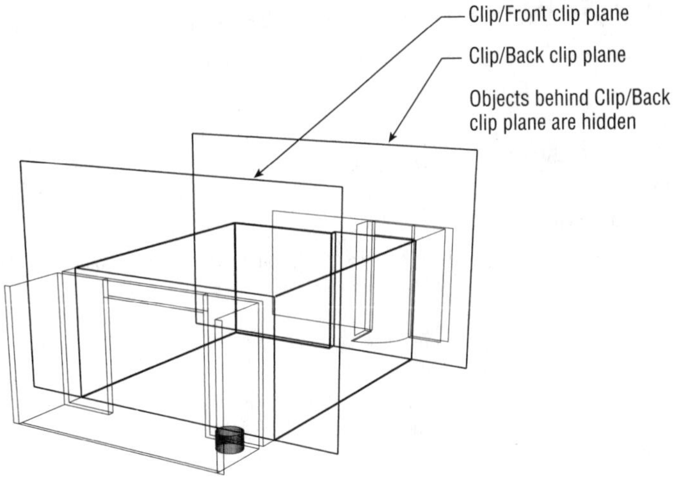

A third option, the Create Slice button, lets you move both the back and front clipping planes in unison. All these options are also on the Adjust Clipping Planes shortcut menu.

Getting a Simple Animation of Your View

The last 3D Orbit option you'll learn about is one that is perhaps more fun than practical. You can get a simple animated view of your model that rotates your view about the target point. Try this exercise to see how it works.

1. To make this animation a bit more interesting, turn on the Gouraud shading mode. While in 3D Orbit mode, right-click and then choose Shading Modes ➢ Gouraud Shaded.

2. Right-click again; then choose More ➢ Continuous Orbit. You can also select 3D Continuous Orbit from the 3D Orbit toolbar.
3. Click and drag to the left just a short distance. Your view begins to spin in a clockwise direction. The distance you click and drag controls the speed of the spin.
4. Click anywhere to stop the rotation; then click and drag to the right. This time the model spins in a counterclockwise direction.
5. Click again to stop the spinning.
6. After you've reviewed the results of this exercise, close the `Setting.dwg` file without saving it.

The 3D Continuous Orbit option is better suited to viewing single objects rather than the interior of a room, but this exercise shows what can be done with this option.

This concludes your tour of the 3D Orbit tool. You've used nearly every option available in this tool. With this knowledge, you should be able to set up practically any view you want. You covered a lot of ground here, so you might want to review this section before you work in 3D again.

If You Want to Experiment...

You've covered a lot of territory in this chapter, so it may be a good idea to play with these commands to help you remember what you've learned. Try the exercise shown in Figure 17.50.

FIGURE 17.50

Drawing a 3D overstuffed couch

Draw the shape shown to the right using a spline curve polyline.

Use Modify > 3D Operation > Rotate 3D to rotate the curve 90 degrees.

Use View > 3D Views > SW Isometric to get a 3D view of the shape.

Copy the shape in the Y axis so it looks similar to this view. Add arcs connecting the bottom endpoints of the shapes.

Make two more copies of the shape and rotate them so they are oriented as shown to the right.

Add more arcs to the endpoints of these new shapes.

Set the Surftab1 system variable to 12 and the Surftab2 system variable to 24

Use the Edgesurf command to create the mesh forming the couch back and arms.

Mirror the meshes to create the arms for the other side.

Draw some cushions and add them to your couch.

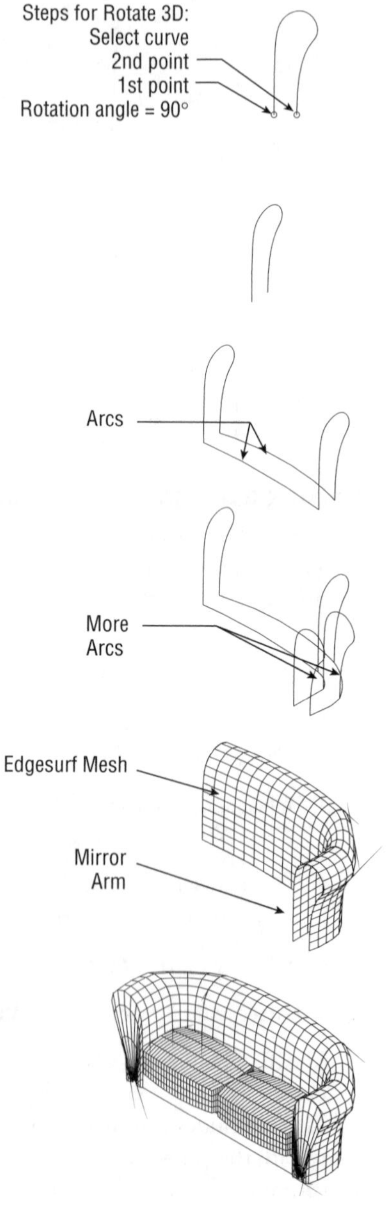

Chapter 18

Rendering and Animating 3D Drawings

JUST A FEW YEARS ago, it took the power of a graphics workstation to create the kinds of images you will create in this chapter. Today, you can render not just a single image, but several hundred images to build computer animations. And with the explosion of game software, the Internet, and virtual reality, real-time walk-through sessions of 3D computer models are nearly as commonplace as word processors.

In this chapter, you'll learn how you can use rendering tools in AutoCAD to produce rendered still images of your 3D models. With these tools, you can add materials, control lighting, and even add landscaping and people to your models. You also have control over the reflectance and transparency of objects, and you can add bitmap backgrounds to help set the mood.

WARNING *AutoCAD 2004 LT does not support any of the features described in this chapter.*

- Creating a Quick-Study Rendering
- Adding a Background Scene
- Effects with Lighting
- Adding Reflections and Detail with Ray Tracing
- Creating and Adjusting Texture Maps
- Adding Landscape and People
- Improving Your Image and Editing
- If You Want to Experiment…

Things to Do Before You Start

You will want to take certain steps before you start working with the rendering tools so you won't run into problems later. First, make sure you have plenty of free disk space on the drive where

Windows is installed. Having 100 megabytes of free disk space will ensure that you won't exceed your RAM capacity while rendering. Also, make sure there is plenty of free disk space on the drive where your AutoCAD files are kept.

Creating a Quick-Study Rendering

Throughout this chapter, you will work with a 3D model that was created using AutoCAD's solid modeling tools. (You'll learn more about solid modeling in Chapter 19.) The model is of two buildings on a street corner. You'll start by creating a basic rendering using the default settings in the Render dialog box.

1. Open the `Facade.dwg` file from the companion CD.
2. Open the Render toolbar from the Toolbar dialog box.

3. Choose View ➢ Render ➢ Render or click the Render tool in the Render toolbar to open the Render dialog box.

   In time, you will become intimately familiar with this dialog box.

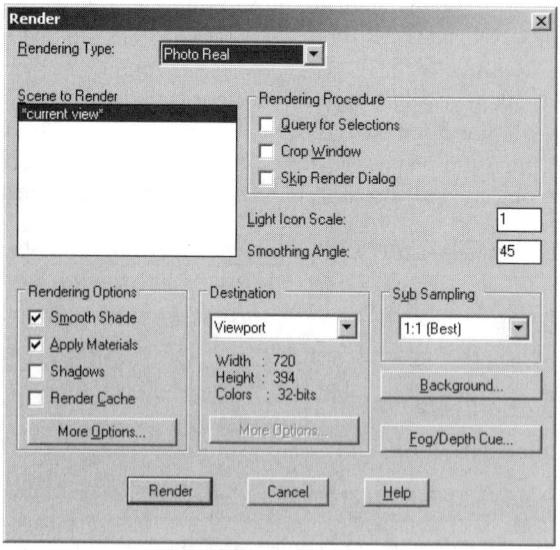

4. Click the Render button. AutoCAD takes a minute or two to render the current view. While it's working, you will see messages in the Command window showing you the progress of the rendering. When AutoCAD is done, the surface-shaded model appears (see Figure 18.1).

When you render a model without any special settings, you get what is called a *Z buffer shaded model*. (A *Z buffer* is like a work area in memory where the distance between surfaces along a view's z-axis can be compared. This helps AutoCAD determine which surfaces overlap.) The surfaces are shaded in their color, and the light source is, by default, from the camera location. This view is much like a Hidden-Line view with color added to help distinguish surface orientation. You can actually get a similar view using the Flat Shade tool on the Shade toolbar.

FIGURE 18.1

The Facade model rendered using all the default settings

Simulating the Sunlight Angle

The ability to add a sunlight source to a drawing is one of AutoCAD's key features. The Sun Angle Calculator tool is used frequently in the design of buildings in urban and suburban settings. Neighboring building owners want to know if your project will cast darkening shadows over their homes or workplaces. You can use the Sun Angle Calculator to accurately simulate the sun's location in relation to a model and its surrounding buildings. AutoCAD also lets you set up multiple light sources other than the sun.

So let's add the sun to our model to give a better sense of the building's form and relationship to its site.

1. Choose View ➢ Render ➢ Light or click Lights on the Render toolbar to open the Lights dialog box.

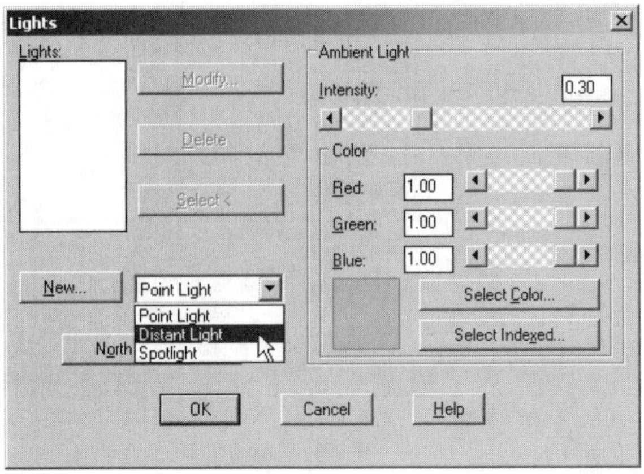

TIP *Whenever you are creating a new light or other object with the Rendering tool, you usually have to give it a name first, before you can do anything else.*

2. Choose Distant Light from the drop-down list next to the New button.
3. Click the New button to open the New Distant Light dialog box. This dialog box lets you control various aspects of the light source, such as color and location.

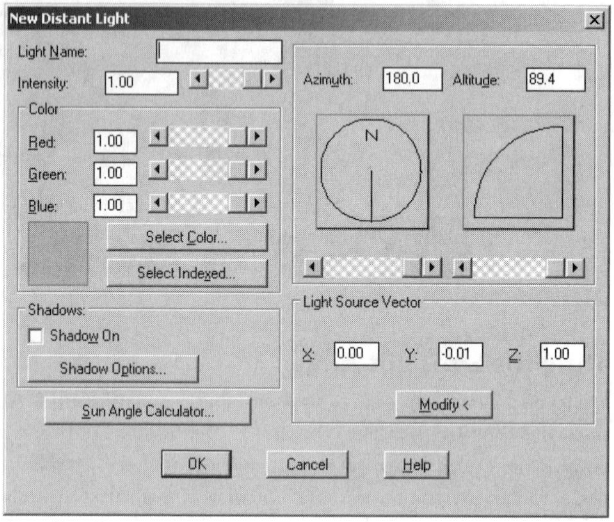

4. Type **SUN** in the Light Name input box.
5. Because you want to simulate the sun in this example, click the Sun Angle Calculator button to open the Sun Angle Calculator dialog box.

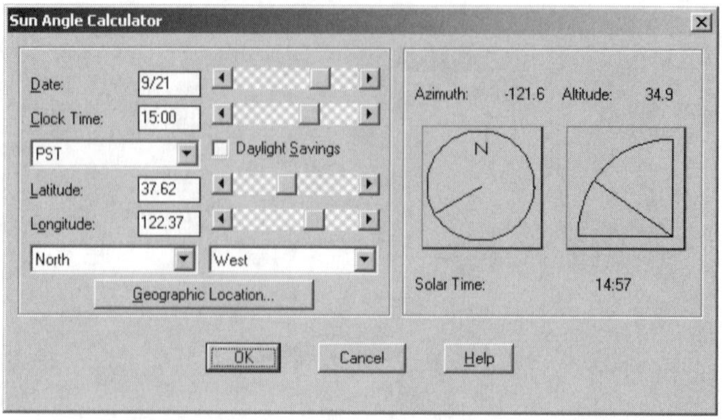

Notice that you have options for setting the date and time to determine the exact location of the sun. In addition, you can indicate where true polar north is in relation to your model. AutoCAD assumes polar north is at the 90° position in the WCS.

6. One important factor for calculating the sun angle is finding your location on the earth. Click the Geographic Location button to open the Geographic Location dialog box. Here you can tell AutoCAD where your building is located in the world.

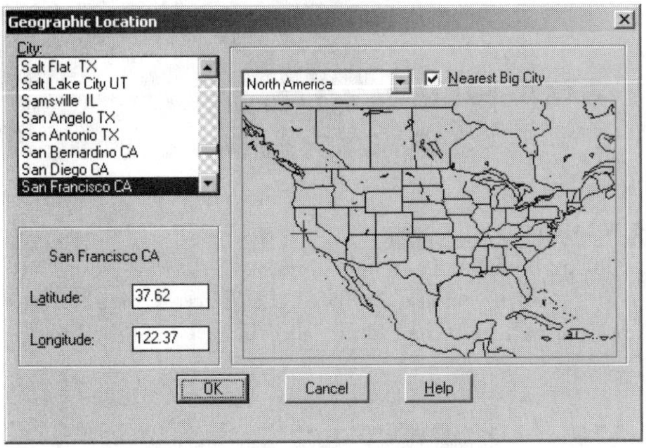

7. For the sake of this tutorial, suppose the Facade model is a building in San Francisco, California, USA. Select North America from the drop-down list above the map.
8. Locate and select San Francisco CA in the scrolling list to the left of the map. Notice that the Latitude and Longitude input boxes below the list change to reflect the location of San Francisco. For locations not listed, you can enter values manually in those input boxes.
9. Now click OK to return to the Sun Angle Calculator dialog box. Set the date for 9/21 and the time for 14:00 hours. Notice that the graphic to the right of the dialog box adjusts to show the altitude and azimuth angle of the sun for the time you enter.
10. Click OK in the Sun Angle Calculator dialog box, click OK in the New Distant Light dialog box, and then click OK again in the Lights dialog box.
11. Choose View ➢ Render ➢ Render or click Render on the Render toolbar, and then click the Render button in the Render dialog box. Your model will be shaded to reflect the sun's location (see Figure 18.2).

Notice that the building itself looks darker than before and that the ground plane is lighter. Remember that in the first rendering, the light source was the same as the camera location, so the wall facing you received more direct light. In this last rendering, the light source is at a glancing angle, so the surface appears darker.

FIGURE 18.2
The Facade model with the sun light source added

SETTING POLAR NORTH

If you are including the sun as a light source in a drawing in order to run shade studies, it's essential to orient your drawing accurately. To set the direction of polar north in your drawing, click the North Location button in the Lights dialog box to open the North Location dialog box, shown in Figure 18.3.

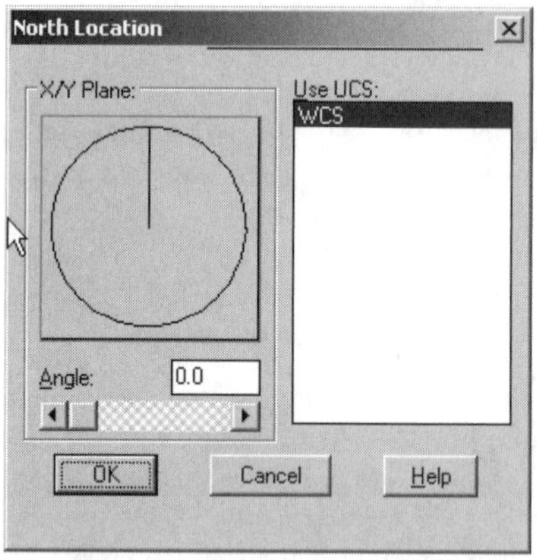

FIGURE 18.3
The North Location dialog box

With this dialog box, you can set true north in any of the following ways:

- Click the graphic to point to the direction.
- Use the slide bar at the bottom to move the arrow of the graphic and adjust the value in the input box.
- Enter a value directly in the input box.

You can also indicate which UCS is used to set the north direction. For example, you might have already set a UCS to point to the true north direction. You only need to select UCS from the list and leave the angle at 0.

IMPROVING THE SMOOTHNESS OF CIRCLES AND ARCS

You might notice that at times when using the Render, Hide, or Shade tool, solid or region arcs appear segmented rather than curved. This may be fine for producing layouts or backgrounds for hand-rendered drawings, but for final plots, you will want arcs and circles to appear as smooth curves. You can adjust the accuracy of arcs in your hidden, rendered, or shaded views through a setting in the Options dialog box.

You can modify the Rendered Object Smoothness setting in the Display tab of the Options dialog box to improve the smoothness of arcs. Its default setting is .5, but you can increase this to as high as 10 to smooth out faceted curves. In the `Facade.dwg` model, you can set Rendered Object Smoothness to 1.5 to render the arch in the entry as a smooth arc instead of a series of flat segments. You can also adjust this setting using the Facetres system variable.

Adding Shadows

There is nothing like adding shadows to a 3D rendering to give the model a sense of realism. AutoCAD offers three methods for casting shadows. The default method is called *volumetric shadows*. This method takes a considerable amount of time to render more complex scenes. The second option is to generate shadows using the *ray tracing* method (described later in this chapter). The third method, called *shadow mapping*, offers the best speed but requires some adjustment to get good results. Shadow mapping offers a soft-edge shadow. Although shadow maps are generally less accurate than the other two methods, the soft-edge shadow gives a level of realism not available in the other two methods.

In the following exercise, you will use the Shadow Map method. It requires the most adjustments and yields a faster rendering.

1. Choose View ➢ Render ➢ Lights or click Lights on the Render toolbar to open the Lights dialog box.
2. Make sure SUN is highlighted, and then click Modify to open the Modify Distant Light dialog box.

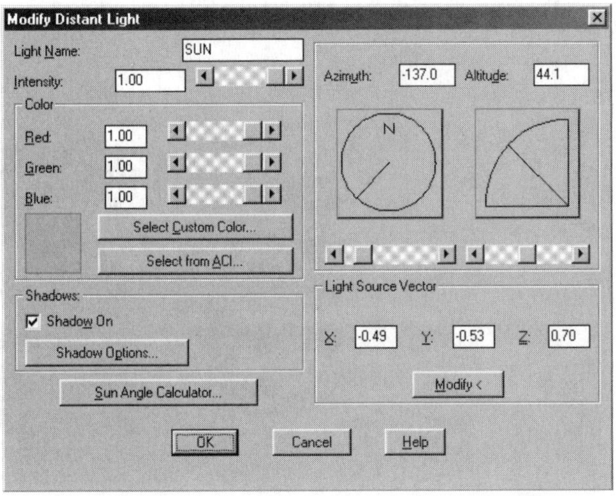

TIP *When adding shadows, remember that you must turn on the Shadow option in the Render dialog box and for each light that is to cast a shadow.*

3. Click the Shadow On check box, and then click the Shadow Options button to open the Shadow Options dialog box.

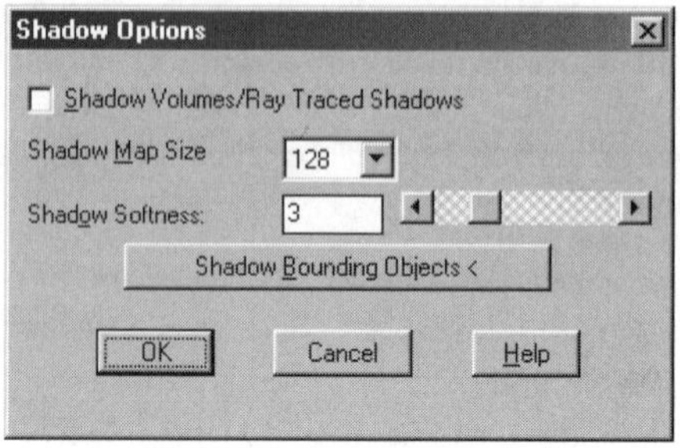

4. In the Shadow Map Size drop-down list, select 512. This is the actual number of pixels used to create the shadow map.
5. Click the Shadow Bounding Objects button. The dialog box temporarily closes to allow you to select the objects on the screen that you want to cast shadows.
6. Select the entire Facade building. Don't select any of the building next to it. When you are done, press ↵. The Shadow Options dialog box reappears.
7. Click OK to close the Shadow Options dialog box, and then click OK in the Modify Distant Light dialog box. It may take several seconds before the dialog box closes.
8. When you get to the Lights dialog box, click OK to close it.
9. Click the Render button on the Render toolbar.
10. In the Render dialog box, click the Shadows check box, and then click the Render button. After a minute or two, the model appears rendered with shadows (see Figure 18.4).

FIGURE 18.4

The Facade model rendered with shadows using the Shadow Map method

Adjusting Shadows for an Accurate Representation

Don't panic if the shadows don't appear correct. The Shadow Map method needs some adjustment before it will give the proper shadows. The default settings are appropriate for views of objects from a greater distance than our current view. The following exercise will show you what to do for close-up views.

1. Open the Render dialog box again, and then click the More Options button to open the Photo Real Render Options dialog box.

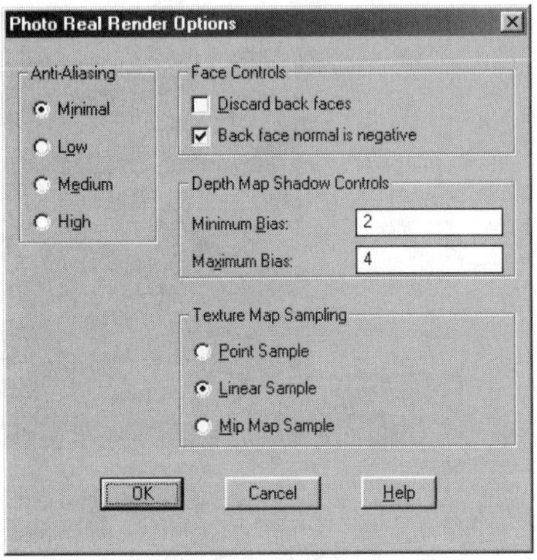

2. In the Depth Map Shadow Controls group, change the Minimum Bias value from 2 to .1.
3. In the same group, change the Maximum Bias value from 4 to .2.
4. Click OK to close the Photo Real Render Options dialog box, and then click Render. Your next rendering will show more accurately drawn shadows (see Figure 18.5).

FIGURE 18.5
The rendered view with the Shadow Bias settings revised

The shadow still looks a bit rough. You can further refine its appearance by increasing Shadow Map Size to greater than 512. This setting can be found in the Shadow Options dialog box in step 4 of the exercise in the "Adding Shadows" section. Figure 18.6 shows the same rendering with Shadow Map Size set to 1024. As you increase the map size, you also increase render time and the amount of RAM required to render the view. If you don't have enough free disk space, AutoCAD might refuse to render the model. You will then either have to free up some disk space or decrease the map size.

FIGURE 18.6
The rendered view with Shadow Map Size set to 1024

Notice that the shadow has a soft edge. You can control the softness of the shadow edge using the Shadow Options dialog box. The Shadow Softness input box and slide bar let you sharpen the shadow edge by decreasing the value or soften it by increasing the value. The soft shadow is especially effective for renderings of building interiors or scenes in which you are simulating artificial light.

Adding Materials

The rendering methods you've learned so far can be of enormous help in your design effort. Simply being able to see how the sun affects your design can be of enormous help in selling your ideas or helping get plans through a tough planning board review. But the look of the building is still somewhat cartoonish. You can further enhance the rendering by adding materials to the objects in your model.

Let's suppose you want a granite-like finish to appear on the Facade model. You will also want the building next to the Facade model to appear as a glass tower. The first step in adding materials is to acquire the materials from AutoCAD's materials library.

1. Choose View ➢ Render ➢ Materials or click Materials on the Render toolbar to open the Materials dialog box.

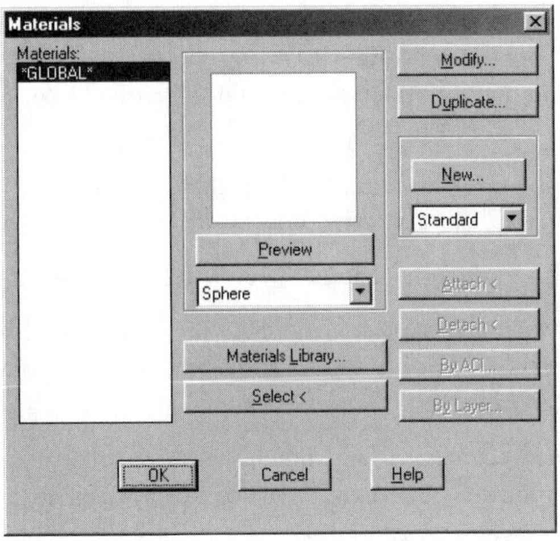

2. Click the Materials Library button to open the Materials Library dialog box.

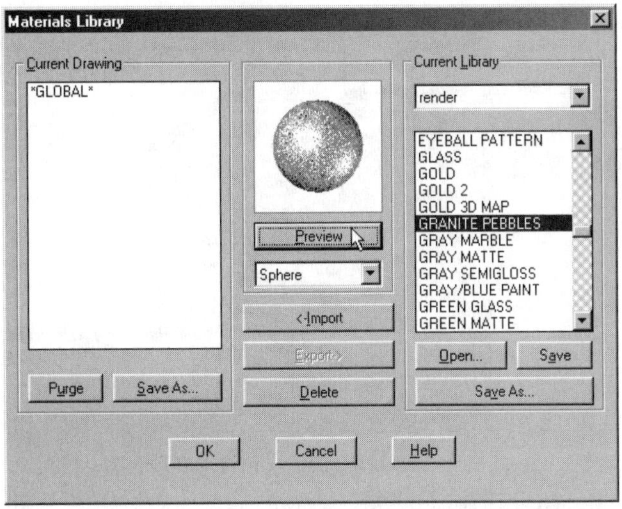

3. In the Current Library list box, find and select Granite Pebbles. This is the material you will assign to the facade.

4. Click the Preview button in the middle of the dialog box to display a view of the material on a sphere, giving you an idea of what the material looks like.

5. Click the Import button. Notice that Granite Pebbles now appears in the list box in the Current Drawing group. box to the left. This list box shows the materials you've transferred to your drawing.

6. Now locate Glass in the list on the right and select it. Click the Preview button again to see what it looks like. Notice that the preview shows a transparent sphere showing some reflected light. You might notice a textured effect caused by the low color resolution of the AutoCAD display.
7. Click the Import button again to make Glass available in the drawing; then click OK to exit the Materials Library dialog box.

Once you've acquired the materials, you will have to assign them to objects in your drawing.

1. In the Materials dialog box, highlight the Granite Pebbles item shown in the list on the left, and then click the Attach button in the right half of the dialog box. The dialog box temporarily disappears, allowing you to select the objects you want to appear as Granite Pebbles.
2. Click the Facade model, including the steps, columns, and arched entrance, and then press ↵. After a moment, the Materials dialog box appears again.
3. Click Glass in the Materials list.
4. This time you'll assign a material based on its layer. Click the By Layer button to the right of the dialog box to open the Attach By Layer dialog box.

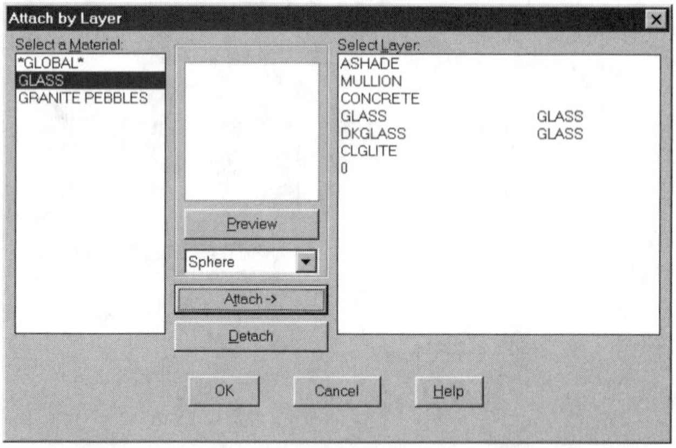

5. Shift+click Glass and Dkglass from the Select Layer list to the right, and then click the Attach button. Notice that the word `Glass` now appears next to the layer names you selected, indicating that the Glass material is now associated with those layers.
6. Click OK to exit the Attach By Layer dialog box; then click OK again to exit the Materials dialog box.
7. Now render your model. You might want to take a break at this point, because the rendering will take a few minutes. When AutoCAD is done, your rendering will look like Figure 18.7.

FIGURE 18.7
The Facade model with the glass and granite pebbles materials added

Adjusting the Materials' Appearance

At this point, the Facade model looks like it has an army camouflage paint job instead of a granite finish. Also, the glass of the office tower is a bit too transparent. Fortunately, you can make several adjustments to the materials. You will want to reduce the scale of the granite pebbles material so it is in line with the scale of the model. You will also want to darken the glass material so it looks more like the tinted glass used in modern office buildings. You'll start with the granite pebbles.

1. Choose View ➢ Render ➢ Materials to open the Materials dialog box.
2. Select Granite Pebbles from the Materials list, and then click the Modify button to open the Modify Granite Material dialog box.

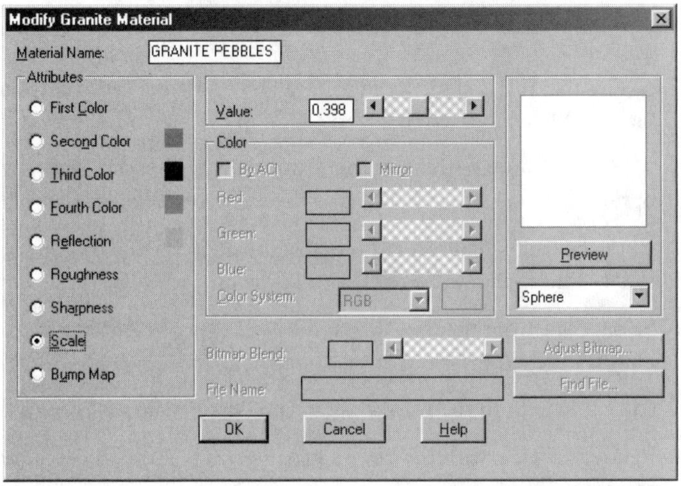

3. Click the Scale radio button in the Attributes area of the dialog box.

4. Change the Value input box near the top of the dialog box from .398 to .010. This reduces the scale of the material.
5. Click OK to return to the Materials dialog box.

The Modify Granite Material dialog box offers a variety of options that let you control reflectivity, roughness, color, transparency, and, of course, scale. Click the Help button to display a brief description of these options. As you'll see when you continue with the next exercise, not all materials have the same options.

1. Select Glass from the Materials list, and then click the Modify button again to open the Modify Standard Material dialog box.

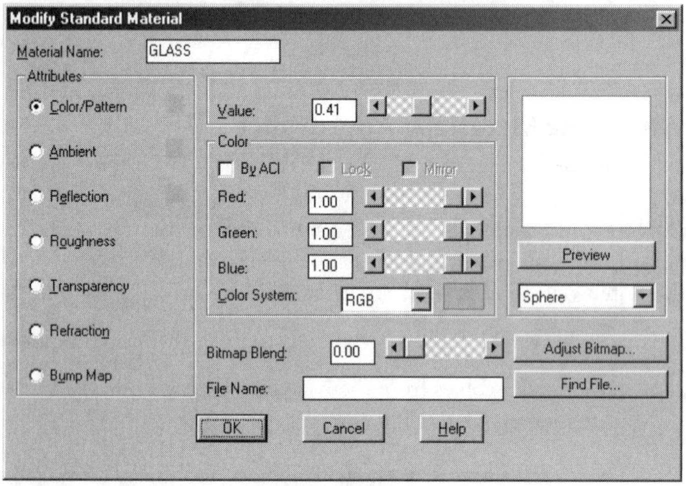

Notice that this dialog box offers a slightly different set of attributes than those in the Modify Granite Material dialog box you edited in the previous exercise.

2. Click the Transparency radio button in the Attributes button group, and then adjust the Value option downward to .55. This has the effect of darkening the glass.
3. Click the Color/Pattern radio button; then, in the Color button group, adjust the Red value to 0.69, the Green value to 0.60, and the Blue to 0.58. This gives the glass a bronze tint.
4. Select Cube from the drop-down list just below the Preview button, and then click the Preview button to get a preview of the color settings.
5. Click OK in both the Modify Standard Material and Materials dialog boxes to exit them.
6. Render the view with the new material settings. After a few minutes, your view will look something like Figure 18.8.

FIGURE 18.8
The Facade model after modifying the material settings

There are four basic types of materials: Standard, Marble, Granite, and Wood. Each type has its own set of characteristics that you can adjust. You can even create new materials based on one of the four primary types of materials. Now let's continue by making another adjustment to the material settings.

The granite surface of the Facade is still a bit too strong. You can reduce the graininess of the granite by further editing in the Modify Granite Material dialog box.

1. Click the Materials tool on the Render toolbar to open the Materials dialog box, select Granite Pebbles from the Materials list, and then choose Modify to open the Modify Granite Material dialog box.
2. Click the Sharpness Attribute radio button. Then set the Value input box to .20.
3. Click OK, and then click OK again in the Materials dialog box.
4. Choose View ➢ Render ➢ Render to open the Render dialog box, and then click the Render button. Your rendering appears after a few minutes with a finer granite surface (see Figure 18.9).

FIGURE 18.9
The rendered image with a finer granite surface

Adding a Background Scene

You could continue by adding and adjusting materials to the other parts of the model, but try dressing up your view by including a sky. To do so, you need to set up the background.

1. Open the Render dialog box, and then click the Background button to open the Background dialog box.

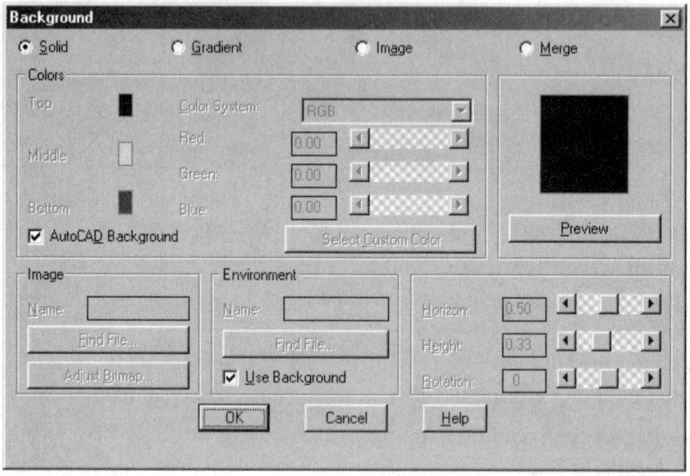

2. In the row of radio buttons across the top, find and click Image. Notice that several of the options near the bottom of the dialog box are now available.

3. Click the Find File button at the bottom left of the dialog box to open the Background Image dialog box.

4. Locate the `Sky.tga` file. If you are using Windows XP, it can be found in the `C:\Documents and Settings\User Name\Local Settings\Application Data\Autodesk\AutoCAD 2004\R16.0\enu\textures 2004\` folder.

TIP *To find the exact location of the textures folder on your system, choose Tools ➢ Options, select the Files tab, then expand the Texture Map Search Path item in the list box. The Textures folder location is listed under this item.*

5. Once back in the Background dialog box, click Preview to see what the file looks like. `Sky.tga` is a bitmap image of a blue sky with clouds.

6. Click OK. Then, once you are back in the Render dialog box, click Render. The background appears behind the model, as shown in Figure 18.10.

FIGURE 18.10
The Facade model rendered with a sky bitmap image for a background

In this example we added a bitmap image for a background, but you can use other methods to generate a background. For example, you might prefer to use a gradient shade or color for the background. This can help give a sense of depth to the image (see Figure 18.11). You can, of course, add a single color to the background if you prefer.

FIGURE 18.11
The Facade model with a gradient color background.

To create a gradient background, click the Gradient radio button at the top of the Background dialog box. You can then adjust the color for the top, middle, and bottom third of the background. AutoCAD automatically blends the three colors from top to bottom to create the gradient colors.

Effects with Lighting

Up to now, you've only used one light source, called Distant Light, to create a sun. You have two other light sources available to help simulate light: point-light sources and spotlights. This section will show you some examples of how you can use these types of light sources, along with some imagination, to perform any number of visual tricks.

Simulating the Interior Lighting of an Office Building

Our current rendering shows a lifeless-looking office building. It's missing a sense of activity. You might notice that when you look at glass office buildings, you can frequently see the ceiling lights from the exterior of the building—provided the glass isn't too dark. In a subtle way, those lights lend a sense of life to a building.

To help improve the image, you'll add some ceiling lights to the office building. You've already supplied the lights in the form of square 3D Faces arrayed just at the ceiling level of each floor, as shown in Figure 18.12.

FIGURE 18.12
The 3D Face squares representing ceiling light fixtures

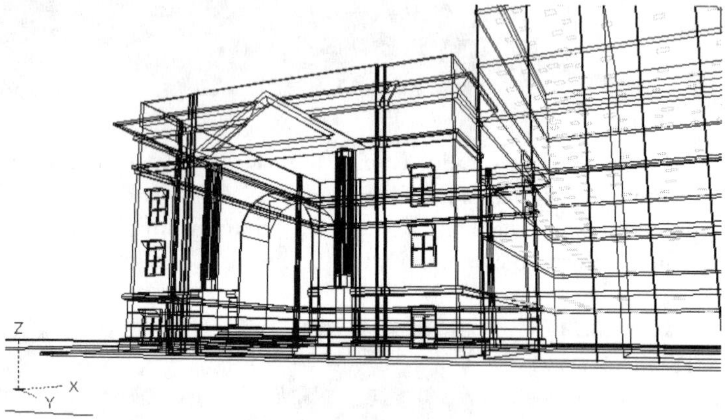

In this section, you will learn how to make the ceiling lights appear illuminated.

1. Assign a reflective material to the squares. Choose View ➢ Render ➢ Materials and then click the Materials Library button to open the Materials Library dialog box.
2. Locate and select White Plastic from the list on the right, and then click Import.
3. Click OK to exit the Materials Library dialog box. Then in the Materials dialog box, highlight White Plastic in the list to the left and click the By Layer button to open the Attach By Layer dialog box.
4. Make sure White Plastic is highlighted in the Select A Material list on the left; then click the Clglite layer in the Select Layer list to the right.
5. Click the Attach button. The words *White Plastic* appear next to the Clglite layer name in the Select Layer list.
6. Click OK to exit the Attach By Layer dialog box, and then click OK to exit the Materials dialog box.

You now have a reflective, white material assigned to the ceiling fixtures. But the reflective material alone will not give the effect of illuminated lights. You need a light source that can be reflected by the fixtures, giving the impression of illumination. For this, you'll use a point-light source.

1. Choose View ➢ 3D Views ➢ SE Isometric to get an Isometric view of the model.
2. Zoom in to the base of the office building so your view is similar to Figure 18.13.

FIGURE 18.13
Selecting the point-light source location in the SW Isometric view

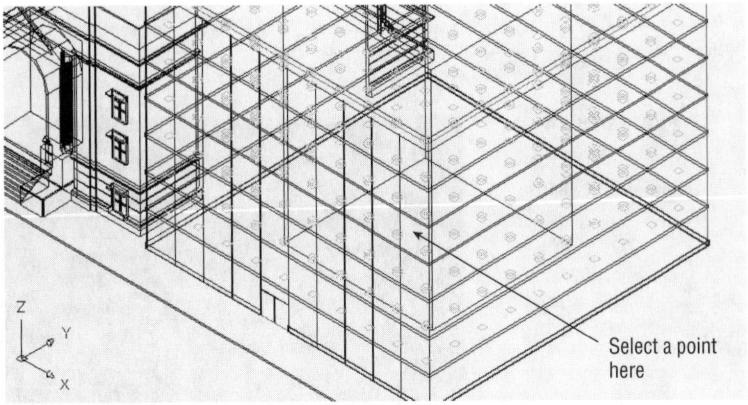

3. Choose View ➢ Render ➢ Light to open the Lights dialog box. Select Point Light from the New drop-down list; then click the New button to open the New Point Light dialog box.

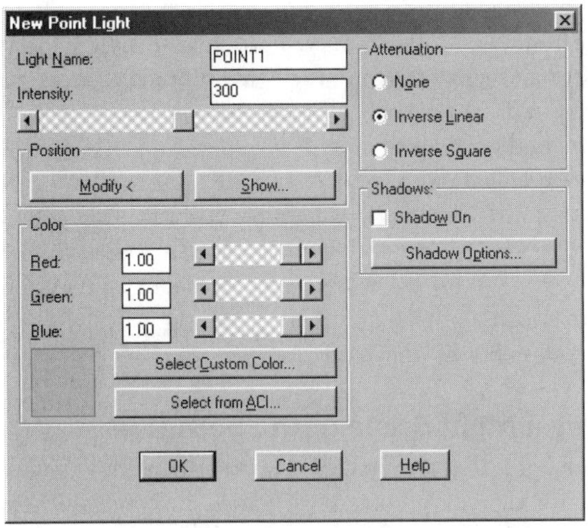

4. Enter **Point1** for the light name. Then enter **300** in the Intensity input box.
5. Click the Modify button, and then select a point at the very center of the office building base, as shown in Figure 18.13.
6. Click OK to exit the New Point Light dialog box, and then click OK in the Lights dialog box.

7. Choose View ➢ Named Views to open the Named Views dialog box. Select 3DFront and click the Set Current button.

8. Click OK to exit the Named Views dialog box.

9. Go ahead and render the view. After a minute, you will have a rendered view similar to Figure 18.14.

FIGURE 18.14
The rendered view with ceiling lights

The new point light in conjunction with the 3D Face light fixture adds a sense of life and depth to the office building. Notice that even though the light is located inside the box representing the office core, it manages to strike all the lights of all the floors as if the floors and core were transparent. Since you didn't turn on the Shadow feature for the point-light source, its light passes through all the objects in the model.

Light is even falling on the granite facade building, illuminating the inside of the arched entrance. This shows that with careful use of lighting, you can bring out some of the detail in the Facade model that might otherwise get lost with the distant light source.

Of course, you can use point-light sources in a more traditional way, representing lightbulbs or other nondirectional light sources. But by playing with light source location and shadow, you can create effects to enhance your rendering.

Simulating a Night Scene with Spotlights

Spotlights are lights that are directed. They are frequently used to provide emphasis and are usually used for interior views or product presentations. In this exercise, you'll set up a night view of the Facade model using spotlights to illuminate the facade.

You'll start by setting up a view to help place the spotlights. Once they are placed, you'll make some adjustments to them to get a view you want.

1. Choose View ➢ 3D Views ➢ SE Isometric; then zoom into the facade so your view looks similar to Figure 18.15.

2. Choose View ➢ Render ➢ Light to open the Lights dialog box. Select Spotlight from the New drop-down list.

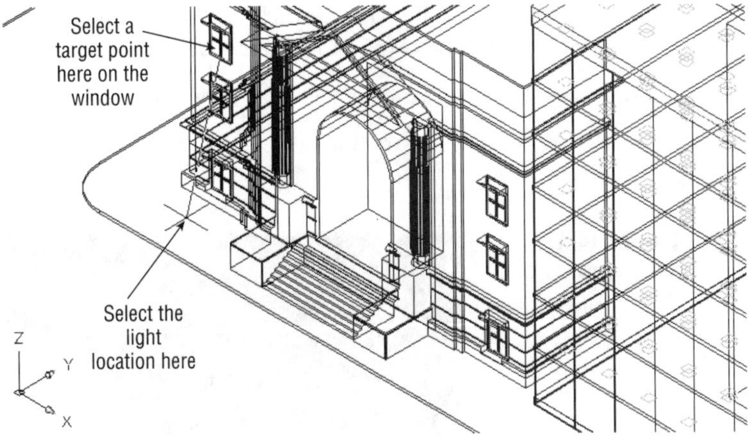
Select a
target point
here on the
window
Select the
light
location here
Z
Y
X

FIGURE 18.15

Selecting the points for the first spotlight

3. Click New to open the New Spotlight dialog box. Enter **Spot-L** to designate a spotlight you will place on the left side of the facade.
4. Enter **400** in the Intensity input box. Then click the Modify button.
5. At the `Enter Target <current>:` prompt, use the Nearest Osnap, and select the point on the window, as indicated in Figure 18.15.
6. At the `Enter Light Location <current>:` prompt, select the point indicated in Figure 18.15. Once you've selected the light location, you return to the New Spotlight dialog box. You can, in the future, adjust the light location if you choose.
7. Click OK. Then, in the Lights dialog box, click New again to create another spotlight.
8. This time, enter **Spot-R** for the name. Enter **400** for the intensity as before.
9. Click the Modify button and select the target and light locations indicated in Figure 18.16.

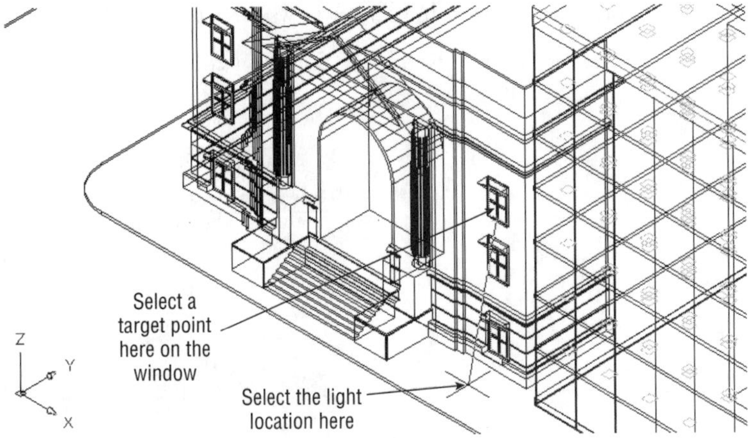
Select a
target point
here on the
window
Select the light
location here
Z
Y
X

FIGURE 18.16

Selecting the points for the second spotlight

10. Click OK to exit the New Spotlight dialog box, and then click OK again in the Lights dialog box. You now have two spotlights on your building.
11. Choose View ➢ Named Views and restore the 3DFront view.
12. Render the model. (You know how to do this by now.) Your view will look similar to Figure 18.17.

FIGURE 18.17

The rendered view of the model with the spotlights

The rendered view has a number of problems. First, the sunlight source needs to be turned off. Second, the spotlights are too harsh. You can also see that the spotlights don't illuminate the center of the building, so you'll need to add some lighting at the entrance. You will solve these problems in the next section.

Controlling Lights with Scenes

The first problem is how to turn off the sun. You can set the sunlight intensity value to 0 using the Modify Distant Light dialog box. Another way is to set up a scene. AutoCAD lets you combine different lights and views into named scenes. You can then quickly select these scenes at render time so you don't have to adjust lighting or views every time you want a specific setup. Here's how it works.

1. Choose View ➢ Render ➢ Scenes, or click the Scenes tool on the Render toolbar to open the Scenes dialog box.

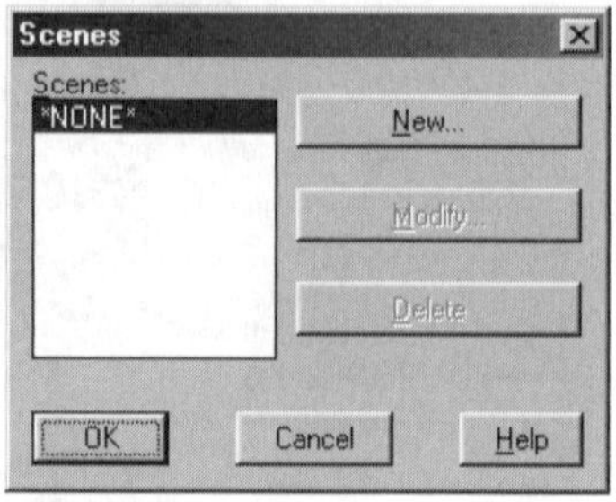

2. Click New to open the New Scene dialog box.

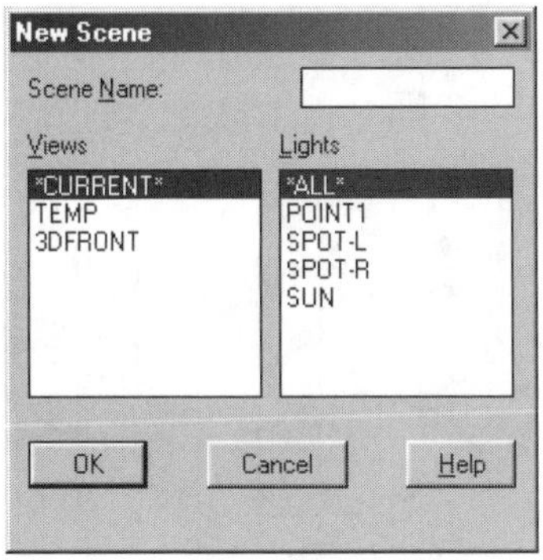

3. Enter **NIGHT** for the scene name. The name appears in the Scene Name input box.
4. Select 3DFRONT from the Views list, and then Shift+click SPOT-L, SPOT-R, and POINT1 in the Lights list.
5. Click OK. Notice that now you have NIGHT listed in the Scenes list in the Scenes dialog box.
6. Click New again, and then type **DAY**.
7. Select 3DFRONT from the Views list, and SUN and POINT1 from the Lights list. Then click OK. You now have two scenes set up.
8. Click OK, and then open the Render dialog box. Notice that you now have DAY and NIGHT listed in the Scene To Render list box.
9. Select NIGHT, and then click the Render button. Your view will look like Figure 18.18.

FIGURE 18.18
Rendering the night scene

Notice that without the sunlight source, your view is considerably darker. You will now add a few more light sources and adjust some existing ones.

1. Choose View ➢ 3D Views ➢ SE Isometric, and then zoom into the office building so your view looks similar to Figure 18.19.

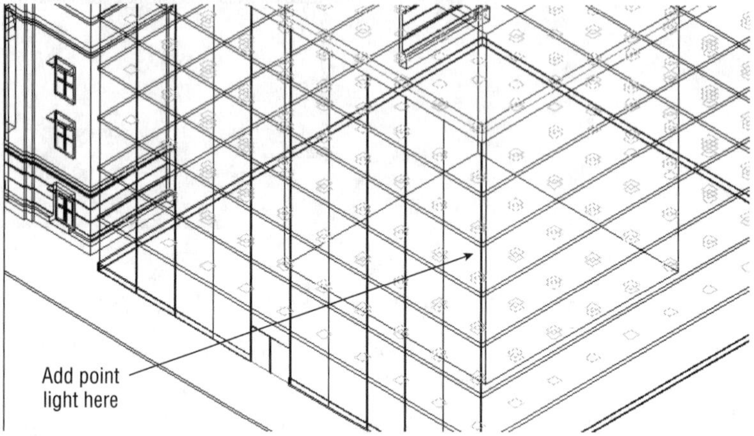
Add point
light here

FIGURE 18.19
Adding another point-light source to the office building

2. Open the Lights dialog box, select Point Light from the New drop-down list, and click New.
3. Enter the name **Point2**, and then give this new point light an intensity value of **500**.
4. Click the Modify button, and place the Point2 light in the center of the office building in the same location as Point1.
5. Click OK; then create another point-light source and enter the name **Point3**. Enter an intensity of **150**.
6. Click the Modify button, adjust your view so it looks similar to Figure 18.20, and then place the light in the facade entrance, as shown in Figure 18.20. Use the .X, .Y, and .Z point filters to select the location of the light.
7. Click OK. Then, in the Lights dialog box, select Spot-L from the list and click Modify.
8. In the Modify Spotlight dialog box, change the Falloff value in the upper right to **80**.
9. Click OK, and then repeat steps 7 and 8 for the Spot-R spotlight.
10. Click OK in the Modify Spotlight dialog box.
11. In the Lights dialog box, increase the ambient light intensity to **50**, and then click OK.

FIGURE 18.20

Adding a point-light source for the entrance to the facade

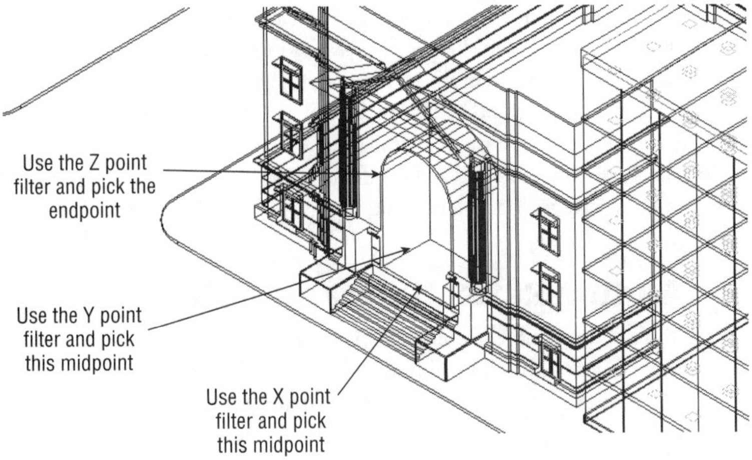
Use the Z point filter and pick the endpoint
Use the Y point filter and pick this midpoint
Use the X point filter and pick this midpoint

You've got the new lights installed and the spotlights adjusted. Before you render your scene, you need to include the new lights in the scene you set up for the night rendering.

1. Choose View ➢ Render ➢ Scene.
2. Highlight Night in the Scenes list, and then click the Modify button.
3. Shift+click Point2 and Point3 in the Lights list, and then Alt+click Point1 to deselect it.
4. Click OK in both the Modify Scene and Scenes dialog boxes.
5. Choose Render and make sure Night is selected in the Scene To Render list.
6. Click the Render button. Your view will look similar to Figure 18.21.

FIGURE 18.21

The night rendering with added lights and an increased falloff area for the spotlights

The new rendering is brighter. You can also see the effects of an increased falloff for the spotlights. They don't have the sharp edge they had in the first night rendering, and the light is spread in a wider radius, illuminating more of the lower portion of the facade.

You also see another by-product of using the Scenes tool. You didn't have to return to the 3DFront view to render the model. Since the 3DFront view is included in the scene information, AutoCAD automatically rendered the model from that view when the Night scene was selected. If you were to issue the Regen command now, you would see that AutoCAD still maintains the SE Isometric view.

Adding Reflections and Detail with Ray Tracing

You've been gradually building up the detail and realism in your renderings by adding light and materials. In this section, you'll learn how using a different rendering method can further enhance your 3D models. Up until now, you've been using the standard AutoCAD rendering method. An alternative technique called *ray tracing* can add interest to a rendering, especially if reflective surfaces are prominent in a model. To make a long, complicated story short, ray tracing simulates the way light works—in reverse. Ray tracing analyzes the light path to each pixel of your display, tracing the light, or "ray," from the pixel to the light origin as it bounces off objects in your model. In this section, you'll use the ray tracing method to render your model after making a few adjustments to the glass material.

Assigning a Mirror Attribute to Glass

Glass is a complex material to model in computer renderings. The AutoCAD standard rendering method simply gives glass a transparency with some "highlight" reflection. But glass has both refractive and reflective attributes that make it difficult to model. Because ray tracing models the way light works, it is especially well suited to rendering views that contain large areas of glass.

To demonstrate what ray tracing can do, you'll use it to render the Facade model that happens to contain an office building with a typical glass exterior. You'll start by making an adjustment to the glass material to make it appear more reflective.

1. Choose View ➢ Render ➢ Materials, and then, in the Materials dialog box, highlight Glass in the list box and click the Modify button to open the Modify Standard Material dialog box.
2. Click the Reflection radio button in the Attributes button group.
3. Click the Mirror check box in the Color button group, and then click OK to close the Modify Standard Material dialog box.
4. Click OK again in the Materials dialog box, and then open the Render dialog box.
5. Choose Photo Raytrace from the Rendering Type list box.
6. Click the More Options button to open the Photo Raytrace Render Options dialog box.
7. Set the Minimum Bias setting to .1 and the Maximum Bias setting to .2. Whenever you change the rendering type, you must reset these settings. AutoCAD does not automatically transfer these settings to different rendering types.
8. Click OK, and then select Day from the Scene To Render list. Click the Background button to open the Background dialog box.

9. Make sure the Use Background check box is checked in the Environment button group; then click OK. This tells AutoCAD to reflect the background image in the glass.

10. Click the Render button. Your view will look similar to Figure 18.22.

FIGURE 18.22
The Facade model rendered with the ray tracing method

The sky bitmap used as a background is faintly reflected in the glass of the office building. The office building has also become brighter from the reflection. Also notice the secondary reflection of the interior ceiling on the west interior wall of the office.

The brightness of the office building is a bit overwhelming, so you will want to adjust the glass material to tone it down.

1. Choose View ➢ Render ➢ Materials. Then with the Glass material highlighted, click Modify to open the Modify Standard Material dialog box.

2. Make sure the Color/Pattern radio button is selected. Then set the Value setting above the Color button group to **.20**. This helps darken the office building.

3. Click OK to close the Modify Standard Material dialog box, and then click OK in the Materials dialog box.

4. Render the scene again. Your view will look something like Figure 18.23.

FIGURE 18.23
The rendering with a lower Color/Pattern setting for the Glass material

You can further reduce the brightness of the office building by reducing the intensity value of the point-light source you added earlier in this chapter.

Getting a Sharp, Accurate Shadow with Ray Tracing

In the beginning of this chapter, you learned how to use the Shadow Map method for casting shadows. Using shadow maps gives you a soft-edge shadow in exchange for accuracy. For exterior views, you might prefer a sharper shadow. The Facade example loses some detail using the Shadow Map method; in particular, the grooves in the base of the building disappear. By switching to the ray tracing method for casting shadows, you can recover some of this detail.

1. Choose View ➢ Render ➢ Light. Then from the Lights list, select Sun and click Modify.
2. In the Modify Distant Light dialog box, click the Shadow Options button.
3. In the Shadow Options dialog box, click the Shadow Volumes/Ray Traced Shadows check box.
4. Click OK in all the dialog boxes to exit them and return to the AutoCAD view.
5. Render the view using the Photo Ray Trace rendering type. Your view will look like Figure 18.24.

FIGURE 18.24
The Facade model using the Shadow Volumes/Ray Traced Shadow option

Notice that you can now see the rusticated base clearly. The shadows also appear sharper, especially around the surface detail of the Facade model.

Creating and Adjusting Texture Maps

You've already seen how you can assign a material to an object by adding the granite pebbles and glass materials to the buildings in the `Facade3.dwg` file. Many of these materials make use of bitmap image files to simulate textures. You can create your own surface textures or use bitmaps in other ways to help enhance your rendering. For example, you can include a photograph of existing buildings that might exist within the scene you are rendering.

Figure 18.25 shows a bitmap image that was scanned into the computer and edited using a popular paint program. Now imagine that this building is across the street from the Facade model, and you want to include it in the scene to show its relationship to your building.

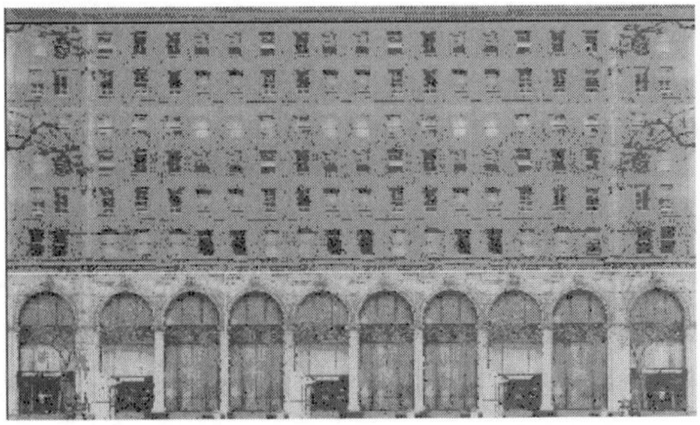

FIGURE 18.25
A photographic image of a building that was scanned into a computer and saved as a bitmap file

The following exercise will show you how it's done.

1. Click Redraw on the Standard toolbar, and then adjust your view so it looks like the top image of Figure 18.26.

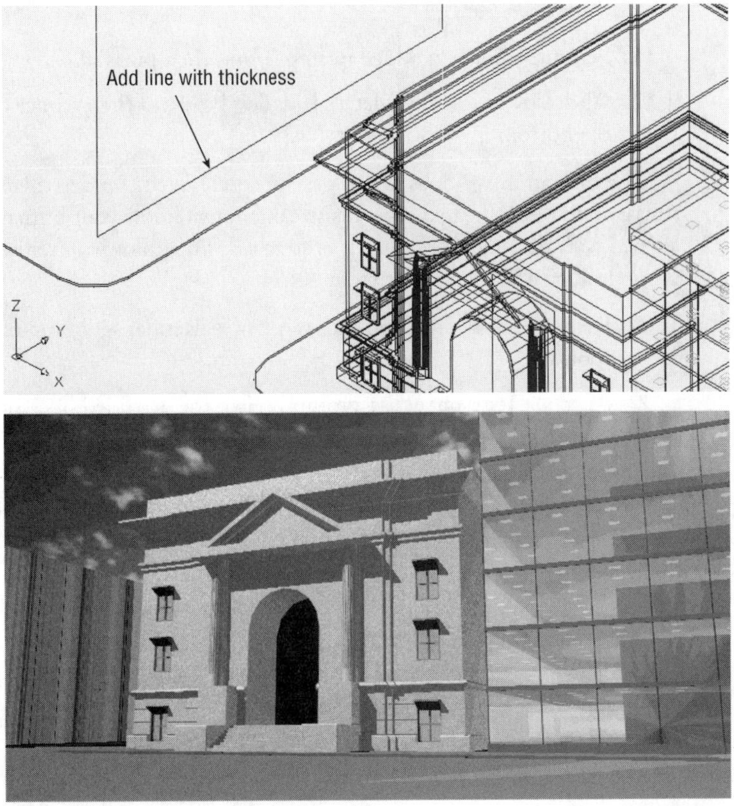

FIGURE 18.26
Adding a bitmap image of a building to your rendering

2. Draw a line 133 feet long, as shown in the top image in Figure 18.26.

3. Change the thickness of the line to 80' using the Properties palette.
4. Choose View ➢ Render ➢ Materials. Then, in the Materials dialog box, click New. Notice that the New Standard Material dialog box is the same as the dialog box for the Glass material. The settings are not the same, however.
5. Enter **Build1** for the material name.
6. Make sure the Color/Pattern radio button is selected, and then click the Find File button in the lower-right corner of the dialog box.
7. Click the List Files Of Type drop-down list. Notice that you have several file types from which to choose.
8. Choose TIF from the list, and then locate the `Market2.tif` file. This file comes with the other sample files on the companion CD.
9. Click Open to exit this dialog box. Then click OK in the New Standard Material dialog box.
10. In the Materials dialog box, make sure Build1 is selected in the Materials list, and then click the Attach button.
11. Select the line you added in step 2, and then press ↵.
12. Click OK to exit the Materials dialog box, and then render the scene. Your view will look like the bottom image in Figure 18.26.

The bitmap image does not appear properly in the rendered view. Instead, it looks like a vertical streak of colors. When you see this streaking, you know your bitmap image or material is not properly aligned with the object to which it is attached. The following exercise introduces the tools you need to properly align a bitmap image to an object.

1. Redraw the screen. Then choose View ➢ Render ➢ Mapping, or click Mapping on the Render toolbar.
2. At the `Select objects:` prompt, select the extruded line you created in the last exercise. The Mapping dialog box opens.

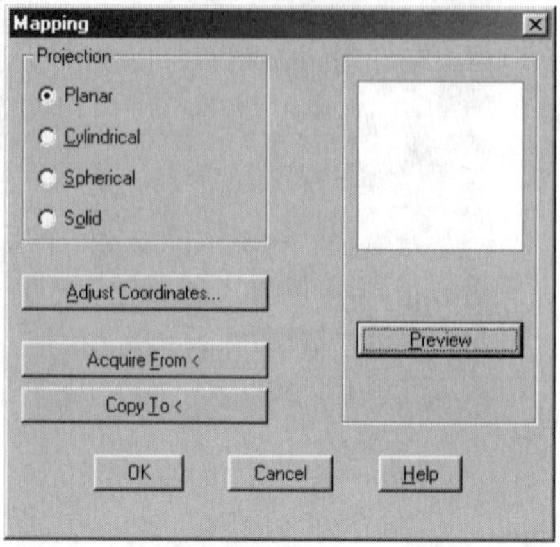

3. Click the Adjust Coordinates button to open the Adjust Planar Coordinates dialog box.

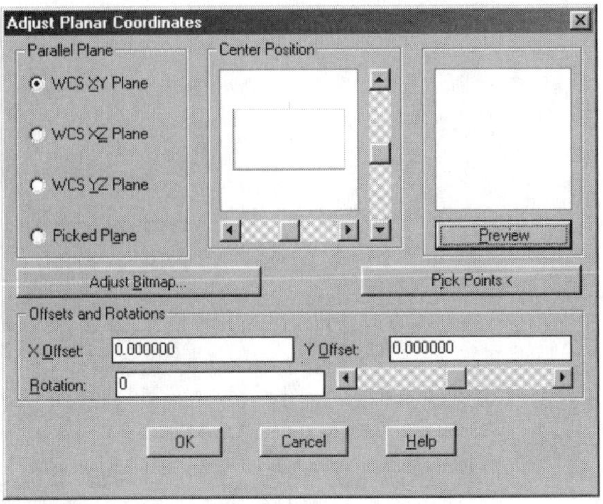

Notice the rectangle in the Center Position area. This shows the relationship of the bitmap image to the object to which it has been assigned. All you can see is a vertical line.

4. Click the WCS YZ Plane radio button. The plane defined by the y- and z-axes is parallel to the surface on which you want the bitmap to appear.

5. Click the Preview button. Now you can see how the bitmap will appear on the vertical surface. You now need to adjust the positioning of the bitmap.

6. You want to increase the size of the bitmap in relation to the surface so the image of the building completely covers the surface. To do this, you need one other dialog box. Click the Adjust Bitmap button to open the Adjust Object Bitmap Placement dialog box (see the first image in Figure 18.27).

7. Enter **.95** in the Scale input box to the left of the U, and then enter **.76** in the Scale input box to the left of the V. The U is the horizontal direction scale, and the V is the vertical direction scale.

8. Click the Preview button to view the effect of the scaling. Notice that the image is larger but still not centered vertically.

9. Use the vertical offset sliders to move the outer rectangle in the graphic upward so it looks like the second image in Figure 18.27, and then click the Preview button again. Now the image fits within the rectangle.

10. Click OK in each of the dialog boxes to close them, and then render the model. Your view will look like Figure 18.28.

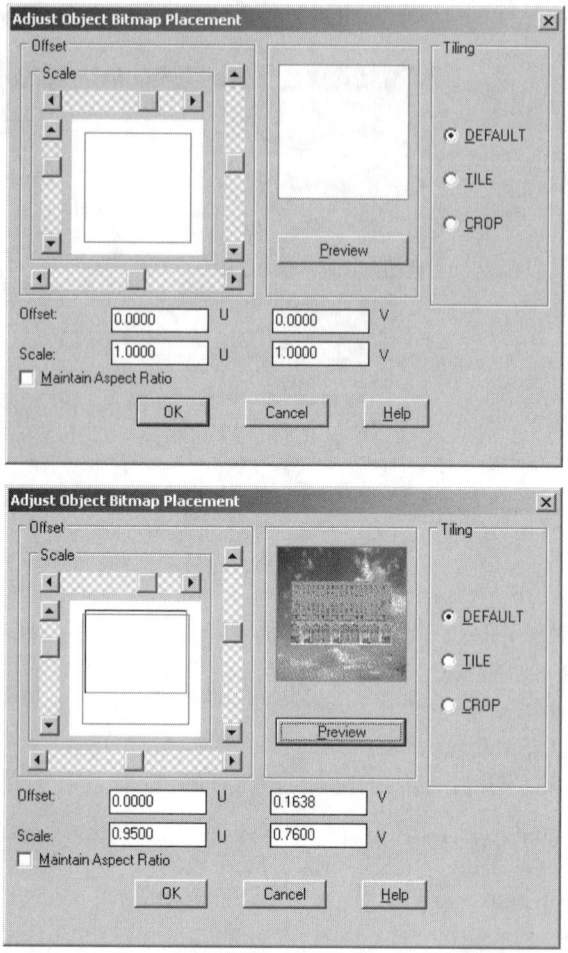

FIGURE 18.27
The Adjust Object Bitmap Placement dialog box

FIGURE 18.28
The rendered view with the bitmap image adjusted

Notice that the image of the building across the street now appears correctly and no longer looks like vertical streaks. The odd blank spaces formerly visible on the building are also gone. As you have seen in the previous exercise, the Adjust Object Bitmap Placement dialog box allows you to stretch the image vertically or horizontally in case the image is distorted and needs to be fitted to an accurately drawn object.

Another option is to use a paint program to refine the bitmap image before it is used in AutoCAD. AutoCAD attempts to place the bitmap accurately on a surface, so if the bitmap is fairly clean and doesn't have any extra blank space around the edges, you can usually place it on an object without having to make any adjustments other than its orientation.

Adding Landscape and People

There's nothing like adding landscaping and people to a rendering to add a sense of life and scale. Computer images, in particular, need landscape props because they tend to appear cold and somewhat lifeless. AutoCAD offers a set of prebuilt landscape objects to help soften the appearance of your rendering. Let's see how you can add a few trees and people to the Facade model.

1. Choose View ➢ Redraw, and then choose View ➢ Render ➢ Landscape New. You can also click the Landscape New tool on the Render toolbar to open the Landscape New dialog box.

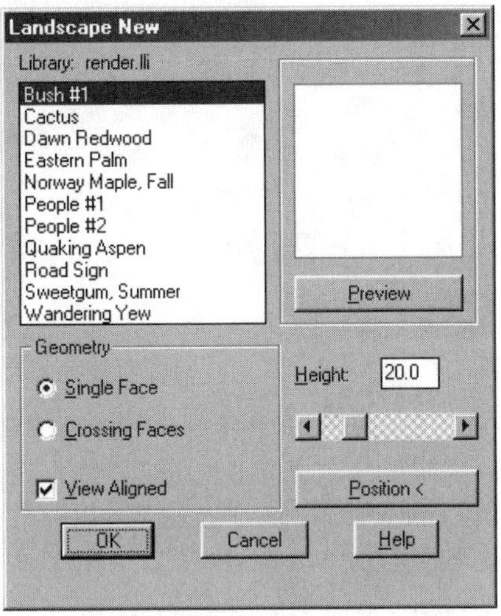

2. Click Quaking Aspen in the Library list, and then click Preview to view the item.
3. Use the slider just below the Preview button and change the Height value from 20 to 100, the highest setting.
4. Click the Position button, and then click the point indicated in the first image in Figure 18.29 to place the tree in front of the buildings. You may have to adjust your view.

FIGURE 18.29

Placing the trees in the Facade model

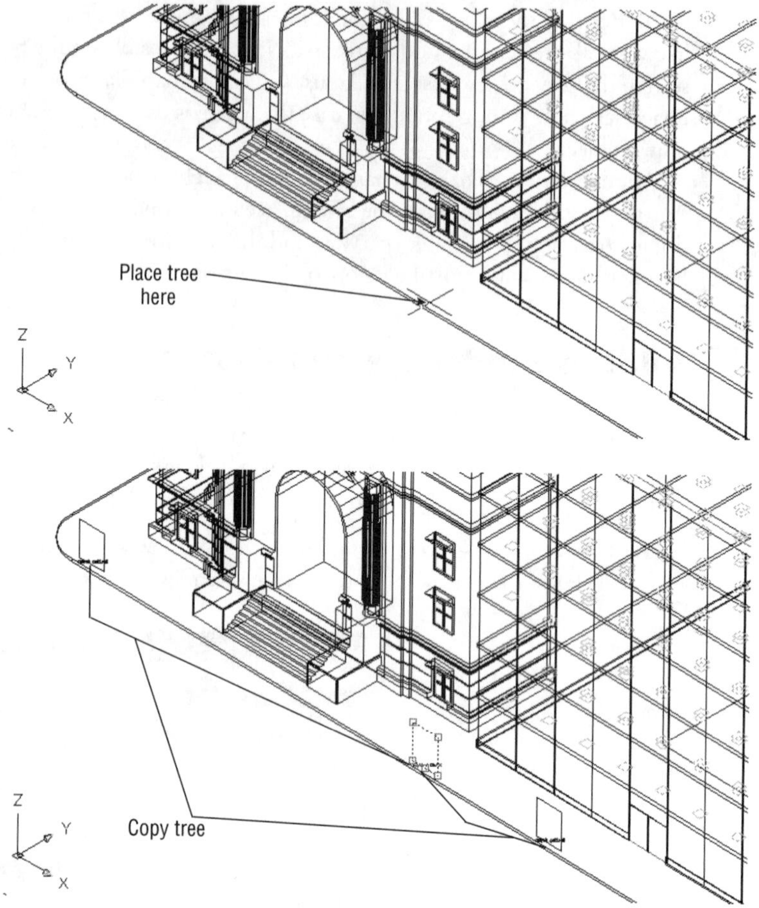

5. Click the View Aligned check box to deselect this option. You'll learn more about View Aligned later in this section.
6. Click OK. The tree appears as a rectangle with a text label telling you what it is, as shown in the second image in Figure 18.29.
7. Copy the tree to the positions indicated in the second image in Figure 18.29.
8. Now render the view. You will see a view similar to Figure 18.30.

The trees you added are actually two-dimensional bitmap images. If you view the model from a glancing angle, the trees will begin to look thinner, and you will see that they are indeed two-dimensional. You can use two options in the Landscape New dialog box to reduce the 2D effect. The View Aligned option you turned off in step 5 forces the tree to align to your point of view, so you never see the object edge-on. Another option, Crossing Faces, creates two images of the object to appear. Each image is crossed over the other, creating an almost 3D look.

FIGURE 18.30
The rendered view of the model with the trees

CUSTOM OBJECT TYPES IN AUTOCAD

If you use the List tool to find out what the landscape objects are, you would find that they are called Plant or People. Does AutoCAD 2004 have some object types you don't know about? The answer is maybe.

Since AutoCAD 14, third-party developers have been able to add new object types that aren't native to the program itself. This is a fairly revolutionary idea. AutoCAD uses this capability by adding Plant and People objects. However, there is a problem with adding new object types: you need the third-party application to view and edit the objects you create. When the application is not present, the new objects become what Autodesk calls *proxies*. You can edit proxies with a limited set of editing tools. The level of "editability" is determined by the application that created the proxies.

As far as AutoCAD's rendering tools are concerned, the application is always present, so you can always edit the trees and people.

The ability to add new object types to an AutoCAD drawing has some far-reaching implications. The possibilities for third-party developers are enormous, and you, the end user, will benefit in many ways. The Landscape tool in AutoCAD is an example of what can be done.

There are a few things wrong with the rendering shown in Figure 18.30. The trees are too small, and they appear to be shaded on the wrong side. The shadows on the trees don't reflect the location of the Distant Light setting in the model. The street is also unusually empty for a daytime scene. You can easily fix the trees using standard AutoCAD editing tools. You can also add some people using the Landscape New tool in the Render toolbar.

1. Redraw the screen, and then click one of the trees to expose its grips.
2. Click the grip at the base of the tree, right-click the mouse, and choose Rotate from the shortcut menu.
3. Type **180**↵ to rotate the tree 180 degrees.
4. Click the grip again, right-click the mouse, and this time choose Scale.

5. Enter 2.4↵ to increase the size of the tree by 2.4 times.
6. Repeat steps 1 through 5 for each of the other trees.
7. Open the Landscape New dialog box again, and select People #1 from the list.
8. Enter a Height value of 66, and then use the Position button to place the people at the entrance of the Facade building (see Figure 18.31). The people will appear as triangles in the Wireframe view. (Make sure you use the Nearest Osnap override to place the people.)

FIGURE 18.31
Placing people in the scene

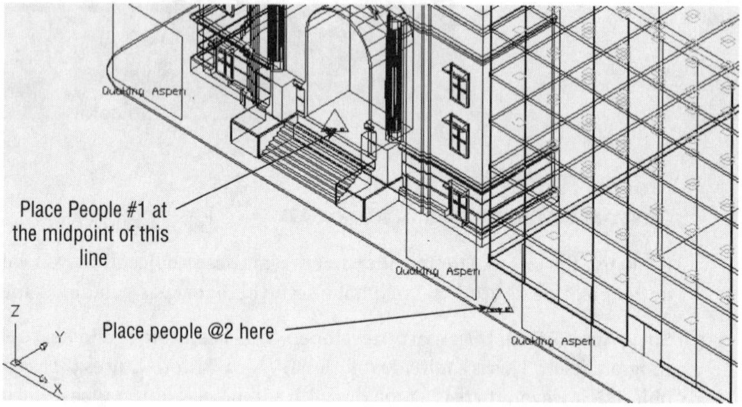

9. Click OK. Then repeat steps 7 and 8 to place People #2 in front of the office building between the trees (see Figure 18.31).
10. Render the view. Your view will look similar to Figure 18.32.

FIGURE 18.32
The view after rendering, with the trees adjusted and people added

The shadows of the trees now match the sun's location, and they are a size better suited to the model. However, notice that the people are not lit very well. This is because you did not turn off the View Align option when you placed them. Therefore, they are facing your view tilted slightly away from the sun. This has the effect of darkening their image.

You can choose View ➢ Render Landscape Edit to change the settings for landscape objects. You will be prompted to select an object. Once you do, the Landscape Edit dialog box opens, which is identical to the Landscape New dialog box. From there, you can change the settings for the selected landscape object.

Other Rendering Output Options

Throughout this chapter, you have been rendering to the AutoCAD drawing area. You can also render to a file, which enables you to recall the image at any time in any application, or you can render to the Render window. From there, you have a number of options for dealing with the rendered image.

Rendering to the Render Window

The Render window lets you control the resolution and color depth of your image. It also lets you save the images that you render in the Windows .bmp format. Another advantage of the Render window is that you can render several views and then compare them before you decide which ones to save.

1. Open the Render dialog box, and then select Render Window from the Destination drop-down list near the bottom of the dialog box.
2. Click Render. After a moment the Render window appears. It then takes a minute or two before the image finishes rendering and appears in the window.

Notice that the image is within its own window. If you render another view, that view will also appear in its own window, leaving the previous rendering undisturbed. You can choose File ➢ Save in the Render window to save the file as a .bmp file for later editing or printing, or you can print directly from the Render window. You can also use the Render window to cut and paste the image to another application or to view other files in the .bmp format.

To set the size of renderings, choose File ➢ Options in the Render window to open the Windows Render Options dialog box (see Figure 18.33). Here, you can choose from two standard sizes or enter a custom size for your rendering. You can also choose between 8-bit (256 colors) and 24-bit (16 million colors) color depth. Changes to these settings don't take effect until you render another view.

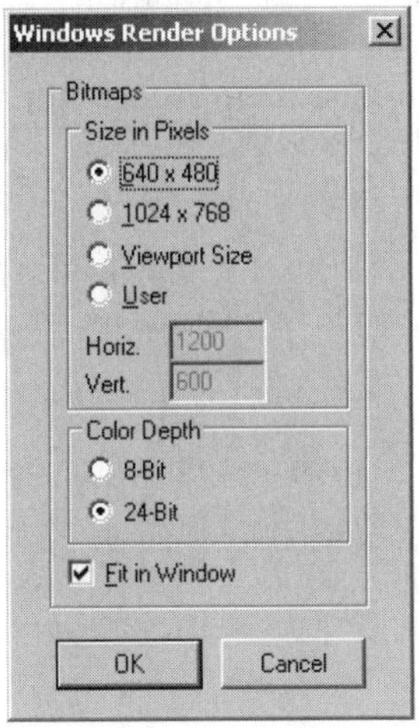

FIGURE 18.33
The Windows Render Options dialog box

Rendering Directly to a File

Rendering to the Render window allows you to view and compare your views before you save them. However, you can only save your views in the .bmp format. If you plan to further edit the image in an image-processing program, this may not be a problem. But if you want to use your image file with a program that requires a specific file format, you probably want to render directly to a file. Here's how it's done.

1. Open the Render dialog box, and then select File in the Destination button group in the lower middle of the dialog box.
2. Choose More Options at the bottom of the Destination button group to open the File Output Configuration dialog box.

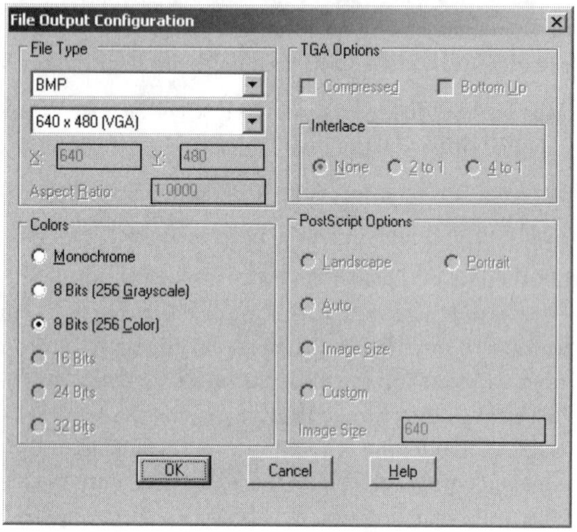

3. Click the File Type drop-down list to see the options. You can save your image in .BMP, .PCX, PostScript, .TGA, .and TIFF format. You might also notice the other options in the dialog box, such as color depth, resolution, and compression. Not all these options are available for all the file types. For example, .GIF, .BMP, and .PCX are limited to 256 colors, so the other color options will not apply to thesefiles.
4. Click OK to return to the Render dialog box, and then click the Render button. The Rendering File dialog box opens, prompting you for a filename for your image.
5. Enter **Facade1**. AutoCAD adds the filename extension for you.
6. Click OK, and AutoCAD proceeds to render to the file.

As AutoCAD renders to the file, the command line tells you how much of the image has been rendered.

Improving Your Image and Editing

At times, you will be rushing to get a rendering done and won't want to wait for each trial rendering to become visible. Several AutoCAD tools can save you time by limiting the resolution or area being rendered. Suppose you want to render just the area where you've added a tree to make sure it is in the right location. The following exercise will show you how this is done.

1. Choose View ➢ Named Views, and then restore the 3DFront view.
2. Open the Render dialog box and set the Destination option to Viewport.
3. Click the Crop Window check box to activate this option, and then click the Render button.
4. The prompt `Pick crop window to render:` appears. Select the area shown in Figure 18.34, indicated by the rubber-banding square. Once you select the window, AutoCAD renders only the area you selected.

FIGURE 18.34

Selecting the crop window

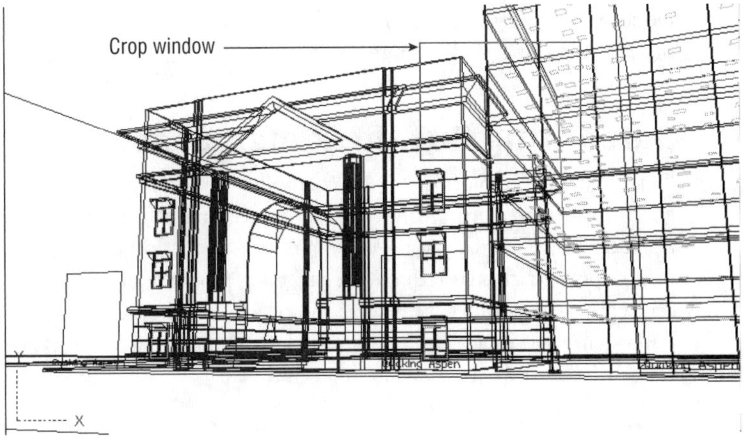

The Crop Window option is a working tool and is not available when File or Render Window is selected as the destination.

You can also select specific objects to be included in the rendering by checking the Query For Selections check box in the Render dialog box. This option asks you to select a set of objects before it proceeds to render. You can render to all three destination options with Query For Selections turned on.

If you want to get a quick rendering with a reduced resolution to check composition, you can use the Sub Sampling drop-down list. Try the following exercise to see how it works.

1. Open the Render dialog box, and then open the Sub Sampling drop-down list.
2. Choose 3:1 from the list, make sure the Crop Window option is unchecked, and then click the Render button. Your view will render faster but will look a bit crude (see Figure 18.35).

FIGURE 18.35
A rendered view with the Sub Sampling option set to 3:1

The different ratios in the Sub Sampling option tell you how many pixels are being combined to reduce the resolution of the image. For example, 3:1 combines three pixels into one to reduce the resolution to a third of the original.

Smoothing Out the Rough Edges

By reducing the resolution, the Sub Sampling option increases the jagged appearance of your rendering. For your final rendering, you can improve the smoothness of edges and thereby increase the apparent resolution by using the Anti-Aliasing option in the Render dialog box. This option performs a kind of computer trick that reduces the jagged appearance of object edges. Anti-Aliasing blends two adjacent contrasting colors. This gives the effect of smoothing out the "stairstep" appearance of a computer-generated image. The improvement to your rendering can be striking. Try the following exercise to see firsthand what Anti-Aliasing can do.

1. Open the Render dialog box, and then click the More Options button.
2. In the Raytrace Rendering Options dialog box, click the Medium radio button in the Anti-Aliasing button group, and then click OK.
3. Select 1:1 from the Sub Sampling drop-down list, and then click the Render button. The rendering takes several minutes, so you might want to take a break at this point. When the rendering is done, it will look similar to Figure 18.36.

Notice that the edges of the buildings are much smoother. You can also see that the vertical mullions of the office building are more clearly defined. One negative point is that the texture effect of the Facade model has been reduced. You may have to increase the scale value for the Granite Pebbles material setting to bring the texture back.

As you can see from this exercise, you trade off rendering speed for a cleaner image. You will want to save the higher Anti-Aliasing settings for your final output.

FIGURE 18.36
A rendering with the Anti-Aliasing setting set to Medium

Printing Your Renderings

When you've decided that your rendering is perfect, you can print a copy directly from AutoCAD. Through a Layout tab, you can also put together presentations that include 2D floor plans and elevations with your rendering on a single sheet. Or you can have several different renderings on one sheet. Try the following to set up a Layout tab to render the 3D model in both a rendered view and a hidden line view.

1. Click the Layout1 tab. Then in the Page Setup dialog box, select your printer from the Plot Configuration group's Name drop-down list and select `Acad.ctb` or `Acad.stb` from the Plot Style Table group Name drop-down list. Click OK to exit the dialog box.
2. Double-click inside the viewport that shows the 3D model, and then enter V↵ to open the View dialog box.
3. Select 3DFront from the Current View list, and then click Set Current. Click OK to exit the View dialog box.
4. Choose View ➢ Render ➢ Render or click the Render tool from the Render toolbar.
5. Select 1:1 from the Sub Sampling drop-down list, and then click the Render button. The rendering may take several minutes, so you might want to take a break at this point. When the rendering is done, it will look similar to Figure 18.36.

You have set up a layout with a single viewport showing the perspective view of the 3D model. Next, make a copy of the viewport.

1. Double-click outside the viewport to go to Paper Space.

2. Click the viewport border to expose its grips, and then use a grip to make the viewport smaller so it is about half the height of the Paper Space layout. Keep the height to width proportions of the viewport as close to the original as possible.

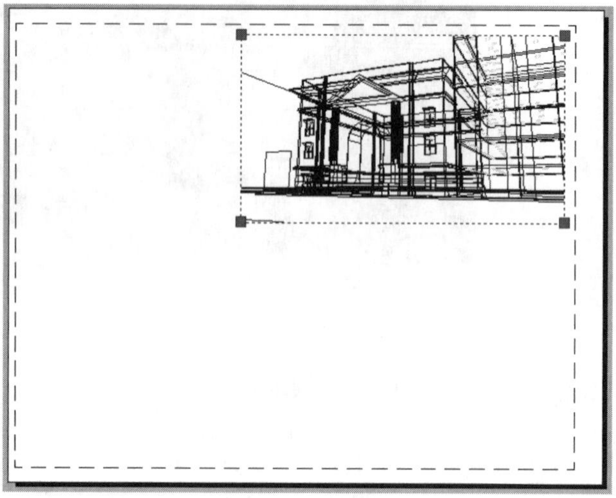

3. Copy the viewport down so you have an identical viewport just below the original.

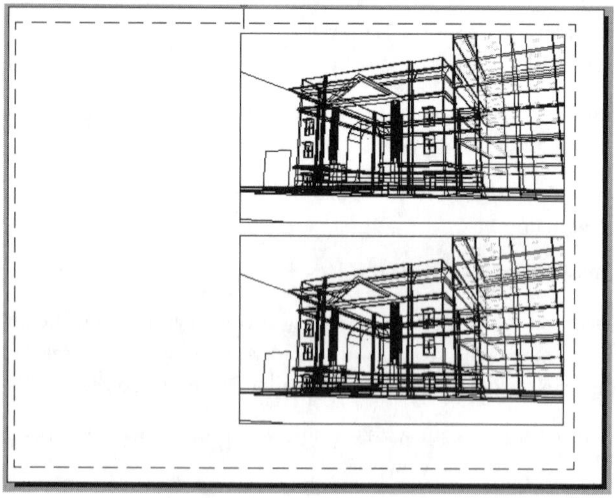

Now you're ready to setup the viewport to render the views in specific ways. For example, you can set one viewport to render as a fully rendered view while rendering another viewport as a hidden line view.

1. Click the top viewport, and then right-click and choose Shade Plot ➢ Rendered.

2. Click the lower viewport, and then right -click and choose Shade Plot ➢ Hidden.
3. Choose File ➢ Plot Preview. After a moment, you see a preview of your plot showing a fully rendered view in the top viewport and a hidden line view in the lower viewport.

You can go on to add additional viewports to include floor plans and elevations if needed. Or you can add isometric views with labels that point out features of the drawing.

You also have control over the quality of the rendered viewport. If you right-click the Layout tab and choose Page Setup, the Page Setup dialog box opens. Click the Layout Settings tab. You can use the Shaded Viewport Options group to select from a set of viewport quality settings.

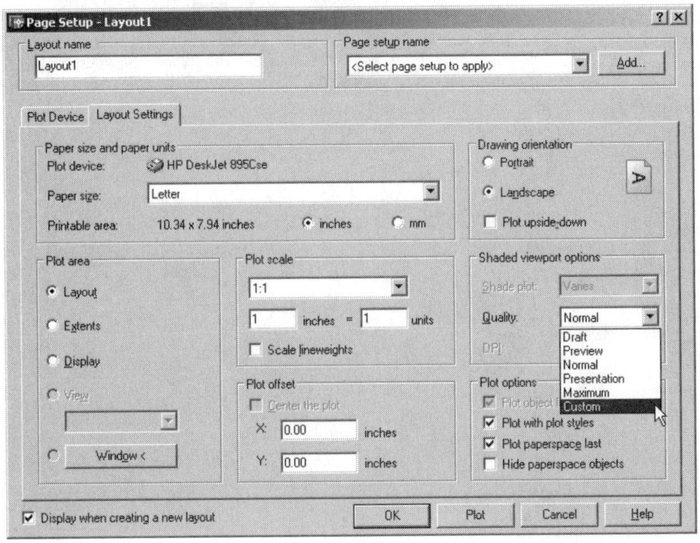

You can choose from Draft, Preview, Normal, Presentation, Maximum, and Custom. These options are described in detail in Chapter 7, so I won't go into detail here. Just remember that the options are available to help you get the most from your rendered printer output.

If You Want to Experiment...

In this chapter, you participated in a guided tour of AutoCAD's rendering tools and saw the main features of this product. Because of space considerations, this chapter didn't go into the finer details of many features, but you now have the basic knowledge from which to build your rendering skills. Without too much effort, you can adapt much of what you've learned here to your own projects. If you need more detailed information, click the Help button found in all Render dialog boxes.

Computer rendering of 3D models is a craft that takes some time to master. Experiment with these rendering tools to see firsthand the types of results you can expect. You might want to try different types of views such as an Isometric or Elevation view, the latter of which is shown in Figure 18.37. With a bit more detail added, this rendered elevation could fit nicely into a set of renderings for a presentation.

FIGURE 18.37

An Elevation view of the Facade model

Chapter 19

Mastering 3D Solids

So FAR, YOU HAVE been creating 3D models according to a method called *surface modeling*: As you drew, you used 3D Faces to give your models form and the appearance of solidity. But you can use another method to create 3D computer models: *solid modeling*.

With surface models, drawing a simple cube requires several steps; with solids, you can create a cube with one command. Having created a solid model, you can assign materials to it and have the computer find physical properties of the model, such as weight and center of mass. It is easier to create models by using solid modeling, and many advantages are associated with the technique, especially in mechanical design and engineering.

Solid modeling was once thought to require more computational power than most personal computers were capable of, but with today's powerful microcomputer hardware, solid modeling is well within the reach of most PC users. AutoCAD offers built-in solid modeling functions, which you will explore in this chapter.

TIP *LT users do not have solid modeling capabilities. However, you can take advantage of the Region objects and their related editing commands described in the section entitled "Using 3D Solid Operations on 2D Drawings" in this chapter.*

Topics in this chapter include the following:

- Understanding Solid Modeling
- Creating Solid Forms
- Creating Complex Solids
- Enhancing the 2D Drawing Process
- Taking Advantage of Stereolithography
- If You Want to Experiment…

Understanding Solid Modeling

Solid modeling is a way of defining 3D objects as solid forms rather than as wireframes with surfaces attached. When you create a 3D model using solid modeling, you start with the basic forms of your model—cubes, cones, and cylinders, for instance. These basic solids are called *primitives*. Then, using more of these primitives, you begin to add to or subtract from your basic forms. For example, to create a model of a tube, you first create two solid cylinders, one smaller in diameter than the other. You then align the two cylinders so they are concentric and tell AutoCAD to subtract the smaller cylinder from the larger one. The larger of the two cylinders then becomes a tube whose inside diameter is that of the smaller cylinder, as shown in Figure 19.1.

Several primitives are available for modeling solids in AutoCAD (see Figure 19.2).

FIGURE 19.1

Creating a tube using solid modeling

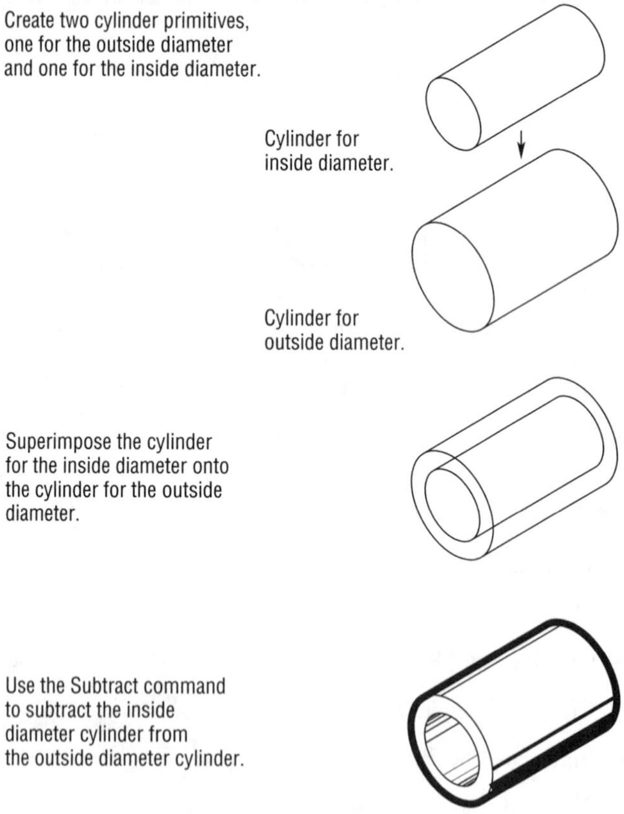

Create two cylinder primitives, one for the outside diameter and one for the inside diameter.
Cylinder for inside diameter.
Cylinder for outside diameter.
Superimpose the cylinder for the inside diameter onto the cylinder for the outside diameter.
Use the Subtract command to subtract the inside diameter cylinder from the outside diameter cylinder.

You can join these shapes—box, wedge, cone, cylinder, sphere, and donut (or *torus*)— in one of four ways to produce secondary shapes. The first three, demonstrated in Figure 19.3 using a cube and a cylinder as examples, are called *Boolean operations*. (The name comes from the nineteenth-century mathematician George Boole.)

FIGURE 19.2
The solid primitives

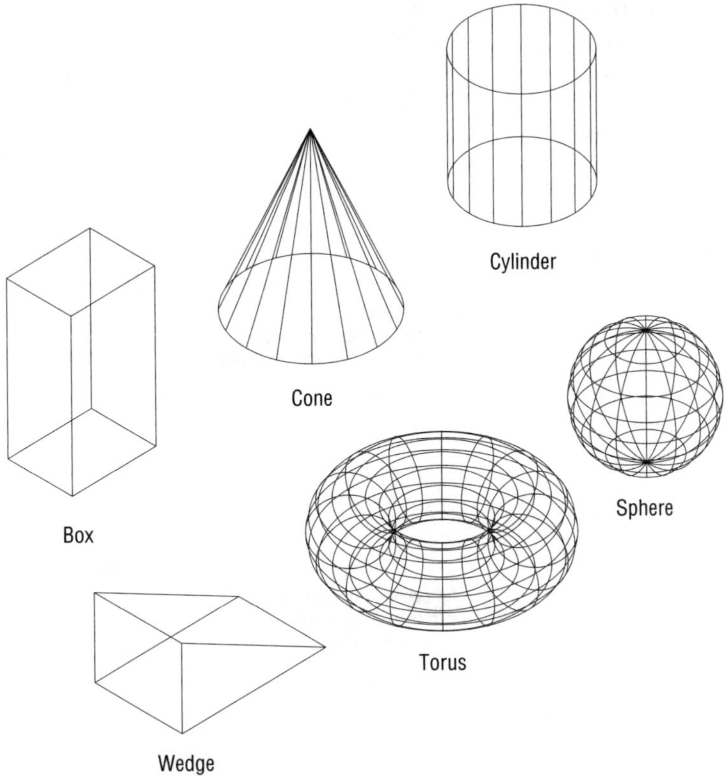

The three joining methods are as follows:

Intersection Uses only the intersecting region of two objects to define a solid shape.

Subtraction Uses one object to cut out a shape in another.

Union Joins two primitives so they act as one object.

A fourth option, *interference,* lets you find exactly where two or more solids coincide in space—similar to the results of a union. The main difference between interference and union is that interference allows you to keep the original solid shapes, while union discards the original solids, leaving only their combined form. With interference, you can have AutoCAD either show you the shape of the coincident space or create a solid based on the coincident space's shape.

Joined primitives are called *composite solids.* You can join primitives to primitives, composite solids to primitives, and composite solids to other composite solids.

Now let's take a look at how these concepts let us create models in AutoCAD.

TIP *To simplify the exercises in this chapter, the instructions don't specify inches or centimeters. This way, users of both the metric and Imperial measurement systems can use the exercises without having to deal with duplicate information.*

FIGURE 19.3

The intersection, subtraction, and union of a cube and a cylinder

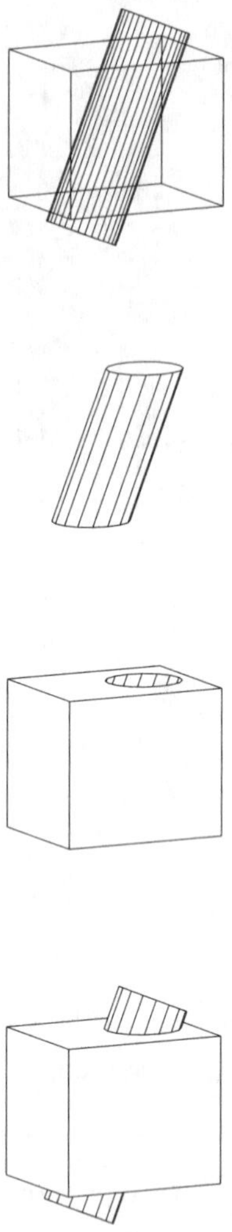

A solid box and a solid cylinder are superimposed.

The intersection of the primitives creates a solid cylinder with the ends skewed.

The cylinder subtracted from the box creates a hole in the box.

The union of the two primitives creates a box with two round pegs.

Creating Solid Forms

In this section, you will begin to draw the object shown in Figure 19.4. In the process, you will explore the creation of solid models by creating primitives and then setting up special relationships between them.

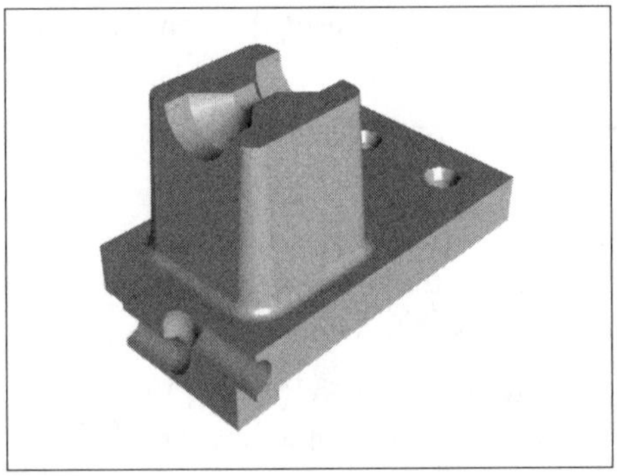

FIGURE 19.4
This steel bracket was created and rendered in AutoCAD.

Displaying the Solids Toolbar

All the commands you will use to create the solid models, and many of the commands you can use for editing solids, are accessible on the Solids toolbar. Right-click any toolbar and choose Solids from the shortcut menu to open the Solids toolbar.

Use the same method to open the Solids Editing toolbar as well; you'll work with it shortly. Now you're ready to begin creating basic solids.

Creating Primitives

Primitives are the basic building blocks of solid modeling. At first, it may seem limiting to have only six primitives to work with, but consider the varied forms you can create with just a few two-dimensional objects. Let's begin by creating the basic mass of our steel bracket. First, prepare your drawing for the exercise.

1. Create a new file called `Bracket`.
2. Right-click the Snap button on the status bar; then, in the Drafting Settings dialog box, set the Snap spacing to **0.5** and turn on the Grid and Snap modes.
3. Press F6 to turn on the dynamic coordinate readout if it isn't already on. You'll use the readout to help guide you in selecting points in the exercises that follow.

Now start building the solid model.

1. Click the Box tool on the Solids toolbar, or enter **BOX**↵. You can also choose Draw ➢ Solids ➢ Box.
2. At the `Specify corner of box or [CEnter] <0,0,0>:` prompt, pick a point at coordinate 3,2.5.

3. At the `Specify corner or [Cube/Length]:` prompt, enter **@7,4↵** to create a box with a length of 7 and a width of 4.

4. The `Specify height:` prompt that appears next is asking for the height of the box in the z-axis. Enter **1↵**.

You've drawn your first primitive, a box that is 7 units long by 4 units wide by 1 unit deep. Now, let's change the view so you can see the box more clearly. Use the Vpoint command to shift your view so you are looking at the WCS from the lower left.

5. Open the Viewpoint Presets dialog box (choose View ➢ 3D Views ➢ Viewpoint Presets), and then enter **225** in the From X Axis input box and **19.5** in the XY Plane input box.

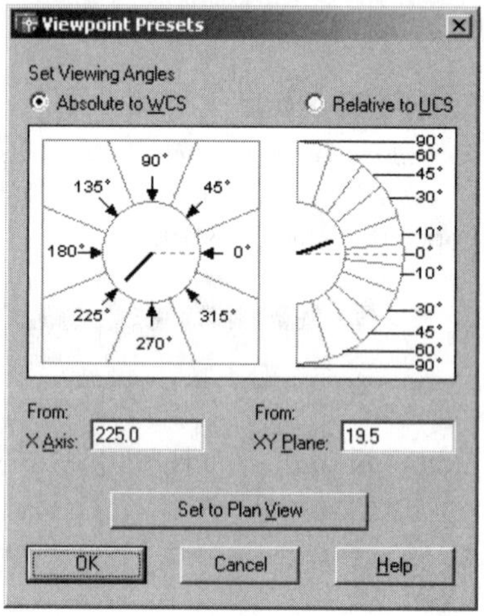

6. Click OK, and then adjust your view so it looks similar to Figure 19.5.

FIGURE 19.5

The first stage of the bracket

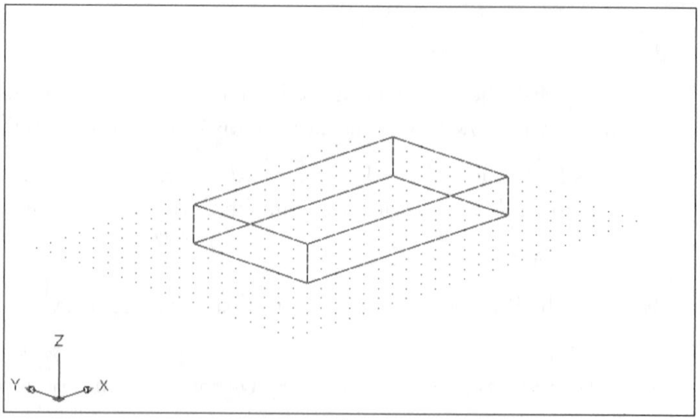

Turning a 2D Polyline into a 3D Solid

Now let's add another box to form the lower lip of the bracket. This time, you'll create a box primitive from a polyline.

1. Click the Polyline tool on the Draw toolbar.
2. At the `Specify start point:` prompt, start the polyline from the coordinate .5,2.5.
3. Continue the polyline around to create a rectangle that is 1 unit in the x-axis and 3 units in the y-axis. You should see a rectangular outline of the smaller box to the left, as in Figure 19.6.

FIGURE 19.6

The converted polyline box

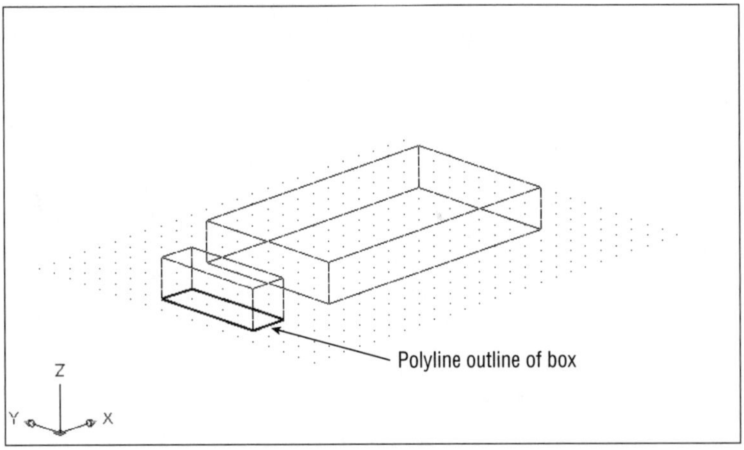

4. Click the Extrude tool on the Solids toolbar, or type **EXT↵**.
5. At the `Select objects:` prompt, pick the polyline and press ↵.
6. At the `Specify height of extrusion or [Path]:` prompt, type **1↵**.
7. At the `Specify angle of taper for extrusion <0>:` prompt, press ↵ to accept the default taper of 0°. (You'll see what the Taper option does in a later exercise.) The polyline now extrudes in the z-axis to form a bar, as shown in Figure 19.6.

You've now drawn two box primitives using the Box and Extrude options on the Solids toolbar. Just for variety's sake, in this exercise you created the smaller box by converting a polyline into a solid, but you could just as easily have used the Box option for that as well. The Extrude option converts polylines, circles, and traces into solids. (Regular lines, 3D lines, 3D Faces, and 3D polylines cannot be extruded.)

OTHER OPTIONS FOR SOLIDS

Before you continue, let's examine the commands for primitives that you haven't had a chance to use yet. Refer to Figures 19.7 through 19.10 to understand the terms used with these other primitives.

Cone↵ (Cone icon on the Solids toolbar) Draws a circular cone or a cone with an elliptical base (see Figure 19.7). Drawing a circular cone is much like drawing a circle, with an added prompt asking for a height. The Ellipse option acts like the Ellipse command (on the Draw toolbar), with an additional prompt for height.

FIGURE 19.7

Drawing a solid cone

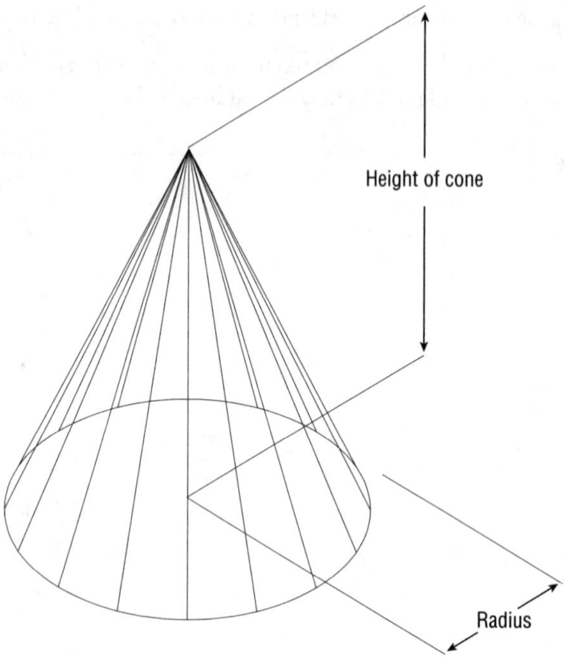

Sphere↵ (Sphere icon on the Solids toolbar) Acts like the Circle command, but instead of drawing a circle, it draws a sphere (see Figure 19.8).

FIGURE 19.8

Drawing a solid sphere

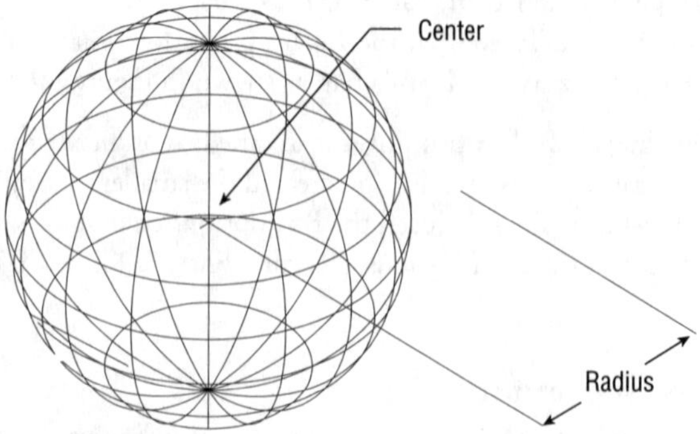

Torus↵ (Torus icon on the Solids toolbar) Creates a donut-shaped solid called a *torus* (see Figure 19.9). You are prompted for the two diameters or radii that define a torus; one for the torus "ring" and another for the "tube" portion of the torus.

FIGURE 19.9

Drawing a solid torus

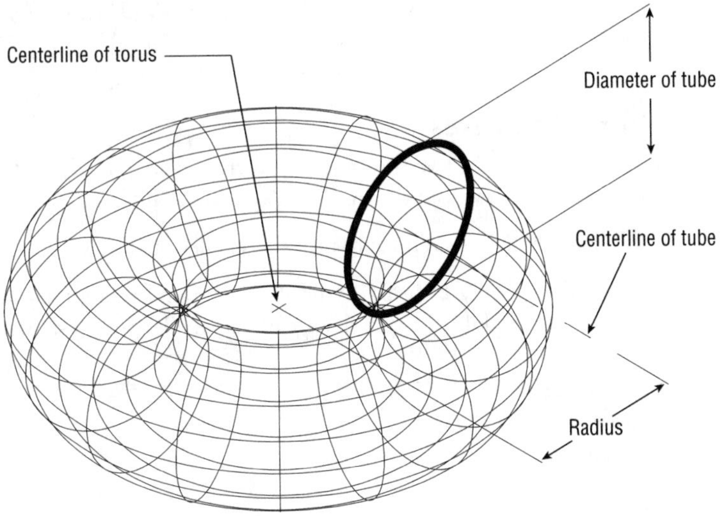

Wedge↵ (Wedge icon on the Solids toolbar) Creates a wedge-shaped solid (see Figure 19.10). This command acts much like the Box command you used to draw the bracket. You have the choice of defining the wedge by two corners or by its center and a corner.

FIGURE 19.10

Drawing a solid wedge

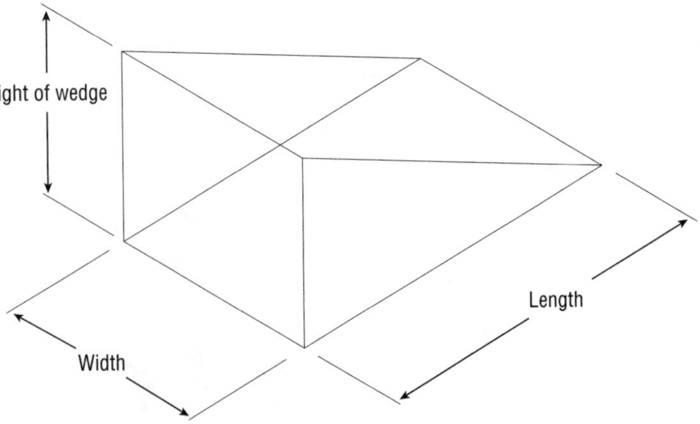

In the following exercises you will be creating and combining solid primitives. The commands required to create complex solids are available on the Solids Editing toolbar.

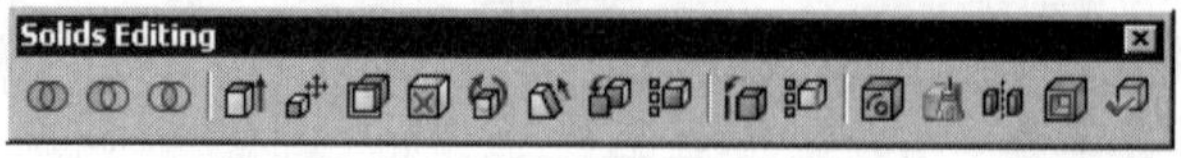

Joining Primitives

Now let's see how the two box objects you created are joined. First, you'll move the new box into place, and then you'll join the two boxes to form a single solid.

1. Start the Move command, pick the smaller of the two boxes, and then press ↵.
2. At the `Specify base point or displacement:` prompt, use the Midpoint Osnap override and pick the middle of the back edge of the smaller box, as shown in the top image in Figure 19.11.

FIGURE 19.11
Moving the smaller box

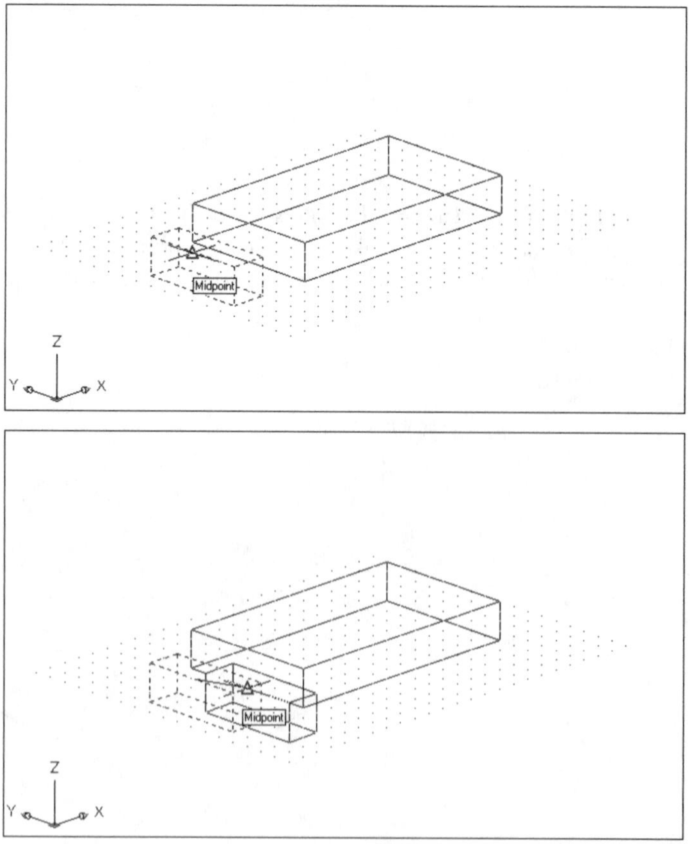

3. At the `Specify second point of displacement or <use first point as displacement>:` prompt, pick the middle of the bottom edge of the larger box, as shown in the bottom image in Figure 19.11.

4. Choose Modify ➢ Solids Editing ➢ Union, or type **Uni**↵. You can also click Union on the Solids Editing toolbar.
5. At the `Select objects:` prompt, pick both boxes and press ↵. Your drawing now looks like Figure 19.12.

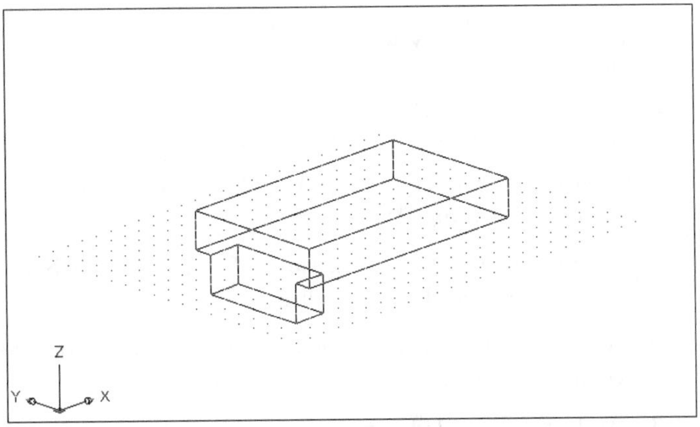

FIGURE 19.12
The two boxes joined

As you can see in Figure 19.12, the form has joined to appear as one object. It also acts like one object when you select it. You now have a composite solid made up of two box primitives.

Now let's place some holes in the bracket. In this next exercise, you will discover how to create negative forms to cut portions out of a solid.

1. Click the Cylinder tool on the Solids toolbar, or type **Cylinder**↵. You can also choose Draw ➢ Solids ➢ Cylinder.
2. At the `Specify center point for base of cylinder or [Elliptical] <0,0,0>:` prompt, pick a point at the coordinate 9,5.5.
3. At the `Specify radius for base of cylinder or [Diameter]:` prompt, enter **.25**↵.

TIP *As with the Circle command, you can enter* **D** *to specify a diameter or enter a radius value directly.*

4. At the `Specify height of cylinder or [Center of other end]:` prompt, enter **1.5**↵. The cylinder is drawn.
5. Copy the cylinder two units in the negative direction of the y-axis so your drawing looks like Figure 19.13.

FIGURE 19.13
The cylinders added to the drawing

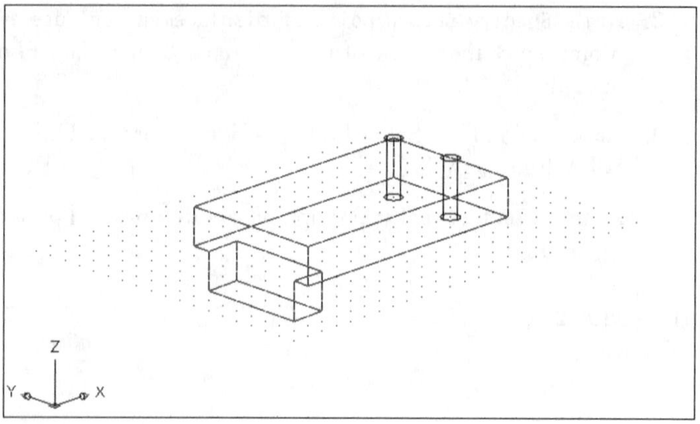

You now have two instances of the cylinder primitive, but you still need to define their relationship to the composite solid you created from the two boxes.

1. Choose Modify ➢ Solids Editing ➢ Subtract, or type **Su**↵. You can also click the Subtract tool on the Solids Editing toolbar.
2. At the `Select solids and regions to subtract from… Select objects:` prompt, pick the composite solid of the two boxes and press ↵.
3. At the `Select solids and regions to subtract… Select objects:` prompt, pick the two cylinders and press ↵. The cylinders have now been subtracted from the bracket.
4. To view the solid, choose View ➢ Hide. You'll see a Hidden-Line view of the solid, as shown in Figure 19.14.

FIGURE 19.14
The bracket so far, with hidden lines removed

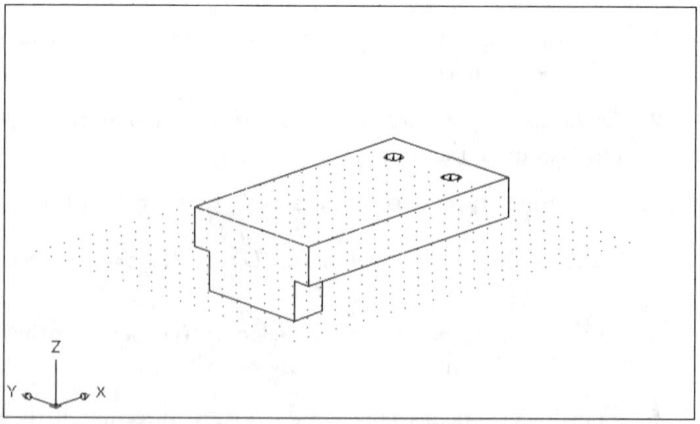

As you've learned in the earlier chapters in Part IV, Wireframe views, such as the one in step 3, are somewhat difficult to decipher. Until you use the Hide command (step 4), you cannot be sure that the subtracted cylinders are in fact holes. Using the Hide command frequently will help you keep track of what's going on with your solid model.

You might also have noticed in step 3 that the cylinders changed shape to conform to the depth of the bracket. You drew the cylinders at a height of 1.5 units, not 1 unit, which is the thickness of the bracket. Having drawn the cylinders taller than needed, you can see that when AutoCAD performed the subtraction, it ignored the portion of the cylinders that doesn't affect the bracket. AutoCAD always discards the portion of a primitive that isn't used in a Subtract operation.

WHAT ARE ISOLINES?

You might have noticed the message that reads:

```
Current wire frame density: ISOLINES=4
```

This message tells you the current setting for the Isolines system variable, which controls the way curved objects, such as cylinders and holes, are displayed. A setting of 4 causes a cylinder to be represented by four lines with a circle at each end. You can see this in the holes that you've created for the Bracket model in the previous exercise. You can change the Isolines setting by entering **Isoline**↵ at the command prompt. You then enter a value for the number of lines to use to represent surfaces. This setting is also controlled by the Contour Lines Per Surface option in the Display tab of the Options dialog box.

Creating Complex Solids

As you learned earlier, you can convert a polyline into a solid using the Extrude option on the Solids toolbar. This process lets you create more complex shapes than the built-in primitives. In addition to the simple straight extrusion you've already tried, you can also extrude shapes into curved paths, or you can taper an extrusion.

Tapering an Extrusion

Let's look at how you can taper an extrusion to create a fairly complex solid with little effort.

1. Draw a 3 × 3 closed polyline at the top of the current solid. Start near the back-left corner of the bracket at coordinate 3.5,3,1, and then draw the 3 × 3 closed polyline to fit in the top of the composite solid, as shown in Figure 19.15.

WARNING *Remember to use the Close option to create the last side of the box.*

2. Click the Fillet tool on the Modify toolbar. At the `Select first object or [Polyline/Radius/Trim/mUltiple]:` prompt, type **R**↵ to set the radius of the fillet.
3. At the prompt for the fillet radius, type **.5**↵.
4. Type **P**↵ to tell the Fillet command that you want to fillet a polyline.
5. Click the polyline. The corners become rounded.

FIGURE 19.15
Drawing the 3 × 3 polyline box

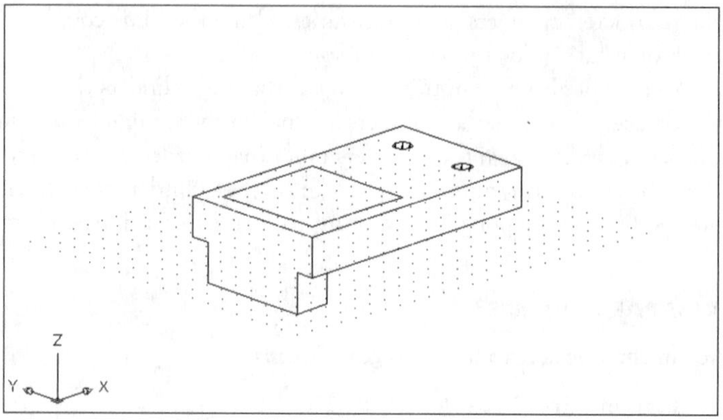

6. Click the Extrude button on the Solids toolbar, or enter **Ext**↵ at the command prompt.
7. At the `Select objects:` prompt, pick the polyline you just drew and press ↵.
8. At the `Specify height of extrusion or [Path]:` prompt, enter **3**↵.
9. At the `Specify angle of taper for extrusion <0>:` prompt, enter **4** for 4° of taper. The extruded polyline looks like Figure 19.16.

FIGURE 19.16
The extruded polyline

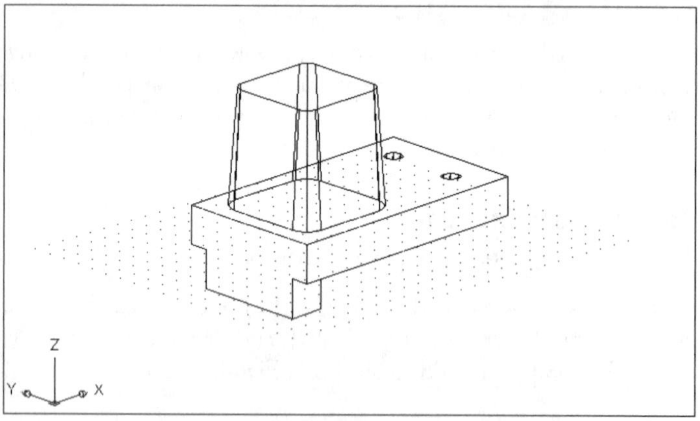

10. Now join the part you just created with the original solid. Choose Modify ➢ Solid Editing ➢ Union, and then select the extruded part and the rectangular solid just below it. Press ↵ to complete your selection.

TIP *In step 9, you can indicate a taper for the extrusion. Specify a taper in terms of degrees from the z-axis, or enter a negative value to taper the extrusion outward. Or press ↵ to accept the default of 0°, to extrude the polyline without a taper.*

Extruding on a Curved Path

As you'll see in the following exercise, the Extrude command lets you extrude virtually any polyline shape along a path that is defined by a polyline, an arc, or a 3D polyline.

1. Choose View ➢ Zoom ➢ Extents and turn off the grid.
2. Choose View ➢ Hide. This helps you view and select parts of your model in the following steps.
3. Place the UCS on a vertical plane perpendicular to the back of the bracket. Choose Tools ➢ Orthographic UCS ➢ Left.
4. Start a polyline at the point shown in the first image in Figure 19.17. Use the Midpoint Osnap to make sure you select the midpoint of the vertical corner edge. After you locate the first point, enter the following coordinates:

```
@2<180
@1<270
@2<180
```

When you are done, your drawing should look like the second image in Figure 19.17.

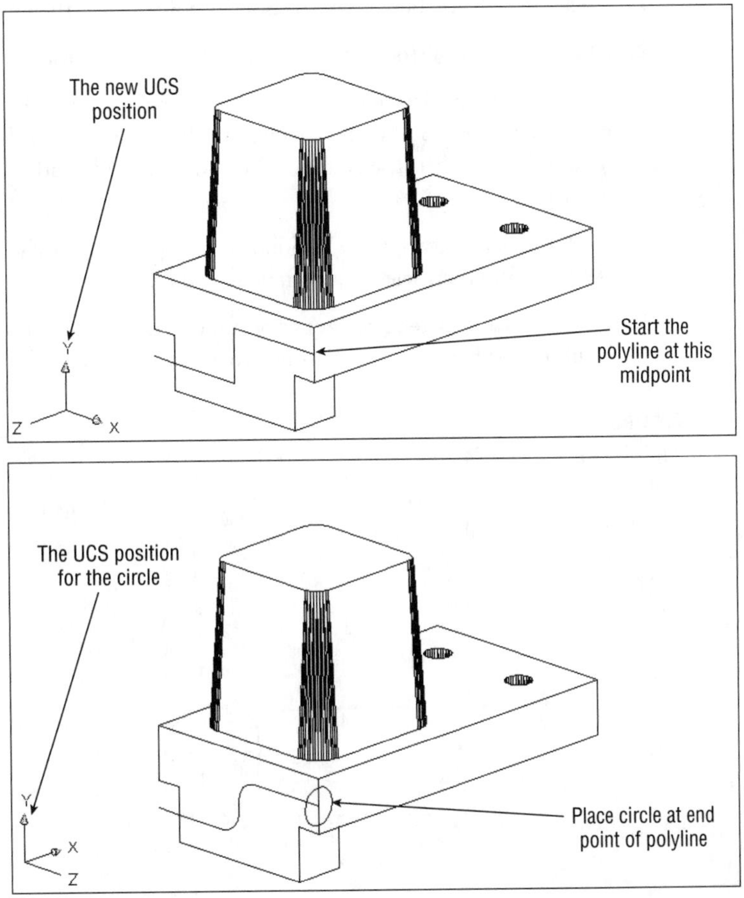

FIGURE 19.17
Hidden-line view showing how to set up your drawing to create a curved extrusion

5. Click the Fillet tool on the Modify toolbar, and then type **R**↵ to set the fillet radius.
6. Enter **.4**↵ for the fillet radius.
7. Type **P**↵ to select the Polyline option.
8. Click the polyline you drew on the back side of the solid.
9. Choose Tools ➢ New UCS ➢ Y, and then enter **90**↵. This rotates the UCS 90 degrees around the y-axis so the UCS is perpendicular to the front face of the solid.
10. Draw a circle with a 0.35-unit radius at the location shown in the second image in Figure 19.17.

TIP *Figure 19.17 shows a hidden-line view to help you see the polyline and circle more clearly. It shows a lot of extra facets on the curved portion of the model. You can set up AutoCAD so these extra facets don't appear. Open the Options dialog box and click the Show Silhouettes In Wireframe checkbox on the Display tab.*

At this point, you've created the components needed to do the extrusion. Next, you'll finish the extruded shape.

1. Click the Extrude button on the Solids toolbar, click the circle, and then press ↵.
2. At the `Specify height of extrusion or [Path]:` prompt, type **P**↵ to enter the Path option.
3. At the `Select extrusion path or [Taper angle]:` prompt, click the polyline curve. AutoCAD pauses a moment and then generates a solid "tube" that follows the path. The tube may not look like a tube because AutoCAD draws extruded solids such as this with for line showings its profile.
4. Click the Subtract tool on the Solids Editing toolbar or choose Modify ➢ Solids Editing ➢ Subtract, and then select the rectangular solid.
5. Press ↵. At the `Select objects:` prompt, click the curved solid and press ↵. The curved solid is subtracted from the square solid. Your drawing will look like Figure 19.18.

FIGURE 19.18
The solid after subtracting the curve

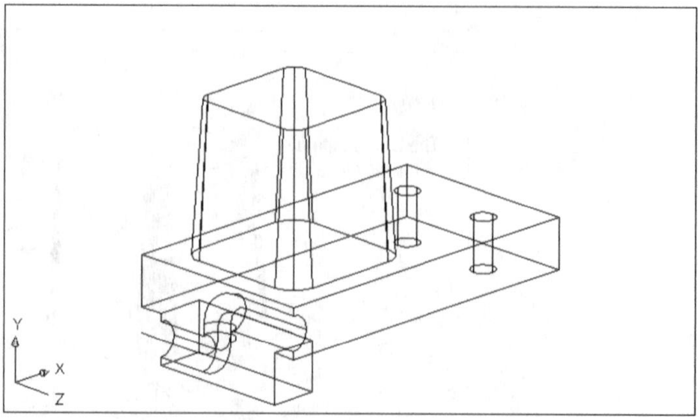

In this exercise, you used a curved polyline for the extrusion path, but you can use any type of 2D or 3D polyline, as well as lines and arcs, for an extrusion path.

Revolving a Polyline

When your goal is to draw an object that is circular, the Revolve command on the Solids toolbar is designed to let you create a solid that is revolved, or swept in a circular path. Think of Revolve's action as similar to a lathe that lets you carve a shape from a spinning shaft. In this case, the spinning shaft is a polyline, and rather than carving it, you define the profile and then revolve the profile around an axis.

In the following exercise, you will draw a solid that will form a slot in the tapered solid.

1. Zoom in to the top of the tapered box, so you have a view similar to Figure 19.19.

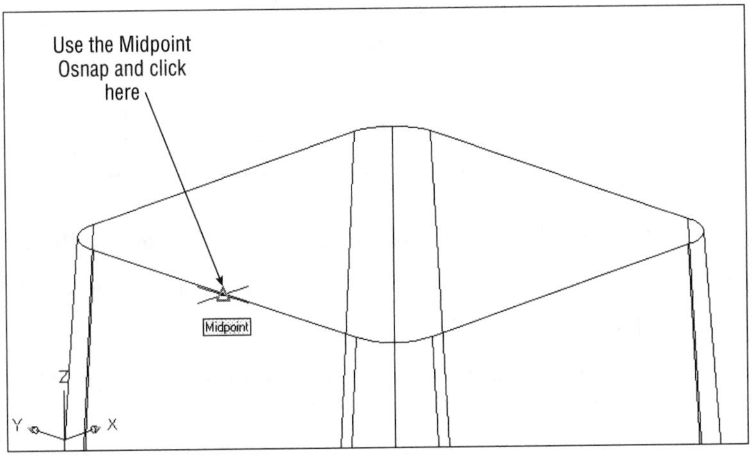

FIGURE 19.19
An enlarged view of the top of the tapered box and the new UCS location

2. Turn off the Snap mode.
3. Return to the WCS by choosing Tools ➢ New UCS ➢ World.
4. Choose Tools ➢ New UCS ➢ Origin.
5. At the Specify new `origin point <0,0,0>:` prompt, use the Midpoint Osnap override and pick the midpoint of the top surface, as shown in Figure 19.19.
6. Set the Snap distance to **0.25** and turn on Polar Tracking.
7. Draw a polyline using Polar Tracking with the following polar coordinates:

```
Start at -0.25,0
@.75<90
@.75<0
@.7071<315
@.5<0
@.7071<45
@.75<0
@.75<270
```

8. When you've finished, type **C**↵ to close the polyline. AutoCAD will not revolve an open polyline. Your drawing should look like Figure 19.20.

FIGURE 19.20
Drawing the polyline

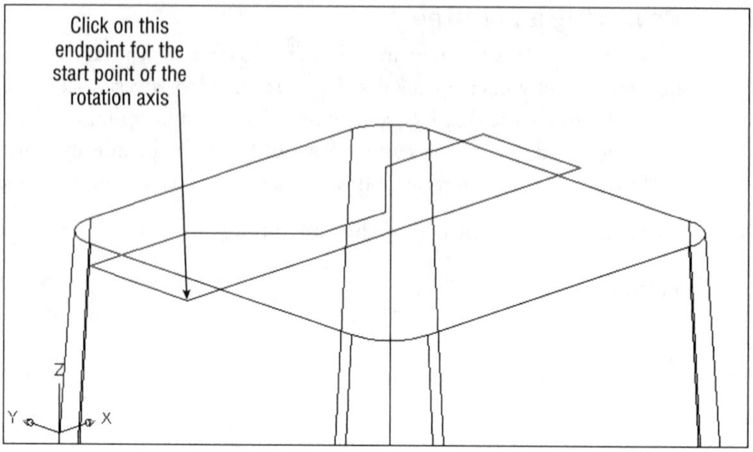

Click on this endpoint for the start point of the rotation axis
Z
Y
X

9. Click the Revolve tool on the Solids toolbar, or type **Rev**↵ at the command prompt.
10. At the `Select objects:` prompt, pick the polyline you just drew and press ↵.
11. When you see the next prompt:

```
Specify start point for axis of revolution or define axis by
-[Object/X(axis)/Y(axis)]:
```

use the Endpoint Osnap override and pick the beginning endpoint of the polyline you just drew.

12. At the `Specify endpoint of axis:` prompt, turn on the Ortho mode (press F8) and turn off the Snap mode (press F9). Then pick a point to the far left of the screen so that the rubber-banding line is parallel with the x-axis of the current UCS.
13. At the `Specify angle of revolution <360>:` prompt, press ↵ to sweep the polyline a full 360°. The revolved form appears, as shown in Figure 19.21.

You just created a revolved solid that will be subtracted from the tapered box to form a slot in the bracket. But before you subtract it, you need to make a slight change in the orientation of the revolved solid.

1. Choose Modify ➢ 3D Operation ➢ Rotate 3D.
2. At the `Select objects:` prompt, select the revolved solid and press ↵.
3. At the prompt

```
Specify first point on axis or define axis by
[Object/Last/View/Xaxis/Yaxis/Zaxis/2points]:
```

use the Midpoint Osnap and click the right-side edge of the top surface, as shown in Figure 19.22.

FIGURE 19.21
The revolved polyline

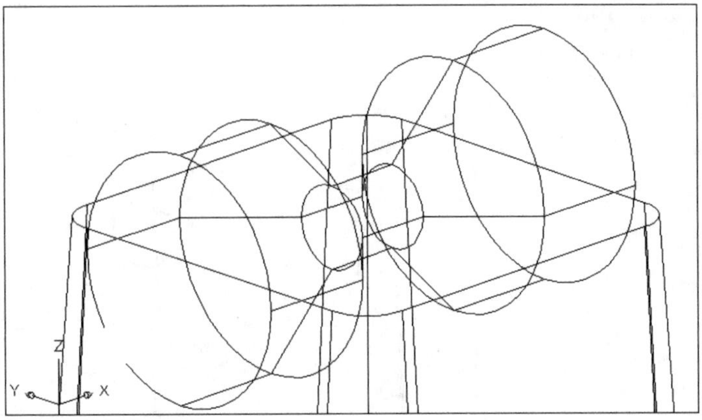

FIGURE 19.22
Selecting the points to rotate the revolved solid in 3D space

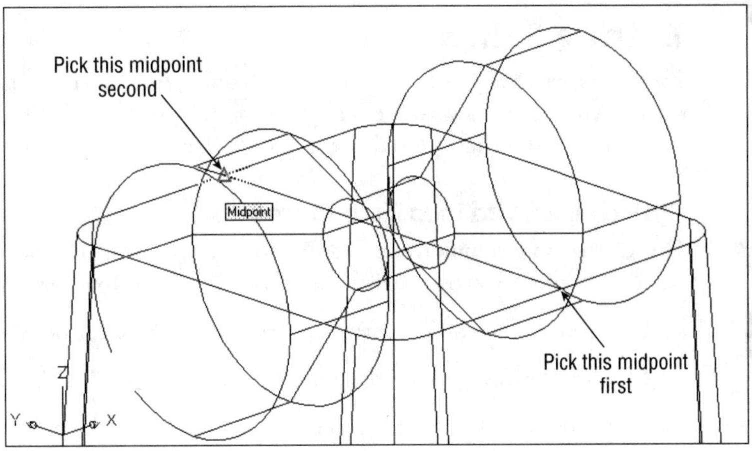

4. At the `Specify second point on axis:` prompt, use the Midpoint Osnap again and click the opposite side of the top surface, as shown in Figure 19.22.
5. At the `Specify rotation angle or [Reference]:` prompt, type **5**↵. The solid rotates 5°.
6. Click the Subtract tool on the Solids Editing toolbar or choose Modify ➢ Solids Editing ➢ Subtract, click the tapered box, and then press ↵.
7. At the `Select objects:` prompt, click the revolved solid and press ↵. Your drawing looks like Figure 19.23.

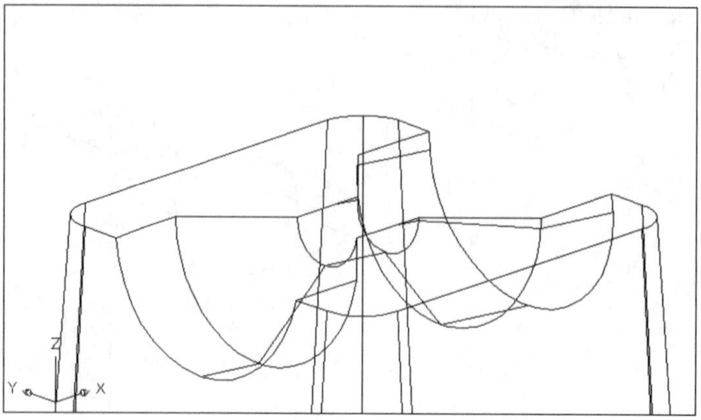

FIGURE 19.23
The composite solid

Editing Solids

Basic solid forms are fairly easy to create. Refining those forms requires some special tools. In this section, you'll learn how to use some familiar 2D editing tools to edit a solid as well as some new tools. You'll also be introduced to the Slice tool, which lets you cut a solid into two pieces.

Splitting a Solid into Two Pieces

One of the more common solid-editing tools you'll use is the Slice tool. As you might guess from its name, Slice allows you to cut a solid into two pieces. The following exercise demonstrates how it works.

1. Zoom to the previous view and return to the World Coordinate System.

2. Click the Slice tool on the Solids toolbar, or type **Slice↵**.
3. At the `Select objects:` prompt, click the part you've been working on and press ↵.

TIP *In step 3, you could select more than one solid. The Slice command would then slice all the solids through the plane indicated in steps 4 and 5.*

4. At the prompt

   ```
   Specify first point on slicing plane by [Object/Zaxis/View/XY/YZ/ZX/3points]
   <3points>:
   ```

   type **XY↵**. This lets you indicate a slice plane parallel to the XY plane.
5. At the `Point on XY plane <0,0,0>:` prompt, type **0,0,.5↵**. This places the slice plane at the Z coordinate of .5 units. You can use the Midpoint Osnap and pick any vertical edge of the rectangular solid.

***TIP** If you want to delete one side of the sliced solid, you can indicate the side you want to keep by clicking it in step 6, instead of entering **B**↵.*

6. At the `Specify a point on desired side of the plane or [keep Both sides]:` prompt, type **B**↵ to keep both sides of the solid. AutoCAD will divide the solid horizontally, one-half unit above the base of the part, as shown in Figure 19.24.

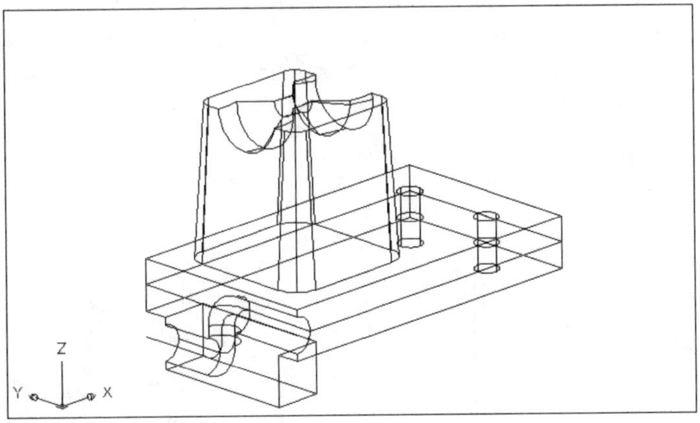

FIGURE 19.24
The solid sliced through the base

THE SLICE OPTIONS

Several options in step 4 of the previous exercise are worth discussing briefly here.

Object Lets you select an object to define the slice plane.

Zaxis Lets you select two points defining the z-axis of the slice plane. The two points you pick will be perpendicular to the slice plane.

View Generates a slice plane that is perpendicular to your current view. You are prompted for the coordinate through which the slice plane must pass—usually a point on the object.

3points The default; lets you select three points defining the slice plane. Normally, you would pick points on the solid.

XY/YZ/ZX Pick one of these to determine the slice plane based on the x-, y-, or z-axis. You are prompted to pick a point through which the slice plane must pass.

Rounding Corners with the Fillet Tool

Your bracket has a few sharp corners that you may want to round in order to give the bracket a more realistic appearance. You can use the Modify menu's Fillet and Chamfer commands to add these rounded corners to your solid model.

1. Adjust your view of the model so it looks similar to the first image in Figure 19.25.

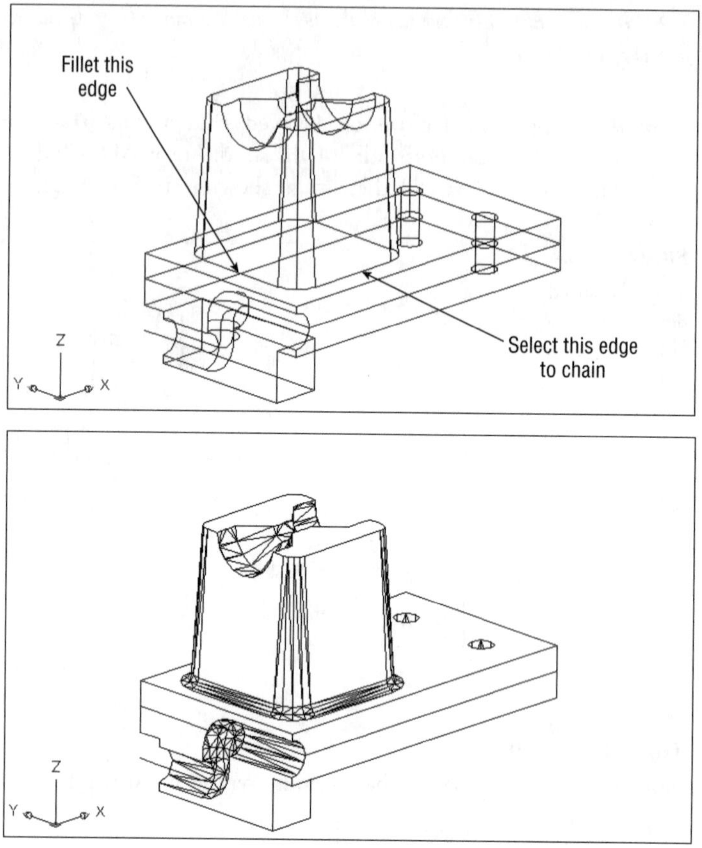

FIGURE 19.25
Filleting solids

2. Click the Fillet tool on the Modify toolbar.
3. At the `Select first object or [Polyline/Radius/Trim/mUltiple]:` prompt, pick the edge indicated in the first image in Figure 19.25.
4. At the `Enter fillet radius:` prompt, type **.2↵**.
5. At the `Select an edge or [Chain/Radius]:` prompt, type **C↵** for the Chain option. Chain lets you select a series of solid edges to be filleted.
6. Select one of the other three edges at the base of the tapered form, and press ↵.
7. Choose Hide from the Render toolbar or type **Hide↵** to get a better look at your model, as shown in the second image in Figure 19.25.

As you saw in step 5, Fillet acts a bit differently when you use it on solids. The Chain option lets you select a set of edges, instead of just two adjoining objects.

Chamfering Corners with the Chamfer Tool

Now let's try chamfering a corner. To practice using Chamfer, you'll add a countersink to the cylindrical hole you created in the first solid.

1. Type **Regen↵** to return to a Wireframe view of your model.

2. Click the Chamfer tool on the Modify toolbar, or type **Cha**.
3. At this prompt

   `Select first line or [Polyline/Distance/Angle/Trim/Method/mUltiple]:`

   pick the edge of the hole, as shown in Figure 19.26. Notice that the top surface of the solid is highlighted, and the prompt changes to `Enter surface selection option [Next/OK (current)] <OK>:`. The highlighting indicates the base surface, which will be used as a reference in step 5. (You could also type **N↵** to choose the other adjoining surface, the inside of the hole, as the base surface.)

FIGURE 19.26

Picking the edge to chamfer

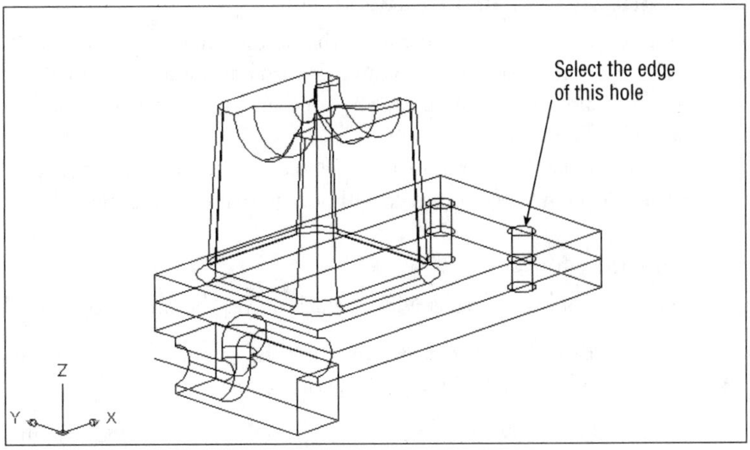
Select the edge
of this hole
Z
Y
X

4. Press ↵ to accept the current highlighted face.
5. At the `Specify base surface chamfer distance:` prompt, type **.125↵**. This indicates that you want the chamfer to have a width of .125 across the highlighted surface.
6. At the `Specify other surface chamfer distance <0.1250>:` prompt, type **.2↵**.
7. At the `Select an edge or [Loop]:` prompt, click the edges of both holes and then press ↵. When it is done, your drawing will look like Figure 19.27.
8. After reviewing the work you've done here, save the `Bracket.dwg` file.

TIP *The Loop option in step 7 lets you chamfer the entire circumference of an object. You don't need to use it here because the edge forms a circle. The Loop option is used when you have a rectangular or other polygonal edge you want to chamfer.*

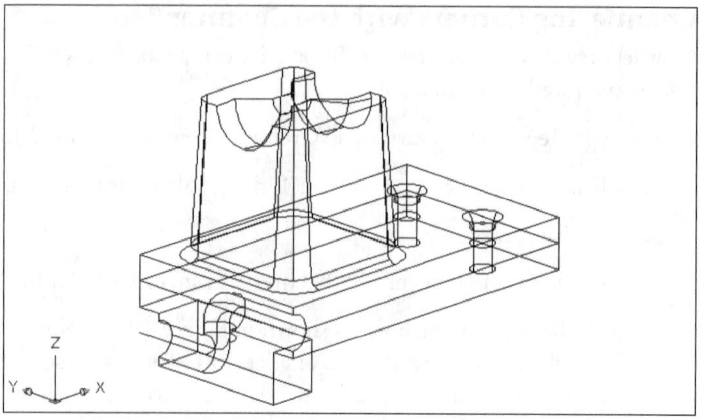

FIGURE 19.27
The chamfered edges

Using the Solids Editing Tools

You've added some refinements to the Bracket model by using some standard AutoCAD editing tools. A set of tools is specifically geared toward editing solids. You already used the Union and Subtract tools found on the Solids Editing toolbar. In this section, you'll explore some of the other tools available on that toolbar.

To help keep the exercises simple and easy to understand, you'll be using an existing 3D model, called `Soldedit.dwg`. This file will help to demonstrate the Solids Editing tools.

MOVING A SURFACE

The first tool you'll try is Move, which moves the surface of a solid.

1. Open the `Soldedit.dwg` file from the companion CD. This file is set up with the Hidden Shade mode turned on so you can see the form more easily.

2. Click the Move Faces tool in the Solids Editing toolbar, and then click the back edge of the model, as shown in Figure 19.28. Notice that two surfaces are highlighted. These are the faces that will be moved unless you indicate otherwise. To isolate the back surface, you will remove the top surface from the selection set.
3. At the `Select faces or [Undo/Remove/ALL]:` prompt, type **R**↵. The prompt changes to read `Remove faces or [Undo/Add/ALL]:`. Now any highlighted object you select will be removed from the selection set.
4. Click the edge of the top surface, as indicated in Figure 19.28. The top surface is removed from the selection set.

TIP *You can enter* ***A***↵ at the `Remove faces or [Undo/Add/ALL]:` *prompt to continue to add more surfaces to your selection set.*

5. Press ↵ to finish your selection.

FIGURE 19.28

Moving the back surface of the model

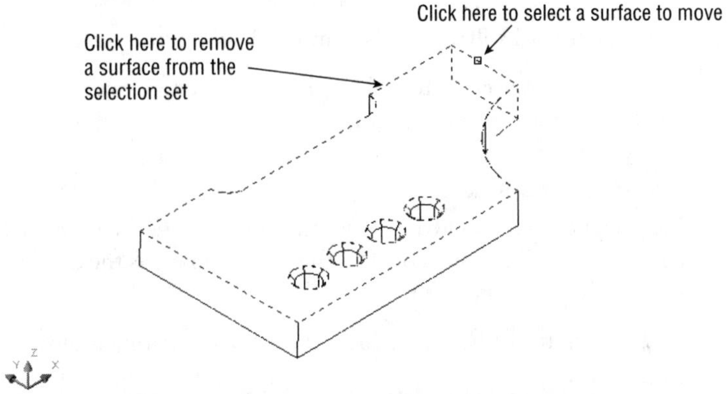

6. At the `Specify a base point or displacement:` prompt, click any point near the back face.
7. At the `Specify a second point of displacement:` prompt, enter **@.6<0**↵ to move the surface 0.6 units to the right.

Once you've selected the surface you want to move, the Move Faces tool acts just like the Move command. Notice how the curved side of the model extends its curve to meet the new location of the surface. This shows you that AutoCAD attempts to maintain the geometry of the model when you make changes to the faces.

Try Move Faces again, but this time, move a set of faces on the interior of the model.

1. Click the Move Faces tool again.
2. Click the countersink hole closest to the foreground, as shown in Figure 19.29. Then click the straight shaft of the hole, as shown in Figure 19.29.

FIGURE 19.29

Moving the countersink hole in the model

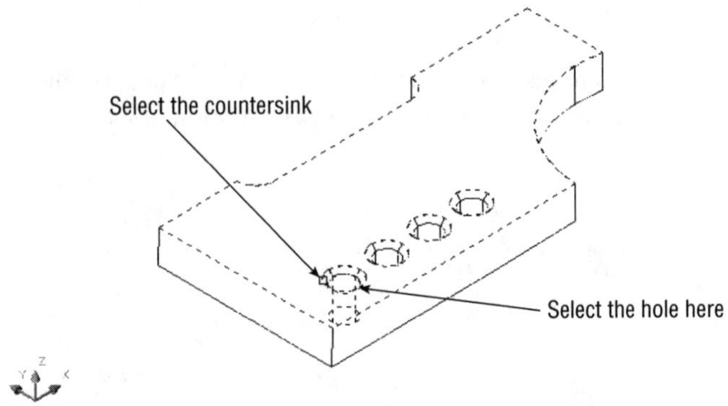

3. Press ↵ to finish your selection; then click any point on the screen.
4. Enter **@1<90↵**. The hole moves 1 unit in the y-axis.

In some instances, AutoCAD will not be able to move surfaces. This usually occurs when an adjoining surface is too complex.

OFFSETTING A SURFACE

Now suppose you want to decrease the radius of the arc in the right corner of the model, and you also want to thicken the model by the same amount as the decrease in the arc radius. To do this, you can use the Offset Faces tool.

1. Click the Offset Faces tool on the Solids Editing toolbar.
2. Click the lower edge of the curved surface, as shown in Figure 19.30. Notice that both the curved surface and the bottom of the model are highlighted. You can add or remove surfaces from the selection set as you did in the previous two exercises. Here, you'll just stick with the selection set you have.

FIGURE 19.30

Selecting a surface to offset

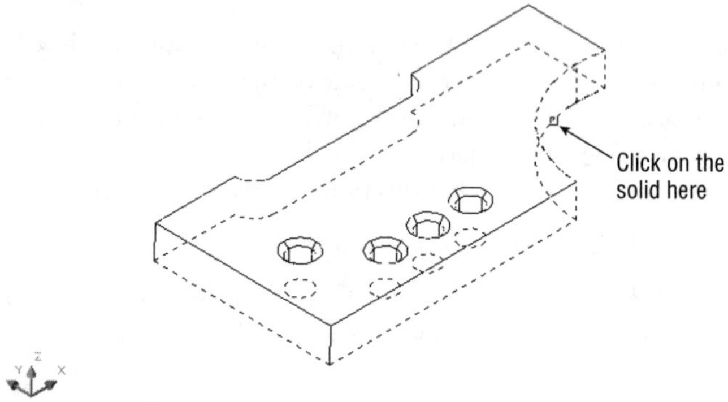
Click on the solid here
Y
Z
X

3. Press ↵ to finish your selection; then, at the `Specify the offset distance:` prompt, enter **.5↵**. The surfaces move to their new location (see Figure 19.31).

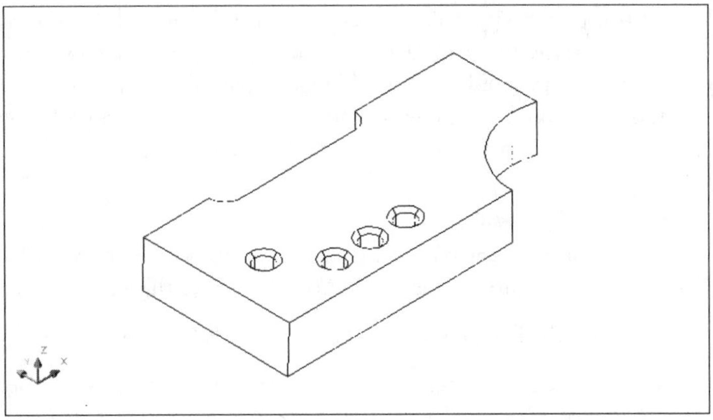

FIGURE 19.31

The model after offsetting the curved and bottom surface

DELETING A SURFACE

Now suppose you've decided to eliminate the curved part of the model altogether. You can delete a surface using the Delete Faces tool.

1. Click the Delete Faces tool on the Solids Editing toolbar.
2. At the `Select faces or [Undo/Remove]:` prompt, click the bottom edge of the curve as you did in the last exercise. You'll need to remove the bottom surface from the selection set; otherwise this operation won't work.
3. Type R↵, and then select the back edge of the bottom surface to remove it from the selection set. The curved surface remains highlighted.
4. Type ↵ to finish your selection. The curve disappears and a corner forms in its place, as shown in Figure 19.32.

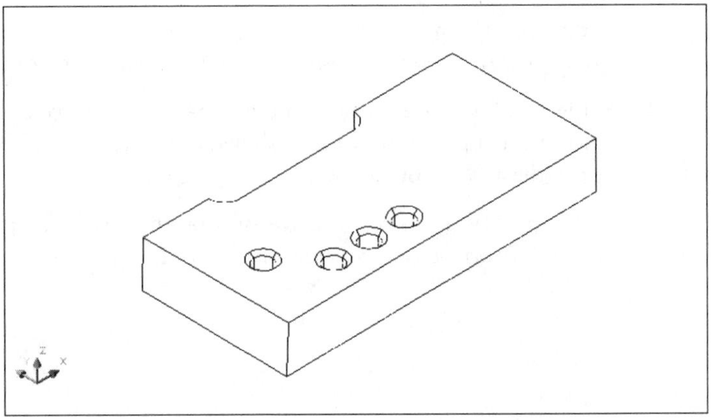

FIGURE 19.32

The model with the curved surface removed

When you attempt to delete surfaces, keep in mind that the surface you delete must be recoverable by other surfaces in the model. For example, you cannot remove the top surface of a cube expecting it to turn into a pyramid. That would require the sides to change their orientation, which is not allowed in this operation. You can, on the other hand, remove the top of a box with tapered sides. Then, when you remove the top, the sides converge to form a pyramid.

ROTATING A SURFACE

All the surfaces of the model are parallel or perpendicular to each other. Imagine that your design requires two sides to be at an angle. You can change the angle of a surface using the Rotate Faces tool.

1. Click the Rotate Faces tool on the Solids Editing toolbar.
2. At the `Select faces or [Undo/Remove]:` prompt, select the corner edge in the foreground, as shown in Figure 19.33, and press ↵. The two surfaces facing you are highlighted.

FIGURE 19.33

Defining the axis of rotation.

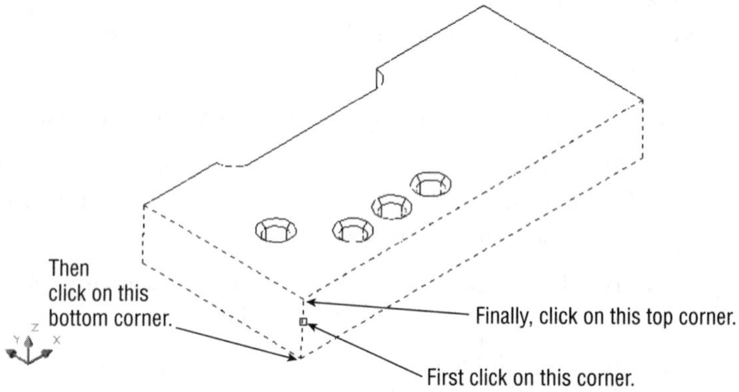

3. At the `Specify an axis point or [Axis by object/View/Xaxis/Yaxis /Zaxis] <2points>:` prompt, use the Endpoint Osnap to select the bottom of the corner, as shown in Figure 19.33.
4. At the `Specify the second point on the rotation axis:` prompt, use the Endpoint Osnap to select the top of the corner as shown in Figure 19.33. The two points you just selected specify the axis of rotation for the surface rotation.
5. At the `Specify a rotation angle or [Reference]:` prompt, enter **4**↵. The two surfaces change their orientation, as shown in Figure 19.34.

FIGURE 19.34

The model after rotating two surfaces

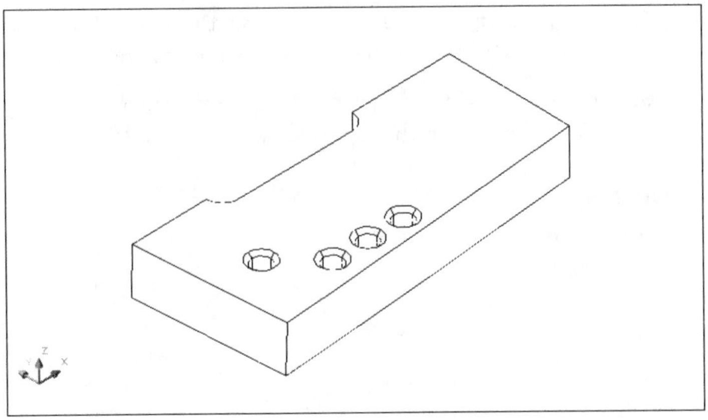

TAPERING SURFACES

In an earlier exercise, you saw how to create a new tapered solid using the Extrude command. But what if you want to taper an existing solid? Here's what you can do to taper an existing 3D solid:

1. Choose the Taper Faces tool from the Solids Editing toolbar.
2. Click the three corners of the model, as indicated in Figure 19.35. You may have to approximate the location of the back corner to select it.

FIGURE 19.35

Selecting the surfaces to taper and indicating the direction of the taper

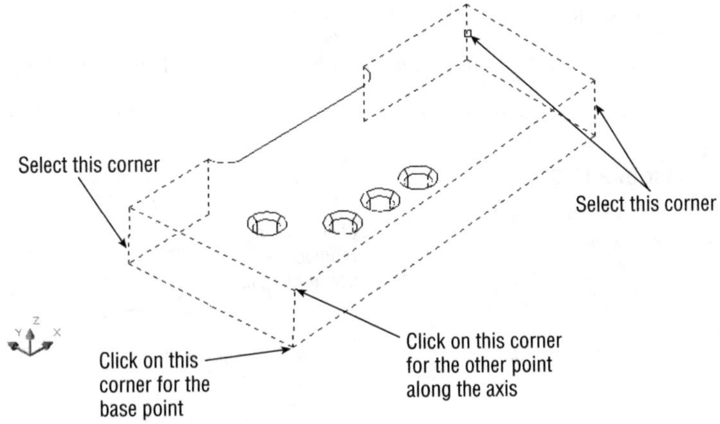
Select this corner
Select this corner
Click on this corner for the base point
Click on this corner for the other point along the axis

3. Press ↵ to finish your selection.
4. At the `Specify the base point:` prompt, use the Endpoint Osnap to click the bottom corner in the foreground of the model, as shown in Figure 19.35.

5. At the `Specify another point along the axis of tapering:` prompt, use the Endpoint Osnap to click the top corner, as shown in Figure 19.35.
6. At the `Specify the taper angle:` prompt, enter **4↵**. The sides of the model are now tapered 4 degrees inward at the top, as shown in Figure 19.36.

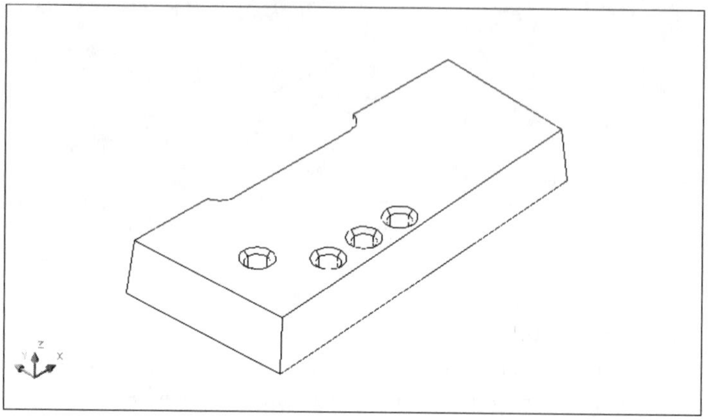

FIGURE 19.36
The model after tapering the sides

EXTRUDING A SURFACE

You've used the Extrude command to create two of the solids in the Bracket model. The Extrude command requires a closed polyline as a basis for the extrusion. As an alternative the Solids Editing toolbar offers the Extrude Faces tool, which will extrude a surface of an existing solid. The following exercise demonstrates how it works.

1. Click the Extrude Faces tool on the Solids Editing toolbar.
2. Click the bottom edge of the front surface of the model, as shown in Figure 19.37.

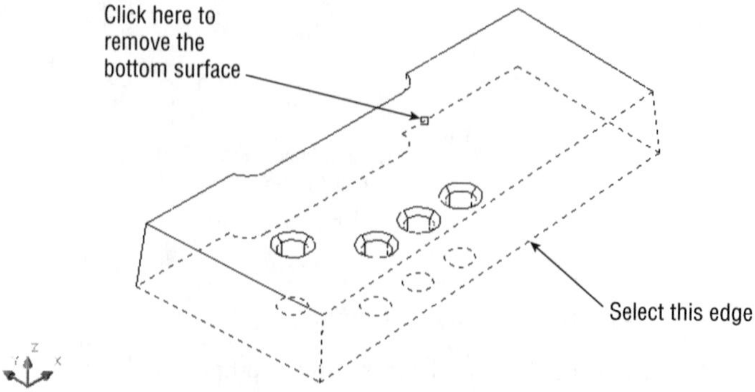
Click here to remove the bottom surface
Select this edge

FIGURE 19.37
Selecting the surfaces for extrusion

3. You don't want to extrude the bottom surface of the model, so type **R↵** and click the back edge of the highlighted bottom surface, as shown in Figure 19.38.

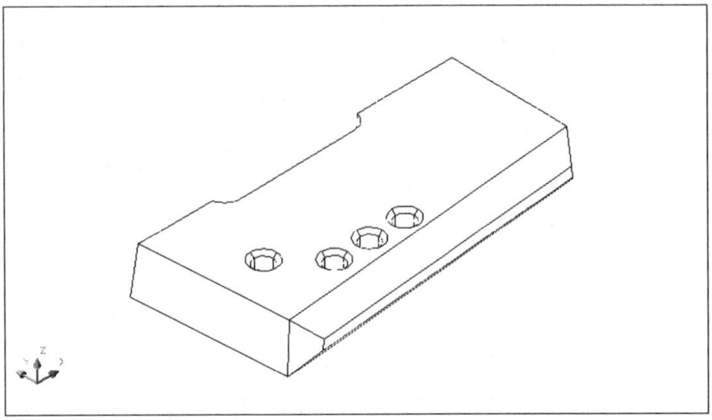

FIGURE 19.38
The model with a surface extruded and tapered

4. Press ↵. The `Specify height of extrusion or [Path]:` prompt appears. Notice that this is the same prompt you saw when you used the Extrude command earlier in this chapter.
5. Enter **.5↵** for an extrusion height of 0.5 units.
6. At the `Specify angle of taper for extrusion <0>:` prompt, enter **45↵** to taper the extrusion at a 45° angle. Your model now adds the extrusion, as shown in Figure 19.38.

You can extrude multiple surfaces at one time if you need to by selecting more surfaces after step 2. In this exercise, you removed a selected surface in step 3 so that only one surface is extruded.

Aside from those features, the Extrude Faces tool works just like the Extrude command.

TURNING A SOLID INTO A SHELL

In many situations, you'll want your 3D model to be a hollow, rather than solid, mass. The Shell tool lets you convert a solid into a shell. Here's an example of how it might be used:

1. Choose the Shell tool from the Solids Editing toolbar.
2. Click the model. The entire model is highlighted. AutoCAD assumes you want to shell the entire object with a few faces completely removed. The `Remove faces or [Undo/Add/ALL]:` prompt appears, and you see the object selection cursor, indicating that you can select objects for removal.
3. Click the top-front edge of the solid, as shown in Figure 19.39, to remove the two surfaces adjoining that edge.

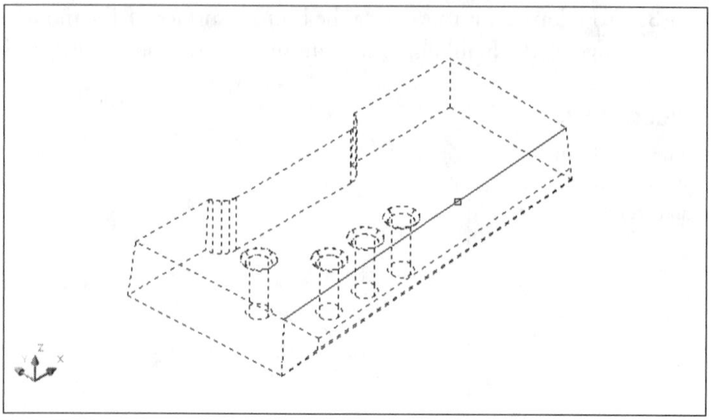

FIGURE 19.39
Selecting the edge to be removed

4. Press ↵ to finish your selection.
5. At the `Enter the shell offset distance:` prompt, enter **.05↵**. The solid becomes a shell with a 0.05 wall thickness, as shown in Figure 19.40.

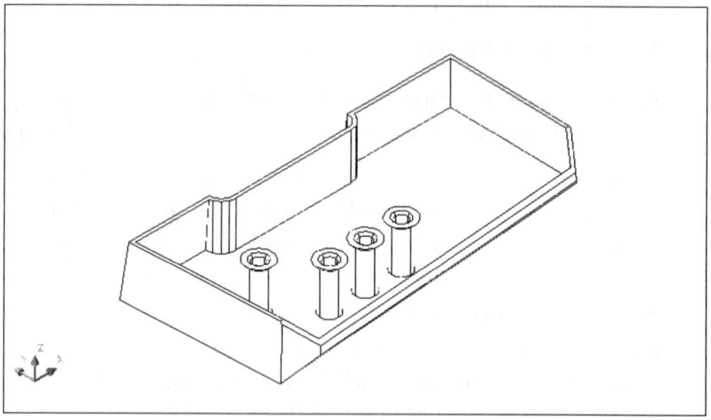

FIGURE 19.40
The solid model after using the Shell tool

6. After studying the results of the Shell tool, type **U↵** to undo the shell operation in preparation for the next exercise.

The shell thickness is added to the outside surface of the solid, so when you're constructing your solid with the intention of creating a shell, you need to take this into account.

COPYING FACES AND EDGES

At times, you might want to create a copy of a surface of a solid to analyze its area or to produce another part that mates to that surface. The Copy Faces tool creates a copy of any surface on your model. The copy it produces is a type of object called a *region*. You'll learn more about regions later in this chapter. Right now, let's see how the Copy Faces tool works.

1. Click the Copy Faces tool on the Solids Editing toolbar.
2. Click the front-top edge of the model, the same edge shown in Figure 19.39 in the Shell exercise. Two surfaces are highlighted.
3. Press ↵ to finish your selection.
4. Click a base point for the copy, and enter **@10<315**.
5. Choose View ➢ Zoom ➢ Extents or type **Z↵ E↵** to view the entire drawing. The copied surfaces appear to the right of the solid.

The copies of the surfaces are opaque and can hide objects behind them when you perform a hidden-line removal (choose View ➢ Hide).

Another tool that is similar to Copy Faces is Copy Edges. It works in a similar way, but instead of selecting surfaces as in step 2, you select all the edges you want to copy. The result is a series of simple lines representing the edges of your model. This tool can be useful if you want to convert a solid into a set of 3D Faces. The Copy Edges tool will create a framework onto which you can add 3D Faces.

Using the Command Line for Solids Editing

The Solids Editing tools are actually options of a single AutoCAD command called Solidedit. If you prefer to use the keyboard, here are some tips on using the Solidedit command. When you first enter **Solidedit↵** at the command prompt, you see the following prompt:

```
Enter a solids editing option [Face/Edge/Body/Undo/eXit] <eXit>:
```

You can select the Face, Edge, or Body option to edit the various parts of a solid. The Face option offers the following prompt:

```
[Extrude/Move/Rotate/Offset/Taper/Delete/Copy/coLor/Undo/eXit] <eXit>:
```

The options from this prompt produce the same results as their counterparts in the Solids Editing toolbar. The Edge option from the first prompt offers the following prompt:

```
Enter an edge editing option [Copy/coLor/Undo/eXit] <eXit>:
```

The Copy option lets you copy a surface, and the coLor option lets you add color to a surface. The Body option from the first prompt offers following prompt:

```
[Imprint/seParate solids/Shell/cLean/Check/Undo/eXit] <eXit>:
```

These options also perform the same functions as their counterparts on the Solids Editing toolbar. As you work with this command, you can use the Undo option to undo the last Solidedit option you used without exiting the command.

Adding Surface Features

You'll start by inserting an object that will be the source of the imprint. You will then imprint the main solid model with the object's profile.

1. Choose Insert ➢ Block to open the Insert dialog box.

2. Click Browse; then locate the Imprint.dwg file in the \Projects\Chapter19\ folder and select it.
3. In the Insert dialog box, make sure that the Explode option is checked, and remove the checkmark from the Specify On-Screen check box in the Insertion Point group.
4. Click OK. The block appears in the middle of the solid.
5. Click the Imprint tool.
6. Click the main solid model.
7. Click the imported solid.
8. At the Delete the source object <N>: prompt, enter Y↵.

You now have an outline of the intersection between the two solids imprinted on the top surface of your model. To help the imprint stand out, try the following steps to change its color.

1. Click the Color Faces tool on the Solids Editing toolbar.
2. Click the imprint from the previous exercise. The imprint and the entire top surface are highlighted.
3. At the Select faces or [Undo/Remove/ALL]: prompt, type R↵; then click the outer edge of the top surface to remove it from the selection set.
4. Press ↵ to open the Select Color dialog box.
5. Click the red color sample at the top of the dialog box; then click OK. The imprint is now red.
6. Press ↵ twice to exit the command.
7. To see the full effect of the Color Faces tool, choose View ➢ Shade ➢ Flat Shaded. The imprint appears as a solid red area.

If you want to remove an imprint from a surface, use the Clean tool on the Solids Editing toolbar. Click the Clean tool, and then click the imprint you want to remove. If the imprint has a color, that color will then "bleed" out to the surface where the imprint was placed.

Separating a Divided Solid

While editing solids, you can end up with two separate solid forms that were created from one solid, as shown in Figure 19.41. Even though the two solids appear separated, they act like a single object. In these situations, AutoCAD offers the Separate tool in the Solids Editing toolbar. To use it, just click the Separate tool and select the solid that has become separated into two forms.

FIGURE 19.41

When the tall, thin solid is subtracted from the larger solid, the result is two separate forms, yet they still behave as a single object.

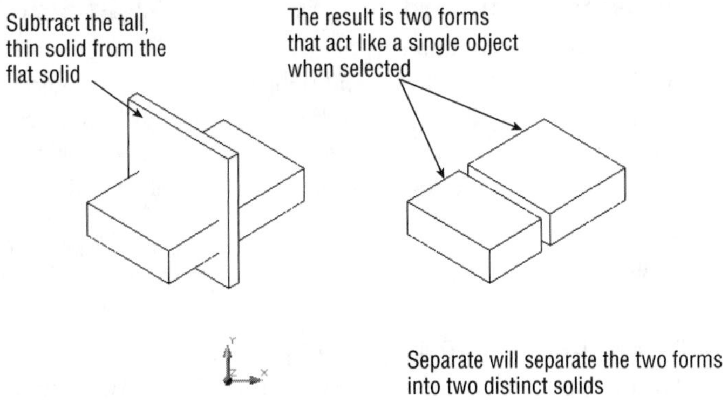

Subtract the tall, thin solid from the flat solid
The result is two forms that act like a single object when selected
Separate will separate the two forms into two distinct solids

Through some simple examples, you've seen how each of the Solids Editing tools works. You aren't limited to using these tools in the way shown in this section, and this book cannot anticipate every situation you may encounter as you create your solid models. These examples are intended as an introduction to these tools, so feel free to experiment with them. You can always use the Undo option to backtrack in case you don't get the results you expect.

TIP *Figure 19.41 is included in the sample figures under the name of* `Separate.dwg` *on the companion CD. You can try the Separate tool on this file on your own.*

This concludes your tour of the Solids Editing toolbar. Next, you'll learn how to use your 3D solid models to quickly generate 2D working drawings.

Enhancing the 2D Drawing Process

Using solids to model a part—such as the Bracket and the Solidedit examples used in this chapter—may seem a bit exotic, but there are definite advantages to modeling in 3D, even if you want to draw the part in only 2D as a page in a set of manufacturing specs.

The exercises in this section show you how to quickly generate a typical mechanical drawing from your 3D model using Paper Space and the Solids toolbar. You will also examine techniques for dimensioning and including hidden lines.

TIP *If your application is architecture, and you've created a 3D model of a building using solids, you can use the tools described in this section to generate 2D elevation drawings from your 3D solid model.*

Drawing a Standard Top, Front, and Right-Side View

One of the more common types of mechanical drawings is the *orthogonal projection*. This style of drawing shows separate top, front, and right-side views of an object. Sometimes a 3D image is also added for clarity. You can derive such a drawing within a few minutes, once you create your 3D solid model. The first step is to select a sheet title block. The title block consists of a border and an area in the lower-right corner for notes and other drawing information.

TIP *If you need to refresh your memory about using Paper Space, refer to Chapter 13.*

SETTING UP A FILE WITH A TITLE BLOCK

The first step is to create a file using one of AutoCAD's template files designed for mechanical applications.

1. If you haven't done so already, save the `Bracket.dwg` file from the earlier exercise, and then Choose File ➢ New to open the Create New Drawing dialog box. If you do not see the Create New Drawing dialog box, select `Ansi D-Color Dependant Plot Styles.dwt` then skip to step 4.

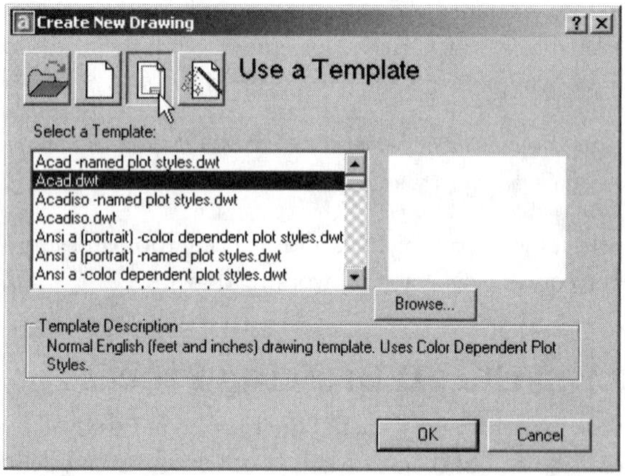

2. Click the Use A Template button.
3. Scroll down the Select A Template list box, and select `Ansi d-color dependent plot styles .dwt`. A title block appears, along with a viewport to Model Space.
4. This template contains a predefined layout viewport that you don't need for this exercise. Click the inside border of the title block to select the viewport; then press the Delete key.

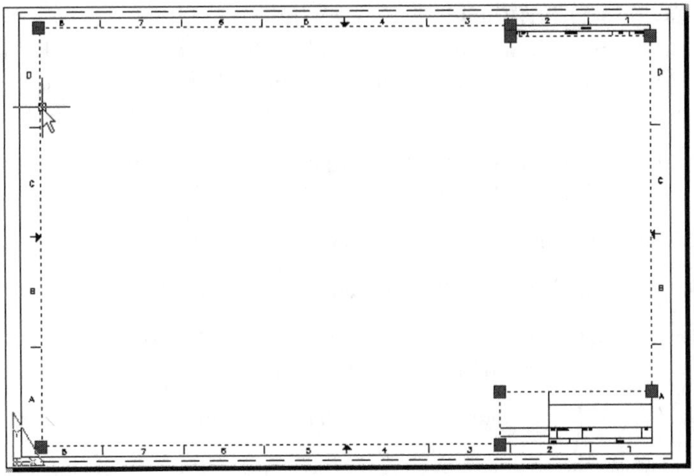

5. Choose View ➢ Viewports ➢ 1 Viewport, and then click two diagonal points to add a single rectangular viewport a little larger than the one shown in Figure 19.42. (However, you won't see anything in the viewport yet.)

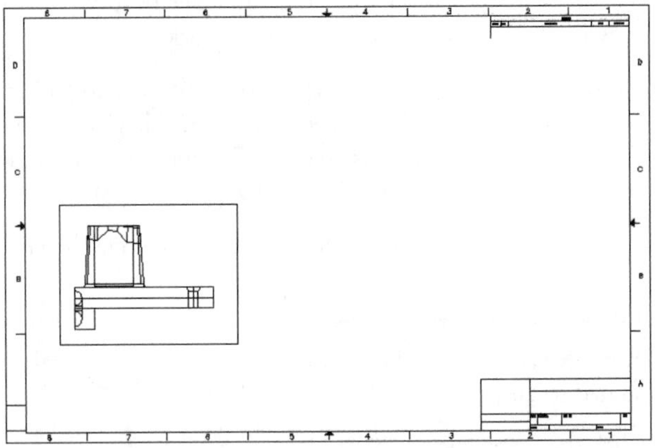

FIGURE 19.42
Resizing the viewport so it is just large enough to contain the view of the bracket

6. Choose File ➢ Save As to save this file as `Bracket_title.dwg`.

You are now in Floating Model Space. Though it may not be obvious at first glance, the title block is in Paper Space, and an active Model Space viewport is inside the title block.

WARNING *If for some reason you do not see a listing of template files in the Create New Drawing dialog box, you will need to set up AutoCAD to look for these files in the right place. Normally, AutoCAD looks in the* `\Program Files\AutoCAD 2004 \Template` *folder for template files. Check the Template Drawing File Location listing in the Files tab of the Options dialog box. See Appendix B for details.*

IMPORTING THE 3D MODEL

The next step is to insert the Bracket solid model into this drawing. Remember that while you are in a floating Model Space viewport, anything you do affects Model Space. So in the next exercise, you will use the Insert tool to import the Bracket drawing into the Model Space of this new drawing.

1. Double-click inside the new viewport to make it active, and then choose Insert ➢ Block to open the Insert dialog box.
2. Click the File button to open the Select Drawing File dialog box.
3. Locate and select the `Bracket.dwg` file, and then click Open.
4. Back in the Insert dialog box, make sure that the Explode check box is checked. If the Specify On-Screen option in the Insertion Point group is turned on, turn it off.
5. Click OK. The drawing appears in the viewport.

You must take one more step before you actually set up the orthogonal views. You want the current viewport to display a front view of the bracket. You can do this easily with a single menu option.

1. Choose View ➢ 3D Views ➢ Front. The Viewport view changes to show the front view of the model.
2. Choose View ➢ Zoom ➢ Scale, and then type **1xp**↵ to give the view a 1-to-1 scale. This has the same effect as setting the Standard Scale property of the viewport to a value of 1:1. The view is now in proper scale to the title block.
3. Double-click outside the viewport or click the Model button in the status bar, and then, using its grips, resize the viewport so it is just large enough to display the model, as shown in Figure 19.42 earlier in this chapter. To expose the viewport grip, click the inner border of the title block, as shown in Figure 19.42.
4. Move the viewport to a location similar to the one shown in Figure 19.42.

CREATING THE ORTHOGONAL VIEWS

Now you are ready to create the orthogonal views. The next part will seem simple compared with the steps you had to take to set up the title block and viewport.

1. Click the Setup View tool on the Solids toolbar, or choose Draw ➢ Solids ➢ Setup ➢ View.
2. At the `Ucs/Ortho/Auxiliary/Section/<Exit>:` prompt, type **O**↵.
3. At the `Specify side of viewport to project:` prompt, place the cursor on the right side of the viewport so that a Midpoint Osnap marker appears, as shown in the first image in Figure 19.43. A rubber-banding line appears.
4. At the `Specify View Center:` prompt, click a point to the right of the viewport, at about half the width of the viewport. The right-side view of the bracket appears, as shown in the second image in Figure 19.43. Click again to adjust the horizontal position of the right-side view.

FIGURE 19.43
Adding the Orthogonal views in Paper Space

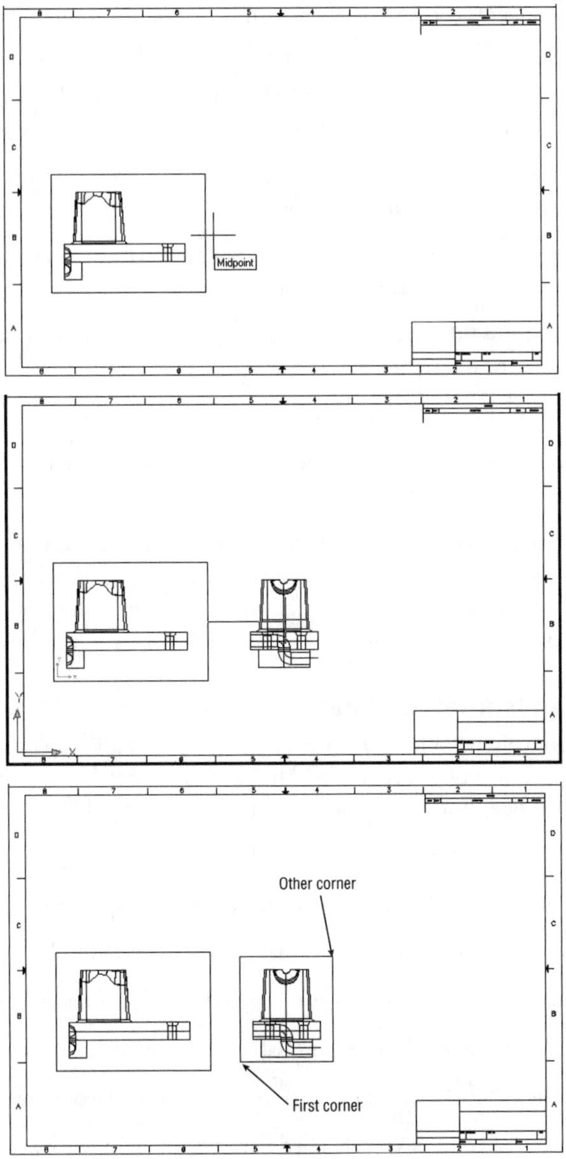

5. Once you're satisfied with the location of the view, press ↵. You don't have to be too precise at this point because you will be able to adjust the view's location later.

6. At the `Specify first corner of viewport:` prompt, click a location below and to the left of the right-side view, as shown in the final image in Figure 19.43.

7. At the `Specify opposite corner of viewport:` prompt, click above and to the right of the view, as shown in the final image in Figure 19.43.
8. At the `Enter view name:` prompt, enter **rightside↵**. Notice that the `Ucs/Ortho/ Auxiliary/ Section/<Exit>:` prompt appears again. This allows you to set up another view.

At this point, you can exit the Setup View tool by pressing ↵, but you need another view. Continue with the following steps to create the top view.

9. Type O↵ again, but this time, at the `Specify side of viewport to project:` prompt, click the top edge of the front-view viewport.
10. Follow steps 4 through 8 to create a top view. In step 4, click a point above the viewport instead of to the right.
11. Name this third viewport **Top**.
12. When you return to the `Ucs/Ortho/Auxiliary/Section/<Exit>:` prompt, press ↵ to exit the command.

Each new view you create using the Setup View tool is scaled to match the original view from which it is derived. As you saw from step 3, the view that is generated depends on the side of the viewport you select. If you pick the bottom of the viewport, a bottom view is generated, which looks the same as the top view until you choose View ➢ Hide to display it as a Hidden-Line view.

Creating an Isometric View

In this section, you will add an Isometric view to your Paper Space layout at a 1-to-1 scale. You can use the Setup View tool to accomplish this, but you'll need to set up a UCS to which the Setup View tool can refer. The following explains how to set up such a UCS for an Isometric view.

1. Click the Model tab to go to Model Space.
2. Choose View ➢ 3D Views ➢ SE Isometric to display an Isometric view of the model.
3. Choose Tools ➢ New UCS ➢ View to set the UCS to be parallel to the current view plane.
4. Choose Tools ➢ Named UCS to open the UCS Control dialog box.
5. Rename the current Unnamed UCS to SEIsometric.
6. Click the ANSI D title block tab to return to the layout view of your model.

Notice that even though you changed your view in Model Space, the Paper Space viewports maintain the views as you last left them. Now you're ready to create a viewport showing the same Isometric view you set up in Model Space.

1. Click the Setup View tool on the Solids toolbar or choose Draw ➢ Solids ➢ Setup ➢ View.
2. At the `Ucs/Ortho/Auxiliary/Section/<Exit>:` prompt, type **U↵**.
3. At the `Named/World/?/<Current>:` prompt, press ↵ to accept the current UCS.

4. At the `Enter view scale<1.0000>:` prompt, press ↵ to accept the scale of 1.
5. At the `View center:` prompt, click a point above and to the right of the original viewport. The Isometric view of the model appears, as shown in Figure 19.44. If you don't like the view's location, you can continue to click points until the view's location is just where you want it.

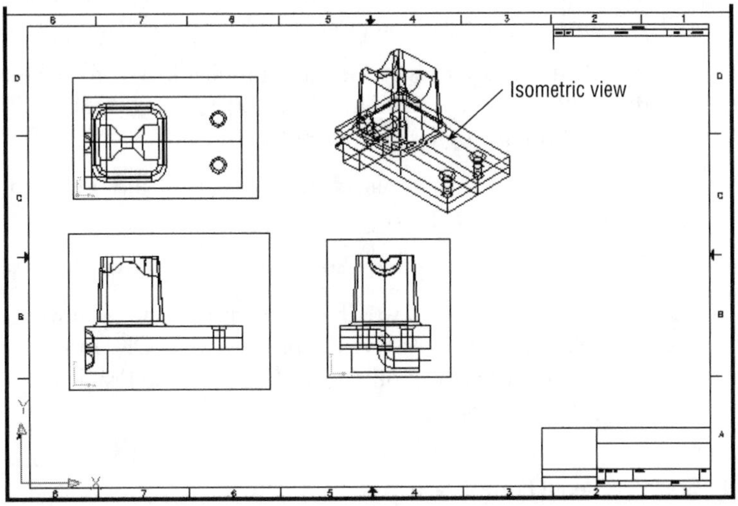

FIGURE 19.44
Adding a viewport for the Isometric view

6. Press ↵ when you are satisfied with the view's location.
7. At the `Clip First corner:` prompt, place a window around the Isometric view to define the viewport border.
8. Name the view `SEIsometric`.
9. Press ↵ to exit the Setup View tool.

A lot of steps were involved in creating these views. However, imagine the work involved if you had to create these views manually, and you'll appreciate the power of these few simple tools.

Creating Hidden-Line Views

You aren't quite finished yet. Typically, orthographic projections, such as the top, front, and right-side view, show the hidden portions of the model with dashed lines. For example, the holes toward the right end of the bracket would be shown dashed in the front view. You could set up the viewports to do a hidden-line removal at plot time, but this would not create the effect you want.

Fortunately, AutoCAD offers the Setup Profile tool to quickly generate a proper Orthographic Projection view of your solid model. Take the following steps to create your first hidden-line view.

1. Go to Floating Model Space by double-clicking the lower-left viewport.

2. Choose Setup Profile from the Solids toolbar, or choose Draw ➢ Solids ➢ Setup ➢ Profile.
3. Click both halves of the solid model, and then press ↵.
4. At the `Display hidden profile lines on separate layer? <Y>:` prompt, press ↵.
5. At the `Project profile lines onto a plane? <Y>:` prompt, press ↵.
6. At the `Delete tangential edges? <Y>:` prompt, press ↵. AutoCAD will work for a moment, and then the command prompt will appear with no apparent change to the drawing.

You don't see the effects of the Setup Profile tool yet. You'll need to make the solid model invisible to display the work that was done by the Setup Profile tool. You'll also have to make a few layer changes to get the profile views just right.

1. Double-click an area outside the viewport or click the Model button on the status bar to return to Paper Space.
2. Zoom into the front view so it fills most of the display area.
3. Turn off Layer 0 (zero). If it is the current layer, you will get a message telling you that you are about to turn off the current layer. Click OK. You've just turned off the layer of the solid model, leaving the profile created by the Setup Profile tool. Notice that you only see an image of the front view.
4. Open the Layer Properties Manager (click the Layers tool in the Object Properties toolbar or choose Format ➢ Layer).
5. Select the layer whose name begins with the "PH" prefix.
6. Change its line type to Hidden. You may need to load the hidden-line type.
7. Once you've changed the line type, click OK to exit the Layer Properties Manager dialog box. The front view now displays hidden lines properly with dashed lines, as shown in Figure 19.45.

FIGURE 19.45
The front view after using the Setup Profile tool

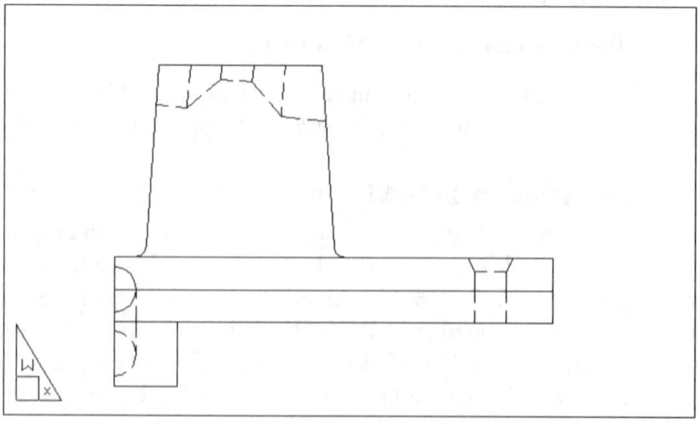

The Setup Profile tool creates a 2D drawing of your 3D model. This 2D drawing is projected onto an imaginary plane that is parallel to the view from which you selected the model while using the Setup Profile tool. To see this clearly, take a look at your model in Model Space.

1. Click the Model tab to go to Model Space.
2. Turn Layer 0 back on. You see the projected 2D view next to the 3D model, as shown in Figure 19.46.

FIGURE 19.46

The projected view next to the 3D solid model

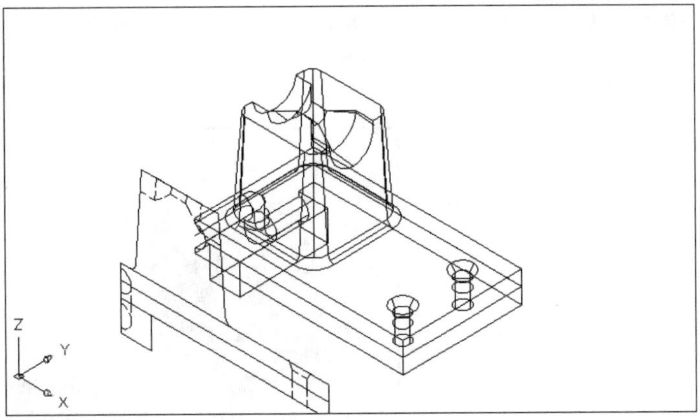

CREATING A 2D PROJECTION FROM YOUR 3D MODEL

Another tool on the Solids toolbar creates 2D drawings of 3D solid models. The Setup Drawing tool does nearly the same thing as the Setup Profile tool, with some differences. First, the Setup Drawing tool works only with viewports that are created by the Setup View tool. It automatically turns off the layer on which the solid model resides. So once it has created a 2D view, you can see the results without having to adjust layer settings. Also, unlike the Setup Profile tool, Setup Drawing leaves the 2D drawing objects as individual objects ready to be edited, instead of turning them into blocks.

Finally, the Setup Drawing tool creates layers whose names offer a better description of their purpose. For example, if you use Setup Drawing to create a 2D drawing of the right-side view, you will get layers entitled Rightside-dim, Rightside-hid, and Rightside-vis. These layer names are derived from the View name from which the 2D drawing is derived. Setup Drawing adds the -dim, -hid, and -vis suffixes to the view name to create the layer name. These suffixes are abbreviations for dimension, hidden, and visible.

Shading a Viewport

In Chapter 16, you saw how you can view your 3D model as a shaded view in Model Space. The shaded view gives you a more realistic representation of your 3D model, and it can show off more of the details, especially in rounded surfaces. You can also view and plot a shaded view in a Layout tab.

To do this, you make a viewport active and then turn on the shading feature you want to use for that viewport. The following exercise gives you a first-hand look at how this is done.

1. Click the Layout tab in the lower portion of the AutoCAD window.
2. Double-click inside the viewport with the Isometric view of the model to switch to Floating Model Space.
3. Choose View ➢ Shade ➢ Gouraud Shaded. The view changes to a shaded view.

NOTE *The view may appear a bit dark due to the black color setting for the object. You can change the color to a lighter one such as cyan or blue to get a better look.*

4. Double-click outside the isometric viewport to return to Paper Space.

You changed the display of one viewport from Wireframe to Gouraud Shaded without affecting the other viewports. This can really help others visualize your 3D model more clearly.

You'll also want to know how to control the hard-copy output of a shaded view. For this, you use the shortcut menu.

1. Click the Isometric view's viewport border to select it.
2. Right-click to open the shortcut menu, and then point to the Shade Plot option to display a set of Shade Plot options.

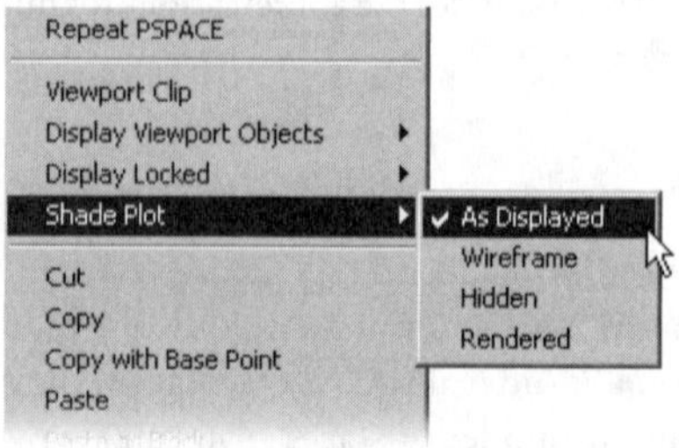

3. Take a moment to study the menu, and then click As Displayed.

The As Displayed option plots the viewport as it appears in the AutoCAD window. You use this option to plot the currently displayed shaded view. Wireframe plots the viewport as a wireframe view. Hidden plots the viewport as a hidden line view similar to the view you see when you use the Hide command. The Rendered option plots the view using AutoCAD's render feature described in Chapter 18. You can use the Rendered option to plot ray-traced renderings of your 3D models.

Remember these options on the shortcut menu as you work on your drawings and when you plot. They can be helpful in communicating your ideas, but they can also get lost in the array of tools that AutoCAD offers.

Adding Dimensions and Notes in Paper Space

Although I don't recommend adding dimensions in Paper Space for architectural drawings, it might be a good idea for mechanical drawings such as the one in this chapter. By maintaining the dimensions and notes separate from the actual model, you keep these elements from getting in the way of your work on the solid model. You also avoid the confusion of having to scale the text and dimension features properly to ensure that they will plot at the correct size.

TIP *See Chapters 8 and 9 for a more detailed discussion of notes and dimensions.*

As long as you set up your Paper Space work area to be equivalent to the final plot size, you can set dimension and text to the sizes you want at plot time. If you want text 1/4" high, you set your text styles to be 1/4" high.

To include dimensions, just make sure you are in a Layout tab, and then use the dimension commands in the normal way. However, you need to be careful to: make sure that full associative dimensioning is turned on. Choose Tools ➢ Options to open the Options dialog box, and then click the User Preferences tab. In the Associative Dimensioning group, click the Associate New Dimensions With Objects option. With associative dimensioning turned on, dimensions in a Layout tab display the true dimension of the object being dimensioned, regardless of the image scale in the viewport.

If you do not have the associative dimensioning option turned on and your viewports are set to a scale other than 1 to 1, you have another option. You can set the Annotation Units option in the Dimension Style dialog box to a proper value. The following steps show you how.

1. Select the Model tab at the bottom of the AutoCAD window, and then choose Dimension ➢ Style to open the Dimension Style Manager dialog box.
2. Make sure you have selected the style you want to use, and then click Modify to open the Modify Dimension Style dialog box.
3. Click the Primary Units tab.
4. In the Scale Factor input box in the Measurement Scale group, enter the value by which you want your Paper Space dimensions multiplied. For example, if your Paper Space views are scaled at one-half the actual size of your model, enter **2** in this box to multiply your dimensions' values by 2.

TIP *To make sure the value you need in step 4 is correct, determine which scale factor you need for your Paper Space drawing to get its actual size; that's the value you need to enter.*

5. Click the Apply To Layout Dimensions Only check box. This ensures that your dimension is scaled only while you are adding dimensions in Paper Space. Dimensions added in Model Space are not affected.
6. Click OK to close the Modify Dimension Style dialog box; then click OK again in the Dimension Style Manager dialog box.

You've had to complete a lot of steps to get the final drawing, but, compared with having to draw these views by hand, you undoubtedly saved a great deal of time. In addition, as you will see later in this chapter, what you have is more than just a 2D drafted image. With what you created, further refinements are now quite easy.

Drawing a Cross-Section

One element of your drawing that is missing is a cross-section. AutoCAD will draw a cross-section through any part of the solid model. In the following exercise, you will draw such a cross-section.

1. Save your drawing so you can return to this stage (in case you don't want to save the results of the following steps).
2. Choose Tools ➢ New UCS ➢ World.

3. Click the Section tool on the Solids toolbar.
4. At the `Select objects:` prompt, click both halves of the solid model and press ↵.
5. At the prompt

   ```
   Specify first point on Section plane by [Object/Zaxis/View/XY/YZ/XZ/3points]
   <3points>
   ```

   enter ZX↵. This tells AutoCAD you want to cut the solid in the plane defined by the x- and z-axes.
6. At the `Point on ZX plane:` prompt, pick the midpoint of the top-right surface of the solid (see the first image in Figure 19.47). The section cut appears, as shown in the second image in Figure 19.47.

The section shown in the bottom image in Figure 19.48, later in this chapter, is a type of object called a *region*. Next you'll learn how regions share some characteristics with 3D solids.

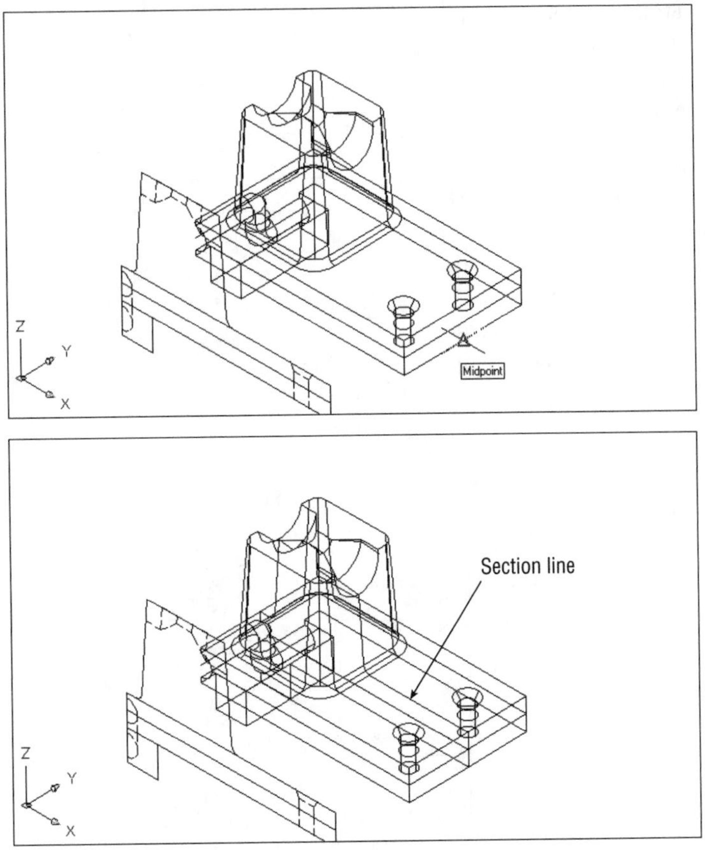

FIGURE 19.47
Selecting the point on the z-x plane to define the section-cut outline

Using 3D Solid Operations on 2D Drawings

You can apply some of the features described in this chapter to 2D drafting by taking advantage of AutoCAD's *region* object. Regions are two-dimensional objects to which you can apply Boolean operations.

Try the following optional exercise, which demonstrates how two Boolean operations, Union and Subtract, work on 2D objects.

1. If you have been working through the tutorial on 3D solids, save the Bracket drawing now.
2. Open the `Region.dwg` drawing supplied on the companion CD. You will see the drawing shown in the first image in Figure 19.48. The objects in this drawing are circles and closed polylines.

FIGURE 19.48
Working with regions in the `Region.dwg` file

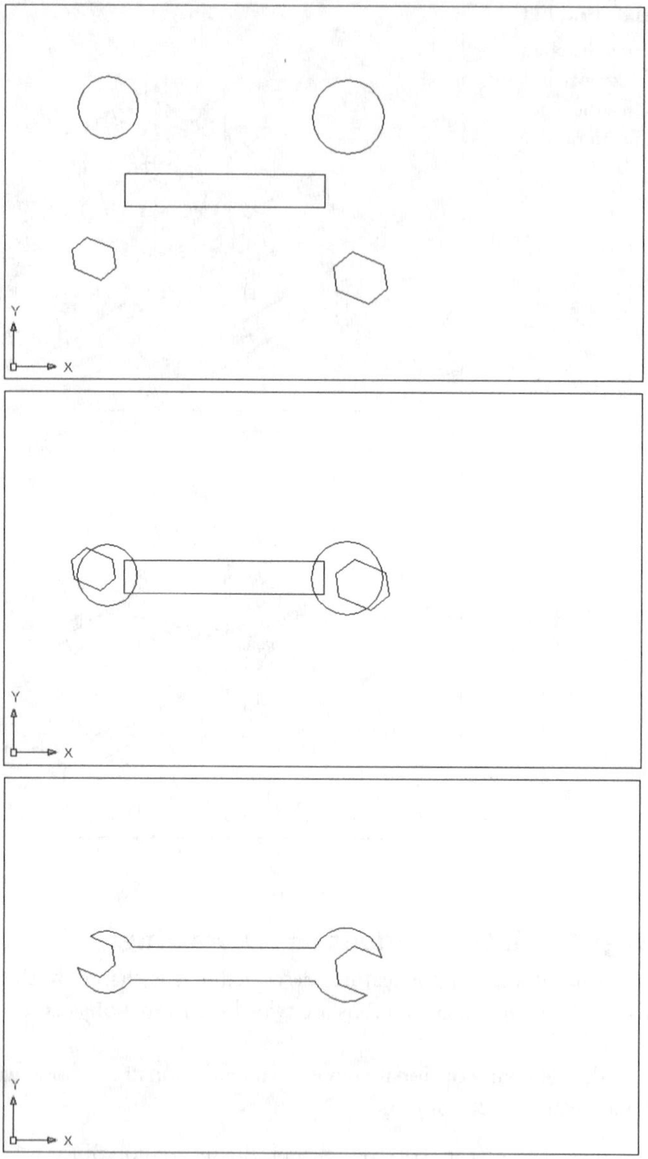

3. Click the Region tool on the Draw toolbar, or type **Reg**↵.
4. At the `Select objects:` prompt, click all the objects in the drawing and press ↵. AutoCAD converts the objects into regions.

5. Move the two circles and the hexagons into the positions illustrated in the second image in Figure 19.48. (For this demonstration exercise, you don't have to worry about matching the positions exactly.)

6. Choose Modify ➢ Solids Editing ➢ Union, or if you are using LT, choose Modify ➢ Region ➢ Union

7. At the `Select objects:` prompt, click the rectangle and the two circles. The circles merge with the rectangle to form one object.

8. Choose Modify ➢ Solids Editing ➢ Subtract (LT users should choose Modify ➢ Region ➢ Subtract), and then click the newly created region and press ↵.

9. At the next `Select objects:` prompt, click the two hexagons. Now you have a single, 2D solid object in the shape of a wrench, as shown in the final image in Figure 19.48.

You can use regions to generate complex surfaces that might include holes or unusual bends (see Figure 19.49). Keep in mind the following:

- Regions act like surfaces; when you remove hidden lines, objects behind the regions are hidden.
- You can explode regions to edit them. (You can't do this with solids.) However, exploding a region causes the region to lose its surfacelike quality, and objects will no longer hide behind its surface(s).

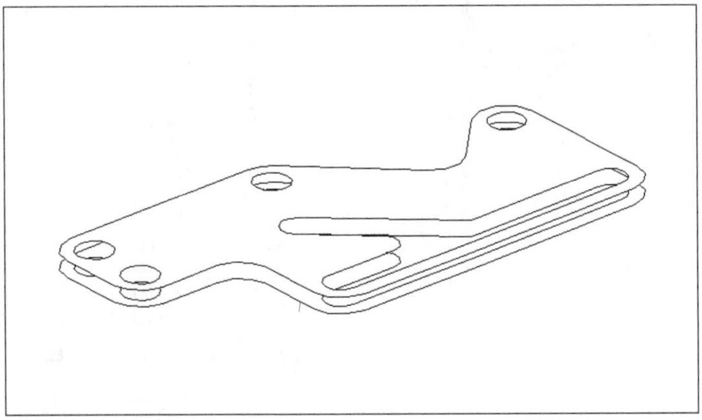

FIGURE 19.49
You can use the regional model to create complex 2D surfaces for use in 3D surface modeling.

Finding the Properties of a Solid

All this effort to create a solid model isn't just to create a pretty picture. Once your model is drawn and built, you can obtain information about its physical properties. In this section, you will look at a few of the commands that let you gather such information.

TIP *LT users can use the Massprop command described here to find the properties of solids that are part of an existing drawing.*

Finding a Model's Mass Properties

You can find the volume, the moment of inertia, and other physical properties of your model by using the Massprop command. These properties can also be recorded as a file on disk so you can modify your model without worrying about losing track of its original properties.

1. Open the Bracket drawing you worked on through most of this chapter.
2. Choose Tools ➢ Inquiry ➢ Region/Mass Properties, or enter **Massprop↵**. You can also click the Region/Mass Properties tool on the Inquiry toolbar.
3. At the `Select objects:` prompt, select the two halves of the solid model. AutoCAD will calculate for a moment and then display a list of the object's properties, as shown in Figure 19.50.

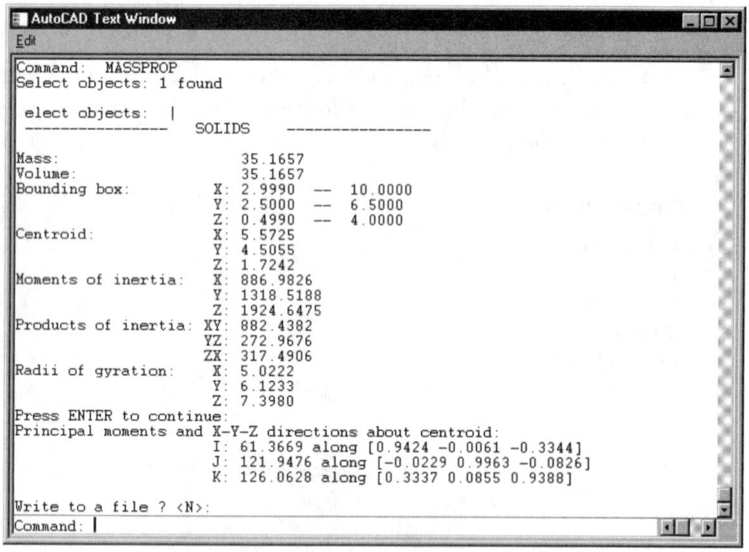


```
Command:  MASSPROP
Select objects: 1 found

 elect objects:  |
 ----------------          SOLIDS     ----------------

Mass:                            35.1657
Volume:                          35.1657
Bounding box:               X:  2.9990   --   10.0000
                            Y:  2.5000   --   6.5000
                            Z:  0.4990   --   4.0000
Centroid:                   X:  5.5725
                            Y:  4.5055
                            Z:  1.7242
Moments of inertia:         X:  886.9826
                            Y:  1318.5188
                            Z:  1924.6475
Products of inertia:       XY:  882.4382
                           YZ:  272.9676
                           ZX:  317.4906
Radii of gyration:          X:  5.0222
                            Y:  6.1233
                            Z:  7.3980
Press ENTER to continue:
Principal moments and X-Y-Z directions about centroid:
                            I:  61.3669 along [0.9424 -0.0061 -0.3344]
                            J:  121.9476 along [-0.0229 0.9963 -0.0826]
                            K:  126.0628 along [0.3337 0.0855 0.9388]

Write to a file ? <N>:
Command: |
```

FIGURE 19.50

The Mass Properties listing derived from the solid model

ACAD only

Taking Advantage of Stereolithography

A discussion of solid modeling wouldn't be complete without mentioning *stereolithography*. This is one of the more interesting technological wonders that have appeared as a by-product of 3D computer modeling. Stereolithography is a process that generates resin reproductions of 3D computer solid models. It offers the mechanical designer a method for rapidly prototyping designs directly from AutoCAD drawings. The process requires special equipment that will read computer files in a particular format.

AutoCAD supports stereolithography through the Stlout command. This command generates an .stl file, which can be used with a *Stereolithograph Apparatus* (*STA*) to generate a model. You must first create a 3D solid model in AutoCAD; then you can proceed with the following steps to create the .stl file.

1. Choose File ➢ Export to open the Export Data dialog box..
2. In the Save As Type drop-down list, select Lithography (*.stl). Click the Save button.

TIP *You can also type* ***Stlout↵*** at the command prompt to bypass steps 1 and 2.

3. At the `Select a single solid for STL output:` prompt, select a solid and press ↵. The solid must reside in the positive X, Y, and Z coordinates of the World Coordinate System. Also note that most stereolithography apparatus cannot produce undercuts like the hole of a donut shape when the donut is oriented vertically.

The AutoCAD 3D solids are translated into a set of triangular-faceted meshes in the .stl file. You can use the Facetres system variable to control the fineness of these meshes. See Chapter 18 for more information on Facetres.

If You Want to Experiment...

This chapter has focused on a mechanical project, but you can, of course, use solids to help simplify the construction of 3D architectural forms. If your interest lies in architecture, try drawing the window in Figure 19.51. (Imagine trying to create this window without the solid-modeling capabilities of AutoCAD!)

FIGURE 19.51

Drawing a window

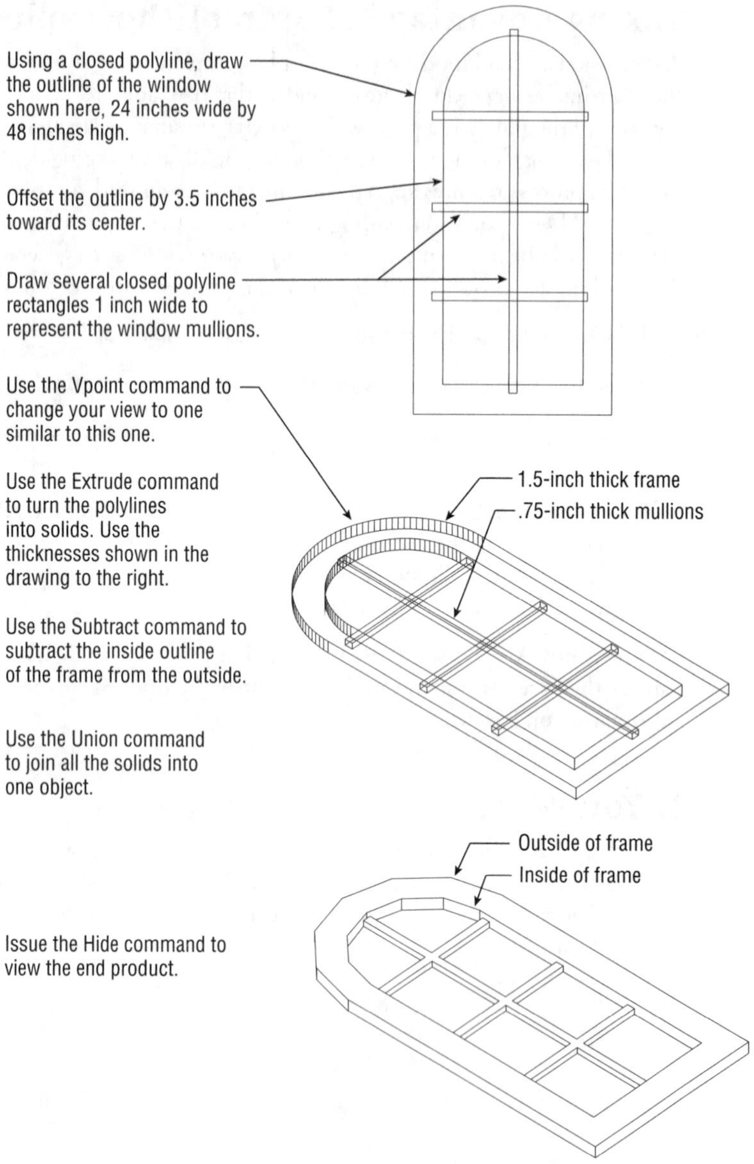

Using a closed polyline, draw the outline of the window shown here, 24 inches wide by 48 inches high.
Offset the outline by 3.5 inches toward its center.
Draw several closed polyline rectangles 1 inch wide to represent the window mullions.
Use the Vpoint command to change your view to one similar to this one.
Use the Extrude command to turn the polylines into solids. Use the thicknesses shown in the drawing to the right.
1.5-inch thick frame
.75-inch thick mullions
Use the Subtract command to subtract the inside outline of the frame from the outside.
Use the Union command to join all the solids into one object.
Outside of frame
Inside of frame
Issue the Hide command to view the end product.

Part 5

Customization and Integration

In this part:

- **Chapter 20: Introduction to Customization**
- **Chapter 21: Integrating AutoCAD into Your Projects and Organization**
- **Chapter 22: Collaborating with Others**

Chapter 20

Introduction to Customization

AutoCAD offers a wealth of features that you can use to improve your productivity. But even with these aids to efficiency, there are always situations that can use further automation. In this chapter, I'll introduce you to some ways that you can enhance AutoCAD with add-on utilities. You'll also learn how you can adapt AutoCAD to fit your particular needs by customizing its menus and toolbars.

First, you'll learn how to load and run the AutoLISP utilities that are supplied on this book's companion CD. By doing so, you'll be prepared to take advantage of the many utilities available from user groups and online services. You'll also see how third-party tools can enhance AutoCAD's role in your workplace. Then you'll learn how you can create keyboard macros and incorporate them into custom menus and toolbars. And, finally, you'll learn how to create custom line types and hatch patterns.

Topics include the following:

- Enhancements Straight from the Source
- Utilities Available from Other Sources
- Putting AutoLISP to Work
- Using Third-Party Software
- Getting the Latest Information from Online Services
- If You Want to Experiment

Enhancements Straight from the Source

If you've followed the tutorial in this book, you've already used a few add-on programs that come with AutoCAD, perhaps without even being aware that they were not part of the core AutoCAD program. In this section, I'll introduce you to the AutoCAD Express Tools: a set of AutoLISP, ARX, and VBA tools that showcase these powerful customization environments. The best part about the Express Tools is that you don't have to know a thing about programming to take advantage of them.

NOTE *Only two tools discussed in this chapter, Wipeout and Revcloud, are available in AutoCAD LT. If you are using AutoCAD LT, you can skip all but the "Finding Former Express Tools" section.*

There are so many Express Tools that I can't provide step-by-step instructions on all of them. Instead, I'll give you details about some of the more complicated tools and provide shorter descriptions of others. Let's start with the Express Layer Tools.

Opening the Express Toolbars

If you don't have the Express toolbars on your screen, here's how to open them.

1. Right-click any toolbar, and then choose Customize from the shortcut menu to open the Customize dialog box.

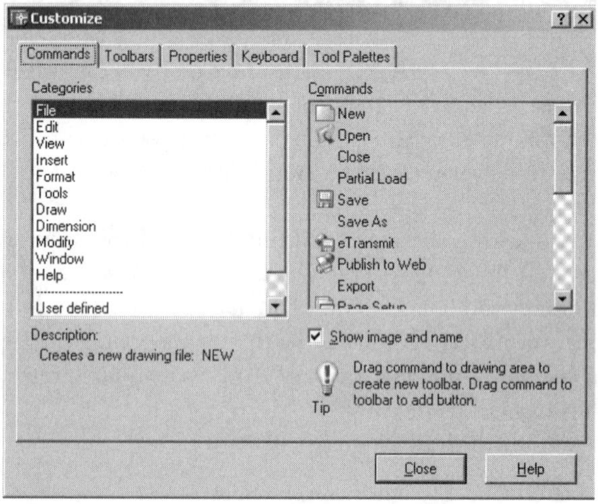

2. Click the Toolbars tab, and then select Express from the Menu Group list. The Toolbars list box will change to show a listing of toolbars available from the Express menu group.

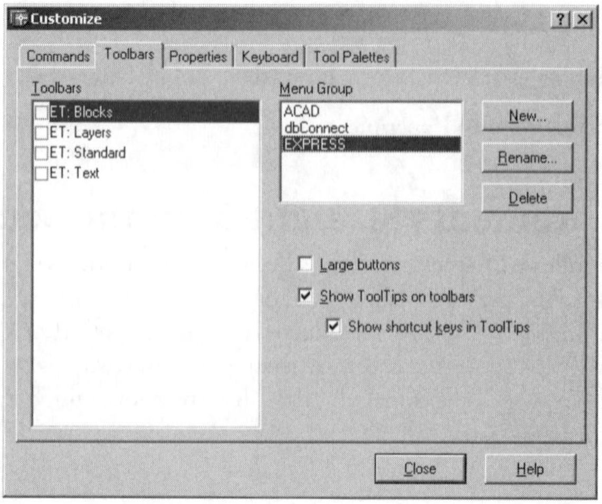

3. Click the check box to the left of each item in the list.
4. Click Close to close the Customize dialog box.

NOTE *You'll get a chance to learn more about the Customize dialog box in Chapter 21.*

You now have all the Express toolbars on your screen. If this is too much clutter, keep only one of them open. When you then want to display any others, right-click the open toolbar, and choose the toolbar(s) to display from the shortcut menu.

Now let's take a look at the Express Layer toolbar.

Loading the Express Tools

If you installed AutoCAD using the Typical Installation option, you may not have installed the AutoCAD Express Tools. Fortunately, you can install these utilities separately without having to reinstall the entire program.

Place the AutoCAD 2004 installation CD in your CD-ROM drive. When you see the AutoCAD 2004 installation window, make sure the Install option is selected. You'll see a set of numbered steps on the left side of the window. In step 5, Install Supplemental Tools, click the AutoCAD Express Tools option. Follow the installation instructions from there. Once you've installed the Express Tools, they will appear the next time you open AutoCAD.

Tools for Managing Layers

In a survey of AutoCAD users, Autodesk discovered that one of the most frequently used features in AutoCAD was the Layer command. As a result, the layer controls in AutoCAD have been greatly improved. Still, there is room for more improvement. The Express Layer Tools offer some shortcuts to controlling layer settings as well as one major layer enhancement, the Layer Manager.

TIP *All the tools discussed in this section have keyboard command equivalents. Check the status bar when selecting these tools from the toolbar or pull-down menu for the keyboard command name.*

Saving and Recalling Layer Settings

The Layer Manager lets you save layer settings. It performs the same functions as the Save State and State Manager buttons in the Layer Properties Manager dialog box that you saw in Chapter 4. The Express Tools Layer Manager is an alternative for users who are more used to its methods. With the Layer Manager, you can turn layers on and off to set up the drawing for a reflected ceiling Plan view and then save the layer settings. Later, when you need to modify the ceiling information, you can recall the layer setting to view the ceiling data. The following steps show you how the Layer Manager works.

1. In AutoCAD, open the `15a-unit.dwg` file from the CD. Open the Layer Properties Manager dialog box and turn on all the layers except the Notes And Flr-pat layers. Your drawing should look similar to the top image in Figure 20.1.

FIGURE 20.1

The view of the `Unit.dwg` file before and after changing layer settings

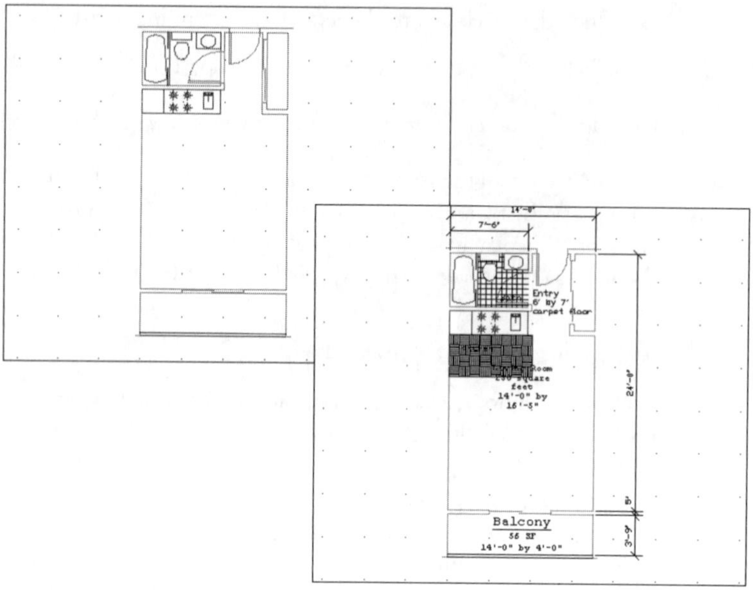

2. Click the Layer Manager tool in the Express Layer Tools toolbar to open the Layer Manager dialog box.

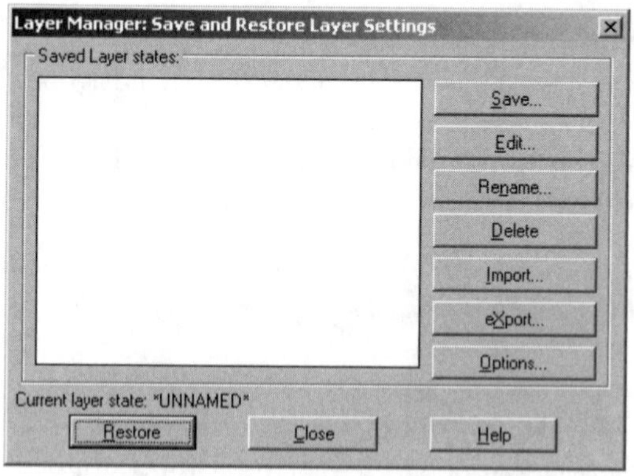

3. Click the Save button to open the Layer State Name dialog box.
4. Enter **blank floor plan**, and then click OK. You return to the Layer Manager dialog box. Notice that the name you entered for the layer state appears in the list box.
5. Click the Close button.

6. Now open the Layer & Linetype Properties dialog box, and turn on the Flr-pat and Notes layers, and turn off the Ceiling layer. Your drawing will look like the bottom image in Figure 20.1.
7. Click the Layer Manager tool again.
8. Select BLANK FLOOR PLAN from the list, and then click Restore.
9. Click Close. Your drawing reverts to the previous view with the Notes and Flr-pat layers turned off and the Ceiling layer on.

The layer states are saved with the file so you can retrieve them later. As you can see from the Layer Manager dialog box, you have a few other options. Here is a listing of those options and what they do:

Edit Opens the Layer & Linetype Properties dialog box in which you edit the settings for a layer state. Highlight the layer state from the list, and then click Edit.

Rename Renames a layer state in the list.

Delete Deletes a layer state from the list.

Import Imports a set of layer states that have been exported using the Export option of this dialog box.

Export Saves a set of layer states as a file. By default, the file is given the name of the current file with the .lay filename extension. You can import the layer state file into other files.

Options Offers a list of the states you can save and restore. When you select Options, the Layer Manager Restore Options dialog box opens with a list of check boxes. You can check the items you want to save as part of the layer state. The list includes all the standard layer properties such as the on/off and freeze/thaw state, lock/unlock, color, line type, lineweight, plot status, and plot style status.

WARNING *The Express Tool Layer Manager does not share layer states with the Save State and State Manager options in the Layer Properties Manager. If you start to save layer states in the Express Tool Layer Manager, you cannot manage layer states using the Layer Properties Manager and vice versa. You can still use both tools, just don't expect to load layer states across tools.*

Exploring Layers with Layer Walk

When you work with a file that has been produced by someone else, you usually have to spend some time getting familiar with the way layers are set up in that file. This can be a tedious process, but the Layer Walk Express Tool can help.

As the name implies, the Layer Walk tool lets you "walk through" the layers of a file, visually isolating each layer as you select the layer's name from a list. You can use Layer Walk to select the layers that you want visible, or you can turn layers on and off to explore a drawing without affecting the current layer settings. The following exercise explores some of Layer Walk's features.

1. While still in the 15a-unit drawing, click the Layer Walk tool to open the Layer Walk dialog box.

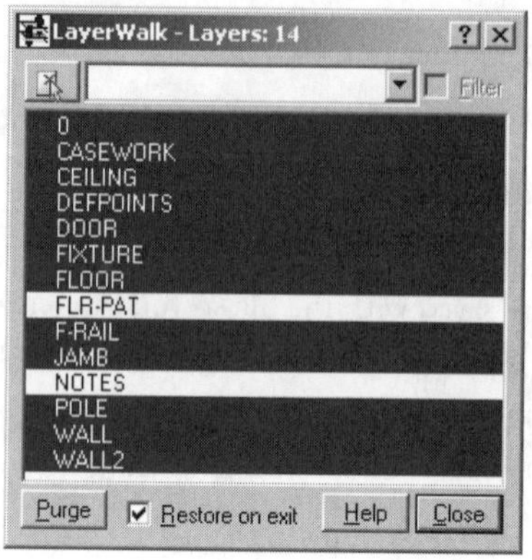

You can click and drag the bottom edge of the dialog box to expand the list so that you can see all of the layers in the drawing. Notice that all but two layers are highlighted in the list. The highlighted layers are currently visible. The two layers that are not selected are not visible.

2. Ctrl+click the Flr-pat layer in the list to add the Flr-pat layer to the selected layers and make the Flr-pat layer visible.
3. Ctrl+click the Flr-pat layer name again to remove it from the selection, and then right-click and choose Inverse Selection from the shortcut menu.

Now the selections in the list are inverted with only two layers selected. The display also changes to show only objects on the two selected layers.

1. Right-click in the Layer Walk dialog box, and choose Select Unreferenced from the shortcut menu. The plan disappears, and two layers are highlighted in the list. There are no objects on these two layers.
2. Click the Purge button to purge these unreferenced layers.
3. Right-click in the Layer Walk dialog box again, and choose Select All from the shortcut menu to display the plan again, this time with all the layers visible.
4. Right-click in the Layer Walk dialog box yet again, and then choose Clear All from the shortcut menu. Randomly click layer names in the list.

Notice that each layer you select from the list appears in the drawing. When you click a layer name, the previous layer turns off so that only one layer is visible at a time.

1. Ctrl+click the Wall, Jamb, and Door layers to make them visible, and then right-click and choose Hold Selection from the shortcut menu. Asterisks appear to the left of the selected layer names.

2. Once again, randomly click layer names from the list. Notice that as you click other layer names, the layers with the asterisks remain visible. The Hold Selection option temporarily locks them on so that other selections do not affect their visibility.

3. Right-click in the Layer Walk dialog box, and then choose Select All from the shortcut menu to display the entire plan once again.

4. Click the Object Select tool in the upper-left corner of the Layer Walk dialog box to temporarily close the dialog box, allowing you to make a selection.

5. Click any dimension and the black line at the bottom end of the unit plan. Press ↵. Now the F-rail and Notes layers are visible along with the Wall, Jamb, and Door layers.

Finally, you can select layers by filtering layer names. For example, you can select all the layers whose name begins with C.

1. In the Filter input box at the top of the Layer Walk dialog box, enter **C*↵**. The Casework and Ceiling layers are the only items shown in the list and visible in the drawing. Notice that the Wall, Jamb, and Door layers are still visible, indicating that the hold status is still in effect.

TIP *To turn off the hold status of a layer, right-click in the Layer Walk dialog box, and choose Release All from the shortcut menu.*

2. Click the Filter check box to turn off filtering. The other layer names reappear in the list.

3. Click the Restore On Exit check box at the bottom of the Layer Walk dialog box to turn off this option.

4. Click Close. The layers are now displayed as they were in the Layer Walk dialog box.

In step 3, you turned off the Restore On Exit option, which caused AutoCAD to keep the layer settings you established while working in the Layer Walk dialog box. Had you left the Restore On Exit option turned on, the drawing would revert to the layer settings that were in place before you opened the Layer Walk dialog box. This gives you the option to use the Layer Walk dialog box as a tool to set up the layers in a drawing or to explore layers in a drawing that is unfamiliar to you.

As an option, before you close the Layer Walk dialog box, right-click and choose Save Layer State from the shortcut menu to open the Save Layer State dialog box in which you can save the layer state under a name. You can then exit the Layer Walk dialog box and restore your saved layer settings using the Express Tools Layer Manager.

CHANGING THE LAYER ASSIGNMENT OF OBJECTS

In addition to the Layer Manager and Layer Walk tools, the Express Layer toolbar includes two tools that change the layer assignments of objects. The Match Objects Layer tool is similar to the Match Properties tool, but is streamlined to operate only on layer assignments. After clicking this tool, you first select the object or objects you want to change, and then you select an object whose layer you want to match.

The Change To Current Layer tool changes an object's layer assignment to the current layer. This tool has long existed as an AutoLISP utility, and you'll find that you'll get a lot of use from it.

CONTROLLING LAYER SETTINGS THROUGH OBJECTS

The remaining Express Layer tools let you make layer settings by selecting objects in the drawing. These tools are easy to use: simply click the tool, and then select an object. These tools are so helpful that you might want to consider docking them permanently in your AutoCAD window. The following list describes what each tool does.

Isolate Object's Layer Turns off all the layers except for the layer of the selected object.

Freeze Object's Layer Freezes the layer of the selected object.

Turn Object's Layer Off Turns off the layer of the selected object.

Lock Object's Layer Locks the layer of the selected object. A locked layer is visible but cannot be edited.

Unlock Object's Layer Unlocks the layer of the selected object.

DELETING A LAYER WHILE PRESERVING ITS CONTENTS

Every now and then, you will inherit an AutoCAD file from some other office or individual, and you'll want to convert its layering system to one more suited to the way you work. This usually involves renaming and deleting layers. The Layer Merge Express tool is a great aid in this effort.

Choose Express ➢ Layers ➢ Layer Merge to start Layer Merge. It works by first moving all the objects from one layer to another existing layer. You can either select objects to indicate the layer you want, or you can type the layer names. Once the objects are moved, Layer Merge deletes the empty layer. Another related tool is Layer Delete (choose Express ➢ Layers ➢ Layer Delete). This tool completely deletes a layer and its contents.

Tools for Editing Text

It seems that we can never have enough text-editing features. Even in the realm of word processors, we see numerous tools for configuring fonts, paragraphs, tabs, and tables. Some programs even check our grammar. Although we're not trying to write the great American novel in AutoCAD, we are interested in getting our text in the right location, at the right size, and with some degree of style. This often means using a mixture of text- and graphics-editing tools. In this section, I'll describe some additional tools that will help ease your way through some otherwise difficult editing tasks.

MASKING TEXT BACKGROUNDS

One problem AutoCAD users frequently face is how to get text to read clearly when it is placed over a hatch pattern or other graphic. The Hatch command will hatch around existing text, leaving a clear space behind it. But what about those situations in which you must add text *after* a hatch pattern has been created? Or what about those instances when you need to mask behind text that is placed over a nonhatch object, such as dimension leaders or raster images?

The Text Mask tool addresses this problem by masking the area behind text with a special masking object called a Wipeout. Try the following exercise on the `14a-unit.dwg` file to see firsthand how it works.

1. In the `Unit` file, make sure the Flr-pat and Notes layers are turned on.
2. Adjust your view so that you can see the kitchen area as it appears in the top image in Figure 20.2. Notice that the Kitchen label is obscured by the floor's hatch pattern.

FIGURE 20.2
Creating a mask behind text

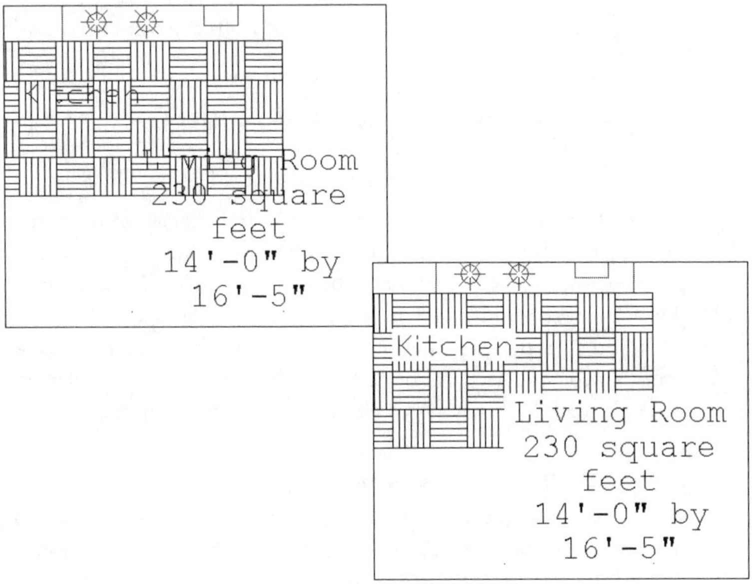

3. Choose Text Mask from the Express Text Tools toolbar. You'll see the following message:

```
Current settings: Offset factor = 0.3500, Mask type = Wipeout
Select text objects to mask or [Masktype/Offset]:
```

4. Here you can enter the amount of space you want around the text as a percentage of the text height, or you can select a different type of object for the mask.
5. Select the Kitchen text, click the Living Room text, and press ↵. You'll see the message

```
Masking text with a Wipeout
Wipeout created.
1 text items have been masked with a Wipeout.,
```

and the text will appear on a clear background, as shown in the bottom image in Figure 20.2.

Text Mask creates an object called a Wipeout that masks other objects behind the text. Wipeout is not a standard AutoCAD object; it is a new object created through AutoCAD's programming interface.

If you prefer to use a 3D Face or Solid to hide the background of text, you can do so by entering **M**↵ at the prompt in step 3. You see a prompt asking you to select a Mask type.

```
Specify entity type to use for mask [Wipeout/3dface/Solid] <Wipeout>:
```

After you enter the mask type at this prompt, you'll return to the previous prompt.

If you want more room around the text, you can enter **O**↵ at the prompt in step 3. You can then enter a value for the margin around the text.

The Wipeout object has its own little quirks that you will want to know about. To get a bit more familiar with Wipeout objects, try the following exercise.

1. Click the Kitchen text. Notice that both the text and the Wipeout object are selected.
2. Click Move on the Modify toolbar.
3. Move the text and Wipeout object to the right about 12 inches. The text seems to disappear.
4. Type **Re**↵ to issue a Regen. The text appears once again.

The text and Wipeout objects are linked; if you select the text, you automatically select the Wipeout object. Also, the display order of the two objects gets mixed up when you move them, so you need to issue a Regen to restore the text's visibility. You can also edit or erase the Wipeout object. The "Express Standard Tools" section later in this chapter describes how to edit Wipeout objects.

If you want to delete the wipeout background, choose Express ➢ Text ➢ Unmask Text. This option prompts you to select an object. Select the masked text to delete the wipeout background.

Next, we'll look at ways to globally change text objects.

ADDING LINKED TEXT DOCUMENTS

One of the more frustrating and time-consuming aspects to drafting is editing lengthy notes. General notes and specifications change frequently in the life of a project, so editing notes can be a large part of what you do in AutoCAD. Frequently notes are written by someone else, perhaps a specifications writer, who doesn't work directly with the drawings.

You can improve the efficiency of note editing by using OLE (object linking and embedding) to cut and paste notes into your drawing (see Chapter 15 for more on OLE). That way, you or the specifications writer can edit the note, and it will be automatically updated in drawings that contain pasted copies of the note. Some drawbacks are associated with OLE linked text documents, however. The biggest problem is that you have little control over the text size and font.

To help make note editing easier, AutoCAD supplies the Remote Text object. This special object is linked to an external text document. Like an OLE object, Remote Text objects automatically update their contents when the source document changes. To use Remote Text objects, take the following steps.

1. Choose Express ➢ Text ➢ Remote Text or type **Rtext**↵ at the command prompt.
2. At the `Enter an option [Style/Height/Rotation/File/Diesel] <File>:` prompt, press ↵ to open the Select Text File dialog box. This is a typical file dialog box that lets you locate and select a file for import.

3. Select a file and click Open.
4. At the `Specify start point of RText:` prompt, position the text in the drawing.
5. At the `Enter an option [Style/Height/Rotation/Edit]:` prompt, enter **H↵**, and then enter the height for the text.

As you can see from the prompt in step 5, you can specify the text style, height, and rotation for the imported text. You also have the option to edit the text from within AutoCAD.

Since the Remote Text object is linked to the original document you selected in step 3, the Remote Text in your drawing will be updated automatically in a way similar to Xref whenever that original document is edited.

Automatically Update Drawing Information Labels

Another way to use Remote Text is to use it to add labels that supply general information about the drawing, such as the name of the file, the date it was last edited, and the person who did the editing. This information is usually placed in the corner of the drawing for reference so that a print of a drawing can be easily associated with a drawing file.

You can also use Remote Text to keep track of this information. Even if the name of the file or its location on the hard drive changes, Remote Text will automatically update labels. Here's an example of how to set up Remote Text to do this.

1. Choose Express ➢ Text ➢ Remote Text or type **Rtext↵** at the command prompt.
2. At the `Enter an option [Style/Height/Rotation/File/Diesel] <File>:` prompt, type **D↵** to select the Diesel option and open the Edit Rtext dialog box.

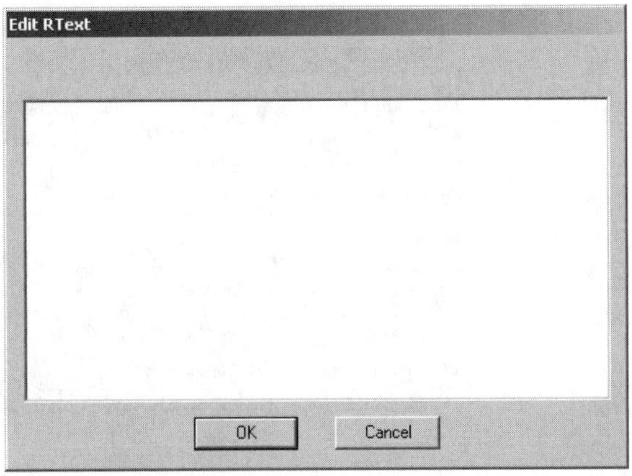

3. Enter the following text:

   `Drawing name and location: $(getvar, "dwgprefix")$(getvar, "dwgname")`

4. Click OK. You'll see the text string appear as a rectangle in the drawing next to your cursor.

5. Click a location for the text, which is usually the lower-left corner of a drawing title block. The text will display the drawing location and name.

6. At the `Enter an option [Style/Height/Rotation/Edit]:` prompt, type **R↵**, and then enter 90 to rotate the text 90°.

This example uses the Diesel option of the Remote Text tool. Diesel is one of many macro programming languages AutoCAD supports. The text `$(getvar, "dwgprefix")$(getvar, "dwgname")` is the Diesel code that extracts the current drawing location and name from the file. This code is translated into the actual file listing and filename of the current drawing. This is how Remote Text reads the dwgprefix and dwgname system variables of the file. If the file is moved to another location or if it is renamed, Remote Text will read the dwgprefix and dwgname system variables and update the label containing this code. You'll learn more about Diesel in Chapter 21.

TIP *You can type* ***dwgprefix*** *or* ***dwgname*** *at the command prompt to see the information that Remote Text is reading.*

OTHER EXPRESS TEXT TOOLS

I've shown you several of the main text editing tools in the Express Text Tools toolbar and Express pull-down menu. There are several more that you might find useful. By now, you should feel comfortable exploring these tools on your own. The following is a brief description to get you started:

Text Fit Lets you visually stretch or compress text to fit within a given width.

ArcAlignedText Creates text that follows the curve of an arc. If the arc is stretched or changed, the text follows the arc's shape. This is one of the more interesting bonus text tools, offering a wide range of settings in a neat little dialog box.

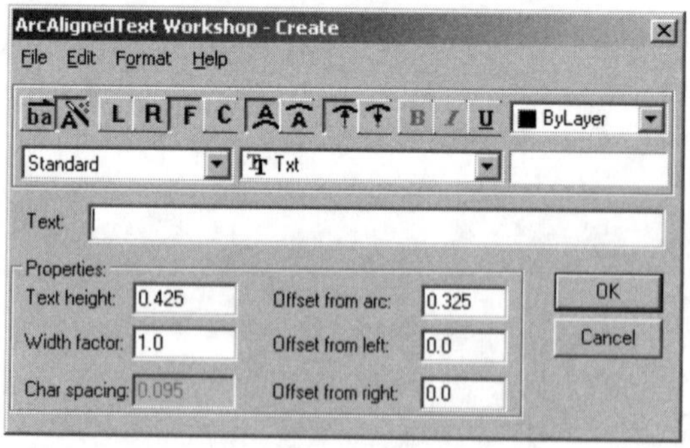

Explode Text Converts the individual characters in a text object into polylines. Beware! This tool can take some time while it works.

Enclose Text with Object Lets you outline text, Mtext, or attribute definitions with a box, a circle, or a slot.

Automatic Text Numbering Lets you append or change text to a set of sequential numbers such as 1, 2, 3, and so on. This is an excellent tool for renumbering a series of notes or other labels.

Change Text Case Lets you change the case of text in a variety of ways. Once you start this tool and select text objects, you are presented with the Tcase dialog box, which offers several options.

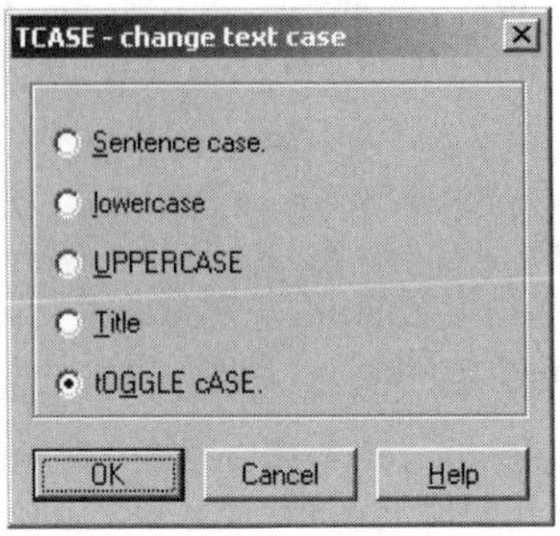

Sentence Case capitalizes the first word and lowercases the rest of the words . Lowercase and Uppercase make all the letters lower- or uppercase. Title capitalizes each word, and Toggle Case reverses the case of the letters.

TIP *If you want text to follow a curved path, take a look at the* `Txtpath.lsp` *utility on the companion CD. It draws text on a spline curve to follow virtually any contour you want. (See Appendix A.)*

Express Block Tools

Every now and then, you run into a situation in which you want to use objects within a block to trim or extend to, or perhaps you want to copy a part of a block to another part of your drawing. In these situations, you can use the following tools. They're fairly simple to use, so the following descriptions should be enough to get you started. You'll find these tools on the Express Tools Block toolbar.

List Xref/Block Properties Displays basic information about an Xref or a block.

Copy Nested Objects Lets you copy single objects within a block. You are only allowed to select objects individually—one click at a time. The copied objects are placed on the current layer.

Trim to Nested Objects Lets you trim to objects in a block. This tool works just like the standard Trim command with the exception that you must select the objects to trim to individually.

Extend to Nested Objects Lets you extend to objects in a block. This tool also works like its standard counterpart with the exception that you must select the objects you want to extend to individually.

Extended Clip In Chapter 6, you saw how to limit the display of an Xref to an L-shaped, rectilinear area. Extended Clip adds the ability to use arcs, circles, and polylines to "clip" the view of an Xref.

Explode Attributes to Text Explodes blocks containing attributes so that the attribute values are converted into plain single-line text.

In addition to the tools on the Express Tools Block toolbar, you can access the following tools by choosing Express ➢ Blocks.

Convert Shape to Block Converts a shape object into a block. You can then explode the block to its component objects if needed.

Export Attribute Information Offers a quick way to extract attribute information from a simple text file. You are prompted to select a file location and name and then select the attributes you want to export. The text file is formatted as a tab-delimited file. You can then edit the exported text file and use the Import Attribute Information tool (described next) to update the drawing with the modifications you made to the text file.

Import Attribute Information Allows you to import changes to the attribute information that has been exported using the Export Attribute Information tool.

Convert Block to Xref Lets you replace block references in your drawing with externally referenced files or Xrefs. For example, you can replace the tub blocks in the apartment plan from earlier tutorials with an Xref of a different tub. When you select this option, the Blocktoxref dialog box opens.

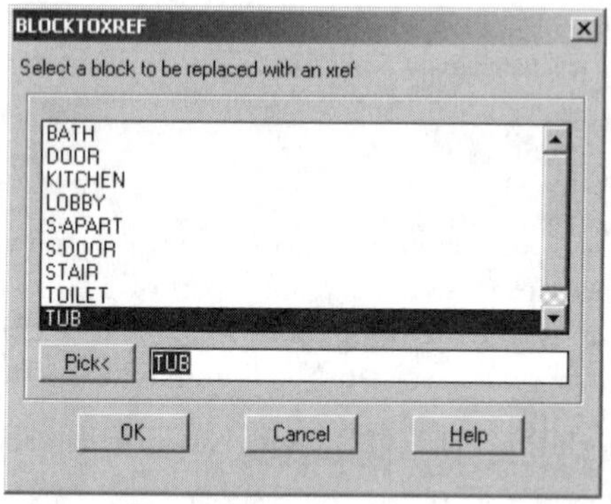

From here, you can select the block you want to replace. You are then asked to select a file that will be the replacing Xref.

Replace Block with Another Block Replaces one set of block references with another. For example, you can replace the tub block in the apartment plan with the door block, causing all the bathtubs to turn into doors. This tool works in a way similar to the Convert Block to Xref tool.

Express Standard Tools

The Express Standard toolbar seems to be the answer to most AutoCAD users' wish lists. As with many of the Express Tools discussed so far, these tools have been floating around in the AutoCAD user community as AutoLISP utilities. We'll start with a look at one tool that has been on my wish list for quite some time.

MULTIPLE OBJECT STRETCH

The Stretch command has always been limited in that you can select only one set of vertices. The Multiple Object Stretch tool removes that limitation and makes stretching multiple objects a simpler task. Here's how it works.

1. From the Express Standard toolbar, click Multiple Object Stretch. You'll see the following message:

```
Define crossing windows or crossing polygons...
Options: Crossing Polygon or Crossing first point
Specify an option [CP/C] <Crossing first point>:
```

2. Start to place crossing windows around the vertices you want to stretch. You can also enter **CP↵** and proceed to place crossing polygons around the vertices.
3. After you select the vertices, press ↵.
4. Go ahead and select a base point and a second point to move the vertices.

STREAMLINED MOVE/COPY/ROTATE

The Move/Copy/Rotate tool combines these three functions into one tool. It's like a streamlined Grip Edit tool without the grips. Here's how it works.

1. Click the Move/Copy/Rotate tool from the Standard Express toolbar or choose Express ➢ Modify ➢ Move/Copy/Rotate.
2. Select the objects you want to edit, and then press ↵.
3. Click a base point.
4. At the [Move/Copy/Rotate/Scale/Base/Undo]<eXit>: prompt, enter the option you want to use, for example, type **C**. You can also right-click and choose Copy from the shortcut menu. The object or objects you selected in step 2 now follow your cursor.
5. Click a location for your copy. You can continue to select more points to create multiple copies.
6. When you are finished making copies, press ↵. The [Move/Copy/Rotate/Scale/Base/Undo]<eXit>: prompt returns, allowing you to make further edits.
7. Press ↵ to exit Move/Copy/Rotate.

The Move/Copy/Rotate tool acts like the Move or Copy command up until step 4. From step 4 on, you can perform any number of operations on the selected objects as listed in the prompt.

CREATING CUSTOM HATCH PATTERNS WITH SUPERHATCH

AutoCAD offers a large variety of hatch patterns from its Boundary Hatch dialog box, but at times none of those patterns will fulfill your needs. This is where the Super Hatch tool comes in. With Super Hatch, you can create virtually any hatch pattern you want. You can use objects in your drawing as a basis for a hatch pattern, or you can import bitmap images and use them to form a hatch pattern, such as tiled wallpaper in the Windows desktop background. The following exercise shows you how to use Super Hatch.

1. Open the `Superhatch.dwg` file from the companion CD. You'll see a block of an arrow on the left side of the screen and a rectangular area to the right. In this exercise, you'll turn the arrow into a hatch pattern.

2. Click the Super Hatch tool to open the SuperHatch dialog box.

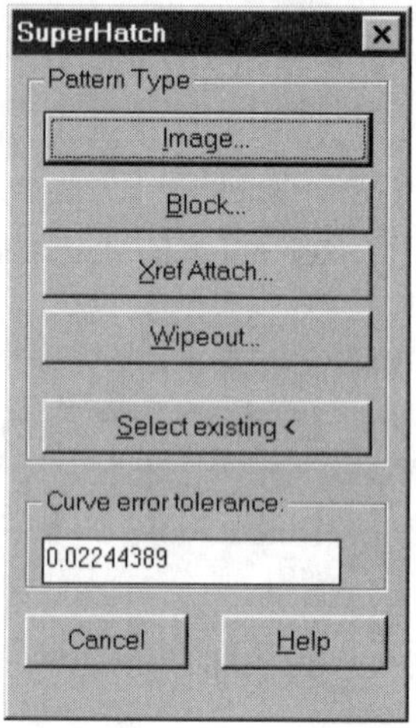

3. Click the Select Existing button. The SuperHatch dialog box closes.
4. Click the arrow. It becomes highlighted, and a magenta rectangle encircles the arrow.

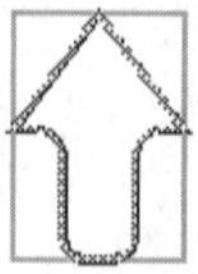

At this point, you can indicate the array you want repeated in your pattern. The default is the extents of the selected item as indicated by the magenta rectangle.

5. Click the two points shown in Figure 20.3 to indicate the area that you want repeated. The rectangle changes to reflect the new area. You can repeat the area selection as many times as you need until you get exactly the area you want.

FIGURE 20.3

Selecting the area to be repeated

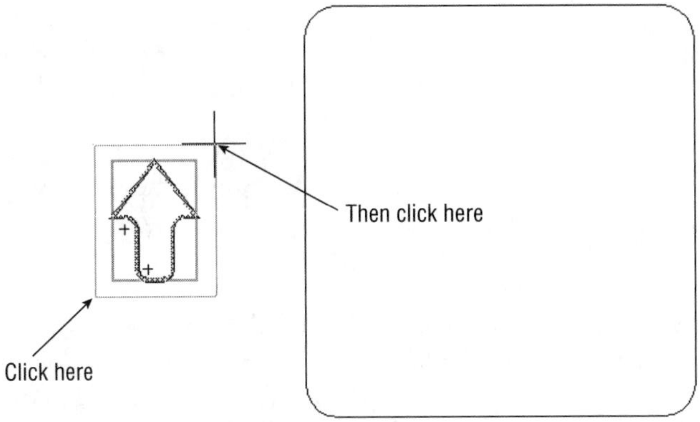

Then click here
Click here

6. Press ↵ to move to the next step.
7. Click the interior of the rectangle to indicate the area you want to hatch. If you have multiple hatch areas, you can continue to select them at this step.
8. Press ↵ to finish your selection of hatch areas. The arrow appears repeated as a pattern within the rectangle, as shown in Figure 20.4.

FIGURE 20.4

The custom hatch pattern

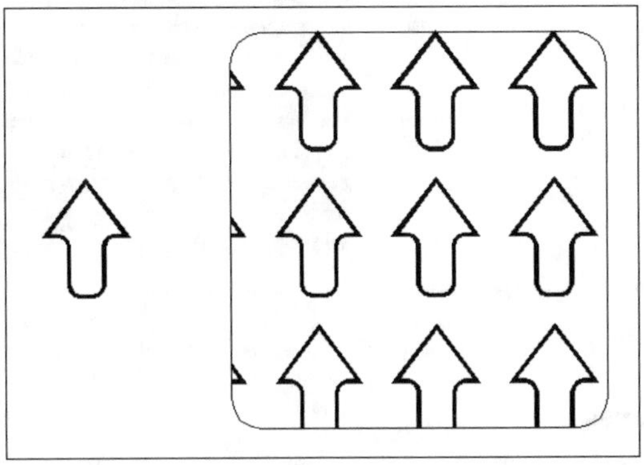

The object you select using the Select Existing option in the SuperHatch dialog box must be a block. You can modify that block using the techniques described in Chapter 6, and the changes will appear in the hatch pattern as shown in Figure 20.5.

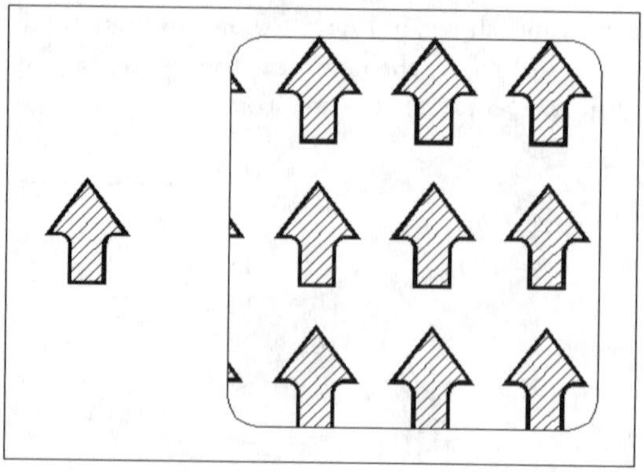

FIGURE 20.5
The custom hatch pattern after the arrow block has been modified to include the diagonal hatch pattern

As you can see from the SuperHatch dialog box, you can incorporate Xrefs, blocks, and even image files into your custom hatch pattern. Each of these options prompts you to insert the object before you convert it into a hatch pattern. You use the usual insertion method for the type of object you select. For example, if you choose the Block option, you are prompted for an insertion point, the X and Y scale factors, and a rotation angle. For image files, you see the same dialog box that you see when you insert an image file, offering the options for insertion point, scale, and rotation. Figure 20.6 shows a sample hatch pattern with an image file used instead of an AutoCAD block.

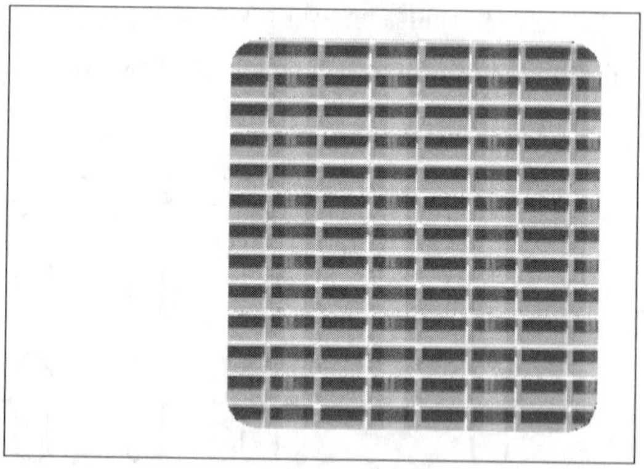

FIGURE 20.6
A custom hatch pattern using a bitmap image

ADDING BREAK LINES

In architectural plans, objects that project beyond the current view are often indicated with a break line. Common examples of this are stairs that extend above the current plan view or views of objects that are shortened to fit on a sheet. Although fairly easy to draw, break lines can be a nuisance if you have a lot of them to place in a drawing. The Break-Line Symbol tool in the Standard Express toolbar is an easy way to add break lines to a drawing.

To use it, click Break-Line Symbol in the Express Tools Standard toolbar, and then select two points close to the ends of the desired break line. At the `Specify location for break symbol <Midpoint>:`

prompt, either press ↵ to place the break line symbol at the midpoint of the break line, or select a point along the line where you want the symbol to appear.

As with most AutoCAD features, you have a lot of options with the Break Line Symbol tool. When you first click the Break Line Symbol tool, you see the following prompt:

```
Specify first point for breakline or [Block/Size/Extension]:
```

At this prompt you can enter **B** for the Block option, **S** for the Size option, or **E** for the Extension option. The Block option lets you use a custom break symbol that you have created as a block. The Size option lets you control the size of the break symbol. The Extension option lets you determine the distance that the break line extends beyond the point you select for the break line.

When you create a block for your custom break symbol using the Block or Size option, you need to follow these steps.

1. Draw the break line symbol, and then turn it into a block.
2. Add point objects to the symbol at the locations where the break lines are to start.
3. Put the point objects on the Defpoints layer.
4. Combine the original break line symbol block and the points you added into another block. This is the block you specify when you use Block option.

The Size option is affected by the Dimscale system variable. For example, if Dimscale is set to a value of 24 and the Size option of the break line symbol is set to 4, the size of the break line symbol will be scaled to 96 (4 × 24) times its original size.

Tools on the Express Pull-Down Menu

Most of the Express Tools we've discussed so far are available as options in the AutoCAD menu bar on the Express menu. There are some additional options on the Express menu you won't see in any of the toolbars. You won't want to miss these additional tools. They can greatly enhance your productivity on any type of project.

Controlling Shortcuts with the Command Alias Editor

Throughout this book, I've been showing you the keyboard shortcuts to the AutoCAD commands. In Windows XP, all these shortcuts are stored in a file called `Acad.pgp` in the `C:\Documents and Settings\User Name\Application Data\Autodesk\AutoCAD 2004\R16.0\enu\Support` folder. (Check the Working Support File Search Path option in the Files tab in the Options dialog box to find the exact location for the support files on your system.) In the past, you had to edit this file with a text editor to modify these command shortcuts (otherwise know as command aliases). But to make our lives simpler, Autodesk has supplied the Command Alias Editor, which automates the process of editing, adding, or removing command aliases from AutoCAD.

In addition, the Command Alias Editor lets you store your own alias definitions in a separate file. You can then recall your file to load your own command aliases. Here's how the Command Alias Editor works.

1. Choose Express ➢ Tools ➢ Command Alias Editor to open the AutoCAD Alias Editor dialog box.

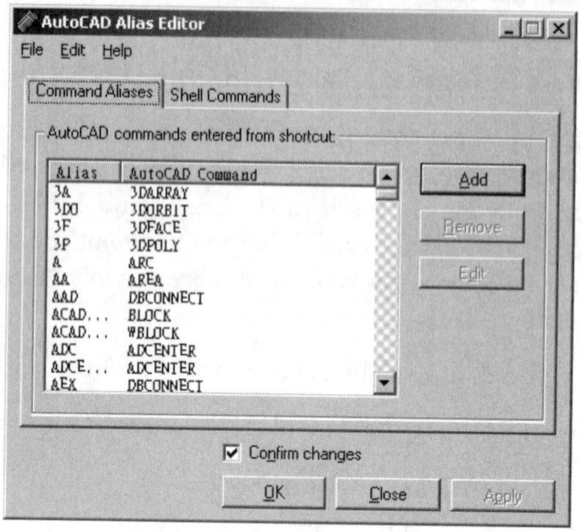

2. As you can see from the button options, you can add a new alias or delete or edit an existing alias. Click the Add button to open the New Command Alias dialog box.

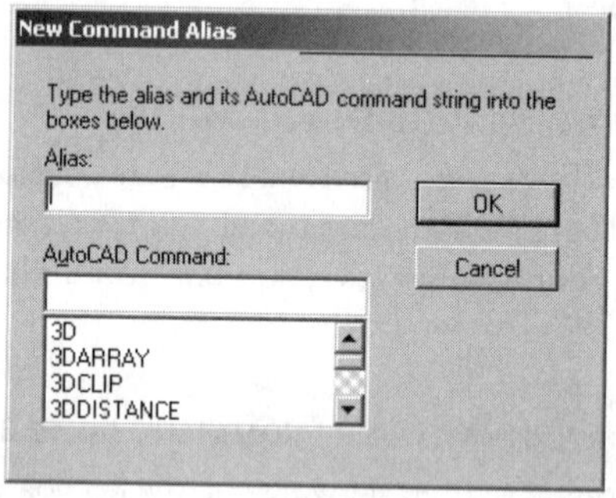

In this dialog box, you enter the desired alias in the Alias input box and then select the command from the list box below. You can also enter a command or macro name, such as Wipeout, in the input box. When you click the Edit option in the AutoCAD Alias Editor dialog box, you see a dialog box identical to this one with the input boxes already filled in.

3. After you create or edit an alias, click OK to return to the AutoCAD Alias Editor dialog box.
4. Click OK to exit the dialog box. You see a warning message that tells you that you are about to overwrite the `Acad.pgp` file.
5. Click No to leave the `Acad.pgp` file untouched. You then see the Save As dialog box. You can enter an alternate filename, such as `Myalias.pgp`, to store your personal set of command aliases.

6. After you enter a name and save your settings, you will see a message telling you that your new settings have taken effect. Click OK to return to AutoCAD.

If you're a veteran AutoCAD user, you may have become accustomed to your own set of command aliases. If so, you might want to leave the original `Acad.pgp` file alone and create your own .pgp file as I suggested in step 5. Then, whenever you use AutoCAD, open the AutoCAD Alias Editor, choose File Open, and load your personal .pgp file. From then on, the aliases in your file will supersede those of the standard `Acad.pgp` file.

Full Screen AutoCAD

AutoCAD users can't seem to get enough drawing space. This tool is for those AutoCAD users who are never satisfied with the amount of drawing area their screen provides.

When you choose Express ➢ Tools ➢ Full Screen AutoCAD, the AutoCAD drawing area is pushed to the maximum available. The AutoCAD title bar is hidden, as well as the menu bar. You can access the menu bar by pointing to the top of the screen. The menu bar will momentarily appear, allowing you to select an option.

To return to the normal AutoCAD window, point to the top edge of the screen to open the menu bar, and then choose Express ➢ Tools ➢ Full Screen AutoCAD to return to the standard AutoCAD view.

Clipping a Raster Image to a Curved Shape with Extended Clip

In Chapters 6 and 12, you saw how you can clip portions of an Xref or a raster image so that only a portion of these objects are visible. One limitation to the Raster Clip option is that you can clip only areas defined by straight lines. You cannot, for example, clip an area defined by a circle or an ellipse.

Extended Clip is designed for those instances when you absolutely need to clip a raster image to a curved area. The following steps show you how it works.

1. Create a clip boundary using a curved polyline or circle.
2. Choose Express ➢ Modify ➢ Extended Clip.
3. Click the boundary.
4. Click the Xref, block, or image you want to clip.
5. At the `Enter max error distance for resolution of arcs <7/16">:` prompt, press ↵. The Xref, block, or image will clip to the selected boundary.
6. You can erase the boundary you created in step 1 or keep it for future reference.

Extended Clip really doesn't clip to the boundary you created, but, instead, approximates that boundary by creating a true clip boundary with a series of very short line segments. In fact, the prompt in step 5 lets you specify the maximum allowable distance between the straight line segments it generates and the curve of the boundary you create (see Figure 20.7).

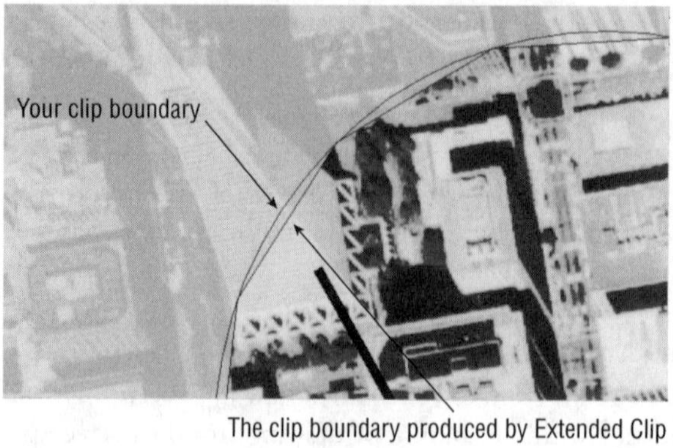

FIGURE 20.7
Extended Clip allows you to set the maximum distance from your clip boundary and the one it generates.

Once you've created a boundary using Extended Clip, you can edit the properties of the boundary by choosing Modify ➢ Object ➢ Clip for Xrefs and blocks or by choosing Modify ➢ Object ➢ Image Clip for raster images.

CREATING A CUSTOM LINE TYPE WITH MAKE LINETYPE

Most of the time the line types provided by AutoCAD are adequate. But if you're looking for that perfect line type, you can use the Make Linetype tool to create your own. Here's how it works.

1. Open the `Customltype.dwg` sample file from the `Figures` folder. The sample drawing is made up of simple lines with no polylines, arcs or circles. When you create your own line-type prototype, make sure the lines are all aligned. Draw a single line and break it to form the segments of the line type (see Figure 20.8). Also make sure it is drawn to the actual plotted size.

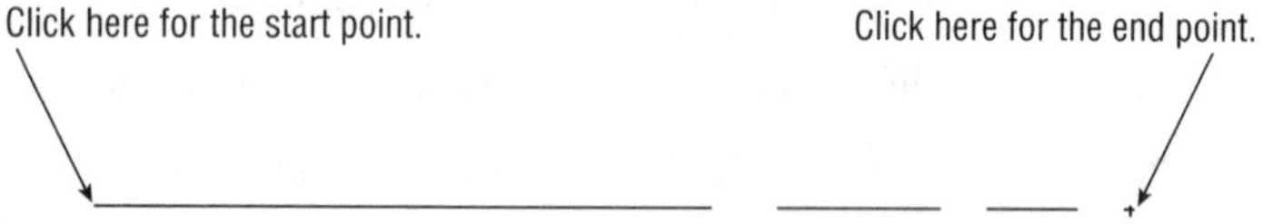

FIGURE 20.8
Creating a custom line type using Make Linetype

2. Choose Express ➢ Tools ➢ Make Linetype to open the Mkltype dialog box.

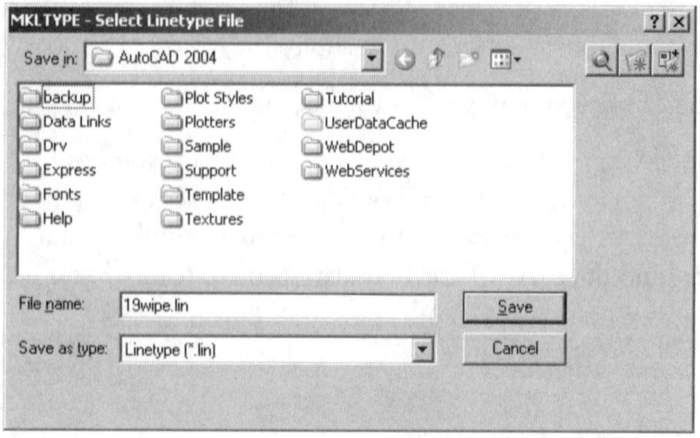

3. Enter **myltype** for the filename, select a location for the file, and then click OK.
4. At the `Enter linetype name:` prompt, enter **MyLinetype** or any name you want to use to describe the line type. The name must be a single word.
5. At the `Enter linetype description:` prompt, enter a description for your line type. This can be a sentence that best describes your line type.
6. At the `Specify starting point for line definition:` prompt, pick one endpoint of the sample line type.
7. At the `Specify ending point for line definition:` prompt, pick a point just past the opposite end of the sample line type. Pick a point past the endpoint of the sample to indicate the gap between the end of the first segment of the line type and the beginning of the repeating portion as shown in Figure 20.8.
8. At the `Select objects:` prompt, select the sample line-type lines. When you're done, press ↵. You now have a custom line type.

To load your custom line type, use the Linetype Manager dialog box (choose Format ➢ Linetype) to locate your line-type file and load the line type. If you send your file to someone else, you need to make sure you include your custom line-type files with the drawing file. Otherwise, anything drawn using your custom line type will appear as a continuous line, and your recipient will get an error message saying that AutoCAD cannot find a line type resource.

The Make Linetype tool creates a single line-type file for each line type you create. The line-type file is a simple ASCII text file. If you end up making several line types, you can combine your line-type files into one file using a simple text editor such as Windows Notepad. Don't use WordPad or Word because these programs will introduce special codes to the line-type file.

Creating Custom Shapes as an Alternative to Blocks

Shapes are a special type of AutoCAD objects that are similar to blocks. They are usually simple symbols made up of lines and arcs. Shapes take up less memory and can be displayed faster, but they are much less flexible than blocks, and they are not very accurate. You cannot use Object Snaps to snap to specific parts of a shape, nor can you explode shapes. They are best suited for symbols or as components in complex line types.

Shapes have always been difficult to create. In the past, you could not create a shape by drawing it. You had to create something called a shape definition using a special code. A *shape definition* is just an ASCII file that contains a description of the geometry of the shape. Creating such a file was a tedious, arcane process that few users bothered with.

With the introduction of complex line types in recent versions of AutoCAD, interest in shapes has revived. To make it easier for users to create shapes, AutoCAD 2004 offers a tool that will create a shape definition file for you based on a line drawing. Try this simple exercise to learn how you can create and use a shape.

1. Open the `Makeshape.dwg` sample file. This file contains a simple drawing of an upward-pointing arrow. It contains lines and arcs.

2. Choose Express ➢ Tools ➢ Make Shape to open the Mkshape dialog box. This is a typical File dialog box that allows you to specify a name and location for your shape definition file.
3. In the File Name input box, enter **Arrow**; then locate the Figures folder and place your new file there.
4. Click OK to create your file.
5. At the `Enter the name of the shape:` prompt, enter **Arrow**↵.
6. At the `Enter resolution <128>:` prompt, enter **512**↵. Shapes are defined with a square matrix of points. All the endpoints of lines and arcs must be on a point within that matrix. At this prompt, you can define the density of that matrix. A higher density will give you a better looking shape, but you don't want to get carried away with this setting.
7. At the `Specify insertion base point:` prompt, select the tip of the arrow as shown in Figure 20.9. This will be the insertion point of your shape, which is similar to the insertion point of a block.

FIGURE 20.9
Creating a shape from an existing drawing

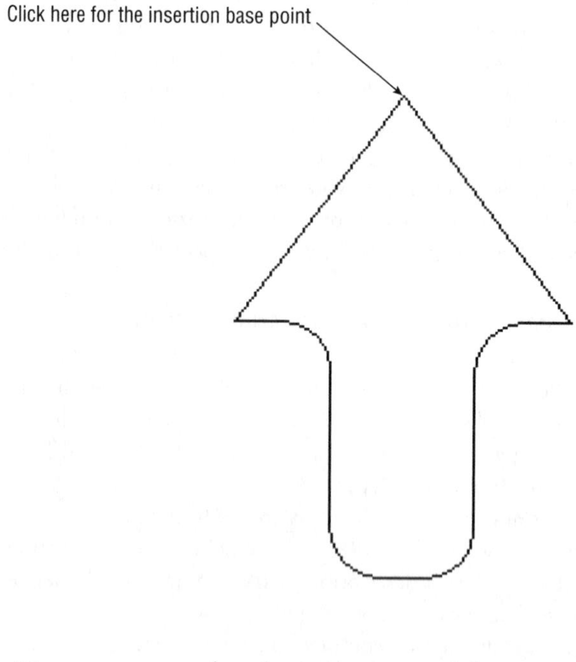
Click here for the insertion base point

8. At the `Select objects:` prompt, select the entire arrow and then press ↵.

You'll see a series of messages telling you what AutoCAD is doing. The last message will tell you whether AutoCAD was successful in creating the shape file, and it will tell you the location and name of the new shape file.

```
Compilation successful.  Output file C:\Documents and Settings\User Name\My
    Documents\Arrow.shx contains 309 bytes.
```

```
Shape "ARROW" created.
Use the SHAPE command to place shapes in your drawing.
```

To see how your shape came out, try the following. Here, you'll learn how to load and insert a shape.

1. At the command prompt, type **Load↵** to open the Select Shape File dialog box. This is a typical File dialog box.
2. In the `Figures` folder, locate the file `Arrows.shx`, and click Open to load it.
3. Now type **Shape↵**.
4. At the `Enter shape name or [?]:` prompt, type **Arrow↵**. Now you'll see the arrow follow the cursor as you move it across the drawing area.

NOTE *If you've forgotten the name of a shape you are loading, you can enter a question mark (?) to see a listing of available shapes.*

5. At the `Specify insertion point:` prompt, click to the right of the original arrow.
6. At the `Specify height:` prompt, press ↵ to accept the default of 1.
7. At the `Specify rotation angle:` prompt, enter 45↵. The arrow appears at a 45° angle.

In many ways, a shape acts like a block, but you cannot snap to any of its points. It is also less accurate in its representation than a block, though for some applications, this may not be a great concern. Finally, you cannot use complex shapes such as splines or 3D objects for your shape. You can only use lines and arcs.

Still, you may find shapes useful in your application. As mentioned earlier, you can include shapes in line-type definitions. See Chapter 21 for a description on how to create a line type that includes shapes as part of the line.

TIP *You might also notice a tool that converts shapes into AutoCAD blocks. Choose Express ➢ Blocks ➢ Convert Shape To Block, and then select a shape. A prompt appears asking for a name for the block. You can accept the default name, which is the same name as the shape you are converting.*

Using the Express Selection Tools

Sometimes it seems that there aren't enough selection tools available in AutoCAD. In Chapter 2, you learned about the various methods you can use to select groups of objects to build a selection set, which is a set of objects selected for an operation such as a move or copy. The Express Tools offer a few more ways to select objects.

The Get Selection Set tool sets up a selection set based on layers or types of objects. When you choose Express ➢ Selection Tools ➢ Get Selection Set, you are prompted to select an object whose layer contains all the objects you want to select. You can press ↵ to create a selection set of all the objects in the drawing. Next, you are prompted to select an object of the type you want. If you press ↵ at the first prompt and then select a line at the second prompt, all the lines in the drawing will be included in a new selection set. You won't see anything happen on the screen, but the next time you use a command that asks you to select objects, you can enter **P↵** to select the lines.

The other selection tool is Fast Select. When you choose Express ➢ Selection Tools ➢ Fast Select, you are prompted to select an object. Once you do so, the object you select plus any object touching it will be selected.

DIMSTYLE EXPORT AND DIMSTYLE IMPORT

Most AutoCAD users really only need to set up their dimension styles once and then make minor alteration for drawing scale. You can set up your dimension styles in a template file and then use that template whenever you create new drawings. That way, your dimension styles will already be set up the way you want them.

But frequently, you will receive files created by someone else who many not have the same ideas about dimension styles as you do. Normally, this would mean that you have to re-create your favorite settings in a new dimension style. Now with the Express Tools, you can export and import dimension styles at any time, saving you the effort of re-creating them. Here's how it works.

1. Open a file from which you want to export a dimension style.
2. Choose Express ➢ Dimension ➢ Dimstyle Export or enter **Dimex↵** to open the Dimension Style Export dialog box.

3. Click the Browse button at the top of the dialog box to locate and name a file for storing your dimension style. AutoCAD appends the .dim filename extension.
4. Click Open in the Open dialog box. If the file you specified does not exist, AutoCAD will ask if you want to create it. Click OK to create a new .dim file.
5. Select the name of the dimension style you want to export from the Available Dimension Styles list box.
6. Click the Full Text Style Information radio button to include all the information regarding the associated text style.
7. Click OK. You will see a message in the Command window telling you that your dimension style was successfully exported.

To import a style you've exported, take the following steps.

1. Open a file into which you want to import a dimension style.
2. Choose Express ➢ Dimension ➢ Dimstyle Import or type **Dimim↵** to open the Dimension Style Import dialog box.

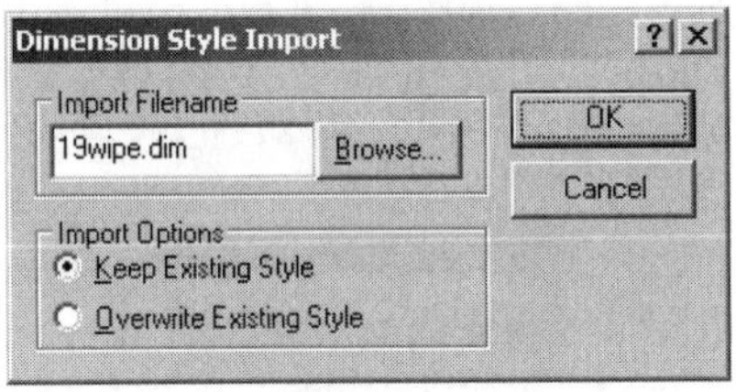

3. Click the Browse button to open the Open dialog box.
4. Locate and select the dimension style file you saved earlier, and then click Open.
5. Click either the Keep Existing Style or Overwrite Existing Style radio button to choose which action to take.
6. Click OK.

OPTIONS FOR ATTACHING DATA TO OBJECTS

This set of options is less likely to get as much use as the others we've looked at so far, so I've included a brief description of them here without going into too much detail. They're actually fairly easy to use, and you shouldn't have any trouble trying them out. You can access both tools by choosing Express ➢ Tools.

Attach Xdata Lets you attach extended data to objects. Extended data is usually only used by AutoLISP, ADS, or ARX applications. You are asked to select the object that will receive the data, and then you are asked for an application name that serves as a tag to tell others who the data belongs to. You can then select a data type. Once this is done, you can enter your data.

List Object Xdata Displays extended data that has been attached to an object.

FILE TOOLS

AutoCAD has always made extensive use of external files for its operation. Everything from fonts to keyboard shortcuts depend on external files. The Express File Tools (choose Express ➢ File Tools) offer options to simplify a few file-related operations. You may find some of these tools helpful on a daily basis, such as Save All Drawings and Close All Drawings. Others, such as Edit Image, might be useful to know about when you need to edit an image.

Move Backup Files Lets you specify a location for AutoCAD .bak files for the current drawing session.

Convert PLT to DWG Converts HPGL plot files to drawing files. You must first set up AutoCAD or Windows for an HPGL plotter and then specify that HPGL plotter in the Plot or Page Setup dialog box. You must also indicate that you want to plot to a file at the time you produce the plot (check the Plot To Tile option in the Plot Device tab of the Plot dialog box).

Edit Image Offers a quick way to open and edit an image file that has been inserted into an AutoCAD drawing. Choose Express ➢ File Tools ➢ Edit Image, and then select the image you want to edit. A File dialog box opens showing the file in a list box. Click Open, and the program associated with the image file type will open the image file.

Redefine Path Lets you redefine the path to external files that are referenced from the current drawing. This includes Xrefs, images, shapes, styles, and Rtext. You can strip a path from a referenced file by using the asterisk option (*) when you see the Enter old directory (use '*' for all), or ? <options>: prompt. When you see the Replace "*" with: prompt, press ↵. If you strip the path in this way, AutoCAD will use the support file search path specified in the Files tab of the Options dialog box. You can specify the type of external file you want to redefine by pressing ↵ at the first prompt. This opens the Redirmode dialog box. From this dialog box, you can select the type of support file whose path you want to redefine.

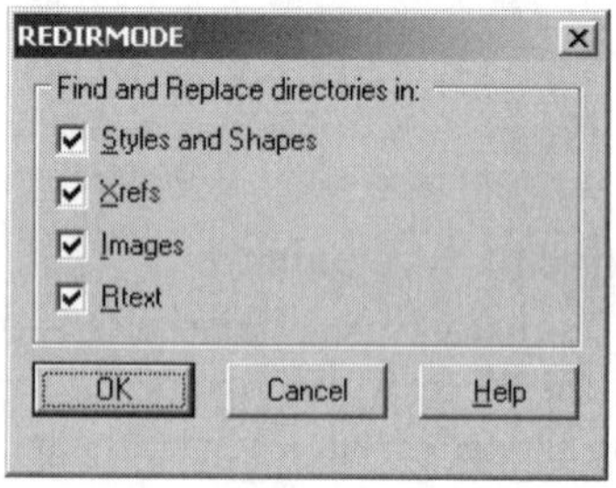

Update Drawing Property Data Drawing property data can be a handy feature of AutoCAD, but to use it requires some discipline. (See Chapter 15 for more on drawing property data.) For one thing, the amount of data you must enter can be a bit daunting. The Update Drawing Property Data Express Tool offers a way to let you quickly add drawing property data by utilizing property data templates. Drawing property data is often the same for a set of drawings, so you can create a template and apply it to similar drawings in a set using the Update Drawing Property Data tool.

To create a drawing property data template, choose Express ➢ File Tools ➢ Update Drawing Property Data. At the Enter an option [Active template/Edit template/List/Remove/Update] <Update>: prompt, enter E↵ to open the Edit Populate Template dialog box.

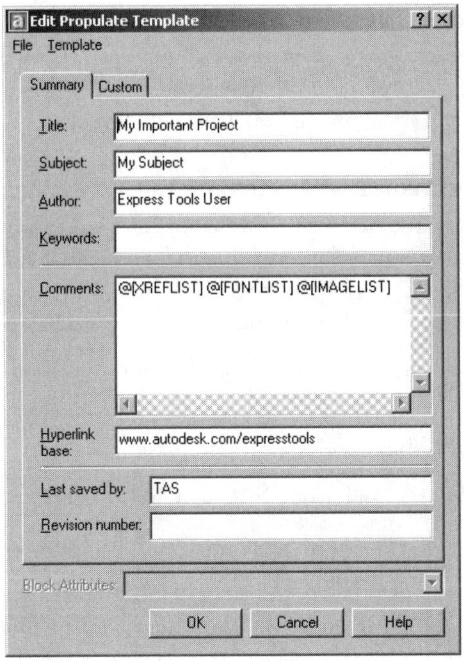

Fill in the data, and then choose File ➢ Save As. Use the Update option to apply the template to a drawing or to a set of drawings in a folder.

Save All Drawings Saves all currently open files. The files remain open for additional editing.

Close All Drawings Closes all currently open drawings. AutoCAD remains open.

Quick Exit Closes all currently open drawings and exits AutoCAD. You are asked if you want to save changes to each file before it is closed.

Revert to Original Causes a drawing to revert to its last saved state. It does so by closing the file without saving any changes (since the last Save) and then reopening the file.

Web Tools

AutoCAD allows you to add URL links to objects. This is a great feature that can help you link drawings to other types of data. The Express Web Tools (choose Express ➢ Web Tools) add some enhancements to the URL linking features of AutoCAD.

Show URLs Displays the URL link attached to an AutoCAD object.

Change URLs Lets you quickly edit an existing URL of an object. You must still choose Insert ➢ Hyperlink to attach a new URL to an object.

Find and Replace URLs Replaces a set of existing URLs with a URL of your specification.

Layout Express Tools

AutoCAD 2004 introduces some new Express Tools that will help make your work with layouts go a lot easier. These tools found in the Express ➢ Layout Tools menu address some of the more common operations you will encounter as you work with layouts.

MOVING OBJECTS FROM PAPER SPACE

The Change Space tool lets you quickly move an object from a layout Paper Space to Model Space and vice versa. It automatically compensates for any differences in scale between the Model Space and Paper Space. This tool is great for moving drawing titles from one space to another and for moving dimensions between Model Space and Paper Space. Change Space is easy to use by taking these steps.

1. Click a Layout tab. Change Space does not work in the Model tab.
2. To move an object from Model Space to Paper Space, double-click inside a viewport that displays the object you want to move. Otherwise, stay in the layout Paper Space.
3. Choose Express ➢ Layout Tools ➢ Change Space.
4. Select the objects you want to move, and then press ↵.
5. You are prompted to select a viewport. If you are moving an object from a viewport to the layout Paper Space, press ↵. Otherwise, if you are moving an object from the layout Paper Space to a Model Space viewport, select a viewport.

ALIGNING MODEL SPACE OBJECTS WITH LAYOUT OBJECTS

If you ever try to align an object in a layout with objects in a Model Space viewport, you know how difficult it can be. This situation often arises when you accidentally pan or zoom a Model Space viewport and objects drawn in Paper Space, such as break lines or dimensional notations, become misaligned with the underlying view.

The Align Space tool helps you quickly align objects in a Model Space viewport with objects in the layout Paper Space. Align Space can even rotate a viewport view to align objects that are at an angle. To see firsthand how it works, try the following exercise. You'll align a Plan view of a set of survey data points to a north arrow in Paper Space.

1. Open the `Alignspace.dwg` sample file from the companion CD.
2. Choose Express ➢ Layout Tools ➢ Align Space. Notice that the viewport automatically becomes active.
3. At the `FIRST alignment point in MODEL space:` prompt, click the upper endpoint of the north arrow in the viewport as shown in Figure 21.10.
4. At the `SECOND point in MODEL space or <Return> for none:` prompt, click the endpoint of the bottom end of the north arrow as shown in Figure 21.10.

5. At the `FIRST alignment point in PAPER space:` prompt, notice that AutoCAD automatically switches to Paper Space to allow for your next input. Click the upper endpoint of the layout Paper Space north arrow.

FIGURE 20.10

Select these points to align the Model Space north arrow with a Paper Space north arrow.

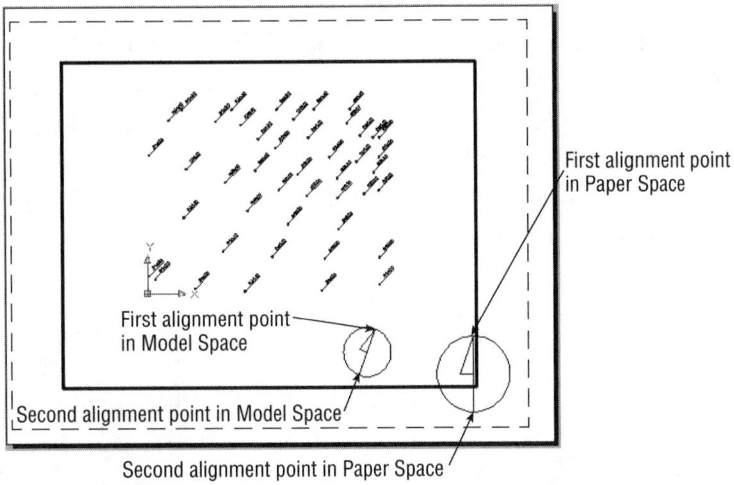

6. At the `SECOND alignment point in PAPER space:` prompt, click the lower end of the Paper Space arrow. The two arrows will align, and you will see a message telling you the scale of the viewport.

In this exercise, you can see that the two north arrows are aligned in both scale and direction. The object you are aligning to in Paper Space does not have to be within the area of the viewport either.

If you prefer, you can align a single point without changing the scale or rotation of the viewport by pressing ↵ in step 4 when you see the `Second point in MODEL space or <Return> for none` prompt.

ALIGNING MULTIPLE VIEWPORTS TO A SINGLE VIEWPORT

The Align Space tool lets you align a Model Space object to a Paper Space object, but what if you want to align two Model Space views? For example, suppose you want to overlap two viewports of the same view, with one viewport displaying graphics while the other displays just the power and signal symbols for a small region of the plan.

The Synchronize Viewports tool lets you do just that. It aligns one or more viewports to another "master" viewport. The Synchronize Viewports tool aligns the coordinates in one viewport with the coordinates and scale of another so that the views are matched like pieces of a jigsaw puzzle. To get a better idea of what this means, try the following exercise. Suppose you have an enlarged plan showing a portion of a building. You want to include the grid lines in your plan, but you don't want to have to include other portions of the plan or redraw the grids. Synchronize Viewports can make easy work of this project.

1. Open the `Synchronize.dwg` file from the companion CD, and then choose Express ➢ Layout Tools ➢ Synchronize Viewports.
2. At the `Select object:` prompt, click the border of the viewport in the lower-right corner.
3. At the `Select viewports to be aligned to master viewport Select objects:` prompt, click the other two viewports and press ↵. The two viewports will change to show the adjacent areas of the first viewport.

Notice that the three views of the layout combine to show a contiguous Plan view instead of three random views.

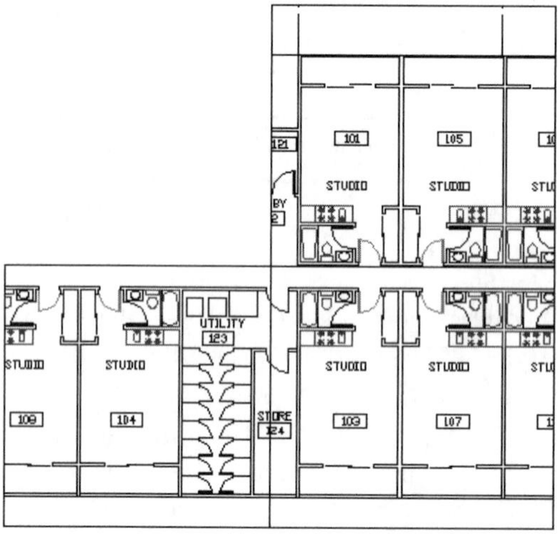

You could use Synchronize Viewports in just this way to piece together parts of a floor plan in a nonrectangular shape.

To finish adding the grid lines, do the following.

1. Double-click in the top viewport, and then click the Pan tool in the Standard toolbar.
2. Shift+click and drag the view downward to bring the grid lines into view. Then Shift+click and drag, and keep the pan motion in an exact vertical direction. Pan downward until you see only the grids and dimensions.
3. Press Esc to exit the Pan tool; then double-click the left viewport, and use the Pan tool to Shift+click and drag the view toward the right. Keep panning until just the grid lines show.

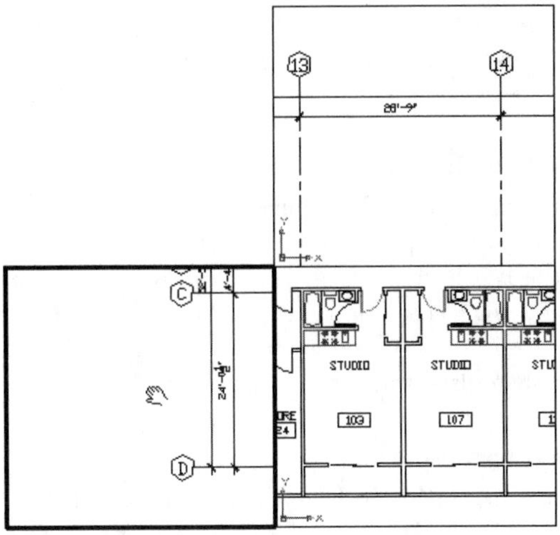

If you've ever tried to do this operation without the aid of the Synchronize Viewport tool, you can see how helpful a tool it is.

FINDING VIEWPORT SCALES AND MERGING LAYOUTS

There are two more fairly simple tools in the Layout Tools category: List Viewport Scale and Merge Layout. List Viewport Scale does just what its name says. Choose Express ➢ Layout Tools ➢ List Viewport Scale, and then click a viewport border to display the viewport scale. Merge Layout combines the contents of one layout with another. This tool is handy if you are exporting files to AutoCAD 14 in which only one layout is possible. Choosing Express ➢ Layout Tools ➢ Merge Layouts opens the LayoutMerge dialog box.

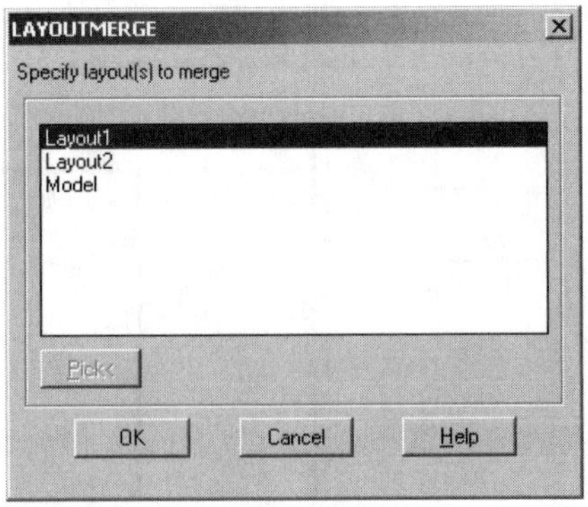

This dialog box lets you select the layout that you want merged with the current layout. Once you've made your selection and click OK, another dialog box appears that looks identical to the first LayoutMerge dialog box. This time you select the destination layout for the merged layouts.

That covers the Express Layout tools. Like many of the other Express Tools, you may find yourself using these tools more than most of the other standard AutoCAD commands, so keep them in mind as you work on the layout of your next set of drawings.

Finding Former Express Tools

If you've been using AutoCAD for some time, you know that some of the Express Tools eventually find their way to the main part of the program. For example, the Find And Replace tool in the shortcut menu of the Text Editor was once an Express Tool. An Express Tool called Pack'n Go became eTransmit in the File menu. This time, you'll find that two more former Express Tools are included as part of the main AutoCAD program—Wipeout and Cloud. If you are using AutoCAD LT, these are really the only tools in this chapter that are available to you.

MASKING AREAS WITH WIPEOUT

Earlier in this chapter, I described a method for masking hatch patterns behind graphics using the Text Mask Express Tool. Another method is to use the Wipeout tool. Wipeout is actually incorporated into the main part of the AutoCAD program; to access it, choose Draw ➢ Wipeout.

Wipeout creates an object called Wipeout, which acts like a mask. If you read the earlier section on the Text Mask tool, you have an idea of how Wipeout works because the Text Mask tool uses the Wipeout object. The following exercise demonstrates how to use this tool in another application.

Imagine that you've set up a Paper Space layout showing an enlarged view of one of the units of the studio apartment building from this book. You want to show dimensions and notes around the unit, but too many other objects are in the way. The Wipeout tool can be of great help in this situation. Here's how.

1. Open the `19wipe.dwg` file. This is one of the sample files from the companion CD. When you open this file, you will be in Paper Space.
2. Zoom in to the typical Unit plan so that your view looks similar to Figure 20.11.

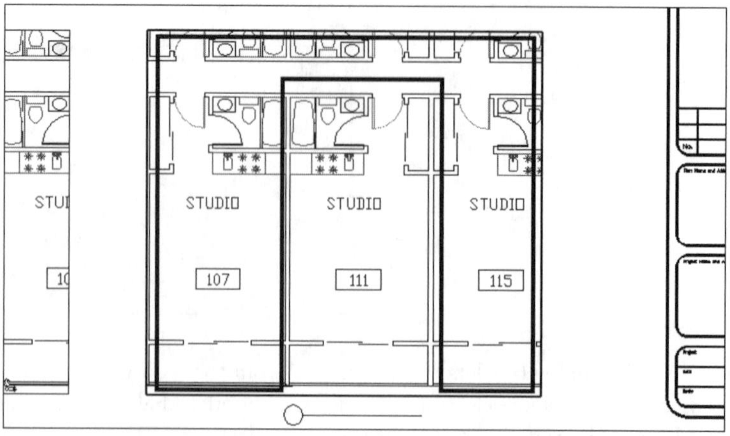

FIGURE 20.11
Adding a polyline to the enlarged Unit plan

3. Create a layer called Wipeout and make it current.
4. Switch to Floating Model Space by choosing View ➢ Model Space (Floating) or by clicking Paper in the status bar.
5. Draw the closed polyline shown in Figure 20.11. You don't have to be exact about the shape; you can adjust it later.
6. Choose Draw ➢ Wipeout.
7. At the `Specify first point or [Frames/Polyline] <Polyline>:` prompt, press ↵ to accept the default Polyline option.
8. At the `Select a closed polyline:` prompt, select the polyline you just drew.
9. At the `Erase polyline? [Yes/No] <No>:` prompt, enter **Y**↵ to erase the polyline. The area enclosed by the polyline will be masked out.

The Wipeout object has a border that can be turned on and off. When the border is visible, you can click the Wipeout border and use its corner grips to reshape the area that it covers. You can also erase, move, or copy the Wipeout object using its border. In the example of the Unit plan, you will want to hide the Wipeout border. Take the following steps to turn off the Wipeout border's visibility.

1. Choose Draw ➢ Wipeout.
2. At the `Specify first point or [Frames/Polyline] <Polyline>:` prompt, type **F**↵.
3. At the `Enter mode [OFF/ON] <ON>:` prompt, type **OFF**↵. The frame disappears.

When the frame is off, you cannot edit the Wipeout object. Of course, you can turn it back on using the Frame option you used in step 2 of the previous exercise. By the way, if you need to edit the Text Mask tool described earlier in this chapter, you use the Frame option presented in the previous exercise to turn on the Text Mask border.

With the Wipeout object in place and its border turned off, you can add dimension and notes around the image without having the adjoining graphics interfere with the visibility of your notes. Figure 20.12 shows the Unit plan with the dimensions inserted from the individual Unit plan file.

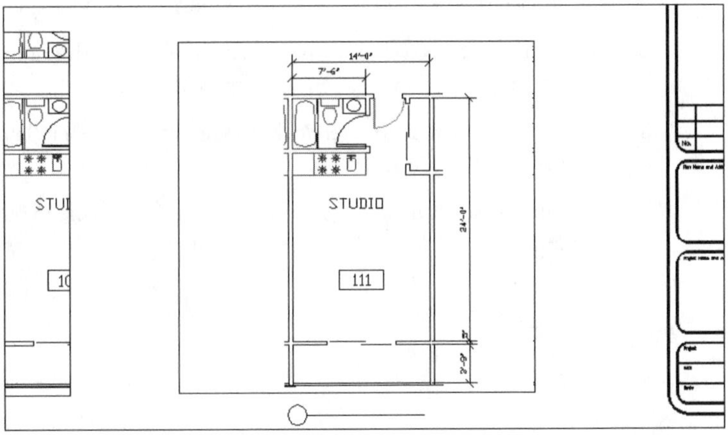

FIGURE 20.12
The Unit plan with dimensions added and the viewport border adjusted to hide the graphics beyond the Wipeout object

I should address one more point here. If you switch to Paper Space and zoom out to view the entire Paper Space drawing, you'll notice that the Wipeout object appears in the overall plan at the top of the screen (see Figure 20.13). Fortunately, you can freeze the Wipeout layer in the viewport with the Overall view to hide the Wipeout object.

FIGURE 20.13

The Wipeout object as it appears in the overall Plan view

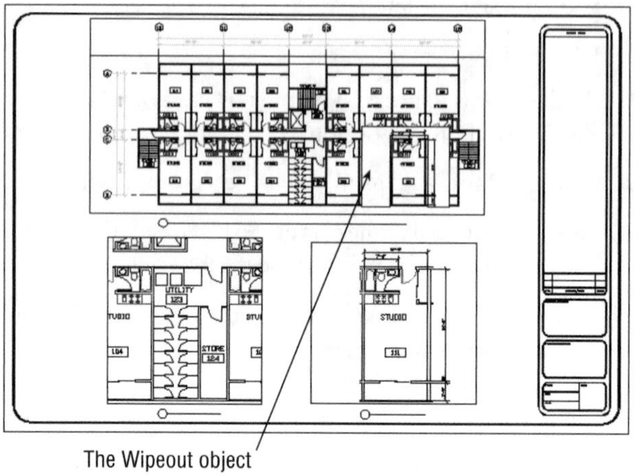

DRAWING REVISION CLOUDS

A revision cloud is a cloudlike outline drawn around parts of a drawing that have been revised. They are used to alert the viewer to any changes that have occurred in the design of a project since the drawings were last issued. Revision clouds are fairly common in most types of technical drawings, including architectural, civil, and mechanical drawings.

As simple as they might appear, revision clouds are difficult to draw using the standard AutoCAD tools. But now we have a single tool that makes them easy to draw. Try using the Revision Cloud tool on the `19wipe.dwg` file from the companion CD by following these steps.

1. If you haven't already done so, switch your drawing to Paper Space.
2. Choose Draw ➢ Revcloud. Then click a point near the right side of the viewport that shows a view of the Unit plan, as shown in Figure 20.14.
3. Move the cursor in a counterclockwise direction to encircle the Unit plan view. As you move the cursor, the cloud is drawn.
4. Bring the cursor full circle back to the point from which you started. When you approach the beginning of the cloud, the revision cloud closes, and you exit the Revision Cloud tool.

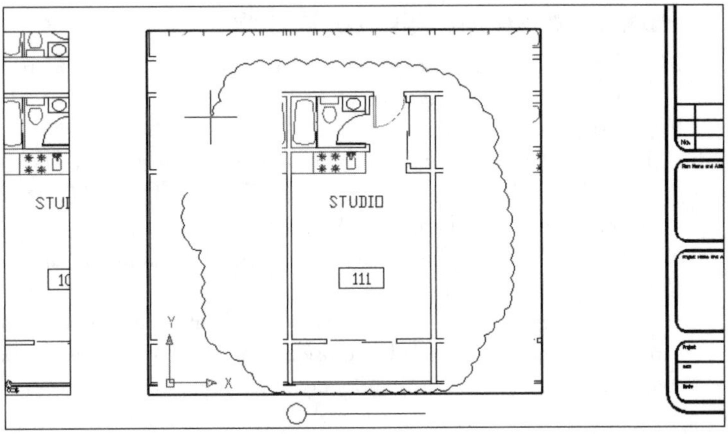

FIGURE 20.14
Drawing a revision cloud

If you need to change the size of the arcs in the revision cloud, you can do so in step 2 by entering A↵. You can then enter an arc length. You can also convert an existing closed polyline or circle into a revision cloud by using the Object option. To use the Object option, press ↵ instead of clicking a starting point in step 2. You are prompted to select an object. You can select a single closed polyline or a circle, which is converted into a revision cloud.

Utilities Available from Other Sources

The utilities discussed in the previous section are just a few samples of the many available for AutoCAD. Other sources for AutoLISP utilities are the AutoCAD journals *Cadence* and *Cadalyst*. Both offer sections that list utilities written by readers and editorial staff. If you don't already have a subscription to one of these publications and want to know more about them, their contact information follows:

Cadence, published by Miller Freeman Inc. 525 Market Street, Suite 500, San Francisco, CA 94105
`http://www.cadenceweb.com`

Cadalyst, published by Advanstar Inc., 131W. First Street., Duluth, MN 55802-2065
`http://www.cadonline.com`

Finally, the companion CD included with this book contains some freeware and shareware utilities.

Also on the CD, I have included my own AEC (architecture, engineering, civil) software offering basic architectural utilities, such as a symbols library, automatic door and window insertion program, and reference symbols. If you're using AutoCAD's 3D features, you'll also want to check out the Eye2eye 3D viewer. Eye2eye lets you easily create perspective views using a camera and target object. For more information about what is included on the companion CD, see Appendix A and on the CD itself.

Putting AutoLISP to Work

Most high-end CAD packages offer a macro or programming language to help users customize their systems. AutoCAD has *AutoLISP*, which is a pared-down version of the popular LISP artificial intelligence language.

Don't let AutoLISP scare you. In many ways, an AutoLISP program is just a set of AutoCAD commands that help you build your own features. The only difference is that you have to follow a different set of rules when using AutoLISP. But this isn't so unusual. After all, you had to learn some basic rules about using AutoCAD commands too—how to start commands, for instance, and how to use command options.

If the thought of using AutoLISP is a little intimidating, bear in mind that you don't really need substantial computer knowledge to use this tool. In this section, you will see how you can get AutoLISP to help out in your everyday editing tasks, without having to learn the entire programming language.

OTHER CUSTOMIZATION OPTIONS

If you are serious about customization, you'll want to know about Autodesk's ObjectARX programming environment that allows Microsoft Visual C++ programmers to develop full applications that work within AutoCAD. ObjectARX allows programmers to create new objects within AutoCAD as well as add functionality to existing objects. ObjectARX is beyond the scope of this book, so to find out more, contact your AutoCAD dealer or visit Autodesk's website at `www.autodesk.com`.

If you are familiar with Visual Basic, you'll want to know that AutoCAD offers Visual Basic ActiveX Automation as part of its set of customization tools. ActiveX Automation offers the ability to create macros that operate across different applications. It also gives you access to AutoCAD objects through an object-oriented programming environment. Automation is a broad subject, so several chapters on the CD are devoted to this topic.

Loading and Running an AutoLISP Program

Many AutoCAD users have discovered the usefulness of AutoLISP through the thousands of free AutoLISP utilities that are available from bulletin board and online services. In fact, it's quite common for users to maintain a "toolbox" of their favorite utilities on a disk. But before you can use these utilities, you need to know how to load them into AutoCAD. In the following exercise, you'll load and use a sample AutoLISP utility found on the companion CD.

1. Start AutoCAD and open the `Unit.dwg` file.
2. Choose Tools ➢ Load Application to open the Load/Unload Applications dialog box.

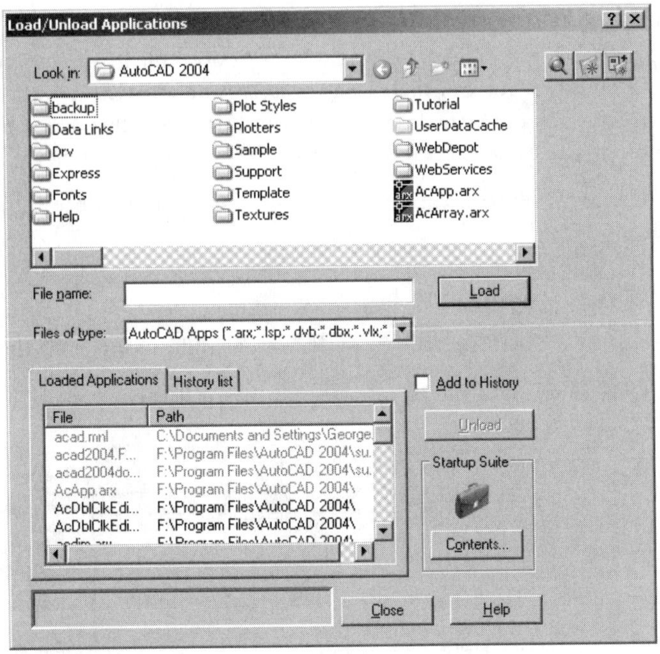

3. Locate and select the `Getarea.lsp` file from the companion CD.
4. Click the Load button. The message `GETAREA.LSP successfully loaded` appears in the message box at the very bottom of the dialog box. If you scroll down the list in the Loaded Applications tab, you also see `Getarea.lsp` listed there, which tells you that it is loaded.
5. Click Close to close the Load/Unload Applications dialog box.
6. Now enter **getarea**↵.
7. At the `Select point inside area to be calculated:` prompt, click inside the Unit plan.
8. At the `Select location for area note:` prompt, pick a point just above the door to the balcony. A label appears displaying the area of the room in square feet.

You have just loaded and used an AutoLISP utility. As you saw in the Load/Unload Applications dialog box, there are several other utilities you can load and try out. I'll introduce you to a few more of these utilities later on in Appendix A, but for now, let's look more closely at the Load/Unload Applications dialog box.

TIP *The functions of some of the more popular AutoLISP utilities have become part of the core AutoCAD program. Tools such as Match Properties and Make Object's Layer Current have been around as AutoLISP utilities since the earliest releases of AutoCAD.*

Managing Your AutoLISP and VBA Library

The Load/Unload Applications dialog box gives you plenty of flexibility in managing your favorite AutoLISP utilities. You can also manage your VBA and ARX applications. As you saw from the previous exercise, you can easily find and select utilities using this dialog box. If you use a custom application often, you can include it in the History List tab of the Load/Unload Applications dialog box.

1. Choose Tools ➢ Load Application again to open the Load/Unload Applications dialog box.
2. Click the Add To History check box.
3. Click the History List tab.
4. Select `Getarea.lsp` again from the list of applications at the top of the dialog box.
5. Click Load. `Getarea.lsp` now appears in the History List.

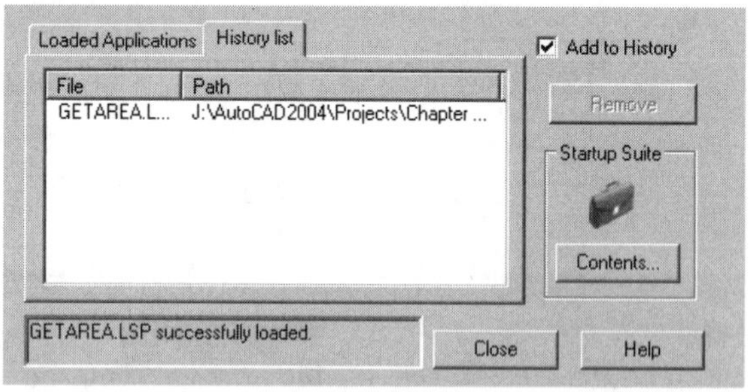

6. Click Close to close the Load/Unload Applications dialog box.

Now when you exit AutoCAD, the dialog box retains the name of the `Getarea.lsp` utility in the History List tab. When you want to load `Getarea.lsp` in a future session, you won't have to hunt it down. You can highlight it in the History List tab and then load it from there. You can add as many items as you want to your History List or remove items by highlighting them and clicking the Remove button. The History List works with all types of applications that AutoCAD supports.

Loading AutoLISP Programs Automatically

As you start to build a library of AutoLISP and VBA applications, you may find that you use some of them all the time. You can set up AutoCAD to automatically load your favorite applications. To do this, you use the Startup Suite in the Load/Unload Applications dialog box.

1. Choose Tools ➢ Load Applications to open the Load/Unload Applications dialog box.
2. Click the Contents button or the suitcase icon in the Startup Suite group to open the Startup Suite dialog box.

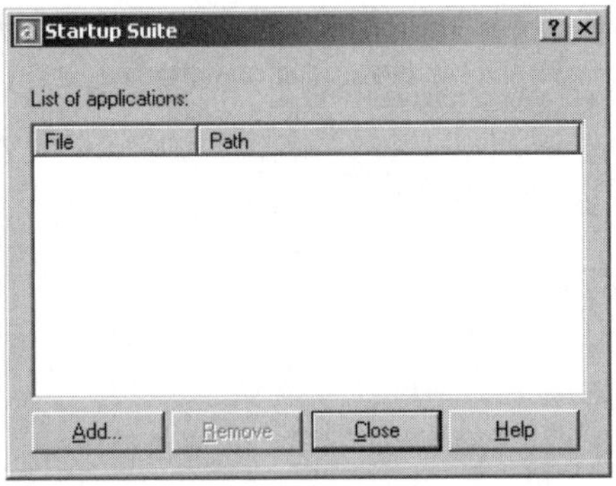

TIP *You can also drag and drop files into the Startup Suite list from Windows Explorer or other drag-and-drop-compatible applications.*

3. Click the Add button to open the Add File To Startup Suite dialog box. This is a typical File dialog box that allows you to search for and select a file.
4. Locate and select the `Getarea.lsp` file in the `\Figures\` folder, and then click Add. The Startup Suite dialog box reappears, and `Getarea.lsp` is listed.
5. Click Close, and then click Close again in the Load/Unload Applications dialog box.

From now on, `Getarea.lsp` will be loaded automatically whenever you start AutoCAD. You can add several files to the Startup Suite list, or you can remove them by selecting them in the list and then clicking the Remove button.

Creating Keyboard Macros with AutoLISP

You can write some simple AutoLISP programs of your own that create what are called *keyboard macros.* Macros—like script files—are strings of predefined keyboard entries. They are invaluable for shortcuts to commands and options you use frequently. For example, you might find that you often use the Break command to break an object at a single point while editing a particular drawing. Here's a way you can turn this operation into a macro:

1. Open the `Unit` file, and, at the command prompt, enter the following text. Be sure you enter the line exactly as shown here. If you make a mistake while entering this line, you can use the I-beam cursor or arrow keys to go to the location of your error to fix it.

   ```
   (defun C:breakat () (command "break" pause "f" pause "@"))↵
   ```

2. Next, enter **breakat**↵ at the command prompt. The Break command starts, and you are prompted to select an object.
3. Click the wall on the right side of the unit.

4. At the `Enter First Point:` prompt, click a point on the wall where you want to create a break, and make sure the Osnap mode is turned off.
5. To see the result of the break, click the wall again. You will see that it has been split into two lines, as shown in Figure 20.15.

FIGURE 20.15
With the grips exposed, you can see that the wall is split into two lines.

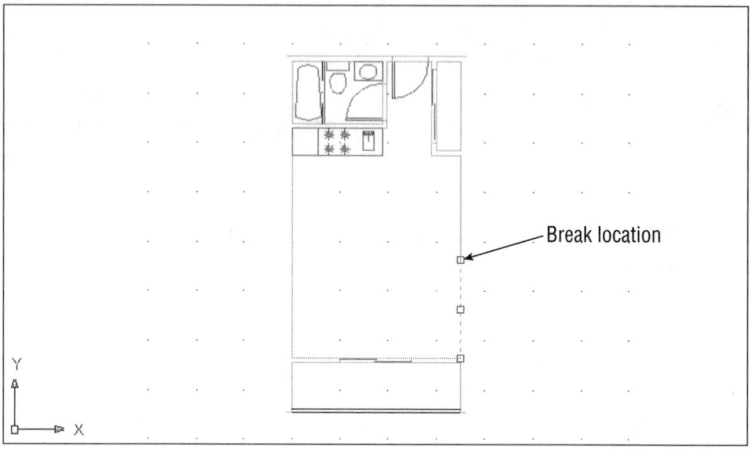

You've just written and run your first AutoLISP macro! Let's take a closer look at this very simple program (see Figure 20.16). It starts with an opening parenthesis, as do all AutoLISP programs, followed by the word `defun`. `Defun` is an AutoLISP function that lets you create commands; it is followed by the name you want to give the command (`Breakat`, in this case). The command name is preceded by `C:`, telling `defun` to make this command accessible from the command prompt. If the `C:` were omitted, you would have to start `Breakat` using parentheses, as in `(Breakat)`.

After the command name is a set of open and close parentheses. This set encloses what is called the *argument list*. The details aren't important; just be aware that these parentheses must follow the command name.

Finally, a list of words follows, enclosed by another set of parentheses. This list starts with the word `command`. `Command` is an AutoLISP function that tells AutoLISP that whatever follows should be entered just like regular keyboard input. Only one item in the `Breakat` macro—the word `pause`—is not part of the keyboard input series. `Pause` is an AutoLISP function that tells AutoLISP to pause for input. In this particular macro, AutoLISP pauses to let you pick an object to break.

Notice that most of the items in the macro are enclosed in quotation marks. Literal keyboard input must be enclosed in quotation marks in this way. The `pause` function, on the other hand, does not require quotation marks because it is a proper function, one that AutoLISP can recognize.

Finally, the program ends with a closing parenthesis. All parentheses in an AutoLISP program must be in balanced pairs, so these final two parentheses close the opening parenthesis at the start of the `command` function as well as the opening parenthesis back at the beginning of the `defun` function.

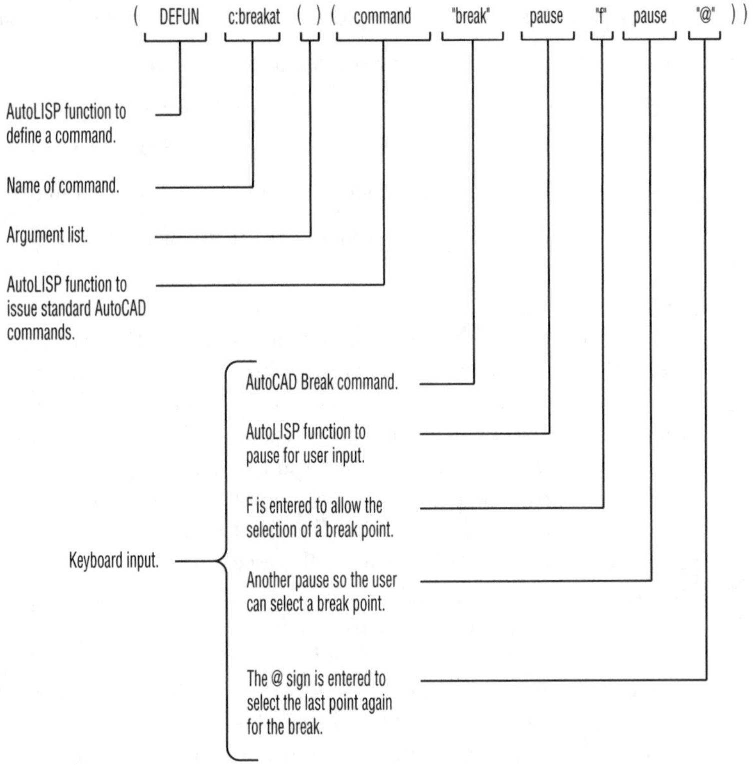

FIGURE 20.16
Breakdown of the Breakat macro

STORING AUTOLISP MACROS AS FILES

When you create a program at the command prompt, such as you did with the `Breakat` macro, AutoCAD remembers it only until you exit the current file. Unless you want to re-create this macro the next time you use AutoCAD, save it by copying it into an ASCII text file with a .lsp extension, as shown in Figure 20.17, in which the `Breakat` macro is saved, along with some other macros I use often.

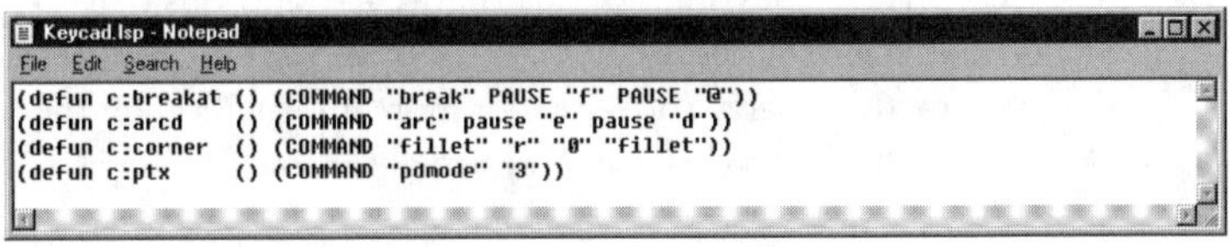

FIGURE 20.17
The contents of `Keycad.lsp`

Figure 20.17 shows the contents of a file named `Keycad.lsp`. This file contains the macro you used previously, along with several others. The other macros are commands that include optional responses. For example, the third item, `defun c:corner`, causes AutoCAD to start the Fillet command, enter an **R↵** to issue the Radius option, and finally enter a **0** for the fillet radius. Table 20.1 shows the command abbreviations and what they do.

TABLE 21.1: THE SHORTCUT KEY (COMMAND ABBREVIATIONS) MACROS PROVIDED BY THE Keycad.lsp FILE

ABBREVIATION	COMMAND OR ACTION TAKEN
`breakat`	Breaks an object at a single point
`arcd`	Draws an arc using the Start, End, Direction sequence
`corner`	Sets the fillet radius to 0; then starts the Fillet command
`ptx`	Sets the point style to be in the shape of an X

Use the Windows Notepad application and copy the listing in Figure 20.17. Give this file the name `Keycad.lsp`, and be sure you save it as an ASCII file. Then whenever you want to use these macros, you don't have to load each one individually. Instead, you load the `Keycad.lsp` file the first time you want to use one of the macros, and they're all available for the rest of the session.

Once the file is loaded, you can use any of the macros within it just by entering the macro name. For example, entering **ptx**↵ will set the point style to the shape of an X.

Macros loaded in this manner will be available to you until you exit AutoCAD. Of course, you can have these macros loaded automatically every time you start AutoCAD by including the `Keycad.lsp` file in the Startup Suite of the Load/Unload Applications dialog box. That way, you don't have to remember to load it in order to use the macros.

Now that you have some firsthand experience with AutoLISP, I hope these examples will encourage you to try learning more about this powerful tool. If you would like to discover more about AutoLISP, the book *The ABCs of AutoLISP* is included on the companion CD. This 400-page book, converted into an electronic document, is a complete resource for AutoLISP, including tutorials and example programs.

Using Third-Party Software

One of the most significant reasons for AutoCAD's popularity is its strong support for third-party software. AutoCAD is like a chameleon; it can change to suit its environment. Out of the box, AutoCAD may not fulfill the needs of some users. But by incorporating one of the more than 300 third-party add-ons, you can tailor AutoCAD to your specific needs.

This section discusses a few of the third-party add-ons that are popular today so that you'll know about some of the possibilities open to you while using AutoCAD. This section will give you an idea of the scope of third-party software. For more information on the myriad third-party tools out there, check out the Autodesk website at `www.autodesk.com`.

Custom-Tailoring AutoCAD

The needs of an architect are far different from those of a mechanical designer or a civil engineer. Third-party developers have created some specialized tools that help users of specific types of AutoCAD applications.

Many of these tools come complete with libraries of parts or symbols; AutoLISP, ADS, or ARX programs; and menus—all integrated into a single package. These packages offer added functions to AutoCAD that simplify and speed up the AutoCAD user's work. For example, most AEC (architectural or engineering construction) add-ons offer utilities for drawing walls, inserting doors and windows, and creating schedules. These functions can be performed with the stock AutoCAD package but usually require a certain amount of effort. Certainly, if you have the time, you can create your own system of symbols, AutoLISP programs, and menus, and often this is the best way of molding AutoCAD to your needs. However, when users want a ready-made solution, these add-ons are invaluable.

TIP *The companion CD includes a basic AEC add-on called AEC On-Screen. This add-on provides the basic tools for creating architectural CAD drawings, as well as some great utilities for your everyday use.*

Specialized third-party add-ons are available for AEC, mechanical, civil engineering, piping, mapping, finite element analysis, numeric control, GIS, and many other applications. They can save you a good deal of frustration and time, especially if you find just the right one for your environment. Like so many things, however, third-party add-ons can't be all things to all people. It is likely that no matter which add-on you purchase, you will find something lacking. When you're considering custom add-ons, make sure that there is some degree of flexibility in the package so that if you don't like something, you can change it or add to it later.

Check with your AutoCAD dealer for information about third-party add-ons. Most AutoCAD dealers carry the more popular offerings. You might also want to get involved with a user group in your area.

Third-Party Product Information on the World Wide Web

The World Wide Web is another good place to start looking for third-party add-ons. In particular, you will want to take a look at the Autodesk Partner Products and Resource website at `http://partnerproducts.autodesk.com/catalog/default.asp`. While you're at it, you might want to check out the other options on the Help ➢ Online Resources cascading menu. It offers links to support, technical bulletins, upgrades, and other valuable information.

Autodesk's Own Offerings

Autodesk also offers a wide variety of add-ons to AutoCAD, from simple symbols libraries to full-blown, industry-specific applications. There are offerings for architecture, civil, mechanical, mapping, data management, and 3D visualization. Check out the Autodesk website for full details.

Getting the Latest Information from Online Services

Many resources are available for the AutoCAD user. Perhaps the most useful resources are today's popular online services and in AutoCAD-related newsgroups. If you don't already subscribe to one, you would do well to explore the AutoCAD newsgroups, departments, or forums on online services.

To start with, check out the `alt.cad.autocad` newsgroup that is devoted to AutoCAD users. Next, check out the many discussion groups found on the `discussion.autodesk.com` news server.

These newsgroups offer a forum for you to discuss your AutoCAD questions and problems with other users. Most Internet browsers let you access newsgroups. For example, you can open a News window from Netscape by choosing Task ➢ Mail. From the Mail panel, right-click News, and choose Subscribe from the shortcut menu. In the Subscribe dialog box, enter **alt.cad.autocad** in the Newsgroup input box, and then click Subscribe. From then on, you can read messages, reply to posted messages, or post your questions. Note that not all news servers have access to `alt.cad.autocad`.

To get to the Autodesk discussion groups, open your web browser and enter **discussion.autodesk.com**. At the Discussion Groups page, select the topic you are interested in.

As mentioned earlier, *Cadalyst* and *Cadence*, the two North American magazines devoted to AutoCAD, both have their own websites. Also, check out the Sybex website at `www.sybex.com` for the latest information on more great books on AutoCAD. Finally, visit my own site—`www.omura.com`—for information concerning this and other books, files, and links to other AutoCAD resources.

If You Want to Experiment...

Try to think of some other keyboard macros you would like to create. For example, you might try to create a macro that copies and rotates an object at the same time. This operation is a fairly common one that can be performed using the grip edit options, but you can reduce the number of steps needed to copy and rotate by creating a macro. Review the "Creating Keyboard Macros with AutoLISP" section for help.

Here are some hints to get you started:

- Use the Copy command to copy an object in place.
- Use the same coordinate, such as 0,0, for the base point and the second point.
- Use the Last Selection option to rotate the last object selected, which happens to be the original object that was copied.

Chapter 21

Integrating AutoCAD into Your Projects and Organization

AutoCAD offers a high degree of flexibility and customization, allowing you to tailor the software's look and feel to your requirements. In this chapter, you will see how you can customize AutoCAD so that it integrates more smoothly into your workgroup and office environment.

The first part of the chapter shows how you can adapt AutoCAD to fit your particular needs. You will learn how to customize AutoCAD by modifying its menus, and you'll learn how to create custom macros for commands that your workgroup uses frequently.

We'll then take a look at some general issues that arise when you use AutoCAD in an office. In this discussion you may find help with some problems you have encountered when using AutoCAD in your particular work environment. I'll also discuss how to manage AutoCAD projects.

Topics in this chapter include the following:

- Customizing Toolbars
- Adding Your Own Pull-Down Menu
- Understanding the Diesel Macro Language
- Creating Custom Line Types
- Creating Hatch Patterns
- If You Want to Experiment...

Customizing Toolbars

The most direct way to adapt AutoCAD to your way of working is to customize the toolbars. AutoCAD offers new users an easy route to customization through the Customize dialog box. With the Customize dialog box, you can create new toolbars, customize tools, and even create new icons. You can also create keyboard shortcuts. In this section, you'll discover how easy it is to add menu and toolbar features to AutoCAD.

Getting Familiar with the Customize Dialog Box

Throughout this book, you've used the toolbar shortcut menu to open toolbars that are normally closed. You may have noticed the Customize option at the bottom of the toolbar shortcut menu. This Customize option is the doorway to customizing toolbars. Let's take a look at what it has to offer:

1. Right-click the Draw toolbar and then choose Customize from the shortcut menu to open the Customize dialog box.

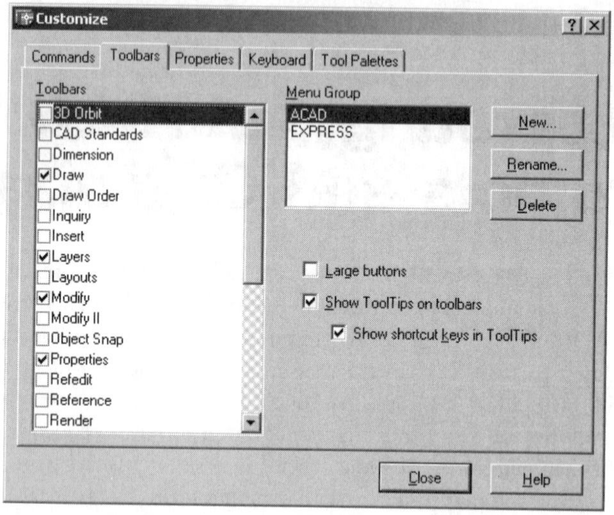

2. Click the Toolbars tab. You see a Toolbars list to the left and a Menu Group list to the right. You'll learn about menu groups in the "Adding Your Own Pull-Down Menu" section later in this chapter.
3. In the Toolbars list, click the Inquiry check box to display the Inquiry toolbar. (You may have to move the Customize dialog box to see the Inquiry toolbar.)

As you have just seen, you can use the Customize dialog box to open a toolbar, but toolbars behave in a different way when you have the Customize dialog box open, as you'll see in the next set of steps:

1. Click the Distance tool in the Inquiry toolbar to open the Customize dialog box at the Button Properties tab. You see the properties of the Distance tool.

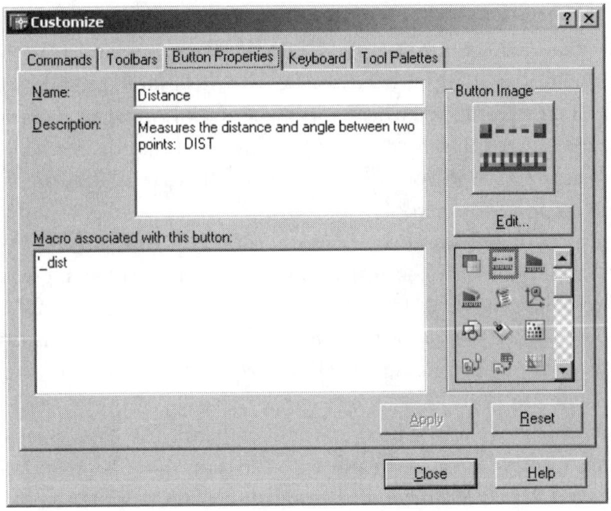

2. Click the Line tool in the Drawing toolbar. The information in the Button Properties tab changes to show you the properties of the Line tool.

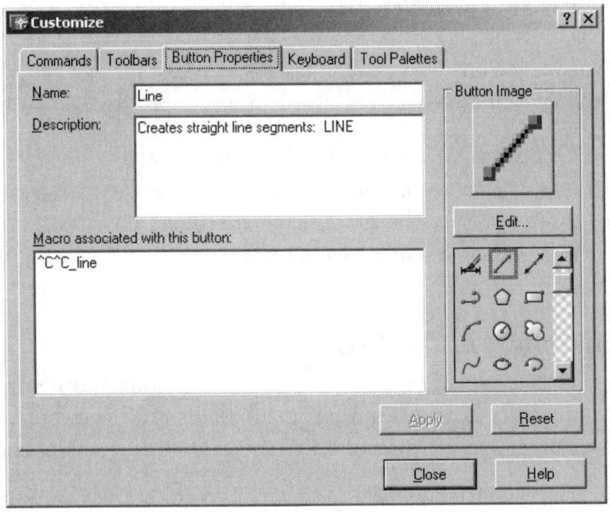

3. Click the Close button to close the Customize dialog box.

As you can see from this exercise, when you click tools in the Customize dialog box, they display their properties instead of performing their usual function. This allows you to change the tools' behavior and appearance.

UNDERSTANDING THE BUTTON PROPERTIES TAB

Let's take a moment to look at the contents of the Button Properties tab. At the top, you see the name of the tool in an input box. You can use this Name input box to create a custom tool tip. Right now, it shows the word *Line*, which appears as a tool tip when you point to the Line tool.

Below the Name input box is the Description input box. Here you can enter a full description of the tool. The description you enter appears in the status bar at the bottom of the AutoCAD window whenever you point to the tool.

The heart of the Button Properties tab is the Macro Associated With This Button input box. This input box contains the explicit instructions that AutoCAD is to execute when the tool is selected. For the Line tool, you see `^C^C_line`. The two `^C`s are a special AutoCAD menu notation indicating the Escape key. In other words, the presence of the `^C`s in the macro is the same as pressing the Escape key. Two are used to ensure that AutoCAD returns to the command prompt even if it is in the middle of another command.

The two `^C`s are followed by the `line` command. You enter this command in the macro just as you would enter it through the keyboard, with the exception of the underline at the beginning. The underline is a special AutoCAD menu notation that ensures that the command is understood by any language version of AutoCAD. You could leave it out if you are certain that you will not be using your macro on a foreign-language version of AutoCAD.

Finally, to the right on the Button Properties tab, you see an enlarged version of the tool icon. Just below the icon, you see a set of predefined icons. When you create your own custom tools, you can select an icon from the set of predefined ones, or you can select the Edit key to create your own custom icon.

Now you've seen how you can gain access to the properties of existing tools. In the next section, you'll learn how you can create new toolbars and tools.

TIP *Typically, AutoCAD stores new toolbars and buttons in the* `Acad.mns` *file (see "The Windows Menu Files" sidebar later in this chapter). You can also store them in your custom menu files. Once you've created and loaded your menu file, as described in the section "Adding Your Own Pull-Down Menu" later in this chapter, choose your menu from the Menu Group list in the Toolbars tab of the Customize dialog box.*

Creating Your Own Toolbar

You may find that instead of using one toolbar or flyout, you are moving from flyout to flyout from a variety of toolbars. If you keep track of the tools you use most frequently, you can create your own custom toolbar containing your favorite tools. Here's how it's done:

1. Right-click any icon in any toolbar, and then choose Customize from the shortcut menu to open the Customize dialog box.
2. Click the Toolbars tab, and then click the New button to open the New Toolbar dialog box.

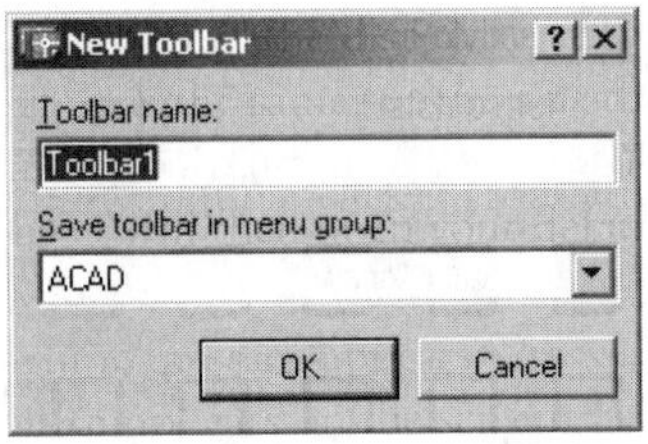

3. Enter **My Toolbar** in the Toolbar Name input box, and then click OK. A small, blank toolbar appears in the AutoCAD window. (You may need to move the Customize dialog box to view the new toolbar.)

Notice that ACAD appears in the Menu Group list box and My Toolbar now appears in the Toolbars list box. You can now begin to add buttons to your toolbar.

4. In the Customize dialog box, click the Commands tab and look at the Categories list. Notice that it contains the names of menus in the AutoCAD menu bar.
5. Choose Draw from the list. The Commands list box to the right displays all the tools available for the Draw pull-down menu. If you scroll down the Commands list, you'll notice that it offers several additional arc and circle tools not found in the Draw toolbar.
6. Click the first tool at the top of the list: the Line tool. You'll see a description of the tool in the Description box below the Categories list box. You'll also see a tip in the lower-right corner telling you what you can do with the selected option.
7. Click and drag the Line tool from the Commands list into the new toolbar you just created. The Line tool now appears in your toolbar.
8. Click and drag the Arc Start End Direction tool to your new toolbar. You will have to scroll down the Commands list to get to Arc Start End Direction.

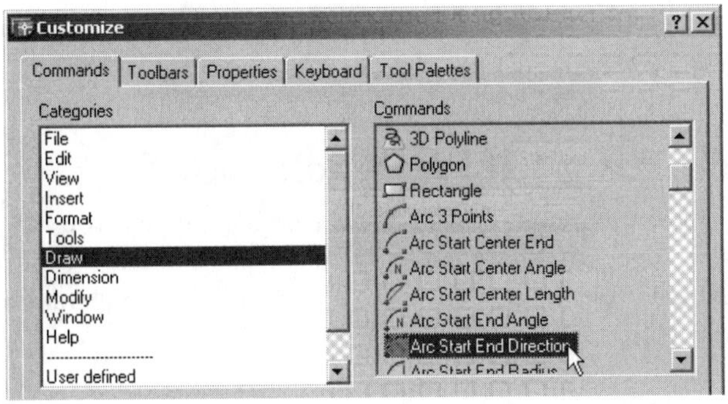

9. Close the Customize dialog box.

You now have a custom toolbar with two buttons. You can add buttons from different categories if you like. You are not restricted to buttons in one category.

TIP *If you need to remove a tool from your toolbar, click and drag it out of your toolbar into the blank area of the drawing. Do this while the Customize dialog box is open.*

AutoCAD treats your custom toolbar just like any other toolbar. It appears when you start AutoCAD and remains until you close it. You can recall it using the steps in the first exercise in this section.

Opening Toolbars from the Command Line

Opening toolbars from the command line can be especially helpful if you want to create toolbar buttons that open other toolbars.

1. At the command prompt, type **–Toolbar**↵. (Don't forget to include the minus sign at the beginning of the Toolbar command.)
2. At the `Enter toolbar Name or [All]:` prompt, enter the name of the toolbar you want to open.
3. At the `Enter an option [Show/Hide/Left/Right/Top/Bottom/Float] <Show>:` prompt, press ↵. The toolbar appears on the screen.

A typical button macro for opening a toolbar might look like this:

```
^c^cToolbar[space]inquiry[space][space]
```

Here, the `[space]` is added for clarity. You would press the spacebar in its place. This example shows a macro that opens the inquiry toolbar. You can use the name that is shown in the toolbar shortcut menu to specify the name of the toolbar in the command-line version of the Toolbar command. For compound names like `Object Snap`, you need to add an underline between the two words in the name like `Object_Snap`.

As the prompt in step 3 indicates, you can specify the location of the toolbar by left, right, top, or bottom. Float lets you specify the location and number of rows for the toolbar.

Customizing Toolbar Tools

Now let's move on to more serious customization. Suppose you want to create an entirely new button with its own functions. For example, you might want to create a set of buttons that will insert your favorite symbols. Or you might want to create a toolbar containing a set of tools that open some the other toolbars that are normally "put away."

Creating a Custom Button

In the following set of exercises, you'll create a button that inserts a door symbol. You'll add your custom button to the toolbar you just created:

1. Right-click any tool in a toolbar and choose Customize from the shortcut menu to open the Customize dialog box again.
2. Make sure the Commands tab is selected, and then select the User Defined option at the bottom of the Categories list. The options in the Commands list will change to two items: User Defined Button and User Defined Flyout.
3. Click and drag the User Defined Button option from the Commands list to your new toolbar. A blank space, which is actually a button, is added to your toolbar.
4. Click the blank space in your new toolbar. The Button Properties tab is automatically selected in the Customize dialog box, and you see the properties of your new tool.

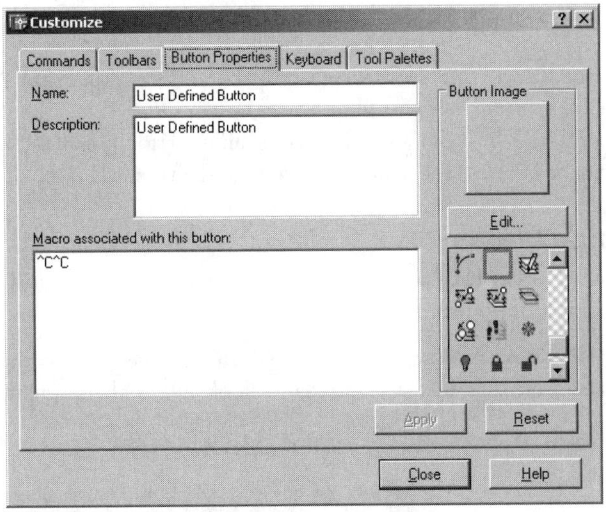

When you were first introduced to this tab, you saw the properties for the Distance and Line tools. Now you see User Defined Button in both the Name and Description input boxes, a blank icon in the Button Image group, and two `^C`s in the Macro Associated With This Button input box. This tells you that the blank tool is waiting for you to add your own properties to it.

Now let's go ahead and add a macro and new icon to this tool.

1. In the Name input box, enter **Door**. This will be your tool tip for this button.
2. In the Description input box, enter **Inserts a single door**. This will be the help message for this button.
3. In the Macro Associated With This Button input box, enter **^C^C–insert door**.

Make sure you include the minus sign before **insert**. This indicates that you want to use the command-line version of the Insert command.

TIP *You can put any valid string of keystrokes in the Macro Associated With This Button input box, including AutoLISP functions. See* The ABCs of AutoLISP *on the companion CD for more on AutoLISP. You can also include pauses for user input using the backslash (\) character. See the "Pausing for User Input" section later in this chapter.*

Note that the two `^Cs` already appear in the Macro Associated With This Button input box. These represent two Cancels being issued, which is the same as pressing the Esc key twice. It ensures that when the macro starts, it cancels any unfinished commands. If you don't need the two `^Cs`, you can delete them as in the case of transparent commands. You follow the two Cancels with the Insert command as it is issued from the keyboard.

WARNING *It is important that you enter the exact sequence of keystrokes that follow the command; otherwise, your macro can get out of step with the command prompts. This will take a little practice and some going back and forth between testing your button and editing the macro.*

After the Insert command, there is a space, and then the name `Door` appears. This is the same sequence of keystrokes you enter at the command line to insert the door drawing you created in Chapters 2 and 3. You can go on to include an insertion point, a scale factor, and a rotation angle in this macro, but these options are better left for the time when the door is actually inserted.

Creating a Custom Icon

You have all the essential parts of the button defined. Now you just need to create a custom icon to go with your Door button.

1. Take a look at the scroll box in the Button Image group containing the icons. Notice that a blank button is currently selected. It looks like a blank square box in the lower-left corner.
2. Click the Edit button to open the Button Editor dialog box.

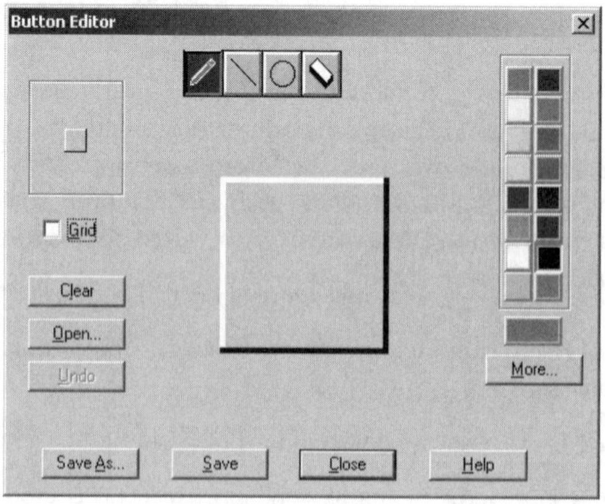

TIP *If you prefer, you can use any of the predefined icons in the scroll box. Just click the icon you want to use, and then click Apply.*

The Button Editor is like a simple drawing program. Across the top are the tools to draw lines, circles, and points, as well as an eraser. Along the right side, you see a color toolbar from which you can choose colors for your icon. In the upper left, you see a preview of your button. The following describes the rest of the options:

Grid Turns a grid on and off in the drawing area. This grid can be an aid in drawing your icon.

Clear Erases the entire contents of the drawing area.

Undo Undoes the last operation you performed.

Open Opens a .bmp file to import an icon. The .bmp file must be small enough to fit in the 16 × 16 pixel matrix provided for icons (24 × 24 for large-format icons).

Save As Saves your icon as a .bmp file under a name you enter.

Save Saves your icon under a name that AutoCAD provides, usually a series of numbers and letters.

Close Exits the Button Editor.

Help Displays helpful information about the features of the Button Editor.

Now let's continue by creating a new icon:

3. Draw the door icon shown here. Don't worry if it's not perfect; you can always go back and fix it.

4. Click Save, and then click Close.
5. In the Button Properties tab, click Apply. You'll see the icon appear in the button in your toolbar.
6. Now click the Close button in the Customize dialog box.
7. Click the Door icon on your new toolbar. The door appears in your drawing ready to be placed.

WARNING *The Door drawing must be in the default folder or in the* `Acad` *search path before the door button will be inserted.*

You can continue to add more buttons to your toolbar to build a toolbar of symbols. Of course, you're not limited to a symbols library. You can also incorporate your favorite macros or even AutoLISP routines that you accumulate as you work with AutoCAD. The possibilities are endless.

Now suppose you've decided that the Door tool is not what you wanted. Here's a quick way to clear the properties of a button.

1. Open the Customize dialog box again. By now, you should know how to do this.
2. Click the Door tool in your custom toolbar.
3. Right-click the Door tool, and then choose Reset from the shortcut menu.

Notice that the Button Properties settings revert to the previous settings when you first added the new tool. You can also reset the tool properties by clicking the Reset button in the lower-right corner of the Button Properties tab, but here we've shown you that right-clicking a button offers some additional options when the Customize dialog box is open. The options in the shortcut menu you saw in step 3 are self-explanatory except for the Begin A Group option. This option adds a vertical bar to the toolbar to act as a visual divider between buttons. Let's see how this works:

1. Right-click the blank tool in your custom toolbar, and then choose Begin A Group. Notice that a vertical line now appears to the left of the button.

2. Right-click the blank tool again. You now see a checkmark to the left of the Begin A Group option.
3. Select Begin A Group again. The line disappears.
4. You don't need a blank tool in your toolbar, so click and drag the blank tool into the drawing area to delete it. You then see a message asking if you are sure you want to delete the user-defined button from your toolbar. Go ahead and click OK.

Setting the Properties of Flyouts

Just as you added a new button to your toolbar, you can also add flyouts. Remember that a flyout is really just another form of a toolbar. This next example shows how you can add a copy of the Zoom toolbar to your custom toolbar and then adjust the properties of the flyout.

1. Click the Line tool in the toolbar you just finished to open the Customize dialog box at the Button Properties tab.
2. Click the Commands tab, and then click the User Defined option at the bottom of the Categories list.
3. Click and drag the User Defined Flyout option from the Commands list box in the Customize dialog box to your custom toolbar.

You now have a blank flyout to which you can assign any existing toolbar. Let's see what options are available for flyout buttons:

1. Click the blank flyout that you just added to your toolbar. You see a message telling you that you need to associate a toolbar with this flyout.
2. Click OK. The Customize dialog box switches to the Flyout Properties tab.

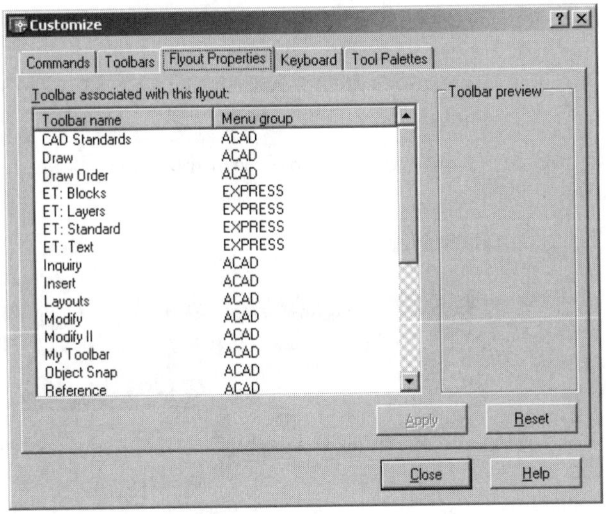

Notice that the Flyout Properties tab has replaced the Button Properties tab and that it contains a different layout.

3. Scroll down the Toolbar Associated With This Flyout list and then select Zoom. You see a preview of the selected toolbar in the right side of the dialog box.
4. Click Apply. The blank flyout you added to your toolbar changes to the Zoom flyout.
5. Click the Close button to close the Customize dialog box.

TIP *To delete a button from a toolbar, open the Customize dialog box and then click and drag the tool you want to delete away from the toolbar.*

Now if you click and drag the flyout that you just added to your toolbar, you'll see that it contains the same Zoom tools found in the Standard toolbar.

So now you've seen how you can create your own custom toolbar, and you've seen how to add new and existing tools. Although you used your own custom toolbar in these exercises, you can also add and remove buttons and flyouts to existing toolbars.

TIP *If you decide that you want to delete a toolbar entirely, click the Toolbars tab in the Customize dialog box, select the toolbar from the Toolbars list, and then click the Delete button.*

Creating Keyboard Shortcuts

The last feature that we'll explore in the Customize dialog box is the Keyboard tab. The Keyboard tab lets you create keyboard shortcuts for any tool, command, or menu option. AutoCAD already has a set of shortcuts that you see displayed in the pull-down menus, usually to the right of the menu option. For example, if you open the File menu from the menu bar, you see that the New option shows a Ctrl+N to the right. This means that, if you prefer, you can use the Ctrl+N keystroke combination to open the New File dialog box. You can add other control key shortcuts to other commands using the Customize dialog box.

Try the following exercise to see how you can set up a shortcut for the Endpoint Osnap option. The first step is to locate the command for the shortcut:

1. Right-click any toolbar and choose Customize from the shortcut menu to open the Customize dialog box.
2. Click the Keyboard tab.

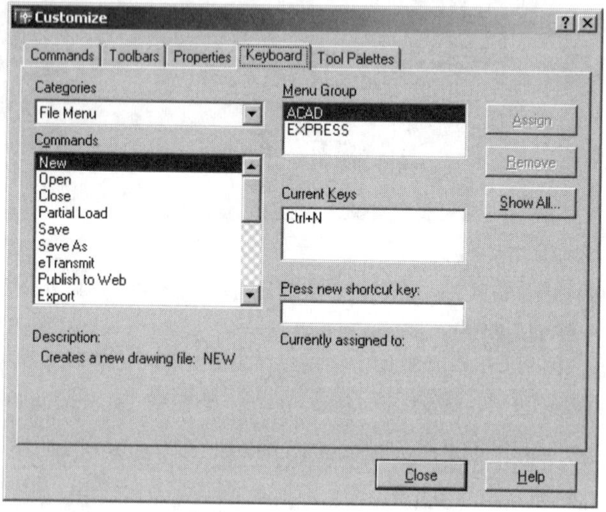

3. Open the Categories drop-down list. You'll notice that it is divided into two groups. The first group lists the options in the menu bar; the second group lists the toolbars.
4. Scroll down the list until you find Object Snap Toolbar and select it. The Commands list, just below the Categories drop-down list, shows the names of the tools in the Object Snap Toolbar.
5. Select Snap To Endpoint from the Commands list. You see a description of the command you selected just below the Commands list.

You've located the Endpoint Osnap. Now you can associate a shortcut key with the command. The shortcut key must start with a Ctrl key, as in Ctrl+N for the New File dialog box. Let's try a couple of shortcuts to see what happens:

1. Click in the Press New Shortcut Key input box and then press Ctrl+E. The Ctrl+E appears in the input box, but you also see a message just below the input box that warns you that Ctrl+E is already assigned to something. (It cycles through the isometric planes.)

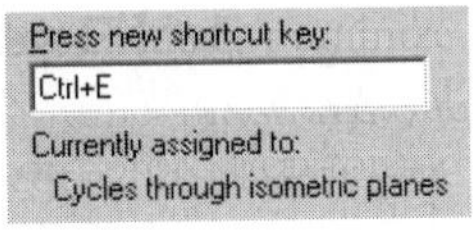

2. Press the Backspace key to remove this shortcut.
3. Press Ctrl+Shift+E. The Ctrl+Shift+E appears in the input box, and the message shows that the shortcut you've indicated is unassigned.

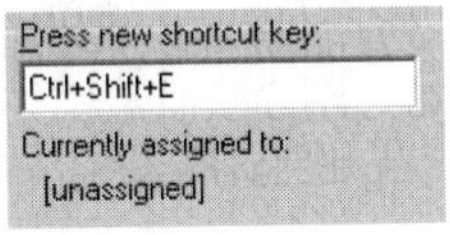

4. Since you know that the Ctrl+Shift+E shortcut is unassigned, go ahead and click Assign in the upper-right corner of the dialog box. The shortcut now appears in the Current Keys list box.
5. Click Close, and then press Ctrl+Shift+E. You'll see `Endp Osnap` appear in the command line along with a message that the Endp is an unknown command. You get this message because Endp is valid only while selecting points.
6. Right-click a toolbar tool and choose Object Snap to open the Object Snap toolbar.
7. Place your cursor on the Snap To Endpoint tool and look at the tool tip. It now shows the Ctrl+Shift+E option.

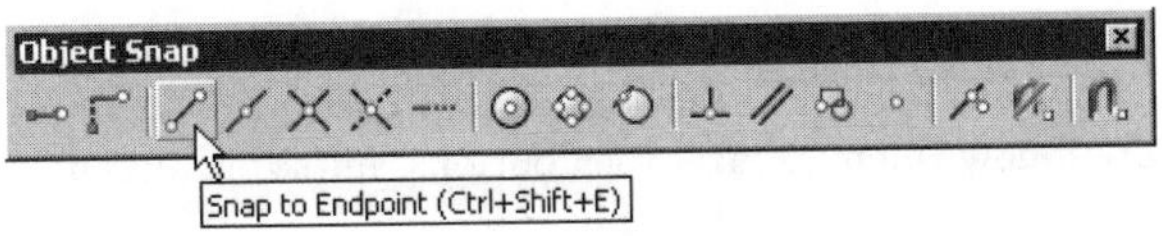

Shortcut keys are great for those options that you use frequently. Perhaps the most commonly used Windows shortcuts are Ctrl+C for Copy, Ctrl+V for Paste, and Ctrl+X for Cut. You won't want to redefine those shortcuts in AutoCAD because you may find them useful for copying, pasting, and cutting objects in AutoCAD.

Several other shortcuts are also built into AutoCAD. Although you are creating shortcuts with the Customize dialog box, you can get a quick list of the existing shortcuts by clicking the Show All button in the Keyboard tab. The Shortcut Keys dialog box appears, listing all the existing AutoCAD shortcut keys that are currently active.

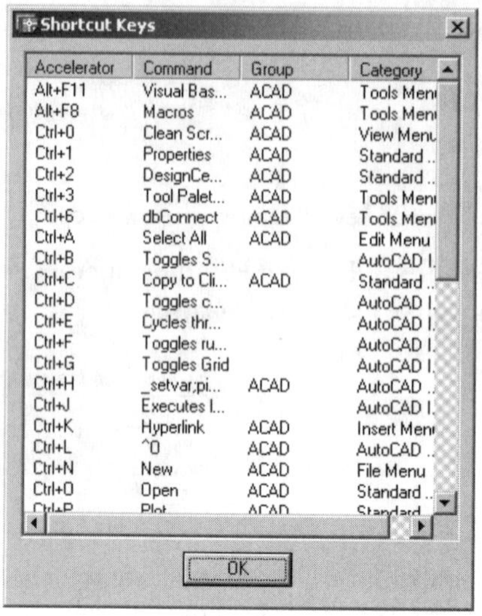

THE WINDOWS MENU FILES

The new toolbars you create are stored in an AutoCAD menu file. This file describes the menus and toolbars in a plain-text format. AutoCAD employs several files to store the menu information. You'll learn how to create custom menu files in the "Adding Your Own Pull-Down Menu" section later in this chapter.

Here's a brief rundown of those menu files:

Acad.mnu The source text file that contains the information required to build the AutoCAD menu. If you are a programmer, you can use this file to customize the AutoCAD menu in detail. Here, you can edit the pull-down menus, image tiles, buttons, and so on. Most users won't have a need to edit this file.

Acad.mnc AutoCAD's translation of the Acad.mnu file. AutoCAD translates, or compiles, the Acad.mnu file so that it can read the menu faster.

Acad.mns A text file created by AutoCAD that contains the source information from the .mnu file plus additional comments. This file is rewritten whenever an .mnu file is loaded. If you make changes or additions to toolbars, you'll want to keep a backup copy of this file to preserve those changes. You can use the Acad.mns file as you would use an Acad.mnu file as a source text file to build the AutoCAD menu.

Acad.mnr The menu resource file. This is a binary file that contains the bitmap images used for buttons and other graphics.

As you create or edit icon buttons and toolbars, AutoCAD first adds your custom items to the Acad.mns file. It then compiles this file into the Acad.mnc and Acad.mnr files for quicker access to the menus. If you reload the .mnu version of your menu, AutoCAD re-creates the .mns file, thereby removing any toolbar customization you may have done.

Continued on next page

THE WINDOWS MENU FILES *(continued)*

You need to copy the Acad.mns file to other computers in order to transfer your custom buttons and toolbars. Also, if you create your own pull-down menu files, as in the Mymenu.mnu example in this chapter, AutoCAD creates the source file and then compiles it and creates the resource files for your custom menu file. You have the option to store new toolbars in your custom menu through the Menu Group drop-down list in the New Toolbar dialog box.

Adding Your Own Pull-Down Menu

In addition to adding buttons and toolbars, AutoCAD lets you add pull-down menu options. This section looks at how you might add a custom pull-down menu to your AutoCAD environment.

Creating Your First Pull-Down Menu

Let's start by trying the following exercise to create a simple pull-down menu file called My Menu.

1. Using a text editor, such as Windows Notepad, create a file called `Mymenu.mnu`, containing the following lines:

```
***POP1
[My 1st Menu]
[Line]^c^c_line
[--]
[->More]
[Arc-SED]^c^c_arc \_e \_d
[<-Break At]^c^c(defun c:breakat ()+
(command "break" pause "f" pause "@")+
);breakat
[Fillet 0]^c^c_fillet r 0;;
[Point Style X]'pdmode 3
***POP2
[My 2nd Menu]
[door]^c^cInsert door
[Continue Line]^C^CLINE;;
```

2. Save this file, and be sure you place it in your `\AutoCAD2004\Support\` folder.

WARNING *Pay special attention to the spaces between letters in the commands described in this chapter. (You need not worry about whether to type uppercase or lowercase letters.)*

WARNING *The Breakat menu item uses AutoLISP which is not supported by LT. It is used in the example to show AutoCAD 2004 users that AutoLISP can be embeded in the menu.*

Once you've stored the file, you have your first custom pull-down menu. You may have noticed some familiar items among the lines you entered. The menu contains the Line and Arc commands. It also contains the Breakat macro you worked on in the previous chapter; this time, that macro is broken into shorter lines.

Now let's see how My Menu works in AutoCAD.

Loading a Menu

In the following exercise, you will load the menu you just created and test it. The procedure described here for loading menus is the same for all menus, regardless of their source:

1. Choose Tools ➢ Customize ➢ Menus to open the Menu Customization dialog box.

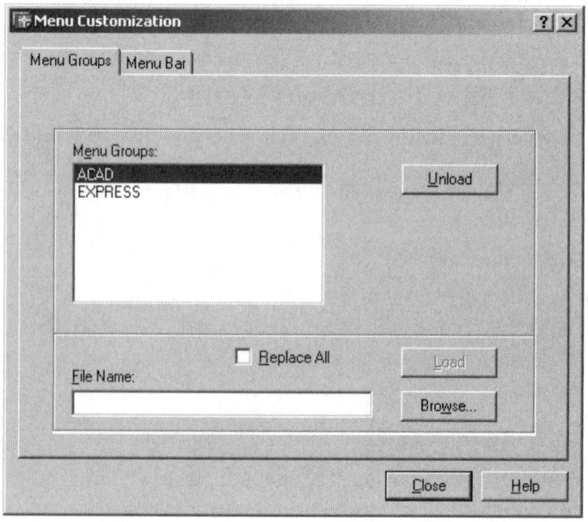

2. Make sure that the Menu Groups tab is selected. Then click Browse to open the Select Menu File dialog box.
3. Click the Files Of Type drop-down list, and then select Menu Template (*.mnu).
4. Locate the `Mymenu.mnu` file, highlight it, and then click Open. You return to the Menu Customization dialog box.
5. Click Load. You see a warning message telling you that you will lose any toolbar customization you have made. This refers only to the specific menu you are loading. Since you haven't made any toolbar customization changes to your menu, you won't lose anything.
6. Click Yes. The warning dialog box closes, and you see the name of your menu group in the Menu Groups list box.
7. Click the Menu Bar tab. The dialog box changes to show two lists.

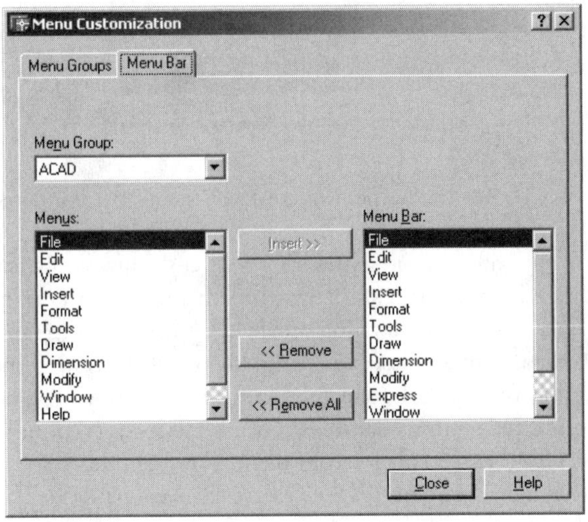

On the left is the name of the current menu group. The list on the right shows the currently available pull-down menus.

8. Click the Menu Group drop-down list, and then select MYMENU. The names of the pull-down menus in your menu file appear.
9. Highlight Help in the column on the right. This tells AutoCAD that you want to add your pull-down menu in front of the Help pull-down menu.
10. Highlight My 1st Menu in the list on the left, and then click the Insert button. My 1st Menu moves into the column on the right, and it appears in the AutoCAD menu bar.

11. Highlight My 2nd Menu from the list on the left, and then click Insert again. My 2nd Menu is copied to the column on the right, and it also appears in the menu bar.

12. Close the Menu Customization dialog box.
13. Draw a line on the screen, and then choose My 1st Menu ➢ More ➢ Break At.

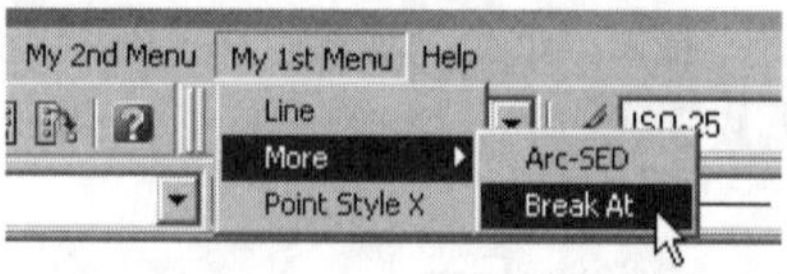

With just a 15-line menu file, you created a menu that contains virtually every tool used to build menus.

In step 5, you saw a warning message about customization changes. When you load an AutoCAD .mnu file, AutoCAD creates a set of new files that it uses to work with your menu. These files have the extensions .mns, .mnr, and .mnc. You usually don't have to worry about the .mnr and .mnc files because AutoCAD manages these files. However, when you load your .mnu file for the first time, AutoCAD creates and uses the .mns file, which is a reformatted copy of your .mnu file. This reformatted file contains additional sections AutoCAD needs for its operation. For this reason, you should make changes and edit the .mns file for your menu. For example, if you want to make additional changes to your Mymenu menu, edit `Mymenu.mns` rather than `Mymenu.mnu`. This way, if you add custom toolbars or custom keyboard macros, you won't lose them when you make changes to your menu file.

Now let's take a more detailed look at how menu files work.

How the Pull-Down Menu Works

Let's take a closer look at the `Mymenu.mns` file. The first item in the file, `***POP1`, identifies the beginning of a pull-down menu. The text just below the first line is `My 1st Menu` enclosed in square brackets. This is the title of the pull-down menu; this text appears in the toolbar. Every pull-down menu must have this title element.

Following the title, each item in the list starts with a word enclosed in brackets; these words are the options that actually appear when you open the pull-down menu. If you were to remove everything else, you would have the menu as it appears on the screen. The text that follows the item in brackets conveys instructions to AutoCAD about the option.

Finally, in the My 1st Menu sample, you see `***POP2`. This is the beginning of a second pull-down menu. Again, you must follow this with a pull-down menu title in square brackets. Below the title, you can add other menu options.

CALLING COMMANDS

Now look at the `Line` option in the `Mymenu.mnu` listing. The two Ctrl+C (`^C`) elements that follow the square brackets cancel any command that is currently operative. The `Line` command follows, written just as it would be entered through the keyboard. Two Cancels are issued in case you are in a command that has two levels, such as the Edit Vertex option of the Pedit command (Modify ➢ Object ➢ Polyline).

The underscore character (_) that precedes the `Line` command tells AutoCAD that you are using the English-language version of this command. This feature lets you program non-English versions of AutoCAD using the English-language command names.

You might also notice that there is no space between the second `^C` and the `Line` command. A space in the line would be the same as ↵. If there were a space between these two elements, ↵ would be entered between the last `^C` and the `Line` command, causing the command sequence to misstep. Another way to indicate ↵ is by using the semicolon, as in the following example:

```
[Continue Line]^C^CLINE;;
```

TIP *If a menu macro contains multiple instances of* ↵, using semicolons instead of spaces can help make your macro more readable.

In this sample menu option, the `Line` command is issued, and then an additional ↵ is added. The effect of choosing this option is a line that continues from the last line entered into your drawing. The two semicolons following `Line` tell AutoCAD to start the Line command and then issue ↵ twice to begin a line from the endpoint of the last line entered. (AutoCAD automatically issues a single ↵ at the end of a menu line. In this case, however, you want two instances of ↵, so they must be represented as semicolons.)

PAUSING FOR USER INPUT

Another symbol used in the menu file is the backslash (\); it is used when a pause is required for user input. For example, selecting the `Arc-SED` option in My 1st Menu starts the Arc command and then pauses for your input.

```
[Arc-SED]^c^c_arc \_e \_d
```

TIP *The underscore character (_) that precedes the command name and option input tells AutoCAD that you are entering the English-language version of these commands.*

The space between `^c^c_arc` and the backslash (\) represents pressing the spacebar. The backslash indicates a pause to allow you to select the starting endpoint for the arc. Once you have picked a point, the `_e` represents the selection of the Endpoint option under the Arc command. A second backslash allows another point selection. Finally, the `_d` represents the selection of the Direction option. Figure 21.1 illustrates this. If you want the last character in a menu item to be a backslash, you must follow the backslash with a semicolon.

FIGURE 21.1

The execution of the Arc menu item

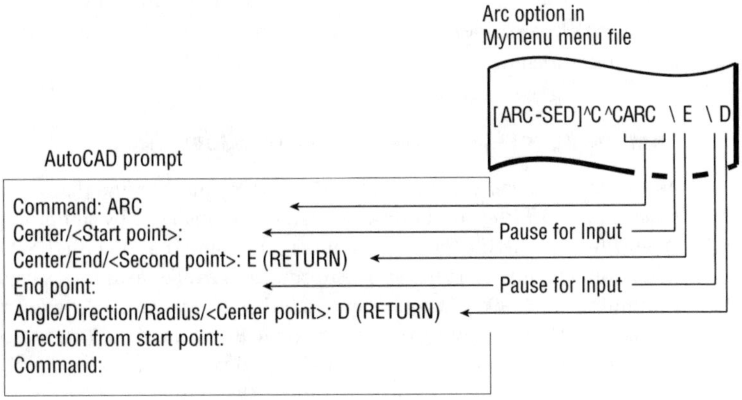

USING THE PLUS SIGN FOR LONG LINES

As you browse through the `Acad.mnu` file, notice that many of the lines end with a plus sign (+). The length of each line in the menu file is limited to about 80 characters, but you can break a line into two or more lines by adding a plus sign at the end of the line that continues, like this:

```
 [<-Break At]^c^c(defun c:breakat ()+
(command "break" pause "f" pause "@")+
);breakat
```

TIP *It's okay to break an AutoLISP program into smaller lines. In fact, it can help you read and understand the program more easily. LT does not support AutoLISP.*

This example showed how to include the Breakat AutoLISP macro in a menu. Everything in this segment is entered just as it would be with the keyboard. The plus sign indicates the continuation of this long item to the subsequent lines, and the semicolon is used in place of ↵.

CREATING A CASCADING MENU

Look at the More option in the File pull-down menu group; it starts with these characters: ->. This is the way you indicate a menu item that opens a cascading menu. Everything that follows the `[->More]` menu item will appear in the cascading menu. To indicate the end of the cascading menu, you use the characters <-, as in the `[<-Rotate90]` menu item farther down. Anything beyond this <- item appears in the main part of the menu. If the last item in a cascading menu is also the last item in the menu group, you must use <-<-, as in `[<-<-.XZ]`.

PLACING DIVISION LINES AND DIMMED TEXT IN PULL-DOWN MENUS

Two symbols are used to place dividing lines in your pull-down menus. One is the *double-hyphen* symbol (--). This is used to divide groups of items in a menu; it will expand to fill the entire width of the pull-down menu with a line of hyphens. The other option is the *tilde* symbol (~). If the tilde precedes a bracketed option name, that option will be dimmed when displayed; when clicked, it will have no effect. You have probably encountered these dimmed options on various pull-down menus in the programs you use. When you see a dimmed menu item, it usually means that the option is not valid under the current command.

LOADING AUTOLISP MACROS WITH YOUR SUBMENU

As you become a more advanced AutoCAD user, you may find that you want many of your own AutoLISP macros to load with your menus. You can accomplish this by combining all your AutoLISP macros into a single file. Give this file the same name as your menu file but with the .mnl filename extension. Such a file will automatically load with its menu counterpart. For example, say you have a file called `Mymenu.mnl` containing the Breakat AutoLISP macro. Whenever you load `Mymenu.mns`, `Mymenu.mnl` is automatically loaded along with it, giving you access to the Breakat macro. This is a good way to manage and organize any AutoLISP program code you want to include with a menu.

Earlier in this chapter, you learned how to include a help message with a button. The help message appears in the status bar of the AutoCAD window when you highlight an option. You can also include a help message with a pull-down menu item.

First, you must give your pull-down menu file a menu group name. This helps AutoCAD isolate your file and its help messages from other menus that might be loaded along with yours. To give your menu file a group name, add the following line at the top of the file:

```
***MENUGROUP=MYMENU
```

in which **MYMENU** is the name you want for your menu group name.

Next, you have to add an ID name to each menu item that requires a help message. The following shows how this might be done for the My 1st Menu example you used earlier:

```
***MENUGROUP=MYMENU
***POP1
[My 1st Menu]
ID_1line    [Line]^c^c_line
[--]
[->More]
ID_1arc-sed [Arc-SED]^c^c_arc \_e \_d
ID_1breakat [<-Break At]^c^c(defun c:breakat ()+
(command "break" pause "f" pause "@")+
);breakat
ID_1fillet0 [Fillet 0]^c^c_fillet r 0;;
ID_1pointx  [Point Style X]'pdmode 3
***POP2
[My 2nd Menu]
[door]^c^cInsert door
[Continue Line]^C^CLINE;;
```

The ID name starts with the characters `ID` followed by an underscore character (_) and then the name for the menu item. Several spaces are added so that the menu items align for clarity. Each menu item must have a unique ID name.

Finally, you add a section at the end of your file called `***HELPSTRINGS`. For this example, it would look like the following code:

```
***HELPSTRINGS
ID_1line    [Draws a line]
ID_1arc-sed [Draws an arc with start, end, direction]
ID_1breakat [Breaks an object at a single point]
ID_1fillet0 [Sets the Fillet radius to zero]
ID_1pointx  [Sets the Point style to an X]
```

The menu item ID names are duplicated exactly, followed by several spaces, and then the actual text you want in the status bar, enclosed in brackets. The spaces between the ID and the text are for clarity.

WARNING *The ID names are case-sensitive, so make sure they match up in both the* `HELPSTRINGS` *section and in the menu section.*

Once you've done this and then loaded the menu file, you will see these same messages appear in the status bar when these menu options are highlighted. In fact, if you browse your `Acad.mnu` file, you will see similar ID names. If you prefer, you can use numbers in place of names.

Creating Accelerator Keys

In the "Customizing Toolbars" section earlier in this chapter, you saw how you can add shortcut keys using the Customize dialog box. If you prefer, you can also add shortcut keys directly into a menu file. The shortcut keys are called *accelerators* in the menu file.

To add accelerator key definitions directly to a menu file, you need to become familiar with some additional code. The following is an example of what you can add to the `Mymenu.mnu` file to define a set of accelerator keys:

```
***ACCELERATORS
[CONTROL+SHIFT+"E"]endp
[CONTROL+SHIFT+"X"]int
ID_1breakat [CONTROL+SHIFT+"B"]
```

The `***ACCELERATORS` line at the top is the group heading, similar to the `***HELPSTRINGS` heading in that it defines the beginning of the section. This is followed by the accelerator descriptions.

Two methods are shown in the previous example for defining an accelerator key. The first two bracketed text items follow the format you've already seen for the pull-down menu. But instead of the menu text in square brackets, you see the keys required to invoke the action that follows the brackets. So in the first line

```
[CONTROL+SHIFT+"E"]endp
```

the `CONTROL+SHIFT+"E"` tells AutoCAD to enter the Endpoint Osnap (`endp`) whenever the Ctrl+Shift+E key combination is pressed. Notice that the E is in quotation marks and that all the characters are uppercase. Follow this format for quotation marks and capitalization when you create your own accelerator keys.

A second method is shown in the third line:

```
ID_1breakat [CONTROL+SHIFT+"B"]
```

Here, the `ID_1breakat` is used to associate a key combination with a menu option, not unlike the way it is used to associate a menu item with a help string. This line tells AutoCAD to issue the Breakat macro listed earlier in the menu whenever the Ctrl+Shift+B key combination is pressed.

You can use either Ctrl or Shift individually or together in combination with most keys on your keyboard, including the function keys. You can also assign keys without the Ctrl or Shift options. Note that the function keys and the Esc key are already defined, so take care that you don't redefine them unless you really want to. Table 21.1 contains a list of some of the special keys you can define and how you need to specify them in the menu file.

WARNING *Although you can use the F1 and Esc keys for accelerator keys, their use is discouraged because they serve other functions for both Windows and AutoCAD.*

TABLE 21.1: KEY NAMES TO USE IN YOUR ACCELERATOR KEY DEFINITIONS

KEY	FORMAT USED IN AUTOCAD MENU
Numeric keypad	"NUMPAD0" through "NUMPAD9"
Ins	"INSERT"
Del	"DELETE"
Function keys	"F2" through "F12"
Up arrow	"UP"
Down arrow	"DOWN"
Left arrow	"LEFT"
Right arrow	"RIGHT"

Understanding the Diesel Macro Language

If you browse through the `Acad.mnu` file, you'll see many menu options that contain odd-looking text beginning with a dollar sign (`$`). In some instances, the dollar sign tells AutoCAD to open a shortcut menu. But in many cases, it is used as part of the Diesel macro language. Diesel is one of many macro languages AutoCAD supports, and you can use it to perform some simple operations. Like AutoLISP, it uses parentheses to enclose program code.

You can actually use Diesel at the AutoCAD command line using a command called Modemacro. The Modemacro command sends information to the status bar. Diesel can be used with Modemacro to perform some simple tasks. Try the following exercise to experiment with Diesel.

1. At the command prompt, type **Modemacro↵**.
2. At the `Enter new value for MODEMACRO, or . for none <" ">:` prompt, enter **$(/,25,2)↵**. You'll see the answer to the equation in the far-left side of the status bar.

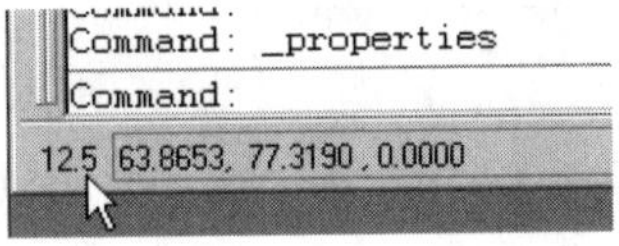

3. To clear the status bar, enter **Modemacro↵.↵**.

The equation you entered in step 2 is referred to as an *expression*. The structure of Diesel expressions is similar to that of AutoLISP. The dollar sign tells AutoCAD that the information that follows is a Diesel expression.

A Diesel expression must include an operator of some sort, followed by the items to be operated on. An *operator* is an instruction to take some specific action, such as adding two numbers together or dividing one number by another. Examples of mathematical operators include the plus sign (+) for addition and the forward slash (/) for division.

The operator is often referred to as a *function* and the items to be operated on as the *arguments* to the function or simply the arguments. So, in the expression (/,25,2), the / is the function and the 25 and 2 are the arguments. All Diesel expressions, no matter what size, follow this structure and are enclosed by parentheses.

Parentheses are important elements of an expression. All parentheses must be balanced; for each left parenthesis, there must be a right parenthesis.

You can do other things with Diesel besides performing calculations. The Getvar function is an AutoLISP function that you can use to obtain the drawing prefix and name. Try the following to see how Diesel uses Getvar.

1. Type **Modemacro**↵ again.
2. Type **$(getvar,dwgprefix)**↵. The location of the current drawing appears in the status bar.
3. Press ↵ to reissue the Modemacro command; then type **$(getvar,dwgname)**↵. Now the name of the drawing appears in the status bar.

In this example, the Getvar function extracts the drawing prefix and name and displays it in the status bar. You can use Getvar to extract any system variable you want. If you've been working through the tutorials in this book, you've seen that virtually all AutoCAD settings are also controlled through system variables. (Appendix D contains a list of all the system variables.) This can be a great tool when you are creating custom menus, because with Getvar, you can "poll" AutoCAD to determine its state. For example, you can find out what command is currently being used. Try the following exercise to see how this works.

1. Click the Line tool in the Drawing toolbar.
2. Type **'Modemacro**↵. The apostrophe at the beginning of Modemacro lets you use the command while in another command.
3. Type **$(getvar,cmdnames)**↵. The word `line` appears in the status bar, indicating that the current command is the Line command.

Diesel can be useful in a menu when you want an option to perform a specific task depending on which command is currently active.

TIP *LT users cannot use AutoLISP to find the location of AutoCAD resource files. However, you can use the Diesel macro language. For example, to find the log file path, enter* ***Modemacro*** *then* ***$(getvar,logfilepath)****. The path will be displayed in the far left of the status bar.*

Using Diesel in a Menu

So far, you've been experimenting with Diesel through the Modemacro command. To use Diesel in a menu requires a slightly different format. You still use the same Diesel format of a dollar sign followed by the expression, but you don't use the Modemacro command to access Diesel. Instead, you use `$M=`. You can think of `$M=` as an abbreviation for Modemacro.

Here's a Diesel expression that you can use in a menu:

```
[Blipmode on/off]'Blipmode $M=$(-,1,$(getvar,Blipmode))
```

This menu option turns Blipmode on or off. Blipmode is a feature that displays point selections in the drawing area as tiny crosses. These tiny crosses, or *blips* as they are called, do not print and can be cleared from the screen with a redraw. They can be helpful when you need to track your point selections.

In this example, the Blipmode command is invoked, and then the `$M=` tells AutoCAD that a Diesel expression follows. The expression

```
$(-,1,$(getvar,Blipmode))
```

returns either a 1 or a 0, which is applied to the Blipmode command to turn it either on or off. This expression shows that you can nest expressions. The most deeply nested expression is evaluated first, so AutoCAD evaluates

```
$(getvar,blipmode)
```

to begin with. This returns either a 1 or 0, depending on whether Blipmode is on or off. Next, AutoCAD evaluates the next level in the expression

```
$(-,1,getvar_result)
```

in which *`getvar_result`* is either a 1 or 0. If *`getvar_result`* is 1, the expression looks like

```
$(-,1,1)
```

which returns a 0. If *`getvar_result`* is 0, the expression looks like

```
$(-,1,0)
```

which returns a 1. In either case, the end result is that the Blipmode command is assigned a value that is opposite of the current Blipmode setting.

Using Diesel as a Menu Option Label

In the previous example, you saw how you can use Diesel in a menu to read the status of a command and then return a numeric value to alter that status. You can also use Diesel as part of the menu option label. The following expression shows the same menu listing , with a twist. It includes Diesel code as the menu option label, as follows:

```
[$(eval,"Blipmode =" $(getvar,blipmode))]'BLIPMODE $M=$(-,1,$ (getvar,blipmode))
```

TIP *When Diesel is used as the menu name, you don't need the* `$M=` *code.*

Normally, you see the menu name within the square brackets at the beginning of this menu listing, but here you see some Diesel instructions. These instructions tell AutoCAD to display the message `Blipmode = 1` or `Blipmode = 0` in the menu, depending on the current Blipmode setting.

Here's how it works. You see the familiar `$(getvar,blipmode)` expression, this time embedded within a different expression. You know that `$(getvar,blipmode)` returns either a 1 or 0 depending on whether Blipmode is on or off. The outer expression

```
$(eval,"Blipmode =" getvar_result)
```

displays `Blipmode =` and then combines this with *`getvar_result`*, which, as you've learned, will be either 1 or 0. The `eval` function evaluates any text that follows it and returns its contents. The end result is the appearance of `Blipmode = 1` or `Blipmode = 0` in the menu, depending on the status of Blipmode. Here's how the option looks in a menu.

You can get even fancier by setting up the menu option label to read `Blipmode On` or `Blipmode Off` by using the If Diesel function. Here's that same menu listing with additional Diesel code to accomplish this:

```
[$(eval,"Blipmode " $(if,$(getvar,blipmode),"Off","On"))]'BLIPMODE $M=$(-
,1,$(getvar,blipmode))
```

In this example, the simple `$(getvar,blipmode)` expression is expanded to include the If function. The If function reads the result of `$(getvar,blipmode)` and then returns the `Off` or `On` value depending on whether `$(getvar,blipmode)` returns a 0 or 1. Here's a simpler look at the expression:

```
$(if, getvar_result, "Off", "On")
```

If *`getvar_result`* returns a 1, the If function returns the first of the two options listed after *`getvar_result`*, which is `Off`. If *`getvar_result`* returns a 0, the If function returns `On`. The second of the two options is optional. Here's how the fancier Blipmode option appears in a menu.

You've really just skimmed the surface of what Diesel can do. To get a more detailed description of how Diesel works, choose Help ➢ AutoCAD Help, to open the Help Topics dialog box. Click the Index tab. Enter **Diesel** in the input box at the top to display a listing of topics that deal with Diesel.

For fun, try adding this Blipmode menu listing to your `Mymenu.mnu` file under the `[Continue Line]` option; then reload the menu file and check the results:

```
[$(eval,"Blipmode " $(if,$(getvar,blipmode),"Off","On"))]'BLIPMODE $M=$(-
,1,$(getvar,blipmode))
```

Make sure the last line in your menu file is followed by ↵.

Table 21.2 shows some of the commonly used Diesel functions. Check the AutoCAD Help Topics dialog box for a more detailed list.

TABLE 21.2: A SAMPLE OF DIESEL FUNCTIONS. TO INDICATE TRUE OR FALSE, DIESEL USES 1 OR 0.

CODE	FUNCTION	EXAMPLE	RESULT	COMMENTS
+	Add	`$(+,202,144)`	346	
-	Subtract	`$(-,202,144)`	58	
*	Multiply	`$(*,202,144)`	29088	
/	Divide	`$(/,202,144)`	1.4028	
=	Equal to	`$(=,202,144)`	0	If numbers are equal, 1 is returned.
<	Less than	`$(<,202,144)`	0	If the first number is less than the second, 1 is returned.
>	Greater than	`$(>,202,144)`	1	If the first number is less than the second, 0 is returned.
!	Not equal to	`$(!,202,144)`	1	If numbers are equal, 0 is returned.
<=	Less than or equal to	`$(+,202,144)`	0	If first number is less than or equal to second, then 1 is returned.
>=	Greater than or equal to	`$(+,202,144)`	1	If the first number is less than or equal to the second, 0 is returned.
`eq`	Equal string	`$(eq,"Yes", "No")`	0	If both text strings are the same, 1 is returned.
`eval`	Evaluate text	`$(eval,"Here I Am")`	Here I Am	Returns text in quotes.
`getvar`	Get system variable value	`$(getvar,ltscale)`	Current line-type scale	
`if`	If/Then	`$(if,1,"Yes","No")`	Yes	The second argument is returned if the first argument evaluates to 1. Otherwise, the third argument is returned. The third argument is optional.

Creating Custom Line Types

As your drawing needs expand, you may find that the standard line types are not adequate for your application. Fortunately, you can create your own. This section explains how to do so.

You'll get an in-depth view of the process of creating line types. You'll also learn how to create complex line types that cannot be created using the Express Make Linetype tool.

Viewing Available Line Types

Although AutoCAD provides the line types most commonly used in drafting (see Figure 21.2), the dashes and dots may not be spaced the way you would like, or you might want an entirely new line type.

FIGURE 21.2

The lines in this list of standard line types were generated with the underscore key (_) and the period (.) and are only rough representations of the actual lines.

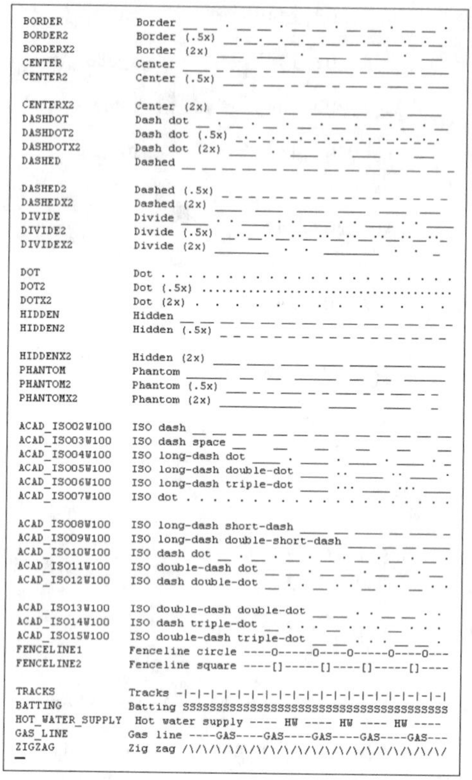

TIP *AutoCAD stores the line types in a file called* `Acad.lin`*, which is in ASCII format. When you create a new line type, you are actually adding information to this file. Or, if you create a new file containing your own line-type definitions, it too will have the extension .lin. You can edit line types as described here, or you can edit them directly in these files.*

To create a custom line type, use the Linetype command. Let's see how this handy command works, by first listing the available line types.

1. Open a new AutoCAD file.
2. At the command prompt, enter **–Linetype**↵. (Don't forget the minus sign at the beginning.)
3. At the `Enter an option [?/Create/Load/Set]:` prompt, enter **?**↵.
4. In the dialog box, locate and double-click ACAD in the listing of available line-type files. You get the list shown in Figure 21.2, which shows the line types available in the `Acad.lin` file along

with a simple description of each line. Figure 21.2 shows a complete view of the standard line types and the ISO and complex line types. Figure 21.3 shows how some of the line types actually look in a drawing or when they are plotted.

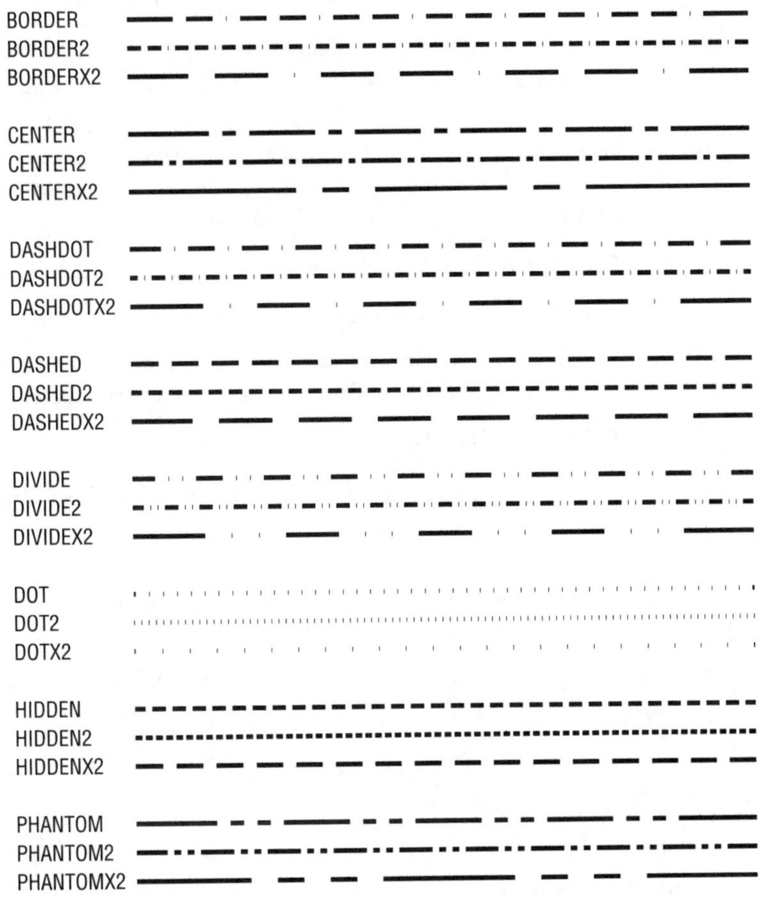

FIGURE 21.3
Some of the more commonly used standard AutoCAD line types as they appear when plotted

Creating a New Line Type

Next, let's try creating a new line type.

1. At the `?/Create/Load/Set:` prompt, enter **C**↵.
2. At the `Enter name of linetype to create:` prompt, enter **Custom**↵ as the name of your new line type.
3. The dialog box you see next is named Create Or Append Linetype File. You need to enter the name of the line-type file you want to create or add to. If you pick the default line-type file,

ACAD, your new line type is added to the `Acad.lin` file. If you choose to create a new line-type file, AutoCAD opens a file containing the line type you create and adds .lin to the filename you supply.

4. Let's assume you want to start a new line-type file. Enter **Newline**↵ in the File Name input box.

TIP *If you accept the default line-type file, ACAD, the prompt in step 5 is* `Wait, checking if linetype already defined...`. *This protects you from inadvertently overwriting an existing line type you want to keep.*

5. At the `Descriptive text:` prompt, enter a text description of your line type. You can use any keyboard character as part of your description, but the actual line type can be composed only of a series of lines, points, and blank spaces. For this exercise, enter

   `Custom - My own center line __________ _ ____________`↵

   using the underscore key (_) to simulate the appearance of your line.

6. At the `Enter linetype pattern (on next line):` prompt, enter the following numbers, known as the line-type code (after the a that appears automatically):

   `1.0,-.125,.25,-.125`↵

WARNING *If you use the Set option of the –Linetype command to set a new default line type, you will get that line type no matter what layer you are on.*

7. At the `New definition written to file. Enter an option [?/Create/Load/Set]:` prompt, press ↵ to exit the –Linetype command.

Remember, once you've created a line type, you must load it in order to use it, as discussed in Chapter 4.

TIP *You can also open the* `Acad.lin` *or other .lin file in Windows Notepad and add the descriptive text and line-type code directly to the end of the file.*

THE LINE-TYPE CODE

In step 6 of the previous exercise, you entered a series of numbers separated by commas. This is the line-type code, representing the lengths of the components that make up the line type. The separate elements of the line-type code are as follows:

- The `1.0` following the a is the length of the first part of the line. (The a that begins the line-type definition is a code that is applied to all line types.)
- The first `–.125` is the blank or broken part of the line. The minus sign tells AutoCAD that the line is *not* to be drawn for the specified length, which is 0.125 units in this example.
- Next comes the positive value of `0.25`. This tells AutoCAD to draw a line segment 0.25 units long after the blank part of the line.

- Finally, the last negative value, `-.125`, again tells AutoCAD to skip drawing the line for the distance of 0.125 units.

This series of numbers represents the one segment that is repeated to form the line (see Figure 21.4). You can also create a complex line type that looks like a random broken line, as in Figure 21.5.

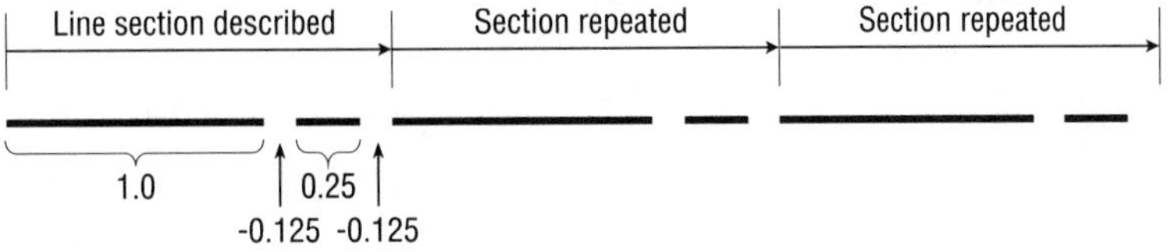

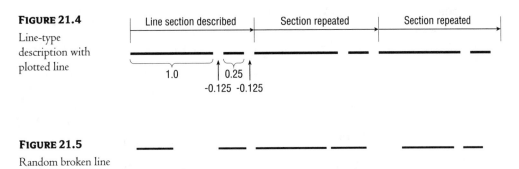

FIGURE 21.4
Line-type description with plotted line

FIGURE 21.5
Random broken line

You may be wondering what purpose the `a` serves at the beginning of the line-type code. A line type is composed of a series of line segments and points. The `a`, which is supplied by AutoCAD automatically, is a code that forces the line type to start and end on a line segment rather than on a blank space in the series of lines. At times, AutoCAD stretches the last line segment to force this condition, as shown in Figure 21.6.

FIGURE 21.6
AutoCAD stretches the beginning and the end of the line as necessary.

TIP *The values you enter for the line-segment lengths are multiplied by the Ltscale factor; so be sure to enter values for the plotted lengths.*

As mentioned in the beginning of this section, you can also create line types outside AutoCAD by using a word processor or text editor such as Windows Notepad. The standard `Acad.lin` file looks like Figure 21.3 with the addition of the code used by AutoCAD to determine the line-segment lengths.

Normally, to use a line type you have created, you have to load it, through either the Layer or the Linetype dialog box (choose Format ➢ Layers or Format ➢ Linetype). If you use one of your own line types frequently, you might want to create a button macro so it will be available as an option on a menu.

Creating Complex Line Types

A complex line type is one that incorporates text or special graphics. For example, if you want to show an underground gas line in a site plan, you normally show a line with the intermittent word *GAS*, as in Figure 21.7. Fences are often shown with an intermittent X.

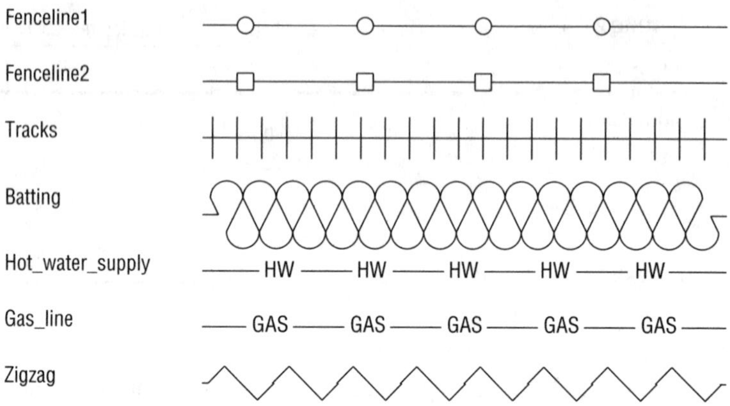

FIGURE 21.7
Samples of complex line types

For the graphics needed to compose complex line types, use any of the symbols found in the AutoCAD font files discussed in Chapter 8. Just create a text style using these symbol fonts, and then specify the appropriate symbol by using its corresponding letter in the line-type description.

To create a line type that includes text, use the same line-type code described earlier, with the addition of the necessary font file information in brackets. For example, say you want to create the line type for the underground gas line mentioned previously using just the letter G. You add the following to your `Acad.lin` file:

```
*Gas_line_G ---- G ---- G ----
a,1.0,-0.25, ["G", standard, S=.2, R=0, X=-.1, Y=-.1], -0.25
```

The information in the square brackets describes the characteristics of the text. The actual text that you want to appear in the line is surrounded by quotation marks. Next are the text style, scale, rotation angle, X displacement, and Y displacement.

WARNING *You cannot use the –Linetype command to define complex line types. Instead, you must open the* `Acad.lin` *file using a text editor, such as Windows Notepad, and add the line-type information to the end of the file. Make sure you don't duplicate the name of an existing line type.*

You can substitute `A` for the rotation angle (the `R` value), as in the following example:

```
a,1.0,-0.25, ["G", standard, S=.2 A=0, X=-.1, Y=-.1], -0.25
```

This has the effect of keeping the text at the same angle, regardless of the line's direction. Notice that in this sample, the X and Y values are a `-.1`; this will center the Gs on the line. The scale value of `.2` will cause the text to be .2 units high, so the `-.1` is half the height.

In addition to fonts, you can also specify shapes for line-type definitions. Instead of letters, shapes display symbols. Shapes are stored not as drawings, but as definition files, similar to text-font files. In fact, shape files have the same .shx filename extension as text files and are also defined similarly. Figure 21.8 shows some symbols from shape files supplied with the companion CD.

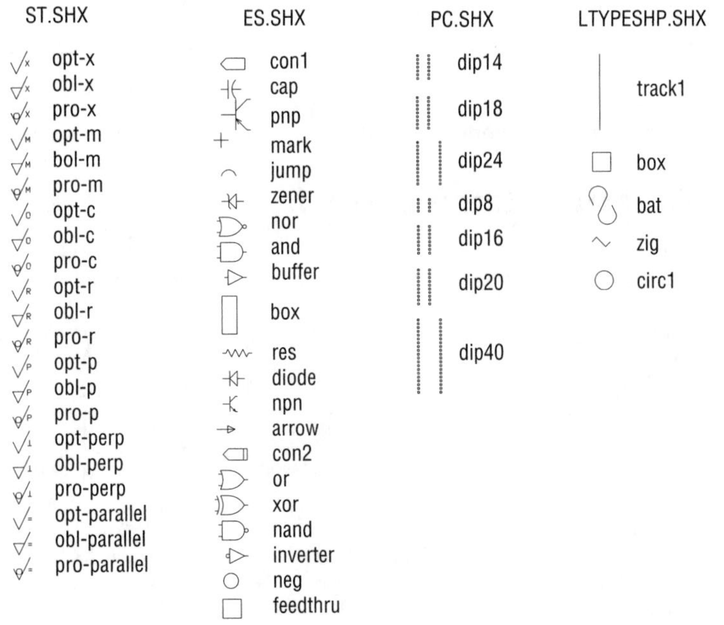

FIGURE 21.8

Samples of shapes available on the companion CD

To use a shape in a line-type code, you use the same format as shown previously for text. However, instead of using a letter and style name, you use the shape name and the shape filename, as in the following example:

```
*Capline, ====
a,1.0,-0.25,[CAP,ES.SHX,S=.5,R=0,X=-.1,Y=-.1],-0.25
```

This example uses the `CAP` symbol from the `Es.shx` shape file. The symbol is scaled to .5 units with 0 rotation and an X and Y displacement of –.1.

Here is another example that uses the arrow shape:

```
*Arrowline, ----|-----|-----|
a,1.0,-0.25,[ARROW,ES.SHX,S=.5,R=90,X=-.1,Y=-.1],-0.25
```

Just as with the Capline example, the `ARROW` symbol in this example is scaled to .5 units with 0 rotation and an X and Y displacement of –.1. Here's what the Arrowline line type looks like when used with a spline.

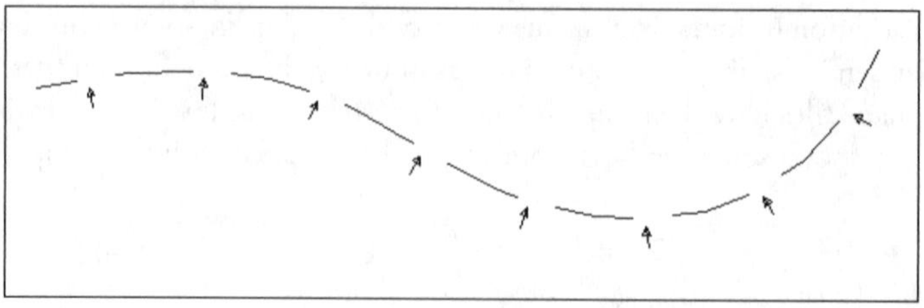

In this example, the Ltype generation option is turned on for the polyline. Note that the arrow from the ES.SHX sample shape file is used for the arrow in this line type.

Creating Hatch Patterns

AutoCAD provides several predefined hatch patterns you can choose from (see Figure 21.9), but you can also create your own. This section demonstrates the basic elements of pattern definition.

FIGURE 21.9

The standard hatch patterns

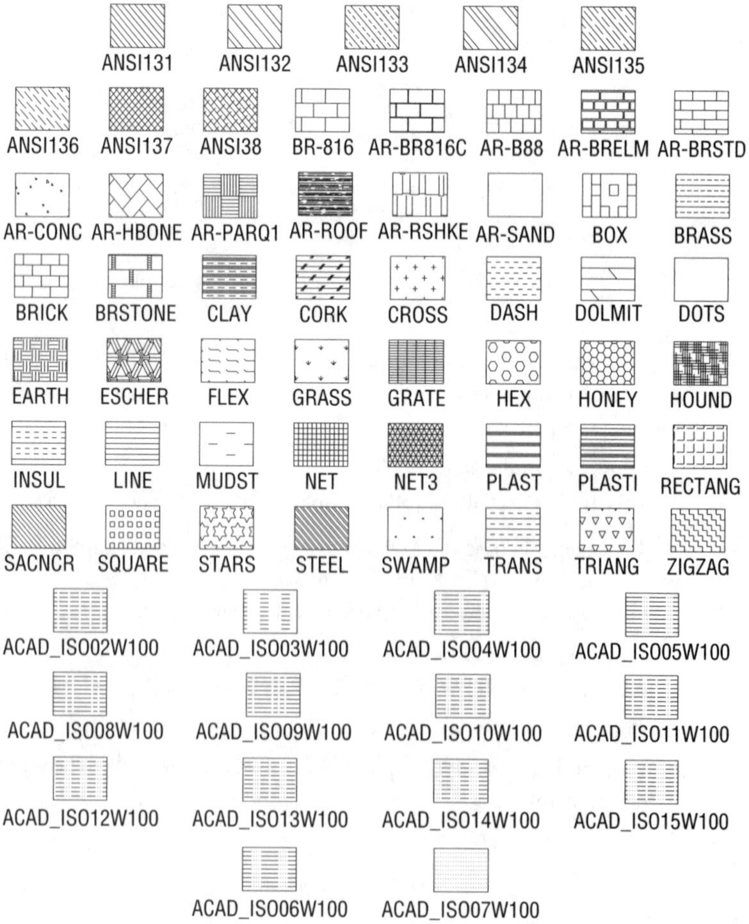

Unlike line types, hatch patterns cannot be created while you are in an AutoCAD file. The pattern definitions are contained in an external file named `Acad.pat`. You can open and edit this file with a text editor that can handle ASCII files, such as Windows Notepad. Here is one hatch pattern definition from that file:

```
*square,Small aligned squares
0, 0,0, 0,.125, .125,-.125
90, 0,0, 0,.125, .125,-.125
```

You can see some similarities between pattern descriptions and line-type descriptions. They both start with a line of descriptive text and then give numeric values defining the pattern. However, the numbers in pattern descriptions have a different meaning. This example shows two lines of information. Each line represents a line in the pattern. The first line determines the horizontal line component of the pattern, and the second line represents the vertical component. Figure 21.10 shows the hatch pattern defined in the example.

FIGURE 21.10

A square pattern

A pattern is made up of *line groups.* A line group is like a line type that is arrayed a specified distance to fill the area to be hatched. A line group is defined by a line of code, much as a line type is defined. In the square pattern, for instance, two lines—one horizontal and one vertical—are used. Each of these lines is duplicated in a fashion that makes the lines appear as boxes when they are combined. Figure 21.11 illustrates this point.

FIGURE 21.11
The individual and combined line groups

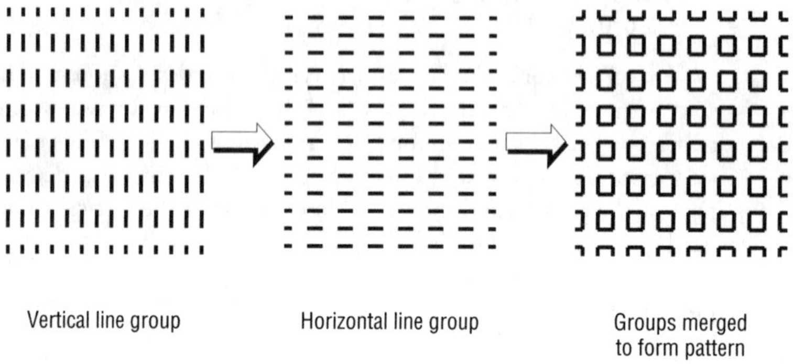

Look at the first line in the definition:

```
0, 0,0, 0,.125, .125,-.125
```

This example shows a series of numbers separated by commas; it represents one line group. It actually contains four sets of information, separated by blank spaces:

- The first component is the `0` at the beginning. This value indicates the angle of the line group, as determined by the line's orientation. In this case, it is `0` for a horizontal line that runs from left to right.
- The next component is the origin of the line group, `0,0`. This does not mean that the line actually begins at the drawing origin (see Figure 21.12). It gives you a reference point to determine the location of other line groups involved in generating the pattern.

TIP *If you have forgotten the numeric values for the various directions, refer to Chapter 2, which explains AutoCAD's system for specifying angles.*

- The next component is `0,.125`. This determines the distance for arraying the line and in what direction, as illustrated in Figure 21.13. This value is like a relative coordinate indicating X and Y distances for a rectangular array. It is not based on the drawing coordinates, but on a coordinate system relative to the orientation of the line. For a line oriented at a 0° angle, the code `0,.125` indicates a precisely vertical direction. For a line oriented at a 45° angle, the code `0,.125` represents a 135° direction. In this example, the duplication occurs 90° in relation to the line group, because the X value is `0`. Figure 21.14 illustrates this point.

FIGURE 21.12
The origin of the patterns

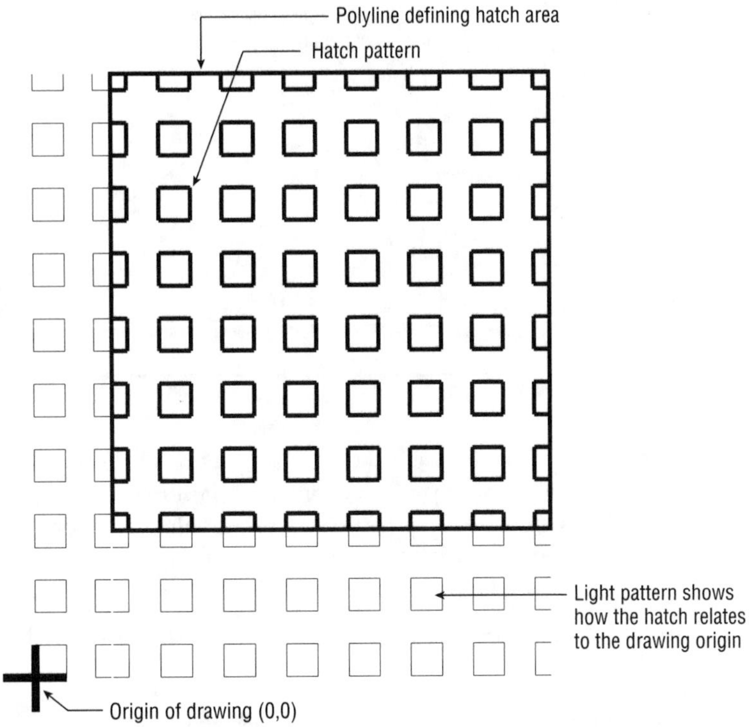

FIGURE 21.13
The distance and direction of duplication

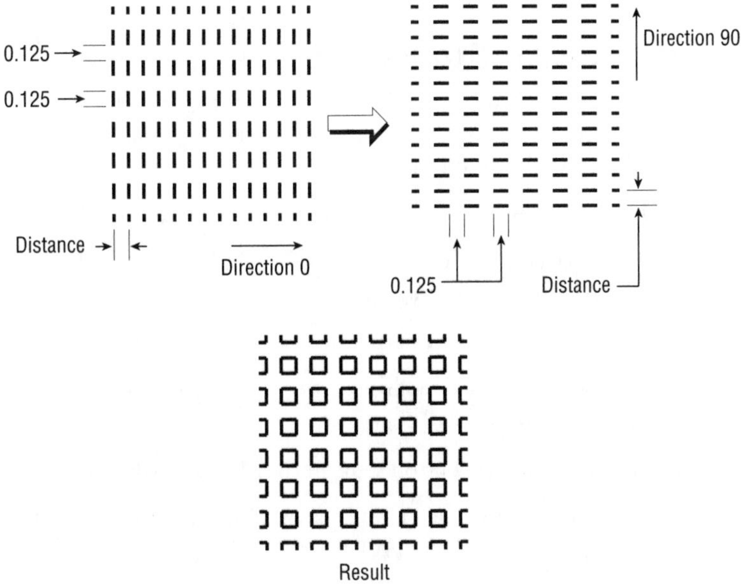

FIGURE 21.14
How the direction of the line group copy is determined

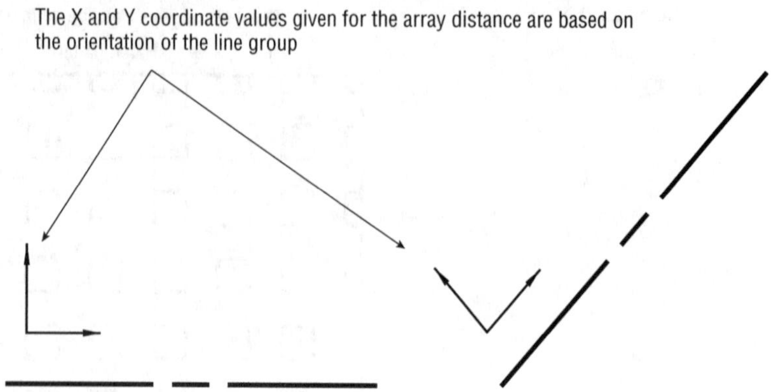

The X and Y coordinate values given for the array distance are based on the orientation of the line group

- The last component is the actual description of the line pattern. This value is equivalent to the value given when you create a line type. Positive values are line segments, and negative values are blank segments. This part of the line-group definition works exactly as in the line-type definitions you studied in the previous section.

This system of defining hatch patterns may seem somewhat limiting, but you can actually do a lot with it. Autodesk managed to come up with 69 patterns—and that was really only scratching the surface.

TIP *If you want to include thick lines in your hatch patterns, you have to "build up" line widths with multiple line-type definitions.*

If You Want to Experiment...

In this chapter, you learned that you can create your own toolbars, and then you went on to learn how to create your own menu. Try adding custom toolbars to the menu you created in the "Adding Your Own Pull-Down Menu" section:

1. If you haven't done so already, load the `Mymenu.mnu` file into the AutoCAD menu bar.
2. Right-click a button in any toolbar, and then choose Customize from the shortcut menu to open the Customize dialog box.
3. Select Mymenu from the Menu Group drop-down list.

Since you don't have toolbars coded into your menu file, the Toolbars list box is empty. The next step is to add a toolbar to your custom menu:

1. Click the New button to open the New Toolbar dialog box.
2. Enter **My Toolbar** in the Toolbar Name input box, and then click OK. A small, blank toolbar appears in the AutoCAD window.

3. Select the Command tab in the Customize dialog box. Notice that the Categories list contains the main categories of commands as they appear in the menu bar.
4. Choose Draw from the list. The Command list box to the right displays all the commands available for the Draw category.
5. Go to the top of the Command list, then click and drag the Line tool from the Command list into the new toolbar you just created. The Line tool now appears in your toolbar.
6. Click and drag the Arc Start End Direction tool from the Commands list of the Customize dialog box to your new toolbar.
7. Exit the Customize Toolbars dialog box.

AutoCAD saves your addition in a file called `Mymenu.mns`. This file contains all the code you wrote when you created the `Mymenu.mnu` file, plus the code needed for the toolbar you added in this last exercise. You can preserve your toolbar additions to your menu file by making a copy of `Mymenu.mns` and renaming it to `Mymenu.mnu`.

Chapter 22

Managing and Sharing Your Drawings

Whether you're a one-person operation working out of your home or one of several hundred AutoCAD users in a large company, file sharing and file maintenance become the focus of much of your time. In a more interconnected world, the volume of messages and files crossing our path seems to be constantly on the rise. In addition, the Internet has allowed us to be more mobile, adding complexity to our file management tasks.

In this chapter, you'll learn about some of the tools that AutoCAD offers to help you manage your files and the files you share with others. You'll also examine some general issues that arise while using AutoCAD in a workgroup environment. In this discussion, you may find help with some problems you have encountered when using AutoCAD in your particular work environment.

- Sharing Drawings over the Internet
- ePublishing Your Drawings
- Managing Your Drawings with the DesignCenter and Tool Palettes
- Establishing Office Standards
- Converting Multiple Layer Settings

Sharing Drawings over the Internet

The Internet has become a major part of the computer industry and everyday life. And the Internet offers AutoCAD users some real, practical benefits through its ability to publish drawings and other documents online. AutoCAD gives you tools that allow you to post drawings on the Internet that others can view and download. In the architectural, engineering, and construction (AEC) industry in particular, this can mean easier access to documents needed by contractors, engineers, cost estimators, and others involved in the design, bidding, and construction of architectural projects. Suppliers of products can post symbol libraries of their products or even 3D solid models.

In this section, you'll learn about the tools AutoCAD provides for publishing and accessing drawings on the Internet (and on any office local- or wide-area network). You'll start by looking at one of the most common uses of the Internet: file transmission.

Sharing Project Files with eTransmit

Perhaps the most common use of the Internet is to send and receive files. Whether you're a one-person office or a member of a 50-person firm, you'll eventually have to share your work with others outside your building. In prior versions of AutoCAD, this meant that you had to carefully examine what you were sending to make sure you included all the ancillary files needed to view or work on your drawings. Xref, font, and custom line-type files all had to be carefully included with the drawings you sent to consultants or partners in a project, and often something was missed.

With eTransmit, you can quickly collect all your project drawings into a single archive file, or you can store the files in a separate folder for later processing. This collection of files is included with a report file as a transmittal. Try the following to see how eTransmit works.

1. In AutoCAD, open a file you intend to send to someone; then choose File ➢ eTransmit to open the Create Transmittal dialog box.

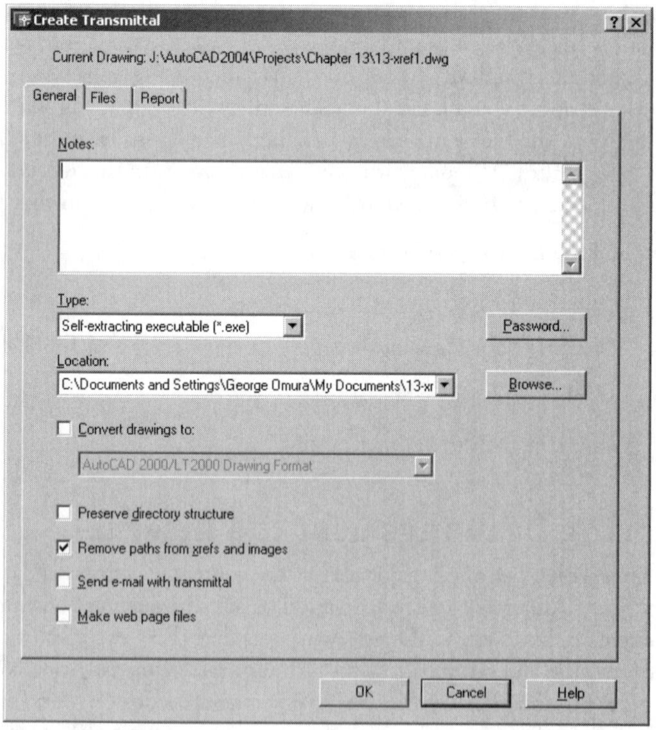

2. With the General tab selected, click in the Notes input box and enter a description or other note.

3. In the Type drop-down list, select the format for your collection of files. You can create a Zip or self-extracting executable archive, or you can save the files in a folder. If you choose the Zip or executable option, you can also add a password using the Password button. The person receiving the transmittal file must then enter a password to extract the files. If you choose the Folder option, you can tell AutoCAD where to place the files using the Browse button. For this exercise, choose Folder.
4. Click the Browse button to open the Specify Location Folder dialog box. This is a typical AutoCAD file dialog box that you can use to select a location for you files. You can use the Create New Folder tool to create a new folder for your files. You'll want to keep your transmittal files in a separate location from other files. Once you select a location, you return to the Create Transmittal dialog box.
5. To add more files to be included in the transmittal, click the Files tab. You'll see a tree structure listing of the files that are included in the transmittal so far. If you need to include more files than the ones shown, you can use the Add File button in the upper-right corner of the dialog box. You can also exclude font files to save space by turning off the Include Fonts option in the lower-left corner.
6. Finally, you can preview the report file by clicking the Report tab.

This report gives you a detailed description of the types of files included in the transmittal. It also alerts you to files that AutoCAD was unable to find but that are required for the drawing.

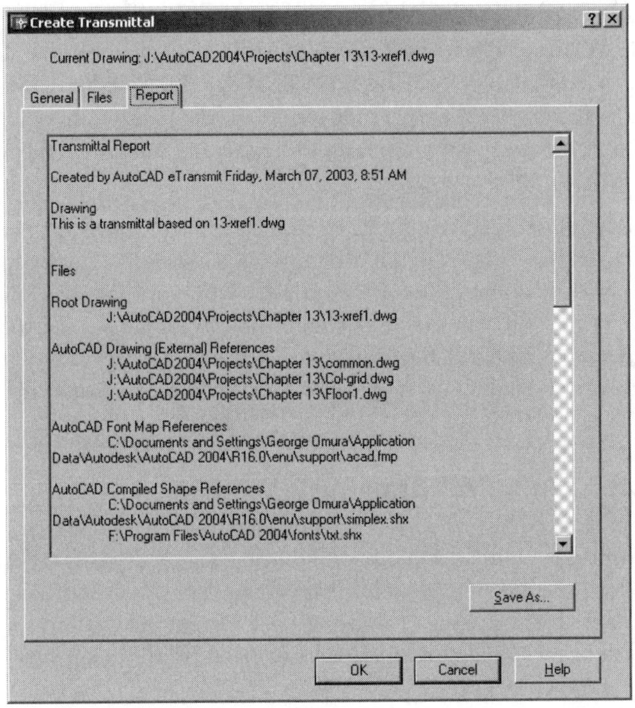

Once you've selected the options, you can click OK in the Create Transmittal dialog box, and AutoCAD will proceed to collect the files into an archive folder or a Zip file. You can then send the files over the Internet or put them on a removable disk for manual transport.

The General tab of the Create Transmittal dialog box offers some additional options you'll want to know about:

Password Gives you the option to password protect the transmittal file. If you click the Password button, you are presented with a dialog box that lets you enter a password and confirm it. The person receiving the transmittal file must then enter a password toe extract the files.

Convert Drawings To Lets you select between the AutoCAD 2004 and AutoCAD 2000 file formats in case your recipient requires an earlier version.

Preserve Directory Structure Preserves the directory structure for the files in the transmittal. This can be important when Xref and other files are located across several folder locations. If the person receiving your files is not able to open Xref files properly, try using this option when you re-send your transmittal files.

Remove Paths From Xrefs And Images Removes path references for Xrefs in the current file. This is useful if you know the recipient of your file will place all the files in one folder to view them. This is best used if the transmittal drawings are only going one way.

Send E-Mail With Transmittal Lets you send an e-mail transmittal with the files included as an attachment. This option streamlines the transmittal process by opening an e-mail dialog box that allows you to enter a message and select a recipient for your transmittal.

Make Web Page Files Generates a web page with a sample thumbnail of the current, open drawing being included in the transmittal. The page also includes a Download button and a button that lets the viewer open the report file generated by eTransmit. If you have a website, you can place this web page file along with the eTransmit report and transmittal files on your web server to allow easy access to your files over the web.

eTransmit gives you a quick way to package a set of drawings to be sent to others working on the same project. But you may have a need to offer a wider distribution of your files. You might want to let others view and plot your drawings from a website without exposing your drawing database to anyone who might visit your site. If this sounds like something you're interested in, you'll want to know about the AutoCAD .dwf file format, which lets anyone view AutoCAD files whether they own the program or not. You'll learn more about the DWF file format in the "ePublishing Your Drawings" section later in this chapter.

Protecting AutoCAD Drawing Files

Since AutoCAD drawings specify the methods and materials used to produce an object or building, the drawings are often treated like legal documents. Once an AutoCAD drawing is issued, it is often archived and guarded as a legal record of a design. For this reason, many AutoCAD users are concerned with the possible tampering of drawings that are sent out to third parties. Even minor, unauthorized changes to a drawing can have major repercussions to the integrity of a design.

AutoCAD 2004 offers some tools that can help minimize file tampering . The eTransmit feature offers a password protection option to reduce the possibility of unauthorized tampering of the transmittal files. AutoCAD also offers password protection for individual files as well as a digital signature feature that helps protect both the author of a drawing and the recipient in the event of file tampering.

ADDING PASSWORD PROTECTION TO FILES

The basic type of file protection is the password protection of individual files. AutoCAD offers password protection through the Save Drawing As dialog box and the Options dialog box.

To add a password to a drawing when you save it, do the following:

1. Choose File ➢ Save As to open the Save Drawing As dialog box.
2. Choose Tools ➢ Security Options from the menu in the upper-right corner of the dialog box.
3. In the Security Options dialog box, enter a password or phrase in the input box.

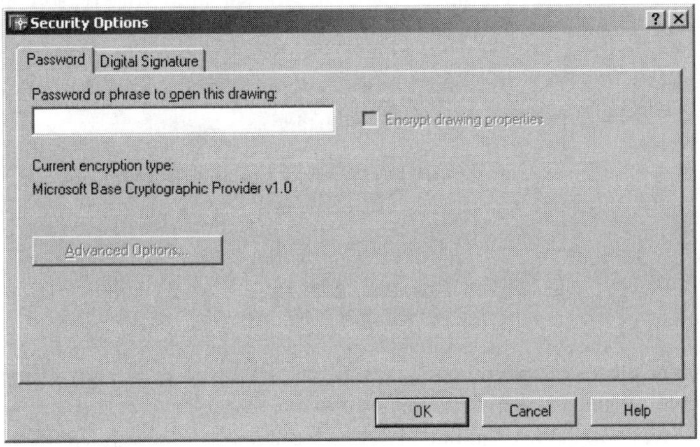

4. Click OK. You are prompted to enter the password again.
5. Enter the password again and click OK to return to the Save Drawing As dialog box.
6. Enter the name and location of your file, and then click Save.

In addition to the Save Drawing As dialog box, you can also add password protection through the Options dialog box.

1. Choose Tools ➢ Options to open the Options dialog box, and then click the Open and Save tab.
2. Click the Security Options button in the File Safety Precautions group to open the Security Options dialog box.
3. Enter your password, select other options as necessary, and then click OK.

As a third option, you can enter **Securityoptions↵** at the command prompt to go directly to the Security Options dialog box.

Once you've added a password, anyone attempting to open the file will be asked to provide the password before the file can be opened. This includes any attempt to use the file as an Xref or a file insertion.

TIP *Once you open a password-protected file and give the password , you can open and close the file repeatedly during that AutoCAD session without having to reenter the password. If you close and reopen AutoCAD, AutoCAD will prompt you for a password the next time you attempt to open the password-protected file.*

USING A DIGITAL SIGNATURE

In addition to password protection, you can use a digital signature to authenticate files. A digital signature can't prevent someone from tampering with a file, but it offers a way to validate whether a file has been modified after it has been saved. This protects you in the event that your file is unofficially altered. It also protects the recipient of your file by verifying the file's authenticity and that it was not altered from the time it left your computer.

The first time you attempt to use the digital signature feature, you see a message telling you that you need a digital ID.

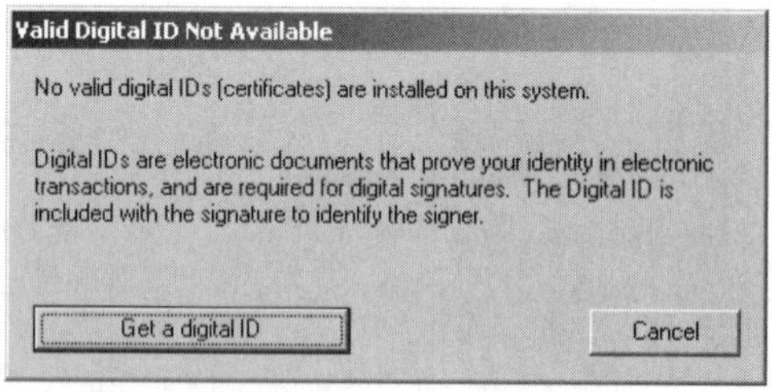

As the message explains, a digital ID is required to use the digital signature feature. AutoCAD uses a digital ID issued by VeriSign, Inc., a company that specializes in Internet security. The ID is fee based with prices ranging from about $15 for a basic one-year enrollment to a professional level ID costing close to $700. A free 60-day trial is also offered.

The following steps offer a general explanation of the process of acquiring a digital ID.

1. Connect to the Internet. During the process, you will log on to the VeriSign website.
2. From the Windows Taskbar, choose Start ➢ All Programs ➢ Autodesk ➢ AutoCAD 2004 ➢ Attach Digital Signature. Or from AutoCAD, open the Security Options dialog box and click the Digital Signature tab. The Valid Digital ID Not Available warning dialog box appears.
3. Click the Get A Digital ID button. Your web browser opens at the VeriSign page.
4. Select the security level you want and follow the rest of the instructions.

Once you've obtained a digital ID, the signature resides in the Registry on your computer. You can then access the digital ID from AutoCAD using the Digital Signature tab of the Security Options dialog box.

1. Open the drawing to which you will attach the digital signature, and then open the Security Options dialog box by entering **Securityoptions**↵ at the command prompt.

2. Click the Digital Signature tab.

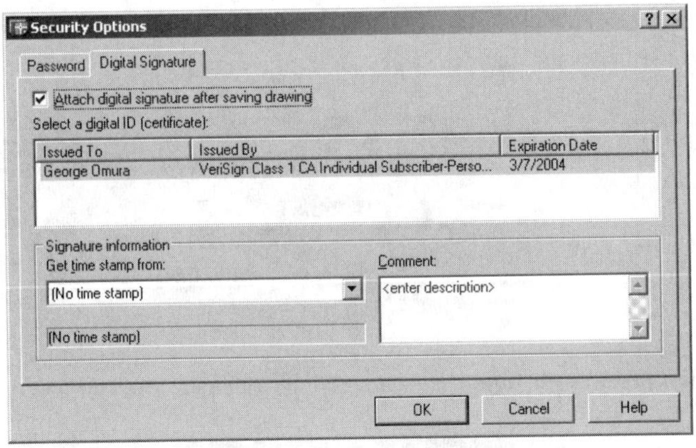

3. Turn on the Attach Digital Signature After Saving Drawing option. The Signature Information options become available. You can add a date stamp and a brief description.

4. Click OK to exit the dialog box.

The next time you save the file, depending on the level of security you choose during the digital ID setup, you may be prompted for a password. Once you enter the password, the file is saved.

The next time the file is opened, you will see the Digital Signature Contents dialog box, which verfies that the drawing has not been tampered with.

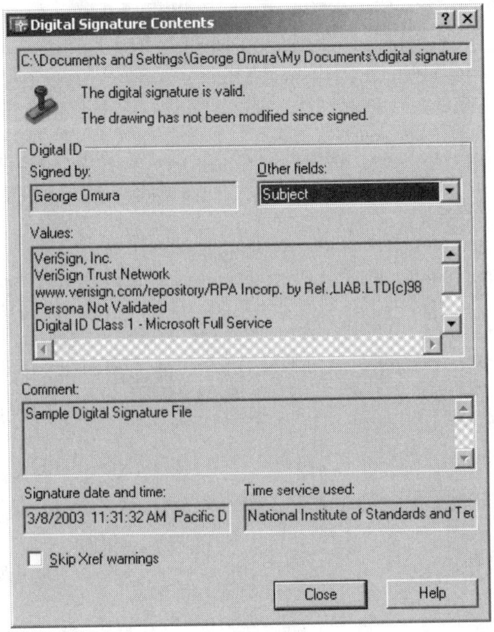

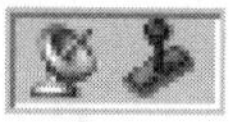

You'll also see a stamp icon in the lower-right corner of the AutoCAD window. You can click this icon at any time to view the digital signature status of the file. You can also issue the Sigvalidate command to view the status. If the file is modified in any way and then saved, a warning message appears the next time the file is opened.

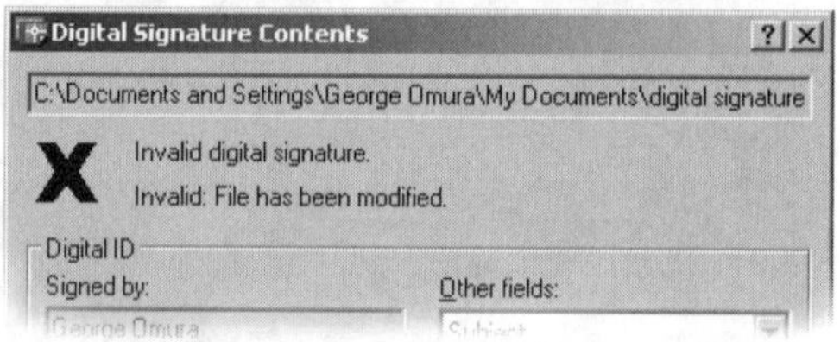

A file containing a digital signature will also display a warning when it is being modified.

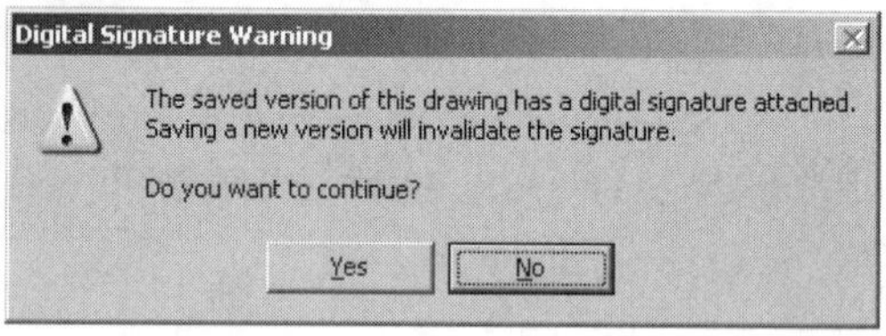

If you need to update a drawing that contains your digital signature, you can do so and then use the Security Options dialog box to reissue the digital signature.

ADDING YOUR DIGITAL SIGNATURE TO MULTIPLE FILES

If you have multiple files to which you would like to attach your digital signature, you'll want to use the Attach Digital Signatures utility. This program runs outside AutoCAD, and it provides a convenient way to attach your digital signature to a set of drawings. Here's how it works.

1. From the Windows Taskbar, choose Start ➢ All Programs ➢ Autodesk ➢ AutoCAD 2004 ➢ Attach Digital Signature to open the Attach Digital Signatures dialog box.

WARNING *If you have not obtained a digital ID, you will see a message telling you that no valid digital IDs are installed on your system. To proceed, you will have to obtain a digital ID from Verisign as described at the beginning of this section.*

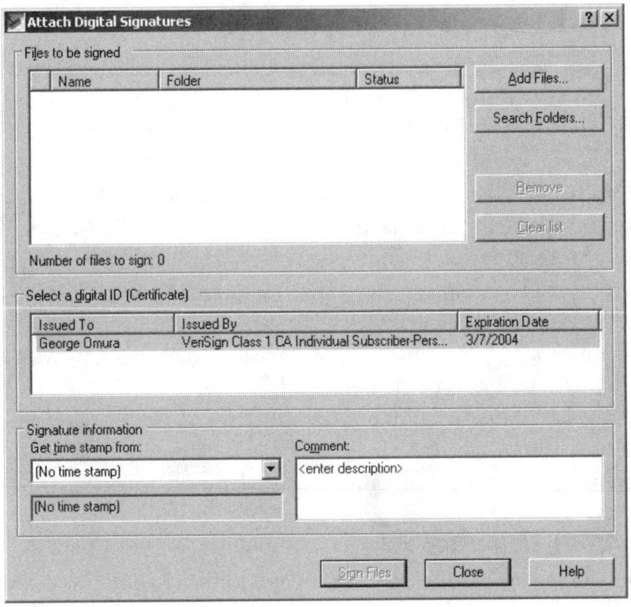

2. Click the Add Files button to locate and select files. You can also search for files in a particular folder by clicking the Search Folders button. The files you add appear in the Files To Be Signed list box.
3. If you decide to remove a file from the list box, highlight it and then click Remove. You can also remove all the files from the list by clicking Clear List.
4. The rest of the dialog box is the same as the Digital Signature tab of the Security Options dialog box. You can enter the date and time and a comment for the files you've selected.
5. Click Sign Files when you are sure you have selected the correct files and entered an appropriate comment.

If you exchange AutoCAD drawings regularly with clients and consultants, you'll want to obtain a digital ID and use AutoCAD's digital signature feature. Be aware, however, that since this is feature is new in AutoCAD 2004, it only works if you exchange files with others using AutoCAD 2004. In fact, a quick way to remove a digital signature from a file is to save the file in the AutoCAD 2002 or earlier file format.

WARNING *If you intend to use the password feature in conjunction with your digital signature, you must add the signature first before adding the password.*

ePublishing Your Drawings

The features discussed so far are mostly intended for exchanging files with others who need to work directly with your AutoCAD files. But there are always associates and clients who only need to see your final drawings and really don't care whether they get AutoCAD files or not. Or you may be working with people who do not have AutoCAD but still need to view and print your drawings. For those non-AutoCAD end users, AutoCAD offers the .dwf file format.

You can think of the .dwf file format as a kind of Adobe Acrobat file for AutoCAD drawings. .dwf offers a way to get your plans and design ideas in the hands of more people more easily. With the help of the free Autodesk Express View, .dwf files can be viewed using the same types of pan and zoom tools available in AutoCAD, thereby allowing greater detail to be presented in your drawings. In addition, you can embed URL links that can open other documents with a single mouse click. These links can be attached to objects or areas in the drawing.

You can also print .dwf files printed using your Windows system printer or plotter, all without having AutoCAD installed. A single .dwf file can contain multiple drawing "sheets," so you can combine a complete set of drawings into one .dwf file.

Exchanging Drawing Sets

Imagine that you are working on a skylight addition to a house and you need to send your drawings to your client for review. In addition to the skylite plans, you want to include some alternate floor plans that your client has asked you to generate. In the next exercise, you'll put together a set of drawings that will become a single .dwf file that you will send as an e-mail attachment to your client.

1. Open the `Sample House.dwg` file from the sample files on the companion CD. Notice that the file has several Layout tabs, each representing a separate drawing sheet.
2. Choose File ➢ Publish to open the Publish Drawing Sheets dialog box. Notice that the dialog box lists all the layouts in its main list box, including Model, which is equivalent to the Model Space tab. (See Chapter 7 for more on layouts). LT users will not see the Plotter Named In Page Setups option at the bottom of the dialog box.

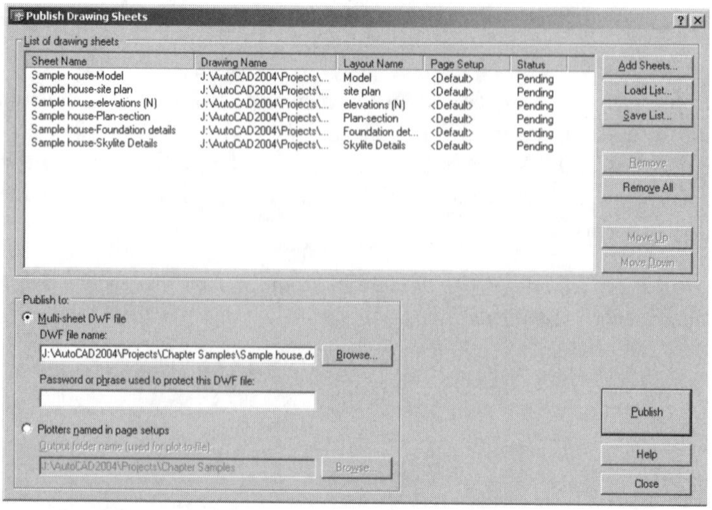

3. In the list box, Ctrl+click Sample House – Model, Sample House – Foundation Details, and Sample House - Skylite Details to select them. You do not want to include these layouts in your .dwf file.
4. Click the Remove button. The items you selected are removed from the list.

At this point, you could go ahead and create a .dwf file, but suppose you want to include layouts from a file that is not currently open. The following steps show you how to accomplish this.

1. With the Publish Drawing Sheets dialog box still open, click the Add Sheets button to open the Select Drawings dialog box.
2. Locate and select the `Sample House Alt.dwg` file. Now you see two new items, Sample House Alt – Model and Sample House Alt – Alternate Plan, in the list box. These are the Layout tabs that are in the `Sample House alt.dwg` file.
3. Select Sample House Alt – Model and click Remove. You don't need the model space view included in your set.

You've got all the sheets that your client needs listed in the list box. Now you're ready to create the .dwf file.

1. In the Publish To group toward the bottom of the dialog box, make sure that the Multisheet DWF File radio button is selected.
2. Click the Browse button and select a name and location for the .dwf file. By default, AutoCAD uses the same name as the current file and the folder location of the current file.
3. Click Publish. AutoCAD will spend some time "printing" the selected layouts to a .dwf file.

When AutoCAD is finished, you'll see the Publishing Complete message box. As this message indicates, you can create a log of the .dwf output, preview the .dwf file, or close the message.

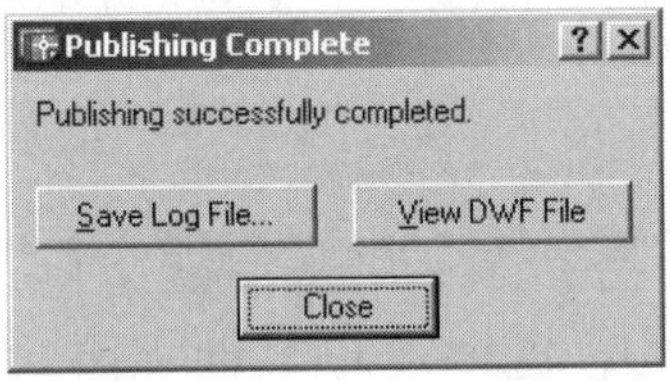

Let's take a look at the .dwf file. In the process, you'll be introduced to the Autodesk Express Viewer.

1. Click the View DWF File button in the Publishing Complete message box. The Autodesk Express Viewer opens and displays the first sheet of your set of sheets. Notice that the Autodesk Express Viewer offers the same Pan and Zoom tools in its toolbar that AutoCAD offers. You can also print the drawings by clicking the Print button in the toolbar or copy the current view in bitmap form to the Clipboard.

2. Open the drop-down list in the Autodesk Express Viewer toolbar and select Sample House-Plan-Section (14 × 8.5in). The view changes to show the plan and section drawing.

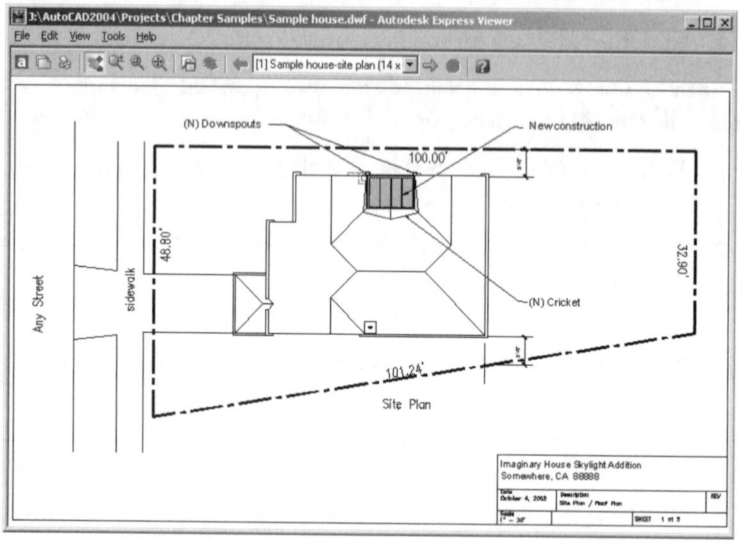

3. Click the arrow icon to the right of the drop-down list. The view advances to the next sheet.

4. Go ahead and experiment with the Pan and Zoom tools.

5. Close the Autodesk Express Viewer, and then close the Publishing Complete message box.

The Autodesk Express Viewer offers a fast and simple way to view .dwf files, and as I mentioned earlier, it is free. It is installed automatically when you install AutoCAD. You can open the Autodesk Express Viewer any time by choosing Start ➢ All Programs ➢ Autodesk ➢ Autodesk Express Viewer.

TIP *If the person receiving your .dwf file does not have a copy of the Autodesk Express Viewer, send them to the Products page of the Autodesk website (`www.autodesk.com`) to download their own copy. The download file is approximately 2.3MB, which is easily downloaded even with a slower dial-up connection.*

You may notice that when you click the Publish button in the previous exercise, AutoCAD behaves as if it is printing the layouts in your list, and that is exactly what it is doing. AutoCAD uses its own .dwf printer driver to "print" your drawings to a .dwf file. AutoCAD uses the layout settings from the Plot dialog box for each layout to produce the .dwf pages. You may recall from Chapter 7 that the layout settings control sheet size, scale, and sheet orientation, among other things. You can also use the Plot Page Setup option to apply a different set of layout settings to an item in the list box. (See the section "Shortcut Menu Options" later in this chapter for a brief description of how to use page setup options.)

OTHER PUBLISH DRAWING SHEETS OPTIONS

Let's take a moment to review some of the options in the Publish Drawing Sheets dialog box that you did not use.

- The Load List and Save List buttons let you save and load the list you've compiled. It is a good idea to save your list in case you need to reproduce the .dwf file at some future date.
- The Remove button removes a selected item from the list. The Remove All button clears the entire list so you can start from scratch to build a list.
- The Move Up and Move Down buttons let you move an item in the list up or down. These are important options because the order of drawings in the list determines the order that the drawings will appear in the Autodesk Express Viewer. The item at the top of the list appears first, the next one down the list is second, and so on.
- In the Publish To group, you've seen what the Multi-Sheet DWF File option does. Notice that when this option is selected, you can include password protection. This works in a similar way to the file and eTransmit password protection options.
- The Plotters Named In Page Setup radio button option lets you print the sheets instead of creating a .dwf file. If the layouts are set up to plot to a .dwf file, you will get individual .dwf files for each layout. This option is not available in AutoCAD LT.

SHORTUCT MENU OPTIONS

If you right-click an item or a set of items in the Publish Drawing Sheets dialog box list box, you'll see a menu with the standard options mentioned earlier plus some additional options. You'll want to know about a few of these options.

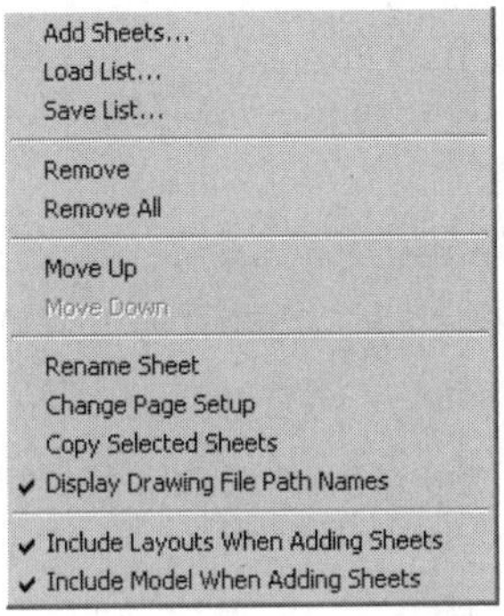

By default, AutoCAD applies the existing layout settings for each layout when it produces the .dwf file. These are the settings found in the Layout Settings tab of the Plot Or Page Setup dialog box and include settings such as the sheet size, scale, and page orientation. The Change Page Setup option lets you use a different set of layout settings for a selected layout in the list. To use this option, you must have saved a page setup in the Page Setup Or Plot dialog box of the file. (See Chapter 7 for more on the Page Setup dialog box and its options.) You can also import a page setup from a different AutoCAD file.

If you happen to have two different layouts with the same name, you can use the Rename Sheet option to rename a layout. The Copy Selected Sheet option will add copies of selected layouts to the list. The copies will have the word *copy* appended to their names. Finally, the last three items in the shortcut menu let you control what is displayed in the list box. Display Drawing File Path Names determines whether path names are displayed in the list box. Include Layouts When Adding Sheets controls whether layouts are automatically imported from a drawing into the list box. Include Model When Adding Sheets controls whether Model Space views are automatically imported from a drawing into the list box.

Creating a Web-Viewable Drawing

Besides being a great tool for sharing plans, the .dwf file format is also a good medium for posting drawings on the Web. With .dwf, drawings can be viewed on the Web with far more detail than with conventional bitmap graphics. Before the .dwf file format, posting drawings on a web page involved capturing bitmap images of drawings and adding them to web pages. Although this method is fairly simple, it allowed for only the crudest of images to be displayed. Drawings had to be limited in size and resolution to make them easily accessible. If you wanted to add URL links (clickable areas on an image that open other documents), you had to delve into the inner workings of web page design.

TIP *URL stands for Uniform Resource Locator and is a standard system for addressing Internet locations on the World Wide Web.*

CREATING A .DWF FILE

In most cases, you will want to create a web-viewable drawing file that looks similar to your printed output. You can think of your .dwf files as plots or renderings that you can post on the Web. So to create a .dwf file, you go through the AutoCAD plot system. The following exercise shows you exactly what to do.

1. In AutoCAD, open the `Plan.dwg` file. You can use the `13a-plan.dwg` file from the companion CD if you didn't create the `Plan.dwg` file on your own.
2. Click the Layout1 tab.
3. In the Page Setup dialog box, click the Plot Device tab and select DWF6 ePlot.PC3 from the Name drop-down list.
4. Click OK to close the Page Setup dialog box; then choose File ➢ Plot or right-click the Layout1 tab and choose Plot to open the Plot dialog box. The Plot dialog box is similar to the Page Setup dialog box. You'll use this dialog box to enter a name for your plot file, since the Page Setup dialog box does not offer an option to name your .dwf file.
5. In the Plot Device tab, enter a name for your .dwf file in the File Name input box. Then click the Plot Settings tab and select the area you want to plot from the Plot area group.

6. Click OK in the Plot dialog box to proceed with the creation of the .dwf file.

You can control the .dwf plot as you would any plot.

Configuring the .DWF Output

In addition to the settings available in the Plot dialog box, you can make some special configuration adjustments to the .dwf plotter configuration file. Here is where to find those configuration settings.

1. Choose File ➢ Page Setup to open the Page Setup dialog box, and click the Plot Device tab.
2. Make sure the DWF6 ePlot PC3 configuration file is listed in the Name list box.
3. Click the Properties button to the right of the Plotter Configuration Name drop-down list to open the Plotter Configuration Editor dialog box.
4. Make sure the Device And Document Settings tab is selected; then click the Custom Properties listing in the dialog box.

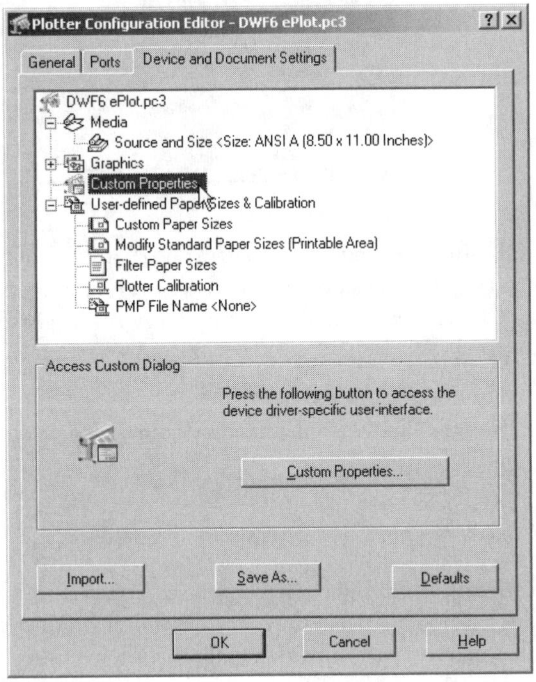

5. Click the Custom Properties button that appears in the lower half of the dialog box to open the DWF Properties dialog box. In this dialog box, you can set the resolution, format, and background color and paper boundary for your .dwf file. You can also specify whether to include layer and font information.

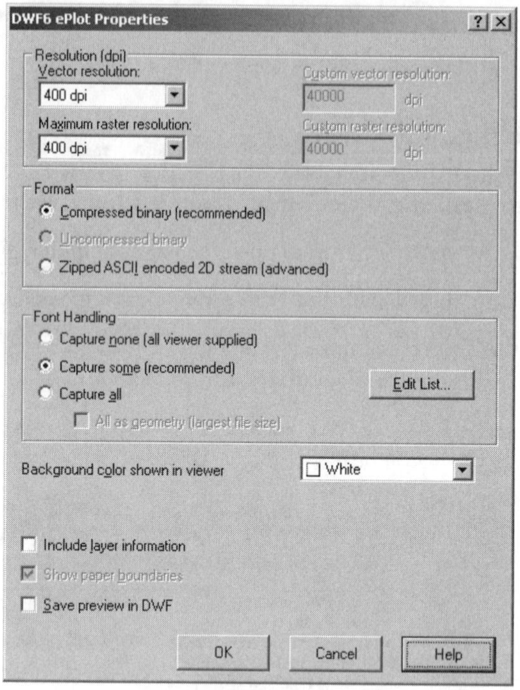

6. Click OK after selecting your settings. The Plotter Configuration Editor dialog box reappears. Once you've set the custom properties, you can save any new settings under the `DWF6 ePlot.PC3` file, or you can create create a new DWF6 PC3 plot configuration file. To save any setting changes, click the Save As button and select the PC3 file in which you want to save the settings.
7. Click OK in the Plotter Configuration Editor dialog box to return to the Page Setup dialog box.
8. Click OK to exit the Page Setup dialog box.

TIP *For more information on PC3 plot configuration files, see Chapter 7.*

After you select your custom configuration settings in step 5, you needn't open the Plotter Configuration Editor dialog box again the next time you plot a .dwf file. If you save your new settings as a new PC3 file, you can select it from the File drop-down list in the Plotter Configuration group. You needn't reenter the custom settings.

Once you've created your .dwf file, you can include it in a web page or use it as an alternate to the .dwg file to send to clients or anyone else who wants to look at your drawings or plot them out but doesn't need to edit them.

TIP *The person receiving your .dwf file will need a copy of the free Autodesk Express Viewer program that lets you view AutoCAD .dwf files. Autodesk Express Viewer is installed with AutoCAD 2004.*

If you just want to use the .dwf file format to post your drawings on a web page, you can use a new feature that creates a .dwf file and a preformatted web page in one operation.

Creating a Web Page Containing .dwf Files

AutoCAD 2004 offers a tool that will automatically generate a web page containing your .dwf files. The Publish To Web Wizard lets you create and edit web pages that contain single or multiple .dwf files. You can then place the pages on your web server without any extra work.

Try the following exercise to see firsthand how easy it is to create a web page.

TIP *As you work through the Publish To Web Wizard, read the instructions provided directly in the wizard dialog boxes. They will give you additional information and instruction.*

1. Choose File➢Publish To Web from the AutoCAD menu bar to start the Publish To Web Wizard.

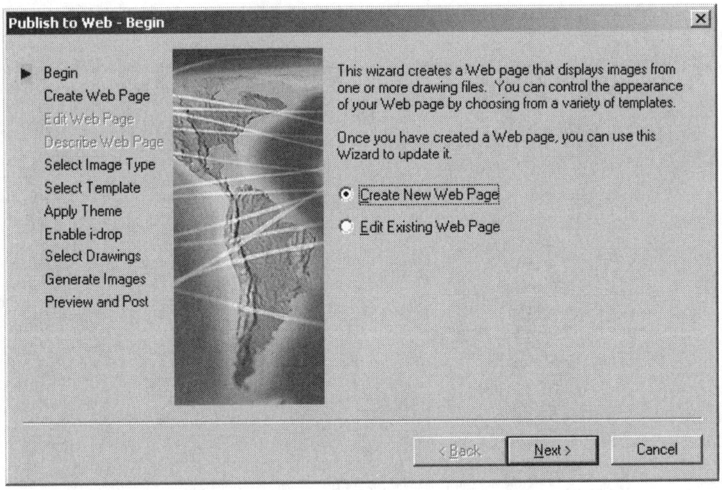

2. Click the Create New Web Page radio button and click Next to open the Create Web Page screen. This is where you enter a name and location for your web page. Enter **Test** in the Specify The Name Of Your Web Page input box. You don't have to enter a filename extension. You can also browse to specify a location for your web page. The default location is your Autodesk Documents And Settings folder.

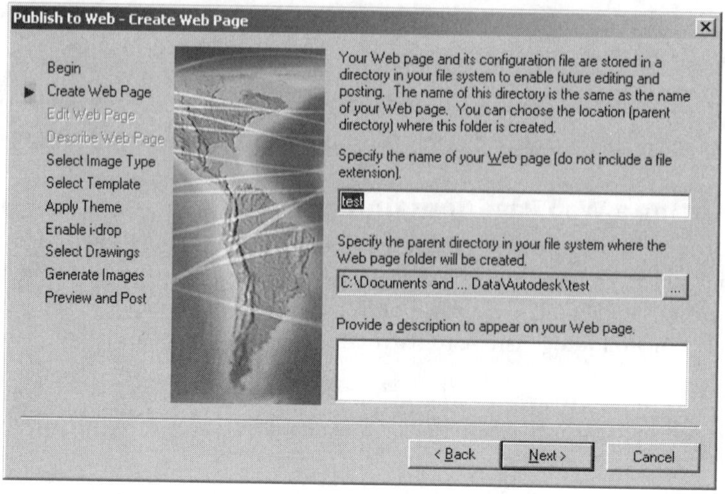

3. Click Next to open the Select Image Type screen. Here you have the option to specify the type of graphics you want to include in your web page: .dwf, JPG, or PNG.

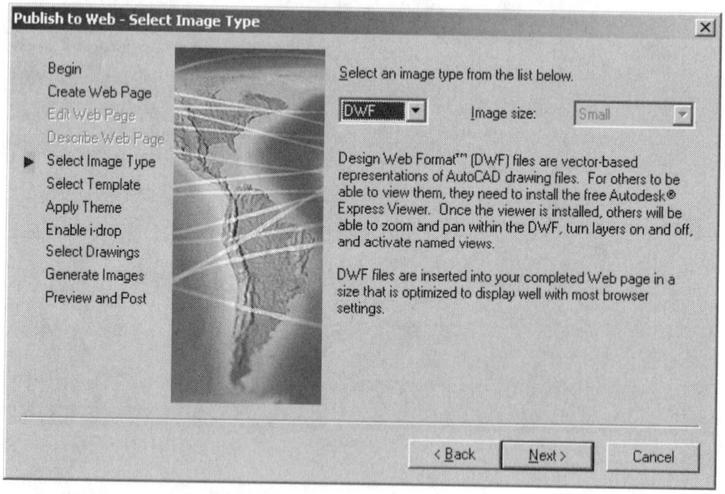

4. Make sure that DWF is displayed in the drop-down list and click Next to open the Select Template screen. This screen lets you choose from four predefined page layouts. The first and the basic is the Array Of Thumbnails. For any option you select, a sample of the layout appears in the graphic to the right of the list.

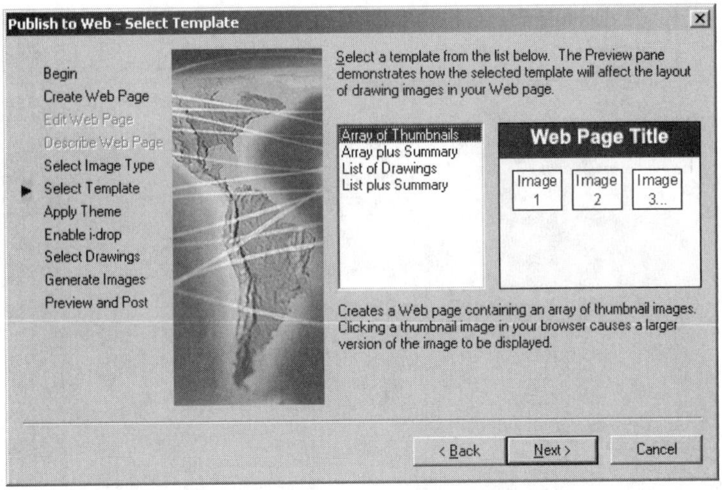

5. For this exercise, select List Plus Summary from the list; then click Next to open the Apply Theme screen. This screen lets you select a color scheme and font for your web page from a drop-down list. When you select a "theme" from the list, a sample is displayed below the list.

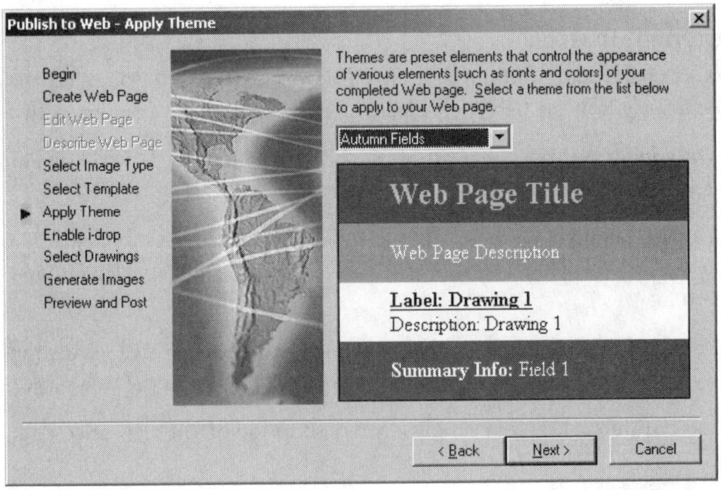

6. Click Next to open the Enable i-drop screen. The i-drop feature allows viewers of your web page to drag and drop drawing files from your page into their AutoCAD session. (See the section "Exchanging .dwg Files Using i-drop" later in this chapter.)

7. Turn on the i-drop feature, and then click Next to open the Select Drawings screen. Here you specify the drawings that you want to include in your web page. You can include several drawings, and you can select between Model Space views and layouts. For example, if you have a

single drawing file that contains four or five layouts, you can set up a web page to show each layout and the Model Space view separately on the page. Let's take a closer look at how the options on the Select Drawings screen work.

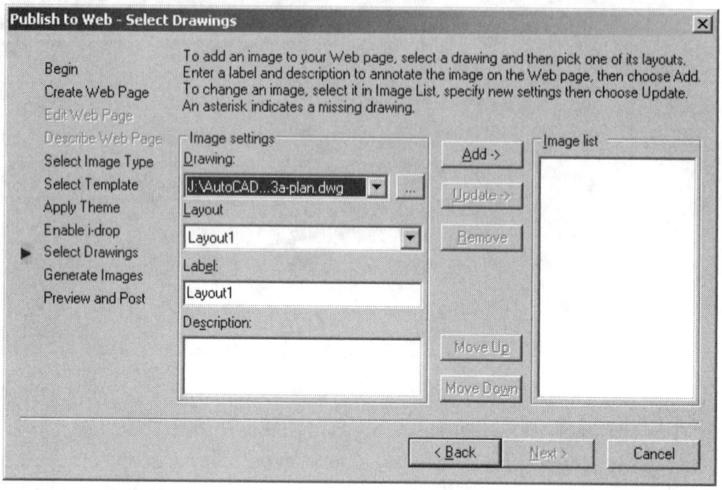

SELECTING AN IMAGE

The Image Settings group in the Select Drawings screen lets you select the drawing file and the layout to be displayed in the web page. Here's a rundown of the four options that are available in this group:

Drawing A drop-down list of all the currently open drawings in AutoCAD. You can click the Browse button (...) to select files that are not currently open.

Layout A drop-down list that lets you select a Layout tab view for your web page view. You can also select the Model Space view. You can include multiple layout views from a single drawing if you like.

Label Lets you supply a label or name for the view you've selected in the Layout drop-down list. The label is useful for identifying the drawing's view in the web page.

Description Lets you supply a full description of the view selected in the Layout drop-down list.

ADDING DRAWINGS TO THE IMAGE LIST

Once you've selected a file and a layout and you've added a label and description, you can click the Add button to add your selection to the Image List in the Select Drawings dialog box. Let's continue using the Publish to Web Wizard by adding a few views to the Image list.

1. With the `13a-plan.dwg` file selected in the Drawings drop-down list, select Model from the Layout drop-down list.
2. Enter **Overall floor plan** in the Label input box.

3. Enter **Model Space view of floor plan** in the Description input box.
4. Click the Add button. The label you entered in step 2 appears in the Image List.
5. Select Layout1 from the Layout drop-down list. Notice that the Label input box changes to show Layout1 and the Description input box becomes blank.
6. Change the Label input box to read **Floor plan Layout1**.
7. Change the Description to **Layout1 view of floor plan**, and click the Add button.

Now suppose you've decided that you don't like the label you provided for the Model Space view. You can go back and change an option before you commit to creating the web page.

1. In the Image List, click Overall Floor Plan. Notice that the options in Image Settings change back to those you entered for that option.
2. Change the Label input box to read **Floor plan MS**; then click the Update button. The name in the Image List changes to the new label.

You can add more drawings and images to the Image List. But for this exercise, let's move on to the next step to complete the web page.

1. Click the Next button to open the Generate Images screen. Here you can choose whether to regenerate all your images or just the ones that have changed. These options are relevant only if you are updating an existing page.
2. Click Next. AutoCAD will take a moment to create the page. If you selected a layout for one of the images but have not set up the layout yet, AutoCAD opens the Page Setup dialog box. This allows you to set up the layout options before AutoCAD creates the .dwf file for the layout.
3. If the Page Setup dialog box is open, close it. The Preview And Post screen opens.

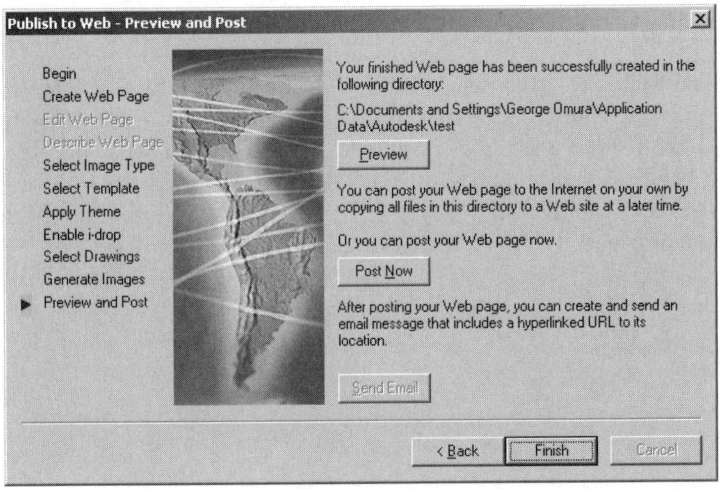

4. Click the Preview button. Your web browser opens and displays the page you created. Notice that you can see your labels and descriptions of the drawings in the web page. You can use the scroll bars to get a better view of the plan.

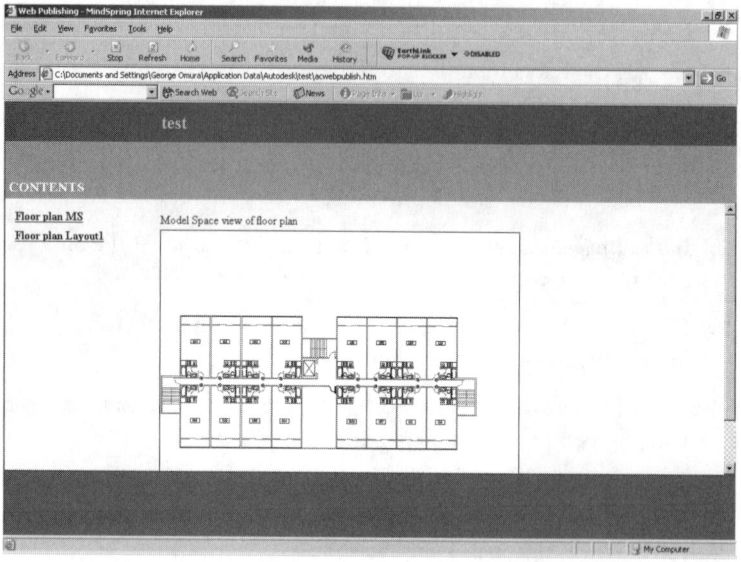

5. Close the preview of your web page; then click Post Now in the Preview And Post screen. You see a file dialog box that allows you to select a location for your web page files.
6. Select a location and click Save. You might want to use the Create New Folder option to create a new folder for your test web page.
7. Click the Finish button to exit the wizard.

The Publish to Web wizard creates all the files needed for the page, including the JavaScript code to allow viewers of the page to drag and drop drawings from the page into their AutoCAD sessions. Figure 22.1 shows a listing of the files for the exercise you just completed.

If you feel creative, you can use the Publish to Web wizard as a starting point to create custom web pages of your drawings, or you can use the pages as is. You can edit the pages using any number of web programs such as Adobe GoLive or Microsoft FrontPage.

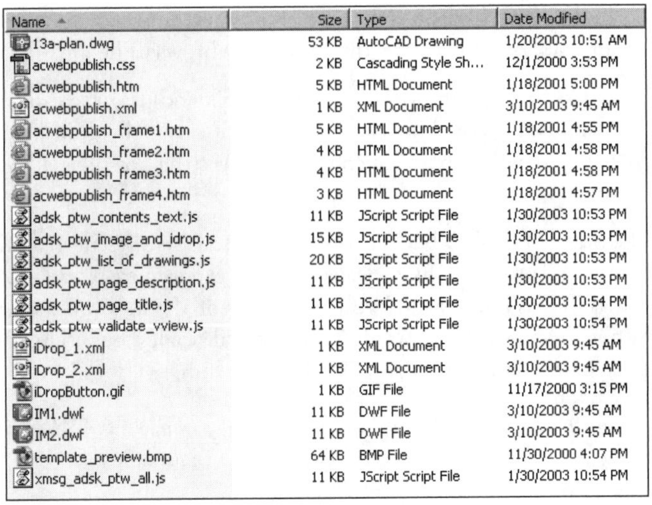

Name	Size	Type	Date Modified
13a-plan.dwg	53 KB	AutoCAD Drawing	1/20/2003 10:51 AM
acwebpublish.css	2 KB	Cascading Style Sh...	12/1/2000 3:53 PM
acwebpublish.htm	5 KB	HTML Document	1/18/2001 5:00 PM
acwebpublish.xml	1 KB	XML Document	3/10/2003 9:45 AM
acwebpublish_frame1.htm	5 KB	HTML Document	1/18/2001 4:55 PM
acwebpublish_frame2.htm	4 KB	HTML Document	1/18/2001 4:58 PM
acwebpublish_frame3.htm	4 KB	HTML Document	1/18/2001 4:58 PM
acwebpublish_frame4.htm	3 KB	HTML Document	1/18/2001 4:57 PM
adsk_ptw_contents_text.js	11 KB	JScript Script File	1/30/2003 10:53 PM
adsk_ptw_image_and_idrop.js	15 KB	JScript Script File	1/30/2003 10:53 PM
adsk_ptw_list_of_drawings.js	20 KB	JScript Script File	1/30/2003 10:53 PM
adsk_ptw_page_description.js	11 KB	JScript Script File	1/30/2003 10:53 PM
adsk_ptw_page_title.js	11 KB	JScript Script File	1/30/2003 10:54 PM
adsk_ptw_validate_vview.js	11 KB	JScript Script File	1/30/2003 10:54 PM
iDrop_1.xml	1 KB	XML Document	3/10/2003 9:45 AM
iDrop_2.xml	1 KB	XML Document	3/10/2003 9:45 AM
iDropButton.gif	1 KB	GIF File	11/17/2000 3:15 PM
IM1.dwf	11 KB	DWF File	3/10/2003 9:45 AM
IM2.dwf	11 KB	DWF File	3/10/2003 9:45 AM
template_preview.bmp	64 KB	BMP File	11/30/2000 4:07 PM
xmsg_adsk_ptw_all.js	11 KB	JScript Script File	1/30/2003 10:54 PM

FIGURE 22.1

The web page files used for the sample page

USING YOUR WEB SPACE

Nearly all Internet service providers (ISPs) offer web space as part of their basic package. Web space is an area on your Internet provider's computer reserved for you alone. You can place your web pages there for others to view. Of course, along with the web space you get your own web address. If you are using the Internet now, but aren't sure whether you can use your Internet account to post web pages, check with your ISP. You may already have the web space and not even know it.

Once you've established your web space, you'll need to know how to post your Web pages. If you need help in this area, try a book such as *Effective Web Design, Second Edition* by Ann Navarro (Sybex, 2001).

Exchanging .dwg Files Using i-drop

If you need to share your AutoCAD drawings with a lot of people, you can post your files on your website and allow others to download them. This is typically done through a web page by assigning a graphic or a string of text to a file. A person viewing your page can then click the graphic or text to start the download process.

AutoCAD also offers i-drop, a way to open files directly from a web page. You'll need to know the name of the file you are downloading, but beyond that, the process is quite simple. Try downloading a sample drawing from my web page at `www.omura.com` to see how this process works.

1. Connect to your ISP and close all open files in AutoCAD.
2. With AutoCAD open, choose File ➢ Open to open the Select File dialog box.
3.  Click the Search The Web tool in the Select File dialog box menu bar. The Browse The Web dialog box opens, with a window showing the selected website (by default, the Autodesk site).

4. In the Look In drop-down list, enter **www.omura.com/autocad/idrop↵**. The web page appears. As you can see, the AutoCAD Browse The Web dialog box acts as a web browser.
5. Go to the bottom of the page; then click and drag the i-drop icon from the page into the blank AutoCAD window. The file is automatically downloaded and opens in AutoCAD. If you have a file already open in AutoCAD, the downloaded file will be inserted in the open drawing.

The Search The Web button you used in step 3 is present in all the file dialog boxes that you encounter in AutoCAD. This means that you can import blocks, Xrefs, and even raster image files from websites, as long as you know the names of the files you want to import.

Although you used the AutoCAD Select File dialog box to import a file using i-drop, you can also use your web browser to accomplish the same thing.

TIP *You can also click and drag a .dwf file from a web page into AutoCAD to download and open a .dwg file, provided that a .dwg file with the same name as the .dwf file exists on the website.*

Adding Hyperlinks to Drawings

The Internet gave the world a tool that is so simple yet so powerful that it has permanently altered the way we look at information. Virtually every web page we view contains a hypertext link—a word, a sentence, or an image that takes us to another web page. Such links allow the viewer to explore the content of a web page or gather more information on a particular topic.

AutoCAD offers a similar tool that you can apply to your AutoCAD drawings, called hyperlinks. With AutoCAD hyperlinks, you can link any document to an AutoCAD object. Then, with a few clicks of your mouse, you can open these links to view other drawings, text files, spreadsheets, or web pages. Once you create a hyperlink in an AutoCAD drawing, you can export the drawing to a .dwf file, and that .dwf file will also contain the same links. You can then post that .dwf file on a web page where others can gain access to those links.

The inclusion of hyperlinks in drawings and .dwf files opens a world of new possibilities in the way that you work with drawings. You can link product specifications directly to the objects in the drawing that represent that product. You can also link to extended data beyond the simple symbol or graphic in a drawing, such as a database table or a spreadsheet.

You don't have to limit your links to HTML files containing AutoCAD drawings. You can link to all sorts of web documents, to drawings on your computer or your company network, and even to documents on other sites.

CREATING HYPERLINKS

The following shows you how to add links to a sample floor plan.

1. In AutoCAD, open the file `houseplan.dwg` in this chapter's folder from the companion CD.
2. Choose Insert ➢ Hyperlink.
3. At the `Select objects:` prompt, click all the hexagonal door symbols, as shown in Figure 22.2.

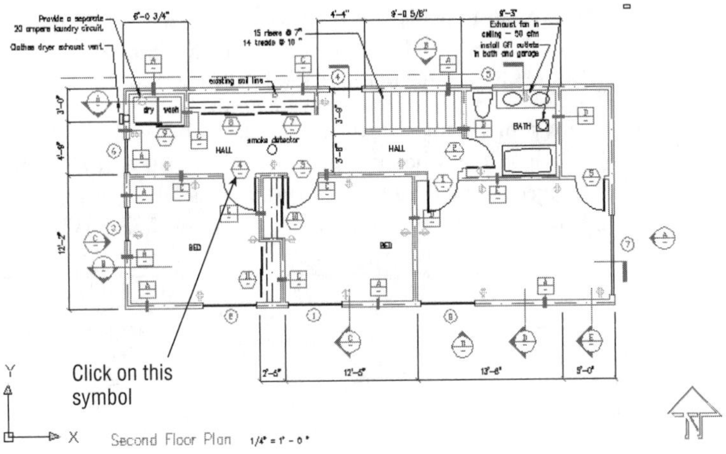

FIGURE 22.2

The door symbol in the `Houseplan.dwg` file

4. When you're done, press ↵. The Insert Hyperlink dialog box opens (see Figure 22.3).

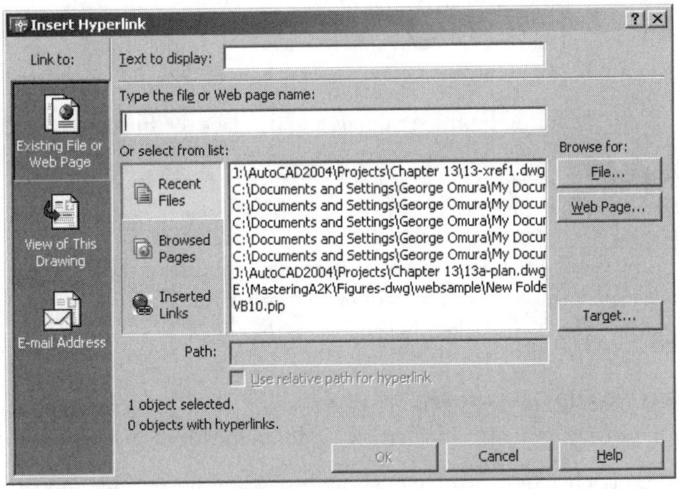

FIGURE 22.3

The Insert Hyperlink dialog box

5. Click the File button on the right side of the dialog box to open the Browse The Web – Select Hyperlink dialog box. It's a typical file window.
6. Locate the `doorsch.html` file in the `\Projects\` subfolder and select it.
7. Click Open. The Insert Hyperlink dialog box reappears. Notice that `doorsch.html` appears in the list box at the top of the dialog box.
8. Make sure the Use Relative Path For Hyperlink option is not checked, and then click OK.

The link you just created is stored with the drawing file. You can then create a .dwf file from this drawing, and the link will be preserved in the .dwf file.

Now let's see how you can use the link from within the AutoCAD file.

1. Move your cursor over the hexagonal door symbol. Notice that the cursor changes to the Hyperlink icon when it is placed on the symbol. It also shows the name of the file to which the object is linked. This tells you that the object is linked to another document somewhere on your system, on your network, or on the World Wide Web.

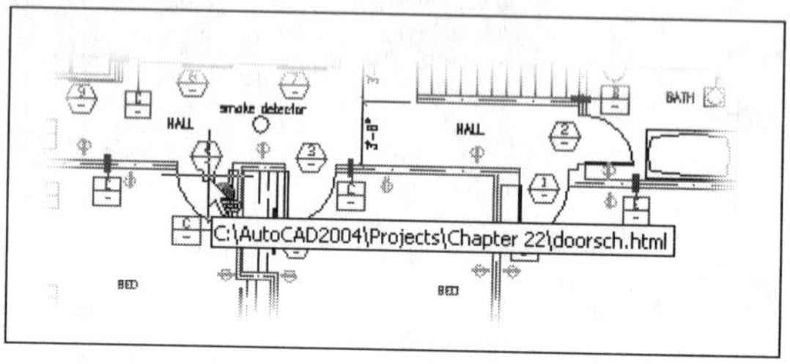

2. Click the hexagonal door symbol to select it.
3. Right-click a blank area of the drawing. In the shortcut menu, choose Hyperlink ➢ Open and choose `C:\ ACAD2004\Projects\Chapter 22\ doorsch.html`.

Your default web browser opens and displays the file `doorsch.html`.

WARNING *If you installed the sample figures from the companion CD on another drive or folder location, the Hyperlink menu option will reflect that location instead of the one shown in step 3.*

You've used the `doorsch.html` file as an example in these exercises, but this could have been a text file, a spreadsheet, a database, or even another AutoCAD file. AutoCAD will start the application associated with the linked file and open the file.

EDITING AND DELETING HYPERLINKS

You can edit or delete a hyperlink by doing the following.

1. Right-click the object whose link you want to edit, and then choose Hyperlink ➢ Edit Hyperlink from the shortcut menu to open the Edit Hyperlink dialog box (see Figure 22.4).
2. You can now change the link, or you can click the Remove Link button in the lower-left corner of the dialog box to delete the link altogether.

When you create a hyperlink that connects to an AutoCAD drawing file, you can set up the link to open a specific view in the drawing. You do this by entering the name of the view in the Named Location In File input box in the Edit Hyperlink dialog box. You can also link to a specific point in a word-processed document by entering the name of a bookmark in this input box. If you're linking to an HTML document, you can enter an anchor name to go to a specific anchor.

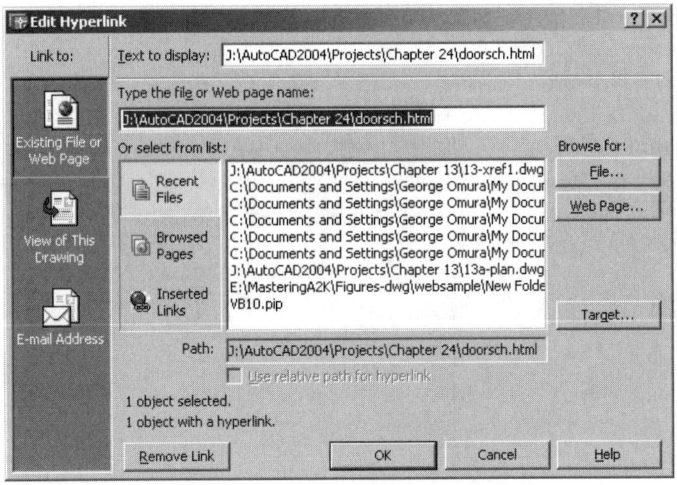

FIGURE 22.4
The Edit Hyperlink dialog box

TAKING A CLOSER LOOK AT THE HYPERLINK OPTIONS

You were introduced to the Insert Hyperlink dialog box, shown in Figure 22.4, in the previous exercises. Let's take a moment to study this dialog box in a little more detail.

To specify a file or a website to link to, you can enter either a filename or a website URL in the Type The File Or Web Page Name input box or use the Or Select From List area, which offers a list box and three button options. When you select one of the buttons, the list box changes to offer further, related options.

Recent Files Displays a list of recently edited AutoCAD files, as illustrated in Figure 22.3. You can then link the object to a file in the list by clicking the filename.

Browsed Pages Displays a list of websites that you recently visited using your Internet Explorer browser.

Inserted Links Displays a list of recently inserted links including files or websites.

You can also use the three buttons to the right of the list box to locate specific files, websites, or saved views within the current drawing. As you saw in the exercise, the File button opens the Browse The Web dialog box, which lets you locate and select a file from your computer, from your local area network, or even from an FTP site. This is a typical AutoCAD file dialog box with some additional features.

The buttons in the left column let you select the location of your file search. You can also select a location using the file navigation tools at the top of the dialog box.

The Web Page button on the right opens a simplified web browser that lets you locate a web page for linking (see Figure 22.3). In this dialog box, you can use the standard methods for going to web pages such as using the Look In drop-down list to select recently visited pages or entering a URL in the Name Of URL input box. The page is then displayed in the main window of the dialog box.

Finally, the Target button in the Insert Hyperlink dialog box opens the Select Place In Document dialog box (see Figure 22.5), which lists the saved views within the drawing that is selected in the Edit Hyperlink list box.

FIGURE 22.5
The Select Place In Document dialog box

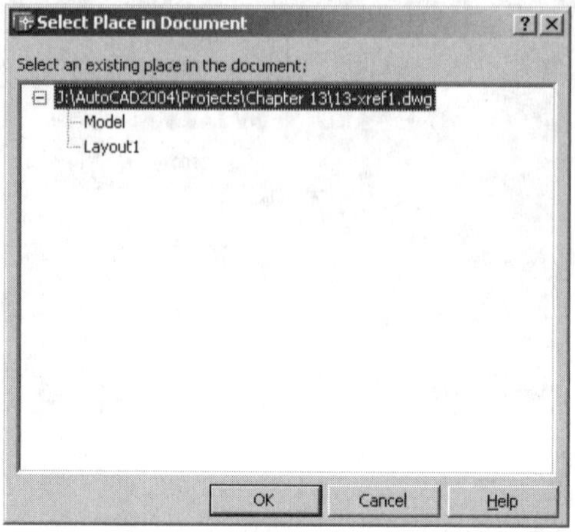

Views are subdivided by Layout tab. At the top is the Model Space tab listing and below that are other Layout tab listings. If the current drawing contains saved views, you'll see a plus sign next to the Layout tab name. Click the plus sign to display a listing of the views in that layout.

At the very top of the Insert Hyperlink and Edit Hyperlink dialog boxes, you have an input box labeled Text To Display. When a hyperlink is added to an object in AutoCAD, AutoCAD will display a hyperlink icon whenever the cursor passes over the object. You can also include a descriptive text that will display along with the icon by entering a description in the Text To Display input box.

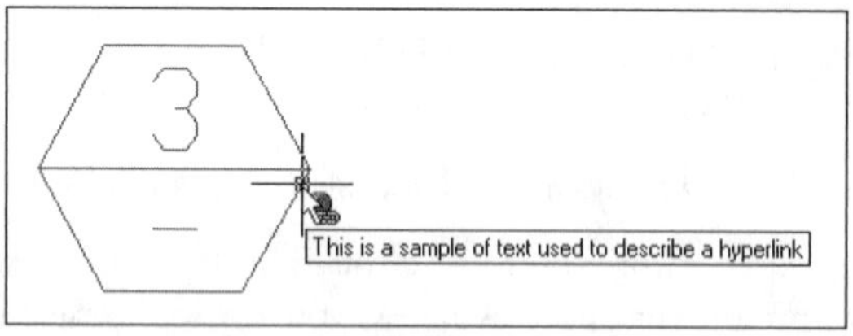

By default, the text is simply the name of the hyperlinked item that you select. You can change the text to provide a better description of the link.

Finally, there is a column of options to the far left of the Insert Hyperlink dialog box, labeled Link To. The top button, Existing File Or Web Page, displays the options discussed so far in this section. The other two buttons change the appearance of the Insert Hyperlink dialog to offer some different but familiar options.

The View Of This Drawing button changes the display to show just the views that are available in the current drawing. This option performs the same function as the Target button described earlier.

The E-Mail Address button changes the Insert Hyperlink dialog to allow you to link an e-mail address to an object. Clicking the object will then open your default e-mail application, allowing you to send a message to the address.

Managing Your Drawings with DesignCenter and the Tool Palettes

As you start to build a library of drawings, you'll find that you reuse many components of existing drawing files. Most of the time, you will probably be producing similar types of drawings with some variation, so you'll reuse drawing components such as layer settings, dimension styles, and layouts. It can be a major task just to keep track of all the projects you've worked on. It's especially frustrating when you remember setting up a past drawing in a way that you know would be useful in a current project, but you can't remember that file's name or location.

AutoCAD 2004 offers DesignCenter to help you keep track of the documents you use in your projects. You can think of DesignCenter as a kind of super Windows Explorer that is focused on AutoCAD files. DesignCenter lets you keep track of your favorite files and helps you locate files, blocks, and other drawing components. In addition, you can import blocks and other drawing components from one drawing to another by using a simple click and drag. If you've been diligent about setting a unit format for each of your drawings, you can use DesignCenter to import symbols and drawings of different unit formats into a drawing, and the symbols will maintain their proper size. For example, a 90-cm door symbol from a metric drawing can be imported into a drawing in Imperial units, and the DesignCenter will translate the 90 cm metric door size to a 35.43-inch door.

Getting Familiar with DesignCenter

At first glance, DesignCenter looks a bit mysterious. But it only takes a few mouse clicks to reveal a tool that looks much like Windows Explorer. Try the following steps to get familiar with DesignCenter.

1. Open AutoCAD to a new file, and then click the DesignCenter tool on the Standard toolbar.

DesignCenter opens as a floating palette (see Figure 22.6).

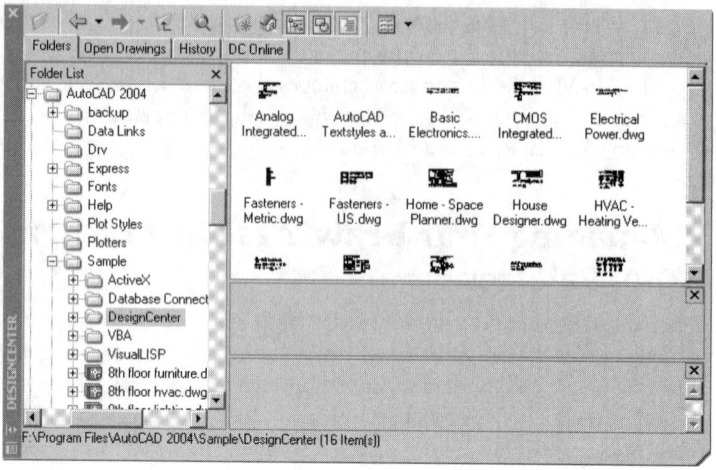

FIGURE 22.6

DesignCenter opens as a floating palette.

TIP *If your DesignCenter view doesn't look like this, with the DesignCenter window divided into two parts, click the Tree View Toggle tool in the DesignCenter toolbar. The tree view opens on the left side of the DesignCenter window. Click the Home tool to display the contents of the* `\Sample\DesignCenter` *folder.*

2. Click the Favorites tool in the DesignCenter toolbar.

DesignCenter displays a listing of the `Favorites` folder. What you are actually looking at is a view into the `C:\Documents and Settings\`*`User Name`*`\Favorites\Autodesk` folder in which *`User Name`* is your login name. Unless you've already added items to the `\Favorites\Autodesk` folder, you see a blank view in the right-hand panel. You can add shortcuts to this folder as you work with DesignCenter. You may also see a view showing the tree structure of the files you have open in AutoCAD.

3. Place your cursor in the lower-right corner of the DesignCenter window so that a double-headed diagonal arrow shows; then click and drag the corner out so that you have an enlarged DesignCenter window that looks similar to Figure 22.7. By the way, the view on the right containing the `DesignCenter` folder is called the Palette view and the view on the left is called the Tree view.
4. Place your cursor on the border between the Tree view and the Palette view until you see a double-headed cursor. Then click and drag the border to the right to enlarge the Tree view until it covers about one-third of the window.
5. Finally, use the scroll bar at the bottom to adjust your view of the Tree view so you can easily read its contents.

TIP *Like the Tool Palettes and the Properties palette, Design Center has an auto-hide feature. To use it, click the double-headed arrow icon near the bottom of the DesignCenter title bar. DesignCenter will disappear except for the title bar. You can then quickly open DesignCenter by placing the cursor on the title bar.*

FIGURE 22.7

The components of the DesignCenter palette

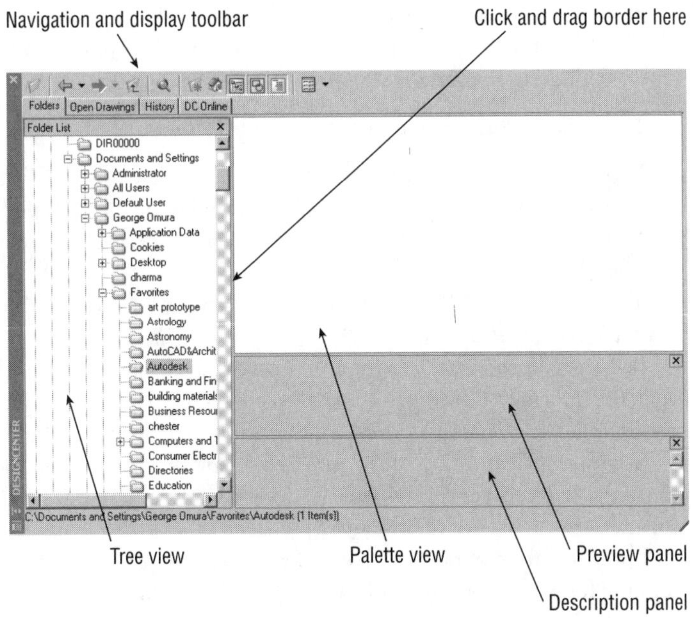

Once you have it set up like this, you can see the similarities between DesignCenter and Windows Explorer. You can navigate your computer or network using the Tree view, just as you would in Windows Explorer. There are a few differences, however, as you'll see in the following exercise.

1. Click the Home tool in the Design Center toolbar. The view changes to display the contents of the `DesignCenter` folder under the `\AutoCAD2004\Samples\` folder.

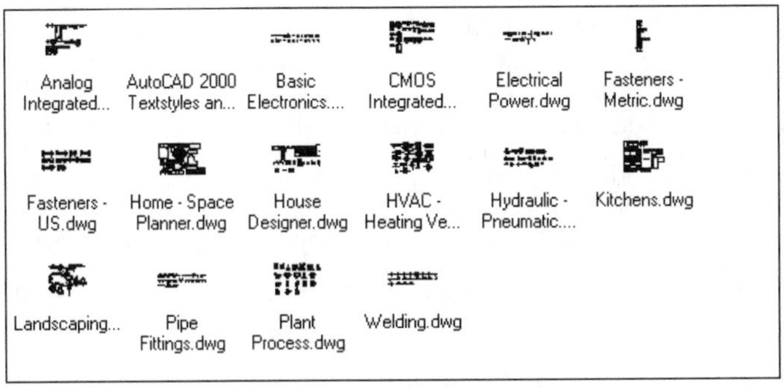

2. Instead of the usual listing of files, you see sample images of each file. These are called *preview icons.*

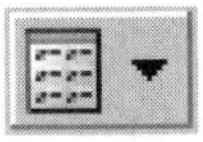

3. Click the Views tool in the DesignCenter toolbar, and then choose Details from the menu.

   The Palette view changes to show a detailed list of the files in the `DesignCenter` folder.

4. Click the Views tool again, and then choose Large Icon to return to the previous view. The Views tool is similar to the Large Icon, Small Icon, List, and Detail options in Windows Explorer.
5. Click the `Basic Electronics.dwg` file to select it.

You see a preview of the selected file in the Preview panel of DesignCenter. You can adjust the vertical size of the Preview panel by clicking and dragging its top or bottom border.

You can also open and close the Preview panel by clicking the Preview tool in the Design Center toolbar.

The preview can be helpful if you prefer viewing files and drawing components as a list in the main part of the Palette view.

Below the Preview panel is the Description panel. This panel displays any text information included with the drawing or drawing element selected in the Palette view. To add a description to a drawing, choose File ➢ Properties; to add a description to a block, use the Block Definition dialog box.

You can open and close this panel by clicking the Description tool in the Design Center toolbar. Since the `Basic Electronics.dwg` file doesn't have a description attached, the description panel shows the message "No description found."

Both the Preview and the Description panels can offer help in identifying files that you may be looking for. Once you find a file, you can click and drag it into a folder in the Tree view to organize your files into separate folders.

You can also add files to the `Favorites` folder under the `Windows` folder by right-clicking and then choosing Add To Favorites. The file itself won't be moved to the `Favorites` folder; instead, a shortcut to the file will be created in the `Favorites` folder. If you want to work on organizing your `Favorites` folder, you can open a window to the `Favorites` folder by right-clicking a file in the Palette view and choosing Organize Favorites. A window to the `Favorites` folder appears.

Since you'll be working with the sample drawings from the companion CD, go ahead and add the `Projects` folder to the `Favorites` folder.

1. Locate the `Projects` folder (the one created when you installed the sample files from the companion CD) in the left panel Tree view and right-click it.
2. Choose Add To Favorites from the shortcut menu.

3. To go directly to the `Favorites` folder, click the Favorites tool in the DesignCenter toolbar.

   The `Favorites` folder appears in the right panel in Palette view.
4. Double-click the Projects shortcut in the Palette view. You see the contents of the `Projects` folder.

You can go beyond just looking at file listings. You can look inside files to view their components.

1. In the Palette view, locate the file named `17b-unit.dwg` in the `Chapter 17` folder and double-click it. You see a listing of its components in the Palette view. The Tree view also shows the file highlighted.
2. Double-click the Block listing in the Palette view. Now you see a listing of all the blocks in `17b-unit.dwg`.

From here, you can import any of the drawing components from the DesignCenter palette into an open drawing in AutoCAD. But before you try that, try a few other features of the DesignCenter.

TIP *If you were to try to view the contents of the file* `17a-unit.dwg`*, you would see that most of the blocks in the drawing do not show preview in the Palette view. This is because the layers for those blocks were turned off when the drawing was last saved. The* `17b-unit.dwg` *file is identical to* `17a-unit.dwg` *except that* `17b-unit.dwg` *has all its layers turned on.*

USING THE FAVORITES TOOL IN THE AUTOCAD FILE DIALOG BOXES

As you use AutoCAD, you may notice the Tools option in the upper-right corner of nearly all file dialog boxes.

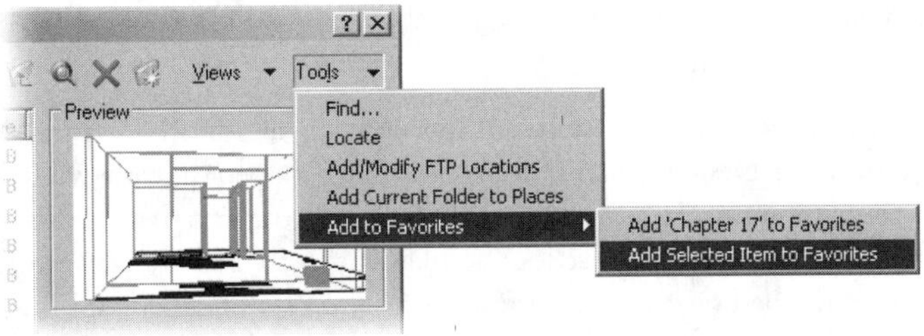

When you choose Tools, you'll find the Add To Favorites option. This option creates a shortcut to the currently selected file and places it in the `Favorites` folder. You can then easily retrieve that file by clicking the Favorites tool in the left column of the file dialog box and selecting the shortcut to the file.

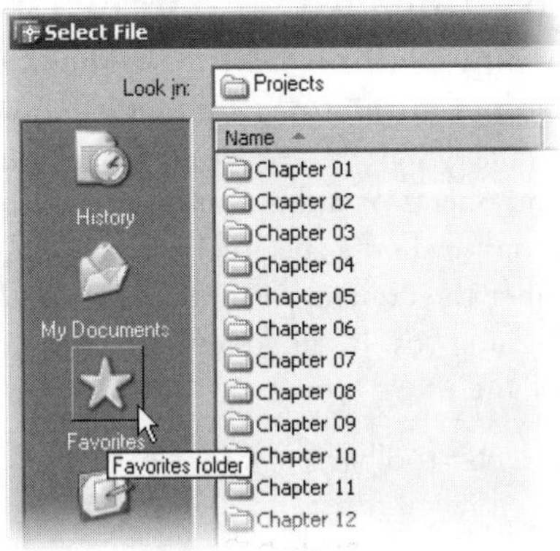

You can use the `Favorites` folder like a collection of bookmarks to those files that you use frequently. Instead of searching your hard disk or your network for a file, use the Look In Favorites tool to go directly to your favorite file. Be aware, however, that if the file is moved from its location at the time the shortcut was made, the shortcut won't work. You'll have to delete the old shortcut and establish a new one using the Add To Favorites tool.

Opening and Inserting Files with DesignCenter

With DesignCenter, you can locate the files you are looking for more easily because you can view thumbnail preview icons. But often that isn't enough. For example, you might want to locate all the files that contain the name of a particular manufacturer in an attribute of a drawing.

Once you've found the file you're looking for, you can load it into AutoCAD by right-clicking the filename in the Palette view and then choosing Open In Window. Try it with the following exercise.

1. Click the Up tool in the DesignCenter toolbar twice. This takes you up two levels in the Palette view from the view of the drawing blocks to the list of filenames.
2. In the Tree view, select the `Chapter 13` folder. Then in the Palette view of DesignCenter, locate the `13c-unit2.dwg` sample.
3. Click and drag `13c-unit2.dwg` to the AutoCAD 2004 title bar. The drawing appears in the AutoCAD window.

If you want to insert a file into another drawing as a block, you can do so by clicking and dragging the file from the DesignCenter Palette view into an open drawing window. You will then be prompted for insertion point, scale, and rotation angle. If you prefer to use the Insert dialog box to insert a drawing from DesignCenter, right-click the filename in the Palette view, and then choose Insert As Block. The Insert dialog box opens, offering you the full set of Insert options, as described in Chapter 3.

Finally, you can attach a drawing as an Xref by right-clicking a file in the Palette view of DesignCenter and choosing Attach As Xref. The External Reference dialog box opens, offering the insertion point, scale, and rotation options similar to the Insert dialog box. This is the same dialog box described in Chapter 6.

Finding and Extracting the Contents of a Drawing

Aside from the convenience of being able to see thumbnail views of your drawing, DesignCenter may not seem like much of an improvement over Windows Explorer. But DesignCenter goes beyond Windows Explorer in many ways. One of the main features of DesignCenter is that it allows you to locate and extract components of a drawing.

Imagine that you want to find a specific block in a drawing. You remember the name of the block, but you don't remember the drawing you put it in. You can search the contents of drawings using DesignCenter's Find dialog box. In the following exercise, you will search for a block named kitchen2-metric among a set of files.

1. In the DesignCenter toolbar, click the Search tool to open the Search dialog box.

   It looks similar to the Search tool that comes with Windows.

2. Select the drive that contains your `\projects\` folder from the In drop-down list.
3. Select Blocks from the Look For drop-down list. As you can see from the list, you can look for a variety of drawing component types.

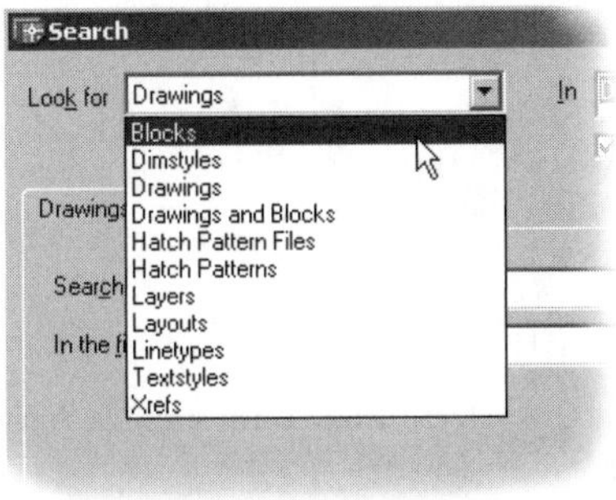

4. Enter **kitchen2-metric↵** in the Search For The Name input box. The magnifying glass icon in the lower-right corner will move back and forth, telling you that it is working. After a minute or two, you'll see the name of the block in the window at the bottom of the dialog box.
5. Double-click the block name. DesignCenter displays the block in the Palette view and the file that contains the block in the Tree view.

Search Options

As you can see from this example, the Search dialog box can be helpful in finding items that are buried in a set of drawings. In the exercise, you searched for a block, but you can search for any named drawing component, including attribute data and text. For example, if you want to find all attributes that contain the name ABC Manufacturing Company in your drawings, you can do so with the DesignCenter Search dialog box. Here is a summary of its features.

In Lets you select the drive you want to search.

Look For Options Lets you select the type of item to search for. The options are Drawings, Drawings And Blocks, Layers, Layouts, Linetypes, Textstyles, and Xrefs.

Browse Lets you locate a specific folder to search.

Search Subfolders Lets you determine whether Search searches subfolders in the drive and folder you specify.

Search Now Starts the search process.

Stop Cancels the current search.

New Search Clears all the settings for the current search so you can start fresh on a new search.

Help Opens the AutoCAD help system to the Search topic.

Additional Hidden Options

When you select Drawings from the Look For drop-down list, you see a set of additional tabs in the Search dialog box:

The Drawings Tab Contains two options:

Search For The Word(s) Lets you specify the text to search for in the Drawing Properties fields.

In The Field(s) Lets you specify the field of the Drawing Properties dialog box to search through, including filename, title, subject, author, and keyword. These are the fields you see when you choose File ➢ Drawing Properties.

The Date Modified Tab Lets you limit search criteria based on dates.

The Advanced Tab Offers three options to further limit your search to specific types of drawing data or to a range of dates:

Containing Lets you select from a list of data to search for, including block name, block and drawing description, attribute tag, and attribute value.

Containing Text Lets you specify the text to search for in the types of data you select from the Containing option.

Size Is Lets you restrict the search to files greater than or less than the size you specify.

Automatically Scaling Blocks at Insertion

Once you've found the block using DesignCenter, you can click and drag the block into your open drawing. In the following exercise, you'll do just that, but with a slight twist. The block you've found is drawn in centimeters, but you'll be inserting the Kitchen2-metric block into a drawing named `13c-unit2.dwg`, which was created in the Imperial measurement system. If you were to insert the Kitchen2-metric block into `13c-unit2.dwg`, the kitchen would be exactly 2.54 times larger than it should be for `13c-unit2.dwg`. But as you'll see, DesignCenter takes care of scaling for you.

1. In AutoCAD, make sure the `13c-unit2.dwg` sample drawing is loaded if you haven't done so already. You can temporarily close DesignCenter to do this.
2. Back in DesignCenter, click and drag the Kitchen2-metric block from the Palette view into the `13c-unit2.dwg` window in AutoCAD. The kitchen appears at the appropriate scale.
3. To see that DesignCenter did indeed adjust the scale of the Kitchen2- metric block, click it in the 13c-unit2 window, and then right-click and choose Properties.
4. Check the Scale X, Scale Y, and Scale Z settings in the Geometry category. Notice that they show .3937 as the scale factor instead of 1.
5. After reviewing the Properties palette, close it.

You may recall from Chapter 3 that you have the opportunity to specify the type of units the drawing is set up for in the Units dialog box under the Drag And Drop Scale drop-down list. DesignCenter uses this information when you drag and drop blocks from DesignCenter into an open drawing. This is how DesignCenter is able to correctly scale a block drawn in metric to a drawing that is drawn in the Imperial format. The same option is offered in the Block Definition dialog box.

Blocks aren't the only type of drawing component you can click and drag from the Palette view. Line types, layouts, dimension styles, and text styles can all be imported from files on your computer or network through DesignCenter's Palette view.

Exchanging Data between Open Files

You've seen how you can extract a block from a file stored on your hard drive and place it into an open drawing, but what if you want to copy a block from one open drawing to another open drawing? You change the way the Tree view displays data so that it shows only the files that are loaded in AutoCAD. The following exercise demonstrates how this works.

1. In AutoCAD, make sure that `13c-unit2.dwg` is still open; then open the `13c-unit2-metric.dwg` file.
2. In DesignCenter, click the Open Drawings tab above the Tree view. The Tree view changes to display only the drawings that are open.
3. Click the plus sign (+) to the left of the `13c-unit2.dwg` filename in the Tree view. The list expands to show the components in `13c-unit2.dwg`.
4. Click Blocks in the Tree view. The Palette view changes to show a list of blocks available in `13c-unit2.dwg`.
5. Locate the Kitchen block in the Palette view.
6. Click and drag Kitchen from the Palette view into the open `13c-unit2- metric.dwg` drawing in AutoCAD. You see the block move with the cursor. Once again, DesignCenter has automatically scaled the block to the appropriate size, this time from Imperial to metric.
7. Click anywhere in the drawing to place the Kitchen block.

In this example, you inserted a block from one open drawing into another drawing. If you prefer to use the Insert dialog box, you can right-click the block name in step 6 and choose Insert Block. The Insert dialog box opens, allowing you to set the insertion point, scale, and rotation options.

Just as with drawings, you can see a preview and descriptive text for blocks below the Palette view. In Chapter 3, you had the option to save a preview icon with the block when you first created a block. This is where that preview icon can be really helpful. The preview icon gives you a chance to see what the block looks like when you use DesignCenter to browse through your drawing files. If you don't save a preview icon, you'll see the same block icon that was displayed in the previous Palette view.

You can also add the text description at the time you create the block. Before saving the block, enter a description in the Description input box of the Block Definition dialog box.

If you're updating older drawing files to be used with DesignCenter, you can add text descriptions to blocks using the Make Block tool in the Draw toolbar. Click the Make Block tool, and then, in the Block Definition dialog box, select the name of a block from the Name drop-down list. Enter the description you want for this block in the Description input box toward the bottom of the Block Definition dialog box. When you're finished, click OK.

Loading Specific Files into DesignCenter

You've seen how you can locate files through the Tree view and Palette view. If you already know the name and location of the file you want to work with, you can use a file dialog box to open files in DesignCenter. Instead of choosing File ➢ Open, you use the Load tool in the DesignCenter toolbar to open the Load dialog box. This is a standard file dialog box that lets you search for files on your computer or network.

If you want to open a file in DesignCenter that you've recently opened, you can use the History tab just above the Tree view.

1. In DesignCenter, click the History tab. The Tree view closes, and you see a list of the most recent files you've worked on.

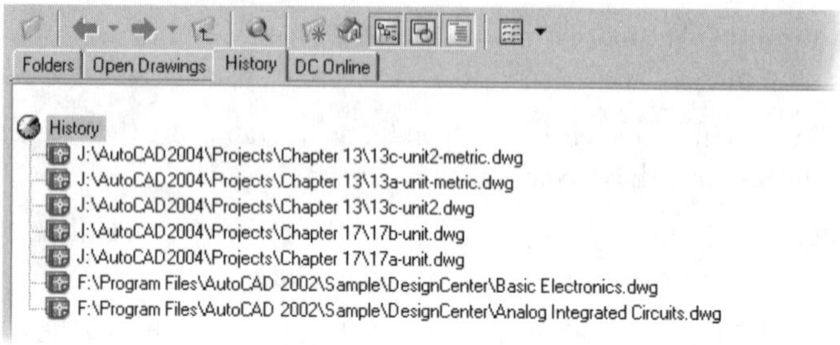

2. Locate `13c-unit2.dwg` and double-click it. The Tree view returns, displaying the file you selected, and the Palette view displays the contents of the selected file.

Downloading Symbols from DesignCenter Online

Besides allowing you to obtain files and blocks from your computer or network, you can also download symbols directly from Autodesk's DesignCenter Online website. This option offers thousands of ready-to-use symbols for a variety of disciplines.

1. Connect to the Internet.

2. Click the DesignCenter Online tab that appears above the Tree view. The DesignCenter Online symbol categories appear in the Tree view, and the Palette view shows the same categories in a text view.

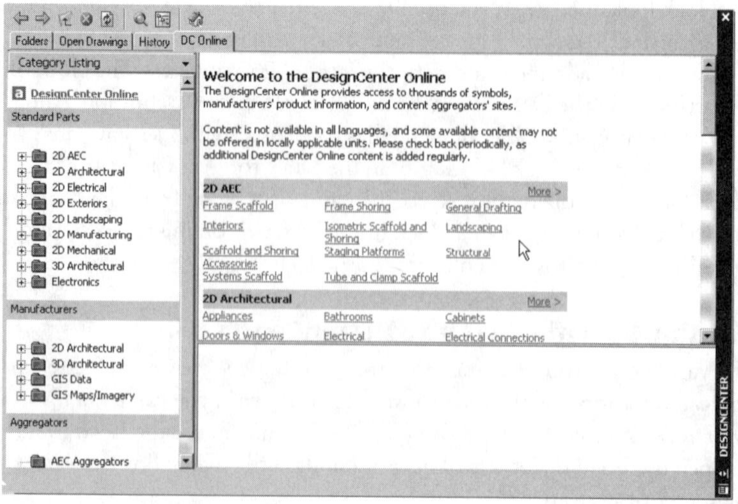

3. Expand the 2D Architectural listing to display a set of subcatgories.
4. Expand the Bathrooms category, and then click Bath Tubs. The Palette view displays a set of bath tubs.
5. Place the cursor over one of the bath tubs. The i-drop icon appears.
6. Click a tub to display an enlarged preview of the tub in the display panel along with a description of the symbol.
7. Click and drag a symbol into the current open drawing. The i-drop cursor appears in the drawing. When you release the mouse button, the symbol appears at the cursor, waiting for you to select an insertion point.
8. Click a location to place the symbol.
9. To return to the opening page of DesignCenter Online, click the DesignCenter Online listing at the top of the Tree view.

Since DesignCenter Online is a website, AutoCAD uses the i-drop feature to bring the symbols into your drawing. As you can see, the list of symbols is fairly extensive. Many of the symbols are samples from third-party vendors that offer expanded symbols libraries.

Customizing the Tool Palettes with DesignCenter

Many AutoCAD users have built their own custom library of symbols and are accustomed to using them in conjunction with custom menus. But creating and editing menus is a bit cumbersome and can become difficult to manage. In Chapter 1, you saw how easy it is to drag and drop a symbol, known as a tool, from the Tool Palettes. At first glance, there is no obvious way to add your own tools to the palettes. Adding tools and additional palettes to the Tool Palettes is actually fairly simple once you are familiar with DesignCenter. The following exercise shows you how it's done.

1. If it isn't open already, click the Tool Palettes tool in the Standard toolbar to open the Tool Palettes.
2. Right-click in the Tool Palettes, and then choose New Tool Palette from the shortcut menut.
3. Enter **My Tool Palette**↵. A new, blank tab is added to the Tool Palettes.

4. Go back to DesignCenter and click the Home tool.
5. In the Palette view to the right, double-click the `Landscaping.dwg` file, and then double-click the Blocks icon that appears in the Palette view.
6. Make sure that the Tool Palettes are visible behind DesignCenter, and then Ctrl+click Clump Of Trees Or Bushes – Plan And North Arrow.
7. Click and drag the selection to the Tool Palettes.

WARNING *If you click a tool in a tool palette, it is inserted in the current drawing; so take care when clicking around in the Tool Palettes.*

You've just created a tool palette and added two symbols. You can continue to add symbols from other drawings to your custom tool palette. Or, if you have a drawing that contains all the blocks you need for a tool palette, you can quickly create a tool palette directly from a file. Here's how that's done.

1. In DesignCenter, click the Up tool to move up one folder level to the `\Samples` folder.
2. Scroll down the Tree view to locate the `Wilhome.dwg` file. You'll use `Wilhome.dwg` as a sample because it contains a lot of blocks.
3. Right-click `Wilhome.dwg`, and then choose Create Tool Palette. After a few moments, a new tool palette called Wilhome appears in the Tool Palettes. This new palette contains all the blocks found in the `Wilhome.dwg` file.

This exercise shows that you can quickly create a palette of all the drawings from a file. You can do the same thing with entire folders of drawings, though you might want to make sure such folders don't contain too many files.

But what if you don't want some of the items in your custom palette? You can remove items easily using a shortcut menu.

1. In the Wilhome palette, select the top three symbols by right-clicking the tool third from the top and then Shift+clicking the top tool. This is a little different from the typical Windows method for selecting items from a list.
2. Right-click, and then choose Delete Tools from the shortcut menu. Click OK to confirm the deletion.

You may have noticed the Cut and Copy options in the shortcut menu in step 2. You can use these options to move symbols from one palette to another. For example, instead of deleting the three symbols in step 2, you can choose Cut from the shortcut menu, open another palette, right-click, and choose Paste. The symbols will move to the new palette location. In the next section, you'll see how you can use the Copy and Paste shortcut menu options to make a copy of a tool within the same palette.

Customizing a Tool

Other shortcut menu options let you delete entire palettes or rename tools or palettes. You can also edit the properties of symbols in a palette. The following exercise shows how you can use the shortcut menu options to create two different scale versions of the same tool.

1. In the My Tool Palette tab of the Tool Palettes, right-click the North Arrow tool and choose Copy from the shortcut menu.
2. Right-click a blank area of the palette and choose Paste. A copy of the North Arrow tool appears in the palette.
3. Right-click the copy of the North Arrow tool, choose Rename from the shortcut menu, and then enter **North Arrow Copy**.
4. Right-click the North Arrow Copy tool, and then choose Properties to open the Tool Properties dialog box.

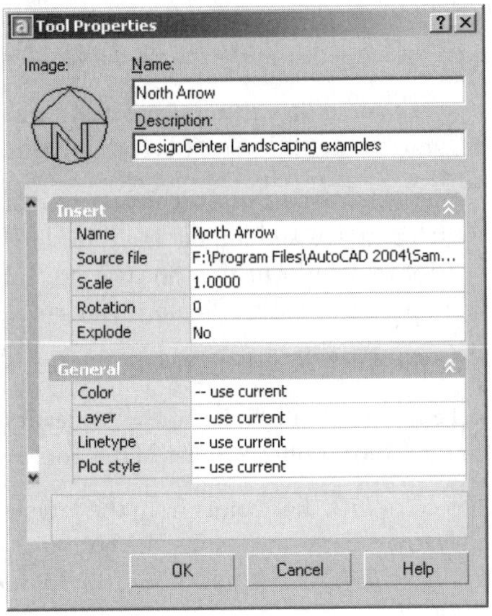

5. Click 1.0000 to the right of the Scale listing and change the value to 4.
6. Click OK, and then click and drag the North Arrow Copy tool into the drawing.
7. Now click and drag the original North Arrow tool into the drawing. Notice that the original North Arrow is smaller than the North Arrow Copy whose scale you changed to 4.

This exercise demonstrates that you can have multiple versions of a tool at different scales. You can then use the tool appropriate to the scale of your drawing. And as you can see from the Tool Properties dialog box, you can modify other tool properties such as color and layer assignments. You can use this feature to set up sets of tools for different scale drawings. For example, you can create a palette of architectural reference symbols for 1/4" scale drawings, and you can create another palette for 1/8" scale drawings.

Adding Hatch Patterns and Solid Fills

You've seen how you can turn blocks into tool palette tools, but what about solid fills? In Chapter 1, you saw that sample hatch patterns and solid fills are available in the Tool Palettes. Here's how you can add your own.

TIP *To find out exactly where support files are located, choose Tools ➢ Options to open the Options dialog box. Click the Files tab. Expand the Support File Search Path listing at the top of the list, and then place the cursor on the item just below Support File Search Path. You'll see the path to the support folder.*

1. In DesignCenter, use the Tree view to locate the `AutoCAD 2004 Support` folder. In Windows XP, it is typically in:

   ```
   C:\Documents and Settings\User Name\Application Data\Autodesk\
   AutoCAD 2004\R16.0\enu\Support
   ```

   (*`User Name`* is your Windows login name.)

2. Double-click the `Acad.pat` file shown in the Palette view. AutoCAD will build a list of the patterns and display the list in the Palette view.
3. You can now click and drag a pattern into any tool palette. You can also click and drag an entire .pat file into the Tools Palette to create a palette of all the patterns in a hatch pattern file.

In this exercise, you used the standard hatch patterns that come with AutoCAD. You can also create your own custom hatch patterns and import them to the Tool Palettes using the method described here. See Chapter 21 for more information on creating custom hatch patterns.

If you want to set up a set of solid fill colors, you can do the following:

1. Click and drag the solid fill pattern from the `Acad.pat` file into the tool palette.
2. Right-click the new solid fill tool, choose Properties from the shortcut menu, and then select a color from the Color drop-down list in the Tool Properties dialog box.

You can select any color including colors from the True Color or Color Book tab in the Select Color dialog box that you learned about in Chapter 4. You can also cut and paste an existing solid fill tool to make copies. You can then modify the color property for each copy to get a set of custom solid fill colors.

MANAGING THE TOOL PALETTES

You can perform other types of Tool Palettes maintenance operations using the Customize dialog box. To open the Customize dialog box, right-click the Tool Palettes and choose Customize from the shortcut menu.

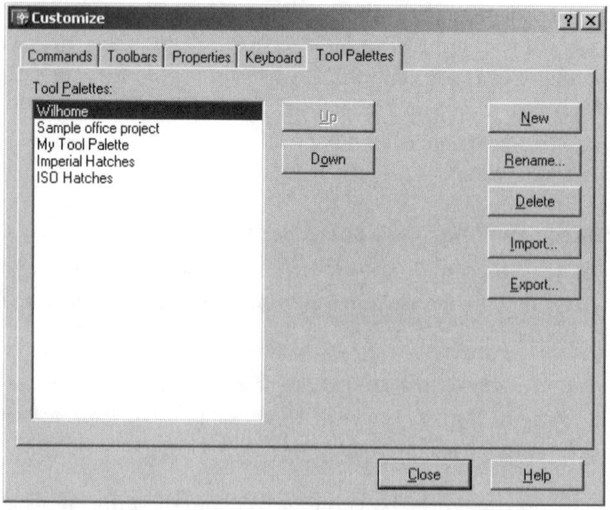

You may recall seeing this dialog box in Chapter 21. Here you can create new palettes or rename existing ones. You can delete palettes or export or import palettes. Click the Up and Down buttons to move a palette up or down the tab list in the Tool Palettes.

WARNING *If you use the Export or Import options to move a palette from one computer to another, be aware that you must also import or export the drawings that are the source files for the palette tools.*

DesignCenter and Tool Palettes offer some great features that will prove invaluable to AutoCAD users. Although these examples show you how to use DesignCenter on a stand-alone computer, you can just as easily perform the same functions across a network or even across the Internet.

This ends our exploration of DesignCenter and Tool Palettes. In the next part of this chapter, you'll look at AutoCAD's tools for maintaining layer-naming and other standards throughout an organization and for converting between your own layering system and those of clients or partners.

Establishing Office Standards

Communication is especially important when you are one of many people working on the same project on separate computers. A well-developed set of standards and procedures helps to minimize problems that might be caused by miscommunication. In this section, you'll find some suggestions for setting up these standards.

Establishing Layering and Text Conventions

The issue of CAD standards has always been difficult to resolve. Standardizing layers, dimensions, and text can go a long way toward making file exchange more seamless between different trades, and standards can also make files easier to understand. CAD standards are analogous to languages. When everyone speaks the same language, communication flows easily; but if you find yourself in a place where everyone speaks a different language, you have difficulty exchanging ideas. Likewise, when everyone follows a standard, the structure of a drawing is more easily understood, and those who have to edit or interpret your work can do so without having to ask a lot of questions. If there are no standards, someone editing your drawing for the first time may have to struggle to know what layers to turn off and on or what dimension style to use.

You have seen how layers can be a useful tool. But they can easily get out of hand when you have free reign over their creation and naming. This can be especially troublesome when more than one person is working on the same set of drawings. The following scenario illustrates this point.

One day, the drawing you are working on has 20 layers. The next day, you find that someone has added six more layers, with names that have no meaning to you whatsoever. You don't dare delete those layers or modify the objects on them, for fear of damaging some organizational scheme you may be unaware of. You ask around, but no one seems to know anything about these new layers. Finally, after spending an hour or two tracking down the purpose of the new layers, you discover that the layers are not important at all.

With an appropriate layer-naming convention, you can minimize this type of problem (though you may not eliminate it entirely). A too-rigid naming convention can cause as many problems as no convention at all, so it is best to give general guidelines rather than force everyone to stay within narrow limits. As mentioned in Chapter 6, you can create layer names in a way that allows you to group them using wildcards. AutoCAD allows up to 31 characters in a layer name, so you can use descriptive names.

Line weights should be standardized in conjunction with colors. If you intend to use a service bureau for your plotting, check with them first; they may require that you conform to their color and line-weight standards.

TIP *If you are an architect, an engineer, or in the construction business, check out some of the CAD layering standards set forth by the American Institute of Architects (AIA) and the Construction Standards Institute (CSI).*

Checking Office Standards

WARNING *The Standards command discussed in this section is not available in AutoCAD LT.*

AutoCAD offers a very open-ended environment that lends itself to easy customization, but this also leaves the door wide open for "on the fly" creation of layer names, dimension styles, and other drawing format options. It's easy to stray from standards, especially when you are under pressure to get a project out on a deadline. So, to help you and your office maintain a level of conformity to office or industry standards, AutoCAD 2004 includes the Standards command.

The Standards command lets you quickly compare a drawing against a set of standard layer names, dimension style settings, line types, and text styles. A dialog box displays any item that does not conform to the standards you selected. You can then adjust the file to make it conform to your standards.

You can create several sets of standards for different types of files, and you can assign the standards directly to a file so that anyone editing that file can make periodic checks against your office standards while the drawing is being edited.

SETTING UP STANDARDS FILES

The first step in using the Standards command is to set up a file to which other drawing files can be compared. Standards uses an AutoCAD drawing file with a .dws filename extension. Here are the steps you take to create a new Standards DWS file.

1. Open AutoCAD and choose File ➢ New.
2. Set up the file with the layers, line types, dimension styles, and text styles you will want as your standards.
3. Choose File ➢ Save As.
4. In the Save Drawing As dialog box, choose AutoCAD 2004 Drawing Standard (*.dws) from the Files Of Type drop-down list.
5. Choose a convenient folder for the location of your standards file and click Save.

As an alternative to creating a new file, you can open an existing file that contains all the typical settings you will want to use on your projects. You can then delete all the graphics in the file and purge all its blocks and shapes. Once you've done this, you can begin at step 3 of the previous exercise to save the file as a .dws Standards file.

You can set up as many .dws files as you need for your office. Often a single set of standards is too limiting if your office is involved in a diverse range of projects, so you might want to set up .dws files on a project basis, drawing on a core of generic .dws files.

USING THE STANDARDS COMMAND TO ASSOCIATE STANDARDS

Once you've created your .dws standards files, you can begin to check other files for conformity. The next step is to assign your .dws file to the drawing file that you want to check.

1. In AutoCAD, open the file you want to check for standards conformity.
2. Choose Tools ➢ CAD Standards ➢ Configure to open the Configure Standards dialog box.

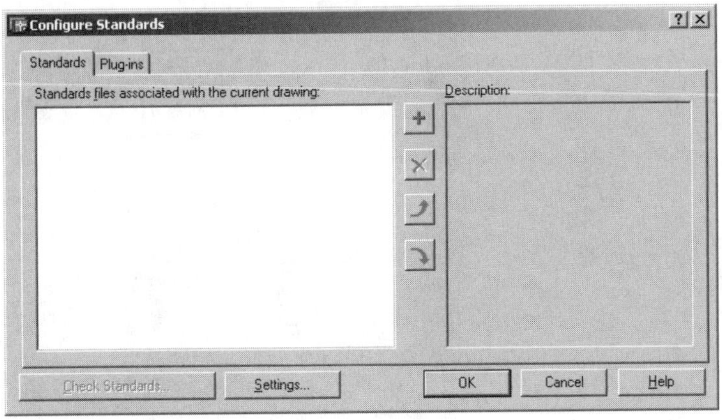

3. Click the Add Standards File (F3) button in the middle column of the dialog box. It's the one with the plus sign on it.
4. The Select Standards File dialog box opens. This is a typical AutoCAD file dialog box. Notice that the Files Of Type drop-down list shows the Standard (*.dws) file type.
5. Locate and select the standards file that you want to use to use to check the current file. After a moment, the name of the file you select appears in the list box of the Configure Standards dialog box. On the right side of the dialog box, you see a listing of the items that will be checked.

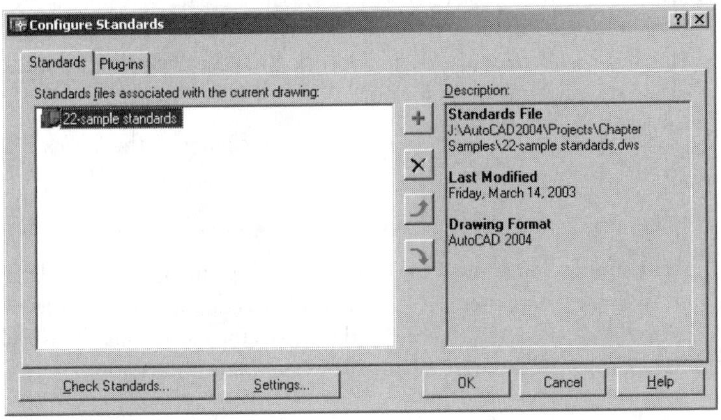

6. Now check the current file against the .dws standards file. Click the Check Standards button in the lower-left corner of the Configure Standards dialog box. AutoCAD pauses while it checks the current file, and then you see the Check Standards dialog box.

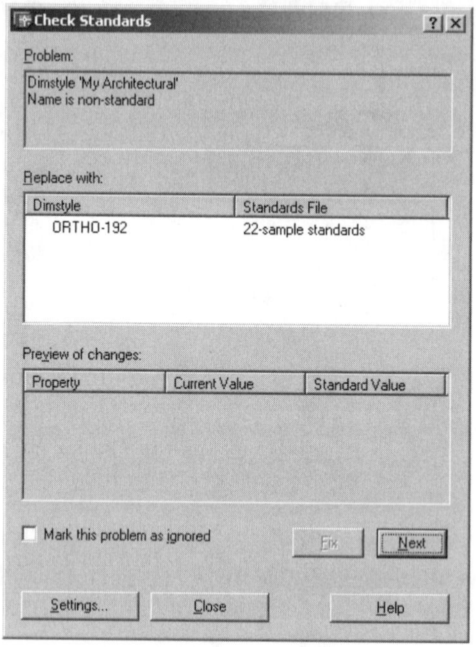

If AutoCAD finds a discrepancy between the standards file and the current file, the problem appears at the top of the dialog box. For example, if a layer name appears in the current file that is not in the standards file, a message appears indicating that a nonstandard layer name exists in the current drawing. If this happens, take the following steps.

1. Below the Problem statement, you see the Replace With list box containing options related to the nonstandard item. You can convert the nonstandard item to an option in the Replace With list box by selecting the option and clicking the check box to the right of the list. Or you can leave the problem alone for now.

2. Click the Next arrow in the bottom-right corner of the Check Standards dialog box to move to the next "problem."

3. Repeat steps 1 and 2 until you see the statement "Checking is complete" in the Problem list box.

In this example, you entered the Check Standards dialog box directly from the Configure Standards dialog box. Once you've used the Check Standards dialog box on a file, the .dws standards file is associated with the checked file. You can go directly to the Check Standards dialog box by choosing Tools ➢ CAD Standards ➢ Check during any subsequent editing session.

TIP *Once you've assigned a .dws standards file to a drawing, you will need to save the drawing, or its association with the .dws file will be lost.*

Checking Standards for Multiple Drawings

The Standards and Check Standards commands are great for checking individual files, but eventually you'll want a method to batch-check a set of files. AutoCAD 2004 provides a utility that does just that. The Batch Standards Checker is a stand-alone utility that audits a set of drawing files and checks them against their associated .dws files. The Batch Standard Checker can also check a set of drawings against a single .dws file of your choice. It then generates an audit report showing the problems it encounters.

Here's how it works.

1. From the Windows desktop, choose Start ➢ All Programs ➢ Autodesk ➢ AutoCAD 2004 ➢ Batch Standards Checker to open the Batch Standards Checker dialog box (see Figure 22.8).

FIGURE 22.8
The Batch Standards Checker dialog box

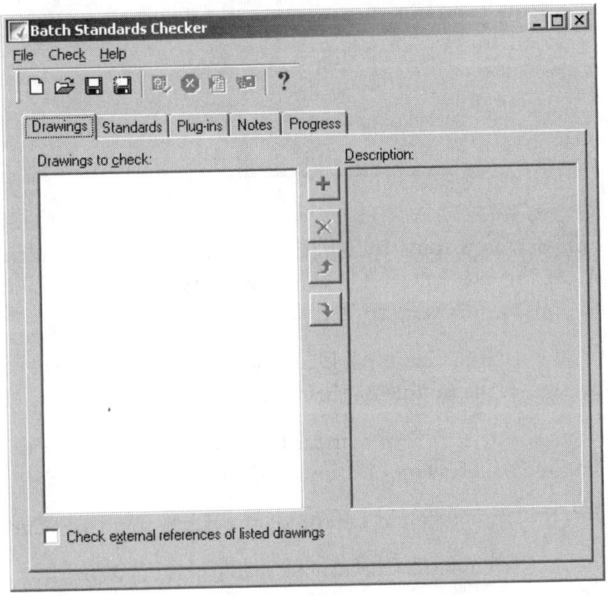

2. Click the Plus button in the middle of the dialog box to open the Batch Standards Checker – File Open dialog box. This is a typical AutoCAD file dialog box.
3. Locate and select the drawings you want to check. You return to the Batch Standards Checker dialog box, and, after a moment, a list of the drawings you selected appears in the Drawings To Check list box.

4. Click the Standards tab. This is where you can select the standards file against which your selection will be checked.

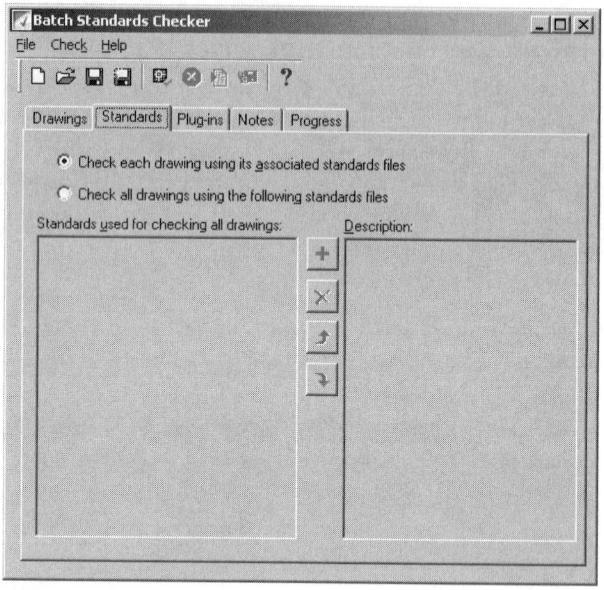

If the drawings you selected in step 3 already have a standards file associated with them, you can use the Check Each Drawing Using Its Associated Standards Files option to check each file. You can then skip to step 7.

5. If you select the Check All Drawings Using The Following Standards Files option, click the plus sign in the middle of the dialog box to open the Batch Standard Checker dialog box.

6. Locate and select a .dws standards file. The file then appears in the Standards Used For Checking All Drawings list box to the left of the Standards tab.

7. Click the Save button at the top of the Batch Standards Checker dialog box.

The Batch Standards Checker file dialog box opens to allow you to specify a Standards Check File name and location. This file will have a .chx filename extension. The Batch Standards Checker file is an audit file that stores the drawing list and the list of standards files in the current session. It also stores the results of the audit.

8. Once you've specified the location and name of a checker file, click the Start Check button.

TIP *The .chx file is an XML-based file. XML is a file format designed to allow data exchange over the World Wide Web.*

AutoCAD proceeds to check each file listed in the Drawings tab list box. The progress is shown in the Progress tab of the Batch Standards Checker dialog box. If you decide to cancel the audit, you can click the Stop Check button (it looks like a stop sign), which cancels the current audit in progress.

When the checking is finished, the data from the audit is automatically saved in the check file you created in step 7. Then the audit file is opened in your web browser, and you see the results of the audit.

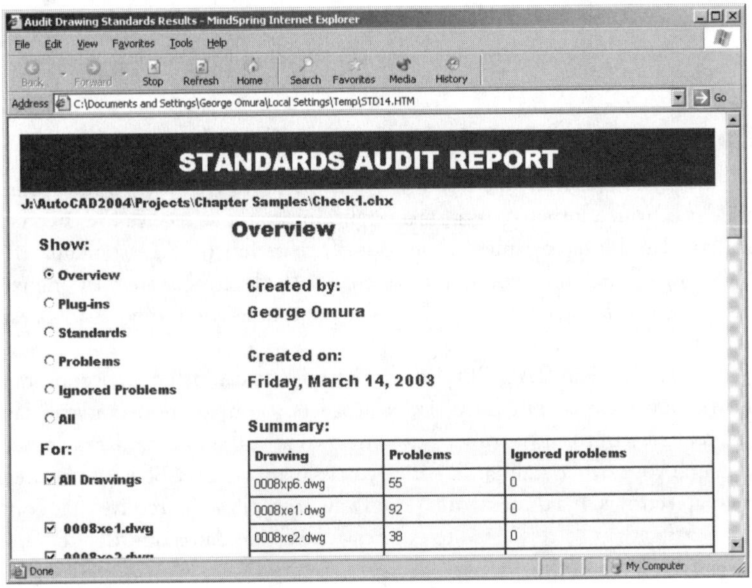

The audit report file displays a number of options in a set of radio buttons:

Overview Displays a simplified view of the problems encountered by the audit. It lists the drawings audited and the number of problems encountered.

Plug-ins Shows the standard plug-ins used to audit the drawings. Autodesk supplies these standard plug-ins, which test for layers, dimension styles, line types, and text styles. Third-party developers can create other plug-ins to check for additional problems.

Standards Lists the .dws standards files used for the audit.

Problems Displays a detailed description of the problems encountered in the audit. It gives the drawing name and the specific item name that is a problem. For example, if the audit discovers a nonstandard layer name, the layer name is listed under the drawing name as a nonstandard layer.

Ignored Problems Displays problems that have previously been flagged as problems to ignore. You can flag problems to be ignored using the Check Standards command within AutoCAD. (See the "Using the Standards Command to Associate Standards" section earlier in this chapter.)

Reviewing Previously Saved Standards Audits

Once you've created a check file and completed a standards audit, you can always return to the audit by opening the Batch Standards Checker utility and clicking the Open tool in the toolbar.

This opens the Batch Standards Checker file dialog box, where you can locate and open a previously saved standards check file with the .chx filename extension. In this file, you'll see a list of the files that were checked in the Drawing tab and the .dws standards file used in the Standards tab. You can then view the results of the audit by clicking the View Report tool in the toolbar.

This opens a web browser and displays the audit results contained in the standards check file.

Converting Multiple Layer Settings

As AutoCAD files flow in and out of your office, you're likely to find yourself working with layering standards from another system. You might, for example, receive files from an architect who uses the CSI standard for layer names, while your office prefers the AIA standard. If your job involves extensive reworking of such files, you'll want to change the layering system to one you are most familiar with. But converting layer settings is a painstaking and time-consuming process, especially if you have several files that need conversion.

Fortunately, AutoCAD 2004 offers a tool that can make layer conversion from one standard to another much easier. The Layer Translator lets you map "nonstandard" layers (that is, those using a different system from your own) to your own set of standard layers. It can then convert those layers to match your office standards. Once you've mapped a set of layers between two files, you can save the map settings in a drawing file. Then any other files you receive that contain the same nonstandard layer settings can be converted to your own layer standards quickly. Let's take a closer look at how the Layer Translator works.

When using the Layer Translator, you must initially match the layers of your incoming file with those of a file whose layers are set up the way you want. Here are the steps to do this.

1. Open the file whose layers you want to convert in AutoCAD, and then choose Tools ➢ CAD Standards ➢ Layer Translator to open the Layer Translator dialog box, which lists the layers from the current file in the Translate From list box.

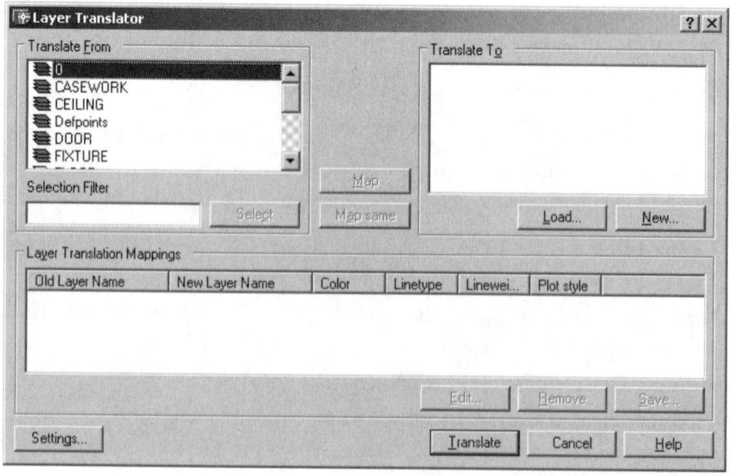

2. Click the Load button in the Translate To group to open the Select Drawing File dialog box. Locate and select a file that contains the layer settings you want to use for this project. The file can be a standard .dwg file, or it can be a .dws standards file or a .dwt template file. Once you've opened a file, its layer names appear in the Translate To list box.

3. Select a layer name in the Translate From list, and then select the layer you want to convert it to from the Translate To list box. When you've made your two selections, click the Map button in the middle of the dialog box. You'll see a listing appear in the Layer Translation Mappings group, showing you the old and new layer names and the layer settings for the conversion (see Figure 22.9).

FIGURE 22.9

The Layer Translator dialog box

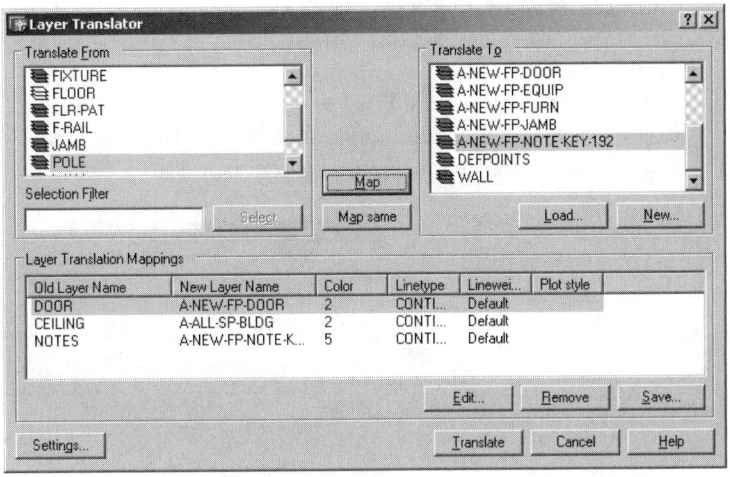

4. Repeat step 3 for all the layers that you want to convert. You can map several layers from the Translate From list to a single layer in the Translate To list if you need to.

5. If there are matching layers in the Translate From and Translate To list boxes, the Map Same button in the middle of the dialog box becomes active. You can then click this button to automatically map layers that have the same names in both the Translate From and the Translate To lists.

After you've completed your layer mapping, you can save the mapping for future use.

1. While still in the Layer Translator dialog box, click the Save button in the Layer Translation Mappings group to open the Save Layer Mappings dialog box. This is a typical AutoCAD file dialog box.

2. Enter a name for your saved settings and click Save. You can save the layer map settings as either a .dws standards file or a .dwg file.

3. Click the Translate button, and AutoCAD will proceed to translate the mapped layers.

Once you've saved the layer mapping in step 1, you can load the saved layer map settings into the Layer Translator dialog box in future layer translations, saving you the effort of mapping each layer individually each time you want to perform a translation. This will work for incoming files that use the same layer settings, but you'll have to create another layer map settings file for each different layer system you encounter.

To use a saved layer map, click the Load button in the Translate To group of the Layer Translator dialog box, and then select the saved layer map file you saved in step 6. You can have several layer map files for each project involving files with nonstandard layer settings.

Other Layer Translator Options

You'll often come across situations in which the layers in the Translate From list do not correspond directly to those in the Translate To list. For these situations, the Layer Translator offers a few additional options.

If you have difficulty finding a match for layers in the Translate From list, you can create a new layer by clicking the New button in the Translate To group. This opens the New Layer dialog box, where you can enter the properties for your new layer.

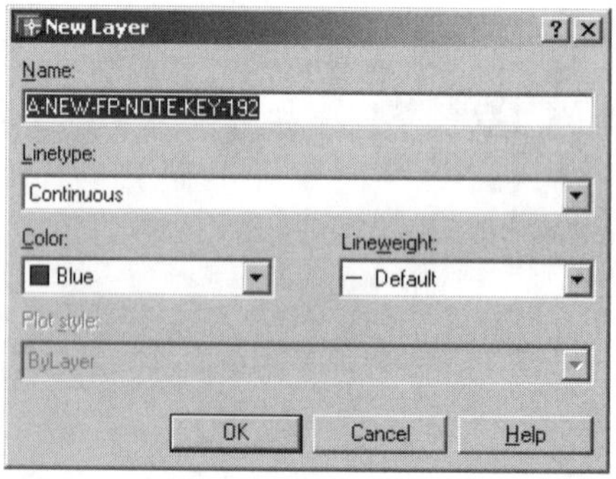

Once you create a new layer with this dialog box, it appears in the Translate To list box, allowing you to map Translate From layers to your new layer.

Another option you'll find useful is the Edit button in the Layer Translation Mappings group. You may find that once you've mapped a Translate From layer to a Translate To layer, the Translate To layer is not exactly what you want. You can highlight the mapped layer in the Layer Translation Mappings group list box, and then click Edit to open the Edit Layer dialog box. From here, you can modify the new layer's settings from their original values.

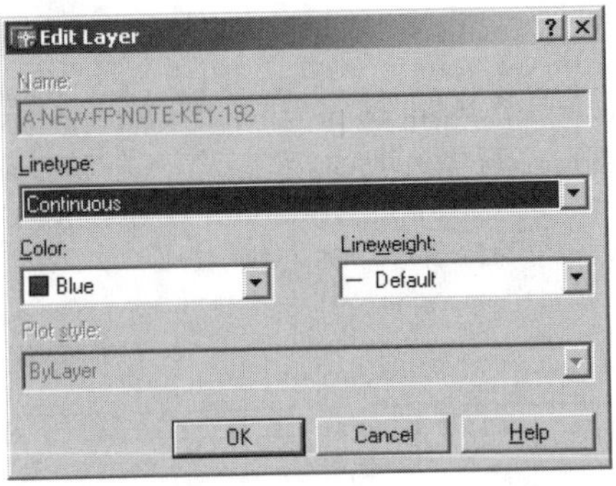

Finally, the Layer Translator offers a set of options that give you some control over the way translations are performed. For example, you can control whether layer colors and line types are forced to the ByLayer setting or whether layer assignments for objects in blocks are translated. You can gain access to these options by clicking the Settings button in the lower-left corner of the Layer Translator dialog box. Figure 22.10 shows the Settings dialog box. The options are self-explanatory.

FIGURE 22.10

The Settings dialog box for the Layer Translator

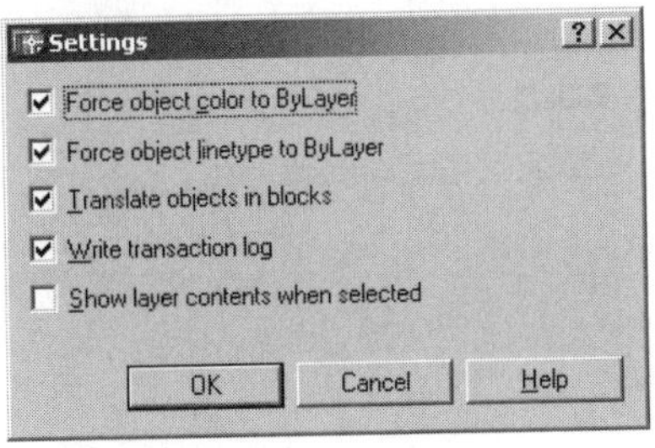

Summary

You have learned how AutoCAD can help you meet your drafting and design challenges by allowing you to visualize your ideas more clearly and by reducing the time it takes to do repetitive tasks. AutoCAD also forces you to organize your drawing process more efficiently. It changes your perception of problems, and the additional accuracy and information AutoCAD provides will minimize errors.

AutoCAD also provides drawing consistency. A set of drawings done in AutoCAD is more legible and consistent, reducing the possibility of errors caused by bad handwriting or poor drafting. In our litigious culture, this is a significant feature.

Finally, because AutoCAD has become something of a standard, especially in the AEC industry, it is easier to find people who can use it proficiently. Training, which was once a major cost in introducing a CAD system, is less of a burden to your company.

As you have seen, AutoCAD is a powerful software tool, and like any powerful program, it is difficult to master. I hope this last chapter has given you the incentive to take advantage of AutoCAD's full potential. Remember, even after you've learned how to use AutoCAD, there are many other issues that you must confront while using AutoCAD in an office environment. AutoCAD is just one link in the chain of office technology.

So now you've come to the end of *Mastering AutoCAD 2004 and AutoCAD LT 2004*. I hope that you have found this book to be a useful addition to your library and that you will continue to use it when you have questions or when you need to hone your skills. I wish you the best of luck and thanks for choosing *Mastering AutoCAD 2004 and AutoCAD LT 2004!*

Appendices

In this part:

- **What's on the Companion CD?**
- **Installing and Setting Up AutoCAD**
- **Hardward and Software Tips**
- **System and Dimension Variables**

Appendix A

What's on the Companion CD?

THIS APPENDIX DESCRIBES THE MATERIALS supplied on the CD that comes with this book. The CD contains a number of useful utilities and resources that you can load and run at any time. Before you use them, however, it's best to get familiar with AutoCAD 2004. Many of these utilities work within AutoCAD from the command line or as options on the pull-down menus, and they offer prompts in a way similar to most other AutoCAD commands. Other utilities are stand-alone applications.

The Mastering AutoCAD Bonus Software

To help you get the most from AutoCAD and this book, I've included a set of programs and files. Once you load the CD, the Sybex interface guides you to the following utilities:

AutoCAD 2004 Trial Version If you don't have AutoCAD 2004, you can use this 30-day trial version to get started. If you need more time, check the Autodesk website for some new, more flexible terms of use.

AutoCAD 2004 provides new productivity tools, an improved user interface, and presentation graphics for faster, more productive data creation. It offers password protection, CAD standards tools, and support for multisheet DWF™ (Design Web Format™) files for easier data sharing. And AutoCAD 2004 provides new network licensing and software inventory tools for more efficient data management.

Projects This folder contains the drawings used in this book. If you follow the tutorial chapter by chapter, you'll create these figures yourself. If you want to do the exercises out of sequence, use these files as needed.

Bonus CD Chapters When you're ready for more advanced topics, you can work with the Bonus Chapters on the CD. These chapters include VBA and ActiveX tutorials and chapters on advanced 3D modeling previously found only in the Premium Edition of *Mastering AutoCAD 2002*. All of the project files for these bonus chapters are included on the CD as well.

The *AutoCAD 2004 Instant Reference* At times, you might want to get a quick overview of a command, or you might just want to know what commands are available. The *AutoCAD 2004 Instant Reference* covers every feature and command in a concise, easy-to-use form for those times when you just need the basics.

On-Screen AEC and On-Screen AEC-LT This is a folder of the set of utilities described later in this appendix. These utilities are mostly aimed at the AEC environment, but any AutoCAD user will find them helpful. I've included three versions of AEC, one for users in the United States, another for metric users, and a version for AutoCAD LT 2004.

Eye2eye This folder contains the Eye2eye add-on to AutoCAD, described later in this appendix. Eye2eye makes perspective viewing of your 3D models a snap.

ActiveX Samples These samples help you get started with ActiveX Automation in AutoCAD. You can use these examples along with Chapter 22 to explore the newest customization features of AutoCAD.

The ABCs of AutoLISP This is a complete tutorial and reference book for AutoLISP, the AutoCAD macro-programming language. This book has been a favorite of users and developers alike, and it's now in an easy-to-use web browser format.

PanaVue ImageAssembler This folder contains PanaVue Image Assembler , a powerful but easy-to-use image-stitching application.

3D AutoLISP Utilities These tools help you construct 3D objects that standard AutoCAD does not offer. With these tools, you can create a solid surface for Boolean operations, extrude shapes along 3D spline curves, and simplify editing tasks.

Clip Art Drawing Libraries of Furnishings, People, and Trees Hundreds of drawings are provided, including many 3D furnishings and kitchen cabinets. Other drawings include trees in both plan and elevation, 2D cars in elevation, and more.

Opening the Installation Program

You can easily install the software discussed in this appendix using the interface and installation program on the CD. Take the following steps to open the installation program:

1. Insert the *Mastering AutoCAD 2004 and AutoCAD LT 2004* CD in your CD drive.
2. The Sybex interface launches automatically. You will first see the License Agreement screen.
3. After you've read the agreement and accepted the terms, click Accept. You then see the Mastering AutoCAD 2004 and AutoCAD LT 2004 software installation interface.

From here, you can select the software you want to install. For details on each of these options, read the following sections.

Installing the AutoCAD Trial Version

If you don't already have AutoCAD, you can use the trial version of AutoCAD 2004 included on the CD. The trial version will enable you to practice the tutorials offered in this book. The AutoCAD 2004 trial version is time-limited and fully functional, so you can experiment with all of AutoCAD's features. It also offers the option to upgrade your current version of AutoCAD or to purchase a full version of AutoCAD 2004. You can extend your trial use of AutoCAD 2004 by taking advantage of Autodesk's rental or lease options. These options offer a flexible and cost-effective way to gain access to AutoCAD when you are not a full-time AutoCAD user. Check the `www.autodesk.com` website for detailed information on these options.

To install the trial, click the AutoCAD 2004 trial button.

Installing and Using the Sample Drawing Files

The `Projects` folder contains sample drawing files for the exercises in this book. These drawings are provided for you in case you decide to skip some of the book's tutorial material. With these files, you can open the book to any chapter and start working, without having to construct the previous drawings. To get to them, follow these steps:

1. Start the Mastering AutoCAD 2004 and AutoCAD LT 2004 software installation program, as described earlier in this appendix.
2. Click the Project Files button.
3. Click Browse. You can now browse and choose which files you would like to open and install.
4. Close the window to return to the main installation program screen.
5. Proceed with another installation or click Exit.

Once you've installed the sample files, you have access to them during the exercises.

Installing On-Screen AEC

On-Screen AEC is a set of AutoLISP macros and architectural symbols, all integrated with a standard AutoCAD menu. This package provides the basic tools you'll need to start creating architectural drawings. In addition, it contains many timesaving tools to aid all users, not just architects, in editing their drawings. Three versions of the AEC add-on are included: one for U.S. users, one for for metric users, and one for LT users.

Follow these steps to install On-Screen AEC:

1. Start the Mastering AutoCAD 2004 and AutoCAD LT 2004 software installation program, as described earlier in this appendix.
2. Click the AEC On-Screen button.
3. Click to install either the AutoCAD 2004 or AutoCAD 2004 LT version. You see the WinZip Self-Extractor dialog box. You have the option to accept the default folder shown in

the input box, or you can enter a different location for the files. I recommend that you install the AEC files in a subfolder called `AEC` under the `\Program Files\AutoCAD 2004\` folder where AutoCAD is installed.

4. When you've entered the location for the AEC files, click Unzip. The files will be installed on your computer.
5. Click Close to return to the main installation program screen.
6. Click Exit, and then start AutoCAD.
7. Choose Tools ➢ Options to open the Options dialog box.
8. Click the Files tab.
9. Click Support Files Search Path.
10. Click the Add button and then click Browse.
11. Locate and select the `\Program Files\AutoCAD 2004\AEC\` folder and then click OK. (If you've installed the AEC files in a different folder, specify that folder and click OK.)
12. Click OK in the Options dialog box.

On-Screen AEC is now installed and ready for use. The next section describes how to load the On-Screen AEC menu.

Loading the On-Screen AEC Menu

Now you are ready to load the On-Screen AEC menu to give you access to the symbols and utilities offered. You will load a partial menu that will give you full access to all the AEC tools. Here's how it's done:

1. Once back in AutoCAD, choose Tools ➢ Customize ➢ Menu, or type **Menuload↵**. The Menu Customization dialog box opens. Click the Menu Groups tab.

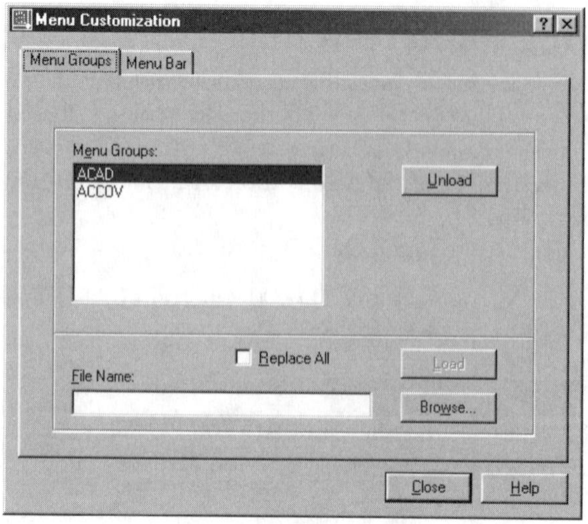

2. Click the Browse button to open the Select Menu File dialog box. This is a typical AutoCAD file dialog box.
3. Locate the `Osaec.mnu` file and then double-click it. You return to the Menu Customization dialog box, and the `Osaec.mnu` filename appears in the File Name input box.
4. Click the Load button. A warning message appears. Press ↵. AutoCAD takes a moment to load the menu. The AEC toolbar appears on the screen.
5. Click the Menu Bar tab.
6. Open the Menu Group drop-down list and select OSAEC.

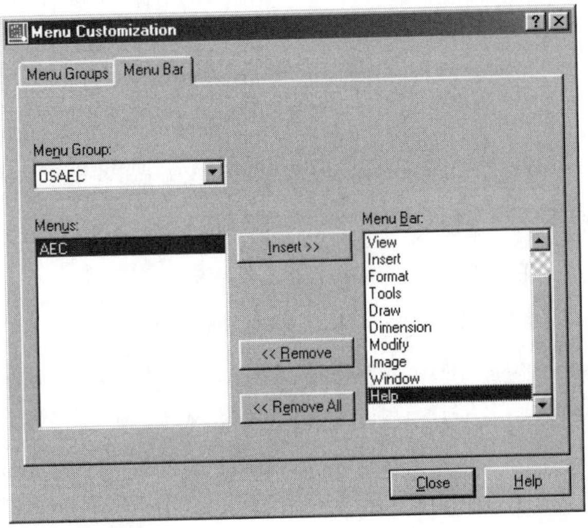

7. In the Menu Bar list box, click Help. This determines where the AEC pull-down menu appears in the menu bar.
8. Click the Insert >> button. AEC appears just above Help in the Menu Bar list box, and you will see AEC in the AutoCAD menu bar at the top of the AutoCAD window.

Using the AEC Utilities

After you've installed On-Screen AEC, make sure you review the `Osaec.PDF` file included with the On-Screen AEC files. The PDF file provides important instructions on how to use the On-Screen AEC utilities.

Installing and Using Eye2eye

Eye2eye is a utility that replaces the AutoCAD `Dview` command with an easy-to-use method for creating perspective views. Eye2eye uses a camera-target metaphor to let you place viewpoints and view directions in a drawing.

Here's how to install Eye2eye:

1. Start the Mastering AutoCAD 2004 and AutoCAD LT 2004 software installation program as described earlier in this appendix.
2. Click the Eye2eye button.
3. Click Install. You see the WinZip Self-Extractor dialog box. You have the option to accept the default folder shown in the input box, or you can enter a different location for the files. I recommend that you install the Eye2eye files in a subfolder called `Eye2eye` under the `\Program Files\AutoCAD2004\` folder where AutoCAD is installed.
4. When you've entered the location for the Eye2eye files, click Unzip. The files will be installed on your computer.
5. Click Close to return to the main installation program screen.
6. Click Exit.
7. Start AutoCAD and choose Tools ➢ Options to open the Options dialog box.
8. Click the Files tab.
9. Click Support Files Search Path.
10. Click the Add button and then click Browse.
11. Locate and select the `\Program Files\AutoCAD 2004\Eye2eye\` folder and then click OK.
12. Click OK in the Options dialog box.

After you've installed Eye2eye, make sure you review the `Eye2eye.PDF` file included with the Eye2eye files. The PDF file provides important information regarding the use of Eye2eye.

The Bonus Chapters and Samples

With AutoCAD 2004, you now have a new way to create custom applications in AutoCAD. ActiveX Automation is a new feature that allows AutoCAD users to take control of AutoCAD, either by creating Visual Basic applications or through other applications that support ActiveX Automation.

The ActiveX Automation chapters on the CD provide an introduction to ActiveX Automation as it relates to AutoCAD:

- "Exploring VBA" begins with an overview of VBA and AutoCAD automation.
- "Using ActiveX Automation with AutoCAD" shows you the basic theory behind ActiveX Automation and how it applies to AutoCAD.
- "Using VBA to Create AutoCAD Applications" brings together the concepts in "Exploring VBA" and "Using ActiveX Automation with AutoCAD" to produce applications in VBA.

You can experiment with some sample applications included when you're reading the chapters. The following steps show you how to access those examples:

1. Start the Mastering AutoCAD 2004 and AutoCAD LT 2004 software installation program, as described earlier in this appendix.
2. Click the Bonus Chapters button. Then open the `Samples` folder.
3. Inside the `Samples` folder are subfolders for each of the bonus chapters. Open the subfolder that corresponds to the chapter you are working with.
4. Click the name of the sample set of files you want to install and then follow the instructions that appear on the screen.

Other Bonus Chapters on the CD include the following:

- "Architectural Solid Modeling," is based on Chapter 19 of *Mastering AutoCAD 2002, Premium Edition*. Using the floor plan of Le Corbusier's Villa Savoye you'll explore the use of regions and 3D Solids to build architectural 3D models.
- "Advanced Surface Modeling," is based on Chapter 20 of *Mastering AutoCAD 2002, Premium Edition*. It shows you how to break out of the flat world and start creating curved objects. To do this, you'll use AutoCAD's surface modeling tools in a new way.

NOTE *The project files for the all of the bonus chapters on the CD can be found in the* `Samples` *subfolder in the same folder as the bonus chapters themselves.*

AutoCAD 2004 Instant Reference

Mastering AutoCAD 2004 and AutoCAD LT 2004 was designed to help AutoCAD users by demonstrating commands in the context of everyday activities that you might encounter in your work. It shows you what commands to use in a given situation. As a result, this book doesn't always show every option or permutation of a command. This is where the *AutoCAD 2004 Instant Reference* comes in.

The *AutoCAD 2004 Instant Reference* is the perfect companion to *Mastering AutoCAD 2004 and AutoCAD LT 2004*. You can think of it as a dictionary of AutoCAD commands that describes each command in detail, including all the command options.

The CD contains an electronic version of the *AutoCAD 2004 Instant Reference*. You will need to install Adobe Acrobat Reader (also on this CD) to use this online book:

1. Start the Mastering AutoCAD 2004 and AutoCAD LT 2004 software installation program, as described earlier in this appendix.
2. Click the AutoCAD Instant Reference button.
3. Click the View button to open the ebook.

The ABCs of AutoLISP

The ABCs of AutoLISP is an in-depth tutorial on AutoLISP starting with the basics and continuing to more advanced topics. *The ABCs of AutoLISP* is a PDF file that can be viewed with Adobe Acrobat 3 or later (also on the CD). Once you've installed Acrobat the following steps show you how to open *The ABCs of AutoLISP* from the companion CD:

1. Start the Mastering AutoCAD 2004 and AutoCAD LT 2004 software installation program, as described earlier in this appendix.
2. Click the ABC's of AutoLISP button. Click the View button to open the ebook.

PanaVue ImageAssembler

The *Mastering AutoCAD 2004 and AutoCAD LT 2004* CD contains a trial version of PanaVue ImageAssembler. This program helps round out your needs as an AutoCAD user.

Click the ImageAssembler button in the Mastering AutoCAD 2004 and AutoCAD LT 2004 CD installation menu and then follow the instructions that appear.

If you decide to remove ImageAssembler, use the Add Or Remove Programs utility in the Windows Control Panel.

3D AutoLISP Utilities

AutoCAD has numerous tools for creating and editing 3D models, but you may find that for some types of objects, those tools are not enough. I've created a few AutoLISP utilities that I've found useful in my own 3D modeling work. You can install them from the installation menu by clicking the 3D AutoLISP utilities button. Here is a listing of those utilities and how they work. If your work involves 3D modeling, you may find them useful.

Editing Polylines in 3D Space with *3Dpedit.lsp*

One of the more annoying aspects of 3D modeling in AutoCAD is having to edit polylines on different User Coordinate Systems (UCSs). Before you can make changes to a polyline, you have to first set the UCS to one parallel to the polyline you want to edit. `3Dpedit.lsp` simplifies polyline editing by eliminating the need to locate a polyline's UCS before editing it. `3Dpedit.lsp` works just like the `Pedit` command. After you load the utility, type **3Dpedit** at the command prompt, and then click the polyline you want to edit. The rest works just like the `Pedit` command.

Importing HPGL Plot Files with *Hpglin.lsp*

Several years ago, I found a need to import HPGL files into AutoCAD drawings, so I wrote `Hpglin.lsp`. You can use `Hpglin.lsp` to import hidden line plots of your 3D models. This is a quick way to generate 2D line drawings of your 3D perspective or isometric views.

`Hpglin.lsp` is fairly straightforward. After you load it, type **Hpglin** at the command prompt. You'll see a file dialog box, which you use to select an HPGL plot file for translation. Once you select the file, `Hpglin.lsp` starts to work. It takes a minute or two while the plot file gradually appears on your screen.

Note that `Hpglin.lsp` only works for HPGL. It does not work for HPGL/2 or PCL files. You can set up AutoCAD to create HPGL plot files by using the AutoCAD Add-a-Plotter Wizard to install the HP 7585 plotter driver. See Chapter 7 for more on the Add-a-Plotter Wizard.

Converting 3D Meshes into Solid Surface with *Mesh2sol.lsp*

One frustrating limitation of AutoCAD is its inability to generate solids with compound-curved surfaces. These are surfaces curved in two directions, such as a saddle shape or the fender of a car. You can create such forms using surface modeling tools, but you cannot perform Boolean operations on surface meshes.

`Mesh2sol.lsp` helps relieve this limitation by converting surface meshes into a series of triangular-shaped solid panels. You can then use the Union, Subtract, or Interfere Boolean operations to create new surface shapes. Here's how it works:

1. After you load this utility, type **Mesh2sol**↵ at the command prompt.
2. At the `Select mesh to convert to Regions/Solid:` prompt, select the mesh you want to convert.
3. At the `Create [Regions/<Solids>]:` prompt, press ↵.
4. At the `Specify height of extrusion <0.001>:` prompt, you have the option to indicate the thickness of the surface. Press ↵ to accept the default 0.001 thickness.
5. At the `Specify angle of taper <30>:` prompt, you have the option to indicate a taper angle for the sides of each surface panel. Press ↵ to accept the default.

The surface mesh will be replaced by a series of triangular shapes. Each triangle is actually a solid with beveled edges. The beveled edges allow the triangular solids to join in a single edge. You can use Boolean operations to cut holes or join other solids to your new surface.

A few words of caution: Use `Mesh2sol.lsp` sparingly because solids can quickly increase the size of your drawing, and you can easily generate large numbers of solids with `Mesh2sol.lsp`. Also, when using Boolean operations on a `Mesh2sol.lsp`-converted object, select only those solids to be affected by the Boolean operation; otherwise you may receive error messages.

You can use `Mesh2sol.lsp` in a variety of ways. For example, you can create compound-curved objects with holes punched through them. You can also *slice* solids with compound-curved meshes by converting a mesh to a solid and then subtracting the converted mesh from an extruded solid form. Once this is done, you can explode the sliced solid, which reduces the solid to a series of regions. You then erase the regions you don't need from the sliced region.

Extruding a Shape Along a Spline Curve with *Splinep.lsp*

You can use the Extrude command to extrude a closed polyline along a path. Unfortunately, that path cannot be a spline curve, and it cannot it lie outside a 2D plane. `Splinep.lsp` is a utility that overcomes this limitation by letting you extrude a closed polyline shape along a spline curve. `Splinep.lsp` does not create a solid; instead, it creates a series of mesh surfaces to simulate an extrusion. Here's how it works:

1. After loading `Splinep.lsp`, type **Splinep**↵ at the command prompt.

2. At the Do you want to change the number of surface segments? [Yes/<No>]: prompt, press ↵ or enter Y↵ and enter the number of surface segments for the extruded shape.
3. At the Pick profile for extrusion: prompt, select the closed polyline you want to extrude. This can also be a circle, an arc, or a polygon.
4. At the Select insertion point for profile <pick point>: prompt, select a point that will be the base point of the extruded object. This is the point that will be placed on the axis of the spline path.
5. At the Pick path for extrusion: prompt, click the spline.

The selected shape will extrude along the spline or polyline. To improve the smoothness of the extrusion, use the Surftab1 and Surftab2 system variables to increase the number of facets for the extrusion. Surftab1 controls the number of facets around the extrusion, and Surftab2 controls the number of segments along the length of the extrusion. Splinep.lsp only works for splines.

Drawing Tubes with *Tube.lsp*

In the CD bonus chapter "Advanced Surface Modeling," you learn how to convert a truss diagram into a 3D model of a truss. Although the methods shown in that chapter are simple enough, the process can become tedious if you have a lot of tubes to draw. Tubes are common enough that a utility such as Tube.lsp can be a timesaver. Here are the steps to take when using Tube.lsp:

1. After you load the utility, type **Tube**↵.
2. At the Select object: prompt, click the line that represents the central axis of the tube.
3. At the [Solid/<sUrface>]: prompt, press to draw a mesh tube or enter S to draw a solid tube.
4. At the Enter tube radius<1.0000>: prompt, enter a radius for the tube.

The tube will be drawn according to your specifications.

Sample Clip Art Files

Some of the more popular accessories for AutoCAD are drawing libraries. I've included my own set of libraries on the companion CD for you to use in your projects. You can access them by clicking the Clip Art Drawing Libraries button. The library includes an extensive set of 3D kitchen cabinets, people, trees, and 3D furniture. The kitchen cabinets are fairly schematic, but you can use them to help design a kitchen layout. They are drawn to standard sizes for commercial, prefabricated cabinets. The people can be used for architectural elevation presentation drawings. The trees are typical architectural "rubber-stamp" trees for plan and elevation views. The furniture includes a few designer chairs as well as some generic items such as beds and tables. I hope you find them useful!

Appendix B

Installing and Setting Up AutoCAD

This appendix gives you information on installing AutoCAD 2004 on your system and describes the system parameters that you will want to set to configure AutoCAD to meet the needs of your operating environment. Throughout this appendix, the system variable associated with a setting, when available, is included at the end of an option description, enclosed in brackets. System variables are settings that allow you to control AutoCAD's behavior when using commands and features. You'll find a detailed description of the AutoCAD system variables in Appendix D.

Before Installing AutoCAD

Before you begin the installation process, be sure you have a drive with at least 220MB of free disk space on drive C plus an additional 170MB of disk space on the drive on which you intend to install AutoCAD. You will also want to have at least an additional 100MB of free disk space for AutoCAD temporary files and swap files, plus another 20MB for the tutorial files you will create. (Temporary and swap files are system files AutoCAD creates as it works. You don't have to deal with these files directly, but you do have to allow room for them. If you want to know more about these files, see Appendix A.) If you are installing AutoCAD on a drive other than the one on which Windows is installed, make sure you have about 220MB free on the Windows drive. AutoCAD also stores temporary files there.

Finally, have your AutoCAD vendor's name and phone number ready. You will be asked to enter this information during the installation. You will also want to have your network and single-user authorization code ready. You can obtain these by calling the toll-free number listed in your AutoCAD package. Single-user systems have a 30-day grace period, so you can install and use AutoCAD without having to enter your authorization code right away.

Installing the AutoCAD Software

Installing AutoCAD is simple and straightforward; AutoCAD uses an installation wizard like most other Windows programs. Here are some guidelines to follow during the installation process:

- Before you start, make sure you have enough disk space and also make sure that no other programs are running. You will also want to have your AutoCAD serial number and CD key on hand. These items are usually on the package label.
- Typically, the AutoCAD installation program starts up automatically when you insert the AutoCAD 2004 CD into your computer, but in the event that it doesn't, do the following:
  1. In Windows, choose Start ➢ Run to open the Run dialog box.
  2. In the Open box, enter **D:setup**. Enter the letter of your CD drive in place of the **D** in this example. Click OK when you are ready. You see the AutoCAD 2004 Master Setup dialog box.
- You'll see a row of options near the top of the Master Setup dialog box labeled Install, What's Inside, Documentation, Support, and Network Deployment. Click Install. The rest of the dialog box will change to show the Install options. Click Install under Install AutoCAD 2004.
- Once the installation starts, follow the directions in the installation wizard. In the Personal Information screen, you are asked for your name, company, and AutoCAD vendor's name and telephone number. This information will be displayed on the opening AutoCAD screen, so don't enter anything you'll regret later.
- You are also asked to select the location for your AutoCAD files. The tutorials in this book assume that you have AutoCAD on drive C and in a folder called `\Program Files\AutoCAD2004\`—these are the defaults during the installation.
- You are given the choice of Typical, Full, Compact, or Custom installation. I encourage you to choose the Full installation so that you can take advantage of all AutoCAD features.
- If you don't have enough disk space, the installation wizard will let you know exactly how much room you need on each drive involved in the installation. You can take steps to make more room using Windows Explorer or the Windows Disk Cleanup utility. If you do this, make sure you close those programs when you've finished making room and before you return to the AutoCAD Setup.
- After the AutoCAD files are installed, you are returned to the Master Setup dialog box. You will also want to install the AutoCAD Express Tools under Install Supplemental Tools.

Once the installation is complete, you will see the AutoCAD 2004 Setup dialog box asking you if you want to restart your computer. It's usually better to restart your computer immediately after installing AutoCAD, if it requests that you do so.

Installing Other AutoCAD Components

If you didn't initially install some AutoCAD components, such as the database tools, and you would like to install them, take the following steps:

1. Place your AutoCAD 2004 CD in your computer's CD drive.
2. If the AutoCAD 2004 Master Setup dialog box does not appear automatically, choose Start ➢ Run to open the Run dialog box.
3. In the Open box, enter **D:setup**, where **D** is the letter of your CD drive.
4. Click Install from the row of options, and then click Install under Install AutoCAD 2004. The installation program will detect that you have AutoCAD already installed on your system and give you the option to add or remove features, reinstall or repair AutoCAD 2004, or remove AutoCAD 2004 altogether. Select Add Or Remove Features, and click Next. At the next dialog box, you see a list of AutoCAD features that you can install.
5. Choose the feature you want to install from the list. A drop-down menu appears, offering a set of installation options. Select the appropriate option.
6. Repeat step 5 for each option you want to include in your AutoCAD installation. When you are finished, click Next.
7. You are asked if you want to proceed with the installation. Choose Yes to install the selected additional features.

The AutoCAD Program Files

The `\Program Files\AutoCAD2004\` folder contains a number of other folders.

Here are brief descriptions of each subfolder's contents:

Backup Contains backup versions for many of AutoCAD's system files.

Data Links Contains the Data Link files for AutoCAD's dbConnect feature.

Drv Contains special software drivers that AutoCAD uses for plotting and display features.

Fonts Contains AutoCAD fonts.

Help Contains AutoCAD help documents.

Plot Styles Contains the plot styles.

Plotters Contains the plotter configuration files.

Sample Contains sample drawing files, as well as sample ActiveX, DesignCenter, VBA, and VisualLISP files.

Support Contains the files that define a variety of AutoCAD's customizable functions.

Template Contains AutoCAD template files.

Textures Contains texture files for AutoCAD's rendering feature.

Tutorial Contains Autodesk's own sample tutorial files.

UserDataCache Contains source files for custom user data.

WebDepot Contains HTML files for AutoCAD's online registration.

WebServices Contains files for AutoCAD's web services such as the communication center.

For customization, you should work with the files in the `C:\Documents and Settings\User Name\Application Data\Autodesk\AutoCAD 2004\R16.0\enu` folder. This is where you'll find the Data Links, Plot Styles, Plotters, and Support folders that work with your login user name.

Configuring AutoCAD

In this section, you will learn how to configure AutoCAD. By configure, I mean set up AutoCAD to work the way you want it to work. You can configure AutoCAD at any time during an AutoCAD session using the Options dialog box.

The tutorials in this book assume that you are using the default Options settings. As you become more familiar with the workings of AutoCAD, you may want to make adjustments to the way AutoCAD works, using the Options dialog box. You can also set many of the options in the Options dialog box through system variables.

Choose Tools ➢ Options to open the Options dialog box, which has the following tabs and settings.

TIP *Many of the options in the Options dialog box show an AutoCAD file icon. This icon indicates that the option's setting is saved with the file, as opposed to being saved as part of AutoCAD's default settings.*

The Files Tab

You use the options on the Files tab to tell AutoCAD where to place or find files it needs to operate. It uses a hierarchical list, similar to the one presented by Windows Explorer. You first see the general topics in the Search Path, File Names, and File Location list boxes. You can expand any individual item in the list by clicking its plus sign.

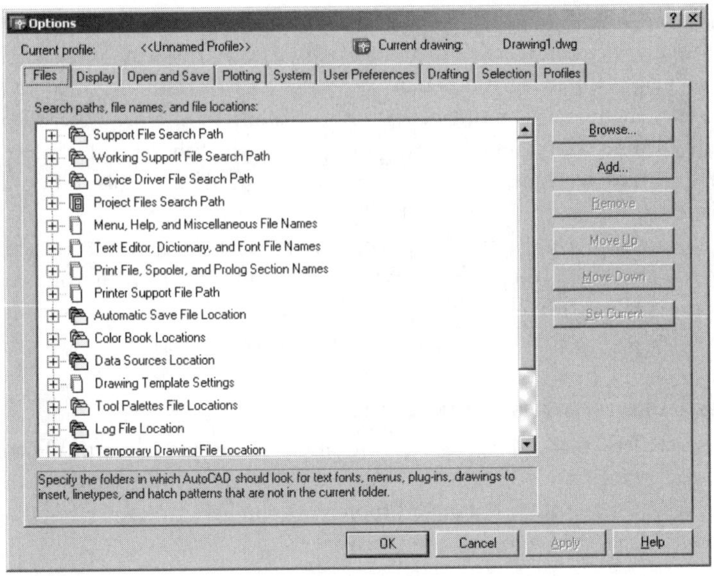

The following explanations describe what each item in the list box is for. Chances are you won't have to use most of them, while you may change others occasionally.

TIP *The related system variable is shown in brackets at the end of the description of each item.*

SUPPORT FILE SEARCH PATH

AutoCAD relies on external files for many of its functions. Menus, text fonts, line types, and hatch patterns are a few examples of features that rely on external files. The Support File Search Path item tells AutoCAD where to look for these files. You can add folder paths to this listing by clicking the Add button and entering a new path or using the Browse button. It's probably not a good idea to delete any of the existing items under this heading unless you really know what you are doing.

If you are familiar with using environment variables, you can include them in the search paths.

WORKING SUPPORT FILE SEARCH PATH

The Working Support File Search Path item contains a read-only list of the support file search path for the current session, including any special settings that may be included with command switches and environment settings.

DEVICE DRIVER FILE SEARCH PATH

The Device Driver File Search Path item locates the device drivers for AutoCAD. Device drivers are applications that allow AutoCAD to communicate directly with the printers, plotters, and input devices. In most cases, you do not have to do anything with this setting.

Project Files Search Path

Eventually, a consultant or other AutoCAD user will provide you with files that rely on Xrefs or raster images. Often, such files will expect the Xref or raster image to be in a particular folder. When such files are moved to another location with a different folder system, Xref-dependent files will not be able to find their Xrefs. The Support File Search Path item allows you to specify a folder where Xrefs or other dependent files are stored. If AutoCAD is unable to find an Xref or other file, it will look in the folder you specify in this listing.

To specify this folder, highlight Project Files Search Path, and then click the Add button. AutoCAD suggests Project1 as the folder name. You can change the name if you prefer. Click the plus sign next to Project1, and then click Browse to select a location for your project file search path. The project file search path is stored in a system variable called Projectname [Projectname].

Menu, Help, and Miscellaneous File Names

This item lets you set the location of a variety of support files including menu, help, automatic save, log, and configuration files. It also lets you set the default Internet address for the Launch Browser button on the AutoCAD Standard toolbar. If you have a network installation, you can also set the License Manager location on your network.

Text Editor, Dictionary, and Font File Names

Use this item to set the location of the text editor [mtexted], the Custom and Standard dictionaries [Dctmain, Dctust], and the alternate font and font mapping files [Fontalt]. Chapter 8 describes these tools in more detail.

Print File, Spooler, and Prolog Section Names

You can specify a print filename other than the default that is supplied by AutoCAD whenever you plot to a file. The Spooler option lets you specify an application intended to read and plot a plot file. The Prolog option is intended for PostScript export. It lets you specify the Prolog section from the `Acad.psf` file that you want AutoCAD to include with exported Encapsulated PostScript files. See Appendix C and Chapter 15 for more information on exporting PostScript files and the `Acad.psf` file [Psprolog].

Printer Support File Path

Several support files are associated with the AutoCAD printing and plotting system. This item allows you to indicate where you want AutoCAD to look for these files.

Automatic Save File Location

You can indicate the location for AutoCAD's Automatic Save file using this item [Savefilepath].

Color Book Location

This item lets you specify the location for the PANTONE color book. This is an optional installation item so if the PANTONE color books are not installed, you can install them through your AutoCAD 2004 Installation CD.

Data Sources Location

This item lets you specify the location for ODBC data link files for linking AutoCAD drawings to database files.

Drawing Template Settings

When you select the Use A Template option in the Create New Drawing dialog box, AutoCAD looks at this setting for the location of template files. You can modify this setting, but chances are you won't need to.

Tool Palettes File Location

This item lets you specify a location for your custom tool palettes resource files. When you create custom palettes, AutoCAD will store it's data regarding those palettes in this location.

Log File Location

With this item you can indicate where log files are to be placed [Logfilepath].

Temporary Drawing File Location

AutoCAD creates temporary files to store portions of your drawings as you work on them. You usually don't have to think about these temporary files until they start crowding your hard disk, or if you are working on a particularly large file on a system with little memory. This item lets you set the location for temporary files. The default location is the `C:\Documents and Settings\`*`User Name`*`\Local Settings\Temp\` folder. *`User Name`* is your login name. If you have a hard drive that has lots of room and is very fast, you might want to change this setting to a location on that drive to improve performance [Tempprefix, read-only].

Temporary External Reference File Location

If you are on a network and you foresee a situation in which another user will want to open an Xref of a file you are working on, you can set the Demand Load Xrefs setting in the Open and Save tab to Enabled With Copy. This causes AutoCAD to make and use a copy of any Xref that is currently loaded. This way, others can open the original file. The Temporary External Reference File Location lets you specify the folder where AutoCAD will store this copy of an Xref [Xloadpath].

Texture Maps Search Path

This item specifies the location for AutoCAD Render texture maps. In most cases, you won't have to change this setting. You can, however, add a folder name to this item for your own texture maps as you acquire or create them.

i-drop Associated File Location

This is where you specify the location of files imported to your computer through the i-drop function in AutoCAD. By default, no location is specified, so the i-drop imported .dwg file is placed in the same folder location as the current drawing.

NOTE *While in AutoCAD, you may want to quickly find the location of a resource file such as a log file or the automatic save file. You can do so by using the Autolisp Getvar function along with the name of the system variable associated with the resource. For example, to quickly find the location of the log file path, enter* ***(getvar "logfilepath")*** *↵ at the command prompt. For the automatic save file enter* ***(getvar "savefilepath")*** *↵. LT users can employ the Modemacro command as in* ***Modemacro*** *↵* ***$(getvar,logfilepath)*** *↵ or* ***Modemacro*** *↵* ***$(getvar,savefilepath)*** *↵. See Chapter 21 for more on Modemacro.*

The Display Tab

The settings on this tab let you control the appearance of AutoCAD. You can make AutoCAD look completely different with these settings if you choose. Scroll bars, fonts, and colors are all up for grabs.

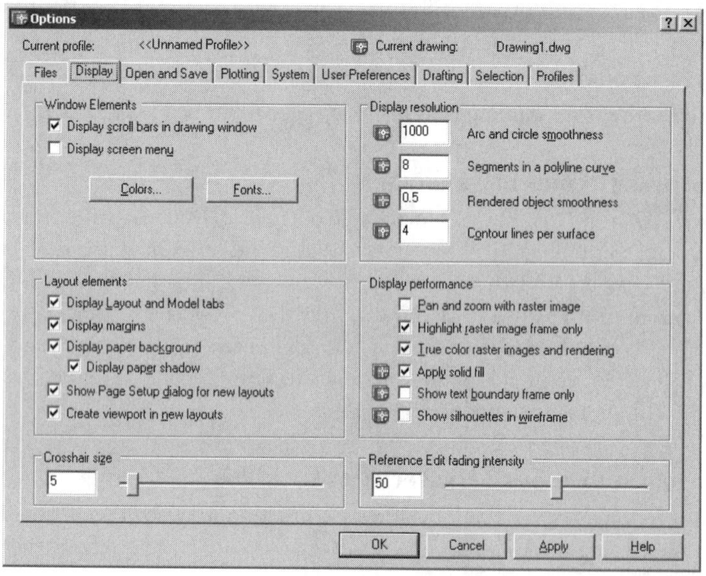

THE WINDOW ELEMENTS GROUP

These options control the general settings for AutoCAD windows:

Display Scroll Bars In Drawing Window Lets you turn the scroll bars on and off. If you've got a small monitor with low resolution, you might want to turn the scroll bars off for a larger drawing area.

Display Screen Menu Turns on the old AutoCAD Format Screen menu that once appeared on the right side of the screen. If you really must have it displayed, this is where you can turn it back on.

Colors Opens a dialog box that lets you set the color for the various components of the AutoCAD window. This is where you can change the background color of the drawing area if you find that black doesn't work for you.

Fonts Opens a dialog box that lets you set the fonts of the AutoCAD window. You can select from the standard set of Windows fonts available in your system.

The Display Resolution Group

These options control the way different types of objects are displayed in AutoCAD. You can choose between display accuracy and speed.

Arc And Circle Smoothness Controls the appearance of arcs and circles, particularly when you zoom in on them. In some instances, arcs and circles will appear to be octagons, even though they will plot as smooth arcs and circles. If you want arcs and circles to appear smoother, you can increase this setting. An increase will also increase memory use. This setting is also controlled by the Viewres system variable [Viewres].

Segments In A Polyline Curve Controls the smoothness of polyline curves. Increase the value to make curved polylines appear smoother and less segmented. Decrease the value for improved display performance. This option is also set by the Splinesegs system variable [Splinesegs].

Rendered Object Smoothness Controls the smoothness of curved solids when they are rendered or shaded. Values can range from 0.01 to 10 [Facetres].

Contour Lines Per Surface Lets you set the number of contour lines used to represent solid, curved surfaces. Values can range from 0 to 2047 [Isolines].

The Layout Elements Group

These options control the display of elements in the Paper Space Layout tabs. See Chapters 7 and 13 for more information.

The Display Performance Group

You can adjust a variety of display-related settings from this group.

Pan And Zoom With Raster Image Controls the way raster images react to real-time pans and zooms. If this option is checked, raster images move with the cursor. Turn this option off for better performance [Rtdisplay].

Highlight Raster Image Frame Only Determines how raster images appear when selected. Turn this option on for better performance [Imagehlt].

True Color Raster Images And Rendering Determines whether raster images and rendered images are displayed in true color. Turn this option off for better performance.

Apply Solid Fill Controls the display of filled objects such as wide polylines and areas filled with the solid hatch pattern. This option is also controlled by the Fillmode system variable. See Chapter 14 for more information on filled polylines and the solid hatch pattern. Turn this option off for better performance [Fillmode].

Show Text Boundary Frame Only Controls the way text is displayed. Turn this option on to display text as rectangular boundaries [Qtextmode].

Show Silhouettes In Wireframe Controls whether surface meshes for solid models are displayed. Turn this option off for better performance [Dispsilh].

THE CROSSHAIR SIZE SLIDER

This slider controls the size of the crosshair cursor. You can set this to 100 percent to simulate the full-screen crosshair cursor of earlier versions of AutoCAD [Cursorsize].

THE REFERENCE EDIT FADING INTENSITY SLIDER

This slider controls the display of nonselected objects during in-place reference editing. See Chapter 6 for more information on in-place reference editing [Xfadectl].

The Open And Save Tab

The Open And Save tab offers general file-related options such as automatic save and the default file version for the Save and Save As options.

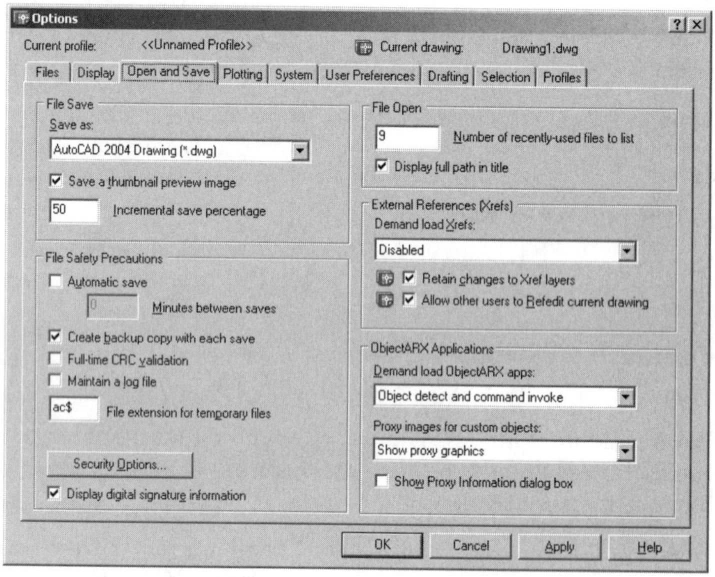

THE FILE SAVE GROUP

You can control how AutoCAD saves files by using the options in this group.

Save As This drop-down list lets you set the default file type for the File ➢ Save and File ➢ Save As options. If you are working in an environment that requires Release 14 files as the standard file type, for example, you can use this option to select Release 14 as the default file type. You can also set up AutoCAD to save DXF files by default.

Save A Thumbnail Preview Image Lets you determine whether a preview image is saved with a drawing. Preview images are used in the AutoCAD File dialog box and the DesignCenter to let you preview a file before opening it [Rasterpreview].

Incremental Save Percentage Controls the degree to which the incremental save feature is used whenever you use the File ➢ Save or File ➢ Save As options. An incremental save improves the time it takes to save a file to disk, but it also makes the file size larger. If you have limited disk space, you can set this value to 25. A value of 0 turns off incremental save altogether, but will reduce AutoCAD performance. This option is also controlled through the Isavepercent system variable [Isavepercent].

The File Safety Precautions Group

These options control the automatic backup features of AutoCAD.

Automatic Save Offers control over the Automatic Save features. You can turn it on or off using the check box or set the frequency at which files are saved using the Minutes Between Saves input box. You can set the location for the automatic save files using the Automatic Save File Location listing in the Files tab of the Options dialog box. You can also set the frequency of automatic saves through the Savetime system variable [Savefilepath, Savefile].

Create Backup Copy With Each Save Lets you determine whether a .bak file is saved along with every save you perform. You can turn this option off to conserve disk space. You can also use the Isavebak system variable to turn this option on or off [Isavebak, Tempprefix].

Full-Time CRC Validation Controls the cyclic redundancy check feature, which checks for file errors whenever AutoCAD reads a file. This feature is helpful in troubleshooting hardware problems in your system.

Maintain A Log File Lets you record the data in the AutoCAD Text Window. See Chapter 15 for more on this feature. You can set the location for log files in the Files tab of the Options dialog box [Logfilemode, Logfilename].

File Extension For Temporary Files Lets you set the filename extension for AutoCAD temporary files. These are files AutoCAD uses to store drawing data temporarily as you work on a file. If you are working on a network where temporary files from multiple users may be stored in the same folder, you might want to change this setting to identify your temporary files.

Security Options Opens the Security Options dialog box in which you can either password protect a file or add a digital signature. See Chapter 22 for more on these features.

The File Open Group

You can control how AutoCAD displays filenames in the File menu or the drawing title bar.

Number Of Recently Used Files To List This input box lets you specify the number of files listed in the File menu history list. The default is 4, but you can enter a value from 0 to 9.

Display Full Path In Title Just as its name implies, this option controls whether the full path is included in the title bar with a drawing's name.

The External References (Xrefs) Group

These options let you control memory and layer features of Xrefs.

Demand Load Xrefs Lets you turn on the Demand Load feature of Xrefs. Demand Load helps to improve the performance of files that use Xrefs by loading only those portions of an Xref drawing that are required for the current open drawing. This option is a drop-down list with three options: Disabled turns off demand loading, Enabled turns demand loading on, and Enabled With Copy turns on demand loading using a copy of the Xref source file. This last option allows others on a network to edit the Xref source file while you're working on a file that also uses the file [Xloadctl].

Retain Changes To Xref Layers Lets you save layer settings of Xref files in the current drawing. This does not affect the source Xref file. With this setting turned off, the current file will import the layer settings of the Xref file when it loads that file. This setting is also controlled by the Visretain system variable [Visretain].

Allow Other Users To Refedit Current Drawing Lets you specify whether others can simultaneously edit a file that you are editing. This option is intended to allow others to use the Modify ➢ In-Place Xref And Block Editing option (the Refedit command) on files that you currently have loaded in AutoCAD [Xedit].

The Object ARX Applications Group

AutoCAD allows users and third-party developers to create custom objects that usually require the presence of a custom ObjectARX application to support the object. These options control the way AutoCAD treats custom objects and their related ObjectARX applications.

Demand Load ObjectARX Apps Controls when a supporting third-party application is loaded if a custom object is present in a file. This option offers several settings that you can select from a drop-down list. The available settings are Disable Load On Demand, Custom Object Detect, Command Invoke, and Object Detect And Command Invoke. Disable Load On Demand prevents AutoCAD from loading third-party applications when a custom object is present. Custom Object Detect causes AutoCAD to automatically load an ARX application if a custom object is present. Command Invoke loads a custom application when you invoke a command from that application. The Object Detect And Command Invoke option loads an ARX application when either a custom object is present or when you invoke a command from that application [Demandload].

Proxy Images For Custom Objects Offers a drop-down list with three settings that control the display of custom objects when the objects supporting ARX applications are not present on your system. Do Not Show Proxy Graphics turns off the display of custom objects. Show Proxy Graphics displays the custom object. Show Proxy Bounding Box shows a bounding box in place of the custom object.

Show Proxy Information Dialog Box Lets you determine whether the Show Proxy Information warning dialog box is used. When this option is checked, the Show Proxy Information warning appears when a drawing with custom objects is opened but the objects' associated ARX application cannot be found by AutoCAD [Proxynotice].

The Plotting Tab

The Plotting tab in the Options dialog box offers settings related to printing and plotting. See Chapter 7 for a description of these options.

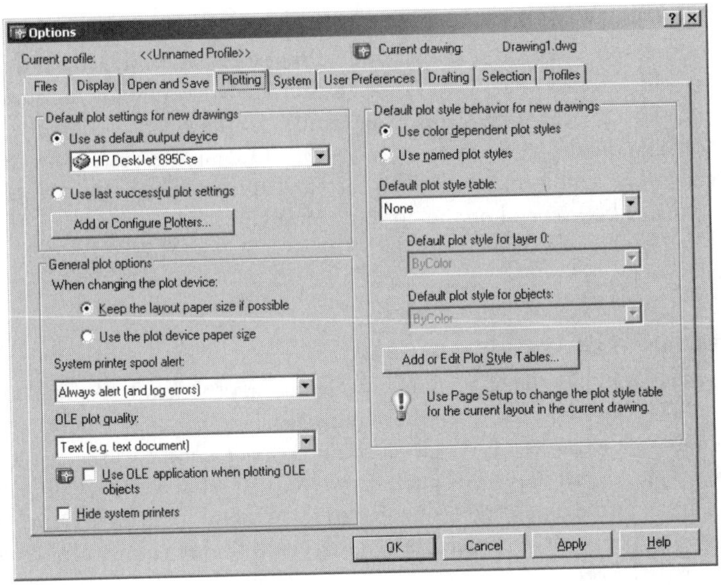

The System Tab

These options in the System tab offer control over some of AutoCAD's general interface settings such as display drivers and pointing devices.

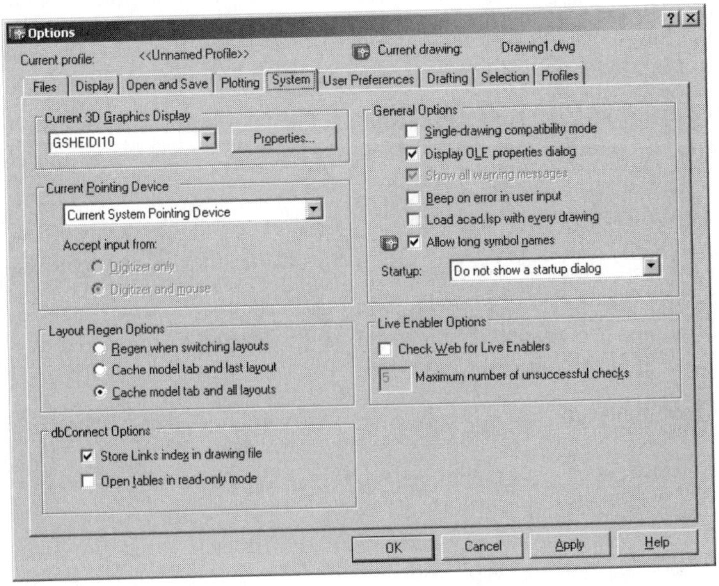

The Current 3D Graphics Display Group

This group offers a drop-down list and a Properties button. The drop-down list offers any available 3D graphics display systems. The GSHEIDI10 default option is Autodesk's own Heidi 3D Graphics display system. Other options may be provided by third-party vendors.

Clicking the Properties button opens the 3D Graphics System Configuration dialog box that offers further options for controlling the 3D Orbit and Shade Mode tools. The options in the Properties dialog box depend on the option selected in the drop-down list. If you are using the default GSHEIDI10 display system, see the "Adjusting AutoCAD's 3D Graphics System" section later in this appendix.

The Current Pointing Device Group

You can choose the type of pointing device you want to use with AutoCAD through the options in this group. The drop-down list offers Current System Pointing Device and Wintab Compatible Digitizer. If you want to use the default Windows pointing device, choose Current System Pointing Device. If you have a digitizer that uses the Wintab driver, you can select Wintab Compatible Digitizer.

You can further limit AutoCAD's use to the Wintab Compatible Digitizer by selecting the Digitizer Only radio button. If you select the Digitizer And Mouse radio button, AutoCAD will accept input from both devices.

The Layout Regen Options Group

This set of radio buttons allows you to specify how regens are applied when working with Layout tabs.

Regen When Switching Layouts This causes AutoCAD to force a regen when you select a Layout or Model tab. Use this option when your computer is limited in RAM.

Cache Model Tab And Last Layout This causes AutoCAD to suppress regens when switching to the Model tab or the most recently opened Layout tab. Other layouts will regen when selected.

Cache Model Tab And All Layouts This causes AutoCAD to suppress regens when selecting any Layout tabs or the Model tab.

The dbConnect Options Group

These check boxes in thie group offer controls over the dbConnect feature.

Store Links Index In Drawing File Lets you specify where database link data is stored. If this option is checked, link data is stored in the drawing that is linked to a database. This increases file size and file-loading time.

Open Tables In Read-Only Mode Lets you limit access to database files.

THE GENERAL OPTIONS GROUP

This set of check boxes allows you to set options related to the general operation of AutoCAD.

Single-Drawing Compatibility Mode Lets you control whether AutoCAD allows you to open multiple documents or limits you to a single document, as in earlier versions of AutoCAD [Sdi].

Display OLE Properties Dialog Lets you control the display of the OLE Properties dialog box, which normally appears when you insert OLE objects into an AutoCAD drawing. You can turn this feature off by clearing the Display OLE Properties Dialog When Pasting New OLE Objects option in the OLE Properties dialog box. You can restore the OLE Properties dialog box using this option.

Beep On Error In User Input Turns on an alarm beep that sounds whenever there is an input error.

Load Acad.lsp With Every Drawing Lets you determine whether an `Acad.lsp` file is loaded with every drawing. If you are used to using an `Acad.lsp` file with your AutoCAD system, you can check this option; otherwise, AutoCAD will load only the `Acaddoc.lsp` file [Acadlspasdoc].

Allow Long Symbol Names Allows you to use long names for items such as layer, block, linetype, and text-style names. With this option turned on, you can enter as many as 255 characters for names [Extnames].

Startup This drop-down list lets you determine whether AutoCAD displays the AutoCAD Startup dialog box when you first start AutoCAD, or the Create New Drawing dialog box when you select File ➢ New. If Show Startup Dialog Box is selected, these dialog boxes appear. Otherwise, AutoCAD automatically opens a default blank file based on the last template file used and the Select Template dialog box appears when you select File ➢ New.

THE LIVE ENABLER OPTIONS GROUP

Since AutoCAD 14, third-party developers have had the ability to create custom objects, also known as *proxy objects*, through a programming tool known as ObjectARX. When this feature was first introduced, you had to have the third-party application installed on your computer in order to view or edit such custom objects. *Object enablers* are small programs, like plug-ins to AutoCAD, that allow you to view and edit custom third-party objects without having the full third-party application present.

These object enablers may be available on the web for free download if the third-party producer has posted them. For example, if you receive a file created in Architectural Desktop that contains a custom object, AutoCAD can automatically go to the Autodesk website and download the Architectural Desktop Object Enabler so that you can edit and view the file. The Live Enabler options let you control how the Object Enabler feature is engaged when AutoCAD encounters custom objects.

Maximum Number Of Unsuccessful Checks This option lets you specify the number of time AutoCAD checks the Internet for object enablers after an attempt to make a connection has failed.

The User Preferences Tab

The options in the User Preferences tab allow you to adjust the way AutoCAD reacts to user input.

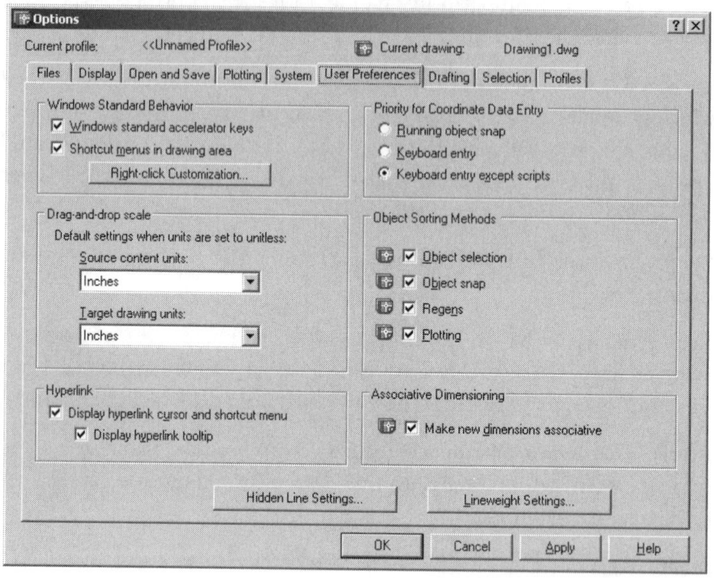

THE WINDOWS STANDARD BEHAVIOR GROUP

These settings allow you to control how AutoCAD reacts to keyboard accelerators and mouse right-clicks.

Windows Standard Accelerator Keys Causes AutoCAD to use the standard Windows behavior for Ctrl+C (Copy to Clipboard) and Ctrl+V (Paste from Clipboard) keystrokes. When this is not checked, AutoCAD interprets Ctrl+C as Cancel and Ctrl+V as Viewport Toggle.

Shortcut Menus In Drawing Areas Lets you see the shortcut menu when you right-click. When this option is not checked, AutoCAD responds to a right-click with an ↵ [Shortcutmenu].

Right-Click Customization Opens the Right-Click Customization dialog box, which offers further options for the behavior of the right-click in AutoCAD.

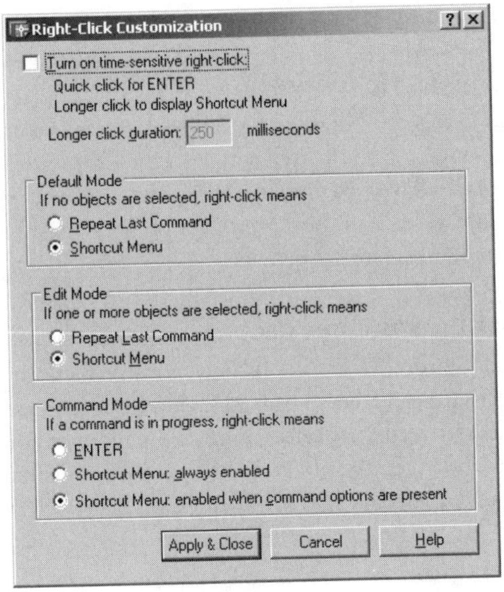

TIP *A new feature in 2004 is the Turn On Time-Sensitive Right-Click option. This option causes AutoCAD to respond differently depending on whether you right-click quickly or hold the right mouse button down momentarily. With this option, a rapid right-click issues an ↵ as if you press the Enter key. If you hold the right-mouse down, the shortcut menu appears. You can further adjust the time required to hold down the mouse button.*

Drag-AndDrop Scale Group

These settings control how the DesignCenter or i-drop feature determines the scale of blocks when blocks are given a unitless setting for their DesignCenter unit type. Each drop-down list offers the standard set of unit types that are available in the Block Definition dialog box under the Insert Units drop-down list. See Chapter 6 for more information on Blocks and Chapter 22 for information on the DesignCenter [Insunits].

The Hyperlink Group

These options control the display of the Hyperlink icon and its shortcut menu.

Priority For Coordinate Data Entry

These options control the way AutoCAD responds to coordinate input.

Running Object Snap Forces AutoCAD to use Running Osnaps at all times [Osnapcoord].

Keyboard Entry Allows you to use keyboard entry for coordinate input. The Keyboard Entry Except Scripts option allows you to use keyboard entry for coordinate input, except in scripts [Osnapcoord].

THE OBJECT SORTING METHODS GROUP

These options let you determine how objects are sorted during the specified operations. If an item is checked, the sort method is based on the order in which objects are drawn. If the item is not checked, the sort method is based on how AutoCAD optimizes the order of objects for display and file performance. For example, if you place a check in the Object Selection check box, AutoCAD offers the most recently drawn of two overlapping objects when you attempt to select the object with a selection cursor. If you place a check in the Regens option, AutoCAD restores the view of the drawing in the order that objects were created [Sortents].

THE ASSOCIATIVE DIMENSIONING GROUP

This area has one option, Make New Dimensions Associative, which you can toggle on or off. This option lets you control whether AutoCAD uses the true associative dimension feature introduced in AutoCAD 2002. With true associative dimension, a dimension will follow changes to an object whenever the object is edited. In the old method, you have to include a dimension definition point during the editing process in order to have the dimension follow changes in an object.

HIDDEN LINE SETTINGS

Click the Hidden Line Settings button to open the Hidden Line Settings dialog box, in which you can control how 3D hidden line views appear. The options presented let you control how hidden lines appear in a 3D hidden line view generated by the Hide command or the Hidden Shaded view. By default, hidden lines are invisible, but you can make them appear in a different color or in a different line type.

The Hidden Line Settings dialog box also lets you control whether intersecting 3D planes are indicated with a line. In past versions of AutoCAD, intersecting planes were not indicated, but with AutoCAD 2004, you have the option to show intersecting planes with a line in hidden line views. You can also control the color of the line.

LINEWEIGHT SETTINGS

Click the Lineweight Settings button to open the Lineweight Settings dialog box. See Chapters 7 and 13 for more information about the Lineweight Settings dialog box.

The Drafting Tab

The Drafting tab offers settings that relate to the drawing cursor, including the AutoSnap and AutoTrack features.

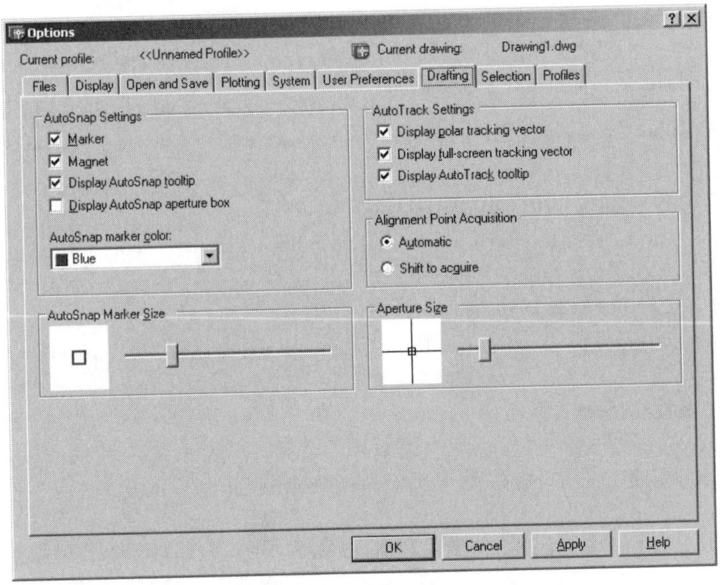

THE AUTOSNAP SETTINGS GROUP

The options in this group control the AutoSnap features that are engaged when you use Osnaps.

Marker Turns on the small, square graphic that appears on the Osnap location. If you prefer not to see this marker, clear this check box [Autosnap].

Magnet Causes the Osnap cursor to "jump to" an Osnap location as the cursor moves close to that location [Autosnap].

Display AutoSnap Tooltip Controls the display of the Osnap tool tip [Autosnap].

Display AutoSnap Aperture Box Displays a square over the cursor whenever Osnaps are active. If you are familiar with earlier versions of AutoCAD, you'll recognize the Aperture Box as the graphic used to indicate Osnaps before the AutoSnap feature was introduced [Apbox].

AutoSnap Marker Color Lets you determine the color for the AutoSnap marker.

THE AUTOSNAP MARKER SIZE SLIDER

Move the slider to control the size of the AutoSnap marker.

THE AUTOTRACK SETTINGS GROUP

These options offer control over the tracking vector used for Polar Tracking and Osnap Tracking.

Display Polar Tracking Vector Turns the Polar Tracking vector on or off [Trackpath].

Display Full-Screen Tracking Vector Lets you control whether the tracking vector appears across the full width of the drawing window or stops at the cursor location or the intersection of two tracking vectors [Trackpath].

Display AutoTrack Tooltip Turns the Osnap Tracking tool tip on or off [Autosnap].

THE ALIGNMENT POINT ACQUISITION GROUP

This option lets you determine the method for acquiring Osnap Tracking alignment points.

THE APERTURE SIZE SLIDER

Move the slider to set the size of the Osnap aperture pickbox [Aperture].

The Selection Tab

The options in the Selection tab of the Options dialog box control the way you select objects in AutoCAD. You can also make adjustments to the Grips feature.

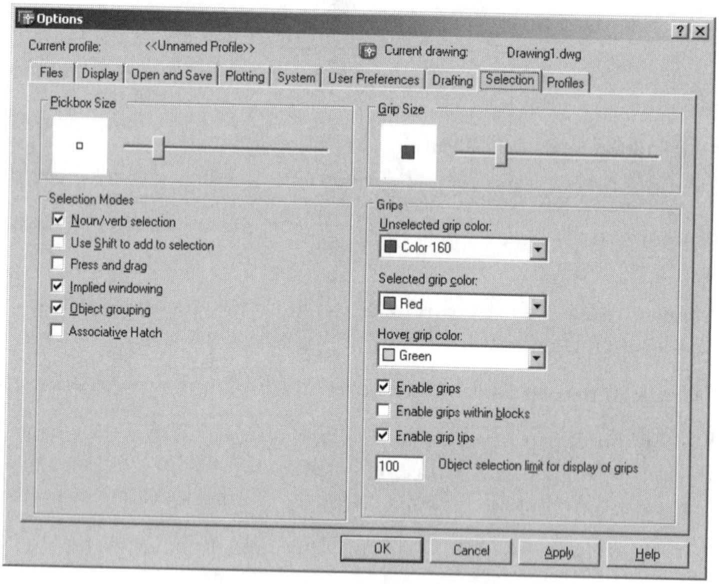

THE PICKBOX SIZE SLIDER

This slider lets you adjust the size of the pickbox [Pickbox].

THE GRIP SIZE SLIDER

This slider lets you adjust the size of grips [Gripsize].

The Selection Modes Group

The Selection Modes group lets you control the degree to which AutoCAD conforms to standard graphical user interface (GUI) methods of operation.

Noun/Verb Selection Makes AutoCAD work more like other Windows programs by allowing you to select objects before you choose an action or command [Pickfirst].

Use Shift To Add To Selection Lets you use the standard GUI method of holding down the Shift key to select multiple objects. When the Shift key is not held down, only the single object picked or the group of objects windowed will be selected. Previously selected objects are deselected, unless the Shift key is held down during selection. To turn this feature on using system variables, set Pickadd to 0 [Pickadd].

Press And Drag Lets you use the standard GUI method for placing windows: First, click and hold down the Pick button on the first corner of the window; then, while holding down the Pick button, drag the other corner of the window into position. When the other corner is in place, you let go of the Pick button to finish the window. This setting applies to both Verb/Noun and Noun/Verb operations. In the system variables, set Pickdrag to 1 for this option [Pickdrag].

Implied Windowing Causes a window or crossing window to start automatically if no object is picked at the `Select objects:` prompt. This setting has no effect on the Noun/Verb setting. In the system variables, set Pickauto to 1 for this option [Pickauto].

Object Grouping Allows you to select groups as single objects [Pickstyle].

Associative Hatch Allows you to select both a hatch pattern and its associated boundary with a single pick [Pickstyle].

The Grips Group

These options control the grips feature.

Unselected Grip Color Lets you select a color for grips that are exposed but not selected [Gripcolor].

Selected Grip Color Lets you set the color for grips that are exposed and selected [Griphot].

Hover Grip Color Lets you set the color for grips when the cursor hovers over the grip [Griphover].

Enable Grips Turns on grips.

Enable Grips Within Blocks Turns on the display of grips within blocks. Although you cannot edit grips within blocks, you can use grips within blocks as selection points [Gripblock].

Enable Grip Tips Turns on the display of grip tool tips for custom objects that have them [Griptips].

Object Selection Limit for Display of Grips Controls the display of grips based on the number of objects selected. If set to 1, grips are not displayed if more than one object is selected. You can select a range from 1 to 32,767. The default is 100 [Gripobjlimit].

The Profiles Tab

In Windows XP Professional, Windows 2000, and NT 4, a user profile is saved for each login name. Depending on the login name you use, you can have a different Windows setup. The Profiles tab offers a similar function for AutoCAD users. You can store different settings from the Options dialog box in a profile and recall them at any time. You can also save them to a file with the .arg extension and then take that file to another system. It's a bit like being able to take your Options settings with you wherever you go.

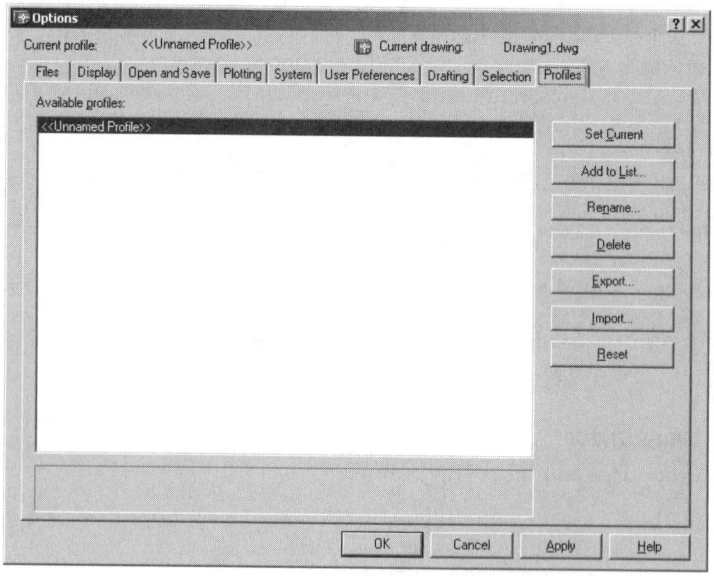

The main part of the Profiles tab displays a listing of available profiles. The default profile is shown as `<<Unnamed Profile>>`. As you add more profiles, they will appear in the list.

To create a new profile, highlight a profile name from the list, and then click Add To List. The Copy Profile dialog box opens, allowing you to enter a profile name and a description of the profile. The description appears in the box below the list on the Profiles tab whenever that profile is selected.

Once you've created a new profile, you can modify the settings on the other tabs of the Options dialog box, and the new settings will be associated with the new profile. Profiles will store the way menus are set up, so you can use them as an aid to managing both your own customization schemes and third-party software. You can also use profiles to manage multiple users on the same computer. Each user can maintain their own profile so they don't have to fight over how AutoCAD is set up. Here is a brief description of the options on the Profiles tab:

Set Current Installs the settings from the selected profile.

Add To List Creates a new profile from an existing one.

Rename Allows you to rename a profile and change its description.

Delete Removes the selected profile from the list.

Export Lets you save a profile to a file.

Import Imports a profile that has been saved to a file.

Reset Resets the values for a selected profile to its default settings.

Configuring the Tablet Menu Area

If you own a digitizing tablet and you would like to use it with the AutoCAD tablet menu template, you must configure your tablet menu. You can open the `Tablet.dwg` file in the Support folder of the AutoCAD 2004 folder and print the tablet menu template drawing to a size that will fit your digitizing tablet. Then do the following.

1. Securely fasten your tablet menu template to the tablet. Be sure the area covered by the template is completely within the tablet's active drawing area.
2. Choose Tools ➢ Tablet ➢ Configure. The following prompt appears:

   ```
   Enter number of tablet
   menus desired (0-4) <0>:
   ```

   Enter **4**↵. For the next series of prompts, you will be locating the four tablet menu areas, starting with menu area 1 (see Figure B.1).
3. Locate the position indicated in Figure B.1 as the upper-left corner of menu area 1. Place your puck or stylus to pick that point. The prompt changes to

   ```
   Digitize lower left corner of menu area 1:
   ```
4. Locate the position indicated in Figure B.1 as the lower-left corner of menu area 1.
5. Continue this process until you have selected three corners for four menu areas.
6. After you select the menu areas, you get the following prompt:

   ```
   Do you want to respecify the Fixed Screen Pointing Area?
   ```

   Type **Y**↵ and then choose the position indicated in Figure B.1.
7. Finally, you get this prompt:

   ```
   Digitize upper right corner of screen pointing area:
   ```

   Pick the position indicated in Figure B.1.

FIGURE B.1

How to locate the tablet menu areas

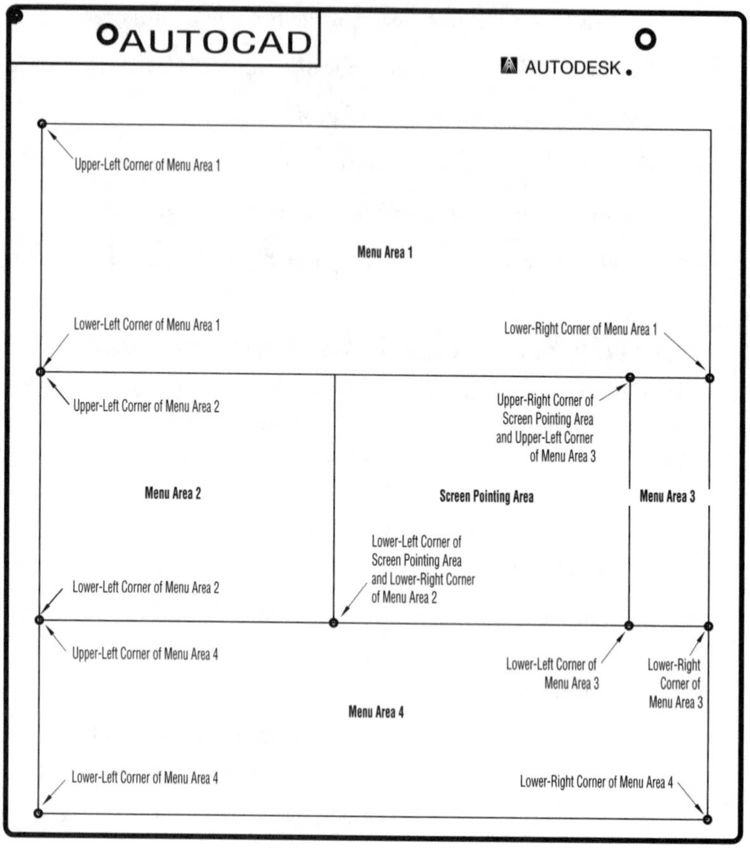

The three prompts that remain refer to a *floating screen pointing area*. This is an area on your tablet that allows you to select menu options and other areas on your screen outside the drawing area. This option is necessary because when you set up a digitizer for tracing, access to areas outside the drawing area is temporarily disabled. The floating screen pointing area lets you access pull-down menus and the status bar during tracing sessions (see Chapter 12).

8. If you never intend to trace drawings with your tablet, type **N**↵ at all three prompts. Otherwise, take the following three steps.
9. At the following prompt:

   `Do you want to specify the Floating Screen Pointing Area? <N>:`

   type **Y**↵.
10. At the prompt

    `Do you want the Floating Screen Pointing Area to be the same size as the Fixed Screen Pointing Area? <Y>:`

type **Y↵** if you want the floating screen pointing area to be the same as the fixed screen pointing area, the area you specified in steps 6 and 7. Type **N↵** if you want to use a separate area on your tablet for the floating screen pointing area.

11. The last prompt asks if you want to use the F12 function key to toggle the floating screen pointing area on and off. (This is similar to the F10 key function of earlier releases of AutoCAD.) Enter **Y↵** or **N↵**, depending on whether you want to specify a different function key for the floating screen pointing area.

AutoCAD will remember this configuration until you change it. Quit this file by choosing File ➢ Exit.

Turning On the Noun/Verb Selection Method

If, for some reason, the Noun/Verb Selection method is not available, follow these steps to turn it on.

1. Choose Tools ➢ Options. Then, in the Options dialog box, click the Selection tab.
2. In the Selection Modes button group, click the Noun/Verb Selection check box.
3. Click OK.

If it wasn't there before, you should now see a small square at the intersection of the crosshair cursor. This square is actually a pickbox superimposed on the cursor. It tells you that you can select objects, even while the command prompt appears at the bottom of the screen and no command is currently active. As you saw earlier, the square will momentarily disappear when you are in a command that asks you to select points.

You can also turn on Noun/Verb Selection by entering **'Pickfirst↵** at the command prompt. At the `New value for PICKFIRST <0>:` prompt, enter **1↵** (entering **0** turns the Pickfirst function off). The Pickfirst system variable is stored in the AutoCAD configuration file. See Appendix D for more on system variables.

Turning On the Grips Feature

If, for some reason, the Grips feature is not available, follow these steps to turn it on.

1. Choose Tools ➢ Options. Then in the Options dialog box, click the Selection tab.
2. In the Grips group, click the Enable Grips check box.
3. Click OK, and you are ready to proceed.

The Selection tab of the Options dialog box also lets you specify whether grips appear on objects that compose a block (see Chapter 4 for more on blocks), as well as set the grip color and size. You can also set these options using the system variables described in Appendix D.

You can also turn the Grips feature on and off by entering **'Grips↵**. At the `New value for GRIPS <0>:` prompt, enter **1** to turn grips on or **0** to turn grips off. Grips is a system variable that is stored in the AutoCAD configuration file.

Setting Up the Tracking Vector Feature

If you find that AutoCAD does not display a tracking vector as described in the early chapters in this book or that the tracking vector does not behave as described, chances are this feature has been turned off or altered. Take the following steps to configure the tracking vector so that it behaves as described in this book.

1. Open the Options dialog box by choosing Tools ➢ Options.
2. Click the Drafting tab.
3. Click all three options in the AutoTrack Settings group.
4. Make sure that the Marker, Magnet, and Display AutoSnap Tooltip check boxes are checked in the AutoSnap Settings group.
5. Make sure the Automatic radio button in the Alignment Point Acquisition group is selected.
6. Click OK to exit the dialog box.

Adjusting AutoCAD's 3D Graphics System

You can adjust the performance of AutoCAD's 3D graphic system through the 3D Graphics System Configuration dialog box. To open this dialog box, click the System tab in the Options dialog box, and then click the Properties button in the Current 3D Graphics Display group.

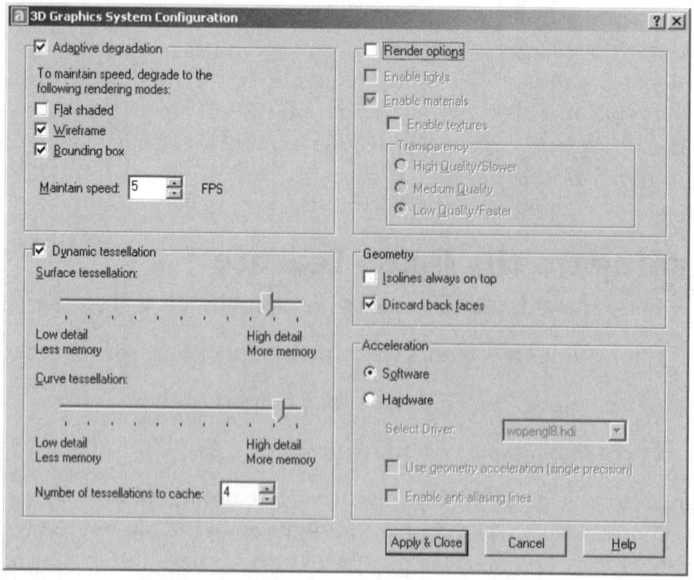

This dialog box offers control over the way AutoCAD displays 3D models when you use the 3D Orbit tool or when you are using a Shade mode. Here is a listing of the options for the GSHEIDI10 3D Graphics System Configuration dialog box.

The Adaptive Degradation Group

The 3D Orbit tool allows you to adjust your view in real time, which places high demands on your display system. To maintain the smoothness of the real-time update of your 3D views, AutoCAD will degrade the display while performing the view transformation. The options under Adaptive Degradation let you set the level to which the view is degraded while using the 3D Orbit tool. You can turn all these features on or off by using the check box next to the group title.

Flat Shaded Causes AutoCAD to degrade the 3D view to flat shaded mode.

Wireframe Causes AutoCAD to degrade the 3D view to wireframe mode.

Bounding Box Causes AutoCAD to degrade the 3D view to show bounding boxes to indicate objects.

Maintain Speed FPS Lets you set the frame rate in frames per second for the real-time display of 3D objects. Higher values require greater performance from your display system.

The Dynamic Tessellation Group

The options in this group determine the smoothness of 3D objects when they are shaded. To simulate smoothness, the AutoCAD Heidi 3D Graphics system divides curved surfaces into triangles called *tessellations*. You can turn all these features on or off by using the check box next to the group title.

Surface Tessellation Controls the amount of detail shown for surfaces. Greater detail requires more surface tessellation, which in turn requires more system memory.

Curve Tessellation Controls the amount of detail shown for curved surfaces. Greater detail requires more surface tessellation, which in turn requires more system memory.

Number Of Tessellations To Cache Controls the number of tessellations that are cached. A cache is a part of memory reserved to store frequently used data. AutoCAD will always cache one tessellation. Caching two tessellations will improve the appearance and performance of 3D objects when you use multiple viewports.

The Render Options Group

If you plan to use AutoCAD's rendering feature, these options can be useful. Once you've applied lights and materials to an AutoCAD 3D model, the settings in the Rendering Options group allow you to conveniently view a rendered version of your model. If your computer's resources are limited, you will want to keep these options turned off, as they use extra RAM.

Enable Lights Allows you to view your 3D model in a shaded mode using lights that have been added using the Light command or the Light tool from the Render toolbar. If no lights have been added, your model will appear normally, as if the Enable Lights option is not turned on.

Enable Materials Allows you to view your 3D model in a shaded mode using materials that have been added using the Rmat command or the Materials tool from the Render toolbar. If no materials have been added, your model will be shaded normally, as if the Enable Materials option were not turned on.

Enable Textures Allows you to view your 3D model in a shaded mode using textures that have been added using the Rmat and Setuv commands or the Materials tool from the Render toolbar. The Enable Materials option must be turned on before this option can be used.

Transparency Lets you control the visual quality of transparent objects in your model when viewing your model in a shaded mode. You have the option to set transparency to a high-, medium-, or low-quality level. Low-quality levels will show transparent objects with a "screen door" effect, while medium and high options will give transparent objects a smoother appearance. The low-quality level allows faster view changes.

THE GEOMETRY GROUP

These options let you control back faces and isoline visibility in 3D models.

Isolines Always On Top If you use either the Flat Shaded/Edges On or Gouraud Shaded/Edges On options of the Shademode command (View ➢ Shade ➢ Flat Shaded/Edges On or View ➢ Shade ➢ Gouraud Shaded/Edges On), you'll see the outlines of surfaces and surface tessellations displayed. With the Isolines Always On Top option turned on, these outlines and tessellations appear on both the front and back faces of surfaces.

Discard Back Faces In most 3D rendering systems, surfaces have just one visible side. The back sides of surfaces are invisible. This doesn't matter for objects such as cubes and spheres because you only see one side of a surface at any given time; but in some situations, you can see both sides of a surface, such as a single surface used as a wall.

If your drawing is composed of mostly closed objects such as cubes and spheres and you will only see one surface, you can check the Discard Back Faces box to improve system performance. If you have many single surfaces that will be viewed from both sides, you will want to leave this option turned off.

THE ACCELERATION GROUP

This option lets you determine whether you use software or hardware acceleration to perform 3D drawing tasks.

Software Causes AutoCAD to use software to draw 3D objects.

Hardware Causes AutoCAD to use hardware to draw 3D objects, when hardware acceleration is available.

Use Geometry Acceleration (Single Precision) Causes AutoCAD to use hardware acceleration for object geometry. This option is only available when the Hardware option is selected and your graphics hardware supports geometry acceleration.

Enable Anti-Aliasing Lines Causes AutoCAD to smooth out lines and remove the jagged appearance of lines and arcs. This option is only available when the Hardware option is selected and your graphics hardware supports anti-aliasing.

Appendix C

Hardware and Software Tips

Because some of the items that make up an AutoCAD system are not found on the typical desktop system, I have provided this appendix to help you understand some of the less common items you may need. This appendix also discusses ways you can improve AutoCAD's performance through software and hardware.

The Graphics Display

There are two issues to consider concerning the graphics display: *resolution* and *performance*. Fortunately, nearly all computers sold today have display systems that are more than adequate for AutoCAD, thanks to the popularity of 3D games. You do need to make sure that your resolution is set to at least 1024 × 768, preferably higher. The higher your resolution, the more detail you'll be able to see in your drawings.

If you have an older system that needs a graphics display upgrade, you will want to consider the following factors in choosing a new display:

AGP Bus Contemporary motherboards use high-speed AGP (Accelerated Graphics Port) expansion slots that offer the fastest video throughput available. Check that yours is a system of this type. Windows 98 and later versions also provide options for using multiple monitors, an approach that has been popular among AutoCAD users. Multiple monitors offer AutoCAD users the option to view multiple documents more easily. PCI (Peripheral Component Interconnect) display cards are also a fine alternative for the budget-minded AutoCAD user.

Video RAM If you are shopping for a display system, you should also make sure that it has at least 8MB of video RAM. Greater amounts of up to 64MB will give you better performance with AutoCAD, and you'll be able to take advantage of larger color palettes and higher resolution for other programs such as 3D studio max or VIZ.

Pointing Devices

Our most basic means of communicating with computers is the keyboard and pointing device. Most likely, you will use a mouse, but if you are still in the market for a pointing device, choose an input device that generates smooth cursor movement. Some of the lesser-quality input devices cause erratic movement. Since AutoCAD relies on precise input, you may want to upgrade to an optical mouse, which is less likely to wear out or accumulate dirt in its mechanism.

The Digitizing Tablet

If you need to trace large drawings, you might want to consider a digitizing tablet. It is usually a rectangular object with a penlike *stylus* or a device called a *puck*, which resembles a mouse. It has a smooth surface on which to draw. The most common size is 4" × 5", but digitizing tablets are available in sizes up to 60" × 70". The tablet gives a natural feel to drawing with the computer because the movement of the stylus or puck is directly translated into cursor movement.

AutoCAD supports Wintab-compatible digitizers. If your digitizer has a Wintab driver, you can use your digitizer as both a tracing device (to trace drawings on a tablet) and a general pointing device for Windows to choose program menu items.

Your Wintab digitizer must be installed and configured under Windows. Make sure it is working in Windows before enabling it in AutoCAD, or you will not be able to use the digitizer as a pointing device (mouse). To enable the digitizer in AutoCAD, choose Tools ➢ Options to open the Options dialog box and click the System tab. Open the Current Pointing Device drop-down list and select Wintab-Compatible Digitizer ADI 4.2–by Autodesk, Inc.

Output Devices

Output options vary greatly in quality and price. Quality and paper size are the major considerations for both printers and plotters. Nearly all printers give accurate drawings, but some produce better line quality than others. Some plotters give merely acceptable results, while others are quite impressive in their speed, color, and accuracy.

AutoCAD 2004 can use the Windows XP or Windows NT system printer, so any device that Windows supports is also supported by AutoCAD. You also have the option of plotting directly to an output device, although Autodesk recommends that you set up your plotter or printer through Windows and then select the device from the Plot Configuration group in the Plot Device tab of the Plot dialog box or the Page Setup dialog box.

Printers

So many types of printers are available these days that it has become more difficult to choose the right printer for your application. This section describes the broad categories of printers available and how they relate to AutoCAD. You will also want to consider the other uses for your printer, such as word-processing or color graphics. Here are a few printing options:

Laser Printers Laser printers produce high-quality line work output. The standard office laser printer is usually limited to 8.5" × 11" paper; however, 11" × 17" laser printers for graphics and

CAD work are now becoming affordable and are commonly used for proof plots. Resolution and speed are the major considerations if you are buying a laser printer. An output of 300 DPI (dots per inch) produces very acceptable plots, but 600 DPI is fast becoming the standard. You should also look for a laser printer with sufficient built-in memory to improve spooling and plotting speeds.

Color Inkjet Printers These printers offer speed and quality output. Some color inkjet printers even accept 17" × 22" paper. Since inkjet printers are competitively priced, they can offer the best solution for low-cost check plots. And the 17" × 22" paper size is quite acceptable for half-size plots, a format that many architects and engineers are using now.

PostScript Printers If you want to use a PostScript device to output your drawings, the best method is to use File ➢ Export or the Psout command. These options convert your drawing into a true PostScript file. You can then send your file to a PostScript printer or typesetting machine. This can be especially useful for printed circuit board (PCB) layout that requires photo negatives for output. If you are an architect who needs presentation-quality drawings, you might want to consider using the Encapsulated PS (*.eps) option in the Export Data dialog box. Often service bureaus that offer a raster plotter service can produce E-size PostScript output from a PostScript file. The uses of this option are really quite open-ended.

Another option is to export your drawing to an illustration program such as Adobe Illustrator and make any refinements to your drawing there. You can save files in the AutoCAD 2004 DXF file format or use the File ➢ Export option to export files to the Windows Metafile format. Most illustration programs accept either of these formats.

Plotters

Printer technology has changed significantly since the early versions of AutoCAD. This is especially true in the area of large format plotters. Output devices intended for CAD were once dominated by pen plotters, but now color inkjet plotters and printers are commonplace. Inkjet technology offers far greater flexibility and speed, giving you many more options in the look of your output.

You can also find laser or electrostatic plotters at a much higher price. Inkjet plotters offer the best value; they are fast and fairly inexpensive compared with the older pen plotters they supersede. For a bit more expense, you can step up to a color plotter. Black-and-white plotters are capable of printing raster images in larger formats, and they can print patterns and screens for highlight effects.

If you need large plots but can't afford a large plotter, many blueprint companies and even some copy centers offer plotting as a service. This can be a very good alternative to purchasing your own plotter. Check with your local blueprinter or CAD service bureau.

Fine-Tuning the Appearance of Output

If you open the Plot dialog box or the Page Setup dialog box and click the Plot Device tab, you'll see the options that offer control over how your plotter or printer works.

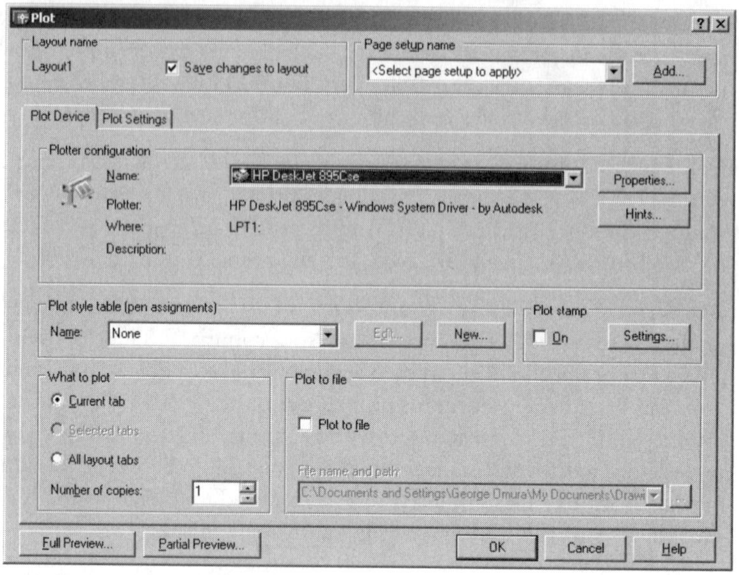

The Plot dialog box shows four option groups:

- Plotter Configuration
- Plot Style Table (Pen Assignments)
- What To Plot
- Plot To File

The What To Plot and Plot To File groups are not shown in the Page Setup dialog box.

These button groups seem innocent enough, but behind two of these groups lies a vast set of options that can be quite intimidating. You've already seen how the Plot Style Table options work in Chapter 7. This section covers the options available when you click the Properties button in the Plotter Configuration group.

Making Detailed Adjustments with the Plotter Configuration Options

The Plotter Configuration options allow you to adjust those printer or plotter settings that you may want to change only occasionally. These settings are fairly technical and include things like the port your printer is connected to, the quality of bitmap image printing, custom paper sizes, and printer calibration, which lets you adjust your plotter for any size discrepancies in output. You won't be using most of these settings often, but you should know that they exist just in case you encounter a situation in which you need to make some subtle change to your printer's configuration. You can also use these options to create multiple configurations of the same plotter for quick access to custom settings.

All the settings in this group are stored in a file with the .PC3 filename extension. You can store and recall any number of configuration files for situations that call for different plotter settings. PC3 files are normally stored in the `Plotters` folder under the `C:\Documents and Settings\`*`User Name`*`\Application Data\Autodesk\AutoCAD 2004\R16.0\enu\`folder. *`User Name`* is your login name.

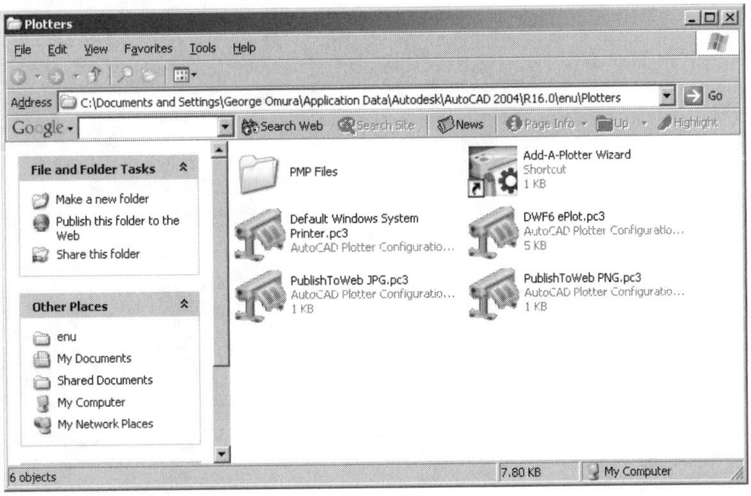

The Plotter Configuration button group offers a drop-down list from which you can select a printer or file output configuration. If a PC3 file exists for a plotter configuration, the drop-down list will display it, and it will display any Windows system printer. Once you've selected an output device from the list, you can click the Properties button to access the Plotter Configuration Editor dialog box.

TIP *You can configure AutoCAD to create bitmap files in the most common file formats (such as TIFF, Targa, and PCX) or to create Autodesk's DWF file format for the Internet. Once you've configured AutoCAD for these types of output, this is where you select the file output type.*

The Plotter Configuration Editor dialog box has three tabs. The General tab displays a list of Windows drivers that this configuration uses, if any, and there is a space for your own comments.

TIP *You can access and edit the plotter configuration settings without opening AutoCAD. To do this, locate the PC3 file in the* `Plotters` *subdirectory under the* `C:\Documents and Settings\`*`User Name`*`\Application Data\Autodesk\AutoCAD 2004\R16.0\enu\Plotters` *directory (where* `User Name` *is your login name), and double-click it.*

The Ports tab lets you specify where your plotter data is sent. This is where you should look if you are sending your plots to a network plotter or if you decide to create plot files. You can also select the AutoSpool feature, which allows you to direct your plot to an intermediate location for distribution to the appropriate output device.

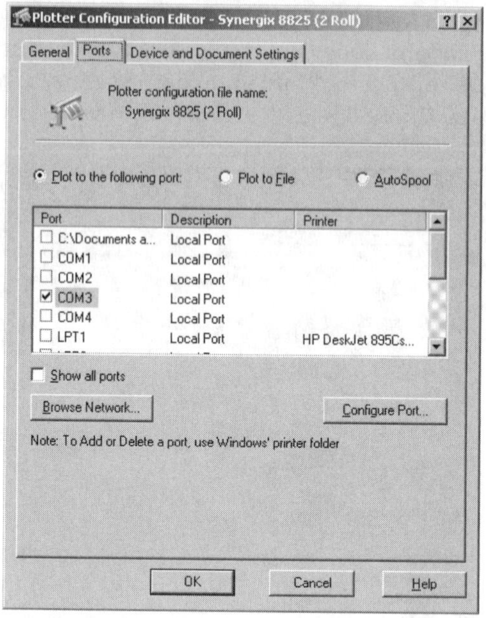

The Device And Document Settings tab is the main part of this dialog box. It offers a set of options ranging from OLE output control to custom paper sizes. The main list box offers options in a hierarchical list, similar to a listing in Windows Explorer. Toward the bottom of the dialog box are the Import, Save As, and Defaults buttons. These buttons let you import configuration settings from earlier versions of AutoCAD, save the current settings as a file, or return the settings to their default values.

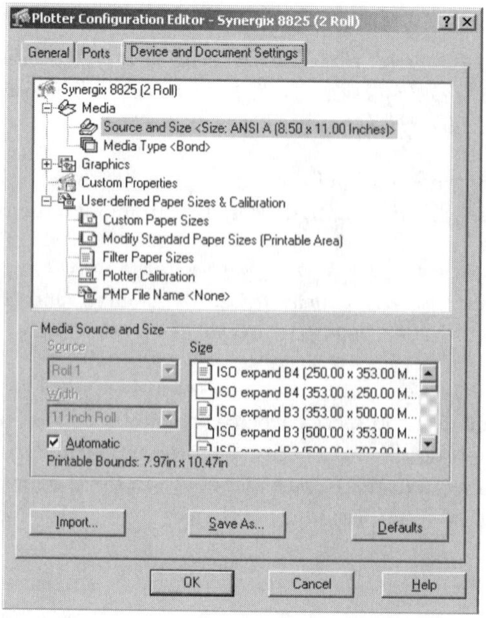

The list has four main categories: Media, Graphics, Custom Properties, and User-Defined Paper Sizes & Calibration. Not all the options under these categories are available for all plotters. When you select an item from this list, the area just below the list displays the options associated with that item. The following describes each category and its options, using the Xerox Engineering Systems XES8825 as an example.

The Media Category

Some plotters, such as the Xerox Engineering Systems 8800 series, offer options for the source and size of printer media and for the media type. If the Source And Size option is available, the dialog box offers a listing of the source, such as sheet feed or roll, and the sheet size. The Media Type option lets you choose from bond, vellum, or glossy paper or any other medium that is specifically controlled by the plotter. Duplex Printing, when available, controls options for double-sided printing in printers that support this feature. Media Destination, when available, lets you select a destination for output such as collating or stapling in printers that support such features.

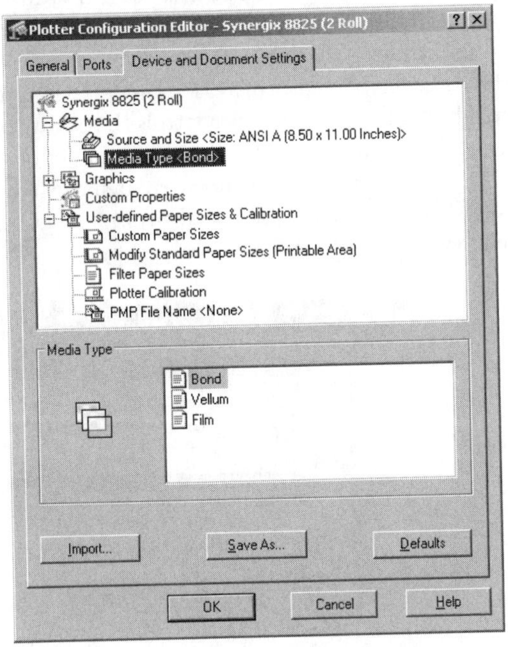

The Physical Pen Configuration Category (Shown Only for Pen Plotters)

Pen plotters have features that diverge from the typical laser or inkjet printer or plotter. When these options are present, they let you control some of the ways that AutoCAD generates data for pen plotters. Here is a listing of those pen plotter feature settings:

Prompt For Pen Swapping Stops the plotter to allow you to switch pens. This feature is designed primarily for single-pen plotters.

Area Fill Correction Tells AutoCAD to compensate for pen width around the edges of a solid-filled area in order to maintain dimensional accuracy of the plot.

Pen Optimization Level Sets how AutoCAD sorts pen movement for optimum speed. AutoCAD does a lot of preparation before sending your drawing to the plotter. If you are using a pen plotter, one of the things it does is optimize the way it sends vectors to your plotter, so your plotter doesn't waste time making frequent pen changes and moving from one end of the plot to another just to draw a single line.

Physical Pen Characteristics Lets you assign plotter pen numbers to AutoCAD colors, adjust the speed of individual pens, and assign pen widths.

THE GRAPHICS CATEGORY

These settings give you control over both vector and raster output from your plotter. The Vector Graphics settings let you control resolution and color depth, as well as the method for creating shading. If you want to configure your printer for virtual pens, select 255 Virtual Pens under the Color Depth option.

The Raster Graphics settings slider gives you control over the quality of any bitmap images. If this setting is placed all the way to the left, raster images will not be plotted. As you move the slider to the right, the raster image quality increases, the speed of printing decreases, and memory requirements increase. The OLE Settings slider controls the quality of OLE linked or embedded files. With the slider all the way to the left, OLE objects will not be printed. As you move the slider farther to the right, OLE image quality and memory requirements increase while speed is reduced.

The Tradeoff slider lets you choose how the Raster and OLE sliders improve speed. You can choose between lower resolution and fewer colors.

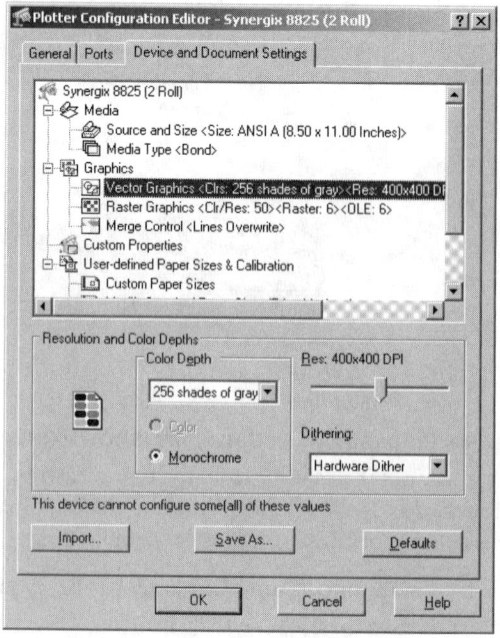

For printers and plotters that support TrueType fonts, the TrueType Text options allow you to select between plotting text as graphics or as TrueType text.

Custom Properties

This is a single option that displays the Custom Properties button in the lower part of the dialog box. Clicking the Custom Properties button gives you access to the same printer or plotter settings that are available from the Windows system printer settings. You can also access these settings by choosing Start ➢ Settings ➢ Printers, right-clicking the desired printer, and choosing Properties from the shortcut menu.

TIP *The options offered through the Custom Properties button often duplicate many of the items in the Device And Documents list. If an option is not accessible from the Device And Documents list, check the options offered under Custom Properties.*

Initialization String

Some plotters require preinitialization and postinitialization codes, in the form of ASCII text strings, to get the plotter's attention. If you have such a plotter, this option lets you enter those strings.

User-Defined Paper Sizes & Calibration

The options in the User-Defined Paper Sizes & Calibration category offer some of the more valuable options in this dialog box. In particular, the Calibration option can be useful in ensuring the accuracy of your plots.

Plotter Calibration

If you find that your printer or plotter is not producing an accurate plot, you should focus on the calibration option. If your plotter stretches or shrinks your image in one direction or another, the calibration option lets you adjust the width and height of your plotter's output. To use it, click the Plotter Calibration listing under User-Defined Paper Sizes & Calibration.

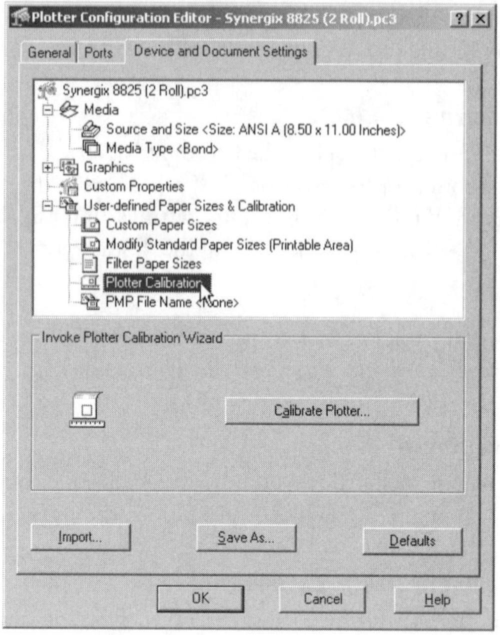

A button appears labeled Calibrate Plotter. Click this button to start the Calibrate Plotter Wizard. You are asked first to select a paper size, and then to select a width and height for a rectangle that will be plotted with your printer. Figure C.1 shows the wizard screen that asks for the rectangle size.

FIGURE C.1

The Calibrate Plotter Wizard lets you adjust the width and height scaling of your plotter output in order to fine-tune the accuracy of your plots.

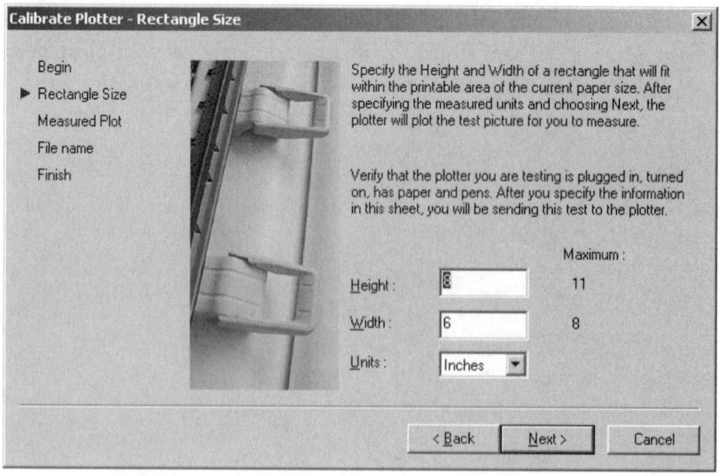

You can use the Calibrate Plotter Wizard to plot a sample rectangle of a specific size. You then measure the rectangle and check its actual dimensions against the dimensions that you entered. If there are any discrepancies between the plotted dimensions and the dimensions you specified, you can then enter the actual plotted size and print another test rectangle. You can repeat this process until your plotted rectangle exactly matches the dimensions entered into the wizard.

Toward the end of the Calibrate Plotter Wizard's steps, you'll be asked to give a name for a Plot Model Parameter (PMP) file that will store your calibration data. The PMP file also stores any custom paper size information that you input from other parts of the User-Defined Paper Sizes & Calibration options. This file is then associated with the PC3 file that stores your plotter configuration data.

If you have more than one PC3 file for your plotter, you can associate the PMP file with your other PC3 files using the PMP File Name option in the Device And Document Settings list box. You only need one calibration file for each plotter or printer you are using. This option is the first item under the User-Defined Paper Sizes & Calibration category.

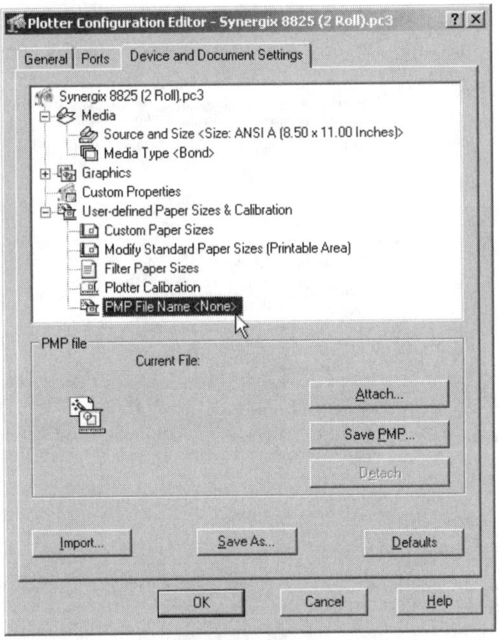

To associate a PMP file with a PC3 plotter configuration file, select the PC3 file from the Name drop-down list in the Plot Device tab in the Plot dialog box. Click the Properties button and then, in the Device And Document Settings tab, click the PMP File Name listing. The PMP options appear in the bottom of the dialog box. Click the Open File button, and then select the PMP file from the Open dialog box. Click OK. You'll see that the PMP file has been added to the PMP file name listing.

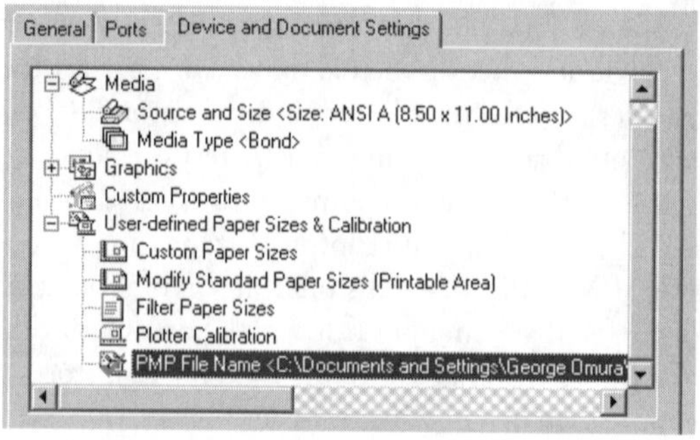

Custom Paper Sizes

Some plotters offer custom paper sizes. This feature is usually available for printers and plotters that you've set up to use the AutoCAD drivers instead of the Windows system drivers. If your plotter offers this option, you'll see a list box and a set of buttons when you select Custom Paper Sizes.

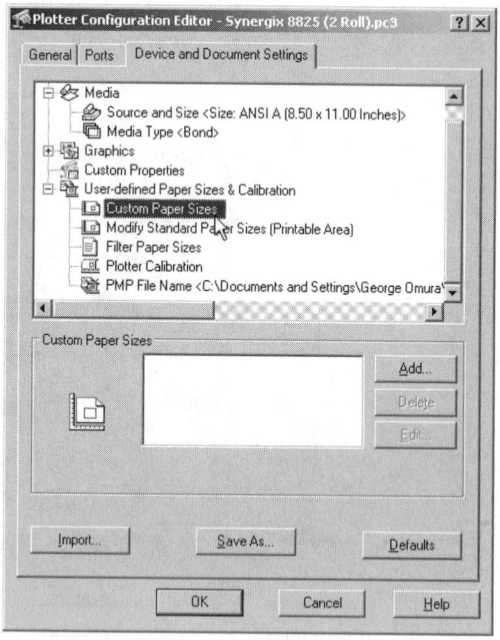

Clicking the Add button starts the Custom Paper Size Wizard, which lets you set the sheet size and margin, as well as the paper source. This information is then saved in a PMP file. You are asked to provide a specific name for the custom paper size, which will be listed in the Custom Paper Size list box.

Once you've created a custom paper size, you can edit or delete it using the Edit or Delete button in the Custom Paper Size options.

Modify Standard Paper Size

The last item in the Device And Document Settings list is the Modify Standard Paper Size option. If this option is available, it allows you to adjust the margins of a standard paper size.

TIP *If you are using an older pen plotter, you will see the Physical Pen Configuration options in the Device And Document Settings list box. These additional options give you control over pen speed, pen optimization, and area fill correction.*

Import, Save As, and Defaults

The Import, Save As, and Defaults buttons at the bottom of the Plot Configuration Editor let you import or save your plotter settings as PC3 files, which you can then load from the Plot Device tab of the Plot dialog box and the Page Setup dialog box, as described earlier in this appendix. The Import button lets you import PCP and PC2 files from earlier versions of AutoCAD. Save As lets you save your current settings under an existing or a new PC3 filename. The Defaults button restores the default settings, if any, for the current plotter configuration.

Plot Stamp

To help cross-reference your printer or plotter output to AutoCAD drawing files, it's a good idea to add a *plot stamp* to your drawings that identifies the date, the time, and the filename of the drawing that generated your plot. To accomplish this, the Plot Stamp feature lets you imprint data onto your plotted drawings, usually in the lower-left corner. In addition, Plot Stamp lets you keep a record of your plots in a log file.

To use Plot Stamp, type **Plotstamp↵** at the AutoCAD command prompt. You can also click the Settings button in the Plot Stamp group of the Plot dialog box (choose File ➢ Plot). The Plot Stamp dialog box opens (see Figure C.2).

TIP *The Plot Stamp group in the Plot dialog box also lets you turn the Plot Stamp feature on and off.*

FIGURE C.2
The Plot Stamp dialog box

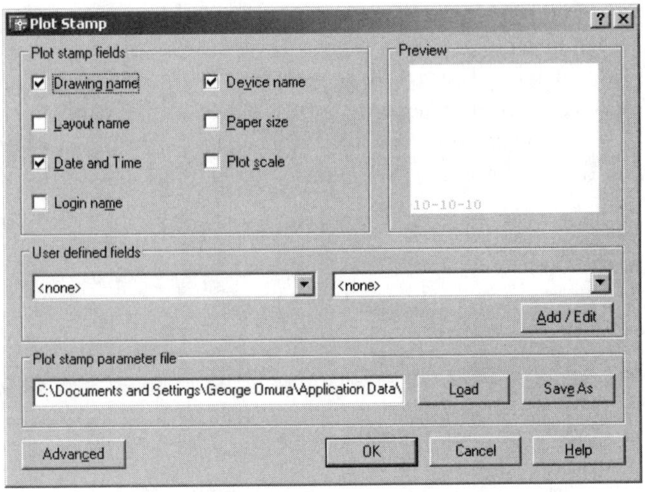

The Plot Stamp dialog box offers a number of options that let you determine what to include in the stamp.

TIP *If you find that the options are grayed out, click the Save As button to save Plot Stamp settings under a new file.*

The Plot Stamp Fields group lets you include a number of predefined options in your stamp, including drawing, layout, and output device name. The User Defined Fields group lets you add custom text to the stamp. To use this feature, click the Add/Edit button in the User Defined Fields group. The User Defined Fields dialog box appears, as shown in Figure C.3.

FIGURE C.3

The User Defined Fields dialog box

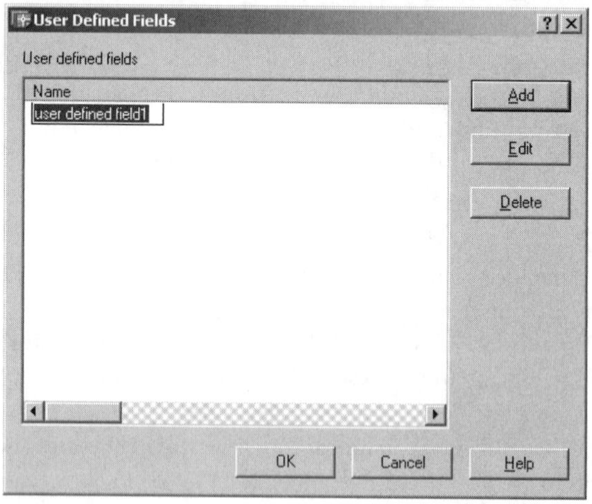

You can use the Add, Edit, or Delete button to add or make changes to the user-defined fields. Once you've added a field, it will appear as a list in both of the list boxes in the User Defined Fields group of the Plot Stamp dialog box.

To control the location, orientation, font, and font size of the plot stamp, you can click the Advanced button in the lower-left corner of the Plot Stamp dialog box. This opens the Advanced Options dialog box, shown in Figure C.4.

This dialog box lets you specify the orientation of the stamp on the page as well as the exact location of the stamp in relation to either the printable area or the paper border. In addition, you can specify whether to save a record of your plotting activities in a log file using the Log File Location group.

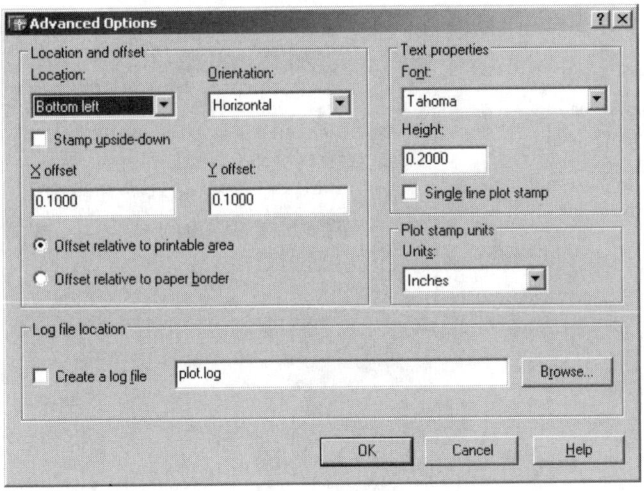

FIGURE C.4
The Advanced Options dialog box

Merge Control

Some output devices let you control how overlapping lines and shaded areas affect each other, a feature known as *merge control*. In versions of AutoCAD prior to 2000, merge control was handled through additional commands such as Hpconfig or OCEconfig. AutoCAD 2004 includes merge control as part of the Plotter Configuration Editor dialog box.

You can gain access to merge control by opening the Plotter Configuration Editor and, in the Graphics And Document Settings list box, clicking the plus sign next to Graphics to expand the list of Graphics options.

If your device supports merge control, you will see it listed under Graphics as shown in Figure C.5.

Filtering Paper Sizes

AutoCAD displays all the available paper sizes for a selected output device in the Page Setup dialog box or the Plot dialog box. For some plotters, the list can be a bit overwhelming. You can filter out paper sizes that you do not need by using the Filter Paper Sizes option in the Plotter Configuration Editor.

Go to the Plotter Configuration Editor and click the plus sign next to the User-Defined Paper Sizes & Calibration listing. You'll see Filter Paper Sizes as an option, as shown in Figure C.6. Once you select this option, you'll see the Filter Paper Sizes area in the lower half of the Plotter Configuration Editor. Remove the checkmark in the box next to any size you won't need.

FIGURE C.5

The location of the Merge Control setting in the Plot Configuration Editor

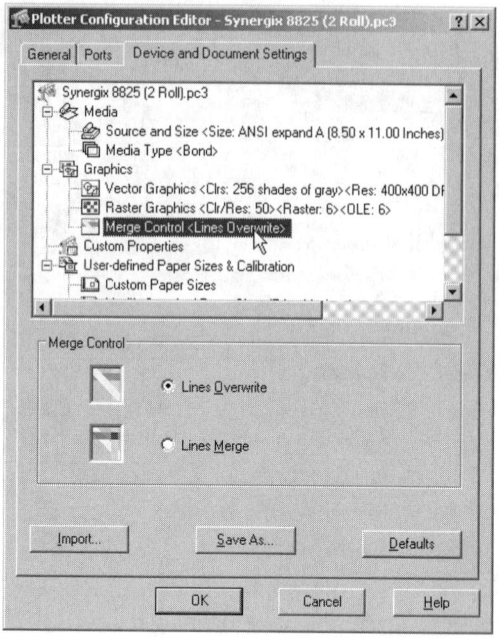

FIGURE C.6

The location of the Filter Paper Sizes option in the Plot Configuration Editor

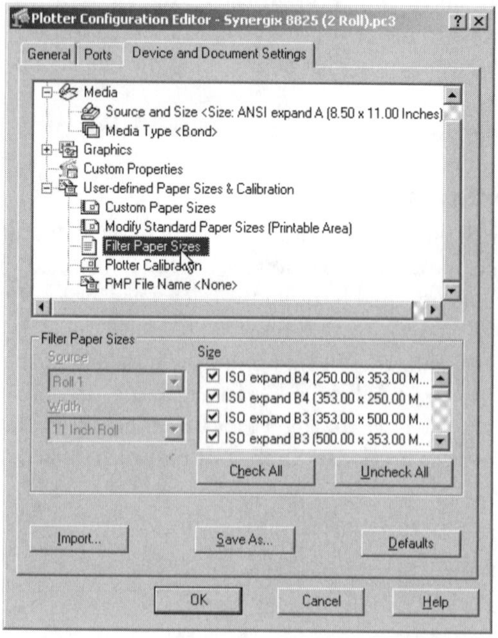

Filtering Printers

In some instances, you might want to hide the Windows system printer from the list of printers shown in the AutoCAD Plot dialog box. For example, there may be several shared system printers on a network that are not intended for AutoCAD use, so you would not want those printers to appear in your list of available printers. You can do this by turning on the Hide System Printers option in the lower-left corner of the Plotting tab in the Options dialog box (choose Tools ➢ Options). This limits the selection of printers and plotters to those that have a .PC3 plotter configuration. You can further limit the plotter selections by moving any unneeded .PC3 file out of the AutoCAD 2002 Plotters folder and into another folder for storage.

Controlling the Plot Preview Background Color

If you prefer to use a color other than white for the plot preview background, you can set the plot preview background color using the Color Options dialog box.

1. Choose Tools ➢ Options to open the Options dialog box.
2. Select the Display tab.
3. In the Windows Elements group, click the Color button to open the Color Options dialog box, as shown in Figure C.7.
4. Select Plot Preview Background from the Window Element drop-down list.
5. Select a color from the Color drop-down list.
6. Click the Apply & Close button.

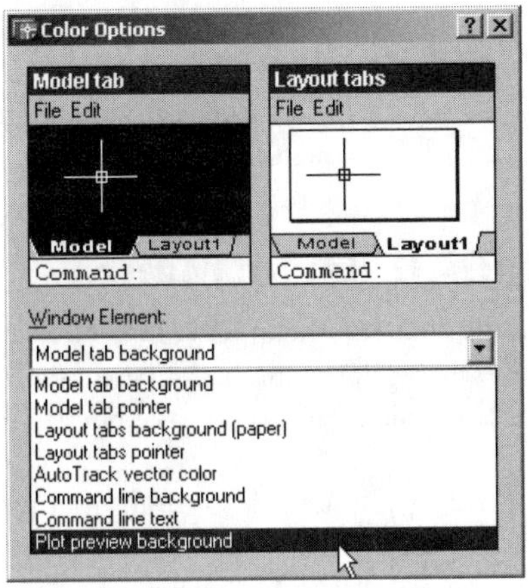

FIGURE C.7
The Color Options dialog box, showing the Plot Preview option in the Window Element drop-down list

Controlling the Windows Metafile Background Color

If you prefer using the Windows metafile file type to export AutoCAD drawings to other programs, you can now control the background color of your exported file. The AutoCAD Wmfbkgnd system variable lets you control the background color of exported Windows metafiles. Wmfbknd offers two settings: 0 (zero) generates a transparent background, and 1 (one) generates the background color of the current view. The initial default value is 1.

Fine-Tuning PostScript File Export

AutoCAD provides the PostScript user with a great deal of control over the formatting of the PostScript file that is output with the File ➤ Export and Psout commands. The options range from font-substitution mapping to custom PostScript Prologue data.

However, you need to master the PostScript programming language to take full advantage of AutoCAD PostScript output. Most of this control is offered through a file named `Acad.psf`. This is the master support file for the Psout command. You can customize the PostScript file created by Psout by making changes in the `Acad.psf` file. `Acad.psf` is divided into sections that affect various parts of the PostScript output. Each section begins with a title preceded by an asterisk: the `*fonts` section lets you control font substitution, for example.

You will also want to know about the Psprolog system variable, which instructs Psout to include your custom prologue statement in its PostScript output. You add your custom prologue to the `Acad.psf` file using a text editor. The prologue should begin with a section heading that you devise. The heading can say anything, but it must begin with an asterisk like all the other section headings. Everything following the heading, up to the next heading or the end of the file, and excluding comments, will be included in the Psout output file.

TIP *A complete discussion of Psout PostScript support is beyond the scope of this book. If you are interested in learning more, consult the PostScript section of the AutoCAD Customization manual.*

You can also add a PostScript plotter to the plotter configuration. When you do this, AutoCAD plots the drawing as a series of vectors, just like any other plotter. If you have any filled areas in your drawing and you are plotting to a PostScript file, the vectors that are used to plot those filled areas can greatly increase plot-file size and the time it takes to plot your PostScript file.

Memory and AutoCAD Performance

Next to your computer's CPU, memory has the greatest impact on AutoCAD's speed. How much you have, and how you use it, can make a big difference in whether you finish that rush job on schedule or work late nights trying. This section will clarify some basic points about memory and how AutoCAD uses it.

AutoCAD 2004 is a virtual memory system. This means that when your RAM memory resources reach their limit, part of the data stored in RAM is temporarily moved to your hard disk to make more room in RAM. This temporary storage of RAM to your hard disk is called *memory paging*. Through memory paging, AutoCAD will continue to run, even though your work might exceed the capacity of your RAM.

AutoCAD uses memory in two ways. First, it stores its program code in RAM. The more programs you have open under Windows, the more RAM will be used. Windows controls the use of memory for program code; so if you start to reach the RAM limit, Windows will take care of memory paging. The second way AutoCAD uses memory is for storing drawing data. AutoCAD always attempts to store as much of your drawing in RAM as possible. Again, when the amount of RAM required for a drawing exceeds the actual RAM available, AutoCAD will page parts of the drawing data to the hard disk. The paging of drawing data is controlled strictly by AutoCAD. Since RAM is shared with both program code and drawing data, your drawing size, the number of files you have open in AutoCAD, and the number of programs you have open under Windows will affect how much RAM you have available. For this reason, if you find your AutoCAD editing session is slowing down, try closing other applications you might have open or close files that you are no longer using. This will free up more memory for AutoCAD and the drawing file.

AutoCAD and Your Hard Disk

You will notice that AutoCAD slows down when paging occurs. If this happens frequently, the best thing you can do is add more RAM. But you can also improve the performance of AutoCAD under these conditions by ensuring that you have adequate hard-disk space and that free hard-disk space has been *defragmented* or *optimized*. A defragmented disk will offer faster access, thereby improving paging speed.

Windows dynamically allocates swap-file space. However, you should make sure that there is enough free space on your hard disk to allow Windows to set up the space. A good guideline is to allow enough space for a swap file that is four times the size of your RAM capacity. If you have 128MB of RAM, you need to allow space for a 512MB swap file (at a minimum). This will give your system 512MB of virtual memory. Fast, high-capacity hard drives are fairly inexpensive, so if you are running out of space, you may want to consider adding another hard drive.

Keep Your Hard Drive Clean

If you are not in the habit of emptying your Recycle Bin, you want to get into the habit of doing so. Every file that you "delete" using Windows Explorer is actually passed to the Recycle Bin. You need to clear this out regularly. If you are a regular Internet user, check your Internet cache folder for unnecessary files. You can employ one of the many hard drive cleaning utilities to do this. Finally, it is a good idea to perform regular maintenance on your hard drive to keep it clear of fragmentation and unused files. The Tools tab of the Properties dialog box for your hard drive offers error-checking and defragmenting options.

AutoCAD Tools to Improve Memory Use

AutoCAD 2004 offers some tools to help make your use of system memory more efficient. Partial Open and the Spacial and Layer indexes let you manage the memory use of large drawings and multiple open files by reducing the amount of a file that is loaded into memory. Using these tools, you can have AutoCAD open only those portions of a file that you want to work on.

Using Partial Open to Conserve Memory and Improve Speed

Use the Partial Open option in the File dialog box when you know you are only going to work on a small portion or particular set of layers of a large drawing. Choose File ➢ Open, locate and select the file you want to open, and then, at the bottom-right corner of the dialog box, click the down arrow next to the Open button and select Partial Open to open the Partial Open dialog box. Note that this option is only available for files created and edited in AutoCAD 2000 and later.

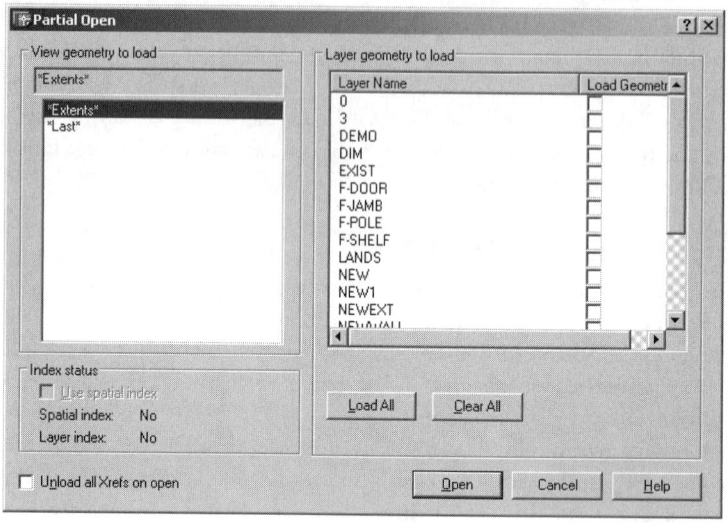

You can use this dialog box to open specific views of your drawing by selecting the view name from the View Geometry To Load list box. Only the geometry displayed in the selected view will be loaded into memory. This does not limit you to only that view as you edit the drawing. Subsequent views will cause AutoCAD to load the geometry of those views as needed.

You can further limit the amount of a drawing that is loaded into memory by selecting only those layers you want to work with. Place a check next to the layers you want in the Layer Geometry To Load list box.

Once a file is opened using the Partial Open option, you can always make further adjustments by choosing File ➢ Partial Load. This opens the Partial Load dialog box, which offers the same options as the Partial Open dialog box. The Partial Load dialog box is not available for files that are opened normally without using the Partial Open option.

Using Spatial and Layer Indexes to Conserve Memory

The Spatial and Layer indexes are lists that keep a record of geometry in a drawing. A Spatial index lists a drawing's geometry according to the geometry's location in space. A Layer index lists the drawing's geometry according to layer assignments. These indexes offer more efficient memory use and faster loading times for drawings that are being used as Xrefs. They take effect only when Demand Load is turned on. (See Chapter 6 for more on Demand Load.) The Layer index allows AutoCAD to load only those layers of an Xref that are not frozen. AutoCAD uses the Spatial index to load only objects in an Xref that are within the boundary of a clipped Xref.

You can turn on the Spatial and Layer indexes for a file through the Indexctl system variable. Indexctl has four settings:

- 0 is the default. This turns off Spatial and Layer indexing.

- 1 turns on Layer indexing
- 2 turns on Spatial indexing.
- 3 turns on both Layer and Spatial indexing.

To use the Indexctl system variable, type **Indexctl**↵. Then, at the `Enter new value for INDEXCTL <0>:` prompt, enter the number of the setting option you want to use.

TIP *The Partial Open option in the File dialog box includes the Index Status button group, which offers information on the index status of a drawing. If the drawing you're opening has Spatial or Layer indexing turned on, you can use it by checking the Spatial Index check box.*

Using the Incremental Save Percentage to Conserve Disk Space

If your disk is getting crowded and you need to squeeze as many files as you can onto it, you can reduce the amount of wasted space in a file by adjusting the Incremental Save value in the Open And Save tab of the Options dialog box. By setting Incremental Save to a lower value, you can reduce the size of files to some degree. The tradeoff is slower performance when saving files. See Appendix B for more information on this setting.

Another related option is to turn off the .bak file option, also located in the Open And Save tab of the Options dialog box. Each time you use File ➢ Save or File ➢ Save As, AutoCAD creates a backup copy of your file with the .bak file extension. When you turn off the Create Backup Copy With Each Save option, .bak files are not created, thereby saving disk space.

When Things Go Wrong

AutoCAD is a complex program, and at times things don't go exactly right. If you run into problems, chances are they won't be insurmountable. Here are a few tips on what to do when things don't work.

Difficulty Starting Up or Opening a File

The most common reason you'll have difficulty opening a file is a lack of free disk space. If you encounter errors attempting to open files, check to see if you have adequate free disk space on all your drives.

If you've recently installed AutoCAD but you cannot get it started, you may have a configuration problem. Before you panic, try reinstalling AutoCAD from scratch. Particularly if you are installing the CD version, this does not take long (see Appendix B for installation instructions). Before you reinstall AutoCAD, use the Uninstall program to remove the current version of AutoCAD. Also make sure you have your authorization code, serial number, and CD-Key handy. Make sure that you've closed all other programs when you run the AutoCAD installation. As a final measure, restart your computer when you've completed the installation.

Restoring Corrupted Files

Hardware failures can result in data files becoming corrupted. When this happens, AutoCAD is unable to open the drawing file. Fortunately, there is hope for damaged files. In most cases, AutoCAD will run through a file-recovery routine automatically when it attempts to load a corrupted file. If you have a file you know is corrupted, you can start the file-recovery utility by choosing File ➢ Drawing Utilities ➢ Recover. This opens the Select File dialog box, allowing you to select the file you want to recover. Once you enter the name, AutoCAD goes to work. You get a series of messages, most of which have little meaning to the average user. Then the recovered file is opened. You may lose some data, but a partial file is better than no file at all, especially when the file represents several days of work.

Another possibility is to attempt to recover your drawing from the .bak file—the last saved version before your drawing was corrupted. Rename the drawing .bak file to a .dwg file with a different name, and then open it. The drawing will contain only what was in your drawing when it was previously saved.

If you want to restore a file that you've just been working on, you can check the file named `Auto.sv$`. This is the file AutoCAD uses to store your drawing during automatic saves. Change the .sv$ filename extension to .dwg, and then open the file.

There may be situations when a file is so badly corrupted it cannot be restored. By backing up frequently, you can minimize the inconvenience of such an occurrence. You might also want to consider a third party utility that performs regular disk maintenance.

Troubleshooting

AutoCAD is a large, complex program, so you are bound to encounter some difficulties from time to time. This section covers a few of the more common problems experienced while using AutoCAD.

You can see but cannot select objects in a drawing someone else has worked on. This may be happening because you have a Paper Space view instead of a Model Space view. To make sure you're in Model Space, type **Tilemode↵**, and then type **1↵**. Or you can turn on the UCS icon (by typing **Ucsicon↵ On↵**). If you see the triangular UCS icon in the lower-left corner, you are in Paper Space. You must go to Model Space before you can edit the drawing. Another item to check is the layer lock setting. If a layer is locked, you won't be able to edit objects on that layer.

Grips do not appear when objects are selected. Make sure the Grips feature is enabled (choose Tools ➢ Grips). See Appendix B for details.

Selecting objects doesn't work the way it appears in this book. Check the Selection settings to make sure they are set the same way as the exercise specifies (choose Tools ➢ Selection). See Chapter 2 for details.

Text appears in the wrong font style, or an error message says AutoCAD cannot find font files. When you are working on files from another company, it's not uncommon that you will encounter a file that uses special third-party fonts that you do not have. You can usually substitute standard AutoCAD fonts for any fonts you don't have without adverse effects. AutoCAD automatically displays a dialog box that lets you select font files for the substitution. You can either choose a font file or press the Esc key to ignore the message. (See Chapter 8 for more on font files.) If you choose to ignore the error message, you may not see some of the text that would normally appear in the drawing.

You can't import .dxf files. Various problems can occur during the .dxf import, the most common of which is that you are trying to import a .dxf file into an existing drawing rather than a new drawing. Under some conditions, you can import a .dxf file into an existing drawing using the Dxfin command, but AutoCAD may not import the entire file.

To ensure that your entire .dxf file is safely imported, choose File ➢ Open and select *.DXF from the File Type pull-down list. Then import your .dxf file.

If you know the .dxf file you are trying to import is in the ASCII format and not a Binary .DXF, take a look at the file with a text editor. If it contains odd-looking lines of characters, chances are the file is damaged or contains extra data that AutoCAD cannot understand. Try deleting the odd-looking lines of characters, and then import the file again. (Make a backup copy of the file before you attempt this.)

A file cannot be saved to disk. Frequently, a hard drive will fill up quickly during an edit session. AutoCAD can generate temporary and swap files many times larger than the file you are editing. This might leave you with no room to save your file. If this happens, you can empty the Recycle Bin to clear some space on your hard drive or delete old AutoCAD .bak files you don't need. *Do not delete temporary AutoCAD files.*

AutoCAD does not display all the Paper Space viewports. AutoCAD uses substantial memory to display Paper Space viewports. For this reason, it limits the number of viewports it will display at one time. Even though viewports don't display, they will still plot. Also, if you zoom in on a blank viewport while in Paper Space, you will be able to see its contents. The viewport regains visibility because you are reducing the number of viewports shown on the screen at one time.

You can increase the number of viewports AutoCAD will display at one time by resetting the Maxactvp system variable. (This is usually set to 64.) Be forewarned, however, that increasing the Maxactvp setting will cause AutoCAD to use more memory. If you have limited memory on your system, this will slow down AutoCAD considerably.

AutoCAD becomes impossibly slow when adding more Paper Space viewports. As mentioned for the preceding problem, AutoCAD consumes memory quickly when adding viewports. If your system resources are limited, you can reduce the Maxactvp system variable setting so that AutoCAD displays fewer viewports at one time. This will let you work on a file that has numerous viewports without causing a decrease in your computer's performance. Try reducing Maxactvp to 8, and then reduce or increase the setting until you find the optimum value for your situation. Alternatively, you can use the Mview OFF option to turn off viewports when you are not working in them.

AutoCAD won't open a large file and displays a "Page File Full" message. AutoCAD will open drawing files larger than can fit into your system's RAM. In order to do this, however, AutoCAD attempts to store part of the drawing in a temporary file on your hard drive. If there isn't room on the hard drive, AutoCAD will give up. To remedy this problem, clear some space on your hard drive. It is not uncommon for AutoCAD to require as much as 10MB of hard-disk space for every 1MB of a drawing file.

The keyboard shortcuts for commands are not working. If you are working on an unfamiliar computer, chances are the keyboard shortcuts (or command aliases) have been altered. The command aliases are stored in the `Acad.pgp` file. Use the Windows Find utility to locate this file and make sure that the `Acad.pgp` file is in the `C:\Documents and Settings\User Name\Application Data\Autodesk\AutoCAD 2004\R16.0\enu\Support` folder.

Plots come out blank. Check the scale factor you are using for your plot. Often, a blank plot means your scale factor is making the plot too large to fit on the sheet. Try plotting with the Scale To Fit option. If you get a plot, you know your scale factor is incorrect. See Chapter 7 for more on plotting options. Check your output before you plot by using the Full Preview option in the Plot Configuration dialog box.

You cannot get your drawing properly oriented on the sheet. If you want to change the orientation of your drawing on a plotted sheet, and the Plot Configuration orientation options don't seem to work, try rotating the UCS to align with your desired plot view, and then type **Plan↵**. Adjust the view to display what you want to have plotted, and then use the View command (choose View ➢ Named Views) to save this view. When you are ready to plot, use the View option in the Plot Configuration dialog box and plot the saved view, instead of rotating the plot.

Dimensions appear as lines and text and do not act as described in this book. The Dimassoc system variable has been set to 0 or was 0 when the dimension was created. Another possibility is that the dimension was reduced to its component objects using the Explode command. Make sure Dimassoc is on by typing **Dimassoc↵ 2↵**. Unfortunately, an exploded dimension or one that was created with Dimassoc turned off cannot be converted to a true dimension object. You must redraw the dimension.

A file containing an Xref appears to be blank or parts are missing. AutoCAD cannot find the Xref file. Use the External Reference dialog box (choose Insert ➢ External Reference) to reestablish connection with the Xref file. Once the External Reference dialog box is open, select the missing Xref from the list, and then click the Browse button and locate and select the file using the Browse dialog box.

As you draw, little marks appear on your screen where you have selected points. The Blipmode system variable is on. Turn it off by typing **Blipmode↵ off↵**.

A file you want to open is read-only, even though you know no one else on the network is using the file. Every now and then, you may receive a file that you cannot edit because it is read-only. This frequently happens with files that have been archived to a CD. If you have a file that is read-only, try the following:

1. Locate the read-only file with Windows Explorer and right-click its filename.
2. Choose Properties from the shortcut menu to open the Properties dialog box.
3. Click the General tab.
4. Click the Read-Only check box to remove the check.

Tracking vectors do not appear in the drawing as described in this book. Make sure that the AutoTrack features are turned on. See the discussion of the Drafting tab in the Options dialog box in Appendix B.

The Hyperlink icon does not appear as described in Chapter 22. Make sure the Hyperlink options are turned on in the User Preferences tab in the Options dialog box.

When you open new files, the drawing area is not the same as described in this book. Make sure you're using the correct default unit style for new drawings. In the Create New Drawing dialog box, click the Start From Scratch button and select the appropriate unit style from the Default Settings button group. If you are using feet and inches, select Imperial (feet and inches). If you are using metric measurements, select Metric. AutoCAD will use the `Acad.dwt` file template for new Imperial measurement drawings and the `Acadiso.dwt` template for metric measurement drawings. You can also use the Measureinit system variable to set the default unit style.

When you offset polylines, such as rectangles or polygons, the offset object has extra line segments or rounded corners. Set the Offsetgap system variable to 0. Offsetgap controls the behavior of the line segments of offset polylines. When Offsetgap is set to 0, the individual line segments of a polyline are extended to join end to end. When Offsetgap is set to 1, the line segments remain their original length and are joined with an arc. If Offsetgap is set to 2, the line segments retain their original length and are joined by a straight-line segment.

The `Slidelib.exe` DOS tool doesn't seem to work. `Slidelib.exe` is a DOS application, so it needs all its files and resources in the same folder where it resides; or you can set a DOS path to those resources. Setting a DOS path is a bit too involved to explain here. To simplify things, make sure your slide files and your text file containing the list of slides are in the same folder as `Slidelib.exe`. If you prefer, you can move `Slidelib.exe` to the location of your slides and slide list.

Your AutoCAD 14 file contains filled areas that were once transparent, but in AutoCAD 2004 the text and line work are obscured by solid fills. Earlier versions of AutoCAD let you adjust the Merge Control feature of your plotter, which in turn allowed solid filled areas to appear transparent. The merge control feature is still available, but it has been moved to the Plot Configuration Editor. See the section on merge control earlier in this appendix for more information.

Another option is to use the Draworder command to move the solid filled area "behind" other objects in the drawing. See Chapter 12 for more on the Draworder command.

When you click a viewport in a Layout tab, the viewport automatically zooms out to show the entire drawing. Change the Ucsfollow system variable to 0 (zero).

Appendix D

System and Dimension Variables

System variables let you fine-tune your AutoCAD environment. Dimension variables govern the specific dimensioning functions of AutoCAD.

You can set a system variable by entering the variable name at the command prompt. Or, if you are in the middle of another command, you can set a system variable by entering the variable name preceded by an apostrophe. For example, if you are drawing a series of line segments, you can enter **'Snapang↵** at the `Specify next point:` prompt to change the Snapang system variable on the fly. You can also access these variables through the AutoLISP Interpreter by using the Getvar and Setvar functions, as well as through ActiveX Automation. LT users can use the Modemacro command and the Diesel macro language to obtain information from the sysem variables. (See Chapter 21 for more on Modemacro and Diesel.)

This appendix is divided into two major sections; the first concerns setting system variables, and the second concerns setting dimension variables. This division is somewhat artificial, because as far as AutoCAD is concerned, there is no difference between system variables and dimension variables—you use both types of variables the same way. But because the set of dimension variables is quite extensive, I've separated them here for clarity.

At the end of this appendix, you will also find a detailed description of the Dimension Style dialog boxes. They are presented here to supplement the main discussion of dimensions in Chapter 9.

Setting System Variables

Table D.1 lists the variables and notes whether they are read-only or adjustable. Most of these variables have counterparts in other commands, as listed in the table. For example, you can adjust Angdir and Angbase using the Ddunits command (choose Format ➢ Units). Many, such as Highlight and Expert, do not have equivalent commands. You must adjust these at the command line (or through AutoLISP).

TABLE D.1: SYSTEM VARIABLES. ITEMS MARKED WITH AN ASTERISK WERE ADDED IN AUTOCAD 2002. ITEMS MARKED WITH TWO ASTERISKS ARE NEW IN AUTOCAD 2004.

VARIABLE NAME	ASSOCIATED COMMAND	WHERE SAVED	USE
Acadlspasdoc	Options	Registry	Controls the loading of the `Acad.lsp` file when present. 0 = load only into first drawing (initial value); 1 = into every opened drawing.
Acadprefix	Options	*NA*	The AutoCAD environment setting.
Acadver	*NA*	*NA*	The AutoCAD version number.
Acisoutver	Acisout	With drawing	Controls ACIS version of SAT files.
Adcstate (read-only)	*NA*	Registry	Indicates the current display state of the AutoCAD DesignCenter: 0 = closed; 1 = opened.
Aflags	Units	*NA*	Controls attribute mode settings: 1 = invisible; 2 = constant; 4 = verify; 8 = preset.
Angbase	Units	With drawing	Controls direction of 0° angle relative to the current UCS.
Angdir	Units	With drawing	Controls positive direction of angles: 0 = counterclockwise; 1 = clockwise.
Apbox	Draw and Edit commands	Registry	Displays AutoSnap aperture box when AutoSnap is activated: 0 = off, 1 = on.
Aperture	Draw and Edit commands	Registry	Sets size of Osnap cursor in pixels.
Area (read-only)	Area	*NA*	Displays last area calculation; use with Setvar or AutoLISP's Getvar function.
Attdia	Insert/Attribute	With drawing	Controls the Attribute dialog box: 0 = no dialog box; 1 = dialog box.
Attmode	Attdisp	With drawing	Controls attribute display mode: 0 = off; 1 = normal; 2 = on.
Attreq	Insert	With drawing	Controls the prompt for attributes: 0 = no prompt or dialog box for attributes (attributes use default values); 1 = normal prompt or dialog box upon attribute insertion.
Auditctl	Config	Registry	Controls whether an audit file is created: 0 = disable; 1 = enable creation of .adt file.

Continued on next page

TABLE D.1: SYSTEM VARIABLES. ITEMS MARKED WITH AN ASTERISK WERE ADDED IN AUTOCAD 2002. ITEMS MARKED WITH TWO ASTERISKS ARE NEW IN AUTOCAD 2004. *(continued)*

VARIABLE NAME	ASSOCIATED COMMAND	WHERE SAVED	USE
Aunits	Units	With drawing	Controls angular units: 0 = decimal degrees; 1 = degrees-minutes-seconds; 2 = grads; 3 = radians; 4 = surveyor's units.
Auprec	Units	With drawing	Controls the precision of angular units determined by decimal place.
Autosnap	Draw/Edit	Registry	Controls AutoSnap display and features: 0 = everything off; 1 = marker on; 2 = Snaptip on; 4 = magnet on.
Backz (read-only)	Dview	With drawing	Displays distance from Dview target to back clipping plane.
Bindtype	Xref	*NA*	Controls the way Xref names are handled when bound to a file: 0 = maintain Xref file name prefix (initial value); 1 = remove Xref filename prefix.
Blipmode	*NA*	With drawing	Controls appearance of blips: 0 = off; 1 = on.
Cdate (read-only)	Time	*NA*	Displays calendar date/time read from system date (YYYY MMDD.HHMMSSMSEC).
Cecolor	Color	With drawing	Controls current default color assigned to new objects.
Celtscale	*NA*	With drawing	Controls current line-type scale for individual objects.
Celtype	Linetype	With drawing	Controls current default line type assigned to new objects.
Celweight	Lineweight	With drawing	Controls the default line weight for new objects: –1 = Bylayer; –2 = Byblock; –3 = Default as set by Lwdefault. Specific line-weight values can also be entered in millimeters.
Chamfera	Chamfer	With drawing	Controls first chamfer distance.
Chamferb	Chamfer	With drawing	Controls second chamfer distance.
Chamferc	Chamfer	With drawing	Controls chamfer distance for Angle option.
Chamferd	Chamfer	With drawing	Controls chamfer angle for Angle option.

Continued on next page

TABLE D.1: SYSTEM VARIABLES. ITEMS MARKED WITH AN ASTERISK WERE ADDED IN AUTOCAD 2002. ITEMS MARKED WITH TWO ASTERISKS ARE NEW IN AUTOCAD 2004. *(continued)*

VARIABLE NAME	ASSOCIATED COMMAND	WHERE SAVED	USE
Chammode	Chamfer	*NA*	Controls method of chamfer: 0 = use two distances; 1 = use distance and angle.
Circlerad	Circle	*NA*	Controls the default circle radius: 0 = no default.
Clayer	Layer	With drawing	Sets the current layer.
Cmdactive (read-only)	*NA*	*NA*	Displays whether a command, script, or dialog box is active: 1 = command active; 2 = transparent command active; 4 = script active; 8 = dialog box active (values are cumulative, so 3 = command and transparent command are active).
Cmddia	*NA*	Registry	Controls use of dialog boxes for some commands: 0 = don't use dialog box; 1 = usedialog box.
Cmdecho	Autolisp	*NA*	With AutoLISP, controls display of prompts from embedded AutoCAD commands: 0 = no display of prompt; 1 = display prompts.
Cmdnames (read-only)	*NA*	*NA*	Displays the English name of the currently active command.
Cmljust	Mline	With drawing	Sets method of justification for multilines: 0 = top; 1 = middle; 2 = bottom.
Cmlscale	Mline	With drawing	Sets scale factor for multiline widths: a 0 value collapses the multiline to a single line; a negative value reverses the justification.
Cmlstyle (read-only)	Mline	With drawing	Displays current multiline style by name.
Compass	3dorbit	*NA*	Controls the display of the 3D compass: 0 = off (initial value); 1 = on.
Coords	F6, Ctrl+D	With drawing	Controls coordinate readout: 0 = coordinates displayed only when points are picked; 1 = absolute coordinates dynamically displayed as cursor moves; 2 = distance and angle displayed during commands that accept relative distance input.

Continued on next page

TABLE D.1: SYSTEM VARIABLES. ITEMS MARKED WITH AN ASTERISK WERE ADDED IN AUTOCAD 2002. ITEMS MARKED WITH TWO ASTERISKS ARE NEW IN AUTOCAD 2004. *(continued)*

VARIABLE NAME	ASSOCIATED COMMAND	WHERE SAVED	USE
Cplotstyle	Plot/Pagesetup	With drawing	Controls the default plot style for new objects. Startup values are ByLayer, ByBlock, Normal, and User Defined.
Cprofile (read-only)	Options	Registry	Displays the current profile name.
Ctab (read-only)	(tabs)	With drawing	Displays the name of the current tab.
Cursorsize	*NA*	Registry	Determines size of crosshairs as a percentage of the screen size (1–100).
Cvport (read-only)	Vports	With drawing	Displays ID number of current viewport.
Date (read-only)	Time	*NA*	Displays date and time in Julian format.
Dbstate**	dbConnect	With drawing	Read-only. Displays the display state of the dbConnect Manager dialog box. 0=closed, 1 = opened.
Dbmod (read-only)	*NA*	*NA*	Displays drawing modification status: 1 = object database modified; 2 = symbol table modified; 4 = database variable modified; 8 = window modified; 16 = view modified.
Dctcust	Spell	Registry	Sets default custom spelling dictionary filename, including path.
Dctmain	Spell	Registry	Sets default main spelling dictionary filename; requires specific keywords for each language. See AutoCAD Help for complete list of keywords.
Deflplstyle	Plotstyle	With drawing	Sets the default plot style for new layers.
Defplstyle	Plotstyle	Registry	Sets the default plot style for new objects.
Delobj	*NA*	With drawing	Controls whether source objects used to create new objects are retained: 0 = delete objects; 1 = retain objects.
Demandload	*NA*	Registry	Controls loading of third-party applications required for custom objects in drawing (0–3).

Continued on next page

TABLE D.1: SYSTEM VARIABLES. ITEMS MARKED WITH AN ASTERISK WERE ADDED IN AUTOCAD 2002. ITEMS MARKED WITH TWO ASTERISKS ARE NEW IN AUTOCAD 2004. *(continued)*

VARIABLE NAME	ASSOCIATED COMMAND	WHERE SAVED	USE
Diastat (read-only)	*NA*	*NA*	Displays how last dialog box was exited: 0 = Cancel; 1 = OK.
Dispsilh	All curved solids	With drawing	Controls silhouette display of curved 3D solids: 0 = no silhouette; 1 = silhouette curved solids.
Distance (read-only)	Dist	*NA*	Displays last distance calculated by Dist command.
Donutid	Donut	*NA*	Controls default inside diameter of a donut.
Donutod	Donut	*NA*	Controls default outside diameter of a donut.
Dragmode	*NA*	With drawing	Controls dragging: 0 = no dragging; 1 = if requested; 2 = automatic drag.
Dragp1	*NA*	Registry	Controls regeneration-drag input sampling rate.
Dragp2	*NA*	Registry	Controls fast-drag input sampling rate.
Dwgcheck	*NA*	Registry	Controls the display of a warning dialog box indicating that a drawing was last edited in a program other than Auto CAD. 0 = suppress dialog box; 1 = display dialog box when needed.
Dwgcodepage (read-only)	*NA*	With drawing	Displays code page of drawing (see Syscodepage).
Dwgname (read-only)	Open	*NA*	Displays drawing name and drive/folder, if specified by user.
Dwgprefix (read-only)	*NA*	*NA*	Displays drive and folder of current file.
Dwgtitled (read-only)	*NA*	*NA*	Displays whether a drawing has been named: 0 = untitled; 1 = named by user.
Edgemode	Trim, Extend	Registry	Controls how trim and extend boundaries are determined: 0 = boundaries defined by object only; 1 = boundaries defined by objects and their extension.
Elevation	Elev	With drawing	Controls current 3D elevation relative to current UCS.

Continued on next page

TABLE D.1: SYSTEM VARIABLES. ITEMS MARKED WITH AN ASTERISK WERE ADDED IN AUTOCAD 2002. ITEMS MARKED WITH TWO ASTERISKS ARE NEW IN AUTOCAD 2004. *(continued)*

VARIABLE NAME	ASSOCIATED COMMAND	WHERE SAVED	USE
Expert	*NA*	*NA*	Controls prompts, depending on level of user's expertise: 0 = normal prompts; 1= suppresses `About to regen` and `Really want to turn the \current layer off` prompts; 2 = suppresses `Block already defined` and `A drawing with this name already exists` prompts for Block command; 3 = suppresses `An item with this name already exists` prompt for the Linetype command; 4 = suppresses `An item with this name already exists` prompt for the UCS/Save and Vports/Save options; 5 = suppresses `An item with this name already exists` prompt for Dim/Save and Dim/Override commands.
Explmode	Explode	With drawing	Controls whether blocks inserted with different x, y, and z values are exploded: 0 = blocks are not exploded; 1 = blocks are exploded.
Extmax (read-only)	Zoom	With drawing	Displays upper-right corner coordinate of extents view.
Extmin (read-only)	Zoom	With drawing	Displays lower-left corner coordinate of extents view.
Extnames	Options	With drawing	Controls the length of names for named objects in AutoCAD: 0 = limits names to 31 characters; 1 = allow up to 255 characters.
Facetratio	Shade, Hide	*NA*	Controls aspect ratio of faceting of curved 3D surfaces. Value is zero or 1; 1 increases the density of the mesh.
Facetres	Shade, Hide	With drawing	Controls appearance of smooth curved 3D surfaces when shaded or hidden. Value can be between 0.01 and 10. The higher the number, the more faceted (and smoother) the curved surface, and the longer the time needed for shade and hidden-line removal.

Continued on next page

TABLE D.1: SYSTEM VARIABLES. ITEMS MARKED WITH AN ASTERISK WERE ADDED IN AUTOCAD 2002. ITEMS MARKED WITH TWO ASTERISKS ARE NEW IN AUTOCAD 2004. *(continued)*

VARIABLE NAME	ASSOCIATED COMMAND	WHERE SAVED	USE
Filedia	Dialog box	Registry	Sets whether a file dialog box is used by default: 0 = don't use unless requested with a ~ (a tilde); 1 = use whenever possible.
Filletrad	Fillet	With drawing	Controls fillet radius.
Fillmode	Fill	With drawing	Controls fill status: 0 = off; 1 = on.
Fontalt	Open, Dxfin, other File ➢ Import options	Registry	Lets you specify an alternate font when AutoCAD cannot find the font associated with a file. If no font is specified for Fontalt, AutoCAD displays a warning message and a dialog box in which you manually select a font.
Fontmap		Registry	Similar to Fontalt, but lets you designate a set of font substitutions through a font mapping file. Example line from mapping file: `romans:c:\ Program Files\AutoCAD2002\fonts\ times.ttf`. This substitutes Romans font with Times True Type font. Font-mapping file can be any name, with extension .FMP.
Frontz (read-only)	Dview	With drawing	Controls front clipping plane for current viewport; use with Viewmode system variable.
Fullopen (read-only)	Open	*NA*	Displays whether the current drawing is fully or partially opened.
Gfshift**	Bhatch	Not saved	Controls whether gradient fills are centered: 0 = centered, 1 = shifted up and to the left.
Gridmode	Grid	With drawing	Controls grid: 0 = off; 1 = on.
Gridunit	Grid	With drawing	Controls grid spacing.
Gripblock	Grips	Registry	Controls display of grips in blocks: 0 = show insertion point grip only; 1 = show grips of all objects in block.
Gripcolor	Grips	Registry	Controls color of unselected grips. Choices are integers from 1 to 255; default is 5.

Continued on next page

TABLE D.1: SYSTEM VARIABLES. ITEMS MARKED WITH AN ASTERISK WERE ADDED IN AUTOCAD 2002. ITEMS MARKED WITH TWO ASTERISKS ARE NEW IN AUTOCAD 2004. *(continued)*

VARIABLE NAME	ASSOCIATED COMMAND	WHERE SAVED	USE
Griphot	Grips	Registry	Controls color of hot grips. Choices are integers from 1 to 255; default is 1.
Griphover**	Grips	Registry	Controls the color of a grip when the cursor hovers over the grip. Values are index colors from 1 to 255; default is 3.
Gripobjlimit**	Grips	Registry	Controls the display of grips based on the number of objects selected. If set to 1, grips are not displayed if more than one object is selected. Range is from 1 to 32,767; default is 100.
Grips	Grips	Registry	Controls use of grips: 0 = grips disabled; 1 = grips enabled (default).
Gripsize	Grips	Registry	Controls grip size (in pixels), from 1 to 255 (default is 3).
Griptips**	Grips	Registry	Controls the display of grip tips for custom objects. 0 = no grip tips, 1 = grip tips; default is 1.
Handles (read-only)	*NA*	With drawing	Displays status of object handles: 0 = off; 1 = on.
Hideprecision	Hide, Shade, Hlsettings	*NA*	Controls the Hide/Shade precision accuracy: 0 = single precision; 1 = double precision.
Highlight	Select	*NA*	Controls whether objects are highlighted when selected: 0 = none; 1 = highlighting.
Hpang	Hatch	*NA*	Sets default hatch pattern angle.
Hpassoc**	Hatch	Registry	Controls associative property of hatch pattern. 0 = not associative, 1 - associative; default = 1.
Hpbound	Hatch	Registry	Controls type of object created by Hatch and Boundary commands: 0 = region; 1 = polyline.
Hpdouble	Hatch	*NA*	Sets default hatch doubling for user-defined hatch pattern: 0 = no doubling; 1 = doubling at 90°.

Continued on next page

TABLE D.1: SYSTEM VARIABLES. ITEMS MARKED WITH AN ASTERISK WERE ADDED IN AUTOCAD 2002. ITEMS MARKED WITH TWO ASTERISKS ARE NEW IN AUTOCAD 2004. *(continued)*

VARIABLE NAME	ASSOCIATED COMMAND	WHERE SAVED	USE
Hpname	Hatch	*NA*	Sets default hatch pattern name; use a period (.) to set to no default.
Hpscale	Hatch	*NA*	Sets default scale for hatch patterns; cannot be 0.
Hpspace	Hatch	*NA*	Sets default line spacing for user-defined hatch pattern; cannot be 0.
Hyperlinkbase	Hyperlink	With drawing	Sets the base location for hyperlink addresses. If left blank, the drawing path is used.
Imagehlt	Options	Registry	Controls highlighting of raster images: 0 = frame only; 1 = entire image.
Indexctl	*NA*	With drawing	Controls whether layer and spatial indexes are created and saved in drawings: 0 = no index; 1 = Layer index; 2 = Spatial index; 3 = both.
Inetlocation	Browser	Registry	Stores the Internet location used by the Browser command.
Insbase	Base	With drawing	Controls insertion base point of current drawing.
Insname	Insert	*NA*	Sets default block or filename for Insert command; enter a period (.) to set to no default.
Insunits	Units	With drawing	Sets the units value for the DesignCenter insert: 0 = unit less; 1 = inches; 2 = feet; 3 = miles; 4 = millimeters; 5 = centimeters; 6 = meters; 7 = kilometers; 8 = microinches; 9 = mils; 10 = yards; 11 = angstroms; 12 = nanometers; 13 = microns; 14 = decimeters; 15 = decameters; 16 = hectometers; 17 = gigameters; 18 = astronomical units; 19 = light years; 20 = parsecs.
Insunitsdefsource	Units	Registry	Sets the default source units. Values are the same as for Insunits.
Insunitsdeftarget	Units	Registry	Sets the default target units. Values are the same as for Insunits.

Continued on next page

TABLE D.1: SYSTEM VARIABLES. ITEMS MARKED WITH AN ASTERISK WERE ADDED IN AUTOCAD 2002. ITEMS MARKED WITH TWO ASTERISKS ARE NEW IN AUTOCAD 2004. *(continued)*

VARIABLE NAME	ASSOCIATED COMMAND	WHERE SAVED	USE
Intersectioncolor**	Hide	With drawing	Controls the color of the intersection of 3D surfaces when Hide or Hidden Shademode are used. The interesting surfaces are displayed by "intersection polylines". 0 = byblock, 256 = bylayer, 257 = entity color, 1 through 255 = AutoCAD index color. Intersectioncolor is only valid when the Intersectiondisplay system variable is set to 1; default = 257.
Intersectiondisplay**	Hide	With drawing	Controls whether the intersection of 3D surfaces are displayed with a line, called an intersection polyline. 0 = no intersection polyline, 1 = display intersection polyline; default = 0.
Isavebak	Save	Registry	Controls the creation of BAK files: 0 = no BAK file created; 1 = BAK file created.
Isavepercent	Save	Registry	Determines whether to do a full or an incremental save based on the amount of wasted space tolerated in a drawing file: (0–100).
Isolines	Curved solids	With drawing	Specifies the number of lines on a solid's surface to help visualize its shape.
Lastangle (read-only)	Arc	*NA*	Displays ending angle for last arc drawn.
Lastpoint	*NA*	*NA*	Sets or displays coordinate normally referenced by @.
Lastprompt	*NA*	*NA*	Saves last string echoed to the command line.
Layoutregenctl*	Options	Registry	Controls the way regens occur when switching between Model/Layout tabs. 0 = Regen at each tab selection; 1 = no regen for Model tab or last used Layout tab; 2 = after initial opening of tabs, no regens while switching between tabs.
Lenslength (read-only)	Dview	With drawing	Displays focal length of lens used for perspective display.

Continued on next page

TABLE D.1: SYSTEM VARIABLES. ITEMS MARKED WITH AN ASTERISK WERE ADDED IN AUTOCAD 2002. ITEMS MARKED WITH TWO ASTERISKS ARE NEW IN AUTOCAD 2004. *(continued)*

VARIABLE NAME	ASSOCIATED COMMAND	WHERE SAVED	USE
Limcheck	Limits	With drawing	Controls limit checking: 0 = no checking; 1 = checking.
Limmax	Limits	With drawing	Controls coordinate of drawing's upper-right limit.
Limmin	Limits	With drawing	Controls coordinate of drawing's lower-left limit.
Lispinit	Load	Registry	Preserves AutoLISP-defined functions and variables beyond current drawing session: 0 = AutoLISP variables preserved; 1 = AutoLISP functions valid for current session only.
Locale (read-only)	*NA*	*NA*	Displays ISO language code used by your version of AutoCAD.
Localrootprefix (read-only)**	Options	Registry	Displays file path for support and custom files. If entered at the command prompt through AutoLISP [as in (getvar "localroot-prefix")], the full path is displayed.
Logfilemode	*NA*	Registry	Determines whether log file is recorded: 0 = log file off; 1 = log file on.
Logfilename	*NA*	Registry	Specifies name/path of log file.
Logfilepath	Options	Registry	Sets the path for the log file.
Loginname (read-only)	*NA*	*NA*	Displays user's login name.
Ltscale	Ltscale	With drawing	Controls the global line-type scale factor.
Lunits	Units	With drawing	Controls unit styles: 1 = scientific; 2 = decimal; 3 = engineering; 4 = architectural; 5 = fractional.
Luprec	Units	With drawing	Controls unit accuracy by decimal place or size of denominator.
Lwdefault	Lineweight	Registry	Sets the default line weight. Values are specified in millimeters (25 = 0.25mm).
Lwdisplay	Lineweight	With drawing	Determines whether line weights are displayed: 0 = not displayed; 1 = displayed.

Continued on next page

TABLE D.1: SYSTEM VARIABLES. ITEMS MARKED WITH AN ASTERISK WERE ADDED IN AUTOCAD 2002. ITEMS MARKED WITH TWO ASTERISKS ARE NEW IN AUTOCAD 2004. *(continued)*

VARIABLE NAME	ASSOCIATED COMMAND	WHERE SAVED	USE
Lwscale	Lineweight	With drawing	Determines whether line weights are scaled with plotter scale settings or are absolute values: 0 = scaled with plot; 1 = absolute value.
Lwunits	Lineweight	Registry	Sets the display of line weight units: 0 = inches; 1 = millimeters.
Maxactvp	Viewports/ Vports	With drawing	Controls maximum number of viewports to regenerate at one time.
Maxobjmem	*NA*	*NA*	Specifies the amount of virtual memory that can be used before AutoCAD starts paging a drawing out to disk.
Maxsort	*NA*	Registry	Controls maximum number of items to be sorted when a command displays a list.
Mbuttonpan	Options	Registry	Determines the behavior of the pointing device's wheel or third button: 0 = behavior determined by menu file; 1 = click-and-drag panning.
Measureinit	Open	Registry	Sets the unit style for new drawings. Determines whether metric or Imperial template file should be used. Determines which default line type and hatch pattern files should be used: 0 = Imperial; 1 = metric.
Measurement	Bhatch, Linetype	With drawing	Sets drawing units as Imperial or metric: 0 = Imperial; 1 = metric.
Menuctl	*NA*	Registry	Controls whether side menu changes in response to a command name entered from the keyboard: 0 = no response; 1 = menu response.
Menuecho	*NA*	*NA*	Controls messages and command prompt display from commands embedded in menu: 0 = display all messages; 1 = suppress menu item name; 2 = suppress command prompts; 4 = Disable ^P toggle of menu echo; 8 = debugging aid for Diesel expressions.

Continued on next page

TABLE D.1: SYSTEM VARIABLES. ITEMS MARKED WITH AN ASTERISK WERE ADDED IN AUTOCAD 2002. ITEMS MARKED WITH TWO ASTERISKS ARE NEW IN AUTOCAD 2004. *(continued)*

VARIABLE NAME	ASSOCIATED COMMAND	WHERE SAVED	USE
Menuname (read-only)	Menu	With drawing	Displays name of current menu file.
Mirrtext	Mirror	With drawing	Controls mirroring of text: 0 = disabled; 1 = enabled.
Modemacro	*NA*	*NA*	Controls display of user-defined text in status line.
Mtexted	Mtext	Registry	Controls name of program used for editing Mtext objects.
Mtextfixed**	Mtext	Registry	Controls how text in the Multiline Text Editor is displayed. 0 = AutoCAD attempts to display the text as closely as possible to the actual size and appearance in the drawing; 1 = text is displayed in a fixed size and location based on the last size and position.
Mtjigstring**	Mtext	Registry	Controls the display of the sample text that is displayed when placing the text boundary for Mtext. The default is abc, but can be set to anything up to 10 characters. Enter a period (.) for no display.
Mydocumentsprefix (read-only)**	Options	Registry	Displays the full path for the current user's My Documents folder.
Nomutt*	*NA*	*NA*	Suppresses message display (muttering): 0 = normal display; 1 = suppress messages.
Obscuredcolor*	Hide/Shade/ Hlsettings	With drawing	Controls the color of obscured lines in hidden or shaded views. 0 and 256 = object color; 1 through 255 = AutoCAD color index. This feature is disabled when Obscuredltype is set to 0.
Obscuredltype*	Hide/Shade/ Hlsettings	Drawing	Controls the line type of obscured lines in hidden or shaded 3D views. At the default 0, obscured lines are not displayed. 1 = solid line; 2 through 11 = various dashed and dotted lines.
Offsetdist	Offset	*NA*	Controls default offset distance.

Continued on next page

TABLE D.1: SYSTEM VARIABLES. ITEMS MARKED WITH AN ASTERISK WERE ADDED IN AUTOCAD 2002. ITEMS MARKED WITH TWO ASTERISKS ARE NEW IN AUTOCAD 2004. *(continued)*

VARIABLE NAME	**ASSOCIATED COMMAND**	**WHERE SAVED**	**USE**
Offsetgaptype	Offset	Registry	Controls how polyline line segments are joined when offset: 0 = extend line segments to join ends; 1 = keep line segments the same length and join endpoints with arcs; 2 = keep line segments the same length and join endpoints with lines.
Olehide	*NA*	Registry	Controls display of OLE objects.
Olequality	Options	Registry	Controls the quality of OLE objects: 0 = line art; 1 = text; 2 = graphics; 3 = photograph; 4 = high-quality photograph.
Olestartup	Options	With drawing	Determines whether the source application of an OLE object is loaded when the OLE object is plotted: 0 = No load; 1 = load.
Opmstate (read-only)	Properties	Registry	Displays the current state of the Properties palette: 0 = not open; 1 = open.
Orthomode	F8, Ortho	With drawing	Controls Ortho mode: 0 = off; 1 = on.
Osmode	Osnap	With drawing	Sets current default Osnap mode: 0 = none; 1 = endpoint; 2 = midpoint; 4 = center; 8 = node; 16 = quadrant; 32 = intersection; 64 = insert; 128 = perpendicular; 256 = nearest; 512 = quick. If more than one mode is required, enter the sum of those modes.
Osnapcoord	Osnap	Registry	Controls whether coordinates entered at the command line use running object snaps: 0 = Running Osnaps settings override; 1 = keyboard entry overrides; 2 = keyboard entry overrides, except in scripts.
Paletteopaque**	Toolpalettes	Registry	Controls the transparency of palettes that offer transparency. Availability of transparency depends on the operating system and whether hardware accelerators are in use. 0 = turned on by user, 1 = off by user, 2 = on by user but unavailable, 3 = off by user but unavailable.

Continued on next page

TABLE D.1: SYSTEM VARIABLES. ITEMS MARKED WITH AN ASTERISK WERE ADDED IN AUTOCAD 2002. ITEMS MARKED WITH TWO ASTERISKS ARE NEW IN AUTOCAD 2004. *(continued)*

VARIABLE NAME	ASSOCIATED COMMAND	WHERE SAVED	USE
Paperupdate	Plot	Registry	Controls the display of paper size warning message: 0 = display warning if the paper size in a Paper Space layout is not supported by the specified plotter; 1 = adjust paper size to conform with plotter configuration.
Pdmode	Ddptype	With drawing	Controls type of symbol used as a point during Point command.
Pdsize	Point	With drawing	Controls size of symbol set by Pdmode.
Peditaccept**	Pedit	Registry	Controls the display of the `Object selected is not a polyine` prompt when selecting nonpolyline object with the Pedit command. 0 = prompt, 1 = no prompt.
Pellipse	Ellipse	With drawing	Controls type of object created with Ellipse command: 0 = true NURBS ellipse; 1 = polyline representation of ellipse.
Perimeter (read-only)	Area, List	*NA*	Displays last perimeter value derived from Area and List commands.
Pfacevmax (read-only)	Pface	*NA*	Displays maximum number of vertices per face. (PFaces are 3D surfaces designed for use by third-party software producers and are not designed for end users.)
Pickadd	Select	Registry	Determines how items are added to a selection set: 0 = only most recently selected item(s) become selection set (to accumulate objects in a selection set, hold down Shift while selecting); 1 = selected objects accumulate in a selection set as you select them (hold down Shift while selecting items to remove those items from the selection set).
Pickauto	Select	Registry	Controls automatic window at `Select objects:` prompt: 0 = window is disabled; 1 = window is enabled.
Pickbox	Select	Registry	Controls size of object-selection pickbox (in pixels).

Continued on next page

TABLE D.1: SYSTEM VARIABLES. ITEMS MARKED WITH AN ASTERISK WERE ADDED IN AUTOCAD 2002. ITEMS MARKED WITH TWO ASTERISKS ARE NEW IN AUTOCAD 2004. *(continued)*

VARIABLE NAME	ASSOCIATED COMMAND	WHERE SAVED	USE
Pickdrag	Select	Registry	Controls how selection windows are used: 0 = click each corner of the window; 1 = Shift+click and hold on first corner, and then drag and release for the second corner.
Pickfirst	Select	Registry	Controls whether you can pick object(s) before you select a command: 0 = disabled; 1 = enabled.
Pickstyle	Group, Hatch	With drawing	Controls whether groups and/or associative hatches are selectable: 0 = neither are selectable; 1 = groups only; 2 = associative hatches only; 3 = both groups and associative hatches.
Platform (read-only)	*NA*	*NA*	Identifies the version of AutoCAD being used.
Plinegen	Pline/Pedit	With drawing	Controls how polylines generate line types around vertices: 0 = line-type pattern begins and ends at vertices; 1 = line-type patterns ignore vertices and begin and end at polyline beginning and ending.
Plinetype	Pline	Registry	Controls whether AutoCAD creates optimized 2D polylines and/or converts existing polylines to optimized polylines: 0 = polylines in existing drawings are not converted, and new polylines are not optimized; 1 = polylines in existing drawings are not converted, but new polylines are optimized; 2 = polylines in existing drawings are not converted, and new polylines are optimized.
Plinewid	Pline	With drawing	Controls default polyline width.
Plotrotmode	Plot	Registry	Controls orientation of your plotter output.
Plquiet	*NA*	Registry	Controls the display of dialog boxes for batch plotting and scripts: 0 = display dialog boxes; 1 = do not display dialog boxes.

Continued on next page

TABLE D.1: SYSTEM VARIABLES. ITEMS MARKED WITH AN ASTERISK WERE ADDED IN AUTOCAD 2002. ITEMS MARKED WITH TWO ASTERISKS ARE NEW IN AUTOCAD 2004. *(continued)*

VARIABLE NAME	ASSOCIATED COMMAND	WHERE SAVED	USE
Polaraddang	Dsettings	Registry	Sets the value of the Additional Angle setting of the Polar Snap tab of the Drafting Settings dialog box. You can enter as many as 10 angles of 25 characters each separated with semicolons.
Polarang	Dsettings	Registry	Sets the Increment Angle setting of the Polar Snap tab of the Drafting Settings dialog box.
Polardist	Dsettings	Registry	Sets the Polar Snap distance.
Polarmode	Dsettings/ Options	With drawing	Sets Polar and Object Snap Tracking settings. The value is the sum of four pairs of codes as follows. Polar angle measurement: 0 = absolute; 1 = relative. Object Snap Tracking: 0 = orthogonal only; 2 = use Polar Tracking settings. Use additional Polar Tracking angles: 0 = no; 4 = yes. Acquire Object Snap Tracking points (Options dialog box): 0 = automatically; 8 = Shift to acquire.
Polysides	Polygon	*NA*	Controls the default number of sides for a polygon.
Popups (read-only)	*NA*	*NA*	Displays whether the current system supports pull-down menus: 0 = no; 1 = yes.
Projectname	Options	Registry	Assigns a project name to a drawing. The project name can be associated with one or more folders.
Projmode	Trim, Extend	Registry	Controls how the Trim and Extend commands affect objects in 3D: 0 = objects must be coplanar; 1 = trims/extends based on a plane parallel to the current UCS; 2 = trims/extends based on a plane parallel to the current view plane.
Proxygraphics	*NA*	With drawing	Controls whether images of proxy objects are stored in a drawing: 0 = images not stored; 1 = images saved.

Continued on next page

TABLE D.1: SYSTEM VARIABLES. ITEMS MARKED WITH AN ASTERISK WERE ADDED IN AUTOCAD 2002. ITEMS MARKED WITH TWO ASTERISKS ARE NEW IN AUTOCAD 2004. *(continued)*

VARIABLE NAME	ASSOCIATED COMMAND	WHERE SAVED	USE
Proxynotice	*NA*	Registry	Issues a warning to the user when a proxy object is created, i.e., when user opens a drawing containing custom objects created using an application that is not loaded: 0 = no warning; 1 = warning displayed.
Proxyshow	*NA*	Registry	Specifies if and how proxy objects are displayed: 0 = no display; 1 = graphic display of all proxy objects; 2 = only bounding box shown.
Proxywebsearch*	Options	Registry	Controls whether AutoCAD searches the web for Object Enablers. 0 = prevent search; 1 = search web for Object Enablers if there is an Internet connection; 2 = specify the number of attempts to find Object Enablers.
Psltscale	Pspace	With drawing	Controls Paper Space line-type scaling.
Psquality	Psin	Registry	Controls how images are generated in AutoCAD with the Psin command. Value is an integer: 0 = only bounding box is drawn; >0 = number of pixels per AutoCAD drawing unit; <0 = outline with no fills, and absolute value of setting determines pixels per drawing units.
Pstylemode	Options	Drawing	Determines the type of plot styles used in new or imported drawings: 0 = color plot styles; 1 = named plot styles.
Pstylepolicy	*NA*	Registry	Determines whether object colors are associated with its plot style: 0 = no association; 1 = association.
Psvpscale	Vports	*NA*	Sets the default view scale factor for new viewports. Values must be positive real: 0 = scale to fit.
Pucsbase	Ucsman	With drawing	Stores the name of a UCS that you want to use as the base for orthographic UCS settings. Paper Space only.
Qtextmode	Qtext	With drawing	Controls the quick text mode: 0 = off; 1 = on.

Continued on next page

TABLE D.1: SYSTEM VARIABLES. ITEMS MARKED WITH AN ASTERISK WERE ADDED IN AUTOCAD 2002. ITEMS MARKED WITH TWO ASTERISKS ARE NEW IN AUTOCAD 2004. *(continued)*

VARIABLE NAME	ASSOCIATED COMMAND	WHERE SAVED	USE
Rasterpreview	Save	Registry	Controls whether raster preview images are saved with the drawing and sets the format type: 0 = No preview image created; 1 = BMP preview image.
Refeditname (read-only)	Refedit	*NA*	Displays the current reference-editing state of a drawing.
Regenmode	Regenauto	With drawing	Controls Regenauto mode: 0 = off; 1 = on.
Re-init	Reinit	*NA*	Reinitializes I/O ports, digitizers, display, plotter, and ACAD.PGP: 1 = digitizer port; 2 = plotter port; 4 = digitizer; 8 = display; 16 = PGP file reload.
Rememberfolders*	*NA*	Registry	Controls the default folder displayed in file dialog boxes. 0 = use Start In Path specification from AutoCAD Icon; 1 = last used path.
Reporterror**	*NA*	Registry	Controls whether errors can be reported to Autodesk as they occur. 0 = no error report, 1 = error report message is displayed with option to send error report to Autodesk.
Roamablerootprefix (read-only)**	*NA*	Registry	Displays the full path name for customizable support files for roaming profiles.
Rtdisplay	Rtpan, Rtzoom	Registry	Controls display of raster images during real-time Pan and Zoom.
Savefile (read-only)	Autosave	Registry	Displays filename that is autosaved.
Savefilepath*	*NA*	Registry	Specifies the folder location for automatic save files.
Savename (read-only)	Save	*NA*	Displays user filename under which file is saved.
Savetime	Autosave	Registry	Controls time interval between automatic saves, in minutes: 0 = disable automatic save.
Screenboxes (read-only)	Menu	Registry	Displays number of slots or boxes available in side menu.

Continued on next page

TABLE D.1: SYSTEM VARIABLES. ITEMS MARKED WITH AN ASTERISK WERE ADDED IN AUTOCAD 2002. ITEMS MARKED WITH TWO ASTERISKS ARE NEW IN AUTOCAD 2004. *(continued)*

VARIABLE NAME	ASSOCIATED COMMAND	WHERE SAVED	USE
Screenmode (read-only)	*NA*	Registry	Displays current display mode: 0 = text; 1 = graphics; 2 = dual screen.
Screensize (read-only)	*NA*	*NA*	Displays current viewport size in pixels.
SDI	*NA*	Registry	Determines whether AutoCAD allows multiple documents or limits user to single document editing: 0 = multiple documents; 1 = single document; 2 = indicates single documents because loaded third-party application does not support multiple documents (read only); 3 = same as 2 with SDI set to 1 by user.
Shadedge	Shade	With drawing	Controls how drawing is shaded: 0 = faces shaded, no edge highlighting; 1 = faces shaded, edge highlighting; 2 = faces not filled, edges in object color; 3 = faces in object color, edges in background color.
Shadedif	Shade	With drawing	Sets difference between diffuse reflective and ambient light. Value represents percentage of diffuse reflective light.
Shortcutmenu	Right-click	Registry	Controls the Default, Edit, and Command mode shortcut menus. For multiple options, use the sum of option values: 0 = restore R14 behavior; 1 = Default mode shortcut enabled; 2 = Edit mode shortcut enabled; 4 = Command mode shortcut enabled; 8 = Command mode shortcut enabled only when options are shown in command line.
Shpname	Shape	*NA*	Controls default shape name.
Sigwarn**	Sigvalidate	Registry	Controls whether the digital signature warning message is displayed when a file containing a digital signature is opened. 0 = warning appears only if a digital signature is present and is not valid, 1 = warning appears if digital signature is present.

Continued on next page

TABLE D.1: SYSTEM VARIABLES. ITEMS MARKED WITH AN ASTERISK WERE ADDED IN AUTOCAD 2002. ITEMS MARKED WITH TWO ASTERISKS ARE NEW IN AUTOCAD 2004. *(continued)*

VARIABLE NAME	ASSOCIATED COMMAND	WHERE SAVED	USE
Sketchinc	Sketch	With drawing	Controls sketch record increment.
Skpoly	Sketch	With drawing	Controls whether the Sketch command uses regular lines or polylines: 0 = line; 1 = polyline.
Snapang	Snap	With drawing	Controls snap and grid angle.
Snapbase	Snap	With drawing	Controls snap, grid, and hatch pattern origin.
Snapisopair	Snap	With drawing	Controls isometric plane: 0 = left; 1 = top; 2 = right.
Snapmode	F9, Snap	With drawing	Controls snap toggle: 0 = off; 1 = on.
Snapstyl	Snap	With drawing	Controls snap style: 0 = standard; 1 = isometric.
Snaptype	Snap	Registry	Controls whether polar or grid snap is current: 0 = grid snap; 1 = polar snap.
Snapunit	Snap	With drawing	Controls snap spacing given in x and y values.
Solidcheck	Solidedit	*NA*	Controls solid validation for 3D solids in current session: 0 = off; 1 = on.
Sortents	*NA*	Registry	Controls whether objects are sorted based on their order in database: 0 = disabled; 1 = sort for object selection; 2 = sort for object snap; 4 = sort for redraws; 8 = sort for Mslide; 16 = sort for regen; 32 = sort for plot; 64 = sort for Psout.
Splframe	Pline, Pedit, 3dface	With drawing	Controls display of spline vertices, defining mesh of a surface-fit mesh, and display of "invisible" edges of 3D Faces: 0 = no display of spline vertices, display only fit surface of a smoothed 3D Mesh, and no display of "invisible" edges of 3D Face; 1 = spline vertices are displayed, only defining mesh of a smoothed 3D Mesh is displayed, "invisible" edges of 3D Face are displayed.

Continued on next page

TABLE D.1: SYSTEM VARIABLES. ITEMS MARKED WITH AN ASTERISK WERE ADDED IN AUTOCAD 2002. ITEMS MARKED WITH TWO ASTERISKS ARE NEW IN AUTOCAD 2004. *(continued)*

VARIABLE NAME	ASSOCIATED COMMAND	WHERE SAVED	USE
Splinesegs	Pline, Pedit	With drawing	Controls number of line segments used for each spline patch.
Splinetype	Pline, Pedit	With drawing	Controls type of spline curve generated by Pedit spline: 5 = quadratic B-spline; 6 = cubic B-spline.
Standardsviolations**	Standards	Registry	Controls whether user is notified when a file contains standards violations. 0 = no notification, 1 = notification when standards violations occurs, 2 = notification via icon in status bar.
Startup**	New/Qnew	Registry	Controls whether the Starup dialog box appears when AutoCAD is first opened. Also controls whether the Create New Drawing dialog box appears when a new document is created by choosing File ➢ New. 0 = Displays Select Template dialog box for File ➢ New, opens AutoCAD with no Startup dialog box; 1 = Displays Create New Drawing or Startup dialog box.
Surftab1		With drawing	Controls number of facets in the m direction of meshes.
Surftab2	ERevsurf, Edgesurf	With drawing	Controls number of facets in the n direction of meshes.
Surftype	Pedit	With drawing	Controls type of surface fitting used by the Pedit command's Smooth option: 5 = quadratic B-spline surface; 6 = cubic B- spline surface; 8 = Bezier surface.
Surfu	3Dmesh	With drawing	Controls surface density in the m direction.
Surfv	3Dmesh	With drawing	Controls surface density in the n direction.
Syscodepage (read-only)	*NA*	*NA*	Displays system code page specified in `Acad.xmx`.
Tabmode	Tablet	*NA*	Controls tablet mode: 0 = off; 1 = on.
Target (read-only)	Dview	With drawing	Displays coordinate of perspective target point.

Continued on next page

TABLE D.1: SYSTEM VARIABLES. ITEMS MARKED WITH AN ASTERISK WERE ADDED IN AUTOCAD 2002. ITEMS MARKED WITH TWO ASTERISKS ARE NEW IN AUTOCAD 2004. *(continued)*

VARIABLE NAME	ASSOCIATED COMMAND	WHERE SAVED	USE
Tdcreate (read-only)	Time	With drawing	Displays time and date of file creation in Julian format.
Tdindwg (read-only)	Time	With drawing	Displays total editing time in days and decimal days.
Tducreate (read-only)	Time	With drawing	Displays the time and date that a drawing was created.
Tdupdate (read-only)	Time	With drawing	Displays time and date of last file update in Julian format.
Tdusrtimer (read-only)	Time	With drawing	Displays user-controlled elapsed time in days and decimal days.
Tduupdate (read-only)	Time	With drawing	Displays the time and date of last update or save.
Tempprefix (read-only)	*NA*	*NA*	Displays location for temporary files.
Texteval	*NA*	*NA*	Controls interpretation of text input: 0 = AutoCAD takes all text input literally; 1 = AutoCAD interprets "(" and "!" as part of an AutoLISP expression, unless either the Text or Dtext command is active.
Textfill	Text	Registry	Controls display of Bitstream, TrueType, and PostScript Type 1 fonts: 0 = outlines; 1 = filled.
Textqlty	Text	With drawing	Controls resolution of Bitstream, TrueType, and PostScript Type 1 fonts: values from 1.0 to 100.0. The lower the value, the lower the output resolution. Higher resolutions improve font quality but decrease display and plot speeds.
Textsize	Text, Dtext	With drawing	Controls default text height.
Textstyle	Text, Dtext	With drawing	Controls default text style.
Thickness	Elev	With drawing	Controls default 3D thickness of object being drawn.
Tilemode	Mspace/ Pspace	With drawing	Controls Paper Space and viewport access: 0 = Paper Space and viewport objects enabled; 1 = strictly Model Space.

Continued on next page

TABLE D.1: SYSTEM VARIABLES. ITEMS MARKED WITH AN ASTERISK WERE ADDED IN AUTOCAD 2002. ITEMS MARKED WITH TWO ASTERISKS ARE NEW IN AUTOCAD 2004. *(continued)*

VARIABLE NAME	ASSOCIATED COMMAND	WHERE SAVED	USE
Tooltips	Icon tool palettes	Registry	Controls display of tool tips: 0 = off; 1 = on.
Tpstate (read-only)**	Toolpalettes	*NA*	Tells whether the Tool Palettes window is active. 0 = not active, 1 = active
Tracewid	Trace	With drawing	Controls trace width.
Trackpath	Options	Registry	Controls the display of the tracking vector: 0 = full screen; 1 = only between alignment points; 2 = no Polar Tracking vector; 3 = no Polar or Object Snap Tracking vector.
Trayicons**	*NA*	Registry	Controls the display of the AutoCAD Tray icons in the lower-right corner of the AutoCAD window. 0 = no display, 1 = display
Traynotify**	*NA*	Registry	Controls the display of service notifications in the AutoCAD Tray. 0 = no notification, 1 = notification
Traytimeout**	*NA*	Registry	Controls how long tray notifications are displayed. Values from 0 to 10 are valid.
Treedepth	Treestat	With drawing	Controls depth of tree-structured spatial index affecting speed of AutoCAD database search. First two digits are for Model Space nodes; second two digits are for Paper Space nodes. Use positive integers for 3D drawings and negative integers for 2D drawings. Negative values can improve speed of 2D operation.
Treemax	Regen, Treedepth	Registry	Limits memory use during regens by limiting maximum number of nodes in spatial index created with the Treedepth command.
Trimmode	Chamfer, Fillet	Registry	Controls whether lines are trimmed during the Chamfer and Fillet commands: 0 = no trim; 1 = trim (as with pre-Release 13 versions of AutoCAD).
Tspacefac	Mtext	*NA*	Sets multiline text line spacing as a percentage of text height. Valid range is between 0.25 and 4.0.

Continued on next page

TABLE D.1: SYSTEM VARIABLES. ITEMS MARKED WITH AN ASTERISK WERE ADDED IN AUTOCAD 2002. ITEMS MARKED WITH TWO ASTERISKS ARE NEW IN AUTOCAD 2004. *(continued)*

VARIABLE NAME	ASSOCIATED COMMAND	WHERE SAVED	USE
Tspacetype	Mtext	*NA*	Controls multiline text line spacing quality: 1 = use tallest letter for basis of line spacing; 2 = use text height specification as basis of line spacing.
Tstackalign	Mtext	With drawing	Controls text alignment for stacked text: 0 = bottom; 1 = center; 2 = top.
Tstacksize	Mtext	With drawing	Sets stacked fraction text height as percent of normal text height. Valid range is 1 to 127.
Ucsaxisang*	Ucs	Registry	Sets the default rotation angle for x-, y-, or z-axis option of UCS command.
Ucsbase	Ucs	With drawing	Sets the name of the UCS used as a basis for orthographic UCS options.
Ucsfollow	Ucs	With drawing	Controls whether AutoCAD automatically changes to Plan view of UCS while in Model Space: 0 = UCS change does not affect view; 1 = UCS change causes view to change with UCS.
Ucsicon	Ucsicon	With drawing	Controls UCS icon: 1 = on; 2 = UCS icon appears at origin.
Ucsname (read-only)	Ucs	With drawing	Displays name of current UCS.
Ucsorg (read-only)	Ucs	With drawing	Displays origin coordinate for current UCS relative to World Coordinate System.
Ucsortho	Ucs	With drawing	Controls whether the UCS follows ortho-graphic views: 0 = does not follow; 1 = follows orthographic view.
Ucsview	View	With drawing	Controls whether a UCS is saved with a named view: 0 = not saved; 1 = saved.
Ucsvp	Vport	With drawing	Controls whether the UCS follows the orien-tation of a new viewport: 0 = current UCS; 1 = follow orientation of view port view.
Ucsxdir (read-only)	Ucs	With drawing	Displays x direction of current UCS relative to World Coordinate System.

Continued on next page

TABLE D.1: SYSTEM VARIABLES. ITEMS MARKED WITH AN ASTERISK WERE ADDED IN AUTOCAD 2002. ITEMS MARKED WITH TWO ASTERISKS ARE NEW IN AUTOCAD 2004. *(continued)*

VARIABLE NAME	ASSOCIATED COMMAND	WHERE SAVED	USE
Ucsydir (read-only)	Ucs	With drawing	Displays y direction of current UCS relative to World Coordinate System.
Undoctl (read-only)	Undo	*NA*	Displays current state of Undo feature: 1 = Undo enabled; 2 = only one command can be undone; 4 = Autogroup mode enabled; 8 = group is currently active.
Undomarks (read-only)	Undo	*NA*	Displays number of marks placed by Undo command.
Unitmode	Units	With drawing	Controls how AutoCAD displays fractional, foot-and-inch, and surveyor's angles: 0 = industry standard; 1 = AutoCAD input format.
Useri1–Useri5	Autolisp/ Diesel	With drawing	Five user variables capable of storing integer values.
Userr1–Userr5	Autolisp/ Diesel	With drawing	Five user variables capable of storing real values.
Users1–Users5	Autolisp/ Diesel	With drawing	Five user variables capable of storing string values.
Viewctr (read-only)	*NA*	With drawing	Displays center of current view in coordinates.
Viewdir (read-only)	Dview	With drawing	Displays camera-viewing direction in coordinates.
Viewmode (read-only)	Dview	With drawing	Displays view-related settings for current viewport: 1 = perspective on; 2 = front clipping on; 4 = back clipping on; 8 = UCS follow on; 16 = front clip not at a point directly in front of the viewer's eye.
Viewsize (read-only)	*NA*	With drawing	Displays height of current view in drawing units.
Viewtwist (read-only)	Dview	With drawing	Displays twist angle for current viewport.

Continued on next page

TABLE D.1: SYSTEM VARIABLES. ITEMS MARKED WITH AN ASTERISK WERE ADDED IN AUTOCAD 2002. ITEMS MARKED WITH TWO ASTERISKS ARE NEW IN AUTOCAD 2004. *(continued)*

VARIABLE NAME	ASSOCIATED COMMAND	WHERE SAVED	USE
Visretain	Layer	With drawing	Controls whether layer setting for Xrefs is retained: 0 = current layer color; line-type, and visibility settings retained when drawing is closed; 1 = layer settings of Xref drawing always renewed when file is opened.
Vsmax (read-only)	*NA*	With drawing	Displays coordinates of upper-right corner of virtual screen.
Vsmin (read-only)	*NA*	With drawing	Displays coordinates of lower-left corner of virtual screen.
Whiparc	*NA*	Registry	Controls the tessellation of circles and arcs: 0 = tessellated; 1 = not tessellated.
Wmfbkgnd	Export/Cut	*NA*	Sets the way backgrounds and borders are generated in exported Windows metafiles: 0 = transparent backgrounds, no borders; 1 = background same as AutoCAD background, border is reverse color of background.
Wmfforeground*	Options	*NA*	Controls the appearance of Windows metafile export from AutoCAD. 0 = ensures foreground color is darker than background; 1 = ensures background color is darker than foreground. This feature takes effect only if Wmfgkgrnd is set to 0.
Worlducs (read-only)	UCS	*NA*	Displays status of WCS: 0 = current UCS is not WCS; 1 = current UCS is WCS.
Worldview	Dview, Vpoint	With drawing	Controls whether the Dview and Vpoint commands operate relative to UCS or WCS: 0 = current UCS is used; 1 = WCS is used.
Writestat (read-only)	*NA*	*NA*	Displays the current drawings read/write status: 0 = read-only; 1 = drawing can be written to.
Xclipframe	Xref	With drawing	Controls visibility of Xref clip ping boundaries: 0 = clipping boundary is not visible; 1 = boundary is visible.

Continued on next page

TABLE D.1: SYSTEM VARIABLES. ITEMS MARKED WITH AN ASTERISK WERE ADDED IN AUTOCAD 2002. ITEMS MARKED WITH TWO ASTERISKS ARE NEW IN AUTOCAD 2004. *(continued)*

VARIABLE NAME	ASSOCIATED COMMAND	WHERE SAVED	USE
Xedit	Options	With drawing	Controls Refedit availability of current drawing: 0 = not available for in-place Xref editing; 1 = available for in place Xref editing.
Xfadectl	Options	*NA*	Controls fading intensity in percent value for objects not selected while using Refedit (in-place Xref editing). Valid range is 0 to 90.
Xloadctl	Xref, Xclip	Registry	Controls Xref demand loading, and creation of copies of original Xref: 0 = no demand loading allowed, entire Xref drawing is loaded; 1 = demand loading allowed, and original Xref file is kept open; 2 = demand loading allowed, using a copy of Xref file stored in AutoCAD temp files folder.
Xloadpath	Xref	Registry	Creates a path for storing temporary copies of demand-loaded Xref files.
Xrefctl	Xref	Registry	Controls whether Xref log files are written: 0 = no log files; 1 = log files written.
Xrefnotify**	Xref	Registry	Determines whether notification appears in the AutoCAD Tray for updated or missing Xrefs. 0 = no notification, 1 = notification that current drawing contains Xrefs. If xrefs are missing, a yellow alert icon is displayed. 2 = same as 1 notification and includes a balloon message.
Zoomfactor	Mouse Wheel	Registry	Controls the amount of zoom applied to a drawing when the mouse wheel is turned. Valid range is between 3 and 100. Default is 10.

Setting Dimension Variables

Chapter 9 discussed the various options for dimensioning available through Dimension Styles and other dialog boxes and mentioned that most of these options have equivalent system variables. Later in this appendix you'll find a complete discussion of all elements of the Dimension Styles dialog box and how to use it.

This section provides further information about the dimension variables. For starters, Table D.2 lists each variable, its default status, and a brief description of what it does. You can get a similar listing by entering **–Dimstyle↵** at the command prompt, and then typing **ST** to select the Status option. Alternatively, you can use the AutoCAD Help system. This section also discusses a few system variables that do not appear in the Dimension Styles dialog box.

TABLE D.2: DIMENSION VARIABLES

DIMENSION VARIABLE	DEFAULT SETTING	DESCRIPTION
General Dimension Controls		
Dimaso	On	Turns partial associative dimension on and off. (obsolete)
Dimassoc	2	Turns true associative dimension on and off. 0 = exploded dimension; 1 = pre-2002 associative dimensions; 2 = fully associative dimensions.
Dimsho	On	Updates dimensions dynamically while dragging.
Dimstyle	Standard	Name of current dimension style.
Dimtmove	0	Sets the way dimension text behaves when moved: 0 = move dimension line with text; 1 = add leader and move text freely; 2 = no leader and move text freely.
Dimupt	Off	Controls user positioning of text during dimension input: 0 = automatic text positioning; 1 = user defined text positioning allowed.
Scale		
Dimscale	1.0000	Overall scale factor of dimensions.
Dimtxt	.18 (approx. 3/16")	Text height.
Dimasz	.18 (approx. 3/16"	Arrow size.
Dimtsz	0"	Tick size.
Dimcen	.09 (approx. 3/32")	Center mark size.
Dimlfac	1.0000	Multiplies measured distance by a specified scale factor.
Offsets		
Dimexo	.0625 or 1/16"	Extension line origin offset.
Dimexe	.18 (approx. 3/16")	Amount extension line extends beyond dimension line.
Dimdli	.38 (approx. 3/8")	Dimension line offset for continuation or base.
Dimdle	0"	Amount dimension line extends beyond extension line.

Continued on next page

TABLE D.2: DIMENSION VARIABLES *(continued)*

DIMENSION VARIABLE	DEFAULT SETTING	DESCRIPTION
Tolerances		
Dimalttz	0	Controls zero suppression of tolerance values: 0 = leaves out zero feet and inches; 1 = includes zero feet and inches; 2 = includes zero feet; 3 = includes zero inches; 4 = suppresses leading zeros in decimal dimensions; 8 = suppresses leading zeros in decimal dimensions.
Dimdec	4	Sets decimal place for primary tolerance values.
Dimtdec	4	Sets decimal place for tolerance values.
Dimtp	0”	Plus tolerance.
Dimtm	0”	Minus tolerance.
Dimtol	Off	When on, shows dimension tolerances.
Dimtolj	1	Controls vertical location of tolerance values relative to nominal dimension: 0 = bottom; 1 = middle; 2 = top.
Dimtzin	0	Controls zero suppression in tolerance values: 0 = leaves out zero feet and inches; 1 = includes zero feet and inches; 2 = includes zero feet; 3 = includes zero inches; 4 = suppresses leading zeros in decimal dimensions; 8 = suppresses leading zeros in decimal dimensions; 12 = suppresses leading and trailing zeros in decimal dimensions.
Dimlim	Off	When on, shows dimension limits.
Rounding		
Dimazin	0	Controls zero suppression for angular dimensions: 0 = display all zeros; 1 = suppress leading zeros; 2 suppress trailing zeros; 3 = suppress all zeros.
Dimrnd	0”	Rounding value.
Dimzin	0	Controls zero suppression dimension text: 0 = leaves out zero feet and inches; 1 = includes zero feet and inches; 2 = includes zero feet; 3 = includes zero inches; 4 = suppresses leading zeros in decimal dimensions; 8 = suppresses leading zeros in decimal dimensions; 12 = suppresses leading and trailing zeros in decimal dimensions.

Continued on next page

TABLE D.2: DIMENSION VARIABLES *(continued)*

DIMENSION VARIABLE	DEFAULT SETTING	DESCRIPTION
Dimension Arrow & Text Control		
Dimadec	–1	Controls the number of decimal places shown for angular dimension text: 1 = uses the value set by Dimdec dimension variable; 0–8 = specifies the actual number of decimal places to be shown.
Dimatfit	3	Controls the way text and arrows are placed when there is not enough room to fit both within extension lines: 0 = place both outside extension lines; 1 = move arrows first; 2 = move text first; 3 = move either text or arrows, whichever is best fit.
Dimaunit	0	Controls angle format for angular dimensions; settings are the same as for Aunits system variable.
Dimblk	" "	Predefined or user-defined arrow block name. You can enter a user-defined block name or one of the following: _DOT, _DOTSMALL, _DOTBLANK, _ORIGIN, _ORIGIN2, _OPEN, _OPEN90, _OPEN30, _CLOSED, _SMALL, _OBLIQUE, _BOXFILLED, _BOXBLANK, _CLOSEDBLANK, _DATUMFILLED, _DATUMBLANK, _INTE GRAL, ARCHTICK.
Dimblk1	" "	Predefined or user-defined arrow block name for first end of dimension line used with Dimsah. See Dimblk for valid options.
Dimblk2	" "	Predefined or user-defined arrow block name for second end of dimension line used with Dimsah. See Dimblk for valid options.
Dimdsep	. (period)	User-defined separator for decimals when dimension units are set to decimal.
Dimfit	3	Controls location of text and arrows for extension lines, if space is not available for both: 0 = text and arrows placed outside; 1 = text has priority, arrows are placed outside extension lines; 2 = arrows have priority; 3 = AutoCAD chooses between text and arrows, based on best fit; 4 = a leader is drawn from dimension line to dimension text when space for text not available; 5 = no leader.
Dimfrac	0	Sets the fraction format for architectural and fractional formats: 0 = vertical; 1 = diagonal; 2 = not stacked.

Continued on next page

TABLE D.2: DIMENSION VARIABLES *(continued)*

DIMENSION VARIABLE	DEFAULT SETTING	DESCRIPTION
Dimgap	1/16" or 0.09"	Controls distance between dimension text and dimension line.
Dimjust	0	Controls horizontal dimension text position: 0 = centered between extension lines; 1 = next to first extension line; 2 = next to second extension line; 3 = above and aligned with the first extension line; 4 = above and aligned with second extension line.
Dimldrblk	0	Sets the arrow type for leaders: 0 = standard closed filled arrow; (period) = no arrow. See Dimblk for valid options.
Dimlunit	Off	Sets unit style for all dimension types except angular: 1 = Scientific; 2 = Decimal; 3 = Engineering; 4 = Architectural; 5 = Fractional; 6 = Windows Desktop.
Dimsah	Off	Allows use of two different arrowheads on a dimension line. See Dimblk1 and Dimblk2.
Dimtfac	1.0"	Controls scale factor for dimension tolerance text.
Dimtih	On	When on, text inside extensions is horizontal.
Dimtoh	On	When on, text outside extensions is horizontal.
Dimtad	0	When on, places text above the dimension line.
Dimtix	Off	Forces text between extensions.
Dimtvp	0	Controls text's vertical position based on numeric value.
Dimtxsty	Standard	Controls text style for dimension text.
Dimunit	2	Controls unit style for all dimension style groups except angular. Settings are same as for Lunit system variable.
Dimension & Extension Line Control		
Dimsdl	Off	When on, suppresses the first dimension line.
Dimsd2	Off	When on, suppresses the second dimension line.
Dimse1	Off	When on, suppresses the first extension line.
Dimse2	Off	When on, suppresses the second extension line.
Dimtofl	Off	When on, forces a dimension line between extension lines.
Dimsoxd	Off	When on, suppresses dimension lines outside extension lines.

Continued on next page

TABLE D.2: DIMENSION VARIABLES *(continued)*

DIMENSION VARIABLE	DEFAULT SETTING	DESCRIPTION
Alternate Dimension Options		
Dimalt	Off	When on, alternate units selected are shown.
Dimaltf	25.4000	Alternate unit scale factor.
Dimaltd	2	Alternate unit decimal places.
Dimalttd	2	Alternate unit tolerance decimal places.
Dimaltu	2	Alternate unit style. See Lunits system variable for values.
Dimaltz	0	Controls the suppression oh zeros for alternate dimension values.
Dimpost	" "	Adds suffix to dimension text.
Dimapost	" "	Adds suffix to alternate dimension text.
Colors and Lineweights		
Dimclrd	0 or *ByBlock*	Controls color of dimension lines and arrows.
Dimclre	0 or *ByBlock*	Controls color of dimension extension lines.
Dimclrt	0 or *ByBlock*	Controls color of dimension text.
Dimlwd	*ByBlock*	Controls the line weight of dimension lines. Valid values are Bylayer, ByBlock, or integer representing 100th millimeter.
Dimlwe	*ByBlock*	Controls the line weight of extension lines. Valid values are Bylayer, ByBlock, or integer representing 100th millimeter.

Finally, for those of you who might want to write macros, scripts, or AutoLISP programs to control dimension styles, you'll learn about using two options of the Dimstyle command to set and recall dimension styles from the command line: **–Dimstyle↵** **S↵** and **–Dimstyle↵** **R↵**.

If you want to change a setting through the command line instead of through the Dimension Styles dialog box, you can enter the system variable name at the command prompt.

Storing Dimension Styles through the Command Line

Once you have set the dimension variables as you like, you can save the settings by using the Dimstyle command. The Dimstyle/Save command records all the current dimension variable settings (except Dimassoc) with a name you specify.

1. At the command prompt, enter **–Dimstyle↵**.

2. At the `[Save/Restore/Status/Variables/Apply/?] <Save>:` prompt, press ↵.
3. When the `Enter name for new dimension style or [?]:` prompt appears, you can enter a question mark (?) to get a listing of any dimension styles currently saved, or you can enter a name under which you want the current settings saved.

For example, suppose you change some of your dimension settings through dimension variables instead of through the Dimension Styles dialog box, as shown in the following list:

Dimtsz	0.044
Dimtad	On
Dimtih	Off
Dimtoh	Off

These settings are typical for an architectural style of dimensioning; you might save them under the name Architect, as you did in an exercise in Chapter 9. Then suppose you change other dimension settings for dimensions in another format—surveyor's dimensions on a site plan, for example. You might save them with the name Survey, again using the Save option of the Dimstyle command. When you want to return to the settings you used for your architectural drawing, use the Restore option of the Dimstyle command, described in the next section.

Restoring a Dimension Style from the Command Line

To restore a dimension style you've saved using the Dimstyle Save option:

1. At the command prompt, enter **–Dimstyle**↵.
2. At the `[Save/Restore/STatus/Variable/Apply/?] <Restore>:` prompt, press ↵.
3. At the following prompt:

   `Enter dimension style name or [?] or <select dimension>:`

   you have three options: enter a question mark (?) to get a listing of saved dimension styles; enter the name of a style, such as Arch, if you know the name of the style you want; or use the cursor to select a dimension on the screen whose style you want to match.

Notes on Metric Dimensioning

The AutoCAD user community is worldwide, and many of you may be using the metric system in your work. As long as you are not mixing Imperial (feet and inches) and metric measurements, using the English version of AutoCAD is fairly easy. With the Drawing Units dialog box (choose Format ➢ Units), set your measurement system to decimal, and set the Drawing Units For DesignCenter Blocks option to the appropriate metric option; then draw distances in millimeters or centimeters. At plot time, select the MM radio button (millimeters) under Paper Size and Paper Units in the Plot dialog box.

If your drawings are to be in both Imperial and metric measurements, you will be concerned with several settings, as follows:

Dimlfac Sets the scale factor for dimension values. The dimension value will be the measured distance in AutoCAD units times this scale factor. Set Dimlfac to 25.4 if you have drawn in inches but want to dimension in millimeters. The default is 1.00. If you want to scale dimension values from millimeters to inches, use a value of 0.03937.

Dimalt Turns the display of alternate dimensions on or off. Alternate dimensions are dimension text added to your drawing, in addition to the standard dimension text.

Dimaltf Sets the scale factor for alternate dimensions (that is, to metric from Imperial). The default is 25.4, which is the millimeter equivalent of 1″. If you are using metric ISO units, the default will be 0.03937, which is the inch equivalent of 1 mm.

Dimaltd Sets the number of decimal places displayed in the alternate dimensions.

Dimapost Adds suffix to alternate dimensions, as in 4.5 mm.

USING THE AUTOCAD METRIC TEMPLATE

If you prefer, you can use the metric template drawing supplied by AutoCAD.

1. Choose File ➢ New. If you see the Select Template dialog box, go to step 2; otherwise skip to step 3.
2. Select the `Acadiso.dwt` file and click Open. You can also select ACADISO – Named Plot Style.DWT if you want to use a named plot style.
3. In the Create New Drawing dialog box, click the Template button. Then select the filename `Acadiso.dwt`, and click OK to open the template. You can also select ACADISO – Named Plot Style.DWT if you want to use a named plot style.

These templates are set up for metric/ISO standard drawings.

You can also use the Metric radio button in the Start From Scratch option of the Create New Drawing dialog box. When you choose Metric from the Create New Drawing dialog box, subsequent new files will be set to metric by default.

If the AutoCAD 2004 Startup dialog box does not appear when you open AutoCAD or if you don't see the Create New Drawing dialog box when you choose File ➢ New, you can turn these dialog boxes on by using the Startup option in the System tab of the Options dialog box. Choose Tools ➢ Options, and then click the System tab in the Options dialog box. In the General Options group, select Show Startup Dialog Box from the Startup drop-down list.

A Closer Look at the Dimension Style Dialog Boxes

As you saw in Chapter 9, you can control the appearance and format of dimensions through dimension styles. You can create new dimension styles or edit existing ones. This section describes all the components of the dialog boxes you use to create and maintain dimension styles.

TIP *You can use the DesignCenter to import dimension styles from one drawing into another.*

The Dimension Style Manager Dialog Box

The Dimension Style Manager dialog box is the gateway to dimension styles. With this dialog box, you can create new dimension style, edit existing dimensions styles, or make an existing dimension style current. You can open the Dimension Style Manager by choosing Dimension ➤ Style.

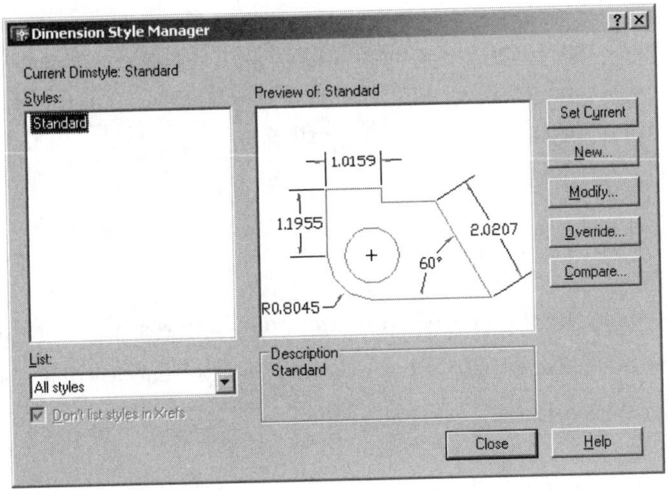

The following sections describe the options in the Dimension Style Manager dialog box.

PREVIEW OF <STANDARD>

The image you see in the right half of the Dimension Style Manager dialog box gives you a preview of your dimension style. It shows a sample of most of the types of dimensions you'll use, formatted the way you specified when you created or modified your dimension style.

THE STYLES LIST BOX

The Styles list box displays the available dimension styles. You can highlight the dimension style names in the Styles list box to indicate a style to be used with the Set Current, New, Modify, and Override options. You can also right-click a style name and then rename or delete the selected style.

THE LIST DROP-DOWN LIST

The List drop-down list lets you control what is listed in the Styles list box. You can display either all the styles available or only the styles in use in the drawing.

DON'T LIST STYLES IN XREFS

The Don't List Styles In Xrefs check box lets you specify whether dimension styles in Xrefs are listed in the Styles list box.

THE SET CURRENT BUTTON

The Set Current button lets you set the dimension style highlighted in the Styles list box to be current.

THE NEW BUTTON

The New button lets you create a new dimension style or modify the dimension type of an existing dimension style. The New button will use the dimension style that is highlighted in the Styles list box as the basis for the new style. Clicking the New button opens the Create New Dimension Style dialog box.

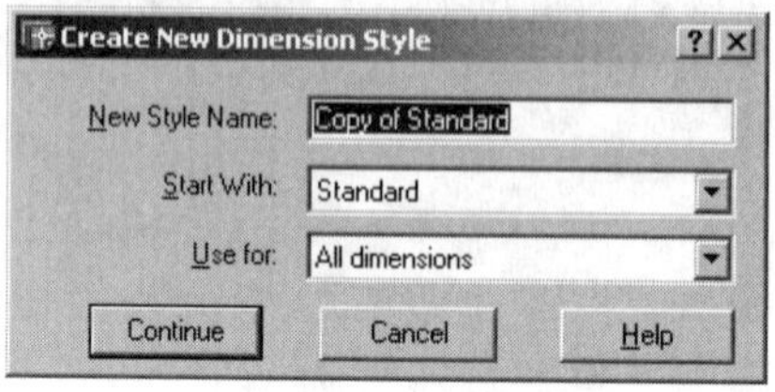

In the Create New Dimension Style dialog box, you can enter the name for your new dimension style. You can also select the source dimension style on which your new dimension style will be based.

New Style Name Lets you specify the name for your new dimension style.

Start With Lets you select an existing style on which to base your new dimension style.

Use For Lets you choose a dimension type for your new dimension style. For a completely new dimension style, use the All Dimensions option in the Use For drop-down list. If you want to modify the specifications for a particular dimension type of an existing dimension style, select a dimension type from this list. Your modified dimension type will appear in the Styles list box under the main style you specify in the Start With drop-down list. Once you've modified a dimension type, the new type will be applied to any new dimensions.

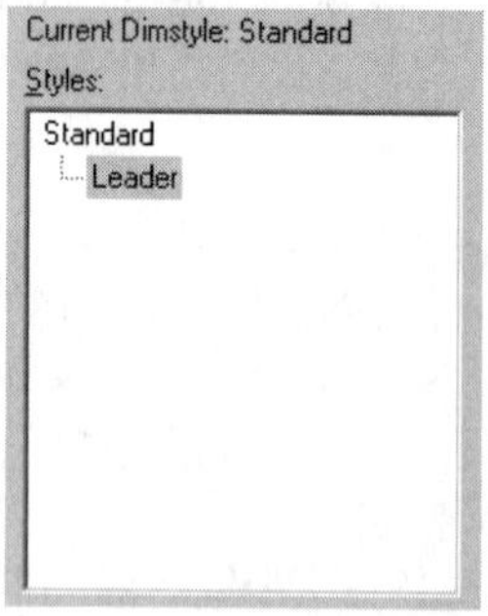

Once you've entered your options in the Create New Dimension Style dialog box, click Continue. You see the New Dimension Style dialog box described in the next section. When you are finished setting up your new style, you will see it listed in the Styles list box.

THE MODIFY BUTTON

The Modify button lets you modify the dimension style that is selected in the Styles list box. This option opens the Modify Dimension Style dialog box described in the next section.

The Override Button

The Override button lets you create a temporary dimension style based on an existing style. You might want to use this option if you need to create a dimension that differs only slightly from an existing style.

To use the Override option, select a style from the Styles list box and then click Override. You'll see the Override Current Style dialog box described in the next section. Once you create an override, you'll see it listed as <style overrides> in the Styles list box right under the style you used to create the override.

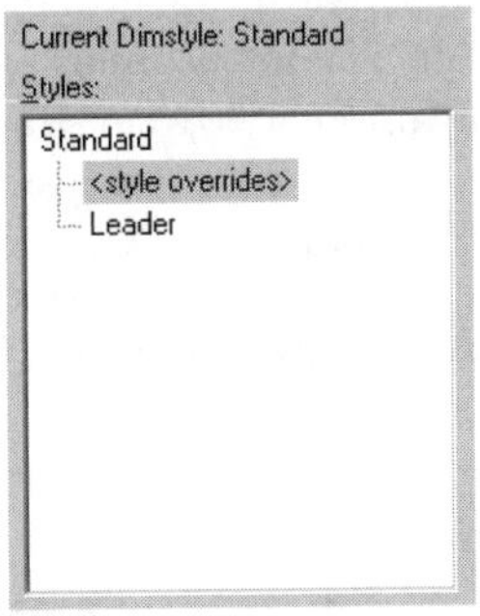

The override then becomes the default dimension style until you select another one from the Styles list. When you select a different style to be current, you will see a message telling you that the unsaved style will be discarded. To save an override style, select the override from the Styles list box and click New. Then click Continue in the Create New Dimension Style dialog box, and click OK in the New Dimension Style dialog box. You can also merge the Override style with its source style by right-clicking the <style overrides> listing and selecting Save To Current Style.

The Compare Button

The Compare button lets you compare the differences between two dimension styles. When you click the Compare button, the Compare Dimension Styles dialog box opens.

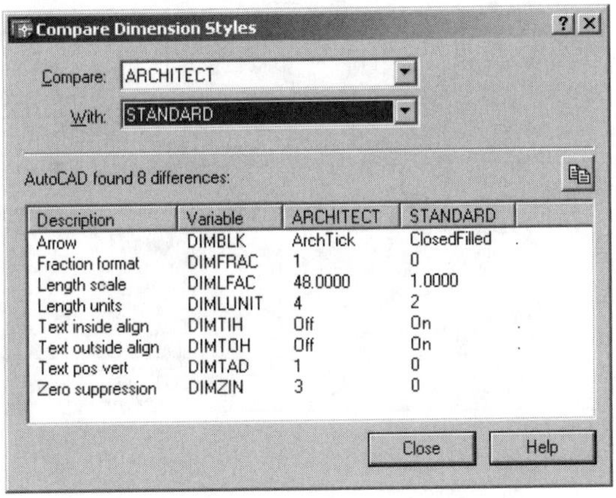

You can select the two styles you want to compare from the Compare and With drop-down lists. The differences will appear in the list box. Just above the upper-right corner of the list box is a Copy button; this copies the contents of the list box to the Windows Clipboard, allowing you to save the comparison to a word-processed document.

The New/Modify/Override Dimension Style Dialog Box

When you select the New option in the Dimension Style Manager dialog box and then click Continue in the Create New Dimension Style dialog box, the New Dimension Style dialog box opens.

You will also see this same dialog box under a different name when you select the Modify or Override button in the Dimension Style Manager dialog box. The options in this dialog box let you determine all the characteristics of your dimension style. The following sections provide detailed descriptions of each available option.

TIP *The equivalent dimension style variables are shown in brackets at the end of the description of each option.*

THE LINES AND ARROWS TAB

The options in the Lines And Arrows tab give you control over the appearance of dimension and extension lines, arrowheads, and center marks. Figure D.1 shows an example of some of the dimension components that are affected by these options. The value you enter here for distances should be in final plot sizes and will be multiplied by the dimension scale value in the Fit tab to derive the actual extension distance in the drawing.

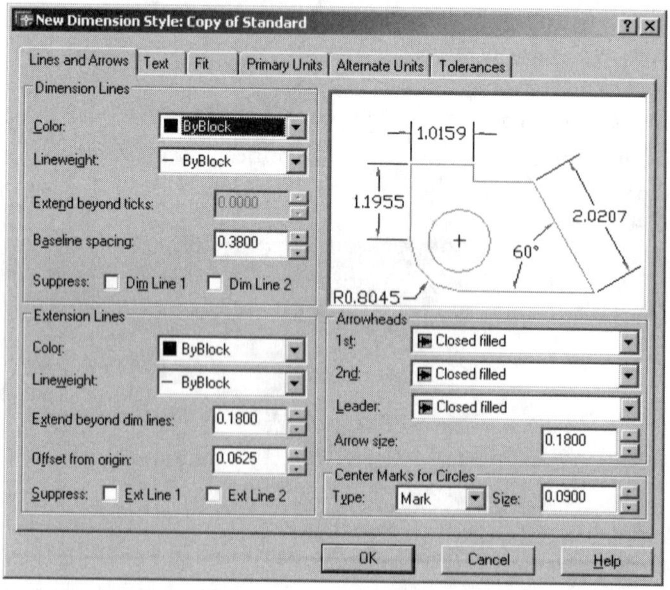

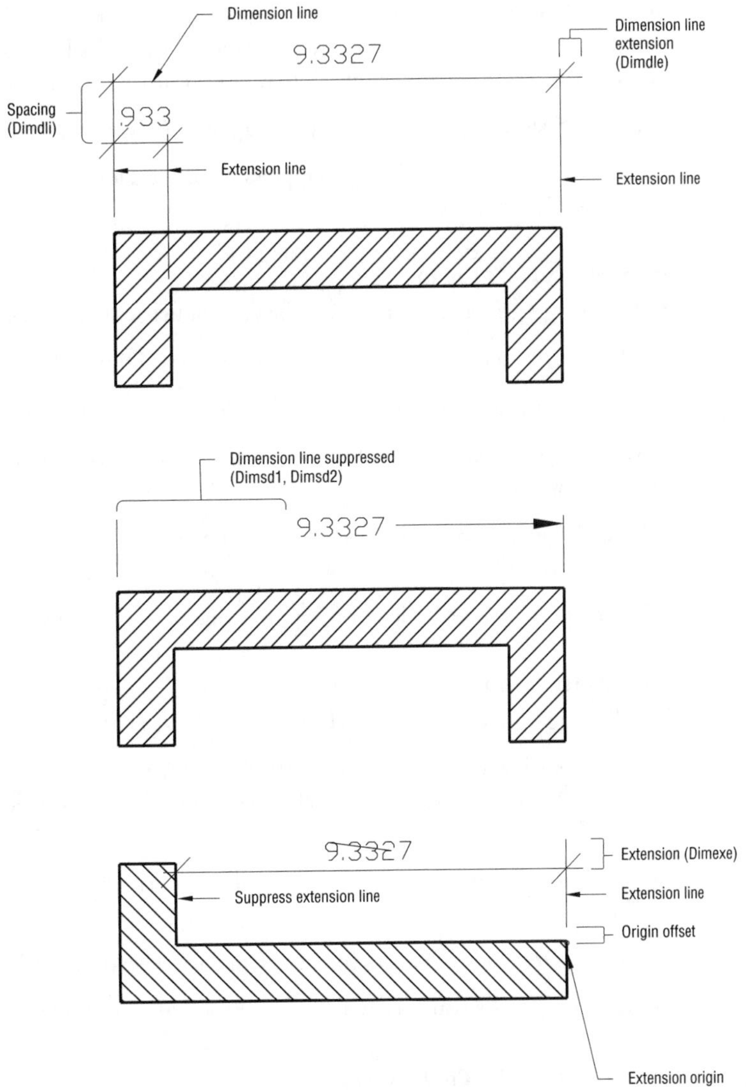

FIGURE D.1
Examples of how some of the Lines And Arrows tab options affect dimensions

The Dimension Lines Group

The following options let you control the general behavior characteristics of the dimension lines:

Color Lets you set the color of the dimension line [Dimclrd].

Lineweight Lets you set the line weight for dimension lines [Dimlwd].

Extend Beyond Ticks Lets you set the distance that the dimension line extends beyond the extension lines. The value you enter here should be in final plot sizes and will be multiplied by the dimension scale value in the Fit tab to derive the actual extension distance in the drawing [Dimdle].

Baseline Spacing Lets you specify the distance between stacked dimensions [Dimdli, Dimbaseline].

Suppress Check boxes let you suppress the dimension line on either side of the dimension text [DimLine1, DimLine2].

The Extension Lines Group

The following options let you control the general behavior and characteristics of the extension lines:

Color Lets you set the color for extension lines [Dimclre].

Lineweight Lets you set the line weight for extension lines [Dimlwe].

Extend Beyond Dim Lines Lets you set the distance that extension lines extend beyond dimension lines [Dimexe].

Offset From Origin Lets you set the distance from the extension line to the object being dimensioned [Dimexo].

Suppress Check boxes lets you suppress one or both extension lines [Ext Line1, Ext Line2].

The Arrowheads Group

The following options let you select the type and sizes of arrowheads for dimensions and leaders:

1st Drop-down list lets you select the type of arrowhead to use on dimension lines. By default, the 2nd arrowhead automatically changes to match the arrowhead you specify for this setting [Dimblk1].

2nd Drop-down list lets you select a different arrowhead from the one you select for 1st [Dimblk2].

Leader Drop-down list lets you specify an arrowhead for leader notes [Dimldrblk].

Arrow Size Lets you specify the size for the arrowheads [Dimasz].

The Center Marks For Circles Group

The following options let you set the center mark for radius and diameter dimensions:

Type Drop-down list lets you select the type of center mark used in radius and diameter dimensions. Mark draws a small cross mark, Line draws a cross mark and centerlines, and None draws nothing [Dimcen].

Size Lets you specify the size of the center mark [Dimcen].

The Text Tab

The options in the Text tab offer control over the appearance of the dimension text. You can set the text style and default location of text in relation to the dimension line. If the text style you select for your dimension text has a height value of 0, you can set the text height from this tab.

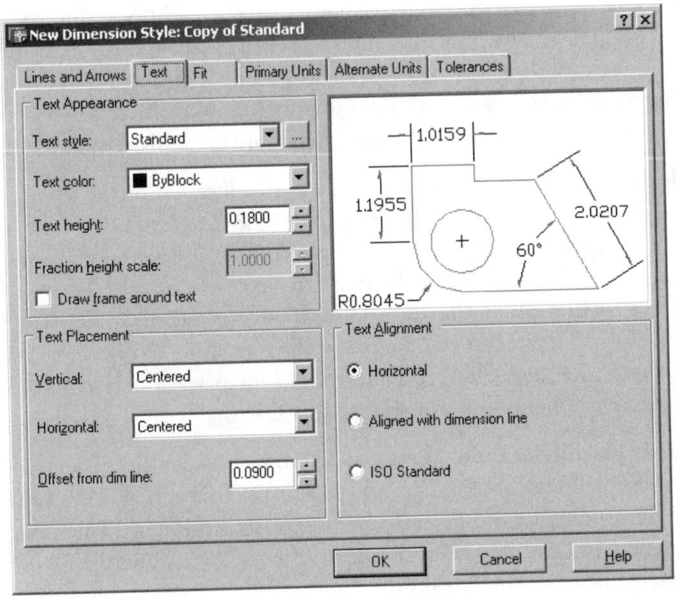

The Text Appearance Group

The following options give you control over the appearance of text:

Text Style Drop-down list lets you select an existing text style for your dimension text. You can also create a new style for your dimension text by clicking the Ellipses button [Dimtxsty].

Text Color Drop-down list lets you select a color for your dimension text [Dimclrt].

Text Height Lets you specify a text height for dimension text. This option is only valid for text styles with 0 height [Dimtxt].

Fraction Height Scale Lets you specify a scale factor for the height of fractional text. This option is only available when Architectural or Fractional is selected in the Primary Units tab [Dimtfac].

Draw Frame Around Text Check box draws a rectangle around the dimension text when selected [Dimgap].

The Text Placement Group

The following options give you control over the placement of text, including the ability to specify the distance of text from the dimension line:

Vertical Drop-down list lets you set the vertical position of the text in relation to the dimension line. The options are Centered, Above, Outside, and JIS. Centered places the text in line with the dimension line. The dimension line is broken to accommodate the text. Above places the text above the dimension line leaving the dimension line unbroken. Outside places the text away from the dimension line at a location farthest away from the object being dimensioned. JIS places the text in conformance with the Japanese Industrial Standards [Dimtad].

Horizontal Drop-down list lets you set the location of the text in relation to the extension lines. The options are Centered, 1st Extension Line, 2nd Extension Line, Over 1st Extension Line, and Over 2nd Extension Line. Centered places the text between the two extension lines. 1st Extension Line places the text next to the first extension line but still between the two extension lines. 2nd Extension Line places the text next to the second extension line but still between the two extension lines. Over 1st Extension Line places the text above the first extension line and aligned with the first extension line. Over 2nd Extension Line places the text above the second extension line and aligned with the second extension line [Dimjust].

Offset From Dim Line Lets you determine the distance from the baseline of text to the dimension line when text is placed above the dimension line. It also lets you set the size of the gap between the dimension text and the endpoint of the dimension line when the text is in line with the dimension line. You can use this option to set the margin around the text when the dimension text is in a centered position that breaks the dimension line into two segments [Dimgap].

The Text Alignment Group

The following options give you control over the alignment of text in relation to the dimension line:

Horizontal Keeps the text in a horizontal orientation, regardless of the dimension line orientation.

Aligned With Dimension Line Aligns the text with the dimension line.

ISO Standard Aligns the text with the dimension line when it is between the extension lines; otherwise the text is oriented horizontally [Dimtih, Dimtoh].

THE FIT TAB

The options in the Fit tab let you fine-tune the behavior of the dimension text and arrows under special conditions. For example, you can select an optional placement for text and arrows when there isn't enough room for them between the extension lines.

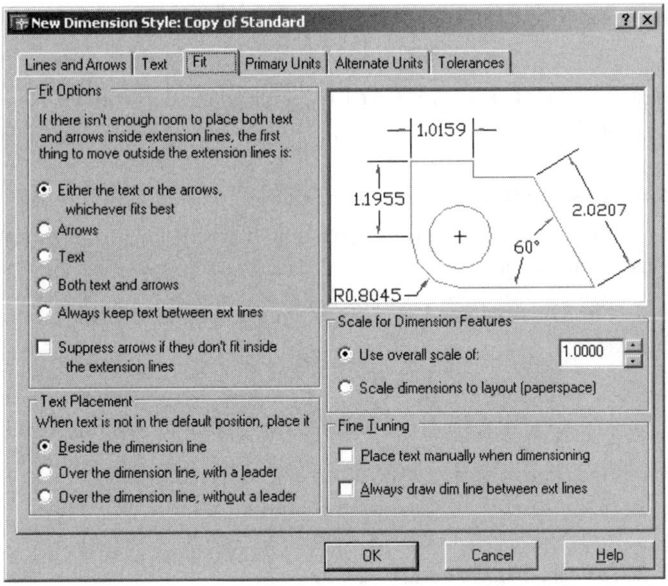

The Fit Options Group

The Fit Options radio buttons let you determine which dimension component is moved when there isn't enough room between the extension lines for either or both the text or the arrows.

Either The Text Or The Arrows, Whichever Fits Best Automatically determines whether text, arrows, or both text and arrows will fit between the extension lines and then places them accordingly. For example, if there isn't enough room for both text and arrows, and the text is wider than the two arrows combined, the text will be placed outside the extension lines. If the width of the arrows is greater than the width of the text, the arrows will be moved outside the extension lines. If the gap between the extension lines is too narrow for either the text or arrows, both the arrows and the text will be moved outside the extension lines [Dimatfit].

Arrows Moves the arrows outside the extension lines when there isn't enough room for both arrows and text between the extension lines. If the gap between the extension lines is too narrow for either the text or the arrows, both the arrows and the text will be moved outside the extension lines [Dimatfit].

Text Moves the text outside the extension line when there isn't enough room for both arrows and text between the extension lines. If the gap between the extension lines is too narrow for either the text or the arrows, both the arrows and the text will be moved outside the extension lines [Dimatfit].

Both Text And Arrows Moves both the text and the arrows outside the extension line when there isn't enough room for both arrows and text between the extension lines [Dimatfit].

Always Keep Text Between Ext Lines Places the text between the extension lines, regardless of whether the text will fit there [Dimtix].

Suppress Arrows If They Don't Fit Inside Extension Lines Removes the arrows entirely if they don't fit between the extension lines [Dimsoxd].

The Text Placement Group

The Text Placement radio buttons determine how the dimension text will behave when it is moved from its default location.

Beside The Dimension Line Keeps the text in its normal location relative to the dimension line [Dimtmove].

Over The Dimension Line, With A Leader Lets you move the dimension text, independent of the dimension line. A leader is added between the dimension line and the text [Dimtmove].

Over The Dimension Line, Without A Leader Lets you move the dimension text, independent of the dimension line. No leader is added [Dimtmove].

The Scale For Dimension Features Group

These options offer control over the scale of the dimension components. You can set a fixed scale, or you can allow the dimension components to be scaled depending on the Paper Space viewport in which they are displayed.

Use Overall Scale Of Radio button and input box let you determine the scale of the dimension components. All the settings in the Dimension Style dialog box will be scaled to the value you set in the input box if this radio button is selected [Dimscale].

Scale Dimension To Layout (Paper Space) Will scale all the dimension components to the scale factor assigned to the Paper Space viewport in which the drawing appears [Dimscale].

The Fine Tuning Group

The following two check boxes offer miscellaneous settings for dimension text and dimension lines:

Place Text Manually When Dimensioning Allows you to manually place the dimension text horizontally along the dimension line when you are inserting dimensions in your drawing [Dimupt].

Always Draw Dim Line Between Ext Lines Forces AutoCAD to draw a dimension line between the extension lines no matter how narrow the distance is between the extension lines [Dimtofl].

THE PRIMARY UNITS TAB

The options in the Primary Units tab let you set the format and content of the dimension text, including the unit style for linear and angular dimensions.

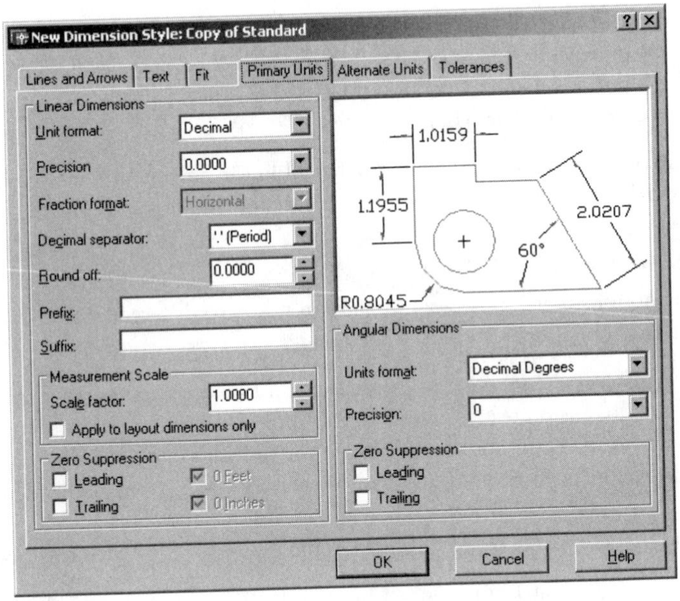

The Linear Dimensions Group

The following options offer control over the unit style and the formatting of dimension text for linear dimensions:

Unit Format Drop-down list lets you determine the unit style of the dimension text. The options are Scientific, Decimal, Engineering, Architectural, Fractional, and Windows Desktop. You must set this option independent of the overall drawing units setting (choose Format ➢ Units) if you want the dimension text to appear in the appropriate style [Dimunit].

Precision Drop-down list lets you set the precision of the dimension text. This option will round off the dimension text to the nearest precision value you set. It does not affect the actual precision of the drawing [Dimdec].

Fraction Format Drop-down list is only available for Architectural and Fractional unit formats. This option lets you select between vertically stacked, diagonally stacked, and horizontal fractions [Dimfrac].

Decimal Separator Drop-down list lets you select a decimal separator for dimension unit formats that display decimals. You can choose a period, a comma, or a space. If you want to use a dimension separator not included in the list, you can use the Dimsep system variable to specify a custom dimension separator [Dimsep].

Round Off Lets you determine the degree of rounding applied to dimensions. For example, you can set this option to 0.25 to round off dimensions to the nearest .25 or 1/4 of a unit [Dimrnd].

Prefix Lets you include a prefix for all linear dimension text. For example, if you want all your linear dimension text to be preceded by the word *Approximately*, you can enter **Approximately** in this input box. Control codes can be used for special characters. See Chapter 8 for more information on control codes [Dimpost].

Suffix Lets you include a suffix for all linear dimension text. Control codes can be used for special characters. See Chapter 8 for more information on control codes [Dimpost].

The Measurement Scale Group

Offers options that can convert dimension values to different scale factors. For example, Dimensions in Imperial units can be scaled to metric and vice versa.

Scale Factor Lets you set a scale factor for the dimension text. This option will scale the value of the dimension text to the value you enter. For example, if you want your dimensions to display distances in centimeters, even though the drawing was created in inches, you can enter **2.54** for this option. Your dimension text will then display dimensions in centimeters. Conversely, if you want your dimension text to show dimensions in inches, even though you've created your drawing using centimeters, you enter **0.3937** (the inverse of 2.54) for this option [Dimlfac].

Apply To Layout Dimensions Only Causes AutoCAD to apply the measurement scale factor to Paper Space layouts only. With this option checked, the Dimlfac dimension variable gives a negative value [Dimlfac].

The Zero Suppression Group

Lets you suppress zeros so they do not appear in the dimension text. For dimensions other than architectural, you can suppress leading and trailing zeros. For example, 0.500 becomes .500 if you suppress leading zeros. It becomes 0.5 if you suppress trailing zeros. For architectural dimensions, you can suppress zero feet or zero inches, although typically, you would not suppress zero inches [Dimzin].

The Angular Dimensions Group

The following options allow you to format angle dimensions:

Units Format Drop-down list lets you select a format for angular dimensions. The options are Decimal Degrees, Degrees/Minutes/Seconds, Grads, Radians, and Surveyor [Dimaunit].

Precision Lets you set the precision for the angular dimension text [Dimadec].

Zero Suppression Lets you suppress leading or trailing zeros in angular dimensions [Dimazin].

THE ALTERNATE UNITS TAB

The Alternate Units tab lets you apply a second set of dimension text for linear dimensions. This second set of text can be used for alternate dimension styles or units. Typically, alternate units are used to display dimensions in metric if your main dimensions are in feet and inches.

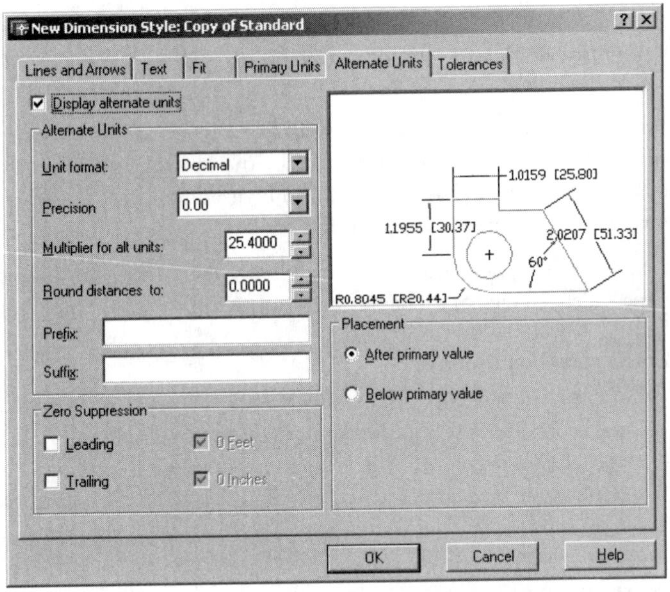

Click the Display Alternate Units check box to turn on alternate units. This causes AutoCAD to include an additional dimension text in the format you specify in the Alternate Units tab [Dimalt].

The Alternate Units Group

The following options offer control over the unit style and the formatting of dimension text for linear dimensions:

Unit Format Drop-down list lets you determine the unit style of the dimension text. The options are Scientific, Decimal, Engineering, Architectural Stacked, Fractional Stacked, Architectural, Fractional, and Windows Desktop. You must set this option independent of the overall drawing units setting (choose Format ➢ Units) if you want the dimension text to appear in the appropriate style [Dimaltu]. You can adjust the size of fractions relative to the main dimension text by using the Dimfac dimension variable.

Precision Drop-down list lets you set the precision of the dimension text. This option will round off the dimension text to the nearest precision value you set. It does not affect the actual precision of the drawing [Dimaltd].

Multiplier For Alt Units Lets you set a multiplier value for the dimension text. This option will multiply the value of the dimension text by the value you enter. For example, if you want your alternate dimensions to display distances in centimeters even though the drawing was created in inches, you can enter **2.54** for this option. Your alternate dimension text will then display dimensions in centimeters. Conversely, if you want to have your alternate dimension text show dimensions in inches, even though you've created your drawing using centimeters, you enter **0.3937** (the inverse of 2.54) for this option [Dimaltf].

Round Distances To Lets you determine the degree of rounding applied to alternate dimensions. For example, you can set this option to 0.25 to round off dimensions to the nearest .25 or 1/4 of a unit [DImaltrnd].

Prefix Lets you include a prefix for all linear alternate dimension text. For example, if you want all linear dimension text to be preceded by the word *Approximately*, you can enter **Approximately** in the Prefix input box. Control codes can be used for special characters. See Chapter 8 for more information on control codes [Dimpost].

Suffix Lets you include a suffix for all linear alternate dimension text. Control codes can be used for special characters. See Chapter 8 for more information on control codes [Dimapost].

The Zero Suppression Group

Lets you suppress zeros so they do not appear in the alternate dimension text. For dimensions other than architectural, you can suppress leading and trailing zeros. For example, 0.500 becomes .500 if you suppress leading zeros. It becomes 0.5 if you suppress trailing zeros. For architectural dimensions, you can suppress zero feet or zero inches, though typically, you would not suppress zero inches [Dimaltz].

The Placement Group

The following options let you determine the location for the alternate units:

After Primary Value Places the alternate dimension text behind and aligned with the primary dimension text [Dimapost].

Below Primary Value Places the alternate dimension text below the primary dimension text and above the dimension line [Dimapost].

THE TOLERANCES TAB

The options in the Tolerances tab offer the inclusion and formatting of tolerance dimension text.

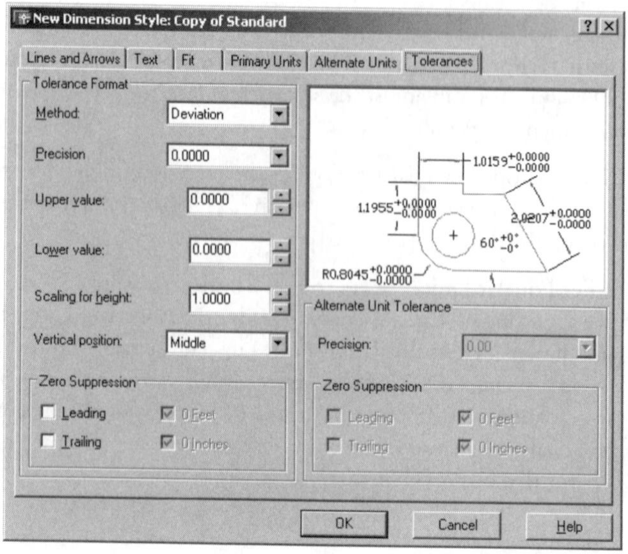

The Tolerance Format Group

The following options offer control over the format of tolerance dimension text:

Method Lets you turn on and set the format for the tolerance dimension text. The options are None, Symmetrical, Deviation, Limits, and Basic. None turns off the tolerance dimension text. Symmetrical adds a plus/minus tolerance dimension. This is a single dimension preceded by a plus/minus sign. Deviation adds a stacked tolerance dimension showing separate upper and lower tolerance values. The Limits option replaces the primary dimension with a stacked dimension showing maximum and minimum dimension values. The Basic option draws a box around the primary dimension value. If an alternate dimension is used, the box encloses both primary and alternate dimension text [Dimtol, Dimlim, (minus) Dimgap].

Precision Drop-down list lets you set the precision of the tolerance dimension text. This option will round off the dimension text to the nearest precision value you set. It does not affect the actual precision of the drawing [Dimtdec].

Upper Value Lets you set the upper tolerance value for the Symmetrical, Deviation, and Limits tolerance methods [Dimtp].

Lower Value Lets you set the lower tolerance value for the Deviation and Limits tolerance methods [Dimtm].

Scaling For Height Lets you adjust the size for the tolerance dimension text as a proportion of the primary dimension text height [Dimtfac].

Vertical Position Lets you determine the vertical position of the tolerance text. The options are Top, Middle, and Bottom. The Top option aligns the top tolerance value of a stacked pair of values with the primary dimension text. Middle aligns the gap between stacked tolerance values with the primary dimension text. Bottom aligns the bottom value of two stacked tolerance values with the primary dimension text [Dimtolj].

The Zero Suppression Group

Lets you suppress zeros so they do not appear in the tolerance dimension text. For dimensions other than architectural, you can suppress leading and trailing zeros. For example, 0.500 becomes .500 if you suppress leading zeros. It becomes 0.5 if you suppress trailing zeros. For architectural dimensions you can suppress zero feet or zero inches, though typically, you would not suppress zero inches [Dimtzin].

The Alternate Unit Tolerance Group

The Precision drop-down list lets you set the precision of the alternate tolerance dimension text. This option will round off the dimension text to the nearest precision value you set. It does not affect the actual precision of the drawing [Dimalttd].

Drawing Blocks for Your Own Dimension Arrows and Tick Marks

If you don't want to use the arrowheads supplied by AutoCAD for your dimension lines, you can create a block of the arrowheads or tick marks you want, to be used in the Arrowheads group of the Dimension Styles/Geometry dialog box.

TIP *To get to the Arrowhead options, go to the Lines And Arrows tab of the New, Modify, or Override Dimension Style dialog box.*

For example, suppose you want a tick mark that is thicker than the dimension lines and extensions. You can create a block of the tick mark on a layer you assign to a thick pen weight and then assign that block to the Arrowhead setting. To do so, choose Dimension ➢ Styles from the menubar to open the Dimension Styles dialog box; then select a style from the Style list and click the Modify button. In the Lines and Arrows tab, select User Arrow from the first pull-down list in the Arrowheads group. In the User Arrow dialog box, enter the name of your arrow block.

When you draw the arrow block, make it one unit long. The block's insertion point will be used to determine the point of the arrow that meets the extension line, so make sure you place the insertion point at the tip of the arrow. Because the arrow on the right side of the dimension line will be inserted with a zero rotation value, create the arrow block so that it is pointing to the right (see Figure D.2). The arrow block is rotated 180° for the left side of the dimension line.

FIGURE D.2

The orientation and size of a block used in place of the default arrow

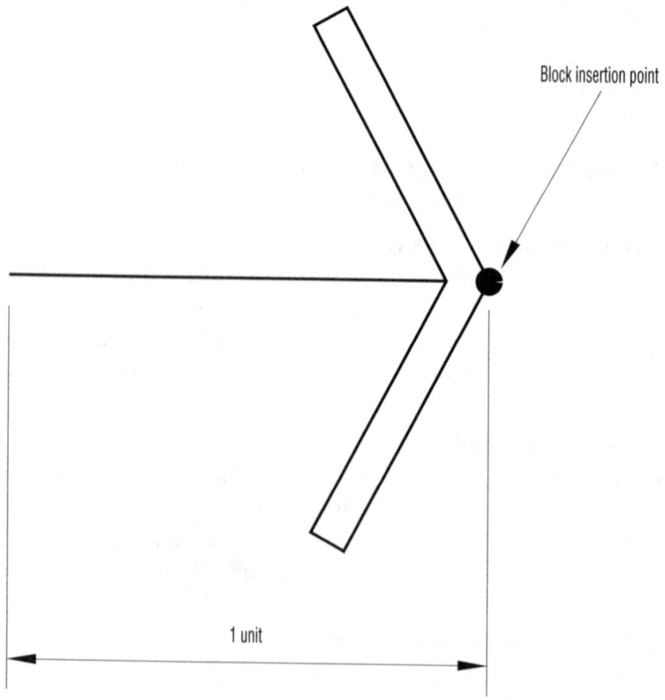

To have a different type of arrow at both ends of the dimension line, create a block for each arrow. Then, in the Dimension Styles/Geometry dialog box, choose User in the drop-down list for the first arrowhead, and enter the name of one block. Then choose User in the drop-down list for the second arrowhead, and enter the name of the other block.

Index

Note to the Reader: Throughout this index **boldfaced** page numbers indicate primary discussions of a topic. *Italicized* page numbers indicate illustrations.

Symbols

Numbers

A

C

G

H

O

Q

R

S

V

W

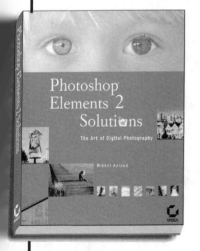

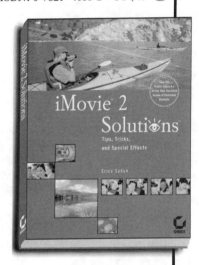

en Your Eyes to
Photoshop
Photoshop Elements 2 Solutions
The Art of Digital Photography
Richard Lynch
THE HIDDEN POWER OF
Photoshop Elements 2
Power-User Tools Dramatically Expand What Photoshop Elements Can Do!
SYBEX
Photoshop® Elements 2 Solutions: The Art of Digital Photography
ISBN: 07821-4140-4 · $40
PHOTOSHOP 7 at Your Fingertips
Get In, Get Out, Get Exactly What You Need™
Jason Cranford Teague
THE PHOTOSHOP REFERENCE YOU'VE BEEN WAITING FOR
The Hidden Power™ of Photoshop® Elements 2
ISBN: 07821-4178-1 · $40
Photoshop 7
Savvy
Photoshop® 7 at Your Fingertips: Get In, Get Out, Get Exactly What You Need™
ISBN: 07821-4092-0 · $40
FREE Book Included! A $50.00 Value!
Photoshop 7
LEARNING STUDIO
Photoshop 7 Savvy book included FREE!
Photoshop® 7 Learning Studio™
ISBN: 07821-4185-4
$119.99
Photoshop® 7 Savvy™
ISBN: 07821-4110-2
$40
Coming Soon
Photoshop Tennis: The Secrets of Winning Digital Design
ISBN: 07821-4191-9 · $44.99
Style. Substance. Sybex.
SYBEX®

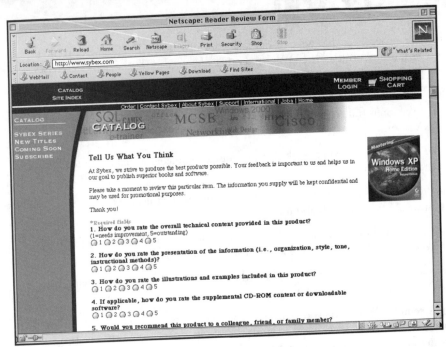

On the CD-ROM

This CD offers valuable resources, including a 30-day trial copy of AutoCAD 2004, electronic books, bonus chapters, add-ons, utilities, the DWG and other files needed for the book's exercises, and more. Specifically, you'll find:

AutoCAD 2004 Trial lets you try the new features covered in this book and practice the tutorials. This trial version is fully functional but expires after 30 days of use and includes the Autodesk Express Viewer.

The ABCs of AutoLISP is an electronic book that provides a complete tutorial for AutoLISP, the AutoCAD macro-programming language.

AutoCAD Instant Reference is the definitive companion to this book as it offers detailed descriptions of AutoCAD's commands and tools.

AEC On-Screen is an architectural add-on that gives you the basic symbols library for drawing floor plans. Versions for AutoCAD 2004 and AutoCAD LT 2004 are included.

Eye2eye is an add-on utility that greatly simplifies the process for obtaining 3D perspective views of your 3D models by using a camera-and-target metaphor.

PanaVue ImageAssembler Trial lets you seamlessly connect two or more bitmap images for large-scale drawing backgrounds. If you have a standard desktop scanner, use PanaVue ImageAssembler to scan those really large aerial surveys or existing renderings that you want to use for backgrounds.

Project files from the exercises in the book are included so you can easily study any topic at any time.

VBA and Active X chapters discuss how Microsoft Visual Basic or Excel interact with AutoCAD. The chapters also show you how to use the VBA programming language and user interface tools to build user-friendly front-ends to your AutoCAD applications. The AutoCAD object model is also introduced, and source code for all the program examples is included.

Architectural Solid Modeling and Advanced Surface Modeling chapters cover more advanced 3D modeling topics. These chapters will teach you how to become a 3D pro with more detailed information on how to accurately model your designs.

3D modeling utilities greatly simplify the creation of complex 3D shapes, such as free-form 3D tubes and surfaces with cut-out openings.

2D and 3D parts library includes kitchen cabinets, furniture, trees, and people.

NOTE *See Appendix A and the Readme file for details on installing the software and files on the CD.*